The Deutsche Bank
1870–1995

The Deutsche Bank
1870–1995

by

Lothar Gall, Gerald D. Feldman,
Harold James, Carl-Ludwig Holtfrerich,
Hans E. Büschgen

Weidenfeld & Nicolson
LONDON

Translated from the German by:

J. A. Underwood: *The Deutsche Bank from its Founding to the Great War 1870–1914*,
Dona Geyer: *The Deutsche Bank 1945–1957: War, Military Rule and Reconstruction*,
Deutsche Bank Language Services (Head Office): *Foreword* and *Deutsche Bank from
1957 to the Present: The Emergence of an International Financial Conglomerate*

With 20 tables and 19 diagrams in the text
and 82 illustrations

© 1995 Deutsche Bank

Reprinted 1999

First published in Great Britain in 1995 by
Weidenfeld & Nicolson
The Orion Publishing Group Ltd
Orion House
5 Upper Saint Martin's Lane
London WC2H 9EA

A catalogue record for this book is available
from the British Library

ISBN 0 297 81606 3

Printed and bound by Butler & Tanner Ltd,
Frome and London

Contents

The Deutsche Bank
from its Founding to the Great War
1870–1914

by Lothar Gall

The Deutsche Bank
from World War to World Economic Crisis
1914–1933

by Gerald D. Feldman

The Deutsche Bank and the Dictatorship
1933–1945

by Harold James

The Deutsche Bank 1945–1957:
War, Military Rule and Reconstruction

by Carl-Ludwig Holtfrerich

Deutsche Bank from 1957 to the Present:
The Emergence of an International
Financial Conglomerate

by Hans E. Büschgen

Foreword

Few institutions in Germany have survived 125 years and become intertwined with the nation's history. Deutsche Bank has travelled the road traversed by the German people, with all its peaks and troughs, since the founding of the Bismarckian empire in 1870. The rise of the bank and the development of German industrial society are indissolubly linked. The bank has been carried along, even driven along, but it is also a driving force itself. Its Annual Reports, detailed in content and precisely and clearly formulated from the very outset, have never been concerned merely with the trials and tribulations of the bank; they have always been a reflection of the nation's economic development.

But this industrial society and the bank, which forms part of it, do not exist for their own sake, nor are they self-sufficient. The parameters within which they operate have always been politically determined – throughout the prolonged start-up phase in the nineteenth century, before and during the First World War, during the brief respite of the Weimar Republic and then, more than ever, under the Nazi dictatorship. This bank is an integral part of the nation and shares the destiny of the people whose name it bears.

Those who rise high can also fall hard. Deutsche Bank has experienced its own descent into the nadir. In 1945 no one would have wagered on its future. The revival of the bank – like that of the country – was a miracle. The Federal Republic became an economic power. Deutsche Bank benefited from this and set the resources that flowed its way to work once again. Who it is who gives and who takes is never decided with finality. By contrast, the decision that democracy is indispensable was final and conclusive. In the bank, as elsewhere, new ways of thinking were increasingly supplanting the old after 1945. Thus, when the idea of this historiographic venture was conceived and given the go-ahead in the spring of 1989, no one imagined that Germany would be united the following year and that the name 'Deutsche Bank' – long infused with a new spirit – would regain its old resonance.

But is Deutsche Bank an institution that has retained a single identity over these 125 years? Can its story be told like that of an individual? The history of the bank breaks off, resumes, and finally broadens out. Today the bank is German only in a limited sense; indeed, if it were otherwise, it would no longer carry much weight in Germany itself, or be able to render the country much service. The history of Deutsche Bank is not cast from one piece. Therefore, it is presented here chronologically through the research of five authors who view the subject each from their individual perspectives. They alone are responsible for what they have written and the manner in which they have tied the bank into its social and political context. No instructions were given nor guidelines laid down. Those members of Deutsche Bank's Management Board who initiated the project were moved only by a single desire – that it should serve the truth.

'Chronicles are written only by those to whom the present is important,' Goethe observed. To us, the present is not merely important. We live in the present and strive to ensure the continuing success of the bank in future. Looking back is not something we indulge in for its own sake or from a mere fascination with things past. The present demands that we understand how Deutsche Bank became what it is today.

Our thanks go to the authors.

Frankfurt, autumn 1994   *Hilmar Kopper*

Introduction

The occasion for the publication of this book is the one hundred and twenty-fifth anniversary of Germany's largest universal bank, the Deutsche Bank. The purpose of this volume, however, is not simply to celebrate this event but most importantly to understand the history of the bank and its place in German history. This book, therefore, is intended for a much broader audience than is usually the case with either a company anniversary publication or a work of scholarship. The employees and friends of the Deutsche Bank do, of course, constitute a large and varied potential readership for this book in and of themselves, and we certainly hope they will find this book interesting and enjoyable and will come away from it with a better and clearer sense of how the Deutsche Bank evolved into the institution it is today. Our larger and primary goal, however, has been to produce a work that will be of interest to the wide body of persons interested in problems of history, economics and public affairs. Included among them should be many of our fellow historians, some of whom tend to treat the history of banking and financial institutions as a specialized and even arcane form of historical knowledge. It need not be, and it is our conviction that the role played by banks and financial institutions has to be demystified, and that they must be viewed as part of the general history in which they are embedded. We do, after all, live in advanced capitalist societies, and the collapse of alternative economic and social systems makes it all the more imperative that we understand how capitalist societies actually function both individually and collectively. The Deutsche Bank, the archetypal German universal bank, provides an ideal subject for studying the interaction of business, society and government between the unification of Germany under Bismarck and the unified Germany of today.

Needless to say, it is a story with both national and international dimensions, and it is not always a happy one. One of the goals of this book is to contribute to sorting out the role of the Deutsche Bank and the other big banks in the disasters as well as the successes of modern German history. This is especially necessary because the role and alleged 'power of the banks' have had considerable significance in German politics, sometimes legitimately and sometimes in a very sinister manner.

Even in an age of user-friendly automated teller machines and credit cards available to a broad public, the business of banking remains rather opaque and mysterious to many persons. There has always been something suspect about lending and borrowing. The reasons are not far to seek and were well expressed by Polonius's pompous advice to his son Laertes, about to go off to France, in Shakespeare's *Hamlet*: 'Neither a borrower nor a lender be; / For loan oft loses both itself and friend, / And borrowing dulls the edge of husbandry.' If an opinion poll were held asking the question, 'Was Polonius right?', one suspects he would come off very well, and would not be treated as the 'wretched, rash, intruding fool' that Hamlet called him after running him through with his sword. If Polonius's advice really were to be followed, international tourism would come to as sad an end as he did and the world economy would break down. It is hard to imagine a modern-day Laertes heading off to France without a credit card of some kind, and credit provides the sinew of international and domestic production and commerce.

Lending and borrowing are, of course, tricky matters, and that is why there are banks. Banks depersonalize credit relations by selling money for interest and commissions that calculate in the element of risk. At the same time, the 'husbandry' of borrowers is maintained by the credit checks and status reports to which they must submit to get the money in the first place and then by the incentive of reducing their interest costs. So far so good. But banks also compete with one another for customers, and seek to win them by offering 'personal service', better rates and special consideration in getting credit. In the process, the banks may risk the deposits of their own creditors. In the mixed or universal system of banking so typical of German banking, the problems of comprehending the activities of banks are further compounded by the role of the banks in financing industrial enterprises through the transformation of short-term into long-term debt, the floating of stocks and bonds on the market, the holding of company securities for themselves and their customers, and the responsibilities they assume on the supervisory boards of companies. Finally, new levels of complexity have been reached in recent years with the internationalization of financial markets and their computerization. One knows what steelmakers, baby carriage manufacturers, and brewers produce, but what do banks produce? The new and most recent answer is 'financial products', but it takes a leap of imagination to understand what a 'financial product' is – especially if it is called a 'derivative' – and why it may be worth producing.

Little wonder, therefore, that the banks have been the target of so much criticism and so many demands for regulation in the modern history of Germany and the industrialized West. The prejudice against interest dates back to early Christianity, and the fact that more scrutiny is usually given to the credit worthiness of the smaller and weaker than to the larger and stronger credit seekers inevitably invites resentment. When big banks make mistakes that attract public attention, usually because they have been overly generous and trusting of big customers, their mishaps are treated with a mixture of *Schadenfreude* and outrage that seldom attends upon the malfunctions of other kinds of enterprise.

Such is the price of engaging in an activity that is always somewhat suspect and yet requires constant 'confidence', to employ a translation of the Latin word 'credit'.

As this book shows, there has often been much to criticize. The German banking system, like every banking system, has peculiar ills to which it is prone that reappear with some frequency. It is worth stating, however, that there is nothing in this record that legitimizes the extremist attacks to which the banks were subjected by right-wing anti-Semites and political and economic cranks who yearned for a return to pre-modern conditions.

Germany was not alone in suffering from such problems, as the assaults on Wall Street in the United States, the City in England, and the so-called Two Hundred Families in France testify. In Germany, however, the assault on the *Börsianer* – that is, stock market speculators and promoters – the distinction between 'productive' and 'grasping' capital, and the idea of 'interest slavery' inevitably carried anti-Semitic undertones and notions of evil conspiracy. Such code words were employed by anti-Semites from the nineteenth-century editor of the *Gartenlaube*, Otto Glagau, to the author of the National Socialist programme, Gottfried Feder, and the pathological anti-Semite, Julius Streicher, and they inspired the political practice of the Third Reich. The terrible consequences of such prejudice and bigotry for German history are well known, and they also blighted the history of the Deutsche Bank. Jewish bankers will appear prominently in the pages which follow as founders and managers of the Deutsche Bank until they were driven out in the deplorable manner also described in this book.

The paranoid attacks on finance capital from the extreme right must be taken seriously because the right was able to put its ideas into practice and because mankind's capacity to generate conspiratorial theories and magical notions seems to be boundless. Hostility to banks, and the tendency to be dismissive of their functions, exist on the left as well. These tendencies are well illustrated by the words of Bertolt Brecht in the *Threepenny Opera*, 'What's breaking into a bank compared with founding a bank', and by the fact that the lately deceased Communist states considered both banks and the entire service sector as 'unproductive' and failed to assess their contribution to the national economy in the manner employed by capitalist societies. Nevertheless, some analyses of banking from the perspective of the Marxist left are significant because they have set some of the important questions which must be addressed as well as transcended in a history such as this one. The crowning figure in this tradition is, of course, the Austro-German theoretician Rudolf Hilferding, whose *Finance Capital* (1910) postulated the growing control over industry by finance capital, the development of an increasingly 'organized capitalism' based on banking control, cartels and trusts, and the drive of advanced capitalism to export capital and promote imperialism. For Hilferding and the Marxists inspired by him, such as Lenin and Bukharin, the developments described were seen as way stations on the road to socialism. The teleological side of Marxist theory is not faring very well these days for obvious reasons, but the issues raised by Hilferding have always had considerable relevance.

Thus, Hilferding's contemporary, the banker and publicist Alfred Lansburgh, lamented the appearance of a Deutsche Bank representative on the supervisory board of the Donnersmarckhütte in 1909 as a sign that one of the very few corporations that had resisted the banks had succumbed, thus demonstrating 'the power of the banks, which no one can escape in our age, which is ruled by large credit'. Decades later, the developmental economist Alexander Gerschenkron emphasized the crucial role of the banking sector and the state in countries that were and are late starters in the process of industrialization. More recently, the German historian Jürgen Kocka and others have picked up Hilferding's notion of 'organized capitalism', and while questioning Hilferding's claims concerning bank control of industry, have nevertheless stressed the peculiar importance of bank influence and power in organizing German 'organized capitalism'. It is significant that the leading big banks have always been singled out, whether rightly or wrongly, as the most important element in the great economic crises of 1873, 1907 and 1931, were made the subject of famous inquiries in 1907 and 1933, and were almost dismantled by the Allies after 1945. Whatever the present status of economic theories of imperialism, no history of the big banks, and especially of the Deutsche Bank, which was founded to finance export trade, can evade the question of their role in German foreign affairs. The Deutsche Bank was the leading financial institution in the Baghdad Railway, was involved in German expansionism during the First and Second World Wars, but was also the major financial institution concerned with German economic relations with the Soviet Union between the two world wars and during the Cold War.

It would be pretentious to suggest that even so large a book as this one will provide a full, comprehensive and satisfactory exploration of all the issues which have been raised. This book is, among other things, intended to encourage future research by showing that serious scholarly investigation of these questions is possible, that theories can be tested, proven, disproved and modified on the basis of research, and that some of the issues can be sorted out in a sensible and satisfactory manner. The five authors of this book are all highly individual scholars, and while we have agreed on a set of issues and problems we wish to see covered in this book, we have always understood that the emphases and character of our respective contributions would be determined by what seemed most pertinent to the period we were covering, our own special interests, and the sources available.

To begin with, this is a history of the Deutsche Bank as an enterprise, and therefore a work of entrepreneurial rather than purely economic history. There are issues raised here which can and should engage cliometricians and econometricians – problems of banks and economic growth, the comparative benefits of universal banks, and the profitability of universal banks, for example – but this book is not written for an audience seeking answers to such questions on the basis of rigorous economic analysis. We believe, however, that those who are concerned with these problems will find useful points of departure in this book. We have devoted considerable attention to the Deutsche Bank's organizational evolution, to those who ran it, to those who worked for it, and to its place in the banking sector. The special qualities of the Deutsche Bank as a company and an institution are at the centre of every chapter in this volume.

At the same time, we understand this book to be a contribution to the economic, social and political history of modern Germany. The evolution of the Deutsche Bank is inseparable from that of modern banking and the German and world economy over the last 125 years. The functions of banks and the clientele they have served have changed dramatically, and while there are startling continuities – in some of the industrial firms associated with the Deutsche Bank, for example – there have also been revolutionary transformations in the scale of transactions, the scope of banking operations, and the relative significance of various domestic and international operations. An effort has been made here to bring this history to life through the actions of some of the remarkable personalities who have figured in the bank's history, the changing character of labour relations in the bank, the actual relations between bankers and industrialists at various points in the bank's history, and the interaction between the bank and Germany's central banks, the Deutsche Reichsbank, the Bank deutscher Länder, and the Deutsche Bundesbank, as well as with government ministries and leaders.

Finally, the history of the Deutsche Bank has been inextricably involved with Germany's political history. Not every special anniversary of the bank has been a pleasant one. The fiftieth anniversary, in 1920, took place in the context of a recently lost war and revolution, a depreciating currency and a very uncertain future for Germany and for the bank. The seventy-fifth anniversary in the spring of 1945 was even more miserable and might well have been its last. That there would be a one hundredth anniversary of a reunited Deutsche Bank with headquarters in Frankfurt am Main and Düsseldorf in 1970 was anything but predictable in the years immediately following the end of the Second World War, and there was no reason to think in 1970 that the Deutsche Bank would be celebrating its one hundred and twenty-fifth anniversary with reopened branches in what was formerly the GDR. The Deutsche Bank was sometimes a more and sometimes a less important actor in the events of German history. Certainly its existence was threatened by its involvement in the finances of the German state during and after the First and Second World Wars, but it was also too significant and powerful an institution to be treated as a mere victim of the forces of history. It is very much to the credit of the present leadership of the bank that it has chosen to encourage historical reflection as well as celebration on this occasion.

The idea for a history of the Deutsche Bank by a group of independent scholars was first proposed by the head of the Historical Archive of the Deutsche Bank, Manfred Pohl, in discussions with the late spokesman of the Deutsche Bank, Alfred Herrhausen, and Professor Knut Borchardt of the University of Munich in 1989, at which time an initial conception of the work was developed. At the same time, initial discussions were held with Professor Gerald D. Feldman of the University of California at Berkeley, who was asked to function as scholarly co-ordinator of the project. Following Herrhausen's tragic murder, his successor as spokesman for the bank, Hilmar Kopper, took up the idea and energetically and enthusiastically promoted its realization.

The decision to pursue the project reflected the long-standing commitment of the Deutsche Bank to historical scholarship, as exemplified not only by the maintenance of a first-class historical archive in the bank, but also by the Deutsche Bank's support of the Historisches Kolleg in Munich. The decision to pursue this project was also an expression of the bank's commitment to promote banking history as a subject of general historical interest as well as of specialized scholarship. Lastly, and most importantly, it attested to the support of free and independent scholarship. At no time, between the inception of this project and its realization in the form of this volume, has the bank sought to censor or influence the content or judgements of the contributors. While Hilmar Kopper and his colleagues have provided us with warm encouragement and hospitality, they have left the business of scholarship to us. Naturally, we are aware that our judgements and emphases diverge at various points from those of the managing directors and their colleagues in the bank.

There will undoubtedly be differing interpretations of certain events and phases in the development of the bank after the publication of this volume. We have, of course, commented on one another's own work in periodic meetings, and drafts of the chapters by Messrs Feldman, James and Holtfrerich were discussed by a group of distinguished scholars invited on the recommendation of the authors to a meeting in October 1993.* We have benefited greatly from their comments and suggestions. The authors, however, are solely responsible for the content of their individual contributions and for any errors which they may contain.

In keeping with the proposition that this book should be a work of general interest, Professor Thomas Nipperdey of the University of Munich was originally asked to write the first chapter, dealing with the period 1870–1914. Unfortunately, because of his serious and rapidly progressing illness, Professor

---

* The scholars present at the meeting in addition to the three mentioned authors were Werner Abelshauser, Theodore Balderston, Knut Borchardt, Christoph Buchheim, Hans E. Büschgen, Lothar Gall, Peter Hayes, Peter Hertner, Theo Horstmann, Christopher Kopper, Karin Lehmann, Dieter Lindenlaub, Gerhard Schulz, Hans-Peter Schwarz and Jonathan Steinberg.

Nipperdey was unable to begin work on his section of the book. We are deeply grateful to Professor Lothar Gall for having completed the first chapter of the book within a far shorter time frame than that available to the other authors.

If those who launched this project considered the perspective of the general historian most desirable for the first chapter of this volume, they also recognized that a very different kind of perspective was necessary for the concluding chapter, namely that of the expert on contemporary banking. Quite aside from the fact that all the sources could not be made available for obvious reasons, and that a historical perspective is very difficult to attain in so revolutionary a period of banking development, an expert account of the current situation and a critical perspective that looked toward the future appeared the most appropriate and interesting way to conclude this book. Professor Büschgen's chapter, therefore, is very different in method and character from the chapters which precede it, and the difference is intentional.

In all other cases, the scholarship in this book is based on unrestricted access to the available sources in the Deutsche Bank and in a variety of public and private archives insofar as their use has not been limited by the rights of living persons or by personal legal testament. Furthermore, the documentary evidence on which the historical portions of this book are based is open and available to all qualified scholars, and thus, as should always be the case in works of historical scholarship, it is subject to the standard of replication and to differing interpretation. A word should be said here, however, about the quality and character of these sources. Until very recently, the Historical Archive of the Deutsche Bank had reasonably good materials on the period before 1914, and very scattered and unsatisfactory documentation for the period after the First World War. However, there did exist a very massive collection of Deutsche Bank papers on the 1918–45 period in the former Central Archive of the German Democratic Republic in Potsdam, now the German Federal Archive, Potsdam Division. When the project began, the Deutsche Bank was negotiating with the former GDR authorities to procure access for the authors to these archives. The problem was solved by the collapse of the GDR. While the Deutsche Bank has claimed the original documents, it has provided the German Federal Archive with a full microfiche of the over twelve thousand volumes in the collection. Messrs Feldman, Holtfrerich and James wish to express their great appreciation to the administrators of the Federal Archive in Potsdam and their colleagues for their assistance well beyond the call of duty during our visits to Potsdam.

While the sources in Frankfurt and Potsdam for the period 1870–1945 are extraordinarily rich in many cases, their limitations should also be made clear. There is an almost total absence of protocols of the board of managing directors, or of meetings of the supervisory board or its major committees. The richest source materials are those that deal with companies on whose supervisory boards the Deutsche Bank played a significant role, and other important areas of investment. The broad policies of the bank, therefore, must often be divined, so to speak, from the way the bank acted in the 'field', or from printed circulars and published policy statements. It is reasonable to assume that much has been lost or, one hopes, is yet to be discovered somewhere. This certainly holds true for the period after 1945. The chaotic early post-war years were not conducive to good record keeping, and sources seem to have been badly scattered because of the tripartite division of the bank. As the contribution of Professor Holtfrerich shows, the Historical Archive of the bank has managed to recover some important documentation, and there are papers in private hands as well as in the archives of the occupation authorities.

We are nevertheless very grateful for what we have. We are especially grateful to Manfred Pohl, for his inspiration, dedication and support of this enterprise in all its aspects. So, too, are we appreciative of the efforts of Angelika Raab-Rebentisch, who has worked closely with Manfred Pohl and with us on all the large and small problems connected with the project. The staff of the archive have been wonderful. Martin L. Müller put at our disposal his remarkable command of the materials in the archive and his genuine imagination for what might and could be found, as well as the physical energy needed to move masses of paper about. Marga-Rose Schuch and Andrea Bauer took care of complicated arrangements connected with our research and visits to Frankfurt and other places with good humour and great patience. We also wish to express our appreciation to Frau Bauer for the great effort and care she exercised in the proofreading and technical standardization of the manuscript.

We wish to thank Lord Weidenfeld for his promotion of the English edition of this work.

Finally, we wish to express our gratitude to the board of managing directors of the Deutsche Bank for its support of this project. We are especially grateful to Hilmar Kopper for his personal interest and the time he spent with us despite his busy schedule.

Berkeley, October 1994   *Gerald D. Feldman*

The Deutsche Bank
from its Founding to the Great War
1870–1914

by Lothar Gall

I. Beginnings

1. Founding

Chairos – a moment favoured by the gods; that was what the ancient Greeks used to call a situation in which plans and opportunities for their realization, future expectations and present circumstances came together in a way that not only promised success but virtually guaranteed it. That kind of *chairos* must, it seems in retrospect, have prevailed at the beginning of 1870, when a small group of men who combined business experience with enormous enterprise decided to set up a German export bank based in Berlin. Following the political revolution of 1848–49 (a failure, but one that had imparted great momentum to historical development), what we call the Industrial Revolution had come to embrace broader and broader areas of the central European economy. The expansion and internal consolidation of the German Customs Union (founded in 1834) in part provided the basis for this, as did liberalization of the law as it related to the economy (for example, by making it easier to set up joint stock companies), the spread of the principles of freedom of trade beyond the confines of Prussia, and the country's adhesion, during the 1860s, to the west European free-trade zone created by the Cobden Treaty of 1860. In the wake of Prussia's victory over Austria in 1866, the resultant dissolution of the German Confederation, and the creation of a federal state uniting the northern part of Germany, the conflicts surrounding the redrawing of the political map of central Europe aspired to a final decision – even though it was not yet entirely clear what that map would look like and above all how it was going to come about. The self-confidence of the German middle class, despite many a political setback since the abortive revolution of 1848, was growing steadily, along with its economic strength and the social influence that that class was simultaneously acquiring as a result of an

The author is deeply indebted to Angelika Raab-Rebentisch and Barbara Wolbring for their generous assistance during the preparation of this work.

increasingly dominant position in the law, in government, and in science and education. Ludwig Bamberger, one of the co-founders and political advisers of what was to become the Deutsche Bank, boldly pronounced Bismarck at the time to be involuntarily paving the way for the efforts of the liberal-oriented middle classes, which would soon achieve political victory on the foundation that Bismarck had laid as well.

The basis of Bamberger's prophecy was the politically useful alliance that Bismarck had forged after 1866 with the right wing of the very party that he had so passionately opposed hitherto, namely with the National Liberals. The domestic political consequences of that alliance made themselves felt first in northern Germany, in the so-called North German Confederation, where they produced a positive thrust towards modernization in virtually all areas of economic and social life, a thrust that saw most of the remaining restrictions on trade and industry fall away. The result was to impart even greater momentum to an economy that could already look back on almost two decades of sustained boom conditions, and to create a mood of general expectation and adventure, since what German historians have dubbed the *Gründerzeit* (the 'flotation years' of rapid industrial expansion; Tr.) in fact began in the second half of the 1860s rather than 'after 1871' (the usual starting point assigned to the period).

Just as the high hopes and venturesomeness of contemporaries, mainly among the middle class but also far beyond that segment of society, were particularly directed during those years towards establishing a national state, so too did those contemporaries, even the professed free-traders among them, quite naturally tend to see and conceive of the economy and economic life in such categories. The terms on almost everyone's lips were '*Volks*wirtschaft' and '*National*ökonomie'. So what could be more appropriate than to establish, for the purpose of financing Germany's foreign trade, which until then had been handled essentially by British and French banks, a *German* bank domiciled in the capital of the supreme power (Prussia) of the German Customs Union and of the old North German Confederation – with the prospect of also assuming other financial functions in what was clearly so egregiously prosperous an economy?

In consequence, the new financial institution was named simply 'Deutsche Bank'. Its founding charter was approved on 10 March 1870 by 'supreme decree of His Majesty the King of Prussia'. The Deutsche Bank was the first joint stock bank in Berlin and only the second in all of Prussia, where joint stock companies still had to be licensed and licences were granted only rarely. Contemporaries were therefore quick to note that for the first time in 22 years, namely since the Cologne-based bank of A. Schaaffhausen had been converted into a joint stock company in 1848, the Prussian government was once again issuing a licence. Even David Hansemann, the important entrepreneur and banker, had had to start up his Disconto-Gesellschaft in Berlin in 1851 as a simple 'commercial company' (*Handelsgesellschaft*), proceeding in 1856 to turn it into a limited partnership with shares (*Kommanditgesellschaft auf Aktien*). The other major banking foundation in Prussia, that of the Berliner Handels-Gesellschaft in 1856, had likewise taken the form of a limited partnership with shares. Only outside Prussia did any pure joint stock banks come into existence at the time: the Bank für Handel und Industrie in Darmstadt in 1853, for example, or in 1856 the Norddeutsche Bank in Hamburg and the Bremer Bank.[1] So why, when the Deutsche Bank was founded, did the Prussian government depart from its former practice and for the second and last time – the requirement that joint stock companies be licensed was abolished on 11 June 1870 – allow a joint stock bank to be established? And who were the people behind the new institution?

The initiative came from two particular experts in the world of banking and finance: Adelbert Delbrück (1822–90) and Ludwig Bamberger (1823–99), the one a private banker, the other a politician, banker and currency specialist. But it is the former, head of the Delbrück Leo & Co. bank in Berlin, who should be regarded as the 'true founder'[2] of the Deutsche Bank. The house of Delbrück was not in fact, at the time, in the very front rank of Berlin private banks (dominated by such names as Bleichröder, Mendelssohn and Magnus), but it enjoyed an excellent reputation.

Adelbert Delbrück, born in Magdeburg in 1822, came from an important family of lawyers and theologians that played an outstanding part in the upper reaches of the Prussian and German civil service and produced numerous states-men, politicians and scholars.[3] His father, Gottlieb Delbrück, was a lawyer who became a privy councillor in Magdeburg and eventually registrar of Halle University. Adelbert's cousin, Rudolf von Delbrück, had headed the Federal Chancellery since 1867 (the Imperial Chancellery since 1871), and as Bismarck's right-hand man until 1876 had played a key role in the liberal economic policy of the German Reich – a family connection that was not exactly disadvantageous when starting up an export bank.

Adelbert Delbrück had begun by studying theology, but had switched to law. Contrary to family tradition, however, he had subsequently declined to enter the service of the state and had gone into private business instead, beginning as solicitor and legal adviser to a recently founded firm of spinners and weavers in Gladbach before moving to Berlin as general agent for Concordia Life Insurance. There, with the collaboration of business and banking associates from the Rhineland, he had founded a bank called Delbrück Leo & Co. in 1854. His son Ludwig further consolidated the bank, which in 1910 merged with the Gebr. Schickler bank to become Delbrück Schickler & Co. Twenty-eight years later, one of the partners of this private bank, Hermann J. Abs, was to become a managing director of the Deutsche Bank and exert a substantial influence on its fortunes. The Delbrück bank still exists today, in fact; it is the only one of the private banks involved in the founding of the Deutsche Bank to have survived.

In addition to his professional activities, Adelbert Delbrück also filled import-ant public offices. Having already been involved in the launching of the Associ-ation of German Chambers of Commerce in 1861, in the years 1870 to 1885 he headed this organization in which the key problems of financial, monetary and economic policy of the day were discussed. As a member of the college of elders of Berlin's mercantile community, Delbrück influenced the development and organization of the Berlin Stock Exchange. He also became involved politically, as a founder member of the Deutsche Fortschrittspartei (German Progressive Party), in the Berlin City Council, though he subsequently turned down a chance to stand for the Prussian parliament and played no further role in the organizational side of party life.

It was in the spring of 1869 that Adelbert Delbrück first conceived the idea of 'creating a big bank, principally for foreign trade, that should make us independent of Britain and the credit granting facilities that a German merchant might seek and find only in London'.⁴ Initially, he tried to get the Berlin banking house of Mendelssohn interested in his idea, though without receiving much of a response. He did, however, find an influential backer for his plans in the cosmopolitan, much-travelled figure of Ludwig Bamberger. Bamberger happened to be involved in various South American and Far Eastern credit transactions at the time, and found himself obliged to conduct the majority of them through London. As he later wrote in his memoirs: 'These experiences were the reason why, when Adelbert Delbrück, head of the Delbrück, Leo & Co. bank, talked to me in the late 1860s, on the occasion of my first stay of any length in Berlin, about the business of starting up a Deutsche Bank and asked me to participate in its formation and organization, I eagerly agreed in the light of the expansion to be won for German banking in transatlantic territories, a realm in which I could claim to have some knowledge.'⁵

The decision turned out, under the circumstances, to be a stroke of luck. This was because Bamberger combined the banker, the politician and the theoretical economist in his person in a way that was absolutely ideal with respect to the task at hand.⁶ At the time of the founding of the Reich, he was not only one of the leading National Liberal politicians; he was also a key authority on all matters of financial and monetary policy.

In his youth, Bamberger had supported the revolution of 1848–49 with great passion as a journalist and public speaker. He had been a committed representative of the political left. As a participant in the Pfalz uprising of May 1849, he had had to leave Germany, fleeing first to Switzerland and subsequently to Holland, Britain and France. He was sentenced in his absence to long terms of imprisonment and in 1852 even to death ('the sentence to be carried out in the marketplace of the town of Zweibrücken').⁷ A qualified lawyer, he had first planned to work in that profession abroad. However, being related on his mother's side to the Bischoffsheim banking family, he followed the family's advice and tried his hand at banking. His mother's two brothers, Louis and Jonathan Bischoffsheim, had founded banks in Amsterdam, Antwerp, London and Paris, and Bamberger learned the business, initially in London, 'starting at the bottom'. As a token of his adjustment to his new trade, the 'offensive' beard that symbolized the revolutionary was promptly shaved off, altering his appearance so dramatically that most of his friends no longer recognized him at first. In 1851 Bamberger started a bank of his own in Rotterdam, though without much success. After this sobering experience, he went to Paris as an authorized signatory (*Prokurist*) in his uncle's firm, where he principally acquired the expertise in foreign business that was to stand him in such good stead later, when he came to found an export bank. One of the most important experiences of that period of Bamberger's career was his involvement in establishing the Banque de Paris et des Pays-Bas, one of the two forerunners of the Banque Paribas, which is still among the leading French banks today.

Events in Germany, including the movement for national unification (something he longed to see) and the liberal change of direction in Prussia, prompted Bamberger to return in 1866. He had already been a supporter of Bismarck's 'little Germany' policy (aimed at a united Germany excluding Austria) while in exile, not least because it also helped the Liberals' ideas of economic organization to find expression. Standing as candidate for his home city of Mainz, in 1868 he was elected to the so-called 'Customs Parliament', the parliament of the Customs Union that was made up of members of the North German Reichstag and representatives of the south German states. Bismarck, who was subsequently to make Bamberger his personal adviser during the Franco-Prussian war of 1870–71 as being one of the most knowledgeable authorities on French political conditions, initially hoped to use him to gain some influence over the Liberal press, which remained far from friendly towards the Chancellor. His keeping company with Bismarck astonished Bamberger's democratic friends, earning him a certain amount of public mockery: 'Oh Bamberger, erstwhile keenest, sharpest penman of Hessian democracy, how old and feeble you have become since, while sipping the champagne of bitter exile in Paris, you have been earning so much money as a banker!'[8]

Following the founding of the Reich in 1871, Bamberger was elected to its parliament, the Reichstag, of which he was to remain a member for more than 20 years, until 1893. As a leading member of the National Liberal parliamentary group, he played a crucial part in unifying the German currency, switching from the silver to the gold standard, and setting up a German central bank, the Reichsbank, which came into operation in 1876. In 1880 Bamberger joined the 'Secessionists', who split off from the National Liberal parliamentary party in the Reichstag during the dispute about Bismarck's demand for the introduction of protective tariffs. Unlike their party colleagues, who were prepared to co-operate with the Chancellor, the Secessionists (who shortly afterwards renamed themselves the Liberale Vereinigung (Liberal Union)) firmly opposed the protectionist economic policy advocated by the conservative majority in the Reichstag, by the 'Central Association of German Industrialists' and by agriculture. It meant at the same time the final break with the Chancellor. From 1883 to 1893 Bamberger belonged to the Deutschfreisinnige Partei (German Liberal Party), which at times was the largest group in the Reichstag. When this split again in 1893, he sided with its right wing, the Freisinnige Vereinigung (Liberal Union), though without seeking re-election to the Reichstag. Numerous texts on currency and other economic policy matters underpinned the high respect in which Bamberger was held as an economic theorist. His academic background, his political and journalistic contacts, but above all his practical experience in politics and business positively marked him out for the role of 'political adviser' in connection with the establishment of a national bank.

Adelbert Delbrück also won the support of the proprietors of some well-known Berlin banks for his project, thus providing it with a broad capital base. At the same time, the reputations of those private bankers gave the new bank the necessary *gravitas*. In addition to Delbrück, the founding committee that was formed in the early summer of 1869 comprised five other members.[9] Delbrück having attached particular importance to involving 'one of the top Berlin banks' and Mendelssohn having proved unobtainable, Baron Victor von Magnus, head of the F. Mart. Magnus bank, joined the committee and in fact became its chairman.

Magnus came of an ancient and respected banking family, his father having helped to found the Berliner Handels-Gesellschaft back in 1856. As Carl Fürstenberg noted in his memoirs, in both business and social terms he was one of the most important people in Berlin. Berlin high finance was also represented by Hermann Zwicker, co-proprietor of the Gebr. Schickler bank. Adolph vom Rath, co-proprietor of the Cologne bank Deichmann & Co., supplied the connection with the banking world of the Rhineland. His firm was at the same time, through its founder Wilhelm Ludwig Deichmann, closely associated with the A. Schaaffhausen'sche Bankverein. Deichmann was in fact the son-in-law of Abraham Schaaffhausen, the proprietor of that institution, which in 1848 had been converted into Prussia's first joint stock bank. Finally, two less prominent members of the founding committee were Gustav Kutter and Gustav Müller. About Kutter, a businessman whose firm Kutter, Luckemeyer & Co. had offices in New York, Lyons, Zurich and Berlin, we know very little except that he was the confidential representative of the Frankfurt Gebr. Sulzbach bank and subsequently subscribed a large number of Deutsche Bank shares on Sulzbach's behalf. Gustav Müller, too, left no very pronounced traces. All we know of him is that the G. Müller & Co. bank he had founded in Berlin in 1866 was taken over as early as 1873 and became the Berlin branch of the Mitteldeutsche Creditbank. However (and this was not without importance), Müller did provide links with Stuttgart, representing as he did both the Württembergische Vereinsbank and the Kgl. Württembergische Hofbank.

With the exception of Kutter, then, the founders of the Deutsche Bank were private bankers; they were joined by Ludwig Bamberger, who gave their cause political and journalistic support. This starting situation was comparable with that of the other two major joint stock banks set up during these years, namely the Commerz- und Disconto-Bank in Hamburg (1870) and the Dresdner Bank in Dresden (1872). Since even large private bankers were no longer able to meet the high capital requirement of expanding industry and international commerce with their own funds, they got together to found new banks on a joint stock basis. They threw themselves unreservedly into this new development in banking without at first recognizing that they were thereby generating their own most powerful competition; rather, they saw the joint stock banks as partners complementing the business of their own institutions, partners whom they believed they could control at will. However, as a result of the rise of these modern joint stock banks, with the power of large-scale capital behind them, many of the classic private banks found themselves in ever-increasing difficulties.[10]

The provisional articles of association of the Deutsche Bank were sent out, together with an initially confidential memorandum, to key banking figures throughout Germany in order to emphasize the founders' intention of setting up an institution with a supra-regional character. The memorandum of July 1869, concerning the aims and objectives of the bank to be established, painted the economic prospects of a 'Deutsche Bank' (clearly the name had already been decided on) in glowing colours. At the same time it deliberately appealed to the national idea: 'The German flag now bears the German name to every corner of the world, and this would be a further step towards doing honour to the name of Germany in more distant lands and carving out at last for Germany a position in the sphere of financial intermediation commensurate with that already occupied by our country in the fields of civilization, science and art.'[11] Since, however, the plan was for a bank that would operate internationally, the document immediately went on: 'But the support of the enterprise need not be exclusively German, since it should adopt a cosmopolitan standpoint.'

Those interested in the project were invited to Berlin, where the foundation meeting took place on 22 January 1870. A provisional administrative board of ten persons was formed to apply for a licence and conduct negotiations with the government. According to the articles of association, the new institution was to devote itself, in addition to 'performing every kind of banking transaction', principally to 'promoting and facilitating commercial relations between Germany, the other European countries, and markets overseas'[12] – that is, to financing foreign trade. Increased industrial production had also resulted in a big growth in the volume of trade since 1850. Whereas between 1800 and 1835 German exports had risen by 40 per cent, by 1873 the total volume of such trade had shot up by 420 per cent. In other words, exports achieved average annual growth rates of around 11 per cent. The largest growth rates were in the 1860s, presenting a private banker like Delbrück with a positive challenge to open up this growing market to a domestic institution rather than leave it all in the hands of foreign banks.

The idea from which the Deutsche Bank sprang was, as Delbrück put it,

essentially an 'economico-political' one; from the outset it pursued 'simultaneously economic ... and national ... objectives'.[13] The very name 'Deutsche
Bank' implied a programme: the founders wished, by setting an equal German
institution in place on foreign markets beside the British banks, to seek freedom
from foreign supremacy.[14] How strongly the founding of the Deutsche Bank was
rooted in the nationalist thinking of the day is clear from the memorandum that
Ludwig Bamberger composed on behalf of the provisional administrative board
and sent to Bismarck on 8 February 1870 with the object of adding extra weight
to the licence application.[15]

The Deutsche Bank, the memorandum declared, had 'taken as its starting
point the restructuring of the national circumstances and drawn its deeper
meaning from the founding of a Germany standing united and strong on the
world stage under the protection of the North German Confederation and the
Customs Union'. The fact that the financial transactions made necessary by a
growing world trade could not currently be handled by a German bank was
detrimental to the national interest – not least because the founding of the
Deutsche Bank sprang from 'truly patriotic ideas': after all, the head office of
the new institution was to be in Berlin.

The decision in favour of Berlin was indeed based on political considerations.
A more obvious location would have been a major port – Hamburg or Bremen,
for instance. Instead, the founders settled on the capital city of Prussia and of
the North German Confederation, soon to become, as the capital of the Reich,
Germany's leading economic and financial metropolis.

The idea of going straight to the Prussian Prime Minister and Chancellor of
the North German Confederation was suggested by the fact that, ever since his
time as Prussian envoy to the German Confederation in the 1850s, Bismarck
had had a deeper understanding of the interconnectedness of commercial and
foreign policy than most of his contemporaries in diplomatic circles. Even then
he had worked very closely with Rudolf von Delbrück in this field, and had
remained constantly aware of the close links between economic interests and
national power interests. This was also (and importantly) true with regard to
domestic affairs. Delbrück's economic policy as head of the chancellery of the
North German Confederation was very much in line with this, as was Bismarck's
close association with a man like Bamberger.

We know of no direct reaction on Bismarck's part to this memorandum, which
so clearly reveals the motives and arguments of the founders. However, only 12
days later they already had a preliminary decision from the Ministry of Commerce, where the licensing process had clearly been expedited under the benevolent eye of Prussian Minister of Commerce Itzenplitz.

The decisive factor behind the ministry's decision had in fact been the founding
of a rival enterprise, the Internationale Bank, in Hamburg. This financial institution, which came into existence on 24 January 1870, only two days after the
Deutsche Bank founders' meeting in Berlin, was also wholly geared to financing

foreign trade. The founding of the Internationale Bank in Hamburg marked the fulfilment of a long-cherished wish of the wholesale merchants of the port cities, who had suffered particularly from the fragmentation of the national capital market. Only to a limited extent could their high-risk international export business be financed through local merchant banks (the Bremer Bank, for example, a joint stock institution dating from 1856). As a result, a substantial proportion of Germany's export business was conducted on the major European money markets in London, Paris and Amsterdam, some of it even in foreign currency. The Hamburg bankers had set out to overcome this structural weakness by founding the Internationale Bank in their city, which was the port of embarkation for much of Germany's foreign trade, and this is in fact the reason why they had not responded to the invitation from the founders of the Deutsche Bank to participate in their institution in Berlin. At the same time, the public perception was that the Hamburg bank had won the race, and sceptics clearly advised against a further commitment in favour of a major bank in Berlin at this stage. In Berlin government circles, particularly in the Ministry of Commerce, there was a fear that it might not be the Prussian metropolis that rose to become the nation's premier capital market, but Hamburg, a city that had not even joined the German Customs Union and in any case did not exactly have a reputation for benevolence towards Prussian policy. The political intention of the Prussian Minister of Commerce to maintain and develop Berlin's status as the principal financial centre in Germany was thus entirely in line with the argument that Ludwig Bamberger had advanced on behalf of the provisional administrative board. 'If the company [the Deutsche Bank] pursues and achieves its purpose, it may indeed come to be of great significance as regards the development of commercial relations. It seems to us to be important that such a company should have its head office in Berlin', Itzenplitz wrote to Bismarck on 10 February 1870.[16]

At the 16 February 1870 meeting of the Royal Staatsministerium, the Cabinet attended by all ministers, Itzenplitz put forward the founding concept and the licence application. The new line that he and the council laid down was that it was not in the interests of the state 'to limit the business scope of sound entrepreneurs of joint stock companies'.[17] Negotiations were already taking place in the North German parliament regarding the abolition of compulsory licensing for joint stock companies. These reached fruition shortly afterwards with the Corporation Law revision (*Aktienrechtsnovelle*) of 11 June 1870. That fact, together with the reputations of the founding fathers of the Deutsche Bank, accelerated the process of granting a licence. The Chief of Police had already confirmed the respectability of the founding committee in his first statement of 1 February 1870: 'All the aforementioned persons are, so far as they are known here, representatives of well-known and reputable commercial firms against whose reliability there is not the slightest objection.' As regards the trustworthiness of the 'non-Prussian members of the founding committee, their association with the domestic figures, who are generally known in the world of commerce, offers sufficient guarantee'.[18]

Within days of the Cabinet meeting, Minister of Commerce Itzenplitz wrote to Victor von Magnus on 20 February 1870 that he was prepared 'to recommend at the very highest level'[19] that a licence be issued, provided that a number of points in the articles of association were amended. The number of objections in fact amounted to 34; however, as the applicants noted with relief, these were 'mainly of a formal nature'[20] and therefore easily met. On two points, though, they were unwilling to concede. The first was where the Ministry of Commerce required the formation of a reserve in the amount of 10 per cent of company profits, which the bankers rejected as excessive. In the end they were able to achieve a compromise, whereby only 10 per cent of the net profit remaining after distribution of dividends had to be transferred to the reserve. Objection was also made to clause 4 of the draft articles, which gave original subscribers the right to acquire shares of subsequent issues at face value. The purpose of the ministry's objection was to prevent any speculators interested only in profits rather than in the success of the enterprise from acquiring the new shares in order to resell them subsequently at the highest possible premium. Here the concession that the founders managed to obtain was to the effect that original subscribers might acquire only as many shares of subsequent issues at face value as they held founders' shares.[21]

The amended articles of association were resubmitted with much haste on 25 February and finally approved on 10 March 1870. It was possible to see the granting of the licence as a signal, and it was no doubt understood as such in that the programme of the new bank combined the national idea with one of the key ideas underlying the founding of the German Customs Union in 1834. Formulated principally by Friedrich List, that idea was to give Germany as much autonomy as possible in commerce and industrial production, which meant above all freeing it from dependence on the premier industrial and financial power of the day, namely Britain.[22] Even if that dependence was not actually so very great,[23] contemporaries like Adelbert Delbrück and Hermann Wallich, one of the first directors of the bank, nevertheless felt it to be so.[24] And there was something else, too – something that made the granting of a licence to the Deutsche Bank even more of a signal. The new institution fitted in perfectly with Bismarck's alliance with the Liberals and with the liberal economic policy adopted in the interests of that alliance. After all, the joint stock bank was *the* 'liberal' corporate form, since it used the principle of association and, ideally, involved broad sections of society in building up national business enterprises.

Its 'national' significance was something the new institution bore before it like a banner with its very name. Even then the Deutsche Bank was often taken for the national bank of issue. As a banking journal noted retrospectively in 1910, the bank had been and continued to be concerned 'to carry its cleverly chosen name (many people at home and abroad saw it as Germany's national bank) into every corner'.[25] This was helped along by the fact that the bank took as its company emblem a bird that bore a more than passing resemblance to the Prussian and subsequently the imperial eagle. The emblem was retained until the merger with the Disconto-Gesellschaft in 1929 and reinforced the impression of a 'state institution'. One managing director of the bank, Carl Michalowsky, felt called upon on one occasion to defend the bank, in a letter to the Central Association of the German Bank and Banking Industry, against the charge that it was using the eagle in an attempt to deceive people as to the private nature of the institution. The eagle, he said, 'has been used by the Deutsche Bank since the time of its founding, that is to say since 1870. There can thus be no question of an intention to give the appearance of a state institution, and in particular to cause confusion with the Reichsbank, since the Reichsbank did not come into existence until several years later. Moreover, as you can see from the attached detail of a cheque form, the eagle is certainly not the imperial eagle, since on a large, brightly protruding breastplate it very clearly bears the letters "DB" and not the Prussian coat of arms.' Furthermore, he pointed out, by law all German manufacturers were allowed to use and portray the imperial eagle provided that the form of a coat of arms was avoided.[26] A glance at an old cheque reveals that the *Kaiseradler* was indeed changed slightly but that the 'DB eagle' did very much suggest the idea of a close tie with the state, which in the light of its customers' need for security will certainly not have been entirely unwelcome to the bank.

A licence having been granted, the first general meeting was held on 21 March 1870, with 76 persons or companies fully subscribing the share capital of the Deutsche Bank in the amount of 5 million talers (15 million marks). The list of subscribers[27] comprised mainly private banks, together with a few joint stock banks and private individuals from the worlds of industry and finance. The shareholders came from the principal German economic centres with the exceptions of Hamburg (whose bankers had, as we have seen, founded the rival Internationale Bank) and Munich, where there was clearly less interest in events in far-off Berlin. A few foreign banks (Bischoffsheim & Goldschmidt in London, for example) were also on the list. On the other hand, such prominent names as Rothschild, Bleichröder, Bethmann and Oppenheim were missing. They took no more part in the institution than did the Disconto-Gesellschaft or the Berliner Handels-Gesellschaft, which as the principal financial institutions in the city presumably wished to have nothing to do with actually cultivating competition for themselves.

On 24 and 25 March 1870 the Deutsche Bank shares were offered to the public. Of the already fully subscribed starting capital of 5 million talers, the first subscribers made 2 million talers available for public subscription, and they did so at the face value of the shares: 'at par course' (*zum Paricourse*), as the first financial advertisement put it on 24 March.[28] They thus dispensed with the quick profit from stock-jobbing known as *agiotage*. The shares offered were eventually oversubscribed something like 150 times. Such oversubscribing of shares was among the deplorable customs of the period. In order to achieve a small premium at least, interested parties subscribed many hundreds of thousands.[29]

The press was predominantly sceptical at first. The fact that the rival Internationale Bank in Hamburg had had a head start was certainly not the only reason for this. The respected Frankfurt financial newspaper *Der Aktionär* cast doubt on the founders' ability 'to run such an institution in accordance with "modern" requirements'. In stock exchange circles, too, the project was received with some scepticism, it being assumed 'that the heart of the matter would be not so much the very finely conceived support for German exports, as far more wholesale *agiotage* on the model of the Viennese and Parisian institutions'.[30] The accusation touched on a central problem of the start-up boom of the so-called *Gründerjahre*: joint stock companies were floated and their share prices initially driven up in order to maximize profits from the sale of shares. Meanwhile, the commercial success of the newly founded company was of only secondary importance to the founders; their main interest was in making a speculative profit. Even after the first Deutsche Bank shares had been offered to the public and massively oversubscribed, *Der Aktionär* doubted that the Deutsche Bank would succeed commercially; the reason for the massive oversubscription, it suggested, lay rather in the speculative intentions of investors. The paper criticized the fact that at the allocation a minimum of 105 shares had to be subscribed in order to obtain a participation, and that smaller subscription amounts were not considered at all. It concluded, surely quite rightly: 'Germany seems due for its banking fever now, as Austria was last year.'[31]

The *Frankfurter Zeitung* nourished the same suspicion in its issue of 25 March 1870. It criticized the administrative board's right, as laid down in the articles of association, to act without the agreement of the general meeting to increase the share capital at its discretion to 20 million talers – four times the original amount. Such a provision was unprecedented, the paper claimed, and the only possible reason for it was the desire of the founders to purchase shares at face value and resell them at a profit.[32] The charge was renewed when as early as 1871 it was announced that the share capital was to be increased from 5 to 10 million talers to make it possible to open branches in Bremen, Hamburg, London, Shanghai and Yokohama. The press considered this reasoning premature, and *Der Aktionär* remarked pointedly: 'There is in any case no need for a doubling of share capital, even if the bank really does have in mind to go into partnership with pirates, kaffirs and Blackfoot Indians.'[33]

On 9 April 1870 the Deutsche Bank opened for business in rented premises at 21 Französische Strasse, not far from the Gendarmenmarkt and the French Cathedral, and two blocks south of the magnificent avenue known as Unter den Linden. The building was a modest one (the days of prestigious bank architecture still lay in the future) but it was in a good location, carefully chosen as being close to the Stock Exchange in what was in the process of becoming the banking quarter of Berlin.

The corporate organs of the bank were the general meeting, the administrative board and the management. The first general meeting of 21 March 1870 elected the administrative board, which initially comprised 24 members, most of them private bankers.[34] In accordance with section 22 of the articles of association, the board was the 'holder of all powers of attorney on the company's behalf',[35] and it was endowed with executive rights far exceeding those of the present-day supervisory board. The management was required to conduct business 'in accordance with the instructions given it by the administrative board'.[36] To give the somewhat unwieldy administrative board effective representation *vis-à-vis* the management, it elected from among its number the so-called Committee of Five, which met regularly every week, whereas the administrative board often met only quarterly.[37] The Committee of Five was the true decision-making body of the new bank. It operated virtually as a 'managing board' and had to approve all major transactions. The founders consciously wished to influence the way the company was run and to control the activities of the management. The arrangement of course involved the risk of clashes between the management and the members of the administrative board or the Committee of Five (nor was it long before such clashes began to occur). Victor von Magnus was elected the first chairman of the administrative board, to be replaced by Adelbert Delbrück in July 1871. Behind the scenes, however, it was Delbrück who pulled the strings from the outset: as Hermann Wallich noted in his memoirs, his first visit to the Deutsche Bank in the autumn of 1870 had brought him to 'President Delbrück'.[38]

The first directors, elected by the administrative board on 23 March 1870, were Wilhelm Platenius and Georg Siemens, with Hermann Wallich joining them in the autumn of that year. However, there could be no question of the new management acting autonomously: as the body of the proprietary shareholders, the administrative board and its Committee of Five intervened forcefully in day-to-day affairs from the very beginning (for instance, the appointed directors could transact no business in excess of 1,000 marks) and put a stop to any initiative that ran counter to their interests as private bankers. Wallich complained that the founders sought 'to reduce the directors to mere clerks'.[39] He therefore thought several times – as did Siemens – of quitting his job in Berlin. Eventually, however, Siemens and Wallich managed to get their way, helped by the revised Corporation Law of 1884. This drew a line between management (henceforth the 'managing board') and the administrative board, which now became known as the supervisory board and had its functions restricted essentially to oversight functions. From this point on, the managing board had sole responsibility for the actual conduct of business.

The bank's emancipation from its founders had begun. There was further evidence of it in 1889, when Delbrück resigned the chair of the supervisory board. The clashes between Siemens and Wallich on the one hand and the administrative board headed by Adelbert Delbrück on the other in the period 1870–84 characterized the transition from 'banker' to the modern 'manager' in the world of banking. The year 1884 may be described as marking the birth of the bank manager. Siemens and Wallich perfectly embodied the new breed in business life.[40] Both men played key roles in the development of the Deutsche Bank during the first decades of its existence.

Georg Siemens[41] was born in Torgau on 21 October 1839, the son of a lawyer and official in the Prussian civil service; he was ennobled in 1899, chiefly for services rendered in connection with the construction of the Baghdad Railway. After completing his schooling at the *French Gymnasium* in Berlin, he studied law at Heidelberg. Civil service exams and military service followed (he took part in the Prussian–Austrian war), and eventually he joined the firm of Siemens & Halske. His contact with Werner von Siemens, the founder of the electrical concern and a cousin of his father, was very close, with the result that in 1868–9 Werner von Siemens gave Georg the job of conducting negotiations on the firm's behalf in London and Tehran concerning the construction of the Indo-European telegraph line. In this the young man acquitted himself so skilfully that when Adelbert Delbrück, who had also been involved in the same business, was looking for a director for the Deutsche Bank in 1870, he thought of Georg Siemens. Although as a lawyer Siemens had no knowledge of banking whatsoever, he had gathered experience abroad of a kind that Delbrück considered useful in view of the business objective of the newly founded bank. In any case, Siemens was to be given an experienced banking expert to work alongside him.

Siemens accepted the offer despite the risk of starting as a newcomer to banking in an untried institution with correspondingly insecure prospects. His doing so involved turning down a job as corporate lawyer with Siemens & Halske, which was already an established concern at the time. Possibly it was the prospect of always playing second fiddle to Werner von Siemens that prompted his decision. With the Deutsche Bank, on the other hand, he would enjoy very much greater creative scope, for he was 'consumed by a burning sense of achieving something truly beautiful and important', as he wrote at the time to the woman who was later to become his wife.[42]

In letters to his family, Siemens was fond of repeatedly stressing, with a certain amount of self-irony, his total ignorance of banking. In an April letter to his cousin Rudolf Siemens, for example, he wrote: 'Though I understand little of American and Indian banking, I nevertheless try to look very erudite, give the occasional shrug, grin from ear to ear – this is my sneering smile – and secretly refer, when I get home, to my encyclopaedia or dictionary or "How to become a banker in twenty-four hours" when I want to find a word I didn't understand. I've already just about grasped the difference between letter of credit and cash.'[43] However, this unconventional way of reading himself into the job soon started to bear fruit. Hermann Wallich, several years older than Siemens and of a calmer disposition, became his colleague's unofficial tutor in banking affairs. But it was not long before Wallich saw his pupil beginning to outperform him.

Siemens quickly recognized that the bank would be able to do its real job of financing exports only if it succeeded in giving itself a broad business foundation at home as well. Accordingly, before the bank's first year was out he began introducing the kind of deposit or investment business that had hitherto been the exclusive province of savings banks, and which was proving to be highly profitable. In the second half of the 1880s, after some initial hesitation, Siemens and his fellow managing directors proceeded to get involved in financing industry. But above all it was the major foreign financial transactions that Siemens conducted so successfully for the bank which formed the basis of his and its reputation. These ranged from financing railway building in North America to setting up the Bank für elektrische Unternehmungen in Zurich, the Banca Commerciale Italiana in Milan, and the Deutsch-Ueberseeische Elektricitäts-Gesellschaft in Buenos Aires, and financing and building the Anatolian Railway and the Baghdad Railway.

Siemens was the 'go-getter' on the managing board of the Deutsche Bank, the man who conceived the big projects, bubbled over with ideas, and was capable of putting things into operation. He hated detailed work; he was concerned with laying out the large canvases, which it was then up to his fellow directors to execute. Hermann Wallich often had to curb his colleague's energy, though at the same time he was fascinated by it. By the time Siemens quit the managing board at the end of 1900 and switched to the supervisory board, he had put the Deutsche Bank in the front rank of Germany's banks in both domestic and foreign business. Siemens was the real driving force and generator of ideas in the first thirty years of the Deutsche Bank's development and the man who set the course for its growth as a credit institution.

Siemens made great demands on both himself and his colleagues and would brook no reference to old age (he had once remarked in jest that 'bank directors should be killed off in their fiftieth year').[44] His work for the company did not prevent him from simultaneously cultivating an upper-class life-style: he kept a country estate in Ahlsdorf, which his father had bought in 1858, and a house in Berlin that he and his wife Elise Görz made into one of the centres of the city's social life. Siemens did not long survive his departure from the bank's managing board in December 1900, dying less than ten months later, on 23 October 1901, at the age of only 62.

Hermann Wallich (1833–1928) was not appointed to the managing board of the Deutsche Bank until October 1870. However, as his biographer noted, 'he was destined, in his existence as a managing director of a major bank, to be overshadowed by a man of genius, and part of his life's work consisted in holding that genius in check'.[45] He did not even meet his future colleague on first joining the bank, because Siemens did not return to his desk in Berlin until after the end of the Franco-Prussian War in March 1871. Previously, Wallich had managed the

Shanghai branch of the Paris-based Comptoir d'Escompte, but on the outbreak of war in 1870 he had been dismissed, along with all the bank's German staff. Although the Bonn-born Wallich was only 37 at the time, he was already regarded as an experienced expert in international banking. Unlike Siemens, he had learned banking 'starting from the bottom', having begun an apprenticeship under Jakob Cassel in Cologne in 1850. After only four years he moved to Paris to work for his uncle, Cahen d'Anvers. Seeing no promotion prospects in his uncle's bank, in 1860 Wallich switched to the Comptoir d'Escompte and worked in various of its overseas branches including Réunion, Mauritius, Yokohama and finally Shanghai.[46]

Wallich had met Bamberger during his time in Paris, and Bamberger introduced his distant relation to the Deutsche Bank as 'an experienced and intelligent practitioner'.[47] Where Siemens was continually taking risks and getting involved in deals that seemed bound to fail, Wallich was the thoughtful one, always advocating caution. But probably it was this very combination of the experienced, prudent Wallich, who carefully weighed the pros and cons, and the adventurous Siemens that produced such magnificent results. Both men were also perfectly aware themselves of how well they complemented each other. 'I recognized his great gifts immediately,' Wallich recalled later, 'and although I had to fight many a battle with him (he frightened me even then with his bold thirst for action), we nevertheless remained friends, and in many instances I gave in to him in response to an inner feeling that he was going to be indispensable so far as the future of the bank was concerned.'[48]

Wallich completely identified himself with the original business objective of the Deutsche Bank: namely, to make Germany's foreign trade independent of financing by British banks. Since he already had extensive knowledge of this field on joining the bank, he subsequently concentrated mainly on building up its foreign business. It was under his aegis that the bank opened branches in Bremen and Hamburg (1871–72) as well as in London, Shanghai and Yokohama (1872–73) and founded the Deutsche Ueberseeische Bank (1886) and the Deutsch-Asiatische Bank (1889). It was because of his experience that the Deutsche Bank was also given the job of selling off Germany's silver reserves after the Reich switched from a silver to a gold standard in 1873. In 1894, at the age of 61, Wallich resigned his position as a managing director on the grounds that, as he put it retrospectively, he no longer wished to participate in the 'perpetual trapeze act'[49] of his colleague's chancy transactions. He moved to the bank's supervisory board, of which he remained a member until his death in 1928. Although he helped to mould a key period in Germany's economic development in an important position, Hermann Wallich tended to operate in secret. When he died at the age of 95 he was not a 'prominent' figure. 'Today's generation hardly even knew his name', the *Berliner Börsen-Zeitung* wrote on the occasion of his death.[50]

Another early member of the bank's management, along with Siemens and

Wallich, was Wilhelm Platenius, a German American who had experience of the American market; however, constant friction with the managing board caused Platenius to resign even before the end of 1870. His successor, Friedrich Mölle, had previously been a privy councillor at the Finance Ministry, where he had 'quarrelled with Camphausen'.[51] In his new role, however, he turned out to be totally miscast. Bamberger's verdict was: 'The man was neither stupid nor inexperienced, but I have never come across a greater degree of incompetence in such a position. The civil service and the world of business certainly are poles apart!'[52] Mölle, too, resigned from the bank early on (in 1872). He was replaced by the 23-year-old Max Steinthal, who took his seat on the managing board in 1873, at the height of the *Gründerkrise*. He concentrated initially on foreign exchange dealing and issuing business before turning increasingly from the late 1880s onwards to the bank's involvement in industry. Steinthal remained a member of the managing board until 1905, when he changed to the supervisory board, on which he was active until 1933.

2. The early years

True to its founding ideal, in the early years the Deutsche Bank engaged mainly in international business.[53] At first the managing board concentrated on financing German exports, foreign investments being added only in the 1880s. Because of its geographical position, Berlin was less convenient for this sort of business than the ports of Hamburg and Bremen, through which nearly all of Germany's export trade passed. Accordingly, Wallich considered it 'absolutely necessary'[54] that the bank should be represented in those cities, and in July 1871 the first branch of the Deutsche Bank was opened in Bremen, to be followed a year later by a second branch in Hamburg.

It was also clear that the bank needed to have a presence in London, the commercial and financial capital of the world.[55] Legal obstacles prevented it from setting up a branch of its own there immediately, so by the end of 1870 the managing board was already conducting negotiations with various German and British banks concerning joint participation in a new foundation. These came to fruition in March 1871 with the establishment of the German Bank of London, of whose starting capital of £600,000 the Deutsche Bank held more than 40 per cent (£250,000). The other shareholders were the Mitteldeutsche Creditbank in Meiningen, the Gebr. Sulzbach bank in Frankfurt am Main, and the British Deinnistown and Rohdewald banks. It soon became clear, however, that because of tight credit restrictions this holding permitted only limited freedom of action. Moreover, the company capital of the German Bank of London was inadequate for certain financial purposes (carrying out acceptance credits, for example). So the Deutsche Bank pursued its efforts (even using diplomatic channels) to have a branch of its own. Eventually it was successful, and in March 1873 the bank was able to open what was known as the Deutsche

Bank (Berlin) London Agency.[56] It sold its holding in the German Bank of London in 1879 at a loss of 117,000 marks.

The Deutsche Bank had set up agencies in Shanghai and Yokohama, the main trading centres of the Far East, by May 1872.[57] However, it was only in 1872 that these were able to show a profit, moving into loss as early as the following year as a result of depreciation of the silver values on which their working capital was based. The Far Eastern branches therefore had to be closed again in 1875. The bank rapidly established a presence in America and France as well. In October 1872 it bought a partnership in the New York bank of Knoblauch & Lichtenstein, and in January 1873 it acquired a holding in Weissweiller, Goldschmidt & Co., Paris.[58] In 1874 it started trying to gain access to what was Germany's most important foreign market at the time, namely South America, by participating in the Deutsch-Belgische La Plata Bank, which operated mainly in Argentina and Uruguay.[59] However, business went so badly as a result of repeated revolutions in South American countries that in 1885 the Deutsch-Belgische La Plata Bank had to be liquidated. The Deutsche Bank suffered further setbacks during these years so far as foreign business was concerned, because the Paris partnership was dissolved in 1877, and in 1882, following unsuccessful speculations in stocks and bonds, the New York partnership had to be wound up as well.

The bank made a fresh attempt to open up the South American market in 1886 with the founding of the Deutsche Uebersee-Bank (renamed Deutsche Ueberseeische Bank in 1893). This subsidiary marked the beginning of a new era in the Deutsche Bank's foreign involvement, because the newly founded institution not only conducted commercial financing, it also performed local banking operations, for which numerous branches were set up in South America. In the years that followed, the bank's foreign business made 'regular, satisfactory progress', as the 1888 business report put it.[60] The founding of the Deutsche Ueberseeische Bank marked yet another change in the business strategy of Siemens and Wallich. From this point on the Deutsche Bank proceeded to open up overseas markets through the medium of subsidiary institutions that were each responsible for a particular country or region.[61] In this it directed its main attention to South America, the Far East (with the founding of the Deutsch-Asiatische Bank in 1889) and, to a very much lesser extent, the German colonies in Africa.[62] It opened overseas branches of its own in Constantinople (in connection with the construction of the Baghdad Railway) in 1909 and in Brussels in 1910. The importance that foreign business was acquiring for the Deutsche Bank was also clear from the fact that in 1890 the profits earned by the Hamburg, Bremen and London branches were even able to balance out a decline in domestic turnover.[63] The chief pillars of the bank's foreign business before the First World War were the London branch and the Deutsche Ueberseeische Bank.

Although the main thrust of the Deutsche Bank's activities was intended to lie and at first did indeed lie in foreign business, domestic business played an important part from the outset. To begin with, admittedly, the bank's maxim in this area was to use its capital only on an interim basis domestically until the money was needed for foreign business.[64] However, as Siemens and Wallich found themselves having to struggle with difficulties on the foreign front, the bank's domestic business soon gained substantially in importance. It quickly became clear to the two men that the status of the Deutsche Bank on the domestic market constituted a decisive criterion as regards its reputation abroad.

In a memorandum addressed to the administrative board in the autumn of 1870, Hermann Wallich named the areas of domestic banking business in which the Deutsche Bank might well become involved. Arbitrage business he considered to be unsuitable in that exploiting price differentials between the various trading centres was tantamount to 'concealed speculation'. He refused to 'look for the centre of gravity of our operation in the stock exchange'. On the other hand, he advocated deposit banking as being a promising line, and after that issuing business, 'for depositors would form the basis of a clientele for the underwriting of financal investments that are secure and carry our recommendation'.[65]

Both Wallich and Siemens backed the idea of deposit or investment business in the bank, the former on the basis of his Paris experience, the latter on the basis of the experience he had gained in London. The brand new institution accepted its first deposits as early as July 1870. Although other banks also had access to customer deposits at the time, the Deutsche Bank is regarded as the originator of deposit banking, since it was the first credit institution in Germany deliberately to seek deposits, which it viewed as a source of refinancing.[66] The established private bankers as well as the older big banks had always refused to do business with deposit money on the grounds that there was not much to be earned in this field. There was also the risk of the money suddenly being withdrawn, plunging the institution into financial difficulties. Instead, they conducted their business solely with their own capital, which in the case of joint stock banks could be increased by issuing more shares.[67] Siemens and Wallich, on the other hand, had learned the advantages of deposit banking abroad. Particularly in Britain it was customary at the time to deposit one's cash with the bank, which in turn formed the basis for that country's lively clearing-house business.

Meanwhile, the Deutsche Bank had given up its somewhat modest head office in Berlin's Französische Strasse and moved into 29 Burgstrasse, in the immediate vicinity of the Stock Exchange. When it subsequently moved to Behrenstrasse, later to become the site of the central bank, in 1879, it turned Burgstrasse into a deposit branch – the very first in the history of German banking.[68] To begin with, of course, deposit business developed only slowly. The business report for 1870 shows only 22,000 talers on the books, remarking by way of excuse that 'all new institutions find their way only after they have been in existence for some time'.[69] In 1899 deposits exceeded starting capital, in 1901 they exceeded total company capital, and soon they formed the crucial basis of the bank's liabilities.[70] As early as 1876 the Deutsche Bank caught up with the two older banks, the Disconto-Gesellschaft and the Darmstädter Bank, in terms of amounts deposited, and by 1895 it had left them far behind. In 1910, for example, the Deutsche Bank's deposits totalled 558 million marks, compared with 313.7 million for the Disconto-Gesellschaft, 286.3 million for the Dresdner Bank, and a mere 148.3 million for the Darmstädter Bank.[71]

At first the bank maintained deposit branches only in Berlin,[72] and in the first thirty years of its existence they increased only slowly in number (from 12 in 1895 to 20 in 1900).[73] Not until the turn of the century did growth begin to accelerate, with 44 branches in 1905 rising to 87 by 1910. The minimum deposit was only 100 marks, in order to make even small capital sums available. That this aim was achieved is clear from the way the average amount deposited went down from 4,138 marks in 1883 to 2,570 marks in the space of ten years.[74]

The first serious crisis that the young bank had to survive was the great *Gründungskrach* of 1873,[75] the deep depression that followed two decades of virtually uninterrupted boom conditions with huge opportunities for company flotations and growth. On 11 June 1870 the North German parliament had abolished compulsory licensing for joint stock companies. This liberalization of company law marked the beginning of a period during which vast numbers of companies were floated, with the influx of money represented by the French Idemnity of 1871 playing an additional (albeit sometimes exaggerated) role. 'Flotation fever' spread to banking, too, and to the temperamentally cautious figure of the private banker. As a result, between 1870 and 1872 a total of 107 joint stock banks were founded in Germany,[76] though most enjoyed only a brief existence. By 1879, 73 of the new institutions had been liquidated as a major collapse followed the overheated boom years with their wild speculations. Shares, still ostensibly a guarantee of affluence and security, began to be discredited. The crisis, which began with the collapse of the Vienna Stock Exchange in May 1873 and spread from there, looked at first like a declaration of bankruptcy on the part of the new economic order and of the capitalism and liberalism that underlay it; the *Gründerkrise* was seen, in fact, as constituting an existential crisis of the bourgeois period at its very outset. Even if the economic collapse (the real fall in production and profits) was less critical and sustained than is often assumed, the social, psychological and political consequences nevertheless ran deep. They led to a complete reversal of future expectations and to an utterly changed outlook on life, particularly among the educated and propertied classes. A mood of pessimism replaced the former enthusiastic anticipation of profits. As the Berlin professor of jurisprudence and long-time Liberal member of parliament Rudolf Gneist put it in later years, an 'era of general dissatisfaction' set in.[77]

The Deutsche Bank survived the *Gründerkrise* very well. It refrained from company-flotation and issuing business for a surprisingly long time and so was less affected by the repercussions of the crisis. Wallich in particular remained sceptical in the face of 'flotation fever'. As he said in his memoirs: 'To me this unhealthy "scramble", which had nothing in common with legitimate business, was unsympathetic and I adopted a negative attitude, never having learned what they called "floating".'[78] The managing directors (including Siemens this time) confined themselves to underwriting national and local government loans and railway stock – 'solid' business not associated with too much risk. The bank's only flotation activities were in connection with foreign transactions, conducted through the German Bank of London and the Deutsch-Belgische La Plata Bank almost as a side-line to the pursuit of its overseas business objectives. Adelbert Delbrück kept an eye on the domestic business, for he was heavily involved in company flotations through his own bank and was anxious to prevent the Deutsche Bank from offering him any competition.

3. Growth and consolidation

The economic collapse that began in 1873 shook the world of banking in Berlin and led to the first significant concentration in the German banking industry. The majority of the newly floated banks got into difficulty as a result of the fall in stock exchange prices. They had either to close down or to merge with other banks. In the period 1873–76, the Deutsche Bank took over five credit institutions altogether, including two sizeable firms: the Berliner Bank-Verein, in whose founding Adelbert Delbrück had been involved in 1871, and the Deutsche Union-Bank, dating from the same year.[79] There was fierce resistance to these mergers within the management and the administrative board as well as among shareholders. But in taking over the Deutsche Union-Bank and the Berliner Bank-Verein in 1876, the Deutsche Bank acquired, at relatively little capital expense, two damaged institutions that were nevertheless massively involved in industrial investment. It thus gave itself a solid basis on the domestic capital market, for the takeovers led to a huge increase in customer contacts. The number of current account holders at head office rose from 885 to 1,384 as a result. 'But the really important thing', Hermann Wallich summed up retrospectively, 'was that by dint of this operation, as a result of the concentration of three banks, we became a major bank overnight. Because that year [1875] marked the beginning of the 'splendid development embarked upon by the Deutsche Bank, which in spite of the inevitable minor hard knocks and incidents was quite unstoppable.'[80]

The year 1875 did indeed represent the first turning point in the development of the Deutsche Bank. Its foreign business had suffered initial setbacks: the closure of the Shanghai and Yokohama branches and the poor business situation and eventual liquidation of the Deutsch-Belgische La Plata Bank in Argentina and Uruguay could only partially be offset by the success of the London branch. Siemens and Wallich remained loyal to their original programme: namely, foreign business. At the same time, however, they engaged themselves more strongly on the domestic market in order to seek profit from day-to-day banking operations.

Here the bank was able to improve its position considerably from 1876 onwards, and unlike many of its competitors it truly prospered. For example, in 1879 its rival, the Internationale Bank in Hamburg, also went into liquidation. The expansion and cultivation of investment business, an extremely cautious company-flotation and issuing policy at home and abroad, confinement to low-risk transactions, and promotion of industrial export business created the conditions for a slow but steady upward development even in the crisis years until 1880. The bank's net profit increased from 1.4 million marks in 1875 to 6 million marks in 1880; profits from bills of exchange and interest ('classical banking business') went up from 2.3 million marks in 1875 to 3.5 million marks in 1888, and profits from commission payments (the so-called 'services' that account for so much of the bank's business today) increased from 1.5 million to 2.6 million marks over the same period.[81]

In 1876, with a balance sheet total of 190.5 million marks following the acquisition of the Berliner Bank-Verein and the Deutsche Union-Bank, the Deutsche Bank overtook the previous leader, the Disconto-Gesellschaft, with a balance of 136.1 million marks, to become the largest bank in Germany. In terms of balance sheet total, the Deutsche Bank continued to present higher figures than the Disconto-Gesellschaft in all years up to 1914, though of course at the time that criterion alone was not sufficient to define the size of a bank. In the eyes of contemporaries, the Disconto-Gesellschaft was still the leading German big bank, its tradition and its market position ensuring that it remained 'number one' in Germany. Carl Fürstenberg tells us how the 'absolute ruler' of the Disconto-Gesellschaft, Adolph von Hansemann, refused until his death in 1903 properly to acknowledge the rise of the Deutsche Bank. As the latter's balance sheet totals leapt ahead of those of the Disconto-Gesellschaft, Hansemann opined simply, in one of many conversations on the subject, that this was due to 'nothing but entry cancellations' – that is, counter-entries – not based on any real business.[82]

Prior to 1876, Hansemann had likewise consistently opposed giving the Deutsche Bank a position in the Prussia Consortium, a consortium for the emission of Prussian state loans and Reich loans, and in which the state-owned Prussian Seehandlung, the Disconto-Gesellschaft and Bleichröder were the leading participants. The Deutsche Bank was admitted in 1877 with a tiny 7.5 per cent quota, which it accepted with an ill grace. Not until 1899 was it able to demonstrate its increased issuing power by taking on and placing single-handed (without the aid of the Consortium) a Prussian loan in the amount of 125 million marks and a simultaneous imperial loan in the amount of 75 million marks. The Deutsche Bank thereby showed itself to be 'Germany's most powerful institution', as was said at the time.[83] And in 1896, in his survey of Berlin's joint stock banks, Paul Model described the position of the Deutsche Bank in the following terms: 'It is interesting to note how the bank, which today occupies the front rank among German banks beside the Disconto-Gesellschaft and has in many respects even overtaken its great rival, was at the time of its founding widely greeted with scorn and derision. No one then had any idea of the splendid development it was shortly to undergo!'[84] One of the leading banking journalists of the day, Alfred Lansburgh, editor of the journal *Die Bank*, similarly concluded in 1914 that since the turn of the century the Deutsche Bank had been the undisputed leader in Germany.[85] It is also interesting in this connection that in 1897 the Deutsche Bank share price for the first time topped that of Disconto-Gesellschaft shares.[86]

All of this had to do with head office. In the period up to 1914, the development of a network of branches was not a prime objective so far as the Deutsche Bank was concerned, any more than it was for the city's other big banks. All important transactions were conducted through head office in Berlin. After the first branches in Bremen and Hamburg (1871–72), it was not until 1886 that the Deutsche Bank opened another branch. That was in Frankfurt am Main, where it took over the business of the Frankfurter Bankverein, founded by Adelbert Delbrück in 1871. A Munich branch was added in 1892, and in 1901 the bank took advantage of the liquidation of the Leipziger Bank to open a branch in that city. These were joined in the same year by a branch in Dresden, which absorbed the deposit office that had existed there since 1889. This expansion extended to Bavaria with the establishment of a branch in Nuremberg in 1905 and a deposit office in Augsburg in the following year.

The growing industrial finance sector and participation in industrial companies made closer customer contact necessary, and this was scarcely possible without a local presence. Accordingly, beginning in the 1870s the Deutsche Bank purchased holdings in key regional banks in the principal centres of German industry and between 1897 and 1911 formed communities of interest with them. These were, in the Rhine–Ruhr industrial area, the Bergisch Märkische Bank in Elberfeld, the Duisburg-Ruhrorter Bank, and the Essener Credit-Anstalt; in the Silesian industrial area, the Schlesische Bankverein in Breslau (Wroclaw); in North Germany, the Hannoversche Bank; and in the Rhine–Neckar region, the Oberrheinische Bank and the Rheinische Creditbank, both in Mannheim, and the Württembergische Vereinsbank in Stuttgart. A series of smaller institutions in a wide variety of locations completed the system.[87]

The communities of interest resulted from the gradually increased share-holdings in provincial banks in the Deutsche Bank portfolio, and were highly advantageous for both parties concerned. They enabled the Deutsche Bank to penetrate key industrial areas while enjoying the benefits of special local characteristics and specific knowledge of the local customer structure. And the communities of interest gave the regional banks the capital backing of a major Berlin bank, because their own resources were no longer sufficient to cover the credit requirements of industry in the areas in which they did business. In the process, their outward independence was preserved. Most community of interest agreements contained arrangements about the pooling and distribution of profits as well as joint administrative guidelines. This administrative co-ordination usually consisted in an exchange of seats on each other's supervisory boards; only rarely did the 'dominant' bank demand a position on the managing board.

So far as the pre-1914 period is concerned, the communities of interest represented the first stage of the concentration process in the German banking industry, a process that took much the same course in all big banks. Subsequently, a second phase of concentration began in which Berlin big banks proceeded to merge with regional banks.[88] The beginning of this fresh wave of concentration was marked by the takeover of the Bergisch Märkische Bank, one of the largest and most reputable of all the regional banks, by the Deutsche Bank in 1914. Following a series of 'dishonoured loans', the managing board in Berlin had reached the conclusion that, while the Deutsche Bank had to help bear the risks of the regional bank's business policy, it had only very limited influence (through the supervisory board) on its decisions. It naturally had very much more influence over the business policy of its own branches. As a result of the merger with the Bergisch Märkische Bank, the latter's head office in Elberfeld and all its branches passed to the Deutsche Bank, which thus suddenly found itself in possession of an extensive branch network and superb customer contacts throughout the Rhine–Ruhr district. At the end of 1913, the Deutsche Bank had only eight domestic branches: in Bremen, Hamburg, Frankfurt am Main, Munich, Leipzig, Dresden, Wiesbaden and Nuremberg; it also had the three foreign branches in London, Constantinople and Brussels. As a result of mergers and new foundations, it now acquired an additional 38 branches (mainly in the Rhineland–Westphalia region but also in Saarbrücken, for example). In 1914, the Deutsche Bank also opened branches in Darmstadt, Hanau and Offenbach. It had taken the decisive step towards becoming a 'branch bank'.

1914 also marked a decisive point in that it was the year in which the Deutsche Bank abandoned the caution that had characterized its policy towards mergers and new branches for so long. By 1925 it had taken over other important regional joint stock banks with extensive branch networks as well as numerous private banks. This signified a switch to a policy that henceforth placed the emphasis on regional expansion.

II. Financing Industry

1. The Deutsche Bank and the development of the system of universal banking

When Friedrich Krupp founded his cast-steel works in Essen in 1811, he borrowed the starting capital he needed from his mother and his siblings. This very common, indeed at the time thoroughly customary, way of financing industry from the immediate family circle is strikingly documented in a letter that Therese

Krupp wrote to her father in May 1819, making a further request for a loan guarantee: 'My mother-in-law, who has already done so much for us, would be happy to put up this guarantee, but I know that owing to domestic circumstances she cannot and should not do so. I therefore beg you to be so good as to furnish the same, because there are no mortgages whatsoever on my husband's property, and I know he always paid you the interest on Varnhorst's capital promptly and will certainly see to it that you never need to advance the interest on the 12,000 thalers, because even now he owes my brother-in-law von Müller no interest.'[89]

Friedrich Krupp never applied to a bank, nor in the early years of the nineteenth century did banks play any more than the most minor role in financing industry. The banking scene was dominated at the time by private bankers, who mainly dealt in government loans. They hardly ever made a spontaneous offer of credit to people founding companies; conversely, it was rare for the latter to seek bank loans. The fact that going into debt was still regarded as immoral or at least dishonourable may also have had something to do with it.[90] Here again the example of Friedrich Krupp is revealing, for in 1824 his indebtedness to his father-in-law had reached such proportions that the latter took him to court to secure payment. As a result, Krupp not only had to sell the remainder of his property, including his house; he also lost all his civic offices and was struck off the list of Essen's 'merchants with rights',[91] the people who, on the basis of the General Law for the Prussian States (which now had validity in Essen, too), held commercial licences from the government.

When Krupp died in 1826, the tiny foundry was to all intents and purposes bankrupt. Therese Krupp did, however, manage to raise fresh loans, again mainly from within the family, in order to keep production going. Very soon her eldest son Alfred took over the management of the company. He was only 14 when his father died, but he had already been working in the factory for some time. For years to come the chief sources of the loans needed for investments remained family and friends. Not until 1834 did the firm of Friedrich Krupp have an account with the Herstatt bank in Cologne, and that came about through the agency of Krupp's cousin, Carl Friedrich von Müller. Around that time the first (mainly Cologne-based) banks began to lend money to steel works and coal-mine proprietors. However, banks were still very reluctant so far as lending money to industry was concerned. This is clear not only from the fact that business connections had to be mediated. The first loans were also in very modest amounts: 8,000 talers were all Krupp received from Herstatt in 1835, and the bank even demanded security for that. As time went on, the line of credit was extended, and when the Oppenheim bank granted a loan in 1849 the amount had already risen to 30,000 talers.

The year of revolutions, 1848, saw the foundation in Cologne of an institution that was prepared to grant industrial loans on an altogether larger scale. This was the A. Schaaffhausen'sche Bankverein, a reorganization of the private bank of Abraham Schaaffhausen, which together with the Herstatt and Oppenheim banks had begun to get involved in industrial business at a very early stage. When the A. Schaaffhausen bank ran into financial difficulties following the revolutionary events of March 1848, and was able to stave off collapse only by converting a large proportion of its liabilities into proprietary shares, the new Liberal government of Prussia feared a worsening of the crisis in the Rhineland. After all, a total of 170 companies employing 40,000 people would have been directly affected by a Schaaffhausen collapse. A key role in rescuing and restructuring the bank was played by the Aachen liberal, David Hansemann, later founder of the Disconto-Gesellschaft, who had become Prussian Minister of Finance in March 1848. He managed to get a licence for a joint stock company issued, a process that was finalized in August 1848. Only weeks later the revolution in Prussia met with failure, putting an end to the Liberal government's period of office. Subsequent Conservative governments rejected joint stock banks as being inscrutable and uncontrollable centres of economic power and approved no further licence applications. So until the Deutsche Bank was founded in 1870, the A. Schaaffhausen'sche Bankverein was Prussia's only joint stock bank.

The governments of the reactionary period, particularly that of Prussia, were of course also keen on economic change, not least in view of the state of their finances and the (potentially revolutionary) poverty of broad sections of their steadily growing populations, which under the conditions imposed by the existing social and economic order no longer found it possible to make ends meet. Consequently, in much of central Europe the period of political reaction became a time of economic change overthrowing every traditional criterion, as well as a time of dramatic economic growth. It was the true beginning of what we call the Industrial Revolution.

In the field of banking, which was becoming increasingly important in this connection, a significant impulse was provided around this time by the Société Générale de Crédit Mobilier, a Paris-based bank founded in 1852 that did not pursue industrial finance as a mere side-line, but placed it, programmatically and in practice, at the centre of its operation. As a finance company for industry, the Péreire brothers' Crédit Mobilier centralized all the credit operations necessary for floating large industrial companies: capitalization, the issue of stocks and shares, and the provision of long-term loans to maintain business operations. Although strictly speaking the Société Générale des Pays-Bas pour favoriser l'Industrie nationale (founded in 1822) was the first bank to operate as a commercial bank,[92] the Crédit Mobilier de Paris is rightly regarded as the true prototype of the later universal banks, because like them it combined several types of business (deposits, exchange and investment) in a single institution. For a long time, in fact, commercial banks operating in this field were known, after the joint stock bank founded by Emil and Isaac Péreire, as 'Crédit Mobilier banks'. The Péreires' system of finance was planned on an European scale from the outset, aiming to concentrate available capital in large amounts and direct it via a network of financial centres into industrial flotations: 'We must ensure that these institutions retain the freedom to adapt to the particular requirements of industry in each country, but at the same time we must be careful to avoid the danger of isolation ... In this way we shall steer capital towards where it will be most useful and give it, when a particular stage has been reached, the broadest and most influential scope.'[93]

The aim of the founders of Crédit Mobilier was to make adequate finance available to industrial companies and thus to promote industrialization. The bank was conceived as a joint stock company and operated as an agency for the collection and focusing of capital that could then be made available to companies in the form of long-term credit. The broad capital base also made it possible to issue stocks and to underwrite and place securities.

These forms of business did not really represent anything new; what was new was that, unlike the major private banks of the Haute Banque, which mainly dealt in government loans, Crédit Mobilier de Paris placed them at the centre of its operation. Claiming adherence to the theories of the proto-socialist Saint-Simon, who had given banks a key role in the non-revolutionary transformation of society, the Péreire brothers wished to create a bank that would be instrumental in steering the economy. As they saw it, the formation of cartels would exclude competition, and the banks would then control the economy. At the same time, the workers, as the true productive class, were through share ownership to participate in the means of production. The new type of bank also represented an assault on the supremacy of the Parisian Rothschild bank, in which the Péreire brothers had previously worked as clerks. This earned the brothers' undertaking the support (worth a great deal of publicity) of Napoleon III, who regarded the Haute Banque as a bastion of his political enemies on the right. Rothschild, of course, took up the idea very quickly and founded his own 'Crédit Mobilier banks', including the Österreichische Credit-Anstalt in Vienna. At the same time the Rothschild bank attempted to use the powerful political 'clout' it possessed in individual countries to prevent the Péreire brothers from founding corresponding institutions (as it succeeded in doing in, for example, the cases of Belgium, the Netherlands and Russia).

The influence of Saint-Simon's ideas was largely confined to France. However, the Péreire brothers' basically Saint-Simonian concept met with a huge response and was quickly imitated in many European countries. This was particularly true of Germany, where the Darmstädter Bank für Handel und Industrie, founded in 1853, was virtually a straight copy of the Crédit Mobilier de Paris. The Berliner Handels-Gesellschaft, founded in 1856 as a limited partnership with shares, and the Disconto-Gesellschaft, which was converted into a limited partnership in the same year, were other so-called 'Crédit Mobilier banks'. The extent of this first wave of joint stock bank flotations is clear from the fact that, in the years 1855–56, 15 such institutions were founded in Germany alone.[94]

Admittedly, there were also massive setbacks. The severe economic crisis of 1857 put an end to what had in some instances been exaggerated expectations, and led to most of the newly founded banks switching their main capital issues back to such traditional securities as railway bonds and government loans. Many of the new banks also turned out to be underfunded but at the same time overdynamic, often showing blind faith in the perpetual continuance of specific economic and political conditions. The warnings of more sober contemporaries, which had often been irresponsibly brushed aside, received dramatic confirmation when in 1867 the great prototype of the new class of bank, the Crédit Mobilier de Paris, virtually collapsed because of mismanagement by the Péreire brothers (even if final liquidation did not ensue until 1902).[95]

Regardless of this, the fresh economic boom that began in the mid-1860s and culminated in the so-called *Gründerjahre* of 1870–73 led to a further wave of company flotations and issues of capital by banks in the industrial sector. Concomitantly with this, a whole series of new joint stock banks were founded that operated as commercial banks, including the Deutsche Bank, the Dresdner Bank, the Bayerische Vereinsbank and the Commerzbank. Just how risky and economically sensitive capital issues continued to be was made abundantly clear in 1873, when the collapse of numerous stock markets drastically reduced the value of new foundations, bankrupting many of the newly floated banks.[96] One result of this experience was that the surviving institutions again turned increasingly to more secure lines of business, principally dealing in government and railway securities.

None of them, however, completely gave up financing industry by granting loans and starting up companies. Unlike in Britain, for example, where the expansion of enterprise was made possible by direct injections of private capital, in the industrialization of Germany the banks played a very prominent role. While a distinction became established in Britain between deposit banks on the one hand and institutions acting as issuing and finance banks on the other, banks in Germany and France operated in both fields and developed into universal banks. In France, following a banking crisis in the 1880s, this mixed system of banking was abandoned in favour of a division of labour between deposit banks and investment banks, but in Germany it has remained intact until today.

Even in Germany, however, the debate about the advantages or dangers of combining banking services in this way has never let up.[97] It has flared particularly in times of crisis, with many vehement assaults on 'the power of the banks' and the possibility of their using seats on supervisory boards and large shareholdings to control whole branches of industry. Up to now, however, the state has never, as we have seen, intervened decisively in the universal banking system.

The first commercial banks saw their function as being on the one hand to mediate between capital that was looking for something to invest in and industries in search of capital. In this, while participating in the foundation of new enterprises, they nevertheless placed the shares of new companies directly with private investors rather than issuing their own bonds. On the other hand, they offered the whole range of regular banking services. This was because the connection between the banks and industry was to be based not on the issuing business, but rather on the current account relationship. This guaranteed a steady flow of capital and created a permanent connection with the companies concerned.[98]

As well as these joint stock banks of the first generation, the second generation of bank foundations that followed in the 1870s played a crucial part in shaping the system of universal banking. In this, the Deutsche Bank played an outstanding role. Although, as has been shown, the institution was originally conceived as a purely specialist bank for financing foreign trade, its articles of association provided from the outset for the performance of 'banking transactions of all kinds'. The founders themselves were aware that foreign business, particularly in the difficult initial stages, would have to be coupled with banking activities in the domestic market. The fact remains that, whereas in the early 1870s nearly all banks fell victim to 'flotation fever', the managing directors of the Deutsche Bank showed impressive restraint, their original declaration of intent operating as a salutary brake in this respect. They confined themselves to floating the Deutsche Jute-Spinnerei und Weberei AG in Meissen in 1872 and to participating in the flotation of the United States Direct Cable Company in the following year. Both companies were unsuccessful: the latter had to be wound up with a loss, and the former was unable to pay a dividend until 1880. Subsequently, the Deutsche Bank participated in no further small industrial enterprises until 1879, confining itself to underwriting lower-risk national and local government loans and railway bonds.[99] The vast majority of business in the early years was made up by the granting of short-term commercial loans and the acceptance of deposits (i.e. similarly short-term investments). In its early years, the Deutsche Bank thus corresponded more closely to the British type of commercial bank than to the universal bank that was becoming increasingly characteristic of Germany in particular.

After 1875 – the climax of the *Gründerkrise* – the Deutsche Bank did in fact change its business policy and, in order to expand its domestic business, also went into conducting issuing and finance business. However, this change of strategy, proposed by Georg Siemens, was at first vigorously opposed.[100] A group of Bremen shareholders led by a lawyer named Johannes Wilckens lodged a particularly vigorous protest against the management's plans. They demanded a reduction of the share capital of the Deutsche Bank by one-third to 10 million talers.[101]

The managing directors thereupon sought the backing of the administrative board. In a memorandum dated 26 October 1875 they outlined the development of the Deutsche Bank hitherto and set out its prospects for the future.[102] They warned against reducing the bank's capital, saying that this would be 'the biggest policy mistake it would be possible to make'. As a result of the stock market collapse and the subsequent economic crisis, they saw few possibilities, currently, for the bank to come closer to its original objective. The bank's own resources were too small to allow it to operate solely on the basis of exchange transactions. It was therefore necessary to develop the deposit side even further. To enable the bank to pay the interest involved, it was 'natural' that such deposit business must be complemented by 'issuing business in respect of high-interest securities'. 'A well-connected big bank will of course always be better placed to secure underwriting deals than smaller banks of the middle rank whose efficiency is not apparent for all to see.'

The directors already very clearly foresaw the imminent process of concentration in banking and predicted that 'only big banks with plenty of capital will be able to derive real advantages from the change in our banking industry'. The argument was intended primarily to prevent a reduction in the share capital of the Deutsche Bank, but at the same time it clearly revealed the kind of objective the directors were pursuing: namely, to transform the bank from being a purely commercial bank to being a universal bank that, in addition to bills of exchange and current account business, also transacted, on a discount basis, the issuing of government and industrial securities.

This change of direction was discreetly announced in the 1876 business report under the heading 'Domestic Business': 'The increased strength of our company as a result of these circumstances [the reference is to the takeovers of the Berliner Bank-Verein and the Deutsche Union-Bank] has given us the ability to participate to a greater extent than heretofore in underwriting deals of our own, and we intend to continue to do so in future.' The report goes on, however, to stress yet again that the Deutsche Bank will remain a merchant bank seeking to concentrate on granting short-term loans. Any financing of industry should be restricted to 'provisional transactions in solid investments that without adversely affecting capital liquidity nevertheless guarantee a high yield in interest'. The object, besides the hoped-for yield in interest, was to offer the bank's industrial customers a comprehensive range of banking services and thus strengthen their connection with the institution.[103]

2. The move into flotation business

In other words, the Deutsche Bank established its relations with industry not primarily through financing company flotations, but by granting loans on overdraft and various forms of short-term credit.[104] The issue of stocks and shares subsequently constituted the 'keystone of the mighty arch of industrial relationships between banks and industry'.[105] The issue of bonds against commission, unlike the risky business of floating companies, actually represented one of the traditional instruments of finance. Until then, however, it had been reserved for public debtors (national and local governments) and for railway companies. The first bond in respect of an industrial company was issued in 1874 when the firm of Friedrich Krupp, which has since become one of the largest concerns in

Germany, took out a loan in the amount of 30 million marks at 6 per cent with an 86 per cent takeover price and a 110 per cent repayment rate. Previously, Alfred Krupp had financed his investments through the medium of short-term loans, which banks had cancelled following the crash. It was a highly precarious situation as far as the steel company was concerned, and the loan was issued in order to stave off collapse. To offset the inferior security of industrial loans as compared with public loans, Krupp was obliged to mortgage his entire steel works. This addition of mortgage security to the classical loan soon gained acceptance in connection with the issue of industrial bonds as well.[106] The underwriting on the occasion of the issue of the 1874 bond was performed by the Seehandlung, which since it was a national body was tantamount to the loan being guaranteed by Prussia.

By 1879 Krupp's financial situation had so far improved that it was able to redeem the old bond with a new issue on more favourable terms.[107] This came to the still unrepaid amount of the first loan, namely 22.5 million marks, with a takeover price of 102 per cent, repayment at 110 per cent and interest at 5 per cent. The annual amortization payment was substantially reduced as a result of a repayment plan extended by six years. The underwriting in respect of this second loan was performed by the Deutsche Bank, which was thus able to establish a connection with the Krupp steel business. A further reason why the deal was a particular success for the Deutsche Bank was that the bank contrived to cut out its greatest rival: where the Disconto-Gesellschaft had occupied second place in the consortium for the 1874 loan, five years later it had no place at all.[108]

In much the same way, Siemens managed in the years that followed to strengthen the connections that the bank had made with the jute industry when it set up the Deutsche Jute-Spinnerei und Weberei AG. Relations with other branches of industry, particularly the rising chemical industry, also became closer. In 1881 the Deutsche Bank helped to underwrite a 5 per cent bond by the Aktien-Gesellschaft für Anilinfabrikation in Berlin-Treptow in the amount of 2.5 million marks. Two years later it led a consortium that was to list the shares of the company formerly named Friedrich Bayer & Co., which was founded in Elberfeld in 1881, on the Berlin Stock Exchange; this it eventually did in 1885. Subsequent Bayer bond and share issues were also handled by the Deutsche Bank acting alone. Completing the bank's involvement in the rapidly growing chemical industry, in 1886 it underwrote a share issue by the Badische Anilin & Soda-Fabrik (BASF) of Mannheim-Ludwigshafen. This shareholding developed into an ever-closer relationship, and in the 1890s the Deutsche Bank eventually became one of BASF's house banks.[109]

From the early 1880s onwards, then, the Deutsche Bank gradually extended its involvement in industrial business. Eventually it was involved in floating joint stock companies that evolved into multinational concerns. It accompanied the rise of the steel tubing works that grew out of a revolutionary discovery by the

Mannesmann brothers, and it lent special support to the development of the German electrical industry.

3. AEG and Siemens

The discovery and harnessing of electrical power was a key element in the scientific, technical and economic progress made in the second half of the nineteenth century. The initial area of application was telegraphy, the first telegram having been successfully transmitted from Baltimore to Washington in 1844. The telegraph and to an even greater extent the telephone revolutionized communications, giving rise to a new branch of industry concerned with the manufacture of cables, insulators, instruments and appliances.[110] Large-scale procurement of raw materials and production of goods became necessary only after it had become possible to exploit for practical purposes not only the weak current used for telegraphy but also heavy-current technology. The decisive breakthrough in this area was made by Werner von Siemens in 1866 with the discovery of the principle of the dynamo, which made it possible to convert mechanical into electrical energy. The spread of electric lighting from the 1880s onwards led to a huge boom in the electrical industry. Already existing companies such as Siemens & Halske (founded in 1847) and the Schuckert-Werke in Nuremberg (founded in 1873) now expanded, and there was a further wave of industrial flotations. The most important company to come into existence around this time was Emil Rathenau's Deutsche Edison-Gesellschaft für angewandte Elektricität (German Edison Company for Applied Electricity), founded in 1883 and renamed AEG in 1887.[111] The result of the flotation boom was that by 1895 the electrical branch numbered not only eight large concerns but more than 1,300 smaller enterprises. From 1900 on, however, the majority of the small and medium-sized companies fell victim to the process of concentration, and by as early as 1910 three-quarters of electrical production was in the hands of the two market leaders, Siemens and AEG. The new industry quickly achieved outstanding importance in Germany, and before the First World War the German Reich led the world in the production of electrotechnical goods with a 34.9 per cent share of the market.

This sudden onset of rapid growth and the enormous capital requirement of the branch made it virtually impossible for companies to expand by their own efforts. The banks were therefore very soon crucially involved in building up and extending the electrical industry. The fact that the Deutsche Bank played a particularly significant part in this was surely due not least to the family tie (they were second cousins) between the spokesman of the managing board and the founder of Siemens & Halske. The development of the electrical industry had been placed in the hands of Georg Siemens from the outset. After all, before he even came to the bank he had worked for Siemens & Halske, conducting negotiations regarding the construction of the Indo-European telegraph line.

Siemens & Halske, however, being like many of the leading industrial enterprises a family firm, made very little call on the services of banks at first.

The Deutsche Bank's initial involvement was therefore in the creation of AEG, which soon became the great rival of Siemens & Halske. The founder of AEG, Emil Rathenau, became interested in the electrical industry in the late 1870s after his mechanical engineering company had failed in the *Gründerkrise*. In 1881 Edison's electric light bulb was presented for the first time in Europe at the Paris international exhibition. It represented a major advance over previous electric lighting methods, and Rathenau determined to market the invention in Germany. For this he not only needed the exploitation rights to the patent for Germany, which were controlled by the French-based Compagnie Continentale Edison; he also required extensive finance. To raise this, in 1882 Rathenau floated a market-research company with a starting capital of 225,000 marks intended mainly to promote domestic electrification.

As early as March 1883 he was able to found the Deutsche Edison-Gesellschaft für angewandte Elektricität (DEG) with a starting capital of 5 million marks. An agreement was reached with Siemens & Halske that recognized DEG's exclusive right to construct lighting systems and produce electric light bulbs using the Edison process. DEG undertook for its part to purchase all machines, apparatus and materials for the construction of lighting systems not directly covered by Edison Group patents from Siemens & Halske. Four-fifths of the share capital of DEG was underwritten by the Nationalbank für Deutschland and by the Landau and Sulzbach banks; Emil Rathenau also took out a major holding himself. To begin with, he was also the sole managing director. Not until the end of 1883 was Oskar von Miller (who had organized the International Electricity Exhibition in Munich the year before) appointed additionally to the managing board.

Until that point, the Deutsche Bank had yet to become financially involved in the electrical industry; in fact, when the Edison-Gesellschaft was founded, Siemens had specifically declined any participation by the Deutsche Bank, following consultation with Werner Siemens. It can surely be assumed that Georg Siemens and hence the management of the Deutsche Bank followed the growth of the new industry attentively.[112] However, the bank did not agree to become financially involved until the Edison-Gesellschaft ran into difficulties only a few years after its founding.

Meanwhile, the terms on which DEG's agreements with the Compagnie Continentale on the one hand and Siemens & Halske on the other were concluded had changed in certain key respects, with the result that DEG was disadvantageously bound to a partner by contract. Also the Städtische Electricitäts-Werke AG (Municipal Electricity Works), a DEG subsidiary that was to develop Berlin's power supply, failed to earn as much profit as expected. With capital of only 3 million marks, the company was unable to meet the commitments it had entered into with the city. Increasing that capital would have seriously overstretched the means of the parent company, because DEG itself had a starting capital of only 5 million marks. In this situation, Georg Siemens worked out a solution with the parties concerned that led eventually, at the Edison-Gesellschaft's general meeting of 23 May 1887, to DEG being refloated as the Allgemeine Electricitäts-Gesellschaft (AEG) (General Electric Company). It was the Deutsche Bank's first successful industrial flotation.

The objects of the reflotation were to get out of the agreements with the Edison Group and also to rearrange the firm's connections with the Städtische Electricitäts-Werke as well as with Siemens & Halske. To extend the capital base, it was decided to increase the share capital from 5 million to 12 million marks.[113] Siemens & Halske took a holding of 1 million marks; the remaining shares, to the value of 6 million marks, were underwritten by a financial consortium under the joint leadership of the Delbrück Leo & Co. bank and the Deutsche Bank, which also handled the accounting. The two leaders of the consortium subscribed for holdings of 1.7 and 1.9 million marks respectively. Other members of the consortium were the Berlin bank of Jacob Landau (1.125 million marks), the Frankfurt bank of Gebr. Sulzbach (675,000 marks) and the Berliner Handels-Gesellschaft, with a holding worth 600,000 marks.[114] In October the consortium offered its shares for public subscription.[115]

As a shareholder and member of the banking consortium, the Deutsche Bank received a seat on the supervisory board of AEG. Initially, Georg Siemens deputized for Adelbert Delbrück, who took the chair, but in 1890 he replaced him. Beyond that, the details of the relationships between the consortium of banks and AEG were governed by an underwriting agreement in accordance with the national and international conventions of the day. In it the company undertook to do its banking business exclusively through the consortial banks: that is, to maintain current accounts with them and to grant them preferential rights in connection with future share issues. The members of the consortium thus became house banks to AEG. As far as banks were concerned, underwriting agreements meant a chance of binding the company to them in respect of other business as well. Such agreements were particularly important with respect to assessing and hence containing what was often, in corporate financing, the very high level of risk, because through their current account connections banks were kept constantly informed about the state of the company.[116] Usually, though, the first result was a long-lasting current account connection between the company and the bank, to which the company then also turned when investments or expansions needed financing. In this way, an ever denser web of relations developed between the two parties over the course of time.[117]

At general meetings, banks often had access to larger blocks of votes than their shareholdings actually warranted. This was the result of the deposited shares voting right that gradually gained acceptance after 1870 (though not enough research has yet been done into exactly how this came about).[118] Even without the express consent of small shareholders, banks often exercised, at general meetings, the voting rights arising out of shares that they held on deposit. The 1884 revision of the Corporation Law had banned this practice, as a result of which, of course, often no more than between 5 and 20 per cent of share capital was actually represented at general meetings.

Emil Rathenau was afraid this might happen at the general meeting of the Edison-Gesellschaft that was meant to approve the reflotation of the company as AEG. In order to ensure that a quorate majority was present, he asked the consortium banks 'to agree to represent, at no cost, those shareholders who intended to vote in favour of the agenda'.[119] It was the first documented use of the deposited shares voting right. The reaction of the banker Jacob Landau makes it clear that the practice was not uncontroversial. He initially rejected Rathenau's proposal because he was afraid of being accused of representing only his own interests rather than those of shareholders.[120] Eventually, however, Rathenau's proposal was adopted. The Hamburg shareholder Felix Friedemann, for example, asked the Deutsche Bank to exercise his right to vote in respect of shares to the value of 10,000 marks.[121] Towards the end of the century, big banks began to enshrine the deposited shares voting right in their general terms of business;[122] as far as the Deutsche Bank is concerned, such a provision is first documented in 1900.[123]

Even beyond the purely technical transaction of banking business, the Deutsche Bank supported the interests of AEG. For example, Steinthal sought to play the role of mediator when in November 1887, only six months after the conclusion of the new co-operation agreement, fresh differences arose between AEG and Siemens & Halske.[124] Negotiations were even put in hand regarding cancellation of the agreement, though these did not come to anything. The agreement was to survive for a few more years, in fact, but tensions between the business partners continued to grow to the point of personal attacks. The co-operation agreement between the two electrical concerns was finally cancelled in 1894, only two years after Werner von Siemens's death. The one-time partners had finally become bitter rivals.[125]

The Deutsche Bank's involvement in AEG became something of a problem when the successors of Werner von Siemens started to pursue a different financial policy. Where the founder had run the firm as a purely family business, his successors, wishing to raise additional outside capital, naturally turned first to the Deutsche Bank. The bank had to decide between the rivals, because it could scarcely offer its services as house bank (and hence as adviser) to both of the two giants of the electrical industry simultaneously. A decision was finally made in favour of Siemens & Halske, and in a letter to Rathenau dated 7 January 1897 Georg Siemens resigned his position as chairman of the supervisory board of AEG; he withdrew from the board altogether in July. Siemens's role as financial adviser to Emil Rathenau was assumed by the proprietor of the Berliner Handels-Gesellschaft, Carl Fürstenberg. Although the Deutsche Bank also withdrew from the consortium, not all connections were finally severed. However, to avoid any conflict of interest, Siemens no longer handled relations with AEG himself, but asked Arthur Gwinner (who had joined the managing board of the Deutsche Bank in 1894) to take care of them.[126]

AEG and Siemens & Halske, which between them dominated the electrical industry around the turn of the century, represented two stages in Germany's industrialization as far as their corporate development was concerned. AEG had been founded in 1887 as a joint stock company with a broad capital base financed purely by the banks. Forty years previously, Werner Siemens had borrowed the 7,000 talers of starting capital with which he set up the telegraph construction agency Siemens & Halske from his cousin Johann Georg Siemens, father of the future Deutsche Bank spokesman. While the founder lived, the company remained in family ownership, although it was clear that a broader capital base would be required at some time in the future. In fact it was in October 1892, only months after Werner von Siemens's death, that his sons Arnold and Wilhelm borrowed their first outside capital in the form of a mortgage-secured loan of 10 million marks at 4.5 per cent. Siemens & Halske needed the funds to avoid losing its market lead finally to AEG, which with its flotation and expansion policy was steadily closing the gap that separated it from the older company. The danger of Siemens & Halske losing its position as number one in the field had been strikingly illustrated in the previous year when, in connection with the Electrotechnical Exhibition in Frankfurt, AEG had succeeded for the first time in transmitting power over a distance of 175 kilometres from the hydroelectric power station at Lauffen on the Neckar to the exhibition site.

It was the almost natural consequence of the Deutsche Bank director Georg Siemens's family and friendly relations with the proprietors of Siemens & Halske that the Deutsche Bank headed the consortium charged with placing the electrical company's bond issue. However, a policy of expansion on the AEG model did not become possible until Siemens & Halske had changed in the summer of 1897 from being a limited partnership to being a joint stock company. It was only from that point on that Georg Siemens felt he had to decide between the rival companies.

Even after Siemens & Halske's conversion to a joint stock company, the majority of shares and hence the power of decision as to future business policy remained in the hands of the family. Whereas in 1892 the firm had had access to funds of its own amounting to 24 million marks,[127] after the conversion to a joint stock company it had capital in the amount of 35 million marks, which by 1900 had been gradually increased to 54.5 million marks.[128] At the time of the conversion in 1897, the Deutsche Bank took shares worth 1.1 million marks, and in the following year, when the company raised an additional 5 million marks in capital, it acquired further shares worth 2 million marks. As yet the Deutsche Bank was the only financial institution involved in these transactions, because so long as the Siemens family held the majority of shares it was able to dispense with the services of a banking consortium.[129] This changed only in 1898, with the issue of a bond in the amount of 20 million marks.[130]

The biggest project that the Deutsche Bank implemented in conjunction with Siemens & Halske was the construction of Berlin's surface and underground railway, which was initiated by Georg Siemens on the bank's behalf and completed after his death by Max Steinthal.[131] The Deutsche Bank joined the Gesellschaft für elektrische Hoch- und Untergrundbahnen (Company for Electrical Surface and Underground Railways) in 1897. The idea was not a new one. Back in 1880 Werner Siemens had planned to build a tramway on the New York model through the Friedrichstrasse. Eleven years were to pass, however, before he was able to present the authorities with a plan that was ripe for execution. Meanwhile, an east–west connection had been conceived, part of which was to run underground.

The Deutsche Bank also acted as adviser and intermediary when in the early years of the twentieth century the electrical industry plunged into deep crisis and various mergers were mooted. On the basis of their knowledge of the people and institutions involved, the Deutsche Bank directors Steinthal, Mankiewitz and Gwinner argued for an amalgamation of Siemens & Halske with the Schuckert works, which duly came about in 1903.[132] Siemens-Schuckert and AEG grew into the market leaders of the German electrical industry during this period, though for a while it looked as if Berlin's Bergmann Elektricitäts-Werke AG might establish itself as a third major contender.[133] Bergmann began to produce steam turbines in 1904, and in 1908 it set up its own cable factory. Between 1900 and 1913 its balance sheet total rose from 10.7 million to 103.9 million marks. Despite this rapid expansion and the extensive investment it involved, over the same period Bergmann paid an average dividend of 18 per cent. This led the company in 1911–12 into potentially fatal liquidity problems. As Bergmann's house bank, the Deutsche Bank led the financial restructuring, and 23 million marks' worth of new shares were issued on the Berlin Stock Exchange. Both Siemens-Schuckert and AEG hoped at that moment to secure their own positions by taking Bergmann over. The success of Siemens-Schuckert in immediately acquiring a major shareholding was undoubtedly due to its Deutsche Bank connection. Legally speaking, Bergmann continued to exist as an independent concern, but in practice it was controlled by Siemens-Schuckert, which appointed the chairman of the board of managing directors and had a seat on the supervisory board.

4. Mannesmann

In addition to the giants of the rapidly developing electrical industry, it was above all Mannesmann in which the Deutsche Bank became more and more heavily involved. The close relationship that the bank maintained with Mannesmann arose out of the financial difficulties in which the company Deutsch-

Österreichische Mannesmannröhren-Werke AG had found itself not long after its establishment. The object of the company was the industrial exploitation of an invention by the brothers Max and Reinhard Mannesmann. They had discovered a process of using oblique rolling to produce tubing from a block of steel without a weld. Previously, steel tubes had usually been welded together from sheet steel, which under tough operating conditions often led to tubes cracking at the weld and hence to boiler explosions that not infrequently cost lives. The sole possibility of avoiding the weld was represented by tubes made from cast steel. However, not only were these very costly to manufacture, but because of their great weight and susceptibility to shock, they gave rise to considerable problems of their own. Clearly, there was a need for a seamless metal tube.

In 1886 the Mannesmann brothers began to exploit their invention industrially. Rolling mills were built in their home town of Remscheid, in Bous on the River Saar, in Komotau in Bohemia (today's Chomutov in the Czech Republic; Tr.) and in Landore in south Wales that operated with the Mannesmann patents. Early investors included, apart from the Cologne industrialist Eugen Langen, above all Werner von Siemens, himself an engineer and inventor, who until his death remained a fatherly friend to the Mannesmanns and who managed to gain his brothers' support for the invention as well as that of his cousin Georg and with him the financial power of the Deutsche Bank.

This became necessary in 1890 when, with the invention of the so-called 'pilgrim step process' (*Pilgerschrittverfahren*), a method was found that in combination with oblique rolling finally made it possible to manufacture the requisite qualities. However, the financial resources of the Mannesmann family were exhausted. Not even Langen and Siemens were willing to make further investments, the works having so far shown nothing but losses. Other financiers would now have to be found to convert the Mannesmann works into a joint stock company. At the request of Werner von Siemens, the joint stock company was duly floated by the Deutsche Bank, Eugen Langen having failed to win acceptance for his proposal that the deal should be done with Schaaffhausen and the Disconto-Gesellschaft, two banks with longer traditions and undoubtedly greater experience in industrial business at the time.[134] The Deutsche Bank hesitated at first and called for detailed expert reports.[135] Eventually, it agreed to the operation on condition that, instead of a consortium, the Deutsche Bank should be in sole charge, and that it grant only a small number of sub-participations.[136] The bank was going out on a limb here because, in addition to the euphoric reports, there were one or two warning voices. Georg Siemens was well aware of the risk, writing to his father on the day of the flotation: 'After much to-ing and fro-ing, the Mannesmann business has finally materialized. Let's hope it turns out reasonably well and we do not make fools of ourselves.'[137]

On 16 July 1890, then, the Deutsch-Österreichische Mannesmannröhren-Werke was founded with what for the time was the substantial starting capital of 35 million marks. Not all of this was paid up in cash because the inventors received bonus stock worth approximately 17.5 million marks for their patents (14 million), for licences already issued (2 million), and for the Komotau works (just under 1.5 million).[138] Only 12.01 million marks were paid in cash, with a 20 per cent premium being transferred to a reserve fund. A further 5.49 million marks were allowed for the tubing works in Remscheid, Komotau and Bous, which passed into the possession of the joint stock company. The Deutsche Bank took 3 million marks' worth of shares for its own portfolio and passed the rest on to sub-participants.[139] It had made a wise choice because initially the invention failed to fulfil the expectations placed in it. The oblique-rolling process turned out to be less than perfect as yet, and it was still not possible to manufacture thin-walled tubing in the larger diameters. Further cost-intensive experiments needed to be undertaken.

In the circumstances, there could be no question of the company paying appropriate interest on its starting capital. Not until 1893 was the 'pilgrim step process' considered far enough advanced technically to make economic exploitation a possibility. Nevertheless, the company's financial and administrative difficulties made some restructuring inevitable if collapse was to be avoided. The two brothers, Max and Reinhard Mannesmann, had concentrated too much on the technical problems of manufacture, neglecting the commercial side. The Deutsche Bank feared for its reputation (as Werner von Siemens did for his), which this loss-making business threatened to damage. The Mannesmann brothers finally agreed to have Julius Franken appointed alongside them as commercial director.[140]

However, this alone was not enough. It became necessary to reorganize the entire management of the company and the way in which it was financed. This led to tensions between the inventors and the investors, led by the Deutsche Bank, which centred initially around the question of a successor to the chairman of the supervisory board, Werner von Siemens, who died on 6 December 1892. Agreement was eventually reached on a compromise candidate, namely Siemens's previous vice-chairman, the banker Karl von der Heydt; he was given two new vice-chairmen, Eugen Langen and Max Steinthal. The latter, who had been a managing director of the Deutsche Bank since 1873, had represented the bank on the company's supervisory board since its inception. Steinthal now became the mastermind behind the restructuring.

In order to reduce the company's capital stock, the Mannesmanns were asked to return a substantial portion of their bonus shares. While the family was prepared to shoulder some of the financial losses, it was unwilling to accept the reduction in its voting power associated with returning the shares, and the resultant diminution of its influence on the company's affairs. Under an agreement that was eventually signed on 2 February 1893, the Mannesmann brothers undertook to return without reimbursement an initial 1,000 shares with a nominal value of 1 million marks and beyond that (irrespective of how the

business developed in the years 1893 to 1895) further shares to the value of
between 6.5 and almost 10 million marks. However, this capital reduction was
to be achieved 'by reducing the nominal value of the shares from 1,000 to 200
marks.[141] The first 1,000 shares were indeed returned by the brothers, but all
further agreements made in this connection became the object of litigation that
dragged on for years.[142]

The simplest method of restructuring the company financially was thus
blocked, making it necessary to turn to production and administration instead.
To reduce the Mannesmann brothers' influence over the company, in February
1893 the supervisory board appointed a technical commission, the powers of
which then steadily increased at the expense of the management. The commission
began by introducing extensive cost-cutting measures: experimental technical
projects were cancelled, the number of personnel was reduced, production was
concentrated on those items that earned a profit, and the head office was moved
away from the grand Pariser Platz address in Berlin to Düsseldorf. As a result of
this curtailment of their powers, the inventors finally quit the managing board
in October 1893 and moved over to the supervisory board. Even from there,
Max Mannesmann tried to retain some influence over the company,[143] while his
brother turned his attention to fresh projects in America.

Although the 1894/95 business report for the first time showed a net profit of
17,000 marks, in its report for the following financial year the management
played down the hope 'that henceforth all obstacles in the way of an economic
exploitability of our patents might be behind us'.[144] As a further restructuring
measure, it was planned to persuade the Mannesmann brothers to return bonus
shares in the (nominal) value of 9 million marks, and thus consolidate the
remaining share capital in a proportion of one to three to a value of 8.33 million
marks.[145] Finally, the decision was made to reduce the asset side of the balance
sheet by 8.1 million marks in respect of the Mannesmann family's unreturned
shares and also to cut the balance sheet value of the patents drastically from
11.5 to 2 million marks. The resultant adverse balance amounted to nearly
18 million marks.

In the years that followed, the company's financial convalescence was helped
along by a growing demand in the steel-tubing market. In 1896/97, sales were up
by more than 50 per cent compared with the previous year, and net profit after
deductions came to 1.3 million marks. This meant that the debt burden could
gradually be reduced and a start finally made on the long-overdue construction
of a new factory in Düsseldorf.[146] In 1900 a settlement was reached at last
between the Deutsch-Österreichische Mannesmannröhren-Werke and the brothers Max and Reinhard Mannesmann.[147] It led to a reduction in the company's
share capital of 6.2 million marks, making it possible at the same time to bring
the balance sheet loss down to 8.4 million marks. The share capital was again
reduced by 2.5 million marks in 1904/05 as a result of the repurchase of shares
for almost 1.5 million, which allowed a further million to be credited to the

profit-and-loss account. In the 1905/06 financial year the restructuring of the company was completed, and for the first time a 5 per cent dividend was distributed. In the following year the dividend was already up to 12 per cent, and in the years thereafter it stabilized at a rather high level.

The restructuring complete, Steinthal largely withdrew from active management of the company's affairs. This is also clear from the correspondence he conducted over the period 1900 to 1919 with Nikolaus Eich, Julius Franken's successor as chairman of the managing board (Franken having died in 1899). Eich kept Steinthal informed and sought advice, though without ever losing the initiative as far as business policy was concerned. Steinthal welcomed this development because he lacked technical expertise himself and had no very precise knowledge of the steel-tubing market. 'The impulse for such measures as increases in capital, the issue of bonds, or the granting of credit did not and presumably could not come from the bank, even if Steinthal may have hinted at the implementation of such measures in conversation. The backing of the Deutsche Bank was more important than its actual or potential influence.'[148]

As a result of the flotations of the major joint stock companies AEG and Mannesmann, and the conversion of Siemens & Halske into a joint stock company, the Deutsche Bank was able to make something of a name for itself in industrial financing. In all three instances, the fact that a business connection with the Deutsche Bank came about was closely bound up with Georg Siemens's relationship with his cousin, the founder of Siemens & Halske. It was through him that the spokesman of the managing board of the Deutsche Bank acquired his familiarity with the burgeoning electrical industry and was quickly persuaded to participate in setting up AEG. Following the death of the founder of Siemens & Halske, the Deutsche Bank carried out the conversion of the firm into a joint stock company. The Deutsche Bank's connection with Mannesmann also came about through Werner von Siemens.

Apart from this involvement, the bank was, as set out above, wary of industrial flotations at first.[149] As far as the coal and steel industries of the Ruhr were concerned, the Deutsche Bank initially took an indirect approach, co-operating with the established regional banks already *in situ*.[150] In 1897 a community of interest was formed with Bergisch Märkische Bank in Elberfeld. After the two institutions had been collaborating for around ten years, the Deutsche Bank took over about three-quarters of its partner's share capital in exchange for shares of its own. In this way, even if the bank did not conduct local business in its own name, it received part of the profits earned by its partner. Relations between the two institutions were facilitated by the friendship that existed between Siemens and Hans Jordan, the leading member of the managing board of Bergisch Märkische Bank.[151] To give itself an immediate presence in the Ruhr district, in 1914 the Deutsche Bank finally decided to take over the Bergisch Märkische Bank completely.

5. Klönne, Thyssen and the Ruhr

The industrial business of the Deutsche Bank received a fresh impulse in 1899, when Siemens managed to obtain the services of Carl Klönne for the institution.[152] Born in Solingen in 1850, Klönne had already reconstructed his first bank (albeit a small one: the Westfälische Bank in Bielefeld) by the age of 25. In 1879 he switched to the managing board of the Cologne joint stock bank, the A. Schaaffhausen'sche Bankverein, which was labouring under the repercussions of the recent collapse. He consolidated the bank, but above all he became the principal contact for the entrepreneurs who were beginning to forge the first big businesses in the Ruhr. In 1891 he became engaged in building up a branch in Berlin and wanted to shift the bank's focus of business to the imperial capital. As a result, however, he found himself increasingly isolated both on the managing board and *vis-à-vis* the supervisory board, and eventually decided to leave Schaaffhausen.

When Siemens heard of this, he at once tried to persuade this distinguished expert to come to the Deutsche Bank and look after industrial finance, particularly in the area of the west German coal and steel industries. Although he also had other interesting offers, in 1899 Klönne initially joined the supervisory board of the Deutsche Bank, but then in the course of the 1900 financial year he switched to the managing board, of which he remained a member until 1914.

Klönne brought with him to the Deutsche Bank his largest and most important industrial customers from the A. Schaaffhausen'sche Bankverein. Among the companies on whose supervisory boards he had sat during his time with Schaaffhausen, and on which he continued to sit after the move to the Deutsche Bank, were the Bochumer Verein, the Schalker Gruben- und Hüttenverein, the Harpener Bergbaugesellschaft, and the Essener Bergwerksverein König Wilhelm.[153] The entrepreneurs set great store by having a relationship based on trust and confidence with their bank, a relationship which was founded on well-developed ties with their contact person and which offered them advice appropriate to their needs. The process of concentration in the west German coal and steel industry further made it increasingly necessary for entrepreneurs to have access to the Berlin capital market. And before long, apart from the big banks, the only regional banks able to give entrepreneurs access to that market were the ones that had formed communities of interest with Berlin institutions. Klönne had seen this development coming for a long time, unlike his colleagues on the managing board at Schaaffhausen, whose impercipience in this regard eventually cost them the independence of their institution. In 1903 the Cologne-based bank did provisionally form a community of interest with the Dresdner Bank, but this failed to develop satisfactorily and was soon dissolved. In the end, the A. Schaaffhausen'sche Bankverein merged with the Disconto-Gesellschaft in 1914.

With his extensive contacts in the Ruhr district, Klönne put the industrial business of the Deutsche Bank on a broader foundation. It was through him, too, that the community of interest with the Essener Credit-Anstalt came about in 1903. This was an important regional bank in the Ruhr district, managed by his close friend Albert Müller. Klönne also had close ties with the steel magnate August Thyssen. For years, the bank manager and the industrialist carried on an intense correspondence that is of great interest with respect both to the relationship between banks and industry and to contemporary economic developments in general.[154] The two correspondents repeatedly indulged in detailed surveys of the overall economic situation; they asked each other for their opinions of particular events, and of course they also discussed specific concrete transactions. Let us take just a few examples. In a letter of 18 December 1902, Thyssen argued strongly in favour of hurrying along the process of concentration in the German economy, something that could not be done without the big banks. Only in this way would German industry be able to remain competitive: 'German industry cannot forever bear the burdens of the expensive railway monopoly, the coal and coke cartel, iron production, and semi-finished and finished manufacturing. We have to work more cheaply and still earn money, which we can achieve only by amalgamating factories and creating bigger businesses and by an improved division of labour.'[155] Klönne for his part was more inclined to see the disadvantages of forcing the pace of concentration. No one should be in too much of a hurry here. He hoped instead that 'it may still be possible, while avoiding the mistakes made hitherto, to retain the cartels. I fear we cannot do without them yet, since the time for achieving what you have for years been describing as the necessary firm amalgamation of all viable industrial works has not yet arrived.'[156]

It was not just in the steel industry that Thyssen argued for the creation of larger units. As a logical consequence of his thinking, he demanded a greater degree of concentration for banks as well. A few days after the death of Adolph von Hansemann, the second proprietor of the Disconto-Gesellschaft and one of the top bankers in imperial Germany, he wrote to Klönne: 'You should merge the Disconto now with the Deutsche Bank. Here too a community of interest is in order. I believe the time is right. Their individual characteristics do not sit well together, though. The Deutsche Bank would definitely have to call the tune.'[157] Here, too, banks and their leading representatives (men like Klönne) were very much more cautious: it was not until 26 years later that a merger between Germany's two largest banks came about.

Most of the letters, of course, dealt with day-to-day business. Klönne was always looking for ways to strengthen the business links between the Deutsche Bank and the Thyssen concern. As early as July 1900, shortly after joining the managing board of the Deutsche Bank, Klönne was assuring his fellow correspondent that 'the Deutsche Bank will be utterly and completely on your side' and discreetly suggesting – 'in order to enhance the mood in your favour as much as possible' – that Thyssen open a deposit account with the Deutsche

Bank: 'I assure you that this advice comes purely on my own initiative; no one,' he assured Thyssen, had thought to 'make such a demand of you'. Evidently, Thyssen had already received a loan from the Deutsche Bank because in his next letter he mentioned that he had transferred his holding of 200 shares in the Gladbeck mine to the Deutsche Bank: 'This covers the loan of Deutscher Kaiser and my firm.' However, his friendship with Klönne notwithstanding, he was not prepared to make a greater investment. He excused himself on the grounds of 'my son's machinations', because of which he feared credit restrictions from other banks.[158]

Two years later Klönne again approached Thyssen with a similar request. It had been noticed at the Stock Exchange, he said, that Schaaffhausen was buying large quantities of Schalker Gruben- und Hüttenverein shares, and the instructions were presumed to be coming from Thyssen. 'My invariable pleasure when you call upon the services of the Deutsche Bank ... is already known to you,' Klönne observed on 4 August 1902.[159] Thyssen thereupon opened a private account with the Deutsche Bank 'that I may also do my business, which as you know is not extensive, with yourselves'.[160] Presumably, however, he did not transact any significant amounts of business through the account because in February 1903 Klönne complained: 'Schalker Verein shares are steadily being bought through the Dresdner Bank; have you nothing for us to do?'[161] This time Thyssen did not respond to the banker's urgings. 'I have not bought any Schalker shares for a long time. The last ones you acquired for me' was his somewhat curt reply.[162]

For all his trust in Klönne, Thyssen was still careful not to show him his cards. For example, it was only afterwards that he confessed that the reason why he had been obliged to sell a colliery to the government at the beginning of 1902 had been the need to reduce what had become the dangerous level of his firm's indebtedness. In January he had written: 'I do not like selling mine property. It was particularly hard for me in the case of the Gladbeck, Bergmannsglück, etc. fields, which in my opinion will probably have the greatest future. What decided me was my desire to consolidate the financial side of my enterprises before my death and do as much as I can to lessen the jealousy felt in important circles regarding my very extensive mine ownership, which is actually bound up with enormous influence and responsibility, and thereby improve their disposition towards me and their appreciation and judgement of me.'[163] Only six months later he was admitting to Klönne that 'for years Thyssen & Co., Gladbeck and Deutscher Kaiser operated with debts of between 30 and 40 million marks. The worry this caused us was sometimes quite unbearable. Eventually, I had to sell Gladbeck, and it was only by selling Gladbeck etc. that I was able to restore confidence once more and survive the crisis.'[164]

The closeness of the collaboration between the industrialist and the banker is clear from Thyssen's projected involvement in Swedish ore extraction, even if the mines concerned were not actually purchased in the end. Thyssen's efforts to acquire a holding in Swedish ore mines began in 1902. The first contact to whom he turned with a request for advice and support in this matter was Klönne. His aim was to acquire two mines that were in financial difficulties at the time and to combine them with a shipping company to form a profitable business. In the first letter (dated 23 June 1902) in which he spoke of a possible deal, he even referred at the same time to the wider economic and political dimension of such an involvement: 'We shall be doing the great iron and steel industry of the Rhineland and Westphalia a big favour and greatly reassure it if we are able to place Europe's largest known ore-mining resource largely in German hands, and I see it as a great and patriotic duty to secure that resource for Germany lest it fall, as I fear it might, into the hands of Britain or America.'[165] The 'German hands' concerned were of course to be Thyssen's own. He therefore asked for the whole matter to be kept in the strictest confidence. 'It is my wish, incidentally, that no other German steel works should be able to participate without my consent, in order to avoid frictions, etc.'[166] On Klönne's initiative, the Deutsche Bank continued to make available to Thyssen all its information and contacts, including those with the Swedish Stockholms Handelsbank; it acted as negotiator *vis-à-vis* the Swedish partners, and it offered advice, all without (at first) being directly involved in any transactions.[167]

6. The role of 'finance capital'

The role of banks as intermediaries between investors of capital and those who take up credit has repeatedly given rise to the questions of how that role should be assessed and what power accrues to the banks as a result. The starting point for this debate is still the theory, put forward by Rudolf Hilferding in 1910, that German industry in particular (and above all the corporate bodies conceived as joint stock companies) came increasingly to be controlled and indeed dominated by the banks. That dominance arose partly through a network of interpersonal relations (and here he referred, as did Lenin, to the study published in 1905 by Otto Jeidels, the later proprietor of the Berliner Handels-Gesellschaft),[168] but partly also as a result of the granting of long-term loans and the acquisition of major shareholdings. 'But the bank is not only able to grant the joint stock company much greater credit than it can to the private company; it can also, for a shorter or longer period, invest part of its capital in shares. In every case, however, the bank receives a permanent interest in the joint stock company, which on the one hand needs to be controlled by the bank in order to guarantee proper use of the credit and on the other hand needs as far as possible to be dominated by the bank in order to secure all the bank's profit-making transactions.'[169] Banks had thus been able to impose their own interests on companies. The result was a process of increasing monopoly and cartel formation, guided by the banks.

These were highly radical conclusions, the empirical foundations for which were already being challenged by many contemporaries.[170] But even a man like Otto Jeidels noted from a quite different standpoint, that of a banker who was in complete agreement with existing circumstances and trends: 'Banks will be obliged to seek closer ties with industry and to give their traditional ties a different form, while industry, with its increasing need for capital, finds itself more and more reliant on the banks and offers them the right ground for extending their power.'[171]

That in the first phase of Germany's industrialization the demand for and shortage of capital enormously favoured the power and influence of the big universal banks was one of Alexander Gerschenkron's central propositions in his now famous 1952 essay on 'Economic Backwardness in Historical Perspective'. In this he took his cue directly from Hilferding, firmly endorsing the latter's key statements. Only after the initial dearth of capital had been overcome (i.e. after 1900) did the 'master–servant relationship' give way to a 'partnership between equals'.[172]

However, numerous detailed studies have since increasingly compromised the convenient simplicity of this view of the relationship between banks and industry, questioning many of its underlying assumptions, including particularly that of a 'dearth of capital'.[173] Attention has been devoted not least to the importance of the principal actors on both sides who either reinforced or mitigated tendencies in the direction of a heightened influence on the part of the banks. Bankers such as Georg Siemens, Adolph von Hansemann, Carl Fürstenberg and Carl Klönne certainly exerted a strong influence in the one direction, while their counterparts, men like Emil Rathenau, Werner von Siemens, Alfred Krupp, Hugo Stinnes and August Thyssen pulled the other way. 'The banks were in no position to dictate a merger policy to the industry. In any case, one did not dictate to either the Siemens family or to Emil Rathenau' is how Hugh Neuburger put it on one occasion.[174]

Neuburger is one of those who have studied Hilferding's and Gerschenkron's ideas in terms of concrete examples, in his case the example of relations between the Deutsche Bank and the electrical industry. Granted, he stresses the close contact that existed between the decision-makers at the Deutsche Bank on the one hand and at Siemens and AEG on the other. The bank was able to exert substantial influence, he concedes, and its services as an adviser were sought both in financial matters and as a broker of transactions. However, any talk of 'bank supremacy' fails to do justice to what was a multifaceted relationship governed by partly identical but also partly contrary interests and objectives, and the particular course taken by the industrialization process in Germany can certainly not be understood from this standpoint alone.

Jürgen Kocka, in his authoritative study of Siemens, also stresses the ambivalent qualities of the reciprocal relationship, in which 'short-term profit interests on the part of the banks were up against long-term calculation as well as staff-policy objectives on the part of the company and the family'. Wilhelm von

Siemens apparently always managed effectively to put forward his point of view and the interests of the firm, at least negotiating favourable compromises. Indeed, one is struck by 'how little, at least in the electrical industry after the turn of the century, companies were dominated by their banks'.[175]

In the case of Mannesmann, bank and company enjoyed a particularly close relationship, which is why the case is often cited as a prime example of the decisive influence that the banks wielded over industry.[176] Basically, though, what was involved here was a clash between two groups of shareholders, because for a long time it was not possible for Mannesmann shares to be listed on the Stock Exchange, which meant that the share capital was not dispersed.[177] The construction of the joint stock company when the Deutsch-Österreichische Mannesmannröhren-Werke was floated suggests that the Mannesmann brothers had assumed they would be able to run the company based on their invention in the manner of a family business; their only interest in the new shareholders was as financial backers. As with all previous flotations, they insisted on being granted, in respect of their patents, bonus shares in the amount of half the share capital. The voting majority and the management of the company were to remain with members of the Mannesmann family.[178] The prime concern of the engineers Max and Reinhard Mannesmann was to develop more and more potential applications for seamless tubing in order to demonstrate the superiority of their invention; rational, profitable exploitation of the process interested them less.[179] When the hoped-for profits failed to materialize and the company recorded only losses in the early years, the company construction started to wobble. Questions were asked not only about the management of the Mannesmann brothers and their relatives, who were accused of crass managerial and accounting errors, but also about the excessive estimate put on the value of the invention.

The financial backers had to intervene if they did not wish to lose the capital invested. After all, Siemens and Steinthal also had to answer to the Deutsche Bank's sub-participants, who had purchased Mannesmann shares on their advice. During the reorganization, shareholders were so confident of the invention's solid value that they agreed to forgo interest payments on capital invested for years[180] – possibly even for longer than was absolutely necessary.[181] The commitment once entered into, the Deutsche Bank could no longer duck the problems it faced without doing permanent damage to its reputation at a time when it was looking to broaden its industrial contacts. So the Mannesmann restructuring is of only very limited use as an illustration of bank supremacy.

Granted, the house-bank principle gave credit institutions full insight into the financial situation of companies, and also enabled them to influence the invest-ment policies of those companies through the medium of financial provision. However, some industrialists contrived to retain their independence by exploiting the competition between banks to their own advantage. This was how in 1879, as we have seen, Alfred Krupp was able, with the aid of the Deutsche Bank, to pay off the loan that he had issued five years before with the crucial participation of the Disconto-Gesellschaft – and in the process obtain substantially better terms. The Thyssen/Klönne correspondence offers a further example of how industry was able to derive advantage from competition between banks. In 1903 Thyssen was planning to take out a major loan for the Gewerkschaft Deutscher Kaiser, the centrepiece of his concern. He first offered the leadership of the consortium to the Deutsche Bank. Klönne agreed immediately 'that the Deutsche Bank will be entirely at your disposal in this respect as well. This is the first deal it has been possible to conclude with you under the leadership of the Deutsche Bank, which is of course particularly welcome so far as we are concerned.'[182] In the very next letter Thyssen qualified his offer, mentioning his obligations *vis-à-vis* other banks. The Disconto-Gesellschaft had made a bid for the consortium leadership on the grounds of its previous involvement, he informed Klönne, adding: 'I find it embarrassing that banks should fight over such trifles.' He was therefore considering dispensing with the loan completely, 'the more so since, apart from yourselves, I have to involve the Disconto-Gesellschaft, the Dresdner Bank, the Rheinische Bank, and most importantly Schaaffhausen. As you know, the Dresdner Bank and Schaaffhausen have at all times shown the greatest confidence in me. Never have these banks found fault with our credit and demanded guarantees, despite the fact that we, i.e. Thyssen & Co., owed up to 3 million marks and more at the most difficult time. It is my duty to take this opportunity to show these banks my gratitude, should it in fact come to a loan.'[183] It did eventually come to a loan, with the Deutsche Bank also getting its share, albeit under terms which clearly reflected the growing competition cleverly brought about by Thyssen among the banks.

Undoubtedly, the banks were more heavily involved in the process of industrialization in Germany than in other countries. Moreover, they took some extraordinary risks. These in turn contributed substantially to the process of concentration that is such a feature of the history of German banking. The risks arose mainly out of the fact that, when industrial companies were floated, substantial funds needed to be made available in advance as well as on a long-term basis – 'on a hunch', as it were: in other words, on the assumption that those investments would pay off in future. Given the scale of the underlying volume of business in each case (one thinks of the financing of the development of the electrical industry, for example), a concentration of funds both on the investor side and on the side of the producers was a virtual prerequisite if success was to be achieved. This distinguished industrial finance from commercial loans, which for one thing were bound up with an already existing equivalent in the form of commodities, and for another were repayable within a relatively short period. A counter-example to the way things developed in Germany was offered by Britain, certainly, but above all by France, where after the failure of the Crédit Mobilier the big banks steered clear of 'industrial speculation', as it was contemptuously termed, until the 1880s. This led, for example, to great French industrial enterprises such as the Schneider works in Le Creusot remaining family businesses, the vast majority of which were self-financed or used sleeping partners.[184] As a result, industrialization proceeded sluggishly – with momentous consequences as far as the country's development and its international ranking were concerned. In Germany, by contrast, as a result of collaboration between the big banks and industry (with shareholdings and interchange of management personnel at board level), the processes of industrialization and concentration forged ahead side by side. What is often regarded as one of the negative consequences of this was the increasing concentration of power, resources and finance, together with the way in which market decisions became centralized in a few large-scale enterprises, for which the emergence of the two electrical giants, Siemens and AEG, and above all, of course, the 'mighty vertical empires' of the coal and steel industry offer particularly striking examples. In the financial sphere, the counterpart of this process of concentration was the centralization of all decisions affecting the credit market in the hands of a few big banks, with the Deutsche Bank at their head.[185]

The Deutsche Bank was able to use the concentration process to its advantage and rose to be the leading big bank in Germany by the beginning of the First World War. For it too, however, this involvement in industry carried big risks. A comment in the memoirs of Hermann Wallich reveals how great the resultant conflicts must have been within the Deutsche Bank management. Wallich, who described himself as a 'cautious, possibly overcautious manager of other people's money', rejected the energy with which Georg Siemens pursued and developed the bank's industrial business because of the high level of risk associated with it: 'The transactions on which my brilliant colleague embarked stood on what were to some extent artificial foundations; they absorbed our liquid funds and often crippled our freedom to move in a different direction. But the public, as I say, had no idea of the weakness of our position, the foolhardy operations embarked upon turned out well, and my colleague was hailed as a genius.'[186]

III. Foreign Business

'Banks are driven to operate abroad not as a result of national enthusiasm but through the need, which at a certain stage of modern capitalist development becomes increasingly pronounced, to create a favourable foreign location for the exploitation of free German capital.'[187] What the future proprietor of the Berliner Handels-Gesellschaft, Otto Jeidels, was also implying when he wrote that sentence in 1905 was an appeal to economic good sense at a time when such good sense threatened to founder in mounting waves of nationalism and imperialism, with the often pseudo-economic justifications that accompanied these phenomena. He was pointing to the difference between the political interests of the state on the one hand and economic interests on the other, and he was indirectly warning against any attempt unilaterally to harness the economy (and particularly the world of finance) in the service of politics. In the age of imperialism then approaching its climax, there was every reason to issue such a warning, particularly in the light of the so-called export of capital and the increasing involvement of banks in foreign business. But what was the attitude of the majority of representatives of the world of banking (and here we are chiefly interested in the Deutsche Bank) to that warning? Were they willing to be 'harnessed in the service of politics'? Had they, as far as foreign business was concerned, become tools of Germany's drive for world power? Or did they (representing a wide variety of political outlooks) allow themselves to be guided primarily by the economic interests that were present at the time – economic interests that, according to Jeidels, had since the early 1890s been largely determined by the increasingly apparent surplus of money on the German capital market and the resultant attempts to export it?

In imperial Germany there were three main points of emphasis as far as banking business in and with foreign countries was concerned: conducting international payment transactions, underwriting foreign government bonds, and finally participating in industrial companies abroad.[188] What is more, in the case of the Deutsche Bank at least, those points of emphasis emerged in precisely that chronological order.

The newly founded bank's first attempts to gain a foothold abroad were wholly geared to supporting the commercial activities of German firms. The aim of the bank was to build up a network of its own for effecting international payment transactions. In the mid-1880s it began to subscribe, centrally and through a subsidiary company, to foreign loans, initially for South American countries. Subsequently, it went beyond this to move into the industrial sector, an involvement in railway construction in the United States of America representing the third form of foreign business: namely, participation in foreign industrial companies. Eventually, with railway building in Turkey and its involvement in the Romanian oil business, it started to play an entrepreneurial role itself.

As well as by function and chronology, we need to break down and look at the Deutsche Bank's foreign business by region, simultaneously bearing in mind the foreign policy interests of the German Reich. The first thing we must establish here is that, even though right from the start of Germany's colonial policy in the 1880s a majority on the managing board counted as 'colonial enthusiasts', the German colonies in Africa and the South Pacific played virtually no part at all (in terms of objects of economic and financial interests) in the bank's business involvement. During the first phase of German colonial policy, the bank steered well clear of all colonial enterprises. Only from the mid-1890s onwards did it play any part in the economic development of the colonies – and even then with tiny amounts of money in comparison with its other areas of business.[189] Initially, most such decision making centred on Latin America and the USA, where significant investments of German capital took place without a corresponding measure of political influence being associated with them. Then, admittedly, a third category of states and regions moved increasingly into the limelight – mainly Turkey, but also China, the Balkans and for a time Morocco. Here there soon came into being a 'web of influences from German diplomacy, military aid and private business that were sometimes in conflict with one another but often backed one another up'.[190]

1. First steps

'While so far as all other branches of business are concerned the German element already occupies a prominent position in all the world's principal trading centres, in banking alone the brokering of overseas transactions is almost exclusively in the hands of British credit institutions.'[191] So ran the opening sentence of the first (as yet confidential) memorandum drawn up in July 1869 concerning the functions and aims of the projected Deutsche Bank. It enshrined the guiding principle under which the bank was to be built up and organized: Financing foreign trade – that was the true objective.

The personnel policy of the new institution was in line with this. As we have seen, the reason why Georg Siemens was appointed to a managing directorship despite his not being a banking expert (indeed, he was a newcomer to banking) was that he had foreign experience. The colleague who joined him soon afterwards, Hermann Wallich, fulfilled even more closely what was expected of a director of a newly founded export bank, for he had already built up that very branch of business for the Paris bank, Comptoir d'Escompte. Comptoir d'Escompte had for the first time offered a French export-financing service that was independent of the British banks.

The aim of the Deutsche Bank in the early years was to offer German merchants the whole range of banking services required to transact foreign trade payments, from advancing money on export articles to providing importers with documentary credit. The bank was to become the contact institution for German merchants who had hitherto had to use the services of the London banks, often on less favourable terms than their British colleagues. A further ambition was to establish the German currency as an internationally recognized medium of exchange. Quite soon after joining the Deutsche Bank, Wallich had set out in a memorandum to the administrative board how the bank should develop its foreign business. The first requirement was to establish branches at the principal trading centres as quickly as possible. The management duly set about giving itself a presence in London initially, since that was the focus of the international flow of money, but also in Bremen and Hamburg. This was because it was through those two North Sea ports that Germany's entire overseas trade was conducted. Holdings in foreign banks in New York and Paris were to follow.

Since the most important international trading centre was London, establishing a branch in the city on the Thames was, as we have seen, a priority from the outset. An intergovernmental agreement with Britain having cleared the way for a branch to be established, the Deutsche Bank London Agency opened on 8 March 1873.[192] The Business Report for that year comments: 'We are in a position to grant those of our business friends who purchase raw materials in overseas markets credit in such a form that they can at their discretion draw either in marks from Germany or in pounds from London and hence take advantage of all the profit opportunities that may arise out of a temporarily greater or lesser demand for mark or pound exchanges as a result of differences in discount rates in London and Berlin, etc.'[193]

The London Agency did indeed develop into the Deutsche Bank's most important branch. In 1873, the year of its founding, it already managed to turn over £4 million, compared with the £2.5 million turnover achieved by the German Bank of London in the previous year. By 1900, total turnover of the Deutsche Bank London Agency had risen to more than £606 million, and by 1913 it was up to almost £1,063 million. Most of the banking business in London consisted of documentary credit, acceptance credit and arbitrage transactions. A crucial factor here was the development of the bill of acceptance, not merely for the success of the London branch, but also for the total acceptance business of the Deutsche Bank.

The Deutsche Bank's ambition to play a part in establishing the German currency as a medium of international exchange (to assist in 'the introduction of the German valuta to overseas marketplaces', as the 1873 Business Report solemnly intoned) was of course unattainable so long as Germany remained fragmented into a large number of currency areas. However, with the founding of the Reich, the introduction of a uniform currency, the gold mark, at last became a possibility. It finally came about in 1873. In anticipation of this step, the Deutsche Bank had set up branches overseas as early as 1872. Their purpose was to establish the mark exchange in addition to the sterling exchange, thus making it possible to examine trading partners more closely *in situ* and reduce credit risks.

The first phase of the expansion of the Deutsche Bank, which lasted until about 1875, also saw an attempt to gain a foothold in the Far East by establishing branches there. The bank's memorandum of foundation, drawn up in July 1869, had already described the Asiatic region of India, China and Japan as a key area for Germany's foreign trade. The Comptoir d'Escompte, it argued, had 'opened establishments in the East Indies, China and Japan in the last 8 to 10 years' and achieved 'brilliant results'.[194] The administrative board deliberately secured, in Hermann Wallich, former director of the French model's Shanghai branch, a prominent Far Eastern expert, and Wallich did indeed, immediately after joining the management of the Deutsche Bank, very energetically set about founding branches in China and Japan.

With their principal export articles of tea and silk, the wealthy countries of Asia had attracted European commerce for centuries. But only since the violent opening-up of China and Japan for European and American merchants from about the second third of the nineteenth century onwards had that commerce assumed dimensions that really stimulated the imaginations of European and American financiers. John Atkinson Hobson, the liberal British business journalist, published a study of imperialism in 1902 that was as influential as it was critical. In it he described China as an absolutely classic example of the new and disastrous form of European and later also North American and Japanese colonialism. His chief criticism was that the colonial powers went in under the guise of a sense of mission, a 'moral trust for civilisation' on the part of the more developed nations, behind which they kept their true economic, political and cultural power interests concealed. Hobson spoke of a 'pirate expedition', the object of which was 'to force trade upon a nation whose one principle of foreign policy was to keep clear of foreigners'.[195]

The giant central Asian realm with its 500 million inhabitants did indeed offer not only a huge potential labour force and almost inexhaustible natural resources, but also undreamt-of prospects for profitable capital investment. For European industry (and above all the British textile industry) it offered access to a new export market, and for free capital it promised excellent investment opportunities in a still underdeveloped communications infrastructure. British merchants had been the first to take advantage of all this, not least because of their long experience in colonial commerce with that part of the world. It was no accident, for instance, that European expansion towards China began from India. British trading companies, having monopolized the opium trade between India and China since the 1830s, gradually sought to bring the internal trade of the central Asian region under their control as well. The consequences of mounting opium consumption and the negative balance of trade resulting from the enormous drain on his country's silver currency prompted the Chinese emperor in 1839 to prohibit the trade in and consumption of opium completely. Foreign importers were threatened with the death penalty for any infringement of the trade ban, and British stocks of opium were destroyed by order of the government. The Opium War of 1840–42 against China and the deployment of the British fleet ended the period of peaceful penetration, the so-called 'informal rule' of the European powers in their colonial territories overseas. More and more often the flag followed trade or, even more commonly, anticipated it; more and more frequently the colonial countries intervened to protect the commercial, economic and financial interests of companies involved in the colonies.

Having lost the Opium War, China was obliged under the Peace of Nanking in 1842 to cede to Britain the virtually uninhabited rocky island to which the British had withdrawn – Hong Kong. This marked the beginning of the period of 'unequal treaties' with Britain, France, Russia and the USA, under which the country was forced to open up further ports, including Canton and Shanghai, to international commerce and to establish extraterritorial settlements in which foreign states enjoyed freedom of trade, consular jurisdiction, and police and customs sovereignty. The colonialization of China reached its peak in the 1890s when the country was carved up into spheres of interest, in which the German Reich was also involved through taking possession of the Gulf of Jiaozhou in Shandong (Shantung) province.

With the more or less violent opening-up of the ports of eastern China and the military protection of bases by the colonial powers, the foundations were laid for an expansion of European trade with China and Japan, which had also had to grant trading concessions after the USA had used gunboats to force it to open up in 1854. In the China trade, agricultural and animal products (chiefly tea, silk, sugar and cattle hides) were imported into Europe at prices dictated by the Europeans, and opium and cotton continued to arrive from India; above all, however, European industrial products were exported to the Far East.

In terms of financial and banking services, almost all of this business was transacted through London, the only exception, as we have seen, being the French bank Comptoir d'Escompte. The managing directors of the Deutsche Bank were anxious to put the experience of Comptoir d'Escompte to good use in building up their own business in the Far East. Accordingly, Wallich turned to his former colleague J. Mammelsdorf, a fellow German who managed the Yokohama branch of Comptoir d'Escompte. His analysis of the market opportunities for the Deutsche Bank in the Far East sounded encouraging: 'I believe, looking to the future as well as weighing Germany's present commercial position, that the time has come to bring German capital into international trade, for the political strengthening and unification of Germany and the imminent introduction of a uniform gold standard make it the duty of German institutions to step out on to the world stage.'[196]

Another reason why Mammelsdorf judged the prospects of a German credit institution in the Far East in a positive light was that 'the monetary surplus stemming from the French war indemnity' would lead to a lowering of the German bank rate, making it competitive with the British rate. 'But in addition to this, the high regard in which Germany is held, the increase in the fleet, and the country's new feeling of strength will be important factors in arousing interest in a German–Far Eastern bank abroad as well as at home, while the silver exports inevitably associated with the introduction of the new currency may immediately present the institution with an opportunity for extensive transactions that will help it to acquire influential status in the East.'[197]

Mammelsdorf suggested that the bank establish branches in the three principal trading centres in Asia: namely, Shanghai, Yokohama and Hong Kong. However, Siemens and Wallich disagreed with him in their report to the administrative board 'because for one thing they [i.e. the management] are able to recommend suitable representatives for only 2 branches and for another thing Hong Kong, being in decline, is a relatively less important location than Shanghai'.[198] Instead, the management requested an increase in capital of 5 million talers in order to set up branches in Shanghai, Yokohama and Hamburg. The board accepted this proposal, and in January 1872 the new shares were issued and the Hamburg branch opened. The Shanghai and Yokohama branches followed in May, the four-month delay being accounted for by 'the time required for travel etc. and a host of other necessary preparations', as the 1872 Business Report explained.

The national impetus that had already been in evidence in the run-up to the bank's foundation also featured in the establishment of its overseas branches. How powerfully it must have been felt by others in addition to the Deutsche Bank directors involved is clear from the fact that in its expansionist efforts overseas the bank was able to count on the backing of the government. The German navy, which until then had met its overseas financial requirements through British banks, financed the fleet in July 1872 through the medium of Deutsche Bank letters of credit. However, for a really good piece of business that would give it a head start in Asia the bank looked primarily to the silver sales that were put in hand as a result of the switch from a silver to a gold standard and that the government in part instructed the Deutsche Bank to carry out.[199]

Nevertheless, only for a brief period did the newly established branches fulfil the expectations that had been placed in them. The stock exchange crisis of 1873 had repercussions beyond Germany and Europe, leading to a sharp decline in the tea and silk trades and a reduced capacity on the part of Asian markets for absorbing European products. An added factor was that the silver price dropped substantially, not least as a result of the surplus of supply engendered by German government sales. Whereas the London branch continued to earn handsome profits from silver sales out of Reich reserves until 1876, for the Far Eastern branches, following the price collapse, such sales resulted in a loss. The fact was, the Deutsche Bank's branches in the Far East had covered their operating capital in silver currency, which was now worth substantially less.

In 1874 it became evident that the recession was going to last for some time, and Berlin drew the consequences. To avoid even greater losses, a decision was made to wind up the Shanghai and Yokohama branches. The dissolutions, which were completed on 1 October 1875, led to losses of 245,000 marks in Shanghai and 191,000 marks in Yokohama. 'Nevertheless,' declared the 1875 Business Report, 'we particularly wish to stress that we are certainly not abandoning our programme of supporting German overseas trade but will in fact continue to pursue the same with the aid of our London branch, which is performing splendidly.' The same report did, however, concede that 'we are obliged, in view of the decline in German exports, temporarily to suspend our efforts to introduce the Germany currency into overseas markets'.[200]

As with its involvement in Asia, the Deutsche Bank also had to take some initial setbacks in South America. In 1874 it took over the Deutsch-Belgische La Plata Bank (founded two years previously by the Disconto-Gesellschaft and the Cologne-based Sal. Oppenheim bank) with the object, as the Business Report for that year expressed it in almost poetic terms, of bringing together 'the world's largest hide emporium' and 'factory-rich Germany'. Although its holding was limited to 1 million of the 3 million talers to which the share capital had been reduced, the Deutsche Bank was granted a majority on the supervisory board. It appointed the management of the Deutsch-Belgische La Plata Bank, the head office of which was then moved from Cologne to Berlin. The fact that the Disconto-Gesellschaft agreed so readily to everything Siemens asked for (Siemens conducted the negotiations on behalf of the Deutsche Bank) ought really to have aroused his suspicions. The very first year brought losses arising out of La Plata Bank's existing commitments. Returns remained poor in subsequent years, largely because following a revolution in Uruguay the new rulers repudiated their predecessors' credit obligations. Not until 1884 was an agreement reached that made it possible for the Deutsch-Belgische La Plata Bank to be wound up in March 1885.[201]

The self-assured vigour with which the young Deutsche Bank had sought very rapidly to build up an effective export-financing service thus met with one or two dampers. Ventures in the Far East and South America met with initial failure, while the bank's holdings in New York and Paris institutions also failed to turn out as hoped and had eventually to be abandoned. Although the branches in Hamburg, Bremen and London were developing satisfactorily, the public assumption was that the Deutsche Bank was about to go bust. For example, the German financial journal *Der Aktionär* wrote in 1875: 'The Deutsche Bank is getting rid of its branches in Shanghai and Yokohama, thus admitting that it is not able to carry out its originally high-sounding programme, for it was in essence founded for the sole purpose of liberating Germany's overseas trade, particularly in China, Japan and the East Indies, from domination by British and French bankers. The question of liquidation is therefore also being considered in respect of the bank itself; at any rate, a reduction in capital is presumably indicated.'[202]

Nevertheless, management and the administrative board did not retreat from the bank's business objective, but sought to continue their overseas involvement with more restricted resources through their branches in London, Hamburg and Bremen. In the 1879 Business Report the management took stock: 'At the close of the first ten years of our operation, may we be permitted, despite many a doubt that has been expressed, to emphasize straight away that we have never, even temporarily, set aside the programme of the Deutsche Bank, namely to facilitate commercial relations between Germany and the other European countries as well as overseas markets. On the occasion of the withdrawal of our Chinese and Japanese branches brought about by the introduction of the gold standard, we stated explicitly that the withdrawal meant only a change in the style of our business operation in that our London branch would take the place of the overseas agencies. The steady increase in our turnover with exporters and importers provides further proof to the contrary.'[203]

2. Worldwide activities: America, the Far East, South-East Europe

The attempt (which the Deutsche Bank was not alone in launching) to gain a foothold in overseas trading centres in the early 1870s having largely proved a failure, most private banks strongly reined in their involvement for a few years. The government of the Reich, however, was still interested, indeed increasingly interested, in an independent method of financing Germany's foreign trade. In 1884 the Chairman of the Reichsbank, Hermann von Dechend, put forward a plan for founding a national overseas bank that should operate under the supervision of the Chancellor and in close collaboration with his institution. Bismarck rejected any direct participation on the part of the Reichsbank, wishing to avoid a resurgence of the debate about government intervention in connection with Germany's colonial policy. He had in mind the parliamentary clashes over the Imperial Subsidies Acts in 1885, when the establishment of a Reichspost steamship line to the Far East and Australia had come in for some heavy criticism. Only by a small majority and in the teeth of the resistance of the Liberal free-traders had the Reichstag passed a bill on 23 March 1885 allowing the Chancellor to assign this task to 'suitable German companies by way of an invitation to tender'. Associated with this were mainly financial subsidies from the imperial government in the amount of up to 4 million marks to the Norddeutscher Lloyd company of the Bremen shipping magnate and member of parliament, Hermann Heinrich Meier, whose ocean-going steamships were considered the fastest and most efficient of the period.[204]

However, more fundamental matters were at stake: namely, the beginning of a German *Weltpolitik* and a new national self-confidence that the Reich proposed to demonstrate particularly in the field of overseas economic, commercial and maritime policy. On 30 June 1886 the German public celebrated the sailing of the *Oder*, the first Reichspost steamer, bound for the Far East. This was treated as a national event, with the President and several members of the Reichstag, members of the Bundesrat or 'senate', and representatives of numerous chambers of commerce among those taking part.

Although the Chancellor was himself definitely not among the 'colonial enthusiasts', as they were called,[205] the Reichsbank chairman thought in the light of the change of mood among broad sections of the public that conditions were now more favourable for a more pronounced merging of politics and private enterprise.[206] Dechend therefore resumed the talks that had already been started with leading Berlin bankers and Hamburg merchants with a view to setting up a German overseas bank on a privately financed basis.

However, this new initiative on the part of the Reichsbank chairman was similarly unsuccessful. The export firms that made up the Hamburg Chamber of Commerce declined to participate. The banks indicated a willingness in principle, but made conditions that ran counter to the new Joint Stock Companies Act. Bismarck and the Foreign Office showed themselves inclined to give the banks what they asked. However, the Prussian Finance Minister and Under-secretary of State at the Imperial Treasury, von Scholz, firmly rejected the idea of any departure from the new legal provisions. With this, the plans to set up a national overseas bank finally collapsed.

It was only four months later, on 2 October 1886, that the Deutsche Bank founded the Deutsche Uebersee-Bank, which was to involve itself particularly in South America. The Deutsche Bank was thus the first institution to react to the government's urgings in this regard. The remark by one German diplomat that the Deutsche Bank had gone to South America 'purely to do the Foreign Office a favour'[207] was doubtless an exaggeration.[208] It was more a matter of the bank taking advantage of an economic upswing to revive an old plan put forward by Hermann Wallich. Back in the autumn of 1872, he had suggested founding a 'Germanisch-Transatlantische Bank', to be a wholly owned subsidiary of the Deutsche Bank with its head office in Berlin. It was to specialize in business with North and South America and to set up branches in the main South American trading centres for that purpose.

In the second half of the nineteenth century, Argentina was seen as a place with great prospects. The enormous, fertile country was at first used very little for agriculture but instead mainly for cattle breeding. Wool and hides were the chief export articles. Then in the 1880s the economy began to grow dramatically. Railway construction having been forced ahead, Argentina already had the most extensive railway network in South America by the middle of the century. That and the simultaneous increase in the influx of immigrants (including many Germans) made it possible to settle the country and ushered in a structural change in the rural economy from cattle breeding to cereal growing. Wheat exports became increasingly significant in the years that followed, and by 1900 Argentina was already producing 20 per cent of the world's wheat.[209]

The end of the constant civil wars and the stabilization of the domestic political situation in the 1880s were further important prerequisites for the rapid economic upswing that set in around that time. Argentina experienced a flotation boom that brought in foreign capital investment on an unprecedented scale.[210] Since in the wake of industrialization and with a rapidly expanding population the German Reich was increasingly becoming an exporter of capital, the two countries had a mutual interest in extending their trading relations. Argentina was seen as a rewarding field for German investment, and interest on the German side increased even further when towards the end of the 1880s relations with Russia deteriorated. However, it was not Germany but Britain that was the principal economic partner of the countries bordering on the River Plate. British trading companies, which brokered the export of wool and hides in exchange for British manufactures and industrial products, had the backing of British banks: namely, the London & River Plate Bank and the Commercial Bank of the River Plate.

The Deutsche Bank's second attempt to gain a foothold in South America, undertaken in October 1886, was successful. The Deutsche Uebersee-Bank (renamed Deutsche Ueberseeische Bank in 1893) represented the interests of the Deutsche Bank in South America until its 1976 merger with the parent institution. Its tasks, according to the articles of association, included 'promoting overseas trading, financial and foreign exchange activity' and, more generally, 'performing banking transactions'.[211] The subsidiary company was thus founded on the same terms as the Deutsche Bank itself back in 1870, and was deliberately not given the fixed status of a bank specializing purely in foreign trade.

The new institution was given headquarters in Berlin and equipped with share capital in the amount of 10 million marks, though initially only 25 per cent of this was paid in. A further 35 per cent payment was made in October 1887, an increase in the bank's operating capital having become necessary after the Banco Alemán Transatlántico opened as a branch of the Deutsche Uebersee-Bank in the Argentine capital, Buenos Aires, on 5 August 1887. Argentina, to which the Deutsche Uebersee-Bank initially turned its attention, remained the bank's principal field of activity throughout the period up until the First World War.[212]

Business in Buenos Aires developed satisfactorily in the early years, despite a serious economic and financial crisis that set in as early as 1890/91 and during which the right to issue notes, acquired in 1887, had to be relinquished. When turnover then rose substantially in 1893, the bank's capital cover proved too thin. However, an increase in capital was not admissible under German company law, since only 60 per cent of the 10 million mark share capital had been paid in. It was therefore decided to wind up the Deutsche Uebersee-Bank and refloat it under the name of Deutsche Ueberseeische Bank with a share capital of 20 million marks. The Buenos Aires branch continued to trade as Banco Alemán Transatlántico.[213]

The bank's volume of business grew steadily in the years that followed. Whereas in 1893 it had turned over just under 1.7 thousand million marks, earning about 500,000 marks profit in the process, in 1899 it was able to record a turnover of 5.6 thousand million marks and profits amounting to 1.4 million marks. By 1913 these figures had shot up: in that year, turnover was nearly 22 thousand million and profits 4.3 million marks.[214] A building occupied in 1894 soon proved too small, so the bank moved again after only two years. The new building, taken over from the old Banco Carabassa, remained home to the Banco Alemán Transatlántico until 1924.[215]

The favourable development of its involvement in Argentina since the 1890s led the Deutsche Bank to hope for a similar upswing in the other countries of Latin America. So when the Disconto-Gesellschaft and the Norddeutsche Bank jointly founded the Bank für Chile und Deutschland in 1895, the Deutsche Bank was anxious not to be left behind in that country. In February 1896, only a month after the Bank für Chile und Deutschland opened its branch, the Banco Alemán Transatlántico also opened a branch in Valparaíso. The more decentralized administrative and economic structure of Chile, in contrast to Argentina, made it necessary to open more branches. In August 1897 one was opened in Iquique, an important port for the country's two main exports, saltpetre and copper, and in November a further branch followed in the capital, Santiago de Chile.

In 1898 the Chilean economy underwent a severe crisis, which for the two rival German banks was a particularly painful experience. Nevertheless, the Banco Alemán Transatlántico continued on its expansion course and in the spring of 1898 opened two further branches in Concepción and Valdivia, which developed satisfactorily. The very next year brought an improvement in the economic situation, from which the Chilean branches of the Deutsche Ueberseeische Bank visibly profited. Overall, the Chilean operation went well until the First World War, so that even the short-term losses occasioned by the severe earthquake that destroyed large parts of Valparaíso in 1906 could be absorbed. More branches were opened, and by 1914 the Banco Alemán Transatlántico had a relatively dense network in Chile.[216]

Since the turn of the century, the bank had also begun to build up a network of branches in Argentina, and in the period up to the First World War six branches opened: Bahia Blanca, Córdoba, Tucumán, Bell-Ville, Mendoza and Rosario. An additional three branches opened in Buenos Aires. The Banco Alemán Transatlántico also proceeded to expand to other Latin American countries, establishing branches in Mexico (1902), in Peru and Bolivia (1905), in Uruguay (1906) and in Brazil (1911); in 1904 a branch opened in Spain. The Mexican branch was abandoned again in 1906, having failed to make its mark against United States influence. To give themselves the capacity to defy the Americans in future, in 1905 the Deutsche Bank and the Deutsche Ueberseeische Bank, acting in conjunction with the Frankfurt bank of Lazard Speyer-Ellissen and the Credit Suisse, set up the Zentralamerika-Bank (Bank of Central America), which was initially to open a branch in Guatemala and later expand to the other countries of Central America as well.

The man behind this strategy of expansion was Ludwig Roland-Lücke, who from 1894 to 1907 (with two interruptions due to illness) sat on the managing boards of the Deutsche Bank and the Deutsche Ueberseeische Bank. He justified his attitude in a note that he wrote on 18 October 1905: 'The knowledge that in economic terms the North Americans will gradually swallow more and more of Central and South America can leave us in little doubt that it is high time we did all we can to strengthen and wherever possible create points of influence such as will be capable of continuing to secure profitable employment for German capital and German labour.'[217] However, the Zentralamerika-Bank failed to achieve its business objective, and in only its second year (1906), in order to avoid what would have been a sensational liquidation for a company that had previously been held in high public esteem, it was converted into a construction company.

Due to its character as a subsidiary of the Deutsche Bank, the Banco Alemán

Transatlántico did not issue loans itself. Although it was invariably involved in preparing such deals with the Argentine provinces and the city of Buenos Aires, and took part in the negotiations, it received only relatively small quotas when the loans were placed. The consortium that floated the Deutsch-Ueberseeische Elektricitäts-Gesellschaft on 12 January 1898 was likewise headed by the parent bank. Nevertheless, this was the most important company flotation in which the Banco Alemán Transatlántico was involved. Following 18 months of negotiations between the bank and the Buenos Aires city authorities, in June 1897 AEG received the concession to build a power station for the city. Only ten years after its flotation, the Deutsch-Ueberseeische Elektricitäts-Gesellschaft that was set up to operate and finance this undertaking was Argentina's largest power-supply company.[218]

Since the closure of the Far Eastern branches of the Deutsche Bank in 1875, German commerce had been thrown back on conducting its business through British banks. Because of this, and in the light of the increasing inter-connectedness of the world economy and the ever harsher competition faced by commercial and colonial interests, beginning in the early 1880s fresh consideration was given in government and banking circles in Berlin to the idea of founding a bank to cover the Far East. These eventually culminated in the Deutsch-Asiatische Bank, which went into operation in February 1889. The starting capital was underwritten by a consortium of 13 well-known joint stock and private banks headed by the Disconto-Gesellschaft.[219] The new institution was based in Shanghai and initially given the task of financing trade. The beginning was not easy, particularly since many German merchants remained loyal for some years to the British banks with which they had worked hitherto. The profit situation improved when in the 1890s the Deutsch-Asiatische Bank switched to underwriting Chinese government loans in conjunction with the Hongkong and Shanghai Banking Corporation. Subsequently, it was also involved in financing Chinese railway construction.[220] By 1914 German capital investments in China amounted to 1,100 million marks or some 5 per cent of all Germany's foreign investments and something like 16.7 per cent of total foreign investments in China.[221] The Deutsch-Asiatische Bank had a significant share in this, and in 1913 maintained, in addition to its head office in Shanghai and offices in Hamburg and Berlin, a network of seven branches and branch offices in China. It had another two branches in the Japanese cities of Yokohama and Kobe as well as branches in Calcutta and Singapore. The bank was the seed from which grew the regional head office in Singapore and its branches which represent the interests of the Deutsche Bank in Asia today.

In the involvement of the Deutsche Bank in South America, political aspects played a part alongside the business aspect from the outset. Government and public both urged that a German institution be established locally. When the Deutsche Bank became involved in the Northern Pacific Railway, however, no such considerations came into play. On the contrary, Georg Siemens complained of obstacles being put in his way by politicians in whose eyes there was nothing to be gained in foreign policy terms from an involvement in the USA.[222] In other words, this was about nothing more nor less than the bank participating in what promised to be a profitable piece of business and beyond that establishing itself in the up-and-coming American market.

Instead of reaping the hoped-for profits, the Deutsche Bank had of course to struggle for years with enormous problems, despite the fact that American railway stock did actually look like a sound investment. Railway construction had been attracting foreign capital since the 1830s. After 1875, canvassing for investors was intensified. For the routes now under construction (which made possible the opening-up and settlement of that vast continent, thus laying the foundations for the meteoric rise of the United States as an economic power), American resources alone were insufficient. Particularly during the last third of the nineteenth century, foreign investors held major shareholdings in the principal railway companies.[223]

Siemens, too, saw the enormous economic potential of the United States: 'I believe that we in Berlin must also take an interest in American affairs', he wrote to Kilian Steiner, his colleague at the Württembergische Vereinsbank. 'America is closer to us than Italy, after all, the Gotthard notwithstanding.'[224] Siemens wanted the Deutsche Bank to have a share of the profits to be expected on the North American continent, so it is entirely understandable that, when he received an invitation to the ceremonial opening of the Northern Pacific railway line in 1883, he should have accepted immediately. However, the involvement with Northern Pacific turned out to be a costly business for the Deutsche Bank and one that brought with it a major loss of prestige. This was the first (but not the last) time that the bank had the wool pulled over its eyes by a man who employed great personal charm and shrewd publicity to win over investors and repeatedly mobilize fresh sources of credit, but whose business rested on thoroughly rickety foundations. The Chairman of Northern Pacific, Henry Villard, was a German immigrant to the USA. Not the least of his intentions in staging this elaborately ceremonial opening was to attract fresh investment for his company, the precarious financial situation of which was by then already known in outline. However, even while the celebrations were running their course, Northern Pacific's shares shed almost half their value. Siemens, though hugely impressed by the grand opening ceremony, was nevertheless aware of the company's financial difficulties. Yet he advocated a commitment to Northern Pacific despite the risk, because in his view a successful consolidation of the company would vastly enhance the international reputation of the Deutsche Bank.

A few months after the opening of the railway line, the Deutsche Bank underwrote 20 million dollars' worth of Second Mortgage Bonds. Before 1883 was out, the Northern Pacific share price fell to a level that forced Villard to resign from the management of the company. However, since the company's prospects were nevertheless positively assessed in the long term, the Deutsche

Bank underwrote further bonds that it listed on the Berlin Stock Exchange from 1886, though it did not gain any possibility of influencing the management of affairs. Then in the late 1880s the financial situation of Northern Pacific began to take another turn for the worse. The money that had continued to flow abundantly into the company even after Villard's resignation had been paid out for unprofitable branch lines and unearned dividends.[225] The bond price slipped considerably, which did the reputation of the Deutsche Bank no good at all. Siemens therefore initiated a company to protect and promote German investments in the USA, and this was founded in March 1890 as the Deutsch-Amerikanische Treuhand-Gesellschaft AG (German–American Trust Company), with a starting capital of 20 million marks.[226]

By 1893 Northern Pacific was on the verge of bankruptcy. In the estimation of Siemens's biographer, Karl Helfferich: 'Probably no other failure among his enterprises ever shook and disturbed Georg Siemens so deeply as did the collapse of Northern Pacific. Not only did he find himself bitterly disappointed in his downright enthusiastic expectations for the future of this company, in his hopes regarding the fruits that should accrue to the German economy from this participation in the development of the American railways, and finally in his personal confidence in Henry Villard; he also felt the whole burden of the responsibility for the hundreds of millions of German capital that had been invested in American railway stock in recent years as resting on his more than on anyone else's shoulders.'[227] In terms of speculative business, railway construction was often the nineteenth-century equivalent of real estate today. Then, too, soberly calculating bankers were 'conned' by men like Henry Villard, whose businesses were financed by loans that had no solid security behind them. Siemens in fact used much of his own money to buy share certificates back from disappointed investors who had subscribed for Northern Pacific securities on the basis of his advice – his behaviour providing impressive evidence of how in this early phase of joint stock banking even an employed bank manager (which is what, in legal terms, Siemens was) saw himself in an almost moral light as bearing the same sort of personal liability as the old-style private banker.

In 1893 Villard finally quit the management of Northern Pacific.[228] Siemens travelled to America to install Edward D. Adams as the representative of the interests of the Deutsche Bank and of the bondholders for whom it acted.[229] At first, however, Northern Pacific continued to slide, until in 1895 the prospect arose of an amalgamation with James J. Hill, chairman of the company's biggest rival. By dint of tight management Hill had made the Great Northern Railway Company, whose track ran largely parallel to that of Northern Pacific, into a profitable company. He therefore struck the Deutsche Bank as a suitable partner. However, in November 1895 the projected merger fell through in the Minnesota Supreme Court, which pronounced it incompatible with current anti-trust legislation.[230] Agreement was eventually reached over a sort of 'defensive alliance' whereby neither company would directly harm its competitor. It meant that

Northern Pacific retained its independence. The reorganization and financial consolidation of the company were finally carried out in conjunction with the powerful private banker, John Pierpont Morgan. By 1896 the bond price had recovered the level of the introductory price, and in 1897 the Deutsche Bank was able to announce in its Business Report: 'The Northern Pacific Railway Company and the Oregon Railroad & Navigation Company have started to pay dividends on their ordinary preferred stock.'[231]

Whereas the participation in Northern Pacific was determined purely by financial interests, with political factors playing no part, the involvement of the Deutsche Bank in the Romanian oil industry (when it took over Steaua Romana) was different: in addition to the positions of its negotiating partners, it also had to take account of the attitude of the Romanian government and people. The German government, on the other hand, although it later took a lively interest in transactions in Romania, initially held back in the run-up to the Steaua acquisition.

The oil market had been in turmoil since the turn of the century. Paraffin sales were declining as more and more households went over to electricity and more and more streets were lit by gas. Although the decline was offset by increasing consumption of petrol, lubricants and fuel oil, given that new oil fields were being discovered and opened up all over the place, the situation as a whole was characterized by fierce competition for markets. A dominant position here was occupied by the Standard Oil Company, headed by John D. Rockefeller.

So when, in the early years of the twentieth century, the Romanian government sought to put its economy (hitherto almost entirely dependent on cereal exports) on to a broader footing by developing the oil industry, it was mainly with Standard Oil and with its traditional creditor, the Disconto-Gesellschaft, that it entered into negotiations. Investment was necessary, initially to substitute mechanical boring techniques for the often primitive method of oil extraction using wells dug by hand and subsequently to improve the transport infra-structure. For this, foreign capital was required. However, the mood in the kingdom of Romania, which had achieved full independence from the Ottoman Empire only recently (1878), was characterized by a nationalism bordering on xenophobia. The anxiety about falling into a fresh dependency that the negotiations with Standard Oil triggered off among the people of Romania was seized on by the liberal opposition to overthrow the government in 1901.

Unlike Standard Oil, which was after an oil concession for government estates, the Deutsche Bank needed to take less account of Romanian nationalism when it took over Steaua Romana in 1903. Deutsche Bank's involvement was even welcome to the Romanian government as counterbalancing American influence.

Steaua Romana had been adding to its refining, storage and transport facilities since the mid-1890s by buying up large tracts of oil-rich territory in the Car-pathians, but following the collapse of the oil price it had been in financial difficulties since 1900. As a result, the Ungarische Bank für Industrie und Handel in Budapest, Steaua Romana's principal shareholder, was put into liquidation in November 1902. The Wiener Bankverein, fearing in turn for its claims against the Ungarische Bank für Industrie und Handel, was on the lookout for a buyer for Steaua Romana. Whereas Standard Oil and the Disconto-Gesellschaft had already been showing interest in Steaua for some years, Gwinner initially placed his services at the disposal of the Wiener Bankverein simply as an intermediary.[232] The offer that Gwinner then made to Rockefeller on 25 November 1902 (through James Stillman, Chairman of the National City Bank of New York) was for Standard Oil to take over two-thirds of Steaua, with the remaining third going to the Deutsche Bank. Two days later a telegram arrived, declining the offer: Standard Oil described the purchase price proposed as too high.[233]

When in March 1903 a signal did come from America that they were prepared to negotiate, Steaua and the Wiener Bankverein were no longer interested in a transatlantic deal. The latter had meanwhile opened negotiations with the Disconto-Gesellschaft. These were subsequently broken off, however, when on 27 June 1903 an agreement was concluded with the Deutsche Bank, which had finally made up its mind to take over the majority of Steaua shares and restructure the company.[234] Two days later Gwinner informed Stillman that 'the Romanian oil deal that had slipped from our grasp has in the end come back to us, and we have decided to take it over and reorganize the company'.[235] Gwinner also referred to the fact that the Romanian people had set their minds against Standard Oil because they feared that the American concern would monopolize their domestic oil industry. This may in fact have been the argument that persuaded the Wiener Bankverein to decide against Standard Oil.

The fact that the Deutsche Bank was eventually chosen in preference to the Disconto-Gesellschaft may have had something to do with financial considerations as well as with the close relations between the Wiener Bankverein and the Deutsche Bank going back over many years.[236] Until shortly before the conclusion of the agreement with the Deutsche Bank on 27 June, the Wiener Bankverein had been in negotiation with both institutions, and Adolph von Hansemann, proprietor of the Disconto-Gesellschaft, consequently reacted with great disgruntlement when, to his surprise, negotiations were broken off. An indignant correspondence ensued between the two Berlin institutions on the one hand and the Wiener Bankverein on the other. In it, Hansemann expressed the suspicion that the Deutsche Bank had been kept informed about the talks with the Disconto-Gesellschaft from the outset, a suggestion that Gwinner of course vehemently denied.[237]

The takeover and restructuring of Steaua were carried out in such a way that the Ungarische Bank für Industrie und Handel could be liquidated without losses to its creditors and Steaua largely freed of debts and substantially improved in terms of its capital structure. The Deutsche Bank had thus acquired 'a company with a big future for a relatively small amount of money'.[238] In the following year, the bank brought together all its oil industry activities, Steaua included, in the Deutsche Petroleum-Aktiengesellschaft (DPAG), which operated as a holding company.[239] With a share of a little over 50 per cent, it secured for itself a majority of votes and hence the leading role; the Wiener Bankverein took 25 per cent, and the rest went to smaller institutions associated with the Deutsche Bank. DPAG thus became closely bound to the Deutsche Bank; 'basically, it was a department that looked after oil'.[240] Emil Georg Stauss, DPAG's first managing director, appointed in 1904, made his career through oil business. He rose to be head of Steaua in 1914 and a year later joined the managing board of the Deutsche Bank.

The bank's involvement in the Romanian oil industry was marked from the outset by competition not only with Standard Oil but also with the Disconto-Gesellschaft. It was not at all the case that, as the Berlin information service *Handels-Signale* reported, 'the advances made by the Standard Oil Company in Europe prompted the two Berlin big banks to mount serious resistance against American attempts to monopolize the oil market'.[241] Rather, the already existing rivalry between the Deutsche Bank and the Disconto-Gesellschaft was aggravated by the collaboration between the latter and Standard Oil.

In its involvement in the Romanian oil industry, the Deutsche Bank did not restrict itself to capital participations, but played an actively entrepreneurial role. Particularly in the face of competition from Standard Oil, Steaua continued to have a hard time of it. Although in Romania itself it managed to win a good market position, in the export markets, particularly in Germany, prices were dictated by the Americans. As Gwinner wrote in his memoirs: 'We had to learn that the main problem is not extracting the oil but selling it. For example, we would bring Romanian petroleum up the Danube in tankers to Regensburg. The Americans promptly set the price in the vicinity of that city so low that there was nothing left for us out of the proceeds; in fact, in the first year we operated at a loss. Our British partners wrote at the time that it would be more profitable "to pour the oil into the Rhine". A joker on our staff answered the letter by saying that transport costs from Regensburg to Mannheim were too dear. It was cheaper to use the Danube.'[242]

In the end, the Deutsche Bank found itself obliged to 'do a deal with the Americans' with the result 'that we shall in future, although we managed to salvage the individuality of our German sales company, be entitled only to supply 12 per cent of German petroleum consumption, and that the Americans dictate the prices', as Gwinner explained to the Chancellor and a Foreign Office representative in July 1907.[243] This arrangement aroused passions in both Germany and Romania, with both governments seeing a threat to their respective national interests. However, the agreement with the Americans related only to oil used for lighting, consumption of which was steadily declining overall; in fact, it amounted to only 30 per cent of Steaua's production.

Nevertheless, Gwinner made it his goal to get a Reich oil monopoly established. Under this, a government-controlled company would have a monopoly in importing and distributing oil. Gwinner first put the plans to the Chancellor in 1907; in 1910 they began to take shape at last, but in 1912 they finally foundered on the resistance of the Disconto-Gesellschaft and Standard Oil. In the fuel-oil and petrol markets the situation looked rather better, and by the outbreak of the First World War Steaua had been able to gain a solid position. 'In the end, the Deutsche Bank even made a lot of money out of the deal', Gwinner noted retrospectively, but he added: 'If I had my time over again I would never, as a banker, touch the oil business.'[244]

3. The Baghdad Railway

Probably the most spectacular foreign venture undertaken by the Deutsche Bank was its crucial involvement (it had overall control) in the construction of the Baghdad Railway. As a result of this, from the turn of the century onwards it found itself right in the middle of diplomatic intrigues in the Balkans and became a factor in Germany's bid for world power. The mere size of the project caused a stir: the first stretch of track was to link Constantinople with Ankara, and the railway was subsequently extended to Baghdad and even beyond, to Basra. Right from the start of the so-called 'Oriental adventure', the fact that the project was to be financed by German banks drew international attention. The reason for this was that the European great powers – France, Britain and Russia – were already pursuing significant interests of a financial, economic and political nature in the Ottoman Empire.

The Sultan, Abdul Hamid II, had commissioned plans for a comprehensive rail network to open up his country back in the early 1870s, but Turkey's national bankruptcy in 1875 had made any implementation of those plans impossible. As developments in Europe and North America had shown, railways laid the foundations for an efficient system of agriculture and often provided the initial impulse for industrialization. Accordingly, Sultan Abdul Hamid II hoped that building a railway would facilitate the economic development of thinly populated Anatolia. 'If railways are capable of boosting a country's economic generative forces and capacity for consumption, this will above all be the case in Anatolia, where all too frequently the lack of transport in the interior means that substantial quantities of fruit decay and huge tracts of land must lie fallow.' Such were the grounds on which the German engineer Wilhelm Pressel, who had drawn up the first Turkish railway plans, continued to argue, ten years after the initial failure, for a resumption of the project.[245]

However, what the Sultan had in mind was primarily the strategic importance of the undertaking. The railway was intended to make it easier to move troops about the vast territory of the Ottoman Empire, which straddled the continents of Europe and Asia. It was also meant to improve the Constantinople government's control over the more remote regions of the country, thus consolidating its power.

When in the mid-1880s the Sultan's attention once again turned to building a railway line across the Asian part of the Ottoman Empire, there was fresh talk of a Baghdad Railway. It began, in fact, with the Anatolian Railway, which was to run from Haidarpasha (a suburb of Constantinople on the Asian shore of the Bosphorus) to Ankara. The Turkish government was anxious to commission British or German banks to finance and carry out the project in order to loosen the country's ties with France, which had hitherto been very close and were sometimes experienced as oppressive. Previously, the Ottoman Empire had covered its financial requirements almost exclusively on the Paris capital market. Moreover, the French big banks exerted enormous indirect influence over Turkey's national finances, for through the French-owned Banque Impériale Ottomane they appointed the top officials of the body that administered the national debt, the Administration de la Dette Publique Ottomane.[246] While the British government was quick to recognize the commercial, political and strategic benefits that building a railway in Asian Turkey would bring to Britain, Britain's banks showed little interest.

Nor was the Deutsche Bank at all keen at first. This time the initiative did not come from George Siemens, who even showed considerable hesitation over embarking on so large and obviously risky a project. Instead it came from one Alfred von Kaulla, a member of the managing board of the Württembergische Vereinsbank, who was in Constantinople at the beginning of 1888, handling negotiations about arms sales for the Mauser works. In the process he became acquainted with representatives of the Turkish government, who eventually held out to him the prospect of awarding the concession for the construction of the Anatolian Railway to a German financial group. The project being too big for the Württembergische Vereinsbank, the provincial institution offered it to the Deutsche Bank, on the supervisory board of which it was represented as a major shareholder. The excellent relations that existed between the two banks were further enhanced by the personal friendship between Georg Siemens and the chairman of the managing board of the Württembergische Vereinsbank, Kilian Steiner. However, in June 1888 Siemens was still saying no to Steiner. It was only when the Turkish government said it was prepared to guarantee payment of interest on the capital by mortgaging part of its tax revenues that the Deutsche Bank showed a greater readiness to agree to the undertaking.

In addition to the financial risk, the Deutsche Bank also shied away initially from the diplomatic complications that might arise from an involvement in the Ottoman Empire, the slow political decline of which had for almost a century led to repeated clashes among the European great powers, and promised to go on doing so.[247] All of them were in one way or another interested in the legacy of the 'sick man of the Bosphorus'. So before negotiating further with the Sultan, the Deutsche Bank wanted to be sure what attitude the German government would take. Accordingly, on 15 August 1888 it directed a formal request to the Foreign Office. The reply came back on 2 September from Bismarck in person:

the Reich had no political objections and would even provide diplomatic support, he wrote, though at the same time indicating the limits of what he was prepared to do in this direction: 'German entrepreneurs investing capital in Anatolian railway construction are indeed taking a gamble. To start with, there are the problems of pursuing legal action in the Orient, but the situation may be further aggravated by military and other complications. The consequent perils for German capital will be incumbent on the entrepreneurs alone, nor may the latter count on the German government bolstering them up against the vicissitudes associated with risky enterprises overseas.'[248]   This was a significant reservation, but in principle it left the way free to proceed, and that same day Kaulla set out for Constantinople to open negotiations with the Turkish government. The German ambassador in Constantinople gave the project diplomatic protection in talks with his British and Italian colleagues. The understanding reached with the British was particularly important because the British government was known to have attempted to implement the project with the aid of British banks the year before. The international situation in fact very much favoured such an understanding: in the eyes of Britain and Italy, whose pact with Austria-Hungary (the so-called Mediterranean or Middle Eastern Triple Alliance) included Germany as a sleeping partner, construction of the railway under German leadership promised to act as a counterweight to French influence in the region.[249]

On 4 October 1888 the Turkish government finally granted a financial consortium headed by the Deutsche Bank the concession to build and operate a railway line from Haidarpasha to Ankara. An initial stretch of that line, which a British company had already constructed, was acquired by the bank for 6 million francs. Hoping to be able to place the financing of the Anatolian Railway on a broad foundation, Siemens offered holdings both to British banks and also to the leading German credit institutions. Although as regards amortizing and paying interest on their capital, the Turkish government was guaranteeing investors an annual income of 15,000 francs per kilometre of railway constructed, Siemens received almost nothing but refusals. In the end, only institutions closely connected with the Deutsche Bank participated in the consortium: in addition to the Württembergische Vereinsbank, through whose initiative the deal had come about in the first place, these were the Berliner Handels-Gesellschaft, Robert Warschauer & Co., and the Deutsche Vereinsbank in Frankfurt.

The Anatolian Railway was built and operated by the Anatolian Railway Company, a company under Turkish law that was set up for the purpose (in Constantinople in the following year) by the Deutsche Bank, the Württembergische Vereinsbank and the Deutsche Vereinsbank. It completed the stretch to Ankara by 1893. Those who profited from the company included not least the industrial customers of the participating banks, who obtained lucrative export orders. All the materials required for building and operating the railway were imported from Germany, while most of the work was done by German companies – the Frankfurt firm of Philipp Holzmann, for instance, which was closely tied to the Deutsche Bank.[250] Other major orders went to the Krupp steel concern for the supply of rails and to the Munich firms Krauss & Comp. and J.A. Maffei, the Hannoversche Maschinenbau Actien-Gesellschaft, and the Maschinenfabrik Esslingen für Lokomotiven. As early as 1890 Siemens was alluding in parliament to the associated benefits to the German economy: 'The result of the new constructions that have fallen to the *modus operandi* of German capital in recent years has led in the present to a very high or relatively high level of activity in our industries,' he said in the Reichstag debate on the Friendship, Trade and Maritime Agreement between the German and Ottoman empires. Siemens argued for adoption of the treaty on the assumption that 'the German Reich will thereby win powerful sympathies in the Middle East', particularly since (as he stressed very much in line with the policy of the Reich's first Chancellor, dismissed only months before) it had no military or colonial ambitions in the region: 'The German Reich and our German nation has nothing to conquer in the Middle East and nothing to desire; we simply have an interest in stabilizing the situation there.'[251]

Siemens attempted to make the Anatolian Railway more profitable by linking it up with the rail network in the European part of Turkey, which at the time still included large tracts of present-day Albania and Greece. There, on the stretch between Vienna and Constantinople, the now legendary Orient Express had been in operation since 1888. But Sultan Abdul Hamid II had only a secondary interest in the railway's being profitable. He was much more keen, for strategic reasons, on extending the line to Baghdad.[252] So in 1891, even before the stretch to Ankara was completed, he once again turned to the Deutsche Bank. However, the crisis of Northern Pacific, which started to become apparent around this time, had meanwhile made Siemens dramatically aware of the risks associated with financing railways, particularly abroad. He also feared diplomatic complications because building eastward beyond Ankara would begin to encroach on the Russian sphere of influence. As a result, he showed little inclination to accede to the Turkish government's request.[253]

However, to meet the Sultan half-way he offered, rather than extending the line beyond Ankara, to build a link running south from Eskisehir to Konya. This promised to be more lucrative economically. For one thing, only a single mountain range needed to be crossed, and for another the line could be joined up with two branch terminal lines to the Mediterranean coast.[254] In 1893 the Anatolian Railway Company received the concession for this stretch, and three years later it was completed. The company was immediately granted a concession to extend the Anatolian Railway beyond Ankara to Kayseri (Caesarea), although it had made no such request.

Still, however, the railway did not go to Baghdad. Further approaches by the Sultan to the Deutsche Bank failed to elicit the desired response, and even the threat of granting the concession to a rival concern, should the Deutsche Bank abide by its refusal, produced no effect. The only possible candidate would have been the Banque Impériale Ottomane, with which the Deutsche Bank was meanwhile collaborating.[255] Furthermore, the Deutsche Bank was now rather less keen on this risky railway project than had been the case in 1891. The Northern Pacific restructuring was taking up much of its energies. Clearly, too, continuing the railway beyond Ankara would be an extremely costly business since it involved crossing two mountain ranges, the Taurus and the Amanus. And lastly, the farther the railway advanced in the direction of Baghdad, the more it attracted the attention of the European powers.

This is precisely the area where the Sultan sought to apply pressure. For if Bismarck had adopted an attitude of sceptical neutrality towards the Anatolian Railway, seeing it as a private business venture of only minor importance in foreign policy terms, under his successors the interest taken by German diplomacy in the project had gradually increased. The prelude to this was probably the first Middle Eastern trip that Kaiser Wilhelm II had made back in 1889. The very next year Germany consolidated its relations with the Ottoman Empire by concluding what it called a Friendship, Commercial and Maritime Treaty. In the following years the foreign policy of the German Reich turned away from Bismarck's more defensive concern with maintaining the European balance of power and towards a steadily more offensive campaign for a 'place in the sun', to use Wilhelm II's famous words. In the wake of this development, railway construction in the Ottoman Empire gained increasingly in political importance.

An entirely new phase of German Middle Eastern policy began in the late 1890s with the appointment of Baron Adolf Marschall von Bieberstein as the Reich's ambassador in Constantinople in 1897, and above all with the Kaiser's second Middle Eastern trip in the following year. Wilhelm II had become keen on the idea of the Baghdad Railway, hoping that it would lead to a big increase in German influence, both economic and political. When the Sultan then proposed to the Kaiser granting a German company the concession for building the line to Baghdad, Wilhelm agreed with delight. Siemens could now no longer refuse without showing the Kaiser up and dealing a substantial blow to the bank's reputation in the process. 'Thus was the Deutsche Bank pushed into its most spectacular foreign venture, a venture in which it had not actually wished to be involved.'[256]

On Christmas Eve 1899 Siemens sent his Berlin colleagues a telegram: 'Baghdad Convention signed here today.'[257] Previously, he had had to agree to granting the Turkish government, which was permanently short of money, an additional loan of 200,000 Turkish pounds, noting laconically in a letter to head office: 'You will think me crazy if despite what we agreed, despite the panic on all the European markets, despite my conviction, which I have been proclaiming since March, of a fall in share prices, American cereal imports, etc., etc., I wish to give the Turks an advance of 200,000 Ltq = 3,800,000 marks at 7 per cent, when it is possible to purchase foreign exchange from reputable German banks at the same rate. The so-called Baghdad Convention is just a piece of paper, yet here am I paying 200,000 Ltq for it!'[258]

Following the granting of this provisional concession to extend the Eskisehir–Konya railway line to Baghdad, Siemens sought at least to postpone construction for a while, and to keep the financial risks to a minimum by means of substantial participation by British, French and Russian companies as well. However, this plan turned out to be more difficult than he had at first assumed. The London banks continued to show no interest in Turkish railway construction, and even the New York bank of J.P. Morgan & Co., with which the Deutsche Bank had collaborated in restructuring Northern Pacific, this time refused the invitation. Banque Impériale Ottomane did agree to participate, however, and positive replies could also be expected from Austria-Hungary and from Italy.

These problems played into Marschall von Bieberstein's hands. Whereas Siemens regarded participation by non-German investors as indispensable (since it was not possible to raise the requisite amount of capital in Germany alone), the diplomat wanted to implement the project under exclusively German colours as 'a German national undertaking, executed, administered and operated as such', as he put it in a report to the Foreign Office on 3 February 1899. In his view, the government should, 'as a precaution, point [private enterprise] in the direction of those undertakings that serve the national interest'. By way of justification, he referred to the importance of the economy in bringing the Reich's foreign policy plans to fruition: 'To resolve its major problems, to develop its colonies, and to create new markets for the products of its labour, Germany needs domestic private capital of a kind that is prepared to take certain risks.'[259] The discrepant approaches and objectives of politics and business could hardly be expressed more clearly!

The result of this attitude, whereby 'the Reich, albeit without defining the aims and limits of what it was after more closely, set about gaining a foothold in the Near East between the Russian and British spheres of influence',[260] was of course to increase the potential risk of tensions and conflicts with those two great powers, which between them called the tune in Anatolia. Berlin, however, was inclined to see this development chiefly in terms of the way it compelled those powers to take no action in the region without first consulting the German Reich. Germany did indeed, as a result of its role in building the railway and of subsequent projects such as extending the port of Haidarpasha, gradually come to be seen by the other powers as 'a factor to be taken seriously in Middle Eastern politics'.[261] Witness, for example, Russia's attempt in 1899 to conclude an agreement with the German Reich in which Germany should give Russia an assurance with regard to the Straits and Russia, in return, should guarantee Germany 'a free hand in Asia Minor so far as its ... industrial and commercial undertakings were concerned'.[262] The German government did stress to Russia that it was pursuing exclusively economic rather than political interests in Turkey, but it declined to sign a treaty to that effect, having no wish to antagonize

Britain, which was following Germany's contacts with Russia (in effect, Britain's opposite number on the world stage) with some suspicion. Above all, however, the feeling a year earlier had been that Germany was in no way dependent on such an offer since this was something it could return to later – on its own terms.

It took the Deutsche Bank four years to secure the finance for the Baghdad Railway, establish the route, and plan the technical details. The death of Georg von Siemens (whom shortly after receipt of the Baghdad Railway concession the Kaiser had for this and other reasons elevated to the nobility) and the Turkish government's chronic shortage of money were further reasons why the preliminaries took so long. The final concession for building and operating the Baghdad Railway was awarded in 1903 to the Baghdad Railway Company, founded in the same year. A construction period of eight years was proposed, with the cost being calculated at 450 million francs. Shortly before the Baghdad Railway Company was set up, Arthur von Gwinner, who since the death of Georg von Siemens had been the man on the Deutsche Bank managing board responsible for the Turkish railway brief, made a further attempt to secure the participation of British banks. The German-born private banker Sir Ernest Cassel and the J.S. Morgan & Co. bank in London[263] both showed some interest. Although the British Prime Minister and his Foreign Secretary backed the proposed participation and even roped in the Baring Brothers bank, once the plan had become known it was heavily criticized in the British House of Commons and in the press. Government and banks bowed to these protests, with the result that, in the end, no British company had a holding in the 15 million franc capital of the Baghdad Railway Company.

The shares were held by the Deutsche Bank (40 per cent), the Banque Impériale Ottomane (30 per cent), the Anatolian Railway Company (10 per cent), the Wiener Bankverein and the Credit Suisse (7.5 per cent each), and finally the Banca Commerciale Italiana jointly with a number of Italian and Turkish banks (5 per cent). Even without the British, international participation in the Baghdad Railway was thus secured. The co-operation of the Banque Impériale Ottomane, incidentally, almost came to grief for political reasons shortly before the Baghdad Railway Company was floated. The French Foreign Minister, Théophile Delcassé, demanded not only that the financing be internationalized, but that British and Russian companies also be considered when it came to awarding supply and construction contracts – a demand to which the German government refused to accede.

When the Deutsche Bank then also showed reluctance to meet Delcassé's demand that it and the Banque Impériale Ottomane be placed on the same footing in the financing arrangements and on the administrative board, the French government recommended that the Banque Impériale Ottomane withdraw, though it declined to do so. The Deutsche Bank insisted on underwriting 50 per cent of the capital in order to be in charge of the project. Arthur von Gwinner became chairman of the Baghdad Railway Company, the articles of association of which provided for one of the two vice-chairmen to be German and the other French. The partnership between the Deutsche Bank and the Banque Impériale Ottomane was further reinforced in 1905 through a mutual agreement to give each other a 25 per cent share of every major piece of business in the Ottoman Empire.

In the years that followed, the whole project in fact came under increasing pressure. The Deutsche Bank wished to continue the railway beyond Baghdad to Basra and the Persian Gulf, since that seemed the only way to make the enterprise a really profitable one. That affected British interests, however, passenger and goods transport between the Gulf and Baghdad being in the hands of a British river navigation company. A tug of war began for the Sultan's favour. The British insisted on Baghdad being made the end-point of the German-built railway. They would not even entertain the compromise proposal from the Deutsche Bank to build the terminal at the confluence of the Tigris and Euphrates rivers, 50 kilometres north-east of Basra, to give Persian pilgrims the chance to use the railway for part of their journey to Mecca.

Things were further complicated for the Deutsche Bank by the shifting political situation. The revolution of the Young Turks, which ended the Sultan's rule in 1908, brought to power a government that was very much less pro-German.[264] If the Baghdad Railway was to be successfully extended to Basra nonetheless, the only way to proceed was through an understanding with the British. Moreover, in the same period (between 1907 and 1910) the former rivals, Russia and Britain, managed to reach a settlement regarding their interests in the Middle East, which considerably restricted the scope of German policy. Instead of looking on as an amused spectator of the struggle without committing itself to either side, the Reich now found itself facing an alliance of two great powers with little to put up against it. As Arthur von Gwinner summed up in his memoirs: 'These were disastrous years, German policy having refused the hand extended to it by Britain around 1900. Eventually, French financiers too were forbidden by their government to participate publicly in the Baghdad enterprise, with the result that the French remained guests at the feast rather than helpers in its preparation.'[265]

The Franco-Turkish Banque Impériale Ottomane reacted to the changed situation by loosening its ties with the Deutsche Bank and turning more towards Britain. This made the Deutsche Bank even more interested in collaborating with British banks. Here it was in possession of a trump card: Mesopotamian oil. This raw material had been gaining steadily in importance since the beginning of the century, and Britain had a bigger interest in it than any other country because in 1910 the Royal Navy had gone over to fuelling its fleet with diesel oil. The Deutsche Bank had a concession to exploit the Mossul oil field, which it had received in conjunction with the grant to the Anatolian Railway Company of the provisional concession to build the Baghdad Railway. Admittedly, since the founding of the Baghdad Railway Company that concession was no longer beyond dispute, but it could still be alluded to and at least used as a starting point for relevant negotiations.

As a result, fresh talks took place between the Deutsche Bank and British banks, and between the German and British governments.[266] Gwinner was prepared to allow the British to head the exploitation of oil resources if the British gave their consent to the extension of the Baghdad Railway to Basra. By the spring of 1914 most of the contentious questions had been cleared up. In exchange for substantial concessions on the oil front, Gwinner obtained the assurance he wanted: namely, that the Baghdad Railway Company might continue the line as far as Basra. The remaining stretch to the mouth of the Shatt al Arab waterway on the Persian Gulf was to be built by a British company. In addition, British capital was to be invested in the Baghdad Railway Company, which further undertook not to grant any national preferential rates. In the summer of 1914, Germany managed to reach agreement with France and Russia as well.

It is one of the ironies of history that the European great powers reached a settlement of their economic and political differences in the Ottoman Empire at the very moment when the First World War broke out, destroying all that had been achieved. By that time the line was complete from Haidarpasha to Jerablus (now Jarabulus in Syria) on the upper reaches of the Euphrates, except for one short stretch in the Taurus Mountains. The Eskisehir–Ankara stretch and a 60 kilometre stretch running north from Baghdad were also already built. The British completed the link to the Persian Gulf during the First World War (the better to exploit the Mesopotamian oil fields). After the war, the section of line in the Mesopotamian region was confiscated, and in 1932 it passed without compensation into Iraqi possession. The railways in Anatolia were likewise confiscated by the Allies in 1919 before passing, after savage clashes, into the hands of the Turkish authorities in 1923. Five years later (in 1928) an agreement was then reached between Turkey and the Anatolian Railway Company. Under this, the company was to receive 440 million Swiss francs in respect of its claims and rights, to be paid within 73 years. The outbreak of the Second World War wrecked this agreement, too.

The First World War thus put an end (if not all at once) to German participation in the rail link between the Bosphorus and the Persian Gulf. Public interest in this stretch of railway, once a focus of international politics, also declined in Germany. And when the last gap in the line was closed in 1940, the news struck the *Frankfurter Zeitung* as being 'a bit like a message from a bygone age'.[267]

In varying degrees, there was a political aspect to nearly all the activities of the Deutsche Bank abroad. However, the bank was more dependent on the co-operation and support of the government of the Reich in the case of the Baghdad Railway than in any other undertaking. Conversely, the government knew that without the Deutsche Bank it could not push this 'most important project of German imperialism'[268] in the direction it wanted and keep it in German hands.

But although neither the Deutsche Bank nor the Foreign Office could achieve its objectives without the backing of the other, it was also clear that the objectives they were pursuing were not the same. Siemens and later Gwinner had in mind mainly the profitability of the railway line, which is why they endeavoured to place the financing of it on the broadest possible foundation by persuading British and French investors to participate in the Baghdad Railway Company. German diplomacy, on the other hand, was concerned above all to exploit the construction of the Baghdad Railway in order to extend German influence in the Ottoman Empire. For these reasons, the German Foreign Office and Ambassador Marschall von Bieberstein in Constantinople were in favour of the project being financed largely through the German capital market; foreign holdings were to be kept as small as possible, serving merely as diplomatic safeguards.

While the Deutsche Bank representatives always took political circumstances carefully into account in negotiations about the construction, route and financing of the Baghdad Railway, they saw themselves primarily as businessmen. Their main problem invariably consisted in guaranteeing the financing and profitability of the venture in order to avoid the kind of fiasco that had occurred with Northern Pacific. 'The Deutsche Bank must not get itself into a situation whereby at any time, possibly ten or twenty years later, the charge can be levelled against it that for the sake of its own profits it placed large amounts of German capital in a dangerous situation', Siemens wrote in a report to his management colleagues in April 1900. Here it was not so much national considerations that guided him; it was chiefly concern about the position of the Deutsche Bank as market leader: 'Given the standing that the Deutsche Bank has achieved in the German credit system, such a charge would have the most detrimental effect not only on the Deutsche Bank but also on the fulfilment of the credit requirements of its enormous present-day clientele.'[269]

In agreeing to the Baghdad Railway scheme, the Deutsche Bank did to a certain extent bow to politics (specifically, to the wishes of Wilhelm II). In the negotiations of subsequent years, however, it sought by contrast to turn the urgings of the Kaiser and his Foreign Office to advantage in order to obtain financial guarantees from the government. For example, in a letter of 11 September 1900 to the Secretary of State at the Foreign Office, Bernhard von Bülow, Siemens pointed out that 'since the start of negotiations concerning the Baghdad Railway we for our part have left it in no doubt that we can venture upon and carry through this vast undertaking only if we are able to rely on the openly declared approval of the German government'. A 'suitable form' of such approval, Siemens added, would be 'that the Preussische Seehandlung participated in the issue of the relevant bonds'.[270] In a letter to his future son-in-law, Theodor Wiegand, he expressed himself even more clearly: 'The German press, which otherwise has so little to celebrate, is currently praising the Anatolian Railway to the skies. But as a piece of business? Good Lord! In that

Adelbert Delbrück, private banker,
initiator and co-founder of Deutsche Bank, Chairman of the
Administrative Board (subsequently the Supervisory Board) from 1871 to 1889

Ludwig Bamberger, co-founder, political advisor
and member of the Administrative Board from 1870 to 1872

Georg von Siemens,
first Spokesman of the Board of Managing Directors from 1870 to 1900

Rudolph von Koch,
Spokesman of the Board of Managing Directors
from 1901 to 1909

Arthur von Gwinner,
Spokesman of the Board of Managing Directors from 1910 to 1919

The formation of AEG in 1887 saw the launch of industrial financing; the cover of an AEG catalogue from 1892

Mortgage-backed bond issued by Siemens & Halske in 1893

A share certificate from the formation of Mannesmannröhren-Werke in 1890

Deutsche Bank's London branch was opened in 1873

The Bahia Blanca branch (Argentina) of Deutsche Ueberseeische Bank
(Banco Alemán Transatlántico) opened in 1903

The Buenos Aires headquarters of Deutsche Ueberseeische Bank, founded in 1886; since 1978 it has housed Deutsche Bank's Buenos Aires branch

A journey on the Baghdad Railway; the welcoming committee for the German Kaiser
Wilhelm II in Hereke (between Constantinople and Ismid) on 20 October 1898

Hermann Wallich,
member of the Board of Managing
Directors from 1870 to 1894

Karl Helfferich,
member of the Board of Managing
Directors from 1908 to 1915

Georg von Siemens
as a signalman
on the Baghdad Railway;
caricature from 1900

Tickets issued by the Anatolian
Railway Company, reserved
for Arthur von Gwinner,
member of the Board of
Managing Directors, in 1907

The Shanghai headquarters of Deutsch-Asiatische Bank, founded in 1889

In 1906 Deutsch-Asiatische Bank, now Deutsche Bank,
was given permission to issue its own banknotes

Deutsch-Asiatische Bank opened a branch in Peking in 1905

The bank's first premises
were opened in Berlin, at
Französische Strasse 21,
on 9 April 1870

The bank's head office in Berlin (opened in 1898) on the corner of
Behrenstrasse and Kanonierstrasse

The entrance to the cashiers' office in Mauerstrasse →

The large cashiers' office in the complex of buildings between Mauerstrasse, Französische Strasse and Jägerstrasse, Berlin, was built in 1907 and 1908

Deutsche Bank Berlin

The classical shot of Deutsche Bank in Berlin with its two *Schwibbögen* (flying buttresses)

respect it is and will always remain a side-show, like the "Club of the Harmless". To me personally, the railway was very useful, because that was when people started to believe in me, and when you are seriously pursuing major affairs that is an advantage, but the railway itself is merely a dead track, and HM's enthusiasm for Mesopotamia has no deeper value as far as German interests are concerned.'[271]

One of the many historians to have looked into the problems surrounding the construction of the Baghdad Railway also comes to the conclusion that the Deutsche Bank was interested 'primarily in securing the capital sums invested in the Baghdad Railway Company': 'There can be no question, on the part of the Deutsche Bank, of a struggle for supremacy for German exports or for German trade in the Middle East.'[272] But when, in 1906, Karl Helfferich moved from the colonial department of the Foreign Office to the management of the Anatolian Railway Company, the broad public perception was that political influence on the undertaking would further increase. Some newspapers assumed that the Deutsche Bank wished to take advantage of Helfferich's contacts; others, including the London *Times*, saw it as a sign of increasing political influence on economic affairs.[273] Helfferich did indeed prove his worth as a link between the Turkish government and the local representatives of German diplomacy on the one hand, and the parent company and the Foreign Office in Berlin on the other. His eventual appointment to the managing board of the Deutsche Bank in 1908 came not least because of his successful brokering work in Constantinople.

In the construction of the Baghdad Railway, the economic and financial interests of investors were closely interwoven with the interests of German foreign policy. In its involvement, the Deutsche Bank sought to take due account of both. Whether positively or critically expressed, the impression that increasingly took root among contemporaries was that the Deutsche Bank had, as the *Frankfurter Zeitung* put it in March 1914, 'long since outgrown its private economic interests'. The newspaper went on: 'The past year in particular has confirmed this view. The Deutsche Bank has not confined itself to concluding financial deals with Turkey in a big way; it is definitely practising politics there by methodically smoothing the way for the German economy. This comes out most clearly in the German–French negotiations just successfully concluded regarding the partition of interests in the Middle East, negotiations that, significantly, were conducted less by diplomats than by a managing director of the Deutsche Bank.'[274] A man like Siemens would not have been happy at all with such assessments. However, his successors already thought very differently on the subject.

IV. Banking and Politics

1. Political attitudes and political involvement of members of the managing and supervisory boards

The complaint about top business people being underrepresented in the political parties and parliament in Germany has a long history. Albert Ballin, chairman of the shipping company Hapag, spoke of the 'painful lack of knowledgeable and experienced managers of industry, banking, shipping, trade and transport in the Reichstag' back in 1907. And the then State Secretary of the Interior, Theobald von Bethmann Hollweg, remarked in January 1909 that 'big business does not have the kind of representation here in the Reichstag that it should have, given its importance as regards our whole economic existence'.[275]

The number of entrepreneurs in the Reichstag reached an absolute peak in 1887 with 14.5 per cent, declining steadily thereafter to a figure of 4.6 per cent in the period 1912–18. The main reason put forward for this political abstinence on the part of the economic élite was that their many business commitments did not permit them to pursue active political careers – what the contemporary observer Max Weber called 'the problem of availability'. There were various other reasons in addition to these occupational demands. The centre of power in the Germany of the Second Empire was not the Reichstag but the government, the executive. Many questions of political principle were decided by circumventing the Reichstag and occasionally even going against it. As a result, the house enjoyed only limited and in many areas even diminishing prestige, which not only caused prominent entrepreneurs to steer clear of it, but also led to a 'general lessening of the social exclusivity of members of parliament as a class'. A further reason could be seen in members' dependence on extra-parliamentary 'pressure groups', which involved a loss of individual freedom of action that represented the very opposite of entrepreneurial autonomy. Finally, German entrepreneurs had a highly organized system of associations with the aid of which they were able to represent their interests more efficiently than through political parties or in national and provincial parliaments;[276] August Servaes, a spokesmen of the Verein Deutscher Eisen- und Stahlindustrieller (Association of German Iron and Steel Manufacturers) (founded in 1873) and one of the most influential men in his position in late nineteenth-century Germany, had already issued the watchword back in 1875 (that is, at a time when there were still Liberal majorities in the Reichstag) to the effect that the association should no longer address itself to parliament but 'as far as possible ... go straight to the Chancellor'.[277]

If the number of entrepreneurs in politics was small, that of proprietors or managers of banks was even smaller. This group seldom sought a public stage on which to present and implement their political convictions. In fact, bankers taking direct political action were very much the exception; as far as most of them were concerned, it was a case of 'the best banker is the one nobody talks about'.[278]

The Deutsche Bank had one or two 'political bankers' among its board members, not that their political involvement was by any means free from controversy. Apart from Adelbert Delbrück, who was a member of the Deutsche Fortschrittspartei but was mainly, as we have seen, active in association politics, the most prominent figure in this respect in the early years was Ludwig Bamberger, although he was more of a 'part-time banker' as far as the period after 1870 is concerned. In any case, it was only for two years (1870–72) that Bamberger sat on the administrative board of the Deutsche Bank. The reason why he resigned his position so soon was that he was afraid his parliamentary effectiveness as a leading member of the National Liberals might be compromised by his business connections. Granted, he did so with some regret: 'I resigned in 1872 because I already foresaw the era of the defamation and disparagement of any kind of business activity that has so powerfully imposed itself since. I wished to protect my parliamentary position on major economic issues against any possibility of attack, no matter how remote. For the same reason I also resigned from the administration of Stolberg Mines. I did both unwillingly, not because of any pecuniary advantage forfeited thereby but because there is nothing more instructive as regards resolving the economic problems of legislation than to be in close touch with the actual running of a business. If one's eyes are trained for it, both practically and theoretically, one learns things every day; out of touch, one suffers a narrowing of one's field of vision.'[279]

Unlike Bamberger, Georg Siemens, the bank's spokesman during the first three decades of its existence, experienced no conflict of interest between profession and politics. For him it went without saying that a leading representative of the business world also played an active role in politics. Siemens had had early exposure to liberal ideas as a child. His father, Councillor of Justice Johann Georg Siemens, standing for the Liberals, had twice represented the Merseburg-Schweinitz-Wittenberg constituency (in which the Siemens family's Ahlsdorf estate lay) in the Prussian lower house. The son ran in the same constituency and in November 1873 was likewise elected to the house of representatives, of which he remained a member until the beginning of 1875. Siemens initially needed to make himself known in the constituency politically and was simply making use of an opportunity; his goal from the outset was a seat in the new national parliament, the Reichstag. He made the mistake, however, of informing neither his fellow managing directors nor the administrative board of the bank. Wallich and Delbrück both voiced misgivings, fearing that his seat in parliament (possibly even seats in two parliaments) might cause Siemens to neglect his work and even cause harm to the bank. The vice-chairman of the administrative board, Eduard von der Heydt, went further still and spoke out against members of the bank's managing board accepting seats in parliament.

In a letter to Wallich dated 1 October 1873, Siemens defended his position vigorously and claimed his candidature as a self-evident right: 'So I cannot agree with you when you say the matter is simply a private desire on my part. I regarded it as a fortunate thing that such a desire, which was indeed present in my case, coincided with the interests of the bank; however, I hardly need assure you that such a private desire would not in itself have decided me had I not believed I was doing a service to the bank thereby, and certainly not if I had thought I was damaging its interests. We have both of us been delighted with the bank far too often and felt furious with the bank far too often not to be totally in love with the dear old thing.'[280] Siemens remained loyal to his convictions, and Wallich and the administrative board eventually came to terms with his political activities.

From 1874 onwards Siemens also represented his constituency as a National Liberal member in the Reichstag. He had joined the National Liberals because, although critical of individual points of the party's programme, he by and large found that it best reflected his own political views. He did not always follow the party line, admittedly, but more than once went his own way on an important question. The parliamentary party was a large one, however, numbering 155 members at that time, and as a political newcomer Siemens did not, on the whole, make much of an impact. Particularly in the debates concerning major decisions on banking and monetary matters, it was Ludwig Bamberger (and with him Eduard Lasker) who dictated the standpoint of the parliamentary party with substantially greater authority. Siemens occasionally complained bitterly about the 'party tyranny' exercised by these two, and he once became involved in so heated a dispute with Bamberger that he 'sent him his seconds'.[281] Moreover, Bamberger was a splendid orator, whereas Siemens tended to speak 'clumsily and disjointedly',[282] with little idea of how to capture an audience.

Siemens was also not given a seat on the consultative committee appointed to discuss the Bank Act, although this was a job for which he felt himself very much cut out. Shortly before, he had published a memorandum on 'The Bank-of-Issue System and the Bank Bill', which tackled the whole question of monetary and central bank policy, and contained a number of fundamental propositions, many of which remain topical today.[283] Bamberger found the brochure 'somewhat under-worked' and brought out his own essay in the same year – twice as long, and entitled 'The Bank of Issue before the Reichstag'. However, the Bank Bill that the government introduced into the Reichstag for its first reading in November 1874 contained nothing about a central German bank of issue.

Among the most vigorous advocates of a 'Reichsbank' were Bamberger and Lasker, who both made key speeches and dominated the debate. Bamberger's speech was more concerned with technical monetary questions, while Lasker dealt more with the political aspects in the context of German unity. However, Siemens too was given the floor and on 18 November 1874 and 28 January

1875 made his first two major speeches in the Reichstag.[284] He supported Bamberger's and Lasker's call for the creation of a national bank and dwelt particularly on the dual function of the bank of issue: deciding the price of money and determining the volume of money. In his view the creation of money by the system known as 'note money' (*Zettelgeld*), i.e. the production of bank notes by many banks of issue, was subject to inadequate control. The coverage provisions were insufficient to deal with an emergency, and the multiplication of notes in circulation did not keep pace with the rise in the national product. He did not even make an exception for the Preussische Bank, Germany's largest bank of issue at the time.[285] But Siemens also opposed any overrating of the functions of the new central bank: 'A bank is quite powerless on its own unless backed by the thrifty population diligently pursuing trade and industry and through its diligence acquiring claims against other countries that those other countries must pay promptly in gold. A bank is no more able to achieve anything without an industrious nation behind it than the famous general we have in our midst [a reference to Count Moltke] is capable of winning a battle without an army.'[286]

Siemens lost his seat in the Reichstag soon afterwards, when in the general election of early 1877 he was defeated by his Conservative opponent. He made an attempt to recover it following the dissolution of parliament in connection with the two attempts on the Kaiser's life and Bismarck's plans for an anti-socialist law in the summer of 1878, but he was again defeated. An appeal to the voters of his constituency shows his political attitude: 'If the last parliament was dissolved because the majority did not agree with a bill directed against the Social Democrats, a bill introduced by the government in the wake of a condemnable attempt on the sacred life of HM the Emperor, then I for my part wish to state that I would support all measures likely to do away with the mounting lack of discipline among certain classes of the people in consequence of Social Democracy.'[287]

Following Bismarck's switch to a policy of protectionism, Siemens quit the National Liberal Party in 1879 and joined the Liberale Vereinigung (Liberal Union) led by Bamberger, Lasker and Forckenbeck, which in 1884 amalgamated with the Deutsche Fortschrittspartei (German Progressive Party) and the Deutsche Freisinnige Partei (German Liberal Party). His position on tariff policy was a thoroughly pragmatic one: 'I am neither a free-trader on principle nor a protectionist on principle and as a pragmatist take as my starting point the proposition that the truth usually lies in the middle; I also know that a thriving industry and a thriving agriculture always go hand in hand ... Accordingly, in 1876 I voted to retain the small customs duty on iron. But knowingly and systematically committing injustices and needlessly favouring individual classes at the expense of all taxpayers ..., that I have refused to do from the outset. For nothing in the life of a people is in the habit of being punished more severely than injustice, which generates distrust and hence destroys the inner equilibrium that is the sole guarantee of peace and with it the steady development of general prosperity.'[288]

Having twice been defeated in parliamentary elections, Siemens devoted most of his energies in the following years to the Deutsche Bank. He turned down a further candidature in 1881 and did not apply again for a seat in the Reichstag until 1884. This time the supervisory board gave its consent, if only for one term initially. He was put up by the Deutsche Freisinnige Partei in the Coburg constituency in the autumn of 1884 and was duly elected. Once again, Siemens rarely stood out in plenary sessions of the new house. On issues of fundamental political principle he kept well in the background, intervening only in debates on legislative proposals of direct concern to banks, the stock exchange, or other financial and monetary matters. A focal point of his parliamentary activity in this respect was the Stock Exchange Taxation Act (*Börsensteuergesetz*).

Under the law of 1 July 1881 'concerning the levy of imperial stamp duty', all securities had for the first time been made subject to an issue tax and a turnover tax, both of modest proportions. In June 1884, prompted by the conservative parties, the government proposed an amendment to the Stamp Duty Act that was to replace the old fixed payment with a percentage turnover stamp. In the first debate in the Reichstag on 21 January 1885, Siemens embarked on a statement of principle concerning the significance of the stock exchange. He began by admitting to a degree of bias in the matter 'in so far as I am part of the management of one of the largest German institutions, to wit the one that, after the Reichsbank, has the biggest turnover figures. Possibly my interest is not quite as direct as that of the large-scale landowner in the future introduction of cereal duties. Nevertheless, I think it right to clarify this question from the outset; you may then consider what value you wish to place on my deductions.'[289]

The image of the stock exchange was far from positive in imperial Germany. It was not only among the vast majority of the population (at all levels of society) that it had a remarkably poor reputation; many economists and politicians held it in similarly low esteem. Lasker referred to the stock exchange in the Reichstag in 1873 as 'an academy for the infringement of our laws', and the Prussian Railways Minister, Albert Maybach, speaking in the Prussian house of representatives in 1879, coined what was to become the widely peddled image of the stock exchange as a 'poison tree ... casting its baleful shadow over the life of the nation'. Terms such as 'casino', 'gambling den' and 'Monte Carlo without music' cropped up frequently as descriptions of the stock exchange.[290] Dealing on the stock exchange was regarded as peculiarly unproductive since it brought no visible results, created no values and basically served no purpose but that of speculation.

Siemens sought to counter this: 'The stock exchange is a place where many people come together to do business, and it is no better and no worse than the public that attends it. The central organ ... in the human organism is the heart; in the economic organism it is the stock exchange, which ensures that mobile capital remains in balance.' In the stock exchange there lay a major political force that ought not to be underestimated: 'When an entire nation and beyond its borders other countries too are used to satisfying their economic needs in a particular place, such an institution may in certain circumstances be capable of assuming in peace the selfsame role in the defence of a country's economic interests as the army assumes in time of war.'[291] At the committee stage, Siemens did in the end manage to achieve one or two improvements, but he could no longer prevent the Stock Exchange Taxation Act as a whole from passing into law.

The Reichstag that had been elected in the autumn of 1884 was prematurely dissolved in January 1887 after the opposition majority threw out the government's bill to increase the peacetime strength of the army. Siemens had voted with his party against the government. In the ensuing election campaign, which was characterized by violent agitation and a marked deterioration of relations between opposition and government, Siemens had a very hard time persuading the bank's supervisory board to let him stand again. He once again asked for his discharge, determined 'to lie on the sofa, read newspapers and await my destiny'.[292] Eventually, the board gave in, and in February 1887 Siemens once again successfully defended his seat. His party, however, suffered huge losses: of its 67 seats in the old Reichstag it retained only 32 and had shrunk to a very uninfluential group.

Siemens frequently criticized the policies of his party colleagues, particularly those of Eugen Richter, the chairman of the German Liberal Party and of the parliamentary group. Richter was becoming daily more irrational, he said, mounting mean and unnecessary attacks not only on the Kaiser but also on the left-wing liberal opponents of Bismarck around Max von Forckenbeck and others, attacks which aroused the greatest displeasure in the party itself. 'Our parliamentary friends,' he wrote in July 1887, 'are too deeply set on petty opposition and too easily lose all sense of judgement regarding the difference between what is important and what is not.'[293] Moreover, Siemens did not once during the whole parliamentary term attend a plenary session of the Reichstag. He devoted his energies unambiguously to the bank.

Even after his 1890 re-election, Siemens rarely spoke in the House. His activities in this term included a role in the consultation process concerning the German Imperial Telegraphy Bill, which in view of his connections with the electrical industry is not surprising. He also gave his opinion once again on the proposed increase in stamp duty. Anyone who like himself as a managing director of a bank saw the stock exchange as 'the heart of the economic organism' naturally defended that institution against attacks from right and left alike. On 19 January 1893 Siemens spoke of the political importance of the stock exchange, sounding a thoroughly national note: 'I have often been laughed at in this House when I have supported the proposition that the stock exchange and in particular mobile capital also constitute a major political force ... In our epoch, every economic question at the same time becomes a political question. Prince Bismarck's theory that one can be the political friend and the economic enemy of another nation has fallen flat on its face; the allied governments have themselves currently abandoned it, as the commercial treaty negotiations show ... Alongside the military war, conducted with powder and shot, a no less ruthlessly conducted economic struggle has emerged in which the nations of Europe are fighting to secure their food supplies. The job of mobile capital is not only itself to play a substantial part in that struggle, but also to make such preparations as are necessary if any military war is to be successful. I should like to compare the role of mobile capital directly to that played by an army's general staff in a military conflict.'[294]

Siemens underlined his comments by citing two examples: the Russian securities that had been sold off in Germany in the late 1880s, when Bismarck imposed the 'Lombard ban' on Russian securities, and the Italian papers taken up by the German people in support of the Triple Alliance policy. 'The vast masses mobilized on that occasion could not have been mobilized except through the medium of active and at the same time ... patriotic speculation.'[295] Again, of course, Siemens failed to get any significant changes made to the bill. The 1885 'imperial stamp duty' rates were doubled by the amendment of April 1894 and in some cases even trebled.

On matters of commercial policy, which in this term gave rise to some lively discussion both in the Reichstag and among the public, Siemens did not comment in parliament. Bismarck's protectionism had been replaced, under his successor Caprivi, by a series of commercial treaties that allegedly signified a turning away from protection as a system. They were therefore opposed by agriculture mainly, but also by a section of industry. In reality they represented a continuation of the protective tariff system in a modified form. Siemens voted with the government over the commercial treaties, even if the reduction in protective tariffs did not go far enough for him. As he wrote to a party colleague in 1891: 'Who would have thought that we should ever be delighted to see commercial treaties concluded that will secure the protective tariff system for 12 years to come – and that we should see their conclusion as a victory for the principle of free trade?! And yet this is a success!'[296]

In 1893, tensions and conflicts occurred within the Deutsche Freisinnige Partei in parliament regarding the line it should adopt on the defence budget. In proposing a new budget that provided for increasing the army's peacetime presence to 72,000 men, Chancellor Caprivi meant to counter the Franco-Russian *rapprochement* that, as far as Germany was concerned, for the first time made a reality of the 'war on two fronts' threat so feared by Bismarck. In order to forestall the opposition expected mainly from the Liberals, Caprivi had proposed two fundamental changes to the constitution of the armed forces, designed to make it easier for opponents to agree to an increase in army numbers. On the one hand, the proposed Army Bill would cut the period of parliamentary approval from seven to five years, thus involving the Reichstag (which since the extension of the parliamentary term had also been elected for five-year periods) more closely in the decisions of the executive with regard to budgetary and military matters. On the other hand, the soldier's period of service was to be cut from three to two years (a change to which Kaiser and generals alike had agreed only with the very greatest reluctance). Despite the readiness to compromise demonstrated by Caprivi in the interests of obtaining parliamentary approval, the Reichstag rejected the proposed increase in army numbers (even in a variant that reduced the figure by 13,000) by 210 votes against to 162 in favour. Not even the Freisinnige group was able to reach a majority decision to accept Caprivi's offer of co-operation. The 'pragmatic minority',[297] to which Siemens and Ludwig Bamberger belonged, and which consisted mainly of former 'Secessionists', voted for the government's bill and regrouped as the Freisinnige Vereinigung (Liberal Union). Even before this, they had been expelled from the party at the request of the left-wing liberal chairman of the group, Eugen Richter. Siemens voted for the army increase 'because I feared the French and the Russians might take fresh heart if the bill was defeated'.

The doctrinaire majority around Richter, with its negative attitude not only to military matters but also to questions of commercial and economic policy, proceeded to found the Freisinnige Volkspartei (Liberal People's Party). For both left-wing liberal parties there now began, following the government's parliamentary defeat and the Chancellor's prompt dissolution of the Reichstag on 6 May 1893, two decades of political decline. At the very next general election in June 1893 (when Siemens no longer stood) they lost a total of 29 seats and consequently a great deal of political weight.

Siemens once again sat with the numerically and politically insignificant Freisinnige Vereinigung (Liberal Union) group in the Reichstag from 1898 to 1901 as the member for his old constituency of Schweinitz-Wittenberg. This time Siemens took part more frequently in proceedings. He spoke on questions of banking, monetary legislation and the increase in stock exchange taxation associated with the Navy Bill, as well as on problems of commercial policy and on the East African Central Railway. One significant action of his was to vote with the party in favour of the second Navy Bill, which the Secretary of State for the Imperial Admiralty, Admiral Alfred von Tirpitz, introduced in 1900. He did so even though the stock exchange had to bear a large proportion of the costs through a further drastic increase in stamp duty. By pushing ahead with the development of a large fleet that would boost the number of German ships of the line to a ratio of 2:3 as against the British fleet, the German government believed it could achieve what it called a 'policy of the free hand' – in other words, one of strength and independence, particularly *vis-à-vis* Britain and all other potential allies.

Unlike his political colleagues, Siemens had advocated a systematic German colonial policy since the mid-1880s and had spoken up in favour of the East

African Central Railway and of subsidies for large mail steamship lines. In his last speech in the Reichstag, on 24 April 1901, he commented on the question of the German guarantee for the railway from Dar es Salaam to Morogoro, a project in which the Deutsche Bank had large-scale financial interests: 'I could recount many a tale from my experiences as a self-appointed fanatic for the colonies about how hard it has become for me to gain even a feeble hearing among my closest friends. Most of them have taken a negative attitude, ... paying insufficient attention to the fact that many changes have since occurred in the international situation. When all other nations are hurrying to occupy the remaining uncivilized parts of the world, it would be clumsiness on our part to wish to hang back.'

And on the participation of the Deutsche Bank in the East African Railway, Siemens summed up: 'It is my firm conviction that the moment the government were to say to the present syndicate: it is important to us that you, the Deutsche Bank, give up your prerogative – some such remark is all that is needed, and you will have the declaration ... Oh, yes! In which connection, I beg to be excused if I put in a quick word for an institution to which I have belonged for thirty years. Suggestions to the effect that these people ever feigned patriotic sentiments in order to earn money were always, if my judgement counts for anything, thoroughly unjust.'[298]

If the managing board of the Deutsche Bank was undoubtedly Siemens's first field of activity and the Reichstag the second, there was also a third component: namely, his work in the business associations and other organizations that represented the banking and merchant professions, or pursued economic objectives outside the political process. Siemens deliberately cultivated this dual strategy both inside and outside parliament. He was active, for example, in the Verein Deutscher Banken (Union of German Banks), in the Korporation der Ältesten der Kaufmannschaft von Berlin (Corporation of the Senior Merchants of Berlin), on the committee of the Deutscher Handelstag (Association of German Chambers of Commerce), in the Verein Berliner Kaufleute und Industrieller (Union of Berlin Merchants and Industrialists) and in the Handelsvertragsverein (Commercial Treaty Association). He made various key statements to these bodies that were closely bound up with his professional activities: for example, on the cheque system in Germany, the importance of the stock exchange, and the question of stock exchange taxation. On the committee of the German Commercial Council, Siemens backed the resolution drawn up by the shipowner Adolf Woermann and adopted unanimously on 27 January 1885, welcoming the government's launching of a practical colonial policy.[299] Siemens and his managing board colleagues Hermann Wallich and Max Steinthal were also members of the Deutscher Kolonialverein (German Colonial Association), founded in Frankfurt in 1882.[300] Siemens, however, resigned from this body in 1896 without ever saying exactly why.[301]

Siemens played a leading role only in the Commercial Treaty Association, which was founded on his initiative in November 1900 and in which he served as chairman. It was this association in particular that Siemens saw as an instrument of the commercial world and a counterweight to the political parties: 'We are today proud of the fact that our ranks include members of a wide variety of parties. We count among our members supporters of the Centre and National Liberal parties; we have friends from the right to the extreme left. We are not a political party; ... let the parties argue amongst themselves over the relationship between the monarchy and parliament and between state and church and over censorship of the theatre and questions of tolerance! Here we are concerned only about the growth of material prosperity and the central question of filling the nation's stomach.'[302] In the autumn of 1901, when Siemens was already marked by illness, he surrendered the chair of the Commercial Treaty Association to his deputy, Adolf Woermann.

In a life that was extremely active in many spheres, Georg von Siemens acquired an exceptional reputation well beyond the world of banking and also beyond his party: that is, among the public at large and in particular among the liberal middle class. The day after his death on 23 October 1901, Theodor Mommsen (the famous author of *The History of Rome*, for which he was awarded the Nobel Prize in 1902, and another man who had long combined a professional life with a political mandate) wrote in a private letter: 'Now we have lost yet another of the few men in whom our poor Germany might still place hope. Had Georg Siemens ever got into government, much would have been avoided and much achieved. The gods, however, would seem to have abandoned us.'[303]

A man who was the exact opposite of Siemens was his colleague Hermann Wallich. He was a bank manager 'pure and simple', at the same time as being very definitely a private man to whom (as his memoirs attest) family life stood above all else in importance. Wallich quit his managing directorship at the age of only 61; he went on to sit on the bank's supervisory board for no fewer than 34 years, until his death in 1928. He was a man who operated in silence, only rarely appearing in public. The other two members of the bank's 'management quartet', Max Steinthal and Rudolph von Koch, were also not active politically.

Among members of the supervisory board of the Deutsche Bank who held parliamentary seats, first mention should go to Karl Schrader, who belonged to the supervisory board from 1895 to 1913 and sat on various other supervisory boards as well, including those of the bank's Middle Eastern ventures. He had two periods in the Reichstag (1881–93 and 1898–1912), where he belonged to the Freisinnige group and worked closely with Siemens. In the 1870s and 1880s, Schrader and his English wife were friendly with the Prussian crown prince and princess, and in 1888 he was allegedly in the running for a seat in government.[304] Two members of the National Liberal group in the Reichstag were Otto Büsing, a privy councillor from Schwerin, and Ludwig Roland-Lücke, who until 1907 had sat on the managing board of the Deutsche Bank and who was elected to the Reichstag in 1912. A further member of the supervisory board, the industrialist Ernst von Eynern, headed the National Liberal group in the Prussian house of representatives from 1886 to 1906.[305]

If the 'first epoch' of the Deutsche Bank was stamped by Siemens and Wallich, in the 'second epoch' (from about 1900) it was Arthur Gwinner who became the dominant figure, flanked by Carl Klönne, the 'industrial financier', and subsequently of course by Karl Helfferich. Owing to the principle of seniority, between 1901 and 1909 the post of spokesman was in fact occupied by Rudolph von Koch, whose principal sphere of activity was the bank's domestic business. But it was Gwinner, Siemens's closest colleague, who took on the big international deals and represented the bank abroad.

Arthur Gwinner (1856–1931)[306] came from a well-known family of Frankfurt lawyers. His grandfather, Philipp Gwinner, was a senator and in 1865 became mayor of Frankfurt. His father, Judge Wilhelm Gwinner, a privy councillor and president of the consistory, was appointed executor to Arthur Schopenhauer and wrote a biography of the philosopher, who had been a regular guest of the Gwinner household. Arthur Gwinner himself completed a banking apprenticeship in Frankfurt am Main before spending several years abroad in Britain, France and Spain. From 1888 Gwinner operated his own private bank in Berlin, which he wound up when he joined the managing board of the Deutsche Bank as successor to Hermann Wallich in 1894. As a result of his marriage to Anna Speyer (connected with the well-known Frankfurt bank of Lazard Speyer-Ellissen), Gwinner enjoyed excellent contacts with British and American banking circles. He took over the major international financial transactions, particularly in the Ottoman Empire, built up the bank's oil concern, and devoted himself to the overseas interests of the German electrical industry. Gwinner was regarded as the bank's 'diplomat', a function for which he seemed peculiarly suited by virtue of his knowledge of the world and the linguistic skills he had acquired during his many foreign postings.

Both the Baghdad Railway and the oil interests of the Deutsche Bank were economic and political undertakings that called for a great deal of diplomatic tact on the bank's part as well as close collaboration with the Foreign Office. They gave rise to numerous personal contacts – for instance, with Chancellor von Bülow, whom Gwinner knew well, but also with Germany's ambassador to Turkey, Baron Marschall von Bieberstein. It was Bülow whom Gwinner had to thank for his seat in the Upper House, Marschall for his title. On the latter subject, Gwinner recorded in his memoirs: 'In the late summer of 1908 Baron von Marschall sent me a telegram inviting me to visit him on his Neuershausen estate near Freiburg im Breisgau. Among the exceptionally lovely rosebeds of his garden he asked me whether like Siemens I should be prepared to accept elevation to the nobility. If for no other reason than the interests of my children I replied in the affirmative, but begged the ambassador to direct the honour at my aged father, who was living as a retired judge and former president of the

Protestant consistory in Frankfurt am Main.'[307] So it transpired, and in the winter of 1908 Gwinner's father was elevated to membership of the hereditary nobility.

Not least in connection with Arthur Gwinner's services in resolving the Bosnian annexation crisis of 1908–09, on 27 January 1910 Wilhelm II appointed him to the Prussian House of Lords.[308] Austria-Hungary had by annexing Bosnia and Herzegovina on 6 October 1908 almost provoked a war among the European great powers. The German government succeeded in defusing the conflict, and in February 1909 the Turkish government recognized the new status quo created by the Austrians, while on the other hand the Dual Monarchy promised Turkey financial compensation.[309] Partly through his good personal relations with the governor of the Österreichische Boden-Credit-Anstalt, Theodor von Taussig, and with the Turkish ambassador in Berlin, Osman Nizami Pasha, Gwinner had fought extremely hard to see that Turkey received such compensation.[310]

On 11 January 1909 Gwinner reported to Bülow in this connection that for the past few weeks he had been exerting influence, through Austrian and Hungarian financial circles, on Austrian Foreign Minister von Aehrenthal and Hungarian Prime Minister Wekerle with a view to settling the conflict over Bosnia by financial means. It had occurred to him while doing so that the largest banks in France, in Belgium and in Britain were headed by men who were represented in the senate or equivalent upper house in their respective countries. Gwinner went on: 'Only in Prussia are banks still not deemed worthy to sit in the House of Lords. And yet German banks have done more for their country than any foreign institutions in the countries concerned. The Deutsche Bank is the largest of the German joint stock companies of which Schmoller says that they have introduced a fresh leading element into the national economy; and the Deutsche Bank is the largest bank in the world: with funds of its own in excess of 375 million marks, it has passed Crédit Lyonnais, and with around 1,400 million foreign investments it recently passed all the British banks as well; in terms of the scale and variety of its operations, it has for several years occupied top place. Should not a director of the Deutsche Bank be empowered and appointed to do the country good service in parliament? My predecessor Siemens, in his younger days, had himself elected to both national and provincial parliaments; very soon, however, he lacked the time and probably also the desire to run again, as is necessary in order to obtain or rather be elected to a seat ... Given our electoral system, our party conditions and the current level of political education among our young people, it is scarcely possible for and scarcely to be expected of a busy man – and good men are kept very busy – to campaign for a seat in parliament. Yet there is an urgent need, particularly in economic matters, to hear from those who, having learned, have something to teach. Under present circumstances, however, that is scarcely possible except through appointment to parliament, to its Upper House.'[311]

Bülow replied on 15 January, thanking him for taking so successful a hand in the Austrian–Turkish settlement. He had always regretted, the Chancellor went on, that leading figures from the banking and business world stayed away from parliament, and he considered it essential that top people from that sphere should be more powerfully represented also in the Reichstag. He continued: 'But I should also very much like to see our leading bankers receive proportionately stronger representation in the House of Lords, and the Deutsche Bank is undoubtedly the first that would justify having one of its top directors appointed to the Upper House. I shall keep the matter in mind and hope to be able to bring it to the desired conclusion, albeit not just at present.'[312]

A year was to pass before Gwinner's appointment to the Upper House, an appointment with which Bülow expressed himself well pleased: 'To see you in our senate is a long-standing wish of mine, and I am delighted that it has at last been fulfilled ... Should you ever come to Rome, we hope very much that you will not pass without calling in at the Villa Malta, into which we hope to be moving some time in February. Then we can discuss many things as we did in Norderney and Berlin, delighting in our agreement over so many issues, and you will see that my love for my homeland has not faded in the southern sun.'[313]

While not the first banker to be appointed to the Prussian House of Lords, Gwinner was the first director of a joint stock bank to enjoy that honour. The world of banking was indeed only poorly represented there by five members, most of them private bankers: in addition to Ludwig Delbrück, son of Adelbert, there were also Richard Koch, former Chairman of the Reichsbank, and Ernst von Mendelssohn-Bartholdy, all from Berlin, Albert von Metzler from Frankfurt am Main, and Albert Schlutow from Stettin.[314] The financial journal *Plutus* commented as follows on Gwinner's appointment: 'Joint stock banks have long been the sun around which our economic life revolves and the brilliance of which makes the old private-bank business pale in comparison. But there has never been a joint stock bank director in the House of Lords before, and Gwinner's entry into the Prussian chamber is thus a historic event.'[315]

According to Gwinner, the Prussian House of Lords consisted at the time 'of some three hundred members, two hundred Conservatives and a hundred others who had banded together in what they called the "New Party"'. There were also a few independents – *Wilde*, as they were called. Gwinner himself belonged to the New Party, which was characterized by 'superior education, practical experience and greater sense', while the Conservatives dominated, as he put it, by 'rank, influence, wealth and political power'.[316] His appointment provided him with 'a welcome opportunity to be able to say what I think on economic matters without being exposed to the irritations of a membership in parliament'.[317]

Gwinner delivered his first major speech in the Prussian House of Lords on 27 May 1910. It was equally sharp in both form and content, attacking the Prussian Finance Minister, Baron von Rheinhaben, and criticizing the Finance Bill, which for the fourth time concluded with a deficit. He slated the government's budgeting and its deficit economics, so damaging to the credit of the Prussian state. In a further speech on 30 May he remarked curtly: 'Everything takes talent, but borrowing requires genius!' – a saying that came to be cited repeatedly in Berlin thereafter. Gwinner asserted that Prussia's financial administration lacked a properly scientific understanding of economics, and he expressed regret that the Deutsche Bank had invested more than half its entire capital in German loans and imperial Treasury bonds: 'A pity, because we are losing a lot of money in consequence.'[318]

However, Gwinner did not expect his critique to bear any practical fruit. It was too late to redraft the budget, and he was eventually to give it his vote in any case.[319] He simply wished to point out that, for example, there were other – and better – ways of borrowing. 'There are certain things we can learn from abroad, notwithstanding that we are the best-governed country in the world.'[320] Alfred Lansburgh commented on Gwinner's remarks in *Die Bank*: 'In other words, the speech was *pour le roi de Prusse* [for the Prussian king]. And he will no doubt have heard it.'[321]

Gwinner had another go at the Finance Bill in the spring of 1911: 'I should like to say, moreover, that in time of peace taxable capacity should be utilized as sparingly as possible. In peacetime one should borrow, for the simple reason that in time of war borrowing is probably out of the question ... In wartime, taxation can if necessary be sharply increased. The next war, gentlemen, will be fought with paper money and forced loans from the taxpayer.'[322] And he repeated the charge that the government was pursuing an unsound financial policy: 'If you want us to become more sound, you must limit expenditure ... There are no Liberal finances, no Conservative finances; there are only good and bad finances. There is only a financial policy that is correct or one that is incorrect.'[323]

In March and May 1912 Gwinner commented in the Upper House on the Saving Banks Act and again on the Finance Bill, and in 1913 he spoke in the general debate on the defence budget: 'It has been a positively edifying spectacle to see how almost the entire nation concurred and continues to concur with this exceptionally high and hitherto – in peacetime, not just in Germany but anywhere else in the world – quite unprecedented demand for an increase in the country's armed forces. The German nation is after all obliged by its geographical position to count less on alliances than on its own might. That an armed force in the amount of one per cent of the population should be fitted out, trained and held in readiness is entirely in line with tradition, with our situation and that of the world, and finally with the desire and the need for independence for our country and its borders. By good fortune, we are also able financially to bear this colossal burden. I state this here deliberately ... that it may be heard and understood in the very widest circles, including abroad.'[324]

In terms of party politics, Gwinner was probably close to the National Liberals. At any rate, the central committee of the National Liberal Party wrote to him on 24 November 1902 with a request that he should 'support our efforts with a contribution that will effectively promote the serious and difficult work of electioneering'.[325] The self-sacrificing assistance of prosperous circles, it said, was indispensable for this purpose.

Following his retirement from the managing board of the Deutsche Bank in 1919, Gwinner continued to be associated with the bank as vice-chairman of the supervisory board. His concern now was more with academic and also political questions. Soon after the signing of the Treaty of Versailles, he launched a campaign against the 'lie of [Germany's] sole blame' for the war. What he sought to show in many articles and lectures was not that Germany had been without blame, but that all the rest had been to blame at least as much.[326] Realistically, he saw at the same time that a recovery of German strength was possible only by agreement with Germany's former enemies. He took up the pan-European ideas of Count Coudenhove-Calergi and as treasurer was a member of the executive of the Pan-European Union from its founding in 1923. The statutes of the German branch of the organization were drafted by him.[327]

Relations between the Deutsche Bank and politics assumed a special kind of importance in the person of Karl Helfferich (1872–1924), who was a member of the managing board from 1908 to the beginning of 1915, and whom Gwinner had intended to succeed him.[328] Helfferich had spent the years 1890–94 studying law and political science in Berlin, Munich and Strasburg, completing his studies with a doctorate in political science. He subsequently worked in Berlin as an academic and journalist, writing on questions of monetary theory, the history of money, and currency policy; in 1899 he qualified as a university lecturer with a study of the reform of Germany's currency that had followed the foundation of the Reich. After working for two years as an external lecturer, in 1901 he received the title of professor from the Prussian government, though he subsequently turned down two chairs that were offered to him. Meanwhile he conducted a journalistic campaign against the introduction of a dual currency in Germany, as called for by the agrarian interests represented in the Bund der Landwirte (League of Farmers). In this early period Helfferich was also, like Bamberger and Siemens, a member of the Freisinnige Partei.

In 1901 Helfferich joined the colonial department of the Foreign Office, which was later (in 1907) to become a separate body, the Reichskolonialamt or Imperial Colonial Department. His job was to reorganize the currency situation in the German colonies, and this occupied him until 1905. During his time at the Foreign Office he continued to lecture at Berlin University, and in 1903 he published what was probably his most important academic work, entitled simply *Das Geld* (*Money*).

Helfferich gave up commuting between the academic world and the Foreign Office in 1906, when Arthur von Gwinner offered him a top job in the management of the Anatolian Railway Company in Constantinople, in the hope that this would unblock the situation with regard to railway construction in the Middle East. Gwinner had met and come to value Helfferich in 1905 during negotiations over East African business. His decision was further encouraged by the special recommendation that came from Siemens's widow. Helfferich was a friend of the Siemens family; in fact, in 1920 he was to marry one of the daughters. He eventually wrote an enormous, three-volume biography of Georg von Siemens based on a great many personal and business documents, notably the man's extensive correspondence – sources that are in large part no longer available today.

In June 1905 Gwinner wrote to Chancellor von Bülow that, in addition to the Swiss Eduard Huguenin, a second civil servant must be found to head the Anatolian Railway Company who combined 'special talent with a certain amount of diplomatic training'. In Karl Helfferich he believed he had found such a man. However, before opening negotiations with him he wanted to have Bülow's agreement. It was undoubtedly in everyone's interests to obtain the services of Helfferich, Gwinner went on, because 'the Emperor's ambassador, Baron von Marschall, said to me on the occasion of my last visit to Constantinople: "The Anatolian Railway is the foundation of our political position here" '.[329]

At a meeting on 14 June 1905, Bülow told Gwinner that he agreed to Helfferich's being transferred to Turkey, and in May 1906 Helfferich joined the managing board of the Anatolian Railway Company in Constantinople as *administrateur délégué*. In business terms he achieved a great deal, for in June 1908 he was able to sign an agreement with the Turkish government securing the extension of the Baghdad Railway through the Taurus and Amanus Mountains to El Helif in Upper Mesopotamia, some 840 kilometres beyond the previous terminus. The financial arrangements were extremely complicated, given Turkey's chronic shortage of money, and the negotiations were subject to repeated political interventions from London, Paris and St Petersburg.

Helfferich was undoubtedly attracted by the political and diplomatic aspects of the railway projects. At the age of 34 he had been appointed to one of the top foreign positions in the Deutsche Bank and found himself at the focal point of political conflicts among the European great powers, which turned every economic undertaking in Turkey into a political issue as well. His Foreign Office contacts came in very useful here and encouraged him to co-operate closely with the German embassy in Constantinople. His 'reward' for the years in Turkey was eventual appointment to the managing board of the Deutsche Bank in March 1908, at first as a deputy and from December 1908 as a full managing director.

In July 1908 Helfferich returned to Berlin, where matters Turkish continued to take up most of his time. But the outbreak of the Young Turks' revolution in that very month and the annexation of Bosnia and Herzegovina by Austria-Hungary in October of the same year necessitated Helfferich's renewed presence at the Golden Horn as early as November 1908. It was important to smooth the billows of Turkish displeasure with Germany, which as Austria-Hungary's closest political ally was held by Constantinople to share responsibility for the annex-

ation decision. At the same time, Helfferich headed the compensation negotiations that, following Bulgaria's declaration of independence and that country's
annexation of the East Rumelian railway lines, became necessary between
Turkey, the Betriebsgesellschaft der Orientalischen Eisenbahnen, and Bulgaria.

A further policy objective of Helfferich's was to open a branch of the Deutsche
Bank in Constantinople. The managing board of the bank was not to be
persuaded at first, fearing that the Turks would regard a Constantinople branch,
even more than they did the Anatolian Railway Company, as an 'inexhaustible
pumping station' (the payment of large amounts of 'baksheesh' was unavoidable
in Turkey, and such sums were allowed for in the accounts from the outset).
Helfferich would not give up, however, and cited other, more general reasons
why such a branch should be established: 'At the present time, which for Turkey
signifies a reappraisal of all it stands for, it seems to me especially important that
the Deutsche Bank should announce, by establishing a branch in Constantinople,
that it has no intention of withdrawing from Turkish affairs following the fall
of absolutism and leaving the field to others, ... and I anticipate the opening of
a branch having a moral effect of very special significance not only for the
position of the Deutsche Bank, but for the position of German concerns in
Turkey generally.'[330] The decision to set up a branch in Constantinople was
finally taken in March 1909, and the branch itself opened on 1 April 1910.

Helfferich continued to spend a lot of time away on 'diplomatic missions'.
When in the summer of 1913 the German government needed to appoint a
delegate to the international financial conference to be held in Paris in an attempt
to settle various matters in the Balkans, its choice fell on him as the man who
knew most about the problems involved. He also, in collaboration with the
Foreign Office, conducted negotiations in the winter of 1913–14 with representatives of the French government and French bankers aimed at sorting out
financial interests in Turkey. At the same time, Gwinner and Helfferich together
conducted what were important talks with British politicians and financiers
concerning the extension of the Baghdad Railway and the concessions in the
Mossul oil field. When after much to-ing and fro-ing the British at last put their
signature to the treaty, the First World War broke out. Gwinner recounts how
the day after the declaration of war, Helfferich laid his papers on the table and
said to him: 'There's nothing more to be done here; it's a mess.' From that
moment on, he is said to have looked for another political position.[331] He found
one only a few months later, when in January 1915 he was appointed secretary
of state at the Imperial Treasury. This was a difficult job, particularly in wartime,
and it was one Bethmann Hollweg had thought of offering him back in 1912.
The Chancellor had changed his mind at the time, presumably because Helfferich
seemed to him to be still too young and in any case doing a more useful job as
a managing director of the Deutsche Bank.

Beginning in 1911 Helfferich also represented the Deutsche Bank on the central
committee of the Reichsbank, and he spoke on the subject of the Reichsbank and

bank liquidity at the Fourth Bankers' Conference in Munich on 18 September 1912. As Jacob Riesser, chairman of the supervisory board of the DANAT-Bank (the product of a merger between the Bank für Handel und Industrie and the Nationalbank für Deutschland), noted in his obituary, this speech made Helfferich 'famous and popular throughout Germany overnight and immediately raised him up as the rightful candidate for the highest offices in the land'.[332] It was couched in very dashing tones: 'Gentlemen, there are some in whom the giant strides currently being taken by our economic life induce a mild sense of panic and who see salvation in a damping down of our industry and trade and even of our burgeoning population figures. This is not, I believe, a party with which we wish to throw in our lot. No nation in history has got anywhere by wearing a hair shirt and tightening its belt. Progress calls for enjoyment of life and for creative enthusiasm, and these are things we have no wish to lose.' The minutes record that his words were warmly applauded.[333]

From 1909 Helfferich was a member of the very large governing body of the Hansabund (Hansa League), founded in that year. This association, which consisted of representatives from the whole spectrum of economic life (industry, banking, commerce, etc.), was directed against the conservative economic and fiscal policy of the imperial government, which one-sidedly promoted the interests of large landowners and was causing particular concern in banking and stock market circles. Helfferich did deliver a number of speeches against budgetary reform in line with the Hansa League's strategy, but the leading figures in the League were Riesser, the mining and steel magnate Emil Kirdorf, and Krupp director Rötger. Moreover, it soon became apparent that the economic policy demands of the branches of the economy represented in the League could scarcely be reduced to a common denominator. A split occurred between a majority of members led by Riesser on the one hand (they were the 'left wing') and the representatives of heavy industry on the other.[334]

In January 1915 Helfferich, as we have seen, quit the managing board of the Deutsche Bank and as Secretary of State at the Imperial Treasury took over the management of the nation's finances. He was helped here by the negotiations he had conducted in Paris in the final years before the outbreak of war, regarding settlement of the Turkish debts, and by the contacts with the world of financial diplomacy to which these had given rise. A year later Helfferich was Secretary of State for the Interior and Vice-Chancellor, though he left the government again in 1917. Finally, a brief stint as ambassador in Moscow (in the summer of 1918) ended the second period of his involvement in politics.

There followed the struggle against the Treaty of Versailles and against the so-called 'policy of fulfilment'. Helfferich's pamphlet Away with Erzberger!, together with his book The World War, of which nearly 100,000 copies were sold, documents this in eloquent fashion. The war gave birth to a new Helfferich: the demagogue. He now found himself as a zealot in the ranks of the Conservatives, who following the collapse of the monarchy had regrouped as the

Deutschnationale Volkspartei (German National People's Party). The war and the defeat of 1918 turned Helfferich, who prior to 1914 had, 'like most bank directors, counted himself a Liberal', into the political opposite of his former self: he became a bitter opponent of the parties of the Weimar coalition. Felix Pinner, editor of the *Berliner Tageblatt*, summed Helfferich up in 1925 when he said that the man's liberalism 'was possibly nothing more, on closer examination, than a penchant for Manchesterism and freedom of trade, or possibly simply opposition to the government bureaucracy inhibiting free economic life and giving preference to landownership'.[335]

2. The bank's connections with Kaiser and government

In the autumn of 1898 Wilhelm II made his great Middle Eastern trip, during which he visited Constantinople and subsequently the Holy Land. Siemens got in touch 'with influential court circles' and on 23 August invited the Kaiser to visit the Anatolian Railway.[336] On 20 October 1898, during a brief journey on the Anatolian Railway, he met Wilhelm II for the first time, though he was not able to have a very long talk with him. He had to content himself with describing the railway's problems to the Secretary of State at the Foreign Office, von Bülow, and asking him to intervene with Wilhelm. Siemens was keen for the Prussian national bank, the Seehandlung, to take a holding in the Anatolian Railway Company, an idea to which Finance Minister Miquel had voiced firm opposition, making 'a great impression on the Emperor'.[337]

Concerning his brief meeting with Wilhelm II, Siemens reported to his wife with detachment and a certain amount of unconcealed irony: 'Actually, the Emperor treated me rather coolly. While with all the others he chatted very nicely, ... with me he confined himself to what was absolutely necessary, whereas the Empress was extraordinarily charming. It appears he had found out a bit about me beforehand. Nevertheless, he was very nice, and a more common mortal than I could and should still have spoken of his "great favour", etc.'[338] Wilhelm liberally distributed decorations among the top men of the Anatolian Railway Company, and even Siemens received the Order of the Red Eagle, Fourth Class (the lowest), against the award of which he was 'powerless to defend' himself, though of course it 'did not particularly excite' him.[339] A year later, even before the signing of the Baghdad Railway Agreements on 24 December 1899, the Kaiser did in fact elevate him to the hereditary nobility in November 1899.

Relations between the spokesman of the Deutsche Bank and Wilhelm II remained slightly uncertain, even if after the 'cool' treatment Siemens had received in Constantinople the Kaiser began to involve him in talks more frequently. In January and March 1899 he invited Siemens to tea, together with Miquel and Bülow, to bring him up to date on the Baghdad Railway but also on railway construction in the African colonies. Concerning the Baghdad Railway, he had the Foreign Office send Siemens a steady stream of detailed reports. Wilhelm often passed him reports and newspaper cuttings himself, inviting his comments. In April 1900 the Kaiser and Siemens met once again over breakfast at the house of Count August zu Eulenburg. Wilhelm was planning a collection for the victims of the terrible floods in India. Siemens agreed with the idea, but was against a public collection on the grounds that anti-British feeling might lead to a fiasco. Instead, he volunteered to raise 500,000 marks 'quietly' in a very short time.[340]

These personal encounters did not fail to leave an impression on Siemens (as was the case with many of his contemporaries). 'Georg took tea with the Emperor today, along with Miquel and Bülow', his wife noted in her diary. 'He came home full of enthusiam for the Emperor's good sense, lucidity and sound knowledge.'[341] In particular, the closeness to the sovereign to which these invitations attested was not without its effect on those around Siemens. As one of his daughters reported: 'The main event is and for the time being remains Father's visit to the Emperor, the social and business repercussions of which are still in evidence. Not for a long time have we seen so many visitors as in the last few days. People who would never have thought of visiting us before suddenly turn up on our doorstep, and after a brief introduction come out with: "Your husband was with the Emperor recently, I hear." '[342]

Wilhelm II's intense interest in the Baghdad Railway continued under Gwinner. In a personal letter to Gwinner written in October 1904, he expressed his 'full recognition of what has been achieved hitherto' and his 'warmest wishes for a successful continuance and completion of the Baghdad Railway enterprise'.[343] Gwinner probably did not meet the Kaiser in person until 1909, as a letter from his father suggests.[344] Rudolf Martin, a contemporary observer of the 'top ten thousand' in Germany, mentions some two dozen businessmen among the advisers of Wilhelm II, including Georg von Siemens and Arthur von Gwinner of the Deutsche Bank. The real strength of the influence that the business community had on the Kaiser is hard to assess. Doubtless he often took in the advice they gave him, but he forgot it again just as quickly when subjected to contrary influences from the other side.[345]

Around 1900, a rumour gained currency to the effect that Siemens was to succeed Miquel as Minister of Finance.[346] The *Berliner Volks-Zeitung* wrote in October 1901 that the Deutsche Bank spokesman had for some time stood so high in the Kaiser's favour that the landowners became nervous when they learned from the court circular that he had received an invitation to Potsdam. According to the newspaper, they trembled at the thought that Siemens might take over Miquel's job. However, not only would Siemens not have fitted into the Bülow–Rheinbaben–Hammerstein cabinet; Prussia had not yet reached the point of entrusting a ministerial post to a member of the Freisinnige Partei.[347] And under the headline 'On the way to becoming Minister of Finance?', *Vorwärts* commented as follows on the news that Siemens was shortly to resign from the management of the Deutsche Bank in order to devote himself full time to public life: 'A straight promotion from bank director to Minister of Finance would in the light of agrarian sensibilities seem rather too bold. So Mr von Siemens will initially become a simple politician until he has marshalled his ideas sufficiently to become Miquel's or Mr von Thielmann's successor.'[348]

Siemens himself did not take these 'offers' very seriously: 'The stupid talk about my becoming Minister of Finance has led to my name being pushed to the fore in connection with a movement to protect the commercial treaties.' And his wife wrote to their daughter on 29 January 1900: 'Last week Father was seriously asked whether he wished to be proposed as Minister of Finance; he declined.'[349] Around the turn of the century, when Siemens resigned from the managing board of the Deutsche Bank and subsequently accepted the chairmanship of the Commercial Treaty Association, his attitude to the government's economic policy, particularly its agricultural policy, underwent such a change that there can scarcely have been any question of a government post for him. 'Serving as a commerical table decoration on a bureaucratic–agrarian–protectionist table is a position he'd respectfully have declined', wrote a close friend, the journalist and Freisinnige MP Theodor Barth, in October 1901.[350]

Like Siemens, Gwinner was also talked of as someone Wilhelm II had his eye on as a future Minister of Finance. And according to notes kept by Ernst Bassermann, in 1909 Bülow was planning to propose either Waldemar Mueller of the managing board of the Dresdner Bank or Gwinner as Treasury Secretary.[351] Again, however, as with Siemens, there was probably not a lot to these rumours of ministerial advancement. Business managers accustomed to independent freedom of action can hardly have felt much inclination to place themselves in thrall to a narrow and relatively rigid system. Furthermore, neither man was any longer in sympathy with government policy on many points. Siemens spent most of his political career on the opposition benches, and Gwinner turned out, on his elevation to the Lords, to be an uncompromising critic of Prussian financial policy. That does not, in his case, mean that he was an opponent of the government, but his standpoint on matters of financial policy was that of a banker who thinks in international terms.

The relationship between the leading representatives of the Deutsche Bank and the political course taken by the country is reflected most immediately in their attitude towards and views about the Chancellor of the day as being, after the Kaiser, the key political figure in the Reich. We must confine ourselves here to a handful of examples. Siemens, in a campaign speech in November 1889, while acknowledging Prince Bismarck as 'the greatest man Germany has produced in a hundred years', and stressing that his foreign policy could be endorsed without reservation, pointed out that in his economic policy he had adopted a thoroughly dangerous line. Here, Siemens said, he disagreed with Bismarck on principle.[352] He was thinking mainly of the question of protective tariffs, on which like most other bankers Siemens followed the Liberal free-traders. But Bismarck's attitude in the *Kulturkampf* also found little favour with him: 'Wars of religion between Protestants and Catholics are not a particularly good idea; and if Bismarck (possibly with reason) does not see the political parties as providing adequate support for his government, he is making a mistake, in my view, if he wants to have a Protestant religious party take their place.'[353] In 1895, however, in a letter to his mother, he took stock in a rather more forgiving way: 'And Bismarck's contribution?! For all the man's mistakes, we must never forget that we should hardly have a German Empire without him; nor should people forget that the advantages of the German Empire benefited each and every one of us ... Now that Bismarck is 80, one is entitled to think only of his good side.'[354]

We have already seen how Gwinner maintained particularly close contacts with Chancellor Bülow, whom he had to thank for his eventual appointment to the Prussian House of Lords. From the turn of the century onwards, a personal relationship developed between the two men that went beyond business matters to reciprocal invitations to tea and even breakfast. Like Gwinner, the Chancellor was an admirer of Schopenhauer, and this in turn engendered numerous points of contact.[355] In the matter of the construction of the Baghdad Railway, Gwinner had to conduct negotiations of enormous political significance, which he regularly discussed with Bülow. In a letter of June 1906, for example, we read: 'On this occasion I take the liberty of humbly beseeching Your Highness for a brief audience. The fact is, I have to make certain decisions regarding the future handling of the Baghdad Railway affair, and given the political nature of this business I dare not put in hand any action bearing on the possible participation of the British without having informed myself as to Your Highness's political views and desires.'[356] Many such letters have survived, similar in content and written in the same sort of tone.

Bülow, too, clearly valued Gwinner's advice. For instance: 'What you say about your Parisian impressions I found most interesting. I am grateful to you for services rendered there in the cause of good sense and peace', Bülow noted in July 1907. And a year later he wrote: 'Your comments interested me greatly and struck me as so noteworthy that I shall be making them the confidential basis for further discussions.'[357] When Bülow resigned the office of Chancellor, Gwinner wrote to him in July 1909: 'Your Highness is leaving the first office in the land, mourned by all men of judgement in Germany, but not forgotten.'[358]

Among the things Fritz Fischer described in his book *Griff nach der Weltmacht* (*The bid for world power*; a book that aroused fierce discussion at the time of its publication) is what he called the 'influential relations' that Gwinner and Helfferich enjoyed with Theobald von Bethmann Hollweg. The war-aim demands put forward by business during the First World War, which were directed at the annexation or at least the economic integration of industrially productive regions by Germany, had found their way into Bethmann Hollweg's 'September Programme'. The economic objectives, Fischer maintained, had been impressed on the Chancellor particularly by memoranda and letters from Walther Rathenau and Gwinner. Helfferich, too, then still a managing director of the bank, had had a hand in this plan, suggesting that the Reich should annex Belgium.[359]

Fischer also alleged in this connection that, at the first wartime meeting of the Mittwochs-Gesellschaft (Wednesday Society) on 2 September 1914, Gwinner, commenting on the war-aims question, had opposed 'blindly embarking on a policy of annexation'. Instead, he had suggested less conspicuous but correspondingly more effective methods: namely, 'establishing Germany's economic supremacy' in Europe. Gwinner's thoughts as expounded to the members of this renowned Berlin forum of top figures from academic, cultural, political and economic life had struck Undersecretary of State Zimmermann as so significant at the time that he had promptly sent a transcript of them to the Chancellor at General Headquarters, where it arrived in time for the drafting of the war-aims programme of 9 September 1914.[360]

However, a recent study of the Mittwochs-Gesellschaft during the Second Empire, which contains a complete list of its meetings from 1863 to 1919, records no meeting for 2 September 1914. In fact, meetings were evidently suspended between May and November 1914. Moreover, it was not until May 1915 that Gwinner became a member of the society.[361] Furthermore, at a very early stage of the war Gwinner had a very different view of its eventual outcome than many of his contemporaries, which again contradicts Fischer's version of events. Even before the end of August 1914 he was expressing the fear that time would work against Germany and for Britain, which was able to count on the assistance of the USA.[362] Gwinner was generally very critical of German policy at the time of the outbreak of hostilities, accusing the government of war-mongering: 'It is true that on 22 August 1914 I had a confidential discussion with the then Undersecretary of State, Admiral von Capelle, about the political situation and the origins of the war ... However, it was my view at the time that certain persons at the Foreign Office had intended war to break out. I am now convinced that those concerned were simply playing a dangerous game with the object of restoring the prestige of Austria, so badly shaken by the assassination of the heir to the throne – rather like in the Bosnian crisis of 1908–09, when Germany had placed itself behind Austria "in shining armour" and averted a threat of war. The whole way in which Germany handled the deeply serious Sarajevo incident was stupid, which in the craft of international politics is a crime – indeed, as a famous saying goes: "Worse than a crime: a mistake".'[363]

3. The bank and the public

'It is a deeply regrettable but alas inescapable fact that, particularly as regards the functions of banks and bankers and as regards the stock market and similar institutions, even in educated circles the very haziest notions prevail; ignorance of these matters has led, especially in times of crisis, to the most distorted of views, nourishing prejudice, envy, and hatred against a useful trade that is called upon to play a prominent role in economic life.'[364] It would be hard to find a more concise expression of the attitude of broad sections of the public towards banks. The author was Jacob Riesser, and the sentence opened the first issue of the journal *Bank-Archiv*, the organ of the Centralverband des Deutschen Bank- und Bankiergewerbes (Central Association of the German Banking and Bankers' Trade), in 1901. The association had been founded in March 1901 to do the banks' 'public relations work', which as expressed programmatically was a matter of 'educating the public about the profession and function of the banker'. But it also sought 'to operate in an informative, premonitory and preventive manner in advance of the enactment of fresh legislative measures and conditions in the field of banking and stock exchange business' – in other words, to exercise political influence. It wished to ensure that in future 'those politicians do not get elected who feel themselves called upon to be legislators in the field of banking and stock-exchange business, too, without knowing any more about it, some- times, than for instance ... Eskimos know about the telephone'.[365]

The creation of a comprehensive professional organization to represent the interests of banking and bankers came about relatively late (compared with industry, for example, or agriculture) partly because of a lack of 'internal coherence and unity within the profession as a whole', but partly also out of consideration for 'current tendencies that, over and over again, make stock exchanges and banks the object of their very primitive attacks, tendencies and agitations that any right-thinking profession must see it as being beneath its dignity to combat'.[366]

Previous banking associations such as the Verein Deutscher Banken (Union of German Banks), founded in 1876, or the Vereinigung von Berliner Banken und Bankiers (Association of Berlin Banks and Bankers), launched in 1885 as Stempelvereinigung, had concerned themselves primarily with such technical banking questions as interest and commission rates, stamp duty and tax prob- lems, and matters to do with cheque and exchange transactions. Their main function had been to defend existing conditions in the banking market and in this way create the surest possible foundations for adequate earning oppor- tunities. They did not 'face the public' like the Central Association of the German Banking and Bankers' Trade, which was founded very much in the wake of the Stock Exchange Taxation Act of 1896.[367] The instigator of the Central Associ- ation (as well as being its first chairman and the leading figure of the early decades of its existence) was Jacob Riesser, then a member of the managing board of the Bank für Handel und Industrie.[368] His vice-chairman was Arthur Salomonsohn, the proprietor of the Disconto-Gesellschaft. The Deutsche Bank was represented on the various committees of the Central Association by Rudolph von Koch until 1909 and by Carl Michalowsky thereafter. Both men (members of the managing board with responsibility for the bank's 'home affairs department') rarely performed public functions on the association's behalf, whether as authors of its publications or as speakers at its conferences. That was done much more by Gwinner and above all by Helfferich.

Every three to five years the association organized the Allgemeiner Deutscher Bankiertag (General German Bankers' Congress). This was attended not only by top figures in the banking profession, but also by many representatives of national, provincial and municipal authorities, as well as by representatives of the press and the academic world. The congress, which dealt with urgent problems facing the profession, quickly developed beyond banking matters as such to become a forum for economic affairs in general. It was where Helfferich, as we have seen, delivered his sensational speech on 'The Reichsbank and Liquidity' in 1912.

However, long before the founding of the Central Association, people had a fairly firm idea of how individual banks should be rated. In official Berlin before the turn of the century, the Deutsche Bank was regarded as 'red' – in contrast, say, to the Disconto-Gesellschaft, which through its participation in protected industries and its activities in the field of public credit (the Prussia Consortium) attached particular importance to good relations with the establishment.[369] Siemens used the term 'red' himself when in 1886 he wanted to participate in some financial business in Bulgaria. Asking his father-in-law, Hermann Görz, to provide him with letters of recommendation to a few influential people in Bulgaria, he explained: 'I cannot turn to our diplomatic service. I have been given a rather bad name "on high" – shrewd rivals having eagerly exploited my political views to our disadvantage – so that not only does no one do the "Red Bank" (that is what they call us) any favours, they are very keen to deal us a blow whenever they can.'[370] However, Siemens's concern turned out to be groundless, and the Foreign Office willingly provided advice, not least with regard to securing funds.

Talk of the 'red bank' was entirely in line with what the journal *Hermes* (subtitle: *An Information Bulletin for Business and Finance*) reported in 1910: namely that, of the big banks, the Disconto-Gesellschaft had formerly been known as the Conservative one, the Dresdner Bank as the National Liberal one, and the Deutsche Bank as the left-wing liberal one. The Deutsche Bank system, it said, was built on the 'broadest democratic foundation', with every depositor, no matter how small, feeling cordially welcome. However, since Messrs Gwinner and Koch had been ennobled, the bank had quit this democratic path. Now its only concern was to attract the 'giants' among depositors. 'The Deutsche Bank has become feudal', was the concluding judgement.[371]

The epithet 'red' in fact described little more than a certain progressiveness in matters of domestic policy. The top men at the Deutsche Bank were seen as middle-class liberals and indeed viewed themselves as such. There could be no question of their entertaining sympathies for parties situated to the left of the Liberals, which mainly meant social democracy – nor, in view of the attitude then taken by social democracy towards 'capitalism' and its principal exponents, the banks, is this at all surprising.

In addition to reporting the bank's large-scale undertakings (the Baghdad Railway, for example, and the oil companies), the major German business newspapers commented on its annual general meetings and the balance sheets presented there. After 1876, however, and the upheavals associated with the takeovers of the Deutsche Union-Bank and the Berliner Bank-Verein, the annual general meeting was increasingly characterized by a mood of passive contentment. There was little criticism of the management, though there was the occasional complaint about the level of dividend. Even *Der Aktionär* (usually given to more biting commentaries) reported 'lively words of recognition' and happy faces 'as proof that the shareholders are in agreement with the management'.[372]

The newspapers confined their reporting either to a sober analysis of the figures (the business supplement of the *Frankfurter Zeitung*, for example) or commenting effusively on the institution's continuous growth, as did the *Berliner Börsen-Courier*: 'The Deutsche Bank has reached a point in its development that leaves all previous ideas regarding the expandability of a banking company far behind, and even foreign countries, where banking had already reached an advanced stage at a time when in Germany it was still in its infancy, can have few creations to show that can be set alongside the Deutsche Bank as being of equal standing.'[373] The *Effekten-Kursblatt* (share-price bulletin) published by the Credit Suisse in Zurich took much the same line: 'In terms of the number of its achievements and the size of its successes, the Deutsche Bank in Berlin undoubtedly occupies front rank in the recent annals of European banks, and the course of its development since its founding in the year of the war, 1870, reflects the massive growth in power of German industry and German commerce over the past thirty years.'[374] And for the *Berliner Börsen-Zeitung* it was hard 'to find the correct and not yet too worn-out superlatives to convey an impression of the phenomenal success of this international institution'.[375]

The *Frankfurter Zeitung* was more objective: 'The Deutsche Bank's final result for 1906, as placed before the supervisory board this afternoon, once again reveals with what powerful energy this institution, which in terms not only of the size of its equity but also of the scale of its revenues stands at the head of the Berlin big banks, continued its inexorable policy of expansion (which for years has been accompanied by ever-greater success) over the year just past.'[376] And in 1912 the same paper reported that the bank was still showing excellent profit figures, despite heavy losses incurred in connection with loans to customers of Bergisch Märkische Bank: 'Last week's results were a further reminder of how, in addition to these reserves in the balance sheet, enormously high hidden reserves continue to play a part so far as the Deutsche Bank is concerned, internal reserves that enable the bank to cause a loss amounting to millions simply to disappear without so much as a trace of it left visible in the end-of-year figures put forward.' The article closed by saying that, even more than was the case with other big bank balance sheets, those end-of-year figures made it clear 'how remote the figures put forward are becoming from an actual year's results, instead appearing solely as components of a pre-established quantity'.[377] The bank had meanwhile achieved a position and gained a reputation in the public eye that were not easily shaken even by heavily loss-making transactions.

In his obituary for Siemens, the liberal journalist Theodor Barth compared the Deutsche Bank in 1901 to a 'major state'. The top levels of management in so powerful a financial institution required 'men with a talent for government'. A leading modern bank (he went on) had, like a major state, to pursue a business policy in which all the various departments needed to be taken into account as power factors and must occasionally be drawn together for wholly power-seeking purposes. Georg von Siemens had been capable of doing this – 'as it were, as prime minister of a bank state'. For Siemens, the supreme charm of his position had lain in the 'sensible exercise of the monetary power reposing in his bank'.[378]

Vorwärts remarked in its obituary that Siemens had as a managing director of the Deutsche Bank had an influence on the economy far exceeding that of a government minister. The big bank that Siemens headed had played so important a part in Germany's industrial development that 'the deceased must be counted among the economic rulers of the country and placed in the front rank of that financial aristocracy'.[379] And the Berlin *Fremdenblatt*, under the headline 'Second Emperor', saw Germany as being already a 'vassal of the Deutsche Bank'. It portrayed 'a future state in which Germany's destiny is guided by the cabinet-in-chief of a few big banks, and the "kings by the grace of God" henceforth play a merely decorative role'.[380] Even that thoroughly serious journal *Die Bank* wrote in connection with the turning-down of the national oil monopoly: 'Mr von Gwinner, who attended the debates in parliament, will now perhaps no longer be quite so firmly convinced that he is the most powerful man in Germany. The fact is, there are still certain things that, despite everything, are still not possible here ... For the Deutsche Bank, the turn taken by events constitutes a severe defeat. It had thought it could pull the wool over the eyes of the government and the entire German nation, indeed it considered its authority great enough for it to be able, by playing this difficult game, to snub and repel the entire competition. Having influence, however, does not yet mean being in the right, nor does it mean always succeeding.'[381]

Of the success or failure of the bank's 'public relations work' it is not, in this context, possible to speak in anything more than limited terms. The fact is that such public relations work, if it existed at all, was on only a very modest scale. There were as yet no press spokesmen, no business reports intended primarily for public consumption, no glossy brochures or advertisements from which anything like a 'corporate identity' might emerge. If we want to know how the bank saw itself, the kind of notion of itself that it sought to convey to others, we must basically go to the programmatic statements on matters of principle made by its leading representatives – foremost among them Siemens, who was so much in the public eye politically as well. We have this statement, for example, that Siemens made in the Reichstag in February 1900: 'What, then, are these institutes called banks? We do not occupy the position attributed to us by the Conservative Party of being minor securities dealers or stock jobbers; the position to which we have always laid and continue to lay claim is that of seeking, as it were, to be leaders of the nation's entrepreneurial spirit.'[382] Elsewhere, he said this: 'I have contrived, by dint of an unshakeable attachment to objectives, to cause our bank, which at the outset looked like becoming a minor lending and agio bank, to jump those rails and indeed achieve a certain glory, with the result that it is now an object of general esteem.'[383] He saw in the bank and in its goal of making German exports and imports independent of Britain an opportunity for him to bring things to pass that would be 'as much a national achievement [as] the conquest of some province'.[384]

Siemens marshalled economic and political arguments principally in order to canvass for German companies and banks to become more involved overseas: 'Every bank or railway established in a foreign land, the shares of which remain in the home country, is at the same time a pioneer for the employment of domestic industry and for the creation of lasting relations between two economic zones ... The times are irrevocably gone by in which one might have thought it possible to maintain pleasant political relations between two governments while those nations are moving in opposite directions economically.'[385]

Siemens and Gwinner were always clear in their minds that every significant expansion of Germany's economic sphere of influence constituted a piece of *Weltpolitik* (i.e. had an international political dimension), even when that expansion stemmed not from the government but from a consortium of banks. They therefore endeavoured from the outset to obtain the collaboration of international financial groups, particularly with British participation as well. But after Wilhelm II's visit to Constantinople in 1898, bankers were no longer able to get their idea of international co-operation accepted by the Kaiser, the German government and the ambassador in Constantinople.

Bismarck's policy, as we have seen, had been to assist the Deutsche Bank in its quest for concessions, while firmly refusing to furnish any kind of political guarantee for economic risks undertaken. The governments that succeeded him, however, were very ready to do so; indeed, they positively forced the pace of economic expansion for political motives. Not only did the government seek to influence the activities of the Deutsche Bank in the Ottoman Empire; the bank's involvement in China likewise occurred at the express behest of the Foreign Office, as the early history of the Deutsch-Asiatische Bank shows.

The behaviour of the top men of the Deutsche Bank (Siemens, Gwinner and Helfferich) abroad and particularly in Turkey was consistently marked by a certain cautious civility. The fact that the first meeting between Siemens and the

Kaiser in Constantinople went off rather coolly was undoubtedly due in part to Siemens's dislike of any form of imperialistic status seeking. Siemens foresaw how his business was irreversibly in the process of being sucked into the wake of politics. And Karl Helfferich later inveighed bitterly against the Pan-German tendency, which ruined business for him.[386]

At the height of the reign of Wilhelm II, any managing director of a major big bank was, willy-nilly, also a spokesman for imperial Germany. In the Business Report for 1914, the managing board described the outbreak of war very much in the patriotic tones prevalent at the time: 'The envy, covetousness and vindictiveness of our foes are to blame for the dastardly war of which all the nations and peoples of the world ... are now victims. Our armies, however, have taken the war to the enemy on all fronts, allowing Germany and its allies to look forward to the future with confidence.' However, they soon reverted to statements of a more sober and pragmatic nature: 'So much has already been written and published about this greatest of all wars and about the causes and effects thereof that we prefer simply to let the figures speak for themselves. They show that the Deutsche Bank, like the German economy as a whole, has survived this great trial of strength victorious.'[387]

Those same top men had very much their own opinions regarding the size and importance of the Deutsche Bank. Siemens, for example, wrote to his wife in May 1896: 'To my mind, the Deutsche Bank has now grown too big ... I'd have made quite a good Elector of Brandenburg, but Chancellor of Europe would be too large a task even for me.'[388] Gwinner, on the other hand, noted with satisfaction in March 1914, in a telegram to Edward D. Adams (the bank's representative in the USA), that, after the proposed takeover of Bergisch Märkische Bank, the Deutsche Bank would not only remain the largest bank in Germany, but would become the world's biggest bank.[389] The phrase 'the world's biggest bank' had in fact been used the previous day in the *Frankfurter Zeitung* article quoted above. The newspaper reported that, for example, the Société Générale in Paris and Lloyds Bank in London had higher levels of equity and borrowed capital. However, these two criteria did not alone determine the importance of a credit institution. The unique position of the Deutsche Bank rested instead (and of course in addition to its high levels of equity and borrowed capital) on its extensive ramifications in all areas of the economy. The bank had long outgrown its private sector interests; in Turkey, for example, it was directly involved in politics.[390]

This was incontestable, and both then and subsequently it drew mounting criticism. Where was the point beyond which sheer size and the political influence that inevitably went with it became a danger, even if the idea of being 'Chancellor of Europe' was far from the minds of those responsible? That question is still being asked in the context of the development of the Deutsche Bank today.

V. The Deutsche Bank in the Life and Society of Imperial Germany

1. The Deutsche Bank as employer and as organization

'Showing a visitor to an engineering works how a machine is built is not difficult because he has the material object before his eyes the whole time ... How a lathe, an automobile or a turbine comes into existence can be described and illustrated in black and white. Anyone viewing the operation of a major bank, however, will undoubtedly see a great many mechanical installations, teleprinter rooms from which cables go out to dozens of branches, pneumatic dispatch systems, four or five telephones on every table, he will see counters, consulting rooms, boardrooms, the mighty vaults with their heavy, armour-plated doors, he will see people in profusion, sitting at desks writing, talking on the telephone – but of the actual business of banking he will see precious little.'[391] That is how the financial journalist and historian of banking Maximilian Müller-Jabusch, writing a biography of Franz Urbig, the future chairman of the supervisory board of the Deutsche Bank, described the difficulty of representing the essence of what a bank does. All anyone can see is the office routine, not the actual business.

Any attempt to describe, in retrospect, the operation of the Deutsche Bank in the Germany of the Second Empire runs into precisely the opposite problem: while the documents (even if only fragmentarily available) provide information about individual pieces of business, about contacts with industry and with other banks, and about capital increases, takeovers and other transactions, there is very little information to hand about the everyday working lives of the people who conducted that business. The first time the Business Report even mentioned staff numbers was in 1894 (24 years after the bank's founding), when the Deutsche Bank employed 1,072 people. And even the few photographs to have survived from the period before the First World War show exterior views of buildings or interiors with not a person in sight. The day-to-day life of bank staff did not seem worth recording, only the architecture of the buildings and views of imposing cash halls.[392]

Of the early years of the institution we know little, as far as employees and their working and living conditions are concerned; we sense only that things were very modest. For his biography of Siemens, published in 1921, Helfferich was still able to draw on oral testimony: 'The offices were on an upper floor of an ancient and dilapidated building in Französische Strasse (no. 21), the dark and almost dangerous staircase of which must by all accounts have acted as a positive deterrent. The manager's office that housed Siemens was a particularly ill-lit "Berlin room" that moved even his father, the Counsellor of Justice, who as a former Berlin public prosecutor will certainly not have been spoiled as regards office accommodation, to shake his head sympathetically on his first visit.'[393]

What departments the Deutsche Bank comprised in its early years, how exactly it was structured, and how many staff it employed are questions we are scarcely able to answer today. All the more interesting, therefore, is the account that Karl Wichmann gave to the monthly staff magazine in 1928 (at the end of his working life, when he had reached the rank of head of department at the Deutsche Bank) regarding the start of his apprenticeship.[394] When the 17-year-old Wichmann joined the Deutsche Bank in 1872, the institution, though only two years old, already had one move behind it: from the Französische Strasse premises to a slightly larger home at 29 Burgstrasse. 'The bank occupied the first floor, part of which had been turned into a single room by removing some of the walls.' Wichmann's account brings the then office and those who worked in it to life; at the same time it shows the departments into which the Deutsche Bank was subdivided in those early days, thus providing a kind of initial organization chart for the institution.

Georg Siemens's rapid assumption of a position of prominence was reflected in the allocation of office space: he was the only one with a room of his own. 'The far room with a single window looking out over Zwirngraben belonged to "Assessor" Siemens, though he was usually away on business. Next to it was a room with two windows occupied by Directors Wallich and Kaiser.' (Kaiser was not long with the bank; he was replaced by Max Steinthal in 1873.) After the two directors' rooms came 'another single-windowed anteroom where the incoming mail was read and discussed by Messrs Wallich and Koch, and then the big room began, with the top desk for Mr Koch separated from the others by a glass partition'. Rudolph von Koch was then a deputy director (deputy member of the managing board in today's terminology). He was promoted to full managing director status in 1878, and from 1901 until his retirement in 1909 he even, as we have seen, served in succession to Siemens as spokesman of the bank, before Gwinner took over that unofficial 'office'.

In the large office overlooking Burgstrasse sat first of all the bank's two stock exchange representatives. Wichmann again: 'Then came the desks for four correspondence clerks, memorial-journal, stock and foreign exchange accounting, daybook and ledger, two current account clerks, bill and foreign exchange department (four men), teller's department (Treasurer Martini and a cashier's clerk). That completed the Zwirngraben-Burgstrasse façade, then the room turned back towards the rear of the building. Next to the teller's department was the foreign currency department: loyal old Sergeant Mogwitz! I see you still in all of your towering six feet six inches, with the shrapnel scar on your head and the Iron Cross (First Class) on your chest, both of which you got leading a platoon of King's Grenadiers that day you captured the first French battery. Young and old addressed you only as Sergeant, and we were all of us proud of you, especially when you sometimes came to work in the uniform of a Crown Guardsman. And you looked after what was at first an unfamiliar area to you so reliably, dispatching our old talers to India and China and receiving gold bars and gold coin in return, flogging bundles of roubles for 180 and 280 and buying "greenbacks" for 3.20. Ah, those were the days; but I must go on, otherwise the editor will cut all my finest memories. After the foreign currency department, then, came the deposit department. Mr Reimer in charge, in the army a first lieutenant of the reserve cavalry, with us a cashier and book-keeper combined. Then came the coupon-paying department, *one* clerk with a tin box for the coupons and another for the cash, then the "live" deposit book, kept by the senior apprentice, and lastly the securities department under Mr Milow, with five men. That ended with the strongroom, where there were four deposit boxes the way they were made then. The windows overlooking the spacious courtyard were all fitted with strong iron bars and metal shutters, which we closed every evening. A side room at the back housed the outgoing mail department, where ... honest old Bach ruled the roost. He used to keep the mail money in his trouser pocket, and when it came to paying he simply stuck a fat hand in his trouser pocket and brought it out brimming with gold and silver coins. *Tempi passati* – gone are the days!'[395]

Altogether our source reckons 'a staff of about thirty persons were employed'.[396] That number soared in the years that followed, and by 1880 it had already reached 341, of whom 270 worked at head office in Berlin.[397] By 1890 the number of employees had passed the thousand mark (1,020), but not until 1894, as we have seen, was it mentioned for the first time in the Business Report. The expansion course pursued by the Deutsche Bank also led to large staff increases. *Beamte* ('bank officials') were continually being taken on. In 1896 there were 1,340 of them, in 1898 there were 1,625, and in 1900 the number stood at 2,063. The expansion in staff numbers continued after the turn of the century, and in 1914 the Deutsche Bank employed 8,475 'bank officials'.[398]

With the advent of the joint stock banks and their growth into big banks, bank employees became (the numbers alone make this clear) a distinct social group. The private banks of the eighteenth and early nineteenth centuries had of course already trained apprentices and employed 'commercial assistants'. In most cases, however, this was the 'young merchant' (often himself from a merchant or banking family) who was taken on for a limited period to enable him to learn the fundamentals of the business before launching into self-employment.[399] With the expansion of the joint stock banks and the displacement of private banks, for a growing number of people the position of bank employee became a permanent condition. The commercial assistant was no longer taken on for a few years, but was a 'bank official' for life.

A common saying before the First World War was that a *Bankbeamter* was five-sevenths civil servant and two-sevenths merchant – in other words, neither one thing nor the other.[400] Even in jest, the hybrid position that the commercial employee (not only in banking) occupied in Germany under the Reich was clearly evident: he was a merchant, yet he operated neither at his own risk nor on his own account; as a salaried employee (*Angestellter*; more usually, nowadays, 'white-collar worker'; Tr.), he was a public servant of some kind without being a government clerk or civil servant (*Staatsbeamter*). The terms *Beamter* and *Angestellter* evolved largely in parallel during the course of the nineteenth century. The latter was someone who drew a fixed monthly remuneration rather than a wage linked to work actually done and hours put in.[401] Since this also applied to the civil servant, in the developing heavy industries such people were referred to as *Privatbeamter* or 'private servants/clerks'. The term *Beamter* raised the salaried employee above the level of worker and (the obvious difference notwithstanding) put him conceptually on a par with the civil servant,[402] which in a German society moulded by bureaucratic traditions at the same time implied respect and a certain social standing. 'The term was thoroughly imbued with an aura of dignity, respect, loyalty and duty that were also invoked, whether wittingly or unwittingly, by anyone who used the term for a section of industrial personnel.'[403]

'Salaried employee' or 'private clerk' eventually came to designate followers of various occupations: not only accounting and office staff, signing clerks, factors, book-keepers, accountants, commercial travellers, engineers and master-craftsmen working in industry, but also teachers, educators, actors and orchestral musicians.[404] Given this variety of 'white-collar' occupations, in one of the first scientific studies of the salaried workforce (published in 1912) Emil Lederer came to the conclusion: 'The endeavour to define salaried employees as a technical entity is therefore doomed to failure; the fact is, they are not a technical entity but (with reservations) a sociological one.' The terms 'salaried employee' and 'private clerk' thus denote membership of a social group situated between the worker and the entrepreneur, a group that was also referred to as the 'new middle class'.

The terms 'salaried employee' and 'private clerk' having originally been coined in the context of the reality of industrial employment, their application to people working in commerce and particularly in joint stock banks led to some blurring of the edges at both the top and the bottom ends of the hierarchy.[405] People employed to perform such mechanical operations as detaching coupons, keeping registers of numbers, copying bills of exchange, or working in dispatch or filing or as collecting clerks were scarcely distinguishable from labourers. At the top of the company, on the other hand, people like directors and members of the managing board, while by virtue of the legal form of the joint stock company they were classed as salaried employees, in practice occupied the position of employer.

Accordingly, in his 1916 study of 'social-structure changes in banking',[406] Oskar Stillich was already talking about three groups of bank employees: '1. the top figures, i.e. directors, authorized agents, authorized signatories, archivists, etc.; 2. *Bankbeamte* proper, "bank officials"; 3. the semi-skilled workers such as messengers of various kinds, post dispatchers, filing clerks, stenographers, etc.'[407] The activities of the 'semi-skilled workers' were usually not specific to banking in any technical sense; they required no actual knowledge of the business. These lower employees were therefore not really entitled to be called 'bank officials'. True 'bank officials' or 'commercial assistants', who had generally completed a banking apprenticeship, naturally attached great importance to the distinction. 'The title "bank official" is still excessively misused,' a *Beamter* of the Deutsche Bank complained. 'Every cashboy and scribbler proudly calls himself a "bank official" and this does nothing to enhance our standing in society.'[408] The technical assistants were rather looked down on by the *Bankbeamter*. Stillich commented: 'Where differences of origin and background, education and behaviour are so strongly emphasized as in banking, this should not surprise us.'[409]

The permanent establishment of white-collar workers as a social class led in turn to the formation of interest groups to improve job opportunities along self-help lines, and to put in place social security systems against accident, sickness and old age. The earliest associations accordingly concentrated from the mid-nineteenth century onwards on organizing employment exchanges, pensions and sickness insurance, and vocational training.[410] Then in the 1880s the big employees' associations began to emerge.[411] The largest of them all was the Deutschnationale Handlungsgehilfenverband (German National Commercial Assistants' Association), or DHV for short, which was founded in Hamburg in 1893 and by 1909 had more than a hundred thousand members. The DHV, which admitted neither Jews nor women, sought particularly to draw a line of demarcation between 'private servants/clerks' and workers and not least for this reason (i.e. to avoid any devaluation of the 'commercial assistant' class) was opposed to female labour. In the 1912 study of the salaried workforce already referred to, Lederer was scornful: 'The DHV seeks ... constantly to maintain a certain exclusiveness. It appears to regard the distinction between entrepreneurs and salaried employees as less fundamental than that between salaried employees and labourers. This view is undoubtedly based on an organic conception of "bourgeois society" ... It is therefore a further endeavour of the DHV to prevent "a large section of the class from sinking into the proletariat".'[412]

Two specialist associations for salaried employees in banking were founded in Berlin in the early 1890s: the Verein der Bankbeamten (Association of Bank Officials) (1890) and the Deutsche Bankbeamten-Verein (German Bank Officials' Association) (1894). The latter, which represented the interests of 'officials' on a trade union basis, was the more important and had most members; on 31 December 1909 a total of 20,448 bank employees belonged to it, as compared with 4,738 for the Verein der Bankbeamten.[413] The founding and establishment of these salaried employees' associations constituted a recognition on the part of members of the middle class that their situation was in principle no different from that of wage-labourers. The enormous popularity of the Deutscher Bankbeamten-Verein undoubtedly had much to do with the fact that it offered its members retirement insurance. Most banks had, like the Deutsche Bank,[414] set up their own pension funds. However, these generally paid out only if the employee did not leave the institution concerned until retirement age, which in practice meant that he could never change his job.[415]

Bismarck's social security legislation of the 1880s provided only for accident, retirement and sickness insurance for wage-labourers. Not until 1911 did the relevant government decree extend these systems of insurance to sections of the salaried workforce as well. Prior to that date, the only possibility for 'bank officials' was to join the pension fund of the Privatbeamten Verein (Private Clerks' Association) or that of the Deutscher Bankbeamten-Verein. The Deutsche Bank had set up its own pensions and benefit fund as early as 1876 – 'to provide support in sickness and non-self-inflicted accidents'. Following the death of Georg von Siemens, in 1901 it was named after him. Also before the government decree came into force, the Deutsche Bank set up a Beamtenfürsorge-Verein (Bank Officials' Welfare Association) for its own salaried employees in 1910. Anticipating the expected legislative arrangements, it offered its staff retirement insurance. After 1911, it became the recipient of the statutory contributions paid by the insured.[416]

In 1909 the Centralverband des Deutschen Bank- und Bankiergewerbes (Central Association of the German Banking and Bankers' Trade), acting in conjunction with the Deutscher Bankbeamten-Verein, set up the Beamten-versicherungs-Verein des Deutschen Bank- und Bankiergewerbes (Employees' Insurance Association of the German Banking and Bankers' Trade). After more than ten years' service, 'bank officials' who became disabled received a pension from this insurance fund that even continued to be paid to surviving widows and orphans after the death of the insured. Contributions were 4 per cent of salary for 'bank officials' and 4.5 per cent of salary for managers.

In 1910 the Deutsche Bank additionally created for its employees what it called the Klub der Beamten der Deutschen Bank (Deutsche Bank Staff Club). The object of this was primarily to offer 'clerks and in particular the unmarried the possibility of good, inexpensive catering'.[417] It was the first Deutsche Bank canteen, if you like, and in it between 550 and 600 'bank officials' ate lunch daily and between 340 and 400 also ate supper.[418] The club was formally separate from the bank. It was run by a committee, and the club's employees (manager, cook, waiters, etc.) were paid not by the bank direct but by the club. Members paid a monthly subscription of one mark, but of course the club was heavily subsidized by the bank on top of that. As well as the canteen, the club also provided leisure facilities. It had rooms for entertainment, billiard rooms, reading rooms and music rooms. It was the bank's way of 'cultivating a spirit of togetherness and conviviality', as Max Fuchs, then the bank's archivist, described the ideological intention of the club.[419]

The leisure facilities provided by the bank expanded as time went on. Choral, orchestral and various sporting associations were formed for staff. In addition, the bank built rest homes where staff could spend holidays or weekends at Johannaberg in the Teutoburg Forest (1918), at Sellin on the Baltic island of

Rügen (1924) and at Caputh, near Potsdam (1917). And in Mariendorf (Berlin) a sports ground was built with two fields for hockey, football or handball, six tennis courts and facilities for athletics.[420]

The overall effect of all this was the transformation of the relationship between staff and management in banking. Of course, strengthening the 'spirit of togetherness' among the various fast-growing groups of bank staff and enhancing their feeling of solidarity did not always, given the tendencies of the time, have entirely happy consequences as far as management was concerned. 'Bank officials' increasingly saw themselves as a separate group with its own interests, which were different from those of members of the management. At the same time, the lower grades of salaried employee took a leaf out of the workers' book and banded together to push through salary increases and other improvements. The initially negative reaction of bank managements is apparent from an incident that took place in November 1913 and evidently continued to make waves for almost six months.[421] The Deutsche Bank dismissed an employee who a few days earlier had headed a delegation that submitted a claim on behalf of bank staff for an increase in salary in the light of rising living costs. The dismissal was officially justified on grounds of mediocre performance by the employee concerned, but the trade union demanded the establishment of a staff committee. This was to serve the employees of the bank as a forum for articulating their interests and at the same time to provide a negotiating partner to meet with management. The Deutsche Bank refused, and the Trades Union Congress cancelled all its accounts with the bank in protest. A large section of public opinion sided with the employees. The *Frankfurter Zeitung* commented: 'It is the general trend nowadays that salaried employees and wage-labourers wish to have some say in matters relating to their employment.'[422] The bank, though, would not give way at first. Talks were held between it and the trade unions, but the bank's representatives refused to give a written guarantee of recognition of and protection for their employees' right of association. Not until 1919 did the trade unions win acceptance for their demand that works committees be set up. The arbitration award that ended Berlin's first bank strike in April 1919 provided for the establishment of works councils that should have a right of co-determination in the appointment, promotion and dismissal of bank staff.[423]

Banks had extremely high demands with regard to their apprentices' schooling. Karl Wichmann, for example, was 17 at the start of his apprenticeship and had passed the 'one-year examination' that entitled him to a reduction in military service to one year. The 'one-year', which was identical to the *Mittlere Reife* (approximately equivalent to GCSE; Tr.), could be taken at secondary schools that normally led to university (either the humanistic *Gymnasium* or the *Realgymnasium*, which was oriented towards modern languages and natural sciences) as well as at the less academic type of secondary school known as *Realschule* that did not prepare students for university. Many bank apprentices had even stayed on at school a year or two longer, and in a few cases they had even taken their *Abitur* (advanced school-leaving examination approximately equivalent to A-level; Tr.).[424] When Carl Michalowsky was asked to place someone in a bank apprenticeship in 1906, he said much the same about educational qualifications: 'In general it is customary, at least among the larger institutions, to demand that the apprentice has his one-year certificate, and often a sixth-form education is required. Even *Abitur* graduates often go in for banking, though it is not usually necessary to have that examination.'[425] On the other hand, a university degree was not expected. Even directors usually had no higher academic education. Siemens, who came to the Deutsche Bank with a doctorate in law, was for a long time the exception. His colleagues Wallich, Steinthal and Gwinner had 'risen from the ranks'; in other words, they, like all their fellow managers, had learned their trade by first completing a bank apprenticeship.

These requirements with regard to the schooling of bank apprentices meant in practice that access to the occupation of 'bank official' was confined to middle-class children: children from working-class families never usually got to any kind of secondary school. For members of the lower classes, there was an additional obstacle in the way of their entering a bank: to gain one of the coveted places as an apprentice it was usually necessary to have personal contacts. Wichmann was able in 1872 to rely on his uncle's personal acquaintanceship with Deputy Director Rudolph von Koch. Georg Obst, a highly regarded author of textbooks on banking, referred in 1921 to written application as a kind of 'way out' for those with no personal contacts that they could exploit: 'Anyone with connections to a director should seek to make use of these; otherwise, apply in writing, setting out the circumstances (curriculum vitae), to the local banks or to banks in another major centre or to the big banks in Berlin.'[426]

The fact that 'bank official' became such an attractive occupation for young Germans under the Reich undoubtedly had a great deal to do with the excellent salaries and career opportunities that went with a job in banking. 'Older friends who had already left school and found jobs in Berlin businesses used to tell marvellous stories of what a young man could earn in a bank, his apprenticeship once completed.' Karl Wichmann admitted that as a 17-year-old he had embarked on an apprenticeship in banking primarily for financial reasons. 'In the civil service you had to have made it at least to "major" before you earned such a salary.'[427] An apprentice, however, earned nothing to begin with, but that was the rule in all branches of business. Not until the third year of his apprenticeship did Wichmann receive a salary of 300 marks a year. After completing his apprenticeship he drew 'the princely salary of 900 marks, though following urgent discussions with Director Koch this was raised after only two months to 1,500 marks' or £75 at that time. [428] Director Michalowsky expressed himself in very similar terms in 1906: 'Apprentices have of course to provide for themselves during their apprenticeship, but after a period of time that may vary in length they usually receive a little pocket money and on completion of their usually three-year apprenticeship are taken on at a salary of between 1,200 and

1,500 marks.'[429] It is clear from these two statements that the salary of a 'bank official' (the numbers refer to annual salary) had risen hardly at all in 30 years. By contrast, the average salary of the commercial assistant (that is to say, not just of the bank clerk, but also of employees in commerce and industry) increased from 1,255 marks in 1887 to 1,672 marks in 1906.[430] Even if the consumer price index did remain relatively constant until around the turn of the century,[431] 'the fact remains that the salaries of bank employees stayed level over a period in which average incomes, based on the calculations of sixty-six trade associations, went up from 1,108 marks to 1,215 marks in the years 1906–13 alone'.[432] Nevertheless, at the beginning of the twentieth century, bank employees still enjoyed a salary that was some 25 per cent higher than that of salaried employees in general.

The reason generally given for this narrowing of the gap between the salaries of 'bank officials' and other white-collar workers is the enormous rush of applicants for jobs in banking. Particularly in the period 1895–1900, banks are said to have attracted more and more people from other branches of the economy. It became increasingly possible for unskilled workers, often with relatively little schooling, and gradually women too, to move up into positions as 'bank officials'. This tendency was of course observed very critically by more qualified banking staff, who feared a loss of status and were concerned about the possibility of 'the level of the profession [being] pushed down too far': 'The bank official continues to occupy a position of trust. He must work correctly (mistakes are very costly), and he must perform his duties quickly and conscientiously. Anyone in the grip of anxieties about his daily bread is clearly not in a position to do this.'[433]

Oskar Stillich described the situation in 1916: 'The struggle currently being played out among bank staff has split people into two camps. Some take the exclusive view that access to banking should be barred to all with only elementary schooling; they cling to the prerequisite of the matriculation exam or at least the one-year certificate for entry into the big banks. Others uphold the democratic principle of freedom of access for all, including those with only elementary schooling behind them, and reject the idea of limiting the profession through the use of examination hurdles.' Stillich himself argued for the abolition of these entry requirements on the grounds that advanced schooling was 'neither formally nor in terms of content likely to be of any use to the individual as regards fulfilling his function in life'. He cited in this connection a Deutsche Bank employee who worked in the coupon-paying department: 'As an *Abitur* graduate [student with A-levels; Tr.], I deeply regret belonging to this profession, which was more or less forced upon me. The one-year certificate or merely elementary schooling is quite sufficient for this mindless work, no matter what scale of business one is dealing with. No value whatsoever attaches to school education.'[434]

That kind of dissatisfaction was a product of the changes that arose for the individual employee as a result of the way in which banks grew in size and a greater degree of division of labour was introduced into their organization. The increasing mechanization of banking also contributed to this development. Punch card machines, which made the first mechanical data processing possible, did not come in until the 1920s, of course; nor did typewriters and adding machines in themselves represent a qualitative change in office procedure (they merely mechanized the performance of secondary operations). Nevertheless, together they marked the beginning of modern office organization, which with its concentration on division of labour and its constant preoccupation with ever-increasing rationalization meant that the individual member of staff no longer understood and executed every aspect of a transaction, but was responsible only for a small part of it.[435]

From about the 1890s onwards, the development of big banks led, as we have seen, to an enormous expansion of bank staffs. The increasingly rationalized organization of the various banking operations enabled banks to supplement their qualified people with growing numbers of less expensive unskilled or semi-skilled workers. As a result, in addition to applicants without secondary schooling and without apprenticeships, women now constituted a further 'new' group of potential employees for banking, as for the world of work in general. However, according to a survey carried out by the Deutscher Bankbeamten-Verein, in 1912 only 2,408 women altogether were employed by joint stock and private banks, about half of them in technical and half in unskilled jobs.[436] It was only with the outbreak of the First World War, when many 'bank officials' were called up and the resultant gaps (as in most other branches of the German economy) proved impossible to fill with male workers, that banks started employing more women. 'We have been able to keep the bank going as it should only by dint of the greatest exertions on the part of the remaining clerks and managers, and we have found ourselves compelled to take on female auxiliary staff', the management informed shareholders in the 1914 Business Report.[437]

Most of the women seeking employment in banking were obliged by their economic situation to earn money at least until they got married. The 'classic' areas of women's work (housekeeping, nursing, education) had meanwhile been joined by other occupations, such as that of shop assistant following the expansion of the retail trade since the 1880s. Office work, which was clean, quiet and socially acceptable, now constituted an increasingly attractive alternative. Women were employed in offices mainly to do general secretarial work or as shorthand-typists and book-keepers.[438]

Among office jobs, working in a bank was even more acceptable in social terms. That went for women too, of course. But although the numbers of women employed in banking also rose, the increase was a long way behind that of other areas.[439] Banks proved very much less welcoming to women than other branches of commerce, and among Berlin big banks the Deutsche Bank showed special reserve: 'The head office of the Deutsche Bank does not, as I have already informed you, employ women,' Michalowsky wrote in October 1910 to a member of parliament who had asked him to find a 'suitable place' for a young lady.[440] Nor was he able, he said, to offer her another position, since 'as far as the branches are concerned the lady is quite out of the question, given the demands that in view of her educational background she would presumably be entitled to make'. While the Deutsche Bank thus clearly drew a distinction between a job at head office and a job in a branch, and employed no female 'bank officials' at the former, the Disconto-Gesellschaft appears to have been less restrictive. At any rate, Michalowsky reported that he had 'made confidential enquiries with the management of the Disconto-Gesellschaft, where ladies are taken on'. There had not, however, been any jobs going there. Only the Bank für Handel und Industrie employed female staff in larger numbers. Some 200 women worked there in various departments before the First World War.[441]

2. Status, origins and self-image of managing directors

At the head of the Deutsche Bank in 1872 there were three managing directors, one deputy managing director, and at the next level of management two *Prokuristen* or authorized signatories. Cashiers, branch managers and correspondence clerks also enjoyed higher status in comparison to the simple 'bank official'.[442] As banking grew and expanded, so too did the number of top positions. On the one hand, that number increased as more and more branches were founded, for all branch managers became managing directors. On the other, the actual managing board at the Berlin head office was itself made larger. From 1878, when Rudolph von Koch was promoted from the position of deputy to become a full member of the managing board, that body comprised four persons. In 1900 there were six managing directors and two deputies. By 1914 the numbers had grown to ten managing directors and a further thirteen deputies. And from 1912 the group of those described in the Business Report as 'management figures' also included nine heads of department. Karl Wichmann, the apprentice of 1872, attained this position in 1917.

One consequence of the legal form of the Deutsche Bank as a joint stock company was that managing directors, like 'bank officials', were employees, whereas in traditional private banks as well as in the Disconto-Gesellschaft, which took the form of a limited partnership based on shares, the company hierarchy was headed by the proprietor or proprietors, who answered for their decisions with their own private fortunes. The people who founded joint stock banks naturally assumed that the proprietors of the company would continue to make the strategic decisions – in other words, that as the actual owners they would retain control of the company and simply delegate the execution of their decisions to the managing board. The managing board was thus conceived of as a subordinate body bound by instructions.

On the distribution of functions and responsibilities between the administrative board as the body representing the shareholders and the management appointed by it, the 1870 articles of association of the Deutsche Bank said this: 'The management conducts the company's affairs in accordance with these articles of association and the instructions given to it by the administrative board' (section 17) and 'The administrative board shall oversee the execution of these articles of association by the management, supervise the latter's activities, and give it instructions' (section 28). The articles of association even laid down in detail which business decisions should be taken not by management alone but by the administrative board: 'The administrative board decides on land purchases for business premises, on the establishing of branches, agencies and subsidiaries and any agreements to be concluded in connection therewith, on amounts of outstanding credit to be granted, and on purchases and sales of shares, bonds and securities of all kinds.'[443]

The managing directors opposed these provisions, which they saw as obstacles to the efficient management of the company. Siemens, criticizing attempts by the administrative board and specifically by Adelbert Delbrück to run the company, used a striking comparison: 'When twenty-four people try to run a bank, it is like a wench with twenty-four suitors. None of them marries her. But she still ends up with a child!'[444] For the most part, of course, the conflict between the administrative board and the management was conducted in less humorous terms, and on several occasions Siemens threatened to resign. Wallich, writing his memoirs, was still complaining that the efforts of the administrative board had been directed at 'demoting the managing directors to the level of mere clerks, who were simply required to execute the resolutions of the administrative board or its committee. They found support for such an endeavour in the bank's articles of association, which laid down that the administrative board was the seat of all powers.'[445] It was in line with the way things were developing generally that the managing directors eventually got their way. The revised Corporation Law of 1884 established a separation between management and administrative board. The latter was renamed the 'supervisory board' and was restricted to its function as a controlling body. Wallich welcomed the underlying intention of 'giving management ... its proper role as executive power' and concluded: 'The present generation of banking management will not understand how fettered were its predecessors.'[446] This was the beginning of the time of employee-entrepreneurs, the 'separation of capital ownership from company control', which in the words of Richard Tilly was 'a fundamental tendency of the period'.[447]

Siemens and Wallich thus belonged to the first generation of bank managing directors. On the one hand, they were employees of the company, as were the growing numbers of 'bank officials'. On the other hand, certain elements remained that distinguished the manager from the ordinary run of employees and put him closer to the private banker who was in business at his own risk. Siemens, as we have seen, although not in principle answerable with his personal fortune for the bank's business result, assumed the traditional obligations of entrepreneurial liability and repeatedly stepped in with his own private means when customers of the Deutsche Bank suffered losses as a result of his decisions.

Socially, managing directors of the larger joint stock banks were evidently on a par with private bankers. This is clear not least from the fact that the overwhelming majority of both groups lived in the same part of the city (broadly speaking, the Tiergarten district), comprising the streets bounded by Pariser Platz and Leipziger Platz (linked at the time by part of Königgrätzer Strasse) to the east, the Zoological Gardens with Lichtensteinallee to the west, Bellevue Station to the north, and the Landwehr Canal to the south. The most popular address was Tiergartenstrasse itself, where Rudolph von Koch and Georg Siemens lived as near neighbours to Paul von Schwabach (of the S. Bleichröder bank), Richard Staudt (of Staudt & Co.), Emil Salomon (of the Emil Salomon Jr. bank) and Adolph von Hansemann, the proprietor of the Disconto-Gesellschaft.[448]

The members of the managing board were also, symbolically, co-proprietors of the Deutsche Bank, the articles of association laying down that each must own at least 25 shares. 'The same shall be deposited with the company during his period of office and may be neither sold nor encumbered.'[449] The pay of managing directors also reflected their position as employees bearing entrepreneurial responsibility. On the one hand, they received a fixed salary, like all 'bank officials'. But the greater part of their income consisted of a bonus based on profits. The total amount of this bonus entitlement was laid down in the bank's articles of association. After deduction of a dividend (5, later 5.5 and from 1907 6 per cent) from the net profit, members of the supervisory board received a total bonus of 10 per cent. Initially, management's profit share was likewise set at 10 per cent, but subsequently the amount was left open (as was the manner of its distribution). In the early, lean years of the Deutsche Bank, managing directors accordingly earned little, and Wallich was later to complain: 'We were very poorly paid; an ordinary stock exchange manager had a bigger income than we did.'[450] Wallich was certainly exaggerating, although precise details of the incomes of individual members of the managing board are not available. At any rate, with the upswing of the Deutsche Bank its managing directors also achieved considerable affluence. They drew additional income from seats on advisory boards that they occupied on the bank's behalf.

Many of the members of the managing board of the Deutsche Bank continued to come from banking or merchant families. This was true of Hermann Wallich, Max Steinthal, Carl Klönne, Gustav Schröter, Paul Millington-Herrmann and Oscar Wassermann. However, as the importance of banking and the numbers of people employed in the sector grew, such men were increasingly joined by the descendants of representatives of other professions: namely, sons of civil servants, teachers, doctors or priests. Where subsequent members of the managing board of the Deutsche Bank did not come from merchant families, in the period before the First World War they mainly sprang from the educated middle class. Ludwig

Roland-Lücke, the son of a papermaker and nephew of a labourer, and Oscar Schlitter, whose father held a postal agency, were exceptions. They were also, however, examples of how anyone might rise to a seat on the managing board who had completed a banking apprenticeship.[451]

Clearly, then, most members of the managing board of the Deutsche Bank in the period before the First World War came from the upper middle class. Moreover, from the turn of the century the business and educated classes began to grow closer and closer together. For Georg Siemens's father there had still been a clear distinction here – even a hierarchical scale. His son could, as a lawyer, have made a brilliant career in the civil service, and Siemens Sr could not at first understand Georg turning down the opportunity and joining the Deutsche Bank instead. He would occasionally refer disparagingly to 'my son, the clerk'.[452]

The crusty old Counsellor of Justice may have been slow to change his mind, but as the joint stock banks grew in size, the social standing of their managing directors rose accordingly. They came to enjoy a level of wealth that, while it could not compete with the fortunes built up over generations by established families of industrialists and bankers, nevertheless enabled them to lead a very pleasant existence. Siemens, Koch and Gwinner may have been ennobled, but their self-image as well as their life-style remained thoroughly 'bourgeois'. It was in line with this bourgeois view of themselves that the person who functioned as spokesman of the managing board did not bear any special title setting him apart from his colleagues. Like Georg von Siemens before him, Gwinner too rejected the term *Generaldirektor* (Chairman): 'The Deutsche Bank has never had such a person, nor will it, so long as I remain on the managing board, ever know one. Ours is a democratic constitution.'[453] Gwinner, who though he had never completed a university course had been awarded many honorary doctorates, also refused to let the bank's publicity material refer to him as 'Dr', asking instead that 'I be listed as plain "Arthur von Gwinner" '[454] – quietly overlooking the fact that the 'von' could hardly be described as 'plain'.

The wealth of members of the managing board was earned by hard work, and their everyday working lives continued to be governed by middle-class principles in this respect. Max Steinthal may stand as an example for many. Born in 1850 into a Jewish family of merchants and academics, Steinthal grew up in Berlin. There he attended the Königsstadt secondary school, leaving with an *Abitur* certificate at the age of 16 and taking up an apprenticeship at the A. Paderstein bank. Within a few years he had sole power of attorney, and in the Paderstein'sche Bankverein that grew out of the private institution in which he had completed his apprenticeship, he even rose to the rank of director. In 1873, Steinthal joined the Deutsche Bank. Siemens greeted the 23-year-old at his interview with the words: 'So you want to become a signing clerk with the Deutsche Bank?' 'No', Steinthal replied, 'not a signing clerk, a managing director.'[455] Steinthal remained a member of the managing board until 1905, afterwards switching (as was usual) to the supervisory board. At this point the *Almanac of Millionaires in Prussia* put his fortune at between 10 and 15 million marks and his income at 600,000 marks.[456] From the 1890s on Steinthal lived in a freehold house in Charlottenburg. He also owned a house in Berlin itself. In 1912 he was the third largest taxpayer in Charlottenburg, after Werner von Siemens and Engelbert Hardt. Gwinner, on the other hand, became wealthy at the time of his marriage to Anna Speyer, daughter of a Frankfurt banking family, who received a dowry of around 6 million marks. As a managing director at the Deutsche Bank, he was able to increase that fortune substantially. His income for 1912 was estimated at close to a million marks, his fortune at just under 14 million.[457]

Despite his wealth, Steinthal followed the tradition of his family and remained personally very modest. Max Fuchs, the first archivist of the Deutsche Bank, wrote in an article in honour of Steinthal's eightieth birthday: 'His generosity has always been coupled with strict conscientiousness, and unstinting fulfilment of the categorical imperative of duty constitutes the solid core of his attitude to life and motivation. He has never left his native city of Berlin for longer than a four-week holiday trip.'[458] Culture and 'keeping good company' were also part of a very deliberately cultivated bourgeois life-style. 'One met not at the bridge table but at the aesthetic tea', noted Fuchs, whose article, for all its stylized prose and penchant for dramatic exaggeration, probably reflects a good deal of 'real life'. 'The works of our great classics' were constantly under discussion, and clearly even managing directors of banks were expected to contribute. Steinthal was specifically said to have by heart 'not merely quotations, which one hears every day, but whole passages such as are memorized only by dint of serious reading'.[459]

The Deutsche Bank did not recruit the majority of its managing directors from among former civil servants, as so many other institutions did; instead, it allowed its own 'bank officials' to rise to the very highest positions. In the early days of the Deutsche Bank (as Ludwig Bamberger related in his memoirs) Delbrück had in fact shown 'a Prussian regard for bureaucracy' in appointing as managing director 'a Privy Councillor with many years of service in the administration'.[460] However, the talents of Geheimer Finanzrat Mölle do not appear to have been particularly convincing. According to his then colleague Wallich, he left the bank again because 'after eighteen months in the post he came to realize that the qualifications of a top civil servant were not sufficient to take over the running of a profit-making institution'.[461] Mölle's failure may have contributed to the fact that, with the exception of Karl Helfferich, the Deutsche Bank appointed no more civil servants to its management. Evidently, this also found approval with shareholders. In 1906 one journal reported that the bank had been congratulated at its general meeting 'for allowing its own employees to rise to the highest rank and not, as other companies are in the habit of doing, appointing former civil servants as managing directors'. The Berlin banker Adolph Jarislowsky even saw in this an explanation of why the Deutsche Bank was so successful: 'This very practice, which has occasioned lively satisfaction not only among shareholders but also on the stock exchange and throughout the world of commerce, will bear rich fruit.'[462]

Banking, like trade, was a branch of the economy in which traditionally many Jews had been involved, and many of the leading private bankers were of the Jewish faith.[463] While the proportion of Jews among the Prussian population remained relatively stable, declining slightly from 1.32 per cent in 1871 to 1.04 per cent in 1910,[464] it dropped very sharply in the money and credit business, though of course still remaining relatively high. From 21.97 per cent in 1882, it went down to only 3.84 per cent in 1925.[465]

The principal cause of this decline in the percentage of Jews employed in banking is to be found in the huge expansion of the sector during the Second Empire. Whereas large areas of traditional private banking had been and continued to be dominated by Jewish names (Rothschild, Bleichröder, Oppenheim), the advent of the joint stock bank led to increasing numbers of sons of Christian families with no previous connection with banking entering the profession. Among private bankers, however, and among the holders of top managerial positions in the big joint stock banks, Jews remained particularly well represented.[466]

This was especially true of the Disconto-Gesellschaft, the Dresdner Bank and the Berliner Handels-Gesellschaft.[467] With Siemens, Gwinner and Koch, the Deutsche Bank was largely headed by Christians. However, a series of important Jewish figures also served on the managing board: Wallich and Steinthal in the early years, and later Paul Mankiewitz, Elkan Heinemann and Oscar Wassermann. Little is known about whether and to what extent their religion played a part in their professional lives. These Jewish bank directors (in the Deutsche Bank as much as in other institutions) were assimilated Jews whose families had been settled in Germany for generations. As we saw from the example of Steinthal, they had attended German schools, they laid emphasis on their patriotism, and they became involved like their Christian colleagues in politics and public life – Bamberger being probably the best-known name in this connection. Unlike the Jews who had immigrated from eastern Europe in increasing numbers after 1871, and who made themselves conspicuous by their dress and habits, these men were members of the German middle class, the educated class, from which apart from their religion they were scarcely distinguishable. Moreover, contemporary biographical appreciations do not usually discuss the religious affiliations of managing directors of the bank; this applies not only to tributes to and obituaries of colleagues, but also to articles about them by journalists of the financial press. And for most of them (Steinthal, Mankiewitz and Heinemann are examples) no private papers have survived that might have told us how they reacted to the increasing anti-Semitism of the Germany of Wilhelm II.

Against this background, Wallich's memoirs assume particular importance because they do not gloss over this aspect of his life. In fact they are permeated with his awareness of belonging, as a Jew, to a marginal group that often suffered discrimination. He also noted, however: 'I clearly foresaw how Jewish arrogance, which was spreading everywhere, must inevitably draw a terrible reaction.'[468] His view, which for the 1890s was eerily prophetic, shows how sharply and pessimistically he saw things. In this context, however, one must, as in the case of Walther Rathenau a short time later, be aware of his own quite ambivalent and anything but objective relationship to his fellow believers. Wallich encountered this growing anti-Semitism soon after his return to Germany: 'German thoroughness has scientifically established that Jewry is a foreign body that has implanted itself in the organism of the other peoples. So long as it behaves in a neutral fashion, it is tolerated. But let it try to stand out or achieve dominance as a result of its special qualities, and it will be shaken off.' Wallich stressed that he was referring here to 'the views of the educated Christian populace, untouched by ordinary anti-Semitism. They scorned to go along with the general howling against Jews, but they were not blind to the errors of their Jewish fellow-citizens, and they sought as far as possible to avoid keeping company with them.'[469] In the bank no anti-Semitism could be detected, Wallich wrote later, and his position as a managing director there and his connections in society had shielded him personally against anti-Semitic attacks. Nevertheless he often, during the 1870s, thought of leaving Germany again. His wife, however, staunchly opposed such a course: 'Born and bred in Berlin, she firmly refused to leave her native land and seek her future abroad, possibly among wealthy and arrogant relatives, who admittedly invited me to join them.' So they stayed in Berlin, and Wallich made even greater efforts in the direction of assimilation. Not being a believer, he declined 'to be martyred for a cause for which one no longer had the feeling'. Nevertheless, he did not convert to Christianity – unlike many of his contemporaries, who used conversion to rid themselves or at least attempt to rid themselves of the 'stain' of Jewishness. Although no longer personally subscribing to the doctrines of the Jewish religion, he felt himself under an obligation to the memory of his orthodox parents. However, he wanted his children to be free of such chains and had them baptized and educated as Protestants. 'Rather than poor believers in the Jewish faith, I wanted to make my children good Christians.' His first concern in so doing was to spare them the problems with which he had had to struggle because of his religious affiliation; he wished to integrate them completely into German society. In this, he failed. Hermann Wallich's son Paul, born in 1882, came to feel the limits of assimilability more and more keenly, and in 1938, to escape imminent arrest by the National Socialists, he committed suicide.[470]

Right from the outset, the leading representatives of Berlin's big banks played an important role in the society, culture and politics of the capital. The Siemens house, for example, became shortly after Georg Siemens's marriage a social meeting place of the first order. In the early years, arrangements were still very modest, as a note from Elise Siemens attests: 'We have worked out a way, thinking about it economically, of having guests without huge extra costs. I tell Georg each morning, when he leaves the house, whether I have a fresh roast that day. Georg has too many claims on his attention at the bank, so in order to be able to discuss important matters thoroughly in peace and quiet, he simply brings the gentlemen he wants to talk to home to dinner.'[471] At these dinners, business was of course not the only topic of conversation. Siemens hoped 'little by little to draw a really interesting group of people around me who will supply me with intellectual comforts outside work'.[472] The first guest was Werner von Siemens, who continued to be a regular visitor. In addition, business colleagues, top lawyers and civil servants, industrialists, academics and above all large numbers of parliamentary friends were invited to dine at the Siemens house. The company Siemens kept was governed by the idea of bringing together, beyond business and professional interests, leading representatives of a new and quite specifically 'bourgeois' élite. A particular concern of his was to get them involved in politics, which he regarded as the proper field for his non-professional activities.

Like many of his colleagues, Siemens also pursued particular cultural interests, stimulated not least by the *soirées*. In his case, it was above all the archaeological excavations being made in Asia Minor that interested him, particularly since he had visited the 'digs' himself during his trips to the region. It was there, incidentally, that his daughters Marie and Charlotte met their future husbands: Theodor Wiegand, who married the former in January 1900, was president of the Archaeological Institute of the German Empire, chief curator of the Pergamon Museum in Berlin and head of excavations at Milet, while his colleague of many years, Hans Schrader, secretary of the Imperial German Archaeological Institute in Athens and later professor of classical archaeology, married Charlotte Siemens in 1901. The two archaeologists 'always found in him [Siemens] a ready ear and a generous hand with regard to their work', according to the tribute published by the bank to mark the centenary of Siemens's birth.[473] In the same spirit, Siemens subsidized the bringing to Berlin of the Pergamum altar, regarded by contemporaries as a major national achievement. Whether he exploited his contacts with the Turkish government for this purpose we do not know.

The Deutsche Bank did not, as an institution, go in for patronage in the first few decades of its existence. This remained the case even under Gwinner, who evinced great personal interest in mineralogy, botany and numismatics, and dispensed not inconsiderable sums of money in order to promote the sciences. For example, he gave 100,000 marks to the Kaiser Wilhelm Society (now the Max Planck Society) at the time of its founding in 1911.[474] He remained a member of the society until his death in 1931, and became one of its senators in 1916. This interest in the natural sciences was even more marked in the case of his son, Hans Gwinner (1887–1959), who became a chemist and in 1929 himself joined the Kaiser Wilhelm Society as a 'Sponsoring Member'. Gwinner made his donation privately, as did Mankiewitz, who gave 40,000 marks. The bank itself became a member of the society only in 1929.[475]

3. The external appearance of the bank before 1914

Whereas industrial companies manufactured products that were plain to see, money as the 'raw material' of banking was something abstract and its operation comparatively difficult for the outsider to comprehend. When showing visitors around the premises of the Deutsche Bank, the institution's first archivist, Max Fuchs, used to point out that 'the work performed here, unlike the noisy business of manufacturing, is mainly done in silent mental operations that cannot be seen, in which not much mechanical plant is involved, and whose purpose becomes apparent to the observer only in financial success'.[476] To an even greater extent than industry, therefore, banks were concerned to use their buildings as a means of self-presentation. The head offices that the up-and-coming joint stock banks of the imperial period erected in the capital and economic metropolis, Berlin, thus became symbols intended to convey to the visitor a feeling of security and an impression of great size and strength on the part of the institution concerned. These 'temples of Mammon' or 'cathedrals of capital'[477] were to be manifestations of the prestige, stability and solid worth associated with money, the object being to gain the confidence of customers in what was becoming an increasingly competitive market.[478]

Even in the ironically deprecatory description given by Werner Sombart, it is clear what sort of impression the 'strongholds of capitalism', as he called them, made on the observer: 'The attentive stroller who directs his steps through the Friedrichsstadt district of Berlin will be struck by a series of huge buildings occupying entire blocks that have sprung up there like mighty fortresses, particularly over the last ten years. The massive pile reposes on enormous blocks of stone, approached by a massive flight of stone steps. Its halls gleam with coloured marble and gilt ornaments. Long rows of counters fill the upper storeys, amidst which elegant boardrooms and nobly decorated reception rooms greet the elect … These are the new focal points of the civilized world: New Sanssouci, New Versailles.'[479]

Such palaces were of course the culmination of a development that had often had very modest beginnings. The Deutsche Bank was no exception in this respect. We have seen how the first offices of the newly founded bank, where perhaps a handful of employees worked at building up the business, were situated on the first floor of an apartment block in Französische Strasse.[480] After only a year the bank needed more space and moved into a building it had purchased in Burgstrasse, within sight of the Berlin Stock Exchange. However, this first freehold home, again quite modest, was itself to be only a transit station as far as the bank was concerned. The core of the future head office was formed by the buildings of the Deutsche Union-Bank and the Berliner Bank-Verein in Behrenstrasse, Mauerstrasse and Französische Strasse at the heart of the emerging bank quarter. The Deutsche Bank took possession of the buildings as part of its takeover of the two institutions in 1876. It moved first into Behrenstrasse 9/10, a building designed by the architects Ende & Boeckmann and erected in 1872, and this became the starting point for expansion on to adjacent sites. From 1883 the two blocks between Behrenstrasse, Französische Strasse, Kanonierstrasse and Mauerstrasse were gradually bought up by the bank and redeveloped. The northern block housed the three cash halls and the head office departments. On the ground floor was the chief cashier's department with the strongroom, the securities teller, and the exchange and foreign currency department. A total of 370 'bank officials' worked in these departments frequented by the public; a further hundred or so were employed in the offices on the upper level, in the stock exchange department, the secretariat and the legal department above.

The southern site between Französische Strasse and Jägerstrasse was set aside for a main deposit department and a central administration for all Berlin deposit business. The year 1906 saw the laying of the foundation stone for the redevelopment of the entire block. The Berlin architect Wilhelm Martens (1842–1910), who had already put up several buildings for the Deutsche Bank, planned the monumental structure in the style of the Italian Renaissance.

The centrepiece was the new cash hall, measuring 75 by 28 metres and accounting for almost half the entire floor area. As the bank's main point of contact with the public, the cash hall naturally received most of the attention as far as interior decoration was concerned. To provide adequate illumination by daylight, the great hall was roofed with a dome of frosted glass. The room extended over two floors and was entirely clad in marble. To temper the monumental impression slightly, the space was divided into a central domed hall with a diameter of 15 metres and two lateral halls each measuring 19 metres in length. The entrance to the deposit department was on Mauerstrasse. Three portals in the rounded, protruding central portion led first into an oval vestibule and thence into the hall itself.

The northern block extended over 6,568 square metres, 5,107 of which were built on. On the southern block, which had an area of 5,309 square metres, 3,444 were occupied by buildings. Whereas the three cash halls in the northern block together covered an area of 682 square metres, the cash hall in the southern block measured 1,056 square metres. To overcome the physical separation that resulted from extending over the adjacent block, the bank planned to link the two buildings by means of a first-floor footbridge over Französische Strasse. As the bank wrote to the Berlin municipal authorities in 1907, requesting permission for the link: 'For the Deutsche Bank, the projected footbridge is necessary if it is to be able to maintain the integrity of its whole extended operation in the way that has been possible hitherto. According to plans now finalized, between six and seven hundred staff are to move into the new building, and since the cashdesks and the accounting and correspondence departments are all closely interrelated and since nearly all those relationships involve oral communication, there has to be a constant movement of people from building to building, on top of which there is all the to-ing and fro-ing of letters, instructions and the like.'

There was also the argument of customer safety: 'It is quite unthinkable that persons wishing to take the usually large sums they have withdrawn at our main cashdesks and immediately transfer them to our deposit cashdesks should be directed out of head office and across the street to our deposit department.'[481] The negotiations were successful, and the first 'flying buttress', as it was called (an arch measuring 21 metres in length spanned the street without intermediate supports), was taken into use on 1 July 1909. Because of its constantly increasing need for more space, at the end of 1909 the Deutsche Bank purchased the Stumm'sche Palais on the other side of Mauerstrasse. It and the adjoining buildings were pulled down in 1912–13 and a new building erected, into which the offices of the management were moved in July 1915. This building too was joined to the northern block by a footbridge over Mauerstrasse. The two characteristic 'flying buttresses', which set their distinctive visual stamp on Mauerstrasse and the corner of Französische Strasse, became something of a symbol of the Deutsche Bank – and possibly also of the way in which it unfailingly contrived to throw bridges across the divide between the centuries and hold its own through shifting circumstances.

The Deutsche Bank
from World War to World Economic Crisis
1914–1933

by Gerald D. Feldman

In the spring of 1914 the *Frankfurter Zeitung* celebrated the Deutsche Bank as the 'greatest bank in the world'. This was not simply because the bank had recently added so formidably to its capital stock – raising its share capital from 200 to 250 million marks and its reserves from 115 to 178.5 million following its fusion with the Bergisch Märkischen Bank. Nor was its greatness to be explained by its more than one and a half billion marks in deposits. The Société Générale could boast a larger capital stock, and both the London, City & Midland Bank and Lloyds Bank had larger deposits. What made the Deutsche Bank extraordinary was that it was the most universal of universal banks: 'There is no bank in the world that can at once dispose of so large an amount of capital and deposits and at the same time also pursue such diverse and manifold engagements in all areas of economic life in almost all the countries of the world.'[1]

The dynamic role of the Deutsche Bank as both a private enterprise and an economic and political actor transcending the bounds of simple corporate interest was evident wherever one turned: the expansion of its network of branches; its role in the long- and short-term financing of some of Germany's most important enterprises; its recent rescue of the Fürstenkonzern, whose collapse might have further destabilized an economy already in recession; the bank's growing engagement in domestic politics through its unsuccessful but impressive effort to promote a petroleum monopoly; its role in the Ottoman Empire and Middle East, both as a financial power and as a pathbreaker for German economic interests; its risky and therefore all the more impressive investments in the chaotic world of the Balkans and involvement in the economic development of the United States and Latin America; and its growing interests in the South Seas, Asia and Africa. The range of investment and entrepreneurship in which the Deutsche Bank engaged itself was indeed remarkable, and it mirrored the growth

I wish to thank Norma von Ragenfeld-Feldman and Jonathan Zatlin for their critical comments and assistance.

and possibilities of the Kaiserreich in the pre-war era. The Deutsche Bank and the ambitious men who ran it were a tangible expression of Imperial Germany's rise to world power status and gave a measure of credibility to that striving for a 'place in the sun' which otherwise found inglorious expression in the vacuous phrase-mongering, aimless power politics and brinkmanship, and irritating mixture of whining, confusion, militaristic posturing and counterproductive bullying that characterized Wilhelmine foreign policy.

The Deutsche Bank's balance sheet of 1914 marked not simply a high point of its growth and prosperity, but also the end of an era. The future of the bank, like that of the Empire, was dependent on the continuation of the long peace since 1871 which, however uneasy it had increasingly become, was squandered away in the summer of 1914. The illusions and waste of war and inflation, the heavy price for both reflected in the brief and very tenuous stabilization of 1924–29, and the horrendous workings of the Great Depression all find expression in the balance sheets of the Deutsche Bank between 1914 and 1933. Even at their most problematic, those balance sheets are not simply the carefully designed self-presentations of a financial institution. They can be read and interpreted in terms of the disappointed hopes and traumatic disasters which engulfed Germany during this unhappy period, but they must also be read in terms of trans-formations in the business of banking, industrial change, and processes of economic and social modernization that took place during these years. An effort must be made to read the balance sheets, both of the bank and the history of which it was a part, in an objective manner.

I. The Deutsche Bank in the First World War

1. The bank and war finance

From the perspective of the banking system, the most revolutionary development brought on by the war was the massive involvement of the banks in the finances of the state. By the end of the war, the private business of the bank in commercial bills and stock market transactions had virtually disappeared, while the enormously increased liquid engagements, as the 1918 Business Report noted, 'quite naturally consist in the largest measure of Reich Treasury bills'.[2] As one of the foremost students of the German credit banks correctly noted, wartime developments 'gave the banks the character of deposit banks lending chiefly to public authorities'.[3]

The great banks had never anticipated such a development, and their rapid and unwelcome engagement with the finances of the state, which brought heavy losses during the war and inflation, remained a problem even after the banks returned to their 'normal' activities. Government borrowing from and through the banks created tense and unsatisfactory relations between the banking system and the government during the stabilization, and played a significant role in the economic crisis of the early 1930s and the banking crisis of 1931. The entire problem, furthermore, is inextricably interwoven with the complex and changing relationships between the Reichsbank and the government, on the one hand, and the Reichsbank and the banking system, on the other.

In contrast to Britain, with its massive London money market and a tradition of commercial bank and discount house willingness to hold Treasury bills, German credit banks had never developed any such sense of involvement and obligation. The British money market was much larger than the German and was heavily engaged in the financing of non-British as well as British international trade, while the German banks devoted their more limited monetary resources to the financing of German business activity at home and abroad.[4] If the German system was more nationally oriented, it was also extremely generous to its business borrowers, a factor of no small importance in Germany's pre-war economic development. Nevertheless, the crash of 1907 and the Second Moroccan Crisis of 1911 had severely strained the banking system and especially its lender of last resort, the Reichsbank. In the years which followed, there was much fretting on the part of the Reichsbank and especially its President, Rudolf von Havenstein, about dubious lending policies of the banks, their undisciplined competition and the inadequacy of their reserves. The situation was dangerous to the economy in time of peace and even more problematic in the eventuality of war because it threatened sudden drainage of the Reichsbank's gold reserves and was not amenable to control through increases of the discount rate.

The Reichsbank's financial planning for war was predicated on an ability to provide the war economy with the necessary liquidity and to maintain faith in the currency despite a suspension of the obligation to convert paper money into gold. It expected to do this by maximizing its stock of gold and maintaining its mandated one-third coverage of gold and first-class bills for its monetary emissions. Rediscountable Reich Treasury bills would function in the manner of commercial bills as primary cover for monetary emissions, as would the notes of loan bureaux to be created for the purpose of providing credit to the private sector and state and local authorities. These credits were to be guaranteed by high-quality securities. The expectation of the Reichsbank and Reich Treasury was that these short-term Treasury bills would then be consolidated into war loans, bonds which could even be paid for with Reich Treasury bills and loan bureaux notes. There was a good deal of monetary sleight of hand in these arrangements, in which the instruments for the reduction of liquidity were financed by instruments designed to increase it, but the assumption was that the war would be short and victorious and that the gold stored in Berlin's famous Julius Tower would persistently reinforce confidence.[5]

Precisely because the war was supposed to be short, the Reichsbank did not anticipate that the banks would have much incentive to trade in their business in commercial bills for Treasury bills, but the Reichsbank was very concerned that the credit banks have sufficient reserves to cover their own obligations and not complicate the tasks of the Reichsbank in its preparations for a national emergency by depleting the gold supply. The Berlin banks were as quick to agree with the need for corrective measures, which they did in all solemnity at the Munich Bankers' Congress of 1912, as they were slow to take them. Indeed, there was an underlying assumption in the banking community that the Reich and Reichsbank were there to serve the private economy rather than that the private economy had something more than an abstract obligation to serve the state by continuing to follow its star. The authoritarianism of the Kaiserreich, such as it was, did not easily extend to state–economy relations, and if German capitalism was more 'organized' than that of other industrial societies, then it was by and for the capitalists.

Havenstein was thoroughly sympathetic with the principles of business self-government, and he was loath to reduce the flexibility of the banks by calling for the legislation of reserve requirements or to yield to pressures for banking legislation by the Reichstag that might lead to the separation of deposit and credit banks and all sorts of regulatory measures that would put a 'Spanish boot' on the banks. Instead he had chosen the path of urging the great Berlin banks to create the 'Condition Cartel', a cartel which was established in 1913 under the leadership of the Berliner Stempelvereinigung, a banking cartel formed in 1900, and which was to put some order in their own house and impose order on the banking sector as a whole. Nevertheless, he remained worried and impatient, and also felt that the depressed business conditions of 1913–14, the relatively high liquidity and the likelihood that the expansion of many of Germany's leading industries had reached a peak provided an ideal opportunity to accelerate the regulation of the banking sector.

On 18 June 1914, only days before the fatal shootings in Sarajevo, he summoned the Berlin bankers to inform them that the Reichsbank expected them to move more quickly and that the great Berlin banks had to accept a 10 per cent liquidity requirement.[6] Their massive growth and disposition over five-eighths of Germany's deposits meant that they had to take the lead, although the Reichsbank intended to impose liquidity requirements on provincial, savings and other banking groups in due course. He charged that German economic life had become 'excessively constructed on credit', and that 'forty years of peace have nurtured a great optimism which even the banking world is unable to resist'.

Havenstein's proposals were greeted with an understandable lack of enthusiasm. Arthur Salomonsohn of the Disconto-Gesellschaft, who was also a member of the Reichsbank Central Committee, objected to the 'strong pessimism' of the Reichsbank, thought that the banker cartel had not been given a chance to show what it could do, and urged that the entire question be put off for a year. At the same time, he protested the singling out of the Berlin banks, suggesting that the provincial banks were even more guilty of having inadequate reserves. This theme was picked up by Arthur von Gwinner, who sharply criticized the liquidity levels of the savings banks and wondered why nothing was being done to regulate the private banks. His fundamental message, aside from raising various technical proposals designed to water down the Reichsbank programme, was that the matter should be left to the big Berlin bankers, who had the strength and power to put the banking sector back in order: 'We the great banks today already control 60 per cent of Germany's deposits. Our power is great, and if we set out to do something, then we can achieve a great deal. Whoever resists a unanimous decision will come to experience serious harm through the reduction of his credit.'

It was precisely the power of the great banks, however, that had moved Havenstein to begin his modest regulatory programme with them, and he was only willing to wait until late August, not the coming year, to get their counterproposals. Gwinner, indeed, saw the handwriting on the wall, and warned Director Walter Bürhaus of the Deutsche Bank's branch in Düsseldorf against encouraging industrialists to protest the new reserve requirements on the grounds that they would receive fewer credits: 'The measure will be pushed through in any case, if necessary through a Deposit Requirement Law, which will be much more oppressive for all concerned ... than that which is now being proposed.'[7]

Gwinner anticipated, undoubtedly with good reason, that the banks could negotiate better terms by accepting Havenstein's basic demands, but the entire affair signalled a potential qualitative change in credit bank–Reichsbank relations. Salomonsohn had made this point by arguing that 'the Reichsbank will for the first time be a controlling authority over the banks'. If it were to dictate their reserve requirements, then it also would inevitably oversee their daily business. Havenstein denied any such intention and claimed his proposed reserve requirements would make the banks 'more independent' of the Reichsbank, but the truth was that greater independence of the Reichsbank and greater control by the Reichsbank were not incompatible since the more control the Reichsbank exercised over the meeting of reserve requirements, the less likely it was to be called upon as a lender of last resort and the more the banks would have to shift for themselves.

This entire debate, above all the issue of bank regulation, was suspended by the outbreak of the war. The danger of a run on the Reichsbank's gold, which proved real enough because of public panic during the week preceding mobilization, was terminated by an illegal but nonetheless effective Reichsbank ban on further payments in gold on 31 July and then by law once war had begun. The decision for war also seems to have brought calm at the tellers' windows of the banks, since on 12 August the Deutsche Bank reported not only that the people had stopped 'losing their heads', but that deposits had exceeded withdrawals during the previous week.[8] At the same time, the Deutsche Bank appears to have been quite nervous about its own liquidity and customer demands for loans at the first stage of the war and placed high hopes in the loan bureaux, where it hoped to turn not only for its own needs but also to refer customers. It was thus very anxious for the Reichsbank to expand the range of securities and assets which could be put up for such loans, and Deutsche Bank Managing Director Michalowsky, who had been appointed to the board of managing directors of the loan bureaux, found it a rather thankless task to be caught between the demands of the banks, with which he privately sympathized, and the resistance of the Reichsbank to the acceptance of securities it thought dubious by the loan bureaux.[9] The tension between the public and the private interest thus continued and even intensified as a consequence of the war.

It would be a mistake, however, to overdo such differences or view them in a one-sided manner. Fundamentally, until they were confronted with military disaster, the German credit banks seem to have been well satisfied with the way in which the war was financed. Gwinner's correspondence, whether with knowledgeable colleagues abroad like the Swedish banker Victor Wallenberg, who was exceptionally friendly to the German cause and provided Gwinner with a great deal of financial intelligence, or with the German press, was persistently upbeat about Germany's finances, while harping on the inflation in Russia and the lack of confidence in its finances, and stressing every sign of weakness in the finances of France and Britain.[10] Gwinner was indeed correct about the strains the war would impose on Britain, and was prescient in noting as early as November 1914 that 'it is quite certain now already that one of the results of the war will be a most serious and irreparable damage to London's position as the world's clearing house'[11] and recognizing that New York might play a new and important role.

He and the majority of his colleagues in the German business world were much less sober about assessing the financial situation of their own country. While they were certainly well aware of the stresses an unanticipated long war was imposing on the German economy and people, there was an all-too-human unwillingness to think the unthinkable until practically the bitter end. The great banks certainly seemed to be prospering throughout most of the war, as Gwinner remarked in response to a newspaper enquiry at the end of 1917 against a background of German victory in the East and hope for coming success in the West. He proudly pointed out that all the German banks were in a healthy state thanks to their profits from interest, 'the backbone of every healthy bank'.

Gwinner's report demonstrated that the virtual disappearance of commercial bills as a result of the government's speedy cash payments for war orders and the decline in international trade had been more than amply compensated for by government paper and fees for the opening of credit accounts and advances. The Deutsche Bank, for example, was having no trouble whatever in profiting from and helping its customers to profit from deposits, which had tripled between 1913 and 1917: 'The results of this year will be favourable for all the banks because the otherwise very difficult placement of deposits in the Treasury bills of the Reich, the federal states, and the larger cities now offers the easiest opportunity to invest every available sum in a short-term and secure manner at acceptable interest rates which run at an average of $4\frac{1}{4}$ per cent to $4\frac{1}{2}$ per cent.'[12] Gwinner made a special point of the fact that the banks had not been called upon to any significant extent to provide advances for the purchase of war bonds, and had not themselves, in sharp contrast to the British banks, found it necessary to hold significant amounts of war bonds. Instead, they were able, 'as was proper in a healthy national economy', to perform their appropriate role as agents for the sale of war bonds – for which they received a modest commission – while satisfying the immediate needs of the war effort through the taking over of Treasury bills. In Gwinner's view, it was this superior organization of the capital market that made it possible for Germany to have such extraordinary success in financing the war through war loans, while her richer enemies were compelled to offer higher interest rates and offer their bonds at lower prices.

Germany's nine war bond drives did constitute an impressive achievement, and were a tribute to the undeniable patriotism of the German people, the extraordinary propaganda campaigns launched by the Reichsbank and Gwinner's protégé Karl Helfferich, who served as State Secretary of the Treasury in 1915 and State Secretary of the Interior in 1916–17, and the less edifying incentive of being able to use the bonds to borrow money at the loan bureaux. During the war, the Deutsche Bank and its branches handled an impressive 6.49 billion marks in war loans, and the big Berlin banks were responsible for 50–60 per cent of the subscriptions.[13] Nevertheless, Gwinner's account was overly rosy. The war bonds had ceased to cover Treasury bill issues by the spring of 1916, and Havenstein was complaining in September that the big banks were not raising as much as expected.[14]

Helfferich had distinguished himself by opposing the taxation or control of war profits and arguing that the costs of the war would be borne by Germany's enemies in the form of a heavy indemnity. There is no record of what his former colleagues at the Deutsche Bank thought of this rather crude approach to the financial problem, but they clearly counted on a German victory to help pay the costs of the war. In any case, the dominant mood among the bankers and the press friendly to them was optimism, and the quantitative increases in the bank balance sheets were interpreted as a vast increase in the wealth of the nation, while the reduced purchasing power of money was treated as a 'temporary phenomenon' resulting from shortages of goods.[15]

2. Expansion at home and abroad

The Deutsche Bank had done much to promote this mood in February of 1917 by taking over through fusion the Norddeutsche Creditanstalt in Königsberg and the Schlesischer Bankverein in Breslau. The Deutsche Bank had a long-standing connection with these banks, Michalowsky having served as the domi-

nant force on the supervisory board of the former since 1905, while most of the
shares of the latter had been in its hands since 1897. Under these circumstances,
the Deutsche Bank had no need to go on the capital market and was able to
engage in only a 'modest' increase of its capital stock by 25 million and of its
reserves by 45 million marks, but this was quite enough to raise its lead in
combined capital from 10 to 80 million marks over its great rival, the Disconto-
Gesellschaft. These fusions also gave the Deutsche Bank a presence in over 80
cities through the acquisition of the 21 branches of the Schlesischer Bankverein
and the 20 branches of the Norddeutsche Creditanstalt.

While anticipated changes in the tax laws played some role in the timing of
the decision to acquire these banks, it was clear to all involved that immediate
financial considerations were secondary to economic and political ones. As
Michalowsky argued to his fellow managing directors: 'Alone the prospect of
large tax increases brings the question of taking over the Schlesischer Bankverein
increasingly into view, and the setting up of our own branches in the other
eastern provinces is becoming more pressing because of the political and economic changes which the war may be expected to bring in the East. We are not
directly represented on the Baltic coast from Stettin up to Königsberg and Libau,
and yet it is precisely the Prussian port cities – Stettin, Danzig, Königsberg as
well as the city of Libau after the annexation of Courland – which will have
increased business importance.'[16] Germany's intended annexation of important
portions of the Baltic provinces of Russia, and the significance of Danzig 'once
Poland is economically joined to Germany', as well as the importance of these
Baltic cities for future trade with Russia, made it essential in Michalowsky's
view for the bank to establish itself in the area, something it could do with 'one
blow' by fusion with the Norddeutsche Creditanstalt. Clearly there was the
danger that the other great Berlin banks would try to compete with the Deutsche
Bank in the region, 'but the chief thing for us', Michalowsky argued, 'is that we
are the first to go East'. Fusion with the Schlesischer Bankverein was the logical
complement to this penetration of the eastern provinces of Germany.

While the Deutsche Bank encountered a certain amount of *Lokalpatriotismus*
in these efforts, the urge toward economic development of these regions, intensified by the wartime centralization in Berlin and Germany's expansionist policies, made fusion with the Deutsche Bank irresistible, and the Deutsche Bank
was quite pleased to bring into its supervisory board important representatives
of the supervisory boards of both banks. Thus it acquired the support not only
of north-east German businessmen and Silesian magnates, but also of important
Centre Party personages like Graf von Ballestrem, whose party had defeated the
Petroleum Monopoly Law in the Reichstag and with which the Deutsche Bank
certainly desired more influence. Informed observers saw this move as an important step in the direction of the industrialization of eastern Germany as well as a
reflection of the advance of German arms and influence in eastern Europe.

Not every businessman, even when admiring of the Deutsche Bank, was as optimistic as its leaders. Geheimrat Witting of the Norddeutsche Creditanstalt's supervisory board was impressed with the Deutsche Bank's farsightedness and supported the fusion, but he believed neither in an independent Poland under German influence nor in the annexation of Courland, and just as he had considered the Battle of the Marne a disaster, so he thought the break in the relations between the United States and Germany, which had taken place at the time of these fusions, was an equivalent disaster.[17] The Deutsche Bank managing directors had in fact discussed the break with the United States at their meeting on 5 February and raised the question of whether they should not either give up or delay the fusion because of the political situation. They decided, however, to go ahead, which was interpreted by the press as another sign 'of the great confidence which the administrations of the banks have in the general political situation' and of their economic strength despite the war.[18]

The fact that the rupture of German–American relations had been 'discussed and considered'[19] in the context of these decisions suggests that the confidence was not as total as these reports pretended. Wilhelmine society, after all, was a society in which one could feel safe saying things in private that would be considered unwise or even unpatriotic to say in public. Just as the Deutsche Bank managing directors knew what Witting thought, so Gwinner knew what Albert Ballin, the head of the Hamburg–America Line (Hapag), a man as well acquainted with the Anglo-American world as himself, believed: 'I have, as you know, been not at all optimistic about the outcome of this war already since 20 July 1914, the day on which I recognized that the war was not to be avoided; but since the days during which we forced America into a state of war with us, I see things very darkly. As I permitted myself to tell you even earlier, one had apparently no sense of the political, economic and military might of this overly rich hundred million people. And when once the first American corpse is transported back from the military theatre to New York and is carried in a solemn parade along Broadway, then the hysteria of the American people will reveal itself fully, and we will find out that there slumbers in this people just as great if not even greater organizational talents than we awakened with such a crude hand in the English people.'[20]

There were plenty of businessmen – among them prominent bankers like Arthur Salomonsohn of the Disconto-Gesellschaft – who dismissed the dangers of unrestricted submarine warfare and supported annexationism. Gwinner, who knew the Anglo-American world but who surely was not as pessimistic as the depressive Ballin, strongly supported the use of German military might to attain economic hegemony in Europe, and thereby counter what he perceived to be a British effort to contain the expansion of Germany's international commercial development. Yet he was associated with those groups which were opposed to extreme annexationism and critical of unrestricted submarine warfare. Directors Weigelt and Millington-Herrmann were well-known colonial enthusiasts, and bankers seem to have been particularly susceptible to notions that overseas expansionism was economically beneficial and necessary for civilized nations. In general, the leaders of the Deutsche Bank seem to have been very reticent about war aims. Being properly hopeful and appropriately cautious, after all, are the traits of good bankers. As patriotic Germans and ambitious businessmen, they participated in war enthusiasm and hopes for victory. As experienced dealers on international currency markets, they warned Havenstein and the Reichsbank against excessive optimism about the exchange rate of the mark.[21]

By 1917, it was in any case too late to turn back, and the only option was to go forward and hope for the best, in war and in business. Even so great a pessimist as Witting thought the Deutsche Bank's move to establish a foothold in the East a good one, just as Ballin sought to secure the future of the Hapag, as shall be shown. If the future might not be quite what the optimists imagined, this did not mean that the bank should not position itself to take advantage of opportunities that might work out in some different form.

The links which the Deutsche Bank had forged with the government, either through its direct involvement in matters bearing on the interest of the state or through its sheer strength and activity as a great bank, inevitably raised the question of the relationship between its public activities and private interests. The 1917 expansion of the Deutsche Bank into eastern Germany caused the noted banking authority and editor of *Die Bank*, Alfred Lansburgh, to reflect on these problems. He argued that the very ambition of the Deutsche Bank to organize and promote this region and the areas that might be annexed or tied to it, inevitably involved collaboration with the state. The bank, through its accumulation of capital and especially its practical expertise, necessarily had certain practical advantages that might lead to a measure of intellectual resignation on the part of those governing the state and, in an obvious reference to Helfferich, to calling banking leaders rather than statesmen to the helm. There was thus the danger that the bank might be as determining of the policies of the state as the state of the banks.

At the same time, Lansburgh also warned, as he had since 1905, that the sheer size and power of the Deutsche Bank made its careful and honest management a matter of national interest and concern, that its competition with the Disconto-Gesellschaft and Dresdner Bank posed the possibility that these three great banks would end up dominating the German money market, and that, unless a responsible reserve policy was imposed on them, there was always the possibility that their private interests would lead to dangerous practices and unwise or irresponsible decisions, and 'that the bank would maintain its readiness to cover its obligations at the cost of its debtors, that is, to cancel or refuse to renew credits in order to remain solvent itself'.[22]

Lansburgh's argument about the importance of regulating the reserve policy of the banks and the danger that banks in trouble presented to their borrowers was an old one whose validity would be demonstrated in the future. His other observations about the power of finance capital and banker domination of the state, however, are interesting precisely because they are insightful in some respects and very problematic in others, and are based on a vision of the role of the great banks that was questionable even before the war and that was becoming even more dubious because of the war.

While Lansburgh certainly was correct about the close relationship that had developed between the Deutsche Bank and the government in a wide range of international and domestic matters, his analysis understates the extent to which the state, especially the military, was autonomous in its policies and demands, and the degree to which its adventuresomeness was dangerous to the interests of the bank and dragged it into risky policies and ventures. Lansburgh rightly detected a tendency for the government increasingly to seek out business experts for high positions, a problem that was to increase in the Weimar Republic. In actuality, however, very few businessmen feel comfortable about going into politics. Also, it is important not to exaggerate the homogeneity of views within the business community or even the banking sector, and it is important to recognize that those who actually sought out or accepted such opportunities – one thinks of Bernhard Dernburg, Karl Helfferich and Hjalmar Schacht – were effectively seeking to move from one career to another. Finally, and most significantly, Lansburgh overlooks the not always explicit competition for power between the banks and industry in the German economy, and the extent to which the accelerated capacity for self-financing created by high wartime liquidity was shifting the balance to industry.[23]

The fate of the Baghdad Railway during the war, and the problems created for Germany and for the Deutsche Bank by Germany's alliance with the Ottoman Empire of October 1914, illustrate many of the complications of government–bank relations and the important role played by personalities in these developments. Indeed, the Baghdad Railway owed its existence to the interplay of government and banking ambition.

It was Helfferich who had, against the 'wish and will'[24] of his mentor Gwinner, concluded the agreement of May 1908 for the expansion of the railway to El Helif. If the 'Baghdad business was a political mistake and a piece of economic nonsense'[25] that one of its chief builders Franz Günther, the Vice-President of the Anatolian Railway Company, adjudged it to be in 1924, then much of the responsibility lay with Helfferich. In Günther's view, 'Helfferich was by his very nature more a politician than anything else and through the influence which he exercised with the Embassy, he was coresponsible for the German policy toward Turkey at that decisive time . . .'. Those political skills certainly served Helfferich in the subsequent negotiations with the French and British and with the combatants after the Balkan Wars of 1912–13 in connection with the politics and financing of the railways. These negotiations, which came to a satisfactory end in early 1914, paved the way for turning to the financial negotiations with the perpetually bankrupt Turks.

The war erupted at a particularly delicate moment in the building of the

Baghdad Railway and in Deutsche Bank operations in the Balkans and Ottoman Empire more generally. In an effort to liberate funds for its Near Eastern railway operations, the Deutsche Bank and its allied Bank für Orientalischen Eisenbahnen had sold their interests in the Macedonian Railway and in other Balkan lines to an Austro-Hungarian group. Relations between the Serbs and the Austrians had been improving, and it appeared that a settlement was near between them on the Orient Railways, which would release more money. As these funds became available, work on the Baghdad Railway which had been virtually suspended since the end of 1912 because of lack of funds, could be renewed. Such instructions were in fact given in May 1914. The company expected that the necessary Turkish Railway bonds could at last be issued and that the outstanding problems with the Turks would be settled smoothly.

Relations with the Turks on the eve of the war, however, were not smooth. Turkish relations with Germany were reaching a deadlock in June because of differences over customs questions, various monetary claims and the status of German schools and hospitals. The Foreign Office, first against Helfferich's advice, but then with his approval, was coming to the conclusion that Turkish wishes for financial support had to be linked to the satisfactory settlement of these questions. The Deutsche Bank, which was involved in assisting the Turks to raise money for economic development and to pay for arms purchases from Krupp, decided that it had to support the German Foreign Office efforts.

At the beginning of July, the situation had been further complicated by the assassination in Sarajevo, rumours of an impending union between Serbia and Montenegro, which further alarmed the Austrians, and the collapse of the railway negotiations between Austria and Serbia. Under conditions where the Balkan peace was unravelling and German relations with the Ottoman Empire were deteriorating, the Deutsche Bank could not help but be cautious, no matter how anxious Krupp was to sell weapons to the Turks. As Helfferich argued to Director Muehlon on 2 July 1914: 'If we now have a situation in which the Foreign Office blows a "stop along the whole line", then it is clear that such a signal cannot be without influence on either the Baghdad negotiations or the business of the Krupp firm; for it would be the reverse of the basic ideas from which our discussions had their point of departure if we were put in the position where the Baghdad negotiations were broken off along with the political negotiations of the Foreign Office in order to put strong pressure on the Turks while with the other hand we had to offer new money to the Turks in order to promote the Krupp deal.'[26] Despite the deepening political crisis, the differences still were not settled by the end of the month, and on 29 July the Berlin headquarters of the Deutsche Bank was expressing its continued suspicion of Turkish financial demands and its unwillingness to provide any advances because of the political crisis.[27]

These events demonstrate the close collaboration between the bank and the government in Near Eastern affairs and the relative unimportance which they seem to have attached to the Ottoman Empire as an ally before the war.[28] Both the parsimonious attitude toward the Turks and the costs and nature of Deutsche Bank involvement changed dramatically once war had begun. The Germans rapidly convinced themselves of the importance of an alliance with the Ottoman Empire and thus delivered themselves up to Ottoman financial demands. The Reich provided its ally with a large gold loan, portions of which had to come from the Deutsche Bank vaults in Constantinople because of the difficulty of shipping gold through the Balkans. Franz Günther and Director Otto Kaufmann of the bank's Constantinople branch were also involved in the truly Byzantine problems of setting up an Ottoman bank to issue paper money, as demanded by the German government in return for its loans. This task was finally achieved in early 1917 after the Germans threatened not to provide more money, but it was the Germans who ended up providing all the coverage in Reich Treasury notes and cash.[29]

For the Deutsche Bank, however, the greatest headaches were to be provided by the Baghdad Railway. Its affairs got off to an unpleasant wartime start when the Ottoman government cut off bank payments and the German personnel in Mesopotamia had to be rescued from their unpaid and rioting Turkish workmen. Conditions improved in October when the Turks entered the war and the railway assumed military importance for the movement of troops and a strategic argument could be made for the closing of the Taurus and Amanus gaps. Geheimrat Riese of the Holzmann Construction Co., which was responsible for the construction work, and Günther now saw an opportunity to accomplish in the Great War what had been blocked before: namely, the closing of these gaps and the completion of the Mesopotamian branch of the line through an accelerated and well-supplied construction programme. The argument with reference to the Mesopotamian question was not lacking in imperialist ambitions of the more fanciful sort, not only by the important German military figure, Field Marshal Colmar von der Goltz, who conjured up visions of a march on Egypt and India, but also by one of the German Embassy officials, Dr Schönberg, who produced a lengthy memorandum which Günther approvingly passed on to Gwinner in September 1915, arguing that Germany should challenge Britain in the Persian Gulf and that the expansion of the railway into Mesopotamia was the best means of doing so. Günther was astute enough to know that the war would not be carried on for such reasons, but he thought that everyone was too 'hypnotized by the Dardanelles'. In his view, 'Mesopotamia loses nothing in its enormous importance from the perspective of its future possibilities as a consequence of the failure to take any measures at all in the present'.[30]

The various crash programmes advocated by Riese and Günther in the initial phase of the war received very tentative support from the Deutsche Bank since Gwinner, and the man who replaced Helfferich in early 1915, Emil Georg von Stauss, wanted advances from the Reich to cover the costs. This, the German civilian and military authorities, including Helfferich, were reluctant to give, since the construction time was felt to be too long for a war they continued to believe would be relatively short. In so far as they were willing to lend to the Turks, the latter were unwilling to borrow on the terms demanded by the Germans and the railway. When the authorities in Berlin finally became genuinely interested in the proposal in early 1916, because the defeat of Serbia enabled them to supply the Ottomans directly by rail and thus made a future major campaign in the Near East feasible, the leadership of both the bank and the railway demanded a Reich guarantee, presented the Turks with extremely sharp terms, and seemed to have lost interest in the entire business. Only when the Ottoman government threatened to build the line itself and cut out the Anatolian Railway Company did Gwinner and Stauss and the railway directors relent and accept an agreement. The document in question was not even properly formulated and signed. It contained contract provisions which the Turks regularly failed to fulfil, and which the Reich Treasury had to cover.[31]

The Baghdad Railway had become a nightmare in every sense, especially as those involved became direct witnesses to the genocidal policies pursued against the Armenians. Pitiful and gruesome reports began to fill the files of the railway headquarters in Constantinople and moved Günther to report to Gwinner on 17 August 1915: 'One has to go far back into the history of humanity to find something comparable in its bestial horribleness as in the extermination of the Armenians in today's Turkey. The pogroms against the Jews in Russia, which I know, are child's play and one has to go back to the expulsion of the Moors from Spain and the persecution of the Christians by Rome to find an analogy to what is taking place here.'

After describing the expulsions and mistreatment which had been witnessed along the lines of their railway, he came to a horrifying conclusion: 'It appears that the government wants to eradicate the entire tribe, root and branch, for this is the only thing that can result from their behaviour, and if things go on this way, they may only too well succeed. There are about 2 million Armenian inhabitants here, and 25 per cent of them are supposed already to have died. The fact in any case is that the eastern provinces have become free of all Armenians.'[32]

A couple of months later, Günther again sent Gwinner reports he had received and included a picture of Armenians packed into a train, concerning which he commented: 'Enclosed I send you a picture illustrating the Anatolian Railway as a bearer of culture in Turkey. These are our so-called mutton cars, in which for example 800 human beings are transported in 10 cars.'[33]

Günther's letter persuaded the Deutsche Bank to provide some money to assist the Armenians, albeit anonymously since the bank did not want to appear hostile to an allied government, and the railway itself managed to protect some of its own Armenian employees and their families. The behaviour of Günther and his colleagues received recognition from the Armenians and from the British at the end of the war.[34] All in all, it was a grim introduction to moral dilemmas that were to take on horrendous proportions in this century, and it constitutes a high point in the otherwise rather mixed record of response by the Ottoman Empire's allies and enemies.[35]

The Baghdad Railway's financial victimization by the Ottoman regime increasingly constituted the major preoccupation of both the managers of the railway and their patrons at the Deutsche Bank, and they responded by focusing their attention on two issues. The first was to ensure that as much of their expenditure for the war effort as possible would be covered by the Reich, whether or not they recovered these costs from the Turks. This effort was regularly rewarded by the receipt of secret subsidies from the Reich, of which the Turks were deliberately kept unaware so as to maintain the claims against them. The second, which dated back to the pre-war period, was to change the archaic 1903 formula regulating how much of the receipts from the operation of the railway could be retained to cover costs and thus were exempted from mandatory surrender to the Turks. Gwinner later privately confessed that this arrangement was the result of the 'insufficiently energetic and incautious policy of Helfferich', and that the railway was in terrible financial straits before the war and was only saved from having to confront possible bankruptcy by its outbreak.[36]

Both the debt of the railway and its operating costs continued to mount during the war, however. By the spring of 1917, Günther and his colleagues at the Anatolian Railway Company were at their wits' end. The Foreign Office, especially State Secretary Zimmermann, was hostile to any immediate solution. Indeed, Zimmermann had bluntly told Günther that 'if Herr von Gwinner is thinking of Reich guarantees for the Baghdad Railway, then he must find another State Secretary'.[37] The most promising 'other State Secretary' was their old colleague Helfferich, but he had come to the conclusion that Baghdad could only be rescued financially when the war was over. The military, German and Turkish, haggled over the amounts for which they were responsible to cover war expenditures and called the patriotism of the Baghdad officials into question. The Ottoman government gleefully paid nothing, and the signals from Berlin encouraged them to continue to do so. Günther's Mesopotamian fantasies of 1916 had evaporated in 1917 because the British had successfully occupied Mesopotamia and were likely to build their own railway to the Persian Gulf and on to India. The wartime victory he now sought was not the conquest of Mesopotamia but the salvation of the Baghdad Railway, and the victory had to be won in war because he and his colleagues were convinced that, once the war was over, the world would not be concerned about the 'downfall of one enterprise more or less', and that even if it was in the interest of the Reich, the parliament would make 'endlessly more difficulties'.

What was one to do? Günther frankly admitted that he had given up on the good will of the Turks and the Germans. The Turks were only interested in extracting what they could from the situation, and Berlin would not help. If the situation was to be saved during the war, then there was only one solution: 'we must attain the strength of decision to give up Baghdad while the war is still on. There is no other means of shaking Germany and Turkey into action. Needless to say, it would not be an agreeable or desirable means, but for our Baghdad Company it would be precisely as much a means of self-preservation as the taking up of full-scale U-Boat warfare was for Germany. It is a difficult decision, but it must be taken, just as the U-Boat war decision had to be taken by Germany to ward off certain destruction.'[38] Günther was certain that his radical proposal would bring both Berlin and the Porte to reason, save the railway and perhaps even make possible the driving of the British out of Mesopotamia after all!

While Gwinner and his colleagues at the Deutsche Bank were absolutely convinced about the dire financial straits of the railway and the necessity of doing something before the war was over, they found it difficult to instigate what Günther had frankly called a 'German Panama' in the midst of the war. There was at least some difference between moral and actual blackmail, and while the bank had prepared a sharply worded petition for the German government, reminding it of the role played by the Kaiser and Germany's highest officialdom in promoting and supporting the Baghdad Railway and pointing out what a disaster its collapse would be for the prestige of the Reich,[39] a decision simply to declare the railway bankrupt and walk away from it was quite a different matter.

Instead, Gwinner proposed that the petition be coupled, as it eventually was, with an alternative solution which had originated with another official of the Deutsche Bank involved in Ottoman affairs, Director Max von Wassermann. The Reich would be asked to provide a prepayment of 100 million marks, for which it would receive as a security the Baghdad Railway bonds Series II and III, which the railway had been waiting for years to be able to sell, as well as the absolute majority of the Baghdad Railway shares. By these means, the railway company would have the money it needed to function during and even after the war until the Turks agreed to revision of the 1903 revenue formula. As Gwinner shrewdly pointed out: 'The Reich would have the possibility at any time when it wants to exercise full control over the Baghdad Company and would by implication be materially interested in the fortunes and fate of the company, especially the servicing of the loans and the results of the operations which guarantee the service on the loans as well as the advance.'[40] Gwinner was able to mobilize not only Ambassador von Kühlmann for this plan, but also the German military officials in Constantinople, especially General von Lossow and, most importantly, the Supreme Command. As a result, the programme was accepted by the German government in July. While this solved the debt problem, however, the mounting operating costs continued to plague the railway and even the intervention of Ludendorff, who wanted to go so far as to threaten not to launch a promised campaign in Palestine, did not move the Turks to change the 1903 formula or even provide payments to compensate the company. Before the war was over, the Baghdad Railway had cost the Reich some 360 million marks.[41]

The Deutsche Bank can hardly be faulted for seeking to protect its interests and cut its losses under the circumstances described, but the entire affair was a classic illustration of the tensions between the acceptable risk allowances and profitability requirements of a private enterprise, on the one hand, and the interests of the public authorities, on the other. In the last analysis, the bank was in a position to threaten the government with a revelation of bankruptcy, and the arrangement finally struck was designed to avoid parliamentary involvement even though it involved a substantial commitment of public funds. Such situations were dangerous, however, and the bank wished neither to overexpose itself to the risks, nor to place itself in positions where it might expose itself to public criticism. Thus, to the irritation of the German administration in Warsaw, it refused in 1916 to participate in the formation of a consortium to establish a bank of issue there because of the unwillingness of the Reich to guarantee the notes. During the same year it declined an invitation to join the supervisory board of the firm of Adler & Oppenheimer because it did not want to become involved in a likely conflict between the firm and the tax authorities over its war profit tax obligations.[42]

Such a desire to avoid what is today called 'the appearance of impropriety' is understandable since it was difficult for members of the bank to perform disinterested service for the government without arousing suspicion. When Gwinner, for example, was called upon to advise the government at the turn of 1914–15 about the financing of the new nitrates factories necessary to replace the Chilean saltpetre from which Germany had been cut off, he strongly urged a Reich guarantee to purchase the production and was immediately suspected of seeking advantage for the Bayerische Stickstoffwerke, in whose financing the Deutsche Bank was heavily involved. Gwinner won the day by mobilizing his friend, the Chief of the Naval Cabinet, Admiral von Müller, and above all because of the support of Helfferich. There is every reason to believe that Gwinner was telling Müller the truth when he claimed that a Reich takeover of the nitrates factories would really have been the best solution to the problem.[43]

The Deutsche Bank, however, hardly owed its position in the world to modesty and self-denial. It vigorously followed the flag and business opportunity throughout the war and certainly did not shy away from doing battle with its competitors. The flag that was followed, however, was one that fluttered with the fortunes of war, and the opportunities were filled with uncertainty. The bank had for long served as one of Germany's wedges into Mitteleuropa as well as the Ottoman Empire, and one of the effects of the war was to make Mitteleuropa more important than ever. In a practical sense, there was nowhere else to go. A blockaded and isolated Germany was by force of circumstances compelled to turn to that portion of the continent that remained friendly and accessible.

Austria was something less than a revered ally. The bank had actually declined to participate in a consortium for a Vienna loan, and when Gwinner received reports in 1917 that the Turks were taking a loan from the Austrians, he expostulated in exasperation that it was 'gross nonsense and in the end means that German money is being used for Turkey via Austria and competes or directly damages German interests'.[44]

While the bank had long participated in the financing of Bulgaria, it opposed a large advance and loan to that country in July 1914 organized by the Disconto-Gesellschaft, claiming that it was a mistake to support Bulgaria when it did not support German policies. A year later, however, Bulgaria was an ally, and the Deutsche Bank informed the Disconto-Gesellschaft and the Foreign Office that it intended to re-enter the business of lending to the Bulgarians.

The war in fact unleashed a ferocious competition between the Deutsche Bank and the Disconto-Gesellschaft in the region which worried the government and the banking community. The noted Hamburg banker Max Warburg, supported by the authorities in Berlin, sought to mediate these differences in the autumn of 1916 by proposing formulas defining where one or the other bank should take the lead or share the leadership in consortia making government loans and financing the industrial development of Austria, Hungary, Bulgaria, Romania and the Ottoman Empire, and where they should be free in their competition with one another. He was especially worried about the failure to reach an agreement on Hungary, pointing out: 'The Hungarians suffer from delusions of grandeur and nothing can please them more than, as has been the case, not having to confront an organized German consortium of the great banks. Such a situation runs against the interest of the German capitalists, but also against the interest of the German banks, who would thereby be ruining their business to the benefit of the Hungarians. It would also be against the interest of German policy, which naturally seeks to avoid any arrangement by which Hungary is treated differently from Austria.'[45]

Warburg's arguments and efforts notwithstanding, it proved impossible to reach an agreement. Salomonsohn of the Disconto-Gesellschaft seemed more willing to compromise than Gwinner, who called for a step-by-step approach to agreements concerning loans to the governments of Germany's allies, and who insisted on a free hand for the Deutsche Bank in industrial business with them. Undoubtedly this was because the Deutsche Bank was the stronger of the two in these regions and had little reason to surrender its advantages. In any case, it had every intention of making itself stronger and opened up branches in Sofia and Bucharest in 1917. Gwinner continued to express great irritation over the Disconto-Gesellschaft's 1914 Bulgarian engagement and efforts to play a role in the Ottoman Empire's Heraclea mines, which the Deutsche Bank had been exploiting in collaboration with the great industrialist Hugo Stinnes. As he angrily told Stinnes, the Disconto-Gesellschaft agreement with Bulgaria of May 1914 'constitutes an intervention in our old territory, not the reverse. Such is also the case with the effort to enter into the Heraclea coal mining area'.[46]

The biggest and most important of the Deutsche Bank's enterprises in the Balkans unquestionably was oil and the industries related to it, and this became a key area of that peculiar combination of contention and collaboration that characterized relations among business, government, the banks and industry during the war. The oil business was the special terrain of the man who had replaced Helfferich on the Deutsche Bank board of managing directors at the beginning of 1915, Emil Georg von Stauss.

The son of a schoolteacher, Stauss had received his education and initial training in the banking business in his native Württemberg before entering the service of the Deutsche Bank in 1898 at the age of 21. Two years later he was in the Secretariat, where he soon specialized in the bank's petroleum interests, becoming director of Deutsche Petroleum AG (DPAG) and a member of the Administrative Council of the Steaua Romana. Had the petroleum monopoly advocated by the bank become a reality, Stauss would almost certainly have been its head. He was talented and adventuresome – ultimately, too adventuresome – and demonstrated a great eagerness as well as a remarkable capacity to enter a variety of fields of activity and master their technical aspects to the point where he could make judgements and decisions with some authority. Gwinner certainly respected his energy and talents, and Stauss was the logical replacement for Helfferich even though he clearly lacked Helfferich's intellectual power and extreme seriousness. Stauss was undoubtedly a more agreeable, albeit more superficial person. But he knew how to make his way in society and politics, having married the daughter of Admiral von Müller before the war. He received a patent of nobility from the King of Württemberg for his services in 1917 and made the most of being 'Ritter von Stauss'. Even more than his predecessor, Stauss's hankering to dabble in politics and his capacity for intrigue were to destroy his historical reputation.[47]

The importance of Stauss's expertise in the petroleum business and the enterprises he managed for the Deutsche Bank was vastly increased by the war, which cut Germany off from overseas sources to the point where Gwinner actually encouraged the government to mass produce available oil substitutes even though it was obviously not in the bank's interest. Of the few oil-producing areas, Romania was unquestionably the most important, especially during the early phase of the war when the Galician fields were occupied by the Russians. The most reliable and important supplier was the DPAG's Steaua Romana, although the Disconto-Gesellschaft-dominated Deutsche Erdöl-Aktiengesellschaft (DEAG), the Astra Romana, which belonged to the Royal Dutch/Shell Group, and the Standard Oil Group's Romana-Americana, which had particularly rich fields, were also sources of supply for Germany prior to Romania's entry into the war on the Allied side in August 1916. Although the British did severe damage to wells and equipment at that point, the conquest of Romania and repair work made the resumption of deliveries possible in the early spring of 1917.

Not only did the Steaua supply oil through most of the war, but the expanding barge fleet of the Bayerischer Lloyd Schiffahrts-Aktiengesellschaft Regensburg, which had been set up by the Deutsche Bank and its petroleum producers in 1913, shipped oil, wheat and weapons up and down the Danube to Germany and Austria and their Turkish allies. Under such conditions, the DPAG prospered and expanded. In 1916, Stauss signed an agreement with the Hungarian government on behalf of a consortium headed by the Deutsche Bank founding the important Ungarische Erdgas-Gesellschaft (UEG) for the exploitation of that country's natural gas production. The DEAG also prospered, which led the DPAG to buy more shares in that company in 1916.[48]

The DPAG interest in the DEAG, however, was not just a matter of dividends; its substantial voting block was a weapon to gain influence over the administration of the DEAG with respect to its oil policies. It was the DEAG's chief shareholder, the Disconto-Gesellschaft, after all, which had opposed the petroleum monopoly, and when the DPAG opposed a proposal to raise the capital stock of the DEAG in the autumn of 1917, informed observers interpreted this as a form of pressure with respect to more basic policy issues. The noted economic journalist Felix Pinner, for example, argued that the quarrels of great banks were often really a prelude to agreements and communities of interest and that, while the government needed the help of the great banks and the firms they stood behind in dealing with the oil question, it also had to look out for the public interest.[49]

The role of conflict as a pathway to collusion is well illustrated by the negotiations over the organization of Romania's oil fields following its defeat and prior to the Treaty of Bucharest of March 1918. The basic question for the Germans was how to make sure that the fields not under the control of the Central Powers already – that is, enemy and Romanian state-owned fields – were made available for German use, and the basic answer was forcibly to liquidate the Allied companies and compel the Romanians to lease their fields to German companies. The task of undertaking this liquidation was given to the four 'D-Banks'. Since neither the Darmstädter Bank nor the Dresdner Bank had any interests in Romanian oil, the government could and did claim that the banks were acting as nothing more than trustees. Most importantly, the arrangement served the interest of some forces in the government to create either a mixed economic enterprise out of the liquidated oil fields or even a government monopoly.

Nevertheless, initially one would have assumed that the chief beneficiaries of this process would have been the DPAG and DEAG and the banks that stood behind them. Suddenly, however, a powerful new competitor appeared on the scene in the form of the Mineralöl-Handels- und Beteiligungs-Gesellschaft, created on 20 December 1917. The driving forces behind this enterprise were Albert Ballin of the Hamburg–America Line, the Ruhr industrialist Hugo Stinnes, whose expanding trading and shipping company was located in Hamburg and who had become a shareholder in the Hapag, and Max Warburg. Wilhelm Cuno of the Hapag served as business manager. This was no provincial operation, however, for it not only included the Ruhr's most powerful industrialist, but also brought together an important group of independent oil-producing and refining companies in Hamburg and Bavaria, and the powerful oil executive Heinrich Riedemann, who had bought up the Standard Oil operations in Germany, which he had headed, and who was the ideal man to organize the takeover of the rich Romano-Americana fields. The entire effort demonstrated that the war and the increased liquidity in the industrial sector were permitting new alliances and alignments in the German business community and encouraging diversification. As Ballin explained to Stinnes: 'It is necessary to secure access to cheap fuel and open up new sources of profit for the Hamburg–America Line so that its earning power is not bound to a single line of enterprise. In this connection the war has taught us much, and to this must be added that I am of the firm conviction that the shipping business will be forced to suffer years of stagnation after a short period of prosperity.'[50]

While the new grouping was denied a place among the banks engaged in the Romanian liquidation, it was assured that this would in no way prejudice its right to participate in such division of the fields as might take place. It manifestly constituted a considerable challenge to the banks, especially the Disconto-Gesellschaft, whose holdings in Romania were quite small in comparison to the Deutsche Bank, but which entertained ambitions of expanding its oil operations elsewhere. Ballin, Stinnes and their allies recognized that the Deutsche Bank had to be dealt with, not only because of the size of its holdings, but also because the new group's ambitions were not limited to Romania but extended to Mesopotamia, Argentina and other areas where the Deutsche Bank had a presence. As for Stinnes, he preferred to keep the banks as much at bay as possible, although he had a certain sympathy for the Disconto, with which he had considerable dealings. Nevertheless, he too thought that it was best to work with rather than against the Deutsche Bank, that 'we have to favour the technically more competent personnel if we want to earn money', and that, 'to speak frankly, I consider the Deutsche Bank and its personnel better than the Disconto-Gesellschaft'.[51]

The new group warned both banks that it was prepared to act alone, and threatened the Disconto-Gesellschaft that it would ally with the Deutsche Bank if Managing Director Solmssen continued to put up resistance, but it became increasingly interested in a consortium in which it would get one-third of the new fields while the remaining two-thirds would be divided on a 2:1 ratio in favour of the Deutsche Bank, and the latter would be granted leadership of the consortium. The chief motive for this collaborative stance was the desire to present a united front against government plans to create a Central European Oil Corporation based on German–Austrian co-operation in the form of a government-controlled monopoly. It was a programme which particularly alarmed Director Nöllenburg of the DEAG, and the government's intentions brought all the parties together on terms that satisfied Stauss, who was able to assert the primacy of his bank and oil company. In an effort to win over the Romanians, the Treaty of Bucharest did provide for a possible government monopoly, which the businessmen feared and which had been opposed by Helfferich, who had participated in the preliminary negotiations. The entire situation infuriated Stauss, Ballin and Stinnes, and they appear to have mobilized Ludendorff as well.[52]

It is difficult to say how the issue would have been resolved had Germany won the war, but the case is important as an illustration of the symbiotic relationship between conflict and co-operation within the German business community and of the growing power and independence of the industrial sector. Competition within the banking sector only strengthened the opportunities for industry to assert itself, play off one bank against the other, and even assume the role of mediator between them. Cuno was very explicit about using precisely these techniques in bringing the banks to terms.[53] At the same time, anxiety over government intervention and involvement acted as a catalyst for co-operation in order to prevent the undermining of their independence and disposition over their production and, as Nöllenburg of the DEAG self-interestedly, but with undoubted sincerity argued, 'a laming of the private economic initiative indispensable for the production and preparation of oil products'.[54]

When all was said and done, however, the most important new projects of the Deutsche Bank during the war involved a high degree of welcome government involvement. The Railway Authorities of the Reich as well as those of Austria and Hungary had to provide long-term concessions to the Central European Sleeping and Dining Car Corporation, or Mitropa, founded by Gwinner and Stauss of the Deutsche Bank in collaboration with the Dresdner Bank at the end of 1916. Mitropa and the Hungarian Natural Gas Corporation were celebrated as 'important contributions to the practical realization of the concept of Mitteleuropa'.[55]

Mitropa was designed to allow the Austro-Hungarians a voice but give the Germans dominance, as was demonstrated again in 1917 when the Deutsche Bank became party to a proposal made by the Austrian Lloyd to the Hapag that its Internationale Luftverkehrs AG, which was pioneering in airmail, be expanded to include Germany. Gwinner immediately thought of Mitropa as a model in this new field, telling Ballin that 'the entire matter should certainly not be under Austrian leadership'[56] and informing him that Stauss was prepared to pursue the project. The government, however, refused to participate or give any guarantees on the grounds that flying according to schedule was still too unreliable and expensive to make economic sense, a view shared by the military. Nevertheless the military did express interest in finding commercial use for the aeroplane plants that had been built during the war, and Stauss's involvement in commercial aviation had really only just begun.

It was the military which got Stauss and the Deutsche Bank involved in a more earth-bound, if purportedly spiritual enterprise – namely, the motion picture business – through their role in the founding and operation of the Universum-Film Aktiengesellschaft (Ufa). There was widespread dissatisfaction among Germany's military and civilian authorities with the inferiority of Germany's propaganda efforts in comparison to those of its enemies, and with the failure to compete in the increasingly popular realm of film. The German film industry was badly fragmented and insufficiently productive. Foreign films and companies dominated the German market, and while the Allies had lost their position because of the war, it was the Danish Nordische Film-Gesellschaft (Nordisk) which filled the gap.

The situation was a source of endless frustration to the military and Foreign Office authorities, especially to Lt.-Col. Hans von Haeften, representative of the Supreme Command at the German Foreign Office. If there was any ray of hope when he took over this position, it was the Deutschen Lichtbild-Gesellschaft (DLG), which had been set up under the auspices of German heavy industry, above all Alfred Hugenberg of Krupp and Hugo Stinnes, at the end of 1916 and placed under the direction of the advertising specialist Ludwig Klitzsch. Intended to propagate German economic and cultural interests both at home and especially abroad, the DLG was not initially to begin operations until after the war, but this changed in early 1917 when it began a major effort in the Balkans.

However, the Picture and Film Office of the War Ministry found the DLG, whether inactive or active, either unapproachable or unsatisfactory in its search for a private partner with which to work in the German cause. While the DLG leaders agreed with Haeften that film was 'a means of influencing the large masses of which there is no other with comparable effectiveness',[57] this was precisely why they wished to maintain as much independence as possible: so they could propagate the views of heavy industry and the Pan-Germans in economic, social and political matters at home and abroad. To Haeften, who was one of the more moderate and sophisticated members of the General Staff, the DLG soon appeared not as a possible partner, but as a dangerous instrument for heavy industry to 'monopolize the German film industry'.

A solution had to be found to satisfy the government's interests and ward off this threat, and the answer Haeften proposed was to take advantage of the hard-pressed condition of Germany's film production and theatre companies and the financial problems of Nordisk to form a massive German film trust. This would take the form of a private corporation founded and financed by leading banks and firms, but it would have significant government financing and control. The new company would then establish a distribution and theatre network throughout the Balkans and Ottoman Turkey, in the neutral countries and in Russia.

Crucial to the success of Haeften's ambitious programme was his access to Ludendorff, to whom he presented it and who then transformed it into an order – often considered the founding document of Ufa – to the War Ministry of 4 July 1917. The matter was then taken up by Major Alexander Grau, the head of

Bufa, who collaborated very closely with Haeften. Haeften and Ludendorff recognized from the outset that a bank would have to play a major role in negotiating with Nordisk, and some of Grau's subordinates had taken up the mention of this in Ludendorff's order to send out feelers to Nordisk with the assistance of the Disconto-Gesellschaft. These had not gone well, and Haeften and Grau believed that 'for such a significant task only the greatest and most respected German banking institute – namely, the Deutsche Bank – could come into question'.[58] It was Haeften who then proposed asking Stauss to take the lead, while Grau supplied the services of the head of his Foreign Section, Karl Bratz.

During the autumn of 1917, these men, assisted by the Deutsche Bank's representative in Copenhagen and the head of the Legal Section of the bank, Johannes Kiehl, hammered out the structure of Ufa, which was formally founded on 17 December 1918 with a capital of 25 million marks. The Reich provided 7 million, which were held in secret trusteeship by the Deutsche Bank, represented by Kiehl, and the private banking houses of Jacquier & Securius, and A.E. Wassermann. They, along with the Silesian heavy industrial firm of Henckel von Donnersmarck, Robert Bosch, the Deutsche Bank, which held 500,000 marks in shares on its own account, the firm of Carl Lindström AG and the banking house of Schwarz, Goldschmidt & Co., formed a 'control group' of 13.4 million marks in shares, with a majority sufficient to ensure that the government's veto power in matters of political concern would be effective. Actually, Carl Lindström AG was a front for the War Ministry, used as a cover by Bratz in his negotiations with Nordisk. Bratz decided to pretend that he was not negotiating on behalf of the Deutsche Bank because foreigners often thought the Deutsche Bank a semi-official institution because of its name. The shares of 'Lindström' were actually backed by Schwarz, Goldschmidt & Co., whose own shares were represented by a rising star in the German banking firmament, Jakob Goldschmidt.

The original idea of taking over the Nordisk had proven too expensive, but the Danish firm did sell its assets in Germany, Austria-Hungary, Switzerland and Holland to Ufa in return for 1.6 million marks in cash and 8.4 million in Ufa shares, thus becoming the largest of the non-control group shareholders. The rest were composed of the two other major film enterprises absorbed into Ufa, the Meester Concern and the Projektions-Union concern; the Dresdner Bank, whose Managing Director, Herbert Gutmann, played a very active role on the executive committee of the supervisory board; the AEG; the Hapag; and Norddeutscher Lloyd. Participations were also held in reserve for Krupp and Siemens, both of which refrained from joining, however, until the relationship between Ufa and the DLG was worked out.

Not surprisingly, Stauss was the chief and only candidate for the chairmanship of the supervisory board, and his appointment had been strongly advocated by the recently resigned Chancellor, Michaelis, as well as by an enthusiastic Ludendorff. Stauss, who certainly bore many burdens, agreed on condition that

Kiehl be appointed to the board to give him some relief, but the records show that Stauss devoted a remarkable amount of effort to the new company. Finally, the ambitious Bratz and Major Grau were placed in charge of Ufa's operations, thus beginning careers in the motion picture business that were to continue after the war.[59]

The founding of Ufa caused a considerable sensation at home and abroad, and Stauss's early performance as chairman of the working committee of the supervisory board is the record of a man determined to bring order to the German film industry and expand its resources and influence. Ufa was a vertical organization intended to encompass all aspects of the industry. Stauss recognized that there might be a wave of concentration in the industry and possible competition, but insisted that 'Universum must be so developed that it maintains superiority with respect to production, leasing and theatres'.[60] Indeed, only two weeks after this statement was made, Bratz was able to report that an effort to form a company with 40 million marks in capital through the participation of other Berlin banks had collapsed because 'Ufa already has the strongest objects in the industry'.[61] A more modest competitive effort directed at dominating the Rhineland and centring around the Bioskop-Gesellschaft, which had a large studio in Babelsberg and a leasing operation, was also being undermined by Bioskop's interest in joining Ufa.

Matters were not to be settled with Bioskop until 1922, and the centre of Ufa film making continued to be the Meester and Projektion-Union studios at Tempelhof, but it was very clear by early 1918 that Ufa ruled the roost in Germany. The most telling evidence of this was the coming to terms with the DLG, or Deulig, as it now called itself. Stauss had intended to make an arrangement with the powerful industrial group behind it all along, and had been empowered to do so at the first meeting of the Ufa supervisory board. The Deulig's activities in Germany and Austria-Hungary were to be limited to films dealing with industry, and it was not to produce 'cultural' films. In order to avoid harmful competition on foreign markets, the two companies agreed to form a community of interest (Auslands GmbH) with Ufa supplying 60 per cent of the capital, Deulig 40 per cent and Agfa, which supplied most of their film, 10 per cent. Ufa was given 'uncontestable leadership' of these operations, while Deulig was guaranteed the opportunity and personnel to produce the industrial films with the point of view it wished to propagate. During the spring of 1918, Ufa set up a host of sister corporations in the Balkans and the Ottoman Empire, and the best comment on the role of Deulig in all this was made by Stauss, who reported on a conversation with Director Klitzsch in October 1918 that 'there was a good deal of annoyance in his voice with regard to the fact that Ufa has apparently not involved the DLG in any way up to now, and that when Herr Bratz is away, there is absolutely no one with whom to negotiate'.[62]

The fundamental purpose of Ufa in the end was to be entertainment, and this indeed is what most cinemagoers at home and abroad were interested in after four years of war. Nevertheless, whether propagating German industrial superiority or the charms of the leading star Henny Porten, Ufa reflected a more general effort by the Deutsche Bank and the German business world to deal with the anticipated economic war after the military war, and to create a firm foothold for Germany and its products wherever possible.

Just as Ufa was intended to compete against the dominance of the French and American film industries in Scandinavia, Holland and the rest of the world, so was the Deutsche Bank's financing a purchase of the Dresden cigarette firm of Georg A. Jasmatzi in 1915 in consequence of a government fearful of an Anglo-American monopoly in that industry.[63] There seemed to be increasing urgency to convince the world that Germany's economy was as productive and inventive as ever, and thus the banks were asked in early 1918 to include more information in their public reports on the 'favourable' economic situation and 'the development of German corporations, especially with respect to new inventions, Ersatz materials, spun paper, etc.'.[64] The banks were more than happy to comply, but pointed out that the censorship had prohibited them from making such reports.

The censors, of course, were concerned about giving an opposite impression, and they had a point. As the Deutsche Bank could demonstrate by its own wartime history, much had been lost that would not be easy to regain under the best of circumstances. Its important and profitable London branch had been seized during the war and placed under forced liquidation, along with all other assets the British could lay their hands on. Moreover, its efforts to strengthen its position in the United States had been a great disappointment even before the disaster of American entry.

Despite its important pre-war engagements in the United States, banking business there was filled with difficulties and restrictions for foreigners. The creation of the Federal Reserve System in 1913 and the war with Britain, however, made the establishment of an office or branch there more attractive, and Hugo Schmidt was sent to New York to explore the matter and work with their old agent, Edward Adams. It rapidly became clear that such a branch would not be welcome in the still provincial and rather Anglophile New York banking scene. There was also little market for German war bonds or municipal bonds in the United States, even among German-Americans, and Gwinner was told that there would not be such a market 'until the conviction gains ground that Germany will not be defeated. One has to concede unworthy conditions and despite that expect only slight success which is not even of significant help to our exchange rate'.[65]

An even unhappier experience was the bank's involvement in the effort to produce benzol and toluol for the German War Ministry through the Lehigh Coke Company in Pennsylvania, which was owned by a German consortium. The contract had been negotiated with the assistance of Franz von Papen, then serving as military attaché in Washington, and was designed also to prevent these products from being sold to the Allies. The entire costly and much delayed construction work proved another illustration of the bank's lack of adequate and reliable interlocutors in the United States, and the Lehigh firm was sold to Bethlehem Steel just before the war broke out.[66] Finally, the bank's efforts to help the German cause in the United States were severely damaged by its being identified in the American press as a repository for moneys used by German intelligence and von Papen in the United States and Mexico.

3. Facing an uncertain peace

The problem of restoring Germany's international connections and trade, which war and blockade had cut off, exercised the German government and business community increasingly in the last years of the war. While the German public suffered from rising prices at home, it had little sense of the increasing depreciation of the mark abroad. The government, bankers and businessmen engaged in commerce were well aware of it, however, and knew that Germany had contracted large debts payable for ore purchases in foreign currencies in order to prevent mark depreciation, and had exported oil from Romania, and coal, iron and steel from Germany to gain foreign exchange. The major banks of Germany, including of course the Deutsche Bank, were used to implement the exchange decrees of January 1916 and February 1917, the first of which gave them the exclusive right to purchase and sell foreign currencies in accordance with the regulations for their use, while the second extended this activity to mark payments to foreigners as well. The banks were thus engaged for the surveillance of foreign trade by the Reichsbank and government. How long, however, were such controls to continue, and what would the role of the banks be in the transition to a peacetime economy and in the restoration of Germany's world trade?

The answers to these questions, obviously, would depend to a large extent on how the war ended, but they would also be determined by changes wrought by the war within the German economy itself. This is well demonstrated by the discussions concerning the transition to a peacetime economy that took place when German military expectations were high. Thus, in November 1917, both the Reichsbank and the banks seemed convinced that exchange controls would have to be maintained immediately after the war in order to protect the German currency from excess or unnecessary imports and ensure a proper use of German capital. This position was strongly opposed by the exporters of Hamburg, who always took the lead in such matters, and Bremen, but also by the leaders of heavy industry, who had their own growing interests in shipping and exporting. Warburg and Stinnes regarded such controls as a menace to the restoration of trade, and Stinnes was particularly blunt in his view of what the banks were up to, arguing that 'the D-Banks are not at all in a position to satisfy the need for private credit sufficiently; this must be left to the individual firms. Actually, there is a great danger in the efforts of the great banks, for they will have a real monopoly if the exchange decree is maintained.'[67]

The leadership of the Deutsche Bank was in fact quite alarmed by the notion that the banks would be unable to fulfil their old functions of providing the capital needed for the recapture of Germany's position on world markets after the war. What made matters worse was that some bankers were taking a similar position, Bernhard Dernburg and Max Warburg, for example, and were joining with the heavy industrialists and the Hanse trading interests to argue that new financial institutions had to be created for the purpose of providing generous amounts of short-term credits and even long-term credits for foreign investment to meet the changed needs of the post-war world.

When such ideas were propagated at the German Economic Association for South and Central America in early 1917, its Deutsche Bank member, Elkan Heinemann, was sufficiently disturbed to write a lengthy and impassioned counterargument. He reminded his colleagues of the high liquidity of the banks and contended that, when combined with the vastly increased liquidity of industry, the effect would be to make the banks more capable than ever of supplying the needs of industry. He contested the notion that the demand for trade credit would be as great as imagined, pointing to the anticipated reluctance of Germany's former enemies to trade with her, and to the import restrictions that would be required by the low quotation of the mark. The demand for credit would also be reduced by the emergence of the United States as a creditor which no longer required capital imports.

Heinemann was particularly critical of the implicit attitude that credit should be given overgenerously and that the banks should become involved in long-term and inevitably risky foreign investments to support German foreign trade, and he stressed that the business of banks was to serve as intermediaries and not as consumers of securities. While agreeing with the need to loosen German stock market regulations, he objected to the idea that foreign securities should be traded outside Berlin, thereby creating the possibility that shares not admitted on the Berlin market would find their way on to a Hamburg market. While stressing that Germans traditionally preferred to make their investments at home rather than abroad, he also emphasized the enormous public debt at all levels of government created by the war and the need to consolidate it. He considered it pointless to talk about the desirability of ending trade and exchange controls, upon which everyone could agree, at a time when it was still not possible, and he was particularly sceptical about Warburg's call for an end to exchange controls while overlooking 'the speculation in currencies which can be expected to continue for as long as the valuation of our mark currency is at such a distance from gold parities'.[68]

There was obviously a good deal of Deutsche Bank self-interest in Heinemann's argument, but there was also a conservative protest against a growing speculative tendency and unwillingness to face the implications of the costs of the war and the depreciation of Germany's currency. On the more immediate level, there was the question of how the bank was to deal with the destabilization of the German business community caused by the war, a destabilization which promoted novel organizational ideas and programmes. The problem became very actual for the Deutsche Bank in the autumn of 1917 when the commercial and shipping circles of Hamburg and Bremen joined forces with some leading bankers, the most active of which was Warburg, and with Stinnes and other major industrialists to form a Corporation for International Enterprises, for the purpose of examining international investment and development possibilities, and providing funds for the launching of such enterprises to serve and complement German trading interests, and for their sustenance until they were viable enough to finance themselves. This was a response in part to the fact that the British could no longer be expected to perform this function for the international commercial world, and in part to the formation during the war of the British Trade Corporation and the American International Corporation to act as centres for international and even domestic investment. Indeed, the German group was interested in domestic investment as well. The new organization, however, also reflected a shifting of financial power and resources in Germany, and the alliance of Hamburg and the Ruhr was bound to make the great Berlin banks uneasy. As Richard Peltzer of the Hapag pointed out to Director Stapelfeldt of the Norddeutscher Lloyd in an effort to bring the latter's company into the new grouping: 'That the new organization was a good stroke by us is demonstrated by the lively resistance of the large banks, which see the new organization to a certain extent as a competitor . . . The situation is namely that large-scale industry has emancipated itself through its enormous profits in the course of the war and has to a large extent transformed itself from a debtor in many cases to a source of money to the banks. The entrepreneurial spirit of industry is thereby no longer bound or as much bound as it was before the war and participation in an enterprise like the one in formation is viewed by industry as a free port from which to sally forth. This increases the chances for the new company very significantly, because it combines the entrepreneurial spirit of industry with the experience of the foreign trade merchants.'[69]

The new corporation claimed that it had no intention of operating in opposition to the banks, and had indeed invited the leading banks to the preliminary discussions that had led to its founding; it was particularly anxious to have the important branch of the Deutsche Bank in Hamburg participate. Furthermore, the Deutsche Bank itself had been asked by the Disconto-Gesellschaft to participate in a parallel plan that it had concocted to join banks and industrial, shipping and commercial firms in a secret corporation that would establish bank-like institutions and trading agencies in the neutral countries, servicing the needs of German trade and circumventing anti-German policies through the use of neutral flags. The Deutsche Bank easily rejected this last 'truly unclear plan' outright, refusing to 'tie our hands now' with respect to what would be needed when the war was over. Heinemann doubted whether so large an organization would be capable of fooling anyone and questioned whether a 'large clique' of big industrial firms and banks could accomplish much.[70]

Heinemann, along with Gwinner, took a similarly negative attitude towards the corporation being set up in Hamburg, but here they ran into great difficulties within the Deutsche Bank itself. Directors von Sydow and Bassermann of the Deutsche Bank's Hamburg branch, who were under great pressure from Warburg, were particularly anxious to join with the other Hamburg banks and bank branches, and participate in an organization in which Hamburg played such an important role. They apparently did not share the negative stance of Gwinner and Heinemann, who did not 'want to be taken in the tow of Herr Warburg in their overseas business',[71] and who felt that 'the great banks should form a front against the increasingly active tendency of the Hamburgers to move the centre of international economic enterprise and its financing to Hamburg'.[72] Interestingly enough, Managing Director Mankiewitz, to whom Warburg appealed directly, did not agree with Gwinner and Heinemann, seeing no reason why the Deutsche Bank and its enterprises would be unable to take the lead in projects of interest to them, and warning that there was a price to be paid for self-exclusion: 'If we do not participate, then possibly we will lose very valuable information, and that seems to me to be the chief thing. We will not hear much about what is going on, and we will regret that.'[73]

Although willing to permit allied firms like the Holzmann AG and Mannesmann to participate in the new corporation, provided it did not bind them with respect to other projects, Gwinner and Heinemann remained insistent that their Hamburg branch follow the boycotting line of the Berlin central office, even if, as Warburg warned, 'it would cause much bad blood in the foremost circles of Hamburg'.[74] In the last analysis, aside from an obvious animus against the pretensions of Hamburg and Warburg, the strong reaction of the Deutsche Bank leadership to the proposed Corporation for International Enterprises reflected a deep and by no means unwarranted suspicion of certain tendencies in the German economy and a desire and capacity to retain a free hand in dealing with them. It was well summed up by Heinemann in a letter to Director Eich of Mannesmann: 'We consider this entire system of concentrating all of Germany into one corporation, which for its part wants to concentrate all the possible business enterprises of the world under its roof, to be false, and for our part we have no desire to run along with the rest of the heap. We want to maintain our freedom of action in this area ... We have worked to the best of our ability for the employment of German capital abroad and overseas in the past and have brought great enterprises to life and developed them, and we will also do this in the future in so far as circumstances allow. But we want to examine for ourselves and decide for ourselves as to for what we wish to employ our labour and our credit and, as already said, do not wish our hands tied in this respect.'[75]

Such autonomy would certainly prove useful as the fantasies of 1917 gave way to the harsh realities of 1918 and the years which followed. The Deutsche Bank could not, of course, either escape or transcend the deeper forces working in the German economy both in the long run and as a consequence of the war, and it could not escape or transcend politics either. This was especially true in the summer and autumn of 1918 as the German war effort collapsed, and the Deutsche Bank, which stood at the forefront of Germany's Mitteleuropa policy, was in a position to note the signs of collapse earlier than most. In June its branch in Sofia was reporting that the 'credit' of 'Detering', a code name for the pro-German Prime Minister Radoslawoff, 'had sunk very sharply', thus signalling the onset of a political crisis that was to lead to Bulgaria's departure from the war in September, the collapse of the German position in the Balkans, and Ludendorff's sudden call for an armistice.[76]

The Deutsche Bank had also played its role in the German eastern policy of encouraging the breaking up of the Russian Empire, and it joined the consortia of industrialists and banks set up to implement the harsh economic terms of the Treaty of Brest-Litovsk and penetrate the successor states economically. In the newly founded Republic of Georgia, for example, it was involved in the plans not only to finance the exploitation of the manganese and other raw materials of the region, but also to set up a State Bank that would issue a 'Markshi' based on the German mark. When Mankiewitz reported to Gwinner on these arrangements in late July, however, he was anything but certain that the Republic of Georgia would survive, and wondered how long the German position there would last. Helfferich was about to go as Ambassador to St Petersburg to replace the murdered Count Mirbach, but there were great doubts that the Bolsheviks could survive Allied and Japanese intervention.

Indeed, things were not going well anywhere: 'In any case, we are today going through a great crisis, also in view of the colossal offensive in the West; it is not to be denied that we have also strongly underestimated the Americans, just as we previously underestimated the English.'[77] The great hope of the Deutsche Bank's ambitions, Mitteleuropa, became the unanticipated catalyst of Germany's collapse in 1918, but in Director Max Steinthal's view, it was no accident that there had been so many false expectations: 'The military arrogance of the Germans also underestimated the numbers and military skills of the Americans and the effects of the tanks: "Inventions which *we* don't discover are inferior" (the tone, for example, at Siemens & Halske in earlier years).'[78]

The collapse of the military effort of Germany and its Allies cut the Deutsche Bank off from its branches and allied firms in the Ottoman Empire and the Balkans. If Ufa was intended to be the propagandistic expression of German interests in these regions and in neutral countries, then its situation in October 1918 as described by Major Grau provides a fitting commentary on what the Deutsche Bank's wartime efforts had come to in every field of endeavour. He began in the East, where he pointed out that the government had asked Ufa to devote particular efforts, since Brest-Litovsk seemed to provide the 'historic hour' for Germany to be the dominant force in that region. He confessed, however, that after numerous visits there, he became convinced that the situation required 'holding back' with respect to the government's wishes. In Scandinavia, little positive had been accomplished against the massive Allied expenditure on propaganda, and he counted himself successful if he had prevented the showing of the worst pieces of Allied agitation. Given the financial situation of Ufa, which was now overstrained, he recommended that the Scandinavians be encouraged to invest in the company. He saw the situation in Holland and Switzerland as more promising. Switzerland, indeed, was the country to which he turned for groups that might take over the German shares of the Ufa subsidiaries in Bulgaria, Romania and Turkey. It was a sad picture indeed, but it would not be complete without some mention of Grau's extraordinary conclusion that it was only a temporary situation, and that Ufa would have to restore its role and connections in these areas and that the German government, 'even if it develops in a very far left direction', could not eschew film propaganda that would express 'the German spirit, German economic power and German science abroad'.[79]

On 4 November, Stauss informed the executive committee of the Ufa supervisory board that an increase of capital would be required and that the Deutsche Bank was prepared to participate in such an effort if the Reich could not put up the money. On 8 November, Ufa entertained the press and prominent guests at a studio preview of Ernst Lubitsch's *Carmen*, which starred the sensuous Pola Negri.[80] The outbreak of revolution in Berlin the next day and the periodic disturbances of the coming weeks, which included strikes by Ufa's employees, sometimes interrupted movie-going. Nevertheless, *Carmen* had a splendid opening on 20 December and was the most popular film of the revolutionary period. As for Pola Negri, she was to be Ufa's most successful weapon against Allied dominance, and there were not many such weapons around.

II. From Inflation to Stabilization 1918–1924

1. Revolution and labour troubles

From the perspective of the Deutsche Bank leaders, real life in Berlin in the winter of 1918–19 was altogether much more exciting than the films that Ufa was producing, and they did not appreciate the fact that it came with sound. As Oscar Wassermann reported to Max Warburg in early January, they were living through 'rather unsettled times, but one gets used to the fact that, when one goes to the bank or comes out of it, a bullet occasionally strikes very near by, and that one's ears are mistreated by infantry fire, machine guns, and periodically also by mine throwers and artillery. If the government does not give in at the last moment, then it will retain the upper hand this time and put an effective end to the nonsense. But who knows if it will remain firm.'[81] Only a few days before these lines were penned, Gwinner had attended an evening gathering where a justifiably confident Gustav Noske and Walther Rathenau had discussed ways and means of raising a military force to maintain order, but Gwinner nevertheless 'viewed the entire situation very pessimistically and spoke of a great bankruptcy to which Germany was irretrievably steering'.[82]

It was indeed to prove easier to put down the Spartacists a few days later than to solve the financial headaches created by war and defeat. One of the worst of these was that, in order to get food and an armistice, the Reichsbank had to pay with a portion of its gold and accept control on its right to use the rest. Mankiewitz had pleaded with the Reichsbank to release its gold earlier so that Germany could pay off the 18.25 billion marks in Swedish ore that it had purchased during the war. The industrial loans had been guaranteed by the banks and had in turn been guaranteed by the Reichsbank, but Mankiewitz was anything but certain that the Reichsbank guarantee was worth much under the circumstances. The situation was driving the value of the mark down and thereby increasing the real value of the debt, and the only way out in Mankiewitz's view was getting a long-term loan from the Netherlands, Scandinavian countries or even the United States to solve these problems and to come to an agreement with the Swedes.

Mankiewitz thought that the financial agreements with the Entente effectively put Germany in the position of a bad bankrupt and that the enemy could make claims on its assets. Nevertheless, Mankiewitz was not totally pessimistic. The Allied threat to German assets would make socialization and nationalization of private property impossible for a long time to come, and he also believed that the situation could be saved if 'commerce, industry and banking march together in complete unity'.[83] Wassermann, in urging the shipping lines to put up their vessels as security for a prolongation of the loans given by the neutrals, went even further than Mankiewitz by claiming that he saw little danger of socialization. The Social Democrats were already discrediting themselves and Wassermann fairly correctly predicted that they 'would drop out as the solely decisive power factor before they get beyond purely theoretical preparations'.[84]

Nevertheless, once the war was lost and revolution had come to Germany, there was little point in pretending that its monetary affairs would be easily ordered. The Annual Business Report of the Deutsche Bank for 1918 spoke frankly of the 'monetary depreciation' as a source of the increase in its volume of business from 188 to 243 billion marks between 1917 and 1918. What had been treated by the press as a 'temporary phenomenon' in 1917 could no longer be handled that way now. Indeed, the symptoms of monetary disease could no longer be denied. The report for 1919, the fiftieth in the bank's history, sadly spoke of a 'heightened inflation' as the cause of a 'passion for playing the stock market' (*Effektenspielwut*) which had forced the closing of the bourse two days a week. As for the Deutsche Bank, it had become a veritable madhouse in the eyes of its stock market specialist, Managing Director Mankiewitz: 'You cannot imagine how burdened our offices are: the correspondence sections, the securities office, and the secretariat hardly find time to work properly through their agendas. There exist conditions in our bureaux which I never would have imagined possible in so orderly a concern as the Deutsche Bank. The day before yesterday we had the tiny task of handling over 13,000 individual orders. Our stock brokers are dropping from exhaustion ...'[85]

The labour situation in the Deutsche Bank had, indeed, exploded in more ways than one since the war and especially since the revolution. The number of employees at the Deutsche Bank had increased from 9,587 in 1913 to 13,529 in 1918–19, an increase which can only partially be explained by the fusions of 1914 and 1917, and which also reflected the increased paper work caused by the war economy and inflation and the hiring of unskilled employees – above all, women – to replace the experienced personnel who had gone off to war, many of whom did not return.

The changed composition of the bank's workforce added to the tensions already created among almost all classes of white-collar workers and civil servants by the war. On the one hand, their salaries and cost-of-living increases were substantially less than those of blue-collar workers in the war industries. On the other hand, inflation had a 'proletarianizing' effect on white-collar workers by levelling incomes, making distinctions between blue- and white-collar workers less easy to maintain, and creating conflicts between traditional bank officials, who identified with the bank and its leadership, and a growing number of white-collar workers and those who performed menial blue-collar tasks, whose pride in working for a bank, in so far as it existed, was tempered by the fact that they received such inadequate amounts of its growing volume of money. It was also difficult for the bank's employees not to note that the bank had paid a 10 per cent dividend in 1914, 12 per cent in 1915 and 1916, 14 per cent in 1917, and 12.5 per cent in 1918 and 1919.

While Managing Director Michalowsky, who was in charge of personnel matters, and his colleagues had sought to provide assistance to the families of bank employees at the front, and various forms of assistance as well as cost-of-living increases to employees during the war, they were inadequate to the circumstances and there was considerable evidence that the old paternalistic way of doing things was no longer working. Shortly before the end of the war, the porters, elevator operators and furnace men of the bank had petitioned the bank management for a supplement to their inadequate pay, which ranged from 43.50 to 49 marks a week. When they were rudely turned down and even denied an opportunity to present their case, union organizers reminded them of the bank's dividends, the high managerial salaries, and the fact the organized workers always got a hearing.[86]

What, however, was to be the new way of doing things? The revolution not only intensified the conflicts between the bank employees and the management, but also brought into the open the conflicts among the employees themselves.

When the bank's newly elected white-collar workers' council, in which the Socialist General Organization of German Bank Officials was strongly represented, made a host of very sharply worded demands, the older bank officials, most of whom belonged to the German Bank Officials' Association, strongly objected to the character of the demands and the tone, both of which they found excessive. As '*Stammpersonal* ... very closely bound up for years and decades with the fate of the bank', these officials, while certainly wanting an improvement of their conditions, rejected the approach of the new employees and insisted that it would also be rejected by their comrades who had not yet returned from the front.[87] The fundamental difficulty was that these bank officials continued to think of themselves as the highest form of commercial employee, a position also taken by the bank's management and reinforced by the fact that many of the directors and managers of the bank had risen through the ranks. The newer employees, however, tended to treat such pretensions with derision, and the gap within the ranks of the bank's employees was made all the greater by the radical leadership of the post-war General Association of German Bank Employees in Berlin, an Independent Socialist named Benno Marx and a Communist named Karl Emont.[88]

At the end of January, Michalowsky and Gwinner negotiated an agreement with the white-collar workers' council to devote three million marks in reserves to supplement the moneys already designated as 'transitional assistance', but refused to grant a 25 per cent bonus increase, exceed the overtime allowance previously negotiated, or immediately agree to employee access to their files. The question of employee council involvement in the hiring and release of workers was a central issue in radical demands for the democratization of work relationships in the banks, and it played a significant role in the strikes which broke out at the banks in early April 1919.

The strike was particularly traumatic at the Deutsche Bank because the bank seemed ready to yield on pay questions, while the role of the councils in hiring and firing was to be regulated by law. The issue became one of solidarity between the Deutsche Bank employees and their striking colleagues at the other Berlin banks. When a slim majority (2,426 to 2,227) of the Deutsche Bank employees – a majority partially created through the exercise of their voting rights by the directors and managers – voted against participating in the strike, the radical leaders held a second meeting outside the bank and procured a majority vote for the strike. The stage was thus set for confrontations between striking pickets and those wanting to go to work on 10 April. These began with insults and ended in physical assaults from both sides, the use of water hoses, and finally the occupation of the bank and surrounding area by Free Corps units summoned by the bank directors. The directors sent home those who were willing to work, until the situation was considered safe. A meeting organized by the German Bank Officials' Association for non-striking Deutsche Bank employees on the following day turned verbally if not physically riotous when many strikers showed up, and the two factions hurled insults at one another and drowned out speakers.[89]

Government mediation rapidly ended the strike, which had little public sympathy. There was a general consensus that the basic material demands of the bank employees were justified, but that the services of the bank were vital for the procurement of food from abroad and the maintenance of economic life, and that the strike organizers, especially Emont, were pursuing political goals. The Majority Socialist *Vorwärts*, for example, bluntly called the bank employees 'victims of Communist agitation'[90] soon after the strike. In the sobering circumstances of the spring of 1919, when Germany was facing the terms of the Versailles Treaty, the radicals were not in a good position to persist in their challenge to the bank.

This became very evident at the General Shareholders' Meeting of the Deutsche Bank on 4 June 1919, where there was a widely reported debate on the labour dispute. Marx and Emont, seeking to play once again on the social changes in the composition of the workforce at the bank, called for equal pay and salary increases for the female workers at the bank. Michalowsky and Mankiewitz flatly rejected such demands, pointing out that the female workers did not have the training of their male counterparts and did not therefore deserve equal pay. They went on to chide Marx and Emont for destroying the traditional values of the employees and undermining the international reputation of the bank at a time when Germany's currency needed every drop of support it could get. As the *Neue Zürcher Zeitung* reported: 'Herr Mankiewitz pointed out that he himself began working for 500 Taler a year at the bank. The majority of the directors have risen from the ranks of the lower officials. Working relationships in the bank have been severely damaged through the new order; he, Mankiewitz, himself does correspondence at night. The Deutsche Bank has always been socially minded; from the very beginning it has had large pension funds. Previously the employees were proud of being business people. Today one does not want to be a business person any more, but rather takes the position of the workers. A worker who does his work is a man worthy of great respect, but a bank employee must be a businessman. The strikes and the agitation contribute to the reduction of Germany's respect and credit in the world.'[91]

Mankiewitz and Michalowsky admitted that the existing situation required many more employees to take care of the vast increase of routine tasks, but here too they took the offensive, arguing that productivity had decreased very sharply and that the seven-hour day (eight hours if one included lunch and pauses) and restrictions on overtime meant that labour costs would increase even further and that the directors and higher officials of the bank would have to labour more at night.

If the radical trade union leaders were not strong enough to mobilize the employees, male or female, for their purposes and effectively challenge the dominant culture of personnel management at the bank, the bank's directors were not in much of a position to develop satisfactory mechanisms to defend that culture and the bank's long-term personnel policies under the bizarre conditions of the inflation either. The number of employees rose rapidly until it reached a peak of 40,000 at the apogee of the hyperinflation in 1923, and most of these obviously were untrained white-collar workers needed to deal with the flood of paper transactions. Like most large employers during this period, the bank found it easiest simply to participate in granting the salary and cost-of-living increases required by inflationary conditions.

Once the aforementioned conflicts of the first half of 1919 were over, the Deutsche Bank leaders faced a problem of fundamental importance with respect to the demands for codetermination raised by the Factory Councils Law of January 1920, which required the presence of employee representatives on the supervisory board. The bank had taken considerable initiative in mobilizing employers against the law prior to its passage, with the argument that it was being used for partisan political purposes by the two Socialist parties and that the trade unions had lost control over their workers because of the partisan struggle. The workers and employees chosen as representatives would, the bank claimed, invariably be those who were most political and least susceptible to the interests of the companies they served.[92] Once the law was passed, the Deutsche Bank sought to be excluded from its provisions on the grounds that such exclusion was in the interests of the state because the bank was involved in so many functions touching upon state activities: Ufa, the recently created banking consortium to take up the war bonds, and the procurement of foreign exchange (*Devisen*).[93]

The issue continued to drag on without resolution until February 1922, when the special law governing the placement of employee representatives on the supervisory board was finally passed. Although the regulations required such representatives to act in the interests of their company and not simply the workers, and also bound them to secrecy, the Deutsche Bank, now joined by the other big Berlin banks, continued to petition for exclusion from the law. There was in fact some support in the Reich Cabinet for doing so, but the Socialists in the Joseph Wirth government and Wirth himself felt that exclusion from the requirements would be dangerous politically; they decided to reject the banks' request with the provision that the banks could renew their petition if serious problems arose.[94] There is no evidence that it ever mattered since the supervisory board of the Deutsche Bank, as became the case in most other corporations, conducted its most important business in committees of which the employee representatives were not members. Indeed, the bank had been advising such quiet circumvention of the law to industrial firms for some time.[95]

2. Credit policies and competition in the inflation

Needless to say, the pacification of the Deutsche Bank's labour force and, indeed, of Germany's during the post-revolutionary inflation contributed to the explosion of costs and prices and added to the uncertainties of the chaotic years preceding the stabilization. The inflation played a very important role in fashioning the development of the Deutsche Bank as an institution during the Weimar Republic and in shaping the complex and multifaceted activities of its leadership.

If one is to understand this development and these activities, it is necessary to bear in mind that the inflation did not develop in any steady, progressive manner, but was rather characterized by leaps of depreciation and plateaux of relative stabilization. Thus, the exchange rate of the mark against the dollar and other highly valued currencies had been deteriorating during the war at a 'creeping' pace and continued to do so until the summer of 1919, when the imposition of the Treaty of Versailles triggered an explosion of inflation that lasted until February 1920. This was followed by a period of relative stabilization between the spring of 1920 and the spring of 1921. In the summer of 1921, especially after the first reparations payment of August 1921, the mark moved into the phase of galloping inflation, which progressed with fits and starts until the summer of 1922. The murder of Walther Rathenau, the repeated failures of reparations negotiations, and the inability of the German government to develop an effective tax collection programme and straighten out its finances fuelled the hyperinflation that began in July 1922. With pauses at some high plateaux, this culminated in the destruction of the mark in the course of the Ruhr occupation, the termination of passive resistance, and the stabilization on the basis of a new currency in the summer and autumn of 1923.[96]

The inflation went on so long and took the peculiar course it did because it served some important functions in the context of desperate circumstances. First, it enabled the weak Weimar governments to deal with the wage and social demands of workers in vital industries and of civil servants, and to maintain high employment levels in a politically unstable, revolutionary and post-revolutionary environment where there were shortages of food, clothing and housing, and where price controls and subsidization of vital necessities appeared to be required.

Second, since domestic prices in Germany were lower than world market prices through most of the inflation, German commerce and industry were able to recover some of their position on world markets and to use either war profits or foreign exchange profits to begin the reconstruction of Germany's industrial plant. The inflation inevitably favoured those with access to foreign exchange and the capacity to control real assets, while it expropriated those with liquid assets and mark holdings. This included, of course, all those who had invested in war bonds and other forms of government debt. A high and socially unjust 'inflation tax' thus lay at the basis of the inflationary process of reconstruction.

Finally, the perpetuation of the inflation was a product of the bitter international and domestic conflict over reparations. The Germans insisted that Allied demands were excessive and that, in any case, Germany could only pay by receiving a large international loan, particularly from the United States, and being given an opportunity to implement effective taxation and other stabilization measures. Without help and a 'breathing space', the German government claimed it had no choice but to print money to maintain domestic peace and keep the economy going. An unspoken effect was to export unemployment to their former enemies and neutrals through underpricing of goods and exchange dumping. The Allies, despite substantial differences between the French and British, argued that the Germans could stabilize on their own through effective taxation, termination of subsidies and deflationary measures. Within Germany, an increasing conflict arose between, on the one hand, those who argued for an honest effort at fulfilment through effective, valorized taxation and the use of the gold in the Reichsbank to effect an internal stabilization in order to qualify for an international loan, and on the other, the leaders of heavy industry and other right-wing elements, who insisted that only a revision of reparations demands and higher productivity through longer working hours at home would pave the way for an end to the inflation.

The Deutsche Bank was a major player in all aspects of the inflation. It is necessary to examine how the bank sought to protect itself against its dangers while taking advantage of its opportunities to participate in the inflationary reconstruction; and also to examine the bank's engagement in the effort to restore Germany's place in the world's financial and economic order and to deal with the problem of reparations.

The leaders of the Deutsche Bank knew that tangible expression of Germany's potential reintegration into the world economy lay in its vaults and those of the other great banks in Berlin, and took the form of speculative investment in marks and mark-denominated assets. The number of accounts at the Deutsche Bank increased from 573,367 in 1918 to 601,921 in 1919, and to 738,869 in 1921. An indeterminate but certainly substantial number of these were foreign, for as the bank stated in its report for 1919: 'since the conclusion of peace, foreign business has increased extraordinarily because foreign entrepreneurs and capitalists, putting their confidence in Germany's productive strength, have bought large amounts of Reichsmark and have sought employment for this money in Germany. A portion has been used for the purchase of securities, but the amount in deposits however remains extraordinarily high.'[97] It has been estimated that as much as 40 per cent of the accounts in the great Berlin banks in 1920 consisted of such deposits, but the foreign speculative engagement in Germany obviously took other forms as well, such as the holding of marks by individuals and companies abroad. The German inflation could never have gone on so long without this foreign investment in the German currency and in the restoration of Germany's old work habits and economic and financial probity.

From the perspective of the Deutsche Bank, the speculation of foreigners constituted an obligation for Germans to live up to foreign expectations as well as the vision of a very solid golden pot at the end of the speculative rainbow. This is well illustrated by a circular sent to its branches at the end of September 1919, a time when international trade was resuming, exchange controls had been lifted, and German businessmen were stocking up on imports while the German government was buying food abroad. The expectation was that such purchases would lead to increased productivity at home and exports abroad. The Deutsche Bank directors were not happy with this policy, complaining about luxury imports, helter-skelter government purchases, and a tendency of German importers to hold on to their foreign currency and to purchase imports with marks instead. The bank urged its branches to dissuade customers from dumping marks in this manner by refusing and restricting credits for imports which were unjustified or conducted in a manner harmful to the exchange rate. The Berlin directors recognized that raw materials were needed, but warned that excessive numbers of individual purchases of foreign exchange could undermine the faith being expressed in Germany by foreigners: 'If the opinion of the world had not been as confident and willing to place its hope in Germany as it is, and if all the countries, North and South America, Spain, Holland, even England and France, had not been willing to buy marks even at their present price, then the German currency would be even much more depreciated than is now the case. But purchases based on feeling also come to an end, and we must take care that moderation is exercised in imports and that there is restraint in the constant offering of marks abroad and in the purchase of foreign exchange ... Every credit taken on an individual basis damages the possibility of the great credit which we so desperately need.'[98]

This restrictive and conservative attitude is also to be found in the general credit policies of the big banks after the war, and caused a considerable amount of bitterness in those portions of the business community dependent on the banks for credit. It reopened the question as to whether the banks would be in a position to meet Germany's post-war credit requirements. The entire debate was triggered by the decision of the Bank Association – that is, the banking condition cartel – to review in December 1919 the conditions it had last set up in 1916. The proposals under consideration and finally passed at a meeting held at the Berlin headquarters of the Deutsche Bank were drawn up by the Berlin banks and involved a very substantial increase of the minimum interest rates and commissions on all manner of bank transactions, and a widening of the gap between the interest charged on overdrafts and that given for deposits. These new terms were justified by increased labour costs, taxes and other expenses, and were presented as a veritable national obligation:

'To compensate for these higher expenses is not only our obligation to preserve ourselves as entrepreneurs and administrators of the capital entrusted to us, but also our duty in the service of the general good and to protect our public credit. We united banks and bankers virtually embody alone today the credit of Germany's economic life, which the Reich, states and municipalities would be incapable of maintaining alone. More than ever dependent on the outside world, our economy and our general welfare has an interest in the maintenance of the earning capacity and profitability of our banking industry. For the reputation of our domestic firms will be evaluated according to the extent of our yearly profits by our investors and depositors and by those who give us credit and accept our bills abroad. Even only transitory unprofitability will deliver incurable wounds not only to ourselves but to German economic life.'[99]

The Deutsche Bank had also sought to restrict, ration and guarantee the repayment of its credits as much as possible. In January 1919 it had warned its branches against granting credits to firms which no longer enjoyed the liquidity provided by wartime contracts and which were faced with heavy taxes, since the bank did want to end up 'paying the levy on assets of our customers'.[100] In March 1920 it warned against the granting of credits for plant expansion, insisting that moneys be provided for materials' purchases and current orders only, and urging the creation of a lien on inventories in the event of inability to repay credits.[101] The bank was also reported to have denied its branches the right to grant credits in excess of 100,000 marks without permission, and its Berlin office almost without exception refused the granting of larger credits.[102]

This combination of credit restriction and high interest and commissions was not without its dangers, as became apparent in March 1920 when the Reich Association of German Industry and the Reich Economics Ministry came up with proposals for a Credit Co-operative for German Industry and then a Reich Economic Bank, whose functions would be the pooling of foreign exchange and the issuing of bonds to channel industrial credit and direct credit for Germany's long-term industrial reconstruction. Two sets of arguments were mobilized in support of such a plan. On the one hand, its proponents argued that the banks lacked the capital necessary for German industrial reconstruction. While they appeared to be 'swimming in money' because of the inflationary liquidity, their situation would abruptly change once real taxes were collected and the Reichsbank ceased to print money. At that point, the speculative foreign investment in the mark would also end, and stabilization would bring a great shortage of capital. A concentrated effort by industry, or by industry and the state, to mobilize and direct capital would, therefore, be better suited to the post-war circumstances. Such a bank was also viewed by Undersecretary Julius Hirsch of the Economics Ministry, a major proponent of the idea, as a means of providing credit to increase employment in times of recession. On the other hand, small and medium-sized firms argued that the big banks were simply unwilling to lend them money on reasonable terms, and were cutting off local sources of capital through programmes of expansion and concentration (see below). They claimed that their survival depended on finding alternative sources of credit.[103]

Happily for the banks, the Reichsbank, Reich Finance Ministry and Chambers of Commerce strongly opposed these ideas because they were seen to be either inflationary or bureaucratic and artificial. Furthermore, there was a genuine contradiction between those who wanted to use the plan to give industry financial autonomy in its search for credit, and those who saw the bank as a potential means of directing investments and increasing state direction of the economy. Nevertheless, the experience was an alarming one. Competition in the banking industry was a serious enough problem, and the banks had been protesting for some time the expansion of savings bank activities, and claiming that such expansion constituted unfair competition because of the tax advantages enjoyed by the savings banks. Now, suddenly, they were confronted with the prospect of competition from a gigantic investment bank which would intensify the self-financing of industry and leave the banks in the cold. The banks warned that the effect of such an institution would be to make unsound investments in firms that were not viable and to produce a credit inflation. Banks were not there to finance expansion directly, but rather to act as intermediaries on the capital market, and they advocated the reintroduction of sound commercial bills as a means of solving current account problems. As far as claims that interest charges and commissions were too high are concerned, the Deutsche Bank instructed its branches to contest such arguments by pointing out that interest rates were even higher abroad and that interest charges under existing conditions were trivial compared to the costs of wages and raw materials.[104]

Manifestly, the advantages in such an economic setting lay with those who enjoyed high liquidity to start with, had access to foreign exchange, controlled raw materials and could afford to meet rising wage demands. It was not the great industrial concerns of the Ruhr who were dependent on the banks for credit. This was well demonstrated by their decision in the autumn and winter of 1919–20 ruthlessly to liquidate their Swedish ore debts by forcing their domestic customers to pay in foreign exchange for coal, iron and steel, and by selling marks to get the necessary kroner. The banks no longer had to worry about their guarantees of these debts, but this show of independence also demonstrated that the great firms were in a position to expand without asking the great banks how and why they should do so. The inflation thus became the heyday of vertical concentration in industry, a process in which the banks played a role as intermediaries in capital share increases and bond and stock flotations, but in which the tone, direction and control were determined by great concern builders like Hugo Stinnes, Paul Reusch, Otto Wolff and Peter Klöckner.

The Deutsche Bank was certainly a major participant in these activities, as demonstrated by the breathtaking and dense five-page list of firms and concerns in its Business Report for 1920, which helps to explain why Mankiewitz was complaining about the chaos at the bank at the beginning of that year. However impressive the list, floating stock and bond issues was not a demonstration of growing influence and neither was the taking of industrialists like Paul Silverberg of the Rhenish lignite industry into the Deutsche Bank's supervisory board.

When Mankiewitz was told that one corporation executive was reluctant to join the board because he feared the bank was thereby trying to gain influence in his company, he responded that 'the great industrial corporations in general dominate the banks and not the other way around. The competition among the banks is much too great for that.'[105]

This competition was very keen indeed, and the speculation promoted by the inflation was not without influence on the composition and character of the German banking world. Not only were outright speculative private bankers like Hugo Herzfeld and Emil Cyprut playing an important role in the operations of Stinnes and other expanding industrialists, but some of the larger banks were also more speculatively involved than had traditionally been the case in the established banking community. The Nationalbank für Deutschland, which merged in 1922 with the Darmstädter Bank to form the Darmstädter und Nationalbank (DANAT-Bank), was especially notable in this regard. In 1916 it had hired away Hjalmar Schacht from the Dresdner Bank to head its credit section, and in 1918 it persuaded Jakob Goldschmidt to leave his private brokerage house, where he had made a fortune in stock exchange speculation, to become head of the National Bank's securities section.

Even before the National Bank became Germany's fourth largest bank through the merger of 1922, the 'activeness' of Goldschmidt and Schacht became a source of concern to the Deutsche Bank leadership. Michalowsky was profoundly irritated when the Rheinische Creditbank, with which the Deutsche Bank had a close relationship, permitted Schacht to be elected to the supervisory board of the Benz automobile firm and thus to lay claim for the National Bank on the Berlin market in the event of a share increase.[106] The Deutsche Bank took more than a 'platonic interest' in the National Bank's use of its huge profits of 1920, made from speculation in foreign exchange and securities, to buy up industrial shares of companies in regions where the Deutsche Bank was also active. Goldschmidt assured Managing Director Wassermann, who was his contact at the Deutsche Bank, that 'he strictly avoids acting aggressively against the Deutsche Bank'.[107] Wassermann believed there was nothing to worry about, but some of his colleagues thought caution was advisable.

The Deutsche Bank always remained on its guard in dealing with its chief rival, the Disconto-Gesellschaft, although there were important signs of a tendency towards a reduction in the sharpness of their competition in 1920. The overtures came from the leaders of the Disconto-Gesellschaft, and the context was the sobering loss of their dominant position in the DEAG to the Bohemian industrialist Baron von Liebieg, who had skilfully acquired a controlling interest in the company before the bank realized what had happened. The Disconto-Gesellschaft now had to share control with Liebieg and two French banking houses, and was thus deprived of its major position in the oil business. Liebieg, however, was anxious to take advantage of German experience in the oil business to set up a large holding company in Holland that would include the DEAG and the DPAG, a proposition that held out the promise of putting Germany back into the international oil business again. This, however, raised the delicate issue of leadership in the company.

Director Nöllenburg of the DEAG was apparently convinced that the new situation made co-operation with the Deutsche Bank and the DPAG in the projected endeavour at once possible and desirable, and that Stauss would have to be given the supervisory board chairmanship. When he met privately with Director Paul Bonn of the Deutsche Bank to discuss such arrangements in September 1920 – apparently without consulting the Chairman of his supervisory board, Georg Solmssen of the Disconto-Gesellschaft – Nöllenburg emphasized that everything had to be done to spare the Disconto-Gesellschaft the appearance of having suffered a 'knock-out'. Bonn agreed that now that 'the Deutsche Bank finally had the upper hand in petroleum matters, it had no interest in having the Disconto-Gesellschaft's defeat take on a shameful appearance to the outside world'. But as Bonn privately confessed to Stauss, 'this well-meaning statement on my part, however, stood in part in undeniable contradiction to the concrete demands which I later raised'.[108]

Very serious negotiations concerning a possible collaboration of the DEAG and DPAG took place in the autumn of 1920, and ultimately failed because of the Disconto-Gesellschaft's insistence on a position of parity with the Deutsche Bank. It was in the course of these discussions that Arthur Salomonsohn of the Disconto-Gesellschaft pointed out to Mankiewitz that the conflicts between the two great banks over 'prestige questions' before the Dutch and French had filled him with 'shame and bitterness'. Salomonsohn also regretted that the Deutsche Bank had shown so little interest in his proposal that the two banks come to mutual understandings with respect to large-scale transactions. The discussion was quite friendly, but Mankiewitz was also quite blunt. He rejected the notion that the Disconto-Gesellschaft deserved parity in the projected oil deal. It had, after all, lost its control over the DEAG. Mankiewitz also expressed irritation over reports that Salomonsohn had claimed that the Disconto-Gesellschaft was the 'top bank' because it had the leading positions in the Central Banker Association and the Berlin Condition Cartel. Salomonsohn denied making such a statement, and while both men agreed that 'one should avoid allowing the rivalry of the two great banks appear in the open too strongly', Mankiewitz had no desire to end it, taking the position that 'the competition between the two banks, for whose activity there is plenty of room, is useful, while an agreement like that proposed could, as in so many syndicates – here we have had sufficient experience – lead to the feeling that the one party is always disadvantaged by the other'.[109]

Clearly it was premature for such an agreement, as the failed effort at co-operation between the bank's oil companies demonstrated. It would also have been very difficult at a time when all the great banks were undergoing a period of great expansion. In this highly competitive and inflationary environment of post-1918 Germany, there was every incentive for the great banks to step up their policy of taking over provincial banks and expanding their network of affiliates and branches. Provincial banks needed to increase their capital to meet the increased credit requirements of their customers and had to turn to the great banks. This gave the latter the opportunity to satisfy such demands by taking over or penetrating the provincial banks still further through exchanges of shares, and thereby gaining access to the capital and silent reserves of the provincial banks. This was necessary if the great banks were to meet the challenge created by the development of large-scale industrial enterprises with increasingly large capital reserves as well as capital requirements.

The role of the inflation in this concentration process was important. The high liquidity at once made possible and encouraged banking concentration, and certainly one of the best inflation hedges available to the banks at this time was the acquisition of the buildings, facilities, personnel and shares of other banks. That this could be done on the cheap only added to its attractiveness. The great discrepancy between the value of the shares of the great banks and that of the provincial banks meant that provincial bank shares could be bought up at low cost even when rumours of an impending fusion suddenly increased their market value. Furthermore, the difference between the internal and external value of the mark enhanced the advantages of the great banks. Although share prices tended to rise whenever the exchange rate declined, the real value of the rise of shares was in no way equal to the depreciation of the mark. The tendency of fusions to occur when the mark fell may have been related to this phenomenon.[110]

3. Expansion at home and retreat abroad

The Deutsche Bank emerged as the champion in this process of capital share increase, fusion and expansion. At its general shareholders' meeting on 29 November 1920, it raised its share capital from 125 to 400 million marks and announced fusion with three friendly banks, the Hannoversche Bank, the Braunschweiger Privatbank AG and the Privatbank zu Gotha, the acquisition of all the shares of the Elberfelder Bankverein, and major exchanges of shares with the Hildesheimer Bank and the Württembergische Vereinsbank. The number of its branches outside Berlin thus increased from 108 to 133. In 1921 it substantially increased its permanent share holdings in the Rheinische Creditbank, which it had assisted in its takeover of the Pfälzische Bank. In addition to opening up new branches independently, the Deutsche Bank had also taken over some Pfälzische Bank branches to attain a high point for this period of 156 branches. Subsequently, it closed branches in eastern territories taken over by Poland and concluded the inflationary period with 146 branches in 1923.[111]

In the case of the Deutsche Bank, therefore, the most important expansion occurred in 1920–21, not only because of the banks actually taken over, but also because its increased share holdings in the banks not taken over prepared the way for their fusion with the Deutsche Bank after the inflation. While one can generalize about the causes and consequences of such expansion, these were often delicate and complicated, and sometimes even dramatic operations, worth considering for what they reveal about the Deutsche Bank as an institution and the business environment in which it operated at this time.

The bank was not always successful when it sought to woo provincial banks. The Deutsche Bank had intended to liquidate the Elberfelder Bankverein and had actually completed this task when the Mayor of Elberfeld, joined by local businessmen, protested that the disappearance of the bank would create a 'serious gap' in the city's banking establishment, since it served as 'the bank of the *Mittelstand*, particularly the solid medium-sized merchants, small and medium-sized industry, and the *Bürgertum* in general'. While the Deutsche Bank claimed that its name had enough drawing power to win over the Elberfelder Bankverein's old customers, the opponents of its liquidation insisted that the name and institution were important. Finally, the Bergisch Märkische Bank, now of course an affiliate of the Deutsche Bank, undertook the re-establishment of the Elberfelder Bankverein while the Deutsche Bank controlled its entire stock.[112]

In the case of its efforts to take over the Siegener Bank by the more genteel technique of fusion without liquidation, the Deutsche Bank faced the doubly irritating situation of having its efforts frustrated in the context of competition from the Siegen Savings Bank. The latter was one of the most aggressive of the savings banks and was the subject of major protests by the big banks for its advocacy of expanding the functions of the savings banks into spheres formerly reserved for the universal banks. In Siegen it claimed that, by taking over the Siegener Bank and its facilities, it could better serve the local business community than the far-away Deutsche Bank. Managing Director Schlitter used all his persuasive powers to try to explain why the Deutsche Bank and the concentration movement its efforts reflected was at once a superior and necessary solution. This movement had the 'explicit purpose of gathering together the forces that lie scattered about at those junctures where they can find the best support in the competitive economic struggle'. Germany's dangerous political situation and her dependence on raw materials along with the depreciation of the mark could create demands which 'the financial strength of the individual enterprise is incapable of meeting'. For this reason, 'economically weak enterprises must seek support more than before from the stronger'. This was as true for banking as it was for industry, both of which were somewhat cushioned against liquidity problems in the relative stabilization of 1920–21. Schlitter warned against believing this situation would last:

'At the present time many industries are still living on a certain excess of cash, so that the banks have increasing means which they can place to some measure at the disposal of other enterprises in need of money. How long this will last, however, cannot be foreseen, and perhaps the Siegerland industry will one day, instead of having the money which it is keeping in the banks at the present time, once again be in need of money. The existing provincial banks are not today any longer in a position to meet such demands on their own. The monetary depreciation today requires sums on short notice that previously were viewed as gigantic.'[113]

When industries were suddenly compelled to pay the costs of raw materials or wages without having immediate buyers, or found it necessary to grant customers longer periods to meet their bills, Schlitter argued, their demands would prove more than the provincial banks could handle and 'only the inner strength of a great bank can do for the nation's industry what is necessary in order to hold out in the great economic struggle'. Schlitter particularly objected to the notion, advocated by some of those in favour of an alliance with the Deutsche Bank, that the city might hold some of the capital of the Siegener Bank and that the Siegener Bank might take the place of the city bank. In his view, private banks should not be in the business of holding small savings and providing small credits to small business, craftsmen, workers and civil servants as a means of increasing municipal income. Such a 'mixing of public and private functions' and a 'confusion of the boundary between savings bank and bank' was 'economically indefensible'.

It would take another four years, until 1925, before the Siegener Bank would surrender to the Deutsche Bank, and yet more years for the transformation in German banking so resisted by Schlitter to gain hold. There can be no question, however, that the leadership of the Deutsche Bank believed that it and the other great banks were on the right path. Furthermore, there were provincial bankers and banks anxious to join forces with them. One of these was the Hannoversche Bank, which had a long-standing relationship with the Deutsche Bank, and its General Director, Paul Klaproth. Founded in 1856 and one of Germany's oldest banking corporations, the Hannoversche Bank's connection with the Deutsche Bank dated back to 1899, and it ranked among the Deutsche Bank's most important permanent share holdings. Klaproth claimed that fusion with the Deutsche Bank would be the culmination of his life's work as the leader – and a very successful one – of the Hannoversche Bank. Although temperamental and vain, Klaproth seems to have been highly regarded by Mankiewitz, with whom he carried on a lengthy correspondence.

It was Klaproth who was first approached at the turn of 1919–20 as the leadership of the Deutsche Bank contemplated using projected capital share increases by the Hannoversche Bank and the Württembergische Vereinsbank, the Mitteldeutsche Privatbank and possibly the Rheinische Creditbank and Pfälzische Bank to make acquisitions for the Deutsche Bank. In short, the Hannoversche Bank was viewed as part and parcel of a package of acquisitions throughout Germany. While Klaproth seemed anxious to have the Hildesheimer Bank and the Braunschweiger Bank included as well, the Deutsche Bank was above all interested in his own bank. Klaproth himself was important enough to be offered a position on the board of managing directors of the Deutsche

Bank, which may have been pro forma given his constant talk of leading a less strenuous life, but he did have to be offered a position on the board of supervisors and its important auditing commission with suitable compensation and a variety of other benefits.

The negotiations took a peculiar and different turn almost as soon as they began because the sheer overwork at the Deutsche Bank made it impossible for the staff of the bank to work through a fusion in early 1920. These problems were compounded by political uncertainties over Allied demands for delivery of those it had named as war criminals and the abortive right-wing Kapp Putsch. Mankiewitz was sincere in his claims as to the overworked condition of the bank, since it was the Deutsche Bank which had called for the shutting down of the bourse for a number of days each week against the objection of the smaller banks, and it could hardly undertake major operations of its own at the same time without appearing hypocritical. Klaproth was deeply disappointed by the delay, however. When the Mitteldeutsche Privatbank merged with the Commerzbank, thus turning the latter into a major bank, Klaproth blamed this on the failure of the Deutsche Bank to act quickly enough in its fusion policy. The argument did not impress Managing Director Wassermann back in Berlin, who retorted, 'if the Commerzbank has now really become a great bank, then I would be extremely happy. We have a national interest in strong banks, but the meal was quite large and will produce digestive complaints.'[114] As for the Deutsche Bank, Wassermann made it clear that it did not wish to be represented everywhere, and he and his colleagues were by no means certain that they wished to acquire the Hildesheimer and the Braunschweiger banks. Klaproth's pressure for them to do so reflected his own bank's interest in these institutions and possibly the desire to mute criticism of his own bank for giving up its independence. While Klaproth certainly had a tendency to exaggerate his difficulties, there is every reason to believe his argument that delay in the fusion only increased particularist objections. Thus, by the autumn of 1920, the local press was criticizing the decision of the Hannoversche Bank: 'It is simply not understood for what reasons so intrinsically well-constructed and distinguished an institution could give up its independence. The economic soundness of the move is contested, and above all much is made of the point that a new attachment to Berlin in the midst of the general cry "away from Berlin" is a first-class tactical mistake.'[115]

The terms offered the shareholders of the Hannoversche Bank were probably irresistible, but Klaproth certainly carried the burden of bringing the Braunschweiger Bank and particularly the Hildesheimer Bank into the arrangement. The former seems to have agreed to fusion relatively easily, while the programme for the Hildesheimer Bank was for a share exchange rather than an outright takeover. Nevertheless there were strong local objections in Hildesheim. Having first brought around Hildesheimer Bank's head, Max Leeser, whose pretensions and demands seem to have irritated everyone, Klaproth struggled to carry the day with Hildesheim's 'big-wig' mayor who, as he sarcastically reported, stormed 'against concentration in general and the hydrocephalous Berlin in particular and declared that a great bank was much more endangered than the wonderful one-and-only-in-this-world Hildesheimer Bank'. Apparently the outcome was uncertain until the mayor made the mistake of saying that 'the Deutsche Bank would certainly try to do in a crooked manner that which was not possible to achieve honestly'. This gave Klaproth and Leeser an opportunity to denounce the opposition, while the District President chairing the meeting, who was on the side of Klaproth, censured the comment, declared that there had been enough talk, and called for those opposed to the project to rise. As Klaproth triumphantly reported: 'and lo and behold, they all remained sitting on their behinds'.[116]

The negotiations with the Württembergische Vereinsbank, which also culminated in an exchange of shares rather than an immediate fusion, lacked these picaresque qualities. They were undoubtedly influenced by the important role which Director Kaulla had played in the affairs of the Deutsche Bank and by Gwinner's presence on its supervisory board, but they may also have reflected a growing sensitivity to the concerns of those surrendering their independence to the great Berlin bank. Director von Stauss, who conducted the negotiations for the Deutsche Bank, certainly played upon the past close relationship. He pointed out that, although the Deutsche Bank had three branches in Bavaria, its big projects there – the nitrogen works, the wartime Krupp plant and the Danube shipping company – had been organized from Berlin. In Stuttgart, however, the Deutsche Bank believed that the Württembergische Vereinsbank offered the opportunity to operate on a more local level. Stauss frankly admitted that the competition of the Disconto-Gesellschaft, which had just taken over the important banking house of Stahl & Federer, had put it in an 'awkward situation', since 'it was not pleasant or useful for the Deutsche Bank to stand by as an observer while the Disconto-Gesellschaft establishes direct relations with the entire economic life of Württemberg, and it is also to be feared that the Württembergische Vereinsbank will be at a disadvantage because of the capital strength of the four Berlin banks now represented in Stuttgart'.[117]

Stauss presented four possible modes of integration between the two banks: community of interest, fusion, taking over of a large block of the Württembergische Vereinbank's shares, and an exchange of the Württembergische Vereinbank's shares for Deutsche Bank shares. Stauss felt that communities of interest had not worked well in the banking field, an opinion shared by his Württemberg colleagues, and he expressed a strong personal preference for fusion. Nevertheless, the Elberfeld experience was fresh in the mind of Stauss and was even held up as a model since he argued that it was important to keep the name of the Württembergische Vereinsbank and then to add 'branch of the Deutsche Bank' in the event of a fusion, and to reconstitute the old bank and its name if an exchange of shares was decided upon. Stauss was also careful to emphasize that the Deutsche Bank desired to promote the independence and sense of responsibility of its branch managers. He pointed out that even in Berlin the managing directors met only one afternoon a week and tried to keep supervision to a minimum and to avoid time-wasting meetings.[118]

Stauss was unable to persuade the Württembergers to accept fusion, however, and both sides agreed on an exchange of shares. The Deutsche Bank was obligated not to undertake a fusion in the coming decade without the approval of the Württembergische Vereinsbank, and to make changes in the Württembergische Vereinsbank's boards of managing directors and supervisors only by mutual agreement. Clearly, however, the way was being paved for the fusion which finally took place in 1924. Thanks to these arrangements, the Deutsche Bank was able to assume the more direct role in the industrial development of Württemberg that Stauss seems to have desired.

It cannot be said that the Deutsche Bank was equally happy with its involvement in the affairs of the Pfälzische Bank, which consumed much of the already strained energies of Michalowsky and especially of Mankiewitz at the turn of 1921–22. The entire situation was a product of the corrupting environment produced by the inflationary currency and stock market speculation that took a quantum leap in the summer and autumn of 1921 when the relative stabilization ended. No major bank could avoid involvement in this speculation, but it was obviously a dangerous business and the Deutsche Bank cautioned its officials that the exchange rate situation could suddenly be transformed at a heavy price to those who made the wrong guess. They were particularly warned against encouraging speculation by people without much capital like 'white-collar workers, officers, widows, orphans, small pensioners and people in general who otherwise have nothing to do with business life'.[119]

Good advice indeed, especially since many of them were to lose their investments when the mark suddenly improved in December 1921 and there was a market crash. But such solicitousness for the small investor did not answer to the problem of how they were supposed to protect themselves against the depreciation of their liquid assets. Furthermore, as small investors of a non-speculative type who had put their money into the 58-year-old Ludwigshafen-based Pfälzische Bank discovered to their horror in December 1921, virtue was not necessarily its own reward. A young and possibly pathological bank official charged with currency dealings at the bank's Munich branch had managed to incur speculative losses totalling 340 million marks. Since the bank had only 75 millions in capital and 33.3 millions in reserves, its rescue had to come from the outside.[120]

It was Managing Director Mankiewitz of the Deutsche Bank who stumbled upon the situation during a visit to Munich in November 1921 when another banker commented that even large banks were now making late payments. Mankiewitz thought that it was his own Munich branch that was meant, but then found out it was the Pfälzische Bank branch. It was a matter of concern because the Rheinische Creditbank, with which the Deutsche Bank was allied, had a community of interest with the Pfälzische Bank. Once further enquiries were made, the cover-up at the Munich branch rapidly unravelled, albeit with periodic unpleasant surprises as to the size of the losses.

The collapse of the Pfälzische Bank would unquestionably have been a substantial blow to the economic life of south-west Germany and Bavaria as well as to the German banking community, and the Deutsche Bank and Rheinische Creditbank agreed to join in the rescue operation. Under the arrangement finally worked out, the capital of the Pfälzische Bank was raised to 240 million with the Deutsche Bank taking most of the stock, while the Pfälzische Bank was taken over by the Rheinische Creditbank along with its branches on the left side of the Rhine. The debts of the Pfälzische Bank were guaranteed by the two banks. The Deutsche Bank took over its Bavarian and Frankfurt branches. Provision was made to provide needy shareholders in the Pfälzische Bank with small compensation for their losses.

The entire arrangement provoked a very stormy meeting between the shareholders and the representatives of the two banks in January 1922. The former not only protested their expropriation, but accused the two banks of taking advantage of the situation. While no one could deny that the Deutsche Bank had made substantial financial sacrifices to save the bank, it was accused of failing to exercise the expected moral leadership by making an inadequate offer to the shareholders, and of using the situation to increase its power. As one representative put it: 'The Deutsche Bank is not simply a purely economic leader, but it also has to take into account that it has moral leadership in the economic realm. There exists the opinion that the Deutsche Bank is swallowing not only the Pfalzbank, which is by and large intact, along with all its facilities and earning potential, but also the Rheinische Creditbank and at the same time the entire capital of a large number of small and medium-sized shareholders.'[121]

Shareholders were furious that Deutsche Bank branch officials had actually torn down the Pfälzische Bank's signs at its branches, and the Deutsche Bank had in fact instructed its officials to stop doing so. For the shareholders, however, this was symptomatic of the ruthlessness that lay behind the alleged sacrifices of the great bank. Director Jahr of the Rheinische Creditbank ably defended his colleagues Michalowsky and Mankiewitz by pointing out that they immediately stepped into the breach without thinking of advantage, while Mankiewitz joined him in complaining that they were getting very little appreciation for their efforts to serve the Fatherland, bind North and South in friendship, and assist an area where they had strong ties with the chemical industry. As far as the shareholders were concerned, he reminded them that the Pfälzische Bank was potentially bankrupt and that little or no claim could be made to compensation under the circumstances.

How is one to evaluate these charges and counterclaims? The Deutsche Bank's response to the crisis of the Pfälzische Bank was almost automatic, and the directors involved began making plans to provide money before contemplating any advantages it might bring. When the managing directors sat down to discuss the situation on the afternoon of 28 November, however, they did contemplate the relationship between sacrifice and entitlement. As Michalowsky reported: 'In the afternoon meeting of the directors, the view was taken that where we are making such monumental sacrifices we should take advantage of the opportunity to gain dominant influence in the Rheinische Creditbank.'[122] Director Jahr of the Creditbank seems to have understood what was at stake, but when he sought initially to resist the terms proposed, Michalowsky threatened to publicize the Deutsche Bank's willingness to save the Pfälzische Bank and, by implication, leave the Rheinische Creditbank with the burden of blame for its failure. While the Deutsche Bank certainly did not approve the open and tasteless removal of Pfälzische Bank insignia, it also privately informed its relevant branches that it was anxious to take over the bank's better customers.[123] To be sure, it was not totally insensitive to the shareholders, and it was Managing Director Wassermann who urged that provision be made for a fund to provide them with a measure of compensation. Whether the Deutsche Bank's reputation would have not been better served by a more generous arrangement and whether the appreciation of its services to the southern German economy would have been less cold are also significant questions which, interestingly enough, were raised even by shareholders friendly to the Deutsche Bank.[124] In any case, the rescue of the Pfälzische Bank is an important case study in the problems of solidarity in the German banking community and the sociology of banking, issues that were to arise in even more dramatic fashion a decade later.

There are obvious lines of continuity with the pre-war and wartime periods in this expansion of the Deutsche Bank and the other great banks into the provinces and in their increasing number of branches. Nevertheless, the conditions of 1920–22 were very different from those of 1914 when the Bergisch Märkische Bank was taken over, or 1917 when the Norddeutsche Creditanstalt and Schlesischer Bankverein were fused with the Deutsche Bank. The post-war expansion was neither consolidation after a long period of growth and expansion nor preparation for further growth at home and abroad. It was a process of compensating for losses and gathering and consolidating forces so as to confront future threats and dangers with maximum effectiveness.

The fact that the Disconto-Gesellschaft briefly became 'number one' among the great banks by raising its capital to 610 million marks in 1922 only to be overtaken by the Deutsche Bank once again in the same year through the doubling of its capital from 400 to 800 million marks and the increasing of its reserves by 450 million to 2.25 billion marks, cannot be construed as one of the grand moments in German banking history, even if it did reflect that splendid combination of 'business and prestige policy'[125] which had characterized the Deutsche Bank for decades. The real worth of all these shares or, to put the matter somewhat differently, the extent to which the banks were watering their shares, was impossible to determine in May 1922 as Germany stood on the brink of hyperinflation. What the capital increase of 1922 really represented was a skilful cutting of losses and husbanding of important assets that had begun in 1919 and culminated in this capital increase, whose special novelty was that it was based on a merger between the Deutsche Bank and the DPAG.

The origins of this merger between the bank and an industrial firm was the need to save the DPAG's Steaua shares from confiscation by the Romanians under the armistice and peace treaty. Director Kurt Weigelt set up a company in Switzerland, EOS (Erdöl Syndikat), for the purpose of selling the shares to a banking syndicate composed of the Romanian Berkowitz Bank, which held 50 per cent, and the London banking house of Stern Brothers and the French Banque de Paris et des Pays-Bas, each of which had a 25 per cent share. At the same time, the DPAG had opened a large credit line with the Credit Suisse and the Skandinaviska Bank. The Steaua shares were initially mortgaged to the Deutsche Bank, which then, with the approval of the Reichsbank, put them up as security for this credit to the DPAG, thereby ensuring that the shares would be treated as neutral property free from Allied seizure. The DPAG then sold the shares to EOS in June 1919, which sought to sell them to American and then to Anglo-French interests. While the Romanians were in a position to hold up the deal so long as the Steaua was under government administration, Weigelt and Stauss found the Romanians willing to make concessions because they were anxious to resume trade with Germany, and Weigelt was able to win over the Administrator and later General Director of the Steaua, Osiceanu.[126] In the end, the DPAG received 72 million Swiss francs for the shares after paying 3 million in commissions. At Mankiewitz's insistence, a small portion was also used to support the mark, while the remainder and other substantial assets of the DPAG, for which there was no proper use under the existing economic circumstances, were turned over to the Deutsche Bank in the fusion. The DPAG shareholders received four new Deutsche Bank shares for each DPAG share. The DPAG itself was reconstituted with a capital of 150 million marks and soon expanded through a community of interest with the Rütgerswerke AG.

The takeover of the DPAG substantially increased the Deutsche Bank's foreign exchange holdings at a very crucial time, but it was clearly a defeat for the bank's efforts to play the great role on the international oil market towards which it seemed to be heading before and during the war. Also, the bank's oil, land and railway investments in Mosul, Mesopotamia and Syria were simply lost without any compensation, although it did manage to retain its interests in the Anatolian Railways by using the same methods of share transfer to a Swiss company – in this case the Bank für Orientalische Eisenbahnen in Zurich – that it had employed in connection with the Steaua Romana. Once the chaos in the region had come to an end and negotiations for a final settlement in Lausanne had begun, these shares were gradually sold off to an English consortium.

This may have been somewhat profitable, but it was an inglorious ending to Germany's dominant role in the region, and some influential Turks thought the Deutsche Bank should make a new beginning. In October 1922, General Director

Günther was approached by the former General Intendant of the Turkish Army, Ismail Hakki Pasha, with the proposal that the Deutsche Bank join him in setting up a bank in Constantinople. When Günther asked why he had 'turned to us poor Germans instead of our rich adversaries', Hakki Pasha responded that he had come to the conclusion that 'one can only engage in large business deals properly with the Germans'. Günther made it clear to Hakki Pasha that Germany was in no position to invest heavily in such enterprises because 'on the one hand, the exchange rate situation hinders the investment of capital abroad and, on the other hand, any investment of German capital outside Germany must, for political reasons, be handled with the utmost caution, inasmuch as the Allies would be quick to point out that, if Germany can find foreign exchange for foreign investment, she should also be able to do so to meet her reparations bill'.[127]   The response of the Deutsche Bank managing directors in Berlin to this and similar proposals from others was well summarized by Mankiewitz's marginal comment, 'out of the question'. At Wassermann's suggestion, Hakki Pasha was put off with the explanation that, so long as the Deutsche Bank branch in Constantinople remained under Allied control, no decisions could be made.[128]

The most striking and painful case of Deutsche Bank disengagement from its foreign investments because of mark depreciation and reparations anxieties was the sale of the Deutsch-Ueberseeische Elektricitäts-Gesellschaft (DUEG) in 1920 to a Spanish banking consortium headed by the Don Francisco de A. Cambó and its transformation into the Compania Hispano-Americana de Electricidad (CHADE). The new company was administered by the man who had actually organized the entire operation, Dannie Heinemann, the Administrator of the Belgian Société Financière des Transports et d'Enterprises Industrielles.

In March 1919, the Deutsche Bank managing directors began contemplating the alienation of this important and dynamic German company which played a major role in the urban electrification of South America. Despite some pressure from the German government, which feared that Germany would lose its presence in South America, the bank leaders came to the conclusion that it could not be saved if they held on to the DUEG. They were moved by three considerations. First, they no longer had the capital necessary to invest in the amounts and with the flexibility required for the company to perform effectively. Second, the shares of the DUEG were denominated in marks, and the depreciation of the mark meant that foreign shareholders, especially the Swiss, who were heavily invested in the company, were receiving no dividend and were holding a depreciating asset. At the same time, foreigners were taking advantage of the low value of the mark to purchase its stock. Almost 50 per cent was believed to be in foreign hands by early 1920. The company could become 'foreignized' and control simply be taken away from the Germans. Finally, there was the danger that the company's German shares could be seized for reparations purposes, a right enjoyed by the Reparations Commission until the final reparations sum was set in May 1921. Indeed, John Maynard Keynes had explicitly mentioned the DUEG, which he characterized as a 'fine and powerful German enterprise in South America' as a candidate for such treatment in his widely read *Economic Consequences of the Peace.*

Once the Deutsche Bank came to the conclusion that it could not afford to hold on to the DUEG, the problem became how to find purchasers with sufficient capital to run the company properly, who were also prepared to give German shareholders a reasonable return on their investments, to maintain German personnel and to promote some German interests, and who would be secure from Allied pressure. The Spanish banks and Dannie Heinemann, who had long been involved with the company, admirably met these needs and even promised that German companies would be entitled to 50 per cent of all contracts for CHADE projects if their prices were competitive, and that Germans could reappear on the supervisory board in due course.[129]

The Swiss, who appeared a logical alternative for the taking over of the DUEG because of their interests in the company, were an unsatisfactory solution because their capital market was overstrained and of insufficient size, and because they were under constant pressure from the Allies not to act as rescuers of German capital.[130] Julius Frey, President of the Credit Suisse, whose Elektrobank was an important shareholder in the DUEG and who had helped to found the DUEG with Gwinner, accepted the situation as gracefully as he could, but expressed considerable unhappiness with the losses that the Elektrobank and the Swiss were taking on their German investments because of the depreciation of the mark. In March 1920, Gwinner, who had retired as a managing director of the Deutsche Bank in 1919, but who remained active now as a member of the bank's supervisory board and on the supervisory boards of other enterprises in which he was involved, sought to console his old friend – and himself – about the end of the DUEG and also tried to put the problems of dealing with Germany in some perspective. He recognized that the Credit Suisse had suffered heavy losses through its German connections, but then pointed out: 'God knows we are not at fault for this. The Deutsche Bank has brought you very fine, solid, splendid business; our creations were able to withstand every assault except that of the lost world war.'[131] Gwinner believed that the Elektrobank would pull through if Europe did not turn Bolshevik, and he reminded Frey that the Polish mark was in even worse shape than the German.

Europe did not turn Bolshevik and the German mark enjoyed a relative stabilization, but the Elektrobank collapsed and had to be reorganized. Frey was utterly fed up with the *Reichsdeutsche* by January 1921 and did not hide his feelings from Gwinner:

'We have to hear almost daily that in German big industrialist circles one is not only quite satisfied with the present exchange rate situation but declares in all seriousness that even an increase of the mark to 15 will eliminate all German competitiveness on the international market. That we foreign creditors are simply going to ruin because of the present German exchange rate, that we once gave our German debtors a good 123.45 gold francs for 100 marks and are now are supposed to be served up with 8 or 9 francs in return, and that even with a 10 per cent dividend on our participations in German enterprises we will not get even a 1 per cent return so that a serious depreciation of those dividends is unavoidable – for these things one does not seem to have any more feeling in Germany. There is no lacking of fine words about work and austerity, but they are not translated into deeds. The government budget is ever more expensive, the inflation is ever larger, and in the end there can be nothing other than a great disaster unless one tries seriously and *as quickly as possible* to bring about a change in these circumstances. Does one still have the strength to do so?'[132]

Gwinner's reply to this sharp criticism was to remind Frey that his own life's work – 'Germany's greatest and most beautiful enterprises abroad' – lay in ruins along with his fatherland. While the mark had improved slightly, the Swiss franc had deteriorated, and the bizarre currency situation from which they were all suffering was the fault of the 'ghastly, unjust peace'. He pointed out that the Germans were working harder and were turning their backs on 'the failed experiment of Socialism', but that German recovery depended on the French changing their ways and the neutrals aiding the process. Since Germany would not raise a foreign loan under the treaty and the existing circumstances, and since its industries had to supply huge amounts of production as reparations in kind for which the government had to pay, 'the only means is the giving of bank notes or the issuance of Treasury notes, which have to be paid for with bank notes when they fall due'.[133]

4. The problem of reparations

There was nothing very novel about Gwinner's response. One of the few points of consensus in an otherwise very divided Germany was that the chief responsibility for the economic problems of Germany and the world were the reparations demands. Furthermore, leading foreign businessmen also questioned the wisdom of the reparations arrangements. In 1922, for example, Francisco de Cambó gave a speech which Gwinner thought 'excellent', arguing that Germany could not pay reparations on the basis of a negative balance of payments.[134] But Gwinner and his colleagues were also aware that many foreign businessmen, as in the case of Frey, were critical of the German business community's attitude towards the inflation and believed that not enough was being done to control it. As Gwinner's cousin, the New York banker James Speyer, asked in February 1920, 'Is there any chance of the Reichsbank stopping the issues of paper money? How can your currency price recover – apart from everything else – if your Government goes on printing bank notes without limit or security?'[135]

While the exclamation mark Gwinner placed beside these lines suggests that he gave his cousin the same kind of answer he was later to give Frey, banks and bankers have an obvious interest in sound money and orderly circumstances. They had a special interest in them after 1918 because the future of the banking business depended upon the reconstruction of Germany's financial and economic role in the world and the gaining of international assistance for this purpose. As Gwinner had predicted in 1914, New York had overtaken London in financial power if not fully as the world's financial centre, and it was to the United States that most bankers looked for aid.

The banking community played a very significant role in the preparations for the peace treaty and in the reparations question which plagued German politics after 1918, as did German industry. While it would be a mistake to overgeneralize about the differences between banking and industry – there were profound individual differences in both camps on political and international issues – the evidence does suggest that bankers were more anxious to achieve a reparations settlement, more willing to take risks and make sacrifices in order to do so, and therefore more anxious to bring about a stabilization of the currency. Risks had to be taken to make Germany a good credit risk, and this long-term perspective helps to explain why bankers tended to be more moderate and to seek modes of accommodation. The industrialists, especially the heavy industrialists, tended to think in more short-run terms, to want to make the most of inflation to increase exports and reconstruct their plants, to fret about the loss of export advantages and the belt tightening that would inevitably come with stabilization, and to resist risking their money and credit to meet reparations demands they thought ultimately unfulfillable. Thus, while bankers and industrialists were in general agreement that Allied demands were unfulfillable, the former were more inclined than the latter to pursue a policy of restraint and accommodation designed to prove that fulfilment was impossible and bring the Allies to reason.

Among the bankers, the most important figures on the reparations question from the very outset were Max Warburg and his colleague Carl Melchior. This was not only because they were very cosmopolitan men with broad international experience, but also because they had excellent connections in Great Britain and especially in the United States. Two of Max Warburg's brothers were American bankers: one was the very influential Paul Warburg, a founder of the Federal Reserve System, and the other was Felix Warburg, a partner in Kuhn Loeb & Co. Franz von Mendelssohn also assumed an important role because of his operations and connections in Amsterdam, which was the major European site for German currency and trade operations during the inflation period. As advisers to the government and participants in the reparations question, directors of the Deutsche Bank unquestionably come next in prominence. Gwinner, Weigelt, Mankiewitz and Wassermann were regularly consulted by the government, as was Stauss, who also served on the Peace Delegation at Versailles and went to the Spa Conference. Alfred Blinzig, who was appointed a managing director upon Gwinner's retirement in 1920, had experience in the United States and concerned himself, among other things, with international issues.

Carl Bergmann was the most notable reparations negotiator connected with the Deutsche Bank. He had joined the Deutsche Bank in 1901, served as a railway expert for the bank in the Ottoman Empire and the United States before the war, and became a deputy director in 1911. Bergmann entered government service during the war, and between 1919 and 1921 served as German representative at the Reparations Commission in Paris and head of the War Burdens Commission. He returned to the service of the bank in September 1921, where he became very involved in dealings with the United States, especially over the return of German confiscated property. Nevertheless, he continued to be used as a negotiator by the government between 1921 and the creation of the Dawes Plan in 1924 and reported on the reparations question regularly to the bank.

While the peace treaty and reparations issues were highly charged questions of international and domestic politics, the Deutsche Bank as an institution and its directors seem in general to have been as circumspect in dealing with it as they had been in the war aims discussion. In its Business Report for 1918, the bank straightforwardly rejected charges that the existence of legislation for the loan bureaux in 1914 constituted evidence of bank complicity in war guilt, as the Allies charged, and the bank quietly supported efforts to combat the war guilt argument. They seem to have been justifiably sceptical about its utility as an argument in reparations matters even when opinion was obviously shifting in favour of Germany. As Blinzig argued in 1927 in connection with a future revision of the Dawes Plan, 'if we mix the debt question with the guilt question, then we will destroy a good deal of our prospects in both regards'.[136]

In contrast to their former colleague Helfferich, who became a leader of the German National People's Party after the war and a noisy supporter of the pernicious stab-in-the-back legend, the Deutsche Bank directors, while understandably opposing socialization ideas and what they felt to be excessive taxes, seem to have been free of such destructive political tendencies. Mankiewitz's understanding of why Germany lost the war was a very sober one: 'Germany went to defeat because it overestimated its strength and believed it could carry on war and do its work from the Caspian to the Baltic and from the Channel to the Duna. That has been our misfortune ...'.[137] He was also a sober adviser to the government with respect to the peace treaty negotiations, warning against trying to determine Germany's capacity to pay before one had the vaguest idea of what that capacity was and tipping one's hand by asking for an international loan under uncertain circumstances.[138]

Bergmann was more representative of the German tendency of trying to enthrone economic reason in a charged political environment by seeking to fix a sum which the Allies would never accept and call for an international loan which no one under the circumstances was prepared to give. Bergmann was playing the Finance Ministry official at this time, however, and it is significant that Stauss, the most politically active and engaged of the Deutsche Bank directors, was more willing to propose a higher sum in reparations payment in an effort to save German territory and come to some kind of accord with the Allies. Stauss, like Warburg and other banking and industrial leaders, ended up opposing the acceptance of the peace treaty, but he had a reputation as a moderate and was untainted by open wartime annexationism. As an active member of the German People's Party, he was the choice of many, including Stresemann, for the Reich list of the party in the June 1920 elections, in preference to Hugo Stinnes, who had an annexationist background and took an openly hostile stance to fulfilment.[139]

Both before and after the May 1921 ultimatum, which set the German obligation at 132 billion gold marks, the Deutsche Bank leaders sought some solution that might avoid catastrophe and create the basis for a large stabilization loan from the United States. This often contrasted sharply with the leaders of heavy industry, upon whose credit and co-operation the government was increasingly dependent, and who used France's dependence on German coal and need for a market for its ore to take a hard line. Prior to the ultimatum, Wassermann urged that German industry place 10 per cent of its production at the disposal of the government for reparations payment, a proposal which the Foreign Office had to drop as a condition for getting any industrial participation in the negotiations.[140] Subsequently, as the German government began its desperate efforts to procure the foreign exchange needed to pay the first reparations instalment of August 1921, Wassermann sharply criticized the hoarding of foreign exchange by private persons and businessmen because of their lack of confidence in the government. At the same time, he had to confess that he did not think that exchange controls could be enforced because of the lack of civic sense in Germany.[141]

Yet, it was also difficult to imagine the German state going bankrupt. Back in May 1920 when Klaproth had asked Mankiewitz whether he thought it was safe to invest in government bonds maturing in 1924, Wassermann had replied on his behalf saying that 'while Herr Mankiewitz sees extraordinarily hard times coming for the private economy, he inclines to the view that the credit of the state cannot be shaken in its foundations and that the possibility of a state bankruptcy is barred for internal reasons'.[142] It was not to prove very good advice, but it must be said to his credit that he and his colleagues at least strove to make it true. Thus, Mankiewitz seems to have particularly distinguished himself when the Reich called upon the D-Banks to guarantee dollar-denominated Treasury bills in a desperate effort to make its first billion gold mark reparations payment of August 1921.[143]

Needless to say, the credit of the Deutsche Bank was intimately bound up with the credit of the German state, as Bergmann observed and reported during a journey to the United States in the autumn of 1921. At a dinner in honour of the former Chancellor of the Exchequer and then Chairman of the Midland Bank, Reginald McKenna, a series of pessimistic remarks about Germany's currency, apparently made in a state of some inebriation, so alarmed representatives of the Equitable Trust Company in attendance that they actually proposed that the German accounts in the United States be established as security for the short-term credits they had been supplying. Sobriety prevailed in the end – obviously not because of Prohibition – but Bergmann found it indicative that a bank which had been so friendly to the Deutsche Bank since the war should succumb so easily to renewed mistrust of the Germans and doubts about the credit of the great banks.

There were other distressing signs. Hugo Schmidt and his staff at the Deutsche Bank office in New York were kept terribly busy selling large amounts of marks to South America, especially to branches of the Deutsche Ueberseeische Bank, but speculative interest in the mark in the important New York market was practically nil. Bergmann was especially disturbed by reports from the various New York houses of regular, large and concentrated offers of marks by the Mendelssohn firm in Amsterdam, which handled Reichsbank business. He felt that the Reichsbank was demonstrating unusual incompetence in this area and inadvertently promoting a decline in the mark notation.[144] Most importantly, the press was full of charges that the Germans were deliberately running down the mark in order to prove they could not pay reparations and accusations, which Bergmann thought 'a quite childish view', that the German government's only financial conception was throwing marks on the market to collect foreign exchange. Mankiewitz, who read these reports, could not, to his sorrow, completely agree that it was all that 'childish', and commented, 'no, so things actually are now!'[145]

While Bergmann sought to counter these charges in the press and among his numerous and growing circle of personal contacts, he was well aware that there were Germans who thought that a collapse of the mark would be the best way to bring about a reduction of reparations, and he warned that they had better 'knock such ideas out of their heads'. His past experience in Paris had shown him that this would have only a negative effect and lead to demands for financial control on Germany and measures against the speculators, who were depriving the government of the foreign exchange it needed. At the same time, he thought that the Reichsbank and the German government had to support the mark actively because 'the indifference of the Americans about Germany's financial misery is astonishing' and he urged that the Reichsbank use its stubbornly held gold for this purpose. This was the only way to secure the American support so desperately needed: 'The Americans expect this self-help from us and will hardly be willing to employ their own money for us so long as they, rightly or wrongly, can accuse us of letting things go their way and keeping our hands in our laps'.[146]

Bergmann had to fight the idea in New York as well as Berlin that it was pointless to support the mark until reparations were scaled down, since this notion was also held by some American bankers. He feared that the mark had fallen too low and that its further collapse would lead to price rises and social disorder in Germany. He placed little hope in a projected credit action by German industry, induced by the fear that its real values would be seized as a guarantee of taxation by the government. Quite aside from the fact that the industrialists were setting impossible conditions – the privatization of the railways and other state enterprises – the amount involved was insufficient. In Bergmann's view, only the use of Reichsbank gold combined with backing by an American consortium could save the mark and pave the way for a change in reparations policy.[147]

Bergmann's lengthy and passionate reports met with a mixed reception from his Berlin colleague Mankiewitz, who seems to have thought a French occupation of the Ruhr more likely than Bergmann, but who was also more despairing because he found Bergmann's position filled with contradictions. Fundamentally, he did not think the situation could be saved without a change in the reparations situation: 'Of what use is buying marks if the situation is all the worse afterward. First, there must be changes regarding reparations.'[148] Nevertheless, Mankiewitz opposed passivity, tried to persuade an increasingly stubborn Havenstein that the Reichsbank should sacrifice some of its gold for political reasons, and complained that the Reichsbank had exchanged its overoptimism of the war years for excessive pessimism in peace. Mankiewitz, however, also thought that Bergmann had underestimated the importance of a large industrial contribution to the cause and agreed with Havenstein's complaints that industry was not supplying the foreign exchange that was needed: 'Naturally industry behaves as selfishly as always and does not deliver enough, and from where else are we supposed to get the foreign exchange?'[149]

A few weeks later, in December 1921, it appeared as if Bergmann's persistence was paying off, and there were signs that the British, the Americans and even important French leaders were moving towards granting a large loan and reparations relief to Germany and raising the value of the mark. Mankiewitz wanted to believe it was true, especially as he looked at what was going on at the Berlin bourse: 'Here one wants the reverse. When the Reichsmark rises, one fears that the securities will fall. For me the most important thing is that there is an end to the frightful game on the bourse, which is ruining all of Germany, driving up wages and inducing the employees to make monstrous demands.'[150] The game, however, only got worse after Poincaré came to power in France in January 1922. The Genoa Conference of April was a failure for those who hoped it would move things forward in the area of reparations, and crisis succeeded crisis as Germany succumbed to hyperinflation in the summer and autumn.

Significantly, some of the Deutsche Bank leaders continued their efforts to find a way out. In the spring, Bergmann seems to have pinned his hopes on a European bankers' plan to stabilize the situation through a combination of internal stabilization measures, and J.P. Morgan seemed ready to head the operation. Indeed, Bergmann was so optimistic that he apparently indicated to a meeting of the Deutsche Bank branch heads that a stabilization of the mark lay in the foreseeable future. This caused considerable excitement, and Mankiewitz, 'who inside himself had been unable to bear the sinking of the mark, saw his hope for a saving of the mark being realized and spoke in enthusiastic tones'.[151] Unfortunately, the bank was soon filled with 'inside information' about an impending stabilization of the mark, which did nothing for its reputation among the customers who acted on it. Then the mark collapsed after Poincaré and the Reparation Commission refused to agree to Morgan's demand for a reduction of reparations and after Foreign Minister Rathenau was assassinated.

If this experience undoubtedly put an end to employing wishful thinking as a basis for currency-investment advice, it in no way terminated the interest of Deutsche Bank officials – above all, Bergmann and Wassermann – in saving the mark and restoring stability. Both served as advisers to Reich Chancellor Cuno in the final unsuccessful efforts in November–December 1922 to ward off the French occupation of the Ruhr which was to begin in the new year. Here, as in the past, there was tension between the approach of the industrialists and that of the bankers, who sought a solution from what their chief critic in industry, Hugo Stinnes, called the 'financial side' rather than his own preferred 'production side'.[152]

Stinnes and his industrial colleagues pursued a policy of risking domestic and international confrontation. On the one hand, they demanded that Germany make herself worthy of credit by ending the eight-hour day, by massive government cost-cutting, and by the privatization of state enterprises and assets so as to run them properly and make them useful security for an international loan. On the other, they made reduction of reparations and termination of Allied occupation of the Rhineland the condition of currency stabilization and treaty fulfilment. The bankers, while certainly not disagreeing with most of these domestic and international goals, had become convinced that Germany had to persuade the international financial community to assist her by undertaking currency stabilization measures through a great domestic effort. Once the Germans became serious about stabilization and did something to satisfy French financial demands, the international financial community would become engaged and force the French to moderate their demands in order to protect the international investment in Germany.

To achieve these goals, Wassermann developed a plan in November 1922 which became the basis of the Cuno government's policy. Wassermann proposed that the Reich issue long-term interest-bearing gold bonds guaranteed by the customs receipts of the Reich. A limited portion of the bonds was to be given to the Allies in place of the reparations to be paid during a projected two-year moratorium, so that Germany could have the breathing space she needed to put her budget and finances in order and negotiate a new reparations settlement. The second portion of the bonds, which was to be unlimited in quantity and amount, was to be placed on the domestic German market, and could be bought by both Germans and foreigners for foreign currency or assets denominated in foreign currency. The proceeds from the sale of the gold bonds marketed in

Germany were to be used to balance the budget and stabilize the currency, while excesses would be used to pay reparations in return for extension of the moratorium.

A major purpose of the Wassermann plan was to lure back such German capital as had flown abroad or was being hoarded in Germany for purposes of capital flight or tax evasion. As an incentive, he proposed to make the entire bond issue free of taxation for all time. This was tantamount to an amnesty for past tax evasion as well as a nullification of taxes that might have been owing, and it was to be guaranteed by a restoration of the secrecy of bank accounts and cancellation of the requirement that all securities and liquid assets be placed on deposit in a bank.[153]

Whatever the morality of ensuring that the rich remained rich and that those who had protected themselves against both inflation and taxation would be guaranteed their gains, the Wassermann plan unquestionably had advantages for Germany in that these gains would be put in the service of the nation in a very advantageous manner. It also had the inestimable advantage for the banks that it would get them out of the hated time- and labour-consuming business of supplying bank account information to the government, and would restore confidentiality between banks and their clients. In contrast to earlier proposals, Wassermann's plan relieved Germany of the need to beg for a loan abroad. In fact, Wassermann suggested that Germany could ride piggyback on Allied efforts to market the bonds in order to pay cash, and, since the reparations bonds and the domestic bonds would be indistinguishable, Allied guarantees of the bonds would have to cover bonds held by German nationals as well. They would thus be acting indirectly in the interest of Germany. Under such circumstances, in Wassermann's judgement, even the use of the Reichsbank gold for purposes of assisting the stabilization effort would no longer be risky. It was all very ingenious, but also too little too late, and the plan foundered on the objections of industry, Allied complaints that the reparations amounts offered were inadequate, and the fact that time had run out.

5. Hyperinflation and stabilization

The Wassermann stabilization proposals also reflected the increasingly desperate and bizarre conditions confronting the banks once the hyperinflation struck in the summer of 1922. They were now discovering that the quantity theory of money was not quite the Anglo-Saxon quirk and product of 'national economists of the old school' that Bergmann, for example, thought it was. A year earlier, he had been trying to drive into 'American brains' that it was not the German 'government that was printing money, but the Reichsbank, that further the needs of the government are covered by the sale of Treasury bills to the Reichsbank, which for its part rediscounts these Treasury bills as much as possible at the banks, so that there can be no talk of a public covering of budget expenses through the printing press, especially since the growth of Treasury bills in the recent past has repeatedly exceeded the note circulation'.[154]

In October and November 1921, the percentage of Treasury bills held outside the Reichsbank was, respectively, 54.7 and 49.7; in the corresponding months of 1922, it was 21.0 and 19.9. The paper mark value of these bills had increased from 226.7 billion in November 1921 to 839.1 billion in November 1922, and rose to 1,495.2 trillion in December. The great banks were finding it impossible to hold these Treasury bills any longer and, as the Deutsche Bank Business Report for 1922 cheerlessly noted, 'the Reichsbank, in order to prevent the immediate total collapse is forced to discount the Treasury bills of the government which are growing to a horrendous degree, and thereby, against its will, to depreciate more and more the money which it gives out'.[155] Bergmann had thus made a mistake. The growing loss of confidence in the mark which had so disturbed him in New York in 1921 had become a world-wide phenomenon by the summer of 1922, and the Germans were now left with their paper money based on dubious Treasury bills.

Germany, of course, did have real assets, and these were in danger too, since it took very little real money to buy up the paper money in which German assets were denominated. Since 1919 many German companies had been issuing preferred shares with multiple voting rights in order to prevent their foreignization. The banks, however, felt particularly vulnerable, and on 28 November 1922 the four Berlin D-Banks signed an agreement pledging mutual support of one another against foreignization efforts by refusing to engage in such transactions themselves, reporting suspicious orders and providing one another with quarterly reports on their stock of deposits.[156] Apparently, this exchange of information served the banks well, since there were attempts to purchase massive numbers of shares in the Berliner Handels-Gesellschaft and the Disconto-Gesellschaft in order to gain influence over those institutions. The Deutsche Bank responded to these experiences in its final capital share increase of the inflation in March 1923. The capital stock was raised by 700 million marks to 1.5 billion, but 400 million of these shares were placed with a friendly institution, the Deutsche Treuhand Gesellschaft, while the remainder were turned over to a consortium headed by the Württembergische Vereinsbank which was instructed to offer the new shares at a ratio of 1:4 of the old to present shareholders and to hold the remaining 100 million for the account of the Deutsche Bank.[157]

Just as the banks had misled others – and themselves – about the non-inflationary character of the Treasury bills issued by the Reichsbank, so they had gravely underestimated the danger of a severe credit crisis and overestimated the feasibility of solving the shortage of operating capital through a return to the use of commercial bills. The disappearance of foreign speculative investment in the mark and the withdrawal of deposits by customers in desperate need of cash, either to pay their bills or to shift their assets into real values, denuded the banks increasingly of worthwhile deposits. At the same time, the demand for credits increased enormously as businessmen calculated in real values and as domestic prices began to approach world market levels. The number of accounts at the Deutsche Bank rose from 780,402 at the end of 1921 to only 804,251 at the end of 1922, while the demand for credits and the costs of doing business multiplied. Thus, the 'banks found it necessary to increase their interest and commission rates very substantially and to try to reduce their unprofitable small accounts'.[158]

The demand for credit and the growing crisis in the economy made it essential for the banks to hold as much cash as possible. While the bank had supported the reintroduction of commercial bills, these had been richly, 'in many cases excessively', used. The amount of commercial bills discounted at the Reichsbank had increased from 1 billion to 422 billion marks between the end of 1921 and the end of 1922, a 400 times over increase as against a 40 times over decrease in the value of the currency. For large corporations, however, the demand for operating capital could not be totally satisfied in this manner, and this produced constant new increases of capital stock. These, to be sure, 'brought the banks good profits', but they also tied up funds at a time when deposits were not keeping up with depreciation. The Deutsche Bank estimated that deposits at all German banks at the end of 1922 amounted to 3 billion gold marks as opposed to 8.5 billion at the end of 1921 and 20 billion in savings banks alone at the end of 1913.[159]

What did this all mean in practice? For the Deutsche Bank itself, it meant considerable anxiety about major engagements, however promising and attractive they may have seemed. Thus, in August 1922, the Rhenish industrialist Paul Silverberg informed Managing Director Schlitter of a proposal that the Deutsche Bank invest 50 million marks to participate in a consortium to take over the banking house of Leopold Seligman. It included the Arbed Concern in Luxemburg and the French concern of de Wendel as well as the Cologne banking houses of Levy and Sal. Oppenheim, and opened up the prospect of the Deutsche Bank eventually taking over the other major private banking houses and forging a link with important international companies. Schlitter was sceptical that the Schaaffhausen'sche Bankverein and the Disconto-Gesellschaft could be excluded from such an arrangement, but he and Mankiewitz agreed that they could not pursue the matter in any case because of the current situation of the bank. Where the amount involved would earlier have been considered a 'trifle' for the bank, it was now a serious matter: 'We unfortunately find it necessary to hold on to our moneys at all costs, because we are already very close to the limit which we have set for the maintenance of our liquidity and ability to speedily meet our payment obligations. We cannot and do not want under any circumstances to come into situations in which other banks already find themselves, and must exercise extreme restraint, even if there is the danger that we will in the one case or the other be sacrificing great future opportunities. You do not realize and I cannot give you a true idea of what has descended upon us ...: withdrawal of deposits by industry, in so far as they are still extant, to the largest extent; credit demands, which increase geometrically from day to day; strikes by partners who collaborate in consortial bank credits, even if they run the danger of giving up old connections as a result. Then there came provincial banks and large, fine private firms which sought dependency on us in one form or another. Thus just yesterday we discussed in great detail the taking over of a firm which does not lie in my domain but that of Herr Stauss, but which has the same significance for him as the Seligman question has for me. After thorough deliberations yesterday, we decided with heavy hearts to drop the project. When I came today with your suggestion, it was impossible for me to get a positive response on the part of my colleagues in view of yesterday's decision.'[160]

So much for the claim of the banks of two years earlier that they were 'swimming in money'! Throughout the spring of 1922, the Deutsche Bank had instructed its branches to review credit accounts regularly and to make sure that credits were being used for necessary purposes, were only being given short term, and were bringing in enough profit to be worth maintaining.[161] The Deutsche Bank supported the Reichsbank's efforts to promote the use of commercial bills, which were stepped up feverishly in the summer. These had always been a more secure form of credit and were thus expected to improve the quality of the Reichsbank's monetary backing as well as the portfolios of the banks. The organizations of industry and commerce had resisted using commercial bills because of their preference for and ability to enforce rapid cash payments through their condition cartels. As Wassermann pointed out at a Reichsbank meeting, businessmen were also reluctant to use commercial bills because it was very hard to form a reliable judgement about the economic condition of their customers under the conditions existing since 1918, especially where foreign trade and foreign exchange were involved.[162] This reluctance was fading, however, as firms were running out of money and were unable to meet payment deadlines, so that commercial bills were the only alternative to ceasing economic life altogether. But such a change of attitude in no way solved the problem which Wassermann had noted, either for businessmen or for the banks, of determining the quality of the borrowers and of the flood of bills which began to be discounted and rediscounted throughout the country.

The Deutsche Bank was well aware of this danger and warned its branches from the outset against accepting acceptances which were not based on actual orders. By late August 1922, the branches of the Deutsche Bank had given a billion marks in credits within only a few days, a 'warning signal' which provoked the Berlin directors once again to call for a reduction of credits of all kinds. They were concerned that control would be lost in the flood of credit requests, and were especially anxious to avoid providing credits for speculative purposes, such as the hoarding of goods in expectation of price increases and the purchase of foreign exchange in anticipation of further mark depreciation. On 23 August they instructed their branches to give no regular current account credits extending beyond 30 November, to remind customers that credits could be called in at any time, and to warn that credits had to be paid off as much as possible since there was no guarantee of prolongation beyond 30 November. While conceding that 'in many cases this will remain a pious wish', they nevertheless emphasized the importance of as much reduction as possible.[163]

They full well understood the implications of these reductions for the growing business in commercial bills and 'how all of a sudden merchants and manufacturers are discovering how useful and valuable it is to draw on their customers'.[164] The bank had no intention of having the rebirth of commercial bills serve as a way of getting around the reduction of current account credit lines, and as a mechanism for sellers to retain or even improve upon their payment conditions while the banks were left stuck with three-month bills. It called on its branches to accept only solid bills based on real orders and limited to six, but preferably to four weeks. Prolongations were not to be given. In this way, 'the recipient of goods will be bound to the short-term payment requirement because he will have the Damocles Sword of the acceptance falling due hanging over him. This will also have the effect of making goods circulate faster and not being hoarded.' The credit officers of the bank were urged to put as much pressure on their clients in this regard as possible, and 'if the one or the other of our friends feels piqued by this and wants to cut his connection with us, then let him do it'. The directors were confident that other banks would take an even tougher line and certain that the Deutsche Bank would benefit from having fewer such customers and greater control over the use of its resources.

The proof that such control was necessary was demonstrated a few months later when the Berlin headquarters reported the case of a watchful credit officer who became suspicious of a very large credit request from an important firm with a previously fine credit record. His 'psychological analysis' of the case presented led him to pursue the matter and discover that the firm had failed to procure foreign exchange in time and was terribly overextended. This demonstrated that it was necessary to take a close look at each case and not simply accept 'monetary depreciation, and increased raw materials and labour costs' as sufficient grounds to grant credits.[165]

All of this in no way prevented the credit explosion which took place, with the Reichsbank at the head, beginning in the summer of 1922. Unlike the Deutsche Bank, the Reichsbank continuously discounted and rediscounted commercial bills for its large customers. A private sector inflation based on commercial bills was thus added to the public sector inflation based on Treasury bills. It was obviously advantageous for those firms to discount bills, especially at the low and always inadequately rising rate charged by the Reichsbank, and then pay them back in depreciated currency. It was good for the banks too, which also employed the services of the Reichsbank. While the Reichsbank was charging 12 per cent on commercial bills in February 1923, the great banks were charging between 30 and 50 per cent, discounting commercial bills in their portfolio at the Reichsbank, and taking the difference between the two discount rates as a profit.[166] Since the autumn of 1922, the Reichsbank had been striving to reduce the number and increase the quality of its commercial bills – a task that became extraordinarily difficult in the midst of the Ruhr occupation – and the Deutsche Bank reacted accordingly, instructing its branches to accept only the best commercial bills, warning against 'moderation' in the discount conditions, and arguing that 'we must always consider in our choice of bills the extent to which our own resources permit us to take them and whether the money we need for other purposes thereby lies unavailable. This would unquestionably be the case if we took bills which, if we find it necessary, we cannot pass on to the Reichsbank.'[167]

It was understandable that the banks would seek to protect themselves as best they could during the protracted agony of the mark in 1923. While doing their share in attempts to support the mark between February and April 1923 and to participate in the purchase of dollar-denominated Treasury bills to assist further the government's efforts to maintain passive resistance, the great banks showed considerable reluctance to participate in the creation of valorized accounts or give valorized loans. Although it was clear that industry and commerce were increasingly calculating in foreign currencies and that both private and public bodies were taking and issuing loans denominated in commodities like rye, coal and even kilowatt-hours, the banks feared that valorized accounts and loans placed them at too great a risk.

It cannot be said that the great banks cut a very impressive figure during this final chaotic period of the inflation. As usual, they were more helpful to the government than big industry, but they seemed panicked and uncertain. In June, for example, they supported establishing a unitary exchange rate for the mark because they wished to ward off attacks on themselves as a source of foreign currency speculation. By late summer, however, it was clear that passive resistance had to end and that drastic measures were necessary. Thus, at the end of August, the Deutsche Bank set up a special section for valorized credits which could be based on foreign exchange, dollar Treasury bills or commodities.[168] While the basic plan for a currency reform was developed by their former colleague, Karl Helfferich, and then carried through with modifications by another banker, Hjalmar Schacht, it cannot be said that the leading bankers who were consulted – Wassermann represented the Deutsche Bank – had much more to offer than qualms and reservations. Indeed, the 1923 Business Report of the Deutsche Bank reads like a confession when it declares that 'only when one looks back at the rushing tempo towards which the fateful developments of the year 1923 finally led and which undoubtedly would have continued even longer, can one form an accurate appreciation of the great deed which the creation of the Rentenmark meant for the German economy'.[169]

The creation of a currency based on all the industrial and landed assets of

Germany was, of course, more likely to be the creation of adventuresome types like Helfferich and Schacht than the by-and-large sober bankers who ran the D-Banks. It was also a 'miracle' bought at a very heavy price, since the final exchange rate of the old paper mark, set on 20 November 1923 at 4.2 trillion to the dollar, constituted a traumatic signature on the expropriation of savings and mark-denominated paper assets both at home and abroad. The re-establishment of the old parity of 4.2 marks to the dollar both for the Rentenmark in 1923 and, after the reconstitution of the Reichsbank in August 1924, for the Reichsmark was a confidence-building measure aimed at assuring the world that the mark was restored rather than at properly determining the real worth of the currency. The stabilization was built on limitations in money issuance, restrictions of credit, massive reductions in the civil service, high taxes and the balancing of the Reich budget. It was also based on the anticipation that an American-led committee of experts would come up with a reparations plan with which the Germans and French could live.

The Dawes Plan imposed strenuous reparations obligations and required the mortgaging of German railway and customs revenues, but it also held forth the promise of liberating the Rhein and Ruhr from French occupation and access to the American capital market. The great banks supported these arrangements because there was nothing else to do. As Carl Bergmann, who at long last had the American engagement for which he had yearned, trenchantly and somewhat ruefully told his colleagues: 'We must pay heavily that we have managed, in the worst chaos through our own strength, to perform the miracle of creating for ourselves a temporarily stable currency and a possibility of survival. The rejection of the plan of the experts from the German side would be suicide since the entire world will stand behind the verdict which the Americans have rendered.'[170]

The legacy of the hyperinflation and stabilization for the German banks was a harsh one. They were severely damaged in their reputations as well as in their substance, and charges were levied against them which kept them on the defensive for years to come. The complaints about 'interest-profiteering' had begun in 1919, but they reached a remarkable crescendo in the last months of 1923 and the first half of 1924. The banks charged a combination of 20 per cent interest and provision at the beginning of 1924, 26–36 per cent at the end of March, and 44–53 per cent at the end of June, before diminishing to 32 per cent in July and 18 per cent in September. The extraordinary charges in the spring were a response to Schacht's decision to insure the Rentenmark against inflation by imposing his famous restrictions on credit in the first week of April, and the Reichsbank apparently felt that the banks were taking advantage of the situation by charging what the traffic would bear. The interest rates being charged were for daily money, since the banks were refusing to grant credit lines until about October 1924 because of the uncertainty of the situation.[171]

During the early part of 1924, bank customers did more than complain. The anti-profiteering laws of the war and inflation period, which had been used primarily to harass retailers, had been extended to services during the hyperinflation, and there were a number of citations against bankers and even arrests for profiteering by authorities responding to complaints of angry would-be borrowers. The Berlin bankers were spared such ignominious treatment, but their branches suffered from these developments and the entire banking industry was under severe attack. Furthermore, there was some movement to use the recently passed Law Against the Misuse of Economic Power – the anti-cartel law – against the banks. The response of the banks, then and later, was that most of the complaints came from those who had received easy credit throughout the inflation, who had taken advantage of the easy credit conditions created by depreciation, and who were now angry that they could no longer have easy access to credit. The costs of the banks had increased enormously, which was easily demonstrable given the enormous increase of employees at the height of the inflation, their unprofitable service for government taxation and exchange control requirements, and their preoccupation with the endless zeros of hyperinflation. The return on stock market transactions, capital increases and loans themselves had deteriorated. Thus, the banks argued, both general conditions and the specific difficulties of the banks justified the extraordinary interest rates they were forced to charge.[172]

While the banks and the organizations representing them won their cases in court, one has the sense that they lost them in public opinion, especially since interest rates, particularly for small and medium-sized business, remained a bone of contention during the coming years. It is significant that the banks still felt it necessary to defend their interest rates of 1923–24 at the banking investigation of 1933, and there can be no question that the episode did much to fuel the radical right-wing war against 'interest slavery'.[173] Nor was the popular image of the banks helped by the fact that they denied all responsibility for losses by customers as a result of faulty service and delays, claiming as an excuse the chaos of the inflation and inexperienced personnel.[174]

Most important from the standpoint of the political image of the Deutsche Bank and the other banks was their opposition to any revaluation of debts in the face of court decisions that the expropriation of creditors through depreciation was a violation of equity and good faith. In alliance with the government, industry and commerce, the banks argued that it was impossible to undo the inflation, that the revaluation of debts would create a legal nightmare, and that the obligation to pay back domestic debtors and the foreign debtors who had speculated on the mark would make stabilization impossible and destroy Germany's ability to gain foreign credits.

Ironically, Germany's future credit depended on a refusal to compensate the creditors of the past. The limited revaluation of mortgage debts and industrial bonds which finally won out did impose considerable labour on the banks, but the creditors felt cheated and betrayed. Bank depositors regularly complained that their small paper mark accounts had been closed down, and initially many seem to have maintained hopes of revaluation. When the Deutsche Bank and other banks rejected such claims with a standardized argument that they had had every opportunity to remove their funds as depreciation progressed, and that the failure to do so was their own fault, it undoubtedly further tainted the banks as parties to the ruthless victimization of the creditors that characterized the inflation and stabilization.[175]

The Deutsche Bank had good arguments on its side, however, when it pointed out to such customers that the banks had also been compelled to accept payment of debts in worthless currency, and that they could not speculate with their customers' money by placing it in valorized accounts without permission. Indeed, the fundamental claim of the banks was that they were victims rather than winners in the inflation, that, if one excepted buildings and equipment, they could not flee into real values and sell abroad for foreign exchange in the manner of industry, and that their costs stood in disproportion to their gains.

The banks *were* severely weakened by war and inflation and constituted the most visible example of Germany's loss of capital. It is significant that they were extremely reluctant to establish gold balances, as required by the government decree of 28 December 1923, and sought to do so as slowly as possible. The trouble was that they were damned if they did and damned if they did not, as demonstrated by the ruminations in their Central Association: 'There was a discussion as to whether it would not be appropriate to have exceptions made for the banking industry, and it was proposed that the banking industry be relieved of the obligation to establish a gold balance by decree. The argument raised against this was that under certain circumstances the credit-worthiness of the German banks abroad could suffer, since one could draw the conclusion that the German banks intended to be silent about their true credit status. There was unity as to the desirability of having the drawing up of balances put off as long as possible especially for the banks so that they could be in a position to evaluate their assets ...'[176]

When the gold balances of the banks finally appeared in 1924, they presented a grim picture. The capital stock and reserves of the banks had dropped from 7.1 billion marks in 1913 to 1.9 billion RM in 1924, and the ratio of stock and reserves relative to deposits had been reduced significantly, from pre-war levels of 1:3.5 to post-inflation levels of 1:15. While the gold mark opening balances were inevitably compared with those of 1913, the comparison did not in fact make much sense since the bases of comparison had shifted radically. What really counted was the extent to which the banks had watered their stock and their fusions with provincial banks. The more they had watered their stock, the more likely it was that some residual substance would be acquired in place of what had been lost. Fusions and acquisitions also served such compensatory purposes.

The Deutsche Bank calculated that the great Berlin banks had lost approximately 30 per cent of their capital and 40 per cent of their reserves as a result of the inflation. In the case of the Deutsche Bank, it opened with 150 million marks in capital and 50 million in reserves, officially a 25 per cent reduction of capital and a 43 per cent reduction of reserves from 1913. The bank had also taken the 40 million Reichsmark in shares from its last capital share increase, which had been turned over to the Deutsche Treuhand-Gesellschaft, and placed them with a foreign consortium headed by the London banking house of J. Henry Schröder & Co., in the expectation that the shares could be marketed in London and, when possible, in New York. The participation of the New York firm of Speyer & Co. made that market seem very promising. Ultimately, thanks to improved conditions on the German market, the shares could be offered for old Deutsche Bank shares at a rate of three to one in 1926.

Thus, the Deutsche Bank emerged from the turbulence, and its losses at home and abroad because of war and inflation, still an attractive investment and a great bank. Significantly, however, it was no longer at the top of German corporations in capital and reserves, but stood ninth behind eight industrial corporations. When one compared the gold mark opening balances of the banks and the great industrial concerns, it was clear that industry's capacity to pay off its debts in depreciating currency, to flee into real values and to hoard foreign exchange had left it in a far stronger position than the banks. More importantly, this changed status reflected what Reich Economics Minister Neuhaus described before the Bankers' Congress in September 1925 as a pushing back of the influence of the banks on industry, and even a penetration of industrial capital into banking through the establishment of concern-owned banks and the taking over of old private banks by industry. It almost seemed as if the great age of the German universal banks had come to an end.[177]

III. The Deutsche Bank and the Perilous Recovery 1924–1929

1. Self-assertion and retrenchment

Neuhaus did not really believe that the dominance of the universal banks was over, and he went on to point out that the 'page had turned again' since the stabilization and that 'industry and banking are more dependent on the help of the banks than ever before'.[178] These remarks were to prove something of a prelude to the keynote speech of the next day by Oscar Wassermann of the Deutsche Bank on preconditions necessary for the private banks to fulfil their general economic tasks.

When Wassermann stepped up to the podium, he had already been serving for over a year as Spokesman of the Deutsche Bank. His predecessor Mankiewitz had retired at the end of 1923 because of ill health, and unexpectedly died in June 1924, a manifest victim of the strains about which he had complained so much. Elkan Heinemann, who had been chiefly concerned with the bank's international operations, had withdrawn into private life in 1924 for health reasons. Apparently, it was not felt necessary to provide more than one replacement on the board of managing directors, and Selmar Fehr, who had risen through the ranks in the Berlin headquarters, was chosen.

Among the men who now emerged at the forefront of the bank, three stand out as its most prominent and dynamic leaders, Oscar Schlitter, Georg von Stauss and Oscar Wassermann. Of these, Schlitter was probably the most powerful and influential, not only because of his long and close relationships with the mighty industrial leaders of the West, but also because his winning temperament and negotiating skills endowed him with natural authority.[179] Stauss, like Schlitter, sat on numerous industrial supervisory boards, but through some combination of natural inclination and the trajectory of his career, he found himself sailing the uncharted seas of new industries and risky ventures. More than any other managing director, he pointed towards the future, but he did so without any clear vision of what it would be and, as shall be shown, was more likely to present problems than find solutions.

Wassermann, in contrast to both of these colleagues, had been born into the banking business. He came from a well-established and distinguished Bamberg Jewish banking family, and had been brought into the Deutsche Bank from a very successful career in private banking by Mankiewitz. While he had carved out important specialities for himself in the areas of mortgage banking and the potash and shipping industries, and played a significant role in cultivating the bank's international connections, Wassermann sat on relatively few supervisory boards. He increasingly devoted himself to representing the bank on broad economic and financial issues and, as has been shown, regularly advised the government. He served as a member of the General Council of the reconstituted Reichsbank. Wassermann was viewed, and apparently viewed himself, as the 'brains' of the Deutsche Bank, and was its natural intellectual leader. He was without doubt a complicated person. A very assimilated and patriotic German Jew who at the same time was deeply supportive of the Zionist cause, a major public figure who nevertheless remained personally distant and kept his own counsel, Wassermann sought to be the embodiment of the grand traditions of German banking. As he told the 1925 assemblage, speculation had a genuine economic function, but it was not the function of the banker to speculate, since 'he who speculates necessarily thinks subjectively, but the banker should always remain objective and cool'.[180] The passion for rationality and objectivity is, of course, itself a passion, and perhaps it provides a clue to the surprising and somewhat controversial decisions that Wassermann was to take in the last years of his career.

Wassermann's speech of 1925, however, was a predictably well-formulated presentation of the predictable views of a great Berlin banker at that juncture in the Weimar Republic's history, and it bespoke the experience and role of the Deutsche Bank as well. The position of the banks *vis-à-vis* industry did indeed appear very much strengthened by post-inflation conditions. The influx of foreign capital in the second half of 1924 and the return of reasonably normal conditions had led to a recovery which lasted until the summer of 1925. At that time, there was a temporary hiatus in the influx of American loans, a tightening of credit conditions by the Reichsbank and the banks, and the news that the Stinnes concern, which was being managed by his heirs following his death in April 1924, was in a state of collapse and liquidation by a consortium of the major banks. These were all signposts on the way to the severe 'stabilization crisis' that was to hit Germany in the autumn of 1925 and last until the spring of 1926. Wassermann thus spoke on the verge of this crisis when it was already clear that credit conditions were tightening and dependence on the banks seemed increasingly unavoidable for both the great and the small.

Wassermann addressed this question very directly: 'One speaks a great deal nowadays of a power struggle between the banks and industry in which banking has allegedly emerged the victor. That is completely misleading. The banking business does not want any struggle and seeks no victory. It does not want to be and should not be the master of industry; it is its servant. The weaker the master, the greater the influence of the servant. That is not the fault of the servant but the fault of the master.'[181] Wassermann, to be sure, admitted that the 'servant' had contributed to the weakness of the 'master' by supplying short-term credits which were then used for long-term investments, and that both had overestimated the possibilities of profits under post-inflation conditions where extremely high taxation and interest rates simply ate them up. The consequence was rising short-term indebtedness in order to maintain operations, and growing loss of confidence because of inflation-inherited irrationalities in the production process. The solution required the transformation of short-term into long-term debt wherever possible, a reduced tax burden, and increased concentration and rationalization in order to reduce the costs of production.

The banks could no longer make the mistake, according to Wassermann, of richly providing credit while failing to control its distribution. Banks not only had a responsibility to direct credit to where it would be most beneficial for the entire economy and to procure sufficient security for the credits which they lent either directly or as an intermediary; the banker had also 'to control where and how the money is used. The recipient of credit is not always inclined to make the necessary distinction between the necessary, the important, and the desirable, and the banker must therefore do so. He must take coresponsibility.' Indeed, the more Wassermann spoke, the more the 'servant' was transformed into something of an overseer: 'One will not be satisfied with the mere presentation of a more or less summarily presented balance, but will want to have a precise knowledge of the bases of the business, the circle of customers, the manner of procuring raw materials, the running contracts or guarantees, in short will have to demand that which had previously been treated as strict business secrets. The banker will thus become the most trusted confidant of the customer, a relationship between banker and customer which was common decades ago and about which neither the bankers, but even much less industry and commerce had cause to complain.'[182]

The purpose of such measures would be to increase the efficiency of the economy and produce profits that would increase the long-term capital available to industry. In Wassermann's view, rationalization had been altogether too much a slogan and too little a reality, and it was essential to begin closing down unprofitable enterprises and concentrating others. And what was true for industry was also true for the banks. He readily admitted, as did his colleagues at the Congress, that an excessive number of banks had been created during the inflation and that there was too much competition in the industry. As usual, however, the complaints were directed against the savings banks and public banks, and he called for a clearer division of labour and a higher degree of concentration, since a doubling of the number of banks over the pre-war period at a time when the available capital had been sharply reduced could only increase the costs of doing business. Nevertheless, he warned against the continued 'hostility to banks', the recurring charges that the banks were 'war profiteers, inflation profiteers and deflation beneficiaries', especially from those who identified themselves with the capitalist system. To drive the point home, and to support his passionate plea for confidence in the banks, he noted that much of the Stinnes borrowing that had got the concern into trouble had been done outside the banks, and that the consortium of banks liquidating the concern were taking no provision for their hard labours.

To the best of its abilities, the Deutsche Bank had in fact been practising what Wassermann preached since the stabilization. The bank had reduced the number of its employees from a peak of 40,000 at the height of the hyperinflation to 16,000 at the turn of 1925–26 and to 14,800 in 1926. These numbers included the banks that had been taken over in the process: the Württembergische Vereinsbank at the end of 1924, and the Essener Credit-Anstalt and the Siegener Bank, which gave up its resistance to a fusion with the Deutsche Bank, in 1925. The first two of these banks had a long-standing relationship with the Deutsche Bank, and their takeover completed a process which appeared logical, while the takeover of the Siegener Bank rounded off the Deutsche Bank's expansion into the Rhenish–Westphalian area. In the following years, there were further fusions with 'friendly banks', primarily in northern Germany, the Lübecker Privatbank in 1927 and the Hildesheimer Bank and the Osnabrücker Bank in 1928. These fusions, however, were very much conditioned by the post-inflation situation, in which these banks found it very hard to continue in the old manner because of the capital shortage, and in which fusion with the Deutsche Bank automatically meant rationalization through the shutting down or consolidation of branches, disposal of superfluous buildings and reduction of personnel. In contrast to the period of the inflation, expansion and contraction now went hand in hand.[183]

Needless to say, this was hard on relations with the bank's employees, and

while retirements were used to cut back staff – the number of directors and
higher bank officials was reduced by almost a thousand in 1924–25 – the
majority of those let go were the relatively untrained and inexperienced personnel
taken on during the inflation, primarily those who were younger and female. A
preference was shown for the retention of married employees with families, who
also tended to be more experienced and skilled and hence more expensive on all
counts. Thus, while staff had been reduced by 60 per cent, personnel costs were
only reduced by 25 per cent, and the bank complained bitterly that it was still
burdened with higher costs for less profit, and that it was forced to employ a
thousand persons to engage in the unproductive tasks connected with debt
revaluation.

The staff reduction policies of the banks bore strong resemblance to those
taken in the civil service in the stabilization, and there can be no question but
that the bank was telling the truth when it argued that its policy was, by the
lights of those times, socially motivated and carried through in collaboration
with the white-collar employee councils. At the end of 1927, 59.2 per cent of
the staff had been working for the bank more than ten years and 49.4 per cent
more than fourteen years. Some 53.3 per cent were older than thirty-five, and
58.3 per cent were married and thus entitled to household and child supplements.
The retained employees also fell within the higher pay categories, 41.7 per cent
in the highest, 43 per cent in the middle, and only 15.3 per cent in the lowest.[184]
The bank seems to have been rather scrupulous about providing a one-time
separation allowance or indemnification payment for the staff it released along
with job relocation assistance. It also appears to have paid valorized or supplemented pensions to its retirees.

Whether it was equally convincing in its defence of its on-going personnel
reductions is another question. The matter inevitably came up at every general
shareholders' meeting, where the representative of the Deutscher Bankbeamten-
Verein (German Bank Officials' Association) Fürstenberg asked when the firings
were going to stop. The bank had promised a substantial end to them in 1926,
but, as Table 1 shows, they continued through the following years, especially in
the branches, to the point where the 'Reduction Commission' in Hamburg, for
example, became known as the 'Murder Commission'.[185] The bank no less
persistently made comparisons with 1913, stressed the reduction of its business,
and emphasized the need to build up reserves for the future.

Obviously, the directors were correct about the loss of capital and reduction
of profit-making business between 1913 and 1924–29, but the gross comparison
of the numbers of employees between those years is problematic. In 1913 the
bank had 92 branches; in 1929 it had 181. The comparison of the number of
persons in the bank and in all its branches made no allowance for organizational
complexity and changing tasks and functions. It is hard to believe that an increase
of 472 persons in Berlin was excessive. Similarly, a 15.8 per cent increase in the
total staff for the entire bank suggests either remarkable success in rationalization

Paul Mankiewitz, Spokesman of the Board of Managing Directors
from 1919 to 1922 (in a painting by Max Liebermann)

Oscar Wassermann,
Spokesman of the Board of Managing Directors from 1923 to 1933

Deutsche Bank's customer hall in Frankfurt am Main in the early 1920s

The main cash office in the bank's Frankfurt am Main branch
during the inflation period (c. 1920)

Hyperinflation in 1923;
banknotes and cheques
with a face value of millions
and even billions of marks
were commonplace

A stock-trading department in the early 1930s

A view of the book-keeping department at the bank's Frankfurt am Main branch (c. 1930)

500 cleaners came early every morning to tidy up the bank's head office
(a photograph by Alfred Eisenstaedt, 1930)

The decision to merge with Disconto-Gesellschaft was taken in the large boardroom of the building in Mauerstrasse

The announcement of the merger on 26 September 1929: Chairman of the Supervisory Board Max Steinthal (*seated left*) and Spokesman of the Board of Managing Directors Oscar Wassermann (*right*); standing (*from the left*): deputy Supervisory Board Chairman Arthur von Gwinner, *Direktor* Johannes Kiehl and members of the Board of Managing Directors Werner Kehl and Emil Georg von Stauss; standing (*from the right*): Board members Oscar Schlitter, Selmar Fehr, *Direktor* Kurt Weigelt and Board member Paul Bonn

In 1929 the bank launched a large-scale advertising campaign for savings accounts and savings certificates

or a very overworked staff, or both. Even among the personnel officers of the bank there was some recognition that it was misleading and exaggerated to claim that the bank had 1,800 more employees in 1929 than it did in 1913, since a good 400 of them were technical personnel – printers, typesetters, mechanics – to whom the bank had contracted work in 1913 and whose employment by the bank constituted a saving rather than an additional expense. The same could be said for the 200 apprentices – as opposed to 13 in 1913 – being trained by the Bank in Berlin, who saved the work of at least 100 employees during their part-time training at the bank. At most, therefore, there was a real growth of 1,300 employees between 1913 and 1929.[186]

Table 1   Personnel of the Deutsche Bank
(including the banks taken over through 1928)

Date	Berlin	Branches	Total	% 1923	% 1913
31.12.13	3,824	7,624	11,448	–	100.0
Highest level, app.	10,300	29,700	40,000	100.0	349.4
31.12.23	10,278	29,201	39,479	98.7	344.9
31.12.24	–	–	20,474	51.2	178.8
31.12.25	–	–	16,240	40.6	141.9
31.12.26	4,525	10,480	15,005	37.5	131.1
31.12.27	4,568	9,771	14,339	35.8	125.3
1. 1.28	4,543	9,464	14,007*	35.0	122.4
1. 4.28	–	–	13,745	34.4	120.1
1. 7.28	–	–	13,681	34.2	119.5
1.10.28	–	–	13,537	33.8	118.2
31.12.28	4,296	9,045	13,341	33.4	116.5
1. 1.29	4,296	8,984	13,261	33.2	115.8

*13,856, if the Hildesheimer Bank is excluded; this lower number is used in the Business Report.
Source: Business Reports of the Deutsche Bank and HADB, file: Personalbestand 1927–29

The employees who did remain were not being paid very much. As Table 2 demonstrates, the only categories of employees whose salaries were higher in 1929 than in 1914 were the lowest category with ten years of service, and beginning employees in the middle range. The nominal pay of employees in the highest class was substantially lower than that of their 1914 counterparts. The cost of living in 1929 was, of course, substantially higher than in 1914. The problem was in no way denied by the leadership of the bank. As Michalowsky bluntly told the branch directors in 1926: 'The bank is well aware that the purchasing power of the income of the officials is today less than the salaries of the individual categories in the pre-war period. But circumstances are stronger than good will.'[187]

*Table 2   Monthly income of contractual employees in Berlin, 1914 and 1929
(numbers in marks (1914) and Reichsmark (1929))*

1914

Group	Employment year	Monthly income	Social contributions of the DB	Total
I	1	140.00	15.86	155.86
	10	200.00	21.50	221.50
	15	270.00	25.38	295.38
II	1	155.00	17.27	172.27
	10	275.00	25.85	300.85
	15	316.00	29.70	345.70
III	1	200.00	21.50	221.50
	10	350.00	32.90	382.90
	15	466.00	43.80	509.80

March 1929

Group	Employment year	Monthly income	Social contributions of the DB	Total
I	1	141.05	11.80	152.85
	10	215.35	17.85	233.20
	15	241.15	18.84	259.99
II	1	165.55	17.74	183.29
	10	273.00	20.06	293.06
	15	312.00	17.30	329.30
III	1	191.65	13.74	205.39
	10	338.05	17.30	355.35
	15	382.80	17.30	400.10

Source: HADB, file: Personalbestand 1927–29

Good will, such as it was, had been tempered by the increasingly formalized determination of salaries, through centralized negotiations of contracts, and state intervention, through compulsory mediation and arbitration. As a conflict over an arbitration decision at the beginning of 1925 demonstrated, the banks had the option of being 'unsocial' in their personnel policy if they felt burdened by salary demands: namely, they would be 'compelled to maintain themselves by replacing ... older employees through younger female and therefore cheaper employees. The possibility of achieving this is easily available through the very far advanced rationalization.'[188]

The bank's leadership was, if anything, even more aggressive in 1928 about complaints that its salaries were inadequate and did not reflect that bank's profits and dividends. In answering criticisms about both the salaries and the dividends, Wassermann admitted that the employees were very devoted and working very hard and that the salaries were 'nothing to go into raptures about', but claimed that the 'Deutsche Bank was not simply there to serve the shareholders, the management, and the employees but also the economy'. Not only had the bank made large profits and set aside large reserves, but it also had large credits outstanding. The reserves were an 'insurance premium' against these turning bad, since 'the German economy and the German banking world to the very least extent are not always placed on a bed of roses'.[189]

Wassermann was hardly alone in making such remarks. Goldschmidt responded to criticisms of DANAT-Bank salary policies by warning that higher salaries for bank officials would produce inflation. The fact was that the labour market situation and the attachment of bank employees to status distinctions continued to play an important role, and it was significant that the 1925 Business Report for the first time makes mention of more modern types of internal company social policy, such as the fostering of sports clubs and the offering of instructional courses for the employees. It would thus appear that an effort was being made to compensate for the potential loss of loyalty and identification with the bank, resulting from expansion and the development of collective bargaining arrangements, through the creation of leisure and educational opportunities within the confines of the bank. The bank had also stepped up its apprenticeship programme.

In September 1927 the bank replaced its rather heavy-handed *News Bulletin* with a *Monthly Journal for the Officials of the Deutsche Bank*, which was intended to 'bring alive the great organism of the Deutsche Bank'. The new publication was intended to provide important news, information about the bank's various departments and serious commentary. The first issue reported the retirement of Michalowsky, who had headed personnel, and another carried a lengthy description of the pneumatic post department, while a later issue compared the Dawes and Young Plans. Nevertheless, it also clearly had the purpose of creating a mood of *Gemeinschaft* by carrying stories, reports and pictures of the 'roaring twenties' at the Deutsche Bank – the 'Black and White Girls' at the party of the shorthand club, the banking regatta at which Frau Fehr and her daughter christened the Deutsche Bank skiffs in the competition, and the female fencers from the bank's fencing club, who provided entertainment at the ball for bank employees in November 1928. The bank hoped the ball would be the beginning of a tradition – such were the ties that were meant to bind those who laboured at the Deutsche Bank.

2. The bank and its industrial clients

Whatever one thinks of the salaries paid at the banks and such modes of compensation for them, there were good reasons for the banks to feel vulnerable. The show of strength and mood of self-assertion at the 1925 Bankers' Congress had much less depth than appeared on the surface. A good illustration is provided by the tense relations between the Deutsche Bank and one of its oldest customers, August Thyssen, following the inflation. The fencing that went on between the bank's directors and August Thyssen was obviously more private and certainly less entertaining than that of the young ladies mentioned above. But it too provided a test of whether and how old relationships were to be reconstituted where, to return to Wassermann's metaphor, strong 'masters' had become stronger and could seek out other 'servants'.

Thyssen owed the Deutsche Bank a pre-war debt of 140,000 pounds sterling, but claimed he could not pay it because of the costs of the Ruhr occupation; he went to the Reich Economic Court and had it reduced to 20,000 pounds. The Deutsche Bank resented both the loss and the manner by which it had been arranged, but became doubly resentful when it discovered that Thyssen had managed to float a twelve million dollar loan in New York, which was marketed with a prospectus that expostulated on the glorious condition of Thyssen's enterprises. The propaganda was made all the more plausible by Thyssen's gold mark opening balance and by the decision of the Reich to compensate the industrialists for their occupation costs. The bank felt cheated. Schlitter made Thyssen aware of the fact by congratulating him on his American loan and his balance, pointing out that the appearance of the gold balances of the heavy industrial firms now made it abundantly clear that 'it was above all the banks which among all the great enterprises had suffered the most serious losses', and that it was a 'requirement of business propriety' to compensate for the mistaken decision of the court.[190]

Thyssen was not a man who gave up money easily, and the bank seriously considered suing as a matter of principle, even if it meant a complete break with Thyssen and probable loss of the case anyway. Ultimately, it decided to make use of the good offices of Paul Silverberg and to appeal to August's son, Fritz Thyssen. The Director of the Düsseldorf branch, Carl Wuppermann, was also mobilized. Finally, in July 1926, Fritz Thyssen settled the matter by giving the bank shares in the United Steel Works at a low price, a matter which they had to keep secret from Thyssen's other partners in the gigantic steel trust.[191] It was an unsavoury end to an unsavoury situation, but Wuppermann accurately spelled out the logic of the situation months before: 'It would be good if the matter is settled in some way, for the Deutsche Bank must over the long run once again gain a connection with this mighty factor in our Ruhr industry. A leadership of the Thyssen Works that judges things objectively will also not easily renounce the advice and collaboration of the Deutsche Bank despite the American loan.'[192]

Not only did the great banks have to come to terms with the autonomy of financially healthy giants of the Ruhr like August and Fritz Thyssen, but they were also unable to prevent the sons of fallen giants like Hugo Stinnes, Jr from escaping the hold which the Standstill Banking Consortium, headed in this case by the DANAT-Bank, had on his enterprises by raising a large loan in the United States in 1926. Thanks to this 25 million dollar 'liberation loan', as one journal called it, he was able to free himself of the bank consortium. Indeed, in 1933 the Deutsche Bank – and Schlitter himself on his own personal account – held $263,000 in Stinnes bonds.[193]

It was one thing to hold bonds and stocks, and to service great enterprises, another to exercise the kind of influence over their formation and activities to which Wassermann alluded in his speech to the Bankers' Congress. Certainly the banks were in no position to do so with a great trust like the United Steel Works (Vestag), which was set up in 1926 out of Stinnes' old Deutsch–Luxemburg concern, Thyssen, Rheinstahl and Phoenix, and whose chief manager was the very influential Albert Vögler. The new concern intended to seek a large credit in the United States, but turned to the D-Banks and a variety of smaller banks for a credit of 120 million marks to bridge the period before getting the American loan. Each of the four D-Banks was to have a 15 per cent share in the project, an obviously attractive one given the business that such a mammoth corporation could offer. In fact, the amount involved soon became 150 million.

The consortium sought a monopoly of Vestag's domestic business and a control over its borrowing for the life of the two-and-a- half-year loan. Managing Director Salomonsohn of the Disconto-Gesellschaft had taken the lead in the matter, and his bank claimed the right to lead the consortium permanently, a pretension which was rejected by Goldschmidt as well as the other two D-Banks. In this instance, the stakes seemed too high for the banks to get bogged down in their traditional rivalries, and an agreement was made to rotate leadership with the Disconto-Gesellschaft starting off the process. Salomonsohn agreed to this compromise 'in the interest of a unified posture by the banks at the founding of an enterprise so significant for the economy'.[194]

The leaders of the Vestag, however, were at once anxious to get even more credit and very disinclined to accept control over their quest for financing. An agreement was finally reached in May 1926, but the Vestag never used any of the loan – 22.5 million marks in the case of the Deutsche Bank – because it managed to get on with a 100 million mark loan it had taken previously from the Reichsbank and was able to secure a large loan in the United States by the autumn of 1927. The banks clearly needed and wanted Vestag more than it wanted them. The Deutsche Bank did play a major role in working out the complex relationship between the major machine construction firm, the Deutsche Maschinenbau Gesellschaft (DEMAG) and Vestag, and the four D-Banks did important business with Vestag and rotated the chairmanship on its supervisory board. In this relationship, however, it was Vestag and its powerful leaders, especially Albert Vögler, who were the masters.

There were, of course, plenty of firms which wanted the Deutsche Bank's money and, to the considerable chagrin of its leaders, were often undeservedly getting it or getting it on terms that its managing directors in Berlin considered too generous. Thus, when the branch directors met in March 1926, Michalowsky, seconded by other colleagues from the board of managing directors, sharply reprimanded them for their alleged generosity at the bank's expense. Bad loans would not have been made if the branches 'had paid more attention to the advice and warnings of the main office'. The branches were exhibiting a 'dangerous independence'. He threatened to have the Auditing Committee issue a report on these unauthorized actions so that the supervisory board would see 'how difficult life is being made for us', and to set up accounts that would charge the costs against the branches. The basic charge was that local and personal considerations were dominating over sound financial decision making: 'An unwarranted consideration is very often shown for the clients, which leads to a situation in which to some degree the client sets the conditions under which he takes the credit, instead of the reverse in which the bank sets the terms for the granting of the money.'

Michalowsky viewed much of this as a legacy of the inflation and the loss of any sense of what numbers meant as well as a provincialism that lost sense of the well-being of the bank as a whole. He warned against an 'unnecessary squandering of resources' and cautioned against companies that liked to get many small credits from many banks. He placed special emphasis on the need for solid security for loans, while both he and Schlitter urged treating the statements of would-be borrowers with the greatest mistrust. Finally, they advised against becoming personally obligated by accepting supervisory board positions. Stauss emphasized 'the dangers which supervisory board positions bring with them and warned that caution be used'.[195]

Stauss was to become a stellar demonstration of this point, and he already knew whereof he spoke thanks to Ufa. Germany's greatest film company certainly holds an honoured place in the history of Weimar culture, especially during its early, most experimental and creative years, but for the Deutsche Bank Ufa sucked money the way Murnau's Nosferatu sucked blood. The bank had taken over the government's 30 per cent share in the company in 1919, and Ufa was thus cut loose from the comfortable moorings of government subvention and involvement. While the company was extraordinarily active and underwent a remarkable period of growth during the inflation, it was more prone than most business enterprises to suffer from the financial opaqueness of that chaotic period. Stauss found the entire situation terribly worrisome: 'In truth Ufa has also meant for me an uncommon amount of work and care. Quite aside from the unfamiliar nature of the entire area, this is primarily because neither the financial endowment nor the internal organizational structure has kept pace with the rapid development of this far-spread and complicated enterprise at home and abroad. Above all, the absence of reliable human material in the industry as measured by the demands of orderly business management has produced particular difficulties.'[196]

These problems were compounded by obligations payable in foreign exchange, municipal efforts to communalize theatres and, most irritating of all in view of the government's promise to nurture the industry even as it withdrew its participation, the heavy entertainment tax levied on cinemagoers. Lastly, while Ufa was Europe's largest film company thanks to its fusions with some of its more important competitors and its expansionist policies, it was clearly no match for the American companies which benefited from an immense market, seemingly endless sums of money, a large reservoir of well-paid talent and great experience. To succeed, Ufa had to come to terms with the Americans and to offer its theatres for the showing of American films in return for the opportunity to market some of its own products in the United States.

The agreements were almost always on terms that favoured that cinematic superpower. It was hard to compete with Charlie Chaplin or Harold Lloyd, and while Pola Negri was a great hit in Lubitsch's *Madame Dubary*, and Murnau's *Der Letzte Mann* was much praised by American critics, it was hard to get the American public enthused about *Fridericus Rex* so soon after the war or, in contrast to the wildly enthusiastic French, to engage their interest with the heroes and villains of Fritz Lang's *Nibelungen* when those of the Wild West were both more appetizing and familiar. Lang understood this and, in a lengthy memorandum on his experiences in America, sought to explain to Stauss that historically young America's Siegfried was the gun-slinging sheriff and that the cowboy film was the American epic. Germans could not compete with Americans on their own cultural terrain for a long time to come, but Lang claimed that Germans could learn from American production and advertising techniques to produce and market more films at lower cost for a mass European market.[197]

After 1924, however, the financial 'sheriffs' of Ufa, Stauss and Kiehl, were having immense problems with this way of doing business in general, and with Lang and his fellow prima donnas at Ufa in particular. In anticipation of a growing market, the company had launched an extensive programme after the stabilization only to face a world-wide overproduction of films. Cutting back, however, was a dangerous business, as Kiehl reported to Stauss, since it would not only hurt future profits from the production in process, but would also create a situation 'in which the reputation of Ufa at home and abroad will be shaken, especially in this business, where everything is known right away and where aura and illusion are mighty powers'.[198]

Both Stauss and Kiehl agreed that the only relief, aside from borrowing money in the United States or Britain, could come from reducing costs and stopping the overruns on production. Here, Fritz Lang's *Metropolis* went unchallenged in exceeding every cost estimate. Stauss pleaded with him to cut down the size of sets and the number of scenes in December 1925, and was even more frantic in September 1926, pointing out that costs were now triple the size of the estimates and that he was having to seek money in America because none was available on the scale necessary in Germany. Lang's ego, however, had grown with his sets. He had stayed with the project and had not accepted other attractive offers, he informed Stauss, 'exclusively out of a sense of responsibility for the German film, which now with respect to the artistic side lies upon my shoulders alone'. He assured Stauss that *Metropolis* would soon be finished and claimed 'that I can say without praising myself, not only that Ufa will do itself the highest honour in the entire world with this film, but also that the capital invested in it will be won back with interest and interest upon interest'.[199]

In the meantime, both the capital and the interest to be won back continued to grow and the problems of Ufa were the subject of regular and embarrassing press commentary. In May 1926, Ufa had taken an American mortgage of 4 million dollars in anticipation that it could cover its debts and pay a dividend. The production director had promised Stauss that costs of the films would not exceed estimates by more than 10 per cent. Instead, an estimated 9 million dollars in costs turned into 22 million thanks to Lang and his fellow directors. The distribution director had estimated revenues of 45 million marks and took in only 15 million. Stauss believed that the estimates were honest, and that the miscalculations were the result of the grandiose sets, the excessive pay for stars and directors, low public purchasing power and the entertainment tax. Nevertheless, the Deutsche Bank held 40 million in Ufa debts and its enthusiasm for the movie business had been substantially reduced.

The dubious joys of reorganizing Ufa would be left to others. Ufa had already taken an American loan in 1926 and there were rumours that American interests would take a commanding share in the company. The Reich government actually considered taking an interest in the company once again to prevent its foreignization, and it did lower the entertainment tax substantially. However, the Finance Ministry objected to further investment and, when the German publishing firm of Scherl bought up a controlling influence in Ufa in April 1927, a Reich investment also became politically impossible.

Scherl was ruled by Alfred Hugenberg and managed by Ludwig Klitzsch, who now became General Director of Ufa. The men of the Lichtbild-Gesellschaft had thus won out after all. The Ruhr industrialist Otto Wolff, who had close relations with the Deutsche Bank, also provided some of the necessary funds. The Deutsche Bank engagement in Ufa was reduced to 3–4 million marks, and Stauss continued to sit on the supervisory board, but it was a very new entity with Hugenberg as chairman and with important industrialists replacing the bank representatives and the Norddeutscher Lloyd – Fritz Thyssen, Otto Wolff, Paul Silverberg and Friedrich Arthur Freundt, who was Vögler's right-hand man at the Vestag.[200]

The Ufa fiasco and the manifest mismanagement which had led to the reorganization of 1927 reflected badly on both Stauss and the Deutsche Bank. While it was a remarkable exercise of the authority of the bank that its balances showed no trace of the losses incurred, while the Ufa shares showed up as an asset, the fact that Stauss had allowed Ufa to continue to pay dividends and had issued optimistic reports under his signature was viewed as the pursuit of a dubious prestige policy in defiance of realities. This, in turn, raised questions about the organization of the bank and the effectiveness of the collegial principle on which the organization of the board of managing directors was based. As Felix Pinner of the *Berliner Tageblatt* argued, while a presidial system had the disadvantage of creating headstrong leaders who might suppress individual initiative, the collegial system had the drawback of fostering compartmentalization into fiefdoms protected by practices of 'unconditional collegiality', thus creating the danger 'of placing consideration of persons above consideration of the issue at hand'. This was, of course, a sharp criticism of Stauss: 'It was just the Deutsche Bank which earlier had the reputation of being a good school for managers. Siemens, its brilliant founder, trained Helfferich; Steinthal trained Mankiewitz; Herr von Gwinner trained Herr von Stauss. But of the qualities which Gwinner possessed, he could only provide Stauss at the most a certain skill in financial diplomacy. The capacity for large-scale industrialization which should never be lacking in the head of a consortial operation of a first-class bank is something that Herr Stauss has never possessed or acquired.'

Pinner pointed out that this was demonstrated not only by the Ufa affair, but also by the DPAG, which had 'vegetated' while the DEAG had moved into petrochemicals in a creative fashion. Similarly, it was reflected in the problems of the Daimler company, whose financial difficulties and situation had also proven problematic. While Stauss was attacked for representing the 'school of vanity' rather than the 'school of wisdom', for Pinner the problem was less Stauss than the leadership of the bank: 'In any case, it lacks the strong hand needed to prevent the unfavourable consequences or to control them with the appropriate barriers. Oskar Wassermann certainly is one of the finest minds and most upright persons in the German world of banking. But he had also lacked the strong hand (or he did not wish to use it, because he is not a man who can bring himself to do something that has the appearance of brutality unless there is an absolute necessity). Perhaps for him also the collegial system has become too much a system of collegiality.'[201]

The Ufa problem was by no means the last or even the worst problem Stauss was to present to the bank, but it is all too easy to personalize these developments and overlook the substantive problems involved for both Stauss and the bank. The men who replaced Stauss, Hugenberg and Klitzsch were in the communications business and had political agendas to which they devoted a great deal more of their time than did Stauss. Whether Wassermann or Schlitter would have had an easier time dealing with the difficult personalities and unique problems of the movie industry is doubtful, although they might have spent less money and got out more quickly. When Wassermann defended the bank's handling of Ufa at the General Meeting in 1927, he pointed out that it was a 'national prestige question'[202] as well as an economic question, and that a ruthless calling in of credits would have saved relatively little in comparison to the damage it would have wrought. Manifestly, the bank had entered the business because the government had asked it to do so, and then the government had abandoned Ufa leaving the Deutsche Bank with the responsibility. From a historical perspective, yet another argument can be made in partial exculpation of all involved: namely, that the German economy was too weak, its resources too limited and its domestic market too small to compete with the Americans and sustain such a massive effort in a new and very expensive field. From this perspective, the degree of concentration achieved by Ufa and its international and domestic impact are quite remarkable. Long-term success, however, depended on government sustenance, and the Weimar regime, unlike its successor, was not in the business of controlling information and entertainment.

There were real parallels between the problems of Ufa and that of the other expensive engagement which Wassermann had to defend at the 1927 shareholders' meeting, where Stauss also had the dubious distinction of being the supervisory board chairman in charge, the large credits given to the Daimler-Benz corporation. The automobile industry was also a new industry which had been – and to a considerable extent remained – divided up among competing companies, suffered from extremely high costs for relatively low production, needed to reach a mass market, and competed with the land of mass production and mass markets, the United States. Just as the film industry complained about high entertainment taxes and asked for government co-operation in setting the contingent of foreign films allowed into the country, so the automobile industry complained about high taxes on cars and an insufficient steadily decreasing 'educational' tariff that left the German industry helpless before its giant competitor. Finally, the public followed the affairs of the automobile industry with the same kind of attentiveness with which it followed the movie industry. 'Automobilization' and motorization were more or less understood to be the great wave of the future for both manufacturing and consumption. Wassermann made no apologies that the Daimler-Benz concern had as much as 35 million marks in credits, of which the Deutsche Bank held some 19 million at the high point, but which had then been reduced to 4 million by December 1926. In fact, he pointed out that the company actually had a positive cash balance with the bank, and the Deutsche Bank was proud that it had helped this 'healthy company' back on to its feet.

The Deutsche Bank had become involved in the affairs of the Daimler and Benz companies shortly after the war through its befriended banks in south-west Germany, the Rheinische Creditbank, which worked with Benz, and the Württembergische Vereinsbank, which dealt with Daimler. While there was much talk of the need to merge the two companies during the inflation, the idea was resisted by Daimler, which was otherwise under very weak leadership, and by von Kaulla of the Württembergische Vereinsbank. The chief proponent of a fusion was Dr Jahr of the Rheinische Creditbank. In 1920 Jahr went so far as to urge Michalowsky and Stauss, both of whom sat on the Benz supervisory board, to withhold credits from Daimler and refuse to participate in a capital share increase for Daimler until it came to terms, a proposal which the Deutsche Bank, having only a small engagement in any case, rejected out of consideration for Kaulla.

The end of the inflation and the fusion with the Württembergische Vereinsbank, which led to Stauss's assumption of the chairmanship of the Daimler supervisory board, changed the Deutsche Bank's role as well as the situation more generally. As Jahr argued in an important memorandum of January 1924, the wartime expansion and inflationary situation had created capacity that could not be used under normal conditions and especially not in an environment of heavy taxation and foreign competition. Rationalization and price reduction were essential, especially in a case like Daimler and Benz, which were the best firms in the business, accounted for 30 per cent of German automobile production, and often competed against one another with similar models. While the ideal solution was fusion, Jahr recognized that this would cause social unrest under the bad conditions of 1924 and that the government might forbid plant shutdowns in the industry for this reason. He thus argued for a community of interest in which there would be consolidation of certain aspects of production and marketing.[203] An added complication was created by the interests of Viennese businessman Jacob Schapiro, the head of the automobile marketing firm of Schebera, who bought up 45 per cent of Benz's shares and 42 per cent of Daimler's in 1922, and apparently had grand ambitions for himself in the German automobile industry.[204]

The community of interest formed in May 1924 did not solve the complicated problems either of production or of ownership, while economic conditions demanded more thoroughgoing measures that culminated in a fusion in the summer of 1926. An increase in the share capital had the effect of reducing Schapiro's role, although he seems to have made considerable difficulty for the Deutsche Bank leadership, while the appointment of Wilhelm Kissel as General Director of Daimler-Benz promised a much more effective and dynamic management for the company and a serious reduction of the debts which Wassermann defended in April 1927, but which inevitably disquieted any sensible banker.

Indeed, the worries only intensified during the coming two years, and it cannot be said that Jahr and von Stauss took their oversight functions lightly. In late August 1928, for example, Jahr complained that the financial return on each worker was only 6,000–8,000 RM when it had to be 10,000–12,000 RM if there was to be a profit. In his view, this proved that there were too many workers at the plant and that his call for a more 'elastic' labour force needed to be implemented. He understood that the concern's directors were reluctant to carry out such strictures 'since worker dismissals, even in not very large numbers, are always connected with great inconvenience'.[205]

A month later, Stauss bore down on Kissel for insufficient quality control and the inadequacies of his sales organization. There was clear evidence that Daimler-Benz's competition was doing better than it was, and the reason was 'the complete disappearance of your reputation through the catastrophic failures of your passenger and truck models'. Stauss made it plain that the bank was getting impatient 'after the bitter experiences of the past three years', and 'sacrifices made in view of your promises of a period of improvement that you would bring about through new models and a faultless programme'. Once again, the bank was ready to help, but Stauss expected Kissel 'to take the bull by the horns in the future without consideration for individual persons in your circle whose activity runs against the common interest'. At the same time, Stauss urged Kissel to cultivate and assist their sales representatives, who had more or less to surrender to the dictation of their customers in the first negotiation 'so that in the second, the competition, which knows the fearful condition of our constructions ... does not take advantage of the situation to your and our own disadvantage'.[206] To help Kissel get matters in hand, Stauss personally ordered the employment of a noted efficiency expert, Otto Max Müller, to survey the organization and labour methods of the plants. Müller's presence caused tremendous anxiety among the workers – and one suspects a considerable amount among the managers as well – but as Stauss told the head of the Daimler-Benz factory council, 'in view of the threatened situation of the German automobile industry no way should go untried through which the profitability of our plants might be improved'.[207]

The evidence suggests that Stauss and the hard-pressed managers at Daimler-Benz did a reasonably good job of driving down the company's bank debts once again.[208] But it was the general problems of the industry as much as the special problems of the company he supervised that led Stauss to tell an official inquiry into the automobile industry in March 1929 that 'The position of the banks *vis-à-vis* the automobile industry is extremely cautious; one has experienced too much. After everything that one has experienced, one cannot think ill of the banks if they are very disinclined to get involved. I am of the view that a firm like Daimler could earn more credit than it actually has ... These are false relationships which do not exist in America as they do with us, where a Ford car is ready in a day, and I have also seen the same at Citroën. Within three hours, where one sees everything in a very large-scale assembly line production, one has the impression that the material is not tied up.'[209]

The question of creating an automobile trust that could consolidate the industry and produce small cars for a large body of consumers in the American manner had been under discussion since the stabilization. Stauss himself had hoped the Daimler-Benz fusion could have also included Magirus and paved the way for a trust. It was essential for such a trust to include one or more of the truly effective producers of small cars in Germany: that is, the Opel firm in Rüsselheim or the Bayerische Motoren Werke (BMW) which had taken over the 'Dixi' company. The dilemma was that there were too many companies and too many players interested in having a hand in such trustification. These included some adventurous types like Schapiro and the Italo-Austrian speculator Camillo Castiglioni, who played an important role in the creation of BMW, but also Otto Wolff, who had important French connections and wanted to create a European trust to combat the Americans, and last but surely not least Jakob Goldschmidt of the DANAT-Bank, who had an interest in Adler, Hansa-Lloyd and the Nationale Automobil-AG (NAG), and who was desperate to play the leading role in such a trust if he could only find a way of doing so.

On 11 July 1928, Goldschmidt visited Wassermann to discuss the automobile trust question. He began by complaining that overtures he had made to Stauss and Jahr had gone without reply, but Wassermann suspected that Goldschmidt had never placed his real cards on the table, and Wassermann accused Goldschmidt of intending to seize the leadership in the matter. As Wassermann described the testy discussion: 'He answered to that, "only the co-leadership", and to my question, "in alphabetical order", no, the Deutsche Bank at the lead. I countered to this that the Deutsche Bank unfortunately cannot say a special thanks for this friendly concession, since it can quite rightfully claim the leadership in a transaction in which Daimler-Benz is involved or even stands at the centre after all it has done for Daimler-Benz in the past and after it had brought the Daimler-Benz fusion into existence through years of effort.'[210]

Actually, both bankers were in a state of some paralysis. Goldschmidt was thinking of an arrangement between BMW and Daimler-Benz, and hoped to use his option on Schapiro's Daimler shares for this purpose. Wassermann was hoping for an arrangement with Opel, which would have meant involving the Disconto-Gesellschaft, which was Opel's chief banking connection, and would have led to its making the kind of leadership demand that Goldschmidt had raised. As Wassermann noted, such a demand would have made things 'formally more complicated than they are now, but naturally objectively much better'. Opel, however, while known to be interested in a connection, was not responding, and this involved the danger of leaving Goldschmidt high and dry in his efforts to play the great role in creating the automobile trust which he had apparently been talking about in public. Wassermann recognized that making an enemy of Goldschmidt was 'something that we will feel in many areas' and that 'it is self-evident that he will have the public on his side if he presents the matter as being one in which his "brilliant" plans, "so useful for the economy", were defeated by the lack of understanding or the stubbornness of the Deutsche Bank'.

Actually, both the Deutsche Bank and the DANAT-Bank were being defeated by the independence of the real prize in the automobile industry, Opel. Goldschmidt had approached Opel in the spring of 1928 with a variety of proposals for mergers with other automobile companies, and with the suggestion that Opel

would benefit from a relationship with the DANAT-Bank. Fritz von Opel saw
no gain from the mergers since they were likely to create a confused and
overblown enterprise which, if it got into difficulties, would end up hurting the
economy in the manner of the Stinnes concern. He was not only quite satisfied
to deal with the Disconto-Gesellschaft alone, but also highly critical of Goldschmidt's 'tendencies': 'The firm of Adam Opel sees the foundation of its rise in
that it has, while practising the most extreme frugality, kept its concentration
on production. It absolutely rejects financial transactions, fusions and similar
things, as they are proposed by Herr Jakob Goldschmidt, because middleman's
profits are certainly attainable by the banks through them, but the actual
production and the unity of their plants are harmed.'[211]

Whether Wassermann was more agreeable to the Opel family is hard to say,
but there is good evidence that it found a union with Daimler quite unattractive
and that Wassermann was hoping for the impossible. Castiglioni had also hoped
for some combination involving Daimler and Opel, and had indeed bought a
large amount of Daimler stock in the expectation of getting a major position on
the Daimler supervisory board. Unhappily, he soon came to the conclusion that
Opel had no interest in 'going together with the sick Daimler works and becoming
infected by them'.[212] Castiglioni, like Goldschmidt, was left holding a large
number of Daimler shares, with the difference that Castiglioni ended up having
to mortgage them because of personal financial troubles and was soon to be
driven out of BMW as well.

The ever-inventive Goldschmidt, however, having been frustrated by Opel and
then by Wassermann, still thought he had one card left. Two weeks after his
meeting with Wassermann, he sent Geheimrat Allmers of the Hansa-Lloyd Werke
to persuade General Director Franz Josef Popp of BMW to become the leader
of an automobile trust that would not stand under the leadership of the Deutsche
Bank or Daimler-Benz. Popp had no intention of playing the pawn in a battle
between the banks and made it clear that 'so long as Herr von Stauss and Herr
Goldschmidt cannot agree over tea-time issues [*Kanapee-Fragen*], he wants
nothing to do with the matter'. Furthermore, he did not think that a 'healthy'
auto trust was possible without Opel, and he knew Opel's views.[213]

The fact was that the Opel firm had always regarded itself as the 'General
Motors' of Germany, and while the Opel brothers had made great noise about
the government's failure to protect the industry and about not buying foreign
cars, they sold 80 per cent of their shares to General Motors in the spring of
1929 at a huge profit.[214] This effectively ended serious discussion of a German
auto trust and intensified what Popp called the 'creeping crisis of the German
automobile industry'. He feared that Germany would now be outclassed in
medium-sized as well as small automobiles, and he saw no point in fusions
among the existing firms: 'The lame will not walk and the blind will not see, no
matter how many of them one brings together.'[215] He could only urge more
concentration and rationalization, although he did agree on the possibilities of

collaboration between Daimler-Benz and BMW in certain areas. Stauss, as supervisory board head of both companies, had always desired such co-operation, and Popp and Kissel sat on each other's boards of managing directors. As Stauss also knew, all was not well at BMW either: his efficiency expert Otto Max Müller had discovered a variety of difficulties in the company's production of aeroplane engines and motorcycles, and there were serious difficulties in the way the company priced and marketed its products.[216] In any case, the dilemma was finding modes for the two car producers under Stauss's oversight to work together in ways that would bring profit.

Another potential type of collaboration, of course, was with European counterparts, particularly at a time when the 'Locarno spirit' had not dissipated and pan-European ideas were in the air. Indeed, the Locarno Treaty had an economic counterpart in a series of agreements among the leading heavy indus-trial firms and organizations of western Europe, and it was quite conceivable that the American penetration of the European automobile market might have produced a European response. There had indeed been some efforts along these lines. In November 1928, Director van Roggen of the Belgian Minerva company offered to buy a large number of Daimler-Benz shares and receive a seat on the supervisory board as a prelude to setting up a European holding company to organize a counterweight to the Americans. A few months later, Otto Wolff discussed the possibilities of collaboration with French car makers.

Both of these projects came to nothing, but they did bring into the open certain aspects of Daimler-Benz's involvement with the German military and the role of international politics. Thus, in the case of van Roggen, Reichswehr officials expressed alarm at the presence of a Belgian on the supervisory board because of certain secret work – most likely in violation of the armaments clauses of the Versailles Treaty – that Daimler-Benz was doing for the army. While Daimler assured the Reichswehr that provision could be made to deny van Roggen such information, and Reichswehr Minister Groener went so far as to suggest that collaboration with European producers was useful as a means of securing information about technical developments in the field, it was clear that military orders would be limited to standard types of vehicle if Daimler-Benz became part of some larger European operation. As far as the French connection, which involved the sale of French cars in Germany, is concerned, discussion never even got off the ground because Daimler-Benz did not feel it could enter into such discussions until the reparations negotiations came to a satisfactory conclusion. Unhappily, while the government could inhibit collaboration with foreign pro-ducers, it was not in a position to provide any help to Daimler-Benz. Groener stressed the desirability of keeping it in German hands, but frankly remarked that 'the financial situation of the Reich is such that he hardly believes there is a prospect of help from the Reich, even if he personally is sympathetic towards it'.[217]

In his capacity as supervisory board chairman of BMW, Director von Stauss ran into much more serious difficulties because of the involvement of Castiglioni in its affairs. BMW had important aeroplane motor and other contracts with the Reich Transportation Ministry, and there were frequent attacks on BMW in the Reichstag because of the difficult Italian.[218] Stauss did whatever he could to use his own political contacts to defend the company, and the problem was ultimately solved when Castiglioni's financial troubles and a falling-out with Popp in 1928–29 provided the banks on the BMW's supervisory board with the opportunity to force him out. The Transportation Ministry expressed great satisfaction with this outcome, but then immediately gave expression to a new alarm with regard to rumours that BMW might allow the American firm of Pratt and Whitney to take over a majority of its shares.

The ministry reminded Stauss of how difficult its plans would be for the development of aeroplane motors with a company that was in foreign hands.[219] This latest government 'inquiry' provided Stauss with a marvellous opportunity to suggest that the government might have some responsibility for the problems about which it was allegedly so concerned. He pointed out that the price of eliminating Castiglioni was that the banks were now saddled with his shares and 'that it naturally cannot be the task of the Deutsche Bank to have large batches of such shares as a permanent holding'.[220] Yet, such shares were very difficult to market domestically because potential investors were being frightened away by reductions in the airline budget. The situation would be improved by more domestic orders, but in the meantime it could only 'be viewed as an advantage that a powerful foreign corporation was showing interest in the company which unfortunately has so few places to go domestically'.

The Deutsche Bank was in fact doubly engaged in the problems of air transport. On the one hand, it was connected with the concerns making aeroplane motors. On the other hand, it was involved in the airline business. As was the case with most of the more advanced industries in Weimar Germany, the airline industry was badly split and irrationally managed after the war. For political and economic reasons, the Reich was anxious to support German airline development and subsidized it, but soon found that its money was being divided in a very irrational manner. Within the industry itself, the two leading companies prior to 1926 were the Aero Lloyd, where the Deutsche Bank was the chief stockholder and Stauss the chairman of the supervisory board, and Junkers, a major aeroplane manufacturer which was also involved in airline transportation. Stauss began pushing for a fusion of Junkers and Aero Lloyd to end the duplication of their efforts, and finally succeeded when the government took over Junkers, which was in financial difficulties, and then worked towards the creation of a single company that would bring together Junkers, Aero Lloyd and a host of local companies.

The end result was Lufthansa, which was established in March 1926, with Stauss as chairman of the supervisory board, and a mix of bankers and private interests, especially shipping, representatives of the Reich and state governments, and municipal leaders. In this last category, especially important roles were played by mayors Landmann of Frankfurt a.M. and Adenauer of Cologne. The purpose of the new company was to consolidate the domestic German lines and expand internationally. The company was to carry both freight and post, but also to expand passenger service, and it included two subsidiaries of Aero Lloyd, 'Deruluft', a joint German–Soviet Russian airline that had been set up in 1921, and the Condor Airline, which ran mail between Europe and South America and within South America. The new company was headed by three of the most experienced people in this new field, Otto Merkel, Martin Wronsky and Erhard Milch, who was later to play a major role in the building up of the *Luftwaffe*.[221]

Stauss frequently made use of his connections with Ufa to promote enthusiasm for commercial aviation, just as he used the film company to promote motorization. But the memories of Ufa's history, of a company founded by the Reich and then abandoned by it, must have been regularly revived as he dealt with the headaches of Lufthansa. If anything, the politics of Lufthansa were more complicated because of the genuine dependence on subsidization, noisy critics and sceptics who challenged the economic viability of the industry and made the most of the frequent accidents that accompanied this early period of aviation, and the weaknesses of German public finance.

It was difficult to plan without knowing what the political attitude and economic situation of the Reichstag would be, and Jakob Goldschmidt, who sat on the supervisory board, was particularly critical of Lufthansa's finances, which were based on uncertain subsidies while requiring periodic credits from the banks. Stauss seems to have been more optimistic, but he too expressed periodic and, with the passage of time, growing concern. For competitive reasons *vis-à-vis* other countries with subsidized airlines and because of the dynamics of the business itself, there was strong pressure on Lufthansa to expand its transoceanic programme and also its collaboration with the Russians in opening up service to Asia. While Goldschmidt kept on arguing that commitments should follow up the actual granting of subventions, the directors spoke optimistically of an 'equity and good faith relationship between the airlines and the Reich authorities'.[222]

That was in August 1927, but such language was inconceivable in 1929 when the Reichstag cut 9 million marks from the 19.25 million mark budget because of the growing budgetary crisis and the need to exhibit parsimony during the Young Plan negotiations. Director Weigelt of the Deutsche Bank urged Milch to point out to the Reichstag that the taxpayer investment of the previous three years was being thrown away, and bitterly complained that one could not run an enterprise like Lufthansa in the manner in which one plays an accordion. Stauss and Director Georg Solmssen of the Disconto-Gesellschaft urged an immediate cutting back of the Lufthansa programme since the company could not behave like an irresponsible bankrupt, and warned against proposals that Lufthansa try to float a loan when the Reich was unable to do so effectively.[223]

While some relief was provided, the credits owed to the banks and the Reichs-Kredit-Gesellschaft AG, which had been established for such purposes, were in excess of what could be afforded, and Stauss agreed with Goldschmidt when the latter argued that 'Lufthansa's drive to expand was much stronger than the means that were available'.[224]

It was nevertheless a bitter situation, since it was the government which had promoted the enterprise in the first place and virtually encouraged it to over-extend itself. There was, however, to be no repetition of the Ufa arrangement and Stauss bluntly informed the Transportation Ministry that 'the carrying out of the measures planned must lead to the liquidation of the German Lufthansa and that one cannot reasonably expect the private economy and private capital to go along any longer with such ill-considered things'.[225] Unfortunately, there was also some similarity with Ufa when it came to internal mismanagement, as a report by the government Austerity Commissar revealed, and Merkel was dropped to reduce costs and tighten management. There was great nervousness about losing Wronsky and Milch, and Weigelt had the feeling that not only Merkel but they would have had better careers in America since 'more and more one gains the conviction that in our small Europe with its 11,000 km of new customs borders and 38 customs areas one cannot accomplish as much practical work as in America'.[226] Indeed, the practical solution to the Lufthansa financial problem in 1929 came from America in the form of credits from the banking houses of Dillon, Read & Co. and Harris, Forbes & Co. taken through the Reichs-Kredit-Gesellschaft and the Finance Ministry.[227]

3. Credits to the USSR and credits from the USA

The problems that Ufa, Daimler-Benz, BMW and Lufthansa each in their own way exposed were the profound difficulties of nurturing the industries of the future under the conditions of the national and international political economy in which they were embedded. The Deutsche Bank stood at the forefront of efforts which, in the last analysis, were beyond its managerial capacities under the circumstances. Similarly, it played a leading role in two of the most important efforts to provide contracts for German industry and to secure the financing of the economy: the so-called Russian credits, on the one hand, and the floating of loans in the United States, on the other.

Doing business in Russia had always been difficult, but the creation of the Soviet Communist regime and general conditions compounded the problem. While Germany's defeat in the war undermined plans to exploit Russia imperi-alistically, Russia's immense problems of industrial development and need for manufactured goods made it an important potential source of raw materials and market for German industry. There was, of course, a significant political dimension to these relations with Russia as well. Since 1920, the Russian connection was important for Germany's secret rearmament, and the Treaty of

Rapallo in 1922 was the first great break in Germany's diplomatic isolation. While Germany's problems could only be solved by coming to terms with the West, the link with the Soviet Union, re-established by a commercial treaty in 1925 and the Treaty of Berlin in 1926, remained an important aspect of German diplomatic and economic policy. The fundamental problem of dealing with the Communist state economically, however, was that it demanded prepayment for its exports while it insisted on prolonged credits for its imports, and these requirements set up significant hurdles for the Germans in their efforts to engage in large-scale trade with the Soviets.

A promising start had been made by German industry in 1921–22, but the hyperinflation had ruined it. After the stabilization, the Reich Association of German Industry had set up a Russian Committee to promote and co-ordinate trade. At the same time, the Deutsche Bank took an important initiative in 1925 by setting up the Export Association East (Ausfuhrvereinigung Ost GmbH), which pulled together a group of major firms for the purpose of offering credit opportunities both to the German firms and the Soviet Trade Monopoly, while preventing the Russians from playing off the various German interests against one another. The Dresdner Bank and the Mendelssohn firm joined the consortium, which offered 20 million RM in credits that had to be paid back by 1927. Additionally, the Deutsche Bank and the Reichs-Kredit-Gesellschaft provided a 75 million RM credit to the Soviet State Bank.[228]

The last-mentioned credit is a good illustration of the complicated forces at play in the Russian credit problem. The Russian commercial delegation in Germany was actually opposed to the credit, which was to be used for consumer items to pacify the Russian peasants and persuade them to deliver their harvest. Foreign Minister Chicherin had pressed for it and argued that it would a useful German gesture at a time when the Germans were making the Locarno Treaty.[229] In the last analysis, it really was hard for the banks not to get involved with the Russian credit operation. In contrast to the Deutsche Bank, which decided to take the lead, the Disconto-Gesellschaft was quite reluctant. While the Foreign Office enthusiasts for the Russian connection expressed surprise that the German banks were not more interested and assured Director Boner of the Disconto-Gesellschaft that things had become 'completely consolidated' politically, Boner told them that the international banking world thought otherwise.[230] Reichsbank President Schacht seemed to be particularly pessimistic, telling Franz Urbig of the Disconto-Gesellschaft that the Russian government was 'a swindler' and that it was 'financially on its last legs'.[231] The Disconto-Gesellschaft leadership, however, was well aware that they could not stand aside when commerce and industry were moving at 'full sail' in the direction of discounting bills with the Russian trade delegation, and Schacht was to give in too.[232] The point was reinforced for the Disconto-Gesellschaft by a representative of the trade delegation, who made it clear that his overtures were to be kept confidential from the Deutsche Bank since the Russians considered themselves 'very closely allied with the Deutsche Bank, have always found it very co-operative and therefore count it among the favoured banks'.[233]

While there was certainly no reason for either bank to find this style of negotiation reassuring, the Deutsche Bank intended to stay in the Russian credit business and to do so as leader. This was demonstrated when Economics Minister Curtius and some industrialists proposed the creation of a special bank – in effect an extended arm of the Reichs-Kredit-Gesellschaft – to act as the intermediary between industry and the Russians in the management of a 300 million RM credit. The alleged goal was to centralize the trade with Russia and have an overview that would prevent the Russians from playing the various firms off against one another. The Reich would have a 20 per cent interest in the projected bank, while most of the money was to be provided by the private banks.

When this scheme was presented at a meeting with industry and banking leaders on 8 April 1926, Deutsche Bank Deputy Managing Director Paul Bonn, who handled the Russian credits and was to become a full member of the board of managing directors in 1928, objected to what he termed 'the socialization of an important and possibly richly promising part of the business of the banks in order to keep industry in tow'. He also could not understand what advantages industry would derive from such an institution, since 'the banks today undoubtedly discount Russian acceptance material to a greater extent than they would like to. But they do it for the important reason of not losing contact with their customers in a very significant category of their business and at the same time to advise them in this regard.' Bonn was pleased to learn that the Reichsbank was taking a more positive attitude towards the Russian credits than it had in the past, but he stressed that if the Reichsbank was going to stand behind the projected government bank in the event of a catastrophe, then it would have to stand behind them as well because of their investment. In that case, however, the private banks were likely to be more objective and careful in the granting of credits than a government bank.[234]

Bonn and his colleague from the Disconto-Gesellschaft effectively killed the government–industry plan. What emerged instead was the idea of using a banking consortium as a means of reviewing credit requests in connection with exports to Russia and keeping the government regularly informed about the status of this activity. On 16 July 1926, an Industry Finance Corporation East (IFAGO) was created with a capital of 1.5 million marks. Carl Duisberg of I.G. Farben served as Chairman and Otto Wolff as Deputy Chairman. Its task was to issue the bills after examination by an inter-ministerial committee and final decision by a rotating committee of the banking consortium headed by the Deutsche Bank. These banks discounted the bills at the Reichsbank rate plus commissions, and the Reichsbank rediscounted and prolonged the bills on the basis of special agreements. The credits were guaranteed up to 60 per cent by the Reich and the states, while the exporter could be asked to provide security for the remaining 40 per cent. Within a year, 561 applications had been granted for a total of approximately 124 million marks, while a Dutch consortium to which the banks belonged had granted another 49.4 million marks in credits. Two-thirds of the total were to run four years, the remainder for two years, and security was required for all because of the length of the credits.[235] This was to be the first of 12 such consortia between 1926 and 1939, although such constant needs for renewal had not been anticipated in 1926. From the very outset, however, it was an important and complicated business for the Deutsche Bank, which had to warn its branches to avoid discounting bills or giving special conditions to the Russians which might then be used with competing banks to gain the same advantages. Every effort was made to concentrate the Russian business in Berlin, where the bank could use its special position in the consortium for all it was worth to benefit favoured customers.[236]

While the Russian credits were to assume unanticipated significance in the years to come, what seemed most consequential during the period prior to the world economic crisis was the import of capital from the United States. The Deutsche Bank acted as an intermediary in providing and marketing American loans for companies in which it had an interest and for municipalities, but it demonstrated considerable restraint in its efforts to restore its own American contacts and reconstruct its position in the United States. This cautious role was especially evident in the extremely tricky problems involved in the liberation of German assets seized during the war and held by the Alien Property Custodian. The Deutsche Bank persistently fought against tying these assets to German obligations to the United States and was outspokenly resistant to the efforts of American lawyers, many of whom were quite shady, to prey upon Germans anxious to get some portion of their assets back on practically any terms. Most importantly, the Deutsche Bank successfully and almost single-handedly opposed schemes in 1921 by the American banker Chandler, supported by Warburg and other German bankers, and by the German industrialist Richard Merton, to use the seized German assets as security for American credits to Germany. Chandler subsequently went bankrupt and Merton became implicated in a nasty, and for the Harding administration not untypical, bribery case involving the Alien Property Custodian. As a consequence of this policy of holding out, a settlement was finally reached in early 1928 and German property-holders received 80 per cent of their holdings while the remainder was to be paid out from Dawes Loan receipts. In general, the Deutsche Bank earned a good reputation for itself in Germany and the United States for its stubborn but dignified and thoroughly honest dealings in protecting German interests in an environment that easily promoted behaviour of a different kind. Its pre-war tradition in the United States was maintained despite the fact that Germany was now a debtor rather than creditor.[237]

Of course, the Deutsche Bank did have an interest in expanding its business contacts in the United States and in encouraging a reform of the Dawes Plan that would reduce German obligations, promote stability through the establishment of a final reparations sum, and liberate Germany from some of the controls and restrictions established in 1924. In April 1927, it sent Director Blinzig to the United States to survey the situation, improve the bank's contacts, and settle some outstanding problems left over from the war. It was an extraordinarily successful trip. Blinzig could scarcely keep up with his invitations, which read like a *Who's Who* of the American banking world, and he was treated with great friendliness and sympathy. This was true even at J.P. Morgan, where he had extremely friendly conversations with Thomas Lamont and a very successful negotiation and settlement of the differences between the Deutsche Bank and Morgan concerning the Northern Pacific contract with Robert Leffingwell. Here, the path seemed to be open to an increase of business between the two banks.

Blinzig also did well in his negotiations on the return of German property and was very satisfied with the general attitude towards a revision of the Dawes Plan, although it rapidly became clear that the time was not ripe for action with a Presidential election coming up the next year and the Americans still quite unwilling to reduce the French debt so long as the franc was inflated. Wassermann was particularly attentive to Blinzig's reports on the reparations question, and while agreeing that the time was not ripe to press the issue, he urged Blinzig in telegrams that were an odd mixture of German and English to press the point that the Germans could not be expected to pay the largest part of their national savings for reparations year in and year out.[238]

There could be no question, however, that the American bankers had buried the hatchet and were anxious to do business with the Deutsche Bank. They praised the results presented in the bank's most recent Business Report. Blinzig was grateful that they paid no attention to the problems of Ufa and Daimler, and noted with interest that they were especially impressed with the great increase in the number of depositors. He felt it important to step up the competition for deposits in the light of the impression they made on the Americans. He also reported that Hugo Schmidt had helped build the Deutsche Bank's reputation both as a person and as a representative of the bank. As Blinzig noted, money was to be had in New York if one offered the right rate of interest, but Blinzig pursued the same policy as Schmidt: 'It is self-evident that I never ask for money. It should not look as if we, as do the others, run after money.'[239]

What Blinzig also learned, however, was that a price was being paid for this self-restraint which seriously limited the power and influence of the banks: 'From various sides I was asked with some bewilderment about how things have developed in such a way that the leading German banks have allowed themselves to be excluded to such a great degree from the handling of German emissions in America. The fact that the Americans have themselves gone to Europe and have made it easy for the German borrowers to circumvent the German banks is not seen to be a sufficient reason given the influence attributed to the banks on their old customers as well as on the cities and states. Just as little is the excuse accepted that the distinguished German banks do not think it correct to emerge abroad as seekers of money, even for a third party. It is certainly true that it must be the task of the banks to function as intermediaries in money matters, even if the flow of money now goes in a direction different from the one in which it went before. On various occasions I was also told that one would give preference here to the direct conclusion of loans in Germany through the intermediation of the German banks and their participation. That we could have practically any partner we wanted for such business is self-evident.'[240]

The pressure for greater aggressiveness was also felt in the realm of selling bank shares on the New York market. The State of New York had made this legal in March 1927, and Dillon, Read & Co., which did a great deal of German business, sought to impress on Blinzig the opportunity this offered the Deutsche Bank. Blinzig wondered whether the American public would really be interested, but he urged his colleagues in Berlin to take the matter seriously. He pointed out that the DANAT-Bank had recently published its Business Report in excellent English and, despite the low value of its shares, might want to take advantage of the advertising value of being the first of the German banks to have its shares on the New York exchange. Goldschmidt and the DANAT-Bank, however, were always more inclined to speculation than the Deutsche Bank, while the latter more accurately reflected the generally held view internationally that stock market speculation was a bad thing.

The spring of 1927 was not in any case a good time to float German shares abroad. On 11 May, Schacht informed the German banks that he would not discount for banks which lent excessively for the purpose of stock market speculation. On the following day, the Association of Berlin Banks and Bankers agreed to reduce Report and Lombard lending by 25 per cent before mid-June as part of a programme of undertaking a 'gradual but significant' reduction of money lent for such purposes. The so-called 'sledge-hammer' communiqué issued by the Association bearing this news triggered the 'Black Friday' collapse on the German stock market, which, appropriately enough, took place on 13 May 1927. Shares fell by 30–40 per cent.

Schacht's approach, which was designed to maintain his low 5 per cent discount rate by redistributing available capital more efficiently and discouraging further short-term foreign borrowing, was seen abroad as an effort to demonstrate the impossibility of carrying out the Dawes Plan. It also suggested that the German stock market was highly vulnerable to unpredictable interventions from on high. Combined with the recent removal of tax exemption for foreign loans in Germany, it at once reduced interest in lending to Germany while demonstrating ultimately that Germany could not go without foreign lending. Matters were not helped by Schacht's suggestion that the currency might be endangered if the situation were allowed to continue, which led to some withdrawal of foreign funds and increased currency anxiety in Germany itself.

Schacht ended up having to raise the discount rate anyway, and the dependence on short-term borrowing only increased.[241]

Schacht was highly criticized both at the time and subsequently for his action. Its unfortunate effects are undeniable, and Schacht was indeed prone to a tactic of causing explosions in order to wake people up without taking into account that the explosion might also kill them. Schacht defended himself in 1953 by pointing out that he was deeply distressed by the illiquidity of the banks and was especially alarmed when Wassermann told him that the Deutsche Bank had 2 billion RM in short-term borrowing. Schacht informed Wassermann that he had only 3 billion RM in reserves at the Reichsbank and urged that the Deutsche Bank consolidate its short-term into long-term debt. Schacht claimed that, when he discovered that similar short-term indebtedness existed among the other banks, he came to his decision to threaten to withhold credits and force such a policy on the banks. He strongly suggested that the banks had overreacted through their 'sledge-hammer' communiqué, and that it was they who had created the explosion.[242]

Schacht was certainly exaggerating what Wassermann could have told him about the Deutsche Bank's short-term debt, which was 1.6 billion RM at the end of 1926 and 1.9 billion RM at the end of 1927, and which obviously had a substantial domestic component. He was also undoubtedly underplaying his own shock tactics by emphasizing the effects of the communiqué. Nevertheless, there is good evidence that there was considerable collusion between the banks and Schacht. The Disconto-Gesellschaft had tried a similar credit restriction at the end of 1926 and had been heavily criticized. The banks were worried about their liquidity and had unsuccessfully urged Schacht to raise the discount rate earlier in 1927. What else was left? As Franz Urbig of the Disconto-Gesellschaft, who, like Wassermann, was a member of the General Council of the Reichsbank, confidentially told his colleagues, he viewed the action of the banks as a 'justified measure', and reported that 'an initiative by the Reichsbank supporting the action of the banks was present. The Reichsbank had certainly not collaborated in the formulation of the decision, but it had approved of the decision itself. Without the participation of the Reichsbank, the bringing about of a common agreement among the banks for a measure of such a type is simply unthinkable.'[243] Indeed, there is reason to believe that Goldschmidt did in fact oppose the measure, or at least its sharp form, but the 'pessimists', undoubtedly influenced by their liquidity anxieties, won out.[244]

Nevertheless, the problem of short-term lending from abroad could not be solved but only made worse by such measures, and the banks did not have much choice if they were to service their customers or even have customers for loans. As has been shown, the great concerns were able to go directly to New York to do their borrowing, and this left the banks with a limited number of companies, primarily of medium size, for whom to act as intermediaries. Manifestly, longer-term loans would have been more agreeable, but where was one to get them? As

Blinzig pointed out to Ferdinand Eberstadt of Dillon, Read & Co. during his visit to New York, since the Deutsche Bank 'has from its beginnings always stood by the principle that it would only use money when it was offered but that it would never and at no time seek it', and since it was of the view that the medium-sized industries could not be financed by means of a trust at reasonable expense, 'nothing else remained than for the German banks, however badly or well they might do it, to finance medium-sized industrial firms themselves'.[245]

Eberstadt decided to respond to this situation by offering a proposal that they float a 25 million dollar loan in the United States for five years for the purpose of financing medium-sized German industry. The idea bore fruition and, in early September 1927, the Deutsche Bank issued a note in the amount of 25 million dollars for which Dillon, Read & Co., joined by Equitable Trust, floated 6 per cent certificates on the American market. The note was to fall due on 1 September 1932. Not only did the Deutsche Bank have the distinction of being the first German company to float an issue on the American market, but also it was praised by Schacht for raising long-term money for genuinely productive purposes.

Praise by Schacht was good advertising, and the confidence of Americans was undoubtedly increased by the way the money was lent. As Blinzig informed Leffingwell, 'the credit has been distributed by us in many single items, and exclusively as dollar credits, against ample security in any and each case, and only to such customers who are producers of foreign exchange and on whom we can depend upon that they will be able to make repayment in the course of the five years'.[246] Leffingwell was impressed, but the Morgan banking house nevertheless came to the conclusion 'that it was better for us to abstain from current financing in Germany'.[247] The Deutsche Bank had exploited the possibilities, but had also discovered the limits of what the Americans would do.

The problem, indeed, was not the condition and practices of the Deutsche Bank, but rather those of Germany. The reports of the Reparations Agent Parker Gilbert, especially that of December 1927, were highly critical of German public finance and of short-term borrowing for 'unproductive' purposes, and called for a new reparations plan and a straightening out of German finances. Blinzig, like many Germans, thought Gilbert's reports first-rate pieces of accountancy, but criticized them for failure to take the 'historical givings' [sic!] into account. German production had increased enormously and Germany had a labour force that was 5 million larger than before the war. Unless the world opened its markets to German goods, the new production would find no market and unemployment would multiply. At the same time, Germany needed more capital and yet was being forced to pay reparations, while the international business community was compelled to wonder about which obligations would have priority in the event of a crisis.

Blinzig could not help be irritated when Leffingwell wrote, on the one hand, that protectionism was unfortunately the national policy of most nations and had to be accepted as a fact and, on the other, that the key question was whether the Germans could produce more and consume less, and thereby store up capital and become more trustworthy. As Blinzig noted, they had to produce not only more than they consumed but also more than they had to pay in reparations, which indeed made it, as Leffingwell claimed, 'a political and social question'.[248] Exactly how were the Germans to deal with these 'historical givings', however, when Morgan was holding back its money and when American capital was inclining more and more to stay at home and invest in the last great speculative boom before the 'Black Tuesday' that would mark the beginning of the end? Liquidity increased slightly at the end of 1928 and the beginning of 1929 because the great lockout in the Ruhr and recession were reducing credit demands, but this hardly constituted a happy circumstance. As negotiations over a new reparations settlement began in early 1929, the cutting off of American capital and the fiscal problems of the government hung like the Sword of Damocles over the German economy.

4. The great fusion

The response of the German economy to its troubles after 1918 had been to build mighty fortresses from which one could sally forth when opportunity arose, and to which one could retreat in security in times of economic tempest. The vertical concerns of the inflation period and the horizontal giants – I.G. Farben and Vestag – created during the stabilization period were illustrative of these tendencies, as was the expansion of the D-Banks in both periods. In October 1929 the high point of this process was reached in the surprising and sensational fusion of the great rivals in the history of German banking, the Deutsche Bank and the Disconto-Gesellschaft.[249]

There were important signs of increasing co-operation and diminishing rivalry between the two banks prior to the actual fusion. The most important illustration of this is to be found in a substantial amount of co-operation in consortial business relating to loans floated by the cities of the Rhineland and credits for various Rhenish enterprises between Schlitter and the head of the A. Schaaffhausen'sche Bankverein, Robert Pferdmenges. Even more significantly, while the Deutsche Bank refused to recognize the old consortial arrangements that had existed for such loans because of changed circumstances, and objected to Disconto-Gesellschaft claims that the A. Schaaffhausen'sche Bankverein and the Norddeutsche Bank be treated as totally independent entities in consortial business when the Disconto-Gesellschaft owned and claimed as its assets all of their shares, an agreement was nevertheless reached between Schlitter and Salomonsohn in April 1925 to consult in all such cases and avoid a 'war of all against all'.

Wassermann not only accepted the proposal, which emanated from Salomonsohn, but took the occasion to remark that 'it is a reflection not only of tradition but also of the attitude of my colleagues and of myself personally that we happily take every opportunity to work in common with the Disconto-Gesellschaft'.[250] It is a measure of Wassermann's seriousness that he took the occasion of these discussions to suggest that the rotating leadership of the Vestag consortium was not really in the interest of the banks. While he thought that the sole leadership of the Disconto-Gesellschaft would hurt the prestige of the other banks, he indicated a willingness to try to change the arrangement at a future date.[251] Finally, in an entirely separate agreement, the two banks promised to keep one another informed about possible fusions with their allied banks in south-west Germany, the Rheinische Creditbank in the case of the Deutsche Bank, and the Süddeutsche Disconto-Gesellschaft in the case of the Berlin Disconto-Gesellschaft.[252]

Another potent factor in making possible a closer relationship between the Deutsche Bank and the Disconto-Gesellschaft was Jakob Goldschmidt and the DANAT-Bank. In an already overcrowded and overly competitive banking system, the presence of Goldschmidt wherever one turned was unnerving on both rational and personal grounds. It mattered little that Goldschmidt was quite conservative in his economic and political views. He appeared as an interloper and a rival. His speculative past and role in financing Stinnes and Friedrich Flick were held against him by a solid banker of the old school like Georg Solmssen of the Disconto-Gesellschaft.[253] In the press, 47-year-old Goldschmidt appeared as the personal rival of the 60-year-old Wassermann, and the latter seems to have transferred some of the sensitivities over questions of status and rank previously reserved for the Disconto-Gesellschaft to the DANAT-Bank. The well-informed observer Felix Pinner thought the differences between the two men more 'personal than objective',[254] but such differences often assume great significance when important decisions must be made. Furthermore, the press played upon the rivalry, both imagined and real, between the two banks.

Goldschmidt was juxtaposed not only to Wassermann but also to Werner Kehl, the young, dynamic former head of the Düsseldorf branch of the Deutsche Bank, who was taken into the securities branch of the Berlin headquarters in 1926 and made a member of the board of managing directors in 1928. Goldschmidt and Kehl were portrayed as lining up an array of major heavy industrial and finishing firms and interests behind them in the battle between the banks. While Wassermann appears to have respected Goldschmidt's abilities, Kehl did treat Goldschmidt as a rival, and the conservative leaders of the Disconto-Gesellschaft were profoundly distrustful of Goldschmidt's views and methods.[255]

If one were to compare the chances of a fusion between the Deutsche Bank and the DANAT-Bank, on the one hand, and the Disconto-Gesellschaft, on the other, however, then the result would seem to have been overdetermined. This becomes evident from the most important source extant on the fusion of the two banks, a memorandum by Solmssen of 16 September 1929 based on the negotiations between Schlitter and Pferdmenges of the A. Schaaffhausen'sche

Bankverein.[256] Pferdmenges and Schlitter had both been vacationing in Pontresina. The two men knew one another well, and Schlitter repeatedly brought up the question of a fusion between the Deutsche Bank and the Disconto-Gesellschaft, and urged Pferdmenges to press the leaders of the Disconto-Gesellschaft to consider the matter seriously. In the course of these conversations, Schlitter reported that there had been serious negotiations between the Deutsche Bank and the DANAT-Bank held at the instigation of the Cologne banker Louis Hagen, but that there had been reservations about working with Goldschmidt from the very start 'for personal reasons', and that the discussions very rapidly ended, apparently to the relief of the Deutsche Bank participants, because of Goldschmidt's 'boundless demands'. It is worth noting that the 'relief' may not have been felt by Wassermann, who is reported elsewhere to have sent a telegram to Goldschmidt declaring that 'what you have rejected in a moment, no eternity will bring back'.[257] There was, of course, no hint of Wassermann's sentiments in Schlitter's discussions with Pferdmenges. Similarly, the Cologne banker Baron von Oppenheim, who was also being used by Schlitter to propagate a fusion by working on Solmssen, confirmed the role Hagen had played in the negotiations with the DANAT-Bank and expressed great satisfaction that they had failed. In Oppenheim's view, a Deutsche Bank–DANAT-Bank fusion would have forced the Disconto-Gesellschaft to join with the Dresdner Bank in order 'not to fall completely behind', and this would have been 'very unpleasant'.

Schlitter's approach to Pferdmenges had not been the first time that the Deutsche Bank had proposed the alliance, but he raised the issue again, despite the lack of Disconto-Gesellschaft response, out of the 'conviction that if nothing along these lines occurs, the position of the Deutsche Bank as well as that of the Disconto-Gesellschaft will have to diminish in a manner that will not reflect the significance of both institutes for our economic life. The concentration of capital in industry has taken on such dimensions and will go on further in such a way that the activity of the banks will be more and more pushed back and it will be made impossible for them to combat this suppression. In order to meet the challenge of industry, it is necessary to create a banking block of such dimensions that its placement capacity will dominate the domestic market and that under-bidding of opposition groups which go beyond the bounds of the reasonable would be pointless.'

While Schlitter admitted that the Deutsche Bank tended to be more generous in its credit policies, he took the view that the two banks were especially suitable for one another because they operated on the same basic principles, managed their branches in the same manner, and were financially sound. This did not mean, however, that their situation was satisfactory. It was impossible for them to raise the capital they needed to compete by increasing their share capital under existing conditions, and the high costs of operation, which could not really be reduced much further in isolation, made their profitability inadequate. Schlitter thought that the banking block he proposed would achieve a yearly profit of 20 million marks and would 'thereby be in a position to develop a force of such magnitude that it could not be circumvented in the securities business and in the reconstruction of the German economy at home and abroad'.

In his discussions with Pferdmenges, Schlitter admitted that the Deutsche Bank had some personnel problems. Stauss, whose credit grants were very expensive, was the worst of these, and Schlitter openly recognized that he was someone the Disconto-Gesellschaft leadership would have to swallow. He was also quite frank about the personnel changes taking place at his bank. Michalowsky, Millington-Herrmann and Blinzig were retiring in the coming year, and Schlitter himself planned to retire in two years. He thought the Deutsche Bank had a promising successor generation – above all, Werner Kehl. Solmssen, however, had the impression that Blinzig and Wuppermann, the director of the Düsseldorf branch, had incurred some very bad losses in western Germany and that this had intensified the interest in fusion. Whatever the case, Solmssen came to the conclusion that the Deutsche Bank intended to exert tremendous pressure on the Disconto-Gesellschaft and was combining intimations of other negotiations and the influence of Pferdmenges and Baron von Oppenheim to force the Disconto-Gesellschaft to take the matter seriously.

The pressure seems to have worked. There is no detailed record of the discussions between the two banks, which were held in the greatest secrecy in Pontresina between Schlitter and Eduard Mosler and among the leading managing directors at their homes in the Tiergarten section of Berlin. The fact that Mosler negotiated for the Disconto-Gesellschaft was of great significance, not only because he was a distinguished banker and head of the Association of Berlin Bankers for many years, but most importantly because he handled salary and contract questions for his bank and had played a leading role in working out the collective bargaining agreements for the bankers' association. There is good reason to believe that considerations of cost reduction and anxieties about the unavailability of long-term capital, rather than the visions of grandeur which Schlitter played upon in his discussions with Pferdmenges, were decisive in bringing about the fusion of these two venerable institutions. It is significant that the Disconto-Gesellschaft, in contrast to the Deutsche Bank, had chosen the 'nobler' amalgamation policy of creating communities of interest with its great partners, the A. Schaaffhausen'sche Bankverein, the Norddeutsche Bank and the Süddeutsche Disconto-Gesellschaft, even though it controlled all their shares. This policy, when combined with the higher salaries paid to directors at the Disconto-Gesellschaft, undoubtedly made operations more expensive.[258]

In this context, it is important to recognize that the managers of the Deutsche Bank central headquarters in Berlin, especially Peter Brunswig and Hans Rummel, who dealt with bookkeeping and accounting, seem to have done very detailed work on cost questions and profitability. Rummel, who was to become a deputy managing director in 1930 and a managing director the next year, was a pioneer in this field for the banking industry and helped introduce entirely new methods of breaking down and analysing the costs of banking operations and the profitability of branches. In the light of the coming fusion, it was of more than a little significance that Brunswig and Rummel met with a small group of branch directors on 13 September 1929 to discuss organization questions and improved efficiency, and that Rummel, who gave the report at the meeting, emphasized how important it was that 'even in the eventuality of a regrouping in the banking industry, the organization of the Deutsche Bank will remain the guiding one'.[259] The competitive problems of post-stabilization banking in Germany showed through again and again in Rummel's remarks. His chief goal was to make sure 'that our costs always press upon us somewhat less or somewhat later than that of our competition'. A particularly significant aspect of the meeting was Rummel's emphasis on the importance of 'taking money' as opposed to the 'giving of money', which had been so much in the foreground of their discussions.

By this time the great credit banks had virtually given up their efforts to contest the expanded functions of the savings banks and, in 1928, had decided to accept small savings accounts themselves and effectively seek to beat the savings banks at their own game. They were especially anxious to tap the resources of professional people, but also of workers and other small savers. As Brunswig emphasized: 'The bringing in of creditors is viewed by all as extraordinarily important. We cannot wait until the customers bring the money to us but must seek the customers.' This was a new business for the credit banks, and they were uncertain about how much they wanted to spend on advertising and on the most favoured approach, the creation of small and convenient deposit-account branches. There was also strong sentiment for the enlivening of the securities business through more effective advising of customers on investment possibilities, and Director Schaefer of the Düsseldorf branch urged the establishment of a central information bureau at the bank to pass along information to the branch officers charged with such activities, and to help create a 'general opinion' of the Deutsche Bank in the investment area.

Characteristic of the meeting, however, was that discussions of building up were always accompanied by anxious discussions of cutting down. Rummel emphasized, for example, that of the bank's 1,200 senior officials, 150–200 were 'more or less superfluous. They cost the bank a pile of money, tie up numerous contractual officials and make difficult the necessary spatial consolidation, and take away the chances of our rising personnel to move upward. Their presence prevents us from paying the really good senior officials the way we would like.' While Brunswig thought that the bank would be capable of replenishing itself from its existing personnel, he expressed concern about the availability of good people for directorships.

These discussions provide an interesting perspective on the condition of German credit banking on the cusp of the great merger of October 1929 – and the great depression so soon to come. It was a business facing an extremely uncertain future. It was gradually recovering its resources, but was perilously dependent on foreign accounts and capital and overpopulated for the capital which was available. On the one hand, it was stepping gingerly into the future by trying to appeal to the small savers. On the other, it was obsessed with rationalization to compensate for its own seemingly irremediable irrationalities. This was the way the bankers viewed not only their own area, however, but the entire German economy. The merger of the two banks clarified the somewhat mysterious meaning of Werner Kehl's widely reported remarks to the Reich Association of German Industry meeting in Düsseldorf, where he spoke of the necessity of a 'conscious policy of consolidation' and went on to declare that 'If the Deutsche Bank is itself now showing the way, then one should immediately recognize in it the *introduction of a new great era of concentration*, which will extend not only to German banking but to the entire business world. The cost problem is the problem child not only of the banks, but of our entire economy.'[260]

It was this 'necessity of rationalization' which Wassermann emphasized to the press when the great fusion was officially announced on 27 September 1929.[261] The new bank was to bring together not only the banks which were to compose its name – Deutsche Bank und Disconto-Gesellschaft – but also the Norddeutsche Bank in Hamburg, the A. Schaaffhausen'sche Bankverein in Cologne, the Rheinische Creditbank, and the Süddeutsche Disconto-Gesellschaft. Despite the many large institutions involved, a capital share increase was not deemed necessary, rumours of an intention to increase the bank's capital with American money notwithstanding. The shares were to be exchanged on a one-to-one basis, and the new bank did indeed emerge as a formidable aggregation of banking capital (see Table 3). It had 800,000 accounts, 289 branches and 77 urban sub-branches. It also constituted an impressive assemblage of human capital, with Georg Solmssen, Eduard Mosler, Gustav Schlieper, Theodor Frank and Franz Boner joining the board of managing directors, and such luminaries as Max von Schinckel, Arthur Salomonsohn, Enno Russell, Franz Urbig and Robert Pferdmenges entering the board of supervisors. Among the new deputy managing directors from the Disconto-Gesellschaft who were to play an important role in the history of the bank were Oswald Rösler and Karl Sippell, and mention must also be made of Karl Kimmich, who came from the A. Schaaffhausen'sche Bankverein, specialized in the affairs of west German industry and undertook a variety of major assignments before being appointed to the board of managing directors in 1933.[262]

While there was much speculation about the potential of the new Deutsche Bank und Disconto-Gesellschaft – the press and much of the public developed the habit of referring to it as the 'Dedi Bank' to the great but helpless irritation of its management – its creation was a terrifying event insofar as its employees were concerned. One of the major purposes of the merger was obviously to consolidate the branches throughout Germany, and profit was anticipated not only from the sale of buildings but most of all from the reduction of personnel.

Table 3   *Deutsche Bank und Disconto-Gesellschaft in the German credit banking system at the time of the 1929 fusion (numbers in millions of RM)*

	Share capital	Reserves	Loans, credits and accept-ances	Liquid assets	Accounts	Reim-burse-ment bills	Securi-ties	Reports and Lombards
Deutsche Bank-Group	150	94	2,982	1,090	1,504	324	45	135
Disconto-Group	135	71	2,075	827	845	309	23	114
Combined bank	285	165	5,057	1,917	2,349	633	68	249
7 great banks	588	309	11,188	4,034	5,141	1,487	179	657
Combined bank as per cent of great banks	48%	54%	45%	48%	46%	43%	38%	38%
101 credit banks	1,066	455	14,829	5,187	7,201	1,857	414	779
Combined bank as per cent of credit banks	27%	36%	34%	37%	33%	34%	16%	32%

Source: *Vossische Zeitung*, No. 456 (27 September 1929).

Indeed, at the general shareholders' meeting of the Deutsche Bank on 29 October, the representatives of the employee associations sharply criticized the merger, which one of them referred to as an 'earthquake' for the 14,000 employees of the Deutsche Bank and the 9,600 of the Disconto, and deplored the forthcoming dismissals, which were estimated in the press to be between 5,000 and 7,000.

As always, Wassermann gave assurances that every effort would be made to spare family men and find employment for those who were let go, and he pointed out that the reductions would hit the high as well as the low, since no fewer than 323 directors and managers were to be retired or let go as a consequence of the fusion. This, however, appeared as small consolation to the contractual employees, and one of their representatives pointed out that the matter was not only socially harmful but politically dangerous: 'I ask you gentlemen to answer for yourselves the question as to from whence it comes that in the large banking enterprises, especially on Berliner Platz, the groups representing extreme political views, the Communists and National Socialists, have found such favourable soil, that here they have found it possible to do practical work among the salaried employees, a phenomenon which is not to be found to the same extent among the salaried employees in private business. I see here a movement towards radicalization as a consequence of the measures conditioned by the fusion whose final consequence I do not want to depict here. I will leave the imagining of its end effect to each one of you.'[263]

It is doubtful that such grim thoughts disturbed the grand dinner held for 127 persons from banking and industry to celebrate the great event that evening. Nor does there seem to have been any openly expressed concern about the events of only three days before on 24 October, the 'Black Thursday' on Wall Street when the stock market crashed. Of course, deep feelings of financial and economic insecurity underlay the fusion that had taken place. The full import of the Wall Street crash, however, was not yet obvious – the German economy had, after all, survived its Black Friday – and far greater significance was attached to the problem of whether Germany could fulfil the obligations she was about to undertake under the recently negotiated Young Plan in view of the growing fiscal crisis in Berlin, the stagnating profits and inability to bring costs down, and the manifest indications of deepening recession. Selmar Fehr, for example, viewed the Wall Street crash as a strong 'technical stock market correction' necessitated by the excessive optimism and speculation. He was more distressed about the messy collapse of the Frankfurter Versicherungsgesellschaft (FAVAG), which was caused by speculations and which had cost the Disconto-Gesellschaft $250,000.[264]

If the rhetoric of business pessimism was reaching new heights – or depths – as 1929 drew to a close, however, the deflationary mood that was to take hold in the coming year was still muted and hope had not yet given way to paralysis. Thus, in mid-November the Deutsche Bank und Disconto-Gesellschaft undertook its first major joint effort by launching a big campaign throughout the country – above all, in small towns to attract the small saver. A big attempt was made to target potential new customers with an illustrated informational brochure, 'What the Deutsche Bank und Disconto-Gesellschaft has to Offer You', and brochures were planned for each of the coming four months, culminating in one urging people to set up savings accounts for their children.

The ideas discussed by Rummel and Brunswig were now put into practice, except that a great deal more emphasis was placed on the use of agents who, as in the American securities business, would go down to the grass roots and persuade people to place their money in a great bank rather than in a savings bank. The bank also offered savings certificates in 50 and 100 mark denominations that would earn interest if held for a minimum of a year and could be held for three years. The moment for such an effort to win over the small saver seemed particularly propitious because the failure of a number of small civil servant banks seemed to show that size mattered. Also, the drive had a social aspect since not only local businessmen but also dismissed bank employees were hired to do the soliciting.[265]

Money from such savings was viewed as some potential compensation for the great decline in money from the United States, but even here the Deutsche Bank had taken some steps to gain capital from that quarter. The amount of long-term American money flowing into Germany had been reduced by more than a half during the first eight months of 1929, and this led the Deutsche Bank to repeat its efforts to secure such money for its customers and reduce dependence on short-term money. In contrast to 1927, however, when the debt incurred to Dillon, Read & Co. had to be taken into the Deutsche Bank's balance sheet, this time the Deutsche Bank joined with the American banking house of Harris, Forbes & Co. and the American Founders Co. to create an investment trust, the United States and Overseas Corporation. The arrangement had been negotiated by Werner Kehl for the Deutsche Bank and E.C. Granbery for Harris, Forbes & Co. The consortium was joined by a number of American and European banks and investment houses. The new company floated 22 million dollars in shares in 1929 and was empowered to go as high as 100 million, and it laid particular stress on the financing of German public securities, which were viewed as a particularly good risk in the United States and of which there were a number in Germany badly needing money. Its initial German loans, however, went to Siemens-Schuckert, Borsig and Ruhrchemie.[266]

It goes without saying that the new enterprise was launched at an extremely difficult time. As Granbery noted to Kehl at the end of the year, the market for foreign bonds in the United States was dead and the stock market had taken a terrible beating. Nevertheless, he remained hopeful for the coming year and even advised the Deutsche Bank und Disconto-Gesellschaft to set up a bond division that would market bonds to a broad public in the American style. He knew the Germans regarded this as expensive, but he pointed out that one attained higher prices through high-powered salesmanship.

Granbery was obviously uncertain about American conditions during the coming months, but tended towards the optimistic side. He was quite naturally curious as to what the situation was in Germany. On the one hand, he was told that businessmen were terribly pessimistic; that unemployment was high and growing; that the government was in disarray and the cities spending too much; that the stock market was continuing to decline; and that money was very dear. On the other hand, his same source assured him that production was the highest it had ever been; that the source of unemployment was higher population rather than declining business activity; that bankruptcies were fewer; and that Germans were borrowing, thereby improving the balance of trade and even making it possible to pay reparations through exports. Granbery wondered what Kehl thought of the situation.[267]

Werner Kehl's lengthy reply provided an excellent illustration of the thinking of a leading banker on the eve of the Great Depression and a fitting climax to this discussion of the Deutsche Bank und Disconto-Gesellschaft during the Weimar Republic's flirtation with prosperity. Werner Kehl characterized 1929 as 'one of the worst years that German economic life had experienced, and there were many people who said on 31 December 1929, "never again 1929" '.[268] The problem, as Kehl saw it, was the tremendous drop in capital imports from the United States, whose effects were compounded by the high interest rates and intensified by the Wall Street crash. What made this turnabout especially harmful was that the economy, wages and costs had been pumped up by the capital inflow in 1928. The standard of living had increased along with public and private expenditure, and now suddenly levels had been reached which could not be sustained because the capital imports that made them possible were no longer there. While the economy had moved into recession, wages, salaries and expenditure had not, and there had been no improvement in profitability.

For Kehl the problem was primarily a political one: 'You see here the power of the state in the hands of the Social Democrats and in part very left-wing bourgeois parties, who out of consideration for the voters demand an economic policy which pays attention to the consumer needs of the broad masses without anyone saying anything in principle against a policy that tries to find the prosperity of the country in a strong domestic market. One can see these things in two ways: If one understands economics as nothing other than a movement of goods from producers to consumers and, from the perspective of national economy, one believes that the optimum is achieved when there is the greatest possible production and the greatest possible consumption, then we have done good work in Germany. But if one understands economics to be something else, if one, in other words, from the standpoint of the businessman asks whether it has paid to pay taxes, to pay wages, to pay salaries, to pay interest, to have taken great risks, then things must be viewed very differently in Germany. Whoever you might ask – and there will be very few exceptions – will answer quite correctly that business has not paid off for the entrepreneur.'

While Kehl typically blamed the problem in part on excessive government expenditure and high wages, he also argued that the third important factor was that of interest charges. If Germany were France or the United States, then the return on business investment would have been billions more. The capital shortage and high interest rates were the crucial problem, therefore, but they could not be dealt with directly and could only be managed by lowering all the other costs so that capital could be liberated and interest rates could be brought down. This brought one back to the political question. Kehl was convinced that high unemployment would continue because labour costs were too high, and that the political situation would have to have 'its final clarification'. He no longer believed, as he apparently had previously, that losses and bankruptcies would not be as high in 1930 as they had been in 1929, but what made him somewhat more optimistic was that the leading people were finally realizing that public policy had to change.

In this regard, he welcomed Reichsbank President Schacht's criticisms of the government, the undermining of a Dillon, Read & Co. loan that the Reich had negotiated, and insistence that revenue be set aside to pay for the public debt. As Kehl almost rhapsodically argued, Schacht's open opposition had 'formed a kind of energy centre to improve what is unhealthy in our development. The historical hour of the banker finds Dr Schacht at the head of this movement, and I believe that the laws of the capital and financial market will be so compelling that what all leading minds want will be carried out.' The political parties had finally recognized the situation for what it was and 'the ultra-radicals in the bourgeois wing have demonstrated their bankruptcy and a movement in the direction of fruitful political collaboration is beginning'. Kehl only hoped that Germany's former enemies would realize the need to relieve Germany of the 'chains' placed upon her, and he warned against overestimating Germany's export capacity.

In the balance, therefore, Kehl expected 1930 to be economically as troubled as 1929, but he looked for an improvement from the political side and hoped that the reduction of foreign loans would lead to a build-up of capital at home: 'I believe that we have already gone a good way on the road to better circumstances. The foundation of our entire economic, political and social situation is healthy, and the development of the past years and of the present situation is only to be explained by the fact that the enormous capital imports of the past years have made it difficult to bring the level of our own capital formation in the entire economic development back to its proper measure.' In the last analysis, Kehl expected that crisis would promote reconstruction and reorganization, and here bankers were indeed specialists. Little wonder, therefore, that Kehl began the fateful year 1930 in the belief that the 'historical hour of the banker' had arrived.

IV. The Deutsche Bank und Disconto-Gesellschaft in Depression and Banking Crisis 1930–1933

1. Scandal, political and fiscal crisis and deflation

The events of 1930–33 were to prove that there was a good deal of wishful thinking in Kehl's notion that the German banking business was about to achieve its finest hour. If anything, there was plenty of evidence, at the very moment he was writing, of the fissures and fault lines that were to produce disaster. One of these was certainly a great tension at the very top of the German banking business. If Wassermann had given the tone to the German Bankers' Congress of 1925, it was the more ebullient, optimistic Goldschmidt who had presented an 'individualistic world view' to that assemblage in 1928. Goldschmidt's mammoth collection of supervisory board seats, which was more than double that of any managing director of the Deutsche Bank und Disconto-Gesellschaft and appeared more a matter of acquiring prestige than earning money, his personal domination of the DANAT-Bank, and his penchant for self-advertisement and pretensions to appear as a spokesman for German banking – which culminated in his reports to the British Macmillan Committee on Finance and Industry in 1929–30 – contrasted sharply with the style and methods of the more traditional bankers in the Deutsche Bank und Disconto-Gesellschaft like Solmssen and Schlitter.

They both were absolutely infuriated by an article which appeared in the January 1930 issue of the *Journal of Commerce* by H. Powys Greenwood, suggesting that the new Deutsche Bank und Disconto-Gesellschaft might be too big and too bureaucratic to be effective, and that 'two plus two might thus possibly equal three rather than four'. At the same time, the article sang 'hymns of praise' to Goldschmidt. For Solmssen, the article was an altogether too transparent effort by Goldschmidt to give the new Deutsche Bank und Disconto-Gesellschaft a black eye while pushing himself to the forefront. Solmssen thought the time had come to demonstrate to Goldschmidt that they 'saw through his game', and that 'we will not have a reasonable relationship with Herr Goldschmidt until we go over to the attack. He has lost all sense of proportion and will only be cured of his megalomania by the opposite of friendliness.'[269]

Solmssen went to some lengths to accomplish this purpose, cutting short a holiday and accepting a Zurich speaking invitation he had previously turned down. In his address on 'Developmental Tendencies and World Economic Tasks of the Great German Banks', Solmssen spoke at some length about the importance of the recent fusion for the rationalization of German banking and industry and meeting the challenges of the Young Plan. He also attacked the *Journal of Commerce* criticisms and stressed the organizational compatibility, the spirit of self-sacrifice and the broad vision that culminated in the creation of the Deutsche Bank und Disconto-Gesellschaft. It was in this context that he made unmistakable reference to the differences between the leadership of the Deutsche Bank und Disconto-Gesellschaft and the DANAT-Bank. The former's leadership had been able to join together because they had 'an identical conception of the business and organizational principles to be followed. These must lead to the point that every official of the bank, including its leadership, views himself as a servant of the bank, and does not view it as a pedestal for personal advantage and as a means of satisfying personal ambition. The avoidance of this evil requires a high measure of traditional discipline and self-control. Where these are lacking and an egocentric go-it-alone policy is pursued under the cover of the so-called expression of personality – which to be sure is allowable in a private business but not in one which is obligated to administer the money of others for future security – there may be momentary successes, especially in times of strong volatility on the markets, but an organism capable of long-term survival will not be the result.'[270]

Certainly all was not blood and thunder between the leaders of the Deutsche Bank und Disconto-Gesellschaft and DANAT-Bank, and there were important areas of co-operation among the great banks as the economic crisis sharpened in the course of 1930. In November, for example, a series of weekly teas for the top leaders of the Deutsche Bank und Disconto-Gesellschaft, DANAT-Bank, and Dresdner Bank was initiated, and the first was held at the Deutsche Bank und Disconto-Gesellschaft with Goldschmidt among those present. Nevertheless, serious differences remained because Goldschmidt's competitive practices pulled the Deutsche Bank und Disconto-Gesellschaft leadership in directions that it thought inappropriate under the circumstances. Thus, Goldschmidt's maintenance of his 1928 dividend for 1929 apparently forced the Deutsche Bank und Disconto-Gesellschaft to do the same, although it would have preferred not to use its reserves to compensate for the reduced profitability in this manner.

By the end of 1930, the Deutsche Bank und Disconto-Gesellschaft was demonstrating much more resolve not to compete with Goldschmidt on the latter's own terms, but the pressures to do so were unpleasant and difficult to counter. When the press compared a reduction in the sum of deposits in the two banks by 240 million RM in the case of the Deutsche Bank und Disconto-Gesellschaft and 47 million in the case of the DANAT-Bank, and argued that the difference demonstrated lack of confidence in the former and the lower interest it paid on deposits, the director of one of the Dresden branches reported anxiety among his customers. His superiors in Berlin urged him to respond to such concerns by pointing out that withdrawal of deposits reflected lack of confidence in Germany's political and economic situation rather than in the bank, that the deposit withdrawals had to be placed in the context of the relative sums of deposits in the two banks – 4.15 billion RM in the case of the Deutsche Bank und Disconto-Gesellschaft and 2.31 in the case of the DANAT-Bank – and that the Deutsche Bank und Disconto-Gesellschaft viewed the high interest paid to keep deposits to be economically unsound: 'Some banks follow the policy of holding on to money which has a tendency to wander away under all circumstances no matter what it costs in interest. We, however, have exercised restraint in giving interest for domestic and foreign money ... in consideration of the fact that every increase of the rates for deposits must have a negative influence on the setting of interest terms for credit customers and must thereby make worse the consequences of the depression for that part of business dependent on credit.'[271]

The Deutsche Bank und Disconto-Gesellschaft worried considerably and understandably about bad publicity that might hurt its standing, and developed a policy of taking the 'high ground' both intellectually and in its public relations. In 1928 the Deutsche Bank had created a 'scientific advisory board' and hired the monetary theorist Melchior Palyi, then a *Privatdozent* but soon to be a professor, to head it. A Hungarian by birth, Palyi had a distinguished career both

in Germany and, after 1933, in Britain and the United States. The appointment of
Palyi was immediately placed in juxtaposition to recent attacks which Goldschmidt had made on the impracticality of some of the economists and the
confusion they were sowing with their theoretical conflicts. Actually, in creating
the advisory board and eventually a section devoted to problems of national
economy, the Deutsche Bank had been acting in consonance with other major
corporations like I.G. Farben and Vestag, which also set up such agencies at this
time.

The Great Depression, however bad for business, was good for economics
and, as Solmssen bemusedly remarked in February 1932, 'there has never been
so much national economy carried on in the banks as now'.[272] One suspects,
however, that the public relations of the bank, which were taken over in 1927
by the economic journalist Maximilian Müller-Jabusch, were even more important. As might be expected, the bank sought to influence the newspapers through
press releases and press conferences, but it also had recourse to the radio. Thus,
Müller-Jabusch gave a broadcast on the history of the Deutsche Bank in 1928,
while managing directors Bonn and Solmssen discussed, respectively, interest
rates and the role of the Reichsbank President in 1930.[273]

These efforts assume particular significance in the context of the very bad
press the banks received as a result of the increasing economic difficulties and
serious scandals which raised questions about the condition of the banks. The
problems that such scandals could cause is well illustrated by the FAVAG collapse,
which is one of the more telling links between the stabilization and the economic
and financial crisis. Almost a year before the Deutsche Bank und Disconto-
Gesellschaft had joined together in the mutual sharing of their profits and losses,
they were already participants, along with the DANAT-Bank and other leading
banks, in the supervisory board of the FAVAG. In December 1928, Managing
Director Bonn of the Deutsche Bank indicated to Director Rothschild of the
Frankfurt branch, who sat on the FAVAG supervisory board, that Solmssen had
privately expressed grave doubts about the guarantees they were supposed to
undertake on behalf of the FAVAG. Solmssen told Bonn that he was
'extraordinarily displeased' by the 'business practices' of the FAVAG, whose
engagements seemed very risky and filled the Disconto-Gesellschaft leadership
with an 'uncomfortable feeling'.[274] Bonn confessed that he had also entertained
such anxieties for a number years. As it turned out, this discomfiture was
well grounded because since 1922 the company had been using its money for
dubious investments that had nothing whatever to do with the insurance
business; the gold mark balance was a vast overstatement of the company's
assets; and the subsequent balances presented to the supervisory board were
fraudulent and landed three of the directors in gaol after the truth was
revealed in August 1929.

One of the major problems highlighted by the FAVAG disaster was that such
a company, which had a considerable number of bank guarantees, had little

difficulty getting foreign loans directly, and that foreign lenders saw no reason to approach German banks either for intermediation or even for advice and information. Thus, when a standstill consortium was created for the FAVAG, it encountered in addition to the 66 million RM owed to domestic creditors, a substantial body of foreign creditors, to whom 37 million RM were owed, for which it and even the Reichsbank might have to assume some liability. Both the banks and the Reichsbank agreed that 'over the long run it is insupportable that foreign bankers without our collaboration give money to business and, as in the Stinnes case, count on the German banks springing into the breach'.[275] While the Reichsbank could be asked to put pressure on domestic creditors of the FAVAG to participate in or collaborate with the standstill consortium, it obviously had no such leverage over foreign creditors. There was also substantial potential for inequity, since some foreign creditors could insist upon and receive their money while those who co-operated with the consortium sacrificed on behalf of a sounder solution. Added to this was the question of a Reichsbank guarantee, which Vice-President Dreyse viewed as a dangerous precedent, since such guarantees were also being asked for by the German co-operative banks and by agricultural banks to cover their loans.

The problem here was not only the relations between the Reichsbank and the banks but also those of the Reichsbank and the government. Thus, at the height of the crisis in November 1929, Economics Minister Curtius summoned Wassermann and Goldschmidt and told them 'in the most severe manner' that 'the banks must make great efforts to prevent a cessation of payments by the FAVAG. The German economy cannot bear its collapse.' Curtius thought that the Reichsbank should intervene by getting the Reich Insurance Supervisory Office to place a ban on FAVAG payment of its obligations until things were worked out. Schacht, however, flatly refused and went so far as to declare that he would intervene against such a payment ban and insist on the FAVAG declaring bankruptcy if payments on its behalf were to cease. His reason quite simply was that such state intervention to stop payments would 'create fear abroad that the same thing could happen with respect to the numerous municipal credits that had been taken abroad'.[276]

This, of course, intensified the pressure on the banks, which were once again at the end of January asked to make sacrifices to prevent political repercussions at home and damage to German credit abroad. The banks thought that the insurance companies should share in the mishaps of their own industry, but the Allianz Versicherungsgesellschaft thought that it was doing enough by taking over the actual insurance obligations of the FAVAG and had little taste for doing more. Goldschmidt, while agreeing that the burdens should be shared more widely, did think it important to reach some kind of temporary agreement with the FAVAG's creditors, and shared the government's concern with the publicity surrounding the problem. As he put it, in words that are pregnant with significance and irony in view of what was to happen to his bank in July 1931, he had all along been for some kind of action that would finally 'permit the curtain to fall over the matter so agitating for the public'.[277]

In the end, it was a curtain that fell all too slowly and that constantly offered the possibility of aggravating encores. There were conflicts between the private banks and the Reichs-Kredit-Gesellschaft, which was unwilling to do its share, problems with the FAVAG's overpayment of taxes on the basis of its bogus overstatement of its profits, and difficulties with the Allianz's digestive problems in swallowing down the FAVAG's business. Most unpleasant was the timing of the trial for the culprits: the matter was dragged out into 1931 and thus became connected in public opinion to other scandals and to the political crisis.

The FAVAG affair confirmed that the bankers were paying a considerable price for taking centre stage in their allegedly 'historical hour'. Where in 1925–26 public interest had focused on Stinnes, Stumm and other post-inflation disasters in industry, the tendency to fix attention on financial problems involving the banks rather than their clients, already evident in the Ufa and Daimler difficulties of the Deutsche Bank, intensified in the increasingly financially troubled environment of the transition to the 1930s. Kommerzienrat Friedrich Manasse, who was charged with writing the report on responsibility for the FAVAG affair, exonerated the supervisory board. He was bewildered to find, however, that the supervisory board was dissatisfied with its own exoneration. Its members knew they had ultimate responsibility since they had blindly trusted the FAVAG's directors. As has been shown, Solmssen and Bonn were suspicious but do not seem to have done very much.[278]

Bonn, however, had worse problems: namely, the 18 million RM losses of the Aktiengesellschaft für Osthandel, a company formed with Eastern and Overseas Products Ltd to handle the purchase and sale of raw materials and food products in Germany and Britain. The world-wide collapse of prices for these goods led to the losses in question, but they were not revealed by the management until the turn of 1929–30, so that Managing Director Bonn, who represented the Deutsche Bank on the supervisory board, found himself in a most embarrassing situation. He had, to be sure, committed no improprieties, and the Deutsche Bank und Disconto-Gesellschaft took the losses involved on its own account. Bonn did, however, draw the consequences and resigned from the board of managing directors in the autumn of 1930. It all appeared quite tasteful, since the bank was reducing the size of its board at this time, and Selmar Fehr also left it to become a partner in the Deutsche Bank und Disconto-Gesellschaft's subsidiary Georg Fromberg & Co. Fehr, unlike Bonn, was given a place on the Deutsche Bank und Disconto-Gesellschaft's supervisory board, but much was made of the fact that Bonn, an expert on overseas trade, was being sent by the bank to explore business opportunities in China.[279]

One cannot help suspecting that Bonn was glad to get far away after the months of scurrilous publicity surrounding the case. Former employees of the Osthandel tried to blackmail the bank with information about alleged improprieties, and a former Deutsche Bank employee, F.C. Holtz, who published a right-wing scandal sheet, *Fridericus*, disseminated charges that Deutsche Bank employees had been involved in violations of customs regulations and that the bank had engaged in tax evasion. The entire bundle of charges was picked up by other right-wing and some left-wing papers throughout the country. Friends of the bank worried that the charges would hurt in the increasingly overheated political atmosphere. While the Deutsche Bank und Disconto-Gesellschaft did react rather sharply to a savings bank that had posted one of the scandal sheets for all its customers to read, it tended to take a somewhat Olympian posture. It was reluctant to sue in court since the fines levied against libellers were usually worth the publicity they were seeking, and the bank thought that efforts to refute the charges had a tendency to give them credence. The furthest it would go was the publication of an informational refutation for the employees of the bank in the November 1930 *Monatshefte* of the bank.[280]

These unhappy incidents touched, of course, on the public functions and responsibilities of the bankers. As Georg Bernhard pointed out, in an article that was somewhat critical of the Deutsche Bank und Disconto-Gesellschaft's unwillingness to answer questions on the aforementioned charges more directly at the spring meeting of the stockholders: 'our bank directors unfortunately still have not realized that they are not simply private people, but that their activities are of great public significance. They have such a major influence on the fate of the entire economy, and such a significant portion of the nation's assets is in their hands, that at the very least their business activity and their relationship to the laws of the state intrude upon the public sphere.'[281]

All this was certainly very true, but there was another side to the problem of the sociopolitical accountability of the banking system to society, and that was the manner in which the chronic fiscal crisis of the state imposed itself upon a banking system which was in no way prepared to deal with it. One does not have to advocate the insupportable thesis that reparations brought Hitler to power to recognize that the preoccupation of Weimar's regimes – and the international financial community – with regulating the reparations question had a profoundly distorting effect on the political, economic and financial management of the Republic, and contributed fatefully to the disasters of 1930–33. Both the Young Plan debate and the requirements of the plan itself exacerbated social tensions and exaggerated the deflationary consensus which developed in 1929 and held sway until the autumn of 1931. The problem of marketing the Young loans, for example, put an end to any consideration of borrowing money to promote work creation in the spring of 1930. While the Young Plan had led to the withdrawal of Allied troops from the Rhineland and the removal of various restrictions and controls on German assets, it had also led to a termination of transfer protection for a portion of reparations payments.

The Germans were thus much more on their own, but the government and monetary authorities nevertheless remained bound by the limitations on their freedom of action imposed by the banking regime created under the stabilization and Dawes Plan. These regulations severely circumscribed the ability of the Reichsbank to assist the Treasury in time of need, and also undermined the traditional relationship between the Reichsbank and the banks because the latter could no longer count on the former to act as a lender of last resort and discount their bills. The way was thus paved for a situation in which the government, once cut off from a sufficient flow of borrowed money from abroad, could suffer from bizarre current account crises, would be unable to call on the Reichsbank, and would have to call on the banks for assistance. The big banks would thus be compelled to take on central bank functions despite what Theodore Balderston has rightly described as 'the absence of a long tradition of regular and instinctive relations between the government and the money market'.[282]

Lurking in the background, of course, was the legacy of the inflation, which left both the Reich's status as a debtor and the currency open to perpetual question. If the banks did lend money to the government and found themselves stuck with unmarketable and non-discountable Treasury bills in their portfolios, then they could only protect their liquidity through credit restrictions and the calling in of loans to their private customers, thereby intensifying the deflationary situation. This was all the more essential because of the volatility of their deposits and the tendency of money to be withdrawn from the banks at every sign of government fiscal difficulty. In short, in so far as they lent to the government, the banks endangered their own liquidity, and public responsibility thus clashed with their obligation to protect their institutions. As Balderston has shown, every time there was a cash-flow crisis, there was a liquidity crisis for the banks as well – the spring of 1929, December 1929, September–October 1930, and the spring of 1931. If the Reich was functioning, or being compelled to function, like a customer incapable of managing its finances, however, it could not easily be treated like one. That is, one could not tell it to seek money elsewhere or tell it exactly how it should shape up because such actions had profound political implications.

The dilemma was especially strong in dealing with the Hermann Müller Great Coalition government in 1929, since most bankers disapproved of that regime's social and economic policies despite its cost-cutting efforts. Thus, when the banks provided the Unemployment Insurance Agency with a one-month advance in March, they warned that the banks were risking their own credit and liquidity, and asked that the state finances be put in order as rapidly as possible. Nevertheless, in April Finance Minister Hilferding asked for a prolongation of the credit, and the banks felt compelled to agree. As they later explained the banks' arguments with Hilferding and negotiating problems: 'The situation is the same as it was with the Reichsbank during the war and inflation, which today one reproaches for having identified itself with the finances of the Reich and thereby ruined itself. One cannot expect the same from the private banking industry, which really ought to follow the example of the Rentenbank at the end of 1923 which refused the Reich its additional credit demands. At the same time, the banks declared that they had to refuse to comment on the Reich's financial mismanagement and to make proposals or set conditions because they would thereby enter the political field.'[283]

The great hope, needless to say, was that the political field would change, which it did in March 1930 with the appointment of the Brüning government. While Schacht, who had resigned shortly before, was no longer at the forefront of the 'historical hour' of the bankers to which Director Kehl had referred at the beginning of the year, the business community welcomed the change and supported the deflationary policies pursued by Brüning and the new Reichsbank President Hans Luther.

The politics, to be sure, would not go away, and the rejection of Brüning's decrees by the Reichstag led to the calling of elections for September 1930. Kehl, nevertheless, was as hopeful in August as he had been at the beginning of the year. As he returned from vacation, it reminded him of his return from vacation seven years before at the height of the hyperinflation: then the country also seemed on the brink of disaster and yet he encountered no 'mood of catastrophe and panic'. He did not think the finances would collapse or that there would be serious unrest, and he was firmly convinced that Germany 'was on the way to putting things in order, probably more quickly than many another land'. It might take a quarter or half a year, Kehl almost light-heartedly noted: 'but the force of circumstances is so unavoidable, and the recognition that it must happen, whether we want or not, is, I believe, so general, that this development will take place more calmly than many have feared would be the case, and when I think back to the problems that confronted us in 1923 and how they were solved, then I really do not think there is any reason to think the game lost. By this I only mean to say that we will succeed in adjusting to the bad economic conditions which I believe, now as before, will continue for a long time. In my view, the whole matter right now is a question of nerves.'[284]

As Kehl was compelled to admit to US Ambassador Sackett in January 1931, however, the September 1930 elections, which brought 107 Nazis into the Reichstag, rubbed the nerves of some of the depositors at the Berlin banks very much the wrong way. Between 15 September and 10 November there had been 900 million RM in excess withdrawals, one-third by foreigners, which 'practically eliminated foreign deposits in Germany', and 60 per cent of the remainder by Jews. While some of the domestic deposits were returning, the banks were actually discouraging foreign deposits since they were 'felt to be a menace to the stability of the German banking situation'.[285] Back in October Wassermann had told the influential State Secretary in the Finance Ministry, Hans Schäffer, that most of the withdrawn domestic deposits were 'Jewish money'. He went on to make the rather extraordinary suggestion that the Nazis be taken into the government since 'the Social Democrats will be now be reasonable anyway'.[286] This rather cynical notion that the Social Democrats were now so scared that they could be ignored, while the Nazis could be neutralized if one co-opted them into the system and implicated them in the Brüning programme was a good illustration of the contempt for parliamentary politics so typical of Weimar's business community. Wassermann, of course, had no sympathy with the Nazis, and around the same time that he was making his naïve proposal to Schäffer, he was also circulating Gottfried Feder's Nazi programme with the points dealing with anti-Semitic measures and economic and financial policy highlighted as a warning to those who might be inclined to sympathize with the movement.[287]

In general, the leaders of the Deutsche Bank und Disconto-Gesellschaft continued the practice of keeping in the political background. The one exception, as always, was the rolling cannon on its managerial deck, Georg von Stauss. Stauss's energy and ambition had often run ahead of his judgement, and while one would have thought he had enough to do with his work for the bank, and his activities as a Wannsee yachtsman, Automobile Club member and Mecklenburg estate owner, he decided to step up his political engagements as well after his election to the Reichstag for the DVP in September 1930.

Stauss, however, had also become impressed with the Nazis. In his capacity as supervisory board chairman for BMW, he had come into contact with Hermann Göring, who served as an adviser to BMW on aviation matters, and Göring had brought Stauss into contact with Hitler. Stauss apparently was impressed and thought the DVP could work with the Nazis. After the September 1930 elections, he organized a luncheon for Nazi Reichstag deputies with the object of having the DVP leader Ernst Scholz replace the venerable Social Democratic leader, Paul Löbe, as President of the Reichstag. The news of the meeting leaked to the press, and Stauss ended up looking like a fool since Scholz's wife was Jewish and much could be made of the fact that the Nazis were hostile to the banks and wanted to do away with 'interest slavery'.

The entire affair certainly damaged the image of the bank. Some Jewish customers withdrew their funds, and the bank had repeatedly to point out that it had no responsibility for the politics of its individual managing board members, and that many of Stauss's colleagues on the board of managing directors were Jews who saw not the 'slightest reason' to sever their relations with Stauss. While one wonders what Wassermann, Solmssen and Frank, and the substantial number of distinguished bankers and businessmen who were Jews or of Jewish origin on the supervisory board, privately thought of Stauss's penchant for playing the devil's matchmaker, the unpleasant publicity must have reinforced those who felt Stauss was a liability.[288]

In the last analysis, however, they worried more about Stauss's business misadventures than his political ones, and issues of religion and 'race' do not appear to have had any significance in the Deutsche Bank und Disconto-Gesellschaft or among the great bankers in general. There is no evidence that anti-Semitism played any role in Stauss's dealings with the National Socialists.

Schlitter thought Frederick the Great wise in luring Jews to Prussia with tax incentives, and he cheerfully worked for the merger with the Disconto-Gesellschaft, which anti-Semites later characterized as 'Jewified'. Men of Jewish faith or origin, however, were no less prominent in the Deutsche Bank, and between a quarter and a third of the leadership of the two banks was composed of such persons. Indeed, their position remained very strong despite the decline of private relative to joint stock banking.

What tended to divide German bankers was not ethnic origins, but rather generation and tradition, as the distaste of Solmssen for the business practices of Jakob Goldschmidt and Stauss illustrates. As the commentary on the deposit withdrawals in the wake of the September 1930 elections demonstrates, the bankers knew who their Jewish customers were and understood the significance of their accounts. Certainly the more prominent members of the German business community were aware of the importance of Jews in German banking and appreciated their talents, even when they harboured some of the more traditional anti-Semitic attitudes or consorted with political racists. The post-1933 despoliation of Jews and mutilation of the German business community through their exclusion were not products of Weimar's big business environment.[289]

There is every reason to argue that most of the leaders of the Deutsche Bank und Disconto-Gesellschaft had political views typical of big businessmen at this time. It is also likely that generational change and the fusion had caused a measure of shift to the right. Steinthal, Mankiewitz, Gwinner and Michalowsky, as well as Wassermann, Fehr and Bonn, were reputed to be more liberal than Salomonsohn, Mosler, Urbig, Solmssen and Honorary Chairman of the supervisory board, Max von Schinckel. Prior to the fusion, Schlitter had been the Deutsche Bank's closest contact with the more conservative industrialists of the Rhine and Ruhr, whereas the Disconto-Gesellschaft's leaders had been closely connected with them all along. Schinckel had actually identified himself with the infamous Young Plan referendum.

It would be reasonable to argue, however, that the real shift had been to the right of the DVP or 'left' of the DNVP, which was hostile to the demagogy of Alfred Hugenberg and wanted a united and conservative bourgeois front. Franz Urbig, for example, believed in the 'necessity of a united front' among the bourgeois parties. Solmssen was a co-founder of the Conservative People's Party which was composed of the national-conservative opposition that had split off from the DNVP. There is solid evidence that the bank answered the call of Carl Duisberg, the head of the Hindenburg Committee, and contributed heavily to his re-election in the contest with Hitler in the spring of 1932. Solmssen and Wassermann were members of the group in the DNVP calling itself the 'German Committee "Hindenburg for Volk and Reich"', which supported Franz von Papen in the November 1932 Reichstag elections.[290] In short, the bankers wanted a regime that was supportive of their economic position and that kept the left and the extreme radicals on the right under control.

Once the shock of the September 1930 elections abated, one could be moderately sanguine about the situation. Thus, in February 1931, Schlitter was asked privately by a colleague whether his firm should not contract its credits for business abroad in marks rather than foreign currencies. While the debts in marks cost him 4.5–5 per cent more, his foreign friends were suggesting to him that debts in marks could be cheaper in the end because Germany appeared to be falling apart and this might affect the currency as well. Schlitter responded by pointing out that conditions in Germany were exaggerated abroad and that 'if a few windows are smashed in Berlin, then there are reports of revolution, etc. in foreign newspapers under large, thick headlines'.

While things certainly were 'not pretty' at the moment, Schlitter felt that the long-range perspective was more promising. The political situation had not only calmed down, but 'Brüning has received the greatest majority in the Reichstag of any minister president – aside from Mussolini – in the world.' If the economic situation remained bad, this was true everywhere in the world, but the flood of deposit withdrawals seemed to have stopped, and Schlitter could see no dangers to the currency. He thought that the government could count on its military and police forces to put down any uprising. He thus concluded: 'I was also truly pessimistic a short time ago, but now I see many rays of hope. I have the feeling that the deepest point of the crisis has passed. Naturally, the road to improvement will be a long one. The most difficult problem is unemployment and the relationship to and attitude of the trade unions. Without the difficulties from that quarter, we would be much further along. In economic life, however, reason does not decide things alone unfortunately, but rather hard, unavoidable distress, and I believe that the distress is now so powerfully evident that reason will prevail in worker and trade union circles also.'[291]

An even greater concern of the Deutsche Bank und Disconto-Gesellschaft leaders was the restoration of reason in international affairs. In a widely noted speech to the shareholders' meeting of 17 April 1931, Wassermann attributed the miserable condition of the world and the German economy to the failure to establish real peace after 1918, the preoccupation of world finance with reparations and war debts, and the resultant overproduction of both raw materials and manufactured goods. The collapse rather than gradual reduction of raw materials prices and the retreat into protectionism were exacerbating the situation, but Wassermann argued strongly that the road to international recovery lay in political rather than economic understanding between the two most hostile of nations, France and Germany. In his view, the 'mutual mistrust' was too great for economic agreements to pave the way for political settlement. It had to be the other away around, and since Germany could only come with 'good will but empty pockets', either France would have to make concessions to pacify Europe or one would have to wait until 'some honest broker' came along to assist the process.[292]

These were not theoretical remarks but rather conclusions drawn from recent experiences. Deutsche Bank und Disconto-Gesellschaft representatives had been involved in negotiations in Paris, where they found that the French invariably put political before economic considerations, and were demanding that the Germans abandon their friendly policy towards the Soviet Union at a time when the Soviet Five-Year Plan was providing Germany with vital export business. At the same time, the bank had also been involved in efforts to bestir the 'honest broker' through Werner Kehl, who with the encouragement of the Foreign Office had visited the United States at the beginning of 1931 to propagate a revision of the Young Plan.[293]

Until there was some breakthrough, however, Wassermann thought it imperative that all sectors of the German economy exercise the deflationary self-discipline and accept the distress that inevitably came with it. The Deutsche Bank und Disconto-Gesellschaft had been contributing mightily to these conditions through its support and implementation of a rigorous policy of austerity and credit restriction. It was a major participant in the general deflation consensus that found expression in the policies both of the Brüning government and of the business world in general.

Furthermore, the Deutsche Bank und Disconto-Gesellschaft did not spare itself in these cost-cutting measures. Thus, between April 1930 and March 1931, the number of employees at the Deutsche Bank und Disconto-Gesellschaft was reduced from 21,600 to 20,051. Even more important was the emphasis on rationalization. Thus, where the elimination of redundancies at the end of the inflation had targeted younger employees and women, the policy that developed during the rationalization wave of the late 1920s was to use machines as much as possible so that, in the words of Solmssen, 'in place of the higher-paid older officials, cheaper, younger or female employees can be employed to work the machines'.[294] Indeed, while one certainly should not play down the manner in which the fusion and harsh economic conditions hit contractual employees at the bank, there is good evidence that senior, non-contractual personnel were especially hard hit. This is certainly the case if the 22 branches and sub-branches in the Rhenish-Westphalian district are any measure. In September 1930, there were 27 directors left out of a total of 28 Deutsche Bank and 7 Disconto-Gesellschaft directors; 39 managers and senior officials out of their 38 Deutsche Bank and 11 Disconto-Gesellschaft counterparts; and 704 contractual employees out of 660 Deutsche Bank and 122 Disconto-Gesellschaft employees at the time of the fusion.

The year 1931 began with major salary cuts for nearly all the directors at the central offices of the bank in Berlin, which ranged between 11.5 and 14.53 per cent, and similar and even higher cuts for branch directors. Directors Schaefer and Wuppermann of the Düsseldorf branch, who were especially well paid, had their 76,300 RM salaries cut by 15 per cent to 64,900 RM, while Director Kraemer of the Dresden branch and Rothschild of Frankfurt were cut from 56,700 RM to 49,496 RM. An apparent effort was made to ensure some equity by reducing higher salaries by higher percentages, and directors entitled to royalties for their service on supervisory boards faced proportionate cuts, so that 1,055,000 RM in advances against such royalties had been saved by November 1930. Finally, the members of the board of managing directors were not spared either. Solmssen's 150,000 RM salary and royalties were cut by 20 per cent, so that he lost 60,000 RM on his advance against royalties.[295]

It would be inane to compare the persons described with the unemployed workers and employees, or the condition of those whose wages and salaries were beginning to be subjected to massive cuts at this time. The important point is to record not the discomfiture of the well-to-do, but rather the extent of the anxiety that had produced such unusual measures. There had, to be sure, been much criticism of the high salaries of bank directors and the costs of royalties to supervisory board members, but the measures do not seem to have had anything to do with placating public opinion. Chancellor Brüning was being urged to persuade the business world to undertake a public and well-publicized voluntary salary reduction in anticipation of the reduction of contractual salaries and wages by decree that was being planned. When Brüning discussed the idea with Wassermann in November 1930, however, the latter pointed out that such cuts were already planned at the Deutsche Bank und Disconto-Gesellschaft, but warned against giving them any publicity since the outside world 'might draw unfavourable conclusions with respect to the credit worthiness of the great German banks'.[296] At the same time, the Deutsche Bank und Disconto-Gesell-schaft did publicly undertake measures of austerity which demonstrated the soundness of its banking practices. In the spring of 1931 it bought back 35 million RM of its shares, a device used by all the banks at this time to maintain the price of their shares. In contrast to the DANAT-Bank, however, which owned 50 per cent of its own shares, the Deutsche Bank und Disconto-Gesellschaft chose to retire the shares and thereby 'reduce its capital, which was considered too large' given its losses under existing circumstances.[297]

This is a useful perspective from which to view the rigour with which the Deutsche Bank und Disconto-Gesellschaft responded to its liquidity concerns in its credit policies, and the deflationary influence it exerted through its presence on the supervisory boards of industrial enterprises. One consequence of the fusion was greater centralization in the handling of consortial credits and munici-pal credits. In the old Deutsche Bank, branches would notify Berlin of such credits as might be necessary, but would then process them on their own, whereas the Disconto-Gesellschaft 'chief of cabinet' reviewed all such credits according to uniform guidelines. In March 1930, the new Deutsche Bank und Disconto-Gesellschaft opted for the Disconto-Gesellschaft procedure as a particularly appropriate means of controlling credit giving.[298] What this meant in practice was demonstrated at the beginning of June, when Wassermann and Schlitter decided that the 7.5 per cent rate for current account credit for municipalities provided 'no incentive to pay back' and raised it to between 8 and 8.5 per cent.[299]

In July, the bank turned its attention to its business credit accounts and noted that debtors of the bank were using credits for personal rather than business purposes, and that they were unaware of the extent of their unprofitability. A month later, the warning was given that the branches should pay more attention to economic conditions, and that too many branches were behaving as if credits would enable the firms in question to keep their heads above water and pay off their debts. Under existing circumstances, this was tantamount to a participation by the bank in the business in such a way that the bank would cover losses while the borrower would take profits. Furthermore, Berlin objected to the borrower being issued prolonged credits and allowed to take out profits without being forced to pay old credits back.[300]

It is difficult to tell how much the bank relied on the reports of the auditing commissions of its regional committees, but the monthly reviews of the Rhenish–Westphalian Committee's commission, which included such important bankers and industrialists as de Weerth, Pferdmenges, Kimmich and Silverberg, certainly must have been influential. In September 1930, because of the crisis, it carefully reviewed every credit over 50,000 RM and considered 'to what a high degree the prosperity and existence of enterprises today depend on the performance of the personalities in charge, and that because of the rapid change in the economic situation a continuous control through intensive surveillance of the credits of the individual enterprise is required to an extent much greater than before'.[301] This committee was concerned not only about private credits, but also about credits to municipalities and the provincial banks. In October, for example, it discussed the Landesbank der Rheinprovinz in some detail, which was well worth doing since the bank was in the business of giving municipal loans and the municipalities were in dire straits.[302]

The dilemma in trying to maintain control of these credits and the affairs of those who took them was that it was easiest in precisely those cases one wished to avoid. Most undesirable were the cases where it was too late. Once the FAVAG had collapsed, for example, the banks knew altogether too much about it. A reconstruction was obviously more desirable than a liquidation, and through the fusion the Deutsche Bank und Disconto-Gesellschaft had acquired a genuine specialist in such matters, Karl Kimmich. His reconstruction of the Cologne confectionery manufacturer Gebrüder Stollwerck is an ideal-typical and almost terrifying case of banker control. While there is no question that the company had been poorly run, Kimmich almost literally took it over in his efforts to rationalize its operation, and meticulously criticized everything from the manufacture of its caramel bonbons and chocolate bars to the layout of its catalogues.[303]

While Stauss could pay considerable attention to the details of Daimler's operation, demonstrating considerable upset, for example, when he discovered that prominent Nazis were buying Horch rather than Mercedes cars, he never sought nor was in a position to exercise the kind of control over Daimler that Kimmich exercised over Stollwerk. Stauss did have to answer for Daimler's debts to his colleagues, however, and the supervisory board over which he presided exercised extremely strong pressure on Director Kissel to reduce inventories and personnel and put an end to wage drift: that is, the paying of workers over and above contractual wages.

Kissel resisted these demands until the summer of 1930, but then he gave way to the exigencies of economic depression. The surrender was truly draconian. The average number of workers was reduced from 11,400 in 1929 to 8,000 in 1930, and the number of white-collar workers from 1,500 to 1,000. Inventories were severely decreased, which eased the debt owed to the Deutsche Bank und Disconto-Gesellschaft. At the same time, Kissel continued to face severe pressure from Stauss to meet his rigid firing ratio for white-collar and blue-collar workers, a difficult task in a business that needed more white-collar staff than average.[304]

An especially telling illustration of the watchfulness of the bank and the pressure it applied to get its customers to reduce wages and staff and rationalize operations is provided by its relationship with the Silesian textile company of Methner & Frahne, whose headquarters were in Landeshut Silesia. The firm was heavily indebted to its German bank consortium as well as to American creditors, and was finding it difficult to cover its costs, but when the bank pressed for wage reductions, its head, Hans Heinrich Frahne, argued that he could not break the collective bargaining contract with his workers. In late September 1930, however, Deputy Managing Director Abshagen of the Deutsche Bank und Disconto-Gesellschaft noted that the Baden firm of S. Fränkel in Neustadt had managed to come to an agreement with its workers, who voluntarily accepted a pay cut, probably in order to save their jobs. Abshagen immediately contacted Frahne and urged him and his colleagues in the Silesian textile industry to look into the matter, since 'one can assume that what is achievable in Neustadt can also be carried out in Landeshut'.[305]

A few weeks later, Frahne's need to get help with his American debt gave Abshagen the opportunity to berate Frahne in connection with critical press reports that the firm was opposed to the consolidation of the industry and for failing to close a plant that was unprofitable. He pointed out to Frahne that firms that were not doing well could not afford bad publicity, and concluded that 'in view of the last reported balance, on the one hand, and in view of the new development in the market, on the other hand, the situation of your company is so threatening that every source of losses must be ruthlessly bottled up'.[306] The Deutsche Bank und Disconto-Gesellschaft had little patience with the firm's reply that it anticipated an improvement of the situation through changes in economic, social, financial and customs policy as well as voluntary price agreements in the industry. It shared the hope that some changes would take place in government policy, but obviously believed that prudent bankers and businessmen were ill-advised to confuse their rhetoric with reality. The reality was that 'certain economic and political actualities in Germany cannot be disregarded by any government for the foreseeable future', and that 'at the moment when productive capacity significantly exceeds normal demand, as is undoubtedly the case in the German linen industry, then no price understanding helps over the long run against ruinous competition'.[307] By the spring of 1931, the combination of economic conditions and bank pressure achieved its purpose, and there was a fusion of the various Silesian textile firms to form the Ostdeutschen Textilindustrie AG. The Deutsche Bank und Disconto-Gesellschaft, which was the chief creditor, imposed rather harsh conditions, so that the firms lost half their capital, the current account liabilities were not transformed into long-term debt, and the capital share consolidation was done at a ratio of 20 to 1.[308]

This was an impressive exercise of banking power, but it should not be thought that the bank always leaped into the breach when it had the opportunity to do so. Thus, in late 1930, leaders of the south German textile industry called on the Deutsche Bank und Disconto-Gesellschaft to establish a consortium to reduce overcapacity and price undercutting, by designating the firms to be shut down, buying them out and blocking credit to new entrants. The industrialists argued that the banks could not be indifferent to the situation, since the industry had already taken a great deal of credit, and that 'the cry for a "strong man" becomes ever louder in the textile industry [which] now seeks him in the banking world after he has not been found in its own ranks'.[309] The Deutsche Bank und Disconto-Gesellschaft's engagement in the textile industry was certainly a heavy one, totalling 97.7 million marks in current account credits in late 1930, but this worried Stauss since 'we see great difficulties in creating so all encompassing an order at a time when no one happily enters into new engagements'. Indeed, this reluctance was particularly evident when Stauss was informed that the trade associations were very much in agreement with the proposal, and he privately wrote to Kehl, 'no wonder, when it is others that are supposed to supply the money'.[310]

At the same time, the great banks were as anxious to continue to supply as much of the money for industrial credit as possible, and to prevent the continued exfoliation of other lending institutions. These concerns were particularly strong in early 1930, when industry began seeking means of financing exports. One proposal that was found particularly irritating was that the Bank für Industrieobligationen, which was set up in 1924 to issue the bonds covering industry's obligations under the Dawes Plan, and which was being used in 1930 to finance the *Osthilfe* to agriculture and small business in the East, should expand its activities to cover export credits for small and medium-sized business throughout the country. While Ludwig Kastl, the Executive Director of the Reich Association of German Industry, had assured Wassermann that the Bank für Industrieobligationen had no intention of competing with the banks, the bankers and their leaders in the Central Association, Mosler and his Executive Director, Otto

Bernstein, were anything but reassured, since they remembered how the Reichs-Kredit und Kontrollstelle, which was meant to deal with government enterprises, had been transformed into the highly competitive Reichs-Kredit-Gesellschaft AG. Ultimately, the plan seems to have been dropped for fear that the government would end up controlling the bank if it undertook such a programme, but it demonstrated how fearful the banks were of industry taking matters into its own hands.[311]

An even more serious threat was presented at this time by a proposal to take the Reichsbank's sister institute, the Deutsche Golddiskontbank, out of its sole control, give the state banks a role in its management, and transform it into an instrument to borrow money abroad so as to finance credit for German exports. The Saxon industrialists, who were by and large the operators of small and medium-sized businesses heavily dependent on exports, were especially interested. Urbig, who served on the Reichsbank General Council and was much experienced in international trade, was particularly contemptuous of the proposal, although he feared he might be playing the 'prophet in the desert', since the industrialists were bound to be enthused 'because it is a matter of indifference to them where the money comes from and how the dividends are procured so long as they have the prospect of getting orders'.[312]

There had already been fiascos enough, with one firm having done construction work in Turkey for 80 million RM under Reich guarantee and standing little chance of payment from the impoverished Turks. Urbig thought the Saxons had demonstrated their incapacity sufficiently in India, where they had circumvented German business firms there and sold directly to natives, who sold their goods in the bazaars! He also found it difficult to comprehend why foreign lenders should buy bonds from such a bank in order to subsidize their competition in the protectionist environment that was taking hold throughout the industrial world. The Reich Association of German Industry also showed interest in the proposition of having industry, the banks and commerce take over the Deutsche Golddiskontbank with industry having the lead, but the banks won out in their effort to keep the Reichsbank in control of the Deutsche Golddiskontbank. In the spring of 1930 the bank was reconstructed to increase government influence over its operations, but its capital remained in the Reichsbank.[313]

This success, however, like the victory of the banks over the Economic Bank schemes in the early years of the Republic, left the now even heavier burden of dealing with the mounting credit crisis on the great banks. Furthermore, the conditions were more uncontrollable than ever and came together in a critical mass in the spring and summer of 1931, thereby dashing Kehl's vision of the 'historical hour of the banks', and Schlitter's belief in early February that 'the deepest point of the crisis has been passed'. Indeed, Schlitter's optimism had already dissipated by the end of the month, as he observed not only the continuous loss of foreign deposits but also the flight of capital from Germany.

Schlitter thought the recent emergency decree requiring every taxpayer to take an oath that he or she had not engaged in capital flight terribly naïve, and he feared that it would only encourage more of the same. While he recognized that high taxes were unavoidable, the chaotic nature of the German tax system and the legal uncertainty connected with it only served to inhibit capital formation. Schlitter's 'greatest concern' was that 'the Young problem will become acute before we have put our own financial situation in order. If that happens, then we will be taken between the pincers of the Entente in a much worse way than before and really get the treatment.'[314]

The Deutsche Bank leaders knew that the German money market was forcing the entire banking system to traverse from the edge of one abyss to another. This was made especially clear in November 1930 when Managing Director Solmssen paid a visit to Director Vocke and Vice-President Dreyse at the Reichsbank to express concern about the capital flight that had taken place during the previous four months, and to enquire what the Reichsbank could do for the banks if they got into trouble. Vocke replied that the Reichsbank would obviously seek to help out the banks as much as possible, but that it was very dependent on its own resources and was uncertain about outside assistance. When Solmssen then enquired as to whether, if the worst were to happen, the Reichsbank could stop payments abroad by refusing to grant foreign exchange for such purposes, Vocke declared that this was impossible because Schacht, very much against the advice of the Reichsbank directors, had made a public declaration of Germany's obligation to pay in gold at the time of the Young Plan negotiations. Although Schacht had initially been disinclined to make such a statement and had even persuaded the British negotiator, Sir Charles Addis, to refrain from demanding it, Schacht had changed his mind from one day to the next without consulting anyone, and had thus fixed the obligation. Dreyse confirmed that 'it is out of the question that the Reichsbank by the method of a partial moratorium against foreign nations can protect the banks against large withdrawals from abroad which cannot be satisfied with their own resources'.[315]

The Reichsbank wanted to be kept informed about the non-renewal of foreign money and to be kept abreast of the situation of the banks so that it could also stop false rumours and take action where appropriate. In October 1930, for example, there had been enquiries about the status of the DANAT-Bank, but it turned out that it had presented the Reichsbank with the least number of bills to discount. Solmssen went away with the impression at this time that all the banks were more or less in the same boat, and with the knowledge that it would be very hard to plug up big leaks.

2. A banking system in eclipse

In the spring and early summer of 1931 those leaks began to be very big indeed as the increasingly stormy sea of financial disorder culminated in the July 1931 banking crisis. The great banking crisis of 1931, like the July 1914 crisis, is one of those events that can keep historians forever arguing about what really happened and the responsibility for the unhappy outcome. On the one hand, there were underlying causes, both structural and historical, which lay partially in the evolution of the German banking system and in the way it functioned under the peculiar arrangements of the post-1918 period. On the other hand, there were the immediate causes and particularities of the crisis. The latter are somewhat more difficult to sort out, since the sequence of events and the motivations of the actors are not always clear or demonstrable, and the entire affair is enveloped in those classic attributes of Weimar politics and of the German political culture which poisoned it: the questions of who bears the most 'guilt' for the extreme nature of the crisis, the Reichsbank or the great banks, and of whether there was a 'stab-in-the-back' that took the form of a refusal of the Deutsche Bank und Disconto-Gesellschaft – above all, Oscar Wassermann – to show solidarity with the DANAT-Bank and Dresdner Bank, and thereby shore up the system rather than allegedly take advantage of the plight of its competitors.

Only a blow-by-blow description of the crisis can answer these questions, assuming they are answerable or are fruitfully posed in this manner, and this is not the place for such an exercise. In the early 1960s there was considerable concern in the higher echelons of the Deutsche Bank about what the former Chancellor Heinrich Brüning, who was known to take a very dim view of the performance of Wassermann and of the great banks, would say in his memoirs, and the bank gathered a considerable amount of material in preparation for a self-defence. The end-of-the-century historian certainly has every reason to be grateful for these efforts, but little reason to frame his or her discussion in terms of what that generation thought most compelling. In any case, the goal here will be to deal with the main aspects of the crisis and their significance for the history of the Deutsche Bank and the banking system of which it was a part. If some of the older debates are made a bit less contentious in the process, so much the better.[316]

On the evening of 11 May 1931, Jakob Goldschmidt learned through Director Max Doerner, who held a high position in the DANAT-Bank, that the balances of the Bremen textile concern Nordwolle had been falsified by its General Director, G. Carl Lahusen. The gentleman in question, who had been invited by Goldschmidt to dine with himself and Doerner, waited in another room while Doerner broke the news to their host. Lahusen was an internationally respected businessman, President of the Bremen Chamber of Commerce, and member of the board of supervisors of the DANAT-Bank. His concern owed 48 million RM to the DANAT-Bank and was also heavily indebted to the Dresdner Bank. Goldschmidt had been worried about the finances of the concern for some time, but had treated Lahusen as the respectable businessman he was supposed to be, and probably would have remained in the dark even longer had not Doerner tenaciously pursued his suspicions. He was able to demonstrate to Goldschmidt that Nordwolle's real losses amounted to about 145 million RM rather than the 45 million that had been publicly reported. It was a shattering blow to Goldschmidt, who repeatedly cried out, 'Nordwolle is finished, the DANAT-Bank is finished, the Dresdner Bank is finished, I am finished.'[317] The men ate their dinner in stony silence; Lahusen subsequently burst into tears and tried to palliate Goldschmidt by explaining that he did it all for the company; then he proceeded to lie once again, this time about the size of his wool inventories. The next day, there was another personal interview with Lahusen at which Goldschmidt threw a chair over his head.

Goldschmidt understood immediately that Doerner's revelations had profound national and international implications. Negotiations were then under way for what was to be the Hoover moratorium on reparations payments, and news of Nordwolle's true losses and of the dangerous condition of his bank and the Dresdner Bank might interfere with the progress of the negotiations. The situation was made all the worse by the news that the Österreichische Credit-Anstalt had collapsed on 12 May, and while the Germans were not directly involved, the event was bound to increase anxiety and lead to further deposit withdrawals from the German banks. It had immediately led to the sale of DANAT-Bank shares, which Goldschmidt sought to counter by purchasing 3 million RM worth for his own account. During the ensuing weeks, Goldschmidt sought desperately to find means of supporting Nordwolle and refused to inform either the Dresdner Bank or the Reichsbank of the situation, despite pressure from his colleagues in the DANAT-Bank to do so.

Goldschmidt was not alone, however, in this effort to 'muddle through' the situation. The Brüning government was in trouble both internationally and domestically. With respect to the foreign policy, it had allowed the Foreign Office to develop and carry through the harebrained scheme for a customs union with Austria, a policy which deeply offended France and undermined the efforts to carry through the kind of policy that Wassermann had advocated with respect to that country. The industrialist Paul Silverberg, who was close to the Deutsche Bank, simply could not understand how the government could undertake such a 'charge of the light brigade' when one had such a 'weak monetary position'.[318] The French were able to use the collapse of the Österreichische Credit-Anstalt and the Hoover moratorium proposal of 20 June 1931 to demand political concessions as the price of dealing with the former and accepting the latter. Foreign policy success came too late to be of preventive help in the banking crisis.

At the same time, the domestic situation, which could never be separated from the international one, was also deplorable. This was demonstrated by the couching of severe reductions of social expenditure in a new emergency decree of 5 June, in a statement of Germany's intention to seek reparations relief. The severity of the decree threatened to lead to a summoning of the Reichstag and the fall of the Brüning government, a danger finally averted on 16 June thanks to the anxiety of the political leadership of the Reichstag.[319]

While all this was going on, the Reichsbank struggled with the consequences of the fiscal and financial crises and the danger that they could become a monetary crisis as well. The calling in of loans and flight of capital as a result of the general political and financial uncertainty, and the reports on Nordwolle and increasing rumours about the DANAT-Bank and other banks and firms, were draining the Reichsbank of foreign exchange and threatening to drive its coverage below the 40 per cent level. On 12 June, Luther raised the discount rate from 5 to 7 per cent despite pleas from the bankers to limit the increase to 1 percentage point.

The Reichsbank's tight policies, and the fact that the government could no longer promise a balanced budget, in no way helped Luther's efforts to procure a bridging credit from the great banks to tide over the government while it sought to meet its obligations to the Bank for International Settlements. Luther's situation in June and more generally was made worse by the fact that he needed help from his fellow central bankers in New York and London; and they would only help him if he kept tight reins on credit, and were even demanding credit restrictions. In late June, Schäffer was actually contemplating using the threat of state bankruptcy to bring the big German banks to terms, but the banks, despite their liquidity problems, recognized what was at stake and yielded.[320]

It is important to recognize, however, that blackmail could cut both ways. On 12 June, Goldschmidt paid a visit to Director Nathan of the Dresdner Bank and pointed out that neither of them had the liquidity to survive a run on their banks. He then suggested that they go to Luther, ask him to discount bills for them on demand, even if they did not meet the Reichsbank liquidity requirements, and, after he refused, threaten to cease all payments the next day. In Goldschmidt's view, this would provide Luther with a great 'political chance' to take measures against a run on the banks. Nathan agreed with Goldschmidt, but would not undertake the step unless the Deutsche Bank und Disconto-Gesellschaft joined the cause, a proposal which Goldschmidt rejected because he felt certain that 'the people in the Mauerstrasse' would never make common cause with him and 'would feel triumphant because they think that I am finished. I will not give them the satisfaction of this triumph. If we both go to Luther, then we will create a *fait accompli* with which the Deutsche Bank must go along.'[321]

This extraordinary proposal says a great deal about the disorganized state of Germany's allegedly 'organized capitalism'. Goldschmidt and Nathan had come to the conclusion that the only way to move Luther to support the banks was by threatening to shut up shop. It is likely that they went so far as to ask for a meeting with Luther, which the Reichsbank President was prepared to hold on 13 June, but which Nathan delayed and which apparently was never held because of Goldschmidt's attitude towards the Deutsche Bank. Perhaps Nathan would have been more interested in holding the meeting if Goldschmidt had seen fit to inform him of the full extent of Nordwolle's losses, which the Dresdner Bank finally discovered for itself at the end of June. The bad news, which Goldschmidt was apparently unwilling to face fully or impart honestly, was leaking out nevertheless. Thus, the textile industrialist, Erich Freudenberg, complained to a friend on the Reichsbank board of managing directors that the Nordwolle was engaging in 'senseless underpricing' but demanding immediate payment for its goods, a clear sign of severe cash-flow problems. Initially, the complaints had been shrugged off on the grounds that 'the Lahusens are clever fellows and Goldschmidt knows what he is doing'. Finally, some enquiries were made with Goldschmidt, who responded that 'his engagement with Nordwolle was as good as if it had been with the Bank of England'. Ironically, it was the Bank of England which was apparently responsible for making the Reichsbank aware that the Nordwolle was in trouble. The information had come to the Bank of England from Franz Koenigs of Delbrück Schickler & Co., who, along with his colleague Hermann J. Abs, were alert to Nordwolle's heavy indebtedness.[322] The result was that directors of the Reichsbank became aware of the existence if not the extent of the Nordwolle problem on 12 June, and Luther brought the matter to Brüning's attention the next day 'without naming names'.[323] The incident is in any case very revealing of the personal forces at play in the banking crisis.

Although there was much talk of liquidity problems by Goldschmidt and other bankers who showed up at the Reichsbank in the second half of June, Luther seems to have stuck sublimely to his passive course with respect to the latent banking crisis. If he failed to take the lead in dealing with the danger, however, he also failed to do anything significant about the massive exploitation of the Reichsbank by the banks to spare their own foreign exchange reserves, and about their role in the flight of capital. The Reichsbank was being made doubly vulnerable by being deprived of the assets needed to intervene in emergencies like Nordwolle, and by having insufficient resources to maintain its credibility to the outside world. The Deutsche Bank und Disconto-Gesellschaft was a prime sinner in this regard, taking 393 million RM in foreign exchange in June and another 139 million RM in the first two weeks of July. During the period 1 June–10 July, however, the Deutsche Bank und Disconto-Gesellschaft used only 25 million of its own foreign exchange reserves to meet obligations payable in foreign exchange. Of the 505 million RM in foreign exchange taken by the Deutsche Bank und Disconto-Gesellschaft between 1 June and 10 July, 266 million were used to cover short-term foreign indebtedness, which meant that 239 million was facilitating capital flight. With respect to foreign exchange, therefore, most of the banks were using the Reichsbank as a lender of first rather than last resort and, to a great extent, for undesirable purposes from the Reichsbank's standpoint.[324]

When the Reichsbank and government became fully aware of the extent of the Nordwolle disaster on 1 July, there was general agreement that it was essential to get Nordwolle back on its feet because of heavy foreign debts and for the sake of the Hoover moratorium negotiations. As was later noted, the entire industrial life of Bremen could collapse as well and thousands of workers be thrown out of work. At the same time, the Reich was in no position to give away the money needed, and Finance Minister Dietrich made the telling point that 'if the Reich continually jumps in, then this will have to lead to a socialization of the banks under present conditions'. Logically, therefore, the banks had to take on the responsibilities that would prevent such an eventuality, and Luther was convinced that this was precisely what should happen. He argued that the Reich had to mobilize the banks to reconstruct the company, and noted that 'the Deutsche Bank has stored up reserves for some time in order to intervene in large collapses'.[325]

While it was clear that the DANAT-Bank and Dresdner Bank were hard hit by the Nordwolle affair, the Reichsbank took the position that it would be cheaper and better to assist Nordwolle than later to have to reconstruct the banks ruined by the firm's collapse, and that a banking crisis would inevitably force the Reichsbank to go below its 40 per cent coverage requirement. In the worst eventuality, the Reichsbank felt committed to maintain the DANAT-Bank because it was considered to be 'a basically healthy bank'.[326] This, at least, was the unanimous decision of the directors on the evening of 2 July. In the first days of July, a scheme was thus devised for the Reich to supply 50 million marks for the issuance of new Nordwolle shares to be used as a basis for partial debt repayment. The fact that the Reich was the source of the money was to be kept hidden and a consortium of banks was to take over the shares with a promise of repurchase by the banks in ten years, and payment of interest and eventually a dividend to the Reich. Nordwolle was placed in a class with the FAVAG, which was about to undergo adjudication in the criminal courts.

The government had a variety of other disasters on its hands, however, where criminality had not been involved but which nevertheless required action: the Borsig concern and Mechernich Lead Mining Company were also in deep difficulty, and the Landesbank der Rheinprovinz had enormous liquidity difficulties whose volume well exceeded that of Nordwolle thanks to its unrecoverable municipal loans. These various problems had pointed to the need for corporation law reform, and legislation was in the making, although Wassermann was urging that it be put off until conditions were calmer. Wassermann thought it most important to establish a small group of persons experienced in economic problems to discuss the situation and advise the government. What interested the government most at this point, however, was not free advice but rather that the business community stand financially behind its efforts to maximize the positive effects of the Hoover moratorium through a 500 million RM credit guarantee to the Reich – a revival of the old RdI credit action plan of 1921.

A decade had passed, however, and the business community was facing a political and economic crisis of unparalleled proportions and a government that was increasingly authoritarian and increasingly impatient. The credit guarantee was instituted by decree on 8 July. Brüning thought that a corporation law reform should also simply be decreed, and was highly critical of what he felt had been gross misinvestment of capital – above all, by the municipalities. In the same spirit, Vice-President Dreyse thought that 'one must use the present embarrassment of the banks to prescribe that in the future foreign debts ought only to be incurred in agreement with the Reichsbank'.[327]

Dreyse made this comment on 6 July, after having been informed a few days previously by Schäffer that the DANAT-Bank was in trouble. Schäffer had this information because Goldschmidt had been warning him privately that the DANAT-Bank was running out of bills acceptable to the Reichsbank. Apparently Dreyse had not understood how embarrassing the 'embarrassment' was. Perhaps the incredible overload of problems confronting the government and Reichsbank helps to explain why the full seriousness of DANAT's difficulties was not realized in the face of such mounting evidence. Whatever the case, on 8 July, Goldschmidt grasped at his last straw and went to Wassermann to propose a fusion of the DANAT-Bank and the Deutsche Bank und Disconto-Gesellschaft. He assured Wassermann that his capital was intact and understated his losses in the Nordwolle affair. Wassermann knew better, asked for time to think about the matter, and pointed out that the Deutsche Bank und Disconto-Gesellschaft would be undertaking a terrible risk unless it knew exactly what the real situation was.

Undoubtedly, Goldschmidt realized that a favourable outcome of this effort was unlikely, which it was, and decided to inform the government instead. Goldschmidt and his colleague Bodenheimer then went to Schäffer's home and told him that they were reaching the end of their discountable bills. Afterwards Schäffer informed Dreyse, and the latter complained that Goldschmidt had only revealed his problems in a very piecemeal way, a charge Goldschmidt denied on the grounds that he was not fully informed himself and feared creating unrest in the bank by researching the matter prematurely. Indeed, Goldschmidt did not know his exact status even then, but it is difficult not to conclude that Goldschmidt had become altogether too practised in not wanting to face the realities, and that the Reichsbank leadership was inept when it came to tending the dykes.[328]

It is also very difficult not to conclude that Wassermann and Solmssen, the two leading actors for the Deutsche Bank und Disconto-Gesellschaft during the critical decision making in the week preceding the suspension of payments by the DANAT-Bank on 13 July and the three-day bank holiday decree on 14 July, showed far greater attention to the pursuit of their own interests than they did to preventing the collapse of the DANAT-Bank and the Dresdner Bank, and the massive government control of the banking system that was its consequence. Most of the controversy has centred about Wassermann, whose behaviour during the crisis was anything but distinguished and is far from easy to interpret.

At a meeting of 6 July with the industrialist and bankers to discuss the guarantee to the Reich, Wassermann was reported to have repeated three times, 'but how are we now supposed to solve the DANAT problem?'³²⁹ On this same day there were leaks about the DANAT-Bank in the Swiss press which were attributed to the Deutsche Bank und Disconto-Gesellschaft. On the morning of 9 July, Bodenheimer informed Wassermann that the DANAT-Bank would have to close its doors the next day, and asked him to summon a meeting of the leading banks. Goldschmidt offered a variation on his proposal of the previous day by suggesting an exchange of shares among the Deutsche Bank und Disconto-Gesellschaft, the DANAT-Bank and the Reichs-Kredit-Gesellschaft. Wassermann was understandably negative on this proposal, but he is also reported to have begun to undermine the DANAT-Bank's position still further. Thus, he proposed directly to Goldschmidt that the DANAT-Bank be liquidated with a guarantee from the Reich to its creditors, a proposal which Goldschmidt refused. At the same time, Goldschmidt gratefully accepted an offer by Wassermann to have the other banks in the Hapag–Lloyd consortium, of which the most important was the Deutsche Bank und Disconto-Gesellschaft, take over the company's credits.

In a meeting with Dreyse, Finance Minister Dietrich and Schäffer, Wassermann, in the company of some other Berlin bankers, bluntly stated that the DANAT-Bank problem could not be solved by the banks, that the DANAT-Bank 'was not to be saved'. Speaking in the name of the other banks as well as himself, Wassermann insisted that, if its creditors received a Reich guarantee, then the DANAT-Bank had to be liquidated because it would otherwise have an intolerable competitive advantage over the other banks. The bankers, who met at the Deutsche Bank und Disconto-Gesellschaft that evening, agreed to the taking over of the DANAT-Bank's Hapag–Lloyd and some of its other credits and, in an effort to prevent the DANAT-Bank from stopping operations – that is, 'to maintain the DANAT-Bank' – agreed to put up 250 million RM in credit to the DANAT-Bank, if the Reichsbank would grant a deficiency guarantee rather than a full guarantee. This was sufficient to keep the DANAT-Bank from shutting down the next day, while all waited to see what the Reichsbank would do and if Luther would be successful in his efforts to get a credit abroad. It is important to note, however, that there is a distinction between 'maintaining' and 'saving' a bank, and it was the former rather than the latter that was involved in this action.³³⁰

This was especially the case because the authorities had begun examining the DANAT-Bank's books and discovered that it had bought large quantities of its own shares and had understated its Nordwolle losses all along. Brüning and Goldschmidt, who kept in contact during their exile in the United States, later complained that the bankers had treated Goldschmidt like a leper and had made him a 'scapegoat'. Brüning also believed that there was something sinister about Wassermann's coming to him on the evening of 10 July and telling him that the situation of the German banks was relatively favourable with the exception of the DANAT-Bank, and that government help to the DANAT-Bank would ease the situation and end the crisis. The context at the time, however, was one in which everyone, including Brüning, was profoundly irritated at the extent of the damage that the Nordwolle scandal had caused. Later, the former Chancellor accused Wassermann of betraying his feelings for a moment by letting a 'smile of triumph' pass over his face after being given the Hapag–Lloyd credits by Goldschmidt. In view of Wassermann's special interest in the shipping field, there may have some element of truth here.[331]

The kindest interpretation of Wassermann's relationship with Goldschmidt was that Wassermann was playing the role of David to Absalom rather than, as Schäffer and other critics of Wassermann thought, Saul to David during the crisis.[332] It is useful to bear in mind, however, that Wassermann was not pursuing a private policy and that Solmssen, who was head of the Central Bankers' Association as well as a senior member of the Deutsche Bank und Disconto-Gesellschaft's board of managing directors, genuinely loathed the way Goldschmidt had violated 'the classic rules of solid banking'.[333]

If Wassermann and Solmssen were satisfied to see the Goldschmidt banking style discredited, to take over some of Goldschmidt's business and to have less competition, they were especially anxious to protect the Deutsche Bank und Disconto-Gesellschaft and avoid new economic disasters. From the standpoint of security, they found Luther more threatening than Goldschmidt because Luther stubbornly refused to give even a deficiency guarantee to back up a banker credit to the DANAT-Bank. Until 10 July, the Reichsbank had been prepared to provide the DANAT-Bank with further help. On the one hand, Luther had flown to London and anticipated a new rediscount credit from the Bank of England. On the other hand, Brüning had agreed to a Reich guarantee of such a credit and the DANAT-Bank had become more credit-worthy thanks to the willingness of the Deutsche Bank und Disconto-Gesellschaft to take over the credits of the Hapag and the Norddeutscher Lloyd. The failure of Luther's efforts in London, the political difficulties he encountered in Paris, and the possibility that risky decisions that might involve going under the 40 per cent coverage requirement would endanger the Hoover moratorium undermined the benevolent attitude towards the DANAT-Bank. On 10 July, the Reichsbank directors decided to sharpen their credit restrictions even though they were aware that this would lead to the collapse of the DANAT-Bank.[334]

On Saturday, 11 July, the DANAT-Bank informed the Reichsbank that it could not open on Monday, and the issue of how much solidarity the banks would show and what Luther would do was thus revived. The result was a rather stormy meeting between the bankers and Brüning and Luther, at which Wassermann and Solmssen declared a willingness to consider a banking consortium to support the DANAT-Bank, but said that they could not enter such an arrangement until they had had a few days to examine the DANAT-Bank's situation. Luther agreed immediately to the idea of a three-day bank holiday. They also declared a readiness to grant a bridging credit of 10–15 million RM provided that the Reichsbank would accept the DANAT-Bank bills. To Solmssen's surprise, Luther refused to accept such bills, and Solmssen pointed out that 'we do not have a money machine in our house and cannot possibly run the danger of losing our own liquidity in order to save that of another bank'. When Hermann Bücher of the AEG spoke out for the banks to take action in solidarity with the DANAT-Bank, Solmssen directly opposed the idea.[335]

Wassermann urged a major change in Reichsbank and government policy. He argued that the coverage requirement should be reduced to 20 per cent, that foreign exchange controls should be introduced immediately to stop capital flight and runs on the banks for foreign exchange, and that the bank holiday should be justified by the capital flight problem rather than the DANAT-Bank problem. He also strongly opposed Luther's plan to introduce new credit restrictions, and warned that a cessation of operations by the DANAT-Bank would lead to a run on all the banks. Wassermann, along with Solmssen, continued to take the position that the DANAT-Bank problem had to be dealt with in isolation from that of the other banks, and rejected suggestions by the Swedish banker and expert adviser to the government Marcus Wallenberg that the banks follow the model of banker solidarity in support of a troubled bank employed in the Swedish banking crisis of 1920.[336]

Wassermann had in fact become suspicious of the reactions of the Dresdner Bank managing directors Frisch and Gutmann at the meeting on 11 July, and had passed a note to Solmssen that the Dresdner Bank was also bankrupt. Brüning had the impression that the condition of the banks was worse than he had thought and that exchange controls were essential, although Luther continued to doubt their effectiveness. The Chancellor had in any case come to the conclusion that a Reich guarantee of the DANAT-Bank had to be given when it shut its doors on 13 July. This was indeed evident the next day, when Wassermann informed Brüning that the Dresdner Bank was also in trouble, a revelation which Frisch regarded as a 'gross breach of confidence'[337] on the part of Wassermann. Frisch told Brüning that Wassermann's statement was unauthorized and untrue, but the incident must only have strengthened Brüning's growing scepticism about the people running Germany's banking system.

It is in fact very difficult to fathom what Wassermann was up to at this point, since he also proposed a fusion of the DANAT-Bank and the Dresdner Bank. Brüning was astonished at the idea that anything could be accomplished by coupling two insolvent institutions. The source of this idea was probably not Machiavellism, but rather Wassermann's conviction that the plan to declare a bank holiday for the DANAT-Bank alone would promote rather than prevent a run on the banks, and that it would thus be 'cheaper' to have a fusion. His biggest concern, as on the previous day, was the Reichsbank's intention to introduce credit restrictions on the banks at this moment, which he felt would 'mean the destruction of the German credit system'. He argued that the banks and credit system were more important than the Reichsbank law, and he was hardly alone in taking this view.[338]

Wassermann was correct about the inadequacy of an emergency decree declaring a bank holiday for the DANAT-Bank combined with a Reich guarantee to its customers posted outside the bank's doors. This was tried on 13 July, but the bankers then requested a bank holiday for all beginning the next day because of their fear of a run on the banks. The decree was thus extended to all of the banks for the next two days, and the government decreed restrictions on bank payouts until they could be lifted in early August. While there had been much talk about using some type of emergency money in the form of loan bureaux notes or Rentenmark, the Reichsbank, under the usual pressure from abroad, opposed such measures, imposed credit restrictions and raised the discount rate to 15 per cent during the coming days. In another one of those remarkable actions that characterized the entire crisis, Solmssen, representing both the Bankers' Central Association and the Reich Association of German Industry, actually went to Reich Chancellery State Secretary Pünder on 15 September and called for the replacement of Luther with Schacht. This would, of course, have been illegal, since the Reichsbank President was chosen for four years and could only be removed for cause by the General Council of the Reichsbank.[339]

Luther stayed on, but the coming weeks did witness a massive transformation of the state's role in the financial sector, with the introduction of control over the banks through the installation of a Banking Commissar, Reich guarantees for the DANAT-Bank and Dresdner Bank, the establishment of a temporary bank transfer association to deal with bank transfers, and then the creation of an Acceptance and Guarantee Bank to replace the old system of interbank drawing of bills on each other which could be discounted at the Reichsbank. After 11 July, the Reichsbank refused such bills, and the purpose of the new bank was to create bills which the Reichsbank could accept in confidence. The Reich held 80 million RM of the bank's 200 million in shares and also gave a deficiency guarantee for the bank's operations. Finally, the Reich was able to negotiate a Standstill Agreement, in which Gustaf Schlieper of the Deutsche Bank und Disconto-Gesellschaft and Carl Melchior of the Warburg bank played leading roles, with Germany's biggest foreign creditors. These agreements, when combined with the foreign exchange controls introduced on 15 July and tightened thereafter, protected the Acceptance Bank and Reichsbank from massive withdrawals from abroad and capital flight.[340]

The Deutsche Bank und Disconto-Gesellschaft emerged from the banking crisis as the leading and strongest representative of a badly battered banking system that was almost permanently on the defensive. The Deutsche Bank und Disconto-Gesellschaft itself was sharply criticized in the press, especially by an article in *Die Bank* which was entitled 'The stab in the back' and recounted some of Wassermann's actions in the crisis. In its usual fashion, the bank avoided much public statement and sought to influence the public by informing its friends on the supervisory board and provincial and local committees of what had happened, and by emphasizing that it had been prepared to act on behalf of the DANAT-Bank if the Reichsbank had come through with a guarantee.[341] On 21 July, the Deutsche Bank und Disconto-Gesellschaft did see fit to inform the public of the 30 million RM it had used to cover the credits of two of the DANAT's biggest customers: that is, the shipping companies.

Its most impressive effort was a 'Memorandum on the July events in the banking industry' which it sent to the Chancellor on 1 October 1931. The major argument made in the memorandum was that the banking crisis was the culmination of what war, reparations and international and domestic mis-management of the economic situation had wrought. The bank pointedly empha-sized the wisdom and importance of its fusion of 1929 in enabling it to weather the crisis, and argued that the crisis would have been much less serious 'if other great institutes had entered on the path of concentration at the right time and thereby made themselves more resistant for times of crisis'.[342]

Most of the memorandum, however, was devoted to attacking the 'sump-tuously fertile garland of legend' surrounding the events of 13 July. On the one hand, it defended the banks which had survived the crisis, especially the Deutsche Bank und Disconto-Gesellschaft. On the other, it more or less laid the blame for the severity of the crisis on the Reichsbank for its failure to recognize the dangerousness of the situation and the rigidity of its policies. The self-defence was the most elaborate of these two efforts. The idea of a fusion with the DANAT-Bank was rejected on the grounds of insufficient time to study the matter, the burden this would place on its employees after the difficulties which the 1929 fusion had caused them, and the undesirability of having even more of Germany's credit business concentrated in one bank.

The Deutsche Bank und Disconto-Gesellschaft above all defended itself against charges made in connection with its refusal on 11 July to consider participating in the 250 million RM loan to the DANAT-Bank without giving the matter proper consideration and without a Reichsbank guarantee. It argued that this was the only responsible policy to follow, and rejected the notion that the banks demonstrated a 'lack of capacity to put things together and imagination'. In the last analysis, it was the Reichsbank which saved the day because only it could do so: 'It has been demonstrated in the course of the crisis that the recipe "pay, pay, pay!" leads with certainty to success in restoring confidence once again. The monetary and confidence crisis was therefore overcome at that moment when the Reichsbank gave up restrictions along with the schematic coverage principle. The precondition for this was that the remaining supply of coverage be insured to some extent through exchange control measures. This security was lacking in the critical days. If the Reichsbank had simply supplied as much credit and quantity of notes as it wished, its coverage would have sunk to 10 or 5 or 0 per cent if the withdrawal of foreign exchange had continued.' Both the banks and the Reichsbank had their hands tied, and the memorandum thus concluded with a prototypical statement of the position that the crisis reflected a lack of freedom of manouevre: 'one can see the enormity of a misfortune coming and still be placed in a position of being unable to avoid it.'

One could argue, however, that something had to be done about a banking system that could get locked into such a situation. The banking crisis marks the great divide between the reassertion of banking power and influence that had taken place after the inflation, and which appeared to reach new heights in the first phase of the depression, and a new period of self-defence and subordination to public authority that began in the wake of the banking crisis, and which continued in various forms well into the post-1945 period. The German credit banking system, which, ironically enough, had received its most spirited endorsement in Jakob Goldschmidt's appearance before the Macmillan Committee a few months before the crisis, threatened to be laid low with him. As State Secretary Trendelenburg noted on the very eve of the revelations about Nordwolle, the economic crisis was 'a crisis of confidence in capitalism', and the financial sector was part of the problem: 'The banking system is overly concentrated. The branch system, to the disadvantage of the entire credit business, has largely suppressed the independent provincial banks. A reorganization is necessary, but it is possible only from inside the system and in a very cautious way, for otherwise there is the danger of a fateful shaking up of the credit structure.'[343]

Once the shaking up had taken place, Trendelenburg could argue that public confidence in the banks had been destroyed and that 'a control of the banks has to be set up and correct information forced out of them through the threat of punishment'.[344] The Reichsbank also called for reforms – above all, in intensifying reserve requirements, reducing competition and artificial overexpansion, and compelling the banks to use their own foreign exchange rather than turning to the Reichsbank all the time. Indeed, the atmosphere was such that the banks could be well satisfied with supervision, since Hilferding, for example, thought the time had come to consider separating the deposit business from enterprise financing, and thus effectively going over to the British system. He was by no means alone in this view.[345]

Brüning was especially ferocious in his criticisms of the big banks and of big business in general. He considered the large enterprises overcapitalized and called for rapid capital consolidation and honest balances. Shortly after the crisis he argued that 'the capital requirements of medium-sized and small business are not given enough consideration. On the other side, capital is being badly invested, as for example the 100 million put into entertainment enterprises in the vicinity of the Kaiser-Wilhelm-Memorial Church. The great banks criticize government expenditure, but then push the City of Berlin into taking credits for the subway and large power works. That has to end. Internal measures and personnel reforms are needed. Otherwise we will get nowhere. It is hard to tell what the banks are up to. At one moment they demand increased security from debtors which cannot be managed even though the companies have contracts.

On the other side they lack the courage to do something about their large bad investments. The government cannot tolerate this ... state capitalism will be unavoidable.'[346]

In answering such charges, the Deutsche Bank und Disconto-Gesellschaft leaders were at their best and most effective when they attributed their failures to the general economic conditions of the Weimar Republic. Solmssen insisted that the events of 13 July were an 'act of God' rather than the guilt of persons or the fault of the banking system, which had been the envy of the world before the war and Germany's impoverishment: 'This unification of financing and deposit banking is a system of which one can say without being arrogant that it built Germany's economy. There was endless experience in this system which rested on an old tradition and which worked well and usefully until the war. At that time one understood instinctively where to draw the line between the money that could be invested and that which had to be kept in readiness. This elastic system cannot be replaced with paragraphs. The hallmark of this system, as it exists today and for whose retention I would like to work for and fight for in the interest of the economy, is its elasticity.'[347]

Solmssen did not deny that the system had not been working well after the war and that a great deal of misplaced credit had been given, but he argued that the alternative to giving the credit would have been massive unemployment. They were compelled to be 'optimists' and hope that the international situation would improve, and that the world economy would work in their favour and begin to mend the damage of war and inflation. Instead, the reverse had taken place. There was indeed much to this argument, and a lance could also be broken for the employment of short-term capital for long-term purposes – provided it was done on a short-term basis. As Schäffer noted in an important memorandum, the banks had always lent a certain amount of short-term money while waiting for the propitious moment to float a capital share issue and thus transform short-term into long-term debts. It was precisely this process which failed in Weimar.[348]

When Solmssen tried to argue that the Deutsche Bank und Disconto-Gesellschaft was doing a good job of caring for medium-sized and small business, he was not very convincing. Thus, in October 1931 he presented the Reichsbank with data showing that 92 per cent of its credits were below 50,000 RM. The effort to confuse the number of credits given with the amount of money given as credit does appear as a rather clumsy effort to make the best of a bad case. If one took the total amounts of credit being given by the bank, then only 16.8 per cent were given in amounts under 50,000 RM, while 26.0, rather than 0.04 per cent, were given in amounts between 1 and 5 million RM, 12.5 rather than 0.01 per cent in amounts over 5 million, and 25.2 rather than 3.9 in amounts between 100,000 and 500,000 RM.[349] Little wonder, therefore, that the Saxon industrialists at their meeting in March 1932 complained that 'the large enterprise feels secure only among its fellows; the large bank tends to the large industrial company and both live off one another and die because of one another'.[350]

One good illustration of why big industry and big banking could work so comfortably together was provided by Friedrich Flick in August 1931, when the Deutsche Bank und Disconto-Gesellschaft became concerned about his status. Flick admitted that some of his engagements were 'very precarious', but then pointed out 'that the breaking up of his holdings would at the same time mean the disintegration of the present leadership of the United Steel Works and this would have consequences for the operation of the United Steel Works which could only be solved from the political side'.[351] This is precisely what happened in the spring of 1932 in the famous Gelsenberg affair, where Flick sold his shares to the Reich. More generally, however, it was unquestionably true that industry had a powerful influence over the banks, as the importance of Paul Silverberg and Otto Wolff on the supervisory board and regional committees of the Deutsche Bank und Disconto-Gesellschaft demonstrated, as well as the fact that it was western heavy industry which took over the shares of the reconstructed DANAT-Bank.

The major concern of the Deutsche Bank und Disconto-Gesellschaft after the crisis of July 1931, however, was what it had been to a great extent all along, self-preservation under the unpleasant circumstances which its leaders confronted with a heavy dose of pessimism. As Solmssen announced to the branch directors at the beginning of September 1931, it was the task of the Deutsche Bank und Disconto-Gesellschaft to take the 'spiritual' leadership in trying to revive the 'healthy old banking principles', and since there was little possibility of increasing profits, the only thing to do was cut costs. By 1 January 1933, the number of employees at the bank had dropped from 20,051 to 16,614. There were rigorous salary cuts of 12 to 14 per cent all along the line in accordance with Brüning's Fourth Emergency Decree, and even more draconian cuts for non-contractual employees. Solmssen himself took another 10 per cent cut and the elimination of prepayments on his supervisory board royalties beginning in January 1932. A further cut was imposed in July 1932.[352]

The Deutsche Bank und Disconto-Gesellschaft also undertook a significant consolidation of its capital for 1931, reducing its share capital from 285 to 144 million RM and its reserves from 160 to 25.2 million RM. It was most successful in maintaining its private character. As part of the consolidation, it took a 50 million mark government credit in April 1932, in return for which it placed an equivalent amount in shares from its own holdings of 72 million with the Deutsche Golddiskontbank. The repurchase began almost immediately thereafter and was completed by the beginning of 1936. An audit conducted by the Reichsbank in connection with this arrangement was extremely favourable, pointing out that the savings expected from the fusion of 1929 had been realized, and that the bank was very well run in that its directors had the necessary information immediately at their disposal. While the bank certainly had its share of 'optimistic' engagements to contend with, and its basis had been severely narrowed by the depression, the auditors believed that it had excellent chances of survival if conditions remained stable.[353]

Not everyone was so satisfied with the management of the bank, and the most vocal of the dissatisfied on record was Paul Silverberg. He was particularly upset that the bank had ended up taking shares for the credits it had given, and thus owning 100 per cent of the Lanz and Maffei firms. Silverberg feared that it would end up owning more industrial enterprises and thus being responsible for them in every sense, a practice that had sealed the fate of the Österreichische Credit-Anstalt and could do the same to the Deutsche Bank und Disconto-Gesellschaft in the event of a crisis. Silverberg was also very unhappy with the role played by the bank in its dealings with Hapag–Lloyd, and rumours going around that Wassermann and Solmssen were in disagreement on basic policy.[354]

Silverberg had a particularly strong dislike of Stauss, whom he considered a great liability. Stauss had proved this point once again in October 1931 when the Schultheiss Brewery scandal broke. The concern was one of Stauss's accounts, and the Deutsche Bank und Disconto-Gesellschaft had played the major role in the Schultheiss–Ostwerke fusion of 1930. Unhappily for Stauss, the General Director, Ludwig Katzenellenbogen, was a swindler, who had taken loans from a variety of banks without telling them of the other loans, and who had falsified the prospectus of the concern. As a result, Stauss was 'kicked upstairs' to the supervisory board in 1932. His political obligations were given as an excuse for his departure from the board of managing directors. The change was made all the more plausible to those who did not know better by the retirements of managing directors Schlitter and Boner in 1932.[355]

As had been the custom of the bank, it proposed to place the three departing managing directors on the special committee of the board of supervisors, but Silverberg protested in no uncertain terms and argued that the time had come to create an Executive Committee that would set the agenda for the board of supervisors and exercise genuine surveillance. He thought this essential given the huge losses of the bank, its reorganization, the dissatisfaction of the share-holders and public criticism. While happy to see Schlitter elected, he objected very strongly to Stauss. While it proved impossible to keep Stauss off the supervisory board, the reorganization proposed by Silverberg did take place. Silverberg's concern with the image of the bank and the importance of control was well taken, as was proven at the end of 1932 by the extraordinary case of Director Schaefer of the Düsseldorf branch, one of the Deutsche Bank und Disconto-Gesellschaft's most trusted and important branch directors. Schaefer suddenly disappeared in November 1932, and it turned out that he had been speculating and embezzling money from the bank to the tune of 8–10 million RM. His malfeasance put an end to the promising career of Werner Kehl at the bank because the Düsseldorf branch was in Kehl's area of responsibility and he felt compelled to resign.[356]

If the bank thus felt very heavy pressure in the management of its own affairs after the banking crisis, the same was true with respect to its public posture on economic and political matters. The departure of Britain from the Gold Standard in September 1931, the increasing call for reflationary measures and the actual introduction of such measures by Papen and Schleicher inevitably raised questions as to where the bank's leadership was to stand on these issues. Through 1931 at least, the stand of the bank's leaders was one that supported deflation, opposed currency experiments, and sought to toughen it out until Germany could compete once more.

Karl Kimmich represented this position most perfectly. After the British devaluation, Kimmich was well aware of tendencies in government circles to use 'doses of inflation' as a means of dealing with the unemployment situation, and he had personally warned Dietrich against notions of not pursuing deflation with continued rigour. Kimmich believed that Dietrich had changed his mind under pressure from Brüning and Luther, and left no doubt where he himself stood: 'I take the view that we must hold on to the gold currency whatever it costs. We must become 15 to 20 per cent cheaper in Germany and the deflation must be maintained until then. The solution of collective bargaining questions must play the decisive role in this. I would consider it the greatest misfortune, even though people from banking circles are already talking about letting the mark go down to 80 pf., if such ideas were to be realized. For us, I think, there would be no halt to the fall because we lack the means to bring the mark into balance again. For that, one needs large monetary reserves which we do not have. And if one is of the view, as I am, that our private enterprises are not yet properly organized, then with what right can one take responsibility for such a defrauding of the people, or, as those people put it, for an inflation in doses? Should Germany then gradually lose credit in each and every area? I think we have lost enough credit in the world by now. Should we now tear away the last anchor of hope from the mark-saving public?'[357]

In 1932, however, there was a growing rebellion against this narrowly deflationary policy, especially as worker reduction ceased to be profitable. In industry there was even some support for the reflationary currency proposals of Ernst Wagemann and others. The Deutsche Bank und Disconto-Gesellschaft encountered such feelings on the supervisory boards on which its leaders sat. The construction programme of the Rhein–Main–Donau AG, for example, which depended on funding by Bavaria and the Reich, suffered from constant uncertainty and irrationality. The minimal programmes into which it was being forced by decreased government infrastructural spending stood in disproportion to the corporation's capacity and required penalty compensations to the construction firms involved for failure to provide funds for the full programme. Indeed, an argument could now be made that funding the full construction programme would save money in unemployment support, since 'things today are now such that for every worker let go from a job, a second becomes unemployed'.[358] How was one to justify unused capacity in the construction industry, where unemployment rates of 59 per cent were reported in 1931, and 1932 promised to be worse?

The Berlin construction firm of Johannes Jeserich complained in January 1932 that it could no longer count on municipal contracts for street building and repair. Previously, these had been given under extra-budgetary allocations whose amortization was then placed in the budget of the following year, but this practice was banned under recent emergency decrees. Indeed, the reduction of municipal expenditure was at the heart of the Brüning–Luther policy, but it was spelling disaster for the private firms servicing urban communities. The only ray of hope appeared to be work creation through credit creation: 'During the last days in the press there has been extensive reporting on the so-called Wagemann currency project. Should this project ... come to be carried out, then conditions could change very much to our favour because the districts and municipalities would then again have financial manoeuvrability and have the possibility of granting contracts.'[359]

While Solmssen had his reservations about the Wagemann Plan, it is worth noting that he too was coming to the conclusion that something needed to be done to fight the radicalism created by high unemployment and the increasing economic irrationalities produced by the continuing deflationary policy. In a speech to the Reich Economic Council in March 1932, he suggested a variety of ways in which bills could be created to support infrastructural employment and pointed to techniques being employed in the United States. This is to suggest not that bankers like Solmssen were turning into monetary radicals, but rather that the radicals in the street were bestirring their imaginations about preventive measures.[360] Furthermore, the Deutsche Bank und Disconto-Gesellschaft had long been in the business of dealing with bills backed by the Reich whose actual status did not always conform to dogma: the Russian bills, for example, and the *Osthilfe* bills, and then the new bills to support the truly reflationary programmes of tax breaks for increasing employment provided by the von Papen and Schleicher governments.

Whatever the causes, there were signs that the depression was bottoming out in 1932, and undoubtedly this brought some hope that, as industry might revive, the banking business might improve with the economy. The two decades since the beginning of the First World War had not been good ones for proud bankers like Solmssen, and he was at once wounded and angry when he learned of objections to his appointment as Chairman of the Supervisory Board of Hoesch because he was 'a banker' and therefore allegedly unsuited to serve in such a position in a pure industrial firm. He insisted he was also an industrialist, and reminded General Director Springorum of his services in the petroleum field and in the electrical power industry. He went on to remind Springorum of what a banker was and should be: 'As I have said, I do not write this to praise myself, but rather in conscious self-defence because I have for a long time found it bitter that one again and again speaks of *the* banks and *the* bankers without making the necessary distinctions. God knows we must now pay for the sins which speculative block traders have committed, who to be sure are called bankers, but who never were in the sense in which I conceive of my profession. They could only behave this way because important representatives of German industry did not confront them with the necessary self-consciousness, but rather allowed themselves to become enmeshed in their rotten business maxims based on indebtedness, self-enrichment and the irresponsible throwing together of industrial plants, only then to end up in the hands of the state.'[361]

Unfortunately for Solmssen, who along with his colleagues at the bank tried to play a leading role in seeking to reform the banking system through self-regulation and to ward off more state intervention,[362] the new age that was dawning when he wrote this letter on 17 January 1933 was not to be his. More predictive of the future was a letter written by Director Kiehl to his client, the cigarette manufacturer Philipp Reemtsma, in January 1932. He had happened to pick up a copy of the *Völkischer Beobachter* and read an article full of praise for Reemtsma, even though he was a big industrialist. He found it all very interesting and lightheartedly concluded: 'In any case, since then I make note of you as my protective patron in the event of the Third Reich, since people from the bank will also have to take care of themselves under the swastika in spite of everything'.[363] If these lines now seem like a bad joke, this is because, unfortunately, they foretold the future.

The Deutsche Bank and the Dictatorship
1933–1945

by Harold James

Introduction

At the end of January 1933, Adolf Hitler became Chancellor of Germany and created a party dictatorship around the monopoly of power of the National Socialist Party (NSDAP) that would last until Germany's defeat by the Allies in 1945. The new regime aimed at complete control of economic as well as social, political and cultural activities. In economics, it interpreted the depression as evidence of the failure of the private market economy and of the necessity of state intervention. Although already earlier in the Weimar Republic there had been a great deal of government intervention – for instance, in the housing market and in wage policy – the depression brought a call for new controls and regulation. The German government imposed restrictions on international capital movement and a partial debt moratorium for agriculture.

The depression, with its enormous human suffering, the almost seven million unemployed, bankrupt farmers and closed banks, seemed unambiguous evidence that the unplanned individualistic market economy and also 'finance capitalism' did not work. Banks had called in many loans in order to protect their severely endangered liquidity, and had earned the hatred of many small and medium-sized enterprises. At the same time, in order to remain in business, banks had demanded, received and become dependent on state subsidies.

The National Socialist New Order inherited from the depression governments a network of controls and proceeded to make it ever more extensive. In 1934 a system of managed trade was inaugurated, as well as the allocation of raw materials and the restriction of dividend payments; and after 1936 came a far-reaching regulation of prices. Jewish property was subject at first to apparently spontaneous attacks from local fanatics, then to official discrimination and, in the end, to expropriation.

With the exception of the racially motivated attack on Jewish possessions, the fundamental principle of private ownership was left untouched. The laws defining what ownership involved, the 'property rights', however, were utterly transformed. Germany remained a private economy, but without the guidance of those signals usually associated with the operation of a market: freely determined (not administered) prices, interest rates and exchange quotations. It was an economy without a market mechanism, which was supposed to behave as its new masters wished. Prices are essential to the market: their suppression and distortion lead to a command economy.

Since the banking system had historically been a transmission mechanism for market signals, in the 1930s it faced potential redundancy as the enthusiasts of new forms of economic organization took over. The crisis of 1931 seemed to teach the lesson that a banking system only harmed the rest of the economy. Would it not, they argued, be more efficient if the state directly realized its objectives by administrative fiat?

In the story of Germany's way out of depression and into the economics of control, it is difficult to distinguish clearly quite what followed more or less inevitably from the financial and economic catastrophes of the depression, and what originated from the political vision of the new masters of Germany. The capital market, for instance, became smaller and less relevant to economic activity. Bank loans recovered much more slowly than did the rest of the economy from the world depression. But both these phenomena were characteristic not only of Germany and dictatorship, but of the development of the whole European economy. Some economists as a result formulated a law of long-term decline in the demand for loans.[1] The capital market seemed to have been destroyed by the experience of depression and by the organizational measures, such as increased cartelization in financial markets, that accompanied the market failure of the 1920s and early 1930s. It required no National Socialist government opposed to finance capitalism to marginalize the German capital market. In this sense, a large part of the macroeconomics of Germany's 1930s experience would have happened anyway, whatever the form of the government.

At first, little bank financing of new investment was required because of the availability of unused capacity. Later expansion could be paid out of high profit levels, or through government credits in the case of firms producing on public contracts.

The Deutsche Bank und Disconto-Gesellschaft[2] gave substantially more new credits in 1933 (118,000) than in 1932 (17,000), but the total volume of credit fell steadily until 1937. As a proportion of the bank's balance sheet, it declined from 55.4 per cent in 1932 to 35.4 per cent in 1937 (Figure 3.1). Though there was a brief recovery of bank lending in 1938, bank loans continued to decline during the war.

Bank lending contracted in part because firms learnt the lesson of the depression as meaning avoidance of indebtedness. But banks also had their own reasons to be cautious in the aftermath of 1931, when they had been obliged to liquidate many loans in a great hurry, and in the process had incurred massive hostility from their clients. Any wise banker would draw lessons from the banking disaster. Time after time the Deutsche Bank urged restraint on its credit

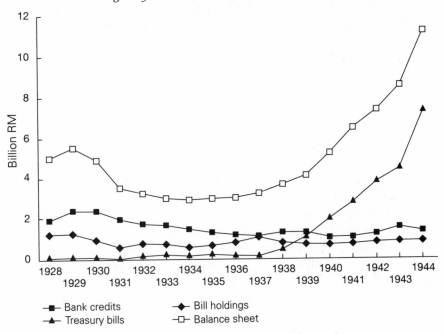

Figure 3.1 Deutsche Bank assets, 1928–44

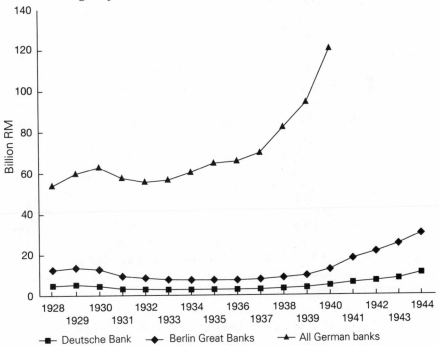

Figure 3.2 Balance sheets of German banks, 1928–44

officers. Thus in a circular to branch managers in August 1933: 'We are interested in as far as possible keeping our liquidity at a satisfactory level in the future.'³ Or Eduard Mosler, the spokesman of the board of managing directors, in October 1936 telling branch managers: 'As a result we need a certain caution in our credit policy. We should not aim at an extension of credit.' Or Karl Kimmich speaking in the board in 1938: 'There is the danger that we will be called on by industry, and we must alter our attitude ... We shall try to convert long- and middle-term credits into short-term loans.'⁴

Deposits of all the major German banks also contracted in the initial phases of the recovery period, as major firms started to use their deposits for investment.⁵ A process of financial disintermediation set in. Foreign deposits dropped particularly sharply, in the case of the Deutsche Bank to 403 million RM at the end of 1933 (compared with 685 million RM in 1931). But after the end of 1934, the total of deposits rose steadily. Faced with low demand for loans, banks found they could do little in the late 1930s except to channel these new funds into state paper. From 1933, holdings of securities shown in the bank's balance sheet rose. To a substantial extent these were government securities. After 1937, as the government became more dependent on short-term borrowing, the number of Treasury bills in the bank's portfolio also rose (see Figure 3.1). This process was described in Germany as the 'silent financing' of a government whose expenditure and deficits rose as it took on ever more tasks. In practice, the result was the financing through the banking system not simply of the government sector of the economy, but of a rearmament drive.

As the traditional business of the bank in taking business deposits and extending commercial credit contracted, its position within the German economy was diminished. In addition, traditionally a major strength of the German great banks, and of the Deutsche Bank in particular, had lain in overseas financing. The dramatic reduction of world trade in the depression, the protectionist environment of the 1930s, and Germany's managed foreign trade regime reduced the scope and significance of foreign economic relations. All these considerations combined to ensure that the Deutsche Bank, along with all the other Berlin great banks, lost its share of German banking business (Figure 3.2).

In the 1930s it was largely the savings banks (*Sparkassen*) that expanded at the expense of the traditional banking giants. Thus from 1932 to 1939 the total assets of the Berlin great banks rose by 15 per cent, while those of the *Sparkassen* increased by 102 per cent. Both in the depression and in the following recovery, the savings banks regained the position they had lost in the post-First World War hyperinflation. This development had its parallel in other European countries, where in the course of the 1930s *caisses d'épargne* (France), cantonal banks (Switzerland), building societies (Britain) and postal savings banks grew rapidly. The fact that the competitive erosion of the position of big commercial banks was a Europe-wide phenomenon suggests that the explanation does not lie solely in German legislation or institutional peculiarities, or a National Socialist favouring of more 'popular banks', let alone in the business strategy of a particular bank. In the first place, a more equal distribution of wealth and income in the inter-war period favoured the savings banks of the little people: although after 1927 the German great banks had taken savings deposits (and the Deutsche Bank was a pioneer in this regard), traditionally they had made little effort to cultivate lower- or lower-middle-class depositors. Secondly, the quasi-cartel arrangements on interest rates which existed in many countries restricted the scope for expanding business, since for many firms the lending rates were often higher than the cost of internal accumulation.

Germany, which had developed an interest rate cartel in 1931, made the cartel's provisions generally binding under the terms of the Banking Law of 1934 (Para. 36). But in Germany in the 1930s, there was an additional factor involved in the relative decline of traditional banking: the rise of large state-owned institutions with a privileged legal status. The Bank für deutsche Industrie-Obligationen (Bank for German Industrial Bonds) and the newly created Bank der Deutschen Luftfahrt (Aero-Bank) could be much more generous in their credit policy as they had an automatic guarantee of being able to rediscount bills at the Reichsbank (*Rediskontzusage*).

If banks existed more and more to channel private savings into state debt, was there any justification at all for their continued independent activity? In the directed economy, did not banks belong to the apparently discredited world of the individualistic nineteenth-century past? Such was the tenor of the arguments put forward by the believers in the new economic doctrines of management and control through party and state. Banking, particularly as it had developed in Germany, is concerned with identifying and assessing risks in a capital market, or (more generally) in evaluating the future. In the 1930s, many politically inspired commentators believed that the state could do all these tasks better – and above all, more closely in accordance with the dominant social and political doctrines of the time. And this is where the character of the new regime made a distinct difference.

The new doctrines had been defined unambiguously by Hitler in a series of programmatic writings and speeches. He frequently declared 'unalterable' the 25-point NSDAP party programme of 1920, which included the demand for the 'breaking of the servitude of interest' and (point 13) 'the nationalization of all businesses which have been formed into trusts'. Again and again he declared that the economy should be subordinated to the good of the people. On the fourth anniversary of the National Socialist 'seizure of power', a few months after the inauguration of the Four-Year Plan for the mobilization of the German economy, Hitler insisted on this demand: 'The will is crucial, by which the economy will be given the role of serving the people and capital of serving the economy. National Socialism is, as we know, the keenest enemy of the liberalistic view in which the economy is there for the sake of capital, and the people is there for the economy. We were thus determined from the first day to break with the false conclusion that the economy could lead an uncontrolled, uncontrollable and unregulated existence in the state. There can no longer today be a free economy, just left to its own devices. Not only would this be politically unacceptable; it would also have impossible economic consequences.'[6]

An elaborate propaganda machine helped to reinforce this picture of the limited role of the entrepreneur, and of his 'social responsibility' before the 'higher good' of the national community. In Veit Harlan's film *The Ruler (Der Herrscher)*, the industrial magnate Clausen, played by the great German actor Emil Jannings, eloquently set out the credo of the National Socialist businessman and a new ethos of 'responsible' business activity: 'The goal of every economic leader who is aware of his own responsibility must be to serve the people's community. This my will is the supreme goal for my work. Everything else must be subordinated to this goal, without contradiction, even if as a result I run the entire enterprise out of existence.'[7]

Germany's business élite should resemble nothing so much as Hagen's vassals in the old Teutonic sagas, with bankers assigned a particularly lowly and subordinate position. Throughout the duration of the National Socialist dictatorship, the party launched periodic attacks on bank and bankers. It associated them with the allegedly defunct economy of 'liberal individualism' and found them to be at odds with its notions of state-led economic activity.

How should banks respond to dramatic changes in political and moral values? Bankers recognized quite well that the new principles of Germany in the 1930s aimed fundamentally at the destruction of the economic system in which and for which they functioned. Yet at the same time, their historic role in evaluating and judging future trends meant that they could not but take seriously the new doctrines. The history of the Deutsche Bank in the Third Reich is the story of the clash of these two strategies of adaptation: on the one hand, self-defence against the intrusions of party and state; but accommodation and compromise on the other. The management of the Deutsche Bank might well have tried to retreat to purely economic activities; but it lived under a regime that had declared economic actions to be political.

Personnel policy, attitudes towards employees defined by new racial criteria as 'non-Aryan', or towards Jewish businesses, or towards economic activity abroad, or even on the subject of what kind of enterprise was most socially desirable: all of these were inevitably affected by bankers' perceptions of the social and political environment in which they moved. Banks do not make their own destiny. In a rather different context, the great Hamburg banker Max Warburg spoke in the early 1920s about the nature of banking history: 'I should set great store on demonstrating how large a role chance plays in the development of such a business, and indeed how much more economic development altogether is to be ascribed to chance opportunities and naturally occurring growth than to the so-called working to a goal of some individual. Throughout the work there should be a certain respect for these spontaneous developments; for most people suffer from exaggerated notions of their importance, and bank directors especially, when they write their annual reports three to six months after year-end, ascribe to their acts after the event a foresight that in fact never existed.'[8]

Modern critics, who, motivated by suspicion of and hostility to capitalism, saw the bank as forming an integral part of the dictatorship's machinery of exploitation, have presented a fundamentally misleading interpretation. The historiography of the German Democratic Republic, and also those who uncritically based their work on the material provided in the post-war US military government (OMGUS) reports, relied on a narration of the banks' and bankers' business and social contacts. Following the unsubstantiated assumption that such connections inevitably meant political pressure, these analyses went on to imply that political leverage was constantly being exercised by business. They took for granted the conclusion that they claimed to be proving, they forgot about the way in which power functioned in a totalitarian state, and they ignored what was really involved in the business of banking. They read even a participation at arm's length in such a body as the South-East Europe Association (Südost-Europa-Gesellschaft) as the hatching of imperialist and annexationist schemes, or presented forced contributions to the National Socialist charity 'Winter Help' (*Winterhilfswerk*) as the provision of subsidies for fascism.

On the other hand, those authors who see in every action of a business or a bank resistance to the new political authorities, and believe that everything not directly politicized must have constituted an act of defiance, are also lacking in historical realism and objectivity. In practice, the financial world offered little direct opposition to the regime. Instead, confronted by a world that no longer appeared to need them, bankers explained their compliant position to themselves by saying that they were doing nothing more than facing realities and then trying, however ineffectually, to mould them as best they could.

I. The Initial Challenge: National Socialist Ideology

1. The bank inquiry

In September 1933, the most focused challenge to the financial world from the party came during the hearings of an inquiry (*Bank-Enquête*) called to reform the banking system in order to avoid a repetition of the catastrophe of 1931. Wilhelm Keppler, on whom Hitler had bestowed the grandiose but ultimately meaningless title of Commissar for Economic Issues (*Beauftragter für Wirtschaftsfragen*), repeated during the inquiry's sessions a long litany of familiar complaints about banks and their position. 'In addition, capital tried to make itself the master of the economy instead of serving. Purchases of blocs of shares, participations and majorities in Annual General Meetings and Supervisory Boards were the order of the day, although this should not properly belong to the sphere of banks' activity.' The banks had become too centralized in Berlin 'in ever larger units ... with an impersonal and bureaucratic character'. They had taken on 'tasks which were concerned with speculation rather than with banking in the strict sense.' They had neglected credits to small and medium-sized enterprise. Keppler called for a 'decentralization of decision making', an extension of the activities of savings banks ('for political reasons') and a general reduction in interest rates.[9]

The newly appointed State Secretary in the Reich Economics Ministry, Gottfried Feder, who had previously distinguished himself as the inventor of a scheme for inflating the money supply by means of a rapidly depreciating unit (*Feder-Geld*), echoed these radical sentiments: 'As a result of the rise of the Jewish, purely trading spirit in banking, the great banks had failed with the result that billions of marks needed to be paid by the state for their rescue.' The conclusion that the new government should 'do something' about the abuses of banking was obvious: 'Of course the banks need to be directed by the state ... One cannot accuse our government of a lack of initiative. Today the greatest initiative belongs to Adolf Hitler.'[10]

But these sentiments did not prevail in the deliberations of the inquiry. Major industrialists testified that they had not felt any 'pressure of the great banks on their customers'. Small businessmen said that they had not been dependent on credit from the great banks, and had had ready access to other sources. Eduard Mosler from the Deutsche Bank und Disconto-Gesellschaft explained how activity on the Supervisory Board involved advice and information, helpful suggestions rather than autocratic control by banks: 'The banker can give the industrialist important advice about filling crucial positions, he can supply experience derived from other branches, experience which could only otherwise be gained with the greatest of difficulty.'[11]

Apparently even the ideologues of state control were convinced by all these arguments from the practical men of business – at least for the moment. Feder admitted rather timidly: 'I am completely satisfied. I have won the impression that in general people want to see closer personal contacts between enterprises and banks.' Perhaps, after all, banks should not be managed as part of a gigantic apparatus of state planning. Hjalmar Schacht, reappointed by Hitler as Reichsbank President, had, it seemed, carefully stage-managed the whole of the inquiry's discussion, as he told a Bank of England official: 'The whole object of the inquiry in his view was to let all the people with new theories talk themselves out, and to bring them face to face with competent experts, who would give the real answers to their theories ... Dr Schacht believed in fact that the party theorists would have no great influence in this affair.'[12]

In the end, the party activists knew they had been defeated by 'the private great banks under the leadership of Reichsbank President Dr Schacht', but wanted to renew the attack in a different forum.[13] The National Socialist movement, they thought, should not let itself be outwitted by smooth-tongued financiers. And indeed the ideological offensive against the banks was launched again, and much more effectively, but only after Schacht had departed from the Reichsbank. In the meantime, the ideologues had to be content with inflicting petty humiliations on Schacht and on the bankers he had protected. At the end of 1934, for instance, the party and the government demanded an emergency donation from businesses. Schacht and the three presidents of the stock exchange committee were obliged literally to hold out collecting boxes in which the leading business executives were personally to deposit banknotes (of a pre-arranged value): the Deutsche Bank was committed to contributing one thousand marks (otherwise Schacht would have been forced to conduct this begging operation in the street). It was a colossal and public symbolic submission of the business community.[14]

The inquiry, however, had left the banking structure untouched: there was no breaking up of the system into a network of regional banks, as had been proposed by many critics of banking in the wake of 1931. The legislative result, in the form of the 5 December 1934 Reich Credit Law (*Reichsgesetz über das Kreditwesen*), created instead a new regulatory environment: the recognition of cartel conditions on interest rates, minimum reserve requirements for banks, limitations on the size of large loans, and supervision through a Supervisory Office for Credit. In practice, it institutionalized the *ad hoc* emergency regulatory system that had developed since the disaster of 1931. The new law also placed savings banks on the same footing as other banks.

2. Credits

Ironically, the new regulations appeared for the moment to be redundant. Bankers now, unlike in the 1920s, needed no persuasion to be hesitant and cautious. The reduced demand for credit during the recovery of the 1930s meant that in the first years of its existence the Supervisory Office 'had not been very effective'.[15] Credit activities were certainly greatly reduced, but not because of legislative or regulatory control.

The profit and loss accounts reveal the contours of the Deutsche Bank's basic business. The immediate legacy of the depression brought bad debts and losses. From 1931 to 1934, write-offs eliminated the bank's operating profit; in the next year, profits were used to pay off the last state's share-holding taken in 1932. In February 1934, the bank still needed an emergency credit from the Reichsbank.[16] After 1936, profit was held at a constant level through declared and undeclared contribtions to reserve funds. Share dividends and thus in practice declared profits were controlled by the state. The revenue side of the accounts shows falling fee income until 1936, and only then a brief recovery, associated with the short-lived revival of the issue business (see below); and revenue from interest only started to recover after 1935. In other words, the decline in banking made itself felt for a long time, while the production figures of the German economy were already surging ahead (Figure 3.3).

The new credit norms restricted banks' activities much less than did a parallel law, issued on 4 December 1934. Through a ceiling imposed on company dividends, the Dividend and Bond Law (*Anleihestockgesetz*) made less attractive both the ownership and the issue of equities. Share issues throughout the 1930s remained at levels below a quarter of that of the later 1920s, and even below the volume of the crisis year 1931. Only in one year, 1938, was there an apparent burst of new issues, but it was provoked by the activities of semi-state companies, not genuinely private corporations: the Reichswerke 'Hermann Göring' and the Hydration Works of Pölitz. Apart from this brief spurt of activity, the new equity market stagnated (Table 1).

Table 1   New issues: bonds and shares in Germany, 1927–38 (RM millions)

	Bonds	Shares
1927	2,854	1,376
1928	2,905	1,339
1929	1,685	979
1930	2,926	555
1931	1,338	635
1932	521	150
1933	1,031	91
1934	338	143
1935	1,646	156
1936	2,718	395
1937	3,408	333
1938	7,851	827

The intention of the Dividend Law was to make bonds more attractive, and in consequence prepare for a conversion of government debt in 1935. The management of the capital market was consciously aimed at improving the market for state paper, and thus enabling a financing of rearmament without a large and unstable short-term debt.[17] The improvement of the fixed-interest market in 1935 generated in the short term a great deal of business, as private corporations followed the state in converting debt to lower interest rates. In 1936 private conversions even exceeded in volume those of public corporations. The Deutsche Bank managed several of these transactions: most importantly the February 1937 exchange of 5 per cent Daimler-Benz bonds for 6 per cents.[18]

In the case of public sector bonds, the holder had a choice between accepting the state's conversion terms, which included a once-only payment of a 2 per cent bonus, or holding on to the old bond, which would, as a result of newly introduced legislation, not be traded or eligible as collateral for bank loans. The private sector conversions were somewhat less egregiously in breach of existing law. The loan was called in, as provided for in the issuing prospectus, and the holder thus had an opportunity to be repaid. Holders who chose conversion received a bonus, as in the case of public sector bonds; the sum required to repay bondholders was raised by issuing new bonds at a new lower rate (Figure 3.4).

There were also some major new private bond issues: in 1937 a 24,500,000 RM 5 per cent issue for Hoesch through a consortium led by the Deutsche Bank; and more after the outbreak of war in 1939: Hoesch, BMW, Daimler, Accumulatoren-Fabrik AG (part of the Quandt concern), and Mannesmann.

Some of the old consortium activities could be revived in a market once again favourable to issues. The Deutsche Bank led jointly with the Dresdner Bank two major credits to finance trade with the USSR: 200 million RM in 1936 and another 200 million in 1939 after the conclusion of the German–Soviet Non-Aggression Pact (Molotov–Ribbentrop Pact).[19]

There were also the major Reich loans (*Anleihen*) in which the Deutsche Bank participated as co-manager in a revised version of the venerable state loans consortium. Its quota was 16 per cent in all except the first 1935 loan, launched after the introduction of universal conscription and the acceleration of Germany's armaments preparations. There were three issues in both 1936 and 1937 and four in 1938. They raised a considerable amount of money, which was largely used to consolidate short-term public debt, and thus indirectly to finance German rearmament.

Of the 3,150 million RM derived from loans in 1937, 2,854.5 million RM were used to provide long-term funding of the short-term financing of armaments that had been conducted through the issue of a special financial instrument (the so-called Mefo-bills).[20] In 1938 another 7,744 million RM were raised through loan issues. But these gigantic issues caused increasing nervousness to authorities which believed that a failure by the public to subscribe to the bond issue could be treated as a vote of no confidence in a regime which permitted no other kind of voting on its record.

The Deutsche Bank's ability to place Reich bonds with its customers gradually decreased, as weariness and suspicions about the build-up of public expenditure set in. While for the first operation in 1935, the Deutsche Bank had sold 24.17 per cent of the total loan stock (well above its quota), it sold only 19.33 per cent of the first 1937 loan and 21.0 per cent of the first 1938 loan. From the Deutsche Bank's internal figures, however, in which the size of the average purchase and the geographic distribution was carefully tabulated for each issue, it is clear that for some time private subscriptions held up rather better. These purchases reflect the symptoms of an already evident inflationary money overhang, caused by increased incomes combined with reduced purchases following the deterioration of quality because of import restrictions in many consumer goods. On the other hand, the Deutsche Bank's industrial customers began to be less willing to buy state paper, although the Four-Year Plan administrators tried to promote the

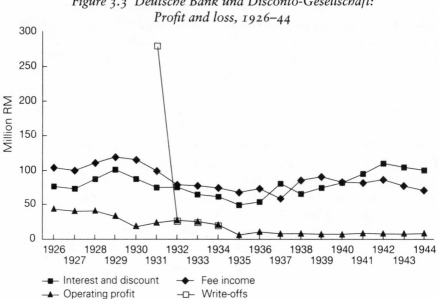

Figure 3.3 Deutsche Bank und Disconto-Gesellschaft:
Profit and loss, 1926–44

Until their fusion in 1929, the Deutsche Bank and the Disconto-Gesellschaft were separate corporations. Their results have been added for the period 1926–29 in this graph.

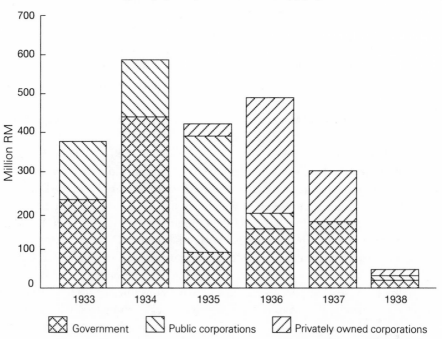

Figure 3.4 Debt conversions, 1933–38

investment of surplus corporate funds in this manner. Whereas industry had bought 48 per cent of the 1935 issue, in the first 1938 loan the share had fallen to a disappointing 34.2 per cent.[21]

It was in 1938 that the big blows came. In October, the third loan issue of that year had been oversubscribed in the wake of a resurgence of political confidence following the Munich agreement with Italy, France and Britain, which brought the hope that the establishment of a greater Germany could be achieved peacefully. The government, desperate to force the pace of rearmament, added an additional 250 million RM bonds to the 950 million originally offered. After Munich, suddenly, there appeared to be no end to the willingness of Germans to hold public debt, and all the doubts vanished. But this mood was short-lived. Soon after the success of this operation came the spectacular failure of the fourth loan of 1938 (of a massive 1,500 million RM), which prompted a major confrontation between the Reichsbank and the government, in which the large banks were drawn in as members of the Reich issuing syndicate. Some 275 million RM were to be sold to the savings banks and credit co-operatives (*Genossenschaften*), while the remainder was to be channelled through the Reich consortium.

In December 1938 the Reichsbank wrote to the Finance Minister that 'We too are of the opinion that the capital market can for the moment no longer accommodate bond issues of this kind, and that the tasks entrusted to your responsibility in the areas of economic rearmament and the Four-Year Plan cannot be accomplished on the scale intended.' The banks had been able to place most of the bonds (900 million out of 1,138 million RM), but the failure to place the rest had shown how Germany had reached her financial limit. The market had gone on strike. Discussion of the implications of this loan led the Reichsbank to prepare for Hitler the fiercely critical memorandum of 7 January 1939, which included the following text: 'The Reich and other public sector enterprises must not take on expenditures, guarantees or commitments that cannot be met out of taxes or out of sums raised through bond issues which do not disturb the capital market.' The 7 January memorandum led to the dismissal on 20 January of Schacht, Vice-President Friedrich Dreyse, and Director Ernst Hülse. Wilhelm Vocke and Karl Blessing together with Carl Ehrhardt were dismissed later.[22]

The Reichsbank directors also involved the leading German bankers in their examination, and criticism, of government policy. On 10 January 1939 the 'narrow' Reich loan consortium of the major banks held a crisis meeting in the Reichsbank building, with the participation of the Reichsbank directorate and representatives of the Finance Ministry. After a long argument, the participants agreed that the 'narrow' consortium should take up the outstanding bonds, but exclude from this operation the 23 smaller banks which had a quota of less than 1 per cent in the consortium. Eduard Mosler of the Deutsche Bank opposed the omission of the smaller firms on the grounds that they should not be exempted from making a sacrifice, but he was overruled on the grounds that 'one should not expose the failure to excessive publicity'. As a result, the Deutsche Bank was obliged to hold a total of 75 million RM of the fourth 1938 loan in its own portfolio.

The consortium also held a very extensive debate about the causes of the failure and listed the following: 'Absence of industrial purchases of government bonds, unwillingness of the public to buy, removal of Jewish purchasers, non-participation of purchasers who are spending money on Aryanization purchases, concern about the demand of the Reichsbahn [State Railways] for funds, an excessive supply of government bonds without the availability of industrial bonds.' The participants reached a general agreement that 'only a limitation of public expenditure will bring about a change'.[23]

The government's financing had also, as the December memorandum made clear, destroyed the market for industrial bonds. An *Emissionsverbot* (ban on issues) was used to protect the market for state paper, and the secondary market was weakened by the extent of new public issues available. The Reichsbank had pointed to 'the lack of confidence' as evidenced 'in the continual fall of prices of industrial bonds'.[24] The industrial market remained extremely restricted in 1939. In the summer an issue by the Deutsche Bank and the Dresdner Bank of AEG bonds placed only two-fifths of the bonds with the public, and the banks fell back on the insurance companies in order to raise the missing sum.[25]

But many of Germany's largest companies were desperate to obtain investment resources, and they tried to approach the banks. The case of I.G. Farben, a business that traditionally had organized itself very independently of banks (and had indeed run its own 'house bank' as an alternative to external financing), is a significant example. Most of the investments of I.G. Farben in the 1930s were financed through some kind of state support, either directly (as in the case of synthetic rubber production), or from the firm's own resources but in response to government orders and contracts. Between 1936 and 1938, about three-fifths of investments in new facilities were managed through the Four-Year Plan.[26] In addition, the costly construction of a synthetic rubber (Buna) works at Hüls near Recklinghausen and at Schkopau near Merseburg was financed through funds provided at 5 per cent by the Raw Materials Office and derived, appropriately enough, from revenue from the rubber tariff.[27]

But by 1939, the firm needed extra funds desperately in order to deal with the costs of absorbing enterprises from Austria and the former Czechoslovakia, and needed the consent of the Deutsche Bank before it could apply to the Economics Ministry for permission to make a flotation on the stock exchange. The bond operation of 1939 was preceded by an intensive discussion with the Deutsche Bank which managed the issue. The bank initially suggested 50 million RM rather than the 100 million that I.G. Farben wanted, and a coupon of 5 per cent, rather than the 4.5 per cent on which the firm insisted.[28] In the end, the Deutsche Bank gave in on both matters to its big industrial customer, on whose supervisory board first Eduard Mosler and then Hermann J. Abs sat as specialists in industrial financing.

Industrial activity by bankers had historically involved the gathering of large quantities of information. One of the most visible activities of bank directors – who had incurred heavy criticism as a result – had been the holding of positions on large numbers of supervisory boards. This time-consuming activity brought gains to the companies on whose boards the bankers sat, as Mosler had pointed out in the 1933 inquiry, because it involved casting the banks' information net as widely as possible; but participation on large numbers of boards made any sort of tight control of firms' management impossible. One common response to the débâcle of 1931 was that banks had been excessively lax in their imposition of financial discipline on their clients because they were too busy on too many boards really to follow a company's affairs. In 1937, any one bank director was limited to 20 seats, and at the same time the size of most supervisory boards was reduced. A big reshuffling occurred in which members of the bank's board of managing directors were replaced on the supervisory board of many smaller companies by *Direktoren der Bank* (Senior Vice-Presidents). (Even this regulation was soon broken: during the war, some bankers were allowed to hold larger numbers of seats on supervisory boards of non-German companies.)

3. Reprivatization

Regulating banking appeared to the regime as a safer and more economically sound alternative to demands from some of the party radicals for direct control of finance through socialization. In fact banks were allowed to reprivatize themselves as their positions recovered from depression losses, and to buy out the state participations built up in the aftermath of the 1931 banking crisis. The Deutsche Bank was the first bank able to do this, because it had received by far the smallest extent of state support during the crisis. In November 1933, it was able to exchange the empty bank building in Berlin of the Disconto-Gesellschaft between the Behrenstrasse and Unter den Linden for government-owned shares.[29] The bank building could be turned into offices for a government whose scope and personnel were both constantly on the rise.

The increased activity of the state worried both the bank and its customers. One of the most important points of contact was in the semi-private environment of the regional Advisory Councils (*Beiräte*), where leading businessmen met to talk about general economic conditions. They presented bankers with an opportunity to dispense information about the bank's policy, listen to descriptions of local conditions and problems, and demonstrate that the bank was in touch with the priorities of its customers. These meetings offer a highly revealing barometer of German business opinion. In the industrial area of Rhineland–Westphalia, Managing Director Karl Kimmich throughout the 1930s presented an account that was consistently critical of the regime's attempts to plan and control. In late 1935, he commented: 'We are living in a state-led boom; we are all in the same boat. Industry cannot live without government orders, since exports cannot be increased adequately ... The German economy cannot do without individual performance. It is extraordinarily difficult to find extremely capable people, and for that reason the *Führerprinzip* [leadership principle] cannot be carried out, as there are not enough leaders.' In the spring of 1936, Kimmich criticized the effects of the armaments boom on the German economy, and argued in very forthright terms that Germany should return as soon as possible to what she was best at – namely, exporting on the world market: 'After we have now become esteemed again in the world through our rearmament, it would be in the interest of a healthy fiscal system to take up again endeavours for a general disarmament. In the long run, it is impossible to keep on con-solidating the short-term unfunded debt of the state through the banks and insurance companies ... As a result, we must restore our links with the world market. It is completely wrong to attempt to expand production for domestic orders.'[30]

After 1936, Kimmich complained that Hermann Göring's Four-Year Plan and its redirection of investment was making impossible that connection with the world economy and export orientation which in past eras had been the key to German economic success: 'It is regrettable that we are forced to take part in an investment boom at a time when we could be selling on an expanding world market.' In 1936 and 1937 many companies experienced acute shortages in the supply of raw materials, and needed to limit their output in consequence. Later the criticism of the planned economy became even more explicit: it was like a 'grafted tree ... whose growth is limited and which eventually dies branch by branch ... The businessman needs room for manoeuvre, otherwise he will become merely an employee.'[31] Even after the outbreak of war, when discussion of public policy became harder, the message was clear, and the planned economy was still blamed for Germany's problems: 'We entered the war with a much less elastic economy than in 1914; and the effects are visible everywhere.'[32]

Such observations had to be kept confidential. To the outside, echoes of the unease over economic policy appeared in the bank's annual general meetings, where shareholders and the press were in attendance, but they were heavily veiled. Eduard Mosler used his opportunity as spokesman of the bank after 1933 to defend the private economy against encroachments, but never directly to criticize state actions. It was, he believed, possible only very marginally to influence government policy, and speeches at the annual general meeting mattered only as statements. Handling the politics of banking became a sensitive, time-consuming and eventually (as we shall see for the wartime period) very dangerous job.

II. Anti-Semitism and the German Banks

In the first months of 1933, politics intruded into banking in two very specific ways. No one would deny that the magnitude of the 1931 crisis revealed severe shortcomings in the German banking system and in the behaviour of its luminaries. The discussion about bank reorganization in the aftermath of 1931 personally threatened the leading figures involved in that débâcle. But by the time of the National Socialist seizure of power, the personnel issues had been by no means completely resolved, and an additional element now entered the calculation. How far should the banks reflect the beliefs of what was thought to be the New Germany, beliefs expressed by the new political leadership and, in the streets, but also in the press, by many of the banks' customers and not least by some of the banks' employees? The NSDAP used the opportunity of bank restructuring to attack the position of Jews in German economic life. The fact that the structure of business organization had been so severely shaken by the Great Depression made a purge much easier.

1. Finance and anti-Semitism

Banks had come under an intense public scrutiny, and many Germans had criticized the 'Jewish' character of banking. It was an opinion widely shared, and by no means restricted simply to the political adherents of the NSDAP. The two men centrally responsible for dealing with the aftermath of the banking crisis, Chancellor Heinrich Brüning and Finance Minister Hermann Dietrich, both expressed such views in private. At the height of the banking crisis in July 1931, State Secretary Hans Schäffer of the Finance Ministry had a 'fantastic row' with his Minister Dietrich when the latter made disparaging remarks about 'Jewish bankers'. At the end of 1931, when discussing bank reorganization with cabinet members, Dietrich had set out the myth of the wish of banks for dominance: 'The banks should support the economy. But they wanted to dominate it and formed industrial trusts, which were then too large for them.'[33] Similarly pernicious prejudices may have underlain the difficult relationship of Brüning with Wassermann.

In the Deutsche Bank, Oscar Wassermann had been in charge of the bank's overall policy in the late 1920s, and was widely blamed for the 1931 crisis. He was also subject to attack as a Jew and a Zionist. Chancellor Brüning, for instance, remained throughout his life convinced that Wassermann had contributed to the catastrophe by refusing to help prop up the DANAT-Bank before its closure on 13 July 1931. Two non-Jewish members of the board of managing directors bore a heavier responsibility than Wassermann for the mismanagement of the Deutsche Bank's business. Werner Kehl resigned from the board because of the large speculative foreign exchange positions of the Düsseldorf branch in

1931, which fell within his regional domain.[34] Emil Georg von Stauss was held to account for the bank's losses on loans to the fraudulently managed Schultheiss-Patzenhofer brewery, over whose supervisory board he had presided.

The lessons of the 1931 banking crisis were drawn in an internal organizational reform of the Deutsche Bank that had originated from an initiative of one of the most dynamic members of the pre-1933 supervisory board, the Rhineland lignite industrialist Paul Silverberg. Silverberg had been bitterly critical of the firm's pre-1931 management, and had suggested an overhaul of the board of managing directors. In response, in early 1932 the Deutsche Bank board tried to push the irritating Silverberg out of the supervisory board, on the grounds that the reformed law on joint stock companies required a reduction of the size of the supervisory board.[35]

Silverberg replied by suggesting the removal of the existing members of the managing board on the bank's credit commission (with one exception: Oscar Schlitter), and the creation of a new more general committee of the supervisory board. It would include eight members, and have the responsibility 'of checking credits and advising the board of managing directors and preparing the decision of the supervisory board'. This body should no longer be called the Credit Commission, but simply 'Committee of the Supervisory Board'.[36] After 1933 the body became known as the Working Committee. Composed eventually of nine members, it laid down central guidelines for the bank's policy, as well as discussing the largest credit operations (credits up to 1 million RM could be approved by individual members of the managing board).

Silverberg had a particular, and strongly personal, motivation in suggesting this change. He wanted to destroy the power and influence of Emil Georg von Stauss: 'The bank is today no longer in the position of being able afford to be in conflict with public opinion, and it has every reason to draw the consequences for its personnel from the general development. This is particularly true of Herr von Stauss.' Stauss's involvement in irresponsible actions before 1931 had been too obvious for him to remain on the managing board, and Kehl had also left. But Silverberg's triumph was incomplete in that Stauss moved to the supervisory board. And in general in 1932 there was still a substantial degree of continuity with the pre-1931 board of managing directors.

Then in May 1933, a new purge of the board began, carried out for very different reasons. Here the New Germany made itself felt. As part of the political concessions made by the bank to National Socialism, the Jewish directors Theodor Frank and Oscar Wassermann resigned from the board.[37] Wassermann as the bank spokesman had been in a particularly exposed position. The internal bank memorandum on the events leading to his departure argued that Was-sermann had failed decisively in the bank crisis. After listing the scandals involving other managing directors, the author asked: 'Where was the man who could not be blind to affairs such as these? Where was the hand that should have intervened decisively before it was too late? Where was the fist banging on the table to bring colleagues back to reason who had lost the understanding for what risks were appropriate? Where was the first among equals, who, less burdened by commitments on supervisory boards, should have kept a supervision over the whole, ensuring continuity, and felt responsible morally to the bank and his colleagues. Where was Herr Wassermann? . . . Whether Herr Wassermann was a Jew or a Christian had nothing to do with all this.'[38] In practice, of course, it had a great deal to do with it.

In the absence of Wassermann, Reichsbank President Schacht had spoken (on 6 April 1933) with two leading figures in the bank, Georg Solmssen and the chairman of the supervisory board, Franz Urbig, and suggested the removal of some of the Jewish members of the managing board. Wassermann initially agreed to leave by the end of 1933, but on 20 May his colleagues decided to announce the resignation before the bank's annual general meeting scheduled for 1 June. The bank's spokesman was thus pushed out prematurely.[39]

The bank clearly found these changes profoundly embarrassing and emphasized the non-racial and non-business grounds for the departures. The press communique pointed out that Wassermann was 64 years old and Frank 62, and stated an intention of electing them to the bank's supervisory board ('suggested for election to the supervisory board'), though neither of them did in fact move upstairs.[40] They were replaced on the board of managing directors by Karl Kimmich, who had been a director of the Disconto-controlled A. Schaaffhausen'scher Bankverein until its merger with the Deutsche Bank in 1929, and Fritz Wintermantel from the Deutsche Bank's Berlin city office. Georg Solmssen, who had been bank spokesman in 1933, and who, although baptized, had been born in the Jewish religion, also moved into the supervisory board. Three additional new members of the managing board in 1933 – Oswald Rösler, Hans Rummel and Dr Karl Ernst Sippell (who took responsibility for the bank's personnel department) – made for an almost complete change of leadership. The only figures remaining from the pre-1933 world were Eduard Mosler, who succeeded Solmssen as spokesman, and the bank's foreign specialist and German delegate on the Standstill Committee (which dealt with the substantial volume of frozen German international debts), Gustaf Schlieper.

The removal of the Deutsche Bank's Jewish directors was an acutely painful process. It was morally and personally repugnant to their colleagues; but even seen from a pragmatic angle, the exercise had dangers. Suppose that the National Socialist revolution was not permanent? When Wassermann and Frank were not made members of the supervisory board, Franz Urbig, the supervisory board chairman, wrote to another board member: 'I feel – as I am sure you do also – uneasy about the thought of going back on a promise made in this way. Other times can come, and we must avoid the possibility of the reproach being made at any time that the bank's decision-making body or its representatives played a role in making non-Aryan members of the board of managing directors leave.'[41]

Georg Solmssen, the spokesman in 1933, saw more clearly than anyone else in the bank what was happening. A letter he wrote on 9 April 1933 to Urbig is both moving and chillingly prophetic. It is worth quoting at length:

'Dear Herr Urbig, The exclusion of Jews from state service, which has now been accomplished through legislation, raises the question of what consequences this measure – which was accepted as self-evident by the educated classes – will bring for the private sector. I fear that we are only at the beginning of a conscious and planned development which is aimed at the indiscriminate economic and moral destruction of all members of the Jewish race living in Germany. The complete passivity of the classes which do not belong to the National Socialist Party, the lack of any feeling of solidarity on the part of those who have up to now worked in business shoulder to shoulder with Jewish colleagues, the ever more evident pressure to draw personal advantages from the free positions created by the purges, the silence about the shame and humiliation imposed on those who, although innocent, see their honour and existence destroyed from one day to the next: all this is evidence of a position so hopeless that it would be wrong not to confront facts straightforwardly, or to make them appear harmless. In any case, those affected have apparently been abandoned by those who were professionally close to them, and they have the right to think of themselves. They should no longer let the enterprise to which they have devoted their lives determine their actions – unless that enterprise treats them with the same loyalty that it expected of them. Among our colleagues too, the question of solidarity has been raised. My impression was that this suggestion met only a lukewarm response in the managing board (perhaps because of its non-homogenous composition); and that if it were to be realized it would take the form of a gesture rather than complete resistance, and as a result would be doomed to failure. I recognize that in the decisive deliberations, differences will be made between different members of the managing board who happen to be on the list of proscription. But I have the feeling that, although I am viewed as someone whose activity is thought of positively, and although I may be honoured as the representative of a now seventy-year-long tradition, I too will be abandoned once my inclusion in a "cleansing action" is demanded by the appropriate outside authorities. I must be clear about this ...'[42]

Soon after, with the same mixture of dignity and desperation, he made an extraordinary suggestion to the man in charge of Hermann Göring's Press Office. In a meeting in his own house in Berlin Wannsee, Georg Solmssen argued that German Jews should defend themselves against the accusations thrown at them by the NSDAP by organizing their own National Council, which would 'examine all complaints against Jews and organize the emigration of those who prove to be harmful or undesirable ... But we do not wish to be treated as second-or third-class citizens, we want to be heard when we are accused. That is a simple human right, and the duty of any cultured state.' He also tried to arrange a personal meeting with Hermann Göring, which however fell through at the last moment.[43]

The reform of the bank's supervisory board became in practice an opportunity to renege on the promises that had been made to Wassermann and Frank. In fact, the supervisory board was not so much purged as expanded (from 16 in 1933 to 25 in 1934), in order to disarm potential criticism by including men from a broader range of business backgrounds. One of the new appointments also held out the possibility of better contacts with the New Germany. Philipp Reemtsma, the Hamburg cigarette magnate, joined not only the supervisory board but also its newly reformed Working Committee. The bank explained to Reemtsma on his appointment that this new body 'would be the focus of the real activity of the supervisory board, and would have a deep insight in the bank's business, and would be composed of the most valued and most intimate friends of the bank, who enjoy the highest confidence'.[44] Reemtsma was particularly valuable not only because of his powerful position in the Hamburg economy, but also because of his good connections with Hermann Göring, which he continued assiduously to cultivate.

The supervisory board's external appearance was also cosmetically retouched for the public view. Revolutions often want to rewrite history, and the National Socialist revolution insisted on a vision that would conceal inconvenient reminders of the past. Georg Solmssen remained on the supervisory board from 1935 to 1938. Max Steinthal, the most obviously historical personality connected with the bank (he had joined the board of managing directors in 1873, and in the depression, at the age of 80, was still chairman of the supervisory board), initially remained on the supervisory board, but he is not listed in the annual statements after the end of 1933 and was dropped from the supervisory board in May 1935. At this time, he noted after a conversation with a member of the current managing board, in which he assured him that he would not make 'difficulties' for the bank, that 'it is painful to see yet another link to the Deutsche Bank cut, but I shall have to come to terms even with this'.[45] He did not emigrate, and seems to have been completely ignored by the bank, although after his death von Stauss tried to secure better living quarters for his elderly and sick widow. The state authorities harassed Steinthal relentlessly, despite his eminence, age and deteriorating physical condition. At the end of 1939 he was obliged to sell his house in Charlottenburg to the Luftgau-Kommando, moved with his family (including a son crippled as a result of injuries sustained in the First World War) to a smaller house, found that that too was requisitioned, and then stayed in a hotel room, where on 8 December 1940 he died.

Meanwhile the supervisory board had to be made to look more representative of the general balance of social forces. In 1937 the bank asked for, and received, permission to expand its supervisory board to 30 members; in 1939 it grew further to 35 in order to continue the policy of making politically useful appointments: 'adding some personalities, who might be regarded as semi-public, and in part may be in connection with the territorial additions accomplished in recent years'.[46]

Silverberg, who had initiated the discussion of supervisory board reform, himself was Jewish and left Germany in 1933, so that he no longer attended the Working Committee he had launched. But Stauss, Silverberg's great enemy, moved on to the new body, and the Committee originally designed to exclude him ironically gave him a new position of influence in the bank. For the rest of his life (he died in December 1942) he played a crucial part in balancing not the bank's financial but its political performance.

2. Bank employees

Responding to Germany's new political order was not just a matter of changes, however dramatic, in the bank's top management and in the supervisory board. A bank is not simply a policy-making institution, but is also driven by internal institutional pressures. National Socialism profoundly altered the climate of work and the internal ethos of the bank. Bank employees, vulnerable in the depression to lay-offs and salary cuts, often hostile to and resentful of their female colleagues, and fearful of a loss of social standing, had provided a capacious reservoir of National Socialist sentiment. At the end of 1932, one-tenth of the bank's employees were reported to have been members of the NSDAP (though the source for this figure may well have wished to exaggerate the extent of party membership).[47] Some of the members saw their party allegiance as a way of altering the behaviour of the firm. After January 1933, the management needed to make concessions to this part of its workforce, to reorganize itself and pay at least lip-service to the notion of a 'works community' (*Betriebsgemeinschaft*). Two National Socialist Factory Cell Organization (NSBO) members were delegated to the supervisory board.

The bank reorganized itself so as to reflect the new German collectivism. On 30 November 1933, the bank's first ever general works meeting started with a parade of those employees who were members of the SA, the SS and the nationalist paramilitary association, the Stahlhelm. The bank's orchestra played 'Deutschland, Deutschland über alles' and the prelude to Richard Wagner's opera *Die Meistersinger von Nürnberg*. Four thousand employees, as well as most of the board of managing directors, were present. A member of the board, Dr Sippell, gave the main address, praising the 'way the new spirit of the age had penetrated the whole bank', promising to take into the Personnel Department 'some gentlemen ... who are especially supported by your confidence', and offering new jobs as a result of vacancies created by the return of female workers to the hearth and kitchen. 'Fortunately there is a healthy turnover of females, who provide for constant fluctuation either through marriage or return to their parental house.' The NSBO representative Franz Hertel also paid tribute to the 324 new positions created by the bank in 1933. Sippell finally stated discreetly that not everyone in the bank should be expected to be a National Socialist. 'Often it is not the worst people who despite recognizing the high ethical stance of National Socialism nevertheless cannot reach a complete acceptance, because they see still in it something that is not yet matured and fully balanced.'[48]

A considerable amount of external pressure was applied regarding the bank's personnel policy. Within the bank, Jewish employees, particularly in prominent positions, were removed either because of direct party pressure (as in Breslau), or in order to forestall the possibility of physical attacks (as in Erfurt, where the co-director and his two most senior subordinates were Jewish).[49] During the first months of the National Socialist regime, bank branches were occasionally assaulted by revolutionary National Socialists. In Pirmasens, an adjutant of the District Commission appeared in order to inform the Deutsche Bank's manager that permission was needed for withdrawals by Jewish customers. In Frankenthal (Palatinate) two SA men demanded to inspect a list of Jewish accounts, but the bank manager refused and appealed for protection to the Lord Mayor.[50] In Duisburg, the local party leadership demanded that the bank take down a swastika flag, on the grounds that 'Jewish enterprises' should not be allowed to raise the banner of the national movement. In Hirschberg in Silesia the local party launched a series of slide lectures with the theme 'How they Fiddled – How they Swindled', which presented a list of 'speculators' from the Deutsche Bank: including Stauss, Millington-Herrmann (who were not Jewish), Steinthal, Michalowsky, Fehr, Wassermann, Nathan (mistakenly – he was at the Dresdner Bank), Solmssen and his father Salomonsohn.[51]

Party hostility came from the centre as well as from local party organizations, but for a while at the central state level it was restrained by considerations of *Realpolitik*. Fundamentally, anything connected with banking and its social world was suspect. In 1934, for instance, the party authorities and the SS turned their attention to a Berlin club, which had traditionally been a meeting place for bankers. The Gesellschaft der Freunde (Society of Friends) had been founded in 1792, and its members included Hjalmar Schacht as well as his predecessor as Reichsbank President, Hans Luther, and almost all the past and present managing directors of the Deutsche Bank. The club's president in 1932 had been Oscar Wassermann; and when Wassermann and Frank left the managing board, they also left the club, and their places there were taken also by their successors in the bank. Rudolf Hess's office had determined that the club represented an 'economic secret society', 'which in the economic area represents an almost unassailable because camouflaged and untransparent bloc – thanks to the composition of its members and their secret cross-contacts'. The SS, however, decided that although this was a sinister and unhealthy organization, it could not be banned under the provisions devised for masonic lodges.[52]

Sometimes, however, pressure came not from the outside but from the banks' own employees. A bank inevitably responds to the sentiments and instincts of the mass of its employees, and to their conception of the way the institution should function. Before 1933 many disaffected men and women had joined the party, and after 1933 came the opportunists. It was clearly tempting to use party membership as part of a bid for promotion. Usually this was not a successful strategy, and the bank's management clearly both resented and resisted it. Karl Ernst Sippell, who had to deal with personnel issues, reprimanded the offenders quite bluntly. He told one ambitious National Socialist in charge of the Bochum branch: 'as a National Socialist he should have increased duties and not merely more privileges', and refused to allow the inclusion of quotations from *Mein Kampf* in the work regulations for the Bochum branch of the bank.[53]

Such conflicts illustrate the extent to which the German *Zeitgeist* had been transformed. The social and political climate encouraged denunciations, not just on racial or political grounds. Very rapidly, Germany became a country of informers who took their knowledge and their tittle-tattle to the Gestapo and the party, but also to business managers.[54] The files of the Deutsche Bank reflect the challenges faced by the institution in the new age. One of the directors of the Leipzig branch complained that the other director had engaged in an affair with his housekeeper, was driving her to meetings and social occasions, was alienating customers, and was also making bad loans. The denouncer quoted the housekeeper involved as saying: 'When Herr V. is sick, she is obliged to lie in bed with him. Herr V. demands the same thing when he comes home drunk. She needs to wean him off bringing street whores back home.' The complaint concluded, 'It is thus not a matter of a "lady", but of a "relationship".' But Sippell took the line that 'the bank cannot concern itself with the personal lives of its branch directors', and obliged the denouncer (and not the alleged fornicator) to move to a much less desirable branch.[55]

Moral, political and racial complaints continued to accumulate. It is hardly surprising that Sippell had soon found the strain of dealing with both the new social climate and the party's personnel demands intolerable. He felt humiliated and burnt out, and believed that he could no longer continue to manage the personnel department. The bank realized that the issues involved required the direction of someone who was himself a trusted party member.[56] At the beginning of 1936, a new Personnel Director was appointed, Karl Ritter von Halt (member of the board of managing directors since 1938), who had come from the Munich private bank Aufhäuser.[57] Halt filled the intended role perfectly: he had been a war hero in the Great War, had been wounded on three separate occasions, and had received a Bavarian knighthood.[58] He also was awarded the Austrian Military Cross, Third Class, and the Bavarian Military Cross, Fourth Class.[59] After the war he had distinguished himself principally as a horseman and athlete; and above all, he was a member of the NSDAP. He organized in 1936 the Winter Olympic games in Garmisch, and attempted to make sports a major part of the life of each Deutsche Bank employee.

Von Halt's appointment seems to have been a rather well-calculated move on the part of the Deutsche Bank. On the one hand, there was no doubt that von Halt would look to the outside world, and to the bank's employees, like a representative of the new movement. On the other hand, he had experience in banking, and it quickly became clear that he considered his primary loyalty as lying with the institution, and not with any external party agency. In this sense von Halt's appointment would bring protection against political pressures for further accommodation. One of his major achievements was to divert party political militancy into athleticism. Some even remember him exhorting the managing directors to become more vigorous physically.[60] Sport was a way of introducing the values of the New Germany, and was accompanied by other attempts to raise the productivity of employees. 'High achievement', von Halt pronounced, 'is the *Führerprinzip* of the German economy.' Internal works competitions would promote knowledge of bank economics, foreign languages, shorthand and typing.[61] Branches also formed sport associations, as well as orchestras and choirs. Von Halt successfully tamed part of the National Socialist threat inside the bank. After protracted negotiations with the German Labour Front (DAF) and the Berlin party leadership, he was allowed to dismiss the NSBO representative Franz Hertel, the keynote speaker of the 1933 works assembly, who had tried to make himself the head of a movement completely to reform the bank politically in the sense of National Socialist revolutionary doctrine. Hertel was not an isolated case: in Stuttgart, Breslau, Görlitz and Magdeburg, other party members of works councils were dismissed.[62]

But a defensive operation alone could not contain the claims of the *Zeitgeist*. In reality, there were many concessions to the New Order. The duties of the bank counter staff were defined so that they became representatives of the state, not the bank, and of what the state taught as propaganda. The clerk was to explain to customers that interest reductions were necessary, were ordered uniformly by the Reich Commissar, and were good for the economy: 'these measures would support the economic development of the Third Reich'.[63] The NSBO participated actively in the redefinition of the workplace. It instructed, for instance, female employees not to dress fashionably and conspicuously – not to be 'fashion ladies'. 'Everyone should know that simple dresses and blouses can be made and altered for relatively little money.'[64]

The change of name and the elimination of the complicated 'Deutsche Bank und Disconto-Gesellschaft' in 1937 may have been intended to help the bank's public and political image. The previous title had been cumbersome and commercial; in the widely used shortened form 'DeDi Bank' it sounded ridiculous, like a 'childish drawl'.[65] As Kimmich noted in 1937: 'The name "Deutsche Bank" is in any case so good that, were it not already there, it would have to be invented.'[66]

3. Banks and 'non-Aryan' business

The government's and party's attitudes, and particularly their anti-Semitic policies, had a major effect on the relationship of banks with the rest of German business. A mixture of official pressure and threats from below led to the removal of many Jewish company directors. Bank directors played their part in this development. In some branches, as in Kassel, they took the initiative.[67] Believed by National Socialist ideologues to be all powerful, represented on many boards of directors, often holding the chairmanship, the Deutsche Bank was inevitably involved in what amounted in practice to a large-scale purge of German economic life.

Two examples will show how the bank became enmeshed in the policies of the new regime. Lorenz Hutschenreuther AG (Selb), where the Deutsche Bank supervisory board chairman Franz Urbig held the chair of the supervisory board, was one of Germany's most famous manufacturers of porcelain, with a substantial and important export market. In October 1933, two NSDAP functionaries replaced representatives of the Weimar Republic works council on the supervisory board. They immediately demanded the dismissal of Jewish members of the board, including the manager of the Mannheim branch of the Deutsche Bank, Ludwig Fuld. The firm felt sensitive because, as it argued, 90 per cent of its domestic sales were made through retailers organized in the National-sozialistische Handels-, Handwerks- und Gewerbe-Organisation (NS-Hago), which might impose a boycott of the firm's products.[68] Urbig responded by attempting to secure the voluntary resignation of the members of the supervisory board who had been attacked, but two refused to give way, pointing out the dangers of compliance (yielding on this issue would be an 'ostrich policy')[69] and adding the commercial argument that obvious and visible acceptance of the National Socialist racial priorities would damage the company's export order book.

For a year, nothing happened and the Jewish supervisory board members stayed in place. Then the party renewed its offensive, through the local party boss. He summoned the manager of Hutschenreuther to come to the town's Brown House and explain himself. When the manager explained that he could not remove a member of the supervisory board, the Kreisleiter (local party director) claimed that this should properly be the responsibility of the Deutsche Bank: 'Herr K. [Kreisleiter Kellermann] then asked the question, whether the Deutsche Bank could not decide by itself as a result of its share-holdings or power of attorney ... Herr K. then explained that one would have to assume that either the Deutsche Bank did not want to intervene – though this was unthinkable – or that because of the capital structure it could not intervene.'[70] The tactic of putting pressure on the central office in Berlin to influence local conditions proved eminently successful. As a result of the renewed, and more insistent, pressure from Urbig, the two members of the supervisory board resigned their seats.

The second example concerns Johannes Jeserich AG (Berlin), a major building firm with road contracts all over Germany, and especially in the north. Dependency on public sector orders made a company of this sort especially vulnerable to political pressure. On 1 April 1933, the day of a nation-wide anti-Jewish boycott, four representatives of the National Socialist Factory Cell Organization walked into a director's office and demanded the immediate dismissal of the company's Jewish employees. The director, Lothar Fuld, who himself was Jewish, responded at once by terminating the contracts of just two workers. But the action of the Jeserich employees turned out to be only the beginning of a much bigger campaign. The company directors were themselves extremely vulnerable. The State Commissar for Building responsible for Berlin, Government Building Master Fuchs, rejected Jeserich bids for road repair work on the ground that 'this was a Jewish enterprise'. The NSBO Charlottenburg then demanded the removal of the Jewish directors – Fuld and Stern.[71] The two directors went without making any protest, and at a meeting of the supervisory board on 13 April the bank representatives, who again included Ludwig Fuld from the Deutsche Bank Mannheim, as well as Director Benz from Berlin, agreed 'that one should agree to the requests of Fuld and Dr Stern in the interest of the company, since otherwise it would no longer obtain public building contracts'.[72] One of Jeserich's remaining directors, Dr Eugen Feuchtmann, then said that it had become clear that the supervisory board required restructuring, and that the five Jewish directors on the supervisory board should resign. They did. Both the supervisory board and the board of managing directors were in consequence almost entirely depleted. Feuchtmann tried to fill the vacancies with obviously politicized figures, which were at first rejected by Benz. But in the end, Benz was pressed into accepting appointments to the supervisory board which included the leader of the NSDAP delegation in the Württemberg Landtag, Hermann Kurz, and, as the representative of the Jewish banking house of H. Aufhäuser Munich, the non-Jewish party member Dr Karl Ritter von Halt.[73]

In both the cases of Hutschenreuther and Jeserich, the initial pressure for the purge came from inside the firm. In the porcelain firm, it originated from the firm's employees as reorganized, after the introduction of a new labour law, in a National Socialist 'Council of Confidence'. With Jeserich the radical agitation by the workforce ultimately had its source in one of the firm's directors, who self-consciously used politics in order to take the management into his own hands.

The use of physical violence in the intimidation that had characterized 1933 diminished as the National Socialist revolution consolidated itself. By the later months of 1933, the anarchical conditions that had marked the early months of the year had been succeeded by the imposition of political centralization and the re-establishment of state authority. For the moment, official anti-Semitism seemed to abate. In the case of the reconstructed department store, Hermann Tietz & Co., where the Deutsche Bank was a member of the bank consortium that ran a participation company (the Hertie-Kaufhaus-Beteiligungs GmbH), many of the Jewish employees were sacked: by August 1933, 500 out of a total of 1,500. But the party then made peace and tried to build bridges to the new managers (although these improved relations were to be paid for by the department store). The SA in Karlsruhe, for instance, suggested that 'our branch there should sponsor some poorer members of the SA Storm Troopers'.[74]

The result of the pressure of 1933 had been that many Jewish firms were purged or sold. More followed in subsequent years. In 1932 there had been approximately 100,000 Jewish firms in Germany (using a religious definition of Jewishness), while in 1935 a contemporary estimate suggested that the number had fallen to 75–80,000.[75] By the end of 1937, two-thirds of small-scale Jewish businesses had already ceased to operate, including five out of six retailers, where Jewish proprietors may have been most visible to the public eye.[76] Many of the larger firms survived until 1938, in part because their disappearance would have jeopardized Germany's recovery from unemployment and depression.

Irrespective of morality and immorality, there were good 'economic' reasons not to 'Aryanize' too rapidly. The forced sale of Jewish firms noticeably weakened the quality of German entrepreneurship. Some businessmen noticed and complained about the development. At the Cologne meetings of the Rhineland–Westphalian advisory council of the Deutsche Bank, for instance, a cotton spinner, Emil Engels (of Ermen & Engels AG) stated that the 'Aryanizations' had reduced the liquidity of firms in the textile branch, and their capacity to keep up payments. 'Until now Jewish elements played a large role in the textile industry. The capacity to pay is sinking rapidly. Aryanization has in part resulted in firms coming under weak management, and he appealed to the bank managements to exercise great caution in managing these transactions.'[77]

Virtual full employment after 1936 weakened the force of pragmatic objections to an economically irrational action. In late 1937, Hitler specified Germany's foreign policy goals at the meeting recorded in the Hossbach protocol, explaining that neither autarky nor integration in the world economy would solve the German economic problem. Only the use of force would create an adequate economic space, or *Lebensraum*. At the same time as foreign policy became much more radical, the regime stepped up the pace in implementing its anti-Semitic programme.[78] The goal that had been frustrated in 1933 by practical considerations, the removal of those the state defined as Jews from German business life, could now be realized without encountering obstacles or objections.

At the end of 1937, Jewish business activity was restricted by a discriminatory tightening of raw material supplies.[79] On 4 January 1938, a decree defined a Jewish enterprise as one owned or dominated by Jews, in the sense that either one managing director or director was Jewish in the sense of the Nuremberg racial laws, or that one-quarter of the supervisory board was Jewish. On 14 June 1938 the Third Ordinance on Reich Citizenship reaffirmed the specific criteria for the assessment of what was a 'Jewish' enterprise. During the course of the year attacks increased until they reached an apogee in the pogrom of Reich Crystal Night, 9 November 1938. This was followed (12 November) by an Ordinance on the Exclusion of Jews from German Economic Life, and the imposition of a 25 per cent tax on assets (cynically termed 'Compensation Measure'). At the same time, Jewish enterprises were threatened with prosecution under existing legislation for actual or alleged 'capital flight' – attempting to bring their assets to safety beyond Germany's frontiers. The transfer of Jewish property into 'Aryan' hands was at first left to private initiative. Reich Economics Minister Schacht had in 1935 defined as one of the tasks that 'the economy should solve on its own', 'the transfer of Jewish business into Aryan hands'.[80]

Throughout 1938, the number of Jewish businesses for sale increased, and banks played a major part in brokering the sales. As was traditional in German business practice, very few of these sales took place on the open market. Bank intermediation made property transfers more discreet. Already before 1938, banks had been involved in some cases of the transfer of Jewish property. In 1935, the owner of the Aronwerke Elektrizitäts-AG, Berlin, was subject to harassment by the party, and was arrested and sent to a concentration camp. He sold his shares in his company to Siemens through the Deutsche Bank.[81] In late 1935, the Mannheim branch of the Deutsche Bank had at its own initiative sent a letter to headquarters asking whether it would not be 'useful' if each branch compiled a list of all non-Aryan firms over a certain value in the district.[82] At the beginning of 1938, a letter of the managing board to branch managers, signed by Hans Rummel and Karl Kimmich, asked for 'a further listing of your non-Aryan debit and credit accounts, and of those that would come into consideration for Aryanization ... In this regard we are interested in how far the Aryanization process of the respective firm has proceeded, and the extent to which you are involved.' The letter added that, in accordance with the decree of 4 January, firms were to be counted as Jewish even if there was only one Jewish member of the managing board.[83]

The additional credit business generated as a result of 'Aryanization' affected the competitive position of the German great banks. At a meeting of the Bavarian branch directors in June 1938, the increased 'generosity' on the part of the Dresdner Bank in giving credits to allow firms to engage in 'Aryanization' was discussed, but the Deutsche Bank's managing directors urged caution: 'Herr Rummel pointed out specifically once more that we should not be driven off track in our credit policy. The aim of the Board of Managing Directors is that in the foreseeable future the demand for bank credit will be so large that we will have plenty of opportunity to make good loans.'[84] But the Deutsche Bank in practice certainly responded to the demand for bank loans – though in some cases, such as Leipzig, it made no 'Aryanization loans' at all.[85] In November 1938, shortly before *Reichskristallnacht*, Kimmich reported that the Deutsche Bank had participated in the 'Aryanization' of 330 businesses. 'The difficulties, particularly regarding personnel, are substantial. Experts with sufficient capital are thin on the ground.' At this time, he estimated the total Jewish capital in Germany to amount to 6–8 billion RM.[86]

In some of these cases, the transfer occurred through the agency of the bank because the old owners wanted the help of a reputable financial institution in preserving their life's work, and also in securing their position should there by some miracle be a change in regime. In addition, they worked hard to protect their old employees. In the case of the banking houses of Mendelssohn, Berlin, and Simon Hirschland, Essen, the Deutsche Bank worked with the management in order to prevent the takeover of the house by the state-owned and hostile bank, the Reichs-Kredit-Gesellschaft.[87] Georg Hirschland, the managing partner of Hirschland, approached the Deutsche Bank after a conversation with a Reichsbank employee. In both the Hirschland and Mendelssohn cases, the NSDAP authorities vigorously opposed a sale to the Deutsche Bank. The Gauleiter (regional party director) of Essen, Josef Terboven, insisted that it would have been far preferable to liquidate Hirschland.[88] From the point of view of the banks, a critical consideration lay in the substantial credit lines extended from foreign institutions, and which fell under the provisions of the agreements on German short-term external debt, the so-called *Stillhalte-Abkommen* (Standstill Agreements). If the partners of the German banks emigrated, they would continue in law to remain personally liable to the foreign (British or American) creditors. It was therefore essential to secure the voluntary agreement of the foreign creditors to the transfer of the credit lines to another institution. But these foreign creditors wanted the best possible security for their claims, through the liability of an institution with a solid reputation, such as the Deutsche Bank, and not a politically run and state-controlled bank such as the Reichs-Kredit-Gesellschaft (RKG). The Deutsche Bank had a particularly powerful position in the standstill negotiations, as its Managing Director Gustaf Schlieper was the head of the German bankers' delegation.

In pre-empting the RKG in 'Aryanizations', the Deutsche Bank assisted the rightful owners of Mendelssohn or Hirschland; but at the same time it also helped to fulfil government expectations of a rapid 'Aryanization' of the banking system. By the beginning of 1939, the SS Security Office (Reichssicherheitshauptamt) was able to report: 'Aryanizations in banking have been accomplished successfully, with the help of the private banks, especially the Deutsche Industriebank, the Reichs-Kredit-Gesellschaft and the Deutsche Bank.'[89]

Another example of a co-operative 'Aryanization' was the Deutsche Bank's involvement with the German portion of the Petschek concern, a vast empire of coal (primarily lignite) fields controlled by four German-Czech brothers, Ernst, Wilhelm, Karl and Frank Petschek. The Petscheks' most important property in Germany lay in Upper Silesia and was administered by a trust company, German Coal Trading Corporation (Deutsche Kohlenhandelsgesellschaft mbH), and its assets attracted Germany's biggest and most powerful mining firms: Wintershall, Salzdetfurth, Central German Steel (Mitteldeutsche Stahlwerke), Bubiag (Lignite and Briquette Company), Henckel von Donnersmarck-Beuthen, Gräflich Schaffgotsch'sche Werke, Deutsche Erdöl-AG, I.G. Farben and above all the Flick group, all approached the trustee. The lignite fields were eventually sold mostly to Flick as part of an exchange of property in which Flick would sell hard coal resources to the Hermann Göring Werke.[90]

But there was also a much smaller Petschek field in western Germany. In this case there appears to have been no rush of interested companies. Of the ordinary shares of the Petschek-owned Hubertus AG, 73.6 per cent were owned by Helimont AG Glarus and Deutsche Industrie AG, which formed part of an extensive industrial empire of the Czech part of the Petschek dynasty. Minority participations included 16.2 per cent held by the Abs family of Bonn: Legal Counsellor Josef Abs, and his sons Clemens Abs and Hermann J. Abs (who in 1938 joined the board of managing directors of the Deutsche Bank). The 'Aryanization' started with an accusation from the tax office (Oberfinanzpräsident Hannover) that the Hubertus AG had organized a flight of 70 million RM. In October 1938, the firm was obliged to present a complete list of accounts, liabilities and assets held abroad.[91] A decree of the Reich Economics Ministry in January 1939 then obliged the Petschek group to sell Hubertus by the end of February. This transaction was managed by the Deutsche Bank, which sold Hubertus AG to the Abs family interests organized in the Erft-Bergbau AG for the not unreasonable sum of 5,750,000 RM. This represented a valuation of Hubertus shares at 205 based on the current stock exchange quotation (the average bourse notation for the period July 1938 to March 1939 had been 203). For a company whose gross profit in 1937 had been 327,000 RM, the stock exchange valuation seems appropriate.[92] In 1950 a West German court established that this sum under-valued Hubertus by some 860,000 RM.[93] There is no doubt that, throughout the sale, the Petscheks had confidence in the character and trustworthiness of Hermann J. Abs, their former junior partner, and that Abs assisted after 1945 in the restoration of their position.

The government also insisted that banks act as its agent in collecting information on Jewish assets. The Deutsche Bank at the same time used the data compiled for this purpose to attempt to buy its own shares from Jewish clients and resell them to other bank customers.[94] By the beginning of 1939, most of the branches of the Deutsche Bank had compiled the lists demanded by the state, although very few of their Jewish customers had actually given the formal notification to their bankers required under Paragraph 11 of the Law on Jewish Property. Some branches refused to give out names, and invoked the principle of bank secrecy, but the violence of the state- and party-initiated November 1938 pogrom helped to break down this attention to legal norms.[95] Some estimate of the scale of this business is provided by figures from the Frankfurt branch, which indicate that in 1938 35 million RM deposits and 15 million RM *Kreditoren* were non-Aryan. Some 16.5 per cent of the overall business of the branch was regarded as non-Aryan.[96] This branch undoubtedly saw 'Aryanization' as a threat to its business, and not in any sense as an opportunity. It weakened the bank, and it brought politics further into the world of finance.

The firm's participation in 'Aryanization' had brought a terrible moral burden.

On the one hand, bank support undoubtedly helped some Jewish owners, especially in Germany in the pre-1938 borders (the *Altreich*): we shall see some occasions in occupied Europe when bank action was much more brutal. Without bank brokerage of property sales, it would have been more difficult for the victims of National Socialist persecution to rescue even the very meagre share that state regulations allowed them to retain and transfer out of Germany. On the other hand, in making these deals, the bank was not only engaged in a relatively well-earning commission business, but also facilitating the state's realization of its political, racially motivated, objectives. In this way, banks were being pushed into the subservient role which the ideological fanatics of the new movement had demanded as early as 1933. An action which in individual cases – as with Mendelssohn or Hirschland or Petschek – may appear to have been motivated by a genuine sympathy for former business partners, in its cumulative effect undoubtedly helped to undermine the principles of property and morality.

III. Emil Georg von Stauss: The Banker as Politician

For the first ten years of the National Socialist regime, the most important high political contacts of the Deutsche Bank were those maintained by Emil Georg von Stauss. He was not 'typical' of the activities of the Deutsche Bank at this time, but he was quite crucial. After 1932, he was not even a member of the managing board, although he did sit on the most important committee of the supervisory board. The leading managing directors – Eduard Mosler, Gustaf Schlieper, Karl Kimmich – concerned themselves with what mattered most to them, the bank's business contacts. They could do this because politics were delegated to Stauss, and because they left the politically most sensitive supervisory board positions held by the Deutsche Bank to Stauss. Stauss was, so to speak, the bank's political alibi until his death in 1942. In his view, developed through extensive experience in Imperial Germany, in the Weimar Republic, and with foreign governments, politics meant building links with government, whatever form that government might take. Although he never became a member of the NSDAP, he was well prepared for a National Socialist government in Germany.

In 1930 he had been elected to the Reichstag as a deputy for the liberal DVP, but he was soon close to the NSDAP and especially to Hermann Göring. His foreign contacts were attractive to a party preparing itself to seize power, and in December 1931 he introduced, in his house, the US Ambassador Frederic M. Sackett to Hitler (who came under the cover name of Herr Wolf). Earlier in 1931, his hospitality had also brought together ex-Reichsbank President Hjalmar Schacht with Göring and Hitler. In 1933, Göring appointed him as a Prussian State Counsellor (*Staatsrat*), and in 1934 Stauss became Vice-President of the

Reichstag, although he was still not a member of the NSDAP and was described as a 'guest' (*Hospitant*) of the NSDAP group.

Stauss's seat in the Reichstag had come to him in a peculiar way. In the election of March 1933, only two right liberal (Deutsche Volkspartei, or DVP) deputies had been elected. One of them, a businessman named Otto Hugo, then wished to dissolve the party and join the NSDAP; while the party chairman, Eduard Dingeldey, who had developed not unreasonable suspicions of the Hitler movement, wanted to keep the DVP as an independent force. In the course of the internal DVP dispute, Hugo had to resign his position within the party; but Dingeldey eventually gave up the struggle to maintain the independence of the party. However, it retained the right to two Reichstag seats as 'guests of the NSDAP parliamentary group'; and Hugo's was taken by Stauss at the suggestion of Dingeldey, as he wrote, 'because for financial and political reasons I place the greatest value on his co-operation at this time'. In other words, Stauss was to act as a bridge between politically and economically active and significant representatives of the old 'bourgeois' parties and the new order – but without joining the party.[97] Stauss consistently ignored later enquiries from the NSDAP as to why he had not joined the movement; and in 1942, when Propaganda Minister Joseph Goebbels suggested that he be awarded the Deutsche Akademie's Goethe medal, the Party Chancellery vigorously objected.[98]

Though not active after 1932 in the conduct of day-to-day business at the bank, Stauss retained an office in the bank's headquarters, and remained very active in the bank's interest. Sometimes he intervened directly to protect the bank's clients. As an example, in March 1933, at the height of the challenge from National Socialist revolutionaries, he was able to contact Hitler's adjutant and the Prussian Interior Ministry and prevent the SA from closing and occupying the Breslau store of the Wertheim department store chain.[99] Most of his duties after 1933 involved him as a supervisory board member and often chairman of a large number of companies, which included the firms that became most politicized under the National Socialist dictatorship. Stauss managed almost all of the Deutsche Bank's most sensitive customers. Films, the air, automobiles, synthetic fibres: these were the high-technology, high-visibility and high-prestige lines of the 1930s. German films, aircraft and racing cars could all function as political propaganda for the new regime. Stauss had the right contacts to exploit the plentiful opportunities offered by these industries, and to play the part of a political liaison man. He intervened decisively in the affairs of the film company Ufa, Deutsche Lufthansa, Bayerische Motoren Werke, Daimler-Benz and the fibre multinational AKU, as well as a range of cultural and academic associations.

1. Films and political education

From its start in 1917, Stauss had been supervisory board chairman of Universum-Film AG, Berlin (Ufa), and had played a major part in its financial reconstruction after the hyperinflation. At the moment of political crisis in 1933, he once more became chairman. Of the 18.8 million RM shares voting at the 1933 annual general meeting, the Deutsche Bank controlled 8.7 million. Another 910,000 RM were registered personally in Stauss's name.[100]

Ufa now stood in a particularly precarious and vulnerable position. Films were obviously political, and the new government had an intense interest in their propagandist use. In the past, however, the business had been heavily dependent on foreign earnings, which accounted for almost two-fifths of revenue. A new political orientation would, and did, ruin this external market. In addition, the firm was concerned that commercial cinemas would face damaging competition from party-run cinemas and from the party's leisure activity organization 'Strength through Joy' (*Kraft durch Freude*). In March 1933, Joseph Goebbels summoned Germany's leading film-makers to the Hotel Kaiserhof and explained his ideas for a reorganization of the film industry. Almost immediately, the Ufa managing board voted to cancel the contracts of its Jewish employees, and as a result deprived the company of many of its best actors, directors and technicians.[101] The combination of all these events and pressures meant enormous operating losses in 1933. Such a performance contrasted with the admittedly small surplus that had been earned even in 1932, the worst depression year. In the case of Ufa, it was clear that it was political adjustment that was causing the losses.

The response was to toe the party line. But even this was difficult. What was the party line? There were many disharmoniously competing voices in the National Socialist choir: rustic utopianism clashed with glorification of modern technology. Then there was the problem of taste, which also rapidly became political. What easier way is there to ridicule a movement than to present its ideas clumsily or unaesthetically? Badly made films on National Socialist themes would appear only as ridiculous. A film with the promising title *Blood and Soil* (*Blut und Scholle*) had to be retitled as *Thou Shalt Not Covet*; and though it was made by a Nazi director on the basis of a Nazi script by a Nazi author (Richard Schneider-Edenkoben), it was attacked by the Agriculture Ministry, by the party press and in internal party decrees. The party ideologues accused Ufa of political opportunism.[102] In the end, 300,000 RM might as well have been thrown down the drain. Even perfectly political topics such as *The Red Death of Riga* (*Der rote Tod von Riga*) were endlessly held up by political interventions.

The list of taboo subjects grew ever longer. Scripts based on books by Jewish authors were obviously out of the question. But party military and paramilitary organizations, the SA and the SS, could not be treated either. A planned film called *The Intoxication of Love* (*Der Liebesrausch*) was called off on the grounds of a 'concern that marital conflicts should not be dealt with cinematically, even if there is no adultery'. What was left? 'Our secure knowledge of what cannot be done unfortunately gives no indication of what can be shown.'[103] The uncertainty made the film-makers ever more hesitant, and above all dependent on guidelines produced by Joseph Goebbels's new Propaganda Ministry. Resulting films were fiercely critical of the vices of the old system: they attacked materialism, individualism, currency speculators, Jews and capital flight (all of these were the ostensible targets of Erich Engel's 1933 film *Inge and the Millions* (*Inge und die Millionen*)).[104] In February 1934, Goebbels tried to solve the problem by requiring the submission of all film synopses to a Reich Film Editor.

Light entertainment offered the easiest solution to the problematical question of subjects suitable for cinematic depiction in the New Germany. It provided the added lure of export earnings in an economy which, in the process of recovering from the depression, had quickly run short of foreign exchange. As a result the fees for multilingual actors who could present an attractive nonchalance exploded. A star system was created. It was not the earnest young men who depicted National Socialist heroes, such as Claus Clausen (*Hitlerjunge Quex*) who did well out of the new cinema, but the frivolous and glittering idols of a new vacuity. Hans Albers had the advantage that he could make films in English or German. Zarah Leander looked like other leading actresses, 'speaks perfect French and English and plays the roles of Greta Garbo and Marlene Dietrich, whom she resembles'. Albers's and Leander's fees shot up. In 1936, Leander received 200,000 RM for three films, two-thirds of which was to be paid in Swedish crowns. In 1933, Hans Albers had been paid 70,000 RM a film, but by 1936 he was receiving 700,000 RM for four films.[105] Film-makers blamed the government for the fees inflation, and pointed to 'the speech of Minister Goebbels, in which he announced that actors should be well paid'.[106] The average cost of producing a film inevitably rose, from 250,000 RM in 1933 and 275,000 RM in 1934 to 420,000 RM by mid-1936 and 537,000 RM in 1937.[107]

Though its managers claimed that Ufa was still potentially profitable in spite of the additional costs, and that the firm could soon resume paying dividends, in practice the demands of party and state for financial support for a Film Academy and Culture Film Institute meant that there seemed no likelihood of operating as a market-minded producer of entertainment. In 1933, the Filmkredit Bank GmbH was created with the participation of the leading banks and Ufa, and with a pledge by the banks to extend credit, as a way of solving the problem of financing a German film industry. Already in 1935 Ufa's rival, the Tonbild-Syndikat AG (Tobis), had been nationalized. The political pressure on Ufa intensified, including an initially unsuccessful demand for the removal of Production Director Ernst Hugo Correll.

In the end, the demands of state and party had their effects. As a result, in March 1937 the majority of Ufa shares held by Alfred Hugenberg's Scherl-Konzern and by the Deutsche Bank were sold at parity to a state-owned trustee company, Cautio Treuhand GmbH. Cautio eventually controlled the whole of the Reich's film business, including Tobis and Ufa as well as a Vienna Film GmbH and Prague Film GmbH. In May 1942 this cinematic empire was eventually reorganized into a single holding company, the Ufa-Film GmbH. But until this moment, and despite an almost complete turnover on the supervisory board, Stauss together with another Deutsche Bank representative, Johannes Kiehl, remained at the helm of the supervisory board of the Ufa AG.[108]

The new cinema did best – at the box office – when it did not try political education. In 1933 the programme had included only a few ideological films: *German Border Land in the East* (*Deutsches Grenzland im Osten*) and *Hitler Youth Quex* (*Hitlerjunge Quex*), as well as *Refugees* (*Flüchtlinge*), (depicting Volga Germans fleeing from the Bolshevik revolution), and instead concentrated rather more on less strenuous themes such as *Viktor und Viktoria* or *War of the Waltzes* (*Walzerkrieg*).

Stauss was more than merely a politically influential figurehead. He involved himself in the commercially critical area of programme choice, but he wanted to make political statements, and sometimes aesthetic ones. Ufa had to make money, but it also had to avoid alienating the politically influential. He passed on Dr Ernst ('Putzi') Hanfstaengl's idea for a film based on the novel *People without Space* (*Volk ohne Raum*).[109] In 1939 he supported the making of a film about a colonial theme, in order to underline German demands for better treatment in the matter of colonies. He made (often inappropriate) suggestions as to which actresses to use.[110]

Even more political was Stauss's involvement with the Deutsche Akademie, founded in 1925 with an educational mission which in the course of the 1930s became a political one. In 1932 the Akademie's 'Practical Department' had created a Goethe-Institut with the aim of promoting German language and culture. After the outbreak of war in 1939, the Goethe-Institut was given a specific charge. The Akademie negotiated a subsidy from the German Foreign Office to conduct German courses for the natives of Germany's allies or potential allies in the new Europe. Its President set out its mission in a personal interview with Hitler in the following way: 'It is most important to work to make the German language *the* world language, or at least a world language.'[111] Thus the Goethe Institute courses of the academic year 1940–41, conducted under the auspices of the Deutsche Akademie, took 600 Italians, Bulgarians, Yugoslavs, Greeks and Spaniards.[112]

The Akademie held out one way of linking politics and the banking world. Stauss was Deputy President, and dealt with the very problematical and highly politicized Presidents of the 1930s. First in 1934 the geopolitician Karl Haushofer, a friend of the Führer's Deputy, Rudolf Hess, was appointed, but it soon became evident that he was mentally and physically sick. He resigned after an outbreak of intense conflict with the Akademie's General Secretary about the institution's political future, and its virtual financial bankruptcy. At this point, Stauss saved the Akademie by arranging for the appointment of a new General Secretary, and by volunteering to take over, if necessary, the presidency for a brief transitional period.[113] Unfortunately Haushofer's eventual successor Professor Kölbl soon resigned too, after being arrested for homosexual activity.[114] Then the Minister-President of Bavaria, Ludwig Siebert, stepped in to fill the breach.

Even the appointment of a prominent National Socialist politician proved an inadequate form of political protection, and Stauss became involved in personal clashes at the highest levels of the party. Rudolf Hess's chief of staff Martin Bormann complained that the Akademie was violating Hitler's instructions in collecting funds from industry as part of an attempt to move into larger and more representative quarters.[115] Stauss, who had served as the main fund raiser, and the organizer of a Berlin association of Friends of the Akademie, could only defend himself by appealing to Siebert; but Siebert's position *vis-à-vis* the central party authorities was not strong. He managed to go right to the top, and persuaded Hitler personally that 'an exception would be justified. He asked Reichsleiter Bormann to inform the Reich Finance Minister as soon as possible'.[116] It was all in vain: despite the green light from on high, the army and the Foreign Office joined the party in limiting the wartime tasks of the Deutsche Akademie to the prosaic task of language instruction.

2. Motors in the air and on the ground

Deutsche Lufthansa AG (founded in 1926 as Deutsche Luft Hansa AG) was another enterprise which kept Stauss as the head of its supervisory board. It was owned by the Reich, some of the German states (*Länder*) and the Reichsbahn, with the Deutsche Bank holding over a quarter of the shares on behalf of Deutscher Aero Lloyd. Like air transport throughout the world, Lufthansa thrived in the 1930s. Its staff increased from 1,232 employees in December 1934 to 2,415 by June 1939. Its route system in Europe and its airmail lines to South America expanded.

The combination of public ownership, public service and new technology would have meant politics in any system: in National Socialist Germany this fate was inescapable. Many German aviators had been supporters of National Socialism before 1933, and regarded Lufthansa as an appropriate base for the German air force that had been prohibited under the terms of the Versailles Treaty. Erhard Milch left the managing board of Lufthansa in 1933 to become State Secretary for Aviation, but he remained on the company's supervisory board. Hermann Esser, a founder member of the NSDAP and in 1933 Minister for Economics (*Staatsminister für Wirtschaft*) and head of the Chancellery (*Chef der Staatskanzlei*) in Bavaria, an uncouth and unsavoury radical National Socialist ideologue, was a new arrival on the supervisory board. At his first meeting he stated that 'as one of the oldest fellow fighters with the Führer he could declare that Lufthansa had long carried within the spirit of the New Germany and could see this as a justification of its previous work'.[117]

Contacts with Milch were crucial for Stauss's other work: the largest part of his time was devoted to being chairman of the supervisory board of BMW (Bayerische Motoren Werke) and Daimler-Benz, which both developed in the

1930s into major producers of aero engines. This was an area of armaments production that posed substantial technical problems, requiring difficult choices between different strategies of development. In a highly politicized system, such issues acquired a political edge as each solution became associated with political clientage networks. Interventions over technical choices of aero-motors reached a dramatic climax during the war, the story of which will be told in part below.

Of all of Stauss's companies, Daimler-Benz most intensively cultivated the National Socialist regime. Stauss had left the supervisory board of Daimler when he had resigned from the managing board of the Deutsche Bank, but he returned quickly to become chairman of the supervisory board (on 4 July 1933), almost certainly because of the extent and the warmth of his political connections.[118] Within the firm, the key figure from the political point of view was Jakob Werlin, initially the director of the Munich sales office and an intimate friend of the new leadership. In 1933 Werlin was selling cars on favourable terms to the new establishment, to Dr Joseph Goebbels, to Ministerial Counsellor Hanke in the Propaganda Ministry, to Julius Streicher, to Wilhelm Keppler and to Staatssekretär Feder. This was, at least from a commercial standpoint, not a futile exercise. It brought influence as well as direct orders.

Werlin was able to extend his contacts with Hitler, and to discuss with him at length the consequences of rearmament. He reported back to the firm: 'If the size of the army were increased to 300,000, motorization would be carried out with the greatest energy; and our prospects in this case would not be bad. I replied that we would start to operate our Marienfelde plant and would expect to obtain particular support from the Reichswehr.'[119] The promised commercial rewards rapidly became a reality: in February 1934, the company received 1.5 million RM in truck orders from the SA.

Werlin was rapidly rewarded with a seat on the managing board of Daimler-Benz, where he behaved part as prima ballerina, part as spoilt child. A letter he wrote in 1935 to Daimler-Benz managing board chairman Wilhelm Kissel with the principal objective of pointing out his indispensability to the company is quite typical of the man: 'I would like to point out to you already today that if I fail to obtain the necessary support from my own firm, I will have no alternative but to point out how conditions lie to another authority. It is not just a matter of the interests of our firm, but of the needs of the state.'[120] As supervisory board chairman, Stauss's responsibilities involved both calming Werlin and using him. Stauss did not hesitate to mix himself in the petty politics of automobile bribery, and to play Werlin's own game. Why, he wanted to know in 1934, were Ernst Röhm and Heinrich Himmler still driving Maybachs rather than Mercedes?[121]

But it would be a mistake just to see Stauss as nothing more than a politics-playing figure-head tolerated by the Deutsche Bank and commercially useless to the firms on whose supervisory boards he sat. The hand of the banker was visible in the development of Daimler in the 1930s in two ways. First, Stauss owed his uniquely authoritative position in Daimler to his skill in making the merger of

Daimler and Benz in the 1920s. The automobile industry was still in the midst of a large-scale shake-out, with the depression only increasing the commercial pressure. Stauss's recipe for survival in the 1930s included a close working relationship – and perhaps an eventual fusion – with the Bayerische Motoren Werke (of which he was also supervisory board chairman). Franz Josef Popp of BMW sat on the supervisory board of Daimler, while Kissel in reciprocation went to the Munich board meetings. There was some collaboration in manufacture. The bodywork for the BMW 315 and 319 was made in Sindelfingen by Daimler.[122] Popp and Werlin both worked together in preparing the plans for the realization of Hitler's dream for a Volkswagen. Most importantly for the two firms (and, it turned out, most dangerously for BMW), Stauss promoted the idea of a division of aero engines into different technologies. Daimler would work with water-cooled and BMW with air-cooled engines.

Second, Stauss was very keen to apply financially realistic criteria to the firm's management decisions. In the light of the economic uncertainty in the automobile industry, and also of the permanent temptation felt by technical experts to undertake interesting but commercially unrewarding innovations, Stauss insisted throughout the recovery period on financial caution. This required a delicate balancing act, between the demands of the firm and the scepticism of the Deutsche Bank bankers. Within the bank, some observers later reported, Stauss was regarded as having used his position on the supervisory board Working Committee to give excessive credit lines to his favourites in the automobile industry.[123] Daimler was – in the 1930s – a bank-controlled industry, and the experience of the 1920s and the depression had made bankers very nervous. The firm staged a spectacular recovery in sales and production after the depression: indeed, it was one of the first German companies to show signs of the upturn, with a significant improvement already evident in 1932. But profitability rose much more slowly, and Stauss insisted on a correction. 'In the long run it is of course insupportable that the works should bring no profit worth speaking of from such a large turnover.'[124] This was the authentic voice of Stauss the banker rather than of Stauss the politician. An economic recovery should mean larger profits, not just a greater market share, more influence and more sales.

3. Multinational business in conflict with nationalism

The roles of banker and politician clashed – less perhaps in the case of Daimler than in the most politically difficult of all of Stauss's operations, the German–Dutch synthetic fibre manufacturer Algemeene Kunstzijde Unie N.V. (AKU). This conglomeration, like Daimler-Benz, had been the result of a bank-inspired merger of the 1920s. In 1929 Oscar Schlitter of the Deutsche Bank had put together a 'community of interest' between the dynamic but highly indebted Vereinigte Glanzstoff-Fabriken AG (VGF) with the Dutch producer Nederlandsche Kunstzijde. AKU was formed through an exchange of shares, so that the new corporation controlled VGF. As a joint German–Dutch company, it constituted the first German multinational (as opposed to transnational) corporation. The AKU supervisory board consisted of four representatives (called 'delegates') of the Dutch and four of the German group as well as one neutral member. The firm owned major foreign subsidiaries: in the USA, the North American Rayon Corporation and the American Enka Corporation and the American Bemberg Corporation, as well as companies in Britain, Italy, Czechoslovakia and Austria. It also held a participation in Glanzstoff-Courtaulds GmbH Cologne. Most of AKU production was still located in Germany, and its output in the early 1930s accounted for 60 per cent of German viscose.

The relationship between the Dutch and German parts of the enterprise would have been strained in any case. The early years of almost all multinationals were filled with conflicts, often with a political edge, about production, sales and taxation, and the constituent companies were frequently seen by outsiders as being at odds with national interests. In the 1930s, as a result of the distortions imposed by trade and exchange control, of technical disparities, and of politics, the climate worsened further. It made work in the AKU difficult. The VGF was highly indebted to the Dutch company, and the debt actually increased in the course of the 1930s as the Dutch bought up VGF bonds issued and owned in the USA. The result was that, in the course of the 1930s, an ever smaller proportion of the firm was in German ownership. At the same time, the Dutch part of the concern lagged in technology, and, despite the installation of faster double-thread spinning machines, remained relatively underequipped.

In 1933 the management of AKU became bitterly divided. An executive director of VGF, Carl Benrath, and Willy Springorum in the supervisory board were accused of manipulating the account books and violating the decree of 19 September 1931 on Share Law and Bank Supervision. Benrath in turn responded by a ferocious attack on Schlitter as one of the delegates on the supervisory board, and appealed to Schlitter's more political Deutsche Bank colleague von Stauss. At this stage, both bankers were no longer active members of the board of managing directors, but both sat on the supervisory board of the Deutsche Bank. Benrath used the new political language as a way of attempting to rehabilitate himself: 'We live in a New Germany in which – thank the Lord – the honour of the individual is protected by a strong hand. I too rely on this protection and I am sure that I will come into my rights,' he wrote to Stauss. 'I am pleased to hear from you that you judge my position favourably from the moral side because of the reasons well known to you.'[125]

Even though the accusations against them were eventually dropped,[126] Benrath and Springorum were forced to resign their positions in the AKU, but – as often happens in bitterly internally divided managements – the position of everyone involved in the conflict was damaged, and Schlitter did not emerge unscathed either. Although still joint chairman of the supervisory board of the Deutsche

Bank, he was moved to a position as the ninth, 'neutral' delegate, and Stauss was placed on the managing German–Dutch supervisory board.

For the AKU, the imposition of Stauss facilitated political contacts, which were crucial for a concern producing synthetic fibres – needed as a substitute for imported raw materials by an increasingly autarkically oriented regime – and faced by a demand that it become more national. Indeed, to many in the government, it appeared strange that a multinational should be in charge of a policy of import substitution. One of the earliest suggestions from the NSDAP textile experts was that the renationalization of Germany's largest producer of artificial silk should be achieved through a takeover by I.G. Farben, which was at least an authentically German corporation.[127]

Instead, the German delegates defended themselves from the political charges of not following a sufficiently German course by shifting production to Germany. German synthetic fibre production benefited from government programmes, particularly from the import restrictions placed on natural cotton and wool under the 1934 New Plan. At the same time, production in the Dutch plants at Ede and Arnhem was cut back.[128] In addition, the Deutsche Bank assisted in buying up Dutch shares for the VGF interests.

All this never seemed enough from the standpoint of the party. After 1936 and the announcement of the Four-Year Plan, the orientation of policy-makers towards autarky became much more explicit. In 1937 Göring's office for raw materials asked whether plans existed to nationalize the firm. Stauss gave a temporizing reply: at present it would be 'tactically wrong' to move until he could be in a position to make 'positive suggestions' on this subject.[129] In order to avoid retaliation against the US subsidiaries, in particular, the firm had to appear as non-German owned with a majority Dutch participation.[130]

But this kind of argument was inadequate for the planners of the Four-Year Plan administration, who saw Stauss and his colleagues increasingly as an obstacle to the implementation of a German solution to the problems raised by the existence of a multinational corporation. In May 1939, the German members of the AKU Delegates Committee, including Stauss, resigned after intensive pressure applied by Hans Kehrl from the Four-Year Plan administration.[131] Göring had reached the conclusion that Stauss had been bribed by the Dutch board members to support an anti-German position, and cited as evidence the gift of a painting (perhaps appropriately, a Dutch old master) to Stauss. The German delegates were replaced by four new figures, including Hermann J. Abs of the Deutsche Bank and Baron von Schröder of Bankhaus Stein, Cologne. The Dutch delegates were surprised and outraged, especially when it appeared that the German government wanted to place the suspect managers of the 1933 vintage back in control, including Benrath. This plan was only abandoned at the insistence of Philipp Reemtsma, the cigarette czar, who worked closely in this manoeuvre with the new men from the Deutsche Bank.[132] In this way, despite the complete change of personnel among the delegates, the AKU survived as a

German–Dutch concern until the war and the occupation of the Netherlands. It became the only Dutch multinational whose management the German authorities could directly control. Shell, Philips and Unilever had moved their headquarters abroad, and were run under the occupation by trustees. In this way they, unlike AKU, were able at least partially to escape the grasping hand of the New Germany.

Stauss's role was as a kind of political insurance for the bank. After his death in December 1942, relations with the state and the party became much more difficult. The new offensive against the world of finance was in large measure a consequence of the rapid ideological radicalization that occurred during the war. But it was also, at least in part, a result of the bank's inability or unwillingness to find another Stauss adept at the game of mixing business and politics. Perhaps too, as the AKU incident indicated, it was not a game that could be played indefinitely. Within the National Socialist state, there were too many competing hierarchies to make it a very simple exercise, even for someone with little sense of morality and a great penchant for expediency.

The case of the business life of Emil Georg von Stauss holds an interesting and important moral. Stauss's objectives were fundamentally all based on a devotion to doing business and making money, and not on a desire for explicit political power. But he wanted to use politics to further his commercial ends. When, however, entrepreneurial capacities become very explicitly a function of a political system, energies that previously were deployed in business activity are increasingly harnessed to the task of capturing political power and influence. In a purely economic sense, considered in terms of an understanding of agents pursuing a rational individual or corporate self-interest, this development is entirely comprehensible. The development of Stauss's activity from technical wizard in the most modern, twentieth-century industries in the air, on the road and on the screen, to his role as a broker of political interests in the Third Reich is natural and self-evident. From a different, moral perspective, however, such a development is infinitely more problematic.

IV. Foreign Expansion

The Deutsche Bank had always been active internationally. Indeed, it had been founded explicitly with the goal of developing German's overseas trade. Before the First World War, it had founded the Deutsche Ueberseeische Bank for financing trade with South America, and the Deutsch-Asiatische Bank, and had participated in the development of Romanian petroleum and Turkish railways. International contacts continued to matter in the 1930s, despite the general movement of that decade away from the international economy and towards strategies of autarkic development. After 1931, the Deutsche Bank led the bankers' committee which annually renegotiated the prolongation of Germany's short-term private sector debts. These discussions of annual Standstill Agreements (called the German Credit Agreements) provided for a gradual and progressive liquidation of the foreign debt; they also dealt with the complex matter of converting frozen debts into other forms of longer-term asset in Germany. The constant rescheduling, together with the possibility of debt to equity swaps, bears an obvious resemblance to the international debt negotiations of the 1980s, with the difference in 1930s Germany that a substantial part of the debt was owed by banks and private corporations. The foreign exchange implications of the Standstill Agreements in a country which had almost entirely exhausted her international reserves by 1933 meant that the government and the Reichsbank not only followed the course of the negotiations, but also frequently intervened directly.

In August 1937 Gustaf Schlieper, the highly respected Director of the Deutsche Bank's Foreign Department, died. His successor, Hermann J. Abs, was a youthful 36, and had been a partner of the leading private bank Delbrück Schickler & Co. Abs's principal attraction to the bank was his expertise in foreign dealings, his linguistic fluency in English, Dutch, French and Spanish, his range of overseas contacts, and his obvious intelligence. Above all, he seemed to the government the obvious choice to replace Schlieper as head of the German Standstill committee. Abs later believed that Reichsbank President Hjalmar Schacht told Eduard Mosler of the likely successor to Schlieper and of the consequence that the Deutsche Bank would no longer run the Standstill negotiations. From the standpoint of the Deutsche Bank, there was, however, a simple way out, and Mosler told his colleagues that the bank's prestige demanded that this rising star of German finance should be added to its board. Abs developed more and more as a generator of contacts, above all abroad, where his reach ranged from the world of New York banking to the corridors of the Vatican. He rapidly became the Figaro of German banking: 'pronto a far tutto, la notte il giorno sempre d'intorno in giro sta. Ahimé, che furia! Ahimé che folla!'

This was the first major change to the board of managing directors since the upheavals of 1933. As long as there had been no new appointments, no one could reasonably complain that there was no party member on the board; but when the very young Abs arrived, it was natural for the bank to encounter questions as to why there was no comrade on the higher floors. Any alteration of the board thus inevitably raised the question of its political composition and balance. The bank needed more political support, and it sought this by appointing to the managing board someone judged to be a relatively 'harmless' party member. The Personnel Manager, Karl Ritter von Halt – usually described by those who remember him as a banker as decent but ineffective ('a nothing') – was the obvious candidate. On the board of managing directors after 1938, he self-consciously took charge of the bank's relationship with the party. He made contributions to a fund supporting the activities of Reichsleiter SS Heinrich Himmler (Sonderkonto 'S' at Bankhaus J.H. Stein, Cologne).[133] He was also a member of a group of around 40 businessmen and officers meeting each month as the 'Heinrich Himmler Circle of Friends'. By April 1943 there had been 38 invitations, of which Halt had managed to miss only six (Dr Rasche, for the Dresdner Bank, had an even better attendance record: he was absent from only five sessions).[134] As a banker, on the other hand, von Halt did relatively little, and took only insignificant positions on other supervisory boards.

Personnel concessions to the party were overshadowed by the much larger political changes in Germany. The military and political expansion of Germany after 1938 fundamentally altered the climate in which the Deutsche Bank operated. In the late 1930s, the international experiences of the past were set to work in the context of present politics, in large part at the insistence of party and state.

1. Colonies

Already in the 1920s, Dr Kurt Weigelt (who in 1928 was appointed as a deputy member of the board of managing directors) had dealt with colonial issues. After 1933 he became a member of the NSDAP Colonial Policy Office, and joined the SS in 1934 and the NSDAP in 1937.[135] His public pronouncements indicated a strident advocacy of Germany's right to her pre-war colonies: criticism of the exploitative imperialism of the western colonial powers, coupled with an economic argument about how colonies would affect Germany's international payments position. 'The German Empire requires raw materials that can be paid in Reichsmark.' He reckoned that within a few years, the old colonies could sell Germany goods worth 400 million RM or 10 per cent of the German trade balance.[136] In 1933, he had tried to discover, through an intermediary, whether the new German Chancellor had an interest in colonies, but found it impossible to obtain a clear answer. He sent a document to Hitler in October 1933 arguing that it would take a long time to create 'the possibility of making room for the German people in the East'. Might not colonies be a more appropriate and realistic goal? In 1934, he asked Rudolf Hess to support a project to sell coffee produced by German planters in Cameroon and Tanganyika in Germany. Later, he suggested the creation of a Franco-German company to increase German trade with France *outre-mer*.[137]

In practice, these initiatives achieved little. The German government had little interest either in overseas possessions or in co-operation with France. Hjalmar Schacht insisted on colonial demands, but found himself isolated in the government and ignored by the party. Germany's overseas colonial plans remained largely on paper. Nor did colonial trade develop as in France or Britain in the 1930s: the major expansion in German overseas trade occurred with independent states in South America. Weigelt recognized and appreciated these realities. He seems in fact to have been a rather cautious businessman. His colonial bark was substantially more impressive than his bite. For instance, he advised Siemens not to go ahead with the construction of a major electricity work in Turkey because of the extent of Turkey's foreign debts and the likelihood that the government would respond by nationalizing Turkish industry.[138] In addition, his position was weakened because of a major scandal in the affairs of one of the colonial companies managed by Weigelt. But in any case, the colonial strategy, though attractive as a long-term ambition, never assumed an immediate priority for the National Socialist leadership, which after all determined the direction of German policy and was quite happy to ignore the advice or suggestions of representatives of 'finance capitalism'.

2. German colonialism in Europe

The immediate objects of German expansionism lay in Europe. The first target for Germany's new-found strength was Austria, joined to the Reich by the *Anschluss* of March 1938. Then came the Sudetenland, ceded to Germany at the Munich conference of September 1938 by a Britain and France who believed that giving way to the clamour of the Sudeten Germans might be a cheap way of buying peace in Europe. The Munich settlement began the economic as well as the political reordering of central Europe. The Sudetenland included a large part of Czech industry, accounting for 37.5 per cent of employment in mining and 57.6 per cent for the textile industry.[139] In March 1939, German troops occupied the defenceless rump of the remainder of Czechoslovakia, and divided it between an occupied protectorate Bohemia–Moravia and a puppet state in Slovakia. In September 1939 the next act of German expansion – into Poland – brought a new European war.

In some of the newly occupied territories, in the Sudetenland, in the area of Poland annexed as the Warthegau, in the Generalgouvernement, and after 1940 in Alsace-Lorraine, German banks took over branches of existing banks. But elsewhere they engaged in a series of strategic links and takeovers of financial institutions in the occupied countries. Viewed in purely business terms, the expansion of Germany recreated that environment long absent, in which, as in the heyday of German universal banking before the First World War, banks could respond to new opportunities and massive transfers of property by organizing huge takeovers and acquisitions.

But the new opportunities were fundamentally unlike those of the pre-1914 world: they were political, and they originated from diplomatic and then, after 1938, from military action. The sphere of bank activity was fundamentally altered. Banks did not bother to attempt to conceal these new acquisitions. In 1944, the US Federal Reserve Board was able to compile an extensive survey of German banking penetration in continental Europe, fundamentally on the basis of published material. The report noted that 'the banks which have been most active in the penetration movement have boasted about their expansion, and it has been an advertising point to show their contribution to the extension of

German influence to foreign countries and to the welding of the banking systems of the annexed territories to that of the old Reich'.[140] The Deutsche Bank took, as we shall see, an exceptionally cautious position in this regard.

After the annexation of the Sudetenland by the German Empire, the Deutsche Bank took over 16 branches of a Czech bank with a large German-speaking client base, the Böhmische Union-Bank, as part of a reordering of Sudeten banking under the direction of the Reich Economics Ministry. It had originally been interested in acquiring the Sudeten German branches of a larger and more successful Czech–German bank, the Böhmische Escompte Bank; but in October 1938 the German Bank Commissar agreed to allocate the branches of the Escompte Bank to the Dresdner Bank.[141] The German government also sent lists of Jewish firms in the Sudetenland to the banks together with a demand that the banks should manage the process of 'Aryanization'. Stauss wrote a short personal response to this list, and included the phrase: 'Both the headquarters of the Deutsche Bank and also the branch in Reichenberg [Liberec] and its local offices will continue to promote Aryanization.'[142] After March 1939, Bohemia–Moravia remained legally separate from Germany, although it was clearly intended to be part of a German economic imperium in which the German people was 'assuring the sources of raw materials necessary for its welfare'.[143] By October 1940, Bohemia–Moravia was linked to the Reich by a customs union. But long before that the banking system had been used to tie the protectorate's economy to Germany through ownership.

The Deutsche Bank continued to work with the Böhmische Union-Bank in Bohemia and Moravia. It took 23 more branches (out of a total of 34 in Rump-Czechoslovakia), 28 branches of the Deutsche Agrar- und Industriebank, and 5 of the Mährische Bank (the Böhmische Union-Bank's Slovakian branches were incorporated into the Unionsbank Pressburg, which was jointly owned by the Böhmische Union-Bank and by the Creditanstalt-Bankverein in Vienna).

The Böhmische Union-Bank in 1939 was in a poor condition, and would have been so even in different political circumstances. Its commercial position had been eroded by the depression. It was illiquid. Politics only worsened the situation. Its management had been in large part German–Jewish, and the departure of its senior managers left the bank effectively leaderless. According to the list drawn up by the Deutsche Bank, eleven of the twenty-two members of the managing board were 'non-Aryan' and three of the eight members of the supervisory board.[144] It remained vulnerable to anti-Semitic purges. At lower levels, in November 1939 the firm was still employing a large number of Jews. It was hard to find replacements. Its managers noted that 'as a result the urgently desired reduction of Jews employed in the bank is delayed and made difficult'.[145] Many of the bank's depositors were Jewish, and many of the credits and industrial assets related to Czech–Jewish firms. The reordering of the Böhmische Union-Bank involved a 10:1 capital reduction followed by an offer from the Deutsche Bank to buy out existing shareholders at a price of 25 per cent of par value. As a result of this transaction, over nine-tenths of the Böhmische Union-Bank's share capital was held by the Deutsche Bank. (In a subsequent capital increase, the Creditanstalt in Vienna took a significant minority participation.)[146] The new management came from the Deutsche Bank in Germany.

Taking over the management of the Böhmische Union-Bank and installing new directors – Walter Pohle from the Sekretariat in Berlin and Max Ludwig Rohde, a deputy director of the Saarbrücken branch – involved substantial costs for the Deutsche Bank. Since the operation had been conducted at the insistence of the German government, the Deutsche Bank demanded a public subsidy. The Reich Economics Ministry eventually agreed on the grounds that 'the Böhmische Union-Bank has . . . always been a German firm. Its collapse would be a significant blow to German interests.'[147] As a result, the German state agreed to meet 55 per cent of the Deutsche Bank's losses arising out of the Böhmische Union-Bank.

From the standpoint of the Deutsche Bank, few aspects of this transaction could hold any attraction. In November 1939 the bank explained to the German government that it would not have been interested in the business 'if we had been completely free in our decisions'.[148] Internally, it justified the takeover on two grounds: first, that the initiative had lain not with the bank but rather with the Reich Economics Ministry; second, that without any response from the Deutsche Bank to the new situation, the expansion of Germany would in reality mean enhanced business for the politically better connected Dresdner Bank.[149]

The extent of the losses tells us a considerable amount about the Böhmische Union-Bank's position. The initial subsidy from the Reich included a provision of 40 million Czech crowns (Kc) (4 million RM) for claims against 'Non-aryans'. In November 1939, the Deutsche Bank estimated its total likely losses as 20.6 million RM, of which 4.2 million were covered through the transfer to the Deutsche Bank of assets from the Agrarbank. The eventual losses were considerably lower than this estimate – 5.9 million RM, of which the Reich guarantee covered 3.23 million.[150]

The uncertainty about the extent of Böhmische Union-Bank losses arose in large measure because of the threat that the party and Sudenten German nationalists would use 'compulsory Aryanizations' (*Zwangsarisierungen*) as a way of stripping the Böhmische Union-Bank's assets. Thus the Reich Food Ministry in April 1939 proposed to seize the Troppauer Zuckerfabrik, on the grounds that the Böhmische Union-Bank, which held a majority of the shares, had remained a Jewish bank. 'The interests of farmers are so crucial that possible bank interests must be subordinated to them.' In 1940, the Four-Year Plan authorities took over in this way the operation of the Bohemia Copper Works (Kupferwerke Böhmen), in which the Böhmische Union-Bank had a 40 per cent holding.[151]

Another 'Aryanized' factory, the 'Bohemia' ceramics works, which had been owned by the Prague investment and banking house of Petschek and which held substantial assets in Germany, was sold by the Böhmische Union-Bank to the SS in 1940. Negotiations for the sale had begun as early as August 1939. The terms were firmly opposed by the only one of the Böhmische Union-Bank's directors who had been part of the pre-1939 management, Josef Krebs; in the end, the sales contracts were signed by the new men from the Deutsche Bank while Krebs was absent on leave. The SS management continued to run the works in Germany as the Porzellan-Manufaktur-Allach-München, with a labour force composed of prisoners from the concentration camp at Dachau. Allach was one of the first parts of what by the end of the war became a gigantic economic empire under the control of the SS.[152]

Initially, however, the economic future of occupied eastern Europe seemed to lie less with the SS than with the gigantic state-run but privately financed holding company, the Reichswerke Hermann Göring. The Reichswerke's initial expansion outside Germany's 1937 frontiers began with large-scale 'Aryanizations' in Austria; it continued in Bohemia with the takeover of the Petschek lignite mines. The Reichswerke's banking connections from its beginnings had been concentrated with the Dresdner Bank. The Deutsche Bank had complained frequently and quite insistently about its relative handicap in what promised to be a very rewarding business, and about the apparent favouritism on the part of the state concern.[153] The Reichswerke manager, Paul Pleiger, told the Deutsche Bank's Karl Kimmich, with some irritation, 'that the differences between the two banks could not be allowed to go on for a long time'.[154] Pleiger in 1937 had asked Kimmich to do the investment banking work connected with the launching of the new firm, to prepare a list of companies that would be prepared to work with the Reichswerke, and to prepare a financial plan for the Reichswerke conglomerate. Kimmich arranged a meeting between Pleiger and Germany's major steel industrialists Flick and Klöckner. But the Deutsche Bank was subsequently ignored, and Pleiger instead promised the leadership of the issuing consortium to Dr Rasche of the Dresdner Bank.

History repeated itself with a surge of investment banking activity in Bohemia–Moravia, and Kimmich again complained bitterly to Pleiger that the big transactions of the Sudetenland and the protectorate had eluded the Deutsche Bank. The sale of the major industrial concerns – Vitkovice Mining and Iron Company (Witkowitz Bergbau- und Eisenhüttengesellschaft) (three-quarters owned by the Rothschilds of Vienna and London), Skoda (where French firms held a significant equity stake) and Brno Munitions (Brünner Waffenwerke, or Ceskoslovenska Zbrojovka) – to the Reichswerke via the Reich Economics Ministry had initially been entrusted to the Dresdner Bank.[155]

The transfer of property by sale was central to the Reichswerke's strategy for the wartime reordering of occupied Europe in preparation for a post-war New Order. A sale would have made the transfer much more permanent than the alternative of a German military imposition of trustees to manage foreign or alien property, but it posed major legal difficulties that took years to resolve. The eventual transfer of Vitkovice to the Reichswerke took place only in 1942, and then under a ten-year renewable contract.[156]

Retrospectively, these operations appear hard to comprehend, a bizarre mixture of astonishingly punctilious legalism and insistence on the following of correct procedures with an underlying simultaneous profound immorality and criminality. It is, for instance, a constant surprise for the historian to discover the amount of time and care devoted to finding and transporting often torn and damaged share certificates in occupied Europe and registering the transfer of ownership, with payments made through the reparations and occupation accounts. From the invasions of 1940, through the Normandy landings, and indeed until the Allied armies had reached the outskirts of Paris, bank couriers shuttled from Paris to Berlin with sealed suitcases in special railway compartments, engaged in the paperwork of creating legality for the New Order. This mixture of correctness, honesty and order (which the historian Jonathan Steinberg has termed the 'secondary virtues') with an ignorance and neglect of the human and moral issues involved was a characteristic of the conduct of institutions and businesses in the National Socialist dictatorship.[157]

In spring 1940, when Göring's prestige in the National Socialist hierarchy temporarily declined, Kimmich believed that there might be a new set of transactions forthcoming as part of a breaking up of the gigantic Reichswerke.[158] But as long as the Reichswerke existed, the Deutsche Bank believed that it was necessary somehow to establish a relationship with it. In April 1939 the Deutsche Bank had sold to the Reichswerke its holding of Bayerischer Lloyd in order to facilitate the integration of transport on the Danube with the strategic and political priorities of the Reich. The Böhmische Union-Bank appeared to be the ideal instrument in managing such a connection of the bank with the monopoly enterprise in eastern Europe, and in the summer of 1939, for this reason, the Deutsche Bank pressed the Böhmische Union-Bank to investigate the possibility of taking charge of the sale of the Vitkovice and the Brno Munitions Company.[159]

In fact, far from breaking up the Reichswerke in 1940, Hermann Göring launched a new phase in its expansion. On 22 June, Göring ordered Reich Economics Minister Walther Funk to prepare the 'inclusion of the occupied areas and those incorporated in the Reich into the Greater German economy' in order to begin a 'new construction of a continental economy led by Germany'. Funk promised that the New Order would bring the 'beginning of an unprecedented economic prosperity'. As part of the reorganization, the structure of industrial ownership in Europe would be rationalized.[160] In the wake of the spring invasion of the Netherlands, Belgium and France, in September 1940, Göring instructed German banks to negotiate the transfer to German control of the major foreign assets of the defeated states. In the National Socialist 'New Europe' the great German banks were to be given back their old function as industrial brokers who built and remodelled vast industrial empires. The difference was that these enterprises were now to be overwhelmingly controlled by the German state.

By 1941 in the Netherlands alone, foreign participations worth over 65 million RM had been acquired 'through *private* negotiations' (original emphasis).[161]

These purchases occurred at such a rate that they began to interfere with government-directed purchases. In April 1941 the Economics Ministry official in charge of banking supervision ordered the banks to slow down the rush of their private customers to seize Dutch assets: 'It is thus the duty of banks to recommend restraint to their customers in the purchase of Dutch shares and bonds.'[162] The private acquisition of shares in western Europe was to be slowed down; and in the meantime, the state-managed programme to reorganize the structure of Europe concentrated on eastern European assets held by residents of western states.

The Böhmische Union-Bank, which had by now established reasonably cordial relations with the Reichswerke in eastern Europe, as well as with the SS, was an ideal agent for this operation. It bought shares of Czech and also Polish works from west European stockholders: Vitkovice, Janina and the Huta Bankowa, which in turn held shares in the Sosnowitzer Bergwerks- und Hütten-AG (Soznowiec Mining), Sosnowitzer Röhren- und Eisenwerke AG (Sosnowiec Pipes), Metallurgia-Werke, Radomsko and Gewerkschaft Renard.[163] These commercial transactions followed quite logically from the extension of German military rule. As the Böhmische Union-Bank's Walter Pohle wrote in 1940, at the height of German successes, concerning the purchase of shares from Schneider-Creusot: 'If we can now buy the shares of Schneider-Creusot, and at a good price, this is in the last result a consequence of the success of German soldiers.'[164]

The shares of central and east European enterprises bought in occupied western Europe were sometimes paid for through the reparations account (*Verrechnungsverkehr*), but some were also bought out of the proceeds of sales of French and Belgian domestic securities that had fallen into the hands of the German authorities. The latter included substantial quantities of securities seized from Jews in occupied Europe, most importantly in the Netherlands, where a formerly Jewish bank (Lippmann, Rosenthal & Co.) took charge of collecting shares turned in to the occupying power on the basis of Decree 148 of 1941 issued by the Reich Commissar for the occupied Netherlands. This business was kept closely guarded, and was generally handled by the Böhmische Union-Bank, as the bank responsible for eastern Europe, and not directly by the Deutsche Bank.[165]

It was the Böhmische Union-Bank rather than the Deutsche Bank that had the closest links with the Reichswerke. At the height of his influence, the Böhmische Union-Bank's Director Walter Pohle was chairman of the supervisory board of Berghütte (Reichswerke AG für Berg- und Hüttenbetriebe 'Hermann Göring', the coal and steel sector of the Reichswerke), and ran the key firms in the Berghütte complex: Berg- und Hüttenwerksgesellschaft Karwin-Trzynietz (Karvina), Berg- und Hüttenwerksgesellschaft Teschen (Decin), and Berg- und Hüttenwerksgesellschaft Wegierska Gorka (near Cracow); and in addition he belonged to the Administrative Council of the explosives factory Böhmisch-

Mährische Stickstoffwerke (Ostrava), Coburg-Werke (Bratislava), Blech-walzwerke AG Karlshütte in Friedeck near Mährisch-Ostrau (Ostrava).[166]

Politics here as elsewhere brought dangers to management. In 1942 as part of the restructuring of Germany's economy to meet the demands of total war, Pohle was pushed out of his influential positions by Major-General Hermann von Hanneken (Director of Department II of the Reich Economics Ministry, Mining, Iron and Energy). Pohle had consulted the Reich Economics Ministry after he had been asked by Max Winkler of the 'Haupttreuhandstelle Ost' to buy the IG Kattowitz and Berghütte for a new Göring monopoly organization designed to encompass formerly Soviet as well as Polish metallurgy works.[167] The Reich Economics Ministry rejected the indirect control of Reichswerke shares by Berghütte: 'The Reich Economics Ministry wishes ... that Berghütte is also given a capital base in the Reich, so that the influence of the Protectorate [Bohemia–Moravia] is correspondingly reduced.'[168] This one false step cost Pohle his functions in the Berghütte industrial enterprise.

After this conflict, Pohle was replaced on the supervisory board of Berghütte by Ambassador Hans Adolf von Moltke, a man of great reputation and decency who was trying to leave the German Foreign Office, but who died within a year as a result of an unsuccessful appendix operation.[169] Moltke was succeeded by someone whose sympathies lay close to the Deutsche Bank, Karl Blessing, director of the strategically important Kontinentale Öl, which had been set up in 1941 as a model for a future private planned economy intended to 'create the position which Germany needs as a Great Power, and which she deserves'.[170] Until 1939 Blessing had been a director of the Reichsbank; he was dismissed after signing the Reichsbank memorandum of 7 January 1939 condemning government policy.

Private capital may have competed with the state concern to acquire east European assets, but the competition was complicated by the fact that both the Reichswerke and its private competitors were producing the same goods, armaments, designed for the same monopsonistic consumer, the German military moloch. In the early phases of the war, even private concerns had to negotiate with the Reichswerke in attempting to build up industrial assets. In 1940, Graf von Ballestrem'sche Güterdirektion Gleiwitz (Gliwice) established a powerful position in Upper Silesia, using the Deutsche Bank and Delbrück Schickler & Co. to repurchase shares in once-German enterprises that had belonged to the Polish state after 1918: the coal field operated by Rudaer Stein-kohlengewerkschaft, Ruda Slanska, Friedenshütten (which had been ceded under the Versailles Treaty to Poland, with Ballestrem retaining a minority of shares) and machine tools and boiler-making plants in Sosnowiec, Dabrowa and Kato-wice.[171] The price paid was 12 million RM, but of this only 4 million was paid immediately, and the rest was to be paid out of future profits; the initial down-payment could be made out of the profits made in Upper Silesian works since 30 September 1939.

After 1941, as Göring's political role came under attack and his importance in the National Socialist hierarchy waned for good, German private capital could attempt to assert itself further. The Reichswerke conglomerate began to break up. Metallurgia-Werke, Radomsko, which bought its raw materials from Berghütte Dombrowa, part of the Berg- und Hüttenwerksgesellschaft Teschen, was now leased to Berghütte, despite opposition from the German Armaments Inspectorate of Cracow.[172] The end of the Reichswerke as an industrial conglomerate came only later, as a result of military developments. It needed to use its complex holdings system to minimize the extent of its financial liabilities, and by the autumn of 1944, the Reichswerke refused to give any guarantee for the debts of companies affiliated in the concern and now being overrun by Soviet armies.[173]

The Böhmische Union-Bank's share-purchasing activities were not confined to central European assets with western European owners. It bought up Jewish shares in Hungary. In Yugoslavia, it built up a participation in the Bankverein für Kroatien AG, Zagreb, and the Bankverein AG, Belgrad. Its position within the Deutsche Bank's south-east European banking system was confirmed through an exchange of shares and seats on the supervisory board with the Creditanstalt-Bankverein Vienna.[174]

Almost all of the Böhmische Union-Bank's investment banking business took place on behalf of state or SS purchasers looking for an apparently respectable financial intermediary to regulate transfers of property. But the war economy, though state dominated, was not entirely socialized, and some private concerns used the same methods. In some cases, the private purchasers deliberately tried to avoid the purchase of Jewish property: the industrial magnate Günther Quandt, for instance, between 1939 and 1941 used the Böhmische Union-Bank to purchase property, preferably but not necessarily non-Jewish property, at favourable prices. Or another example: in June 1941 the largely non-Jewish-owned Metallwalzwerke AG, as well as other shares that had been owned by Czech Jews, were sold by the Böhmische Union-Bank to Mannesmann.[175]

As the course of the war changed, and German defeat appeared ever more probable, and as the intense involvement of the Böhmische Union-Bank in the economics of imperialism in the East became ever clearer, the Bohemian bank appeared as more and more of an embarrassment to the Berlin managers of the Deutsche Bank. The Berlin bank had been dragged in on the crest of the wave of expansionist euphoria in 1938–39, and could now see no way out. In July 1943, Oswald Rösler of the Deutsche Bank, the chairman of the Böhmische Union-Bank's supervisory board, wrote an extensive memorandum about the poor quality of the Böhmische Union-Bank's business, which he attributed to the disruptive consequences of 'Aryanization' and the impossibility of finding adequate management. He noted how 'the extension of the German business depended entirely on the Aryanization of previously Jewish businesses, which

have been taken over in many cases by persons who have only political recommendations, but who unfortunately lack technical knowledge and especially
the necessary financial resources'.[176]

And how poor was the business of the Böhmische Union-Bank! In November
1943, the list of the bank's 'unstable credit accounts' amounted to 943,584,000
crowns (or 94 million RM), which included Emigration and Resettlement
Accounts (of expelled and 'resettled', i.e. murdered, Jews) worth 271,527,000
crowns, and an account of 284,109,000 crowns in the name of the 'Jewish Self-
Administration' of the concentration camp of Theresienstadt.[177] It demonstrated
clearly how the Böhmische Union-Bank's major business lay in the administration
of the property of the victims of National Socialism for the benefit of the German
state. Again, most of the true owners of this account were the murdered victims
of the National Socialist genocide. A final balance sheet produced for 28 February
1945 showed assets consisting mostly of government paper, and liabilities
still shown as 287,693,000 crowns held by Theresienstadt.[178] A few months
later, the chief architect of the Böhmische Union-Bank's wartime strategy,
Walter Pohle, died of starvation in a Czech prison. A pathological over-eater
suffering from 'dumping syndrome', he could not survive on the meagre prison
food.

By the last years of the war, the Deutsche Bank's foreign connections, especially
with the Böhmische Union-Bank, looked incriminating. But foreign involvements
in a period of tension and war had always posed intense problems. Even at the
beginning of the war, when the success of German arms had seemed to most
observers inevitable, the head of the Foreign Department of the Deutsche Bank,
Hermann J. Abs, had tried to set some distance between the bank and its affiliated
foreign institutes. They were not to be mentioned in bank advertisements: 'Herr
Abs has personally explained to Herr Dr Kimmich the reasons for which he
believed that the listing of foreign affiliations, especially during the war, was
inopportune.'[179] The relationship should be kept quiet in order to minimize the
possibility of enemy retaliation.

On the whole this principle of avoiding direct involvement was defended
consistently and semi-publicly by Abs. For instance, in September 1941 he told
the Reichsbank's Stock Exchange Committee that, 'according to his opinion, it
was preferable to develop banking in south-east Europe through national circles,
rather than to attempt to create explicitly German banks. Apart from that
there were already in these countries sufficient banks under a decisive German
influence.'[180] German banks could clearly be influential and powerful without
appearing to be directly involved.

This calculation underlay the Deutsche Bank's dealings with banks in the
Netherlands and Belgium. In 1936 the bank tried to disguise its Netherlands
subsidiary Handel-Maatschappij H. Albert de Bary & Co. N.V., Amsterdam, as
a Dutch company through the transfer of stock to nominally Dutch hands.
After the outbreak of European war in September 1939, the bank dismissed a

substantial part of its German staff. Only after the invasion of the Netherlands were the shares repurchased by the Deutsche Bank, and did the Germans return to their positions.

Almost immediately after the occupation of the Netherlands, the Reich Economics Ministry asked the Deutsche Bank to take over shares in the Rotterdamsche Bankvereeniging, but the bank responded very hesitatingly. Karl Kimmich replied 'that since at present the Dutch are rather stiff in their attitude to German influence, such co-operation can only be imagined with great difficulty and can only be achieved very slowly in a voluntary way'.[181] The Economics Ministry then tried to divide up the newly occupied countries between German companies and allocated Dutch banks to the Deutsche Bank and Belgian banks to the Dresdner's sphere of influence. The plan was to divide Europe between the banks, rather than permit bank competition.

Again the Deutsche Bank protested. Kimmich told the State Secretary in the Economics Ministry, Neumann, that 'such a process is contrary to any commercial view, and can only lead to a fiasco'.[182] The Deutsche Bank's main interest lay in Belgium, not the Netherlands, and the bank remained cautious about attempts to generate a greater German direct participation in Dutch business. One year after the German invasion, the Deutsche Bank's director in Den Haag wrote sceptically that 'a German–Dutch economic interpenetration on a larger scale can only be accomplished if the Dutch no longer believe in a final victory of the English'.[183] But the Deutsche Bank did engage in some major share purchases in the Netherlands, buying for instance most of the Dutch shares of the Algemeene Kunstzijde Unie and the 75 per cent of the Norddeutsche Lederwerke AG that before 1940 had been held by Dutch owners.[184]

The Economics Ministry's attempts to make banking spheres of influence and to award the Deutsche Bank but not Belgium was particularly irritating because Kimmich believed that the dominant Belgian bank, the Société Générale, wished to work closely with the Deutsche Bank, but not with the more politicized Dresdner Bank.[185] The Société Générale's Governor, Alexandre Galopin, had been the exponent of the theory of the 'lesser evil' (known in wartime Belgium as the 'doctrine Galopin'), that it was better to work with Germany and supply products (even semi-military products such as boots or steel), rather than to allow the Belgian population to starve. In order to do this, he needed to have a reliable and non-political German partner. At the same time, from September 1940 through the Vice-Governor of the Société Générale, Félicien Cattier, Galopin kept contacts with the Belgian exile government in London. From 1941, the bank tried to reduce the extent of its collaboration with the Germans, and in February 1944 Galopin was assassinated on his own doorstep by a member of a Flemish fascist group, the Veiligheidskorps, that specialized in counter-reprisals against attacks by the Belgian resistance.

The Société Générale was a vast holding company, with a wide range of assets both in Belgium and abroad. By the summer of 1940, it had ensured that an important part of its overseas assets, notably the important mineral holdings at Katanga and elsewhere in Africa, had been transferred to management in London and New York. On the other hand, the bank was not at all unwilling to dispose of its holdings in south-east and Balkan Europe, which had brought enormous losses and had substantially contributed to the very poor performance of the Société Générale in the 1930s. After 1940, in consequence, it rapidly sold to Germany its shares in the Österreichische Eisenbahn-Verkehrs-Anstalt, the Creditanstalt in Vienna, the Istituto Nazionale di Credito per il Lavoro all'Estero, the Allgemeiner Jugoslawischer Bank-Verein, and the Banca Commerciala Romana.[186] On the other hand, the deal proposed by the Société Générale for a sale to the Deutsche Bank of half of the shares of the Banque Générale du Luxembourg, with an option on the purchase of the other half, was much more complex, with tacit provisions for annulment at the end of hostilities.

In late August 1940, a race for Belgian contacts and assets between the German great banks took place. Carl Goetz of the Dresdner Bank believed that he could rely on Funk's order and on the sympathy of Major von Becker, the German occupation official in Brussels in charge of banking. Goetz visited Galopin and the Société Générale's President, Willy de Munck, but was told by Galopin that he could make no arrangement as 'political conditions did not allow him to form a clear idea about the future of Belgium and the Société Générale'.[187] Suddenly on the evening of 27 August, Hermann J. Abs appeared unexpectedly in Brussels and set out the details of his own bank's negotiations with the Société Générale. The Deutsche Bank's local representative noted: 'His unexpected appearance caused visible confusion in the office of the Commissariat.'[188] Abs's intervention apparently was not enough. Ex-Economics Minister Schacht, still officially in the German government as a Minister without Portfolio, was called in by the Deutsche Bank, spoke on the telephone with Goetz and Funk, and then wrote a letter to Funk in which he explained that the two German banks had come to an agreement: 'The banks agreed with him in thinking it right to leave individual deals in Belgium and the Netherlands to themselves, but to inform the Reich Economics Minister about "larger business".'[189]

After this initial skirmish had apparently been won by the Deutsche Bank, major German industrial firms visited Galopin, expecting to acquire their own Belgian assets: Vereinigte Stahlwerke, Mannesmann, Otto Wolff. Some German firms, notably I.G. Farben, had drawn up their own preliminary studies of the Belgian economy in the summer of 1940. Otto Wolff had made an agreement in August with the metal-exporting firm Société Commerciale d'Ougrée, with which Wolff had worked before 1939, in which Wolff took over export shares to central and eastern Europe. But Galopin criticized the Wolff agreement, and stated to the Deutsche Bank that it would never come into force during the war.[190] Even for those firms such as Mannesmann which had historically been very intimately connected with the Deutsche Bank, the bank's representatives in Brussels were strikingly unhelpful. Director Kurzmeyer made it clear that the

Deutsche Bank could not help with the task of acquisitions. They were, it soon appeared, simply too complex for the bank to handle.

The biggest single transfer of industrial ownership in the case of occupied Belgium involved the Luxemburg steel works Arbed, which had French, Belgian and Luxemburg owners. In November 1940 the Société Générale proposed to the Deutsche Bank the transfer of half of its shares in a holding company for Arbed stock, as well as a sale of some of its shares in the German Bergwerksgesellschaft Dahlbusch to I.G. Farben. But in practice the transaction was postponed to the end of hostilities. Instead of the legally highly complicated process of rearranging a jumble of interlocking holdings, Arbed was run throughout the war by a German military commissioner.

Would direct banking participations be any easier? On 20 September 1940, the Economics Ministry authorized 22 German firms to undertake capital participations (*Kapitalverflechtung*) in the Netherlands, Belgium and occupied France. But the political circumstances of the occupied countries remained unclear: King Leopold of Belgium visited Hitler in Berchtesgaden in November 1940, but the Führer disliked the monarch, and no peace treaty resulted. As a consequence, even Comte de Launoit of the Banque de Bruxelles, generally thought to be more sympathetic to the Germans than Galopin, explained to the Dresdner Bank that a German participation in a large Belgian bank would be counterproductive, as it would undermine the confidence of the population in that bank.[191]

In November 1940 the German Military Bank Commissariat in Brussels produced a paper recommending greater commitment by German banks. They should, it suggested, establish subsidiaries in Belgium to give credits to factories producing armaments for German orders, and to deal with the 'the task of penetration' arising in the question of the readjustment of the ownership of European industry. This exposé was followed by negotiations in the Economics Ministry in Berlin, in which the banking expert suggested that there should be a series of joint German–Belgian banks. These would acquire the assets of 'enemy property' in Belgium, such as branches of British and French banks, as well as 'Aryanized' banks (Phillippson et Cie, Banque Lambert, Banque Cassel). The Dresdner Bank responded by creating a 'Banque Continentale' in the offices formerly occupied by the Banque de Paris, and the Commerzbank used the Brussels 'Hansabank'. The Deutsche Bank declined to engage in this exercise, and to take over the Banque de Commerce as the German authorities suggested, because it believed it needed no subsidiary. Abs pointed out that the Deutsche Bank intended 'to base its business in Belgium on its very old and good relations with the foremost Belgian bank, the Banque de la Société Générale, and before making further decisions to wait for further political development'.[192]

In south-eastern Europe, the Deutsche Bank also preferred to act in agreement with other banks rather than on its own: but in this case the extent of its control was in reality much greater than in the case of the much more equal relationship

Georg Solmssen, Spokesman of the Board of Managing Directors in 1933

Eduard Mosler, Spokesman of the Board of Managing Directors
from 1934 to 1939

Karl Kimmich, Spokesman of the Board of Managing Directors
from 1940 to 1942

Oswald Rösler, Spokesman of the Board of Managing Directors
from 1943 to 1945

The *Schwibbogen* (flying buttress) in Berlin showing propaganda
for the referendum on Germany's intention to leave the League
of Nations in November 1933

Bank staff listening to the radio broadcast of Reich Chancellor Adolf Hitler's speech on
10 November 1933 in the large cashiers' office in Berlin

The bank's first staff meeting under the new political regime was held in the *Neue Welt* assembly rooms, Berlin, on 30 November 1933

Franz Hertel, *Betriebszellenobmann* (factory cell representative), held a keynote speech at the staff meeting

Bank advertising in the 1930s

GROSSE REICHSAUSSTELLUNG 1937

Schaffendes Volk

ÜBERREICHT DURCH:

Deutsche Bank und Disconto-Gesellschaft

FILIALE DÜSSELDORF

DÜSSELDORF-SCHLAGETERSTADT MAI OKT

below:
Emil Georg von Stauss
member of the Board of
Managing Directors from
1915 to 1932 and member
of the Supervisory Board
from 1932 to 1942 (*left*);
Karl Ritter von Halt,
member of the Board
of Managing Directors
from 1938 to 1945 (*right*)

Deutsche Bank's severely damaged building in Berlin after a bombing raid
in November 1943; the main entrance and the *Schwibbogen* (flying buttress)
are visible in the middle of the picture

with the Belgian Société Générale. An Austrian bank, the Creditanstalt-Bankverein (which was not fully controlled by the Deutsche Bank through capital participation until 1942) played a much more crucial part in the re-ordering of the economy of south-east Europe than did the Böhmische Union-Bank. Its historical roots lay in two of the major universal banks of the Austro-Hungarian Empire, which had never adequately adjusted to the new economics of the 1919 peace settlement. After the 1931 banking crisis in Austria, the banks required extensive reconstruction and passed into state control: the merger of the Rothschild-owned Creditanstalt and the Wiener Bankverein took place as part of a government-managed reorganization of the Austrian banking system.

During the banking crisis of 1931, the Deutsche Bank had participated in a support operation for the Creditanstalt, and already before 1938 there had been a representative of the Deutsche Bank on the supervisory board of the Creditanstalt, Gustaf Schlieper, and then after his death Hermann J. Abs. Immediately after the *Anschluss* of March 1938, the Creditanstalt announced that it should like its shares to be sold to the Deutsche Bank, but instead the bank's ownership was transferred from the Austrian state to the German state holding company VIAG (Vereinigte Industrie-Unternehmungen AG). The government had probably always envisaged an eventual privatization, but it had wanted to control the initial transfer on the grounds that 'a gain resulting from an appreciation of share prices as a result of the territorial inclusion of the Ostmark [Austria] into Germany should not accrue to individuals or a bank, but rather to the Reich through the VIAG, since the economic development is a result of the initiative of the Reich, paid for out of general tax revenue'. In December 1938, the VIAG sold a 25 per cent share to the Deutsche Bank; and, after the Creditanstalt had divested a major part of its industrial holdings to the Reichswerke in May 1942, the Deutsche Bank became the majority share owner.[193] Already in 1938, the VIAG had agreed to leave the practical management of the Creditanstalt to the Deutsche Bank, since as an industrial holding company it had little experience in day-to-day banking.

Abs had initially seen the Creditanstalt's role as part of a Europe-wide investment banking network, in which the Creditanstalt would work closely with the Deutsche Bank as well as with the Société Générale de Belgique. His first efforts, before the outbreak of war, involved urging the Creditanstalt to sell shares in Zorka (First Yugoslav Chemical Company) to the Belgian chemical giant Solvay.[194] The Société Générale had large holdings in the Jugoslawischer Bank-Verein, which the Göring authorities wished to transfer to German banks, but Abs resisted this business and the matter rested until the occupation of Belgium.[195] Then the memory of the apparent sympathy of the Deutsche Bank to Belgian interests subsequently led the Société Générale to try to deal with more enthusiasm with Abs in disposing of east and south-east European assets than with rival German bankers.[196] The Société Générale eventually gave up its Yugoslav holdings. Payments for the sale of the Yugoslav Banking Company (Jugoslawischer Bank-Verein) were made, in the usual fashion, over the German–Belgian clearing account. The Creditanstalt took 51 per cent of the Yugoslav stock, and German banks held minority stakes: the Deutsche Bank and the Dresdner Bank each had 12.5 per cent, the Commerzbank and the Reichs-Kredit-Gesellschaft 6.25 per cent each, and the Böhmische Union-Bank 4 per cent.[197] The Yugoslav bank was subsequently divided up along the lines of the new political settlement into a Bankverein für Kroatien and a Bankverein AG, Belgrad.

The division of south-east Europe into spheres of influence between competing banks was carefully planned and calculated by the Reich Economics Ministry.[198] It reflected expectations about the future trading as well as financial connections of a reordered Balkan Europe. Trade with south-east Europe was complicated by systems of exchange control: payments were made by means of clearings through the central banks of the countries involved in trade. Managing these payments meant in effect directing the pattern and course of trade.

The Creditanstalt also expanded its direct Yugoslav operations, lending to Südost-Montan and the Mines de Bor, a major source of copper (with substantial reserves of zinc, lead, antimony and chromium ores). By March 1941 a majority of shares had been bought from their previous French and Belgian owners.

In addition, the Creditanstalt moved into formerly Polish territory: in the Generalgouvernement, it opened branches in 1940 in Cracow and Lvov, and took over the Deutsche Bank's business there.[199] In the Polish territories annexed to Germany, the Deutsche Bank operated in its own capacity, with branches in Gdynia (Gotenhafen), Bialo (Bielitz) and Poznan (Posen). It had already operated a branch in Katowice (Kattowitz) before the war. In Hungary, the Creditanstalt acquired a minority holding of the Pest Hungarian Bank of Commerce (Pester Ungarische Commercial Bank).[200]

In the same way as Böhmische Union-Bank was to do the investment business of the Reichswerke in eastern Europe, the Creditanstalt was to manage the financing and commerce of the Balkans. In a meeting of the Creditanstalt's directors in August 1940, Abs spelt out the strategy. Vienna should have 'an enlarged sphere of activity'. He suggested 'that the Creditanstalt should be the bank in charge of relations with south-east Europe. Whether this should be done through subsidiaries or through a branch network depended on the political conditions.' In the course of this discussion, when the Creditanstalt's Dr Fritscher argued that the Reich Economics Ministry would treat the Creditanstalt with suspicion if it were to be too obviously closely associated with the Deutsche Bank, Abs replied 'that the Deutsche Bank had no reason to take the initiative in the question of participation. But before it could give up one area, there should be a declaration making this possible – since in principle the bank should be represented throughout the world.' He demanded, in other words, either a formal division between the Creditanstalt and the Deutsche Bank of Balkan

Europe into spheres of influence, or a capital participation of the kind eventually established in 1942.[201]

Greece lay outside the Creditanstalt's area. In the summer of 1941, the Deutsche Bank worked with the Reich Economics Ministry in buying the Société Générale's shares in the leading Greek commercial bank, the Banque Nationale de Grèce, while the Dresdner Bank was left to build up a participation in the much smaller Banque d'Athènes.[202]

Romania and Bulgaria also lay outside the economic orbit of the Creditanstalt. Here too the Deutsche Bank acquired a major direct equity participation. By 1941, it controlled 88 per cent of the Banca Commerciala Romana SA (formerly owned by French and Belgian banks) and over 90 per cent of the Bulgarian Kreditbank Sofia, historically an associate of the Disconto-Gesellschaft which had financed German–Bulgarian trade. In the August 1940 meeting with the board of the Creditanstalt, Abs had spoken quite candidly about obtaining an 'enrichment of the Deutsche Bank' in Romania.[203]

Romania had played a major role before 1939 in German economic diplomacy *vis-à-vis* south-east Europe. She had had a powerful bargaining advantage, in that Germany was dependent on petroleum imports and found the development of a substitute through synthetic gasoline to be both extremely slow (and thus useless from the standpoint of Germany's military ambitions) and highly uneconomic. Romania attempted to use her strategic advantage as a major oil producer by increasing her refining capacity, so that four-fifths of native petroleum would be exported as refined products.[204] In 1935 the Deutsche Bank participated in negotiations to establish a joint German–Romanian refining company which would pay for the import of German machinery with petroleum products, but the plan ran into the hostility of the German authorities.[205] Instead, Romania cut back on exports to Germany and imposed a special tax to compensate for the overvaluation of the RM in the clearing arrangements. Only after September 1938 and the Munich conference did Romanian policy become more sympathetic to the Reich: in November 1938 King Carol spoke with Hermann Göring about a 'systematic co-operation for the development of economic relations'.[206]

At the beginning of 1939 Helmut Wohlthat of the Reich Office for Foreign Exchange led a mission charged with the expansion of German–Romanian trade. It produced an agreement after the fall of Czechoslovakia which was widely regarded as a model for future economic relations in the 'greater economic area'. Germany would sell agricultural equipment, tractors and seeding machines, in exchange for oil. Already before the outbreak of war, Wohlthat promoted the establishment of companies in which banks and industry as well as state and party would work to develop relations with the states of south-eastern Europe. The Dresdner Bank's director Professor Meyer was to become President of the German–Yugoslav Society, and Abs of the Deutsche Bank, President of the equivalent Romanian Society.[207]

By the end of 1940, a ten-year plan had been agreed in which Germany would provide long-term credit for the delivery of machinery to Romania. The argument was now made that 'Romania will in the long run only be able to solve the pressure of rural overpopulation through industrialization.'[208]

This scheme provided the basis for a much more elaborate proposal worked out after consultations between businessmen on both sides, and eventually incorporated into a new German–Romanian agreement of 2 February 1943. A German–Romanian Experts Committee included on the German side Abs, Karl Blessing, formerly a director of the Reichsbank and after 1941 head of Kontinentale Öl AG, and (as chairman) Max Ilgner of I.G. Farben. The Committee drew up an 'Immediate Programme', whose main features were the relocation of consumer production from Germany to Romania, the production of synthetic fibres from reeds in the Danube delta and from beechwood, the production of artificial fertilizers (phosphates and nitrates), natural gas, bauxite and aluminium production, hydroelectric works and electrification of major railway lines. The total cost of this ambitious industrialization drive was estimated at 150–200 million RM, of which half would be financed from Germany and would cover the supply of German equipment and expertise; the rest would be raised in Romania, where the German-owned Romanian banks would play the major role.[209] Kontinentale Öl had by this stage become the major Romanian petroleum producer, thanks to the purchases by the Deutsche Bank of the French Romanian holdings in the Colombia and Concordia companies.[210]

The Deutsche Bank also bought holdings in other foreign countries on behalf of a variety of private companies. The Otavi metallurgy company required inputs of aluminium and rare metal ores, but found its African mines useless because of the military conflict. As substitutes it acquired Zinnbergwerk Sudetenland GmbH, the Bauxit-Trust AG (which had substantial Hungarian ore sources), Donautal-Tonerde AG Budapest and the Gravia bauxite mine in Greece. It also tried to buy Romanian companies from the portfolio of the liquidated Romanian Jewish bank, Marmorosch Blank & Co., but found it difficult to circumvent Romanian legislation limiting foreign ownership of industrial enterprise.[211] And despite the war, Otavi also purchased mines in the Congo from Belgian owners.[212]

3. The New Order

Especially in the period between the defeat of France in May 1940 and the launching of Operation Barbarossa in June 1941, business saw and enthused about the dramatic reordering of Europe to Germany's advantage. Businessmen and bankers envisaged a speedy shift into a post-war world that would learn the lessons from the inter-war years, from the failure of internationalism and from the 1930s restriction and bilateralization of trade. The new post-war period would be centred around the fact of German economic power.

Economics Minister Walther Funk developed the familiar National Socialist idea of a Co-Prosperity Sphere or *Grossraumwirtschaft* into a future European trading and currency bloc in which fixed exchange rates and free convertibility would replicate some of the certainties of the gold standard world, but in the context of integration of the European continent. Funk maintained his position long after it seemed to most others unrealizable. As late as 1944, when German clearing balances had built up to staggering amounts, when repressed inflation led to misallocations and the development of a black market, and of course when Germany was very obviously losing the war, he was explaining that 'one of our basic principles for the recasting of the economy in the new Europe is the stability of exchange rates and price stability'.[213]

These were themes that Hermann J. Abs had raised in a speech of 17 July 1941 to the Trade Policy Committee of the Reich Economic Chamber on the theme 'Europe and the USA from an Economic Viewpoint'. The main message of his presentation was that the clearing system created in the 1930s had damaged the development of trade and the spread of prosperity, and that payments should be made in convertible currencies through an international banking system; but that because of the differences in economic performance between Europe and the USA, the liberalization should first be attempted on a continental basis. Looked at in one way, it was a version of the European Payments Union of the 1950s; looked at through the political lens of 1941, however, it was a defence of German imperialism. 'The perspectives for the German economy at the end of the war, which suggest a closer integration of the European economies, in regard to the external economy justify a consideration which counterpoises continental Europe with the American continent.'[214]

The vision of a reordered Europe that formed an economic community controlled by German interests appeared most compelling in the wake of the easy military victories of 1940. But long after the euphoria had passed, the mechanism of international payments remained acutely problematic. The difficulties were frequently debated in the Reichsbank, as well as in the Working Group on External Economic Relations created in 1944, which was composed of bureaucrats from the Reich Economics Ministry and businessmen, including Abs.

Already in December 1939 Abs had criticized the clearing mechanism as inefficient, ineffective and restrictive of trade, and appealed for a return to multilateral trade.[215] This theme remained quite consistent in Abs's statements on trade policy: whether they were made when Germany appeared to be winning the war, or when she was losing.

In the course of 1943, Abs became involved in a rather intriguing international discussion of the likely shape of the post-war order. In May 1943, the Economic Adviser of the Basle-based Bank for International Settlements, the Swede Per Jacobsson, spoke with Abs as well as with Emil Puhl of the Reichsbank and Carl Goetz of the Dresdner Bank. In the setting of the Zurich Hotel Baur en Ville, the bankers discussed the currency plans developed by John Maynard Keynes and Harry Dexter White (in part conceived as a response to Funk's New Order).

The Germans expressed a strong preference for the British version: 'Puhl seems to think that the American plan was too much US hegemony. Abs said unitas [the unit of account in the US Treasury Plan developed by White] was a fig-leave [*sic*] for the dollar.' But quite surprisingly, the German bankers also criticized the German practice of clearings, and described the German currency regime as simply an emergency solution (*Notlösung*). The discussion resumed one month later in Berlin, when Jacobsson arrived to set out the details of the White and Keynes plans to a broader financial circle, again including Abs.[216] Should not – Abs believed – Germany develop a more satisfactory response than that laid out in the speeches of Economics Minister Funk?

In 1943 in the Reichsbank's Council (Beirat), Abs urged that Germany should sell more to the countries of continental Europe and in this way avoid the building up of large clearing balances: 'The publication of the Keynes plan and the White plan have provided an interesting vision of the differences in opinion between the English and the Americans. Germany hardly has the possibility of putting forward any similar plan. But we could show what advantages would be brought by a generous trading policy.'[217] In the defence of a liberal trade policy, Abs was speaking against one of the most important and characteristic elements of National Socialist economic foreign policy; but it was impossible to discuss in a similar way the much broader complex of National Socialist economic thought and the extension of state control.

V. The Expansion of State and Party during the War

In dealing with the foreign activity of the Deutsche Bank, we saw the gradual expansion of state influence: in directing the armaments economy of occupied Europe, in the extension of direct ownership of public sector corporations, and in dividing banking activity into geographic spheres of influence. Only occasionally was this momentum interrupted, usually when one of the figures at the top of the public sector enterprises suffered a personal reverse in the complex and dangerous faction politics of National Socialist Germany. The same tendency – an increase in state and party authority mitigated only by the effects of political factionalism – characterized the development of the German economy on the home front. Wars create considerable opportunities for private business, but also a very powerful demand for the limitation of illegitimate private gains and the extension of state control over the economy. In the case of National Socialism at war, there was no doubt that the latter took the upper hand.

1. The expansion of the state

In the early years of the war, the bank's business included not only purchase of assets in occupied Europe, but also a continuation of privatizations in Germany.

A unique investment climate combined increasing inflationary pressure (as a result of government deficits financed through the printing press) with imposed ceilings on stock prices. This made real assets especially attractive to speculative natures who remembered the inflationary experiences of Germany's first twentieth-century war, and the profits to be made from rapid industrial expansion and the acquisition of real assets (*Sachwerte*) with paper money. Some important debit accounts with the Deutsche Bank suddenly expanded: above all, that of the tobacco empire of Philipp Reemtsma, and the Accumulatoren-Fabrik AG of Günther Quandt. Both used bank borrowing to expand their industrial holdings. Reemtsma, a major shareholder of the bank, had drawn 46 million RM credit by October 1944, and was the bank's largest debit account.[218]

Hapag was privatized in as inconspicuous a fashion as possible in 1941 by a consortium led by Philipp Reemtsma, and financed by the Deutsche Bank. Reemtsma purchased 4 million RM of shares, with an option on another 4 million, without any consultations whatsoever with the supervisory board (which merely recorded its 'regret ... that the supervisory board only discovered this fact and the further details through the press').[219]

Also in 1941, the bank carried out a privatization of 120 million RM shares in Vereinigte Stahlwerke (the leading private German steel concern). Göring, now a much less significant figure in the power hierarchy of the Third Reich, and who had previously fought bitterly with the management of the Stahlverein when he had been setting up the state Reichswerke, agreed rather meekly. His consent came, the Deutsche Bank believed, 'since at present the higher authorities are leaning towards the private side'.[220] But this observation was made just at the moment when the course of the war, and with it the nature of economic policy, began to change in a newly radicalized direction.

After the failure of Operation Barbarossa to achieve an immediate victory over the Soviet Union, a complete reordering of the war economy took place. On 3 December 1941, a Führer command restricted the output of consumer goods and ordered the concentration of war-related production in the most efficient and economical plants. In mid-January 1942, Germany started to restructure the economy to meet the demands of a long conflict. Rationalization initiatives later produced a Central Planning administration, created in April 1942 under Albert Speer, which allocated raw materials centrally and worked with the industrial committees already established by Speer's predecessor as Minister of Armaments, Fritz Todt.[221]

At the same time as Speer's ministry built up its position, the party's influence expanded through the institution of control at a regional level by Gau Economic Chambers (Gauwirtschaftskammer), which replaced the old system of chambers of commerce, and the appointment of Gau Economic Leaders (Gauwirtschaftsführer).

Industrial reorganization also brought a much more powerful involvement of the state in the financing of war production. The major armaments producers expanded their capacity by means of consortia put together out of several commercial banks, but with a leading role taken by public sector institutions. For instance, the newly established German Aero-Bank (Bank der deutschen Luftfahrt) took this role in the highly capital-intensive aircraft-manufacturing industry. Commercial credit played a significant but fundamentally subordinate role in the increase of munitions output. The companies historically connected with the Deutsche Bank were no exception when it came to the financing of expanded munitions production. In 1944, the aero-engine works of Daimler-Benz Motoren GmbH Genshagen, which had originally been 95 per cent owned by the Luftfahrtkontor, the predecessor of the Aero-Bank, had liabilities of 17,750,000 RM, of which 7,000,000 RM was an operating loan of the Aero-Bank, and 3,125,000 RM was a government-provided mobilization credit (*Mob-Kredit*). BMW's Eisenach works were similarly in part state owned,[222] and the state's share of credits increased during the war. In July 1939, out of a total of 43.5 million RM of credits, 19.5 million came from the bank consortium (in which the Deutsche Bank participated with two-thirds, the Dresdner Bank with one-third), and 17.0 million from the Luftfahrtkontor, with another 7.0 million from another public sector bank, the Bank for Industrial Bonds. By 1941, credits had risen to 77 million RM, of which the two commercial banks between them accounted for only 13.5 million RM.[223] In 1942, the Aero-Bank demanded to participate in circulating credit as well as *Mob-Kredite*.[224] Another example is the Junkers aero-works, where out of an investment credit of 65 million RM in 1941, the Aero-Bank provided 29 million RM and the Deutsche Bank 11 million RM; and of its operating credit, the Aero-Bank had 40 million RM and the Deutsche Bank 12 million RM.[225] The public sector banks – the Aero-Bank and the Bank for Industrial Bonds – had the advantage over the commercial banks that their credits could automatically be rediscounted at the Reichsbank (*Rediskontzusage*), while other credits needed to be discussed in the Reichsbank's Credit Committee.[226]

2. Criticism of banks

If industry were to be rationalized and commercial banks were to be squeezed out by government-controlled lending institutions, then there might also be an opportunity for those in the party hostile to finance capitalism to reassert the original radical elements of the National Socialist programme. The old slogans reappeared. 'The credit industry is not an end in itself, but is only justified in as far as the economy requires it.' The consequence was that 'simplification measures' would be needed.[227] Proposals for a regionalization of the German banking structure emerged once more.[228]

There were complaints about interest rates; that there were too many branches in the major cities; that banks had abused their right to vote the shares of their customers (*Depotstimmrecht*); that they exercised an unhealthy influence through their supervisory board presence. The National Socialist party newspaper *Völkischer Beobachter* believed that the bank provision of industrial credit had led to a distorted economy: 'If the banks and in particular the investment banks had not mixed themselves up in financing in the course of the second half of the nineteenth century, economic development would have been much smoother and simpler, and less crisis prone ... All financing through credit is speculative.'[229] The SS Security Service used public opinion surveys to justify its call for action against finance capitalism: 'There is an overwhelming rejection of the idea of great banks, but many emphasize the usefulness of credit institutes that would serve a wider regional base.'[230] By the beginning of 1944 the SS had begun a general attack on the principles of the private economy, claiming 'in the last analysis it is a matter of indifference, whether in future economic investment is carried out by the private economy or by the public sector'.[231]

The bank supervision system built up in 1931–34 was attacked as ineffective, and progressively dismantled. In 1942, control of local bank branches was transferred from the Reich Supervisory Office for Credit to the Reichsbank, which thus took over the day-to-day invigilation of banking activity. In 1944 the supervisory body was dissolved altogether.[232] The abolition was justified primarily in terms of a wartime economy drive. But it also formed part of a general attack on the position of banks. Since their position had become essentially administrative, in dealing with payments transactions and in channelling private savings into the state's coffers, banks might well be pruned back in the same way as the public fiscal administration had been.[233]

The offensive began with a letter of Martin Bormann to Reich Economics Minister Walther Funk on the subject of credit costs and excessive bank profits in wartime: the Deutsche Bank, it was claimed, had managed to quadruple its profits between 1939 and 1940.[234] The Party Chancellery responded by demanding a limitation of supervisory board seats for bankers, and the replacement of bankers by technicians.[235] Rationalization, the major slogan of the winter of 1941–42, and applied across all areas of administration and the economy, could be used by the party to produce a reordering of German finance, and a reduction of its power.

In May 1942 all banks were instructed to close 10 per cent of their branches. The party did not think this sufficiently radical. The Reich Economics Ministry official responsible for the Banking Section, Ministerial Director Joachim Riehle, noted that 'with the Reich Administrators and the Gauleiters the impression has been created that the Berlin authorities are not pursuing rationalization measures with appropriate emphasis'. Later in the year, he told journalists that banks had become too concentrated: 'The fact that *one single Great Bank* [original emphasis] had collected roughly one-third of all credit bank deposits was a political issue. "The fate and attitude" of a great bank must be treated as a political affair.'[236] One immediate result was a further list of branches to be closed.[237] In

1942 the Deutsche Bank closed 21 branches and 24 city deposit offices; in 1943, 61 branches and 30 offices.

In October 1943, the government ordered a simplification of supervisory boards, in which the number of bankers on the board would be reduced, and the majority of its business delegated to a five-man committee. The Deutsche Bank responded by trying to reduce the number of bank representatives on supervisory boards of associated companies to one-third of the total board membership.[238]

Banks and their political allies tried to mount some defence. Banks may have looked superfluous to the requirements of a wartime economy – but what about peace? In a speech of December 1942, Wilhelm Zangen of Mannesmann, the leader of the interest association Reich Group Industry, pointed out that banks would play a vital part in the conversion of military production facilities to peaceful use.[239] By early 1944, even a convinced National Socialist banker such as Otto Christian Fischer, who had been Führer of the Reich Group Banks, was circulating a memorandum on 'reconstruction of the peacetime economy', in which he called for the restoration of 'pure economy', 'which operates on the basis of supply and demand determined by competition and the calculation of cost'.[240]

The Deutsche Bank was especially vulnerable to the new attack because of Stauss's death in December 1942: the bank no longer had a prominently situated political protector. He needed to be replaced, urgently. An initial consequence was greater party involvement in the supervisory board. In March 1943, while the supervisory board's Working Committee discussed the issue of bank rationalization, Albert Pietzsch, President of the Reich Economic Chamber and a member of the Deutsche Bank supervisory board since 1939, was invited to present the views of the party. The minutes record only 'a lively discussion'.[241] In April 1943, the Gau Economic Leader of Middle Silesia, Otto Fitzner, was added to the Deutsche Bank supervisory board.

Modifying the supervisory board alone would not be enough to forestall political pressure. Should the board of managing directors not also include a committed and active National Socialist, and not merely the ineffective and inoffensive Ritter von Halt?

The political balance of the board had already been disturbed in 1940 by the addition of an outsider to the bank (coming from the board of Rudolph Karstadt AG) who was a practising Catholic, Clemens Plassmann. Since there were already three Catholic members of the managing board, Abs, Rösler and Bechtolf (the latter, however, was a non-practising Catholic), critics in the party began to call the Deutsche Bank the 'Catholic bank'.[242] In May 1943, an additional party member besides Halt was taken on after the party started to attack the presence of two Catholics, Plassmann and Abs. The new man was Robert Frowein, head of the Frankfurt branch since 1938 and a member of the NSDAP since 1936.[243] But Frowein also remained in his Frankfurt position, and was rarely in Berlin, only moving there in February 1945.[244] He was hardly an effective National Socialist presence.

An initial suggestion that came from the party was that Landrat Börnicke, Director-General of the public sector Girozentrale Brandenburg and a militant party member, should be the new commanding figure in the Deutsche Bank. But this proposal for a more intimate involvement of the party in the affairs of the bank was vetoed by the Party Chancellery. Hitler and Bormann made it clear that they agreed with the general aim of a 'pushing back of bank influence', but for this reason they should not allow the party to take direct responsibility for running the nerve centres of finance capitalism. 'He [Hitler] believed that these plans [of the Deutsche Bank] could not be carried out, because there could not be any question of the party taking responsibility for banks.' The banks should certainly appoint and promote party comrades, but this should not be interpreted as the state supporting private capitalism. 'If the Deutsche Bank had itself suggested Herr Börnicke for the board of managing directors, there would on the other hand have been no objections.'[245]

Eventually, the Deutsche Bank chose as the party man on the board Professor Heinrich Hunke, the editor of the journal *Die nationalsozialistische Volkswirtschaft* (*The National Socialist Economy*), a civil servant (Ministerialdirektor) in the Propaganda Ministry of Joseph Goebbels, and in the late 1930s the most influential of National Socialist economic theorists. Hunke had been educated as a primary school teacher, and only later entered the university and eventually obtained a doctorate (Dr. rer. nat.) with a dissertation on 'The acoustic measurement of intensity'. He was in the odd position of only completing the university matriculation requirements in 1929, after finishing his doctorate. In 1935 he was awarded the title of honorary professor at the Berlin Technische Hochschule. From 1927 to 1933 he had worked in the Army Ministry. He had joined the NSDAP in 1928,[246] and in 1932 became a Reichstag deputy. In 1933 he became Vice-President of the Werberat der deutschen Wirtschaft (Advertising Council), an institution created in 1933 as part of the new autarkic stance and intended to use advertising in order to influence consumer behaviour. In 1934 he wrote an article advocating the nationalization of the great Berlin banks.[247] In the Propaganda Ministry after 1940 he was responsible for the Foreign Department, and propagated Funkian schemes for a new European economic order and economic community.[248]

The Deutsche Bank Working Committee, when discussing Hunke, explicitly considered the dangers of a political appointment, and the implications for the functioning of the board of managing directors: 'In particular, the board of managing directors has always maintained the principle of collegiality, which is the only system possible for a private bank, and in particular our bank, rather than the *Führerprinzip*.' Hunke had been informed about the duties and obligations of a spokesman ('Even the office of spokesman brings no privileges, but is only a matter of confidence, in order to make easier the process of forming an opinion on the board of managing directors, and representing it to the outside'); and he had declared himself 'in solidarity with the views of the board'.[249] The Deutsche Bank's press representative, Morgenstern, explained Hunke's move in private in the following way: Hunke had wanted to establish himself as a major figure in economic life by becoming President of the Gau Economic Chamber of Berlin, and the 'precondition for this was a corresponding position in the private economy'.[250]

What about the rest of the bank? Party membership figures have often been used by historians as measures of the extent of political commitment and the politicization of business. They may also be used to indicate the extent to which businesses were able to disengage from politics. For a bank such as the Deutsche Bank to have had no managing directors or leading managers who were members of the NSDAP would clearly have been impossible, as the debates about the appointments of von Halt and Hunke revealed. It is equally clear that most of the Bank's directors preferred to avoid direct political commitment.

Below the board level, among the leading managers the extent of party membership was much higher. A list prepared towards the end of the war gives details of 84 branch directors. Of these 44 were party members. None of them had joined before 1933. Most branches at this time had two directors, but there seems to have been no attempt to make a balance. In a few branches, such as Danzig (Gdansk), both were party members; in others, such as Kattowitz (Katowice), neither were.[251] This statistic seems not untypical of German business life in general. It certainly makes it clear that neither party membership nor non-party membership were prerequisites for a successful career in banking. Apart from the three party managing directors, von Halt, Frowein and Hunke, I have been unable to find a case of anyone promoted because of party membership who otherwise would not have been. Neither did party membership offer bankers any kind of protection from attacks by party militants. It is difficult to avoid the conclusion that those of the Deutsche Bank's managers who joined the party wanted to be members.

The party in fact was quite suspicious of business converts, and even of the new managing directors. The Reich Labour Trustee (*Reich Treuhänder der Arbeit*), whose approval was required for the contract, spent several months attempting, in the end unsuccessfully, to limit their income from supervisory board positions.[252]

Hunke's appointment established a link between business and the party's new economic organizations. Hunke had just set out his economic philosophy in an address to the Berlin Society of Friends of the German Academy (an institution, incidentally, created by von Stauss). It appeared at least to leave a limited role to private enterprise and to reject complete socialization: 'We support the principle of the politically directed economy ... A guided economy, however, is not a planned economy, steered in every detail according to a central will.' An international orientation was required, but this – for the foreseeable future –

meant state control: 'Even after the war, Germany will not buy on the principles of a liberal trading policy, but rather according to the demands of the European economic community.'[253]

Such discussions about the future and about the relationship of the German to the rest of the European economy were inevitable in a bank which wanted to think in long-term strategies. But they were deeply problematic, for the very obvious reason that by 1943 it looked unlikely that the world war would be won by National Socialist Germany. The extent of political criticism of banking, and the existence of a terror regime, made it almost impossible for the bank to function in the traditional way, as a network of economic intelligence.

3. Relationships with firms

Traditionally, bankers on the supervisory boards of companies had been called to play the role of a wise uncle, who might arbitrate internal disputes and bring a fresh and impartial eye to the personal divisions inevitably arising in business life. During the war, such an arbitrating role necessarily brought political ramifications and imbroglios.

Stauss had been a master of intrigues involving the party. In 1939, as deputy chairman of the supervisory board of the brewery of Schultheiss, he had to deal with the case of a 'workers' steward' who built up a patronage and bribery system within the firm and the German Labour Front. The management upheaval that followed resulted in the reappointment of Stauss to his old position from the Weimar Republic of supervisory board chairman.[254]

Other cases of companies in political difficulties rapidly involved not just one executive of the bank, but the whole board of managing directors. In 1942, the party and the Munitions Ministry attacked the director of a family managed firm with strong connections with the Deutsche Bank, the United West German Waggon Works (Vereinigte Westdeutsche Waggonfabriken AG Köln-Deutz, known simply as Westwaggon). Director Jackowski's failure to meet supply schedules was interpreted as sabotage. But it soon appeared that behind the accusations lurked an intrigue. The Gau Economic Adviser of Cologne, the politically active and energetically National Socialist banker Kurt von Schröder, accompanied the party's attack with a raid to purchase Westwaggon shares. The party began to say that it was the Deutsche Bank, and its Cologne manager Jean Baptist Rath (incidentally, a party member), who were responsible for the inadequacies of Westwaggon. Westwaggon had been highly indebted in the later 1920s, and its wartime failure to supply sufficient rolling stock was attributed to bank credit policies, since 'Westwaggon was very heavily influenced by banks'. Westwaggon required an active defence, and Abs, the managing director responsible for the Cologne area, circulated a note to the rest of the board asking for nominations for a new managing director.[255]

The most difficult case for the bank as a holder of the chairmanship of a supervisory board arose in the Bayerische Motoren Werke AG. It had been founded as the Rapp-Motorenwerke in 1913, and in the First World War developed rapidly, primarily as a manufacturer of aero-engines, a line of production to which it returned in the 1930s. Since 1917, the firm had been managed in high autocratic style by an Austrian engineer, Franz Josef Popp. It had been rescued in 1928 by a major cash infusion of the Deutsche Bank, and Stauss played a leading role in pushing it to closer co-operation with Daimler-Benz. In the depression, Popp had tried to keep BMW alive by moving to the production of cheaper automobiles.

After 1933, the firm had initially derived major gains from motorization as well as from the expansion of Lufthansa,[256] although Popp pointed out that the Entente countries had already moved far ahead technically in aero-engines. The problem from his viewpoint was that producing for the state meant accepting the imposition of external control. Already in January 1934 a State Commissar (Dr Höfeld) was appointed by the Reich Air Ministry to invigilate BMW, with the result that Popp was 'not especially happy about it'.[257] In 1936 a major expansion began, substantially financed by the Deutsche Bank, with a credit of 8 million RM and a purchase of 1 million RM shares.[258] But the major part of the expansion was paid for by the state: through the provision of Mefo-bills, and through participations of the Luftfahrtkontor in two new works. The Aero-Engine Factory (Flugmotorenbau GmbH) at Munich-Allach and the Aero-Engine Factory at Eisenach (Flugmotorenfabrik Eisenach GmbH) existed as non-public limited liability companies in order to disguise the extent of military production.[259] BMW's historical expertise had been in lighter air-cooled motors, which initially were regarded as less powerful and hence less important to Germany's air rearmament than water-cooled motors. Later, when combat height became a more important consideration in air war, air cooling suddenly became crucial as water-cooling systems were in danger of freezing at high altitudes. The intention of the Reich Air Ministry in 1936 was to rationalize production of types, 'so that BMW and Siemens will be the two factories in Germany for air-cooled motors, while Junkers and Daimler-Benz will continue to concentrate exclusively on water or liquid cooling systems'.[260]

The other air-cooled engine producer was another limited liability company, the Siemens-Apparate-und-Maschinen GmbH in Berlin-Spandau. As part of the reorganization of production in 1936, Siemens gave up control of this factory, because it required excessively high investments, and meant a 'technology that is foreign to our own real specialty in electro-technical matters'.[261] The works continued as the Brandenburgische Motorenwerk Gesellschaft mbH, and the Deutsche Bank worked intensively to secure its sale to BMW. The transaction was completed in 1939, again with a majority of the financing coming from public institutions (Luftfahrtkontor and the Bank for Industrial Bonds).

As a result BMW had three aero-engine works, in Spandau, Eisenach and Munich-Allach, and a German monopoly on air-cooled engines. Its performance became critical for the conduct of the German air war. The firm's turnover increased from 32.5 million RM in 1933 to 280.0 million RM in 1939 (of which 190.0 million RM came from aero-engines).[262] As in 1933, Popp viewed the dramatic expansion with some scepticism: he later noted that, although he had not wanted 'expansionary policy involving the purchase of other firms', 'we were more or less forced by purely external circumstances'.[263] At the time of the deal, Popp claimed that he had been pushed into the deal by his deputy Fritz Hille: 'For over 25 years, it has been his principle to keep BMW from expanding. It was really a great strain to have one development plant in Munich and another in Spandau.'[264]

Such a dogmatic statement about the limitation of the size of an ideal business already appeared dated to BMW's supervisory board, and to the two Deutsche Bank members, Stauss and Hans Rummel, the deputy chairman of the supervisory board. It was even more hopelessly antiquated in the circumstances of the world war, during which the demand for state control, intervention and large-scale enterprise appeared as an overriding military necessity. During the war, BMW expanded its production to plants in Alsace, in occupied France, in Denmark and in the Generalgouvernement. At the same time, output in the German works was increased through 'systematic personnel planning ... in particular the quick supplementation of the Allach workforce with foreign workers', as well as the use of concentration camp labour in Allach and Eisenach.[265]

Co-ordination of the activities of the three German motor plants never worked well. The Munich research and development plant worked painfully slowly, and did not have sufficient resources for the star-piston motor project on which now depended Germany's fortunes in the air. The fundamental technical problem was that funds were divided between two projects, the 800 motor in Spandau (a one-star piston arrangement) and the 801 double-star arrangement in Munich. The 800 was initially stopped, and then – at a time of desperate shortage of motors – made out of 801 parts. By the middle of 1940, the output of motors had become the major constraint on aircraft production, and on the fighting of the air war.[266]

Göring personally insisted on the stepping-up of output, addressing a fierce personal letter to Popp: 'Once again I wish to entreat you how urgently necessary the new two-star motor is for us, and how no hour must be lost in bringing this motor into action on the front.'[267] BMW predictably blamed shortages of labour and machine tools, but also the procurement policies of the Reich Air Ministry: 'The 800 was down-graded in urgency at the beginning of the war, because this motor was not intended for use in [what was planned to be a short] war. This motor was to be used after the war as a basis for developing the 132 Model.'[268] But then the Reich Air Ministry demanded production of the 800 at the rate of 200 a month in Eisenach and 170 in the French factories. Popp continued to complain: 'We had the bad luck that, because of the war situation, our motor suddenly appears as the most urgent priority, although only half a year ago the

Air Ministry spoke in very different tones.'[269] The ministry replied by attacking Popp's record ('a disturbing lack of knowledge of the real technical conditions and an irresponsible carelessness');[270] and eventually, at the beginning of 1942, by replacing Popp by his deputy Hille.

The removal of Popp, who had long exercised a kind of personal dictatorship over the firm, did not help either BMW or the *Luftwaffe*. Instead increasingly politicized conflicts within the senior management multiplied. Then Stauss died, the man who always ensured that the firm greased the right party wheels,[271] and who might have been able to deal with the politics of wartime Germany. His successor as chairman of the BMW supervisory board, Hans Rummel, a far less political figure, was completely out of his depth in the politically charged struggles over engine output.

In order to recapitalize the firm without incurring a total dependence on the state, in May 1942 United Steel Works (Vereinigte Stahlwerke, generally known as Stahlverein) was invited to take a substantial minority stake in BMW. The Stahlverein tried to pay off the government credits and to provide long-term credit of 50–70 million RM in the hope of building a basis for automobile and tractor production in the post-war period.[272]

Hille felt that his position might become vulnerable, and demanded a firm five-year contract as managing director; when Stauss refused, Hille unsuccessfully encouraged the Stahlverein to take a majority of BMW and exclude the Deutsche Bank from intervening in its management.

By the end of 1943, BMW's failure to supply the agreed quantity of aero-engines to the *Luftwaffe* again became critical. Eventually, at the end of May 1944, Field Marshal Erhard Milch demanded the restructuring of BMW's management within 48 hours, and the removal of Hille from any technical responsibility within BMW. The new direction of the firm was entrusted by Milch to the technical manager of the Eisenach works, Schaaf, a man who had originally been appointed at the suggestion of Albert Speer's Munitions Ministry. But the problems of the firm in maintaining production levels remained acute, and by November 1944 Hille was predicting a further shortfall of 1,500–1,800 motors for the period October–December.[273] Not content with pessimistic forecasts, Hille turned to the Berlin Party Chancellery to denounce Schaaf for sabotage and high treason. Faced with a crisis, Rummel on 11 December raced to Munich despite the physical difficulties of travelling at this stage in the war; he found a letter dated 9 December from Hille to Schaaf, which denied Schaaf's authority and attempted to reassert control over the firm's management. Hille said that he would carry out 'all measures ... necessary in order to deal with the unrest, disorder and redundant organization arising out of your behaviour and from the failure of the supervisory board chairman, as well as with the direct and indirect rumours which undermine the exercise of any authority'.[274]

Rummel placed Hille on immediate leave. Hille replied that the government had placed a wartime ban on taking holidays. Rummel then dismissed him. Hille tore up the letter, and accused Rummel and the Deutsche Bank of high treason.

In dealing with BMW's management, Rummel initially thought he could look for allies in the Munich party leadership. It was an unsuccessful manoeuvre. Gauleiter Paul Giesler refused to receive Rummel, and Hille shouted, 'Only my Gauleiter can give me directions. Please take note, Herr Rummel, that I am a National Socialist.' Giesler saw an opportunity, less to support Hille (whose claim that Giesler was his 'Paladin' embarrassed him), than to turn BMW back into being a Bavarian firm and thus part of his political fiefdom. Giesler suggested that either the Bavarian State Bank (Bayerische Staatsbank) or the Flick concern should finance the 'Bavarianization' and reorganization of BMW.

Rummel's seriously threatened situation was rescued in Berlin by the intervention of the Deutsche Bank's political contact man.[275] Heinrich Hunke worked at the highest level, with the party official Reich Leader Philipp Bouhler, and urged Rummel to prepare a memorandum in self-defence: 'In our opinion you should begin as soon as possible to draw up a comprehensive memorandum, which will also be useful for your verbal presentation. On the other hand, we do not believe that, as the situation lies, the composition of the supervisory board and in particular your own position as chairman will be exempt from discussion.'[276] But despite this pessimistic and stern warning, Rummel and the Deutsche Bank seem to have won at least a technical victory: on 2 February 1945 the supervisory board of BMW appointed Schaaf as chairman of the managing board.[277]

The episode showed how inexorably tangled industrial politics had become as a result of National Socialist ideology and the waging of total war. It is also quite typical of the bank's conception of how it should respond to the challenges of the political situation and the offensive of a new and radical vision of state-run capitalism. In the light of the virulence of the attack, and the fanaticism of its perpetrators, it is perhaps regrettable but by no means surprising that the bank's major policy-makers thought only of defensive, damage-limiting responses.

4. Political dangers

The operation of the advisory councils (Beiräte), in the past a key part of economic intelligence gathering and distribution, became practically impossible. Many economic subjects – including notably the prospects for the post-war order – became taboo. When, for instance, Hermann J. Abs presented the bank's view to the Rhineland–Westphalian advisory council in Cologne, he avoided the kind of criticism of state actions that had been characteristic of Kimmich's addresses. Instead he confined himself to the details of the driest, most unrevealing and most technical sides of the bank's activities.

In the course of 1943 the political dangers associated with banking became frighteningly clear. In November 1943, the Working Committee heard without comment a report by Ritter von Halt, still responsible for the bank's personnel, that the directors of the Deutsche Bank's branches in Hindenburg (Zabrze, Upper Silesia) and Stuttgart had been sentenced to death for 'defeatist remarks'.[278]

The Stuttgart manager, Hermann Köhler, then aged 67, had been the Deutsche Bank's most senior branch director. On a rail journey from Munich to Stuttgart after a business meeting, shortly after the collapse of Mussolini's regime, he had told some of his colleagues travelling with him that 'Fascism had disappeared without a murmur; the same would happen with us; National Socialism was in any case nothing more than a fart.' These remarks were reported by a passenger in the same compartment; Köhler was arrested and tried in Berlin before the People's Court (Volksgerichtshof). His defence that he had drunk too much beer because of the hot weather and that he could not remember the words he had used in the train was rejected; and on 8 October the court pronounced the death sentence (as well as a 100,000 RM fine). Relatives of Köhler later reported that von Halt had made considerable efforts to save him, but he was not successful. One month after the verdict, on 8 November 1943, Köhler was executed in Brandenburg prison.

Only three weeks before Köhler's conviction, Georg Miethe from Hindenburg had similarly been condemned, as a result of an accusation brought by employees of his own bank branch. Two bank clerks had complained about Miethe's 'whining': he had allegedly called Goebbels an 'ape' and a 'shit', Göring a 'stuffed belly' and Hitler a 'swindler'. In the Volksgerichtshof's judgment these reported remarks are followed by the comment, in the authentically demagogic and chilling language of the court's President Roland Freisler, 'This was said by a man in a high position of authority, by an educated man.' Miethe's social position clearly played a part in the court's sentence. But the court also heard about Miethe's views on the progress of the war in Russia, and of the air war, and that he had asked the question: 'Well, and when will the end come with us?'[279]

There can be no doubt that the senior managers of the bank knew about their environment, about the course and conduct of the war, and also about some of the criminal aspects of the regime. They were aware of the network of concentration camps across Germany: this was no secret. On the other hand, the regime kept a veil of mystery and euphemism around its genocide directed against racially defined minorities: Jews, Slavs, gypsies. At least one of the purposes of this semi-secrecy was to bind the perpetrators of crimes, and those who acquiesced in them, more closely to the regime. Documents that survive from this period as a result often give the historian little direct evidence about the extent of knowledge about the holocaust. In the case of the Deutsche Bank, for instance, there are numerous files relating to the accounts and property of ethnic Germans (*Volksdeutsche*) resettled in Lodz (known as Litzmanstadt under the Germans), but no written indications whatsoever about the fate of the previous owners of the property transferred, or of the fate of the inhabitants of the Lodz ghetto. Did no one at the time give any thought to this? We also know that Hermann J.

Abs sat on the supervisory board of I.G. Farben, but we do not know whether this body discussed the establishment of a plant in Birkenau, using labour from the concentration and annihilation camp at Auschwitz. Might he not have wondered about what was going on? The public culture of Germany under the dictatorship required an avoidance of discussion, and as a result partial acquiescence and complicity.

Undoubtedly many by 1942 were profoundly disenchanted with the regime. Some of the Deutsche Bank's directors, such as Abs and Clemens Plassmann, possessed as a result of their Catholicism a world-view fundamentally at variance with that of National Socialism, and in the course of the discussions on bank reform of 1943 the party unsuccessfully demanded their removal. Abs had some contacts with the resistance, and there are reports that he was asked by Adam von Trott zu Solz to join the conspiracy but refused, because, as he later said, of his commitment to the bank and to his family. He also once attended a meeting of the Goerdeler circle, but saw Goerdeler taking notes and resolved never to court danger in this way. Leaving a paper trail of conspiracy seemed a sure path to the cells of the Gestapo. In fact the paper trail did reach wartime Washington, though not apparently the Gestapo centre in the Prinz-Albrecht-Strasse of Berlin. The US Treasury Foreign Funds Control noted in its reports on banks in occupied Europe that Abs was 'one of the most prominent lay Catholic leaders in Germany and rumors persist that he is a potential leader of the Catholic opposition in the country. However, no reference to his political activities is available and it may be concluded that his preoccupation arising from affiliation with forty banks and commercial enterprises had prevented any appreciable contribution to the work of the opposition.'[280] This seems a not inappropriate verdict on Abs.

There are, perhaps surprisingly, buried in the Deutsche Bank's archives, some records of Abs's contacts with the German resistance. In June 1940, Abs's secretary noted that Trott had called ('on the basis of your arrangement with him') and 'regretted very much that you were so pressed for time, and hoped that you might have a quarter of an hour for him'.[281] Trott, a member of the German Foreign Office, had recently returned from a trip to the USA, where he had visited prominent German émigrés and also tried to persuade the US administration that a substantial anti-Nazi opposition existed within Germany which might be encouraged by a conciliatory foreign policy. Once back in Germany, he tried to find men of reputation whom he could present to American and British contacts as representatives of an anti-Hitler opposition. He contacted Hjalmar Schacht and Hans von Dohnanyi as well as Abs.[282] From 1940, Abs repeatedly met the lawyer Helmuth James von Moltke in Berlin, almost always in the company of Peter Count Yorck von Wartenburg. Moltke liked Abs, and wanted to draw him closer to the conspiracy, inviting him to meetings in Kreisau. He wrote to his wife: 'Abs has improved. He has arrived to such an extent that he no longer needs to be vain and ambitious. He is simply now the *primus inter pares* of German bankers.' The meetings became much more frequent after June

1941, when Moltke was quick to recognize the difficulty of defeating the USSR. In May 1943, Abs was invited to visit Kreisau, but for one reason or another could not go.[283]

In October 1943, the Deutsche Bank was providing funds for the support of Frau von Moltke (Davida née Yorck, the widow of Ambassador Hans Adolf von Moltke, Helmuth James's uncle); and Yorck von Wartenburg was the intermediary in making the financial arrangement.[284] But there are no records of any closer contacts in 1944, and the July bomb plot did not involve any directors or employees of the Deutsche Bank. In the proposed government under the Chancellorship of Carl Goerdeler, the German opposition in 1944 envisaged as Economics Minister and Reichsbank President not Abs but Karl Blessing of Kontinentale Öl (another friend of Peter Yorck's).[285] One managing director of the Deutsche Bank, Oswald Rösler, was tried before the Volksgerichtshof because one of Goerdeler's acquaintances claimed he had told him about the plot, but there was no clear evidence of any involvement of Rösler, and he was acquitted.[286] The case made it clear that bankers' contacts, of which there were bound to be many, could lead to the suspicion of the security authorities.

The fundamental dilemma of the bank under the National Socialist dictatorship had involved the extent to which it should fit in with and adapt to the new spirit of the times. To a considerable extent the bank was driven by forces it could not control. Bankers did not after all – despite the fantasies held by conspiracy theorists of the National Socialist Party regarding the power of finance capitalism – make German politics. In some cases, however, some individual bankers made the consequences and repercussions of German political decisions more damaging and pernicious for the victims than they would otherwise have been: this was especially true when relatively junior bank officials operated in occupied Europe, seizing goods and assets whose loss made their legitimate possessors even more vulnerable. The bank, especially after September 1938, became part of the machine of German imperialism, and its employees the agents of a brutal political process. In other cases, particularly within the territory of pre-1937 Germany, the actions of the Deutsche Bank may have assisted some of the victims of the regime. In particular, in helping to carry out the official policy target of 'Aryanization', there are cases both of the bank taking the initiative (especially on the local level), and also of the bank and its officials quite actively and positively assisting old business partners.

In conscious or unconscious calculations of how its adaptation to the New Germany would affect the financial and social standing of bankers, most financiers could only come to the conclusion that, whatever happened, they were bound to lose as representatives of a world and a style of business that the new regime had declared to be obsolete and discredited. German banking had traditionally depended on large networks of contacts, both formal and informal, both national and international, in which commitments were made on the basis of trust and honour. This social and cosmopolitan environment corresponded to one of the primary economic functions of banks, as collectors and transmitters of large quantities of information. To the National Socialists this appeared simply as a discredited old-boy network; but this new ideology (which had a substantially egalitarian dimension) was not just something that came from the outside, from the state or the party organization. The new doctrine convinced many of the bank's employees, and at least a substantial part of the National Socialist revolution in this financial corporation was driven by a dynamic internal to the bank as a bureaucratic structure.

Faced by this change of intellectual climate, bankers became more and more passive. The bank's leading figures did not participate in the resistance or in plots against Hitler. It is interesting that, of Germany's old élites, soldiers, diplomats and civil servants, and to some extent churchmen, were involved in the resistance; but there were almost no businessmen and no bankers. It seems to me too easy to say that this was because bankers simply kept their heads down and wanted to make money. Unlike generals and diplomats, who still felt valued and important under the dictatorship, bankers were fundamentally regarded as parasitical. To the extent to which they internalized this criticism, it constituted a brake on effective political action.

Soldiers and generals occupied a more prominent position. Correspondingly, many committed greater crimes than any banker sitting at a desk, dealing with the balance of debit and credit, could possibly undertake; but their moral possibilities and choices were greater too. They were more likely than bankers to be villains, but more likely also to have the historic chance of being heroes. Their moral spectrum was longer: it encompassed the ruthless brutality and the atrocities of the Eastern Front, but also the heroism of 20 July 1944. The two Deutsche Bank managers who were condemned by the People's Court, on the other hand, were not heroes: they were simply very unlucky. Hermann J. Abs, without doubt the most dynamic and imaginative of the Deutsche Bank's managing directors during the war was happy to attack, in only a slightly veiled form, the entire trading policy of National Socialist Germany. But when he had contacts with the men of the resistance, he self-consciously decided not to be a hero. Should it be the historian's role to condemn him for this?

In the course of their progressive marginalization, many bankers retreated into that world with which they were most familiar: the comfortable certainties of a rational economic world. They went on behaving in a traditional way in a world that had become strange and irrational. It may seem to many subsequent observers extraordinary that what bankers, businessmen and civil servants criticized most vehemently about the regime in the 1930s were relatively mundane characteristics – such as its tendency to run large budget deficits – and not its spectacular inhumanity. There can be no doubt that this vision was the product of an extreme moral shortsightedness. The banking world was in this trapped by the regime, and by the way it presented itself to Germans. National Socialism claimed insistently and militantly that it was the embodiment of the common good, and that others represented merely narrow self-interest. Told repeatedly that they had nothing to say about the social and political ordering of society, that the social vision of the business community was nothing more than rampant egoism, bankers tried ever harder not to look beyond the ends of their own noses. The result was that bankers too played their part in Germany's moral catastrophe.

VI. The End of Dictatorship

The course of the war profoundly affected the bank's day-to-day operations. In 1939 there had been 17,805 employees. At the beginning of 1941, 5,900 had been called up for military service; by February 1942, 7,300; and by October 1944, 9,705 (out of a total of 19,343 regular personnel and 1,400 auxiliaries).[287] The proportion of women in the workforce rose to 27.6 per cent in 1941 and 33 per cent in 1943. At the same time, the opening of large numbers of new accounts increased the strain on the functioning of the bank.[288]

By 1943 the physical environment had deteriorated. Air raids damaged and destroyed records and buildings, and killed employees. By the summer of 1943, the bank's branch offices in Lübeck, Mainz, Barmen and Cologne had been completely destroyed, as well as eight *Stadtdepositenkassen* (subsidiary offices).[289] On 22 and 23 November 1943, the central Berlin office was almost completely destroyed, and 3,000 employees had to be moved to alternative quarters. The simple maintenance of normal business began to require an extensive decentralization. Already in late 1942, the Deutsche Bank's Cologne director, Jean Baptist Rath, suggested, partly in response to party criticism, that the bank's regions should be run independently as separate regional banks.[290] In September 1943, as part of the push to increased regionalization, ten major branch managers were appointed as 'Directors of the Bank with Power of Attorney for All Branches'.[291]

In the first ten months of 1944 another 26 branches were completely destroyed by bombing, and 19 more were seriously damaged. In Berlin, in spring 1944, the bank's emergency quarters (*Ausweichstelle*) on the Hausvogteiplatz were also destroyed. Nevertheless by July, the bank's operations were shown off to the Berlin press as an example of how reconstruction after severe bombing damage was possible.[292] Only in the last days of the war did discipline break down and was large-scale bomb damage, as in the extensive raid on Würzburg in March 1945, followed by looting.

In 1943, three-fifths of the staff were simply engaged in 'maintaining payments'.[293] As the bank's centre disintegrated, the leeway possessed by branches in making new credits also fell, and investment credits were restricted by policy to the construction of new raw materials industries (especially cellulose and hydrogenation) and to the financing of inventories. The drop in credit business already evident in the 1930s continued at a more rapid rate during the war. By 1942, credits and advances on goods represented only 18.7 per cent of the balance sheet; by the end of 1944, this ratio had fallen to 13.4 per cent.

Even ordinary business began to collapse. Eventually in the summer of 1944 the physical movement of money became difficult as petrol allowances were cut.[294] Then came the invasion of Germany, and the evacuation of branches.[295] In areas close to the fighting, there were runs on the banks as customers tried to close their accounts before being evacuated.[296] Three regional evacuation centres (*Verbindungsstellen*) were established in Hamburg, Wiesbaden and Erfurt, which continued to operate after the military defeat.

In October 1944 the bank modified its operating rules to allow 1,000 RM to be paid out to the private customers of 'the cut-off branches'; in February 1945 further payments were authorized. But the regulations for dealing with the occupation of parts of Germany and the breakdown of communication brought tensions with industrial customers. Wilhelm Zangen of Mannesmann, the leader of the Reich Group Industry, demanded that the bank in Berlin should pay out Mannesmann's Kattowitz account. Rösler refused completely: he noted angrily that 'The gentlemen are in short demanding that all the accounts that they have with the Deutsche Bank should, for instance, be paid out in Miesbach [in Bavaria] if industry thinks fit in current circumstances to evacuate to there.'[297]

On 16 March 1945 Reich Economics Minister Funk presided over a meeting to discuss the evacuation of banks and their managing boards from Berlin in the 'Ivan case' – if the Soviet army rather than the Western Allies took Berlin. The suggestion was that the bank's main office with six or seven managing directors and about 25–30 others should be moved to Hamburg.[298]

On 9 April 1945 the bank celebrated its seventy-fifth anniversary. The board sent a congratulatory circular to those branches still in contact with Berlin: 'Events do not permit us to look back on this important anniversary with a quiet feeling of pride in our successes and a secure possession of that for which we and our predecessors have worked.' Employees received a bonus of a half month's pay, although the result made little difference because of gathering inflation.[299]

One week later, on 16 April, the battle for Berlin began. The last wartime meeting of the board of managing directors took place on 18 April 1945, with four directors present and von Halt excused to command the reserve militia (*Volkssturm*) in its defence of Berlin. By the 21st, Soviet troops were fighting in the streets of the German capital. But bank business went on with a quite astonishing attempt to make believe that circumstances were normal. Customers were still trying to withdraw deposits, but the chaos and dislocation, and the impossibility of travelling in the city, meant that many of the safe keys were missing. Rösler managed to obtain 500,000 RM from the Reichsbank. When, on 2 May, Russian troops occupied the bank's buildings in the Mauerstrasse, they confiscated the 498,130 RM still in the emergency cash reserve (*Notkasse*).

The bank's Berlin activities only stopped on 11 May when Soviet soldiers temporarily arrested Rösler and other leading employees for questioning, and used explosives to open the bank's vaults.[300]

A day before the final Soviet attack on Berlin began, Hermann J. Abs left for Hamburg at the request of the rest of the Berlin board;[301] and from Hamburg a directing office composed of Abs and Bechtolf, and Plassmann (for the time being in Erfurt) attempted to continue the activities of the Deutsche Bank in the circumstances of a military defeat they had long foreseen but had not dared publicly to contemplate. Stauss and Hunke may have believed in the triumphs of National Socialism; but by 1945 Stauss was dead and Hunke was cold-shouldered by the senior managers of the Deutsche Bank. Bankers, it has already been pointed out, adjust to realities – that is their mission. The reality of 1945 was that National Socialism, and National Socialist economics, was militarily as well as morally bankrupt.

The Deutsche Bank 1945–1957:
War, Military Rule and Reconstruction

by Carl-Ludwig Holtfrerich

Considering the complexity of the post-war history of the Deutsche Bank, it is necessary to concentrate on those topics that clearly characterize the role of the bank within the political and economic framework of this period. Consequently, I have selected four broad topics. The first section focuses on the issue of continuity and discontinuity during the transition from the war to the post-war period, with regard to bank personnel as well as to economic policy and business practices. In the second section, the big banks are examined as *objects* of occupation policy of the Western Allies from 1945 to 1948. The third section looks at the continually growing influence of the Deutsche Bank on the political decision-making process in the Federal Republic, as far as banking policy was concerned. This influence culminated in the period between the 1952 legislation on big banks and the preparation for the legislation of 24 December 1956, which not only enabled the reunification of the big banks in 1957, but also provided for a tax exemption decree. And finally, the fourth section addresses the rebuilding of business and the actions taken by the bank in view of the economic and social problems and challenges between 1945 and 1957.

I. The Transition from the End of the War to Occupation Rule

1. Continuity and discontinuity in the membership of the board of managing directors and the supervisory board, and in the conduct of business

In April 1945, the members of the board of managing directors of the Deutsche Bank were Hermann J. Abs, Erich Bechtolf, Robert Frowein, Karl Ritter von Halt, Heinrich Hunke, Clemens Plassmann, Oswald Rösler, Hans Rummel, Karl Ernst Sippell and Fritz Wintermantel. Of these ten men, only one did not survive the war. Dr Karl Ernst Sippell (b. 4 February 1889) had been left physically unscathed during his active military service. When he left the military with the rank of major in the autumn of 1944, he became head of the bank's legal department. He was not in the habit of attending board meetings and appears to have been a gentleman in the traditional sense.[1] In the last week of April, from 23–28 April 1945, Sippell found himself barricaded in his home in Grunewald, a district of Berlin still being defended by German troops, although it was surrounded by Russian tanks. On 28 April, the German troops retreated in the direction of Kurfürstendamm through a break in the Russian lines, followed by Sippell, members of his household, his house guest – namely, his secretary Miss Liermann – and other civilians from the district. Sippell wanted to seize the apparent opportunity to escape to the head office of the Deutsche Bank in the centre of Berlin. Although many German troops and civilians lost their lives to Russian tank fire during this retreat, both Sippell and Liermann managed to reach the subway station at Kurfürstendamm. There Sippell learned that access to the city centre was once again blocked. He and his secretary found refuge in a basement shelter at Schiller Strasse 10a in Charlottenburg from 28 April to 2 May. During these five days, this section of the city was under heavy fire day and night as the fighting grew closer. Finally the German troops retreated and the Russian troops occupied the district. Following a check of their identification papers, Sippell and another man were arrested on the morning of 2 May and temporarily placed under guard in the same basement shelter. Both men were shot that same day as they attempted to escape. Miss Liermann was more fortunate. She used another avenue of escape and subsequently reported the events leading to Sippell's death.[2]

In general, professional qualifications played a greater role than did political considerations in appointing members to the board of managing directors, the exceptions to this being the appointments of von Halt (1938) and especially that of Hunke (1943–44). However, in both cases, the Deutsche Bank was obviously attempting to ward off more extensive political intervention by the Nazi regime. These small concessions made it possible to get through appointments of highly qualified but politically insignificant men, such as Hermann J. Abs (1938), Johannes Kiehl (1938, d. 1944), Clemens Plassmann (1940), Erich Bechtolf (1942) and Robert Frowein (1943).

Dr Karl Ritter von Halt (b. 2 June 1891), son of the Munich master mechanic Karl Halt, volunteered for service during the First World War and ended his career as a lieutenant in the reserves and head of the Third Company of the Bavarian Infantry Life Guard Regiment. On 24 February 1921, he was dubbed a knight of the Bavarian Military Max-Joseph Order retroactively to 27 October 1917, 'because he captured the Monte Madlessena on his own courageous initiative during the Italian campaign on 27 October 1917, thereby freeing the Natisone pass and enabling an early and strategically crucial descent of the Alpine Corps into the plains of Cividale'.[3] The certificate was signed by Count Bothmer, the deputy Grand Master of the Order. During this military operation, Count Bothmer had been the major under whom Lieutenant von Halt had served.[4]

Von Halt began his banking career as an apprentice at the Deutsche Bank in

Munich. Following the First World War, he entered the banking establishment H. Aufhäuser in Munich, where he advanced to the position of executive manager. In other words, he learned the banking business from the bottom up. However, it appears that, in 1935, the bank offered von Halt the position of director of personnel at the head office of the bank in Berlin, primarily because he obviously enjoyed the favour of the Hitler regime. Not only had this former German decathlon champion become 'Leader of German Track-and-Field Athletics' in 1933, but von Halt had also become president of the organizing committee of the 1936 Olympic Winter Games in Garmisch-Partenkirchen. Due to his involvement in the sports world and his international connections as a member of the International Olympic Committee since 1929, he was considered a valuable asset to the bank. Ideologically he was regarded as relatively harmless. Upon his appointment to the board of managing directors in 1938, he was also given the semi-political office of the 'enterprise leader' (Betriebsführer). Von Halt had been a member of the NSDAP since 1933, and was a member of the SA (with the rank of Oberführer, the rough equivalent of a colonel, since 1942), and of the Freundeskreis der Wirtschaft beim Reichsführer der SS Himmler (Business Friends of SS Reich Leader Himmler).[5] In a post-war evaluation by the bank for the Allies, which is still on record in the personnel files of the Deutsche Bank, he was defended as follows: 'As a respected party member, Ritter von Halt was also in a position to stand up to ambitious and fanatic employees and party sympathizers. In this capacity he was very valuable for the Deutsche Bank, particularly since he could also shield the board ... from the party ... It was chiefly to the credit of von Halt that the attacks carried out by the NSDAP against the Deutsche Bank were not more severe and thorough.' Within the bank itself, von Halt's influence remained restricted to his department from the very start, making him more limited in power than any of the other board members, as is evident in the fact that originally he was not given any supervisory board positions.[6]

Although he had been apparently conscripted into the *Volkssturm*, the home defence guard, on 13 April 1945,[7] this is not how he came to be imprisoned at the end of the war. During the chaos of the battle for Berlin, he had been in search of his wife Grete, who spent days in other people's basements until he found her in their shared second home in the bombed out 'House of the Reich Sport Leader', or more specifically in the bunker of the embattled Reich Athletic Field. They moved in with acquaintances in Charlottenburg who lived at Bayernallee 47. On 7 May 1945, Ritter von Halt left this residence to register, as the Soviet military authorities in Berlin had ordered leading figures in business to do. He never returned, reported his wife. After having been taken under guard once to the head office of the bank, he was held prisoner by the Soviets for nearly five years in Buchenwald. He was not to return home to his wife and son in Munich until early in 1950. That same summer he was classified as Category V (exonerated) by the Munich denazification court.[8] Because he had done more to protect the Deutsche Bank from National Socialist intervention than to subject it to political party interference, he was once again entrusted with a prominent position in one of the successor banks: namely, as a member of the supervisory board of the Süddeutsche Bank in Munich from 1952 to 1957.

Prof. Heinrich Hunke (b. 8 December 1902) was a far graver concession to the political rulers. His appointment to the board of managing directors was made by the supervisory board on 16 September 1943, and became effective on 1 February 1944: that is, at a time when German defeat was foreseeable. Hunke possessed no experience in the banking business.[9] In 1933 he became vice-president of the Werberat der deutschen Wirtschaft (Advertising Council of German Business) and in 1938 its president. This was a supervisory office for business advertising, established by law in 1933, which also organized its own advertising campaigns designed to steer consumer demand and encourage the frugal use of scarce resources.[10] In December 1940, he was given the position of Ministerialdirektor, the equivalent to deputy under-secretary, in the Reich Ministry of People's Education and Propaganda by Goebbels, in whose diaries he is often mentioned then and in the years preceding this appointment. Hunke headed the foreign department there and was chiefly responsible for the 1943 intensification of propaganda abroad. The propaganda campaign was specifically aimed at making the economic and political successes of National Socialist Germany and its economic concepts for the post-war period palatable to the occupied European countries as an alternative to the liberal post-war proposals of the Anglo-American powers. He propagandized the concept of a 'European economic community' both on his own and through the Advertising Council.

Not only did the size of the population and the economic strength of Germany legitimize the country's claims to leadership in such a community, argued Hunke, so did its aim 'to eliminate all powers alien to the region' from European politics. This German equivalent to the Monroe Doctrine was also used as a justification for the entire war. Thus in a positive sense, Hunke differed from those National Socialists who used racist justifications to rationalize the German claim to power.[11] In addition, he was the chief lector of the Parteiamtliche Prüfungskommission zum Schutze des NS-Schrifttums (Official Party Examining Board for the Protection of National Socialist Writings) and a member of the joint executive board (Gesamtvorstand) of the German Chambers of Commerce abroad.[12] He had joined the National Socialist movement as early as 1923, but did not become a party member until June 1928. Later that same year he became the economic adviser for the NSDAP *Gau* (district) of Berlin, and in 1936 president of the Union of Berlin Merchants and Industrialists after the *Gleichschaltung* (forcing into line) of this organization and in 1944 of the economic chamber of the *Gau* (*Gauwirtschaftskammer*, as the chambers of industry and commerce were called during the Nazi period). Due to the intercession of Goebbels, Hunke became a member of the Reichstag for the NSDAP in 1932.

In 1935, he was awarded an honorary professorship at the Technical University of Berlin.[13]

Martin Bormann, head of the party headquarters, had been intensively campaigning since 1941 for increased Nazification of German business. In October and November 1942, the economic advisers from the 13 most important NSDAP *Gaue* (districts) formed a committee on banking with the aim of helping place Nazi cadre in leading management positions. Bormann assumed the auspices of this banking committee, of which Hunke was a member.[14] As the economic adviser for the *Gau* of Berlin, Hunke immediately took the initiative to change the make-up of the board of managing directors at the Deutsche Bank in accordance with the wishes of the party.

On Hunke's instructions, his acting deputy, Dr Karl Heinrich Heuser, held a two-hour meeting on 17 November 1942, at the Hotel Fürstenhof on Potsdamer Platz in Berlin, 'among party comrades in order to discuss the personnel make-up of the board of managing directors of the Deutsche Bank'. Attending this meeting were the Vice-President of the Reichsbank, Kurt Lange, the head of the special office on banks and insurances at the German Labour Front, Rudolf Lencer, a representative from the Advertising Council of German Business (who only stayed for the first quarter of an hour), and Ritter von Halt as the representative of the Deutsche Bank.

During this meeting, the question was raised whether all of the board members who held key positions would be suited for an economy organized strictly along National Socialist lines, the type of economy which both the party and the Reich Economic Minister wanted the soldiers to find upon their return to civilian life following a victorious war. Von Halt was the only one to answer 'yes'. After he was told that he was laying his reputation and his credibility as a party comrade on the line, he then remarked 'that the board of managing directors of the Deutsche Bank shared a comradeship that could not be destroyed by any sort of external influence'. It was pointed out to him 'that the Deutsche Bank is known throughout Germany as the Catholic bank'. Besides Rösler and Abs, Plassmann and Bechtolf were also Catholic, and they were 'brought in as board members from outside the bank, although there was no cause'. Such criticism may well have evolved from the discontent growing among party comrades working at the bank, who at the time made up 46 per cent of the managerial employees in positions ranging from Oberbeamter, as high-ranking bank employees were then called, to senior vice-president.[15]

Von Halt even had to answer the contention that his appointment to the board had been an effort by the bank to provide itself with a 'National Socialist cloak'. He protested against being labelled a 'token appointment' and pointed out that the bank was fulfilling the wish of the party by entrusting him with 'the leadership of the personnel and thereby with full responsibility for National Socialist education for the entire organization'. He would consider it a gesture of mistrust in him to expand the board with other party members.

Hunke's deputy, Dr Heuser, countered that the intent was not to increase the number of board members, but to remove those who 'had to be deemed unacceptable for the National Socialist cause', meaning 'Abs and Plassmann, who could never become National Socialists due to their deep Catholic convictions'. Not a single board member (excluding von Halt) had joined the party, he continued. The party would not chase after anyone for membership; it was above having actively to seek party members. 'Whoever wishes to become a party comrade must come to us. Whoever does not express this wish will be suspected of harbouring anti-party sentiments', threatened Hunke's assistant in a nearly perfect illustration of political logic in a totalitarian system. At the end of the two hours, the meeting was classified as secret: 'Whoever talks about it will be thrown out of the party.'[16]

Dr Hellmut Börnicke, the chairman of the banking committee, economic adviser for the *Gau* of Brandenburg, and also President of the Provinzialbank und Girozentrale there, initially proposed himself for a place on the board, in fact even for the position of chairman. Following a 'tough struggle', von Halt and his colleagues on the board succeeded in preventing this.[17] In the course of these events, Abs and Rösler asked Hunke during an overnight train ride to Vienna shortly before Christmas 1942, if he would be interested in being appointed to the board. In 1934, Hunke had argued in several published articles for the nationalization of major banks and insurance companies and had thus aroused protest within the party. But such views were merely youthful folly, for immediately after the war he described his economic–political premise as follows: Instead of a capitalist market economy, he favoured a planned economy under the direction of the state, featuring a control apparatus that would, however, permit leeway for individual initiative. The state needed to be creative, not didactic in its approach.

At first, Hunke declined the offer to join the board, claiming that his political offices placed him under enough strain.[18] Besides him, the bank directors favoured only one other candidate: Gustav Schlotterer, Ministerialdirigent in the Economics Ministry. But he also turned them down when they approached him.

By January 1943, things had reached the point between the bank and the banking committee where it was clear that the bank would have to co-opt someone in any case. The chairman of the supervisory board, Karl Kimmich, interpreted this to mean that at least one appointment to the board of managing directors could be made from within the bank on the basis of professional qualifications, as long as the appointee was a member of the party. As a result, Robert Frowein, previously head of the branch in Frankfurt a.M. and party member since 1936, was appointed to the board on 1 May 1943.[19]

By the summer of that year, Hunke had apparently become so frustrated with his work at the Propaganda Ministry that he submitted his resignation. A few days later, Walther Funk, who was President of the Reichsbank, Minister of Economics and a person with whom both Hunke and Abs had particularly good connections, offered to arrange a place for Hunke on the board. Hunke agreed to accept it on the condition that the bank again ask him to join. Only days later, Ritter von Halt did precisely this on behalf of the board and in place of supervisory board chairman Kimmich, who had been taken ill. The Bormann committee apparently raised no objections.[20] The supervisory board decided in favour of Hunke's appointment at its meeting on 16 September 1943.

Originally Hunke planned to leave his post at the Propaganda Ministry on 30 November 1943, in order to assume his position on the board. However, Goebbels personally refused to accept his resignation 'until the issue of a successor has been completely settled'.[21] The fact that the National Socialist leadership was nevertheless greatly interested in having Hunke on the board is demonstrated by the actions of the Reich Trustee for Labour Dr Leon Daeschner, whose responsibility it was to approve the contracts of all board members. Daeschner waited until 4 February 1944, four days after Hunke had been given his new contract, to drop his demands to have Frowein's earnings cut. Naturally, Hunke's contract was approved at the same time.[22]

Unlike Börnicke, Hunke was considered acceptable to the board because of the position he took in the debate over war aims that followed the military setbacks in the USSR. Unlike many others in the party leadership, he did not favour an unconditional confrontation to the very end, but preferred a strategy of conciliation with the Western powers in order to avert the looming catastrophe for Germany, especially if the Red Army would be victorious.[23] Hunke was described by the chairman of the supervisory board at the time, Hans Oesterlink, during his interrogation by the American Paul J. Brand, co-author of the OMGUS investigation of the Deutsche Bank, as follows: 'He was a man of high intelligence and moderate political views … he worked in a business-like manner and did not attempt to employ party members at the bank.'[24] Nevertheless his role as watchdog for the party in banking is also demonstrated by the fact that he was the second representative of the Deutsche Bank, in addition to Abs, to be appointed to the advisory board of the Reichsbank.[25]

Hunke's willingness finally to join the board was certainly prompted by the tensions in the relationship between him and his powerful patron Goebbels, whose fanaticism during the second half of the war conflicted more and more with Hunke's increasing desire for conciliation and pragmatic solutions. Shortly before Berlin fell to the Red Army, the once patronizing relationship developed into quite the opposite. When the Soviet troops surrounding Berlin were on the verge of taking it, Hunke had to leave the city 'in the morning of 23 April on an official mission', to use the wording of the Deutsche Bank.[26] Actually, Hunke was fleeing Goebbels, who had become enraged after discovering that, since the beginning of the year, Hunke had been attempting to convince the military and political leadership of the economic futility of defending the capital.[27] Three days later, on 26 April 1945, he arrived in Hamburg. Immediately he was dismissed from the bank in accordance with the 'Instructions to Financial

Institutions, No. 3, and to Government Financial Agencies'[28] that had been issued by the military government.

On 19 July 1945, it was reported from Hamburg that Hunke was free and to be found not far from Detmold.[29] The next day he was taken into custody in Schothmar near Lemgo. Like many others, he was arrested because he was among the group of individuals whom the Allies interned automatically. The initial interrogation was conducted by British investigators in July–August 1945. In their report, they concluded 'that Hunke be released as soon as possible after re-internment and given work by Mil Govt'. On 23 September 1946, he filled out the standardized personal data sheet of the military government while being held in an internment camp at Berlin-Wannsee in the American sector of the city. Later he was transferred to Nuremberg.[30]

There are two indications that the top managers at the Deutsche Bank never fully accepted Hunke, that they had even considered his presence at the bank as temporary. First, he was not assigned any specific function. Second, he was the only member of the board who was not given a single supervisory board position; even Ritter von Halt finally managed to obtain three by the end of the war.[31] It had been Hunke's expressed wish 'that he be given time to familiarize himself with the job, whereas he envisioned a period of two years. It was agreed upon that he be able to carry on the highly demanding work of his full-time position outside the bank as president of the Economic Chamber of the *Gau*', wrote the directing office (Führungstab) in Hamburg in a letter dated 7 February 1947. This letter was addressed to Hunke's wife Hildegard,[32] in answer to her request for a statement from the bank that would help vindicate her husband, who was under arrest in the American zone at the time. In a certified statement dated 27 June 1947, and presented to the denazification trial against Hunke, Wintermantel declared that the decision had been made to grant Hunke only one year to familiarize himself with his new position at the bank. However, developments so late in the war had deprived Hunke of the opportunity to assume any business responsibilities at the bank.[33] On behalf of Hunke, the acting chairman of the supervisory board, Hans Oesterlink, wrote in an affidavit dated 5 September 1947, concerning this introductory period: 'Mr Hunke adjusted to this role – not an easy one for a member of the board – without any difficulty and with a clear understanding of the situation, although he could have attempted to use his influential position at the time as economic adviser of the *Gau* to push his demands. He fitted in well with the other board members; he also adjusted to the interests of the bank. He remained collegial ... I had several conversations with Mr Hunke about the future rebuilding of the destroyed cities, a topic which interested him as president of the Chamber of Commerce. Thus I came to the conclusion that he had his feet firmly on the ground and that he maintained an objective and sound judgement, free from party doctrine.'[34]

Apparently some time between late 1947 and 2 March 1949, Hunke was released from internment and returned to his wife in Detmold. On this very day in March he wrote to inform Wintermantel of his upcoming visit. At the time, Wintermantel was at the Rheinisch-Westfälische Bank in Düsseldorf, one of the successor banks of the decentralized Deutsche Bank. In the period that followed, the only issue Hunke addressed in his communications with the bank was that of his compensation settlement.

Thanks to what might appear as foresight on the part of the bank, Hunke was not granted the pension rights included in the contracts of the other board members when he accepted his position at the bank. Upon leaving the board prior to the end of a five-year term, he was only to receive a single compensation payment of 24,000 RM for every commenced year of service. He was not to acquire pension rights until the sixth year of service, by which time the outcome of the war would have settled many such political matters anyway. Hunke was finally entitled to a payment of 24,000 RM for each of the years 1944 and 1945, as well as a sum of 30,000 RM, representing half of his yearly income. Due to the currency reform, this compensation amounted to 7,800 DM, which he received in 1952. He invested in a company manufacturing elastic bands and was considered by the Deutsche Bank to be a thoroughly creditworthy businessman. Other developments were reported from inside the Chamber of Industry and Commerce in Hanover on 17 November 1953: 'Just recently H. [Hunke] succeeded in becoming recognized as a 131er, namely as "Ministerialdirektor", the highest possible rank in the civil service for non-political positions. He is therefore in a very advantageous position to be reappointed to government service. The budgetary considerations are reason alone for the state to see to it that he is reappointed as soon as possible in order to avoid paying out support. However, in view of the earlier "achievements" of the applicant, this seems alarming.'[35] Hunke was indeed accepted into government service again as an assistant secretary (Ministerialdirigent) in the finance ministry of Lower Saxony.[36]

An example of how useful Ritter von Halt and Hunke were for the Deutsche Bank is illustrated in the following episode. In the spring of 1944, board members Abs and Wintermantel (then 62 years old!) and Josef Adam, head of the stock exchange department at the head office, were ordered to report to the Kriegsführer (war leader) of the SA unit 1 in order to be examined for possible conscription as anti-aircraft gunners in the home guard. SA-Oberführer von Halt wrote in his capacity as 'enterprise leader' (Betriebsführer) to Professor Heinrich Hunke in his capacity as president of the economic chamber of the *Gau* on 27 March 1944, and asked him to seek an exemption for Wintermantel due to health reasons and for the other two men on the grounds of their indispensability for business – with obvious success.[37]

The fate of the other seven members of the board at the end of the war differed greatly, depending on which of the three original occupation forces they were forced to deal with. The bank's branches located in the regions east of the Oder–Neisse Line had been systematically evacuated just prior to the occupation by Soviet troops. This meant that all important bank records, such as accounting books, deposit ledgers and account cards, were shipped to cities located further west. Even some of the bank personnel were sent west with these documents. Auxiliary offices were set up for the 'eastern branches' in cities such as Leipzig, Jena and Coburg – to name three – and were usually located in the building of the local branch office.[38] In 1947, the directing office in Hamburg confirmed that 'the bank branches located in areas under Russian and Polish occupation as well as in the former Sudetenland have all been completely liquidated'.[39] Several of the bank's branches in western Germany were also moved to other locations as the Allies advanced. The branch in Aachen was the first to be evacuated; it was moved to Bielefeld in September 1944.[40]

In order to be prepared for the likelihood that military developments would destroy the established structures of authority, the bank began to decentralize its business operations or, more precisely, to disperse them. At the same supervisory board meeting on 16 September 1943, at which the bank bowed to political pressure and appointed Hunke to the board of managing directors, measures were also taken to ensure that bank operations of the branches could continue in the face of any eventuality, including that of total military defeat. In addition to the four executive vice-presidents in the Berlin head office who already possessed general power of attorney for the bank as a whole (namely Dr Joachim Kessler, Alfred Kurzmeyer, Dr Kurt Weigelt and Dr Hans-Alfons Simon), ten branch managers were appointed as executive vice-presidents of the Deutsche Bank and were thus equipped with the same powers. The men appointed were Hermann Kaiser, Berlin; Dr Max Jörgens, Wuppertal-Eberfeld; Heinrich Klöckers, Mannheim; Ludwig Kruse, Essen; Arnold Maser, Munich; Jean Baptist Rath, Cologne; Dr Felix Theusner, Breslau; Paul Vernickel, Reichenberg; Hermann Willink, Hamburg; and Dr Carl Wuppermann, Düsseldorf. These men remained at their local offices.[41] Since the obligatory second signature for a legally binding transaction involving the entire bank could be provided not only by a board member or someone holding general power of attorney, but also by 'an assistant vice-president or any bank official authorized to co-sign',[42] the head office in Berlin was indeed turning over actual decision-making authority to the managers of the head branches so that they could 'operate on their own *without instruction from Berlin*'.[43]

By taking this step, the Deutsche Bank was also complying with the demands made by the party and the Bormann committee in their attempt to decentralize the big banks. Hans Oesterlink described this during his interrogation by the Americans: 'The Party wanted to strengthen the regional banks, that is to say, the *Gauleiters* [party district leaders] wanted to control the banks in their *Gau*. They could better influence such decentralized banks than the larger banking houses with headquarters in Berlin. There was a certain tendency to dismantle the larger banking houses, which could have been done by reinstating the autonomy originally possessed by such banking institutions before they were merged by the big banks.'[44] By bestowing general power of attorney for the entire bank upon these managers of head branches, the Deutsche Bank temporarily took the wind out of the sails of National Socialist plans for extensive decentralization. The bank officially explained this organizational reform as a measure to counterbalance the competition with regional banks. Reference was also made to the 'state of war and its unpredictable events ... without having to mention all of the technical problems which make it necessary for the branches of big banks to be allowed to act independently'.[45] Following the war, 12 of the 14 executive vice-presidents still held their positions.[46] Abs called them 'the twelve apostles', and indeed, they were the ones who shouldered most of the responsibility for the bank during the turbulent years after the war when the members of the board of managing directors had been arrested, suspended or fired.

On the eve of Germany's defeat, the bank prepared itself for the now inevitable occupation of Berlin by the Soviets and the closure of the big banks. Three 'intermediary offices of the board' were established 'in order to create a degree of decentralization that would enable the entire board to retain control of the bank operations of all branches during the temporary break in communications between the individual branches and the head office in Berlin which was to be expected due to the impact of the war'.[47] Purely by accident, the bank had selected a city in each of the three planned occupation zones to set up such an office, namely in Wiesbaden, Erfurt and Hamburg.[48]

In early 1944, prior to the determination of the borders of the occupation zones, the department for the credit business of the branches was transferred in part from the head office in Berlin to the 'Wiesbaden branch office', apparently due to the increasing breaks in long-distance communication resulting from the war. From this point on, it served the credit business of the southern and southwestern districts of Germany, including Hessen and the Saar. However, decisions on major credits starting at about 1 million RM continued to be made at the head office in Berlin until its closure; during the period from the end of the war until spring 1946, such decisions were made by the directing office in Hamburg.[49] The 'Wiesbaden branch office', which would later also be referred to as an 'intermediary office', temporarily served as the bank's headquarters in the American zone. It was headed by Director Dr Walter Schmidt, the chief of the Wiesbaden branch and co-manager of the Frankfurt branch.[50] Robert Frowein, member of the board of managing directors, was also in Frankfurt during most of this period, but he left for Berlin shortly before the end of the war. The American military government seized the bank's office facilities, located on Friedrichstrasse at the corner of Wilhelmstrasse,[51] in order to set up an office in early July 1945 to investigate crimes against humanity.[52] This action prevented the Wiesbaden office from becoming more important within the newly decentralized structure of the Deutsche Bank.

During this period the bank was trying to survive in an increasingly chaotic situation while attempting to retain as much centralized control over its organization as possible. Rumours that the river Elbe[53] would become the border between the Soviet zone and the other zones prompted the bank in February 1945 to decide to transfer the central cash office to Hildesheim – for what would a bank be without money? – and shortly thereafter, to set up an intermediary office for the board in Erfurt and, not long after that, the directing office in Hamburg. As a result, the bank would have two major banking operations in cities that would be in the British zone: namely, the Hildesheim cash office and the directing office in Hamburg.

On 10 February 1945, one day before the conclusion of the Yalta Conference during which the future partition of Germany was finally settled, the Deutsche Bank informed both the Reichsbank and the Reich Economics Ministry of its intention to establish the 'Hildesheim cash office' and to transfer the funds of 27 named branch districts (representing all of southern and north-western Germany, including Meiningen and Erfurt in the future Soviet zone) to Hildesheim. Therefore, it planned 'to deposit the security accounts comprising of Reich bills and non-interest-bearing Treasury notes corresponding to the funds of the branches in question in the collective securities depository in Hanover and to have these credited to the Hildesheim cash office'.[54] It was to be headed by Director Hermann Ermisch; the directors in Hildesheim, Heinrich Rauschert and Gustav Sommer, were also to have signatory power. By transferring its cash office from the head office in Berlin that February, the bank managed to save nearly 7 billion RM by the end of the war, placing this significant sum at the disposal of the directing office in Hamburg.[55] This included 3.376 billion RM in Treasury notes, 1.478 billion RM in Treasury bills, and 0.325 billion RM in Reich bonds.[56] In July of that year, the cash office in Hildesheim replaced the office in Berlin as the main clearing office for all western branches. It was transferred later to Hanover and in 1947 moved from there to Hamburg.[57]

The decision to set up an 'intermediary office of the board' in Erfurt was made by the board of managing directors in early March 1945, following a meeting in Berlin held by Assistant Secretary (Ministerialdirigent) Walther Bayrhoffer from the Finance Ministry and attended by Oswald Rösler on 1 March 1945. Bayrhoffer, who was also a director on the board of the Reichsbank, had called the meeting in order to inform the major banking houses and insurance companies about the measures being taken by the Finance Ministry, the Reich Debt Administration and the Reichsbank to ensure payment transactions should any disruption in communications with Berlin occur. An auxiliary office was to be established in Meiningen for the Reich Debt Administration, the Reich Central Cash Office and the bond issue department of the Finance Ministry. Linked to this auxiliary office was to be a money market department. The Reichsbank board of managing directors was to establish its own auxiliary office in Erfurt.[58] The Deutsche Bank board must have decided that very day to send Robert Frowein to Erfurt in order to investigate the possibilities for creating an 'inter-mediary office of the board' in the local branch building. In any case, Frowein sent a telegram from Erfurt on 2 March 1945, stating: 'Easy to make spacious office in branch building – stop – ... Emergency quarters can be arranged in the bank without difficulty ...'.[59] Shortly afterwards, the board decided in favour of Erfurt. The decision was made known in a confidential circular dated 6 March 1945, and sent to the managers of the branches: 'Members of the board will rotate their presence in this auxiliary office, so that two, eventually even three of them will be available to advise the branches in their affairs and make decisions, *as long as the head office in Berlin is not reachable* ... No other department from the head office will be transferred, with the exception of the cash office, which has set up a branch office in Hildesheim in connection with the collective giro depository in Hanover so as to ensure cash payments to the branches in western and southern Germany.'[60] The Dresdner Bank set up an auxiliary office in Erfurt as well.[61]

On 13 March, Dr Clemens Plassmann (b. 2 February 1894) joined Frowein in Erfurt. Frowein received a telegram on 28 March 1945, asking him to return to Berlin. Plassmann was promised that another colleague would replace him in early April,[62] namely Abs. Plassmann was sitting on pins and needles in expectation of his arrival, especially as the war front moved closer and closer to Erfurt and long-distance communication became next to impossible.[63] On 5 April 1945, Plassmann reported: 'The "directing office" of the Reichsbank here in Erfurt left the city yesterday headed in the direction of Weimar carrying a backpack.' On 7 April he wrote to the board: 'One week ago today I was to be replaced by Mr Abs, yet he has not appeared ... It was decided yesterday to defend Erfurt "down to the last brick" ... All bridges just east of Erfurt have been blown up.' On 11 April, Plassmann succeeded in sending a telegram to Berlin, informing the head office that Abs had still not yet turned up. He asked whether he should wait out the situation or undertake 'the by now difficult attempt' to return to Berlin. The next day, the board telegraphed the branch in Weimar asking that a message be sent to Plassmann, if necessary by courier, informing him that his rapid return to Berlin would be 'greatly welcomed'.[64] Too late! American troops took Erfurt on 12 April,[65] and four days later the Red Army began its attack on Berlin.

On 16 March 1945, Hunke and Sippell joined Dr Otto Christian Fischer, the head of the Reichsgruppe Banking, at a meeting with Walther Funk, the Reichsbank President and Minister of Economics, to discuss preparations for the *Iwanfall* (Ivan eventuality), meaning the occupation of Berlin by the Soviets instead of by the Western powers. It was agreed that the securities located in collective depositories would be destroyed. Funk stated that previous plans requiring the members of all bank boards to remain in Berlin had only been valid for an occupation by the Western powers; he now ordered 'all board members to leave Berlin without exception'[66] in view of the pending *Iwanfall*. However, in a meeting with Hunke on 20 March 1945, Funk's Deputy Under-Secretary (Ministerialdirektor) Dr Joachim Riehle made it clear that 'contrary to the opinion of Reich Minister Funk, he took the position that all of the board members could not leave Berlin'.[67]

It was then that the Deutsche Bank decided to set up a directing office in Hamburg. Erich Bechtolf (b. 8 April 1891) wrote a letter on 21 March 1945, to Plassmann in Erfurt, informing him about the planned creation of a directing office in Hamburg. 'In a few days I will be leaving for Hamburg,' he wrote. 'In case it becomes necessary to assemble a management apparatus outside of Berlin in order to continue a centralized management of the bank, we have decided that, first and foremost, we need a metropolis complete with transportation facilities. Hamburg is the most suitable of the remaining metropolitian options. For the time being, we want to continue the practice of decentralization in so far as the office will be staffed with two members of the board, as is done in Erfurt. This ensures that three or four members are always outside of Berlin while the others remain there. My own task in Hamburg is to determine whether everything needed to create a small directing office is available. In view of these new considerations, we have asked Mr Frowein to remain in Erfurt temporarily.'[68] Two days later, Rösler wrote to the 'intermediary office of the board' in Erfurt about the meeting with Walther Funk and his instructions for *Iwanfall*. Should it become necessary for the entire top management staff of the bank to operate outside of Berlin, 'something we hope we are spared', it would be necessary to find a location which already had a large organization and a staff experienced in the type of banking operations done at the head office. The only place like this would be Hamburg.[69] Bechtolf had been in Hamburg since 28 March 1945, trying to obtain the proper authorizations for establishing and accommodating the directing office.[70]

Hermann Josef Abs (b. 15 October 1901) escaped Berlin in a delivery van from the department store Karstadt[71] before the Soviets attacked Berlin on 13 April, and he later reported to Bechtolf in Hamburg. According to his own testimony, he had learned from Zeiss-Jena in early April 1945 that Thuringia would become part of the Soviet occupation zone,[72] and therefore did not attempt to relieve Plassmann in Erfurt. He did, however, arrive safely in Hamburg on 14 April – the last person to bring news directly to Hamburg from the head office in Berlin. The next news from Berlin would not be relayed until the end of the first week in July 1945 when Dr Günter Keiser, a top executive of the Association of Private Banking Business,[73] arrived from Berlin.[74] According to Abs's own account, he registered himself with the local Hamburg authorities, living first in the home of Michel Opladen, Marie-Luisen-Strasse 48, and later in the home of Casimir Prinz zu Sayn-Wittgenstein-Berleburg, Leinpfad 73. The latter was the stepson of Richard Merton, the chairman of the supervisory board of the Metallgesellschaft AG and president of the German section of the International Chamber of Commerce. During the months of May and June 1945, Abs was repeatedly interrogated by representatives of the British military government and by a British–American panel, namely by the British Colonel

Sutton and the American officer Clark; Clark would later work for the Federal Reserve Bank of New York. More interrogations would follow by British, French and Dutch investigators.[75]

Abs and Bechtolf were not able to get word to Plassmann in Erfurt until 23 May 1945. They urgently requested him to come to Hamburg to help support the directing office. Plassmann managed to leave Erfurt before the Americans pulled out of Thuringia and arrived in Hamburg on 12 June.[76] This trip, and the others he took throughout Germany from 20 June–31 July 1945, to make business contacts with various companies, branches of the banks and members of the supervisory board of the Deutsche Bank, and to visit his family for four days at their long-established home in Ettal in southern Bavaria, were made under the guise of official business trips for the company Karstadt AG. As a major retail business, this company was not suspected by the Allies of having been involved in the armament industry, and therefore it proved relatively safe to travel in its vehicles.[77] Plassmann's use of Karstadt vehicles was not accidental; he had served on the board of managing directors of Karstadt from 1932 to 1940, and thereafter on the supervisory board.

It proved very opportune for the Deutsche Bank to have in the British zone their two most important central facilities outside of Berlin: namely, the directing office in Hamburg and the cash office in Hildesheim. The British were more sympathetic to German efforts to retain a centralized system of banking, since the British had a similar centralized banking structure. And as the creditors of loans to Germany during the Weimar period, it was in Britain's own interest to ensure an efficient operation of the banks so that Germany could resume repayment of these loans, which had been frozen since 1931. As the nation with the largest private stockholder banks in the world, Great Britain would have found itself hard pressed to attribute the central cause of National Socialism and its aggressive war policy to such institutions and therefore disband them, as the Soviets would do through nationalization of the big banks and the Americans through decentralization.

The three board members present in Hamburg were automatically suspended from their positions, regardless of their personal reputation, as was prescribed by the 'Instructions to Financial Institutions, No. 3, and to Government Financial Agencies'.[78] This ordinance was immediately enacted by each of the Western Allies upon the occupation of German territory. Although these men were not allowed even to enter the offices of the Deutsche Bank,[79] they managed to continue directing the bank informally. Officially, the directing office in Hamburg was structured as follows. The branch bank office was headed by Senior Vice-President Arnold Schwerdtfeger, the legal department by First Vice-President Dr Hans Paschke, the areas of organization, auditing and central accounting by Vice-President Georg Steinmann, the foreign department by Assistant Vice-President Dr Johannes Feske, and the secretariat by Vice-President Franz Heinrich Ulrich, who had previously served Abs as a personal assistant and would later play an important role as a member and spokesman of the board at the Deutsche Bank. Additional members of the directing office in Hamburg were First Vice-President Max Ott, Vice-President Dr Lauer, Cash Deposit Manager Werner Herhold and Paul Walsen, authorized with limited power of attorney.[80]

A plan was also drawn up on 20 June 1945, which 'temporarily divided the responsibilities of the board members in the areas occupied by the Western powers'. The plan assigned responsibilities not only for territorial areas, but also for subject areas, to each of the four suspended board members, including Hans Rummel in southern Germany. At the time, the geographical areas still included the districts of Saxony and Thuringia (assigned to Plassmann).[81] Of course, such a plan was illegal and had to be kept secret from the military authorities. Since the British military government, contrary to the Soviet and the American governments, showed no interest in 'beheading' the big banks, they may very well have just turned a blind eye to this practice. A letter sent by Dr Günter Keiser on 19 July 1945 to Dr Erich Trost, managing director of the Association of Private Banking Business and Keiser's boss, illustrates just how little significance the British military government actually attached to the act of suspending of board members. Keiser, who had been sent from Berlin to Hamburg with reports on the Soviet bank policy that were apparently meant to be turned over to the British, wrote from Hamburg to Berlin that 'contrary to the scepticism expressed by Mr Rösler, Mr A. [Abs] has already established close contact with the leading English authorities ..., and indeed, the reports are well on their way to the proper address, so that I can consider the first – and probably most important – task of my mission to be completed'.[82]

Abs, Bechtolf and Plassmann named two of the 'twelve apostles' to head the directing office in Hamburg: namely, Executive Vice-Presidents Dr Max Jörgens from Wuppertal-Elberfeld and Ludwig Kruse from Essen. The directing office was located at Alter Wall 37. Before April 1946, Dr Victor-Albin von Schenk, the director of the Hamburg branch of the bank, also advanced to the ranks of top management in that office, where he was still serving in December of that year.[83] However, he was forced to leave some time after that, apparently at the insistence of the British military government.[84] In May 1946, Wintermantel was permitted to become active as head of the directing office. Dr Joachim Kessler from Berlin, one of the executive vice-presidents with general power of attorney for the entire bank, joined the staff in the summer of that year.[85] In April 1946, the secretariat, together with the department for syndicate affairs, was headed by Senior Vice-President Dr Ernst Wienands and the personnel department by Senior Vice-President Emil Gossmann.[86] In order to remain active in their districts, Jörgens and Kruse rotated their stays in Hamburg.[87]

The directing office tried to keep the branch network intact and to establish common business principles by snowballing the branches with courier-delivered information circulars.[88] Obviously, the responsible authorities in the British military government not only accepted this practice in their own zone, they even tolerated it being extended into the American and French zones until it was explicitly forbidden on the basis of agreements made by the four powers in March 1946.[89] However, the suspension of the members of the Deutsche Bank board did not stop the Banking Branch of the British military government from seeking advice from Abs on a nearly regular if at first informal basis, starting on 8 May 1945. This office described Abs in May 1945 as being 'extremely knowledgeable, wholeheartedly professional and possibly less political than it is the fashion at present to presume'.[90]

Charles Gunston, who was responsible for the German desk at the Bank of England and was at the time head of the Banking Branch, had first met Abs and come to regard him highly in the 1930s during the negotiation of the Standstill Agreements. He described how he had approached Abs at their first encounter following the war: It was 'like old times. I didn't ask him about the war. It didn't matter. They had been financing their war efforts, like we had been financing ours. Politics just didn't come into it.' His successor, Edward Hellmuth from the Midland Bank, the bank which had represented the Deutsche Bank in London, commented on the difference between the British and American evaluations of Abs: 'The Americans wanted to be rough with him. They didn't appreciate his banking experience. They believed him to be a Nazi. But he wasn't a member of the party, so we gave him protection.'[91]

In August 1945, Abs became the *primus inter pares* of the four-member German Bankers Advisory Board of the British Banking Branch that was created on the impetus of Gunston. The other three board members were Alfred Hölling from the Dresdner Bank and Ernst Hülse and Wilhelm Vocke, both former managing directors of the Reichsbank who had been dismissed by Hitler in 1939. The Financial Investigation Section of the American military government, headed by Bernard Bernstein, a close adviser of Henry Morgenthau, intervened. Following an interrogation of Abs, Hülse and Vocke in Hamburg, the Americans indicated in late September 1945 that they intended to request the British authorities to arrest Abs and try him as a war criminal in Nuremberg, and to have Hülse and Vocke testify as witnesses in the war crimes trial against Schacht and Funk. This meant the demise of the Advisory Board.[92]

According to the British, the Americans wanted to support their charges against Abs with the following five points. First, his income had increased tenfold in the years between 1933 and 1945. Second, as one of the leading members of the board of the Deutsche Bank, he had also been responsible for bank financing of the war industry. Third, he had held positions on the supervisory boards of many armament manufacturers. Fourth, several of these companies had probably profited from the transfer of property and other assets from the occupied territories. Fifth, he had been one of the owners of the bank Delbrück Schickler & Co., where Hitler, Rosenberg and other leading Nazis had maintained bank accounts.[93] In October 1945, Abs was once again interrogated by two American investigators, this time concerning the I.G. Farben conglomorate.[94]

One member of the Banking Branch, Colonel Rose, had always been against co-operating with Abs. Now he demanded that Abs be dismissed from the Deutsche Bank and pressured Gunston by threatening to make the case public in an article for the *Daily Mirror*. On 11 December 1945, the Financial Investigation Section of the American military government also demanded from the British that Abs be extradited as a war criminal.[95] Abs, along with many other leading names from the German world of business and finance, was listed both in July and December 1945 on the so-called CROWCASS list (Central Registry of War Criminals and Security Suspects), which was based on information collected and compiled by the 'United Nations' (as the countries at war with Germany called themselves at the time) while the war was still raging.[96]

On 20 December 1945, the Allied Control Council passed Law No. 10, which prescribed the 'punishment of war crimes, crimes against peace or humanity'.[97] Now there was little even the British could do to evade their commitments as stipulated in this four-power law. As Gunston told Abs: 'There is political pressure to get you and I can't stop it.' It was left to Hellmuth to inform Abs that he was being stripped of his approximately 45 supervisory board seats.[98] Hellmuth recollects: 'I did it with dignity, in my best German. He appreciated my approach.'[99] Gunston's return to London in early January meant that Abs had lost his most important protector. In fact, he was taken into custody on 17 January 1946, probably in connection with the investigation into allegations against the Deutsche Bank about its business practices in the occupied territories, practices that were directly linked to the foreign business department headed by Abs. The conviction and sentencing *in absentia* of Abs to 'ten years' imprisonment with hard labour' by the Zagreb People's District Court in Yugoslavia on 19 November 1945 appears to have played a role in this turn of events. Abs and others were declared guilty because they 'co-operated in business with the enemy and occupation forces between the years 1942 to 1945 while holding responsible positions at the Bankverein für Kroatien [Croatian Bank Association] in Zagreb . . . as members of the managerial board and in this way financed trade with Germany to a great extent . . .'. Several observers viewed this conviction as the outcome of a political trial in a region recently freed from the yoke of Nazi domination, where the population had collaborated especially closely with the Germans. In any case, the Yugoslavian government declared Abs 'exonerated . . . from carrying out the sentence' based on a decision made on 9 April 1956, by the Federal Executive Council in Belgrade on the eve of Abs's first visit to the country.[100]

Abs was at first imprisoned for several days in Altona; then he was transferred to a camp in Bad Nenndorf near Hanover, where the bathing cabins of this health resort had been transformed into cells for the prisoners. The Allies called this camp the 'Dustbin'. The élite of the Ruhr industry were being interned here, among them Otto Wolff, Hans-Günther Sohl, Hans Reuter and even Günter Henle, who had been forced to leave the top managerial position of the Klöckner conglomorate during the Nazi era because he was half-Jewish. Abs shared his cell with Carl Luer, a member of the board of managing directors of the Dresdner Bank, and worked the fields together with Sohl, the future President of the Federal Association of German Industry.[101] He was finally released on 18 April 1946.[102] This was in compliance with the three-month minimum period of internment prescribed by Control Council Law No. 10, during which the authorities from other zones or foreign governments were to present extradition requests if they wished to prosecute the person for war crimes, as defined by the Control Council Law, or if they needed him as a witness in such a trial. However, it was left to the authorities of the zone in which a prisoner was being held to decide whether to grant such extradition requests; they also reserved the right to determine whether the prisoner would be brought to trial in their own zone. Thus, the fate of Hermann J. Abs lay in the hands of the British. John R. Kellam, an officer in the Banking Branch and in civilian life an auditor at the Bank of England, had worked within the British military government to have Abs released.[103]

Following the interrogation of Plassmann in Hamburg on 28 December 1945, and of both Bechtolf and Plassmann on 5 February 1946, the British military government surprised the Deutsche Bank on 19 February 1946, with instructions to dismiss both men. After his dismissal, Plassmann responded in a letter dated 25 February 1946, which was written during a hospital stay in Hamburg's Marienkrankenhaus following a tonsil operation, and was addressed to the directing office of the bank: 'For anyone who knows my political views and actions, the directive against me must remain an enigma, unless ... he is of the opinion ... that what is taking place here is not the purge of National Socialism, but the elimination of Germany's élite regardless of political outlook ... Since I held the apparently mistaken view that the political stance of the Deutsche Bank and its board members was publicly known, I have not attempted to obtain any political character references, especially since I had mentioned the campaign by the NSDAP against me on my questionnaire submitted to the military government.'[104] Plassmann also suffered economically from his dismissal. For 21 months he had to go on the dole.[105]

About the time Plassmann and Bechtolf were dismissed in mid-February 1946, the British asked Wintermantel, who was in Berlin, to join the directing office in Hamburg.[106] Following the closure of the big banks in Berlin by the Soviets in the spring of 1945, Wintermantel had no longer been permitted to assume any further functions there except those necessary to close out business as stipulated by the ordinances of the occupation powers. The head office of the Deutsche Bank in East Berlin was closed down completely on 4 March 1946, and Wintermantel arrived in Hamburg on 6 March 1946.[107] The general plight in Germany also took a heavy toll on him. For months he lived in the Pension Döcke, located at Moorweidenstrasse 34 in Hamburg, which he described as 'lacking any form of comfort, and the supply of food is absolutely pitiful'.[108] Plassmann recalls that

Wintermantel usually visited him in the hospital at noontime 'in order to eat the rest of my noon meal'.[109] The informal 'board meetings' of the suspended or dismissed managing directors in Hamburg were often held in the modest private quarters of Plassmann, Bechtolf, Abs and Wintermantel. Plassmann lived in a small room of only about ten square metres in the half-destroyed Karstadt store located at Mönckebergstrasse 18. Many of the circulars of the directing office for the branches of the bank were formulated here by Abs, Bechtolf, Plassmann and Wintermantel. E.W. Schmidt, the bank's chief economist, who was also in Hamburg at the time, wrote in 1957: 'Because they had been suspended from their positions, they could only compose the text of the circular and suggest it to the bank's management, which at the time consisted of Executive Vice-Presidents Dr Max Joergens (Wuppertal) and Ludwig Kruse (Essen), but they were not permitted to sign it.'[110]

On 6 May 1946, the British military government, at the behest of the Americans,[111] instructed the Deutsche Bank also to dismiss Abs, who subsequently returned to his family to become a fruit farmer on his 250-acre estate 'Bentgerhof' near Remagen in the lower Rhine valley: that is, in the French zone. A few days later, Wintermantel's suspension was lifted, enabling him officially to assume the management of the directing office. In connection with this, the Banking Branch of the British military government also announced, in a letter addressed to the Deutsche Bank on 9 May 1946, that it was unblocking his assets.[112] However, this move meant little financial relief for Wintermantel, since it did not grant him access to his assets in Berlin. Despite his poor health and the dismal food supply in a big city like Hamburg, he continued to shoulder the full responsibility for the entire bank as the only member of the previous board of managing directors throughout this difficult period until early 1948. On 1 November 1946, he was finally able to move into a three-and-a-half room apartment in the home of Victor-Albin von Schenk at Heilwigstrasse 93, in which Joachim Kessler and his wife also lived. Therefore, the three colleagues also became closely involved in each other's private lives. Wintermantel and Kessler regularly received charitable gifts and CARE packages containing food, medicine and alcoholic beverages in the years from 1946 to 1948, thanks to Kurzmeyer in Switzerland, to friends in France and the USA, and to the Riedel-de Haën AG in Seelze near Hanover.[113]

In March 1947, Wintermantel wrote of Abs: 'I have spoken several times recently to our friend Hermann Josef; he is in good spirits, thriving and looks healthy.'[114] Abs was informed in August 1947 at Bentgerhof that he was to testify as a witness at the Nuremberg trials. He applied for the necessary travel papers from the French occupation authorities. From 1 to 21 October 1947, he was in Nuremberg for questioning.[115] Plassmann and Bechtolf were reinstated at the bank following the successful completion of their denazification trials in December 1947; Plassmann was classified as Category V (exonerated).[116] From this point on, they were part of the management at the directing office in

Hamburg until the big banks in the British occupation zone were decentralized on 1 April 1948. A diagram of the organizational structure of the bank from 19 January 1948 indicates that Wintermantel was responsible for the foreign department, the cash office and the central accounting and organization department; Bechtolf headed the stock exchange and legal department; Plassmann directed the personnel department; and Kessler was responsible for the general secretariat, the secretariat of the Stempelvereinigung and the economic research department.[117] The denazification trial of Abs was concluded on 19 February 1948, and he too was classified as Category V.[118] However, he retired temporarily, retroactive to 1 January 1948, with an annual pension of 24,000 RM: that is, with less than his retirement contract called for. In return, he was asked to advise all the bank's branches in the three Western zones without extra compensation.[119]

All four pre-1945 board members were among the most important and significant promoters of continuity. It was also to their advantage that Abs, Bechtolf and Plassmann were among the youngest members of the board. But only Abs would become a close adviser to Adenauer. Adenauer had confidence in Abs, even though Adenauer felt he had been tricked by the Deutsche Bank regarding his private property rights in 1945–46, and despite the fact that in the summer of 1946 his compensation demands were strongly opposed by the bank's directing office.[120] Adenauer wanted to appoint Abs as under-secretary of state responsible for foreign policy in the Federal Chancellery in October 1949, and later as Foreign Minister in the 1950s. These appointments and the plans to have Abs act as chief German negotiator at the Schuman Plan negotiations did not materialize due primarily to the opposition of the French government, as well as to American objections.[121] Yet Abs was able to contribute significantly to foreign policy once he was permitted to head the German delegation to the negotiations conducted from 1951 to 1953 that led to the London Debt Agreement of 27 February 1953.

Hans Rummel (b. 9 March 1882) had been the board member responsible for the entire region of southern Germany, and as such he had sat on the supervisory boards of BMW and Daimler-Benz. Rummel had also been in charge of the department for 'organization, including balance sheets and overhead'.[122] In numerous publications, he had introduced many innovations into the business of banking, such as the practice of calculating interest rate margins for assessing the rate of return on investment and the then seemingly revolutionary concept of 'dividing the banking business into the three areas of credit, money transactions and securities trading, each of which should earn its own overhead'.[123] Rummel had been living in his home town of Krautostheim in Franconia since the summer of 1944. From there he could better pursue his responsibilities as 'supervisory board chairman of various companies vital to the war effort', as he himself wrote on 5 August 1944, to Berlin.[124] By the war's end, health problems also kept him in Krautostheim. Rummel was suspended from his board duties by the American authorities, just like his colleagues in Hamburg had been on instruction of the British military government. He was ordered by the Finance Division of the American military government to appear in Nuremberg on 20 June 1945, for a meeting about agreements on foreign assets. He also hoped to use this opportunity to have his travel permit extended beyond the 50-kilometre radius of his home to which it had been limited. To his surprise, Rummel was arrested on the day of that meeting. About a week later, a wave of arrests of leading names in German business began in the US zone.[125] At first, these were justified by the American directive for the prosecution of war criminals and later by Article II, Law No. 10, issued by the Allied Control Council on 20 December 1945, according to which 'crimes against peace' were defined in so far as 'participation in a general plan' for conducting an aggressive war was a punishable offence for those individuals holding top positions in financial, industrial, economic and political circles in Germany.[126]

For about nine weeks, Rummel was placed in a camp in Freising near Munich 'with about 200 persons, mainly generals and government officials'. His son was allowed to visit him there in mid-July and related afterwards that his father had only been interrogated once in the first three weeks. His interrogators had been interested in bank business with Istanbul and Prague. A few weeks after his release, he was again arrested in Stuttgart on 8 November 1945, and was transferred to Darmstadt in the following week. On 31 January 1946, word spread that Rummel was living in a hotel in Frankfurt '*de facto* under house arrest', that he was taken care of and was being provided with food by the bank's local branch.[127] Temporarily Rummel was imprisoned in Bad Mergentheim, and in August 1946 in Karlsruhe.[128] In April 1947, he was set free.[129] Following this, Rummel began to prepare for his 'denazification trial' in Stuttgart. However, the charges against him were dropped in October because he did not fall under Law No. 104 ('liberation law') of the military government.[130] He declined to accept an active position as board member with the bank, but did agree to advise all branches of the bank in the three Western zones, and was paid the same retirement pension as Abs starting on 1 January 1948.[131] From 1952 to 1957, he was once again active as vice-chairman of the supervisory board of the Süddeutsche Bank.

Oswald Rösler (b. 26 May 1887), a committed Catholic, was in the bank on 24 April 1945, as the Red Army commenced its shelling of Berlin. Wintermantel recalled in 1948: 'Mr Rösler and I left the city centre together by car as the shelling began. Mr Rösler had accommodation in Wannsee, I had a house in Gross-Glienicke near Gatow ... All men holding leading positions were ordered to report. Mr Rösler was able to walk to Berlin on 4 or 5 May, reported, was placed under observation, and was required to remain available to the Russians at the bank at all times.'[132] He was permitted to work actively in the head office in Berlin until mid-June. The banking commissar of the Soviet military government, Winikowsky, then offered him a top position at the Reichsbank, which was still operating as the city bank of Berlin.[133] Yet soon afterwards, on

17 June 1945, he was arrested by the Soviets,[134] moved around several times, and eventually interned in Buchenwald for four years until late January 1950.[135] It is possible that his arrest was connected with his reaction to the position offered to him by Winikowsky. This turn of events was in a way rather tragic, since Rösler had been suspected of being involved in the conspiracy to assassinate Hitler on 20 July 1944. In September 1944, he was arrested on charges of belonging to the Goerdeler circle and brought to trial in the infamous People's Court. Then he got off lightly; he was 'proven not guilty' in November 1944 and released from prison.[136]

In February 1950, the denazification committee for the district of Düsseldorf confirmed that Rösler had 'neither belonged to the party nor to one of its affiliations and had not furthered the cause of National Socialism in any way'.[137] He re-entered management immediately in the Düsseldorf successor bank and, starting in 1952, sat on the board of managing directors of the Rheinisch-Westfälische Bank AG. Once the post-war banking institutions were again reorganized into the Deutsche Bank in 1957, Rösler continued to participate actively as chairman (1957–59) and honorary chairman (1960–61) of the supervisory board of the Deutsche Bank. He also contributed significantly to the economic recovery of the Federal Republic in the 1950s, while serving on the supervisory boards of important industrial manufacturers, including his service as supervisory board chairman for Bayer and Mannesmann, for example. On his personal initiative, the Ausfuhrkredit AG was founded in March 1952, for which he acted as chairman of both the Credit Committee and the supervisory board. He was also a member of the board of the Bundesverbandes des privaten Bankgewerbes e.V. (Federation of Private Banking Business) from its founding in 1951.

Fritz Wintermantel and Dr Robert Frowein were also still in Berlin as the Red Army took over the city. Together with Rösler, Fritz Wintermantel (b. 26 April 1882) directed the new and exceptional business left to the head office. He had left the bank with Rösler on 24 April 1945, and was at first placed under 'basement arrest' in his weekend house in Gross-Glienicke by the Soviets following the invasion of the Red Army in Berlin. However, he managed to return to the bank by foot on either 13 or 14 May 1945, in order to help Rösler. Although he was interrogated by the Soviets, he was not arrested. In 1948, he described his own situation starting in mid-May 1945 thus: 'Mr Rösler was in the bank under quarantine – that was the expression used. I myself could move about the city without any obvious supervision after about fourteen days, during which time I also spent the night in the bank. It is quite a mystery as to why I was not arrested. Rösler and I became convinced that my decision not to run the risk of registering myself had proved to be the right one.'[138] At the time, Wintermantel lived at Bayernallee 10 in Charlottenburg. In the period between Rösler's arrest on 17 June 1945, and the complete closure of the head office on 4 March 1946, Wintermantel was the only acting board member in this Berlin office. Afterwards, he moved to Hamburg in order to head the directing office there, again as the only acting board member. Following the creation of the Rheinisch-Westfälische Bank as one of the ten successor banks to the Deutsche Bank, he moved to Freiligrathstrasse 13 in Düsseldorf on 17–18 September 1948.[139] There he received a letter dated 11 October 1948, from Custodian Dr Robert Lehr, who was performing board functions for this bank in the name of the British military government. Lehr placed Wintermantel in the position of 'executive vice-president with general power of attorney to represent the Rheinisch-Westfälische Bank in all business matters'.[140] Following the partial reconsolidation of the old Deutsche Bank into three successor institutions in 1952, the then 70-year-old Wintermantel acted as chairman of the Rheinisch-Westfälische Bank supervisory board until his death in July 1953.

Dr Robert Frowein (b. 4 January 1893) was taken by the Soviets from his home in Berlin-Neuwestend and brought to the bank on 8 May 1945. This had been initiated by Rösler, who was urgently waiting for support by a board colleague in the bank's head office in Berlin. From there, Frowein was deported by the Soviets on 11 May 1945,[141] and interned in the camps at Frankfurt an der Oder and at Jamlitz near Mühlberg until 20 August 1948. Due to ill health, he did not resume work until October 1949, now as a managing director at the Hessische Bank, one of the ten institutions created in the *Länder* by decentralizing the Deutsche Bank.[142] In 1952, Frowein joined Abs and Dr Walter Tron as a member of the board of managing directors at the Süddeutsche Bank. Once the three successor institutions were legally reconsolidated into the Deutsche Bank AG on 2 May 1957, with its headquarters in Frankfurt a.M., Frowein was one of the carryovers on the board of managing directors from those who had also served at the end of the Second World War, the others being Abs, Bechtolf and Plassmann. However, he died soon afterwards in December 1958.

The members of the supervisory board of the Deutsche Bank were also subject to the 'Instructions to Financial Institutions, No. 3, and to Government Financial Agencies' in the Western zones following the war, and were suspended regardless of their personal reputation. The Business Report for 1944 was a brief, type-written report presented by the board of managing directors on 14 April 1945, and approved in a simplified procedure by the board and three members of the supervisory board, one of whom was only a deputy member.[143] According to this report, the following 27 men sat on the supervisory board: Dr Karl Kimmich, Berlin, president; Hans Oesterlink, Berlin, vice-president; Dr Albert Pietzsch, Höllriegelskreuth near Munich, vice-president; Gustav Brecht, Cologne; Werner Carp, Hahnerhof near Ratingen; Dr Wolfgang Dierig, Langenbielau; Dr Hugo Eckener, Friedrichshaven a.B.; Otto Fitzner, Breslau; Richard Freudenberg, Weinheim (Baden); Franz Hasslacher, Vienna; Hermann Ludwig Fürst von Hatzfeld, Duke of Trachenberg, Trachenberg (Silesia); Dr Hugo Henkel, Düsseldorf; Dr Florian Klöckner, Dortmund-Löttringhausen; Dr Artur Koepchen, Essen; Dr Emil Kreibich, Schluckenau; Hermann R. Münchmeyer, Hamburg; Dr Günther

Quandt, Berlin; Philipp F. Reemtsma, Hamburg-Bahrenfeld; Dr Wolfgang Reuter, Duisburg; Dr Ernst Enno Russell, Berlin; Karl Schirner, Berlin; Max H. Schmid, Berlin; Dr Hermann Schmitz, Heidelberg; Dr Ernst Schoen von Wildenegg, Leipzig; Dr Hermann von Siemens, Berlin; Rudolf Stahl, Berlin; and Wilhelm Zangen, Düsseldorf.[144] The real power within the supervisory board lay in its Working Committee, created in 1935, which as a rule convened monthly, while its chairmen met nearly daily, in order to supervise the board of managing directors. The supervisory board had delegated decision-making authority to this committee for granting major loans (1 million RM or more). At the end of the war, its members were Kimmich as chairman, Pietzsch and Oesterlink as vice-chairmen, and Fitzner, Hasslacher, Reemtsma, Reuter, Russell and Zangen.[145]

As East–West tensions increased, the denazification policy of the Western Allies in general changed,[146] and both Bechtolf and Plassmann were permitted to regain their positions as managers of the directing office of the Deutsche Bank in Hamburg. About the same time, in late 1947 and early 1948, the suspended supervisory board members were informed that they could also resume their functions if they 'first, can obtain a special confirmation of non-incrimination, which can be issued by the government of the *Land*, or second, have either been given an exoneration certificate from the denazification committee and thus belong to Category V (exonerated) or have been listed in Category IV (nominal party member) without having their assets blocked or restrictions placed on their employment.'[147] There were several men who would never be in a position to fulfil these criteria due to their Nazi past, including Albert Pietzsch, who had been a friend of Hitler's starting back in the 1920s, had been an economic adviser to Hess beginning in 1934, and had served as President of the Reich Economic Chamber starting in 1936. Two others were Rudolf Stahl, chairman of the board of managing directors of the Salzdetfurth conglomoration and deputy head of the Reichsgruppe of Industry, and Philipp Reemtsma, tobacco manufacturer and Hermann Göring's close friend and financier. Others could not fulfil all the requirements at first and thus found substitutes to represent them: namely, Hermann Schmitz, the former boss of the I.G. Farben corporation, Wilhelm Zangen, chairman of the board at Mannesmann and head of the Reichsgruppe of Industry, Ernst Enno Russell, and Hermann von Siemens.[148] Some of the men had died by then: namely, Otto Fitzner as a forced labourer in Poland following the war, Karl Kimmich on 10 September 1945, who had accepted the chairmanship of the supervisory board following his resignation from the board of managing directors in 1942, Wolfgang Dierig in the spring of 1945, Wolfgang Reuter in late January 1947, and Florian Klöckner on 10 May 1947.[149] After the death of Werner Carp on 18 January 1950,[150] the supervisory board consisted only of the following 12 members living in the Federal Republic in February 1950: Oesterlink, Brecht, Fürst von Hatzfeld, Henkel, Kreibich, Münchmeyer, Quandt, Schirner, Schmid, Schoen von Wildenegg, von Siemens and Zangen. When Münchmeyer died a couple of months later, on 20 June 1950, Hermann

Schmitz was finally permitted to assume his seat once more, so that there were
again 12 supervisory board members to invite to the important board meeting
of the Deutsche Bank on 7 April 1952, at which it was deliberated how the old
Deutsche Bank could be dismantled into three successor institutions. Of these
12, only 9 were in attendance; Fürst von Hatzfeldt, Quandt and Schmitz asked
to be excused.[151] Up to this point, there had been only two meetings of the
supervisory board, at the headquarters of the Rheinisch-Westfälische Bank: the
first was on 14 October 1948, in Wuppertal-Elberfeld, and the second on
19 December 1949, in the bank's new head office in Düsseldorf.[152]

In February 1948, the chief economist at the Deutsche Bank, E.W. Schmidt,
was apparently in Berlin to discuss supervisory board matters with the then
presiding chairman, Hans Oesterlink, who would move from Berlin to Oldenburg for business reasons in early 1949. The letter Schmidt wrote to Oesterlink
on 19 February 1948, upon his return to Hamburg, demonstrates that there
were serious problems of a totally different kind to face besides those dealing
with the functioning of legal bodies within the bank: 'I was not able to start my
trip to Hamburg until four o'clock in the afternoon with the normal interzonal
train. The trip proceeded as always: after Magdeburg the train became extremely
overcrowded, in Hanover at midnight, changed trains into an even more overcrowded train, which after a stop in Uelzen lasting an hour and a half reached
Hamburg at about seven o'clock in the morning. All this in unlighted train
compartments and thus a trip of more than twelve hours in the dark. It is not
an exaggeration to describe travel under such conditions as human torture.'[153]

2. Berlin at the end of the war and the bank policy of the Soviet military government and of the Berlin Allied Kommandatura

The last normal working day at the head office of the Deutsche Bank was
Saturday, 21 April 1945. Around noon, the first Russian grenades blasted the
city centre. On the following Monday, very few bank employees reported for
work. The city centre and with it the banking district had become a battle-
ground.[154] On 28 April 1945, two days before Hitler committed suicide, Colonel
General N. Bersarin officially assumed control of Berlin. In his capacity as
military commandant of the city and head of the new occupation regime, he
issued Order No. 1,[155] which contained stipulations for banks: 'The owners of
banking houses and bank directors are to temporarily halt all financial business.
All safes are to be sealed immediately. Reports are to be submitted immediately
to the military commandant concerning the state of affairs at the banking
institution. It is categorically forbidden for banking officials to remove any
assets.' Infractions were to be severely punished 'according to martial law'.
Further it was stated: 'In addition to the currency of the Reich in circulation, it
is mandatory to circulate the occupation currency issued by the Allied military
authorities.'

The war ended somewhat later for the assistant vice-president (Prokurist) Martin Rosenbrock. During these critical days in Berlin, he was one of about 20 people who maintained a well-run emergency service in the Deutsche Bank offices located on the Mauerstrasse in the city centre. These people even slept in the bank building.[156] Rosenbrock noted in his diary:

'1 May: Extraordinarily heavy shelling continues. Counterattack by German artillery. Can hear machine-gun fire. The Russians are supposed to have reached the corner of Kochstrasse and Hedemannstrasse already. Tensions are rising. It cannot continue much longer like it did today. An SS-unit appears about nine o'clock this evening, completely exhausted from the intense fighting on Hedemannstrasse. We give the men something to drink. Around 11 p.m. we notice that German troops are continually moving in the direction of Friedrichstrasse. It looks like everything is about to fall apart ... The shelling lessens, then stops. It is the second night of our vigil. Only now have we learned that Hitler committed suicide on 30 April.

2 May: At 8:30 a.m. the Russian vanguards appear on Mauerstrasse and at the gates of the bank. They behave well, ask whether there are armed units in the building ... I am ordered to bring out a *Volkssturm* unit, which was camping out in our basement, unarmed, and to urge them to surrender, which the men are eventually convinced to do. New units are constantly following the first ones, with the former being much rougher. About noontime, Commissar Ivanow arrives with his staff. Confiscates our cash resources of 498,130 RM as well as several items of value from the safe in the steel vault of the manager's office.'[157]

The items of value consisted of a Zeiss-Ikon cinema projector, a camera, two radios, two watches and a brown suitcase. A list was typed up noting both the sum and the denomination of the money taken, the items confiscated and the names of the three owners of the items. This was then signed by four members of the Soviet commission and a receipt given.[158] Such correctness would prove to be an exception, however. Arbitrary confiscation was a daily occurrence in the following weeks, including the use of explosives and welding tools to open steel vaults and safes for which no key was available. In all, the Soviets confiscated 39 million RM in cash from the Deutsche Bank in Berlin,[159] namely German currency amounting to 7.7 million RM from the head office of the Berlin branch, 8.56 million RM from the main cash office, and 19.45 million RM from the deposit-taking branches (*Depositenkassen*), as well as 3.57 million RM in gold and foreign currency taken primarily from customer safety deposits. Compared to the 7 billion RM that had been transferred in time to the central cash office in Hildesheim, the amount confiscated is rather insignificant. However, all foreign stocks, bonds and debentures were 'packed up in boxes and bags and taken away' by the Soviet commission.[160] Although the Soviets had not obtained possession of these securities legally, western banks also participated in putting them back on the market. The Soviets were also interested in confiscating documents with more political value. On 16 May, Rosenbrock wrote: 'two generals appeared this afternoon ...; documents were taken from von Papen's safe'.[161]

The number of employees working regularly at the bank in Berlin had dwindled from nearly 6,000 to almost 3,000 by the end of the war due to military call-ups.[162] Of these, only 40 people showed up for work on 9 May.[163] As the days and weeks passed, more and more reported back until there were nearly 1,200 at the bank by 28 May. Unless commanded by Russian troops to help out elsewhere, the bank employees spent their time taking inventory of the remaining valuable items and, for the most part, clearing away debris in the bank and its immediate vicinity. The board members Wintermantel and Rösler directed the clean-up during this period and handled the remaining bank business, which consisted chiefly of following Soviet military instructions on what was to be done for the requisition of valuables still found in the bank facilities.

On 7 May, a high-ranking Russian officer, a bank director from Leningrad, demanded that all safes be opened, but at the same time instructed the bank to return the contents of these safes to their private customers. This was to be done within ten days.[164] Everything was to be registered: the deposited valuables and the safe contents belonging to customers as well as bank employees. On 15 May, Rosenbrock noted: 'At 6 p.m. it was posted on our building that the private owners of deposited valuables and safe contents were to pick up their valuables by 23 May, between 9 a.m. and 6 p.m, daily. Any items not claimed by then would be declared as forfeited. The technical plausibility of this demand – there are about 8,000 strongboxes alone – appears impossible.'[165] Another source lists 14,500 rented strongboxes and 7,538 deposited valuables, although for 31 December 1943.[166] By 6 p.m. on 23 May, '458 safes and 248 deposited valuables for customers, 877 safes and 644 deposited valuables for employess, a total of 2,227' had been registered, in addition to 29 safes and 31 deposited valuables for the August-Thyssen Bank.[167] This list was submitted to a Russian commission on the following day.

No one was certain what the future would hold for the bank, either at the head office of the bank or at the headquarters of the Soviet commandant. Final instructions were anticipated from Moscow. For the time being, the bank was forbidden to permit its customers access to 'old' deposits, meaning those accumulated prior to the end of the war. No funds were provided for bank employee wages at first, and only insufficient amounts were made available starting in June. 'On the other hand, cash transactions have been authorized for "new" deposits and withdrawals, according to press and radio announcements. Troublesome are the new independent "district" banks like those in Spandau, Wilmersdorf, Friedenau and Schöneberg, which are being set up in part through the confiscation of our deposit-taking branches.'[168] At any rate, Dr Erich Siebert, the city treasurer of the new Berlin City Council, installed by the Soviets, obliged the banks in a memo dated 15 May 1945 to accept money from their customers.[169] This contradicted the wording of the Soviet commandant's Order No. 1 quoted above.

There were also marked differences of opinion among the Soviet officers in the bank. One permitted the continuation of the registration action, another stopped it the next day. On 28 May, a notice was posted at the bank that the registered valuables would not be returned to their owners before 1 June. On that day, the Soviets drove off with 20 truckloads of deposited valuables from the safes of the Deutsche Bank, apparently without having made any distinction between registered and unregistered valuables. On 2 June, the bank was instructed not to return any registered deposited valuables to their owners.[170] And finally, two days later, the Soviet officer in charge informed Rosenbrock and the bank 'that all deposited valuables and safe contents – regardless of whether registered or not – were being "confiscated", that no distinction would be made between German and foreign property, and that the valuables that had been shipped off were to be distributed to the inhabitants of Russian territory plundered by the Germans. The response to my question on how to handle Jews and former prisoners of concentration camps: they should take up the matter with the district commandant.'[171]

On 4 June, the new rulers in Berlin, including the city council installed by the Soviets, apparently decided temporarily to prohibit the Deutsche Bank and numerous other private banks in Berlin from conducting business altogether, even transactions on 'new' deposits. This was announced unofficially in the bank the following day. Officially, the decision was made public later in an ordinance of the City Council of Berlin, Department of Finance and Taxation, dated 5 June 1945, on 'The Reorganization of Banking in Berlin'.[172] The following is an excerpt:

'With regard to the resumption of cash transactions, especially at banks and savings institutions, experience to date has shown that the large and complex machinery of the many various banks is too complicated for reconstruction within the city district of Berlin. Furthermore, most of the Berlin banks are the head offices for all of Germany, namely for regions for which the city of Berlin is not currently responsible and with which it does not yet have any contact. In order quickly and effectively to provide for the economy within the city of Berlin, and in order to be able to control currency circulation, the banking system must be simplified and standardized.

The City Council of Berlin has therefore decided, in agreement with the Commandant, that only one bank will be permitted to conduct cash transactions, namely the Berlin City Bank.

The Reichsbank has been designated as the new Berlin City Bank. From this day forward, it will operate under the name "Berlin City Bank" (Berliner Stadtbank) and is thereby subordinate to the City Council and the responsible department head of the Council, Dr Siebert.

One district bank has been established within each of the twenty-one administrative districts (Friedenau counts as an independent administrative district). These are the former sub-offices of the Reichsbank or, where such an office did not exist, newly established banks. The former city banks, Giro-savings banks and their deposit-taking branches will all be retained as branches of the new Berlin City Bank. All other banks and banking institutions in Berlin, public, co-operative and private, must halt their cash transactions immediately. They are temporarily on hold. All cash funds of the closed banks must be turned over immediately to the new Berlin City Bank.

This ordinance also clarifies the issue of the release of deposits at the banks. Release is not possible as long as the banks are in abeyance. All applications to grant funds for wage payments, rebuilding purposes, the provision of food and goods for the Berlin population are to be submitted from now on to the district banks of the Berlin City Bank, which will open an account if the work and goods are deemed necessary.'

The Sparkasse der Stadt Berlin (Savings Bank of Berlin) was thus not included in this 'abeyance ordinance'. In 1945, it was the only remaining credit institution in business besides the chief office of the renamed Reichsbank and its sub-offices in Berlin, if one does not take into account the reinstated Wohnungsbau-Kreditanstalt (Home Building Credit Bureau). In order better to distinguish the Berlin City Bank from the Sparkasse, also commonly called the 'Stadtbank' earlier, the former was renamed the Berliner Stadtkontor later that year. The Sparkasse was only permitted to conduct new business and merely administer its earlier assets. Its former Giro affiliation, the Berliner Stadtbank-Girozentrale der Stadt Berlin, which had taken over the actual banking business from the Sparkasse in the 1920s, was also placed in abeyance by the ordinance. As a result, the Sparkasse not only had to handle such business in its branch offices once again, it was now also charged with managing the former business of its Giro affiliation.[173] Although the ordinance ordered the other banks to close for business, the personnel were still permitted to work in the bank buildings, not only to secure the premises and furnishings, but also to produce the closing balance as of 30 April 1945, and to supply the occupation authorities with all the information and data they demanded.

Rosenbrock wrote on 13 June: 'Letters from the City Council, Department for Finance and Taxation, signed Dr Siebert, dated 4 June, arrive on 12 and 13 June by messenger and by post, in which we are notified to suspend temporarily all business transactions and to submit the cash balance, including funds from new deposits made since 14 May.'[174] The next day the bank tried to influence the situation when Wintermantel went to see the Berlin City Council and Rösler talked to the Soviet commissar responsible for the Reichsbank, Captain Winikowsky.[175] By the following day it was evident to the bank management that these efforts had failed and that all hope was lost for a revision of this decision, which affected all banks in Berlin except the newly established Berlin City Bank. On 16 June, Rosenbrock noted: 'A black day in the history of the Deutsche Bank. It has been posted that the employees in Berlin are being temporarily laid off, those exempted from this will be notified. It is recommended to seek new employment elsewhere. The situation is very grave. Hopes for a brighter future waning.'[176]

The arrival of Soviet military occupation was not the only indication that power had changed hands in Berlin. German citizens who had been stigmatized as political enemies during the Hitler regime were now also gaining power and influence. This became obvious both in the external affairs of the head office as well as in the internal matters of personnel. The Soviet commission, which had first appeared at the bank on 3 May and had since controlled it, was helped 'in part by German communists'[177] for such tasks as bringing in employees for interrogation, ordering the opening of safes and vaults, and transporting the contents of these away. On 22 May, Rosenbrock's diary entry indicated the development of a new power structure within the bank: 'The antifascist committee created a few days ago at the bank is in contact with the Russian commandant.'[178]

The Soviet troops who had been stationed in the bank for weeks and had protected it against looting pulled out on 17 June. They took Rösler with them. He had already been taken into custody twice for interrogation; this time he remained in Soviet detention until late January 1950. Frowein had also been arrested on 11 May 1945. In his first letter to the directing office in Hamburg on 18 July 1945, Wintermantel complained not only that he had received almost no word from Abs and Bechtolf in Hamburg, and that he had no idea where Plassmann could be currently found, but also that he had been the only board member present in the Berlin head office for more than four weeks. 'I am constantly surrounded by Dr Kessler, Kaiser, Günkel, Ulbricht, Wieland, Schirmer and others.' Every day he was 'being bombarded with thousands of questions, making the work far more than my physical strength can endure'.[179] Wintermantel, Kimmich and Oesterlink wrote numerous letters from July to September 1945 imploring Plassmann and particularly Abs to return to Berlin. However, the three board members in Hamburg felt that the Western zones needed their presence more urgently. They were also well aware of the threat of their arrest should they return to Berlin, as the fate of their colleagues von Halt, Frowein and Rösler had demonstrated. In response to this expressed concern, Wintermantel called on the men to show 'some civil courage ... But perhaps the bank will be closed soon anyhow, and then you will have been right in the end.' And indeed they were.

News from other branches of the bank arrived in Berlin in late June. 23 June: 'The first news from a branch: Director Otte (Görlitz) reports on the local situation, which is no better than here.'[180] Then, a few days later on 29 June: 'News from Meiningen, Magdeburg [both still occupied by the Americans at the time], Dortmund, Hamburg [both in the British zone]: all report that the banking and cash transactions are functioning far better than they are here. At almost all locations, withdrawals are permitted from "old" accounts in maximum amounts ranging from 200 to 500 RM.'[181]

In anticipation of the arrival of the Western powers in West Berlin, truckloads of bank documents were now being smuggled past Soviet guards at the head office and the deposit-taking branches in the Eastern sector of the city, and transported to such branches available in West Berlin. Even the customer account sheets that had been deposited in the vaults of the Reichsbank could later be worked on 'under somewhat dangerous conditions' because a German watchman, who was in possession of the keys to the vaults, granted employees access to the documents 'for weeks'.[182] Otherwise, the bank employees spent most of the second half of 1945 in complying with the directives of the Berlin City Council, the Soviet occupational authorities, the Kommandatura – that is, the Allied military government of Berlin – and the Control Council – the Allied government of Germany as a whole – on locating and confiscating the property belonging to Nazi leaders, organizations and committed sympathizers, to governments and to leading names in public life, big business and finance (Law No. 52), and with directives on reporting and surrendering foreign assets belonging to German nationals (Law No. 53).[183]

On 2 July 1945, American troops entered Berlin in exchange for handing over to the Soviets Thuringia and other western regions of the Soviet occupation zone.[184] However, there was still uncertainty at the bank concerning the boundaries of the occupation zones within the city. Rosenbrock wrote on 11 July: 'For the first time it has become known that our bank district will be included in the American zone, which will extend from the west to Friedrichstrasse and thus include the Reichsbank complex.'[185] This turned out to be a false rumour. That same day, the Allied Kommandatura took over the administration of the city and decided: 'All orders and directives previously issued by the garrison chief and the Red Army military commandant of the city of Berlin and from the German authorities subordinate to Allied control ... are to remain in effect until further notice.'[186] Yet hope was rekindled at the head office by the Potsdam Tripartite Conference, which took place from 17 July to 2 August 1945. Rosenbrock expressed it in this way on 2 August: 'it is hoped that the agreements from the Potsdam Conference, which ended today, will relax the monetary and credit apparatus: for us this is *the question of survival*'.[187]

As it turned out, of course, the centre of Berlin and thus the head office located on Mauerstrasse remained in the Soviet sector of the occupied capital. And although it had been agreed at the Potsdam Conference to treat Germany as a single economic unit during its occupation and to hand the Allied Control Council jurisdiction over financial matters expressly for this purpose, the banking policy of the Soviet-occupied sector of Germany, on one side, and that of the three Western occupation zones, on the other, were never unified. It took time just for the three Western powers finally to agree upon a common policy. Granted, the banking system in the Soviet zone was decentralized, as also later happened in the Western zones. But beyond this, all private bank property was practically abolished, except for a few remaining smaller private banks and agricultural and commercial credit co-operatives, which were allowed to resume business starting in mid-1946.[188] Instead, the economy was supplied with credit and cash through a new network of *Land* and provincial banks, upon which savings institutions were dependent at the district, city and community level. This reorganization was based on Order 01, issued by the supreme commander of the Soviet military administration in Germany, Marshall G.K. Shukow, on 23 July 1945. The following is an excerpt from this order, known as 'The Reorganization of the German Financial and Credit Institutions':

'1. In order for provincial governments and the governments of the united *Länder* uniformly to administer urban and communal finances and organize the banking system, provincial banks are to be established, financial departments set up in administrations, and city and community banks created. The financial departments and the banks must be organized by 5 August 1945. Special guidelines are to be followed for the operations of the banks and financial departments ...

3. Industry, commerce and the economy as a whole are to be supplied with a steady flow of credit and cash.

Funds are to be transferred from the budgets of the provinces in order to ensure the proper operation of the banks to be established.

4. In view of the bankruptcy facing German banks, no withdrawals can be made from current accounts ...

8. No payments are to be made on loans of any sort that were issued before the capitulation of Germany (debt cancellations, interest payments, bond drawing).

9. No withdrawals may be made from old deposits of the savings banks if the assets of these banks have been exhausted by the fascist state.

10. Savings banks are to be opened in the provinces, unified *Länder*, cities and communities. Deposits and withdrawals may be made freely in these institutions at an interest rate of 2.5 per cent for demand deposits and at the previous interest rate for all other types of deposit.'[189]

Whereas the newly established institutions were being financed out of the funds of the various governmental units, point 8 of this order, namely the halting of debt service for all pre-armistice debentures, meant the demise of the older institutions, be it the big banks, savings banks or other previously established banks. During the war, these had been forced by the national government to underwrite the war bonds of the Reich. Because the banks could not pass these commitments on to the public or anywhere outside the banking system, an increasing percentage of their means were tied up in such paper, 'whether they wanted to or not', according to the *Tägliche Rundschau*, the Red Army publication for the German population in an article entitled 'The German people financed Hitler's war' (no. 39, 28 June 1945). 'The banks and savings banks were robbed of their autonomy. They were not allowed to grant credit where they wanted, could not loan money to commerce and industry without reporting it to Hitler's appointed commissar for credit (Reichsbank).' The big banks, too, were explicitly mentioned as targets and victims of such coercive measures by Hitler's regime.[190]

At this point in time, it was emphasized that the banks and thus the head offices of the big banks in Berlin were only 'currently' or 'temporarily' closed. Although the Soviets were indeed then in the process of reorganizing the banking system into a decentralized structure with state and communal institutions, they were probably still receptive to forming a common banking policy with the Western Allies which would have enabled the big banks to survive with their private ownership intact. It has been argued that the closure of the old credit institutions and the creation of the new ones were motivated less by the ideological aim of quickly nationalizing the economy in the Soviet occupation zone than by a pragmatic goal: by confiscating currency and simultaneously stripping the private bank customers of their claims to currency, the occupation authorities intended to increase their purchasing power and ensure that a greater percentage of the demand for goods and services from German production was paid for with the newly issued occupation currency, 'the Allied military mark', which was legal tender like the Reichsmark.[191] The Soviets were in a position to issue the occupation currency in unlimited amounts because they had demanded and eventually been given duplicates of the plates.[192] Unlike the Western Allies, they had objected to having the Allied military marks printed solely in Washington, DC, for all four powers starting in the spring of 1944. The complementary effects of this step in 1944 and the closure of the banks in the Soviet zone in 1945 enhanced the ability of the Soviets in the post-war period to place massive demands on the German national product simply, quickly and without any control from its allies. Since the Soviet Union had suffered the most from the war in comparison with its allies, and since its zone proved to be the most costly to occupy, the behaviour of the Soviets in the banking issue is understandable from economic and financial perspectives that transcend ideological considerations.[193]

The Soviet side retreated into its ideological shell only after it became increasingly clear in the years to follow that the Western powers were neither going to fulfil the great expectations of the Soviets for resource transfers from western Germany to both the Soviet zone and the USSR itself, nor willing to pay any price to ensure that Germany was treated as a single economic unit. In this regard, the Marshall Plan probably came three years too late. This plan provided for huge resource transfers from the United States to European countries, and might well have been accepted by the Soviet Union had the plan been launched before the Cold War froze East–West relations in a state of hostility.

It appears that the closed private banks in the Soviet sector of Berlin were optimistic that the arrival of the Western Allies in the city would result in a reopening of the banks, for they continued to retain employees and to conduct internal business in preparation for this long-awaited day. On 1 March 1946, the Deutsche Bank Senior Vice-Presidents Hermann Kaiser and Karl Günkel submitted the bank's application at the Department of Banking of the Berlin City Council (with translations of the application for the financial committee of the Allied Kommandatura) to reopen the Deutsche Bank and its remaining 38 deposit-taking branches in Berlin for 'new', i.e. post-armistice, business. They stressed the advantages this would have for the rebuilding of the Berlin economy, which the bank could achieve thanks to its previously prominent presence in the city's economic life and the goodwill thus linked to its name. Hermann Kaiser and Karl Günkel also attempted to convince the Soviet occupation authorities to reopen the Berlin head office and deposit-taking branches by pointing out that assets in all of the zones would back up the liabilities of the Berlin branches. They tried to win the consent of the Western powers by arguing that the reopening of the bank in Berlin would improve the position of the bank's foreign creditors.[194]

The initiative for this application had been prompted 'by British and American advice'[195] in order to discover which direction the Soviet side would pursue in its banking policy. The reaction of the Soviet military administration to the application was quick and clear. It felt compelled to enforce its former closure order of 28 April 1945, by again occupying approximately 30 banks in the eastern sector of the city in March 1946 and by firing all bank employees.[196] This action also included the head office of the Deutsche Bank. The bank was closed completely by the Soviet occupation authorities on 4 March 1946. The employees were not allowed even to enter the premises on Mauerstrasse from that point on. Thereupon they moved their business quarters to the deposit-taking branch at Victoria-Luise-Platz 9 in the western part of Berlin.[197]

The complete shutdown of the headquarters of the big banks in Berlin had been agreed upon with the Western Allies. This is proven by the fact that Lieutenant-Colonel George H. Auffinger, Jr from the Finance Division of the American military government in Frankfurt summoned representatives of the three big banks and the Reichsbank director of Frankfurt on 8 March 1946, in order to notify them of the telegraphed instructions he had received from Berlin: namely, that the banks, now that their head offices in Berlin had been closed, must make sure that their branch operations neither requested nor followed any decisions or instructions from places outside of the US zone. Similar orders were issued for the British zone in early March, except that the emphasis was placed at the other end: the directing office in Hamburg was explicitly forbidden to issue instructions beyond the boundaries of the British zone.[198]

Following the final closure of the Deutsche Bank headquarters in Berlin, Wintermantel moved to Hamburg to work with the directing office there. Since it was still thought that the 'dormant' bank would someday reopen, the staff in Berlin were not fired, but were suspended without pay until the number of employees had been reduced to 450 people who could work in the Western sector of the city. The income at the time for a simple employee ranged from 225 to 300 RM; for vice-presidents, assistant vice-presidents and senior vice-presidents, 325–450 RM. The funds to pay these wages were provided primarily by the central cash office in Hildesheim. Local income came from renting bank facilities. The building on Mauerstrasse was rented to the Social Democratic daily newspaper *Vorwärts* in 1946.[199]

The only issue yet to be settled was that of bank property rights. The forerunner in this case proved to be Saxony, where the communist idea had attracted more support, starting in the nineteenth century, than in other regions of the Soviet zone. On 24 October 1946, the *Land* government issued an ordinance empowering the Saxon State Bank (Sächsische Landesbank), itself established by ordinance on 14 August 1945, and the new savings banks to take over the property of the closed credit institutions. Not until early 1948 were laws finally passed in each of the *Länder* of the Soviet zone, stipulating that ownership of the land, buildings and inventory of the closed banks was to be transferred without compensation to each of the respective *Länder*, retroactive to 8 May 1945.[200]

In 1946 the Berlin City Council undertook an initiative that might have led to the reopening of the 'dormant' banks, although under completely different conditions. On order of the Allied Kommandatura, the Berliner Volksbank, a credit co-operative, was granted permission to resume business on 5 January 1946, in the various facilities of the previous Volksbanks, then in abeyance, which the new institutions would manage as branches. This was the first and for many years the only case in which a closed private institution of credit was allowed to reopen after the war.[201] On 28 January 1946, the deputy treasurer, Willi Rumpf, summoned Günkel from the Deutsche Bank in order to discuss with him his plans for reopening the 'big three' banks. He proposed that these banks consolidate into one, as had the Berlin Volksbanks, and solicit from their customers new liable equity capital, to which the city of Berlin would itself contribute 25 per cent. But Rumpf rejected the idea of integrating the capital of the Berlin banks with the capital of the branches in West Germany. Despite the decision at the Potsdam Conference to treat Germany as a single economic unit, regional cash transfers were to be organized not by the banks themselves, but by military administrative agencies. However, Günkel and the Deutsche Bank were not at all interested in the prospect of creating a mammoth bank in Berlin that would operate under state tutelage and remain decoupled from the network of branches in the West.[202]

On 28 August 1946, Rumpf summoned two representatives from each of the three big banks for a 'meeting on the issue of the banking business'. Attending this meeting for the Deutsche Bank were Günkel and Kaiser. The central topic this time focused on how the banks could collect on their outstanding loans.

Again, Rumpf proposed a solution based on the public sector instead of the private sector. The banks were to be combined into an administrative agency. This plan was developed further in the months that followed and was finally accepted at the four-power level. On 22 May 1947, Communiqué No. 65 was issued by the four Allied commanders-in-chief, instructing the finance committee of the Allied military government of Berlin to set up a 'commission for collecting on previous loans made by the banks in abeyance', the so-called Collection Commission. This commission was answerable only to the Allied Kommandatura, and its four members were selected by the occupation authorities. These four men were Otto Kuhn, Willy Huhn, Robert Zoeller and Rudolf Gleimius.[203] The banks were obligated to submit their accounts-receivable ledgers to the commission. Payments made since the summer of 1947 were credited to the banks on blocked accounts at the Berliner Stadtkontor (the renamed Reichsbank). However, the banks were never given access to these accounts.[204] The funds were used, in fact, to boost the liquidity of the Stadtkontor, the foster-child of the Soviet occupation power, at the expense of the dormant banks and their old customers.

By 1 July 1946, the Soviets had created a banking commission at the Deutsche Zentralfinanzverwaltung (DZFV: Division of German Central Finances), which was responsible for the Soviet zone. The purpose of this commission was to 'secure the business documents and securities from the head offices of the closed German banks', but at first only for the state credit institutions in the Soviet sector of Berlin; the commission was also to function as a trustee or administrator with full signatory power in place of the usual signatories. This practice was tolerated by the three Western powers. On 3 November 1947, however, DZFV President Henry Meyer announced publicly that the practice would be officially extended to include specifically named private banks, including all of the big banks.[205] The losses in securities that the banks suffered due to the activities of this commission, which itself was strictly prohibited from giving the banks involved any information on accounts and deposited securities, contributed greatly to the chaos that made it necessary later to pass the Securities Settlement Act (*Wertpapierbereinigungsgesetz*).[206]

Starting on 17 December 1946, and continuing throughout the following weeks, the Soviets transported truckloads of documents, chiefly securities, from the head office of the Deutsche Bank (and other banks in the centre of Berlin) to the Berlin Stadtkontor. Karl Günkel sent three memoranda, delivered both by mail and in person, with detailed information on this action to Hans A. Adler, the head of the banking section at the Finance Division of the American military government. The military governments of the Western powers considered the Soviet action to be a violation of the four-power status of Berlin. American financial experts had known since early December 1946 that the complete lists of certificate numbers of all securities administered by the head office of the Deutsche Bank until 19 April 1945 were kept in a deposit-taking branch of the bank in the American sector of the city. However, following the founding of the Collection Commission, the Soviets began again to remove business documents from the closed banks in their sector in order to undermine the demand for retaining any further employees in the closed banks. They turned over these documents to a German agency answerable only to the Soviet military administration (SMAD) and not to the Allied Kommandatura of Berlin; this action finally prompted the three Western powers to lodge official protests to the financial committee of the Allied military government of Berlin on 5 August 1947. Contrary to their position in creating the Collection Commission, the Soviets now argued that only the 'new' banks and not the old, closed ones fell under the jurisdiction of the Allied Kommandatura.[207]

The Soviet member of the Finance Directorate of the Allied Control Council presented a report on 13 November 1947, concerning allegedly illegal activities of the three big banks in the Western sector of Berlin. The Americans, in turn, reported that the Deutsche Bank maintained its head office at Viktoria-Luise Platz 9 in the American sector and that the 30 deposit-taking branches with about 190 employees operated chiefly in the American and British sectors; yet these were only preparing for final liquidation, managing the remaining investments, and providing information, often for the military government on behalf of customers from Allied countries. The other two big banks were similarly active in both the scope and magnitude of their activities. As of 17 December 1947, the banking committee of the Finance Division could not determine any illegal activities by the big banks in Berlin. This quickly blocked Soviet efforts to have all branches of the big banks in West Berlin closed completely, as they were in the Eastern sector of the city.[208]

The currency reform and the partition of Berlin in 1948 led the three remaining Western commanders in the Allied Kommandatura to attempt to prevent the Collection Commission from collecting bank debts from West Berlin residents, and from thereby obtaining the new Deutschmarks. This was particularly necessary after the East Berlin magistrate confiscated the property of the big banks in that half of the city, including the funds in the blocked accounts at the Berlin Stadtkontor, by issuing on 10 May 1949 an 'ordinance for the transformation of private companies and other economic enterprises into public property'.[209] The losses incurred by the Deutsche Bank through this action amounted only to about 350,000 Ostmarks. But this sum included nearly 2.5 million RM that had been converted by the currency reform to Ostmarks at a ratio of ten to one. Another difficulty was that the payments in Deutschmarks by West Berlin debtors were to be made no longer to the blocked accounts of the respective creditor banks, but to a post office account of the Collection Commission in West Berlin, thus not discharging the debtor of his obligation to any degree.[210]

Therefore the Allied Kommandatura disbanded the Collection Commission on 14 June 1949, and replaced it with a 'committee for the dormant Berlin credit institutions'.[211] The six men appointed to this committee were Karl Günkel

(Deutsche Bank), Dr Ottomar Benz (Centralboden), Dr Erich Trost (Federation of Private Banking Business), Fritz Tuve (delegated by the French administration), Dr Henning (public banks) and Martin Groepler or Dr Claus (Berliner Zentralbank). This committee worked out the guidelines that would enable the dormant banks to collect on outstanding loans themselves, as well as guidelines for other activities; it also supervised these activities. Debtors could now pay off their loans only to their creditors and would thus be legally discharged. In addition, the dormant banks were authorized (a) to register 'grandfather accounts' (*Uraltkonten*), meaning accounts that had existed before 8 May 1945; (b) to collect and register ownership claims to securities for their later settlement; and (c) to review ownership claims to securities in a validation process.[212]

Once the 1949 ordinances on regulating pre-armistice accounts had been enacted and the Securities Settlement Act had taken effect on 1 October of that same year, these authorizations became very important for the work facing the dormant banks. On the basis of this Act, destroyed or lost securities were declared void and replaced by new ones. The validation of claims required considerable work. Between 1 October 1949 and 1 January 1951, the number of employees at the Deutsche Bank in Berlin increased from 130 to 537 as suspended employees were reinstated. This was by far the greatest number of people the bank had employed since its total shutdown in March 1946.[213] For the first time since this shutdown, the dormant Berlin banks had once again been given functions to perform.[214]

Following the separate elections in the Western sectors of Berlin in December 1948, in which Ernst Reuter became mayor, Karl Günkel proposed at a bank 'board' meeting in Elberfeld on 18 December 1948 to seek permission from the Western Allies to establish a bank in Berlin from financial resources available in the regional institutions of the Deutsche Bank in West Germany. The 'board' approved the measure, and Karl Günkel received the go-ahead from the Allied Kommandatura, followed by the permission of the supervisory board for banking of the West Berlin City Council on 1 September 1949 – that is, after the lifting of the Berlin Blockade – to establish the Berliner Disconto Bank AG with capital stock totalling 500,000 DM. The capital stock was provided from the bank's regional institutions in the newly established Federal Republic. The Berliner Disconto Bank opened on 1 October 1949, with initially 18 employees. By the end of 1956, this number had risen to 1,234, and the bank was operating more than 24 deposit-taking branches.[215] At about the same time, both the Commerzbank group and the Dresdner Bank group were doing nearly the same thing; the former founded what was later to be known as the Berliner Commerzbank AG, while the latter established the Bank für Handel und Industrie AG in Berlin.

On 16 June 1950, the Allied Kommandatura issued an ordinance that placed the power to license private banks generally in the hands of German authorities: namely, the supervisory board for banking of the West Berlin City Council in agreement with the Berliner Zentralbank. This step simplified the licensing process considerably.[216] The Berliner Zentralbank had been established on 20 March 1949, with capital amounting to 5 million DM, raised by the city of (West) Berlin. It assumed the majority of the functions previously performed by the Currency Commission that had been set up by the Allied Bank Commission in June 1948 in conjuction with the currency reform. Among these functions were the issuance of bank notes, which were at first still marked as special Berlin notes, and the handling of payments with West Germany, which was still subject to authorization until 25 January 1950. Rudolf Gleimius became president of the executive board. The bank performed the same functions in Berlin that the Land Central Banks did in the Federal Republic.[217]

Just about the time that the authority to license banks was being transferred from the Allied Kommandatura to German officials, the Berliner Stadtkontor West was re-established on 21 June 1950, no longer as a public bank, but as a private one, and renamed Berliner Bank AG. This bank had been founded in conjunction with the partitioning of Berlin *de facto* with the currency reform in Berlin of 24 June 1948 and *de jure* since the end of 1948. Capital stock amounting to 10 million DM had been provided solely by the West Berlin City Council then in office, and therefore its officials were granted the corresponding degree of influence on the bank's supervisory board.[218]

The Berlin *Altbankengesetz* (Old Bank Act) and the *Altbanken-Bilanz-Gesetz* (Old Bank Balance Sheet Act) did not go into effect until 15 December 1953, following a two-year period of preparation and of overcoming objections by both the Allied authorities and the Federal Finance Minister. These laws guaranteed old banks the right to be relicensed for 'new' business under certain conditions. The degree to which these banks were actually interested in being relicensed was usually in direct proportion to the amount of equalization claims awarded to them in place of the devalued Reich bonds by the public officials in Berlin and Bonn.[219] However, neither the Deutsche Bank nor the other two big banks were interested in having their original establishments reopened in West Berlin, since they were already operating subsidiaries there of their new West German banks, which by then had already been legally decoupled from the original Berlin banks in accordance with stock company law.

3. The position of the banks in the Western zones during the initial phase of occupation

As early as 1944, the forces fighting in the British–American regions were equipped with straightforward guidelines on the measures to be taken immediately in occupied German territory. The officers of the occupation forces had undergone actual instruction on the matter. The *SHAEF Handbook for Military Government in Germany Prior to Defeat or Surrender* served as their textbook and manual. It had been composed during March–May 1944 in London by the German Country Unit, a unit within the Supreme Headquarters, Allied Expeditionary Force (SHAEF), that had been set up primarily for this purpose. However, six months passed before it was finally approved by the proper American and British authorities, once some small changes had been made.[220] It had been published as a loose-leaf manual in order to facilitate changes and updates in policy and procedure. In December 1944, General Dwight D. Eisenhower, Allied supreme commander of the armed forces, ordered it to be distributed among the troops. This handbook and the Technical Manuals that were published in conjunction with it on special political matters each contained several hundred pages of instructions on how to enforce military government in the civil sector. These instructions were specific to the point of dictating the wording of laws, instructions, permits, questionnaires and forms that were to be used and indeed were used in the occupied territories.[221] The manual pertinent to banking was the *Financial and Property Control Technical Manual*.[222]

The most important passage in the guidelines for bank policy stated that it was imperative 'to utilize, in so far as it is consistent with Military Government politics, the financial machinery already operative in Germany'.[223] This was the precise opposite of what the banks were experiencing at the hands of the Soviets in their occupation zone and in East Berlin. It was also worded almost identically in both publications that 'banks should be closed by Military Government only if absolutely necessary and then only long enough to introduce satisfactory control by Military Government, to remove objectionable personnel and to carry out instructions for the blocking of certain accounts and other instructions contained in the "Instructions to Financial Institutions". Consistent with the foregoing, banks, if closed, will be permitted to reopen as soon as possible.' It was also instructed, 'to make fullest possible use of the Reichsbank and its subordinate offices in the supervision of the banking system and as a medium for distributing orders and instructions to all involved financial institutions ...'.[224]

The Technical Manual also included the complete wording of what would later become the laws of the American military government pertaining to banking. These included: Law No. 51, in which the Allies declared the military mark to be legal tender in addition to the valid German currency; Law No. 52 with General Order No. 1, which listed the names of individuals and institutions whose property was to be blocked and who were to be placed under supervision by the military government; and Law No. 53, which stipulated foreign exchange controls and required assets in foreign currency to be reported and turned over to the authorities. The Technical Manual also included specific instructions to banks, entitled 'Instructions to Financial Institutions, No. 1', which explained in greater detail how the Laws 51–53 should be enforced and ordered credit institutions to submit several reports and business papers within a period of seven to thirty days. Instructions No. 2 included further instructions on how the banks were to participate in blocking accounts and other assets of incriminated institutions and individuals, and stipulated the reports that the banks were to submit to the military government.

Important for personnel policy were the 'Instructions to Financial Institutions, No. 3, and to Government Financial Agencies', the purpose of which was defined as follows: 'It is the policy of the Supreme Commander to remove active Nazis and ardent sympathizers from office and authority in the financial system, public and private.'[225] Every employee who had 'held any position above that of clerk or other non-policy making functionary',[226] was required to fill out a specific questionnaire and submit it to government agencies within three days.[227] Within seven days, the institutions themselves were to submit a list of the names and addresses of all employees, regardless of position, who were known – from documented evidence or otherwise – to have held certain higher positions in the hierarchy of the Nazi organization.[228] No. 3 also stipulated which employees were to be fired and suspended. The institutions were immediately to fire all employees and functionaries who were on the arrest lists of military governments. One such person arrested was Rummel, who was the only board member in the American zone as the war ended. Like seven of his fellow board members (the exceptions were Rösler and Hunke!), his name had been on one of the lists, compiled by the Americans in late June 1945, of German industrialists and bankers to be arrested.[229] The banks were also to fire anyone who was known to have held a higher position in certain Nazi organizations, as was the case for Hunke and Ritter von Halt. In general, the three big banks were to suspend the board of managing directors, the supervisory board and the local advisory councils. Investigations were to be conducted into possible incrimination of these and all others in top management positions,[230] thus affecting the remaining six board members of the Deutsche Bank.

Why did the British, against all expectations and under pressure from the Americans in 1946, instruct the bank to remove Bechtolf, Plassmann and Abs in Hamburg, although they had held no prominent positions in a Nazi organization? The reason may be easier to understand in light of the following excerpt from the Technical Manual: 'Many of the persons who must be removed may not have conspicuous Nazi Party ties. The absence of such ties, however, does not mean that they are not active Nazis or ardent Nazi sympathizers. From the point of view of occupation authorities, they represent as dangerous and unreliable elements as do notorious Nazi Party members. Because control in the financial field is highly centralized, it is probable that no person holds a key financial post unless he is acceptable to the Nazis, has been found by them to be dependable and has acted in support of Nazi aims.'[231] Although such argumentation reflected a certain inherent logic, it did not mirror the reality of the situation, at least not with regard to positions in the private economic sector.

Since Law No. 52 stipulated that the assets of all those arrested, fired or suspended had to be blocked, one general exception was listed in the Technical Manual, labelled General Licence No. 1. Money could be transferred or withdrawn from blocked accounts 'as may be necessary for the actual living expenses of such natural person and the members of his household'.[232] The total monthly sum was not allowed to exceed 300 RM for each account holder, plus an additional 50 RM for every household member up to a limit of 200 RM, so that the maximum amount of money available each month totalled 500 RM.

On the one hand, this detail is important because the banks apparently applied this rule also to accounts that were not blocked in order to protect their liquidity in the face of severe difficulties in securing and transporting cash.[233] On the other hand, this monthly cash restriction placed on blocked accounts proved advantageous to the Allies due to the magnitude of individuals and institutions involved. In addition, these accounts usually belonged to the relatively wealthy and the balances were well above the average. In practice, this restriction resulted in diminishing the money supply at precisely the moment when the Allied military mark was also being brought into circulation. Therefore, the impact of its introduction into the market was less inflationary than would have been the case had complete access to bank accounts been permitted. In this way the Allies were also able to ensure a higher seignorage profit[234] for a certain amount of military marks than they could have had otherwise. Although this advantage may not have played much of a role in the decision to block the accounts of incriminated individuals and institutions, the Allies profited from the impact of this practice nonetheless.[235]

The degree to which these detailed plans, drawn up in 1944, actually shaped banking in West Germany in the initial weeks and months of its occupation by Anglo-American troops is documented in a report by Dr Günter Keiser, a leading employee of the Association of Private Banking Business. In order to report first hand what was developing in Hamburg, he left Berlin on 22 June 1945,[236] travelling under extremely risky conditions, sometimes by foot. Fourteen days later he arrived in Hamburg. His assessment of the information passed on to him from the directing office of the Deutsche Bank and other sources appeared in a memorandum entitled 'The Situation of the Banks in the Anglo-American Regions as of mid-July 1945'.[237]

In this memorandum he reported that the credit institutions were reopened 10–14 days at the latest following the arrival of Allied troops. He had not been told of any restriction of business operations except the ordered blockage of assets and foreign currency accounts. Control and supervision of the banks was carried out by Allied officers with financial expertise, who used the institutional machinery provided by the network of Reichsbank offices for their dealings with the banks. Co-operation ensued 'in a thoroughly loyal, correct and pleasant manner'. There were, however, numerous reports to be submitted; the work was in fact so extensive that it currently preoccupied entire departments at the banks.

Keiser described the withdrawal restrictions for blocked accounts mentioned above and the initially similar withdrawal practices for all bank accounts in general. These restrictions were already being relaxed, however. In Hamburg and many other places in the Anglo-American regions there were practically no restrictions left, he added. All told, the business community had been permitted to make withdrawals from the very beginning as long as the need for cash could be justified, such as for wage payments. In certain cases, the finance officers had explicitly instructed the banks to act generously. At no point was the public's trust in the credit institutions shaken, Keiser maintained. This resulted in the fact that on the whole more deposits were registered than withdrawals. The liquidity of the banks was improving continually. The current priority was to re-establish transfer operations. Each of the big banks had attempted to create special facilities for their banking network. He reported further: 'The furthest developed of these is the Deutsche Bank, supported by its central cash office in Hildesheim. Accounts have been set up at this central cash office for all main offices based on their preliminary balance sheets as of 30 June (including self-calculated interest). These accounts are substitutes for those at the Berlin head office. Bank transfer payments are made through the reciprocal accounts of the main offices, whereas Hildesheim provides only the balance settlements of the main offices starting at 1 million RM. With regard to customer transfer payments from the region under Russian occupation, it is only possible to post these on a special blocked account. If the balance sheet being prepared for the Western zones shows that the disposable funds at Hildesheim exceed the sum total of obligations of the Western branches, it could result in an unfreezing of these blocked accounts. Bank transfer payments within the West are posted on a proviso account, meaning that the transferred funds only become available once it is certain that they can be cleared over the above-mentioned reciprocal accounts; however, usually the customers are offered an advance on funds transferred to proviso accounts and in some cases to blocked accounts – The Dresdner Bank must manage its business in this area with more caution since it apparently could not transfer a sufficient amount of its Berlin assets to the West.'

Due to the uncertain situation prevailing legally and economically, which also affected attempts to secure collateral for loans, banks were developing their credit business with some hesitation. 'Only smaller, short-term loans with very liquid collateral are to be granted (according to instructions of the Deutsche Bank).' In order to grant larger loans, branches first had to have the loans authorized by the directing office of the Deutsche Bank in Hamburg or by the Wiesbaden branch office. The banks especially recommended basing the credit business on bills of exchange, with 0.5 per cent over the Reichsbank discount rate. Naturally, the banks in the West were aware of the instability of the situation that evolved from uncertainty over the value of their most important assets: namely, the debentures and guarantees of the Reich. But until that situation was clarified, they were right to insist on maintaining the fiction that these assets existed or at least that they would have to be reassessed at some point together with the liabilities of the banks. Therefore, the banks in the Western zones thoroughly rejected the view that the banks were bankrupt, a view maintained in Berlin and especially by the Deutsche Bank there. Several Reichsbank offices helped support the standpoint of the banks in West Germany by accepting Reich securities as collateral for the credit they gave the banks.

Characteristic of the prevailing opinions in the Western zones, argued Keiser, was the fact that securities trading had already been re-established. In more remote locations, such business was conducted by telephone. In Hamburg, the stock exchange was reopened in the form of a controlled over-the-counter market for actual securities. The price index fluctuated greatly, mirroring the current political situation. Keiser reported shortly before the Potsdam Conference began that the market trends were extremely bullish. The quoted price of I.G. Farben had risen again from 90 per cent to 135 per cent of par value despite announcements that the Americans planned to confiscate it. Mining and steel shares were listed consistently at 145–150 per cent, and the big banks at 100–105 per cent, except the Hamburger Vereinsbank which was at 155 per cent. In general the Hamburg securities were valued rather high and often reached the wartime stop price, which was now to be used as the maximum for over-the-counter sales. The stock prices apparently reflected a greater trust of the traders in the economic policy of the British occupation power as opposed to that of the other two Western powers.

The price of bonds also remained relatively good, reported Keiser. Hamburg and Lübeck mortgage bonds were traded between 75 and 85 per cent, Braunschweig bonds for as much as 102 per cent. The price index for industrial shares fluctuated between 80 per cent for BMW and 101 per cent for the Hamburg Electrical Works. In the meantime, Hamburg had made contact with Düsseldorf and Frankfurt in order to establish uniform procedures in the stock exchange business. But the necessary conditions were still missing in the latter two cities. This shows that Hamburg had developed into the most important financial centre in West Germany at the time.

Keiser described the developments in the producing sector of the economy as a contrast with those in the banking industry. Manufacturing improved only slowly. The reasons why few factories were operating were twofold, explained Keiser. First, the occupation authorities were slow to issue the necessary work permits, as only they could. Second, businesses were having liquidity problems due to financial losses from debts owed them by the Reich; they were also facing a severe shortage of coal. His description of the British occupation rule in particular was positive: 'Our people [of whom Abs was certainly the most important], who have been able to establish closer contact with the English, are also under the general impression that the responsible English offices sincerely intend to help the German economy return to fairly normal working conditions.'

When the Soviets closed the banks in Berlin and in the Soviet occupation zone, the losses suffered by the Deutsche Bank were less than those of its competitor, the Dresdner Bank. Compared to early 1944 when the Deutsche Bank was still operating 227 branches throughout the 'Greater German Reich', the bank was conducting its business in May 1946 in 153 branches (67 per cent) throughout the Western zones, with 30 in the American zone, 88 in the British, and 35 in the French. The Dresdner Bank, in comparison, shrank during this same period from 154 to 91 branches (59 per cent), also with 30 in the American zone, 46 in the British, and 15 in the French. These statistics do not reflect the actual financial losses suffered when banking operations were closed in the Soviet zone because they do not account for the extremely important loss of the head offices. By late 1944, 51 per cent of the total assets of the Deutsche Bank were in the Western zones, as opposed to 45 per cent of the assets of the Dresdner Bank.[238] However, the Deutsche Bank transferred bank assets from Berlin to the central cash office in Hildesheim in February 1945. Therefore, it seems that approximately two-thirds of the total assets of the bank were available for the branches in the Western zones, which also constituted two-thirds of the former total of branches.

Whereas the Deutsche Bank branches in all of the Western zones had been managed during 1945 by the directing office in Hamburg with little interference from the Allies, developments and conflicts ensued in late 1945 and early 1946 in conjunction with the announcement of the so-called Dodge Plan for decentralizing German banking, as is described in the following section.

II. The Banking Policy of the Western Allies

1. Internal controversy over the fundamental orientation of occupation policy

The restructuring of Germany's banking system developed in a distinctly different way in the Western occupation zones than it did in the Soviet zone and Berlin. The basically positive approach towards banks in Great Britain and the USA was incorporated early into Allied occupation planning. On 28 April 1944, the Combined Chiefs of Staff (CCS) of the Anglo-American troops issued directive CCS 551 containing political instructions for the occupation.[239] In conjunction with guidelines on economic policy and hunger relief, special guidelines concerning finances and financial institutions, specifically on banking policy and currency matters, arrived at Eisenhower's headquarters in Europe as a supplement to this directive on 31 May 1944.[240]

Eisenhower was instructed in CCS 551 to resume the service of internal public debts as quickly as possible.[241] This was precisely the prerequisite to reviving the liquidity of the banks, and it was precisely what the Soviets would later prohibit in their zone of occupation.

The famous controversy within the American administration and with the British over the Morgenthau Plan and over occupation policy in general was sparked in September 1944 by the protests of Treasury Secretary Henry J.

Morgenthau, Jr, to President Roosevelt against the lenient tenor of the SHAEF Handbook, the drafts of which he had seen in London during a trip to Europe in early August.[242] Within the American administration, three departments were involved in this controversy: the Treasury Department, which supported the plans to turn Germany into a deindustrialized, agrarian nation, the State Department under Cordell Hull, which favoured a long-term economic and political reintegration of Germany into the community of democratic and peaceful nations, and the War Department under Henry L. Stimson, which demanded a pragmatic approach in occupying Germany that addressed the specific problems of military government there. As early as April 1941, Churchill proposed to make Germany 'fat but impotent' after the war – a nearly clairvoyant slogan from today's perspective.[243]

The final version of the American occupation directive JCS 1067 was not completed until 10 May 1945, more than four weeks after Roosevelt's death and two days following the surrender of Germany. It reached Eisenhower four days later. The content of this directive indicated that both the State Department and the War Department had regained much of the political influence on the German policy that they had lost to Morgenthau in August and September the year before, especially at the summit conference between Roosevelt and Churchill in Quebec. Although the Treasury Secretary was not directly responsible for the German issue, his close personal contact with the President had given him an edge at the time.[244] This new directive laid the official groundwork for American occupation policy for the next two years. It was published on 17 October 1945.[245]

From that point on, the authority over banking policy was placed in the hands of the Allied Control Council. In practical terms this meant that a banking policy modelled on the American system would not be fully institutionalized, even in the US zone, for the next two years because the four powers were to prove incapable of agreeing upon a common policy in the Control Council. JCS 1067 included the following authorizations for the area of finance:

'46. Subject to any agreed policies of the Control Council, you are authorized to take the following steps and to put into effect such further financial measures as you may deem necessary to accomplish the purposes of your occupation;

a. To prohibit, or to prescribe regulations regarding transfer or other dealings in private or public securities or real estate or other property.

b. To close banks, but only for a period long enough for you to introduce satisfactory control, to remove Nazi and other undesirable personnel, and to issue instructions for the determination of accounts to be blocked under subparagraph 48e below.

c. To close stock exchanges, insurance companies, and similar financial institutions for such periods as you deem appropriate.

d. To establish a general or limited moratorium or moratoria only to the extent clearly necessary to carry out the objectives stated in paragraphs 4 and 5 of this directive.

47. Resumption of partial or complete service on the internal public debt at the earliest feasible date is deemed desirable. The Control Council should decide the time and manner of such resumption.'[246]

One source of permanent aggravation for the banks in the American zone was the fact that the authorities responsible for financial affairs in the American military government were practically all people appointed by the Treasury Department. In September 1944, President Roosevelt advised his Secretary of War that this recruitment practice was to be implemented even for the planning phase of occupation policy.[247] This meant that, for all practical purposes, the interpretation and implementation of the directive on financial policy remained in the hands of the Treasury Department. Much to the irritation of their immediate military superiors, the Treasury appointees in Germany maintained special and often direct contact with the Department.[248] This explains why the Finance Division of the US military government tried with such tenacity to decentralize the German banking system and thereby to weaken it. The recurring friction between the Finance Division and the Economic Division, which within its areas of responsibility preferred a more pragmatic approach to decentralizing German industry and breaking up cartels, was in a sense the continuation of the tensions that had flared up between the Treasury Department and the other departments in Washington beginning in August and September 1944 during the planning phase of occupation policy for Germany.

For a short while, the Treasury Department was able to retain its hold over American occupation policy in the financial sector after Harry S. Truman became President on 12 April 1945, even though Secretary Morgenthau was not personally close to the new President. Slowly the Department's influence in this area waned as President Truman increasingly sought the more traditional avenues of advice from the departments directly responsible for occupation policy: namely, the State Department and the War Department. In early July 1945, Morgenthau finally resigned in protest over the fact that he was not appointed to the American delegation attending the upcoming Potsdam Conference.

The tripartite conference in Potsdam, officially called the Berlin Conference by the USA, took place from 17 July to 2 August 1945. It was interrupted from 26 to 27 July on account of the national election results in Great Britain. Although Churchill had led his country from the edge of defeat to victory over Germany, the Conservatives were defeated in the parliamentary elections by the Labour Party on 5 July. The new Prime Minister, Clement R. Attlee, who also had been a member of Churchill's delegation during the first half of the conference, took Churchill's place in Potsdam on 28 July 1945. The Potsdam Agreement represented the second comprehensive agreement of the Americans with the British following CCS 551 on common guidelines for occupation policy in Germany. It was to be the first and only understanding on occupation directives reached at the tripartite level.[249]

Compared to the directive JCS 1067 from 14 May 1945, on which the American negotiating position in Potsdam rested, the Potsdam Agreement represented another step away from Morgenthau's concepts of a harsh peace and a step towards the more moderate proposals of the War Department and the State Department. With regard to politics, 'democratic' parties were now permitted and encouraged in Germany, whereas under JCS 1067 such parties had been required to obtain special permission of the zone commander in order to pursue their activities. In the economic sphere, two notable changes were made. The first of these pertained to reparation payments. Under JCS 1067, the Germans were allowed to have a standard of living equal to the lowest living standard of Germany's neighbouring countries before her resources were to be made available for reparations. In Potsdam it was decided that the standard of living to be attained in Germany before reparations commenced should be equal to the 'average' living standard of its neighbours. Second, the zone commanders were explicitly ordered to undertake the following constructive economic and political measures for the purpose of improving the German economy: to repair the transportation system, to increase coal production, to maximize agricultural production and to make the necessary emergency repairs to housing and essential public utilities.[250]

The Potsdam Agreement provided for the decentralization of the political structure, meaning the federalization of Germany, and for the development of local self-government. However, the highest governmental authority pertaining to 'Germany as a whole' was given to the Allied Control Council. In the economic sector, German unity was stressed even more emphatically: 'During the period of occupation Germany shall be treated as a single economic unit.' With regard to financial policy, 'currency and banking, national taxation and customs' were specifically listed as the areas in which it was the responsibility of the Control Council to determine a common policy. Yet at the same time a common decentralization policy, to be applied also to banking, was agreed upon in order to ensure the development of the economic pendant to federalism: 'At the earliest practicable date, the German economy shall be decentralized for the purpose of eliminating the present excessive concentration of economic power as exemplified in particular by cartels, syndicates, trusts and other monopolistic arrangements.'[251] This clear commitment to a common economic policy would later give the leading representatives of German banks and the British military government, which was concerned about the efficiency of the banking system, the leverage they needed to prevent the worst excesses of American (and French)[252] efforts to decentralize banking.

General Lucius Clay, who arrived in Paris on 7 April 1945, in order to assume the leadership of the American military government in Germany, considered directive JCS 1067 unacceptable because it restricted his authority to take charge of developing the German economy. During the period from October 1945 to July 1946, he campaigned for a revision of the directive. With time it became clear that it was very difficult to get the Control Council to make any binding decisions. Clay wanted to obtain greater leeway for the American military government. But the prevailing mood both in Congress and in public opinion at the time was critical of the US military government for allegedly being too easy on defeated Germany. In light of this and the outcome of the Potsdam Conference, no effort was made to reword the directive. Not until the Republicans gained the majority of seats in the newly elected Congress in early 1947 did they turn their attention to reducing government spending by implementing a more pragmatic and liberal occupation policy.

The impetus to do this was even greater after the Foreign Minister Conference in Moscow in March 1947 dashed all hopes of developing a functioning co-operation with the Soviets in the Control Council, and the conflict between these political systems was becoming increasingly competitive in the battle to win the allegiance of the German population. The Cold War between East and West began on 12 March 1947, the day the Truman Doctrine was announced.[253] Clay himself, who had now become Eisenhower's successor as Supreme Commander of the American occupation troops, wrote the new directive JC 1779. This was deliberated in Washington and altered slightly before it was officially sent to Clay on 11 July 1947, and published four days later. This new directive replaced JCS 1067, thus purging policy of most of the remaining relics of the Morgenthau Plan.[254] However, it stipulated very specifically that the big banks in Germany were to be decentralized.

The Potsdam Conference had served as the springboard for the implementation of banking policy among the Western Allies. At this conference, the three Western victors committed themselves to developing a common policy for the big banks in the Allied Control Council. In the meantime, each of the military governments was required to decide if and to what extent the big banks were to be subjected to the Potsdam postulate of decentralization.

By August 1945, the American military government had not yet decided at what level the Reichsbank and the other big banks should be decentralized. When General Clay arrived in Europe in April, he discovered that the Finance Division was being run by Bernard Bernstein, a close colleague of Treasury Secretary Henry Morgenthau. Bernstein had surrounded himself with other colleagues from the Treasury Department in Washington who also favoured the type of *Carthaginian peace*[255] that Morgenthau envisioned for Germany, or, as the *Wall Street Journal* once criticized, preferred revenge over reconstruction.[256] Throughout America a general debate was ensuing as to whether a policy of repression or rehabilitation could best ensure that Germany remained peaceful in the future.[257] Clay's ambivalent position arose from his evaluation of the directive JCS 1067 shortly after his arrival in Europe: 'We were shocked – not at its punitive provisions but at its failure to grasp the realities of the financial and economic conditions which confronted us.'[258] Clay was speaking not only for himself, but also for his new financial adviser Lewis Douglas, an insurance entrepreneur who also served on the board of directors of General Motors.[259] Douglas labelled the authors of the directive as 'economic idiots' and added: 'It makes no sense to forbid the most skilled workers in Europe from producing as much as they can for a continent which is desperately short of everything.'[260] Clay appointed Douglas as Bernstein's supervisor and then sent Douglas back to Washington immediately, where he was able to have several smaller modifications made to the directive by early May. Two months later, however, Douglas resigned out of frustration with the final version of JCS 1067.

Like the entire community of American big business, the two other top advisers Clay had brought with him from America were vehemently opposed to the Morgenthau policy: William H. Draper from the banking establishment Dillon, Read & Co., New York, as economic adviser, and Robert Murphy from the State Department as political adviser. These two men used what leeway for interpretation there was to make constructive use of the occupation directive. In October 1945, 'Morgenthau's man' Bernstein resigned from the military government after Clay had stripped him of much of his authority by making Bernstein chief of the new 'Division of Investigation of Cartels and External Assets' and by appointing a man of Clay's choice from Washington to succeed Douglas in heading the Finance Division in September 1945. This new top adviser was the respected banker Joseph M. Dodge, chairman of the board of Detroit Bank and Trust Co. and president of the American Bankers Association. Until he was succeeded by his deputy Jack Bennett on 1 June 1946, Dodge was the decisive American for conceptualizing the reorganization of the banking business, currency relations and financial structures in West Germany.

Starting in June 1945, before Douglas left his post, the financial experts in the American military government were divided into two camps, each camp supporting a different plan for the decentralization of the Reichsbank and the big banks. The plan that best concurred with Douglas' own ideas called for a decentralization of the Reichsbank at the level of the occupation zones. The Reichsbank chief office in Frankfurt was to become the central bank of the American zone and to assume the supervision of the banks in the entire US zone. The second plan mirrored Bernstein's vision of decentralization on a *Land* basis in conjunction with the American plans for creating a federal, *Land*-oriented political order in Germany.[261] In both cases, the decentralization of the big banks was not stated explicitly, but the practical application of these plans to big banks was implied by analogy of the situation.

Following the agreement in Potsdam, the financial experts from the American military government even developed plans that provided for a central bank for all of the zones, and for the continued existence of the big banks with new head offices to replace the closed ones in Berlin. Such plans corresponded to their interpretation of the commitment made at Potsdam to treat Germany as a single economic unit, especially in the areas of currency and banking. In their opinion, they also facilitated greater economic and adminstrative efficiency.[262]

Shortly after he took office, in late September 1945, Dodge chose the plan he preferred. Surprisingly, the plan he chose was the one based on Bernstein's concept of decentralizing the banking system at the *Länder* level, while his staff favoured the model of zonal decentralization.[263] At most, he was willing to concede the creation of an inter-*Länder* Bank Council that would co-ordinate the Land Central Banks in the American zone. Dodge was determined to subordinate the creation of a new banking system to the same political goals of federalization decided upon at Potsdam. Another influence on Dodge's decision was the 'home model': in the United States banking was decentralized at the level of the individual states, except for the US Federal Reserve System. It operated on the basis of 12 Federal Reserve banks, each in districts superimposed on the state banking system.[264] Dodge was also borrowing from this 'home model' when he proposed to dismantle the universal banking system in favour of a division of labour among banks, so to speak, in which banks would do business either in long-term securities, or in short-term deposits and credit. He also wanted to ban the use of supervisory board positions to interlock industrial and banking directorates.

Even more remarkable was the similarity between the American and the National Socialist perception of the power of the banks, and the measures they took to limit the influence of the banks on the economy. In its role as the occupier of Germany, the American government – pursuing the traditional Jeffersonian ideal of a maximum degree of local self-determination – demanded what the National Socialists had demanded earlier: namely, to limit the proxy voting power, to restrict bankers from sitting on the supervisory boards of business enterprises, and, contrary to the centralized character of the National Socialist state, to regionalize or decentralize the banking system.[265] But the big banks were successful in parrying similar attacks on their established structures first from the National Socialists and later from the Americans. In my view, this can be attributed to the fact that the respective holders of power during the war and post-war period had to assign temporarily a higher priority to economic efficiency than to long-term goals of economic reform.

The wave of arrests that took place in October 1945 also played a role in finally bringing about the dismantling of the centralized structure of the Reichsbank and the big banks. Twenty-seven leading executives from the big banks were taken into custody in the American and French zones either to be charged with war crimes or to act as witnesses in war crimes trials. The British authorities had refused to implement such a sweeping measure in their zone.[266] Dodge described his policy of bank decentralization in a letter to the deputy director of the 'Division of Investigation of Cartels and External Assets', Russell Nixon, on 8 November 1945, in this context: 'I received your letter of 31 October 1945, regarding the arrest of certain financial figures from the "Big Six" banks. I am in complete agreement with the steps which have been taken to investigate and punish culpable elements in the world of German finance. The policies agreed upon at Potsdam and the principles outlined in JCS 1067 require the kind of action which your Division is taking. I have applied the same principle in the proposals I have submitted to the Finance Directorate [of the Allied Control Council] for consideration. These proposals would eliminate the excessive concentration of economic power in banking and destroy the intimate relationship between German banks and large corporations ... These proposals are an integral part of our program to ensure that the German financial hierarchy will never again play any part in disturbing world peace.'[267]

The Dodge Plan, as it stood on 1 November 1945, was first presented to the German public in a newspaper article that appeared on 17 December 1945. Members of the staff of the Deutsche Bank had already learned of the plan beforehand.[268] In fact, they had even been able to see it. The newspaper article appeared in connection with instructions issued by the American military government to the minister-presidents of the three *Länder* in the US zone, namely Bavaria, Greater Hesse and Württemberg-Baden, 'to begin immediately to decentralize the banking system and bank supervision and control in order to destroy the financial monopoly of the Reichsbank and the big banks'. The *Länder* were then instructed in detail to undertake the following measures:

'*First:* A central bank is to be established in each *Land*. Each central bank will make arrangements for clearing transactions with the other two central banks, with the central banks established in the other occupation zones, and with a bank or banks in Berlin. *Second:* The central banks will function as a bankers' bank and as a banker for the *Land* government; however, they are neither banks of issue nor commercial banks. *Third:* Commercial and savings banks will keep a per cent of their deposits as a reserve with the central bank of their respective *Land* to be used for settlement of clearing balances. *Fourth:* An official from the *Land* ministry will supervise the central bank in each *Land*. *Fifth:* A banking council will coordinate bank operations and banking supervision with the three central banks. *Sixth:* All banks and credit institutions must comply with the principle of decentralization. No branches may be established outside of the *Land* in which the principal office is located. *Seventh:* The number of banks will be reduced to correspond with diminished economic demand. After a certain period of time, decentralization will be continued and the regional scope of banking operations reduced to municipal and rural districts.'[269]

As the last point shows, Dodge considered the decentralization of private banks at the *Länder* level only to be a way station to further decentralization at the level of municipal and rural districts. At least on this issue the Dodge Plan concurred with Soviet concepts for reorganizing the German banking system.

In paragraph 7 of the Dodge Plan pertaining to the big banks it was stated:

'7. With respect to paragraph 3a. above, it is recommended that:

a. The principle of decentralizing banking to the *Land* level will be applied to all classes of banking and credit institutions in the same manner as for the central banking institutions.

b. No bank or credit institution will establish or have branches outside of the *Land* where its principal office is located. Establishment of new branches within the *Land* shall be subject to the approval of the bank supervisory authority of the *Land* government.

c. Banks which formerly maintained nation-wide branch banks will reconstitute one branch in the *Land* as a head office for the already established branches in that *Land*. Branches in the *Land* will be related solely and directly only to the head office located within the *Land*. The head office will be completely independent of any control, direct or indirect, of any banking institution outside the *Land*.

d. Reconstitution of head offices, central credit pools, *Girozentralen*, or other credit centralizing institutions will take place only within the *Land*.'[270]

The British pursued a banking policy that differed completely from the American and Soviet policies. They considered an efficient, even centralized banking system to be the prerequisite for a rapid revival of the German economy. The British zone was dependent on this much more than were the Soviet, American or French zones. The Ruhr valley was the industrial heart of Europe, and the recommencement of coal shipments was considered essential for the revival of industry in the neighbouring countries as well. It was for this reason that the British national budget had been burdened after the end of the war with large subsidies which were needed just to commence the mining of Ruhr coal again. The British zone was also the most densely populated and therefore least able to feed itself. So another heavily burdening cost to the British national budget was the food it imported into its occupation zone.[271] There was only one solution to this dilemma for financially crippled Great Britain: the German economy had to be revived to the extent that its industrial exports earned the foreign currency needed to finance the importation of foodstuffs and the subsidization of coal mining as long as coal prices were regulated.

There was another factor influencing British banking policy. The British banking system itself was similar to the German one in that its structures were also centralized, within both the central bank and the commercial banking system. The British system was similar to the American banking structure only in that a differentiation was made between commercial banks and investment banks. Therefore, in contrast to the Soviets, the Americans and finally even the French, the British refrained from morally condemning a centralized banking system as having been the support system of the National Socialist war machine.

The liabilities of German banks to the British that had arisen from the Standstill Agreements of the inter-war period provided another motive for the British desire to retain as centralized a banking structure as possible in Germany. Also, the British financial community had learned to respect personally German bankers like Abs, who had become increasingly involved in negotiating these agreements up to the time of the Second World War.

The head of the British Finance Division was S.P. Chambers, for whom Charles Gunston from the Bank of England had served as chief of the Banking Branch until January 1946. At the first talks among the Western military governments in June 1945, prior to Potsdam, Chambers argued for a centralized Reichsbank in all Western zones or for zone central banks, which would be subordinate to a central co-ordinating agency responsible for all fundamental decisions in credit policy. He also warned against dismantling or weakening the big banks.[272] Chambers felt that the agreements made at Potsdam confirmed his standpoint that Germany needed to be treated as a single economic unit precisely in the area of banking and finance. In preparation for an interzonal banking system, he was active in getting new directing offices set up for the Reichsbank and the big banks in Hamburg instead of Berlin. In September 1945, the British military government officially ordered the big banks to establish a directing office in Hamburg for their banking operations in the British zone, something the Deutsche Bank and the Commerzbank had already done. The Dresdner Bank considered the order disruptive to its plans for creating a directing office for all Western zones in Frankfurt a.M., and therefore did not take any action to comply with this order until its plans for the Frankfurt office were destroyed by the previously mentioned arrest of 27 members of executive management from the big banks, including Carl Goetz and Hugo Zinsser from the Dresdner Bank, in the American and French zones in October 1945.[273]

On 24 November 1945, practically as a reaction to the Dodge Plan, the British military government ordered that a Reichsbank chief office for the British occupation zone be set up in the existing branch office of the Reichsbank in Hamburg.[274] The British appointed the former Reichsbank board members Ernst Hülse and Wilhelm Vocke to the board of the new chief office. Both had been fired by Hitler in January 1939 because they had initiated protest against the inflation policy of the Reich.[275] In the years that followed his renewed appointment, Vocke in particular sided with the big banks in controversies with the Allies over the banking structure.[276]

Due to the informal personal communication network that existed among the big banks in the Western zones, Hamburg had become the financial capital, albeit a rudimentary one, of West Germany by 1945. And this fact could not be changed by co-ordinated, specific instructions sent out by the military governments of the three Western zones through the *Land* finance ministries or Reichsbank offices to the big banks in the first half of March 1946. These instructions forbade orders on business policy from being sent between zones. Characteristically, the banks in the British zone were informed of this through the Reichsbank chief office in Hamburg, and the instructions were formulated so:

'No bank may send instructions regarding banking policy to any of its sister or branch banks or subidiaries in *other* occupation zones.'[277]

The American military government, however, informed the banks in its zone through the *Land* finance ministries. Here the instructions were worded as follows: 'that banks in the American zone of occupation in Germany may neither request nor accept instructions from other banking institutions' and that 'a curtailment to the level of the respective *Land* and not the zone' was demanded.[278] In order to comply with this, the Deutsche Bank limited the authorization of the Wiesbaden office to the US zone, established similar offices in Mainz and Ludwigshafen for the French zone to be supervised chiefly by Executive Vice-President Heinrich Klöckers, and reorganized the head offices accordingly.[279]

Although they tapped telephones and opened mail, neither the American nor the British authorities were able to prevent Hamburg from sending instructions out to the field under the guise of exchanging information. Couriers were sent in abundance, and the exchange of verbal 'information' left absolutely no trace of evidence. And as long as the British refused to participate fully in the American campaign for decentralization, it proved impossible to curb effectively the influence of the directing office in Hamburg on the business practices of the branches throughout West Germany.[280]

In mid-December 1945, the American military government instructed the *Länder* governments in its zone to prepare to set up Land Central Banks. Since late October, Joseph Dodge had been urging the Finance Directorate of the Allied Control Council to discuss his proposals to strip the big banks of their power by introducing decentralization on a *Land* basis. He had submitted a proposal to it on 23 October that would have forbidden the banks from doing business in securities. Seven days later he submitted yet another proposal to decentralize the three big banks on a *Land* basis.[281]

The discussion in the Finance Directorate began on 6 November.[282] The only ones against the American proposals were the members of the British delegation, led by Chambers with his familiar argument that a unified banking system would be more efficient and would correspond to the Potsdam Agreement to treat Germany as a single economic unit in the area of banking and currency, just as the issue of reparations was to be handled. Furthermore, a system of big banks with a network of branch operations could not evolve into a dangerous concentration of economic power if controlled by the military governments. On the contrary, a centralized banking system would aid the Allies in implementing their plans for monetary and credit policy. Such a system would be less susceptible to crisis and would prevent any possibility of creating local monopolies.[283] Compared to the American government, the British military government was far more diligent anyway in exercising its supervisory and control rights over the banking business in its zone.[284]

By April 1946, Dodge felt compelled to propose a compromise in order to find a solution to the stand-off that had developed. He proposed establishing a

Länder Union Bank that would act as a central bank for all four zones placed above the Land Central Banks. This bank would co-ordinate the measures needed to treat Germany as a single economic unit, namely the fundamental decisions in monetary and credit policy, and the balancing of the financial requirements of the German economy: that is, the savings-investment relations between surplus and deficit areas, reparations, foreign trade and reconstruction. The organization of the bank would also be mirrored by its functions: it was proposed to create a department for issuing bank notes, a separate one for the usual banking business, a department of reconstruction finance, and one for exports and imports.[285]

The British reacted favourably to this concession by agreeing to the decentralization of the big banks and bank supervision on a *Land* basis, to the creation of Land Central Banks in place of the Reichsbank, and to the liquidation of the head offices of the big banks and the Reichsbank in Berlin. Now the Soviets and the French rejected the idea of a Länder Union Bank because they felt it would be a far too centralized institution; yet the British refused to back down on their demand for the creation of some sort of suprazonal institution such as the Länder Union Bank.

Before Dodge resigned and his colleague Jack Bennett took over the Finance Division in June 1946 (until May 1949), Dodge proposed yet another compromise in May, featuring a 12-member Länder Central Bank Commission, which would comprise three Land Central Bank presidents from each zone who would be appointed by the respective military governments. All decisions made by this commission were first to be approved by an Allied Banking Board, which would be made up of one representative each from the four military governments.

This proposal became the basis for an agreement in the Banking Committee of the Finance Directorate on 21 June 1946, to decentralize the banks on a *Land* basis, including the liquidation of the big banks' head offices in Berlin.[286] Yet a month later, as the Finance Directorate itself met to deliberate the plan proposed by the Banking Committee, only the three Western powers were still willing to agree to it. At the meeting held on 24 July 1946, the Soviets now rejected this proposal because it would not truly break up the power of the German 'monopolies' in the banking sector. Instead, they recommended a solution that corresponded to the practice in the Soviet zone, where – except for the co-operatives – the only credit institutions still permitted to operate were state owned.

As a result, the issue of socialization was introduced into the talks alongside that of decentralization. The inflexibility of the Soviet position in the negotiations was certainly related to the failure of the second conference of the Foreign Ministers Council in Paris on 12 July 1946; this council had been created by the Potsdam Agreement. The other factor was the concurrent announcement of the US Secretary of State, James F. Byrnes, that if it became necessary to consolidate the zones in order to administer them as a single economic unit, this step would be taken – and indeed the USA and Great Britain did agree on 5 September 1946 to create what would become the Bi-Zone.[287] After the Soviets refused to treat Germany as an economic unit according to the Anglo-American interpretation of the agreement made in Potsdam, and after they then proved only to be interested in free reparation transfers from the Western zones, Clay had all such transfers from the US zone to the USSR stopped in early May 1946.[288]

Due to the irreconcilable differences that had arisen in the Finance Directorate, the policy decision was handed up to the Coordinating Committee,[289] the next highest political authority at the four-power level; from there it was finally passed on to the Allied Control Council itself, where all attempts to arrive at an agreement among the Allies finally failed on 21 October 1946.[290] As a result, the job of structuring the banking system once again reverted to the commanders-in-chief of the respective zones. At the four-power level, talks continued on other measures to curb the power of the German big banks, such as by restricting trade in securities and proxy voting,[291] but these further efforts achieved nothing.

Because the Americans and their Western Allies had no authority over the head offices of the big banks in East Berlin, decentralization in each zone was merely a provisional set-up, a legal torso without the necessary appendages of stock corporation law. This also held true for the Soviets, who could physically close the head offices of the big banks, but could not legally liquidate them because the Commercial Register of the lower district court of central Berlin was located in Berlin-Charlottenburg in the British sector.[292] As would eventually become evident, the resistance put up by the Soviets provided the big banks with a chance for survival that they were able to use later to recentralize the banking system when the political conditions became more favourable.

2. The decentralization of the big banks and the Reichsbank
   by the Western Allies

On 15 April 1949, Garland S. Ferguson, the chairman of the Committee Appointed to Review the Decartelization Program in Germany, presented the final report of the committee to the Secretary of the Army, Kenneth C. Royall. In this report, the committee concluded that efforts to reduce the concentration of economic power in Germany had made little progress during the four years of occupation rule because policy had not been implemented effectively. The only important exceptions in this respect were the cases of I.G. Farben and the banking sector. In light of the fact that it had become a priority of American occupation policy to rebuild the economy of Germany, General Clay had even stopped decartelization measures in the areas of heavy industry and capital goods in March 1948. This is undoubtedly the reason why, in December 1948, he drew the committee's attention specifically to the decentralization policy in banking by claiming it to be 'the biggest single step taken with respect to the elimination of excessive economic power in Germany'.[293] The banks had become the shining example of the success of American deconcentration policy.

The initial efforts of the military government in the American zone to decentralize the banking system were aimed at the Reichsbank. Parallel to his suprazonal decentralization proposal to the Control Council, Dodge had ordered the *Länder* in the US zone in mid-December 1945 to pass their own legislation to establish Land Central Banks and decentralize the big banks.[294]

In a meeting held on 5 January 1946, in Stuttgart, two representatives of the American military government, Major Manuel Gottlieb and First Lieutenant Edward A. Tenenbaum, justified the decentralization orders to the attending finance ministers, the Reichsbank directors, top ministerial aides and bank representatives from the *Länder* of the US zone: 'By establishing [Land] central banks and decentralizing the big banks, it will no longer be possible in the future for the Reich to issue orders that gain it access to the assets of the banks, or more specifically, to the public's savings, as happened during the war.'[295] Such an outlook was not only too retrospective, it was naïve and incorrect, for the Reich had financed the war by using the *Girozentralen* to tap the resources of the savings bank sector, which was highly decentralized, much more than it had used the assets of the big banks.[296]

Bavaria, spearheaded by Economics Minister Prof. Ludwig Erhard and Finance Minister Prof. Fritz Terhalle, opposed the plans proposed by Dodge, although these plans seemed to appeal to the strong Bavarian tradition of federalism. But Erhard was of the opinion that 'political federalism and economic centralism were not mutually exclusive'.[297] Both Erhard and Terhalle believed it was more important to ensure the establishment of an efficient banking system with possibilities for supraregional capital equalization than it was to pursue any specific political aims.

Hesse also opposed the plans to decentralize the Reichsbank, but it was willing to reach a compromise with the Americans concerning the big banks. The senior vice-president of the Commerzbank in Kassel, Köhler, spoke with local representatives of the other two big banks late in 1945 about a plan to decentralize the big banks at the *Land* level, although they were not authorized by their directing offices in Hamburg to do this. Köhler was assured of the backing of the Hessian government, for the Hessian finance ministry was very enthusiastic about the plan at first. The plan called for dividing Hesse into regional banking districts, each of which would be dominated by one of the three big banks. In detail this meant that the Commerzbank would have thirteen banks operating in the Kassel region, the Dresdner Bank would have eleven in the Darmstadt region, and the Deutsche Bank would have eight in the Frankfurt region.[298]

The Hessian government even went a step further. On 11 January 1946, the finance ministry of Hesse presented to the head offices of the three big banks a legislative bill, drawn up three days earlier, for the decentralization of the big banks. This bill would have legally decoupled all of the branches of the big banks in Hesse from their mother banks and fused them together into another organization to be named the Vereinigten Banken AG. Had such a plan of regional concentration in banking been implemented, it would also have stymied American ambitions to weaken the big banks. But when the big banks and business leadership came out strongly opposed to the plan, the finance ministry withdrew its proposed bill.[299]

The fact that the Deutsche Bank reacted so strongly against this proposal demonstrates the firm resolve of the top management to retain the identity and unity of the bank. 'We consider such a course of action as completely unacceptable, as a treasonous act against our own institution and as a thoroughly untenable and unfortunately destructive position held by unauthorized individuals who lack a complete grasp of the situation,'[300] insisted the bank in a statement which then went on to list explicitly the most important arguments that the big banks would later use to persuade both the political decision-making authorities and the public of the necessity to maintain if not restore the big banks. During the talks at the Finance Directorate on decentralizing the banks on 24 July 1946, the French delegate used this statement of the Deutsche Bank to illustrate how firmly opposed the biggest of the big banks would be to the policy being considered.[301]

The only *Land* to favour the Dodge Plan was Württemberg-Baden. Fritz Cahn-Garnier, finance minister of Württemberg-Baden, and Otto Pfleiderer, head of the department for currency and banking there, signalled their approval.[302] Pfleiderer, who would become president of the Land Central Bank in Stuttgart in 1948, was particularly convinced that it was necessary to decentralize the German banking system. His strong commitment to federalism fired this conviction even during the years to follow.

In mid-February 1946, the Finance Division ordered the *Länder* to develop within a period of four weeks a common plan for decentralizing the banks in the US zone. During the following month, the division took an administrative step of its own towards decentralizing the big banks by issuing the aforementioned ban against receiving instructions from places outside the borders of the *Land*. Once the proposal for a Land Central Bank law for the US zone had been drawn up following consultations in the Länderrat (Länder Council) in June 1946, the big banks were put under pressure by the American military government, in part directly, in part through the *Land* governments, to present their own proposals for decentralization. But the banks categorically refused to do this, despite the given political realities. They wanted to avoid any appearance of having participated in their own destruction, not only because they considered the move legally difficult and economically stupid, but also because they would then be in an even better position to justify modifying if not discarding the decentralized banking system, which they anticipated would be imposed upon them by the Allied decree, once the interest of the occupation powers in the issue waned and German autonomy waxed.

On 15 October 1946, the finance ministers of the *Länder* of southern Germany received a memorandum that had been carefully prepared in Munich by the local representatives of the big banks there in close co-operation with the finance minister of Bavaria, the Reichsbank branch in Munich, and the directing offices in Hamburg. This memorandum presented the first official position of the big banks on the issue of decentralization. In it, the big banks justified their existence as universal banks with industrial equity holdings and proxy voting[303] as being an economic necessity rooted in the history of economic development in Germany. The pending challenges, including currency reform, required a consolidated and intact banking machinery. The issue of excessive concentration of power could be addressed by effectively supervising the banks, continued the memorandum. In any case, it was further argued, decentralization was currently impossible due to insurmountable legal and technical difficulties.[304]

Although the governments of each of the *Länder* supported the big banks in their efforts to ward off decentralization, they worked closely with the American military government to decentralize the Reichsbank. They recognized that their influence would grow once Land Central Banks had been established at the expense of the Reichsbank. Before the *Länder* in the US zone were equipped with parliaments in late 1946, which would have had to deliberate a law on Land Central Banks, each of the *Land* governments issued identical Land Central Bank laws at the behest of the American military government. The Land Central Banks thus opened for business at the beginning of 1947. Charles A. Gunston, the expert on Germany at the Bank of England, was pleased to note on 17 January 1947 that the British military government had not also implemented this 'lunatic idea of the American Dodge'.[305] The French military government, however, followed the American example and issued 'Ordinance No. 78 on the Liquidation of the Reichsbank and the Establishment of Land Central Banks' on 18 February 1947,[306] in which the *Länder* in the French zone were required to establish the Land Central Banks by 1 March 1947.

In early December 1946, the *Report on the Investigation of the Deutsche Bank* was submitted by the Financial Investigation Section of the Finance Division as one of several reports on the big banks that were intended to be a basic source of information for the war crimes trials soon to follow. According to this report: 'Investigation of the Deutsche Bank has revealed it to be an excessive concentration of economic power and a participant in the execution of the criminal policies of the Nazi regime in the economic field.' The report recommended that 'first, the Deutsche Bank be liquidated', as was already foreseen in American decentralization policy; that 'second, the responsible officials of the Deutsche Bank be indicted and tried as war criminals', which was the task of the prosecutor at the Nuremberg Trials anyway; and that 'third, the leading officials of the Deutsche Bank be barred from positions of importance or responsibility in German economic or political life', something Clay considered to be the task of the denazification measures.[307]

The Deutsche Bank thus got off lightly compared to the case of the more politically incriminated Dresdner Bank, where the organization as such was found to have been 'a war criminal'. As a result, the report on the Dresdner Bank recommended that, in addition to the measures suggested for the Deutsche Bank, 'the Dresdner Bank and its responsible officials, including entire membership of the Aufsichtsrat [supervisory board] and Vorstand [board of general managers] and certain department heads and branch or affiliate managers be indicted and tried as war criminals'. In the case of the Deutsche Bank, not one case was brought to trial because the Legal Division of the American military government, which was responsible for formally charging businesses and their top management with war crimes, felt that the evidence in the Finance Division report, one imbued with the Morgenthau spirit, was far too shaky to be used in court.[308] Nevertheless, the report served as an additional impetus to decentralize the banks quickly.

On 27 December 1946, at a meeting of the Technischer Beratungsausschuss bei der Reichsbank (Technical Assistance Committee at the Reichsbank), the French military government informed representatives from the banks in its zone of its 'definite decision' finally to start decentralizing the big banks on a *Länder* basis according to the guidelines that had been discussed by the Control Council. The military government asked the banks to submit their recommendations by 20 January 1947.[309] Two days before this deadline, the Freiburg branches of both the Deutsche Bank and the Dresdner Bank presented a comprehensive joint statement that described the level of decentralization already existing, and expressed opposition to any further demolition of the big banks. Property rights, stock corporation legal requirements, including bank obligations to creditors, and the familiar economic arguments were the reasons given for their opposition. They also did not hesitate to point out the disadvantages that would result for foreign creditors of German banks, to whom they owed the foreign currency equivalent of approximately 650 million RM in guarantor liabilities and another 160 million RM in standstill loans.[310]

As the Americans pressed the Germans in late 1946 for their ideas on decentralizing the big banks, it became apparent that only the government of Württemberg-Baden was willing to discuss in the Länderrat a compromise proposal offered to the Americans: namely, the plan to liquidate the big banks, to reorganize the banks into legally separate regional institutions, and to compensate old shareholders with shares of the new institutions. Bavaria wanted to win over the support of the big banks with a less far-reaching solution, one which would forgo liquidating the big banks, but would create regional banks by decoupling all branches within a *Land* from the business policies of the head offices of the old banks in Berlin, while regional trustees would safeguard the voting rights of the owners of the big banks.

The evolving constellation of co-operation between the *Land* governments and various interest groups prompted Arnold Maser, the Deutsche Bank executive vice-president from Bavaria, to note at a meeting of managers of head branches in Hamburg on 10–11 December 1946 that they were fighting a war on two fronts, 'not only against the Americans, but also against our own German authorities and other interested German parties, such as savings banks, trade unions, etc.'[311] On 14 March 1947, the three big banks once again issued a statement expressing the legal and economic reasons for their unconditional rejection of the plans for decentralization. The statement concluded somewhat provokingly: 'Should these arguments not be recognized, then we believe it would be more correct by all accounts to leave it entirely to the occupation powers to regulate authoritatively the matter as they see fit, than to have such a regulation carried out by Germans and in the name of Germans.'[312]

Such dissent was also shared by the Deutsche Bank employee councils in the American zone. These passed a resolution at their conference in Stuttgart on 18 January 1947, stating their opposition to any form of bank decentralization, even if only because they viewed it as detrimental to the planned economy they demanded. Even within the United States, criticism of occupation policy was being voiced. On 25 January 1947, the *Chicago Daily Tribune* reported on a special mission of former President Hoover in Germany and commented that the desolate food shortages Hoover found there had been caused by the Allied policy of booty and revenge. The United States had to spend $300 million yearly to ensure the Germans a subsistence diet. 'The Germans could be made self-supporting in a year and a half, and European recovery could be greatly hastened if private property were made secure and private initiative were given a chance to show what it can do.'[313]

The big banks enjoyed a measure of real protection from the General Custodian of British and USA standstill credits in the British zone, Friedrich Wilhelm von Schelling, who described in a letter to the Accepting Houses Committee in London on 7 March 1949 the serious financial repercussions for the standstill creditors should German banks be decentralized. Although the representatives of the British military government could see the political and psychological advantages to decentralizing the big banks, in their view these were balanced out by the financial and general economic disadvantages, precisely those emphasized by the big banks in their opposition to such plans.[314]

Jack Bennett and his colleagues at the Finance Division now lost all patience. In mid-March 1947, they began to urge the military government to issue a law that would prescribe the desired decentralization to the recalcitrant German *Länder* governments and the big banks.[315] Clay and the Civil Administration Division expressed their reservations that such a step would not correspond to the priority of developing German self-administration in the *Länder*. The Finance Division pushed all such reservations aside and argued that it was necessary to clarify the situation quickly. In order to administer the financial affairs of the growing foreign trade of the Bizone, which were handled since 1 April 1947 by the new bizonal institutions JEIA (Joint Export–Import Agency) and JFEA (Joint

Foreign Exchange Agency), the foreign correspondent banks needed partner institutions in Germany which were not tainted with an incriminating political past and could be accredited as 'foreign trade banks' by the military government in good conscience. This prompted Clay to issue Military Government Law No. 57 on 6 May 1947, entitled 'Custodians for Certain Bank Organizations'. The Finance Division summoned the presidents of the Land Central Banks and the finance ministers in the US zone that same day to meet in Stuttgart at the Land Central Bank of Württemberg-Baden in order to have this law explained to them.

'Art. I 1. Pending final determination of the future financial structure of Germany, an independent and disinterested custodian shall be appointed by the State Government of each State for each of the following banks: a) Deutsche Bank; b) Dresdner Bank; c) Commerzbank.

Art. II 2. Each custodian shall manage and administer the property of the respective banks within the respective States. He shall preserve, maintain, and safeguard the property, and maintain accurate records and accounts with respect thereto and the income thereof.

3. Changes in the present management of each bank may be made by the custodian for good cause and subject to the approval of the State Government.

Art. III 4. The actions of the custodian are in no way to be influenced by the present shareholders or the Directors of the several banks.

Art. IV 5. The custodian shall change the names of the banks listed in Article I.

6. The new name shall not contain, and shall not be related in any way to, the old name of the banks listed in Article I, nor shall the new name be related in any way to the new name of these banks, outside the respective State. The new name shall be subject to approval of the appropriate State Government.

Art. V 7. The Ministers-President of each State shall issue administrative regulations necessary to implement this Law.

8. This Law shall become effective on 6 May 1947.'[316]

At least this law did not take the Deutsche Bank by surprise. At the opening ceremony of the Land Central Bank in Munich on 31 March 1947, Executive Vice-President Arnold Maser, head of the Augsburg branch, was asked by Richard P. Aikin, the head of the Financial Institutions Section of the Finance Division, to attend a meeting on the decentralization issue. Others attending the meeting were the vice-president of the Land Central Bank and the top officials of the Bavarian finance ministry. A week later, on 8 April, Maser described the event to Wintermantel at the directing office in Hamburg:

'I explained to the gentlemen that – for whatever reasons – it is not possible for the banks to make proposals for their own dismantling because of their responsibilities to their depositors, foreign creditors, and shareholders ... After Mr Aikin repeatedly pointed out the political necessities, I explained that our position was not to be interpreted as resistance, but that the great responsibility bestowed upon us meant that we could only follow orders.

The next day there was a meeting lasting several hours between the Americans and the men from the Finance Ministry. Mr Hartlieb informed me that during this meeting three possibilities for decentralization were discussed:

1) voluntary action by the banks themselves,
2) a law of the Bavarian state government,
3) a law of the military government.

The second possibility was dropped in view of the deliberation that would be necessary in the *Land* parliament. The first was the option favoured most, but since the banks have stated that they are not capable of this – a point one did understand – the only remaining possibility was a law of the military government. This plan will now be pursued; it would be welcomed if such action was taken simultaneously in all of the zones. In this sense, the Americans want to be active in Berlin.'[317]

However, the other two Western Allies still refused to fall into line with the Americans. On 12 August 1947, Sir Eric Coates, chief of the Finance Division of the British military government, and Sir Otto E. Niemeyer from the Bank of England called the decentralization of the big banks in the American zone 'a hangover from previous Morgenthau ideas'. Coates specified three conditions under which he would swallow the bitter pill of decentralization in the British zone: namely, if a common budget with the other zones was agreed upon, if a single central bank responsible for more than one zone was established, and if a joint institution for long-term reconstruction loans was created.[318]

The decentralization forced upon the three big banks in the US zone was a fleeting phenomenon in every respect. Despite the new business names, no new institutions were legally created. With regard to property rights and taxes, the regional banks did not become new, legally autonomous institutions.[319] They remained coupled to the old banks, which legally still existed. The custodians, who were deliberately labelled *Verwalter* instead of *Treuhänder*[320] in the official German translation of the law, were only appointed temporarily to direct and supervise the business management of the regional banks in place of the former boards of managing directors and supervisory boards, until decentralization could be permanently implemented by way of stock company law. The measures were deliberately implemented so as to avoid any permanent solutions, thus forcing the issue of decentralization to reappear on the political agenda of the occupation powers later.

For the time being, the British were at least glad that the big banks, and above all the regional institutions of the Deutsche Bank, had been accredited by the military governments as foreign trade banks responsible for carrying on the foreign trade of the Bizone for the JEIA and JFEA, for this brought them one step closer to their long-term goal 'of linking up the German banking system with the rest of the world'.[321] But foreign trade was bogged down in such a bureaucratic swamp that the British zone threatened to drown 'in a welter of forms'. Yet, 'Western Europe needs a healthy Western Germany,' summed up Sir Otto E. Niemeyer in his report of 9 July 1947 following a visit to Germany. 'Her industry is essential for European reconstruction.'[322]

The French were the first of the two Western Allies to join the Americans in their campaign against the big banks. Two months after the Americans had closed the Reichsbank offices and established Land Central Banks in their zone, the French military government had followed suit in the spring of 1947. But in the big banks' case it took them a little less than five months to issue the French counterpart to the American Law No. 57. On 29 September 1947, Ordinance No. 25 'Sequestration and Renaming of Various Banks', a nearly literal duplicate of the American law, brought decentralization of the big banks to the French zone as of 1 October 1947.[323]

The British did not comply with American concepts for reorganizing banking until the spring of 1948 when they finally closed the Reichsbank offices, established Land Central Banks, transferred the supervision of the banks to the *Länder* and decentralized the big banks. In the British Ordinance No. 133, 'Decentralization of the Big Banks', which went into effect on 1 April 1948, a custodian was appointed for each of the regional banks. Unlike in the American zone where the custodians were officially called *Verwalter* in German, or in the French zone where they were labelled *Zwangsverwalter* (*administrateur séquestre*), the title of this office in the British zone remained 'custodian' – even in German translations – which offered the Germans the flexibility also to interpret this term as meaning *Treuhänder*, to the benefit of the former owners.

The British were also careful to be more precise in stipulating the tasks of the custodians ('management and administration' of the regional banks) than the Americans had been, in order to avoid the long court battles that had ensued over this in the US zone.[324] Contrary to their counterparts in the US zone, the British custodians were assisted from the very beginning by an advisory board of German citizens that was responsible for overseeing the 'management and administration' much like a supervisory board. Similar to its American counterpart, the British ordinance had been deliberately formulated to emphasize the temporary nature of this measure.

Why did the British finally conform to the American line? Reichsbank Director Ernst Hülse summoned Wintermantel and Bechtolf to the Reichsbank chief office on 9 December 1947, to hear his answer to this question. Hülse implied that the British would indeed give up their resistance to bank decentralization. It was to be expected that a political unification of the Bizone would soon occur in which 'the Americans, who shouldered the greater financial burden of the occupied territory – roughly in a ratio of 70:30 to the English [earlier 50:50] – would also gain the corresponding influence in solving this problem. In another context the English had told him that in the future everything would have to be seen from the standpoint of the distribution of burdens, so that the Americans would always have the upper hand in solving future issues.'[325] As a matter of fact, on 17 December 1947, the British and Americans signed a supplementary agreement to the 1946 Bizone treaty in which the USA assumed all financial obligations for imports into the Bizone for the period from 1 November 1947 to 31 December 1948, and the British were obligated to import a maximum of £30 million (approx. $120 million) from the sterling area.[326]

Since Hülse was convinced that decentralization could no longer be avoided under these circumstances, he suggested to the banks that they offer their own proposals to the Americans in order to get as much power out of their 'punch' as possible. He proposed assigning each of the three big banks a district in which that bank alone would operate: for example, Bank A with its headquarters in Hamburg would operate in northern Germany, Bank B with its head office in Munich would have the areas of southern Germany under American occupation, and Bank C with its head office in Frankfurt would operate in the French zone and in Hesse. The banks needed to agree among themselves how the districts would be divided up. However, all three were to be present in the Ruhr region.[327] This proposal varied little from the plans once suggested for Hesse, except that it was now being applied to all of West Germany.

The big banks had vehemently opposed the Hesse plans in early 1946, and Hülse's proposal for a nationwide application was also immediately rejected by Wintermantel and Bechtolf. They argued that it did not sufficiently take into consideration the traditions of the three banks. The banking system would be weakened in the transition phase, but the coming currency reform required a 'powerful banking sector'. And finally, it would prove practically impossible for the banks to agree on a partition and allocation of districts due to the differences in economic strength. However, they agreed to meet again with Hülse, then also with representatives of the other two banks, and to present their own proposal at the next meeting.

The plan presented later by the Deutsche Bank, with the approval of the other two banks, proposed that the branches in southern Germany be transformed into independent subsidiary companies, something the Commerzbank had also once proposed to Hülse. In addition, the Deutsche Bank was also to be split up into two or three independent banks in the British zone. The crucial difference between this proposal and the plans of the Allies was that the Deutsche Bank was allowed to exist as such, and to take over and administer all shares from these subsidiary companies.

In a meeting held on 16 December 1947, Hülse stated that he could not support the Deutsche Bank proposal. There were two points of controversy. The first was whether public institutions, such as the Land Central Banks, should not act as intermediary trustees of the shares, and if this were the case, then how the mother banks could retain a decisive measure of influence. The other controversial point was whether the capital of the subsidiaries should be raised through redeeming Reich Treasury bills or by providing new capital from the public sector, which would present the danger that this would be used to justify a demand for the nationalization of the big banks. It was agreed that the three banks should submit a new plan, one which further developed both the ideas of the Commerzbank as well as those of the Deutsche Bank. Bechtolf concluded: 'Our general impression from the discussion so far is that we should not expect to get much support from Mr Hülse in any negotiations.'[328]

On 15 January 1948, the three big banks submitted to Hülse in the Reichsbank chief office their approved plan for decentralization, and requested a personal hearing by the British military government.[329] However, the matter never got that far.[330] The plan was presented in a nine-page memorandum labelled, 'The Future Structure of the Big Banks' and supplemented by the memorandum written on 14 March 1947, listing the objections of the banks to American plans for decentralization at the time. The memorandum contained the results of deliberations on 'how a new banking system, which makes allowances for such political considerations [meaning the demands for decentralization] could best incorporate as many of the advantages of the old system as possible and at the same time avoid any discriminative treatment of creditors and shareholders that would cause financial losses to either of these groups'.[331] The alleged concentration of power held by the big banks had been dealt a much greater blow by the war than it would ever suffer from any organizational measures, maintained the banks in the memorandum. The closures and confiscation in Berlin and the Eastern zone had cost each of the banks nearly half of their business. They had also been weakened by the loss of all foreign investments, which in late 1944 were valued at 54 million RM for the Deutsche Bank and 46 million RM for the Dresdner Bank; however, in actuality the losses were much greater. Among all institutions handling short-term credit, the percentage of the big Berlin banks in the balance sheet total had already begun to decrease in the 1930s and had probably fallen to around 11–12 per cent during the war. It was vital to retain the trust of business, private customers, savers and foreign investors in order to finance Germany's reconstruction. Decentralization would endanger such trust. With regard to the interests of the *Länder* in decentralization, continued the memorandum, the banks were willing to concede the *Länder* governments more influence in banking policy as long as 'it was not of a political nature'.[332] The ultimate responsibility had to continue to lie in the hands of the various bodies within the banks themselves.

The following proposal was then put forth. Decentralization should not be implemented at all in the British zone. The economic structure of this zone and the resulting need for credit required banks of this size. In southern Germany and Hesse – that is, the French and American zones, excluding Bremen – the big banks were to be reorganized into independent shareholding companies in each of the *Länder*. But the mother banks would possess 100 per cent of the shares in these subsidiaries. The capital would be provided by the mother banks. About half of the assets of the old banks in Berlin was available in the Western zones anyway. In order to curb the influence of the mother banks on the banking policy of their subsidiaries, they would only be granted the right to nominate candidates to the boards of managing directors of the subsidiaries. Each of the *Land* governments was to possess veto power, and the supervisory boards of the subsidiaries were to be given voting rights for board membership.

Despite the fact that they would provide all of the share capital, the mother corporations would obligate themselves to have no more than minority representation on the supervisory boards, and to fill the remaining supervisory board positions with only those leading names from the business proposed by the board of managing directors in agreement with the *Land* government and later with the supervisory board. Political or partisan considerations were not to play any role. The mother corporation would be obligated to obtain the approval of the *Land* government, or more specifically the Land Supervisory Office, before making any major decisions – major decisions being defined as those requiring by law a three-quarters majority of the represented shareholders at the general meeting. However, the mother bank would have a representative with veto power on the committee that would be formed to authorize all credit and assumptions of risk. According to this plan, the branches of the Deutsche Bank and the Dresdner Bank operating in the British zone – the Commerzbank already had its corporate seat in Hamburg – would each be organized into a shareholding corporation. In order to retain the private character of the banks and not to run the risk of encouraging nationalization, capital investment by the state was to be avoided at all costs.

This proposal was ignored completely. Two weeks after it was presented, on 2 February 1948, the Reichsbank chief office informed the big banks in Hamburg that the British military government had decided to issue an ordinance corresponding to the American Law No. 57 very soon.[333] Preparations for decentralization commenced immediately. Wintermantel, Rummel, Plassmann, Bechtolf and Kessler met on 11–12 March 1948 in Hamburg, for a 'joint conference' in order make the most important personnel decisions for the new boards of managing directors. Each of the three regional institutions of the Deutsche Bank planned for the British zone was to have at least one member of the directing office in a leading management position: Plassmann would be at the Rheinisch-Westfälische Bank in Düsseldorf, Bechtolf at the Norddeutsche Bank in Hamburg, and Kessler at the Nordwestbank in Hanover. Wintermantel was to remain in Hamburg as 'Generaltreuhänder', a type of executive trustee or co-ordinator for the entire bank. If the British military government did not permit him to act in such a capacity, then Wintermantel planned to go to the Rheinisch-Westfälische Bank in Düsseldorf. Abs and Rummel were to retire, retroactively to 1 January 1948, with a yearly pension of 24,000 RM. They would be called upon to advise all of the banks in the three zones without additional compensation. 'Joint resolutions should be made for all important decisions within the bank by all of the former board members available.'[334] In fact, the old board of managing directors continued to meet regularly after the bank was decentralized. Frowein, Rösler and even Ritter von Halt also participated in these meetings following their release from internment.[335] This body made all of the important decisions for the entire Deutsche Bank group. This was not legally sanctioned, even though the Sonderausschuss Bankenaufsicht, a special committee for bank supervision in the bizonal Länderrat, considered in 1949 'a certain exchange of experience' between the regional institutions to be 'safe', in recognition of the fact that the 'former' big banks still existed as entities in legal terms and with regard to liability.[336] Once the three successor institutions were decoupled from the former Deutsche Bank in 1952, the central co-ordinating function of the former board of managing directors was taken over by the *Gemeinschaftssitzungen*, joint sessions of the boards of the successor institutions.

Both the British military government and the *Land* governments, which were to appoint custodians and approve new bank names, gave the banks relatively free rein in selecting the bank names and even the individuals who would become their custodians.[337] The Rheinische-Westfälische Bank commented later on the results of this leniency: 'The attitude of the various custodians can be summed up by saying that the vast majority of them tend to agree with us completely, whereas one group, comprising of Mr Lust and Dr Eichenlaub, favours a strict interpretation of the pertinent laws and ordinances.'[338]

From this point on, the Deutsche Bank developed other initiatives to retain a minimum of its centralized structure. On 10 February 1948, the Deutsche Bank board of managing directors wrote to the Reichsbank chief office, specifically Mr Hülse, that the big banks still needed head offices to handle business affairs involving all of the regional banks. It was suggested that these be labelled co-ordination offices and that they be prohibited from making any input into business policy and management, as was stipulated by the ordinances of the military governments. Such co-ordination offices would handle, for instance, social and retirement issues, information regarding the closure of the former branches in the East and the Berlin head office, questions concerning the assessment of bank assets located outside of the Western zones, and service to foreign creditors. Their existence would also serve to instil in depositors and shareholders a certain sense of stability and trust. It was also argued that the experienced staffs of the Hamburg directing offices were needed to prepare for *de jure* decentralization, which would someday replace the temporary *de facto* decentralization now in the process of being implemented. The military government could appoint a special trustee (*Generaltreuhänder*) to supervise each of these offices and, in order to reduce the costs of such control, they could require one of the leading men of the big banks to assume such a position.

On 14 February 1948, the Dresdner Bank also petitioned the Reichsbank chief office for the creation of such a co-ordination office. The bank emphasized that this had not been a pressing matter following decentralization in the American and French zones because the affairs that had to be handled by such a co-ordination office, among which was the compilation of an overall balance sheet, could be done by the Hamburg directing offices. These petitions were never officially answered. On 1 April 1948, the Reichsbank chief office ceased its operations.[339]

Even after decentralization had been implemented and the directing office in Hamburg closed, the Deutsche Bank continued its efforts to obtain a head office, again in Hamburg, for the co-ordination of matters affecting all of its successor banks. At first Wintermantel remained convinced that the military government might very well appoint a general trustee for the bank, especially after Friedrich Wilhelm von Schelling was named the trustee for the Reichsbank, and Wintermantel was prepared to assume such a position within the Deutsche Bank.[340]

In early April 1948, not long after the banks had been decentralized in the British zone, the custodian of the Südwestbank, Dr August Neuburger, recommended at meetings and later in correspondence with bank officials in Hamburg that the bank distance itself from the idea of a general trustee appointed by the military government. Instead, the board of managing directors and the supervisory board of the bank should name an executive vice-president with general power of attorney who would manage the affairs of the entire bank as had the directing office. Such an executive vice-president would be responsible for administering and attending to those bank assets that were not under the supervision of the custodian, for compiling the overall balance sheet, and for preparing and handling all of the matters that aimed at 'organically' decoupling the regional banks now established in the Western zones.[341] The Deutsche Bank accepted Neuburger's recommendations, and Wintermantel was supposed to take over this job. Therefore, he remained in Hamburg while his colleagues from the directing office assumed their positions in the new regional banks in the British zone in April. However, by August 1948, it was finally clear that such a position would not be created.

When the directing office in Hamburg was closed on 1 April 1948, staff members were distributed among the three new regional banks. The majority of them were transferred to the Rheinisch-Westfälische Bank, including Plassmann and Senior Vice-President Ernst Wilhelm Schmidt, the chief economist at the bank. In August they were joined by Wintermantel, Fritz Gröning and the head of the legal department, Hans Paschke.[342] At first, the offices of the new bank were located in Wuppertal-Elberfeld because the bank facility there was the largest one not to have been damaged in the war.[343] The bank's central administrative offices (*Hauptverwaltung*) moved there from Hamburg and opened for business on 21 April 1948.[344] In early April 1949, the head office of all of the branches in North Rhine-Westphalia moved to Düsseldorf, following the rebuilding of the facility at Königsallee 45.[345] The Rheinische-Westfälische Bank was by far the largest of all of the Deutsche Bank regional institutions and, in fact, the largest bank in all of West Germany. Following his release from Buchenwald in early 1950, Rösler also joined the managerial staff in Düsseldorf.

Bechtolf remained in Hamburg in order to head the Norddeutsche Bank. Kessler assumed responsibility for managing the Nordwestbank in Hanover. However, he died soon afterwards, on 1 November 1951, at the age of 60.[346] Frowein joined the management of the Hessische Bank in Frankfurt in October 1949, after a convalescence following his release from Soviet imprisonment in August 1948. Rummel was retired but remained an official adviser to the regional institutions, especially in southern Germany. The Rheinisch-Westfälische Bank assumed the functions of the defunct directing office, albeit unofficially and in so far as this could be hidden from the Allies, especially from the Americans and the French. The fact that this bank also took over the central cash office in Hildesheim, headed by Senior Vice-President Hermann Ermisch, illustrates just how important it was compared with the other banks. Therefore, it is worth taking a closer look at the make-up of its executive management.

In the second half of 1948, the management of the Rheinisch-Westfälische Bank was comprised of the following men appointed by Custodian Robert Lehr: Plassmann and Wintermantel from the board of managing directors, as well as the three executive vice-presidents Max Jörgens (previously Wuppertal branch), Ludwig Kruse (previously Essen branch) and Jean B. Rath (previously Cologne branch). The departments at the head office were directed by the following men: Foreign, Wilhelm Regling; Branch Office, Kaiser and Schwerdtfeger; Cash Office, Ermisch; General Secretariat and Economics Department, E.W. Schmidt; Central Accounting Office, Ulbricht; Organization, Richard Ahlborn; Personnel, Ott; Legal, Wilhelm Heitzeberg and Paschke; Secretariat, Gröning and Wienands; Central Auditing Office, Gerhard Polfers; and Building, Friedrich Kirchhoff.[347] Custodian Lehr named four men to the Advisory Council, which existed in the British zone. These were Niels von Bülow (Gerresheimer Glashüttenwerke, Düsseldorf), Gustav Brodt (Pfeifer & Langen, Cologne), Bernhard van Delden (M. van Delden & Co., Gronau) and Dr Günter Henle (Klöckner & Co., Duisburg).[348]

Like the Deutsche Bank, the other two big banks also transferred their top management and key departments from Hamburg to Düsseldorf.[349]

Although not legally liquidated, the Deutsche Bank was decentralized after 1 April 1948, for all practical purposes. It operated in the three Western zones and their Länder under the firm names shown in Table 1.

The regional banks were permitted, as were all other banks, to allay the disadvantages of decentralization through common banking practices. Inter-regional borrowing between banks, which previously occurred internally in the big banks, was usually continued through interbank accounts between the regional institutions without resorting to the money market and the Land Central Banks. This practice was officially sanctioned in the US zone in January 1948, even though balance settlements were still required to be handled through the

Table 1   The ten regional banks of the Deutsche Bank Group
after 1 April 1948
(firm name, custodian and balance sheet totals as of 31 May 1950)

AMERICAN ZONE

Bavaria	Bayerische Creditbank, Munich Custodian: Dr Hans Karl von Mangoldt-Reiboldt Balance sheet total: 159 million DM
Bremen	Disconto Bank, Bremen Custodian: Hermann Tepe/Wolf von Igel/Carl August Reiss Balance sheet total: 62 million DM
Hesse	Hessische Bank, Frankfurt a.M. Custodian: Eugen Lust Balance sheet total: 213 million DM
Württemberg-Baden	Südwestbank, Stuttgart/Mannheim Custodian: Dr August Neuburger Balance sheet total: 327 million DM

BRITISH ZONE

Hamburg	Norddeutsche Bank, Hamburg Custodian: Dr Edgar Wiegers Balance sheet total: 206 million DM
Lower Saxony	Nordwestbank, Hanover Custodian: Dr Hans Fiehn Balance sheet total: 146 million DM
North Rhine-Westphalia	Rheinisch-Westfälische Bank, Düsseldorf Custodian: Dr Robert Lehr/Dr Günter Henle Balance sheet total: 891 million DM
Schleswig-Holstein	–

FRENCH ZONE

Baden	Oberrheinische Bank, Freiburg Custodian: Dr Friedrich Janz Balance sheet total: 114 million DM
Rhineland-Palatinate	Rheinische Kreditbank, Ludwigshafen Custodian: Dr Otto Eichenlaub Balance sheet total: 112 million DM
Württemberg-Hohenzollern	Württembergische Vereinsbank, Reutlingen Custodian: Dr Eduard Leuze Balance sheet total: 44 million DM

Source: Balance sheet totals as of 31 May 1950, Pohl, *Konzentration*, p. 437. Other information from HADB, RWB file 7 and file: Nachfolgebanken 1947-1952 (1).

Land Central Banks. In 1949, E.W. Schmidt commented, 'it can be assumed that the old relations among the now individually functioning parts of the former big bank in each of the *Länder* are proving to be an advantage for the indispensable lending between banks'.[350] Banks could also still float large loans to both the private and the public sectors by creating consortiums of several regional banks, a different and more costly method of financing major loans. Decentralization could not even hinder banks from reaching agreements on business policy with their sister institutions in other *Länder*.

The Allied attack on the existence of a banking structure that had been evolving since 1870 actually strengthened the sense of loyalty and personal attachment not only of the executive management, but also of the other employees to their banks. And this loyalty proved more durable than the legal measures introduced by the Allies. Plassmann, who referred to the 'Balkanization of German banking', described the solidarity between the regional banks at a supervisory board meeting on 19 December 1949: 'We continued to consider it our duty to the German economy as a whole to maintain the solidarity between the ten sister banks in West Germany, naturally while abiding by military regulations, so that not only each individual successor bank could profit most from it but all business circles linked to us as well ... What we are operating is the collective business of associated banks. All of the sister banks exchange their most important business statistics with one another every month. Each institution ... can draw its own conclusions and can adjust its business policies if needed. The sister banks are the born consortium for floating major loans ... I am pleased to note that the collective business of the sister banks has got off to an excellent start and proven so successful.'[351]

However, the opponents of the banks in the decentralization issue, namely the Allied occupation powers, were also co-operating more and more closely. The military governments in the three Western zones standardized their respective decentralization ordinances and reissued them without any substantial changes to go into effect on 15 April 1949.[352] Both sides recognized that decentralization had created a legal torso that needed to be legally restructured on the basis of German stock company law in order to clarify such issues as liability – including the interests of foreign creditors – the future of the old banks, and requirements for the new banking institutions to publish balance sheets. Such reform remained on the political agenda.

3. The Bank deutscher Länder, the Reconstruction Loan Corporation and currency reform

'Unfortunately, we deal in a commodity that just is not worth much right now,' wrote Anton Heringer, the manager of the Bielefeld branch, to Wintermantel in Hamburg on 19 April 1947. Heringer regretted not being able to supply Wintermantel with a bicycle for his long-time secretary, who had also left Berlin to work for the bank in Hamburg, and reassured him that 'someday the situation will be different in this regard'.[353] But more than a year passed before it was.

At first, very little did change in the practical operations of the traditional German banking system within the British zone. The existence of the Reichsbank chief office and the Hamburg directing offices of the big banks provided a framework of continuity in banking relations. The American decentralization scheme was evaluated as being completely unsuitable for the German system of banking, as was emphasized in reports submitted on 27 November 1946, and again on 29–30 April 1947, by the finance committee of the Zonenbeirat (Zonal Advisory Council), a body of German citizens appointed by the British military government. These reports had been written by Ernst Hülse and a representative from the Deutsche Bank directing office.[354]

Although in principle the British Finance Division shared this view fully, in practice it wanted to remain politically more flexible in dealing with the Americans. This was necessary since both the agreement on the founding of the Bizone of 5 September 1946 and the Potsdam Agreement had explicitly specified finance, and thus the banking system, as one of the political areas in which the policy of the occupation powers was to be uniform. The banking issue was deliberated in a banking subcommittee of the Bipartite Finance Committee/Panel, which was composed of the heads of the Finance Divisions in the British and American military governments, and to which was also assigned a Gemeinsamer deutscher Finanzrat (Joint German Council on Finance) with its subcommittee, 'Money and Credit'.

In return for their willingness to decentralize the big banks in their zone, the British not only demanded a bizonal budget, which would commit the Americans to sharing the heavy financial burden of subsidizing the British zone, but also asked that a type of bizonal central bank be established in order centrally to direct monetary and credit policy. The British had been advocating such a central bank for quite some time in the negotiations on the institutional framework of the Bizone since October 1946. Following the announcement of the Marshall Plan in June 1947, they also wanted American co-operation in establishing a Reconstruction Loan Corporation for the purpose of financing industrial reconstruction, especially in the Ruhr region, through long-term credit from outside their zone.

Sir Eric Coates, who succeeded Chambers as head of the Finance Division in June 1947, presented this package of demands to his American counterpart, Jack Bennett, in late August 1947, nearly six weeks after American decentralization policy, also for banking, had been explicitly spelled out in the new occupation directive JCS 1779 issued by Washington on 15 July 1947. Although this directive acknowledged more than its predecessors the necessity of making reconstruction a priority over revenge, the British pushed for more. Bennett, whom the British did not think highly of and considered obstinate and doctrinaire,[355] balked at the idea of creating a bizonal institution with the functions of a central bank. At most he was willing to concede the setting up of a co-ordination office above the Land Central Banks of the Bizone, so that the responsibility and decision-making power in monetary and credit policy would actually remain decentralized at the *Länder* level.

However, Clay wished to reach a compromise with the British quickly and was now convinced himself that a central bank was a prerequisite to bringing urgently needed economic stabilization to the Bizone. On 16 September 1947, he took up the matter with Washington,[356] and on 3 October 1947, he received the go-ahead to set up a central bank, the Länder Union Bank. This predecessor to the Bank deutscher Länder had already been under discussion at the four-power level. The 'doctrinaire' Jack Bennett was forced to relent.

The British now convinced the Americans that a bizonal central bank should be headed by a board of managers with a president or general managing director. From this would later evolve the Directorate of the Bank deutscher Länder. The board of managers was to carry out the decisions on monetary and credit policy made by the board of directors, the later Central Bank Council (Zentralbankrat). This body was composed exclusively of the presidents of the Land Central Banks, as the Americans had originally proposed, and functioned independently of any instructions by the governments, similar to the Board of Governors of the Federal Reserve System and unlike the Bank of England since 1945.

The Bank deutscher Länder was established on 1 March 1948, by both military governments of the Bizone.[357] The new legal residence of the bank became Frankfurt. At the same time, the Allied Bank Commission was also formed, comprising the heads of the finance divisions of the military governments and later of the High Commissioners. This new commission had veto power over the decisions made by the bodies of the Bank deutscher Länder.[358] France, which wanted to support currency reform in the three Western zones, integrated its three Land Central Banks into the new central bank and joined the Allied Bank Commission by issuing Ordinance No. 155a of the French military government on 19 June 1948, retroactively to 25 March 1948. The founding of this central bank made it possible to implement currency reform in the Western zones on 20 June 1948.

Initally there were difficulties in filling the top positions of the new institution. Abs and Karl Blessing, who was at the time being held in a Frankfurt prison by the Americans, had been suggested to head such a central bank by Charles A. Gunston as early as 6 August 1947.[359] At its third meeting, on 2 April 1949, the Central Bank Council, namely the presidents of the Land Central Banks, did actually elect Hermann J. Abs president of the Directorate by a vote of seven to four, and Otto Schniewind president of the Council by a vote of eight to three. In a letter to the Central Bank Council on 9 April 1948, Abs and Schniewind agreed to accept the new positions only under certain, specified conditions. They did not feel that the political independence of the Land Central Bank presidents was safeguarded sufficiently from the influence of their respective *Länder* governments, and therefore asked for a special joint veto of the two presidents over Council decisions on extending credit to the public sector. This veto could only be overturned by a three-quarters majority.

The Zonenbeirat, which had opposed the entire reorganization of banking in the British zone in the first place, had already expressed these concerns as their own in a resolution drawn up on 25 February 1948 by E.W. Schmidt. This resolution stated that the decision-making bodies of the Bank deutscher Länder 'comprise of representatives of future debtors, exclusively'. It was to be feared that 'constant pressure would be exercised' by the Central Bank Council, 'leading to excessive expansion of credit. The guardian of the currency will be seduced by its own bodies into endangering the currency.'[360]

The Central Bank Council was prepared to accept the amendments demanded by Abs and Schniewind, but the Allied Bank Commission rejected them.[361] As a result, Karl Bernard was elected president of the Council on 5 May 1948, and Wilhelm Vocke president of the Directorate on 19 May 1948.[362] However, American government documents tell this story differently. First, the French delegate to the Allied Bank Commission opposed the election of Abs in the first half of April 1948.[363] Second, the Bizonal Vetting Party, under pressure from the Americans and most likely in opposition to the British, objected to the choice of Abs for a leading position at the Bank deutscher Länder.[364]

Abs had been long respected by the British, and his abilities had earned him great recognition among German financial experts as well, as his election demonstrated. At last even the American military government stopped viewing Abs strictly as one of the top business leaders in the German war economy, and began considering him as a leading financial figure with extraordinary talents, whose expertise should be applied to the economic reconstruction of Germany. In September 1947, Richard Whitehead, an envoy of President Truman, and Dr Richard Merton, who had once again assumed the chairmanship of the supervisory board of the Metallgesellschaft in 1948, met with Abs at his farm Bentgerhof near Remagen at the behest of the American military government. They discussed the allocation of Marshall Plan funds for the economic reconstruction of Germany and the role in such development of a new organization, the Reconstruction Loan Corporation, which the Americans and British had been considering establishing since July 1947.[365]

Not until 1948 did the planning for such a reconstruction credit institution truly begin. Following the currency reform, several drafts for legislation were drawn up in the Bizonal Finance Administration and Economic Administration. The final version became the Reconstruction Loan Corporation Act (*Gesetz über die Kreditanstalt für Wiederaufbau*) and went into effect on 5 November 1948. The Verwaltungsrat (Administrative Council) of the bank was made up of a broad spectrum of individuals from business and politics, including Schniewind and Abs, who were elected as chairman and deputy chairman of this supervisory board, respectively. Not long after that, Abs was delegated by the Administrative

Council to assume the position of chairman, or more specifically spokesman, of the bank's board of managing directors. On a recommendation by Abs, Dr Walter Tron joined the board of managing directors in early 1949. He had formerly been a senior vice-president at the Deutsche Bank and the managing director of the Leipzig branch. The new institution officially opened on 2 January 1949 in Frankfurt, with a capital of 1 million DM, supplied by the *Länder*. By the end of 1953, the Reconstruction Loan Corporation had channelled about 3 billion DM of Marshall Plan funds into the German economy.[366]

Once the Bank deutscher Länder had been founded and the French zone had been retroactively integrated on 19 June 1948 into the British–American agreements concerning this bank, everything was set for the long-discussed and well-planned currency reform in the three Western zones. The very next day, on 20 June 1948, the three Western military governments enacted identical legislation for the immediate introduction of the currency reform so long awaited by the population and business. The Western Allies had attempted one last time in early 1948 to implement such reform in conjunction with the Soviets, but these efforts had failed.[367] This came as no surprise to C.A. Gunston, who had commented on 15 January 1948 that the government experts in London were all aware that quadripartite currency reform was not realistic. 'The problem is how to offer it to the Russians in such a way that the Russians will reject it without putting us in the wrong.'[368]

The Soviets reacted to the currency reform in the West by implementing their own currency reform in the Soviet occupation zone and all of Berlin three days later, on 23 June 1948. They first introduced a makeshift currency known as the coupon mark or Klebemark; due to the lack of new bills, coupons were simply glued on to the old Reichsmark, devaluing these at a ratio of 10:1 in East German marks. Every individual could exchange up to 70 RM into the new currency at a ratio of 1:1. Savings deposits in savings banks and other institutions were exchanged at the rate of 1:1 for the first 100 RM; at a ratio of 5:1 for the next 900 RM; and at 1:10 for amounts above this and for any other bank liabilities and debts.

This step forced the three Western sectors of Berlin to introduce a day later the new Deutsche Mark, the currency in circulation in the Western occupation zones, so that the city would not lose its economic connections to the Western zones, or sacrifice its economic and political future to the Soviets.[369] Because so many people still travelled back and forth between East and West Berlin, the East German mark continued to be treated as legal tender to a limited extent in the Western sectors of Berlin at an exchange rate of 1:1 with the Deutsche Mark until 20 March 1949, but only for items under price control, such as foodstuffs and rent, for taxes and other fiscal charges, as well as for fees for postal services, public transportation, electricity and gas. Otherwise, the rate of exchange for the new East German currency sank quickly against the Deutsche Mark in the following months to a rate of 4:1.

These developments sealed the fate of Germany as a partitioned land, at least as far as currency was concerned. The Soviets immediately reacted to the currency reform in West Berlin by blockading all access routes (streets and waterways) and by cutting off the electrical supply to West Berlin. Not until the airlift to West Berlin had gone on long enough to convince the Soviets that the Allies were determined to support West Berlin and its connections to the West did they end this blockade on 12 May 1949. The Soviets also reacted to the currency reform introduced in West Berlin by leaving the Kommandatura, the four-power administration governing the city, on 1 July 1948. After this, the political tensions within the joint municipal administration of Greater Berlin grew worse. Municipal elections could only be held in the Western sectors in December 1948. The new City Assembly for the Western sectors elected Ernst Reuter as mayor. By then the municipal administration had already been partitioned, and it had been decided to establish the Free University in West Berlin in September 1948 as a result of the Communist interference in the freedom of research and teaching at the Humboldt University in East Berlin.

On 20 June 1948, two laws were enacted in the Western zones, the Currency Act and the Currency Issue Act. The former legislation defined the new legal tender, the Deutsche Mark, regulated the process of turning in and registering the old currency, and stipulated the inital allotment for individuals (*Kopfgeld*), enterprises (*Geschäftsbeträge*) and the public sector. Individuals received 40 DM per head at first and were permitted to exchange another 20 DM at a rate of 1:1 two months later. Although the original intent had been to link currency reform immediately to an equalization of war burdens, so imperative for social reasons, this was not done. It was merely stipulated in the preamble of the Currency Act that German legislative bodies were 'assigned the pressing task of regulating the equalization of war burdens by 31 December 1948'.[370] However, provisional legislation was not enacted until August 1949 and the final Equalization of War Burdens Act not until July 1952.

In the Currency Issue Act, the issue of bank notes and coins was regulated through the Bank deutscher Länder. For the first time a German central bank was delegated authority in determining minimum reserve requirements. The most important legislation in the currency reform package was the Currency Conversion Act of 27 June 1949, and the numerous ordinances issued afterwards to implement it. In order to reduce the excess money supply that had resulted from financing the war, and thereby make the level of prices set by control correspond to fair market prices, monetary assets were generally converted at a rate of 1 DM for 10 RM. To prevent prices from plummeting, a conversion ratio of 1:1 was set for regularly recurring obligations, such as wages and salaries, rental payments and retirement pensions, as well as liabilities resulting from purchase and work contracts, from disputes between companies, and in family matters and inheritance cases.

As it was, deposits at banks (including savings banks), into which cash had to be placed in order to be converted, had an even lower rate than the 10 per cent prescribed for other financial assets. All Reichsmark liabilities between banks were cancelled, declared void. Deposits of non-banks were credited at a rate of 1 DM for 10 RM, but the depositor only had free access to half of this; the other half was deposited in a blocked account, known as a *Festkonto*. On 4 October 1948, both the Fourth Currency Reform Act (*Viertes Gesetz zur Neuordnung des Geldwesens*) in the Bizone and the corresponding ordinance of the military government in the French zone went into effect. These stipulated that 70 per cent of the deposits on each *Festkonto* were to be voided, 10 per cent were to be transferred into medium-term and long-term securities, and 20 per cent were to be released. Thus only 6 per cent of Reichsmark cash and deposits at the banks were directly accessible in Deutsche Marks, and 93.5 per cent of the Reichsmark deposits were lost completely.[371]

This discrimination against liquid assets in the form of cash and bank deposits resulted in part from the disproportionate losses which banks (and insurance companies) incurred because one stipulation of the Currency Conversion Act declared the liabilities of the Reich, including the Reichsbahn (State Railways), the Reichspost (Postal Service) and the Reichsbank, to be null and void (para. 14). Since these outstanding debts of the Reich represented the major portion of the assets of credit institutions (and insurances), these financial businesses would have gone bankrupt had they not been granted somewhat equivalent financial relief. On the liabilities side of their balance sheet, relief came in the form of the reduced conversion rate of 6.5 per cent mentioned above. On the assets side these financial businesses also received some compensation: 15 per cent of their Deutsche Mark demand deposits and 7.5 per cent of their savings and time deposits were credited to them on giro accounts by the Land Central Banks. The Land Central Banks also credited them the full amount of the *Geschäftsbeträge*, i.e. the initial allotment in Deutsche Marks that the banks had payed out or credited to businesses.

If these credited funds and their other assets were still not sufficient to secure a 'suitable equity capital' and cover the converted liabilities, the banks were granted equalization claims against the public sector at 3 per cent interest from the *Länder*. However, para. 28 of the Currency Conversion Act prohibited budget deficits in the public sector. In order not to overburden the public sector from the very start with debts incurred through such equalization claims, a significant proportion of the losses suffered by the banks as a result of the nullification of Reich debts was passed on specifically to the depositors at the banks by granting a currency conversion rate of only 6.5 per cent at most instead of the normal 10 per cent.[372]

The Fourth Currency Reform Act of 4 October 1948 must also be considered in connection with the inflationary trends that followed currency reform. These trends were easier to spot than those of the earlier period of suppressed inflation because Ludwig Erhard, who was at the time director of the Economics Administration and later became Federal Economics Minister, ordered the decontrol of prices in tandem with an end to rationing on most markets. Erhard had been given the authority to take such action by the Bizonal parliament, comprising of the Economic Council and the Länderrat, in the *Gesetz über Leitsätze für die Bewirtschaftung und Preispolitik nach der Geldreform* (Act on Guidelines for Rationing and Price Policy following Currency Reform) passed on 24 June 1948.

The price increases that occurred during that summer may therefore have been an important reason why, on 4 October 1948, the military governments passed the Fourth Currency Reform Act, which greatly diminished the purchasing power on the *Festkontos* of the banks. In order to combat inflation further, the Bizonal administration prohibited profiteering by enacting laws that went into effect on 7 October 1948 and 28 January 1949.[373] In late October 1948, the Bank deutscher Länder placed restrictions on credit, which were gradually lifted once prices began to stabilize in late May 1949.[374] In the meantime, wage controls had been lifted by law on 3 November 1948. The fact that aid from the Marshall Plan began during this critical period helped stabilize the situation.[375]

Decisions made in connection with currency reform also simplified foreign business relations. On 1 May 1948, the exchange rate for 1 RM was uniformly set at 0.30 US dollars. Subsequently this rate was also valid for the Deutsche Mark. Step by step, this exchange rate replaced a multitude of differing settlement rates in foreign trade that had been used by the Joint Foreign Exchange Agency (JFEA) and the Joint Export–Import Agency (JEIA) of the Bizone.[376] Due to the dollar gap, foreign exchange controls had to be continued, of course.[377]

The Currency Conversion Act also set guidelines for handling the demands of foreign creditors against German banks. Reichsmark debts to foreigners could be converted into Deutsche Marks along the same lines as domestic debts (para. 15). However, the creditor had the right to refuse to accept this, i.e. to file an objection. Should he choose to exercise this right, the *Land* involved (meaning one of the later federal states) was required to free the debtor of all additional obligations. Paragragh 15 also stipulated that debts in foreign currency, including those of the Standstill Agreements, could only be paid in Deutsche Marks if the creditor agreed to such an arrangement. Thus, Germany's foreign creditors had left all options open for a later debt agreement.

The Currency Conversion Act was spelled out in detail by numerous regulating ordinances issued by the Allied Bank Commission. The second of these, called the Bank Ordinance, went into effect on the same day as the law itself, on 27 June 1948. The three big banks were mentioned explicitly in this ordinance, in order to place their successor institutions at a disadvantage in calculating their equity capital in the conversion balance sheet, compared with other credit institutions.[378]

The big banks were discriminated against even more in the 35th regulating ordinance of the Currency Conversion Act, the so-called Relocation Ordinance of 9 September 1949, which stipulated the conversion procedure for banks whose head office was located outside of West Germany although its branch offices were found within its borders. In such cases, a credit institution could only be eligible for equalization claims if it was considered a relocated bank. This involved a special procedure including the Bank deutscher Länder and bank supervisory officials. Once a credit institution was granted this relocated status, it was allowed to have a second legal head office within the Federal Republic. As a result, residents of the Federal Republic could assert their old Reichsmark claims against banks with head offices outside of the currency area, and foreign creditors could bring their claims to bear, in both cases against the relocated institutions to the extent to which the loans they had granted were invested in West Germany.

The banks for which the option of relocation applied found this attractive because the revived liabilities were offset by the advantageous acquisition of equalization claims against the *Länder*, and because new business opportunities resulted in the process of regulating the claims. However, the big banks were explicitly excluded from this relocation option, since no one wanted to anticipate the final decision in the decentralization issue. Therefore, the procedures for currency conversion for the western branches of the big banks remained a major point of controversy until 1952, in the political tug of war for the legal decoupling of the successor institutions and the recentralization of the big banks.[379]

The big banks in Berlin were dealt another blow when the Allies implemented currency reform in West Berlin: accounts maintained in East Berlin for West Berliners and for the members of the United Nations, i.e. non-Germans, had to be converted through other, non-dormant banks, and the person entitled had some say in selecting which bank this would be. The only accounts remaining for the 'old banks' were the inconvertible ones belonging to account holders in East Berlin, the Soviet occupation zone, and foreigners from countries that were not members of the United Nations and later from those countries that were not formally recognized by the Federal Republic. The 'old banks' would experience a similar blow in the course of the 'securities settlement'.[380]

E.W. Schmidt, who had since become the chief economist at the Rheinisch-Westfälische Bank, completed a rather lengthy review of the consequences of currency reform on 30 August 1948, and sent it to Abs at his home, Bentgerhof near Remagen. In Schmidt's opinion, the initial psychological impact of the new currency had been exceptional: 'People have regained their trust in money and therefore their willingness to exchange goods for money has increased or been fully restored.' Industrial production in the Bizone had risen in July by 20 per cent over that of June 1948, thus reaching 60 per cent of the production level of 1936 as opposed to 50 per cent in June. During the initial weeks following currency reform, Schmidt continued, the supply of goods on the market was reflecting not current levels of production, but current levels of warehouse inventory. This was leading several 'sceptics' to fear that a new inflationary 'backlog' was unavoidable once inventories had been exhausted. However, 'the favourable supply of consumer goods on the market is not only dependent on the productivity of the domestic economy, but is also greatly influenced by the amount of foreign raw materials available to the economy. This is the crucial link between the success of currency reform and the help offered by the Marshall Plan.'

Schmidt was particularly critical of the excessive exchange rate of 30 cents per Deutsche Mark, with which the German export industry could not survive on the world markets. He also criticized the fact that currency reform had been decoupled from an equalization of war burdens, 'because it is imperative for economic reconstruction that everyone in general and each individual in particular clearly perceive the basis on which to build their future'. Last of all, Schmidt viewed the distribution of the new money with scepticism. By giving out money in lump sums per head, and 'by supplying the public sector with billions in new money', the link had been broken between the production of goods and the earning of income. The result of this was an oversupply of long-term funds for the consumer goods industry, and a shortage of the same for production industries. On the one hand, 'commerce and the consumer goods industry obtained great cash resources by emptying their warehouses and were therefore not dependent on bank loans to the degree expected, so that even the banks are relatively liquid'. On the other hand, the problems of financing the majority of industry remained completely unsolved. In addition to foreign help, only the creation of new savings capital could offer relief. However, in order to do this it was first necessary to reduce the tax burden, 'to a much greater extent than that resulting from the completely insufficient, "provisional" tax reform'.[381]

III. Recentralization of the Big Banks

1. The success of German initiatives partially to recentralize the big banks 1949–1952

The historical developments after 1945, both world-wide and in Germany, changed the priorities of the Western powers completely. Whereas they had initially shared common cause with the Soviet Union in uprooting National Socialism in Germany, by 1946–47 at the latest they viewed the expansionist efforts of the communist sphere of influence throughout the world as the greatest threat to Western democratic and economic systems. The Cold War was raging. Currency reform was introduced separately in East and West Germany, followed immediately by the almost year-long blockade of Berlin. Led by the Americans, the Western powers redirected their foreign policy priorities to containing communism. One important aspect of this containment policy was to strengthen the productive power of the economies and raise living standards in the nations of the Western world, so as to destroy the breeding ground of communist ideology. This was also true for Western countries such as Italy and France, where communist parties enjoyed considerable popularity and political strength due in good part to their anti-fascist past.

In this context, the economic reconstruction of West Germany and its integration into the western European economic market became a top priority. The American government and especially the French government were slower than the British to recognize the indispensable role of German business. However, in 1947, both the American and British occupation powers eased the restrictive regulations imposed on the reconstruction of German industry.[382] As a consequence, it became a greater political priority in the West to attend to the needs of both the West German and the western European economies than to fulfil Soviet reparation claims with shipments from the Western zones.[383] As a result of differences with the Soviet Union in the Allied Control Council and in other four-power agencies, the goal of unifying all of Germany into a single economic and political unit, as specified by the Potsdam Agreement, was only pursued for the Western occupation zones and for West Berlin. In a certain sense, one of the highpoints of this development was the founding of the Federal Republic with a government based on Western democratic principles that had extensive autonomy in its political affairs.

Against this background of world politics, the Germans discovered new possibilities for political initiative. They found they were able to influence the political framework of the banking structure, even though the Occupation Statute signed in connection with the founding of the Federal Republic explicitly reserved decision-making authority over legislation dealing with banking to the three Western powers. This authority was conferred upon the Allied Bank Commission, which continued to exist as a body of the Allied High Commission following the founding of the Federal Republic. The attitude of the Western powers to the political suggestions of their gradually emerging new ally, the Federal Republic, was characterized by goodwill, co-operation and a willingness to compromise. The banking authorities of the British occupation power, who had only reluctantly conceded to the American plans to decentralize the big banks, now became the most important partners of the Germans in reconciling the American and French representatives in the Allied Bank Commission to the idea of recentralization.

The public relations campaign for recentralization of the German big banks began in the Anglo-American countries in March 1949. A British editor from the *Economist*, Walter A. Everitt, visited the Western zones, accompanied for part of the trip by the renowned German radio commentator Peter von Zahn. Everitt was gathering material for a major series of articles on the German economy and banking system. E.W. Schmidt from the Rheinisch-Westfälische Bank supplied him with an extensive exposé on the negative effects of bank decentralization. When Schmidt told Abs this, the latter replied: 'Last week I had a three-hour talk late at night with Mr Everitt about the financial situation in West Germany in general and am now curious to see how the series of articles in the *Economist* will turn out.'[384] Before the article entitled 'The German Banking Reorganisation' appeared in the *Economist* on 29 October 1949, Everitt published a similar one entitled 'Germany's Capital Needs' in the London journal *The Banker* in July 1949, which dealt with the weaknesses of the decentralized German banking system. Abs was pleased: 'I noted with interest that the night hours spent with the author were not wasted.'[385] After this Abs was in close contact with the British Banking Committee for German Affairs, a committee comprised of leading members from the London world of finance which represented the interests of British banks in British banking policy in Germany. On 19 July 1951, Abs even attended consultations of this committee in London on the proposed recentralization legislation.

In the summer of 1949, deliberations began in the Allied Bank Commission on replacing the existing interim form of bank decentralization with a final, legally unambiguous and permanent solution. More specifically, this meant that the old Berlin banks were to be liquidated and their assets and liabilities transferred to new joint stock banks with regionally restricted business operations in West Germany.[386] The Allies wanted this wrapped up before the first administration of the new Federal Republic took office in Bonn.[387] Whereas the Americans and the French were chiefly interested in anchoring the decentralization of the big banks as a permanent element of the new political federalism in the Federal Republic, the central British objective was to protect outstanding claims against the German big banks dating back to the pre-war period. In 1931, the British government had pressured the British banks, the main creditors of the short-term loans to German banks in the banking crisis at the time, to accept the Standstill Agreements, although these were hardly to their advantage. Therefore, the government now felt compelled to protect strongly the interests of the British banks.[388]

By mid-1950, the German debts in foreign currency from these Standstill Agreements, dating back to the banking crisis of 1931, amounted to about 425 million DM, of which 293 million DM were owed to British banks, 114 million DM to the Americans, and 15 million DM to the Swiss. Some 51 per cent of the debtors were located in the British zone, 11 per cent in the American, and 5 per cent in the French. Eight per cent were located in Berlin and the rest were either in the Soviet occupation zone or in territory no longer belonging to Germany.[389] These figures clearly show why the British military government in Germany, encouraged by the banks of the City of London, proved to be much more interested in establishing a strong German banking system than were the Americans.

Yet even the Americans were beginning to criticize the decentralization policy which they had implemented. In May 1949, Shepard Morgan became head of the Finance Division of the American military government, replacing Jack

Bennett, who had advocated bank decentralization for three years. With regard to the tasks involved in reconstructing Germany's economy, Morgan stated then: 'We have already gone too far in endeavoring to force Germans to adopt American practices and procedures.'[390] The day the first Adenauer cabinet took office, 21 September 1949, the military governments were replaced by civilian High Commissioners: namely, Sir Brian Robertson for Great Britain, André François-Poncet for France, and John McCloy for the USA. Due to the reorganization of the American bureaucracy resulting from this change, Morgan's influence waned, and he resigned in November 1949. But by then, the Americans had become willing to reconsider their more extreme positions.

Although the Allies wanted to have the big banks issue settled, the solution codified, and the fact of decentralization chiselled into the stone of reality before a new federal government took over the affairs of state, differences of opinion prevented them from accomplishing this in the autumn of 1949.[391] It was the British who used legal arguments in October to prevent the realization of what was foreseen as the definitive solution.[392] This solution was based on the decentralization that had been implemented up to that point. The British wanted to postpone the final settlement of this issue until after the new Federal Republic could be incorporated into the negotiations, for Great Britain had the most to gain from a tug of war with the Americans and French over decentralization. The British were counting on the political weight of this new 'lean and hungry' – meaning highly motivated – partner to help tilt the scale in favour of re-establishing strong German joint stock banks.

As if previously arranged with the British bank authorities, the three big banks began an initiative themselves in October 1949 to have the dismembered banks reunified. Leading figures from each of the regional institutions of the big banks met in Düsseldorf that month to develop a strategy for initiating legislation in Bonn to recentralize the big banks. Three men, one board member from each of the three banks, were placed in charge of this initiative: Paul Marx, member of the board of managing directors at the Commerzbank, Carl Goetz, president of the supervisory board of the Dresdner Bank, and Hermann J. Abs for the Deutsche Bank. E. W. Schmidt was assigned the task of compiling the arguments for recentralization into a memorandum. The 15-page paper, presented on 2 November 1949 and entitled 'The Decentralization of the Big Banks', systematically listed the various arguments against bank decentralization, including those used earlier, and culminated in calling for the re-establishment of the status quo ante: 'The complete restoration of the previous capabilities cannot be achieved by makeshift constructions of any sort, such as a holding company, but only by reuniting the established successor institutions into a single large banking organization.'[393]

On 7 November 1949, Abs had Franz Heinrich Ulrich, since 1948 director of the Wuppertal branch and a future board member, telephone Schmidt and inform him that, although the paper corresponded with the decisions made at the

Düsseldorf meeting and although Abs agreed with its content in principle, he was concerned 'that in the present situation, 100 per cent solutions will not be accepted'. Therefore, it would be better not to aim for full recentralization of the banks, 'because if the re-establishment of complete centralization is suggested but cannot be achieved, the proposal for partial centralization is no longer credible'. The British had given Abs the impression 'that they would not support proposals for a full re-establishment of centralization in the Western zones; but on the other hand, they also would not argue in favour of maintaining decentralization in the current form of ten institutions'. In agreement with Plassmann and Bechtolf, he therefore suggested that the paper be rewritten to propose a form of partial recentralization. They had to act quickly because the British were pressing for a final, 'meaning a legal solution to the issue of the big banks very soon'. He himself would propose 'five or six institutions, at the most; one in northern Germany, one in the west, one in the south-west and two in the south. And each of these institutions should be self-supporting.'[394]

On 11 November 1949, Abs summarized his ideas on recentralization at the time in a four-page memorandum and personally presented this to the President of the Bank deutscher Länder Directorate, Vocke, so that Vocke could act on it in his official capacity. Vocke sent an English translation of Abs' memorandum, with a letter dated 12 November, to the American and the British members of the Allied Bank Commission, S. Morgan and D.H. McDonald.[395] In this paper, Abs argued that a reorganization of the banking system was necessary for two main reasons. First, the laws of the military governments broke up the big banks into regional institutions with regard to business organization. However, they did not decouple the banks with regard to legal status, tax liabilities or stock corporation law. Therefore it was appropriate 'to underpin the decoupling that has taken place *de facto* but not *de jure* as required by legal regulations'. Second, the successor institutions had been set up along the rather randomly determined borders of the *Länder*: for example in south-west or northern Germany. This precluded the creation of a truly viable and stable regional banking system. 'Larger banking units should be introduced within which it is possible to guarantee a better system of borrowing between institutions, a healthier mixture of debtors and thus a more reasonable distribution of risk. This would go hand in hand with a considerable simplification of the bureaucratic apparatus and would reduce expenses to a significant degree.' Perhaps the existing goodwill enjoyed by the mother banks could also be used for certain major business transactions, primarily for foreign business, for the business of underwriting, and for syndicate transactions. The mother banks could assume these specific functions as *banques d'affaires* without violating the rights of the successor banks also to take part in such business. Abs argued that it did not appear to be advantageous to have a large number of more or less unknown regional banks represent German interests abroad, especially in credit transactions.

After this paper was submitted, Abs and Vocke left for the United States, where they travelled separately until mid-December 1949, talking about credit possibilities on behalf of business in the Federal Republic. In Washington, DC, Abs' impression was confirmed that the Americans would not accept a complete revision of the decentralization policy for political reasons.[396] During his trip to the USA, Abs was honoured at a dinner by the renowned Council on Foreign Relations in New York on 5 December 1949, and he met with Allen Dulles, a lawyer and diplomat who had once been president of this council himself. He had been stationed in Switzerland as US intelligence chief for central Europe during the war, later practised law in New York, and would head the CIA from 1953 to 1961.

Abs' trip provoked an outcry among certain sectors of the American press and in the American government, which led to a renewed investigation of Abs by the US Department of State to determine if he should be considered as *persona non grata* in the USA due to his activities during the Hitler regime. Although the investigation found nothing to hang on Abs, he was contacted repeatedly in the spring of 1950 by the office of the US High Commissioner for Germany and given a list of questions to answer about his past. He willingly did this in March and April, submitting his answers as a signed statement.[397]

In December 1949, a series of articles appeared in the German press, undoubtedly prompted by deliberate leaks, which addressed the possibility of a pending recentralization of the big banks. On 3 December 1949, the *Frankfurter Allgemeine Zeitung* ran an article with the headline, 'Big Banks Again?'[398] The same day an article appeared in the *Mannheimer Morgen* with the headline, 'Recentralization of Banking Pending?' which revealed that 'The possibility of reinstating the German big banks is reportedly being considered now by experts of the American High Commission. It has become necessary to review this issue because the four-power agreement on the dismantling of the German big banks from 1945 is also being reconsidered as part of the revision of various laws enacted by the military governments.' On 28 December 1949, *Die Welt*, the *Frankfurter Allgemeine Zeitung* and the *Rheinische Post* reported on the following news release by the Vereinigte Wirtschaftsdienste (United Economic Services) two days before: 'A leading economic expert of the Allied High Commission stated recently in Frankfurt, that in the coming weeks the occupation authorities were expecting German proposals for the re-establishment of big banks in the territory of the Federal Republic. Dr Hermann Abs, a member of the board of the Reconstruction Bank, and other German officials have been encouraged particularly by the British to work out such plans. The reason given for the Allied willingness to revise the bank situation is that the four-power agreements from 1945 on dismantling the German big banks have not proven fully efficient. Throughout the years, banks in several *Länder*, especially in Schleswig-Holstein, Rhineland-Palatinate and North Hesse have experienced serious problems in several areas, including the general profitability of the institutions. Therefore, a reorganization of the scope of business of private banks is being considered. For example, there might be banks with head offices in Hamburg, Düsseldorf or Munich that would operate solely in northern, western or southern Germany, respectively.'[399] The Finance Division of the American High Commissioner identified Abs as the originator of this press campaign.[400]

Abs had his memorandum to Vocke sent to E.W. Schmidt. He requested Schmidt to make all the necessary changes to the extensive proposal he had authored, so that the two documents would correspond before Abs entered into negotiations with German and Allied officials on 3 January 1950. Schmidt was finished with his revision by 30 December 1949. Although in a letter accompanying the paper he again expressed his preference for advocating total recentralization, he dropped this proposal in the paper in favour of partial recentralization.[401]

In a special vote, the British adopted Abs' proposals nearly verbatim as their own when the Allied Bank Commission decided, on 14 December 1949, to request political guidelines on how to handle the bank issue from the next highest authority, the Finance Committee of the Allied High Commission. One American expert noted then: 'Obviously, the UK member of the Allied Bank Commission has accepted the substance of the Abs proposal lock, stock, and barrel.'[402] The Americans and the French did not want to renegotiate the central facet of the existing plans for a permanent solution to the bank decentralization issue; the existing territorial divisions were to be retained.

However, in February the American position began to change. An expert from the Finance Division of the US High Commission, Fred H. Klopstock, analysed the Abs proposal and recommended in a memorandum dated 2 February 1950 that parts of it be accepted: 'The emergence of four or five regional banking areas through amalgamation of existing successor banks appears to be a desirable development that should be welcomed if not encouraged by HICOG.'[403] Klopstock used economic considerations similar to those used by the Germans to support his recommendation. But he totally rejected any type of proposal for retaining the mother banks in Berlin. He also recommended prohibiting, or at least restricting, the traditional proxy voting rights of banks in order to diminish their 'excessive' control over industrial enterprises, especially since some German circles had also made this demand, albeit over the strong objections of the banks. However, the Allies had missed the chance to introduce the institutional division of banking functions characteristic of the American system, meaning the separation of investment banks and commercial banks, and thus to ban 'universal' banks. This should have been done before Allied military rule ended.

A.J. Warner from the Public Finance Section agreed in general with these conclusions. In his 9 February memorandum, he even named four possible banking districts: (1) Bremen, Hamburg, Schleswig-Holstein and Lower Saxony; (2) North Rhine-Westphalia and Rhineland-Palatinate; (3) Hesse and Bavaria; and (4) Württemberg-Baden with southern Württemberg and southern Baden. He also argued that the three big banks could have been kept in their previous form only if the separation of commercial and investment banking had been introduced in time. Now it was too late. Therefore, there was no real alternative but to liquidate the old banks, and he had already developed proposals for this two years previously in co-operation with the legal department as an amendment to the military government Law No. 57. The 'delicate' issue of direct and indirect foreign debts of the banks also needed to be solved, 'which seems to have exerted such important influence on the British position'.[404] He called the decentralization of bank supervision at the *Länder* level an unfortunate result of the 'enthusiasm of the early days'. In his opinion, the US High Commissioner should not block the initiatives of the German Federal Government to re-establish a central body for bank supervision if such a proposal was presented as one of many bank reform proposals.

Immediately after this, the American Finance Division agreed to adopt this political position. It categorically rejected any form of retaining the old Berlin banks as *banques d'affaires*, and thus opposed the continued use of the old business names. However, it was now willing to restructure the banking system into four or five banking areas, since the existing division had indeed created uneconomical banking districts. The enhanced power of the banks resulting from larger banking areas would have to be compensated by restricting their proxy voting power.[405]

In February 1950, political instructions solicited from the London government practically confirmed the position of British financial experts from the Allied High Commission that Great Britain had never been interested in destroying the big banks, that the first preference in the pending reform would be completely to recentralize the banks within the Federal Republic, and that, in view of the expected objections of the Americans and the French, the second preference would be to strive to establish banking areas which would be as large as possible. It was recommended that German proposals on bank restructuring be considered seriously, and no matter what solution was found, it was imperative to pay special attention to the debt service on pre-war loans and on new credit anticipated in the future.[406]

In early January 1950, both the Federal Government and the parliament in Bonn officially took up the issue of the big banks. In early November 1949, Adenauer had created the Economic Committee of the Federal Chancellor, composed of Ministers Erhard, Schäffer and Blücher, Presidents Vocke (Directorate) and Bernard (Central Bank Council) from the Bank deutscher Länder, the banker and Christian Democratic member of parliament Pferdmenges, and Abs. This committee met in January 1950.[407] The Bundestag Committee for Money and Credit also met on 12–13 January 1950, to discuss a possible reorganization of the banking system for the first time. Authorities from the Länder bank supervisory boards were asked to speak at these hearings, while Abs, Marx, Goetz and Zinsser represented the interests of the big banks. Presidents Vocke and Bernard from the Bank deutscher Länder also attended.

Two members of this parliamentary committee were also custodians of regional institutions of the big banks, Neuburger (Südwestbank) and Lehr (Rheinisch-Westfälische Bank). Little was accomplished in this committee: neither details for the desired reorganization were discussed nor memoranda or concrete plans presented. Its sole achievement was to urge the Federal Government to attend to the problem as soon as possible.[408] Shortly thereafter, Finance Minister Schäffer contacted representatives of the big banks, even though it was not clear within the Adenauer administration then, or for some time afterwards, whether he or Economics Minister Erhard was responsible for the area of money and credit.[409]

At this point, Dr Fritz C. Kempner began to work on behalf of the big banks. Kempner, a lawyer who had been forced to emigrate from Berlin because of his Jewish origin, was apparently brought to the attention of the banks by Abs. The special connection between Abs and the Kempner family dated back to late 1938. Paul Kempner, Fritz Kempner's father, had been one of the owners of the banking establishment Mendelssohn & Co., in Berlin.[410] When this bank was liquidated in 1938 as part of the Nazi policy of Aryanization, Abs had worked with Rudolf Löb on the acquisition agreement regarding the banking business, bank employees and pension liabilities of Mendelssohn. In the spring of 1950, Löb wrote to Abs: 'I was grateful for the twist of fate that allowed me to negotiate with you on the matter, since I thought I knew your true feelings.'[411]

When the war ended, Fritz Kempner went to Paris to represent the New York law firm of Cahill, Gordon, Zachry & Reindel. It is presumed that he conducted an investigation of Abs for the American military government even before the war ended.[412] But if Abs did not know Fritz Kempner personally before the latter emigrated from Berlin, then certainly at the latest he had made Kempner's acquaintence by the time Abs returned from his visit to the USA in March 1939.[413] Until September 1949, Kempner worked for the American military government in several capacities, one of which was as a financial expert in the bizonal Joint Export–Import Agency. He also worked closely with the Allied Bank Commission.[414] His other activities have been described thus: 'He negotiated with the Federal Finance Ministry as a representative of the American High Commission concerning the bank issue, and was at the same time the legal counsel of the British standstill creditors.'[415] He therefore had the contacts and experience necessary to help him develop proposals for recentralization that the Americans would accept. According to the final billing, his law office in New York was to receive a total of $50,000 plus $2,003.13 in expenses for his legal counsel on behalf of the three former big banks in 1950 and 1951. This fee was very high for the time and mirrored the value that the banks attributed to Kempner's services and contacts. The cost was divided among the bank groups of the Deutsche Bank, the Dresdner Bank and the Commerzbank at a ratio of 40:40:20, respectively.[416]

On 12 February 1950, Kempner presented Abs with a 15-page, 'strictly confidential' first draft of a plan entitled, 'The Future Structure of the German

Joint Stock Banks'. In it, he described the fundamental problem of the current situation in the following terms: 'Although the old banks are no longer involved in the banking business, as is anticipated by their by-laws, they have also not been liquidated; the successor banks, on the other hand, are legally still branches of the old banks, but in actuality they operate as if they were independent joint stock companies.'[417] In order to create stable successor institutions, efforts had to be made to initiate partial recentralization. Business for the regional institutions in Schleswig-Holstein, Lower Saxony, southern Württemberg and even Bavaria was less profitable than in the highly industrialized regions of the country. 'Yet up to this point, all of the regional banks have had exceptionally large profit margins.' But if these should shrink back to the pre-war level, the business of regional banks in the above-mentioned *Länder* would no longer be lucrative. During a recession this could even lead to bankruptcy, which in turn would topple the entire structure of credit institutions: 'The banking system of a country is just as strong as its weakest joint stock bank.' For this reason, and because of seasonal fluctuations in the demand for credit in some regions, a stable banking system requires banking districts so large that regional liquidity balancing could automatically take place within one successor institution. With regard to the argument that the same could be achieved in the existing central banking system, Kempner pointed out that the existing system was considerably more expensive. In his plan for partial recentralization, he proposed creating three groups from the 11 *Länder* that then comprised the Federal Republic: a northern group with its head office in Hamburg; a western group including North Rhine-Westphalia, Rhineland-Palatinate and Bremen, with its head office in Düsseldorf; and a southern group, for which he suggested having more than one head office, in light of the well-known rivalry between Munich and Frankfurt.

In his paper, Kempner also addressed several other issues, including the relation of such partially recentralized banks to the central banking system, which would continue to be organized on a *Länder* basis, the planned conversion of regional banks into joint stock banks, the handling of the foreign debts of the old banks in creating new institutions, and questions pertaining to the liquidation of the old banks and their relations to the new joint stock banks in the West. On the issue of foreign debts, so crucial to the British, Kempner felt that the foreign creditors had to agree to a distribution of the debt load among the successor banks once these had been transformed into joint stock banks: 'It is strongly recommended that a committee be formed, which is authorized to negotiate such an agreement with the foreign creditors as soon as the principles of the new banking structure in West Germany have been decided and before the successor banks have been converted into joint stock banks ... The creditors of the old banks, whether foreign or German, have the undeniable right to demand that all assets of the old banks, including the net value of the successor banks, are applied to fulfilling their claims against the old banks.'

Kempner visited Abs on 6–7 March 1950, in Frankfurt, in order to discuss his exposé. Abs wrote to Bechtolf in Hamburg, Plassmann in Düsseldorf and Rummel in Stuttgart, on 7 March, that Kempner would be visiting the Rheinisch-Westfälische Bank in Düsseldorf on 14 March, in order 'to discuss with everyone' how the bank issue could be handled further. E.W. Schmidt kept Kempner, who was in Paris, informed by providing reports from Düsseldorf during the second half of February.[418]

Following his initial contact with officials from the big banks, Finance Minister Schäffer invited representatives from the finance ministries of the *Länder* and the bank supervisory boards, from the Bank deutscher Länder, and from the big banks to Bonn on 13 February to discuss the big banks issue. He also included the Minister of Economics, who was still sulking over the clash with Schäffer over responsibilities. Schäffer wanted to use this meeting as preparation for his regular meeting at Petersberg with the financial advisers of the Allied High Commissioners, scheduled for 23 February, at which time the bank issue was to be discussed. At the meeting on 13 February, the representatives of the big banks must have presented the proposal to reorganize the banking system into three major districts, which Kempner had included in his paper, submitted to them the day before. In any case, the group attending this meeting tended to support the three-district solution with head offices to be located in Hamburg, Düsseldorf and Frankfurt.[419]

As a result of the meeting on 23 February and a subsequent one on 30 March 1950, between the finance ministers and the financial advisers of the Allied High Commission, the Allies officially requested Schäffer to submit a German proposal for reorganizing the big banks. This represented a great success for the Germans, for in the cases of I.G. Farben and the iron and steel industry, the Allied authorities had taken charge of developing plans for reorganization.[420] 'We have passed the ball to the Germans,' commented the British financial adviser Eugene Melville in his report to London.[421]

In early March 1950, experts from the ministries of finance, economics and justice, from the Bank deutscher Länder, and from the special committee for bank supervision at the bizonal Länder Council met for the first interministerial session to prepare a legislative proposal. Ministerialrat Dr Ferdinand Kremer, head of the department of Money and Credit at the Federal Finance Ministry, and his section chief, Oberregierungsrat Dr Ernst vom Hofe, organized this meeting and the future work on a legislative proposal.[422] The general attitude towards the idea of recentralizing the banks was positive, especially with regard to improving Germany's credit standing abroad. Not until the Federal Government, the Länder, the Bank deutscher Länder and the interested banks had reached complete agreement on a proposal was it to be presented to the Allies. In the meantime, the participants were to specify their ideas and present them in writing.

The Central Bank Council had already begun to take action. At the first regularly scheduled Council meeting on 26 January 1950, following the hearings on the bank issue at the Bundestag Committee on Money and Credit, which Presidents Vocke and Bernard had attended, the two men reported on the developments taking place. They used this opportunity to invite Abs to the next meeting on 10 February 1950. At this February meeting, Abs discussed his concept of a reorganization of banking with the presidents of the Land Central Banks, who were sceptical of the fact that larger banking districts would no longer correspond with the jurisdictions of individual Land Central Banks. They represented the federalist interests in the bank issue, whereas the Directorate of the Bank deutscher Länder, headed by Vocke, was in complete agreement with the view of the big banks, which advocated centralization. This held true for both the reorganization of the big banks and the constitutional stipulation found in Art. 88 of the Basic Law, requiring the establishment of a federal bank. At any rate, on 10 February 1950, the Central Bank Council charged the Directorate with the responsibility of 'submitting proposals for reorganizing the big banks in the Federal Republic'.[423]

Dr Rudolf Eicke, head of the bank department in the Directorate, completed an 18-page draft proposal on 27 February 1950, which at Vocke's behest had received the approval of Abs, Goetz and Marx and proposed the same three-district solution.[424] Nine of the eleven Land Central Bank presidents commented on this paper, only one of whom, President Klasen in Hamburg, expressed a positive opinion. Klasen, who had been a senior vice-president at the Deutsche Bank before becoming president of the Land Central Bank in Hamburg, and who would later serve on the board of managing directors of the Deutsche Bank, even went so far as to propose a two-district solution. The eight other banks rejected the proposal because of the incongruence between the planned banking districts and the existing districts of the Land Central Banks. The fiscal interests of those *Länder* where there was to be no head office of a bank were also put forth as arguments against the plan.

At its meeting on 19–20 April 1950, the Central Bank Council voted eleven to two (Vocke and Klasen) against accepting the proposals, because 'the regional scope of a credit institution should neither fundamentally nor permanently exceed that of the Land Central Bank which is responsible for the head office of the institution'.[425] Although Vocke and Klasen fully defended the position of the big banks, the majority of the Council, including President Bernard, opposed the three-district solution.

This prevented the Germans from quickly agreeing on a plan for reorganization. The Land Central Banks turned out to harbour federalist sentiments that were even stronger than those of the powers who had prescribed federalism in Germany, namely the Allies, especially the USA. This was a severe setback for the representatives of the big banks, for the Directorate of the Bank deutscher Länder, and for the federal ministries involved, all of which had an interest in introducing a form of recentralization and had set their sights on the three-district solution.

Nevertheless, the Central Bank Council again asked the Directorate of the Bank deutscher Länder to state its position, instructing it this time to ensure 'that the decentralization principle clearly be sustained not only in form but also in content', should the eventual proposal suggest a reduced number of banking districts.[426] In late May 1950, the Directorate submitted the requested position paper in which it reviewed the expedience of recentralizing the banks into six, four or three banking districts. Even the Allied High Commission announced on 1 May 1950 that it considered a recentralization of the banking districts to be appropriate for the smaller *Länder*. However, such centralization should occur congruently for the big banks as well as for the Land Central Banks.[427]

The attitude of the Central Bank Council and the Allies did not lead to a feeling of resignation on the part of the Deutsche Bank representatives, quite the contrary. Fritz C. Kempner had written a four-page memorandum in March that made additional proposals to the paper by Dr Eicke, and Abs had sent this with a letter dated 23 March 1950 to his colleagues Bechtolf in Hamburg, Plassmann in Düsseldorf, and Rummel in Stuttgart. Among the new proposals was one to intensify the participation of the *Länder* in drawing up plans for bank decoupling, evidently in order to counter the opposition of the Land Central Banks.[428] Kempner also spoke directly with Ferdinand Kremer, the responsible official at the Finance Ministry, and with representatives of the Allied High Commission. He reported at a board meeting on 5 May 1950 that he had the impression the Allies would permit the amalgamation of the successor institutions on the basis of the three-district solution. Abs added that, in his opinion, the US military government was willing to do this, and the British would even favour a complete recentralization, meaning a one-district solution, in West Germany. It was agreed that the three-district solution would remain the goal unless the opportunity arose during further negotiations to achieve a two-district solution. In order to overcome the opposition of the Land Central Banks to recentralization, it was agreed 'that regardless of the composition of the successor institutions, the land central banking system would remain functional in so far as the head branches would receive a certain degree of autonomy with regard to their transactions with the Land Central Banks, so that it would not be necessary to introduce a similar amagalmation of the Land Central Banks'.[429]

On 17 May 1950, Deutsche Bank board members and Kempner were to meet with Goetz and Dr Richter from the Dresdner Bank in order 'to agree upon a joint strategy, or more specifically, the formulation of the petition to be written. Kempner offered to compose a draft petition and to submit it in time for the meeting.'[430] Kempner's 37-page 'Proposal for the Future Structure of the German Joint Stock Banks' (strictly confidential) was completed 12 May 1950. Small, rather superficial changes were made to it at the meeting five days later (participants: Abs, Bechtolf, Goetz, Dr Hermann Richter, Kempner, and Dr

Hermann Herold as minutes keeper) and again at a meeting on 2 June with a representative of the Commerzbank (Dr Hanns Deuss); each meeting was held at the Reconstruction Loan Corporation in Frankfurt. The final version of the proposal was completed on 31 May 1950, and 'submitted by: Hermann J. Abs, Carl Goetz and Paul Marx'. It adopted the title and text of the Kempner draft verbatim in the first section and reflected the content of the draft nearly completely in the second section.

The plan proposed to divide the Federal Republic into three banking districts. It also explicitly stated that this was considered the second-best solution, which was only being suggested because the best solution, meaning complete recentralization, was currently not attainable. It proposed locating the head offices of the successor banks in Hamburg for northern Germany, in Düsseldorf or Cologne for the Rhineland and Westphalian regions, and Frankfurt for southern Germany. The arguments used to press for the urgent replacement of the current set-up, which both the American and British military governments had implemented merely as an interim solution, cleverly played upon the interests of both the Germans and the Allies in reconstructing the German economy also with the aid of foreign loans. The existing 11 regional banks were being 'automatically disqualified from international business transactions. No foreign institution can co-operate closely with banks that have no legal identity, no by-laws, and no supervisory board, that do not publish a balance sheet or a profit and loss account, and that are liable for each other without exercising any mutual control'. Well-known arguments were used to advocate the enlargement of the banking districts: the creation of more stable joint stock banks with a larger regional distribution of risk and sufficient profit-yielding capacity; the necessity of balancing money and capital requirements between regions, a function that neither smaller private banks nor state credit institutions could perform; and the necessity of fulfilling the legitimate need for credit by the regular customers of joint stock banks at the best possible terms, especially during seasonal fluctuations.

The proposal addressed the view prevailing in the Central Bank Council and the Allied High Commission that any new banking districts for joint stock banks had to correspond with the districts of the Land Central Banks. This view was not directly negated. It was stated instead that the creation of a healthy and stable banking system, which would encourage economic development, could not be postponed or prevented by the existing land central banking districts. Whether these should be revised was another matter. This was neither vital nor urgent to the German economy and would only create political problems that would take time to resolve. 'Therefore, this proposal strongly opposes coupling these two problems.' The second half of the paper was concerned with the specific measures for implementing the proposal.

Abs submitted this memorandum, on 5 June 1950, in person to the Federal Ministries of Finance and Economics, and made it available to the Hessian

Finance Minister Dr Werner Hilpert and the Hamburg Finance Senator Dr Walter Dudek. Two days later he send additional copies to the Federal Ministries of Finance and Economics and to Vice-Chancellor Blücher, who headed the Federal Ministry of the Marshall Plan. Abs left it to the Minister of Finance to pass it on to the *Länder* finance ministries, the bank supervisory boards and the Allies. For the latter, Abs announced that additional copies of the memorandum would be sent in English, so that the Allies 'would have an authentic version of this paper at their disposal'.[431] In addition, this memorandum was sent to many German and Allied politicians.

Unexpectedly, the big banks were now suddenly able to find support for their three-district solution among some of the Land Central Bank presidents. Otto Pfleiderer, the president of the Land Central Bank of Württemberg-Baden, had supported the original American plans for decentralization because he was personally convinced that this was a suitable means to control the power of the big banks. But in April 1950, in light of the prevailing opinion among the Land Central Bank presidents that any future districts of joint stock banks needed to correspond with those of the Land Central Banks, Pfleiderer proposed the creation of six districts that would simultaneously act as the districts for both the Land Central Banks and the joint stock banks. These districts would exceed the borders of the *Länder* and would be modelled on the Federal Reserve districts in the USA. Pfleiderer was seeking a compromise solution, and he apparently recognized that economic factors necessitated the creation of larger joint stock banking districts.

However, in practice this would have meant that the smaller *Länder*, especially the city-*Länder* of Bremen and Hamburg, would not have been able to maintain Land Central Banks of their own. These *Länder* were also concerned that this proposal was the beginning of a reorganization of the *Länder* themselves at their expense. Therefore, they began to view the three-district solution as a way to avoid this danger, since the larger Land Central Banks would certainly not sacrifice their own existence in order to create three land central banking districts congruent to the three proposed banking districts. A stand-off ensued in the Central Bank Council, weakening its opposition to the three-district solution considerably.

On 1 June 1950, the Office of the US High Commissioner also expressed its preference for the six-district solution with congruent districts for banks and Land Central Banks over the proposal put forth by Abs, Goetz and Marx.[432] However, that same month the Korean War broke out. As a result, American commitment to the principles underlying its original occupation policy took a backseat to American interests in creating an effective, productive West German economy.

The British welcomed the memorandum by Abs, Goetz and Marx, to no one's surprise. They did not see any problems with implementing the three-district solution. As the largest standstill creditor, they would have supported, even preferred, complete recentralization. This would also have re-established a banking structure more similar to theirs. As ever, the British considered the danger of 'excessive concentration of economic power' (Potsdam Agreement) to lie not in the territorial scope of business operations of the big banks, but in their industrial investments, supervisory board seats and proxy voting rights.[433] However, the British did not support the American proposals to restrict proxy voting rights because they thought these were inordinate.[434]

The recentralization plans of the banks found support not only in the Federal Economics Ministry, but also in the economic ministries of the *Länder*. On 29 June 1950, their representatives in the Economic Committee of the Bundesrat passed a resolution urging the Federal Government to advocate the repeal of Allied decentralization regulations or at least their amendment. In late June 1950, an informal meeting was initiated by the Ministers Erhard and Schäffer and took place at the private home of the banker Robert Pferdmenges, with Vocke from the Bank deutscher Länder, Abs, Goetz and Kempner also attending. Each of these men also supported the three-district solution.[435]

Where opposition to this solution was strong was in the Länder of southern Germany, especially in Hesse, Württemberg-Baden and Bavaria. Bavarian Minister-President Hans Ehard argued against implementing a banking district for southern Germany as a whole, with a head office in Frankfurt, 'because in this case, money management will be conducted by a head office whose location is considered peripherial from the standpoint of the Bavarian economic sphere'.[436] It is no accident that the *Länder* most strongly opposed to recentralization were those in the American occupation zone. The Americans had placed Germans whose views and convictions were more federalist than centralist in key political positions, including the top management of the Land Central Banks. A federal law to reorganize the banking system needed the approval of the Bundesrat. And it was not possible to establish a banking district for southern Germany against the will of all three major *Länder* of this district. Even in the Directorate of the Bank deutscher Länder, which otherwise fully supported the position of the big banks in the recentralization issue, there were those in July 1950 who advocated a compromise solution to create five instead of three banking districts.[437]

The fissure between the fronts became particularly clear during a discussion of the issue in Unkel on 28 July 1950, between the finance ministers of the Federal and Länder governments, the Bank deutscher Länder, the Land Central Bank presidents, and bank representatives including Abs and E.W. Schmidt from the Deutsche Bank Group. The Bank deutscher Länder emphatically supported the three-district solution, as did Land Central Bank President Klasen from Hamburg. Klasen acted on behalf of the central banks in northern Germany and was backed by Hamburg Finance Senator Dudek and by the banker Pferdmenges, a close associate of Adenauer. The delegate from Rhineland-Palatinate approved of the plan, as did the others from the French occupation zone, once Abs deviated from the original plan and conceded that the districts Koblenz and Trier did not necessarily have to be incorporated into the banking district of North Rhine-Westphalia, so that all of Rhineland-Palatinate could belong to the district of southern Germany. After this, only the delegates from the US zone seriously opposed the plan, albeit with varying nuances. For example, 'Dr Veit [Land Central Bank President, Hesse], Frankfurt, qualified his endorsement with certain safeguards and restrictions, whereas Mr Pfleiderer [Land Central Bank President, Württemberg-Baden] and Grasmann [Land Central Bank President, Bavaria] expressed their total opposition – Mr Grasmann giving special emphasis to the federalist aspects.'[438] Federal Finance Minister Schäffer was in favour of the three-district solution, but did not want to disregard the objections of the three *Länder* in the US zone.

The Germans were pressed for time. The Allies were waiting for a legislative proposal from the Federal Government that could be incorporated into the planned liberalization of the occupation statute, particularly in the area of deconcentration policy, which was to be decided on at the conference of the Allied foreign ministers in September 1950 in New York.[439] Again the big banks acted. On 23 August 1950, Abs, Goetz and Marx submitted a paper with additional details concerning their original proposal of 31 May to the responsible authorities. In this paper they pointed out from their perspective the weaknesses of the alternative solutions being debated publicly in connection with the pending bank reform, and argued vehemently against the egoism of the *Länder* in southern Germany. It would endanger the central aim of their three-district solution, namely to create 'vigorous and fully efficient institutions', should Bavaria and Württemberg-Baden decouple themselves from the southern group of *Länder* and five banking districts emerge instead of three. 'By no means' could they agree to this. In August 1950, Economics Minister Ludwig Erhard, who had always opposed bank decentralization for economic reasons, took position against the federalists at the opposite side in this tug of war. He enquired whether the Allied High Commission would be willing to consider favourably a German legislative proposal to recentralize fully the big banks in West Germany. The Americans and the French found this unacceptable, as was to be expected, whereas the British reserved the option of giving it favourable advisement.[440]

In October 1950, representatives of the big banks requested the Federal Ministry of Economics to exert pressure on the Federal Minister of Finance finally to submit a legislative proposal for reorganizing the big banks – which was also in the interest of the Allies. They criticized Finance Minister Schäffer (a member of the Bavarian Christian Social Union Party) for being 'extremely hesitant' in handling the issue, and attributed this to the 'weight he gave Bavarian arguments, which could not hold up under objective, critical evaluation'.[441] Schäffer was indeed in a dilemma, since he favoured the three-district solution but did not want to cross his party colleagues in Bavaria. Therefore by early September he had only proposed federal legislation that would not have demarcated banking districts, but would have handed the authority to determine the regional scope of banking districts to the *Länder*, which were to work closely with the big banks on this issue. The only specific stipulation set down by this legislative proposal was that the balance sheet total of the successor bank in North Rhine-Westphalia was to be the maximum for the banks in the new districts, which would be created by amalgamating other *Länder*.[442]

Starting in July 1950, the Deutsche Bank Group spearheaded a campaign to activate support from industry for their proposal.[443] In the Bundesverband der Deutschen Industrie (Federal Association of German Industry) a new committee was formed under the name 'Money, Credit and Currency' and the chairmanship of Dr Otto Reuleaux. However, not a single member of this committee possessed any competence on the big banks issue. One member, Dr Hans Dichgans, director of the cellulose factory Waldhof, actually turned to E.W. Schmidt at the Rheinisch-Westfälische Bank and Dr Kurt Hunscha of the Rhein-Main-Bank – that is, experts from the Deutsche Bank and Dresdner Bank groups – to provide the arguments to be employed in the Bundesverband resolution on the big banks question. By the end of July, he had received precisely worded material from both of them, from which he composed a draft resolution which began with the sentence: 'Decentralization of the former big banks has proven very detrimental for the entire German economy.'[444] He sent this to E.W. Schmidt on 2 August for his evaluation.

Schmidt agreed with all the points made by Dichgans and was particularly pleased that the three-district solution was perceived as an interim solution until the banking system could be completely recentralized. However, the resolution that was actually passed jointly by the Deutsche Industrie- und Handelstag (Association of German Chambers of Industry and Commerce) and the Bundesverband der Deutschen Industrie in September 1950 did not include the concession to political decision-makers of support for a 'second-best' solution that the banks and Abs in particular were willing to make. Dichgans proudly explained to E.W. Schmidt: 'In the new version, the resolution advocates unconditionally a uniform re-establishment of the former big banks throughout the entire Federal Republic.'[445]

At the same time, the Bayerische Creditbank, the regional bank of the Deutsche Bank Group in Bavaria, mobilized representatives from local industry, such as Otto Seeling, the chairman of the executive board of the Verband der bayerischen Industrie (Association of Bavarian Industries); Dr Karl Beichert from the Gesellschaft für Linde's Eismaschinen AG, Wiesbaden, which had an important sector of its production in Bavaria; Director Heinrich Schindhelm of the managing board of the porcelain manufacturer Kahla in Upper Franconia; Director Hanns Grewenig from the board of managing directors at BMW; and the president of the Munich Chamber of Industry and Commerce, Reinhard Klöpfer. These and other industrialists who were customers of the Deutsche Bank Group were asked to exert their influence on Bavarian Minister-President Ehard on behalf of the three-district solution. 'In order to minimize the work this entails,

we have taken the liberty of sending you a proposed draft of such a letter.'
Enclosed was a two-page draft which presented the well-known arguments for
recentralization in different versions appropriate for the industrialist in question.
The men addressed were asked to send Abs in Frankfurt a copy of their letter to
Ehard, which obviously identifies Abs again as being the prime mover of the
recentralization campaign.

In September Abs succeeded in pulling Hesse from the ranks of south German
opposition. He was able to make the proposed three-district solution more
attractive to Hessian Finance Minister Hilpert by pointing out that Hesse would
increase its tax revenue by having the head offices of the big banks located in
Frankfurt and by allowing that city the chance to become the financial capital
of the Federal Republic. At this point, Baden and Rhineland-Palatinate also
preferred to implement the three-district solution throughout all of the Federal
Republic, as opposed to having three banking districts in southern Germany
alone.

Finally, Bavaria and Württemberg-Baden began to signal their willingness to
come to an agreement. But they wanted to get as high a price as possible for
their local patriotism and federalist convictions. Throughout September, both
the Deutsche Bank Group and Bavaria launched articles in the press debating
the alleged advantages and disadvantages that a larger banking district would
bring Bavaria.[446] Early in the month, Bavaria demanded that the price for its
support of the three-district solution be the stipulation that only one big bank
could have its legal seat in Frankfurt; another was to be located in Stuttgart and
a third in Munich. On 6–7 September 1950, a meeting was held in Frankfurt
between Abs, Kempner, and Goetz and Richter from the Dresdner Bank, at
which Abs and the two representatives from the Dresdner Bank agreed that this
proposal should be rejected. However, Abs was willing to compromise: 'The
issue of head office locations must be reconsidered ... only if this issue is turned
into a *conditio sine qua non* for the entire three-district solution.'[447]

In contrast to the Dresdner Bank, the Deutsche Bank had in Abs a person
whose willingness to compromise would become characteristic for him and his
numerous negotiated successes. He wanted to take the kettle from the fire before
the patience of the Allies boiled over and they imposed big bank legislation upon
the Germans, as they had in breaking up I.G. Farben and in restructuring the
iron and steel industry. For in doing so, the Allies would also finally set the
conditions for the pending negotiations in London over the standstill debts.[448]

In light of this situation, Abs and Dr Tron, the head of the Deutsche Bank
regional institution in Munich, the Bayerische Creditbank, met on 29 September
1950, with Bavarian Minister President Hans Ehard, who had also invited
the president of the Bavarian Land Central Bank, Dr Max Günther Grasmann,
to attend. In the course of this meeting, Ehard agreed to accept the three-district
solution on the 'indispensable' condition that one of the major banks, preferably
the Deutsche Bank, establish its head office in Munich.[449] At the meeting that

followed on 13 October, Grasmann met with Abs at the Reconstruction Loan Corporation in Frankfurt to discuss the details of this proposal. Frowein from the Deutsche Bank Group and Zinsser from the Dresdner Bank Group were also there. At this meeting, Grasmann was presented with conditions put forth by the Deutsche Bank for complying with the Bavarian demand to establish its head office in Munich, presumably with four board members, two of whom would live in Munich and two in Frankfurt:

'a) The provision must not evoke any similar requests in the region of northern Germany.

b) Should Württemberg continue to demand that a bank establish its head office in Stuttgart and succeed in getting its demand adopted, the Commerzbank must agree now that it is willing to move its head office to Stuttgart.

c) Should the bank discover in two or three years that this provision has not proven successful, it has the right to take up again the issue concerning the head office of the bank.

d) It remains the prerogative of the bank to operate sections of the central administration in Frankfurt should it deem this necessary.'[450]

Grasmann indicated his approval and stated that he would do what he could to ensure that these conditions of the Deutsche Bank proposal would be accepted in northern Germany and by his colleague Pfleiderer in Stuttgart.[451] Apparently Stuttgart did not insist that a successor institution of the Commerzbank establish its head office there.

Once an agreement had been reached with Bavaria, the road was clear to formulate a draft law in the Federal Ministry of Finance. Consultations were held between 5 and 24 October 1950 on the various versions. Kremer, who by then had been promoted to Ministerialdirigent at the finance ministry, received help in formulating the draft law from Fritz Kempner, who was still working on behalf of the Deutsche Bank on this issue. The final version produced by the responsible branch of the ministry was debated by the Federal Cabinet on 27 October and 2 November 1950. After minor changes were made, it was passed by the Cabinet following the final debate on 28 November 1950, as the Act on the Regional Scope of Credit Institutions (Big Banks Act). Politicians from the Free Democratic Party, such as Vice-Chancellor Blücher, felt that a one-district solution was more sensible and expressed their concerns that a German law implementing the three-district solution would ruin any possibility for the complete recentralization of the banks. However, the advocates of this law were able to prevail by pointing out the political realities of the situation, the economic urgency of creating larger banking districts, and the danger that the Allies would intervene and preclude any German input into the matter.

The legislative bill passed by the Cabinet provided the big banks with a certain degree of flexibility in implementing the three-district solution. The bill did not prescribe which banks were to operate in which *Länder*, but it did stipulate that they were to operate 'branches in no more than six *Länder*' in the Federal Republic. 'Credit institutions established in North Rhine-Westphalia' were not allowed to operate in any other *Land*. It would thus be possible, but not required, for each of the big banks to establish a banking district in the four *Länder* of northern Germany and in the six *Länder* of southern Germany. The successor banks would be created in the three banking districts by legally decoupling them from the mother banks. To do this, resolutions to this effect were to be passed by the decision-making bodies of the 'dormant' old banks in compliance with German stock company law. This would mean that both assets and liabilities would be transferred to the successor banks, which were to compensate the holders of old bank shares with shares from the new banks. The successor institutions of a big bank had to be completely independent of one another and were not permitted to be coupled with one another through capital or personnel. The big banks were to be exempted from most of the taxes and fees that normally fell due in such transactions.[452]

Since the Allies still had the right to approve legislation dealing with banking policy, the legislative bill had to be presented to them 21 days before it was to be voted on in parliament. It was officially handed to the Allied High Commission on 21 December 1950, although Finance Minister Schäffer had already sent it to Allied financial advisers in early November. None of the Allies was content with the plan, but each for a different reason. Washington and Paris once again demanded that five to seven banking districts be created. The British financial expert Eugene Melville countered by calling for an end to all territorial limitations. The most important factors for him were the legal steps of decoupling the West German network of branches from the Berlin big banks and transferring liability for the standstill debts to the new institutions in the West. Not until December 1950 was Washington prepared to accept three banking districts, under the condition that these be specified by the law.[453]

The Allies criticized a series of other points, including the plan to implement the legal transformation of the big banks according to stock corporation law, meaning under the direction of the boards of managing directors and the supervisory boards of the old Berlin banks. Instead, the existing custodians should take charge of the legal transformation process. The Allies also felt the measures to prevent excessive concentrations of financial power were insufficient. They demanded that bank mergers and mutual participations by banks in one another be prohibited, that stock be registered in order to control the stock-holdings, that maximum limits for stock-holdings in banks be set (the French and Americans wanted 5 per cent, the British 10 per cent), that industrial investment by banks be restricted, and that foreign banks also be subjected to the Big Banks Act. The British were especially adamant about including in the law an explicit provision concerning the handling of the standstill debts.[454]

In agreement with the Federal Chancellery, the Allies formally suspended their 21-day appeal period, which otherwise would have been over on 12 January 1951. They informally notified the German government, the Bank deutscher Länder and the big banks of their objections to the proposed law, and invited them to participate in a meeting with experts from the Allied Bank Commission in Frankfurt on 19 January 1951.[455] The Germans had decided that they would be willing to give in only on the point that the three banking districts should be specified by the law, but would reject all other demands put forth by the Allies. During this meeting the position of the British member of the Allied Bank Commission, R.G. Beerensson, was presented in what would later be known as the Beerensson Plan. This plan provided special measures to protect the interests of foreign creditors in the process of decoupling the new joint stock banks from the old Berlin banks, a process to which the Allies objected in the form proposed by the Germans.[456]

As a result of the 19 January meeting, the Germans were requested to present a paper stating their position on the demands raised by the Allies. This was compiled by the Federal Ministry of Finance and sent to the Allied Bank Commission in late March 1951. In it the Germans agreed to the definitive specification of three banking districts and to the inclusion of foreign banks. Their most important concession was that the successor banks would provide certain guarantees and assume complete liability for the foreign debts of the old Berlin banks. This satisfied the British, who had been the main ally of the Germans in staving off more extensive demands by the USA and France, which were categorically rejected in the German memorandum. The stiff resistance of the Germans prompted the American High Commissioner to obtain permission from the Department of State on 30 March 1951 to inform the Germans that the Allies were prepared to issue legislation if the Germans remained unwilling to make concessions.[457]

In the months that followed, concessions were bartered. The Germans were in a relatively strong negotiating position because the threat of imposed Allied legislation was becoming more and more of an anachronism in view of the growing sovereignty of the Federal Republic, the raging Korean War, and the world-wide constellation of the East–West conflict. Everyone recognized the need for a solution to the legal status of the big banks in Germany, and since realities dictated that the problem be resolved by the passage of German legislation, it became imperative to co-operate with the Germans. In the numerous negotiations between Finance Minister Schäffer and the Allied financial advisers that took place between May and August 1951, the Germans agreed to accept the clearly defined banking districts, the 5 per cent limitation on holdings in successor banks, and the ban on interlocking directorates and capital participation. The Allies agreed to have the liquidation process carried out by the previous bodies of the big banks, as stipulated by German stock company law, instead of by the custodians. They also dropped their demand for registered

The remains of Deutsche Bank's Mönchengladbach branch amid advancing
American troops, 28 February–1 March 1945

John McCloy, US High Commissioner to Germany

Clemens Plassmann, Spokesman of the Board of Managing Directors
of Rheinisch-Westfälische Bank AG/Deutsche Bank AG West (1952–1957)

Hermann J. Abs, Spokesman of the Board of Managing Directors
of Süddeutsche Bank AG (1952–1957)

Erich Bechtolf, Spokesman of the Board of Managing Directors
of Norddeutsche Bank AG (1952–1957)

Süddeutsche Bank, Rossmarkt, Frankfurt am Main

Rheinisch-Westfälische Bank, Königsallee, Düsseldorf

Norddeutsche Bank, Alter Wall, Hamburg

The head office of the remerged Deutsche Bank (1957) on the corner of
Rossmarkt and Junghofstrasse, Frankfurt am Main

The bank's first high-rise building:
the tower in Grosse Gallusstrasse,
Frankfurt am Main,
was completed in 1972

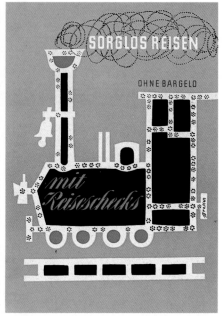

Bank advertising in the 1950s

shares once the Germans guaranteed that each shareholder would be required to submit a written confirmation at the general meeting of the successor banks which stated that his stock holdings did not exceed 5 per cent. A restriction on proxy voting rights was accepted in principle by the Germans, but was not included in the Big Banks Act. Until such a provision would be included in the pending reform of the German stock company law, the Federation of Private Banking Business was to obligate its membership to comply with the wishes of the Allies in restricting proxy voting rights.[458]

Following these compromises, the British surprised everyone with proposed improvements to the legislative bill. Up until this point, the British had been interested only in securing their demands for foreign creditor guarantees, and had hardly supported the more extensive changes to limit permanently the power of the banks called for by the Americans and the French. The standstill creditors in London had lodged massive numbers of complaints with the Foreign Office because they were not willing to accept the fact that the Germans alone were to be allowed to decide how foreign obligations were to be distributed among each of the successor banks during the decoupling process. Left by the Americans and the French to fend for itself, the British government accepted the compromise proposed by the Germans to give standstill creditors the option of changing the registration of their claims to the successor institution of their choice, within a year after the successor banks had been entered into the commercial trade register.

In early October 1951, the Allied High Commission gave the Federal Minister of Finance its formal approval of the 8 July 1951 version of the legislative bill on big banks, in which the above-mentioned compromises had been incorporated. Once this law went into effect, the Commission would surrender all appropriated authority in the area of banking decentralization.

First, this legislative bill was sent to the Federal Cabinet for debate on 7 November 1951, where it received approval nine days later. This was followed by the approval of the Finance Committee of the Bundesrat. Finally it was presented to the Bundestag on 8 December 1951. Following the initial reading of the bill in the Bundestag on 12 December, it was sent to both the Committee for Money and Credit and the Committee for Finance and Taxation (due to the tax exemption provisions), where there were a total of six hearings on the bill before it was returned to the Bundestag for its second and third readings. On 28 February 1952, the bill was passed by the votes of the ruling party coalition. Present at the passage of the bill were the Deutsche Bank representatives Rösler, E.W. Schmidt, Ulbricht, Herold and Hellmuth Pollems.[459] During the debates on the bill, members from the Free Democratic and Social Democratic parties criticized the fact that it did not introduce complete recentralization. Moreover, Social Democratic politicians sharply attacked the tax exemptions awarded to the big banks in Article 11.

Since hidden reserves of the banks would have to be disclosed during the decoupling process, the purpose of the tax exemptions was to protect these reserves from the revenue authorities as much as possible, so that the funds would be available to the banks to strengthen their relatively weak equity capital. On 1 November 1947, the directing office in Hamburg had calculated that the Deutsche Bank was keeping hidden reserves at the Berlin head office amounting at the time to 209 million RM, as opposed to 87.5 million RM in open reserves and 160 million RM in capital stock. Even then it recognized the need for tax exemptions, should successor institutions be established.[460] The hidden reserves that were finally disclosed in 1952 amounted to nearly 110 million DM for all three big banks. Normally the 70 per cent tax due on this would have been about 76 million DM, but according to Art. 11 of the Big Banks Act, the banks were exempted from paying 70 per cent of these taxes, thus reducing the amount owed to 23 million DM.[461] The tax savings of 53 million DM equalled 22 per cent of the capital stock of all nine successor banks and 17 per cent of their own capital resources, including the legally prescribed reserves and the free reserves.[462] The supporters of the tax exemptions argued that this means of strengthening the equity capital base was economically necessary in order to acquire credit standing abroad, because the successor banks were once again required to publish balance sheets, which potential lenders abroad would study.

This argument was not incorrect, but it ignored the fact that by this point other, very similar tax exemptions had been implemented for all credit institutions for the purpose of securing equity captial: namely, so-called overall contingency reserves or general bad-debt provisions. So the big banks profited twice. In light of the fact that it was now possible to create overall contingency reserves, Abs apparently expressed his doubts about the justification for special tax exemptions for big banks to Finance Minister Schäffer during a meeting in January 1952.[463] Because of these tax provisions, the Social Democratic Party regarded the law as a superfluous gift to the big banks. However, advocates of the law could point out that the Allied laws for breaking up the I.G. Farben syndicate (Law No. 35) and the iron and steel industry (Law No. 27) also included such tax exemptions.[464] The equity capital base of the successor banks was to be built upon the tax breaks resulting from the overall contingency reserves and the dotation capital of the mother banks, in addition to these special tax savings. Yet even then, the ratio of equity capital to external funds at the Deutsche Bank, like the other two big banks, amounted to only 3 per cent, compared to 6.7 per cent for the six leading American banks and 12.5 per cent for the five leading Swiss banks.[465]

The Bundesrat unanimously accepted the bill on 14 March 1952. Only Bremen, the smallest *Land*, had expressed reservations because it feared the law would weaken the economic strength of northern Germany.[466] The Act on the Regional Scope of Credit Institutions (otherwise known as the Big Banks Act) of 29 March 1952 was published two days later and went into effect on 1 April 1952.[467] The main clause concerning the three-district solution read as follows:

'Credit institutions, engaged principally in deposit banking and short-term lending within the country as either a legally established stock company or limited commercial partnership, are permitted to operate branches in the country in only one of the following three districts:

1. in the *Länder* Bremen, Hamburg, Lower Saxony and Schleswig-Holstein, or
2. in *Land* North Rhine-Westphalia, or
3. in the *Länder* Baden, Bavaria, Hesse, Rhineland-Palatinate, Württemberg-Baden and Württemberg-Hohenzollern.'

The provisions that followed this one in the law reflected the chief concern of the Allies to prevent the re-emergence of the supposed concentration of economic power enjoyed by the old Berlin big banks. No successor institution was allowed to invest in another successor institution. Interlocking directorates were forbidden. Shareholders with holdings amounting to more than 5 per cent of the capital of one successor institution were not allowed to hold more than 5 per cent of any other successor institution. The shares of the successor institutions were to be registered shares, but they could be issued with freely disposable dividend coupons. The shares were to be turned over to the Bank deutscher Länder, which was then to transfer them to the shareholders of the mother bank. Each old shareholder was entitled to shares in the capital of a successor bank proportionate to the capital he had held in the old Berlin institution. The exchange transaction was to take place between 15 December 1953 and 15 March 1954, for the shareholders of the Deutsche Bank.[468]

The three Berlin banks had a period of six months in which to get the resolution passed by their general meetings to establish successor institutions with regional scopes that complied with the provisions of the new law. Within a period of another 12 months, the successor institutions had to be entered into the commercial trade register. Afterwards, the mother banks were only to engage in banking transactions pertaining to their liquidation, including the liabilities and assets in the Soviet occupation zone and the former eastern regions of the Reich.[469] However, the original institutions were not liquidated by this law. The Deutsche Bank, for example, was not liquidated until July 1983 when the old Berlin bank was finally stricken from the commercial trade register, long after the old bank's shareholders passed a resolution on 12 December 1974, at an extraordinary general meeting in Berlin, stating that all liquidation business had been completed.

Once the old banks in Berlin had been transferred to West Germany, the Old Banks Act and the Old Bank Balance Sheets Act, both from 10 December 1953, went into effect. These laws required the Deutsche Bank to prepare a balance sheet for the old bank for 1 January 1953, which was to serve as a Deutsche Mark opening balance for the government to use in allocating equalization claims. This old bank balance sheet listed a total of 39.9 million DM for 1 January 1953. Equalization claims amounting to 30.8 million DM constituted most of the assets, while 27.1 million DM in pension commitments and 10.6 million DM in currency obligations comprised most of the liabilities.[470] The old bank balance sheet continued to be drawn up to show the latest status in the liquidation process until 1973–74. Based on these calculations, the final compilation of equalization claims for the old Deutsche Bank was set in July 1974 at 11.2 million DM.[471]

As early as 22 November 1951, the Central Bank Council of the Bank deutscher Länder approved the 'recognition of the Berlin offices of the big banks as monetary institutions in liquidation that had been transferred to the territory of the Federal Republic'.[472] In a circular issued on 17 March 1952, the Federation of Private Banking Business honoured the commitment made by the Germans to the Allies to impose restrictions on proxy voting rights voluntarily until the stock company law could be reformed. The Allies published their Law No. A-24, 'Repeal of Legislation on Decentralisation of Banks', on 8 April 1952. This law repealed their previous legislation on decentralization, namely Law No. 57 for the American zone, Ordinance No. 25 for the French and Ordinance No. 133 for the British, retroactively to 1 April 1952, thus ending the role of the bank custodians and the exclusion of the big banks from the 35th regulating ordinance of the Currency Conversion Act (Relocation Ordinance).

However, before the Allies took this step, they again secured confirmation from Chancellor Adenauer, in an unpublished document dated 27 March 1952, of the agreement made with the Federal Minister of Finance on 25 July 1951, to change the proxy voting rights, first through the voluntary commitment of the bank association and subsequently by reforming the stock company law. Before the end of March, the resolution of the bank association was to go into effect, which stated 'that the banks are obligated to follow all instructions issued by the shareholders and that they are only permitted in the future to exercise opposition in the name of shareholders for whom they act as proxies in a general shareholders' meeting if the shareholders have given their explicit approval in each specific case to do so'.

Adenauer also gave his assurances that the Federal Government would not change the act for a period of three years, starting with the completion of the decoupling process and the transfer of the shares of the successor banks to the Bank deutscher Länder.[473] The Deutsche Bank was the first to be informed about this three-year moratorium, which actually began in late 1953. Apparently Abs received a copy of Adenauer's written assurances directly from the German Foreign Office in July 1954.[474] This document was a solution acceptable to all sides. It was therefore no longer necessary to include the big banks issue in the contractual arrangements, known as the Bonn Conventions, that were signed in May 1952 to end the Occupation Statute and enable the Allies to turn over other areas of policy completely to the Federal Republic.[475] Had legislation on big banks been incorporated into these contractual arrangements, it was feared that such legislation could not have been amended until a peace treaty was signed.

Naturally this is what the Germans wanted to prevent because they intended to continue striving for complete recentralization of the banks.

A period of legal uncertainty had finally come to an end for the big banks, which had been decentralized on a *Länder* basis. The rights of the custodians reverted to the regulating bodies stipulated by German stock company law (general meetings, supervisory boards, boards of managing directors), which were once again solely responsible for determining and implementing the decoupling process. From this point on, regulations governing currency, including the important 35th regulating ordinance for the Currency Conversion Act, known as the Relocation Ordinance, were also binding for the big banks. On 24 April 1952, the finance ministry of North Rhine-Westphalia in Düsseldorf officially recognized the relocation of the Deutsche Bank AG, Berlin, to its new legal residence in Düsseldorf. The date of relocation was stipulated as having been 18 July 1947.[476]

In order to co-ordinate the decoupling of the successor institutions from the mother banks, a co-ordination committee was formed under the direction of Dr Hermann Herold, a legal counsellor under contract with the Deutsche Bank. From the first committee meeting in early May 1952 until the last one on this matter on 24 October 1952, representatives from all three big bank groups took part in discussing complicated legal and accounting problems. Usually the committee met in the offices of the Rheinisch-Westfälische Bank in Düsseldorf. The persistence of this committee also paid off with regard to its petitions for exemption from land transfer taxes at the finance ministries of the *Länder,* a matter that could not be regulated at the federal level in the Big Banks Act because such taxation fell under the jurisdiction of the *Länder.*[477] According to Abs, the co-ordination committee of the three big bank groups also discussed matters of common interest, such as legislation on regulating banking and capital markets.[478]

Hans Oesterlink, deputy chairman of the Deutsche Bank supervisory board since 1942, opened an extraordinary general meeting of the Deutsche Bank AG in Berlin on 25 September 1952, the same day as did the other banks. It was the first such meeting to take place since 1943. The Deutsche Bank called this meeting in order to pass a resolution on the establishment of the three successor banks: namely, the Norddeutsche Bank AG, Hamburg, for northern Germany; the Rheinisch-Westfälische Bank AG, Düsseldorf, for North Rhine-Westphalia; and the Süddeutsche Bank AG, Munich, for southern Germany. In order to demonstrate solidarity, the shares of these three banks were designed to be identical, featuring portraits of Georg von Siemens and David Hansemann, significant personalities in the history of the Deutsche Bank and the Disconto-Gesellschaft; the only visible difference was the different bank names on the shares. The mother banks transferred to the successor institutions what capital they had in West Germany as of 1 January 1952, meaning the difference between their assets and liabilities based on the partial balance sheet drawn up for the planned banking districts on 31 December 1951, as a contribution in kind. Since the banks were required by law to have at least five founders, four individuals also each invested 1,000 DM plus premium. The opening balance sheets of the successor institutions of the Deutsche Bank for 1 January 1952 are shown in Table 2.

Table 2   Capital base of the three successor banks of the Deutsche Bank on the date of their founding as of 1 January 1952 (DM millions)

	Norddeutsche Bank AG, Hamburg	Rheinisch-Westfälische Bank AG, Düsseldorf	Süddeutsche Bank AG, Munich	Total
Assets	747.5	1,549.1	1,460.9	3,757.5
Liabilities	719.4	1,492.9	1,404.7	3,617.0
Capital resources consisting of:	28.1	56.2	56.2	140.5
a) share capital	20.0	40.0	40.0	100.0
b) legal reserve	5.0	10.0	10.0	25.0
c) special reserve	3.1	6.2	6.2	15.5

Source: Franz Seidel, *Die Nachfolgebanken in Westdeutschland. Ihre Entstehung und Entwicklung auf Grund ihrer Bilanzen* (Vienna 1955), p. 19.

The three big banks distributed their capital resources to the successor institutions to varying degrees, depending on the regional distribution of business. The Deutsche Bank had enough assets located in West Germany to establish also special reserves for the successor institutions in the opening balance sheet, contrary to the other two big banks, which did not have balance sheet totals, capital stock and legal reserves for their successor banks as large as those of the Deutsche Bank. This was due to the fact that the old Deutsche Bank lost relatively less capital outside West Germany following the war than did the other two big banks. This was also the reason why the Deutsche Bank shareholders received a better exchange rate of old shares into new ones: namely 10:6.25. This ratio was calculated from the ratio of the Deutsche Mark capital stock in the opening balance sheet of the successor banks to the previous Reichsmark capital stock of the mother bank at the end of the war, which in the case of the Deutsche Bank amounted to 160 million RM. Therefore, 1,000 RM of old shares were exchanged nominally for 125 DM of shares in the Norddeutsche Bank AG and 250 DM of shares in the Rheinisch-Westfälische Bank AG and the Süddeutsche Bank AG each, a total of 625 DM. In addition to these registered shares, they also received newly printed bearer shares labelled 'Deutsche Bank Issue 1952' in Reichsmark denominations for the remaining portion of the par value of their former holdings. These bearer shares represented the value of the assets possibly remaining to the old Deutsche Bank, particularly in the territory under communist rule.[479] In the jargon of the stock exchange these were called *Restquoten* (salvage shares), and they were traded on the West German stock exchanges in addition to the shares of the successor institutions starting on 15 December 1953.[480] Their market quotations tended to fluctuate greatly depending on the ever-changing perspectives for German reunification (see Table 7).

The exchange rate for the shareholders of the big banks, even those of the Commerzbank where the ratio was only 10:5, was significantly better than the conversion rate during the 1948 currency reform for the holders of cash assets, especially when the favourable development of the market price of big bank shares in the 1950s is taken into consideration. In mid-October 1954, the shares of the nine successor institutions were already listed at about 180 per cent and even the *Restquoten* at between 10 and 13 per cent.[481]

'Human capital' at the management level of the Deutsche Bank from the period prior to 1945 was also available to the successor banks in nearly the same proportion as the percentage of capital stock from the mother banks. This is well illustrated by the make-up of the boards of managing directors:

Norddeutsche Bank AG: Erich Bechtolf (spokesman), Dr Karl Klasen and Franz Heinrich Ulrich. Dr Edgar Wiegers became chairman, and Kurt Beindorff and Georg Waldthausen became deputy chairmen, of the supervisory board.

Rheinisch-Westfälische Bank AG: Clemens Plassmann (spokesman), Oswald Rösler, Fritz Gröning (since 2 February 1953, as deputy member), Dr Hans Janberg (since 2 February 1953) and Jean Baptist Rath. Fritz Wintermantel assumed the chairmanship, while Hans Oesterlink (successor to the deceased Wintermantel as of summer 1953) and Günter Henle were deputy chairmen of the supervisory board.

Süddeutsche Bank AG: Hermann J. Abs (spokesman), Robert Frowein, Heinz Osterwind and Walter Tron. The industrialist Otto Seeling became chairman of the supervisory board, Richard Merton (successor to the deceased Seeling as of March 1955) and Hans Rummel were deputy chairmen, and Karl Ritter von Halt was a member. Rummel also assumed the chairmanship of the three- or four-member working committee of the supervisory board. At its first meeting on 27 September 1952, the supervisory board assigned this committee its authority to supervise the credit transactions subject to registration and consent according to stock company law and in particular Art. 14, para. 4 of the German Banking Law.

The successor banks also continued the tradition of the advisory boards. These were now created for certain branch districts in a decentralized manner. According to company by-laws, their official task was to advise executives of the branches in matters of management. However, the real motivation for continuing this practice was to motivate important customers to strengthen their business ties with the Deutsche Bank Group. Characteristically enough, the files of the advisory board of the Süddeutsche Bank contain more papers concerning table seating, invitations and declined invitations to business meals than any other issue.[482]

A true innovation over the pre-war period was the membership of employee representatives on the supervisory boards of the successor institutions of the Deutsche Bank, as stipulated by the Industrial Constitution Law. The supervisory board of the Süddeutsche Bank noted with approval that the employee councils of the Deutsche Bank did not intend to appoint representatives who were not Deutsche Bank employees to the supervisory board. The minutes of the supervisory board meetings do not indicate that conflicts arose between the employee representatives and the other members of the supervisory board.[483]

Starting in November 1952, joint sessions of the boards of managing directors of the three Deutsche Bank successor institutions were held every two months on a rotation basis in Hamburg, Düsseldorf, Frankfurt or Munich. Starting in mid-1955, these occurred every month in order to co-ordinate matters ranging from personnel and business policies to social and donation policies.[484] As of 1952, the separation and autonomy imposed on the banks by the Allies no longer existed in actuality. Therefore, the legal reunification that would follow later was only a cosmetic improvement on reality. Its sole significance for business was the fact that, by reviving such a traditional name in banking as the Deutsche Bank, trust in the institution increased, especially abroad, and more business was generated.

2. Total recentralization under German management 1952–1957

Long before the three-year waiting period that had been conceded to the Allies was over, preparations to have the Big Banks Act amended were well under way in the Deutsche Bank Group. During the prior period of concessions to the Allies, there was never any doubt that the final goal of the Germans was to re-establish a centralized Deutsche Bank under its former name; the only controversy revolved around the question of how to bring this about. A memorandum of 24 June 1954, written in Hamburg, discussed two ways in which the successor institutions of the Deutsche Bank could be reunified. The first way was legally to create a unified Deutsche Bank, and the second was to maintain the legal autonomy of the successor institutions, but to integrate them into a holding company under the name 'Deutsche Bank'. Variations of these two proposals were also debated:

1a) To reintegrate the successor institutions into the old Deutsche Bank (and relocate the head office from Berlin to the Federal Republic).

1b) To merge two of the successor institutions into the third and rename this the 'Deutsche Bank AG'.

1c) To reunite the three successor institutions into a newly established Deutsche Bank AG.

2a) To use the old Deutsche Bank as a holding company.

2b) To establish a new Deutsche Bank AG to use as a holding company.[485]

The merit of each of these alternatives was weighed against the criteria of how well it would improve the credit standing abroad and avoid any further liabilities to foreign creditors from pre-armistice debts in addition to those that had already been assigned to the bank by the Relocation Ordinance (35th Regulation Ordinance). The two holding company variations did not fare well in the evaluation for many reasons, among which were the tax disadvantages; nor did variation 1a compare favourably with the relatively similiar variations 1b and 1c. The solution that was later agreed upon was actually based on variation 1b.

Abs also proposed another alternative that would become an important interim solution. He suggested combining the three successor institutions into a community sharing common interests (*Interessengemeinschaft*), a syndicate. In Abs' opinion, the purpose of such a syndicate would be not only to enable mutual profit and loss adjustment, but also to standardize the bank names (Deutsche Bank Süd, West and Nord AG) and to reintroduce interlocking directorships in the otherwise legally independent boards of managing directors and supervisory boards.[486] However, the argument against such a proposed permanent solution was that, 'on the whole, the value of such a syndicate contract would only consist in equalling out the different levels of earning power that now exist, whereby normally it appears possible to preclude deviating stock prices'.[487]

On 16 September 1954, Abs again presented a proposal from the Süddeutsche Bank, this time for an interim solution. The banks would create a 'profit pool' to balance out their profits and losses, and the bank names would be standardized.[488] In a memorandum enclosed with this proposal, it was deliberated in great detail whether the name Deutsche Bank, 'with or without the suffix AG', could be used by an amalgamation of the successor institutions in the Federal Republic if the old banks, which existed in abeyance in Berlin, were not included in such a merger. In the end it was concluded that the name could be used.[489]

The Paris Treaties were signed on 23 October 1954, and went into effect on 5 May 1955, following a long process of ratification by the occupation governments. These treaties granted full sovereignty to the Federal Republic.[490] In this context, the issue was raised at the Rheinisch-Westfälische Bank shortly afterwards, specifically on 27 October 1954, of whether Adenauer's guarantee to the Western powers that the Big Banks Act would not be revised for a period of three years was invalidated by the signing of these treaties. The conclusion reached was ambivalent.[491] The fact that the issue arose demonstrates how great the desire was among the successor institutions to re-establish the Deutsche Bank as a unified organization. However, the Federal Government felt committed to its previous agreement.

Therefore, in 1955 an interim solution was finally found and a contract was signed by the successor banks providing for a 'profit pool', meaning the mutual equalization of profits and losses among the three. The legal department of the Süddeutsche Bank had already studied the legal feasibility of such a contract and approved it on 3 November 1954.[492] In February 1955, the initial draft of this contract was presented to the Federal Ministries of Economics and Justice in Bonn in order to ensure that it was not viewed as an infraction of the Big Banks Act. The federal authorities advised caution. Therefore, Rösler asked the banker and Adenauer's close friend Pferdmenges on 22 February 1955 if he would present the matter to Adenauer. Adenauer prompted Pferdmenges to take up the matter with his close political associates Herbert Blankenhorn and Walter Hallstein at the Chancellor's Office, who in turn emphatically asked that the syndicate contract not be signed before France had ratified the Paris Treaties. The successor institutions did as they were requested.

By the time the Paris Treaties went into effect on 5 May 1955, preparations for the syndicate contract were complete and the banks were merely awaiting the green light from Bonn, which they hoped to get when Chancellor Adenauer met with Abs on 15 July 1955. There were two draft contracts for establishing a syndicate. The first was a comprehensive one, which provided not only for a profit pool, but also for an association of the three institutions under the label 'IG Deutsche Bank' and for the creation of a joint committee (Gemeinschaftsausschuss). The second was not quite so comprehensive and reflected the reservations expressed by the ministries. It provided solely for the profit pool and left everything else to daily business practice or internal business regulations. In anticipation of the developments, the banks had made all the preparations necessary to hold simultaneous yet separate extraordinary general meetings in order to decide on the contract, as prescribed by law. Should the meeting between Adenauer and Abs go against the interests of the banks, the Rheinisch-Westfälische Bank AG planned to put the issue to the test by renaming itself as the Deutsche Bank. Judge Wendel, the lower court judge in charge of the Commercial Register of Düsseldorf, had already signalled his willingness to accept a test case.[493]

The meeting between Adenauer and Abs did *not* end negatively, but the contract was to be sent back once more for approval by both the Ministry of Justice and the Ministry of Economics. The latter was involved because Economics Minister Erhard had finally succeeded in 1952 in taking over the department for money and credit from the finance ministry and had appointed Ministerialdirektor Dr Arnold Kramer to head this department. On 26 July 1955, Hans Janberg, managing director of the Rheinisch-Westfälische Bank AG, sent a letter to his colleagues Bechtolf in Hamburg and Frowein in Frankfurt, which is an exemplary illustration of tactical skill in dealing with the Federal Government:[494]

'In order that the meeting with Ministerialdirektor Kramer and Ministerialdirigent Dr Gessler on 4 August at ten o'clock produces the desired results and that the gentlemen do not subject the plan again to the scrutiny of their staff, it seems advisable to send them the plan for the syndicate contract now so that they can use it in preparing for the meeting. Only one plan should be sent to them for this purpose, namely Plan 1, so as to avoid having them even consider Plan 2. Naturally the plan sent must be labelled "Plan for a Syndicate Contract" and not Plan 1.'

At the meeting on 4 August 1955, the representatives of both ministries expressed their objections to the plan with which they had been confronted. The proposed joint committee and the intended co-ordination of business policy issues would violate the Big Banks Act. Since Bechtolf and the three other representatives from the Deutsche Bank Group failed to dispel the concerns of the ministerial officials, they then presented Plan 2, which they had been careful to bring with them, should the need arise. There were no significant objections to this plan. However, the officials did reject the idea of using the name 'Deutsche Bank' to link all of the successor institutions; therefore, they were also opposed to the plans to hold the general meetings simultaneously. The reasons for their objections closely resembled those they had used against Plan 1.

As a result, the supervisory boards of the three sister banks decided on 24 August 1955 to present a shorter version of Plan 2, entitled 'Contract on Profit and Loss Equalization among the Successor Institutions of the Deutsche Bank', for approval at the general meetings scheduled for 26 September in Düsseldorf, 27 September in Frankfurt, and 28 September in Hamburg. In addition to the profit pool, the syndicate was to specify guidelines and pass joint resolutions regarding the preparation of annual financial statements. It would also guarantee the payment of uniform shareholder dividends and the creation of uniform reserves. This arrangement was designed to strengthen each of the banks financially, and protect the shareholders from any economic disadvantages resulting from the division of the Deutsche Bank. The contract was to become effective retroactively to 1 January 1955. The press was also notified that this contract represented an important step towards amending the Big Banks Act and revising the Allied policy of decentralization. It was also presented as an important step in cultivating the foreign business in which the Deutsche Bank had traditionally engaged. The general meetings of each of the three sister banks approved the contract unanimously, as had been expected. In compliance with a resolution passed at the next regular general meeting, the Rheinisch-Westfälische Bank AG changed its firm name on 18 April 1956 to Deutsche Bank AG West, thus making at least a small move towards standardizing the bank names.

In order to implement and supervise the syndicate contract, the boards of managing directors from the three successor banks met every other month on a rotating basis for so-called 'pool meetings'. According to the internal rules of procedure passed by this body at its first meeting on 12 November 1955 in Frankfurt, it was to handle the following business matters in addition to the tasks specified in the syndicate contract: joint credit transactions of the three successor institutes with individual borrowers of sums exceeding 5 million DM, underwriting commitments in the stock-issuing business or the acquisition of securities over 3 million DM, the acquisition of a participation on one's own account, real estate transactions involving more than 1 million DM and by-law changes. Nine pool meetings were held in the period between the signing of the syndicate contract and the reunification of the successor banks in April 1957. And most of the time was spent discussing credit transactions.[495] During this period it was never necessary to use the profit pool that the syndicate had set up because each of the three banks made enough profit to pay the same size of dividends and to allocate proportionally the same amount to reserves.

All that now remained was the complete legal reunification of the successor banks. The influence exerted by the big banks – above all, by the Deutsche Bank Group – on the origins of the Law to Remove Limitations on the Regional Scope of Credit Institutions (24 December 1956) is a classic example of the successful lobbying of private economic interests in the political arena. The Deutsche Bank Group went so far as to have its experts largely determine if not actually formulate the clauses of the law, the pertinent tax exemptions, and the minutes of the meetings held at the Ministry of Economics. Naturally the influence of the private business sector could not have been so great if political circles had not viewed reunification as the removal of an obstacle imposed upon the West German economy by the occupation policy of the Western Allies. Consciousness of the recently reacquired sovereignty increased the readiness of German politicans to assent to the pressure of private economic circles for the revision of the consequences of Allied policy.

At a meeting on 4 August 1955 at the Ministry of Economics on the profit pool contract, the representatives of the Deutsche Bank Group were asked even then 'to submit the name of a gentleman to the Economics Ministry with whom discussions can be held concerning the bill for the Big Banks Act which is currently being prepared'.[496] On 20 September 1955, the first departmental meeting was held there with representatives of the three big bank groups under the chairmanship of Oberregierungsrat Ernst vom Hofe. The Deutsche Bank Group was represented by Managing Director Janberg from the Rheinisch-Westfälische Bank AG, and the tax experts Dr Georg Siara (Süddeutsche Bank) and Dr Wilhelm Vallenthin (Rheinisch-Westfälische Bank AG).

Due to the three-year moratorium on amending the Big Banks Act, vom Hofe requested that 'the negotiations now being initiated on repealing the law be handled as strictly confidential'.[497] He warned against taking measures that would violate the existing law and once again expressed his reservations concerning the profit pool contract of the Deutsche Bank Group: the ministerial departments had managed to tolerate the contract 'because although it violated the spirit of the Big Banks Act, it did not violate the wording'.[498]

Since no one contested that the limitations on the regional scope of banking operations should be repealed, the bank representatives only stressed the urgency of a new law and presented in detail their requests for exemption from various taxes and fees. The ministerial officials accepted the basic premise that reunification of the big banks should be viewed as a correction of a division forced upon them, and should not result in any burdens in taxes and fees. The three bank groups were instructed to present their requests in written form. Following this meeting, the banks agreed among themselves that the paper to be submitted 'should be composed by the Deutsche Bank Group and approved by the other two banks'.[499]

This paper was submitted by the three bank groups to Ernst vom Hofe, who in the meantime had apparently been promoted to Ministerialrat. It was dated 3 October 1955 and signed by Plassmann and Janberg for the Deutsche Bank Group. As an introduction, the repeal of the Big Banks Act was depicted 'as the final act to make amends' for the hardship resulting from the Allied dismantling of the big banks. Granted, the three-district solution of 1952 had been proposed by the bankers Abs, Goetz and Marx themselves in 1950. But the banks had embraced this plan solely out of necessity, for the occupation powers would never have approved of a re-establishment of the old banks at the time. Otherwise the paper addressed the issues of exemptions from taxes and fees:

'In the interest of avoiding any later confusion in interpretation, we would like to request that the proposals compiled in the enclosed paper are incorporated into law. Regulation by law does not need to be provided in cases where exact clarification can be established by a binding decree from the Federal Ministry of Finance or by identical decrees from the Finance Ministries of the *Länder* – if need be by applying Art. 131 of the Federal Revenue Code. If federal regulation cannot be passed due to problems of jurisdiction, for example in the case of land transfer taxation, we would like to request that the Federal Ministry of Finance exerts its influence upon the Finance Ministries of the *Länder* to create uniform regulation that corresponds to our proposals.'[500]

Enclosed was a detailed list of requests for exemption from several different taxes: namely, the capital transfer, land transfer and turnover taxes, corporation income and wealth taxes, income taxes for shareholders, and court and notary fees.

At the invitation of August Neuburger (formerly the custodian of a regional bank, the Südwestbank in Württemberg-Baden), Georg Siara and Dr Adolf Schäfer (the latter from the Rhein-Ruhr-Bank of the Dresdner Bank Group) attended talks in Bonn on 12 October 1955, at which the issue of reunifying the successor institutions was also addressed. Neuburger and Hugo Scharnberg, an executive of the Hamburger Kreditbank (Dresdner Bank Group) who was also in attendance, were Bundestag representatives for the Christian Democratic Party and members of the Committee for Money and Credit, the committee responsible for bank issues. Scharnberg was even committee chairman. These two men offered the bank representatives who attended the meeting 'to regulate the entire problem, especially the tax issue, by initiating a bill from the floor of the Bundestag, which they believe even Dr Seuffert (Social Democratic Party) would sign. They are in any case ready to do this.'[501] Walter Seuffert was the vice-chairman of the committee. The bank representatives expressed their gratitude for such an offer, but preferred to wait for the reaction of the federal and *Länder* finance authorities to their paper. They also preferred to regulate as little as possible through legislation, 'but to aim for strictly administrative solutions by way of decrees and recommendations for the greater majority of the taxation issues'.[502]

When the boards of managing directors of the Deutsche Bank Group met on 12 November 1955, they were presented with the first draft of a 'Law to Repeal the Big Banks Act'. This was neither a draft from the Federal Ministry of Economics nor the proposed bill from the Bundestag, but a draft from the legal departments of the Rheinisch-Westfälische Bank AG (Dr Wilhelm Vallentin) and the Süddeutsche Bank (Dr Georg Siara). Vallenthin, who would later advance to the board of managing directors of the Deutsche Bank, emphasized that he labelled the draft law a 'Law to Repeal the Big Banks Act' rather than to amend it, which was the terminology of the Ministry of Economics. The title should make it clear to all that the Big Banks Act had been 'one of the last measures enacted of a Morgenthauian nature', and that it was actually to be eliminated, not just changed.[503]

The second session of talks on the Big Banks Act at the Economics Ministry with Ministerialrat vom Hofe took place on 14 November 1955, with Siara and Vallenthin representing the Deutsche Bank Group, Schäfer the Dresdner Bank Group, and Prof. Philipp Möhring the Commerzbank Group. Vom Hofe informed the bank representatives in 'strictest confidence' that Finance Minister Schäffer had 'made several negative notes in the margin' of the bank paper submitted on 3 October, contrary to the overwhelmingly positive evaluation of it at the department level of the ministry.[504] The bank representatives then offered vom Hofe to formulate a legislative bill in order to 'facilitate his preparations'. He 'did not consider that to be immediately necessary, since in his opinion it would not be difficult to formulate the law'. Later in the discussion, the banks pointed out that they would be very interested in having the title of the legislative bill include the words 'repeal of the Big Banks Act', in order to stress that this was the elimination of a Morgenthauian relic.

Vom Hofe also expressed his reservations concerning the bankers' proposal to have the law stipulate that the reunified institutions could again use the old business names. There was concern that the successor institutions might then be forced to compensate the shareholders of the old banks, meaning the owners of salvage shares, for the right to use the old business name. Vom Hofe felt it would not be permissible to strip 'the old banks of their original business names, i.e. their last remaining asset, by a legislative act'. Instead of going into this issue any further, the bank representatives announced that they would bring up the question again in detail, on the occasion of the presentation of the legislative draft they proposed to formulate. At this point, vom Hofe no longer appears to have opposed the offer of the banks to formulate the legislation. At the end of the meeting, the bank representatives agreed among themselves that the two other banks would comment individually on the existing first draft of the Deutsche Bank Group.[505]

In early January 1956, Vallenthin proposed to the other banks a few small changes to the draft legislation and a new title: 'Act to Restore the Freedom of Regional Scope for Credit Institutions'. He argued that this new title would at least have the same 'propagandistic value' as the earlier version. He asked for a quick response to his proposal, since vom Hofe had again urgently requested to receive the draft legislation from the banks.[506]

After he had received the joint legislative draft of the banks, Ministerialrat vom Hofe invited all of the successor institutions of the big banks to a meeting on 1 February 1956, at the Ministry of Economics. This time it was vom Hofe who showed little regard for the spirit of the Big Banks Act, if not its tenor, by leaving it to the discretion of the banks 'to send someone to represent each bank group'.[507] Besides the officials from the Economics Ministry, there were representatives of the Federal Finance Ministry, the Federal Justice Ministry, the Bank deutscher Länder and the city of Berlin present at this meeting. The Deutsche Bank Group was represented by Siara and Vallenthin. The officials from the ministry presented their own draft legislation, much of which closely resembled the content of the bank's own proposal, sometimes even verbatim. The title had been changed to read, 'Act to Remove Limitations on the Regional Scope of Credit Institutions', which eventually did become the title of the law. By using the word 'remove', the new title offered the banks the propagandistic value they had sought. The important tax matters of the banks were acknowledged, but the issues of corporation income tax, wealth tax and individual income tax were to be settled by decree not by legislation. The requests that were not granted dealt with exemption from turnover and securities taxes. Several *Länder*, especially Bavaria and North Rhine-Westphalia, opposed the exemption from land transfer taxes or transaction taxes. Nor were all the requests granted for exemption from fees.[508]

The objections to the land transfer tax exemption were dispelled at a meeting of bank representatives at the North Rhine-Westphalian finance ministry on 17 February 1956.[509] But the issue of transaction taxes remained a problem. Bavaria stubbornly refused to consider a land transfer tax exemption, supposedly because it 'was not being considered as a possible location for the legal seat of one of the future big banks and as a result will lose corporation income tax'.[510]

In the meantime, another discussion of the legislative draft took place at the Economics Ministry on 18 February 1956. It was announced here that North Rhine-Westphalia had petitioned to have all tax issues regulated by way of a decree according to Art. 131 of the Federal Revenue Code instead of by legislation. The bank representatives were happy to agree with this; their chief concern was content, not the legal form. However, they did insist that they be involved in formulating the decree, and that the content be clarified before the first reading of the legislative bill in the Bundestag, 'so that the option is still open to initiate from within the Bundestag legislation on this issue if the ministerial departments have not sufficiently taken our requests into account'.[511] The Economics Ministry agreed to help the banks get what they wanted, but not just because of this concealed threat. The efforts of the bank representatives to take part in formulating a tax exemption decree were successful. A meeting on this issue took place at the Federal Ministry of Finance on 27 February 1956. The bank representatives were asked to submit written proposals for the formulation of the decree. Instead they presented a fully formulated draft.[512]

The Finance Ministry agreed to hold further meetings and to proceed quickly on the matter, so that a tax decree would exist before the law on removing regional limitations went into effect. But the Finance Ministry created new difficulties: it took the position that tax reductions should only be granted on the condition that the old banks be incorporated into the merger within a period of about two years. The old banks had received equalization claims up to full compensation of their pension liabilities, half of which they would have been forced to pay back if, following the merger, they had been given the same status as banks that had been permitted to reopen. The Justice Ministry agreed with the Finance Ministry that, unless the old banks were reunited with their successor institutions, the latter would have an economic advantage over other old banks that had reopened for business, due to the complete exclusion of their Berlin pension liabilities.

A syndicate meeting of the boards of managing directors of the Deutsche Bank Group was called in order to discuss how the opposition of the Finance Ministry could be overcome.[513] Apparently the opposition of the ministry was based on an initiative of the 'commissioner for old bank issues'. Therefore, the big bank groups in West Germany called upon their subsidiaries in Berlin to exert their influence on the Association of Berlin Banking, so that it would do no more than approve the repeal of the Big Banks Act with no ifs, ands or buts, and support the requested exemptions from taxes and fees.[514]

Whether it was this cover fire or the quality of the arguments put forth by the bank representatives, the fact of the matter is that the Finance Ministry indicated its willingness to compromise in a meeting held on 26 March 1956. The link-up between the inclusion of the old banks in reunification and tax exemptions was dropped. Yet because of the actual reallocation of the pension burdens from the old banks to the public sector, the Finance Ministry did want to reach an agreement with the banks that, regardless of when a reunification with the old bank occurred, the recalculation, meaning also the return of the equalization claims for pension liabilities, was to be handled as if the reunification had taken place on 1 January 1958, at the latest.[515] The banks and the Finance Ministry did come to an agreement on this, but with an extension of the deadline to 31 December 1958.

By the end of March 1956, the legislative draft – compiled officially by the Finance Ministry, unofficially by the banks – and its purpose and justification, to which bank representatives had also contributed greatly, were ready to be presented to the Cabinet. It was argued above all that such legislation was justified because the banks had been coerced into the present situation by the Big Banks Act of 1952. There was no obvious reason why 'in the Federal Republic, as opposed to the other European countries, limitations should be placed on the freedom of the regional scope of operation for individual credit institutions, thereby impairing their efficiency and international competitiveness ... An excessive economic concentration of power of individual banks will not result from such a reunification because the three big banks have always been in stiff competition with one another, with the large regional banks, and with many other credit institutions.'[516] The bill was approved by the Cabinet on 18 April 1956, and sent to the Bundesrat exactly a week later.

At this point, the Berlin Senate began demanding that the Berlin subsidiaries of the successor institutions be included in the reunification.[517] This action by the Berlin Senate was motivated by the hope that the big banks would be able to establish a second legal residence in Berlin. If this could be accomplished, the benefits would be twofold in nature: it would enhance the position of Berlin politically, for one, and would generate more tax revenue and offer other economic advantages, for another. The Senate exerted its influence in the Bundesrat with the result that the bill was amended to include the stipulation that the planned reduction of fees would only go into effect if the banks reunited with their Berlin subsidiaries within a period of two years. This amendment had been introduced by Bremen in the finance committee, where it passed with five votes to four.

Now the bank executives mobilized their influence to topple the bill amendment favouring Berlin. The board of managing directors of the Norddeutsche Bank AG intervened at the Office for Economics and Transportation in Hamburg as well as at the finance ministry of Lower Saxony.[518] Frowein in Frankfurt and Goetz or Richter from the Dresdner Bank Group aimed to use their personal contact to persuade Hessian Finance Minister Dr Heinrich Tröger, who was chairman of the finance committee, to put forward a motion in the plenum of the Bundesrat to revise the amendment so as to exclude the mandatory reunification with the Berlin subsidiaries. Vallenthin from the Deutsche Bank Group and Schäfer from the Dresdner Bank Group also spoke with Ministerialdirektor Dr Arnold Kramer, vom Hofe's superior at the Economics Ministry, and convinced him to support their efforts to block the amendment. Kramer promised that Deputy Minister Ludger Westrick, for whom the banks had written a short memorandum, would speak out against the amendment at the Bundesrat meeting on 18 May 1956. Abs himself had also contacted Westrick about this matter, and had supposedly even threatened that the successor banks would not make use of a law with such an amendment. Westrick then decided to avoid having to make a difficult decision by not attending the Bundesrat meeting at all.[519] Neither did Hessian Finance Minister Tröger make the desired motion.

Although the plenum approved the bill with the controversial amendment of the finance committee, it also decided, on a motion that Tröger did put forward, to ask the Cabinet to study whether the Berlin institutions were to be treated as branches or as subsidiaries. In this way the Bundesrat left it to the government to decide whether fee reductions would be linked to unification with the Berlin institutions or not.[520] Soon after this, a meeting was held at the Economics Ministry on 24 May 1956, headed by Deputy Minister Westrick with representatives from Berlin and Bremen and with bank representatives. Abs considered this meeting so important that he postponed other appointments and went to Bonn himself. During this meeting, Abs managed to get Bremen and Berlin to come around to the banks' point of view. Certainly Abs argued very convincingly that the issue of removing the stipulations of the Big Banks Act, which only held for the territory of the Federal Republic and not for Berlin, had nothing logically to do with the issue of an eventual fusion of the banks with the Berlin subsidiaries.[521]

Berlin was willing to give in to Abs's demands only if it received the stated assurances of the big banks that they 'would feel responsible for their subsidiaries and would not abandon them'.[522] Such assurances, which were to be included as a statement in the minutes of the meeting, would possibly incur extensive financial obligations for the West German mother institutions should Berlin ever be separated from the Federal Republic. Therefore, other, less prominent representatives from the three bank groups who attended the meeting, Vallenthin, Möhring and Schäfer, were careful to get permission from Oberregierungsrätin Dr Irene Wolff, who was in charge of recording the minutes of meetings at the Economics Ministry, to help in wording the minutes. As it turned out, the Commerzbank Group and especially the Dresdner Bank Group were very concerned about the statement that was originally included in the minutes, namely 'that the successor institutions would be fully liable for the subsidiaries'.[523] Abs did not consider the wording of this statement to be a problem at all. However, Vallenthin managed to get Dr Wolff to include in the minutes the wording on not abandoning the Berlin banks, as cited above, even though she 'harboured strong objections to this wording – which meant something completely different than a statement accepting full liability – because Dr Klein [Federal Senator of the Land Berlin] had apparently given great import to the liability of the mother institutions at the meeting ... Naturally it is possible that Dr Klein will reject this version of the minutes as not being representative of the negotiations that took place. Therefore, we have to run the risk that another meeting with Dr Klein could result in having to interpret the submitted statements. Compared with the suggestion of assuming full liability, both of the other banks appear to consider this the lesser of two evils.'[524]

However, as Senator Dr Günter Klein expressed in a letter to Deputy Minister Westrick dated 30 May 1956, he had to back away completely from the willingness to compromise which he had demonstrated at the meeting; instead he now had to support the amendment to the bill passed by the Bundesrat. The Berlin Senate had not approved his recommendation to accept the compromise solution.[525]

The Deutsche Bank Aktiengesellschaft West,[526] known as the Rheinisch-Westfälische Bank AG until 17 April 1956, sought ways to counter these developments. Vallenthin saw three options for action: first, to hold further talks with Deputy Minister Westrick; second, to approach the authorities in Berlin immediately; third, to concentrate efforts on having the bill changed in the Bundestag debates. He favoured the second option since it was an unofficial approach and 'the entire problem can be more openly discussed'.[527] During a telephone call to Vallenthin on 14 June 1956, Abs approved of the second option, although at this point he was also willing to concede to the Berlin request to change the Berlin subsidiaries into branches. Vallenthin emphasized that the main objective was to defend the freedom of the banks against the imposition of mandatory measures by the 'public sector' (or by 'High Authority', as he tended to call both the Allied and German political decision-makers of the post-war period). 'There will still be time to consider the branch solution if our efforts in the Berlin matter fail.'[528]

Option two was implemented on 20 June 1956. In Bonn, Schäfer from the Dresdner Bank Group and Vallenthin presented the 'factual basis of the reunification issue' to both Senator Klein and Dr Paul Hertz, the Berlin senator for economics and credit. The bank representatives concentrated on the question 'whether any pressure should be exerted from outside in order to influence this decision'. Both senators acceded to this; although Berlin would like to see such a reunification take place, they maintained, it 'did not intend to force the hand of the big banks in their decision concerning the incorporation of the subsidiaries'. It would be possible to word the requested position of the Cabinet on the issue of incorporating the subsidiaries in such a way that the big banks could not be forced to take any sort of measures. He, Senator Klein, would promise that Berlin would then forgo any further intervention in parliament. However, he thought it would be appropriate for the banks to give Senator Hertz the same written assurances that they had given Deputy Minister Westrick during their meeting with him previously.

This was precisely what the bank representatives wanted to avoid, since the inclusion of the statements in the minutes of the meeting with Deputy Minister Westrick had given rise to so many problems. All agreed that any further resistance from the Berliner Zentralbank would no longer be important, since the bank representatives had learned 'that in connection with the federal reserve bank law [the later Federal Bank Law of 1957] the Berliner Zentralbank argues for its autonomy for the same practical reasons that we prefer to keep subsidiaries'.[529] About this time, Franz Amrehn, the mayor of Berlin, was wavering in his position. This was probably due to the influence exerted by Hertz and Klein, who felt a meeting between Amrehn and the banks would be advantageous in order to safeguard the compromise against subsequent opposition from other sources.[530]

On 5 July 1956, when Vallenthin, Schäfer and two representatives from each of the Berlin subsidiaries visited the Berliner Zentralbank for talks, they discovered that the position of the banks was quite welcomed. At their meeting the next day with Mayor Amrehn, he explained to the bank representatives that 'it is the policy of Berlin to give the appearance that West Berlin is a part of the Federal Republic, and to avoid anything that could one day cause the Russians to suggest a solution to the Berlin problem that would place a unified Berlin under a four-power statute as a special third unit in addition to the Federal territory and the East Zone. This is the reason why the Berlin Senate favours converting the subsidiaries into branches even though the big banks argue against it out of practical considerations.'[531] Amrehn did admit, however, that these were strictly political considerations, and conceded the arguments of the bank representatives that the big banks should not be forced against their will to implement organizational measures that they felt were detrimental. He then also promised to help get the Cabinet bill passed without any changes.

Senators Hertz and Klein did not repeat their original request for a second written statement of the assurances given Deputy Minister Westrick by the bank representatives. During a meeting on the Ufa law – a law stipulating the break-up of the Universum-Film AG, Berlin – at the Deutsche Bank in Düsseldorf in late August, they did call for the proposals that Abs had outlined on 20 June at his meeting with Westrick. These proposed to have the number of interlocking directorships between the board of managing directors of the Berliner Disconto Bank and those of the successor institutions increased, and to have the Berlin institution renamed something similar to 'Deutsche Bank AG Berlin'.[532] Abs approved of implementing both proposals.[533]

Consequently, the Economics Ministry again took up the matter of the bill in July by urging the Cabinet to circumvent the Bundesrat; instead it should pass a resolution that exempted the bill from approval by the Bundesrat and rejected any attempt to link fee reductions to the stipulation that the successor institutions must reunite with their Berlin subsidiaries within a period of two years.[534] Since no objections by the ministers to the Cabinet resolution were registered before the deadline of 28 July 1956, the resolution was accepted without dissent and passed on to the Bundestag together with the legislative bill in August. The parliament planned the first reading of the bill shortly after the end of summer recess in September.

Following the first reading of the bill in the Bundestag, it was sent to the

Committee for Money and Credit, which began deliberations on the bill on 25 October 1956, under the chairmanship of Scharnberg. Roughly a week prior to the start of these deliberations, the Deutsche Gewerkschaftsbund (DGB: German Trades Union Congress) petitioned the Economics Ministry to have the law apply also to those banks which had been founded as separate institutions due to the Allied regulations on decentralization, and which planned to merge in the future. Specifically, the DGB was representing the interests of the six Banken für Gemeinwirtschaft located in Düsseldorf, Frankfurt, Hamburg, Hanover, Munich and Stuttgart.[535] It was argued that these banks should also enjoy the same tax advantages once they were unified that the successor institutions of the big banks were going to have. Vom Hofe objected at first because, contrary to the successor institutions of the big banks, the Gemeinwirtschaft banks did not all have the same founders. Vallenthin considered this position to be too formalistic. It would also not be in the interests of the big bank groups to oppose this petition. And certainly it was clear that the chances for the still controversial tax exemptions would improve if the DGB and consequently the Social Democratic Party had an immediate interest in its passage.

What was important to him was that the passage of the bill not be delayed. The Social Democratic member of parliament Seuffert presented the necessary amendment to the bill concerning the Gemeinwirtschaft banks in the Committee for Money and Credit, which approved it. The committee also complied with the recommendations of the Cabinet resolution. On 9 November 1956, the amended bill was passed unanimously and sent back to the Bundestag with the committee report of 22 November 1956, for the second and third readings of the bill. On 6 December 1956, the bill was unanimously passed there and sent to the Bundesrat, which raised no objections to it at its session on 21 December 1956. The Act to Remove Limitations on the Regional Scope of Credit Institutions was signed into law by the Federal President on 24 December 1956, and published on 29 December.[536] The next day it went into effect.

Although the new law was quite specific in regulating the reductions of fees incurred in handling the legalities of merging the banks, there was no mention of tax exemptions. These were to be established by a decree issued by the Finance Minister far from the glare of the public eye. The Federal Finance Ministry had forwarded copies of the draft of such a decree, which had been compiled by the tax advisers of the Deutsche Bank Group in the spring of 1956, to the finance ministries in each *Land*. Tax exemptions required the approval of the *Länder* in cases where they held exclusive jurisdiction, such as the land transfer tax, or where they received part of the tax revenue, such as from individual income and corporation income taxes. The problem facing the big bank representatives was to get every *Land* to approve the requested tax exemption package. Particularly controversial was the request for exemption from transaction taxes in general, and from the land transfer tax in particular. For example, North Rhine-Westphalia did not want to give more preferential treatment to the big banks than had been given to the iron and steel industry, whose restructuring had only been supported with a reduction of transaction taxes, not an exemption.[537]

On 29 June 1956, the transaction tax authorities met with tax advisers from the banks and representatives from the Economics Ministry in Bonn to discuss the entire issue, but soon they got entangled in the sticky problems of jurisdiction.[538] The issue of taxes posed particularly difficult problems for the *Länder* because some of them were not only going to lose the one-time revenue that they otherwise would have received through the reunification process of the banks; they were going to be sacrificing a permanent source of revenue once head offices of the successor institutions were closed. This was especially critical in the case of *Länder* revenue from the corporation income tax, which only Hesse would profit from as soon as the banks moved their legal residences to Frankfurt from Munich, Düsseldorf and Hamburg, leaving Bavaria, North Rhine-Westphalia and Hamburg with nothing. Therefore it is not surprising that the strongest opposition to the tax exemption plans came from North Rhine-Westphalia and Bavaria, with the former stonewalling the otherwise uncontroversial transaction taxes with the above-mentioned argument and the latter fighting the land transfer tax exemption.

The banks lost to North Rhine-Westphalia when it shot down an identically worded *Länder* decree for tax exemption. On 24 October 1956, the Deutsche Bank AG West wrote to the Norddeutsche Bank AG and the Süddeutsche Bank AG that the new strategy was to have each individual bank group submit a petition for tax exemption at the moment of their unification to each of the responsible *Land* finance ministers, so that a decision on the petitions would be made by individual decree from each of the *Länder* in question. North Rhine-Westphalia referred the banks to the future home state of Hesse for the controversial issue of transaction taxes. Otherwise, the negotiations with the *Länder* over the requested tax exemptions in general progressed, 'whereby the Federal Ministry of Finance acts as a co-ordinating authority in supporting us. In light of the current situation, it can be assumed that the issues of corporation income tax, trade tax, and the Berlin emergency relief tax will be settled according to our requests, including also the issues involving wealth tax and income tax.'[539]

Yet it was still expected to be very difficult to secure a land transfer tax exemption. It was passed in September 1956 by the Conference of Land Finance Ministers, with Bavaria abstaining. Bavaria reserved the right to lodge a formal protest against the measure until 25 October 1956. And in fact, the events to follow kept all in suspense. Bavaria did lodge a protest, although it disclosed at the time that the Bavarian government had not yet made its final decision on the matter, and that the formal protest had been lodged because the October deadline was nearing. Should the Bavarian government decide finally to agree with the resolution of the finance ministers' conference, it would naturally withdraw the protest. The Bavarian finance ministry asked the Deutsche Bank AG West to specify again in writing the reasons for its request for a land transfer tax exemption.

The three bank groups complied by offering a joint petition to Friedrich Zietsch, the Bavarian finance minister, on 13 November 1956.[540] In this, the Big Banks Act of 1952 was once again labelled as the 'last involuntary application of Morganthauian reasoning' and the new, pending law as an 'act of compensation'. The process of reunifying the banks should now be exempted from land transfer taxation just as the process of decoupling them in 1952 had been. Bavaria was asked to withdraw its protest against the resolution of the finance ministers' conference. At about the same time, Managing Director Janberg from the Deutsche Bank West asked his colleague Tron in Munich 'to approach, with the help of former Minister Seidel, Bavarian Finance Minister Zietsch in order to influence his opinion in favour of our petition'.[541] By the end of the month it was clear 'that Mr Seidel is politically the adversary of current Finance Minister Zietsch. It is not clear from here whether his intervention under these circumstances might have a negative effect on Mr Zietsch.'[542] Shortly before Christmas, Seidel, Zietsch and Tron did meet to discuss the matter, but the meeting did not produce the desired results.[543]

In the meantime, tax advisers of the Deutsche Bank West in Düsseldorf had estimated for the first time the extent of the tax savings that the Deutsche Bank Group could expect from an exemption from transaction taxes. By amalgamating the Norddeutsche Bank and the Süddeutsche Bank into the Deutsche Bank AG West, they had estimated that the bank group would save 7.2 million DM in capital transfer taxes, 1.8 million DM in land transfer taxes, and 0.22 million DM in stock exchange transfer taxes, a total of 9.22 million DM. Vallenthin's comment: 'What surprises me about these calculations is that the land transfer tax does not amount to as large a sum as we always assumed it would. The saving on capital transfer tax, for which an exemption is fairly certain, is much higher. Of course, this should not mean that we want to relax our efforts to get a decree for the land transfer tax.'[544]

On 20 November 1956, the tax department raised the estimated savings on land transfer taxes to 3 million DM and thus the entire sum of transaction tax savings to 10.42 million DM.[545]

On 7 November 1956, the Deutsche Bank Group and the Dresdner Bank Group had submitted a joint petition to Hessian Finance Minister Tröger. They had been referred to him by North Rhine-Westphalia, since Frankfurt was to become the legal residence of the reunified institutions. They also included a draft for the desired tax decrees and requested a preliminary tax assessment for the purpose of securing the tax exemptions. Contrary to Bavaria and North Rhine-Westphalia, the former governed by the Christian Social Union and the latter by a Social Democratic government that had entered office the previous spring, Hesse, also a *Land* governed by the Social Democratic Party, did not hesitate to comply with the tax requests of the banks. The loss or gain of tax revenue from the bank fusions was apparently now more important to the safeguarding of their interests than ideological proximity and traditional partnerships.

Hesse wanted to grant unconditionally the preliminary tax assessment that North Rhine-Westphalia had refused to issue. But it was pointed out at a meeting of transaction tax authorities from the Federal Finance Ministry and the other *Länder* that a preliminary tax assessment could not be issued before the law went into effect. This prevented Hesse from issuing the preliminary tax assessment, but in order to pay respect to the banks whose head offices and tax revenue would be in Frankfurt, it notified the banks that, as soon as the law went into effect, then the tax exemption issue would be settled according to the banks' requests.[546] On 4 December 1956, the Hessian finance ministry sent the assessment in question to the Deutsche Bank AG West.[547]

By February 1957, the tax problems had still not all been resolved. With regard to direct taxes, Hamburg and North Rhine-Westphalia, the two losers as far as head offices were concerned, did not want to transfer the wealth tax liability from the successor institutions to the new Deutsche Bank on the date of merger set retroactively for 1 January 1957; instead they wanted to transfer it exactly a year later.[548] They were granted this. Bavaria was still stonewalling against a land transfer tax exemption, and began to demand in late 1956 and early 1957 that it be allowed to keep at least the corporation income tax revenue from the Süddeutsche Bank for 1957 instead of turning it over to Hesse, and, if necessary, to postpone the reunification for this long.[549] This prompted Tron and his board colleagues in Munich, Düsseldorf and Hamburg to decide in the last ten days of January 1957 to let Bavaria run the course of its protest.

The lawyers at the Norddeutsche Bank also decided to work out another solution for the merger. The solution was to have the Süddeutsche Bank become the new Deutsche Bank that would incorporate the other two, instead of the Deutsche Bank AG West as had been planned. However, before the amalgamation became legally binding, the Süddeutsche Bank had to move its head office from Munich to Frankfurt.[550] In this way, no property of the Süddeutsche Bank was to be transferred for which Bavaria could have collected land transfer taxes. And according to this plan, the unification of the successor institutions was actually effective retroactively to 1 January 1957, so that no corporation income taxes for 1957 would have to be paid to Bavaria.

On 5 March 1957, the successor banks of the Deutsche Bank, represented by the 12 members of the board of managing directors, signed the notarial amalgamation agreement.[551] The Norddeutsche Bank and the Deutsche Bank AG West were incorporated into the Süddeutsche Bank, which would then change its name to 'Deutsche Bank Aktiengesellschaft' and move its legal residence from Munich to Frankfurt. Rösler was the only former board member not to take a seat on the board of managing directors of the new Deutsche Bank. Instead he assumed the chairmanship of the 48-member supervisory board. The registered shares of the former successor banks were exchanged for bearer shares 'gratis and tax free' at a ratio of 1:1. On 22 March 1957, the Hessian finance minister notified the Süddeutsche Bank AG in Frankfurt of the government's preliminary decision on tax exemptions; the matter was finally settled as the bank had petitioned on 23 April 1957.[552]

On 26, 29 and 30 April, the regular general meetings of the three successor institutions took place in Hamburg, Düsseldorf and Munich, respectively. At each, the amalgamation was approved unanimously, and it became legally binding on 2 May when the new institution was entered into the commercial trade register. The business still remained somewhat decentralized in so far as Düsseldorf and Hamburg each continued to maintain a central administrative office in addition to the one in Frankfurt.[553] The new board of managing directors unanimously elected Hermann J. Abs as their new spokesman. In the next decade, Abs would become the major figure in the German world of business and finance, furthering the development of business at the Deutsche Bank with his experience, his expertise, his inexhaustible energy and his contacts with high-ranking politicians at home and abroad.

For the organizational development of the Deutsche Bank, like the Dresdner Bank, the year 1957 represented the closing of the chapter of post-war history, just as it did for many other areas of the economy and economic policy. (The Commerzbank did not undergo similar changes until a year later.)[554] Full employment was achieved, thus solving the chief problem facing the economy in the post-war period. On 21 January 1957, the Bundestag passed the pension reform law that introduced pensions, dynamically adjusted to current wages. This was a milestone in social policy. That same year the Deutsche Bundesbank was founded, bringing with it the partial recentralization of the federal reserve banking system in West Germany. Thanks to the success of the German export industry and the influx of foreign capital, the international balance of payments was so positive that the foreign exchange controls could be lifted. The Deutsche Mark became fully convertible *de facto* in 1957 and *de jure* in 1958. The West German Antitrust Law (*Kartellgesetz*), still today the Magna Carta of competition policy in the Federal Republic, was announced on 27 July 1957. On 10 July 1958, a final court decision was handed down, stipulating that the right to engage freely in business also held for banking, and that the banking supervisory authorities could no longer demand proof of need before issuing licences to establish banks. However, it took until 1965–67 before the two-step process of deregulating debit and credit interest rates was finished. At the same time that the successor institutions of the Deutsche Bank and the Dresdner Bank were undergoing the process of reunification, the Rome Treaties were signed on 25 March 1957, uniting the Federal Republic, France, Italy and the Benelux countries into the European Economic Community.

These were important signposts for further internationally oriented development of German business; the newly unified big banks in Germany – above all, the Deutsche Bank – were again in a position to contribute significantly to this development in both domestic and foreign business transactions. Yet with regard to the relative living standard in the Federal Republic, Abs was correct in stating, at the general meeting of the Süddeutsche Bank in Munich on 30 April 1957, that 'compared with most of the other developed industrial nations, we are still a poor country despite all our advances'.[555]

IV. The Deutsche Bank and Economic Reconstruction

1. Reviving business

Traditionally, the Deutsche Bank had engaged in two types of business: it had financed investment of German industry by granting credit and placing securities on the capital market; and it had financed foreign trade. In the era of West German economic reconstruction, both of these financial services were very much in demand. This explains in part the high proportion of business growth enjoyed by the big bank groups as compared with the average of all banks in the period immediately following currency reform. The three big banks had 10.4 per cent of the balance sheet total of all German banks at the end of 1936, [556] and on the eve of currency reform, in March 1948, they had even less: 9.4 per cent.[557] With the rapid growth of the German economy in general and of German foreign trade in particular that followed the currency reform, the percentage of the total volume of bank business in Germany cornered by the big bank groups was approximately 19.5 per cent at the end of 1950 and 1951. This began to decrease at a steady rate in the years to follow and dropped to 13.8 per cent by the end of 1957. By 1963, it had finally fallen to about 10 per cent, a level that had been the normal rate prior to the war; there it stabilized for many years.[558]

In early 1950, an American financial expert for the American High Commissioner explained the above-average growth of the big banks this way: 'As a result of currency reform, most banks started out with very few earning assets, since most of their liabilities were backed by low-yielding government securities (3 per cent equalization claims). The earnings benefits of credit expansion since June 1948 have been unevenly distributed among the various groups of banks, with the former *Grossbanken* receiving the highest share, but many others lagging behind.'[559]

Following the currency reform, credit to non-banks, which represented by far the largest portion of the business volume, developed as is shown in Table 3.

Compared with their normal place in the German banking business as a whole, the big banks cornered a disproportionately large share of the credit market in the six months following the currency reform, as Table 3 indicates. Not until 1949 did the savings banks sector and the credit co-operatives sector begin to

Table 3   *Credit to non-banks granted by the sectors of big banks,*
savings banks and credit co-operatives in West Germany
and West Berlin, 1948–58 (DM millions)

End of year	Big banks sector	Savings banks sector	Credit co-operatives sector
1948	1,558	1,201	527
1949	4,149	6,042	2,029
1950	6,020	8,962	2,643
1951	7,411	10,968	3,003
1952	8,629	14,126	3,850
1953	10,079	18,455	4,693
1954	12,042	24,061	5,744
1955	13,465	28,962	6,504
1956	14,524	32,526	7,092
1957	15,289	37,003	7,850
1958	15,591	43,023	8,808

Source: Deutsche Bundesbank (ed.), *Deutsches Geld- und Bank-wesen in Zahlen 1876–1975* (Frankfurt a.M. 1976), pp. 166, 174–80.

get more heavily involved, and not until 1952 did they expand their credit business to a greater degree than did the big banks sector.

By comparing the development of the big banks prior to and following the Big Banks Act of 1952, it is also obvious that they experienced an extraordinarily high rate of growth from 1948 to 1952: that is, the period in which they were subjected to the greatest decentralization. This holds true particularly for the Deutsche Bank Group, as is shown by the development of their customer deposits in Figure 4.1.

The astonishing finding of these statistics is that the big banks sector in general experienced a far greater rate of growth than did the sectors of savings banks and credit co-operatives in the period from the currency reform until the Big Banks Act went into effect in 1952: that is, during the period of the greatest regional fragmentation. However, as the 1950s progressed, the latter sectors grew at a clearly faster rate than the big banks. In light of these findings, one could be tempted to maintain that the arguments of the big banks against the Allied decentralization policy were empirically weak. But this conclusion is by no means logically compelling. Before such an argument could be supported, it would have to be known how business would have developed had bank decentralization been continued at the *Land* level after 1952. The big banks might have lost their business lead even sooner.

Perhaps the simple truth is that the banks did not experience the detrimental effects of decentralization because it was not being practised, although legally

Figure 4.1 Development of deposits from the end of 1945 to the end of 1957, on a logarithmic scale

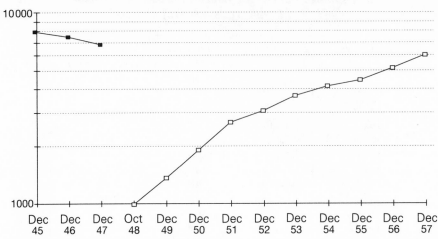

Source: Dec. 1945–Dec. 1947: Savings and current deposits in the RM (without the clearing accounts of the branches) of the three big banks in the British Zone, from Table 5; Oct. 1948–Dec. 1957: customer deposits in DM for the Deutsche Bank Group, 1948–50: from Table 9; 1951–57: from HADB, RWB, 47.

in force. And this is the interpretation I tend to accept, since the big bank groups were generally managed as centralized enterprises in a more or less informal manner, even between 1945 and 1957. There was a regular exchange of correspondence on business matters within the old Deutsche Bank organization,[560] the directors met regularly regardless of *Land* and zonal borders,[561] and there were even numerous meetings of the previous board of managing directors,[562] which refused to surrender any of its competence and which could count on the loyalty of the management of the regional banks and most of their custodians.

There is yet another, more significant factor that explains why the big banks experienced a major surge of growth soon after the war, and why such growth did not begin at the savings banks and credit co-operatives until later. This is a factor that has nothing to do with formal or informal forms of managing business. Wolfgang Stützel has discerned three types of structural change in the credit sector. The first is secular structural change, resulting from long-term processes of development or modernization of the economy in technical and organizational areas. The second is structural change caused by economic policy. This results when the credit sector adapts to changes in the institutional framework that are usually made by law-makers. And the third is structural change caused by regeneration. Such change is a result of major upheavals in the credit structure: for example, by war or currency collapse. A dramatic change occurs both in the structure of institutions themselves as well as in the structure of the banking business. This is gradually corrected in a regeneration process, whereby the 'replenishing phase' differs depending on the type of credit business involved. The phase does not last long 'where the turnover rate of stock of business is relatively high. However, for all durable items such as fixed assets, buildings, or long-term loans, it naturally takes a long time until the wounds of war and currency collapse have not only been scarred over but have been fully healed in the structure of the existing stock of business, especially in its age structure, its age "pyramid".'[563]

Traditionally, a relatively large percentage of the deposits in savings banks and credit co-operatives had been savings deposits: that is, funds tied up in relatively long-term commitments. In turn, the assets of these institutions were invested for the most part in medium-term and long-term credit. At big banks and other joint stock banks, the percentage of sight deposits and relatively short-term time deposits was traditionally much greater. Correspondingly, the assets of these institutions also included a greater percentage of relatively short-term credit in the form of bills of exchange and advances on current accounts. Therefore, after the upheaval of war and currency reform, the replenishing phase of the big bank groups was much shorter, due to the type of business they conducted, than that of the savings banks or credit co-operatives, let alone that of the mortgage banks, which raised their very long-term funds through issuing mortgage bonds.[564]

Of the three big banks, the Deutsche Bank Group could better maintain or expand its volume of business in the first five years after the war than the other two. Whereas in 1936 the business of the Deutsche Bank had represented 44.6 per cent of the balance sheet total of all three institutions, by the end of May 1950 this figure had risen to 50.3 per cent, but by the end of 1957 it had again fallen back to 42.6 per cent.[565] The profits earned in this period between the currency reform and the end of 1951, in which balance sheets were not published, also reflect similar ratios: the Deutsche Bank Group led with about 30 million DM, followed by the Dresdner Bank Group with 23 million DM and the Commerzbank Group with 11 million DM.[566]

There is little available information on the business development of the regional banks in the period prior to the legal decoupling of the three successor institutions from the old big banks in Berlin in 1952, since balance sheets and business reports were not published and only sporadic data exist in the Central Archives of the Deutsche Bank. For the West German branches of the Deutsche Bank, the closing balance sheet compiled for the purpose of currency conversion amounted to 8.4 billion RM.[567] This was significantly less than the balance sheet total of 11.4 million RM that the Deutsche Bank had at the close of 1944.[568] If it is assumed that two-thirds of this sum, 7.6 million RM, was transferred to the Western zone, specifically to the central cash office in Hildesheim at the end of the war, and that, of the other third, part was in the 'East Zone' and part was lost with the eastern territories,[569] then the growth of the business volume of the

Deutsche Bank in the three and a half years between the end of 1944 and currency reform was a very modest nominal total of about 10 per cent.

Of course, this does not preclude the fact that there were major fluctuations in the business volume of banks during this period. For example, in the second half of 1946, bank liquidity suffered from 'a clear channelling of funds from financial institutions to the accounts of the treasuries of the public sector and of the American military government at the Reichsbank'[570] due to increased tax rates and the procedural stipulations for financing imports from the USA. In July 1946, a large prepayment of individual and corporation income taxes was due for the first time since a major rise in the tax rates had been implemented on 1 April 1946. The chief office of the Reichsbank in Hamburg considered this rise in taxes and the rumours about the pending currency reform to be the reasons why the sight, time and savings deposits decreased in the British zone in the summer of 1946.[571] Evidently this was true also for deposits at the Deutsche Bank branches in that zone, for in this situation, the branches in southern Germany propped up the banks in the north by lending them 100 million RM to stabilize their liquidity.[572]

The difficulties that banks were experiencing with their liquidity, including banks in Hesse, prompted the Bavarian finance ministry to issue an ordinance on 22 November 1946 to credit institutions in Bavaria, prohibiting them from any type of credit transactions with banks outside of Bavaria, without the authorization of the chief office of the Reichsbank in Munich (as of early 1947, the Land Central Bank). The weekly newspaper *Die Zeit* commented on this in its 23 January 1947 issue, under the headline 'Blue & White Borders for Foreign Exchange': 'The only thing that is still missing is a maximum limit on the number of bank notes one can take when crossing the Bavarian border – then the Bavarians have truly created a foreign exchange border.'[573]

Thanks to the existence of the chief office of the Reichsbank in Hamburg and its total of 21 monthly Business Reports ranging from May 1946 to February 1948, we have access to more accurate information on the development of the banking business in the British zone before the currency reform.[574] The first report lists the number of credit institutions there and their branch offices at 5,000; in view of the economic realities existing at the time, the credit sector was considered to be overcrowded. The balance sheet total of all credit institutions on 31 March 1946 was reported to have amounted to 80 billion RM in the British zone, as opposed to 74 billion RM in the American zone and 12 million RM in the Soviet zone; however, the latter figure only comprises new business since the end of the war.[575] Table 4 shows that the savings banks and their *Girozentralen* (central giro institutions) comprised 62 per cent of the balance sheet totals, while the big banks and credit co-operatives each had 15 per cent.

Of the 80 billion RM balance sheet total, 37 billion RM were reported to be invested in government securities, 'which are the most important asset item for all credit institutions'.[576] A further 10 billion RM were reported to be deposits

Table 4   Balance sheet totals of the credit institutions in the British zone on 31 March 1946 (RM billions)

Savings banks	34.0
Central giro institutions	15.5
Big banks	12.0
Credit co-operatives	12.0
Regional banks	2.5
Public banks	2.0
Private banks	1.0
Special banks	1.0
Total	80.0

Source: HADBB, Economic Report No. 1 of the Reichsbank chief office in Hamburg.

at the former head offices in Berlin, which were also invested in government securities. 'The fate of the Reich's debt is therefore also decisive for the German credit business.' Some 15 billion RM were attributed to the financial linkage between the banks, and 8 billion RM were reported to be cash balances as well as the balances on Reichsbank Giro accounts and postal checking accounts. This left only 10 billion RM as actual business of the credit institutions in the British zone: that is, less than the 12 million RM balance sheet total registered just as new business by the banks in the Soviet zone. And from this 10 billion RM, only 6 billion RM were invested in business and mortgage loans, securities, bills of exchange and cheques. The savings deposits amounted to 34 billion RM and current account funds to 17 billion RM in the British zone.

In the American zone, however, only 29 billion RM of the 74 billion RM balance sheet total for the credit sector were tied up in government securities. The difference between the two zones amounted to roughly 7 billion RM that the Deutsche Bank had transferred to the central cash office in Hildesheim shortly before the war ended (see p. 368 above). The amount of savings deposits was also much less in the US zone, only 19 billion RM, whereas the current account funds at 16 billion RM and the interlocking bank deposits at 24 billion RM just about equalled those in the British zone.[577]

The chief office of the Reichsbank in Hamburg compiled monthly statistics on the development of the savings and giro deposits of the sectors of big banks, savings banks and postal savings institutions from the end of 1945 to the beginning of 1948.

Table 5 shows that deposits tended to be on the decline at the big banks and the savings banks throughout the entire period. The decrease in savings deposits was remarkably steady for both banking sectors. But the decline is also obvious

Table 5   Monthly development of deposits in the sectors of big banks, savings banks and postal savings institutions in the British zone from 31 Dec. 1945 to 31 Jan. 1948 (RM millions)

	Three big banks		Savings banks and giro institutions		Postal savings institutions
End of month	Savings deposits	Current account deposits	Savings deposits	Current account deposits	Deposits
December 1945	1,545	10,198	26,432	18,500	–
January 1946	1,554	10,169	26,960	19,749	480
February	1,545	10,241	27,020	20,286	683
March	1,528	10,237	27,018	20,330	825
April	1,508	10,247	26,860	20,219	918
May	1,495	10,226	26,759	20,026	984
June	1,470	10,293	26,609	20,045	1,059
July	1,443	10,145	26,392	19,281	1,106
August	1,422	10,117	26,192	19,080	1,142
September	1,402	6,293[a]	26,009	18,987	1,166
October	1,377	6,237	25,780	18,706	1,184
November	1,355	6,199	25,566	18,801	1,198
December	1,332	6,115	25,354	18,970	1,195
January 1947	1,267[b]	5,832[b]	25,263	18,752	1,205
February	1,256	5,852	25,134	18,917	1,208
March	1,239	5,956	24,966	18,980	1,205
April	1,219	5,969	23,945[c]	18,230[c]	1,198
May	1,188	5,978	23,771	18,431	1,188
June	1,153	6,029	23,485[d]	5,760[d]	1,177
July	1,131	6,026	23,261	5,944	1,167
August	1,110	5,971	23,046	5,904	1,160
September	1,089	6,041	22,825	5,838	1,156
October	1,067	5,972	22,569	5,885	1,143
November	1,045	5,924	22,332	5,825	1,132
December	1,013	5,795	22,118	5,744	1,124
January 1948	1,006	5,820	22,047	5,684	1,147

[a] Without the clearing accounts of the branches. These amounted to 3,807 million RM in August 1946.

[b] As of January 1947 without the branches in the *Land* of Bremen (US zone).

[c] As of April 1947 without the savings banks and giro institutions in the *Land* of Bremen. These equalled a total sum of 800 million RM in savings deposits and current accounts.

[d] As of June 1947 without giro institutions, which only accounted for about 50–75 million RM in savings deposits in the three previous months, but did represent the majority of the current accounts, e.g. 12,825 million RM in May 1947.

Source: HADBB, 21 monthly reports of the Reichsbank chief office in Hamburg.

in the current account figures, especially from the second half of 1946 until the end of January 1947. The liquidity crisis mentioned above is mirrored in these statistics. The special development of deposits at the postal savings institutions could not compensate for the declining trend within the other two major groups of credit institutions because the volume of deposits was too small. Unlike the savings deposits, the more dominant current account deposits at the big banks rose rapidly immediately after currency reform. While this reflected the economic upswing that West Germany was experiencing during this period, the shrinking bank balances before early 1948 do not offer any indication of economic recovery at that time.

This finding is also apparent in the development of the stock exchange. The first exchange to resume trade in securities was Hamburg in July 1945. In the British zone, Düsseldorf and Hanover were the next ones to follow suit in April 1946. In the US zone there were also three stock exchanges operating by the end of May 1946, in Munich, in Stuttgart and the biggest in Frankfurt. In the second half of that year, Mainz and Freiburg i.B. also began 'with very little trading'. In 1946, the total trading for all the exchanges amounted to 400 billion RM, of which Hamburg alone totalled 300 billion RM, and Frankfurt, the most important exchange in the south, totalled only 45 million RM. Of the former circulation of old German securities that were not Reich securities, only 0.5 per cent were traded in this period. The reason for this was that the majority of all such securities were deposited in collective safe deposits and were not recallable. Only actual securities were traded on the stock exchanges.[578] The general development of stock prices is illustrated in Table 6.

Table 6   Monthly stock price index of the Reichsbank
chief office in Hamburg 1946–47
(stop prices in 1944 = 100)

Monthly average	1946	1947
January	83.38	84.17
February	88.59	82.54
March	77.27	80.53
April	70.77	82.73
May	62.48	82.11
June	60.04	79.99
July	62.95	83.53
August	70.59	87.72
September	72.65	91.81
October	75.76	90.64
November	83.65	92.11
December	81.50	93.81

Source: HADBB, 21 monthly reports of the
Reichsbank chief office in Hamburg.

Deutsche Bank shares were also traded at the time. The 1944 stop price for these shares, which could not be exceeded in the first years following the war, was 152 per cent of nominal capital, that is at 152 RM for a nominal share value of 100 RM. The bank shares were traded at a monthly average price of 93 per cent in December 1946, 78 in June 1947 – probably as a result of the American decision to decentralize the banks – 107 in September 1947, and 104 in October 1947. By the end of December 1947, the price had reached 132, and by 22 January 1948 it had climbed to 137 RM.[579] Then the price of Deutsche Bank shares began to fall to 97 RM until currency reform.[580] In the reports of the Reichsbank chief office it was pointed out repeatedly that in general the movement in stock prices mirrored the impact of political developments more than current business developments. The upswing that began in the autumn of 1947 was considered to be a result of the anticipation of currency reform in the near future, and of the increase in the demand for real assets caused by such anticipation.

In the second half of 1948, the price of Deutsche Bank shares fluctuated between a high point of 9.75 per cent of nominal capital, which corresponded exactly to one-tenth of the last Reichsmark quotation prior to currency reform, and a low point of 5 (see Table 7). In 1949 the price fell to a low of 4.75 in April, recovered moderately to a level of 7.50 by the end of September, and then skyrocketed to 30 per cent by the end of the year. The probable causes for this were the founding of the Federal Republic, the high expectations for the economy associated with this, and, specifically for the big banks, the prospect of regulating the de- or recentralization issue through stock corporation law. In 1950 the share price tended not to be so strong. But in 1951, especially in the second half of that year, the quotation rose at a spectacular rate from 25 per cent at the end of 1950 to 72 per cent by the end of 1951. From this point on, the development of the price for Deutsche Bank shares can be compared with the development of the average stock value of all authorized common stock on all of the stock exchanges in the Federal Republic (see Table 7). They rose from 55 to 120 per cent in the same period of time. The relatively larger increase in the price of Deutsche Bank shares may be attributed to the imminent passage of the Big Banks Act, which ended the shroud of uncertainty enveloping the legal status of the bank. This is substantiated all the more by the fact that the greatest jumps in price occurred in the second half of the year as it became clear that the law would be passed.

In 1952, the year the three successor banks were founded and the shares of the old Deutsche Bank were converted into Deutsche Mark shares of the new banks at a ratio of 10 : 6.25, the market value of all these shares remained rather stable. At the end of May in the following year, the general meetings of the three successor institutions decided to pay out dividends of 6 per cent for the business year 1952 on the converted capital stock totaling 100 million DM. This was the first time since the war that dividends had been paid. This revived prices on the

Table 7   Dividend payments and share prices of the Deutsche Bank Group 1948–57, compared with the average share prices and average dividend payments of domestic joint stock companies (in parentheses)

	1948	1949	1950	1951	1952	1953	1954	1955	1956	1957
Dividends in %	0 (.)	0 (.)	0 (.)	0 (1.3)	0 (1.9)	6 (3.0)	8.5 (4.8)	9 (6.3)	10 (7.5)	12 (8.6)
Share prices (in % of RM/DM nominal capital) End of										
1st quarter		5.25	21	27	66	59	141[a]	253	251	215.5
2nd quarter		6.0	20.5	37	58	56	146	226[b]	198.75[c]	193.25
3rd quarter		7.5	23	60	64	74.75	174	257	202	209
4th quarter	6.5 (.)	30 (.)	25 (55)	72 (120)	60.5 (95)	91.5 (104)	204 (181)	238 (203)	200.5 (181)	220 (186)
Highest level	9.75	30	32	73.5	83.5	91.5	205	299	263	220
on	–	29 Dec.	2 Jan.	22 Nov.	18 Jan.	31 Dec.	28 Dec.	3 May	18 Apr.	31 Dec.
Lowest level	5	4.75	18.5	25.5	51	56	126.5	195.5	189	193.25
on	–	25 Apr.	14 Jul.	2 Jan.	19 Jun.	26 Jun.	6 Jan.	9 Feb.	8 Aug.	28 Jun.
Salvage shares (in DM for nominal 100 RM) End of										
1st quarter							10	14	20.5	18
2nd quarter							9.5	25	20.5	13.63
3rd quarter							11.75	25.5	21	14.5
4th quarter							14.25	22	22.25	13
Highest level							16.63	30	27.25	25
on							28 Oct.	5 Sept.	18 Jan.	11 Jan.
Lowest level							7.75	12	16	12
on							13 Jul.	7 Feb.	11 Apr.	4 Jun.

[a] As of 1954 price of RWB, later DB-West shares.

[b] Following a markdown of 60 percentage points for subscription rights from the capital increase of 1955.

[c] Following a markdown of 36.375 percentage points for subscription rights from the capital increase of 1956.

Source: Rheinisch–Westfälische Bank, *Die deutschen Börsen im Jahre 1948*, as well as *Das Börsenbild des Jahres, 1949–1957*, published annually by the various successor institutions of the Deutsche Bank, available in HADB. For the averages of common stock admitted to the exchange: Deutsche Bundesbank (ed.), *40 Jahre Deutsche Mark. Monetäre Statistiken 1948–1987* (Frankfurt a.M. 1988), p. 229.

stock exchange enormously during the last six months of 1953. Deutsche Bank shares were quoted at 56 per cent by mid-year and reached their annual maximum of 91.5 by the year's end. This was far above the average price increase of all shares quoted on the exchange for all of 1953, which only amounted to about 10 per cent.

In the years to follow, the Deutsche Mark shares of the successor institutions were quoted separately from the Reichsmark salvage shares of the old bank. Like the dividend payments, the development of the price of the shares of all three successor institutions was practically identical, so that the price of shares of the Rheinisch-Westfälische Bank, later the Deutsche Bank AG West, fully represents the development of the entire group. In 1954, the German stock market rose almost as sharply as it had in 1951. And again, the price of shares of the Deutsche Bank Group rose at a rate well above the average, especially when the value of the salvage shares is taken into consideration. Between 1955 and 1957, the value of the shares fluctuated roughly in tandem with the overall stock market price average: there was a small boom in 1955 that was interrupted in 1956 and 1957. This reflected the decline of economic growth in the Federal Republic, which dropped continually from a real rate of +12.2 per cent in 1955 to +3.4 per cent in 1958. The prices of salvage shares developed along similar lines; but it was probably another factor that played an important role in influencing the bullish market in 1954 and 1955, and the stagnation and slump in the two years that followed: namely, the disappointment over the lack of a profitable rate of return for the old Deutsche Bank shares, which had been expected to result from transferring the good name of the company to the Rheinisch-Westfälische Bank in 1956 and to the new, reunified Deutsche Bank in 1957.

It is also apparent from the development of share prices over time that decentralization neither hindered the payment of sizeable dividend earnings, which since 1952 were considerably higher than the average dividend payments of all domestic joint stock companies (see Table 7), nor prevented investors from regaining their trust in the bank, even in the period prior to the founding of the successor institutions when no dividends were issued. The person who purchased a 1,000 RM share of the Deutsche Bank for 1,000 RM shortly after the war or for 50 DM some time during the first 15 months after currency reform, had increased his investment to the tax-free sum of 1,788 DM by mid-1955 – disregarding salvage shares, dividend payments and transaction costs.[581] This value increase on the original investment of 50 DM represented an average annual rate of return of 66.7 per cent in the seven years from mid-1948 to mid-1955. Yet even the person who purchased shares at the end of 1949 roughly tripled his investment in the following four years, which still equalled an average annual rate of return of 32 per cent. Despite the continued favourable development in the decades to follow, investing in Deutsche Bank shares would never again be as profitable a venture as it had been before recentralization.

On the eve of currency reform, 68 per cent of the assets of the West German branches of the Deutsche Bank still consisted of Treasury bills, Treasury notes, and bonds of the Reich, which were not compensated for in the course of currency reform along with the balances in cash, on bank accounts at the Land Central Banks and on postal checking accounts. Thus the balance sheet totals of the Deutsche Bank's branches in the West shrank to 'no more than approx. 650 million DM' during the currency conversion.[582]

On 14 October 1948, not even four months after the currency reform, Plassmann, the spokesman for the board of managing directors at the Rheinisch-Westfälische Bank, presented the information summarized in Table 8 concerning

Table 8   Equity capital and other balance sheet items for all
of the regional banks of the Deutsche Bank Group
in September 1948 (DM millions)

	Equity capital	Deposits	Accept-ance credit	Cash advances	Bills of exchange
Rheinisch-Westfälische Bank	10	400	44.2	65	147.6
Südwestbank	4	139	33	12	24.5
Bayerische Creditbank	3.7	100	19	11.3	12.3
Norddeutsche Bank	3.25	124	17	21	20
Hessische Bank	2.3	90	10	11	15
Nordwestbank	1.9	76	14.2	13.1	13.4
Oberrheinische Bank	1.7	53	5.8	4.5	4.2
Rheinische Kreditbank	1.5	67	8	8	13
Disconto-Bank	0.6	40	5	3	4
Württembergische Vereinsbank	0.4	16	3	2.4	–

Source: HADB, Aufsichtsrat der Deutschen Bank, vol. III.

the business conditions of the ten decentralized sister banks of the Deutsche Bank Group to the supervisory board members from the old Deutsche Bank who had gathered in Wuppertal.

As this table shows, the equity capital of the ten regional institutions shortly after the currency reform was calculated to equal 29.35 million DM. Deposits in all ten institutions equalled 1,105 million DM. In both cases, slightly more than a third of these belonged to the Rheinisch-Westfälische Bank. The second largest regional institution of the Deutsche Bank Group, namely the Südwestbank, listed the following totals in millions of Deutsche Marks on three dates between the currency reform and the end of 1948 (21 June, 30 September, 31 December) for the following balance sheet items: for advances, 4.2/79.0/98.7;

for sight and time deposits 42.9/126.6/133.0; and for savings deposits 9.7/4.8/6.4, respectively.[583]

Also typical for the other regional institutions of the big bank groups were the massive surpluses of deposits over lendings on the day of the currency conversion, meaning that the banks had an enormously high liquidity. Most banks then typically experienced a dramatic increase in lending, which already by late September 1948 had jumped nearly twenty-fold, while sight and time deposits grew only three-fold and savings deposits decreased in conjunction with the rise in private consumption. Not until October 1948 were the surplus cash balances depleted, so that the Südwestbank was dependent on discount credit from the Land Central Bank. Protests were heard over the enormous additional costs caused by the currency conversion, which in the first few months immediately succeeding the reform required nearly a quarter of the bank's administrative staff to handle this unproductive work. The level of equity capital was also considered to be too low. At the end of 1948, the equalization claims of the Südwestbank against the _Land_ Württemberg-Baden equalled approximately 40 million DM.[584]

At the next meeting of supervisory board members of the Deutsche Bank on 19 December 1949, Plassmann announced that in 1949 new regulations had been issued for calculating the equity capital of banks, according to which the banks were credited with 7.50 DM in equity capital for every 100 DM of converted liabilities. Under these new regulations, the preliminary sum of equity capital for all ten sister banks of the Deutsche Bank totalled 36.5 million DM, of which roughly 14 million DM belonged to the Rheinisch-Westfälische Bank, the largest institution in this group, and 0.4 million DM to the Württembergische Vereinsbank, the smallest institution. After 70 per cent of the credit balances on the so-called _Festkontos_ established at the time of currency reform had been cancelled in early October 1948, the total amount of customer deposits at all of the sister banks equalled only 976 million DM by the end of that month. By the end of November 1949, these had risen to 1,331 million DM. Compared with the total sum of deposits in 1938 at the branches located in what would later be the Federal Republic (1.633 million RM), 81.5 per cent of this sum had been attained by then, compared to nearly 60 per cent in the period shortly after the Deutsche Mark was introduced. Of course, Plassmann conceded, the purchasing power of the Deutsche Mark was only about half as large as that of the Reichsmark in 1938.

At this same meeting with supervisory board members, Plassmann also presented the other balance sheet items for the ten sister banks of the Deutsche Bank, compared with the West German branches of 1938, as listed in Table 9.

The explosive expansion of credit between September–October 1948 and November 1949 by two- or three-fold was far greater than the 36 per cent increase in customer deposits during the same period. This can be explained by the high liquidity mentioned earlier, which acted as a protective padding for the

*Table 9   Credit items and customer deposits of the Deutsche Bank Group
in West Germany in 1938 and 1948–51
(RM/DM millions at the end of each month/year)*

	1938	Sept. 1948	Oct. 1948	Nov. 1949	1949	1950	1951
Acceptance credit	170	159	158	487	490	530	342
Cash advances	597	151	220	582	554	815	1,105
Bills of exchange	364	254	261	531	616	874	1,127
Customer deposits	1,633	1,105	976	1,331	1,353	1,894	2,393

Source: HADB, Aufsichtsrat der Deutschen Bank, vol. III, and HADB, RWB, 409.

regional institutions of the big banks and the banks in general for some time following the currency conversion. On 25 June 1948, shortly after the currency reform, Ludwig Erhard, director of the Bizonal Economic Administration, lifted the restrictions on most prices of finished industrial products and phased out a great many of the rationing controls.[585] This broke the dam of a pent-up demand for consumer goods, on the one hand, and for production and investment goods on the other. Now the deregulated markets could develop freely with prices alone dictating the distribution of goods.

The degree to which this demand could impact the markets was determined not only by the initial distribution of Deutsche Marks to private households, enterprises and the public sector, but naturally also by the expansion of credit and thus the money supply by the banks. During the course of the liberalization of regulations, restrictions were also lifted here: for example, in early August 1948 the ban on granting current account advances was dropped. The result was a rapid rise in cash credit until late October 1948. In the following year, credit based on the use of bills of exchange increased particularly. Contrary to current account (cash) advances, bills of exchange expanded the banks' possibilities for rediscounting at the Land Central Banks; therefore these were preferred. Even more dramatic was the rise in acceptance credit, which was used to finance a good percentage of the greatly expanding business of foreign trade.[586]

Although industrial production rose by 50 per cent during the second half of 1948, neither the growing domestic supply nor foreign sources of supply by then available in conjunction with the start of the Marshall Plan could meet the effective demand. The result was a sharp rise in prices. Workers were hit especially hard by this due to the freeze on wages that lasted until early November. These developments convinced the trade unions that their rejection of a free market economy was justified. On 12 November 1948, they organized a general strike. In light of this situation, the Bank deutscher Länder implemented rigorous restrictions on credit for roughly six months, especially by freezing the banks' volume of credit at the level of late October 1948,[587] by raising the required minimum level of reserves, and even by exercising selective credit controls. And indeed, the level of prices began to drop gradually starting in early 1949, until by mid-1950 it was again equal to that of the first month after currency reform. The other side of the coin was that unemployment rose from 760,000 persons at the end of 1948 to 1.56 million by the end of 1949. After the last credit restrictions had been lifted in the summer of 1949, credit was expanded tremendously, according to the report by Plassmann: 'In the months of August through October, the volume of banker's acceptances doubled. The increasing demand for credit was evident in November, primarily as a result of the required cash deposits made for the growing volume of imports, which have become highly irritating for all banking businesses.'[588]

Plassmann also saw indications of structural change in the bank balance sheets that was due to regeneration, as explained above. In October 1948, 92.5 per cent of all deposits matured daily and only 7.5 per cent were time deposits. By the end of November 1949, these percentages had already shifted to 81 and 19, respectively. Plassmann also had good news to report concerning the growth of savings deposits during 1949: 'At the Rheinisch-Westfälische Bank, for example, we have been able to calculate with nearly mathematical certainty from the beginning of the year that each week savings deposits increase by 200,000–250,000 DM.' Plassmann reported that, on the whole, business at the Deutsche Bank had been very good. The first quarter following the currency reform was the only period in which the bank operated in the red. Then the banks began to break even, starting with the Rheinisch-Westfälische Bank. Like the banking districts of Hamburg and south-west Germany, but unlike the French zone, the Rhineland-Westphalian district was of particular economic importance. Contrary to expectations, this district was able to transform its financial deficit of late October 1948 (35 per cent of the deposits and 41 per cent of the credits of the entire Deutsche Bank Group) into a financial surplus by the end of November 1949 (41 per cent of the deposits and 37 per cent of the credits), and to obtain an especially high percentage of rediscountable commercial bills, on which the other *Länder* could also increasingly rely to help meet the credit needs of the economy. The fact that North Rhine-Westphalia had become a region of credit export ran somewhat contrary to the concerns British financial experts had held when they demanded that a central bank be established for all of West Germany; at the time, they foresaw North Rhine-Westphalia as a region that would need to import substantial sums of credit.

Plassmann strongly recommended that the following economic measures be adopted as policy:

  1. In order to make the banking system more stable, it would be advisable to create hidden reserves, which were as yet non-existent. It was hoped that for this purpose the state would grant the banks the creation of a tax-free valuation adjustment amounting to 3 per cent of their outstanding credit

volume. This would serve to create a hidden reserve of 48 million DM in addition to the equity capital amounting to 36.5 million DM.

2. In order to enable the German economy to calculate future costs and profits with more accuracy, it was strongly recommended that further steps be taken, beyond the immediate help that had already been implemented, to settle once and for all the issue of the equalization of the burden of war debts.

3. In order to encourage capital formation, especially of partnerships (associations without independent legal existence), a thorough tax reform was necessary. The top rates of income tax were actually still far above those of the corporation income tax rate of 60 per cent.

4. Due in part to the short-term character of their deposits, credit banks were only in a position to grant short-term credit. It was still nearly impossible to transform such credit into shares or obligations to any great extent because there was no real capital market yet in West Germany. Therefore it was crucial to develop possibilities for granting long-term credit, such as at the Reconstruction Loan Corporation.

Plassmann reported on the few bond issues that had been floated since the end of 1948, such as those by the Reichsbahn (State Railways), electrical utility companies and the Reconstruction Loan Corporation. The bank syndicates had only been able to sell these to the public in small, sometimes extremely small, amounts. The Deutsche Bank Group led this market with a total of only 22 million DM. It was also not able to place more than 4 million DM in mortgage bonds outside the banking system. Due to the large sums that had not yet been placed, the capital market would remain blocked for a longer period of time, stated Plassmann. The prospects for new bond issues, for example by the Industriekreditbank (Industry Credit Bank) were dismal. This bank had been established in 1949, to a great extent with the financial backing of business firms in Düsseldorf, and specialized in providing enterprises that were not traded on the stock exchange with medium-term and long-term investment credit, from Marshall Plan funds supplied to the banks by the Reconstruction Loan Corporation, on the one hand, and by issuing stocks and bonds, on the other.[589] It wanted to place bonds amounting to 50 million DM in 1949, but by the end of March 1950 had only been able to dispose of 1.7 million DM, despite tax advantages.

As a contrast to such dismal news, Plassmann described the revival of foreign business of the Deutsche Bank Group as being a major success. Once the Bank deutscher Länder had permitted the banks to establish so-called intermediate clearing accounts abroad, the Rheinisch-Westfälische Bank had opened a total of 42 bank accounts in Belgium, Denmark, France, Finland, Holland, Luxemburg, Norway, Sweden, the semi-autonomous Saar region, the United Kingdom and the United States. The figures for the foreign business being conducted by the other sister banks in each of their respective *Länder* were very good everywhere.[590]

The next meeting of the supervisory board members of the old Deutsche Bank did not take place until 7 April 1952: that is, immediately after the Big Banks Act was passed. Table 9 shows the figures on customer deposits that were reported at this meeting. From the end of 1949 until the end of 1951, customer deposits rose by a total of 77 per cent, which corresponded almost exactly to the credit increase in the big banks sector in general during this period (see Table 3). The normalization in the structure of deposits due to the 'regeneration' mentioned above had also progressed further. At the end of 1951, 30 per cent of the customer deposits were time deposits and another 8 per cent were savings deposits, meaning that the percentage of sight deposits had dropped to 62 per cent and was thus approaching the 50 per cent mark typical for the pre-war period. As the volume of credit increased for the Deutsche Bank Group, cash advances and bills of exchange roughly doubled from the end of 1949 to the end of 1951, while banker's acceptances became less significant (see Table 9). In addition to this, there were still 181 million DM in credit from earmarked funds, 96 million DM in old currency advances, and 272 million DM in export drafts and export promissory notes, so that the group's total volume of credit at the end of 1951 equalled more than 3 billion DM. Business was also going well for the Berliner Disconto Bank, a subsidiary which had been established in August 1949 with capital that at first amounted to 0.5 million DM. The bank's equity capital was raised in several phases to 5 million DM, and by the end of 1951 the balance sheet total had reached approximately 100 million DM.

In his address to this meeting on 7 April, Plassmann reported on the extensive 'job creation and housing construction programme' that had been passed by the Federal Government on 9 February 1950. A sum of 2.5 billion DM had been budgeted for the housing construction programme, and another 950 million DM for a special programme. The Bank deutscher Länder was to provide the advance financing. This programme was slow to get started; then a dramatic change in economic development occurred in connection with the outbreak of the Korean War in the summer of 1950. In the Federal Republic, the surge in demand caused by this led to both an exhaustion of all capacity reserves and a 'truly alarming rise in prices'. From the autumn of 1950, the Bank deutscher Länder was attempting to counter this by implementing a very restrictive credit policy, which included issuing a decree on 12 February 1951, with 'guidelines for normalizing the volume of short-term lending of credit banks'. These guidelines stipulated: '1. The total volume of short-term lending is not to be more than twenty-fold of the liable equity capital of a bank. 2. The sum of cash advances and banker's acceptances is not to exceed 70 per cent of the deposits and the liable equity capital of a bank. 3. Acceptances of a bank based on immediate business in foreign trade and crop financing should not exceed seven times the sum of a bank's liable equity capital, all other acceptances no more than three times this sum. 4. The total of the liquid funds of a bank should not fall *beneath* 20 per cent the sum of borrowed funds.'[591]

However, it was not possible to contain the volume of credit due to the influx of foreign currency that arose from the major increase in exports, which caused a foreign trade surplus. At the end of July 1951, the Bank deutscher Länder tightened the credit controls further, so that short-term lending was restricted to a sum that was 18 instead of 20 times that of a bank's liable equity capital, and so that cash advances and acceptances were only allowed to reach a maximum of 60 per cent of the deposits and liable equity capital instead of 70 per cent. But the deposits of the big banks increased due to the influx of foreign currency. Therefore the banks' capacity for the extension of credit rose despite these restrictions.

Plassmann could also announce that the capital resources of the Deutsche Bank Group had risen to 38.7 million DM through the incorporation of the deposits in Berlin belonging to customers who resided in West Germany. He could report further that the narrow capital base had been expanded once again by creating additional hidden reserves. In June 1950, the state not only granted the banks a tax-free overall valuation adjustment to provide for contingency reserves; it also required such reserves. These were to amount to 1.5 per cent of discount credit and credit by way of bank guarantee, and 3 per cent for cash advances and acceptances. By the end of 1951, these hidden reserves amounted to more that twice the equity capital of 38.7 million DM.[592]

Plassmann again reprimanded the state for having done little or nothing to pass a long overdue law to regulate the equalization of the war debt burden, to reform the tax laws so as to encourage private initiative, and to help normalize the capital market, which was still unable to function properly. Granted, the capital market had been helped in the areas of long-term investment financing by the infusion of 3.5 billion DM in long-term capital that the Reconstruction Loan Corporation had made available in part through the banks and in part directly to German business and by the Investment Aid Act, which was to direct 1 billion DM from the rest of the economy to certain basic industries.[593] However, there was still no demand on the capital market for fixed-interest securities, such as 5 per cent mortgage bonds and 6.5 per cent corporate bonds, especially due to the price increases resulting from the Korean War. The only item for which there was a growing market in recent months was 6.5 per cent convertible bonds, and here the Deutsche Bank Group led the market. Since the currency reform, only two joint stock companies had been able to increase their capital significantly. These were the Theodor Goldschmidt AG and the Deutsche Continental-Gas-Gesellschaft AG. In both cases the underwriting consortium was headed by the Deutsche Bank Group.[594]

Plassmann reported further that improvements had been made in financing the export business. The Bank deutscher Länder had made up to 726 million DM available to the Reconstruction Loan Corporation in order to discount the promissory notes of the exporting firms, on the condition that these notes had the endorsement of the house bank and that certain stipulations had been met regarding federal guarantees to cover risk. This was a reference to the well-known Hermes export credit guarantees, which had been reintroduced on 26 August 1949, in a law passed by the Economic Council (Wirtschaftsrat), the precursor to the Bundestag in Bonn.[595] Since the Bank deutscher Länder was not willing to expand the already strained credit framework, the West German banking business, led by the Deutsche Bank, founded the Ausfuhrkredit-Aktiengesellschaft (Export Credit Corporation) in March 1952, through which at first 250 million DM in new funds were made accessible to finance the medium- and long-term credit needs of the German export industry. Oswald Rösler, whose personal initiative had led to the founding of the bank, assumed the chairmanship of its supervisory board.[596] Thus, the Deutsche Bank was continuing a tradition that it had maintained before the war with its 70 per cent holding in the Exportkreditbank AG (Export Credit Bank). This 'dormant' institution in Berlin was not reactivated in West Germany, but liquidated in the 1950s.[597]

Business developments between the currency reform and 1951 are easier to follow for the Rheinisch-Westfälische Bank, the chief bank among the ten regional institutions, than for the entire Deutsche Bank Group due to the availability of better statistics.[598] One such source is a detailed comparison of the Reichsmark closing balance sheet of the Rheinisch-Westfälische Bank from 20 June 1948, with the Deutsche Mark opening balance sheet of the bank calculated according to the conversion guidelines in effect for 1951.[599] The hidden reserves had been totally dispersed at the time of the conversion. A total of 2,072 million RM, i.e. 76 per cent of all assets, was completely lost. This was balanced out only by equalization claims of 3 per cent against the *Land* of North Rhine-Westphalia, which amounted to 142 million DM. This equalled a compensation rate of 6.9 per cent, which is slightly more than the 6.5 per cent that private households received when their deposits at the banks were converted. (See page 436 above.) The initial provision of Deutsche Marks allotted to the Rheinisch-Westfälische Bank only equalled 5.9 per cent of the funds that the bank had lost at the Land Central Bank. A detailed review of the balance sheets of the Rheinisch-Westfälische Bank between 1948 and 1950 compared with the corresponding banking district of the Deutsche Bank in 1938 is shown in Table 10.

Here some of the structural changes caused by regeneration become obvious again. As of 1948, short-term items dominated at first, while other longer-term items gained importance only gradually, and this on both sides of the balance sheet. It is also interesting to note how equalization claims, with their low interest rates, quickly became less important, while claims against debtors at far higher rates gained in significance just as rapidly.

Table 11 shows a breakdown by branches of advances of the Deutsche Bank Group from 1948 to 1951, divided into the three banking districts that would later be established.

Table 10   Balance sheet structure of the Rheinisch-Westfälische Bank,
1948–50, compared with 1938 (RM/DM millions and percentages)

	End of 1938	%	End 1948	%	End 1949	%	End 1950	%
Assets								
Cash, giro account balance and interest coupons	20.3	2.6	118.6	21.1	77.3	9.1	134.9	10.8
Bills of exchange and cheques	125.2	16.3	74.0	13.2	157.0	18.5	291.8	23.2
Securities	40.4	5.3	1.1	0.2	1.7	0.2	3.0	0.2
Nostro balances								
in D-Marks	2.9	0.4	11.2	2.0	11.4	1.4	22.8	1.8
in foreign currency	1.5	0.2	–	–	21.8	2.5	45.0	3.6
Advances and lendings								
in D-Marks	322.2	41.9	145.7	26.0	323.7	38.0	531.8	42.3
in foreign currency	49.4	6.4	56.5	10.1	58.8	6.9	61.0	4.9
Holdings	1.4	0.2	0.3	–	0.6	0.1	2.3	0.2
Bank premises	12.5	1.6	10.0	1.8	10.8	1.3	12.4	1.0
Other real estate	4.8	0.6	1.7	0.3	1.9	0.2	1.7	0.1
Balance at head office	185.5	24.2	–	–	–	–	–	–
Balances at sister banks	–	–	–	–	43.6	5.1	6.4	0.5
Equalization claims	–	–	142.1	25.3	142.1	16.7	142.1	11.3
Other assets	2.1	0.3	0.1	–	0.1	–	1.5	0.1
Total	768.1	100	561.1	100	850.9	100	1,256.7	100
Of which currency assets	50.9	6.6	56.5	10.1	80.6	9.5	106.7	8.5
Liabilities								
Customers' credit drawings at other institutions	0.1	–	0.1	–	0.2	–	0.1	–
Nostro liabilities	45.4	5.9	56.9	10.2	59.2	7.0	63.2	5.0
Accepted earmarked funds	–	–	–	–	14.5	1.7	65.8	5.2
Deposits of German credit institutions	25.6	3.3	19.0 28.7[a]	8.5	64.9	7.6	44.0 1.4[a]	3.6
Deposits of foreign banks	2.7	0.4	2.1	0.4	3.1	0.4	17.4	1.4
Other creditors								
Short-term funds	290.0	37.8	361.6	64.4	478.1	56.2	572.3	45.5
Long-term funds	237.3	30.9	21.5	3.8	63.7	7.5	255.4	20.3
Savings	81.6	10.6	16.0	2.8	29.8	3.5	55.1	4.5
Acceptances	67.4	8.8	7.7	1.4	80.3	9.4	99.1	8.0
Uncompensated reserves	0.1	–	3.2	0.6	10.3	1.2	29.3	2.3
Other liabilities	17.8	2.3	1.1	0.2	2.7	0.3	3.5	0.3
Pension reserves	–	–	29.2	5.2	30.0	3.5	30.7	2.4
Equity capital	–	–	14.0	2.5	14.0	1.7	19.3	1.5
Total	768.1	100	561.1	100	850.9	100	1,256.7	100

[a] Sister banks.   Source: Manuscript of Erhard Ulbricht, 'Die Rheinische-Westfälische Bank', July 1951, HADB, file: Nachfolgebanken 1947–1952 (I).

Table 11   Breakdown of advances to different economic branches
for the Rheinisch-Westfälische Bank, the northern and southern
groups of the Deutsche Bank, 1948–51, at year's end (%)

Cash advances, acceptance credit plus bills of exchange	Rheinisch-Westfälische Bank				Northern Group[a]				Southern Group[b]			
	1948	1949	1950	1951	1948	1949	1950	1951	1948	1949	1950	1951
Coal mining	5.4	4.6	2.8	2.5	0.6	0	0	0	0.1	0	0	0.1
Iron and steel, metal and electrical industries	31.0	24.8	25.0	26.9	15.1	11.1	8.6	9.5	25.3	22.8	19.6	25.6
Chemical industries	7.7	6.6	5.3	4.3	10.8	9.8	4.6	6.6	7.4	6.3	4.8	3.7
Textile and leather industries	7.8	12.3	18.9	20.1	3.8	3.7	5.4	5.6	10.3	17.3	24.4	23.5
Paper and wood industries	3.6	3.9	3.4	3.4	2.1	1.9	1.8	2.6	10.5	6.0	4.5	5.0
Food industry	4.4	4.1	6.8	4.6	10.9	12.5	14.0	11.4	6.3	10.0	11.1	8.5
Construction	3.3	1.9	3.6	2.8	1.9	1.9	1.9	1.9	2.9	2.6	2.6	2.1
Other branches of industry	5.9	5.9	2.4	2.6	3.4	3.4	3.6	3.2	4.3	3.6	3.7	2.4
Trade	23.4	20.7	24.5	23.8	47.0	52.3	57.0	55.1	24.9	23.9	23.4	21.7
Credit institutions	4.6	11.4	3.9	6.2	1.0	1.1	0.5	1.3	4.1	5.3	2.7	4.7
Other	3.1	3.5	3.4	2.8	3.6	2.3	2.5	2.7	4.0	2.7	3.2	2.8
Total (%)	100	100	100	100	100	100	100	100	100	100	100	100
(DM millions)	365	700	964	1,161	177	335	472	544	310	722	881	1,138

[a] Disconto Bank, Norddeutsche Bank, Nordwestbank.
[b] Bayerische Creditbank, Hessische Bank, Oberrheinische Bank, Rheinische Kreditbank, Südwestbank, Württembergische Vereinsbank.

Source: Report of the Treuverkehr Wirtschaftsprüfungs-AG, 28 Aug. 1952, on the ten regional banks, pp. 10–14, HADB, file B, Banken, inländische, Deutsche Bank Berlin, until Dec. 1961.

Three general aspects of the lending practices of the Deutsche Bank Group are evident in Table 11. The first of these pertains to the group as a whole: characteristically, the involvement of the bank group in financing industry greatly outweighed the volume of credit in the trade sector. At the same time, the group was not very involved in the construction industry, which was a particularly important sector of the German economy at the time.

The second aspect illustrated by the table pertains to the typical differences between the three banking districts: namely, the large amounts of credit granted to the coal, iron and steel industry (Ruhr region) by the Rheinisch-Westfälische Bank, to the metal and electrical industries by the southern group where those industries dominated the economic landscape, and to trade (usually more than 50 per cent) by the northern group, which included the port cities of Hamburg and Bremen.

The third aspect pertains to the development of economic structures over time. It is highly interesting to note that the involvement in financing the consumer goods industries – especially the textile and leather industries, but also the food industry – in all three banking districts at the start of West Germany's 'economic miracle' rose relatively faster than in the production and investment goods industries, whose share in total bank advances dropped. This supports the argument that the consumer goods industry was the main beneficiary of the accelerated depreciation allowances that existed at the time (especially those in Art. 7a of the Income Tax Law for capital goods up to 100,000 DM, in which 50 per cent could be written off in the first two years after purchase).[600]

The development of the volume structure of credit also reveals much about the nature of the business in which the Deutsche Bank Group was involved at the time. At the end of 1949, when it was still possible to purchase a decent house for around 20,000 DM, the percentage of all cash advances and acceptance credits granted by the Rheinisch-Westfälische Bank for up to this amount only made up about 10 per cent. The category for 20,000 to 100,000 DM accounted for 17.2 per cent, 100,000 to 500,000 DM for 27.5 per cent, 500,000 to 3,000,000 DM for 32.6 per cent, and over 3,000,000 DM for 12.4 per cent. By the end of 1951, the three lowest categories had each lost two to three percentage points, whereas the top two categories had gained three to four points. The development was the same at all of the sister banks with only minor deviations.[601] Business on a massive scale with small customers did not become very significant for the Deutsche Bank until the 1960s.

The Deutsche Bank Group was also linked to important sectors of the German economy in ways other than its involvement in financing. For one thing, leading representatives of German industry sat on the supervisory boards of the three successor institutions. At the Rheinisch-Westfälische Bank, for example, the following men held such positions: Günter Henle of the Klöckner concern; the leading textile manufacturer of Westphalia, Bernhard von Delden; Ulrich Haberland, the president of the board of managing directors of Bayer; Jost

Henkel from the Henkel concern; Hans Reuter, president of the board of managing directors of DEMAG, a machine tool producer; Werner Söhngen, president of the board of managing directors of the Rheinische Stahlwerke; Otto Wolff von Amerongen, a partner of the iron and steel company Otto Wolff; and Ernst Hellmut Vits, president of the board of managing directors of the Vereinigte Glanzstoff-Fabriken AG.

For another, the leading men from the Deutsche Bank Group in the 1950s

Table 12   Structure of the combined balance sheets of the Deutsche Bank Group from 1 Jan. 1952 to 31 Dec. 1956, and of the Deutsche Bank on 31 Dec. 1957 (%)

	Opening balance sheet	End of	End of	End of	End of	End of	End of
	1.1.1952	1952	1953	1954	1955	1956	1957
Assets							
Cash balance	0.9	0.9	0.6	0.6	0.7	0.7	0.8
Balance at *Land* central bank (LCB)	9.9	9.1	8.6	8.7	7.4	8.2	9.7
Postal chequing account balance	0.3	0.3	0.2	0.2	0.2	0.2	0.2
Bills of exchange rediscountable at LCB	13.1	20.7	22.0	21.7	19.7	23.3	22.4
Securities (eligible as security for LCB advances)	0.0	0.1	0.7	3.9	4.8	4.0	4.3
Securities (other)	1.6	1.7	3.4	1.8	2.5	2.7	2.5
Nostro balances	8.2	4.9	5.6	6.6	5.7	4.5	3.8
Cheques	0.7	0.6	0.6	0.4	0.5	0.3	0.4
Bills of exchange (other)	2.8	2.3	1.4	1.4	1.8	1.5	1.2
Treasury bills	1.7	0.1	0.7	0.5	0.0	0.7	5.5
Equalization claims	11.1	9.3	7.7	6.7	7.0	6.2	5.9
Syndicate holdings	0.1	0.2	0.3	0.8	1.9	2.3	2.1
Debtors	39.8	39.1	36.9	35.7	37.0	35.8	33.3
Long-term loans	6.2	6.5	7.2	7.1	6.7	5.6	4.5
Participations	0.2	0.3	0.3	0.4	0.6	0.7	0.7
Real estate, office furniture and equipment	2.1	2.1	1.8	1.6	1.5	1.5	1.6
Accruals and deferrals, other assets	0.0	0.3	0.6	0.4	0.4	0.5	0.2
Loans on a trust basis	1.3	1.5	1.4	1.4	1.3	1.1	0.9

Table 12 continued:

	Opening balance sheet	End of	End of	End of	End of	End of	End of
	1.1.1952	1952	1953	1954	1955	1956	1957
Balance sheet total (DM millions) (=100%)	3,757	4,488	5,431	6,473	6,725	7,621	8,357
Liabilities							
Sight deposits	51.1	44.1	40.7	45.0	44.4	41.2	42.4
Time deposits	21.1	29.9	32.9	27.4	25.1	29.6	29.1
Savings deposits	5.2	6.9	8.9	11.7	13.8	12.6	13.8
Nostro liabilities	3.6	2.8	1.9	1.5	1.4	2.1	1.9
Acceptances	3.2	0.9	0.3	0.2	0.3	0.2	0.2
Long-term loans	5.1	5.1	5.7	5.6	5.5	5.1	4.1
Pension and other reserves	5.0	4.3	4.1	3.2	3.4	2.7	2.4
Accruals and deferrals, other liabilities	0.7	0.5	0.5	0.9	0.4	0.4	0.4
Loans on a trust basis	1.3	1.5	1.4	1.4	1.3	1.1	0.9
Capital resources	3.7	4.0	3.6	3.2	4.3	4.9	4.8
Consisting in DM millions of:							
Capital	100.0	100.0	100.0	100.0	150.0	200.0	200.0
Legal reserves	25.0	25.0	25.0	25.0	25.0	25.0	25.0
Special reserves	15.5	50.0	60.0	75.0	100.0	125.0	155.0
Profit	–	6.2	8.8	9.5	15.7	25.3	25.2

Source: Franz Seidel, *Die Nachfolgebanken in Westdeutschland. Ihre Entstehung und Entwicklung auf Grund ihrer Bilanzen* (Vienna 1955), appendix I. Business Reports of the Deutsche Bank Group 1952–56 and of the Deutsche Bank 1957.

once again held numerous positions on the supervisory boards of industrial concerns, often as the chairmen of these boards. The association between bank and business was very close in those cases in which there were interlocking directorships, meaning that the company had a representative sitting on the supervisory board of the Rheinisch-Westfälische Bank, for example, and the bank had someone sitting on the supervisory board of the company. This was the case for such companies as the Otto Wolff conglomerate, Bayer, where Rösler was deputy chairman of the supervisory board, DEMAG and several of the companies belonging to the Klöckner conglomerate, where Plassmann sat on the supervisory boards. In the Rhineland–Westphalian district, the bank had representatives on the supervisory boards of companies primarily in the following branches of the economy: mining and heavy industry, mechanical engineering and the chemical industry, and the textile industry and trade. In the southern banking district, Abs was chairman of the supervisory board for BASF, the Metallgesellschaft, and Siemens & Halske AG. In the mid-1950s, Abs held positions on about 30 supervisory boards, Rösler, Plassmann and Rath on roughly 15 each.[602]

In the period between the passage of the Big Banks Act in 1952 and the reunification of the successor banks in 1957, the Deutsche Bank Group continued to return to its traditional business structure. This is particularly clear in Table 12 under the category of liabilities, especially with regard to the replenishing of savings and time deposits conditioned by the 'regeneration' described above. At the end of 1951, sight deposits accounted for 51.1 per cent of the balance sheet total of the Deutsche Bank Group, while time and savings deposits together amounted to 26.3 per cent: that is, only about half of the sight deposits. By the end of 1957, this ratio had shifted to 42.4 per cent for sight deposits and 42.9 per cent for time and savings deposits.

One important factor in the sharp rise in savings deposits from 197.3 million DM at the end of 1951 to 1,150.6 million DM by the end of 1957 was the introduction of tax breaks for the savings of private households, which had been included in the government's economic policy in several revised forms since 1949. At the end of 1954, the volume of savings deposits with tax benefits had reached 96.3 million DM at the Süddeutsche Bank, representing about 37 per cent of all its savings deposits.[603] Not until the second half of the 1950s did the banks make concerted efforts to encourage a more modern form of saving through investment funds. Thus in 1956, the Deutsche Bank Group was the largest investor, holding 30 per cent, in a bank consortium that brought about the founding of the Deutsche Gesellschaft für Wertpapiersparen m.b.H. (German Society for Saving through Securities).[604] It was founded in December 1956 with its principal residence in Frankfurt, just at the time when it was becoming clear how tax issues and other questions concerning capital investment companies would be regulated by the Act on Capital Investment Companies, which would eventually be passed on 16 April 1957.

The upswing in the bank's business since the currency reform is also mirrored in the increase of personnel, as shown in Table 13. Among the female staff members of the Rheinisch-Westfälische Bank, not one was acting as an *Oberbeamter* (supervisor), assistant vice-president or member of the top echelons of management, at least not by the end of 1951. Among the other banks, only two women had managed to reach the level of *Oberbeamter*, one at the Norddeutsche Bank and one at the Oberrheinische Bank.[605] By the end of 1957, when the higher managerial staff made up just about 10 per cent of the total number of persons employed by the Deutsche Bank, there were eleven women among the *Oberbeamte* and two women who held positions at the level of departmental head and assistant vice-president; but there was still not one who had become a director or deputy director.[606]

The number of persons employed by the Deutsche Bank Group, as shown in

Table 13, also confirms the finding of Figure 4.1, that in the period of the greatest decentralization from the currency reform of 1948 until the passage of the Big Banks Act of 1952, the Deutsche Bank Group experienced a growth rate which

Table 13   Number of persons employed by the Deutsche Bank Group,
1937–57

	RWB-DB West		SDB	NDB	DB Group	
	Total	Percentage of women			Total	Percentage of women
End of:						
1937	–	–	–	–	17,462	13.0
21 June 1948	2,248	20	2,902	1,149	6,299	.
End of:						
1948	2,548	25	3,171	1,272	6,991	24.4
1949	3,327	30	3,996	1,733	9,056	28.4
1950	4,091	34	4,722	2,075	10,888	31.0
1951	4,601	35	5,160	2,319	12,080	32.7
1952	5,011	37	5,577	2,627	13,215	.
1953	5,337	38	6,117	2,891	14,345	36.0
1954	5,864	39	6,483	3,249	15,596	.
1955	6,159	.	6,614	3,493	16,266	.
1956	6,256	.	6,680	3,661	16,597	37.9
1957	–	–	–	–	16,839	38.3

Source: Manuscript of Erhard Ulbricht, 'Die Rheinisch-Westfälische Bank', July 1951, HADB, file: Nachfolgebanken 1947–1952 (I). Enclosure to letter RWB to SDB board of managing directors, 15 November 1952, HADB, Frowein, 13. Manuscript of Erhard Ulbricht, 'Die Deutsche Bank Ende 1937 und ihre Nachfolgebanken Ende 1953', May 1954, HADB, file: Fortführung der alten Bank. Evaluation of the balance sheet and profit and loss account of the Deutsche Bank AG for the business year 1957, HADB, Frowein, 18. Report of the Treuverkehr Wirtschaftsprüfungs-AG, 28 Aug. 1952. Business Reports 1952–57, File: B, Banken, inländisch, Deutsche Bank Berlin, until Dec. 1961.

was significantly higher than it was in the period to follow. It is also interesting to note that the Rheinisch-Westfälische Bank/Deutsche Bank AG West had a smaller staff and therefore fewer personnel expenditures than did the Süddeutsche Bank, although it always yielded a greater profit and had a higher balance sheet total until the end of 1955 than did its sister bank in southern Germany.[607] This was due primarily to two factors: a smaller volume of retail banking than was the case at the Süddeutsche Bank, and a better set of terms in North Rhine-Westphalia, particularly for turnover commissions and service charges.[608] In 1949 and 1950 the Rheinisch-Westfälische Bank realized the interest rates listed in Table 14 for its various business transactions.

The total interest margin resulting from this was 2.71 per cent at the end of

*Table 14   Average realized interest rates of the Rheinisch-Westfälische
Bank as of year's end, 1949 and 1950 (%)*

	End of 1949	End of 1950
On the asset side		
Discounted customers' acceptances		
Rate cap	6.93	9.02
Other rates	5.25	6.79
Acceptances of other banks	3.89	6.14
Cash debtors		
Normal rates	8.50	10.50
Reduced rates	4.69	7.52
Acceptance credits	7.07	8.79
Nostro balances	0.92	0.66
Equalization claims	3.00	3.00
On the liabilities side		
Commission-free short-term funds	1.00	1.00
Commission-obligated short-term funds	1.51	1.50
Time deposits		
Agreed period up to 3 months	2.37	4.16
Agreed period more than 3 months	3.36	4.77
Savings deposits		
With legally required withdrawal notice	2.51[a]	3.01[a]
With agreed withdrawal notice	3.70[a]	4.26[a]
Tax privileged	4.03[a]	4.58[a]
Rediscounted bills of exchange	3.84	6.02

[a] Including the employee balances with preferential conditions.

Source: Manuscript of Erhard Ulbricht, 'Die Rheinisch-Westfälische Bank', HADB, file: Nachfolgebanken 1947–52 (I).

1949 when the discount rate stood at 4 per cent; by the end of 1950, this margin had risen to 3.27 per cent, following the post-war high of 6 per cent for the discount rate in late October due to the Korea boom. That was a very high margin, not only from today's perspective but also compared with the inter-war period. In connection with the great expansion of the volume of business, this led to a tremendous increase in profits for the Deutsche Bank Group. Whereas during the two and a half years from the currency reform to the end of 1950 the bank group's total profit after taxes had amounted only to 6.7 million DM, this exploded to the sum of 26.5 million DM for the year 1951.[609] The total interest margin for the Süddeutsche Bank at the end of 1951 was calculated to have been

Table 15   Development and structure of the tax burden of the
Deutsche Bank Group, 1952–57 (DM millions)

	Total taxes paid	Of this: Corporation income tax	Other taxes 1957
July 1948– end of 1951	54.2[a]	52.3	
1952	70.6	49.0	
1953	79.7	51.1	
1954	83.9	54.3	
1955	87.9	53.7	
1956	99.8	60.2	
1957	96.8	54.6	26.5 Trade tax 5.5 Berlin emergency relief 5.2 Wealth tax 5.0 Other taxes

[a] Only corporation income tax, Berlin emergency relief tax (1.8 million DM) and wealth tax (0.097 million DM).

Source: 1952–57: Memorandum of 28 February 1958, HADB, Frowein, 18. July 1948–end of 1951: Memorandum by Ulbricht, 30 April 1955, HADB, file: B, Banken, inländische, Deutsche Bank Berlin, until Dec. 1961.

3.15 per cent and a year later to have been 2.59 per cent. The decrease was attributed to the two-step lowering of the discount rate from 6 to 4.5 per cent in 1952.[610] For the entire Deutsche Bank Group, the interest margin was calculated to have been 2.61 per cent at the end of 1956, and 2.41 at the end of 1957,[611] while the discount rate was 5 and 4 per cent, respectively. Such a positive correlation between the earnings position of the banks and the level of money market interest rates, which the central bank determined by its discount policy, also corresponds with recent research findings on banks in the United States during the inter-war period.[612]

Between 1949 and 1950, the receipts of the Rheinisch-Westfälische Bank that were derived from 'other foreign trade commissions', meaning that they were earned by handling foreign trade transactions for customers, rose from 0.54 million to 2.01 million DM. The amount of export business financed by the bank equalled US$340,000 in 1949 and US$454,000 in 1950. The import business increased even more, from US$93,000 in 1949 to US$ 241,000 in the following year. It is also interesting to note that most of the export credit business of the Deutsche Bank Group apparently took place in the southern region of the Federal Republic of Germany. In 1953, the value of export credits for the entire Deutsche Bank Group totalled 196 million DM for 497 entries. Of

Table 16   Earnings structure of the Rheinisch-Westfälische Bank for 1950 and 1951 and of the Deutsche Bank Group for 1953, 1956 and 1957 (%)

	1950	1951	1953	1956	1957
Total earnings	100.0	100.0	100.0	100.0	100.0
Interest	13.1	9.1	3.3	}36.6	}33.9
Discount	20.8	30.4	27.5		
Commissions from					
Credit business	26.6	23.3	28.9	24.3	22.6
Payment transactions	32.8	30.4	27.8	21.3	21.5
Securities business	4.9	3.7	5.8	6.0	6.0
Foreign exchange trading	1.5	2.0	3.0	3.7	4.6
Securities and underwriting	0.3	1.0	2.1	3.9	6.2
Underwriting and stock exchange admission fees	–	–	0.4	3.6	4.3
Holdings	–	–	–	0.5	0.7
Irregularly recurring transactions	–	0.1	1.1	0.1	0.2
Commissions breakdown					
From credit business:	100.0	100.0	100.0		
Credit and overdraft commissions	61.3	63.3	64.1		
Bill brokerage	13.9	18.0	18.1		
Acceptance commissions	16.5	9.6	6.4		
Commissions from settlements of standstill credits and old monetary claims	–	0.8	2.1		
Guarantee commissions	7.2	6.9	6.9		
Other credit commissions	1.1	1.4	2.5		
From payment transactions:	100.0	100.0	100.0		
Account turnover fees	59.1	58.7	44.3		
Service charges	0.9	0.8	3.1		
Collection charges and fees for redrafted bills	1.7	1.5	1.8		
Foreign exchange commissions	8.4	7.9	10.1		
Documents and accreditation fees	21.2	23.0	27.4		
Other commissions in foreign trade	8.0	7.3	13.3		
Other commissions	0.7	0.8	–		

Source: Enclosure to letter RWB to SDB board of managing directors, 15 November 1952, HADB, Frowein, 13. Manuscript of Erhard Ulbricht, 'Die Deutsche Bank Ende 1937 und ihre Nachfolgebanken Ende 1953', HADB, file: Fortführung der alten Bank. Evaluation of the balance sheet and profit and loss account of the Deutsche Bank AG for the business year 1957, HADB, Frowein, 18.

these, 122 million DM for 319 entries alone were handled by the Süddeutsche Bank.[613]

As the 1950s progressed, the foreign trade business developed on the whole so well for the Rheinisch-Westfälische Bank, the Deutsche Bank Group and the Federal Republic that, as early as 1953, significant reserves in gold and foreign currency had been accumulated,[614] and the Federal Republic had become a major creditor in the European Payments Union. Restrictions on the convertibility of the Deutsche Mark in foreign exchange were relaxed: for example, for the purpose of transferring returns on capital investment. In this connection, the exchange rate for one hundred inconvertible Deutsche Marks in blocked accounts (*Sperrmark*) increased by 20 per cent to 77 Swiss francs in 1953 and during 1954 further approached the level of official parity, which was 96 Swiss francs at the time. From this point on, the reintroduction of convertibility was actually dependent solely on strengthening the other European currencies.[615]

Whereas Table 12 illustrates how extraordinarily favourable the 1950s were for the Deutsche Bank Group with regard to profits, voluntary special reserves (i.e. the open as opposed to the hidden ones) and balance sheet totals, which more than doubled from the end of 1951 to the end of 1957, Table 15 shows that the amount of taxes paid by the bank group only rose from 70.6 million DM in 1952 to 96.8 million DM in 1957. The chief explanation for this may well lie in the tax breaks for companies that were granted in the 1950s under pressure from the business community.

A detailed listing of statistics on the earnings structure of the Rheinisch-Westfälische Bank for 1950 and 1951, and of the Deutsche Bank Group as a whole for 1953, 1956 and 1957, is presented in Table 16. It is interesting that the discount business contributed significantly more to the total earnings than did the actual interest earnings, and that the earnings from commissions were considerably higher than those from discount and interest together. One reason for this was certainly the fact that the bank had to use commissions as a flexible source of earnings until interest rates were deregulated in 1967. It is also quite obvious just how important the securities and underwriting business and foreign exchange trade became, starting in 1953. This indicates that the bank had once again resumed its traditionally predominant role in foreign trade financing and in capital market transactions. Whereas the foreign trade business of the Federal Republic was producing quite spectacular yields during this period, the development of the West German capital market remained disappointing well into the second half of the 1950s, due in part to the distortions resulting from the tax policy and tax-subsidizing policy of the Federal Government.

2. Business policy positions and actions

In section I of the 1952 Business Reports for the Rheinisch-Westfälische Bank, the Süddeutsche Bank and the Norddeutsche Bank, each bank included an identically worded, positive evaluation of the enormous jump in economic growth since currency reform, and of the nearly 25 per cent investment rate of the West German economy. However, pointed out the reports, the source of capital formation had been earnings retained by the business sector, i.e. self-financing, and public sector funding; the private capital market had played a minor role. Now that the bottlenecks of supply for coal, steel and other raw materials had been removed, it was time to remove the bottleneck of the supply of capital. A fundamental reform of the tax system was considered to be crucial to eliminating this problem. It was argued that, by lowering taxes, free capital surpluses would be created both by businesses and private households, the amassing of public funds at public institutions of credit would be reduced to the benefit of the private banking business, and shares would no longer suffer the discrimination caused by twice-taxed dividend payments, thus making them more competitive with tax-subsidized bonds. In 1953, the rate of corporation income tax was 60 per cent for retained profits and 30 per cent for distributed profits.

In these reports, the banks also called for the 'full restoration of truth in interest rates and securities prices', which did not exist due to the distortion of capital market conditions caused by current tax policy. Typically, the nominal interest rate from bond issues was kept below the level of interest that should have resulted in capital markets that were not distorted by taxes. In such a situation, the private demand for such bonds could only be stimulated by offering tax breaks for earned interest income. This was the purpose behind a law passed on 15 December 1952, the First Act for the Encouragement of the Capital Market (*Erstes Kapitalmarktförderungsgesetz*); it was later amended on 15 May 1953. This law exempted from taxation any interest earned from issues of mortgage bonds and communal debentures (*Kommunalschuldverschreibungen*) if the capital accumulated was being used for the construction of publicly assisted housing. Interest earned on federal and *Länder* bonds was also exempted from taxation.[616] Tax privileges had also previously been granted in the form of special depreciation allowances for the creditor of non-interest-bearing loans or subsidies to non-profit housing firms (Art. 7c of the Income Tax Law) and to shipbuilders (Art. 7d); these had made it possible to write off the entire sum as operating costs or business expenses in the year that the credit or subsidy was given. Similar provisions went into effect on 15 May 1953, for contributions to the Bank for the Equalization of War Burdens (Lastenausgleichsbank) (Art. 7f of the Income Tax Law).[617]

In their published Business Reports as well as internally, the three banks of the Deutsche Bank Group expressed their strong opposition to these provisions, arguing that the public sector gave preferential treatment on the capital market to their own bond issues and only to a small number of those from the private sector. For example, it was pointed out that in 1953 nearly 40 per cent of the turnover in securities consisted of public sector bonds and communal debentures, so that the government had soaked up more capital market funds than it needed to finance public investments. Such hoarded capital market funds were desperately needed in the private sector of the economy. The banks went on to argue that the goal of the Capital Market Encouragement Act had not been attained because private households were not investing in the privileged bond issues, despite the extensive tax benefits for earned interest income; instead, the capital was coming from institutional buyers and other major investors.[618] Although the volume of securities placed on the capital market as a whole nearly doubled from 1.6 billion DM in 1952 to 3.1 billion DM in 1953, the stock market only represented 9 per cent of this volume in 1953, since it did not enjoy such tax benefits.[619] At the supervisory board meeting of the Süddeutsche Bank, held on 10 March 1954 in Munich, Abs referred 'again to the disastrous effects of the Capital Market Encouragement Act, which in connection with high taxes, had prevented broad sectors of the population from engaging in any genuine capital formation'.[620]

The story was about the same in 1954. Although the volume of securities placed rose sharply, especially in the area of housing construction, the stock market profited little from this. In the view of the three successor banks, the important prerequisites for a normalization of the situation on the capital market were not laid until the following year, when a major tax reform went into effect on 1 January 1955 and the Capital Market Encouragement Act with its 'dubious' tax breaks expired. The banks viewed it as their job to offer incentives to the private investor not only to save in deposit accounts, as had been done already, but also to invest in securities. In April 1955, the Deutsche Bank Group stated: 'By comparison with the overall level reached by the country's economy, the task of bringing order into the capital market is still in an initial stage.'[621]

In its Business Report for 1955, the Deutsche Bank Group finally referred to 'remarkable progress on the capital market'. For the first time since the end of the war, it had been possible to place large issues of shares, amounting in value to 1.7 billion DM.[622] Included in this was the first increase in share capital of the successor institutions of the Deutsche Bank from a total of 100 million to 150 million DM in April 1955, followed by a second increase of another 50 million DM for a total of 200 million DM exactly a year later.

However, the bond market did not develop as well as expected. In early October 1954, Abs had expressed the opinion that the desired interest rate for industrial bonds and mortgage bonds would be 6–6.5 per cent once the Capital Market Encouragement Act had expired.[623] In 1953 and 1954, the nominal interest rate for public bonds with tax privileges, including the 'social mortgage bonds' for publicly assisted housing, was usually 5 or 5.5 per cent, and for other public bonds 7.5 per cent.[624] As a result of the restrictive credit policy pursued by the Bank deutscher Länder since the summer of 1955, the nominal interest rate on the capital market actually rose; in 1956 it usually hovered around 8 per cent. The banks again complained that the tax privileges for capital investments benefiting publicly assisted housing still distorted the capital market to the disadvantage of private investment. The debt–equity ratio also still left a great deal to be desired because of this.[625]

For the first time, there was no mention of a distortion of the capital market in the Business Report of the Deutsche Bank for 1957. In that year, the bank had a turnover in securities equalling a total of 4.14 billion DM, of which exactly 50 per cent was in bonds. Of these, 323 million DM were in mortgage bonds, 156 million DM in communal debentures, and 539 million DM in industrial bonds. The industrial bonds found many buyers abroad, a good 25 per cent, while other types of bond found few such buyers. Private investors had bought 186 million DM of industrial bonds, which was more than twice the sum of capital invested by insurances, businesses and public authorities put together; however, it was still considerably less than the 270 million DM of the credit institutions.[626] Such 'normalization' shows that the structural distortions that had been caused by the war and the resulting 'regeneration', and later by federal economic policy, had apparently lessened.

Participations also enabled the Deutsche Bank Group, first, to compensate for losses and disruptions caused by the war and, second, to expand these lucrative lines of business.[627] Participations of the first kind included the 100 per cent holding of a newly founded subsidiary, the Berliner Disconto Bank AG, and a two-thirds participation in the Saarländische Kreditbank AG, the former branch of the Deutsche Bank in Saarbrücken. The total holding of the Trinitas Vermögensverwaltung GmbH in Düsseldorf was also related to the war, since this company had assumed the old assets of the Deutsche Bank at the time of decoupling in 1952. These old assets were depreciated in value and therefore caused only losses for Trinitas.[628] The foreign trade business of the bank group was revived with the help of the group's holdings of more than 30 per cent in the Ausfuhrkredit Aktiengesellschaft (with a total of 20 million DM in equity capital), which took over the tasks of the Exportkreditbank AG, the old pre-war institution. As early as 14 August 1950, the foreign interests of the bank were discussed at a meeting of the board of managing directors in connection with three names: 'a) Istanbul, b) de Bary, c) Deutsche Ueberseeische Bank'.[629] Abs had felt it to be very important to invest in a roughly 20 per cent holding in the Dutch bank Handel-Maatschappij H. Albert de Bary & Co., N.V., Amsterdam, in order to normalize the business relations with this internationally reknowned bank, relations that had been strained for political reasons during the war.[630]

The Deutsche Ueberseeische Bank, a subsidiary of the Deutsche Bank, had been one of the 'dormant' credit institutions in Berlin, like the Deutsche Bank itself. However, unlike to the Exportkreditbank AG, this bank was not liquidated. Instead the board of managing directors of the entire Deutsche Bank decided at a meeting on 8 December 1950 to reactivate it. On 20 November 1952, the Deutsche Ueberseeische Bank received its standing as a credit institution, was relocated to Hamburg by the Bank deutscher Länder, was authorized to operate as a foreign trade bank, and began conducting 'transactions on a normal basis with regions with which we had traditionally done business, namely Latin America, Spain and Portugal' in February 1953.[631] In 1954, a representation of the successor banks was established in Istanbul under the direction of Edmund Goldenberg, who had been the head of the former branch of the Deutsche Bank there. Equipped with general power of attorney, he had also represented the bank in Istanbul on instruction of the directing office from 1946 until his recall in early 1951.[632]

Among the second kind of participations of the Deutsche Bank Group, those for the expansion of lucrative lines of business, was a minority holding in the Banco Español en Alemania, which handled the important foreign trade transactions with the Iberian peninsula and with Latin America from the other side. The Süddeutsche Bank and the Rheinisch-Westfälische Bank decoupled themselves from investment management functions by each having full equity holding in the Süddeutsche Vermögensverwaltung GmbH in Munich and the Matura Vermögensverwaltung m.b.H. in Düsseldorf, respectively. The full equity holding of the GEFA Gesellschaft für Absatzfinanzierung mbH in Wuppertal-Elberfeld served to facilitate the quickly expanding business of customer financing with capital equalling 12 million DM in 1956. In addition to these participations, the Deutsche Bank Group also had several holdings in mortgage banks and shipping banks, through which the bank group was well integrated in the expanding businesses of housing construction and shipbuilding.[633] And as mentioned above, the bank group used its 30 per cent holding in the Deutsche Gesellschaft für Wertpapiersparen mbH to encourage more modern forms of saving.[634]

In a much broader scope, the business policy of the bank also included its involvement in general politics, social policy and cultural policy. Politically, the top echelons of management of the Deutsche Bank Group were very critical not only of all proposals for nationalization, but also of the idea of employee co-determination, which was so vehemently debated in the early 1950s. In a speech on 4 November 1950, Plassmann, the spokesman of the Rheinisch-Westfälische Bank, explained: 'We mistrust the catchphrase "economic democracy" … We are of the opinion that the term "democracy", which originates from the political realm, cannot be applied to many other realms of human activity because it is alien to these.' He advocated a hierarchical structure of business organization built upon the foundation of expertise, decisiveness and a sense of responsibility. A ship can better ride out a storm, he argued, if the navigation of the ship is not undertaken in a democratic fashion, but is placed in the hands of an experienced captain, who is aware of his responsibilities. However, Plassmann did want employees who brought initiative and energy to their workplaces; he considered it necessary that they 'exercise the highest degree of responsibility and co-determination possible in those areas defined by their jobs'. The more the people who work for a firm identify with it and feel responsible for it as a whole, the better this is for the firm 'as an economic unit and as a human community'. In this sense, he welcomed the passing of an industrial constitution law (*Betriebsverfassungsgesetz*) but warned against 'undermining the economic and human communities existing in businesses through outside forces'.[635]

Plassmann made these comments in a speech to a gathering of the staffs of the entire Rheinisch-Westfälische Bank at a so-called community hour, which would from then on be held annually in order to foster solidarity and improve the atmosphere at the workplace. The immediate occasion for Plassmann's speech was the establishment of the Franz Urbig and Oscar Schlitter Foundation in honour of the two men who had each served as chairman of the supervisory board in the years between 1930 and 1942. A committee consisting of representatives from the bank staffs and one from management were to distribute vacation allowances to employees from the income of the foundation's capital base of 500,000 DM. In the charter of this new foundation, mention was made of 'the strong feeling of solidarity of our company family' and of the necessity of vacation in order to 'revive body and soul'.[636] Aside from this, one of the major social benefits given employees was aid in obtaining housing; actually this took the form of non-repayable contributions to building costs, low interest rates on loans to purchase housing and household effects, as well as interest-free loans to property owners who were to use the funds to restore housing that would be rented at a reduced rate to employees of the Deutsche Bank Group.

The 'company family' had also already volunteered to pay out support to the 'East retirees', meaning the former employees of the head office in Berlin and the 'East Zone', as it was called then, 'who are left in dire poverty without work and retirement pensions'.[637] However, it had taken a great deal of pressure from those affected to make this happen, and the promise to pay out support was made explicitly without any legal commitment.[638] The funds for this support were at first raised through the *Treuopfer*, a type of solidarity contribution which in 1949 cost the employees of the Deutsche Bank Group in West Germany 1 per cent of their wages and salaries. The ten regional institutions matched the funds of their employees. Starting in 1950, the regional institutions alone carried the cost of supporting the 'East retirees', for which they provided funds amounting to 1 per cent of all salaries and wages until 31 March 1950, 2 per cent as of 1 April, 4 per cent as of 1 October, and finally 6 per cent as of 1 January 1951. In 1949, the amount transferred equalled 222,000 DM and went to support 1,375 retirees and widows in both East and West Berlin and in the 'East Zone'. In 1950 it was 840,000 DM to support 2,319, and in 1951 it amounted to 2,470,000 DM to support 2,734 persons.

On 1 January 1951, these very small payments were increased to equal 40 per cent of the regular pension claims, and they were raised again six months later to equal 80 per cent. However, where it applied, deductions were made for the often very modest public assistance payments, social insurance benefits and pension payments from the Beamtenversicherungsverein of the former Centralverband des Deutschen Bank- und Bankiergewerbes. Twenty per cent of this was paid out in Deutsche Marks, the rest in East marks.[639] By the end of 1955, the successor institutions had incurred costs equalling 30.2 million DM for these payments.[640] In 1956, the three successor banks had accumulated a total of 23.3 million DM in pension reserves for the so-called Berlin pensions and a total of 21.9 million DM for the so-called 'pay-as-you-go' pensions (*Umlagepensionen*) for beneficiaries in the Soviet-occupied territories.

In the area of cultural policy, the Deutsche Bank Group spent a far from insignificant sum on contributions to various causes. In 1956, the Süddeutsche Bank contributed a total of 95,000 DM, just in contributions of at least 1,000 DM, to various organizations for the purpose of supporting scientific research. For example, the Stifterverband für die Deutsche Wissenschaft (Foundation for German Scientific Research) received 69,000 DM, while smaller sums were contributed to the societies supporting universities and individual institutes. The Gesellschaft für Epilepsieforschung (Epilepsy Research Society) in Bethel was given 8,000 DM and the Chemotherapeutische Forschungsinstitut Georg-Speyer Haus (The Georg-Speyer Institute for Chemotherapeutic Research) in Frankfurt received a donation of 5,000 DM. The 59 contributions made by the Süddeutsche Bank to non-profit organizations and for charitable purposes amounted to a total of 433,400 DM in 1956, of which the largest beneficiaries were the Staatsbürgerliche Vereinigung 1954 e.V. (Citizens Association 1954) in Cologne with 120,000 DM, the Deutsche Caritasverband (German Caritas Association) and the Hilfswerk, the relief organization of the Evangelical Church in Germany, each with 64,000 DM, the Gesellschaft zur Förderung des Schutzes von Auslandsinvestionen (Society for the Promotion of Foreign Investment Protection) in Cologne with 20,000 DM, and the 'Ungarnhilfe', the Help for Hungary campaign as it was called, also with 20,000 DM. Smaller contributions were made to help support the church conventions of both the Catholic and Evangelical Churches, the Europe Union (which promoted the European unification process), artistic activities, and organizations promoting foreign exchanges, youth programmes and education, etc.[641] However, it still took several decades before the Deutsche Bank grew into the major patron of art and science that it has become today.

Deutsche Bank from 1957 to the Present: The Emergence of an International Financial Conglomerate

by Hans E. Büschgen

I. Deutsche Bank: An Open, Sociotechnical System

1. Organization and technology: the foundations of business

In its Annual Report for 1973, Deutsche Bank states the following under the heading 'Changing Bank Organization':

'Dynamic – typical of the market for bank services – applies also to the running of the bank. Those responsible for organization, accounting and planning must not merely react to the continuous process of change in the technical field and in living patterns, they must take it into account in their arrangements in advance. During the last decade the development of electronic data processing has influenced and changed operations of our bank decisively. It largely contributed to keeping the rise in staff and material costs as low as possible. Data processing also provided the technical basis for building up the retail business and carrying it through efficiently. The centralization of electronic data processing into three large computer centres – Düsseldorf, Frankfurt and Hamburg – which was started three years ago, was completed. Some of the former computer centres were closed down and some were converted into concentrators with tasks relating to feeding in and printing out data. The three large computer centres are equipped with the most modern systems, permitting figures received to be evaluated quickly and extensive information to be compiled for decisions on business policy. Thanks to these technical improvements it was also possible to expand and refine the accounting system. In addition to the larger branches' drawing up independent balance sheets and the check, in the form of special sub-branch accounts, on smaller branches, which do not compile financial statements of their own, we introduced accounting for the different lines of business divided up according to special fields. Accounts statistics were already being compiled and this is being extended to include a comprehensive earnings and cost analysis of customers. The bank also enlarged its corporate planning on the basis of this improvement in the flow of information. The short-term one-year plan is increasingly being complemented by long-term strategic planning. This is intended to show earnings-related alternatives for longer-term targets in the individual sectors of business, based on foreseeable trends in national and international economic developments.'

This informative and programmatic statement marks a turning point in the significance of accounting, organization and data processing as operating areas in the bank. Though there was no direct impact on their position in the bank's organizational structure, their role in its business policy was changing from that of purely internal functions only marginally related to business areas and operating primarily as settlement units in the various departments. As this quotation illustrates, the idea of a market-oriented bank as documented by the development of departments – from a business-line orientation to a customer-group orientation – also brought the bank's operations closer to the market and gave them clearly identifiable service functions.

a) *Structural organization*

When the three successor institutions merged to form a single bank in 1957, personnel and management structures as well as departmental organization, technical infrastructure and workflow organization had to be adjusted to the new entity. Administrative centres were set up at the domiciles of the pre-merger successor banks (Hamburg, Düsseldorf and Frankfurt am Main), the aim being to combine the advantages of decentralized and centralized organization structures. Three central offices controlled a total of 24 regional head branches, which in turn ran the branches, deposit-taking offices and sub-branches in the Federal Republic of Germany.

The remerged bank's management comprised the members of the boards of managing directors of the three successor institutions. Oswald Rösler, formerly member of the board of managing directors of Rheinisch-Westfälische Bank (which was renamed Deutsche Bank AG West in 1956) became chairman of the supervisory board. The board of managing directors consisted of eleven members: Clemens Plassmann, Fritz Gröning, Hans Janberg and Jean Baptist Rath from Deutsche Bank AG West; Erich Bechtolf, Karl Klasen and Franz Heinrich Ulrich from Norddeutsche Bank; and Robert Frowein, Heinz Osterwind, Walter Tron and the already well-known Hermann J. Abs from Süddeutsche Bank. Abs became the post-merger bank's first spokesman. It is worth noting that the responsibilities of the members of the board of managing directors for individual business areas were not centralized, but remained the responsibility of a board member at the three central offices in Düsseldorf, Frankfurt and Hamburg. Members of the board of managing directors responsible for the central offices were thus responsible there for all the various departments and shared responsibility for specific areas. Hence three board members shared responsibility on the overall board for each department. Each board member also had a regional competence reflected in his responsibility for certain branch areas in the territory covered by the central office in his charge.[1]

This combination of regional and departmental responsibility formed a responsibility matrix which remained typical of the board in subsequent years. The board of managing directors of the whole bank had overall responsibility; specific competences, such as for profitability, could not be derived from the way responsibilities were arranged. So it is not surprising that, from an outsider's point of view, the individual board members seemed to have no direct responsibility for specific areas, departments or divisions. Concrete allocation of responsibility – first mentioned in the Annual Report for 1988 – seems to have been unknown, especially in the first few years of the reunited bank. In particular, the still inadequately adjusted accounting system probably made it impossible to distinguish between responsibilities in this way. The matrix structure which was discernible nevertheless, and which determined the functional and regional responsibilities on the board of managing directors, was to be retained in principle over the next 30 years. It underwent considerable change, however, particularly because of the growing importance of international business and the differentiation of the bank's management tasks.

The organization of responsibilities was laid down in the board of managing directors' internal standing orders, but it was handled very flexibly. Areas of responsibility often seemed to be characterized by members' preferences or by their career in the bank, or arose from the necessity to reallocate personnel owing to new problem areas. A rigorous structural blueprint was not apparent. These specific responsibilities were also of more secondary importance owing to the board of managing directors' overall duties as defined in the bank's internal standing orders and the Articles of Association.

In 1957 the three central offices retained the same organization as the various successor institutions had used until the bank's remerger. The only exceptions were Central Accounts and the Accounting Department as well as the General Secretariat, which were located at the domicile of the overall board of managing directors, i.e. in Frankfurt. But by 1959 the first obvious steps towards organizational streamlining were already being taken. Justified by the cost savings that came from combining duties, these steps were still based on the idea that three central offices with equal rights would be retained. This was formulated in a memorandum as follows: 'Streamlining the structure of the three central offices will undoubtedly cut costs. These changes will not, however, entail returning to the former tightly centralized system. In view of the division of responsibilities between the three central offices, all measures aimed at simplification and cost reduction should be based on the principle that one of the central offices should be in overall charge at any one time. In order to avoid mistakes they should not be taken under time pressure, and should be well prepared.'

In the reamalgamated bank's first decade, the accent was not on organizational or structural considerations, although its division into three central offices was becoming a problem from the point of view of control. Organizational changes during this new start were initially of secondary importance, since new developments in customer business, technical developments and their integration into banking business were making great demands on organizational capacities. Finally, in 1967 it was announced that management would be recentralized and, therefore, the first structural reform begun.

The first 'victim' was the central office in Hamburg, which had to move to Frankfurt, although some board members stayed behind initially. This centralization was intended to make the considerably larger bank even stronger and reduce the inefficiencies stemming from the decentralization of the central offices. At the same time as departments were centralized, however, the discretionary powers of regional management units were increased so that divisional and management responsibilities were delegated further to branch managers. In this way, the organizational structure was streamlined, horizontal management responsibility increased and the depth of management reduced. The ongoing centralization of departments and the decentralization of local market responsibility continued apace in the following years until strict centralization, flatly rejected in 1959, predominated by 1990.

Changes in the organizational structure also had an impact on business operations. Abolition of the state restriction on interest rates in 1967 – in addition to the repeal of the so-called Competition Agreement of 1936 – required the bank to devote more attention to the market, especially in retail banking, if it was to expand its market position in this field. Concentrating the Deposits/Small Personal Loans Department – for retail customers – at the Frankfurt central office reflected the greater orientation towards this area of business. The renaming of this unit as Market and Sales Department highlighted the changes in its mission and importance. The increased internationalization of the bank already taking place in the 1960s found its organizational counterpart in the recentralization of the foreign departments in Frankfurt in 1969, which occurred early in comparison to other functional areas. This took place against a background of important events in the monetary field and international business, which had marked effects on the bank's activities.

Improving market proximity and streamlining the bank's organizational structure were also the objectives of its fundamental restructuring in 1974. This reorganization aimed initially to reshape the bank's management structure and redefine customer service at the branches. 1 January 1975 saw the introduction of the 'OM model' (organization and management) at regional head branches. The central element in this new structure was the new concept of target-group banking, embodied in separate departments for corporate and retail customers. In addition, orientation towards the overall customer relationship was to replace the divisional and, therefore, purely product-oriented view of customer relationships. The idea was for the customer's banking relationship to provide him with one-stop financial services. The concept of cross-selling and the possibility of finding cross-selling potential by analysing the overall customer relationship played a key role in the reorganization. The Credit Department thus took on service functions for Corporate Banking, and the Asset Management Department was responsible for providing a comprehensive service to those private customers and institutional investors whose relationship with Deutsche Bank centred on personal investment advice. Serving retail customers, small corporate customers and the self-employed finally became the responsibility of Retail Banking.

A structural consequence of the OM model was a cut in the number of regional head branches from 23 to 14. Strong regional head branches, the size of which guaranteed capacity as highly qualified departments, were to ensure customer services of high quality – the first steps towards quality management for financial services. The geographical areas covered by the regional head branches were measured in such a way that they would be comparable in size and customer structure.

The streamlining of the management structure was accompanied by further delegation of responsibility to the market areas. The expansion of regional head branches' discretionary powers helped further their independence, as planned, as decentralized management and profit centres in such a way that, in their regions, they had a positioning and market penetration comparable to that of a local regional bank.

While this more or less gave the branch network for almost the next two decades a management structure stemming from an evolutionary process linked with the gradual growth of the bank as a whole, what for the banking community was a virtually revolutionary change was taking place in the organization of customer service through the move towards target-group banking. The organization model, introduced with the reorganization of the bank's market areas for the regional head branches and right down to the smallest branch offices, featured a clear allocation of responsibility for customer (target) groups. The business-line organization prevalent until then was not discarded completely, but levels of organizational priority were changed.

Business-line responsibility was no longer primarily a market function; business departments, such as Credit, assumed support responsibilities for markets classified by target group. Business lines were set up in different ways according to customer structure and the size of branches. Hence, specialists in securities business, domestic and foreign payments, and lending, for example, could stay at the branches if the volume of business warranted retaining their expertise. Regional head branches received full discretionary powers and highly qualified staff for all business lines, which offered support in those areas to all subordinate units in the respective catchment areas. Typical of the organizational structure was having few hierarchical levels and a substantial transfer of responsibility to the next hierarchical level. It enabled much information to be conveyed in a short time within the strongly expanding bank and its complex system of organizational units.

Acceptance and implementation of the OM model were not, however, fully achieved over the next few years. The 'Mannheim Model', introduced almost at the same time with a construction slightly different from, but basically in line with, the OM model, as well as branch egotism meant that in 1986, when a second OM model was developed, the failure to achieve the target of uniform and comparable structures at regional head branches had to be admitted.

The mechanisms for steering the bank, the regional head branches and the Group were reorganized in 1986 in a Group restructuring as an extrapolation of the OM model. The aims were more transparency in costs and income within the Group and better co-ordination of business activities. Also Group-wide cross-selling and the 'resource employee' – as it is called in the 'Organization Manual' – were to receive greater emphasis. In particular, the way in which management co-operated at regional head branches was to be redefined. Here, the management philosophy was defined by principles expressed in three pairs of concepts:

- overall/primary responsibility;
- management/operational responsibility;
- regional/divisional responsibility.

As with the assignment of responsibility on the board of managing directors, the joint responsibility principle still applies today in regional head branch management. The 1986 OM model set new accents in that the competence arrangements were expanded into a regulation of responsibilities. The basic incompatibility between the principle of overall responsibility and that of primary responsibility was resolved by individual reporting within the management body that bears overall responsibility.

Management responsibility includes responsibility for achieving business targets based on agreed objectives (management by objectives), motivating staff, management by delegation, and control. Operational responsibility refers to responsibility for relations with important customers and for all decisions in the business areas and in day-to-day business management. The principle of matrix organization was developed with the OM models. The parameters 'region' and 'business area', which had governed the matrix structure since 1957, were joined by the 'customer group' criterion in 1974. In 1986 this dimension was further specified by the operational responsibility principle with regard to customers served directly by members of management.

Greater importance was attached to internal business acquisition, i.e. optimizing the exploitation of cross-selling potential. Customer connections were defined not only bank-specifically, but also in relation to the Group. For this purpose, the personal customer relationship was emphasized by the account officer, who was referred to jokingly as 'Mr Deutsche Bank'. This person assumed a two-tier responsibility for the market. First, he was responsible for exhausting potential in the relevant market. Second, he had to ensure that the market he was in charge of was tapped for the whole Group and its products. A two-tier profit responsibility for the account officer was derived from this dual market responsibility. The extensive transfer of market responsibility for specific bank products and for the entire range of Group services to the account officer led to a new orientation in central office OM management departments, consisting mainly in ensuring support for locally operating account officers.

Concurrent with implementation of the OM model at regional head branches, there was a need to adjust central office structures. Here, central staff departments which showed a high degree of uniformity in their assignments were combined to form divisions. Besides the increase in co-operation and co-ordination within the divisions, the board of managing directors was relieved of purely operational duties – as mentioned in the Annual Report for 1986 – so that it could 'find more time for strategic matters' without reducing its proximity to the bank's business and customers.

One result of the board's attempt to find more time for strategic tasks was the appointment of central office senior managers as executive vice presidents with responsibility for co-ordinating the work done in the departments. Although the bank had had executive vice presidents since the 1930s, they had been assigned to the three central offices since 1957, with two or three at each central office. What was different about the new structure was that the central office divisions were managed by executive vice presidents, which meant including an additional level in the management structure.

The co-ordination of Deutsche Bank Group developed in the 1970s and early 1980s into the largest management task in the bank. Alongside the original banking business of the parent company, the sharply increasing number of branches, subsidiaries and departments substantially increased the complexity of Deutsche Bank Group. One answer to this problem was the installation of co-ordinating committees assembled for different areas under both functional as well as problem- and business-oriented aspects. The co-ordination of the committees' work was the job of executive vice presidents. The basic line/staff organizational principle underlying the bank's organigram was thus extended by a further element.

In the meantime, there had also been shifts of responsibility within the board of managing directors. The allocation of regional responsibility, which hitherto had only covered Germany, was extended to include international regions. In addition to their responsibility for product groups, the board of managing directors assumed responsibility for customer groups in the wake of the organizational reform, although this responsibility was mainly merely one of management. It did not involve direct profit responsibility for the area in question; rather the bank ran the individual units – branches, regional head branches and subsidiaries – as independent profit centres which were responsible for profit and costs in all areas. Responsibility for profit was borne more or less completely by the board; there was no direct assignment to any particular area. The decisive, structurally formative criterion was thus the regional profit responsibility to the board of managing directors for the (in regional terms) relatively autonomous units.

The progressive internationalization of business and the development towards the European Common Market demanded that banks adapt their business strategies and organizational structures. Deutsche Bank endeavoured – this time, it seems, as the first of the German big banks – to find an organizational form suitable for running an international banking group as well as a European universal bank in an efficient and uniform fashion. In 1988 Alfred Herrhausen defined the aims of the European and worldwide markets with which the bank's structures should be aligned. This was to turn the bank in Europe into a universal bank in the broadest sense, while on a global scale its image was to be that of an extended investment bank.

Against this background, the objective was to give the bank a forward-looking, fundamental strategy that would enable it to use specialization advantages and stimulate flexibility and entrepreneurial thinking at all levels. Factors identified as being important for tomorrow's success were product ranges more geared to target groups, effective distribution and cost efficiency. The aim of these changes was, therefore, to give the bank's structures even greater market proximity and stronger profit orientation. For this purpose, a comprehensive strategy for the reorganization of the bank was devised under the overall responsibility of the spokesman of the board of managing directors and, directly subordinated to him, the Group Strategy Department in co-operation with head office and branch executives and with the occasional involvement of external firms.

Whereas the previous organization had been dominated by the regional principle, which stipulated collective responsibility for all business activities at executive board and regional head branch level, the new structure posited divisional responsibility based on the following principles:

- creation of management structures and systems to guarantee bank-wide implementation of business policy targets;
- specialization in products and internal functions or services which allow the bank to match the performance of specialist suppliers;
- clearly defined profit responsibility at all levels as an incentive and to promote entrepreneurial thinking and behaviour;
- discretionary powers that allow the individual employee to exercise his or her profit responsibility;
- modern reporting systems as control instruments that make the individual services transparent, highlight strengths and weaknesses and allow suitable countermeasures to be taken in good time as and when necessary.

Starting from the basic fact that the bank transacts business with private customers, corporate customers and institutions and, in doing so, uses its material and human resources and its accounting function, three corporate groups were created: Private Banking, Corporate Banking and Resources & Controlling. Business and service divisions were established within these corporate groups.

The Private Banking group was split up by customer group into two business divisions, with Retail Banking Division being responsible for business with the majority of private customers and small corporate clients, and Private Banking Division serving all high-net-worth clients. The business divisions in the Corporate/Institutional Banking group, again defined by customer group, were Corporate Finance, Corporate Banking, Securities Trading & Sales/Asset Management, FX, Money and Precious Metals Trading (combined since mid-1993 in Trading & Sales Division), Treasury and the business division Morgan Grenfell/Mergers & Acquisitions. The Resources & Controlling group comprises the four service divisions Credit Control, Personnel, Organization & Operations and Controlling.

While at corporate group level the respective members of the board of managing directors were responsible for overall co-ordination of the activities of the individual corporate group and for the formulation of its strategy, the business and service divisions, each headed by a board member, were responsible for the profits from their respective customers and/or product group and for the quality and cost efficiency of the services provided. The only deviation from this principle is in the business division Corporate Banking, where the member of the board of managing directors responsible for the region continued to have primary customer responsibility (distribution responsibility). Relationship management and personal contacts – not least through the board members as account managers – were recognized as the decisive factors for the success of this business.

Like the board of managing directors, the managers of regional head branches also headed business divisions. Depending on the size of a head branch region, there were generally three to five managers. Where a head branch had five managers, two each were responsible for Private Banking and business with corporates and institutions, and one was in charge of the Resources and Controlling Division. The Private Banking and Corporate Banking groups were also represented at regional branch level, i.e. regional branches were managed by at least one Private Banking manager and one Corporate Banking manager. Responsibility for Resources and Controlling at regional branches was given to one of the two managers, usually the manager responsible for Private Banking.

The new structure was tested in the summer of 1990 in the Frankfurt, Freiburg and Cologne regions. Its final approval by the board of managing directors took place in December 1990, and its implementation in the domestic bank began on 1 January 1991, with the Group Strategy Department in charge of the project. The structural adjustment of foreign branches was carried out up to autumn 1992 on the basis of experience gathered in the domestic sector.

Linked with the new organization, a largely final centralization of the board of managing directors and staff departments was carried out. The three board members domiciled in Düsseldorf until 1991 moved to Frankfurt by 1993. Regional responsibility was not affected by the move and Düsseldorf remained a central office, albeit only with symbolic character, since all important functions and divisions were now centralized in Frankfurt.

One of the bank's international objectives, as defined by Herrhausen, namely to operate as a leading investment bank world-wide, was also reflected in the divisional structure of the 1990s inasmuch as the structure of the Corporate/Institutional Banking group corresponded to that of an investment bank. The impact of the bank's internationalization on its organizational structures was also reflected in the fact that the business divisions received names well known internationally, but unusual to the German ear. According to Michael Endres, member of the board of managing directors responsible for organization: 'What is new above all, besides the described segmentation, is that three partially autonomous business units have come into being with their own distribution, marketing and processing capabilities and most importantly with responsibility for their own profits and control.'[2] The banks were now also using the term 'lean production', and this led to a 'reduction' of 3,000 staff at Deutsche Bank in 1993 alone. Technical infrastructure, underpinning the three corporate groups, was established as an independent service division. It evolved ultimately from payments business and consisted of five levels used by all Group units:

- The first level is the Private Corporate Network on which language, data and pictures are transferred.
- The second level is that of the computer centres. Deutsche Bank Group, which had over 50 computer centres, began to reduce their number and network them.
- The third level is software production. The Group has a standardized technological platform beginning with hardware and ending with data communication standards. All Group units must comply with these standards. This enables software to be developed decentrally.
- The fourth level comprises the common basic services of payments and securities services.
- The fifth level is information dissemination within the Group. Deutsche Bank has an office communication system with over 50,000 users. It allows the exchange of individual news items, information management in business divisions and increasingly also transaction processing by members of staff.

Head office was left with primary tasks such as co-ordination, corporate strategy, controlling, personnel policy, risk management and resource allocation. The secondary functions at head office – staff and other services – were retained only in so far as they could not be obtained more inexpensively and efficiently on the market. The aim of this outsourcing was to reduce production depth and approach the market for non-core services. Where the bank supplied such services itself, certain service functions were hived off into legally independent units. According to Endres, 'What is then left is a head office which today, in a group like Deutsche Bank with more than 74,000 employees, comprises fewer than 2,000 people.'

Divisionalization also affected the regional head branch and regional branch levels, creating a structure that permeated the bank's entire market and service operations. The organizational structure of the regional branches was determined by their specific customer profile, depending on whether their principal orientation was towards private or corporate business. Business divisions sharply differentiated at head office were combined at regional branch level and subordinated to individual branch managers, with an appropriate business volume being taken as the yardstick for the degree of aggregation at individual branch levels.

Besides the customer-group orientation in the Private Banking and Corporate/Institutional Banking corporate groups, the competence and responsibility of regional head branch managers for regional branches was incorporated into the regional head branch organigram as a dimension of regional structure. However, the criteria by which responsibilities for individual regional branches were established were redefined under the divisionalization strategy in 1991. This made the customer-related business emphasis at regional branches a major factor in the allocation of responsibility for those regional branches to a particular manager of a regional head branch. Regional branches where the emphasis was on private banking were thus assigned to the regional head branch manager responsible for private banking.

Besides these basic trends, there were also special developments in the structural organization of Deutsche Bank *Group*. In 1957 a banking group arose under the leadership of Deutsche Bank AG which was linked by equity holdings but did not declare itself to be a group. Thinking in group dimensions did not begin until the second half of the 1970s, and it was only in the mid-1980s that this finally led to Group structural decisions on a large scale. The 1965 amendment to the German Joint Stock Corporation Act led to all big banks drawing up consolidated financial statements for the first time for the 1967 financial year. In the case of the big banks, however, the dominance of the parent bank in each group was still too great for the latter to have any shaping influence on their self-image. The parent's share in each group's total assets in 1967 was 89 per cent at Deutsche Bank, 90.7 per cent at Dresdner Bank and 92.4 per cent at Commerzbank.

The Annual Report for 1967 marked the emerging change in the bank's Group identity with publication of the first consolidated financial statements; 21 direct and indirect national equity stakes were included in the consolidated entity, and this may be seen as 'the first stage in the process of becoming a Group'. This first phase also comprised the restructuring of the mortgage banks in 1971 (pp. 707–8), after which the bank had a majority stake in Deutsche Centralbodenkredit and Frankfurter Hypothekenbank. Consolidation of Compagnie Financière de la Deutsche Bank AG Luxembourg in 1974 signalled the change from a national to an international group. The Annual Report for 1971 outlined the principles for the Deutsche Bank Group structure:

'This expansion of the Deutsche Bank Group, which has been proceeding for years, must be seen as a parallel development to important changes in our economic and social structure and the growing integration in the world economy. Firstly rising incomes and general prosperity are bringing growing demands from our customers, and we must adjust and expand our range of services accordingly. And secondly we must think ahead and be ready to meet – both in specialisation and size – the specific demands of the international business, where service to multinational companies is an important factor ... Institutionally and in our organisation we have met this continual challenge in four ways: By a continuous expansion and improvement of our own services ... By founding subsidiaries to which special functions are transferred ... By acquiring majority participations or joining in the establishment of specialised institutions, where the bank may work in fruitful combination with the particular knowledge and ability of qualified partners ... By working with other European banks in founding joint subsidiaries in Europe and overseas. Attention should be drawn here to the activities of the EBIC Group.'

This effort also found expression in the publication of the first global annual statement of accounts for 1980, in which for the first time all foreign subsidiaries were consolidated (this became law in 1981). It underlines the bank's aspiration to appear as a company operating as a world-wide group. Since the first Group financial statements in 1967, the bank's total assets had increased almost eight-fold from 22 billion DM to 175 billion DM; by 1993 they had risen more than 25-fold to 557 billion DM. Over the same period, Deutsche Bank AG's share in Group business volume decreased from 89 to 67 per cent in 1990, hitting an all-time low in 1980 of 60.3 per cent. These figures also clearly show the strategy pursued by the bank in the 1970s and 1980s. The tendency towards international, global business became earnest during this period and could only be realized on a group basis – due among other things to divergent basic conditions in individual countries.

During the 1970s, the growing number of the bank's equity participations led to the organizational integration of their managements. Up to 1977 this had been done through the Investment Banking Department, after which co-ordination was handled by a newly formed Participations Department. The final emergence of the Group philosophy, and with that the start of the most recent phase in the bank's development into a group, came in 1986. This became evident and was more or less programmatically described when the Participations Department was renamed Group Strategy Department. The bank's development into a European and international banking group was accelerated under Herrhausen's aegis, and this necessitated greater emphasis on planning and structuring tasks in the Group. Thus the renaming of the department coincided with a redefinition of its mission, away from administration and towards planning and structuring.

The increasing priority of the Group over the once dominant parent company also led to a new definition of the Group management structure in relation to changes linked with divisionalization in 1991. While Group companies with their own management and supervisory bodies corresponding to their legal structures and the legal situation in the country of domicile had previously been embedded in a complex matrix of responsibilities, divisionalization transferred the dominating principle of divisional responsibility to executive board competences at subsidiaries as well. Regional and product-group responsibilities had predominated hitherto on subsidiaries' executive boards, but it was not possible to implement a strict principle of management.

Besides the equity participation, the link between subsidiaries and Deutsche Bank AG was cemented visibly through the supervisory bodies. The responsible members of the bank's board of managing directors were prominently represented in subsidiaries' supervisory bodies; other equity shareholders were also included in accordance with their holdings. In some cases, business associates were also appointed to the supervisory bodies of subsidiaries where the bank had a qualified majority or a 100 per cent stake. With the reorganization of the bank in 1990/91, the supervisory bodies of subsidiaries wholly owned by the bank consisted almost entirely of members of the board of managing directors or the bank's management staff.

Even when the bank's influence was exerted directly on subsidiaries' business policy through the supervisory board, these were allowed business freedom in their markets. This accorded with the bank's general organizational and management maxims:[3] to have management 'as decentralized as possible, as centralized as necessary', even if the maxim, which sounded hackneyed, remained undefined both qualitatively and quantitatively. Qualitative characteristics can be recognized only in indicators: thus organizational changes reflecting a stronger tendency in the bank towards customer orientation as a philosophy made it absolutely essential to transfer responsibility to units active on the market – in particular, to subsidiaries. Similarly, outsourcing functions and centralizing them at subsidiaries, a development which took place on a large scale in the years after 1986, led to a concentration of know-how which meant that a corresponding transfer – and thus increase – of responsibility to those units made sense. The Group's ongoing internationalization also underpinned the tendency towards decentralizing responsibility. First, there was a growing realization that the various national cultures which are an inevitable part of any international group in terms of both staff and customers can be integrated efficiently and adequately only within the framework of a decentralized management structure with closer market contact. Secondly, it appeared that sufficient attention could be paid to specific economic conditions only through decentralized decision-making powers in the countries where the bank operated. At the same time, central office responsibility for planning, controlling and monitoring within the Group increased considerably, one important reason being an improved and much-expanded system of reporting, communication and monitoring with appropriate instruments.

1989 saw the start of a new phase leading to major changes in Group structure. The processes known as Group restructuring can be seen as an expression of the final change in the bank's own perception of its Group identity, and they represented Group-wide implementation of a European and global business strategy. Besides measures to round off the Group's product and service range, divisions were hived off and established as independent entities and international consolidated subsidiaries were wound up and their activities reintegrated into the parent company (pp. 735–83).

An organizational variant, interesting from a market policy standpoint, was introduced in 1991 which must have appeared almost revolutionary to the banker of the classical school. In 1986 the subsidiary Deutsche Bank Bauspar AG had begun to use a field service for new business acquisition and customer service. All field-service activities in retail banking were combined in 1991 in a new company called Vertriebsgesellschaft mbH der Deutschen Bank für Privatkunden. This new entity, a consequence of the current *Allfinanz* (one-stop financial service) strategy, severed the close link between production and sales typical of the banking industry. Because of the prescribed legal separation of functions (property finance, insurance and banking), production responsibility lay with those originally providing the individual financial services, i.e. banks, building and loan associations, and insurance companies. In contrast, sales activities – particularly the field service distribution channel not usual for banks – were integrated into a distribution company whose sole task was to control the field sales activities.

The bank's research activities were concentrated as from 1 January 1992 through the foundation of DB Research GmbH, Frankfurt, which comprised the Economics Department, degab (Deutsche Gesellschaft für Anlageberatung mbH) and parts of the Investment Research Department, especially the staff department Fixed Income Research from the Securities Trading and Sales/Asset Management Division.

The organizational development of the bank's *branch network* has already been referred to. In 1957 the reamalgamated bank began its business activities with 307 branches, all of them domestic. Those in the eastern part of pre-war Germany had been lost through the country's partition and the creation of the German Democratic Republic. In the Federal Republic, a branching boom lasting until the early 1970s was triggered by the big banks' orientation towards broad retail banking as well as the Federal Administrative Court's decision in 1958 to stop checking whether there was really a demand for bank branches before allowing them to be opened.

From 1972 to around 1987, the number of branches remained more or less constant. During this period, in addition to some newly opened outlets which helped to realign the network, there were also branch closures which, apart from cost problems, showed that the market was somewhat overbanked. In 1988 a consolidation phase finally came about. In spite of the renewed wave of openings resulting from German reunification, consolidation continued in western Germany, offset in quantitative terms, however, by the number of branches opening in the five new federal states. At mid-1994, Deutsche Bank Group had 2,477 branch offices, 748 of which were abroad.

For Germany, which in the banks' perception has been overbanked since the 1970s – a statistic often quoted is the population-per-branch ratio, which has been relatively constant at around 1,400 and is thus higher than that of comparable industrial countries – a more sophisticated branch policy became a goal for the 1990s, which would lead to a certain thinning out of the network. One result of this strategy, however, was that the *concept* of branches was reviewed. At the beginning of 1992, the idea of separating the 'advisory bank' and the 'technical bank' was implemented – at first on a trial basis. Areas for fast service as well as self-service areas were introduced at branches. Firstly, self-service areas allowed occasional and regular customers to transact their business without entering the advisory area. Secondly, the self-service areas, which were physically separate from the private-banking advisory area, permitted introduction of a 24-hour service. Especially from the point of view of cost, it was no longer considered possible to provide both normal retail and high-net-worth clients with identical services and advice by the same staff members in every single branch.

A major development took place on 1 July 1990 when monetary union between West and East Germany allowed branches to be set up there. Through the joint venture with Deutsche Kreditbank signed before monetary union was concluded, under which Deutsche Kreditbank contributed 122 branches to the new Deutsche Bank-Kreditbank AG, Deutsche Bank already had a strong branch base from which to penetrate the market in the new federal states. At the end of 1990, Deutsche Bank-Kreditbank AG was merged with Deutsche Bank after the latter's equity stake had gradually risen to 100 per cent following German unification. The bank thus started a new market offensive, first through the joint venture and then by opening a number of its own outlets. At the end of 1991, only 15 months after unification, there were more than 200 new branches in the former German Democratic Republic.

On 1 April 1991, Deutsche Bank Berlin AG merged with Deutsche Bank AG. The former, which had hitherto been seen as a legally independent subsidiary, was 'demoted' to regional head branch and given control of the northern area of the new federal states. The Leipzig branch became regional head branch in charge of the southern area so that, following the unification of the two Germanies, the number of regional head branches rose by only 2 to 16. In 1992, the bank had almost 300 outlets in the new federal states, including all of Berlin.

b) Procedural organization

In 1929, Hans Rummel, manager of the bank's Munich branch and, from 1930 to 1945, member of the board of managing directors, explained the term 'bank organization' to branch managers as follows: 'The nature of organization in the banking business [is a] problem which cannot be solved using machines and formulae by central accountants, rather by properly organizing and using staff available to us in order to bring about a completion of business in as prompt and inexpensive a way as possible, involving work sharing and rational exploitation of technical aids. Business is of the utmost importance. Every organizational action must serve it, and hence organization must remain in the hands of those completing the business. It cannot be left to those people solely in charge of organization.'[4] Although it has been expressed in different ways, this interpretation of bank organization has remained unchanged over the years.

In Deutsche Bank's three successor institutions and in the first few years after the merger of 1957, the organizational duties were taken over by a working group called Central Office/Organization Group at the three central offices. At the individual branches, heads of internal operations were responsible for procedural organization, although the heads of internal operations at the larger branches met to consult each other on organizational strategy. The co-ordination of joint procedural organization was carried out by the Central Office/ Organization Group in close consultation with the heads of internal operations. This created an organizational regime which started more or less below, i.e. in the branches, and went up to central office's organization group.

Its duties show that, besides the personnel responsibility which it still had at that time, the main emphasis – a Central Organization Department did not yet exist in the first few years after 1957 – was on the integration of office technology and the burgeoning use of electronic data processing (EDP) in banking business. The Central Office Organization Group's lack of discretionary powers could therefore be regarded as problematic, since the major organizational tasks were allocated to head branches. Problems of organizational procedure were discussed at regular meetings between the heads of internal operations and the Central Office Organization Group; decision-making powers and responsibility for performance remained, however, with the heads of internal operations.

The organizational tasks which had to be solved in the early 1960s were mainly related to payments business – in particular, how to overcome the problem of large quantities caused by the mass introduction of wage and salary accounts. The decision of competitors, especially the savings banks and co-operative banks, to speed up the introduction of cashless wage and salary payment, and thus to offer salary accounts, made it impossible for the bank to avoid this development. That it was not exactly happy about this can be seen from a memorandum from the Central Office Organization Group in 1959:

'We have to reckon with the fact that cashless salary payments will become widespread. However, it appears that fulfilling the conditions will take companies a long time, so that this will happen only gradually. To what extent our bank will be involved in having payroll accounts is not yet clear. Wage earners working with big companies ... who usually live scattered over a very large area, might have to consider the fact that the number of payroll accounts which we will have will not be very high, relatively speaking ... There should be no doubt that running payroll accounts is generally not a very lucrative business, especially when a suitable equivalent cannot be attained from the firm in question – something which, from previous experience, is possible only in a small number of cases.'

Procedural organization arrangements, which were intended to standardize settlement while accepting the possibility of greater risks, were to rein in the cost of maintaining payroll and salary accounts. It can be seen from such arrangements that special features were being introduced – if only internally – as early as 1960/61 for this specific type of account which distinguished it from normal accounts.

In addition to strategic considerations on how to maintain payroll accounts and how to minimize the costs they generate, the procedural organization of this business required a number of organizational measures in the first half of the 1960s. Handling the large number of new accounts had to be constantly reorganized.

Another main reason for standardizing these procedures was that the central offices in Hamburg, Düsseldorf and Frankfurt, which despite the legal remerger of the three successor banks were still relatively independent in 1957, were again intended to present a united front on the market. Hence, the uniformity of procedural organization was to be established by a central Organization Department. This was resolved on 1 October 1964. When it was being established, attention was focused primarily both in internal operations and in interbank discussions on the standardization of payments structures and the more efficient processing of national and international payments linked to this. The more efficient processing of the bank's payments which, in 1965, reached a volume of 26 million cheques and 82 million transfer slips, paying-in vouchers and cheque presentation forms, as well as the desire to provide the customer with a uniform service, were achieved by standardizing the bank's forms; this was seen as an essential part of a new corporate design.

Moreover, the increasing availability of EDP, both on the part of clients and in the bank, demanded a standardization of vouchers and procedures. Thus a major part of the Organization Department's work had already been laid down in 1964. A further aspect of its work at central office was to look after the technical infrastructure, especially the EDP within the bank as well as other related tasks. Before 1964, the individual head branches and central offices had built up their own infrastructures in this area, which were largely independent of each other. Different makes of computer were used simultaneously in the bank and gave rise to substantial compatibility problems, for example in the bank's internal clearing and accounting. Furthermore, as software increased in importance, the development of a standardized system became increasingly necessary. Hence, in addition to market observation in the area of technological developments and examination of its feasibility in the bank, the aforementioned tasks of both internal and external standardization became the Organization Department's central duties. Tasks in EDP, which had already been assigned early on to the Central Office/Organization Group and subsequently to the Organization Department, increased in importance throughout the following three decades.

Procedural organization arrangements, which also affected the bank's structural organization, became more important at the start of the 1990s. A case in point was a reorganization introduced in the wake of a public debate on insider trading by the bank's staff in 1991. It was shown that monitoring and behavioural recommendations within the bank were not sufficient to prevent incorrect behaviour by staff in securities business or even to spot it in retrospect. In order to prevent staff from using their insider knowledge to trade and make profits for their own account, the bank became the first in Germany to set up a department whose brief was to ensure that both internal regulations and international insider-trading rules and practices were adhered to. 'The watchdog brigade', as they were called in the press, were to ensure that the treatment of market-relevant information was improved and that conflicts of interest were excluded. The department, called Compliance in line with Anglo-American practice, was positioned sufficiently high in the bank's hierarchy to give it adequate responsibility, and was headed by a senior vice president (p. 720).

German unification had an extremely strong impact on the organization of banks in general, and of Deutsche Bank in particular. The large number of branches which within one year had to be built, restructured or quickly brought up to something approaching western standards is a clear indication of the technical and organizational problems which had to be overcome in these years. The almost total lack of any communication and banking infrastructure called for patience, personal commitment and the ability to improvise with internal communication and settlement procedures.

Although communication channels between the new branches and Deutsche Bank's head office were established within a short time with the aid of state-of-the-art technical equipment, the settlement of interbank payments, for example, had to run for some time on the archaic systems of the former East Germany, so that by West German standards in terms of service, transfer times, etc., considerable concessions had to be made. Although rules governing organizational procedure at former East German banks were adopted, the somewhat chaotic conditions, especially during the first few months after unification, resulted in considerable deviations from the bank's normal standards of security and monitoring.

c) EDP and its development into automated information processing

Deutsche Bank presents a true picture of how the methods and technology of data and information processing have developed in modern banking. The system generally used for processing large quantities of data up to the late 1950s and beyond was the punch-card method (conventional data processing phase). Although the technology of the legendary Hollerith machines was by then almost 70 years old, the punch-card method was not introduced into the bank until 1958. This had been preceded by years of discussion, initially producing only negative results.

The Stuttgart branch of Süddeutsche Bank finally experimented with the punch-card machine in safe-custody business from March 1957; by 1958, all safe-custody accounting was being handled by this method. A report to the Central Office Organization Department on the bank's experiences with the punch-card method in 1958 was almost euphoric about the rationalization achieved; the setting up of the new punch-card department necessitated only an insignificant number of new staff and ultimately considerable costs were saved – particularly in personnel. On this basis, the punch-card machines were introduced throughout the bank. It was, however, to be a very short interlude, for in 1961 the era of *electronic* data processing began in the bank; the punch-card machines in use at the time were gradually taken out of operation, a process which lasted until around 1968. Nevertheless, it was some time before the bank recognized the importance of the information and communication technology deriving from electronic data processing for its competitiveness.

The development of electronic media in the bank can be divided into different phases, starting with the support of intensely arithmetic procedures using non-electronic instruments towards the end of the 1950s. In this phase, securities business and safe-custody procedures were automated first.

The second phase saw the automation of standardized retail banking and to improve internal procedures. The principal objective behind deciding to use this technology was to secure the bank's competitive position by reducing costs. In this phase – in the mid-1960s – data processing was carried out centrally at computer centres using mainframes, with mostly internal data being processed.

Remote data processing introduced at the start of the 1970s overturned the principle of centralization, which had been predominant until then, and heralded the start of a third phase involving the growing decentralization of data processing. In this phase, *qualitative* criteria also determined the structure of data processing, and then information processing too. In 1974, on-line processing in the bank was adopted using the IBM 370 and the Siemens 4004 systems. Specialist interactive processing facilitated the integrated processing of business transactions 'on the spot' at branches. The installation of terminals in day-to-day business, right down to the counter, did not begin until 1983. They were used for computer-aided specialist work, and also opened up the possibility of

EDP-based customer advisory services. In what was tantamount to an internal revolution, the step was taken from pure electronic data processing as such to EDP-based information processing.

The fourth and – for the time being – last phase of electronic data and information processing began with the strategy of installing terminals, and was known as the 'intelligent bank automation phase'. It featured an attempted symbiosis of text, language, pictures and data. Intelligent systems, which mainly used fourth- and fifth-generation software (expert systems), led to a change in the bank's business which can only roughly be described by terms such as computer-based customer advisory, customer self-service, electronic banking services and systems permitting 24-hour global trading.

When the bank's board of managing directors held a closed session on 22 March 1983, the third item on the agenda was 'technology and banking services'. Ulrich Weiss reviewed developments in new technology and their effects on the bank. For the first time, the board of managing directors dealt in detail with electronic banking. Some services had been developed on the basis of electronic media and were being used in the form of automated teller machines (ATMs) at the customer/bank interface; however, no uniform strategic line or goal was linked to the development and introduction of these banking services. The discussion at executive board level was based on the realization that the bank could not remain competitive without considerable investment in this technology.

A working group consisting of staff from the Organization Department, Corporate Banking, Retail Banking and the Accounting and Planning Department was to put forward proposals for future strategy, particularly with regard to small and medium-sized corporates. Within a few months it produced detailed proposals which, based on market observation and prediction of technological developments, concerned the institutionalization of a project group called Electronic Banking. These suggestions were also influenced by the German Post Office's videotext system (Btx), which was being tested at that time. This system was regarded by the bank as an important communication system for the future.

A typical electronic banking service where the bank once again did not *react* until the product had been introduced at other institutions was the cash-management system 'db-direct'. In 1980, three years before the aforementioned meeting of the board of managing directors, activities at American banks, which were aggressively canvassing German corporate customers with cash-management products, were mentioned in an internal discussion paper:

'It has been observed recently that
– German groups are increasingly being courted by US banks,
– both neighbouring banks (Dresdner Bank and Commerzbank) are exploring diverse cash-management systems,
– we are being asked by customers and banks to feed account information for these customers into external cash-management systems,

– various foreign banks are asking for account statements for their accounts in Frankfurt to be supplied through a cash-management system.

Although our position on the CMS [cash-management system] question is still very cautious, we will be unable to avoid offering something of this nature. Banks can already transfer account information via SWIFT. A reaction from our side, possibly in response to the competition's behaviour, in other words offering our own CMS, could be used selectively as an advertising measure, particularly for banks without a SWIFT connection. Moreover, all attempts to induce us to join other CMS or rather account information systems could be countered by reference to our own system.'

The development of a cash-management system for international use was not decided until the meetings of the board of managing directors on 14 June and 16 August 1983. At their meeting on 29 May 1984, the board of managing directors approved the introduction of 'db-direct'. At the same time, efforts were made to persuade domestic and foreign banks to join a global cash-management solution based on the Deutsche Bank standard and under its leadership. These plans, however, were doomed to failure right from the start, since other banks had already launched similar activities and had invested substantially in developing their own systems or adapting ones already purchased, and had already entered the market with their systems one or two years previously. They also used a world-wide network infrastructure built up with their support by American banks, which meant that for these banks there could be no question of a system change, as envisaged by Deutsche Bank. Deutsche Bank's claims to leadership prompted at least passive resistance; in some cases, *open* criticism was to be heard from the banks approached.

In 1988, the range of services for cash-management systems was extended. 'db-connect' made it possible to give companies payments data via data media or data communications, allowing them to process raw data in their own data-processing systems. The possibility for companies to deliver their payments data to the bank for further processing was also integrated. When the Post Office released videotext for general use in 1984, the bank decided to expand the product range it had already introduced during the videotext trial period. In addition to the general service of obtaining account information directly from the bank's central computer, software was developed to enable customers to carry out computer-based payment transactions using the videotext link; this program was introduced to customers as 'db-dialog' in 1987.

In addition to cash management, which forms part of payments business, the bank launched a new database enquiry service in 1985, a field not typical of banks. A good reception induced it to step up its activities in this sector: the bank developed an institutional basis for the database service, offered as 'db-data', by founding Deutsche Wirtschaftsdatenbank GmbH, Frankfurt, in 1986. Shortly after this company was founded, it joined Business Datenbank GmbH, which was started jointly by ONLINE GmbH and the bank; through Deutsche Wirtschaftsdatenbank, the bank owned 51 per cent of Business Databank's share capital. The idea quickly attracted the interest of other banks and in the years to follow other banks acquired an equity stake in it; however, Deutsche Bank remained in charge. In the development of database services offered, a decisive change in the bank's attitude towards electronic-banking services can be seen. Whereas before 1983 it pursued – rather unwillingly – an adaptive strategy, by 1985 this had changed completely with the introduction of database services. In this market sector at least, the bank became market leader and a protagonist of the new banking database services.

There was also a change in strategy in retail banking after 1983. Although the services offered via videotext did not have the anticipated success, the bank did not retract this service. Other services offered as part of the substantial growth in customer self-service were also expanded at Deutsche Bank: account-statement printers and ATMs, which at the start of the 1980s were few and far between, were standard in every branch by the 1990s. This development was emphasized by the new branch design started in the early 1990s, where self-service areas with separate entrances were set up. Incorporating data terminals into customer business was not confined to Germany; as part of the bank's European strategy, all foreign branches involved in retail banking were integrated into the network for electronic-banking services. Thus, self-service via electronic banking became a standardized European service and was an integral component of the strategy to promote customer self-service.

The bank's technical infrastructure and hence communication systems could be summed up at the end of the 1980s by terminalization, the internet strategy and 'db-trader'. The internet was an integrated system capable of covering all major business areas of a foreign branch. It was installed at the bank's large foreign branches. 'db-trader' covered the administration and processing of securities and the technical side of accounting in investment banking on an international level. For business, terminalization has certainly been the most important development in the field of EDP in recent years. Since 1987, the bank's entire domestic organization has been converted. Today, all 25,000 terminal workstations and all other data terminals, such as account-statement printers, ATMs and cash adaptors, are networked. World-wide, over 40,000 staff members use the bank's office communication system.

The system behind the terminal concept is based on the building-block principle with IBM, Siemens and Nixdorf computers. Computers are used at Head Office, regional head branch and branch level with clearly defined functions, but they are fully compatible and interactive. This has allowed the differentiation of information flows, greater flexibility and independence, and also a more differentiated distribution of data-processing tasks. This concept, which envisaged different hardware at each level, also guaranteed independence *vis-à-vis* hardware suppliers.

Terminal workstations, self-service elements and automatic cash adaptors are managed by terminal controllers at the lowest of the three levels. Second-level computers function more or less as buffers at the larger branches and central offices; they are used mainly for short-term database support. Databases, transactions and other information which can be retrieved from the terminals are kept available on these computers. Actual entries and data updates are effected on mainframes at the Eschborn, Düsseldorf and Hamburg computer centres. The basis of Deutsche Bank AG's and the Group's communication system is 'db-fastnet', an international data and communication network consisting of leased lines – partly using satellites – and public networks. Including language, i.e. the telephone, all communication world-wide is handled via this network.

The development of electronic data processing in the bank into an integrated global electronic-information processing system underlines the growing importance of information and communication technology. The role of EDP, its risks and its importance for handling business can be elucidated using a trivial example – one which posed considerable problems for the bank. On 31 December 1980, none of the terminals worked any more, causing long queues to form at the counters. On investigation, a simple software mistake was found: 1980 was a leap year and hence had 366 days. In the standard software obtained by the bank from EDP suppliers the possibility of a leap year had not been taken into consideration, so that the software closed all accounts at the end of the 365th day of the year. Hence, no files could be opened for the last day of 1980.

The growing importance of EDP was also reflected in the bank's organigram. In the meantime, EDP organization had been developing into a large section within the Organization Department. In addition to the EDP organization section, which maintained the existing EDP systems and supervised new projects, the bank decided at the end of the 1980s to set up a system of departments which – comparable to research and development departments – were to investigate the potential for integrating new developments in EDP technology. Here, a purely adaptive strategy towards technological developments was abandoned in favour of a more pro-active, user-oriented approach. In relation to this, possibilities for using new technology in the bank were critically defined and requirement catalogues produced for suppliers. Moreover, Group efficiency was increased by the fact that uniform standards were devised for hardware and software to ensure internal systems compatibility.

d) Accounting, controlling and planning

The development of internal accounting at Deutsche Bank over more than 60 years, from pure documentation into a set of management and controlling instruments, was determined more by people than by exciting or major events. Here, names such as Hans Rummel, Klaus Mertin and Jürgen Krumnow stand out as the authors of major changes in this period. Besides change initiated by people, significant progress in accounting and hence in information exchange came from technological developments and the introduction of an integrated EDP system. In 1957 accounting was structured in more or less the same way as in the 1930s. Up to the 1970s, the departments in question were called – in keeping with tradition – 'Accounts' and at Head Office 'Central Accounts'. That accounting should form the basis of a bank-wide or Group-wide information system – based on internal accounting data – was largely unheard of. Only at the beginning of the 1960s did important changes in the bank and its environment bring about modifications in accounting.

In 1986, under the heading 'Accounting at a big bank in a changing environment', Mertin outlined the modern perception and tasks of internal accounting as follows: '[Adapting to changed environmental conditions] is easiest for those who are working from an organic management philosophy and balanced business norms. It should shortly become apparent that expanding companies need basic norms of this type for decision-making if they would prefer not to run the risk of losing their balance. After interest-rate deregulation in 1967, management responsibility grew to new proportions. The basic requirement for meeting these challenges properly is to have continually adapting accounting. The expectation of such a system must be that new questions of a fundamental nature are examined and processed in terms of the bank's own basic conception.'[5]

Interest-rate deregulation represented a decisive turning point in the duties of 'Accounts' in the bank, and hence in its accounting function. In spite of the proliferation of branches in the 1960s, which considerably raised the complexity of information being processed, the interest margin was determined mainly externally by the blocking of borrowing and lending rates; commission income did not accumulate in any volume worthy of mention, so that a closer analysis of the bank's income and cost situation over and above the process used up to then was not necessary. Furthermore, the EDP system did not offer sufficient capacity for making further analyses. The relatively simply structured analyses necessary until then could be implemented using existing technical systems; nevertheless, compared with earlier years, the use of data processing saved much time since only a small amount of manual revision was necessary.

While the termination of the Interest Rates Order precipitated intensive efforts to expand bookkeeping into meaningful and transparent accounting, the organization reform of 1975 elucidated the need for a sophisticated accounting system which could also deliver information for bank controlling purposes. The new organization structure, which was based on the principle of decentralized management and which transferred greater responsibility for decision-making and profits to the market function, had to be supported by a meaningful and transparent accounting system, which was also to take on the functions of controlling and steering. For this, the components of success, its location and source had to be identified in order adequately to control and steer the activities of the market function in relation to its goal.

Operating profit, which was 2.66 DM billion for the Group in mid-1994 (after risk provisioning) and 1.906 DM billion at Deutsche Bank AG, became a central unit for measuring the steering, monitoring and motivation function in internal accounting. Only by publishing the operating profit figure, which also includes own-account trading – nowadays an integral part of any universal bank's business – could the increasingly unsatisfactory meaningfulness of partial operating profit by counteracted.[6] At branches, operating profit was also used as being representative of individual business success. The operating profit's control function was supported by figures and size of profit.

Using a sort of three-dimensional adaptation of the accounting function, questions such as where, how and from whom could be answered in relation to operating profit. The first dimension consisted of head office and the 14 regional head branches with the branches below them. Total operating profit is arrived at by adding the individual results from each reporting branch. The second dimension portrays the individual results of all business lines; the addition of these should also give the operating profit for the whole bank. The final dimension consists of the results per customer or customer group, the sum of which also gives total operating profit less own-account trading. Calculations for branches and sub-branches answer the question of 'where', calculations for the (eight) business lines answer the question 'how', and the customer-group calculations show from whom the operating profit was achieved.

This three-dimensional picture of the bank forms the basis for further part-calculations which facilitate the provision of information: for example, on the profit from a customer group in a particular business line, on the profit contribution from a customer group at a certain branch, or the result achieved by a branch in a particular line of business. With the aid of these calculation processes, a profit-centre calculation is possible: for individual areas – branches, business lines or regions – isolated profit and loss accounts can now be drawn up. In this way, the instrument of a short-term profit and loss account can be fully implemented in the bank. The introduction of the profit-centre concept laid the basis for better profit-oriented control of the bank. With the help of this concept, the profit-oriented control of the Group can also be broken down into individual accounting units. The resulting transparency of each unit's contribution to Group profit is a motivating factor, particularly for branch managers, in addition to performance control.

In addition to the termination of the Interest Rates Order, amendments to the German Banking Act in 1976 and 1984, which resulted in groups being obliged to consolidate their domestic and foreign subsidiaries, and the related question of Group-wide Principle I capital adequacy ratios, the effects of the international debt crisis on the bank's income situation, the effects of greater interest-rate risk and innovative financial instruments had an important influence on the tasks of the bank's internal accounting system in the 1970s and 1980s. The demands placed on this also grew to the extent that the information needs of the bank's decision-making bodies increased too. The accounting system's technological support, which facilitated the compression, evaluation and processing of large amounts of data within a very short time, provided a permanent information base which could quickly access information necessary for controlling, planning and monitoring.

The danger of the bank's decision-makers being flooded with too much information, a distinct possibility given technical developments, was countered by an information selection and compression system, which was implemented as part of a management information system. This step, taken in the second half of the 1970s, meant that the step towards expanding the accounting system into an information and controlling system had finally been taken. In addition to this, the basis for Group-wide controlling had been provided.

By controlling, Krumnow[7] understands the process of obtaining and processing information, from which comprehensive, targeted and up-to-date information can be generated for decision-makers, thus contributing to optimum bank controlling. 'This information is geared primarily to the categories of banking business in terms of product and customer. Hence, terms such as market potential, market share, all types of revenue, expense and costs are used, as are classifications by the characteristics of our customers and their specific product demands.' Today, instruments such as management accounting, resource controlling and marketing controlling, as well as actual-analysis, planning and variance analyses are used, based on data provided by internal accounting. In this way, the information supplied by the accounting system extends far beyond the pure recording and documentation of business transactions, since the imputed figures also influence the analyses within the framework of controlling, but particularly the accounting for planning and control.[8]

The importance of controlling at Deutsche Bank can be seen in its organizational embedding in the 1990/91 reorganization: as a result of this, controlling became an independent division together with accounting, under the corporate group Resources and Controlling. Krumnow assumed responsibility for Controlling/Accounting on the board of managing directors. Here, too, the growth and structural changes to which the bank had been exposed over the past 30 years or so, for internal and external reasons, justified extending the scope of controlling. The isolated view, formerly restricted to the parent company and individual subsidiaries, gave way to an integral Group approach which included all Group units in a uniform strategic business policy and hence an integral management framework.

Another important factor which determined the organization of the controlling system was the bank's management philosophy. Its preferred decentralization philosophy, i.e. the delegation of discretionary powers and responsibility by setting up profit centres, was uniformly adopted throughout the Group. In 1975, when the first OM model was realized, a profit-centre organization was also introduced into the bank. Within the framework of this organization concept,

120 branches became independent units which drew up their own balance sheets; this included the 14 regional head branches. The managers in charge of these profit centres were given responsibility for profits in their business area. In addition to the independent units drawing up their own balance sheets, there were over 1,000 outlets which did not draw up their own balance sheets. They were informed about the development of their profits in the form of selected figures broken down by individual unit. The bank regarded drawing up a rudimentary profit and loss account as being sensible from a controlling point of view, particularly for the sub-branches, which did not draw up their own balance sheets, since this also achieved a motivating effect as well as controlling the unit concerned.

Controlling's results were collated in notifications, analyses and reports, depending on the purpose of the investigation and the intended recipient of the information. The basis and starting point of controlling were the recording and documentation of each individual transaction in the form of a value-added chain, which showed calculations of all transactions throughout the bank and Group. From this set of figures from accounting, information is derived for internal and external rendering of accounts and for reports to banking supervisory bodies and the Bundesbank. It also forms the basis for business management analyses, which in turn provide the basis for recommendations for action to be taken and, further down the line, allow success to be monitored. In 1990 Krumnow commented as follows on the nature and use of controlling: 'It has enabled us to give precise information on each individual transaction. These are calculated according to responsibility and compressed into business lines, regional profit centres and product groups. These partial calculations, though difficult to follow in some cases, are compatible with the information requirements set forth in German joint stock corporation law, commercial law and supervisory regulations. Each result being reported is thus accounted for and allocated to its respective sources, i.e. to the basic functions production, financing and the sale of banking services in the various sectors of our interest and services business, in our trading activities and in the specific products offered by our specialized institutions.'[9]

All instruments could be used at Group level as well as for every profit centre. This means that controlling tasks were assumed functionally at *all* levels of the bank. Controlling was institutionalized in terms of its considerable importance for the Group at Head Office and for the regional and service-oriented units at the respective managerial levels. Thus, the regional head branches and subsidiaries assume specific controlling functions in their own regional market or in the specific products they offer.

Closely related to what was described above was the idea of a systematic *business plan*. The deregulation measures starting in the late 1960s, such as the termination of the Interest Rates Order, put an end to the times when – as was often ironically pointed out – bankers already knew at the start of the year what income they would have at the end. In addition, changing market conditions required a planning strategy to improve the bank's ability to react to foreseeable changes in the market and to intervene actively in the bank's organization in changing markets.

In the early 1970s, the banks had just started efforts to incorporate the formalized planning instrument into their management practice. Especially Herrhausen, who was a member of the VEW board of managing directors before he joined the bank, propagated the introduction of planning as a management instrument also at banks; the first time he really stated this publicly was in a lecture on 'Long-Term Planning at Credit Institutions' on 14 July 1971 in the Banking and Stock Trading Department at the University of Cologne. Herrhausen's particular concern was that planning should not be regarded as a mere technique or procedure, but as a specific attitude of mind, way of thinking and corporate philosophy, as an unmistakable and – for the future – essential mentality. In Herrhausen's view, planning meant rationalization of the recognition and decision-making process in the bank on the basis of a specific way of thinking for making decisions.[10] Characteristic of the relevance and importance which Herrhausen attached to this concept in banks was the initiation of a bank working group on 'Planning Problems at Banks', chaired by himself and Hans E. Büschgen, in which top-ranking bankers worked together, discussed and developed ideas informally. This working group – later chaired by Herbert Zapp and subsequently, with particular commitment, by Krumnow – still exists today and bears testimony to the ongoing need for banks to develop planning strategies.

Herrhausen's thoughts on institutionalizing planning at banks were based on the bank's multi-variable target system. He formulated this strategy – the first time it was so explicitly mentioned by a leading bank manager – in the 1971 Cologne lecture as six return targets in the form of a 'set of objectives' for Deutsche Bank, although he did not consider this list to be exhaustive:

1. A particular profit growth rate and, linked to this, a particular return on equity on a continually rising equity capital.
2. Guaranteeing dividend requirements with sufficient allocation to reserves.
3. A certain growth in business volume and in services business with a view to expanding market share.
4. Maintaining the universal-bank character of Deutsche Bank.
5. The broadest possible geographical representation of the bank in Germany and a presence at the principal international centres.
6. The maintenance and expansion of Deutsche Bank's position among German banks.

To be suitable as a practical benchmark for company management, these bank return targets were made concrete in a planning context, and implemented in relation to each other. For this, use was made of the information basis provided by the internal and external accounting system, whose basic figures made up the planning figures relevant for controlling purposes and hence the operative target variables. The basic concept of profit maximization was not given up, but was made relative through target returns which could be made more concrete. According to Herrhausen, the following could serve as concrete goals for long-term planning:

1. A certain absolute and relative profit.
2. A certain absolute and relative equity ratio.
3. Certain horizontal and vertical structures in the balance sheet and the profit and loss account.
4. A certain amount of total assets and business volume.

This set of objectives was enlarged for planning reasons to include certain competition- and stability-related criteria, which further enhanced the nature and meaningfulness of the planning figures. Further target figures within the framework of planning were assets and liabilities as inventory amounts, expenses and income as service-related amounts, and expenditure and revenues as liquidity-related monetary flows. In the 1970s, Mertin introduced the previously mentioned 'operating profit' as a main way of quantifying the bank's operative and strategic controlling and planning.

The use of figures from the accounting system, whose reporting had previously only looked back into the past, and their enhancement as target *planning* figures caused the bank's accounting functions to be expanded and put them in a position to monitor the achievement of these figures. This laid the theoretical and practical foundations of an integrated controlling system with planning, controlling and monitoring tasks.

The task of bank planning was to establish target figures, i.e. target returns calculated on the basis of planning figures. In addition to this, it offered the functional framework to simulate the effects of changes in data on chosen target figures using forecast calculations. Planning formed the starting point of each one of the bank's strategies. Through long-term planning and its further development, strategic planning, the longer-term goals of its actions were laid down. Operative planning figures were derived from strategic planning. The planning procedure moved more or less from the outside towards the inside. Forecasts on data concerning the market, competition and the national economy formed the set of figures within which strategic planning worked. Budgeted balance sheets, in particular, were the object.

An integrated system was developed institutionally in which decentralized interests could influence decision-making for a target return. Responsibility for devising and carrying out the plan was assigned to head office, which had the advantage of all business activities and organization units being strongly geared towards the strategic concept. In this way, the use of uniform planning methods could also be guaranteed and 'a proliferation of planning' – to quote Zapp – could be avoided. The integration of decentralized elements in the bank's planning concept occurred by incorporating decentralized decision-makers in the planning process. Particularly in the formulation and clarification of auxiliary conditions under which the target performance resulting from the planning was to be achieved, the decentralized units' market knowledge was taken into consideration.

The concrete organization of the institutionalized planning process at the bank at the start of the 1970s proposed the establishment of planning groups and planning representatives at the head branches who, together with a central planning department at the Frankfurt central office, would devise such plans and integrate, compress and extrapolate them. This procedure was intended to implement the planning process and the philosophy behind it throughout the bank and to make it acceptable. Nevertheless, the decision on planning results – especially for long-term planning – came under the board of managing directors' task area. Since the organization reform of 1990, strategic planning has been handled by the Group Strategy Department and operative planning by Controlling.

Only in the early 1970s did the bank also begin to introduce a system of *operative* planning. The one-year plan was to help break up the longer-term target performances into smaller, operational, periodic components. The task of devising and realizing the plans became the responsibility of the branches. They drew up a plan for the bank's interest business with its components loans and deposits and interest rates, for services business including securities business, foreign business, payments business and own-account trading, as well as administrative expense.

In the mid-1970s, the instrument of a regional market analysis provided branches with the information they needed to forecast business development on a more secure basis. On the basis of economic analyses, specific development forecasts were made for the first time for each individual market based on identical data to start with. These markets were not identical with branch areas, but were based on economic criteria.

The bank identified around 300 markets for corporate customers and roughly 1,200 for retail customers within West Germany. Both markets were related to each other inasmuch as the corporate customer markets' wider catchment areas covered the smaller catchment areas of the retail customer markets. A scale for the existing market shares was estimated from which concrete market targets were derived in conjunction with market potential. The market targets were converted into quantitative figures from the balance sheet and profit and loss account, so that the bank officer responsible for a particular market had an exact idea of its target. Performance targets were discussed with those responsible for each market in a two-dimensional manner; targets were agreed at both a regional level and a functional level (the branches in a region with the head of Corporate Banking for that region).

In addition to agreeing a profit target, planning measures (marketing planning) for the different business levels were worked out to tap new markets and develop existing ones in order to ensure that the financial targets were met. Operative planning basically meant profit planning. The basis of this planning was thus the profit and loss account, which was extrapolated using number systems and simulations.

2. Labour and capital: factors behind success

a) From personnel administration to international human resources policy

Banking is a personnel-intensive industry. Statements made by Deutsche Bank repeatedly emphasize how its success and competitive position are increasingly being shaped by the quality and know-how of its staff. Besides the *qualitative* aspect of personnel work, the importance of the bank's staff for its business success can also be illustrated in *quantitative* terms (Figure 5.1).

At the end of 1957, Deutsche Bank AG had total assets of around 8 billion DM and just under 17,000 staff. By the end of 1992 – within 35 years – the bank's total assets had increased by a good 40-fold to 334 billion DM at the parent company and to 496 billion DM in the Group, and the number of staff had risen more than threefold to 56,702 at the parent company and 74,256 in the Group. In 1993, the number of people employed by Deutsche Bank AG fell by 2,835. In the Group, the staff count in the same year was 73,176, and in mid-1994 it was 73,093, of whom 18,241 worked outside Germany. By far the largest share of the bank's administrative costs relates to personnel. Roughly two-thirds of administrative expenses are wages and salaries including social insurance contributions and pension benefits.

An attempt to highlight the main lines of development and new directions in the bank's personnel policy, and at the same time putting them in a time frame, reveals three phases:

- In the 1960s the accent was on personnel administration.
- The 1970s saw the onset of systematic personnel management and development.
- In the 1980s and early 1990s management training was intensified and personnel policy internationalized.

The classification is somewhat nebulous, as the introduction of personnel instruments also requires a certain lead time, as does a new direction in personnel policy.

The dominating functions and areas of activity in the bank's human resources in the 1960s can be illustrated by looking at central business developments and staff statistics. These years are characterized by the start of broad retail business. Linked to this is a considerable expansion of the branch network. This fundamental shift in business policy is reflected clearly in the parent company's staff

Figure 5.1 Development in the number of Deutsche Bank AG staff

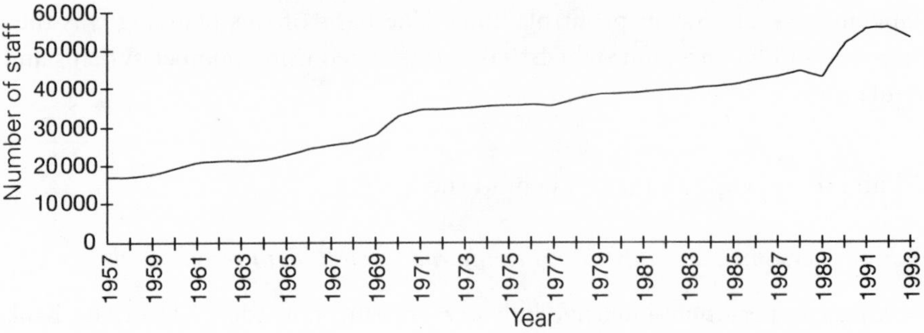

count, which rose by just over 73 per cent between 1960 and 1970, from 19,106 to 33,070 (Figure 5.1).

Staff policy was presented with the task of finding the necessary employees in a tight market where quality was at a premium. A problem directly related to the strong staff expansion was that of training and qualifying new staff; the bank had to employ a large number of untrained and inexperienced staff whose banking knowledge and skills were insufficient or non-existent. Hence, the training of new staff and workplace-specific qualifications became another focal point of personnel work in the 1960s.

It is also worth noting that in the 1960s the bank first started to employ part-time staff. In 1970 these amounted to almost 7 per cent of total staff (not including staff from representative offices abroad, trainees and temporary staff). In 1992, the proportion of part-time staff in the domestic bank was 12.2 per cent. This shows clearly that the hiring of part-time staff in the 1960s was far more important than in later years. Although the hiring of staff was motivated primarily by organizational and, ultimately, business requirements, in later years the expansion of part-time employment, especially for female staff, was driven primarily by personnel-policy considerations. The aim now was to make it easier for women to combine having a career with running a family.

Despite the growing problems of procuring and qualifying personnel in the 1960s – which, however, because of the largely simple nature of the work processes and tasks was usually limited to imparting purely workplace-specific knowledge and skills to new staff, and thus basically consisted of on-the-job training – human resources work in this decade primarily meant mere personnel administration. What was lacking was a systematic, self-contained staff development concept which included all staff. The predominance of administrative activities was reflected, among other things, in the fact that, at the time, the salary-calculation system provided the essential information and the basis for staff statistics and planning.

Staff policy in the 1960s is interesting from an institutional point of view in that, even after the merger of the three successor banks, responsibility for personnel policy was initially placed decentrally at the former central offices in Hamburg, Düsseldorf and Frankfurt. Although in the former western sectors of Germany staff decisions were co-ordinated among the three central offices so that a certain consensus was reached between the three, staff policy in the 1960s was characterized by the lack of a central personnel department which would take over responsibility for staff in the bank as a whole.

In view of the *decentralized* aspect of these staff responsibilities, the establishment of the head office Personnel Department in Frankfurt in 1969 signalled the start of a far-reaching reorganization within the bank in the 1970s. This can be described as the establishment of systematic personnel management and development. The major novelty here was that important human-resources functions were integrated into a uniform and self-contained staff management and development system. The most important measures here were the introduction of training schemes in 1971, the remodelling of the appraisal system in 1971, a staff planning system in 1973 and a special staff database in 1976, as well as the explicit formulation of the 'Principles for Staff Management' in 1980. This phase also saw the further development of the staff database into a computer-aided personnel planning and training system, which was not fully implemented throughout the bank until 1987.

These measures were aimed at putting personnel management and development on a bank-wide basis that was uniform and self-contained. This was intended to combine measures which had previously been pursued somewhat unsystematically and had been more or less unrelated to each other so that they could be better geared to the basic aims of staff policy and the use of staff management and development instruments could be better co-ordinated. This is also to be seen against the background of legislation: in March 1969 – a socio-political milestone – the Employment Promotion Act was passed by the German Parliament to prevent unemployment and promote vocational training; also in 1969 it passed the Vocational Training Act; in 1971 the new Federal Training Promotion Act regulated the promotion of secondary and tertiary education; in 1981, the Vocational Promotion Act replaced the Federal Training Promotion Act, which was declared unconstitutional.

The introduction of a training scheme was based mainly on the realization that, as a result of the shifts in the bank's business strategy, the *quantitative* aspect of staff procurement was becoming less important compared to the *qualitative* dimension. Whereas the number of staff dealing directly with customers was relatively low up to the late 1950s, and the number working in administration and bookkeeping was relatively high, this changed fundamentally in the 1960s as a result of the considerable expansion of the bank's branch network, its decision to commence retail banking and, not least, the increasing use of EDP.

The various departments in the bank were unable to cope, purely from a personnel point of view, with this shift in the bank's business policy aims. In view of the need to open new branches, it became a primary task for the bank's personnel strategy to train teams for this purpose, to instruct staff who had previously had administrative tasks in customer service and familiarize them with new services as well as provide specialists for EDP settlement. What was needed was a departure from a directly demand-oriented, primarily casuistic handling of short-term succession and deployment problems towards long-term, strategically driven personnel planning and staff training.

In the 1970s a further structural change took place in banking. This was characterized by business becoming increasingly international, by an expansion in the banks' range of services to make them into full-service financial institutions and by stepping up the introduction of new technology (the installation of terminals and electronic banking). These developments also had a direct impact on staff. First, there was a sharp increase in staff numbers. In spite of forecasts to the contrary based, among other things, on the assumption that the introduction of EDP would produce considerable rationalization effects and thus cause large numbers of staff to be laid off, the number of those employed in the banking industry increased as a result of the positive ongoing business development, whereas the number of those employed in other industries decreased. Second, these changes in banking brought about a shift in the quality of the work performed by staff and a qualitative change in the demands place on them. Above all, there was an increasing emphasis on the selling aspect, which had already become apparent in the 1960s and resulted mainly from the bank's commencement of retail business. On top of this, the 1970s and 1980s saw the market partially develop from a seller's to a buyer's market – at least in the eyes of the banking industry staff – and, as a result of this, the marketing philosophy of the consumer-goods industry was adopted.

In October 1966 the bank's first special sales seminar was held at its training centre in Jugenheim, with 30 members of staff taking part. Over the following years, many other seminars took place along the lines of this one, so that by 1976 some 20,000 members of staff had attended around 1,000 of these seminars. Moreover, the sharp increase in the need for training, caused by the expansion of the bank's branch network and its wider range of services, was covered by standardized seminars held in the branch regions, which were the responsibility of the department concerned – the sales seminar, for example, was run by the marketing and sales department.

In the late 1960s, however, it became increasingly evident that the growing volume of training and the various business activities in the different divisions made the systematization and centralization of staff development work inevitable. In mid-1969 Training was set up as a separate group within the central office Personnel Department; this took over the co-ordination of training in the years to follow. Although initially certain seminars continued to be held mainly independently of and parallel to seminars organized by the Training group and were hence less co-ordinated, the latter took on the task of designing a uniform staff development concept and implementing it throughout the bank.

One of the first results was the design of a training and staff development system which included all targets, principles and guidelines of staff development as well as the organization and systematic offering of training. At the same time, an overall staff development plan was in progress which was to record the medium-term need for staff. The personnel development system, requirement planning and past experience of practical staff development work formed the basis for the training centre in Kronberg, which from 1973 added substantially to the activities of the training centres in Jugenheim, Düsseldorf (David Hansemann-Haus) and Hamburg (Hermann J. Abs-Haus). This system, introduced in the 1970s, had two prime objectives that still apply today; firstly, to provide for all training needs for the many different tasks at all levels within the bank by developing staff members' skills and personalities and, secondly, if they are suitable candidates, to advance their careers.

What was basically different about this training scheme compared with the 1960s was that responsibility for the content and methods of training was transferred to the central office training group and that the training offered by the various branch regions and departments, which up to then had been mainly decentralized and unco-ordinated, was combined into a uniform training and development system. In addition, the basis for the bank's succession and personnel development planning and for staff members' personal career and development planning was created by the differentiation between various functional levels and the allocation of certain development measures to these levels. This was especially the case since the training system was designed from the start as a building-block system, so that the various seminars, workshops and other courses could be combined into training programmes and hence became modular components of individual training phases which ran for lengthy periods.

Whereas in the 1950s and 1960s on-the-job training was predominant and training independent of the workplace was rare, the new system underscored the importance of off-the-job training in seminars, behavioural learning, planning games, etc., but continued to give priority to practical training at the workplace. Training requirements were to be met whenever possible by a co-ordinated combination of on-the-job and off-the-job training. Hands-on programmes, acting as independent components of the training scheme, were intended to include the latest teaching/learning methods, rationalize learning processes, optimize staff learning skills, reduce the workload on staff in the departments and help staff to train themselves. Since the 1970s, this hierarchical staff development system has provided the bank with a training scheme which offers staff in all areas and at all levels in the bank substantial facilities for vocational training and career advancement.

The establishment of the management trainee scheme, which today remains a central element in the bank's basic training programme, can be seen in direct relation to the development of training in the early 1970s. This scheme goes back to 1966, when the first Management Trainee Group – consisting of two trainees – was set up. The Foreign Department was primarily in charge of this group, since it was realized very early on that the bank's internationalization, which had begun in the 1960s and was expected to increase, would lead to considerable demand for qualified staff – especially at foreign branches.

Only at the end of 1972 was the trainee group allocated to the central office Personnel Department and the unit responsible for the procurement, deployment and management of staff. This was linked to the philosophy that management trainees were provided mainly to meet the demand for personnel at central office. Today this has changed considerably, so that the scope of use for the management trainee programme is viewed much more broadly. In accordance with the increasing emphasis on managerial training in the 1980s, in 1986 the management trainee scheme became the responsibility of the unit responsible for the development of senior executives and management potential, which was now run as a separate group within the Personnel Department.

Basically, the management trainee programme is a personnel development instrument which is used only for university graduates, who are groomed for managerial positions by taking part in systematically planned, tailor-made and mostly short-term learning and activity phases in various functional areas. The predominant principle of training on the job was expanded off the job by internal and/or external measures, such as seminars, workshops and role-plays. Given the short period of training spent in each job, the management trainee bore little or no responsibility in his or her position.

At first, the management trainee programme's target group was almost exclusively graduates in economics, business and law. As a result of internationalization graduates from other disciplines – such as industrial engineers, computer scientists and mathematicians – as well as graduates with knowledge of particular languages (Arabic, Chinese, Japanese, Russian) have increasingly been hired since the early 1980s. At the same time, the number of law graduates among the management trainees has continually decreased. Whereas in the 1970s there was an average of 50 to 60 management trainees, by 1992 this group had been expanded to 382 (including branch trainees).

The staff appraisal system formed a further component of the staff management and development system introduced in the early 1970s. Until 1970, the bank did not have a uniform system; appraisals, which were normally given only for particular reasons – promotions, transfers or upon termination of employment – were made as free qualification reports. Almost simultaneously with the introduction of the training system, appraisal was also modified fundamentally to make it into a self-contained, uniform system of staff planning and development for the entire bank in conjunction with training, development and personnel planning.

The new appraisal system led to standardization of the reasons for appraisal.

In addition to the special reasons mentioned above, a regular appraisal was introduced, usually to be carried out every two years. There was also a considerable improvement in the standardization of the appraisal's content, with valuations based on a numerical scale – usually from 1 to 9. Each assessment was made easier to understand in that the individual value was explained by a brief description of what was expected. Through the inclusion of 23 pre-defined personality- and performance-related criteria, the staff appraisal was placed on a much sounder basis. It also allowed the appraisal to take account of the specific demands on staff at various functional levels of the bank. Involving staff in the appraisal process was also new, since the superior had to explain the appraisal to the employee personally, and the staff member had the opportunity to comment on the appraisal in writing.

This personal talk with the staff member has been a central element since the development of the appraisal system in 1978. However, the appraisal was now made up of only 17 criteria under the headings job performance, social behaviour, work results, development potential and staff management. This appraisal was based on a scale of 1 to 7. This system was especially important in terms of staff development, since basic data for quantitative and qualitative personnel planning were taken from the appraisal.

In 1973 the personnel management and development concept was supplemented by a special personnel planning system and was given the self-contained form which it has today. At this time, personnel was the responsibility of Horst Burgard, who headed this department until 1988. The introduction of this personnel planning system was initiated by two basic influences. Firstly, it reflected economic considerations, since the substantial rise in personnel costs and the greater demands made on staff qualifications highlighted the need for a systematic personnel plan from a quantitative and qualitative point of view. Secondly, it resulted from the growing importance of personnel planning in sociopolitical terms. Staff councils and trade unions saw it increasingly – over and above its formal establishment in §92 of the Labour Management Relations Act – as a suitable instrument to make human resources work more transparent, more continuous and smoother. On the other hand, the bank's personnel planning system enabled it to prove the necessity for certain personnel measures by providing the relevant documents. Prior to its introduction, there had been no overall planning of the bank's personnel; until 1973, the main basis for producing personnel statistics and individual aspects of human resources was the salary calculation system. As a result of the personnel planning system, this was expanded to include information on the qualifications of each staff member, their career in the bank, further training courses taken, appraisals and assessments of their potential by their superiors, etc.

The system was thus suitable not only for quantitative and qualitative personnel planning from the bank's point of view, but also – at least in part – for staff members' individual career planning. The bank developed this into an integrated system for personnel planning and development in the following years by setting up a personnel database and, subsequently, combining this with the staff planning system to form an integrated personnel planning and training system.

The personnel database was set up in 1976 in addition to the computer-based salary calculation system to provide a further EDP-aided information basis for staff administration and planning. It was designed as a mainframe solution, with processing in batch form. Its most important uses were analyses of the bank's staff headcount and fluctuation; *ad hoc* analyses were also possible.

From 1976 there was a growing realization that the personnel database would not be able to meet future requirements either in terms of its size or type of processing. Hence, in 1984 preliminary work began on the implementation of a new personnel planning and training system (PPT), and a pilot version was introduced in the Munich branch region. In 1986 the test run of this revised system was expanded, and one year later it was implemented throughout the bank. It combined and modified the personnel management instruments by linking the personnel planning system with the computer-based personnel data-base concept, and hence went well beyond the systems introduced in the early 1970s.

Over and above the components taken from the original system, i.e. manpower capacity planning, staff procurement and succession planning, the PPT system, which worked online with largely decentralized access authorization, has since 1987 aided the search for candidates, development planning and specific partial functions of personnel administration and reporting as well as seminar planning. If one takes an overall view of these instruments, it can be seen that their introduction in the 1970s has largely turned personnel management and develop-ment into a self-contained unit and can be regarded as *the* central reform in personnel policy during this decade. In this respect, the bank has shown itself to be the innovative driving force in German banking.

The 'Principles for Staff Management' which were formulated in 1988 and round off the set of personnel management instruments, are also to be seen in the direct context of the aforementioned instruments. In contrast to the procedures occasionally adopted by other companies, the bank decided not to stipulate concrete instructions for behaviour and, for the first time, put down on paper the management philosophy which up to then had simply been 'practised' and implicitly experienced.

At the heart of the Principles was the maxim that staff were to be given the opportunity, within their area of competence, to act largely independently and autonomously in order to fulfil the increasing demands for independence, per-sonal responsibility and self-development. The principle of common agreed targets corresponded with that of personal responsibility to enable the broadest possible mutual agreement between company and individual goals and hence a high degree of staff identification with their bank's goals ('management by objectives'). The aspect of control is, however, directly linked to giving staff their own room for manoeuvre: the possibility to act independently not only led to an increase in their rights – it also increased the responsibility of each individual.

From 1980 onwards, these Principles were given to every staff member with management responsibility, who were told to use them as a basis for their own management behaviour. Firstly, this was an appeal to managers' exemplary function; secondly, it was guided by the idea that managerial competence and qualifications should not only be measured by tangible business success, but also by to what extent executives manage, within their own area of responsibility, to groom competent managers for the future and promote their careers.

Although the employee representatives' potential involvement was considerably changed by the legislation on co-determination in the 1970s, the bank had already been trying to involve staff and their representatives at an early stage in many personnel, social and business arrangements – in so far as these concerned staff. The bank's objective here was to inform staff and their representatives on important business changes, and not to take measures concerning personnel policy without their agreement – or at least not against their wishes.

In the 1970s there was a large degree of *legal* regulation of co-operation between managers and employee representatives. Under the Labour Management Relations Act, a new staff council or steward was elected in April 1972 in 220 bank branches; on 16 June 1972, a general staff council was constituted. Under the Employee Co-determination Act of 1976 and the equal parity representation system anchored in the supervisory board, the voting in question took place in March 1978. The general youth and trainee representation was set up on 12 December 1988; in 1981 the Group Staff Council was set up; this was followed in 1990 by the Company and Group Committee of Spokesmen for Senior Executives.

Until the 1960s, the bank's vocational training was largely characterized by the dual system. Basic conceptual changes in its training were not made by the bank during this time. During the 1970s, however, there followed what in some cases could be described as fundamental changes in training which were primarily caused by far-reaching changes in the conditions governing the bank's work, i.e. the considerable influence exercised by the authorities and the state. At the start of the 1970s, training centres were set up in the area of every regional head branch, and these were run by experienced full-time instructors. In line with the bank's basic philosophy of largely decentralizing its personnel work, vocational training in the 1970s was mainly the responsibility of the regional head branches. Responsibility for vocational training in the regional head branches and subordinated branches was placed with the training centres there.

Only functions and tasks affecting other Group units which required central office, bank-wide approval came under the responsibility of the central office Personnel Department, more specifically the Training section or – after the restructuring of central office Personnel in 1986 – the Training Policy section.

The Training section was responsible for co-ordinating all training related to vocational training, evaluating the experiences of training centres and producing training materials, instructions and recommendations to promote and improve vocational training.

In the early 1970s a career aptitude test was introduced which was to provide a psychological basis for the selection process and considerably improve the quality of selections made. Almost simultaneously with the redesign of staff appraisal in 1971, a special appraisal procedure was introduced for apprentices. In the wake of the Instructor Suitability Order of 1972, the bank was faced with the additional problem of having to find a sufficient number of highly qualified instructors by 1975. Even today, it also makes use of seminars offered by external trainers, who induct its staff in labour law, didactics/methodology, psychology and youth studies.

Since the 1980s, the bank's personnel policy has followed two major paths: the expansion of management training and – in line with general economic developments – the internationalization of its human resources.

The growing importance of management training was reflected by the fact that in 1986, during a reorganization of sections within the central office Personnel Department, the section entitled Personnel Development for Senior Management and Management Potential was removed from the sections Training and central office Staff Procurement, Deployment and Management, and since then has been run as an independent section. The importance attached to management training was emphasized by extending the range of management training on offer and – of much greater significance – establishing special 'development pools'.

As early as 1978 the bank set up regional development groups to promote young qualified staff at regional level. These were joined in 1981 by the Regional and Supra-Regional Development Groups, and in 1987 by the EDP Development Group as a specialist development group. The Regional Development Group was established to meet the branches' need for qualified staff, which was anticipated to increase in the years to come. The Supra-Regional Development Group was set up to develop high-potential young staff. This was to present an interesting alternative to university and hence help to reduce the staff fluctuation among young, qualified bank employees – in the early 1980s the bank faced the problem that around 50 per cent of them left within five years of qualifying. In addition to this, the Development Group was intended to illustrate – in accordance with the principle that management positions should be filled, where possible, from the bank's own ranks – that staff with a bank apprenticeship had the same career opportunities as university graduates.

The Supra-Regional Development Group, like the management trainee group, was looked after by the central office Personnel Department. Training at the branches was done mainly on the job, supplemented among other things by seminars. Even with the introduction of the development groups, however, the bank could not sufficiently reduce the number of apprentices leaving for university after successfully completing their training, Therefore, in 1990 an additional training and development programme was instituted to give young staff members the opportunity to study at university after their bank apprenticeship and obtain a degree while gaining further vocational experience.

The bank's specific interest in offering special career opportunities to those trainees and young bank employees who, after their training, consider going to university, becomes even more comprehensible when one looks at the development in trainees' educational background between 1957 and 1992. The number of trainees with secondary-level qualifications decreased considerably, whereas those with university-qualifying exams almost continually increased and, at the end of 1992, stood at 71 per cent.

In addition to the intensification of young executive training, the internationalization of human resources and training were focal points of personnel policy in the 1980s. This became clear when, during a reorganization of the sections within central office Personnel Department in 1986, Staff Deployment and Development Abroad was separated from Domestic Staff Deployment and Development, and was run independently. Although the internationalization of the bank's personnel policy gained importance as early as the 1970s as a result of staff being delegated abroad, it became much more urgent following the strong expansion of the bank's foreign presence in the 1980s.

During the first phase of personnel policy internationalization, which took place between 1976 and the mid-1980s and can be seen as the 'pioneering age' of sending staff abroad, human resources and, in particular, delegation policy was limited almost completely to meeting the need for staff at the newly established foreign branches on a strictly short-term, case-by-case basis. The staff delegated were chosen more or less on an *ad-hoc* basis. In the late 1970s, the bank increasingly recognized the need to introduce some form of system into its delegation policy, development planning and the training of suitable staff. The second phase in the internationalization of the bank's human resources was thus marked by the introduction of systematic personnel training and development, whose aim was long-term staff development planning and specific training of staff for their subsequent deployment at foreign outlets.

In international secondment policy since the 1970s, the development and subsequent expansion of the bank's foreign branch network initially followed a strategy which entailed filling almost all commercial staff posts with expatriates, i.e. German staff sent abroad for a number of years. In subsequent years there was a clear reorientation as foreign staff came to be used more frequently, and today these make up the majority of staff at most foreign branches and subsidiaries. Correspondingly, in recent years there has also been a distinct localization of management at foreign subsidiaries and branches, and managerial positions have been filled, where possible, by local staff (Figure 5.2).

Figure 5.2 Deutsche Bank Group staff abroad

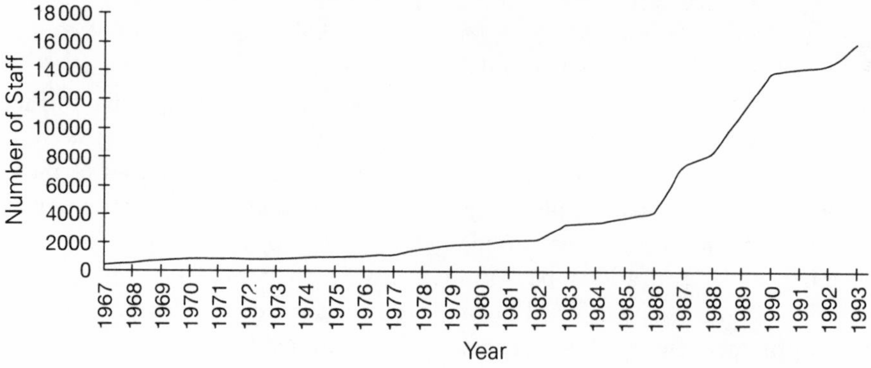

A further result of the internationalization of business was the growing recognition of the need to internationalize training. One of the first measures taken here was the introduction of an international reserve. This meant that in 1980 and subsequent years, a reservoir of staff was formed who were earmarked for deployment abroad and trained accordingly. The internationalization of personnel was also furthered by the start of international recruitment in 1985. First in New York and later in London, Italy and Japan, suitable staff – especially graduates – were recruited from the labour markets and earmarked for deployment at units abroad, but also throughout Deutsche Bank Group.

The bank took the necessary internationalization of training into account in two ways. Firstly, the increasing importance of international business was reflected in the content of domestic training courses; secondly, the bank established training centres at various foreign branches (Buenos Aires 1985, Singapore 1986, New York 1990). The fact that these seminars in Germany and abroad were open to participants from all over the world and the international nature of seminar topics reflected this new orientation. The globalization of personnel was also underlined by the setting up of the international staff exchange programme in 1986. This supplemented the bank's development groups and, in contrast to them, showed a much stronger international orientation. The bank established 100 positions at over 30 branches world-wide for this programme.

In 1989 it expanded the range of training offered at foreign branches by starting training seminars in London. The thinking behind this was that personnel development work in Europe could, in the long term, be conducted in such a way that vocational training at the various European locations could be combined into a uniform concept and thus lead to a qualification recognized equally by all European branches: the 'Euro-trainee' and the 'Euro-manager'.

The high regard for vocational training based on the German dual system – under which the company and school, as places of learning, complement each other perfectly – can be seen from the fact that the bank exported this system increasingly in the 1980s. At the beginning of 1980, vocational training was started by the central office Personnel Department at foreign outlets in the Group. This management training based on the German system was aimed at qualifying staff from around the world because the bank's staff deployment policy since the mid-1980s had sought to fill as many positions as possible in foreign centres with qualified native staff. In doing so, the bank aimed to achieve greater internationalization of its staff and more interdependence between its foreign outlets and the local markets.

Even if stepping up management training and internationalizing human resources and training were the prominent features of personnel policy in the 1980s, one should not overlook the bank's efforts in the mid-1980s to reduce youth unemployment – for which purpose the German parliament sanctioned a package of immediate measures in 1976 – and its activities to promote employment for women as further important aspects of personnel policy during this period. For sociopolitical reasons, the bank expanded its training capacities in the mid-1980s over and above what was required by its business. The bank's policy of taking on more trainees, together with the efforts of several other companies and institutions, made it possible to provide a number of young people with vocational training and, therefore, some sort of career prospect. The bank took its social responsibility very seriously. By increasing the number of trainees in the 1980s, it achieved its target of giving roughly 10 per cent of its permanent staff vocational training. As a consequence of this, there was a sharp increase in expenses for vocational training and further staff training during the 1980s (Figure 5.3).

At that time, the more modern view of women's role in working life was in the air. Hence, in 1981 women went to court to enforce their rights under §3 of the Basic Law; and the Federal Labour Court ruled in one particular case that female staff should receive the same excess bonuses as their male colleagues. The

Figure 5.3 Costs of vocational and advanced training at Deutsche Bank

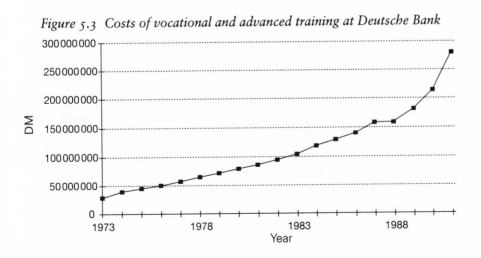

measures taken by the bank in this regard must be seen within the overall context of its personnel development, since it was not only meeting demands made by its female staff and taking into account sociopolitical changes but also pursuing direct personnel-policy objectives. The desire to retain in the long term the services of qualified female employees wishing to make a career break to look after a child stemmed from the experience that, without appropriate personnel policy measures, a large proportion of them would leave the bank altogether.

Personnel statistics show that, in recent years, the bank has been filling more highly qualified positions with women. In 1975 it employed three women in managerial positions. In 1992 there were 39. The number of female assistant vice presidents also rose from 16 in 1975 to 174 in 1992. It is particularly noteworthy that, since the appointment of Ellen R. Schneider-Lenné to the board of managing directors in 1988, there has been a woman in the bank's top management – a real rarity in the extremely conservative German banking industry, and unique among the big banks.

The absolute figures are relativized, however, when one looks at the percentage of female employees in the bank in relation to the total number of staff at a functional level. It then becomes clear that even today the majority of managerial positions are held by men. The opinion, often aired, that women hardly have equal career opportunities at banks is at least not disproved by such figures, even at Deutsche Bank. Many factors could be responsible for these empirically substantiated facts which are not exclusively due to either female employees or the bank.

In view of the increasing desire for women to have better opportunities to combine a career with having a family and growing demands for the equality of women and men in society and, particularly, in business, the bank formulated specific principles and guiding ideas for equal opportunities and better integration of career and family in an agreement between the board of managing directors and the Staff Council in 1990. This is to be seen within the context of all personnel development activities. The agreement, which applied to all domestic branches in the bank, had two main principles:

- 'The bank demands and advances equal achievement on the part of men and women.'
- 'The bank provides male and female staff members with the same facilities for the development of their individual talents and aptitudes.'

While these general principles were primarily aimed at creating equal opportunities in the bank, the agreement also contained concrete measures to improve the possibility of combining career and family. The bank's intention here was to reduce the fluctuation rate among female employees in order to have access to their qualifications later on. Experiences with this agreement between management and Staff Council showed a strong response to the schemes for working flexible hours and for taking statutory and extended childcare leave. Since statutory childcare leave was extended to three years in 1991, basically rendering the bank's facility invalid, the individual re-employment guarantees, subject to certain conditions, were replaced at the end of 1991 by the offer to extend the statutory childcare leave by one year.

Important implications and consequences for personnel arose from the start-up of business in the new federal states. In 1989/90, the number of staff in the Group rose by 11,972 to 68,552, the highest absolute increase within one year in the history of the Group. Decisive factors in this increase were the merger with Deutsche Bank-Kreditbank AG (8,518 staff), the inclusion of Morgan Grenfell Group (2,479 staff) and further increases in personnel at domestic and foreign subsidiaries. Despite this, in 1991 there were 5,589 resignations from the bank (excluding turnover of staff in Group companies). In relation to the average number of people employed, there was a total resignation quota of 11.4 per cent for 1991 (the previous year had 10.3 per cent). These figures show clearly that the bank reduced staff considerably in 1991 in the new federal states.

In taking over staff from Deutsche Bank-Kreditbank, the bank faced the problem that the majority were inadequate for a position in a widely diversified and international universal bank. Considerable efforts regarding basic and advanced training were needed to provide them with the necessary qualifications. A specific problem was also delegation policy, i.e. finding staff for the new branches. While at first many staff members declared their willingness to go to the new federal states, there were increasing problems in finding such persons subsequently.

The bank's personnel policy in the 1990s was geared towards the further development of those personnel management and development instruments which had already been introduced. Concurrent with the particular emphasis on talks between superiors and staff – the 'annual talk' was introduced for the first time – on the bank's business development and on the personal career development of staff, there was a new version of 'Principles for Staff Management'. With the new 'Guidelines and Objectives for Leadership and Co-operation' there was a shift in emphasis from staff management, in the sense of superiors managing staff, to the need for constructive co-operation between superiors and staff for the success of the bank's business. Once again, the Guidelines remained general platitudes. Hilmar Kopper celebrated their introduction in the staff magazine *Forum*: 'It is possible that some people may not view these Guidelines as the source of all wisdom. I believe, however, that such ambitious projects can only offer general solutions. What is important is that the Guidelines are brought to life ... They are meant to provide fixed points of reference at a time when Deutsche Bank is in many respects undergoing radical changes.'[11] And Ulrich Weiss comments in the same magazine: 'The Guidelines grew out of our corporate culture. They describe that culture, but at the same time they provide a stimulus for further development. To that extent they already form part of our corporate culture of the future.'[12]

A development which began to appear in the 1980s but which only really had an impact during the 1990s was the adoption of a marketing philosophy in personnel. Although the bank had been trying for years to have a direct influence on its image as an employer with current and potential staff, this intention was only reflected in the bank's organizational structure in mid-1991 in the form of a Staff Marketing Section within the head office Personnel Department. It was not the task of this section to initiate or realize any personnel marketing measures; its task was firstly to co-ordinate existing activities concerning the hiring of new staff, and only later to introduce new personnel marketing measures.

The radical organizational reform at the start of the 1990s also produced a new job and staff profile, which was outlined by Michael Endres as follows: 'Today we are trying to create the all-round workplace where jobs are completed in one step, where no paper is used any more, one medium is used and decisions are generally made more quickly ... Experience has shown that staff usually like such workplaces despite the great change. They like the greater freedom and room for creativity, they appreciate the higher value added and no longer feel like human interfaces between two programmed processes. This also means, however, that the kind of employee needed for this type of organization is different. Flexible working hours, more job rotation, diverse forms of training as well as team spirit and teamwork are necessary.'

Successful personnel work required continuous improvement and adjustment. This applied above all to management behaviour, since the shift in values made young staff more demanding. At the same time, however, emphasized Ulrich Weiss, the board member responsible for human resources, the bank had to step up its recruitment and training of high-potential young staff, as almost 50 per cent of all senior vice presidents and first vice presidents would have to be replaced by the end of the century owing to retirement. The grooming of excellent executive potential could be expressed in one sentence: 'You can't park high-quality young managers.' At least two to three candidates should be available for important assignments. What employees of the 1990s were looking for was more involvement, more responsibility, interesting work with scope for self-development, broad-based communication and information, scope for creative activity, and more freedom to structure their own working hours.[13]

Finally, a look at the bank's *top management* body, the *board of managing directors*. Since 1957 there have been between 9 and 13 members at any one time, with no particular system being evident. Their number is probably determined firstly by the number of business areas to be looked after, and secondly by personnel considerations. Board members' contract of employment stipulates that they must retire at the bank's first Annual General Meeting after their 65th birthday. Before a board member retires, a new one must therefore be appointed to maintain continuity within the board.

As at other big banks, Deutsche Bank also has the function of spokesman of the board of managing directors, sometimes also known as spokesman of the bank. At times, two members of the board of managing directors have shared this position. Karl Klasen and Franz Heinrich Ulrich succeeded Hermann J. Abs, who for over 10 years had been sole spokesman (also known to insiders as 'ruler of the board') and had exerted a dominating influence during this time. After Klasen became President of the Bundesbank and retired from the board of managing directors, Ulrich was sole spokesman and was succeeded by another 'tandem solution' with Wilfried Guth and F. Wilhelm Christians. When Guth became chairman of the supervisory board, he was succeeded by Alfred Herrhausen as spokesman, so that the bank again had two spokesmen until Christians retired in 1988. After the assassination of Herrhausen on 30 November 1989, it was decided that Kopper should be sole spokesman.

The question of whether the bank is better represented by one spokesman or two is a moot point. One undoubtedly important advantage of the 'tandem solution' is that two board members can share the additional workload. Moreover, the aspect of division of power can also be considered an advantage, since the fixation on one spokesman is avoided. The two-spokesmen solution has the disadvantage (perhaps merely theoretical) that it makes agreement and co-ordination between the two necessary. Apart from this, the division of the function of spokesman can lead to problems where interests diverge. The one-person solution also has the advantage that the board of managing directors and the bank as a whole present a more unified and integral front. The decision on the number of spokesmen also depends on the power factors in a body which – even if not visible externally – has many facets and is thus characterized by a multitude of diverse attitudes and ideas, self-images and self-assertion needs as well as different personalities.

The spokesman has always been elected by the board of managing directors itself and not, for example, by the supervisory board. This procedure underlines the spokesman's position as first among equals on the board; he is not chief executive officer in the real sense of the term. Much earlier, when hierarchical questions still played a substantial role, Arthur von Gwinner commented on this. In 1912 he wrote to the *Berliner Tageblatt* newspaper: 'With reference to your article yesterday ... I should kindly like to ask you not to call me general manager of the bank. Deutsche Bank has never had such a position and never will as long as I am a member of its board of managing directors. Our constitution is democratic.'

To what extent strong, highly competent personalities exercising the function of spokesman from an internal power base actually amount in terms of function and self-image to a chairman of the board of managing directors must remain open here. There is no reason to doubt this completely, since behind the modesty which the word 'spokesman' conjures up, there is hidden a whole array of duties and functions. For all the external display of good co-operation on the boards of managing directors at the big banks, it repeatedly becomes evident that the spokesmen play important roles. They are seen in the public eye as the real representatives of their banks.

While the spokesmen of the two other big German banks have evidently been the *de facto* chairmen of the board, at least from time to time, the position of Deutsche Bank spokesman has repeatedly been claimed to be 'merely' that of first among equals. This was apparent not only from the procedure for electing the spokesmen, and from the fact that the spokesmen earned the same as their board colleagues, but also in matters more to do with protocol. Whereas at the other big banks the spokesmen are usually listed in the Annual Report at the top of the alphabetic list of members of the board of managing directors, or are set apart in some other form, since its foundation in 1870 Deutsche Bank's board members have been listed alphabetically in most years. After 1957 only Abs, who 'could not be beaten' alphabetically, was named first; all subsequent spokesmen were listed in purely alphabetical order.

Even more than the way the spokesman is elected and how the board of managing directors presents itself outwardly, the board's working methods reflect its internal make-up. The board of managing directors follows the clear maxim that no majority decisions are taken; all decisions must be unanimous. Every member has the right of veto. According to Kopper: 'When we decide something at Deutsche Bank, we come up with one opinion that is shared by everyone. Some people call this a unanimous vote: I always say we never vote. We discuss. And if, at the end of the discussion, no one knows any better, we say: "That's it." ... Sometimes it is a consensus that has been achieved after a very hot debate. But it has worked for 120 years. It has served Deutsche Bank well.'[14]

It is worth noting that, of the 37 members of the board between 1957 and 1991, only five transferred directly from another company or institution to the bank's board of managing directors, namely Abs, Guth, Herrhausen, Craven and Schmitz. All others had held various positions in the bank or in the Group before their appointment to the board. This illustrates, even at the highest hierarchical level, that the bank usually tries to fill management positions from within its own ranks. The examples mentioned above prove, however, that it is also possible to switch from another company.

The internationalization of business also seems to have influenced the choice of members of the board of managing directors in recent times. Whereas experience abroad did not play a vital role from the 1950s to the 1970s, it has become increasingly important since the 1980s, the main examples being Cartellieri, Endres, Schneider-Lenné and Schmitz. In appointing Craven to the board of managing directors, the bank charted new territory as he was the first and so far the only non-German on the executive board of a big German bank.

b) Shareholders: divided and conquered

Relations between Deutsche Bank and its shareholders should be seen in terms of a social system. The history of its current shares, denominated in deutschmarks, began on 1 January 1952 with the first part-reunification of the former big banks.

The basis for the conversion of shares in the old banks into shares in the successor institutions was provided by deutschmark opening balance sheets. Deutsche Bank's equity capital was reduced from 160 million RM to 100 million DM (Norddeutsche Bank 20 million DM, Rheinisch-Westfälische Bank 40 million DM, Süddeutsche Bank 40 million DM). For old shares, worth a nominal 1,000 RM, shareholders received new registered shares in the successor institutions worth a total of 625 DM: one Norddeutsche Bank share worth 125 DM and one share in each of the other two institutions each worth 250 DM. Whereas domestic shareholders each received three new shares, there was a special arrangement for foreign shareholders: they were able to choose shares in *one* of the successor institutions.

In addition to the new shares, shareholders of the old bank received bank shares denominated in Reichsmarks in the amount of their original shareholding issued in 1952, which were also traded on the stock exchanges, albeit quoted in deutschmarks: so-called residual quotas. In 1957, when the three successor banks were merged, the absorbing institution raised its equity capital to 200 million DM in order to convert the shares of the two banks being absorbed. From 8 November 1957 to 7 February 1958, the registered shares in the three successor institutions were converted 1 for 1 into bearer shares in the remerged bank.

The amount of the bank's *equity* or *subscribed capital* as a central equity component has shown a sharp increase since then (Figure 5.4): it rose from 200 million DM in 1957 to 2.357 billion DM by the end of 1993. This enormous increase reflected the strong expansion in the bank's national and international business and represented one of the most important developments in the relations between the bank and its shareholders.

After the German Joint Stock Corporation Act was amended in 1965, the minimum par value of a Deutsche Bank share was lowered to 50 DM. In 1966 its shares were no longer quoted in percentages, but price per share. After the bank once again issued new shares at par during its capital increase of May 1966, in 1968 it started fixing the subscription price in line with the balance sheet price and, subsequently, approximating it to the market price. This change in subscription price formation was the subject of intensive public and media discussion. As a result of this the bank was able to realize considerable premiums so that, mainly in recent years, allocations to the capital reserve resulting from this have far exceeded the respective increases in subscribed capital. The fact that after 1968 the bank fixed the issuing price for new shares in line with the

Figure 5.4 Deutsche Bank's equity capital (subscribed capital)

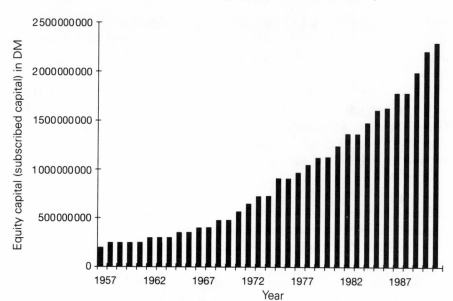

market price resulted in shares becoming increasingly 'heavy': whereas, with the capital increase of 1968, the issuing price for a share with a par value of 50 DM was 125 DM, in 1989 new shares were issued at 600 DM. Today, Deutsche Bank shares are among the most heavily traded equities on the German stock exchanges, and options on them are among the most briskly traded derivatives on the DTB (German computerized futures and options exchange).

In addition to external capital procurement, on average around one-quarter of equity capital was gained by retaining profits as part of the bank's self-financing. Accordingly three-quarters of the equity capital was provided by shareholders. Of interest here is the decrease in subscribed capital as a proportion of 'hard' equity, and hence the increasing importance of disclosed reserves for the bank's capital and reserves (Figure 5.5). Whereas fixed equity capital made up roughly half of total core capital in 1957, by mid-1994 it accounted for 12.3 per cent.

With this development, however, the bank remained clearly within the parameters of an international structural norm, which was rational but hardly justifiable and stipulated that the ratio of disclosed reserves – which were 16.778 billion DM in mid-1994 – to subscribed capital – 2.363 billion DM in mid-1994 – should be at least 1 to 1. In addition to the bank's growing self-financing, this development stemmed mainly from its ordinary capital increases, which were increasingly carried out at high premiums. That this was regarded very critically by the shareholders is shown, for example, by the comments of a shareholder at the 1981 General Meeting: in fixing the conditions for the capital

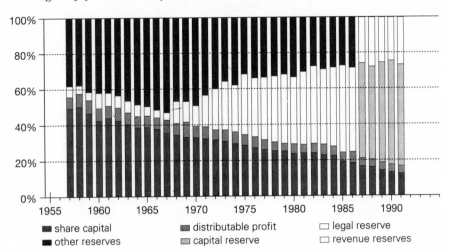

Figure 5.5 Structure of Deutsche Bank's 'hard' equity (core capital)

increase, he claimed, the bank had followed the principle of 'dole it out and rake it in again – or even double the amount'.

As a result of the German banks' inherent tendency to try to conform as far as possible with group-specific equity ratios, however, they regarded the equity ratios as more important than the *absolute* amount of equity. Deutsche Bank aimed to avoid an equity ratio of under 5 per cent, which is internationally considered to be insufficient. Whereas in the 1960s the bank managed to meet this standard for the most part, this ratio did not quite keep pace with the bank's expansion of business in the 1970s. As statutory requirements increased, the ratio only improved again in the 1980s. In 1991 the bank had a 'core' equity ratio of just under 6 per cent, which is considered sound.

To offset potential losses the bank also had substantial undisclosed reserves as hidden equity components, which resulted from the almost infinitely admissible and practised technique of underpricing assets and overpricing certain liabilities and were not externally visible. The extent of these reserves remained – like the 'real' income situation – top secret. A question on this subject put by a shareholder at the 1986 General Meeting was shot down by Herrhausen with the reply that information on undisclosed reserves had never been publicized and that they would lose their character if they were discussed. Abs referred programmatically to the necessity of building up undisclosed reserves at the last General Meeting of the predecessor Süddeutsche Bank in 1957:

'Accumulating undisclosed reserves in preparation for economically hard times seems to us to be very important. Similarly, it serves the continuity of banking business and hence the shareholders' interests, as well as the economy as a whole. The banks must help to cushion possible losses in the case of an economic depression and to soften damaging repercussions on the general economic development. We cannot allow the level of business, which has been good for a long time now, to strengthen the illusion that there will never be losses in the future. To avoid possible recourse by banks to reported liable capital is one of the things which must be the ambition of any banker, if only because of the unfavourable psychological consequences of such a step.'

Just how correct this way of thinking was – not only in the reconstruction phase of the reunified bank, but also in the long-term future – was reflected not least by the international debt crisis of the 1980s which, despite the previously unheard-of scale of the risk, passed over the bank's creditors and shareholders without a trace as a result of its undisclosed-reserves policy, if one disregards the fact that 'throwing good money after bad' did not leave anything for higher profit distributions to shareholders or higher interest payments to investors. This was a point of view which, although articulated in public, was dismissed by the banks as 'academic', in line with their traditional attitude towards such a policy, which ran counter to their striving for conformity. In an attempt to make things look better, Guth commented at the 1982 General Meeting: 'In any case, shareholders don't "lose out", since value adjustments and provisions become free again and are then available more or less as income in the profit and loss account. Our crisis provisions will not go off.'

As far as changes in subscribed capital are concerned, mention should also be made of the increase resulting from the exercise of option and conversion rights by shareholders. In 1977 the bank issued its first bond with warrants: a 4.5 per cent bond for the Compagnie Financière de la Deutsche Bank AG, Luxembourg, for $125 million. At the 1977 General Meeting, Guth justified this issue by mentioning the growing volume of international business, which was to be refinanced by this bond. The range of instruments used by the bank to finance itself was again enlarged at the beginning of 1991 with the advent of participatory certificates with warrants.

Even in 1984 Christians, the 'promoter of equities', pointed out that participatory capital had the disadvantage that the holder of participatory rights bore the same risks as a shareholder, but without having the same powers and without being able to exploit the growth opportunities attached to shares.

Herrhausen's statement at the 1981 General Meeting made clear that the bank was still very ambivalent towards participatory rights: 'In the past we have not been great advocates of using participatory certificates to procure capital for banks. We have also stated this clearly. We are still not great advocates of participatory certificates. Only we cannot avoid utilizing the same opportunities for raising capital as our competitors.' In 1991 the bank therefore issued bearer participatory certificates with warrants totalling 1.2 billion DM, which fulfilled the requirements of §10(5) German Banking Act regarding liable equity capital. In mid-1994 it had 2.7 billion DM of participatory capital. At the same time it also had subordinated liabilities of 4.250 billion DM (Group figure 5.489 billion DM), which also counted as 'soft' equity capital.

The listing of the bank's share on major international stock exchanges became increasingly important for its relations with its shareholders during the 1970s and 1980s. The accompanying internationalization of the bank's shareholder base after its share was listed on the Paris Stock Exchange – in 1994 it was officially quoted on eleven foreign stock exchanges – is to be seen within the context of its business becoming more international. The listing of its share in Paris in 1974 was followed by listings in Vienna (1975), Zurich, Basle, Geneva (1975), Amsterdam (1976), London (1976), Luxemburg (1978), Brussels, Antwerp (1978) and Tokyo (1989). The success of these stock market listings and other efforts to achieve a broad international placement of the bank's share was reflected by the promotion of the bank's subscribed capital in foreign ownership. Whereas in 1970 the proportion of share capital in foreign ownership was 4.5 per cent for equity held in custody by the bank and at least 10 per cent including shares held in other banks' custody, by December 1991 the figures had risen to 12.3 and 48 per cent respectively.

As far as relations between the bank, as a very big public limited company, and its shareholders are concerned, the shareholder structure is also interesting. It can be seen here that the number of private shareholders has increased sharply since 1957. Particularly in the 1970s and in 1987, the bank saw this group increase substantially: their number rose from 121,312 in 1973 to 312,500 in 1987; after this, however, they decreased slightly. At the end of 1991 the bank had 300,300 private shareholders.

There was a changeable development in the number of *institutional* and corporate shareholders. After 9,688 in 1973, it decreased considerably: in 1983/84 only 2,000 institutional investors held shares in the bank, although this number increased again in the late 1980s. In 1990/91, however, there was again a noticeable reduction from 7,300 to 5,700; by 1993 this had risen again to 6,800.[16]

Wage and salary earners among the shareholders had a major impact on this development from 1973 to 1990, since their number increased disproportionately: whereas in 1973 there were 46,750 shareholders in this group, by the end of 1993 there were 167,400. A similar development can also be seen in the number of pensioners and retired employees among shareholders: this increased from 9,212 in 1973 to 45,000 in 1991.

The proportion of private shareholders rose from 92.6 per cent in 1973 to 98.1 per cent in 1991. The fact that the group of wage and salary earners contributed considerably to this can be seen even more clearly in percentages than in absolute figures: they rose from 35.7 per cent in 1973 to 48.3 per cent in 1991. The proportion of pensioners and retired employees rose from 7.03 to 14.7 per cent. The proportion of institutional shareholders decreased sharply in this period from 7.4 to 1.9 per cent. Two opposing developments contributed to this overall trend. On the one hand, the proportion of industrial and trading companies among shareholders decreased from 5.3 to 0.9 per cent, although at the start of the 1980s their proportion was even lower, at 0.6 per cent. On the other, the number of investment companies rose from 121 to 1,250 in 1991, so that their proportion increased from 0.09 to 0.4 per cent.

The various shareholder groups' proportion of total Deutsche Bank shareholders is in some cases significantly different to their share in the bank's capital: although *institutional* shareholders made up only 1.9 per cent of shareholders in 1991, they held 51.5 per cent of subscribed capital; conversely, although 98.1 per cent of shareholders were *private*, their share in the bank's capital was only 48.5 per cent (Figure 5.6).

Figure 5.6 Shareholder groups and their shares in Deutsche Bank's equity capital

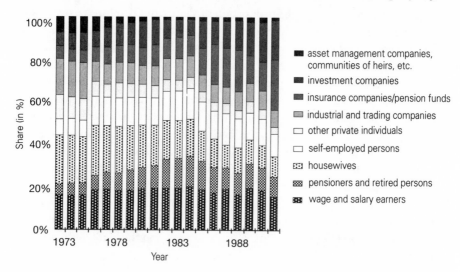

As with other German banks, Deutsche Bank's *dividend policy* is characterized by the basic principle of *consistency*. The payment of bonuses in 1967, 1969 and 1985 suggests that the bank only increased its dividend if it could assume, after estimating its income, that it would be able to pay this increased dividend in the years to follow (or also if there was no better way of 'hiding' profit to be disclosed, despite its various attempts at window dressing). Whenever this expectation appeared too uncertain, the bank seemed to favour the instrument of paying bonuses.

This is also clear from the fact that the payment of bonuses – in addition to cash dividend payments – was always motivated by extraordinary events. In 1967 the bonus payment resulted from the fact that the Federal Constitutional Court ruled that the branch tax was unconstitutional. The reimbursement of tax already paid by the bank up to 1967 was passed on to its shareholders in the form of a bonus of 2 DM. In 1969 the bonus of 3.5 DM was also induced by a particular event: the bank was just approaching its centenary. The high bonus payment of 5 DM in 1985 resulted from considerable revenue which the bank had earned from the Flick transaction (pp. 594–5, 629–30, 687–8). In 1994 tax savings resulting from the Business Location Act were passed on.

Following the public debate on employees' wealth formation, particularly of productive capital, and the (increased) efforts to promote equities in the 1970s, the bank issued staff shares for the first time in 1974. For a price of 115 DM – the market price at the time this resolution was adopted being 230 DM – staff were able to buy two staff shares each with full dividend entitlement for 1974. Although these shares could not be sold until the end of 1978, many staff members availed themselves of this offer, a total of 64 per cent buying staff shares.

Since then, the bank has offered new staff shares every year. For tax reasons, the subscription price is always 50 per cent of the shares' market price at the time it is decided to issue them. The number of shares that may be bought depends on how long the member of staff has worked for the bank. In order to prevent the immediate sale of these stock options, which are bought at a preferential price, the bank blocked their sale for a certain period: up to 1985, the end of this period was 31 December of the fourth calendar year after the year of issue; since 1985 it has been 31 December of the fifth calendar year. The bank also makes a similar offer to the staff of its domestic subsidiaries. Retired bank staff are also entitled to purchase a smaller number of such shares.

Acceptance of this offer is high: with the exception of 1974, the purchase ratio has been between 70 and 80 per cent. This response, which has been high in comparison to companies from other industries, can mainly be explained by the fact that bank staff are more familiar with shares than staff from non-banks. This probably also explains the discrepancy between the old and the new German federal states. In 1991 the offer to purchase staff shares was accepted by 73.6 per cent of staff in the western federal states, but by only 57.3 per cent in east Germany.

The reason for the substantial decline in the proportion of staff exercising stock options in recent years is probably that the subscription price of these shares has risen considerably since 1985. The proportion of staff shareholders among the bank's total shareholders rose from 17.1 per cent in 1975 to almost 19 per cent in 1986, and decreased again to around 15 per cent in the late 1980s. These high rates are, however, put in perspective by the percentage of staff shareholders in the bank's total share capital: whereas their share in 1977 was only 1.1 per cent, this rose at first in the 1980s to 3.9 per cent and then decreased again to 2.6 per cent in 1991.

In examining the relations between Deutsche Bank and its shareholders, one should also mention the introduction of the maximum voting right where it is not absolutely necessary, for this is a construction which contradicts the basically democratic principle of a joint stock company. At the 1975 General Meeting, Ulrich commented on this, saying that the limitation of voting rights to 5 per cent of the bank's share capital 'is intended to maintain the traditional structure of the bank as a public company in future. The supervisory board and the board of managing directors are convinced that it would not be in the interests of either the bank or its shareholders if a major shareholder were to have an influence on the fortunes of the institution. Also, in the interests of the economy as a whole, a wide and constantly expanding shareholder group with no person or group holding a controlling position seems to be correct and desirable ... The property and assets of our shareholders will not be affected by our proposal. The bank's shares are widely spread among roughly 168,000 shareholders. 5 per cent of the bank's share capital, which has been increased to 900 million DM, represents a value of over 250 million DM. We are not aware of a share capital of anywhere near this amount. Thus our shareholders do not lose any voting rights; they gain additional protection.' This was not seen as very convincing.

Although public criticism was considerable, the bank managed to ensure that the introduction of the maximum voting right was passed by the General Meeting, as usual by a large majority, since the institution of proxy voting rights on Deutsche Bank shares – exercised by representatives of the bank itself and 'associated' institutions – had proved itself once again. However, the fact that this measure was 'only' adopted with 94.28 per cent of votes represented, a majority substantially lower than the usual voting results at the bank's General Meetings, indicates that the decision at the 1975 General Meeting – and not only at this one – was highly controversial. It should also be pointed out that, in the case of a dispute, the goals envisaged by Ulrich could not have been achieved anyway by using the maximum voting right. However, it also seems significant that at the same time, maximum voting rights were also introduced at other joint stock companies where the bank was represented on the supervisory board – usually as chairman – and held an equity stake in the company.

The maximum voting right remained a subject of discussion, and its abolition was often demanded by many shareholders. However, the board of managing directors always defended its existence, as did Herrhausen at the 1989 General Meeting, although even he had no new arguments: 'We have not considered dropping our maximum voting right. That this is not in line with the current situation arises from the fact that neighbouring institutions are looking at introducing a modified maximum voting right to enable them to fend off hostile takeover bids. We will not give a general recommendation to introduce a maximum voting right to prevent hostile takeovers. This is not advisable for the very reason that every individual case is different, and a general rule might not be applicable to each individual case. The introduction of a maximum voting right is, at best, one of a number of methods that can be used to fend off hostile takeovers.'

Against the background of the discussion on voting-right restrictions at German companies which resurfaced in the late 1980s, a more liberal position was intimated in Kopper's speech at the bank's Annual Press Conference on 29 March 1990: 'In a market economy, the maximum voting right basically represents an alien philosophy. Before it can be discarded, there must be more transparency in the anonymity of shareholder structures so that investors will be able to recognize changes and the intentions of potential takeover parties at an earlier stage. There is a chance of achieving this in the foreseeable future.'

Despite the initial signs here of a rejection of the maximum voting right – a shift from the original position at the time of its introduction was evident – its abolition was only decided at the 1994 General Meeting. The reason given for this late about-turn was the duty to disclose participating interests as laid down in the Second Financial Markets Act. Although the reason for previously maintaining maximum voting rights had been to prevent hostile takeovers, the new law provided little protection here – at best, takeover intentions had to be indicated earlier on. Hence the law was seen as a welcome opportunity to abolish voting-right restrictions. The real reason is likely to have been the bank's guilty conscience as a protagonist of the market economy – especially at a time when other German companies were also getting rid of their voting-right restrictions.

A similar problem was the exclusion of the bank's shareholders' subscription rights in capital increases, since this also curtailed their rights in a manner which ran counter to the market economy. Capital increases with subscription rights were clearly in the majority. Subscription rights were only excluded for two specific purposes: to issue staff shares and to place shares abroad. A placement in Japan of shares totalling 60 million DM, which was linked to the listing of Deutsche Bank's equity on the Tokyo Stock Exchange, was carried out using the 75 million DM of capital authorized by the 1987 General Meeting with the exclusion of shareholders' subscription rights.

When in 1991 authorized capital of a nominal 75 million DM – again for a share placement abroad – was resolved with the exclusion of subscription rights, the German Association for the Protection of Securities Holdings contested the decision which had been passed, as usual, by an overwhelming majority, mainly thanks to the proxy voting rights of the bank and associated banks. The Association initiated a test case on behalf of three of its members at the Frankfurt Regional Court. The case was dismissed. The judges ruled in favour of the bank's argument that the exclusion of subscription rights only referred to the modest amount of 3.4 per cent of subscribed capital. Moreover, a decisive factor was that the bank had expressly stated at the General Meeting that the issue price of the new shares would be determined by the market price at the time and that a deviation of only 1 per cent maximum would be tolerated to protect shareholders against their assets being diluted. None the less, the Frankfurt Higher Regional Court agreed with the plaintiffs: it ruled that the exclusion of subscription rights was inadmissible because it was not clear to what extent the bank actually intended to be present on foreign markets and what volume of shares the bank would need on the various stock markets in order to achieve its objectives. The successful appeal against the exclusion of subscription rights meant that the entire capital increase resolution was null and void.

A further development in the relationship between the bank and its shareholders concerns changes in investor relations. For some time this had largely been restricted to institutional investors. Starting in the 1960s teams were set up to cultivate and develop relations with selected investors who, because of the capital they held or managed, were important to the bank. An attempt was made to meet the specific information needs of this group over and above the information distributed to the general public by means of advisory talks, presentations and special publications.

In the early 1980s a special project was initiated to improve General Meeting attendance. By writing to shareholders directly, the bank aimed to awaken their interest in specific business-policy decisions facing the bank and to motivate them to exercise a direct or at least – in the form of proxy voting rights – indirect influence on decisions made at the General Meeting. This was intended to raise attendance, which in some years had fallen dramatically. After it had decreased markedly between 1966 and 1979 – from 76 to 61.5 per cent – there was a further rapid decrease in capital represented at the General Meetings in 1979 and 1980: within one year, attendance fell from 61.5 to 52.1 per cent. As a result of the measures taken to improve attendance in the early 1980s, the proportion of capital represented rose again from 52.1 to 66.9 per cent within three years. Since the mid-1980s, however, this has decreased again sharply.

If one looks at the number of shareholders or shareholder representatives present at the General Meetings, shareholders' lack of interest in directly influencing resolutions becomes even clearer. A total of 412 shareholders and shareholder representatives attended the 1967 General Meeting. Although the rising attendance in the following years seems to indicate a growing interest on the part of shareholders in 'their' bank – at the 1970 General Meeting there were over 1,100 and in 1990 almost 4,500 – the response actually remained very low in relation to the total number of shareholders. In spite of the higher number of participants than in previous years, less than 1.5 per cent of a total of 306,000 shareholders were present at the General Meeting in 1991.

Apart from the realization that small and medium-sized shareholders could not influence events anyway at General Meetings, another reason for the large decrease in attendance after 1965 was the increasing internationalization of the shareholder base, which had been furthered by the bank itself. Since foreign shareholders only had a small interest in taking part in General Meetings in Germany, it was only understandable that the increasing placement of the Deutsche Bank equity abroad would have consequences for General Meeting attendance.

As a consequence of its growing number of shareholders – particularly abroad – and the resulting necessity for the bank to cultivate its relations with them, the bank finally saw the need, in November 1988, to set up an Investor Relations Department at central office to systematize and co-ordinate its dealings with its shareholders. Moreover, this department was designed to enhance the international profile of the bank and the Group as a whole, and to facilitate a better understanding of their policies. Investor Relations was made part of the Communications division, since its work required close co-operation with the other departments responsible for shaping the bank's image as part of their communication strategy. Responsibility on the board of managing directors lay with the spokesman.

The target groups of Investor Relations were shareholders, investors, fund managers and, above all, analysts from investment banks, brokers, rating agencies and other banks which give investment advice. Its activities focused not so much on satisfying short-term information needs as on maintaining an ongoing dialogue in addition to the General Meetings and other regular but less frequent road shows and presentations to establish, shore up and strengthen confidence and commitment towards the bank through more regular and closer contacts. By improving communication with institutional investors and analysts, Investor Relations was to enhance the bank's position in the awareness of national and international capital market players and to improve access to new markets. The bank saw the major guiding principles of its communications and investor relations as being the need for reliability and credibility.

The main instrument of Investor Relations is the Annual Report. Since 1988, the bank has been making greater efforts to improve the design of the Report to suit investors – in addition to its function as an instrument of the bank's corporate identity and public relations. By making full use of the reporting scope allowed by statutory requirements, it tries to present itself individually and to show its shareholders an unmistakable profile. For this reason it is understandable that its investor relations strategy should be incorporated into its overall communications strategy. Between 1986 and 1992 the bank also published an annual review in English, which was aimed mainly at foreign investors and analysts and provided information on the business policy of the bank and the Group. On top of further print media, presentations, press conferences, business meals and round-table discussions with selected participants play a large role in investor relations.

It is clear from this outline of the functions performed by investor relations that the bank is not following a completely new path but is reverting to activities related to traditional investor relations which in some cases have been used for some time. One new aspect, however, is that this department ties the bank's investor relations into a uniform communications concept and co-ordinates them with other public relations activities. However, even the concept of investor relations has only managed to a certain extent to intensify relations with private, small and medium-sized investors.

3. Deutsche Bank in its economic and social environment

a) Criticism of the power of banks – Deutsche Bank's position

Owing to their continuing relevance over several decades, the discussions on 'the power of banks' show, on the one hand, the possible forms of social and political criticism with regard to banks' activities; on the other hand, they also show a change in the form of Deutsche Bank's internal and external communication on this question, from initially cautious statements to pro-active, public statements.

This subject has increasingly featured in public debate since the big banks reamalgamated in 1957/58, and has led repeatedly to suggestions as to how their power could be limited by legislation. Their power potential was mainly seen in the peculiarities of the German universal banking system, which was also exposed to criticism aimed at fundamental change. This whole complex took on new dimensions in the late 1960s through the politicization of this discussion and proposals for the nationalization or 'socialization' of the banking sector. Apart from this, potential problems were certainly hidden behind the general criticism of the banking system in regard to the mass of retail customers. The indisputable conflicts of interests inherent in any universal bank can, without 'fault' ever having to be proved, lead to a bank being able to organize its business activities in individual cases at the expense of customers with *less* influence.

The discussion became more urgent following reports from the Monopolies Commission, which have been published every other year since 1976 and examine the level of corporate concentration in the Federal Republic and its foreseeable development from an economic and competition point of view. Also in relation to the power of banks, in 1992 the Social Democratic Party in the German Parliament called for the abolition of the banking industry's privilege under the Restraint of Competition Act ('Exception', § 102).

The discussion also gathered momentum when the cross-shareholding between Dresdner Bank and Allianz AG, which was seen as having enormous potential power, caused the Federal Cartel Office to examine its effects on competition. In this context, the President of the Federal Cartel Office described a conceivable link between Deutsche Bank and Allianz as the 'greatest possible catastrophe' from an anti-trust point of view, whereas the actual link with Dresdner Bank was a 'smaller catastrophe'.

Deutsche Bank became involved in another direct conflict with the anti-trust authorities around the same time at the bank's 1992 General Meeting when Kopper, in reply to a shareholder's question on the base rate for savings deposits, retorted that the bank would consider raising it when the savings banks, as the market leaders, did the same. Massive criticism was forthcoming from the public banking sector, and an official inquiry was made by the Federal Cartel Office to Deutsche Bank's spokesman. He was asked whether there was an anti-trust arrangement or a market-dominating position with respect to demand for savings deposits at statutory notice, as a result of which Deutsche Bank – in accepting a leading position for the savings banks – would be prevented from making an independent decision to raise the base rate on savings deposits. This conflict between Deutsche Bank and the Federal Cartel Office, with the latter asking the former to clarify its interest rate policy, continued for some time.

The discussion about the power of the banks within the business community was also intensified most recently in 1993 with respect to their profit situation and earnings policy. Although the Bundesbank reported new record earnings year after year at the banks, which were still reducing their staff, the recession led to losses and redundancies in many other industries. Kopper commented: 'Unfortunately there is much prejudice, misjudgement and demagogy in public feeling towards the banks. The media and partly politicians, too, are trying to turn the banks into the whipping boys of the 1990s.'[17]

The attempt to retrace the sources and results of the 'cyclical' power discussion reveals that sensational financial transactions – such as Flick's sale of its Daimler package to Deutsche Bank in 1975, or the merger of Daimler and Messerschmitt-Bölkow-Blohm in 1986 – have often caused the issue to re-emerge and attract attention.

As the largest German universal bank, Deutsche Bank has naturally always stood at the centre of public criticism with respect to the power question, since its comprehensive portfolio of industrial holdings as well as the other features constantly mentioned with reference to banking power seem to be particularly evident in its case: supervisory board mandates, proxy voting rights and self-representation at its own General Meetings, conflicts of interest between lending, deposit and securities business along with the aggregation of these characteristics, and insider information. Consequently, the negative effects of this criticism had a particular impact on the bank's image.

As a result, statements were made by representatives of the bank in which they set forth their position – not always with the most fortunate of arguments – on the points used in public discussion as evidence of the power of banks. In a lecture to the Frankfurter Gesellschaft für Handel, Industrie und Wissenschaft in 1974, Guth commented in no uncertain terms on this issue. Referring to the 'sterile, clichéd discussion', he preferred to speak of the bank's 'responsibility' rather than 'power' in the sociopolitical discussion. To illustrate this he cited 'the bank's support of economic goals and helping wealth formation ... the bank's support of large public financing tasks, such as infrastructure, regional support ... environmental protection and energy supply'. The bank's responsibility towards society, according to Guth, also included 'broader public relations work in the sense of disseminating information about the bank's role in our economic system, eliminating mistakes and getting rid of prejudice'. Guth also commented on the 'real or supposed conflicts of interests between banks and customers ... However, it is wrong to believe that the banks could wield power over healthy companies by denying them loans. One only has to look at the competition to realize that this assumption is not true. Equally absurd is the idea that banks could force loans on to companies that really needed capital . . . When universal banks are criticized, the supposed conflict between securities advisory business and the bank's own interest is repeatedly exaggerated . . . Competition prevents these conflicts from arising.'[18] It was well known that the conflict existed for systemic reasons. The question was how to solve it, and this was ultimately accepted by the bank when, reacting to specific internal cases, it became the first German institution to set up a Compliance Department. In 1994 the Second Financial Markets Act concerning securities trading sought for the first time to impose statutory control on the insider trading problem and the issues surrounding 'Chinese walls' in the banks' securities business.

In a lecture in 1979, Herrhausen analysed the discussion of banks' power more realistically, but also took a firm 'official Deutsche Bank' position:

'The idea that the German banks have power has become a popular theory. It seems that it needs no further proof to gain credence everywhere. The criticism of this power even unites those who otherwise have nothing or very little in common . . . Of course banks have power. Anyone who denies that is not telling the truth. But . . . having power is not the same as abusing power . . . We never seek to obtain and keep equity participations in the form of deposits, only by using our own funds, i.e. within the scope of our equity capital . . . We never try to gain a majority holding in a company and, finally, we neither want nor are we able to assume responsibility for other companies . . . Banks do not control supervisory boards. This was established in 1970 in the Co-determination Commission report . . . We are not clinging to the proxy voting right. But if you abolish it, you have to put something better in its place.'

Over and above this objective analysis, however, Herrhausen also took a self-critical view of the way banks presented themselves, especially in this discussion:

'We are better than people think. But it seems sometimes that many people don't know this . . . It has something to do with the way we portray ourselves and how we communicate with our environment. I don't think we've hit the right note yet. Perhaps we are still too much an institution and not sufficiently personal. Perhaps there is not enough naturalness, directness and joy in our approach. Some things appear to me to be too perfect and too sterile. Our advertising probably puts too much emphasis on what we can do for our customers, and too little on what our customers can do for us. The slogan "Ask Deutsche Bank" is undoubtedly a good one, but we should see it more as a call to assist each other – more along the lines of "Let's talk".'

At the 13th German Banking Congress in 1979 – though in his capacity as President of the German Banking Association – Christians expressed similar thoughts and concluded that banks had not done enough to enlighten the public, or in the political sphere, to highlight the positive aspects of this system and the contribution made by the banking industry. On the one hand, representatives of the bank admitted quite freely that they had power. As Christians said in a 1979 interview: 'Of course we have power and influence. Bankers give advice. That is our main job. As banks we have to make things happen. And to that extent I would define power as influence and the obligation to be a driving force.' On the other hand, they occasionally put forward arguments which were difficult to follow, as did Christians, for example, on the subject of participating interests: 'If we did not have the income from our equity participations, we could not provide our customers so cheaply with cost-intensive services such as payments.'

These statements show that the early recognition of the central problem – namely, public acceptance of the bank's arguments – did not in any way coincide with a more active public relations policy by the bank. Right from the beginning, the slow process of the bank opening up to the outside gave more attention and even credibility to critics' positions. A clear statement was given by the bank in its 1986 Annual Report. The sentence chosen to prompt an objective discussion on the subject was: 'Power as such – it is indisputable that banks have it.' The well-known pros and cons raised the central question of how to avoid the excessive accumulation or abuse of power within the economy. The most important corrective was identified as the supposed competition between banks, supported by legal provisions and the necessary controls to regulate and supervise banks' business: 'Whatever one does to remove power, power never disappears – it is only shifted.' On a critical note it should be pointed out here that the constantly repeated argument of tougher competition had little public impact. It also seemed overdone, as competition on the domestic banking market at that time was evidently not very intensive.

In 1987 Herrhausen again took a clear standpoint in an interview: 'Of course banks, too, have power. In our social structure there is a wide variety of power potential ... The 100 largest German companies, not all of them joint stock corporations, have 1,466 supervisory board mandates. 8.3 per cent of them are held by various banks. This is not a uniform front. There is competition here, too. Around 15 per cent are held by trade unionists, the rest by industry, i.e. businessmen and managers ... That we sometimes participate in concentration measures is true. This is not, however, an explicit policy.' Herrhausen concluded that 'It cannot be said that banks have excessive influence or steering potential. The power structure in our democratic society has not been thrown off balance by the banks. Critics have produced no proof of the contrary.'

Deutsche Bank's reaction to the discussion on banks' power in the summer of 1989, which was again initiated from political quarters, was equally unequivocal. The topic was dealt with in discussions, lectures and interviews, and an objective view was sought. Since the bank's staff and Deutsche Bank as an institution were confronted with the accusations concerning banks' power, a set of arguments was compiled as an extension of the statement in the 1986 Annual Report which was intended as a response to the main points of criticism. It concluded: 'Criticism of the banks is not supported by the facts – it is unfounded. This criticism could undermine confidence in the German banking system.

Industry and society, however, need banks that are efficient and internationally competitive.'

Abs commented on the *proxy voting right* in 1965, after publication of the government inquiry on concentration. Leaving aside the central problems, however, he said that the proxy was a written power of attorney given by the customer to his or her bank for a certain period of time. Furthermore, the banks had formulated principles to supplement the legal provisions. It was typical that the shareholder could decide freely whether to exercise his or her rights as a shareholder personally, or whether to be represented by his or her bank. The shareholder's main interest, Abs went on to say, was in dividend payments – 'and that this type of shareholder exists cannot be changed by any amount of fanatic or romanticizing sociopolitical ideas,' and that was why the shareholder gave his bank such a power of attorney. This also ensured that, in comparison to other countries, General Meetings were well attended – 70 to 80 per cent – and chance majorities were avoided.

The amendment of the proxy voting right in the German Joint Stock Corporation Act of 1965 could not, however, quell public criticism. The argument was constantly repeated that the members of the boards of managing directors at joint stock banks, as public companies, ratified their own acts of management at General Meetings through the proxy voting rights transferred to them as a result of their own bank's shares they held in safe custody, and through the concurring behaviour of other banks present that could be 'firmly relied on' in the expectation of 'reciprocity'. In other words, the provisions of company law presented practically no restrictions given the passive behaviour of small shareholders. Hence, in 1992 Deutsche Bank represented 11.8 per cent of its own capital at the General Meeting, with an attendance of 46.79 per cent. Taking into consideration that shares represented by other banks using proxy voting rights also add votes in favour of management's proposals, one can say that banks have a dominating influence at their own AGM.

At the 11th German Banking Congress in 1968, Christians expressed his position on criticism of the modified proxy voting right and noted – not without criticism by leading representatives of private banks on his seemingly unequivocal message, which had, nevertheless, almost certainly been agreed upon beforehand: 'If there are viable alternatives, we should give up proxy voting rights today rather than tomorrow. The banks do not cling to proxy voting.' He particularly referred to the fact that there was no automatic representative power with custodianship; rather, the bank could exercise the voting rights from the securities account of the customer in question only after it had been expressly empowered by the customer in writing for a limited period of time. In practice, however, this was completely routine, and in fact presented no restriction for the bank.

In the 1974 General Meeting, Ulrich reiterated the bank's position on this topic in answer to shareholders' questions:

'We banks believe that, in exercising proxy voting rights on the basis of an explicit mandate, we are providing a service from which we gain absolutely nothing except costs ... Four years ago, my colleague Dr Christians explained at the Bankers' Congress at that time that the banks do ... "not cling" ... to proxy voting rights. We are rather weary of this, but we have to admit that up to now no better solution has been found which would be practicable and which would work in the interest of the shareholders, but also in the interest of companies and the economy as a whole.'

Regarding proxy voting rights, Guth argued in 1974:

'Criticism that banks exercise too much power as a result of proxy voting rights stems solely from the fact that the majority of shareholders do not, or cannot, attend the General Meeting and, in mandating the banks, usually agree with their proposals – either because they trust these banks or because they are not interested ... We have stated repeatedly ... that we are open to better solutions ... I believe that if criticism continues to centre on this point, one in which we have no personal interest, only a responsibility towards companies and shareholders, we might have to consider whether our responsibility for our own sociopolitical reputation should come before these other responsibilities.'

In the results of a survey of custodian customers carried out by the Federal Association of German Banks in 1974 – criticized because of the wording of the questions – the banks found confirmation of the existing arrangement for proxy voting rights. Nevertheless Christians, as President of the Federal Association of German Banks, emphasized again that they did not 'cling' to these proxy voting rights. At the same time, an alibi position was adopted again to the effect that, if the existing arrangement were abolished, a 'better' one would have to be guaranteed – and so far nobody had come up with one. The idea that future AGMs might be dominated by chance majorities due to low shareholder attendance was a totally unacceptable solution.

The fact that members of the board of managing directors and management staff of the banks sat on the *supervisory boards* of non-banks was repeatedly criticized in public – also referring to 'the power of banks' – with special reference to Deutsche Bank. At the beginning of the 1960s, this practice had already been strongly criticized using the example of the more than 20 supervisory board posts – in addition to those not included in the figures for the bank's Group companies – held by Abs. The limit of ten supervisory board mandates per person, imposed with the 1965 amendment to the Joint Stock Corporation Act, was thus referred to as the 'Lex Abs'. From the bank's point of view, this 'power argument' was considered unjustified and was refuted with the same arguments used today: that members of supervisory boards were elected by shareholders, that bank representatives were appointed to supervisory boards at the special request of companies, that supervisory board functions did not include a specific influence on company policy, and so on.

In 1974 Guth commented on the banks' supervisory board mandates: 'To what extent do supervisory board posts confer power? They are powerful in the sense of the old saying "knowledge is power" – none of you would be able to cite examples of healthy, well-managed companies in which the supervisory board could exercise power with a specific aim in mind which did not conform with the company's interests ... The supervisory board is held responsible when it does not exercise this power to bring about a change in management. Ultimately it has power ... in appointing the board of managing directors.'

Since the mid-1980s various suggestions have come from political quarters regarding a further limitation on the number of supervisory board mandates per person and/or a ban on holding mandates on the supervisory boards of competing companies. These proposals, some of which concern only bank representatives, could not, however, win majority support in the current political situation. In early 1992 the Social Democratic Party in the Bundestag again called for the number of supervisory board posts to be limited to five per person and for the exception made for subsidiaries to be abolished. In addition, representatives of banks and insurance companies were not to be allowed mandates on the supervisory boards of competing companies, since considerable conflicts of interest could arise for the mandate-holders. This again showed that critics knew how to stimulate public debate on the 'power of banks', but failed to put forward any constructive or *feasible* proposals for improvements.

Deutsche Bank discovered at the start of the 1990s that holding supervisory board posts can also have disadvantages. This related to industrial restructuring within its sphere of influence. In the merger negotiations between Continental AG and the Italian Pirelli Group, and in the Hoesch–Krupp merger, the publicly observable behaviour of the supervisory board chairmen, who at the same time were members of Deutsche Bank's board of managing directors, caused considerable irritation. In the Continental–Pirelli conflict, criticism resulted particularly from the fact that, in Weiss, the bank supplied the supervisory board chairman at the same time as its subsidiary Morgan Grenfell was mandated to devise a concept on how to fend off the takeover of Continental by the Pirelli Group. The takeover was successfully withstood as a result of a 5 per cent maximum voting right at Continental, which was confirmed in the General Meeting in 1992.

In the case of the Hoesch–Krupp merger, Zapp, as supervisory board chairman at Hoesch, felt compelled to clarify his position at the Extraordinary General Meeting in June 1992:

'In response to various comments to the effect that Deutsche Bank should have prevented Krupp's takeover of Hoesch, I would like to state quite categorically once again that Deutsche Bank is not, and has never been, a Hoesch shareholder. It would not be in keeping with market principles for a house bank to take it upon itself to prevent changes in a company's shareholder structure. This could only be considered in the case of a major new shareholder if, instead of being based on sensible industrial considerations, such measures could be detrimental to the company, its shareholders or staff. In the Hoesch–Krupp case, the yield potential created by the merger is so great that it is also in the interest of Hoesch shareholders to make use of the opportunities offered by the merged company.'

The corporate links resulting from participating interests in non-banks still justify today the 'traditional' supervisory board mandates permanently held by members of the bank's board of managing directors. If one assumes that they exhaust the legal limit on mandates – which is probably realistic – then the total number of supervisory board seats held by the bank's board of managing directors alone is well over 100. In the mid-1970s, bank representatives were on the supervisory boards of 240 companies. In 1991 surveys showed that the bank was represented on the supervisory boards of 43 of the 100 largest industrial and commercial companies, and it held the chairmanship on one-third of these. Moreover, the bank was represented in a large number of small and medium-sized companies – on advisory boards, supervisory bodies, etc.

The numerous mandates held by board members also led to the public criticism that they could not carry out the respective duties satisfactorily – a criticism which inevitably became more vocal when, unnoticed by the supervisory boards, such companies ran into difficulties which threatened their existence as a result of mismanagement. The spectacular cases of Klöckner and Metallgesellschaft[19] – with members of Deutsche Bank's board of managing directors as the supervisory board chairmen – are recent examples.

Participating interests in non-banks have long been a favourite target of public criticism. Deutsche Bank commented on this early on at its General Meetings and to this day has maintained its previously formulated line of argument on its equity participation policy. In an interview in 1972, Ulrich commented on the bank's participating interests, stating the 'official view':

'The banks have held some blocks of shares for a long time, so that they have assumed the character of permanent assets, which for business and tax reasons they would be unwilling to part with. Sometimes the bank is asked to hold a block as a neutral partner; sometimes it is asked to buy an equity stake temporarily to use it for specific purposes – for example, in co-operation deals and to form larger company units. In many cases, the bank itself takes the initiative accordingly. The wish to withstand the threat of excessive foreign control can also play a role; in recent times there have been a few examples of this. In such cases, the banks should not refuse to enter into co-operative partnerships. On the contrary, they should make a responsible and active contribution to planned restructurings in industry if this appears necessary in the wake of structural changes in German industry and the international competitive situation. These solutions should, however, always be sensible from a business and economic point of view, and the banks should always remain liberal in their thinking and behaviour. Moving away from these general considerations, however, I would like to point out that the banks' traditional industrial holdings are of great importance as a source of finance and sustained revenue. To deprive them of this basis would be to weaken their ability to face the demands made of them in the interest of the economy and their own dynamic development.'

Ulrich stated in 1973: 'Naturally the profit aspect is important for a bank when it acquires equity stakes. This should not be held against the bank any more than against other companies. The profits generated in particular by tax-privileged minority holdings contribute substantially to a stable earnings situation.' Guth argued in 1974: 'It is well known that we are in favour of gradually reducing all banks' industrial holdings, that we do not have or want any industrial majorities but, on the other hand, that we must be prepared to acquire holdings temporarily in the interest of companies ... In addition, we have a "permanent stock" of industrial holdings ... Now, in answer to the question: what power do industrial stakes confer? ... Firstly, the power to sell them ... and ... the power to provide the chairman or deputy chairman of a supervisory board ... What we are not aiming for – some bankers have had this ambition in the past – is to participate in industry.'

Apart from its indisputable business interests, which were certainly not illegitimate, there were signs here that the bank was increasingly pointing to overriding general economic or particular customer interests to explain its substantial portfolio of industrial holdings to the public. At the 1973 General Meeting, the spokesman of the board of managing directors gave a programmatic address on the theme of the banks' ownership of industrial shares in the form of a 'philosophy' and business policy:

'First, I would like to repeat our frequent statement that we at our bank do not think it right to buy blocks of shares for personal industrial interests, or to control industrial companies or other firms – with the exception of financial institutions – or to exert influence on their management. This is why we have no majority stakes nor any controlling block of shares in any company. On the other hand, we consider two things to be necessary and absolutely legitimate, namely:

1. as part of investing the bank's own funds – to hold shares as investments, just like every private individual, entrepreneur or joint stock corporation. That this is in the interest of the bank and hence its shareholders is confirmed not only by the development of the underlying asset value of our holdings and by their market valuation, but also by the substantial contribution of investment income to our profit and loss account;

2. to be active in so-called block trading – a job for the banks in our economy which we consider to be very important and indispensable. When equity holdings come up for sale, when companies seek to avoid excessive foreign control, when production ranges are to be expanded, in the event of capital restructurings, regroupings, mergers or the withdrawal of partners, successions and other situations, it proves to be necessary time and again to find a buyer or partner with the financial strength to help provide a constructive solution. This is exactly what the banks are for, and for them it is an interesting business activity.

Thus not industrial ambition, but rather portfolio investment and block trading for the purpose of solving business problems must determine the size of our equity holdings in non-bank sectors ... Since 1952, the bank has resold around four-fifths of all blocks of shares which it has acquired in those years. We want to reduce the present number even further. This goal is also consistent with the restructuring of our business and participating interests with a view to our international tasks.'

In 1976, finally, Ulrich again formulated the basis of the bank's participation policy:

'1. Investment holdings should ... not exceed the bank's capital and reserves, i.e. they should not be financed by bank deposits. 2. No such participations should be held at non-banks, and hence no majorities. 3. Ownership should serve as an investment, and not further industrial or other interests, except in cases of temporary assistance, especially with restructurings, capital increases and similar transactions.' These principles are based on the realization that: 'If a bank uses its block holdings for initiatives or for a substantial involvement in mergers, this can certainly be problematic if the concentration process in question appears dubious for competition reasons. Unfortunately there have been various such transactions. For this reason, the banks must always be aware of their special responsibility when restructuring their portfolio, and should carefully examine their decisions in this light.'

Krumnow stated in 1990 that the bank always asked itself whether by selling its industrial holdings it could achieve a higher return from the proceeds than from the participations themselves. If this were the case, the bank would reduce its portfolio accordingly, at least according to this statement. Furthermore, it sometimes proved necessary – and lucrative – for the bank to act as a financially strong partner in the search for a constructive solution when companies sought to prevent 'excessive foreign control', to expand production ranges, in the case of restructurings, corporate start-ups, mergers or the withdrawal of partners, successions, share price management, sustaining the capital market's efficiency, and other situations. According to the bank, however, this also presented it with the constant obligation not to 'hoard' industrial holdings, but rather to sell them again with the same readiness as when it bought them. Thus in December 1993 the bank reduced its most spectacular industrial holding, in Daimler-Benz, from 28.1 to 24.9 per cent, in order to facilitate trading in Daimler shares in New York, where they were newly listed on the stock exchange. As late as April 1993, however, all plans to sell had been denied.

The clearly formulated ideas regarding participating interests in non-banks remained the basis of the bank's participation policy, but found little general acceptance, as frequently recurring public criticism showed. Moreover, it was partly Deutsche Bank's own fault inasmuch as an open information policy which went beyond legal requirements was not introduced until later on, at a time when the public's negative opinion of banks was already firmly established and seemed irreversible.

It is interesting to look at the development of the bank's participations, as reflected in the balance sheet, in as far as this is possible for the external observer. While in 1957 it had holdings in other companies with a balance sheet value of 58 million DM over which it exerted a business influence, according to their balance sheet disclosures, in 1991 it reported over 150 major holdings with a balance sheet value of 11,879 million DM. Measured in terms of the total volume of the bank's participations, holdings in other banks and financial institutions – owing to the practice at the time of only reporting those in financial institutions under 'Subsidiaries, associated companies and trade investments' – accounted for by far the largest share: 66 per cent in 1991. The share of holdings in other companies was 34 per cent. This structure of the participation portfolio was compatible with the above-mentioned bank philosophy on industrial share-holdings.

If one looks at the relative significance of the item 'Subsidiaries, associated companies and trade investments', its share of total assets grew from 0.7 per cent in 1957 to around 4 per cent in 1991. Hence the growth in the share of participations – particularly those in banks – in the parent company's total assets could be regarded as a clear sign of the Group's expansion and the decreasing share of the parent company in the Group as a whole. The acquisition of new consolidated participating interests and capital increases at existing ones were reflected in the balance sheet items 'Participating interests' and 'Shares in related companies' in the parent company's financial statements, but on a far smaller scale compared with the consolidated financial statements.

The growth of this item in relation to total assets occurred mainly in three phases. In the first phase, from the end of the 1960s to the mid-1970s, it doubled from 1 per cent to almost 2 per cent. This reflected what could be called a round of swapping between the three big banks, in which their tax-privileged minority holdings in mortgage banks were realigned by the sale of old holdings and the purchase of new ones in such a way that, from then on, each of the eight mortgage banks involved in this transaction belonged to only one majority bank shareholder.

In the second phase in the mid-1980s, the share of participations doubled again from 2 per cent to almost 4 per cent of total assets. There were various reasons for this growth. First of all, there was a change in the legal position. A ruling passed by the Federal Supreme Court in 1987 forced the bank to report as participating interests any holdings in non-bank joint stock companies equal to or larger than 20 per cent of the respective company's capital and – irrespective of this percentage – all holdings in non-bank private limited companies and partnerships, in so far as participatory intention could not be disproved. Considerable book transfers were necessary, since the bank had hitherto considered a participatory intention as the fundamental precondition for reporting under participating interests to exist only in the case of holdings in banks and financial institutions conducting the same business or business supplementing it, and in the case of stakes in management companies which, as independent ancillary operations, relieved the bank of administrative tasks.

At the 1982 General Meeting, a shareholder called for the acts of management of the board of managing directors and the supervisory board not to be ratified, since the annual financial statements were incorrect in some items, despite the auditor's unqualified certificate. Participations in non-bank companies were incorrectly reported because they were not included under 'Subsidiaries, associated companies and trade investments'. His remarks culminated in the popular accusation that it was 'a very grave matter' for a firm of auditors to 'tolerate incorrect reporting and not qualify their certificate'.

The growth in the participations ratio in the third phase, from the end of the 1980s, to around 4 per cent of total assets in 1991 can be attributed mainly to the acquisition of the Morgan Grenfell Group.

The high profile and size of the companies in which the bank held stakes as well as certain spectacular events ensured that public criticism of the bank's industrial holdings repeatedly resurfaced. Hence the bank once again became the target of public criticism in 1975 through the purchase and subsequent placement of a 29 per cent share package in Daimler-Benz AG, which until then had been held by Friedrich Flick KG. In agreement with Daimler-Benz and after clearing the transaction with the German government, the bank acquired the shares with effect from 1 January 1976 – in a 'midnight deal' – to prevent them from being sold abroad and to ensure the independence of Daimler-Benz. At least this was the reason given.

The basis of the agreement reached with the previous owner of the block of shares was to effect a private placement and to sell the shares to long-term institutional and industrial investors. To this end, Mercedes-Automobil-Holding AG, Frankfurt, was established. It purchased from the bank a block of shares representing 25.23 per cent of the capital in Daimler-Benz AG. The package included 6 million shares, for which the holding company paid a purchase price of 1.83 billion DM. Deutsche Bank owned 50 per cent of Mercedes-Automobil-Holding, and Stern-Automobil-Beteiligungsgesellschaft mbH and Stella-Automobil-Beteiligungsgesellschaft mbH, both in Frankfurt, owned 25 per cent each. The reason given by the bank for its stake in this holding company was that it subsequently intended to place the shares widely on the market.

In December 1975, Mercedes-Automobil-Holding AG shares worth a nominal 100 million DM were broadly placed with around 50,000 shareholders on the stock market, each share of this holding company being equivalent to one Daimler-Benz share. In April 1976 the rest of the bank's stake in the holding company, with a nominal value of 50 million DM, was also placed on the market in the form of a warrant issue with subscription rights for the bank's shareholders and those of Mercedes-Automobil-Holding. Stern's and Stella's participating interests were divided into four equal tranches and placed with institutional investors, which included Allianz Holding, Bosch, Dresdner Bank and Commerzbank. The completion of this transaction, the bank's largest at that point, made it temporarily the majority shareholder in Daimler-Benz with 57.5 per cent.

Ulrich, as chairman of the supervisory board of Daimler-Benz, commented on this subject at the 1975 Daimler-Benz General Meeting in response to shareholders' questions. He reiterated the bank's position that its equity participations in non-banks were not intended to serve any industrial objectives or to exert any influence on their management. A further statement on the bank's equity holdings and securities at its General Meeting highlighted the general direction of its participation policy. Ulrich said:

'1. Holdings in banks are reported under "Subsidiaries, associated companies and trade investments" ... In accordance with our traditional principles, the fact that they are reported in the balance sheet underlines the bank's declared intention to exert influence on the business of the individual companies.

2. The situation is quite different with respect to our equity holdings outside the banking sector, which are intended solely as financial investments and are in no way linked with the intention of entrepreneurial involvement or influence ...

  a) These holdings represent an investment of our own funds, i.e. they are not financed by deposits.

  b) We do not intend to increase our portfolio overall, but rather to treat it restrictively, i.e. to sell when a suitable opportunity arises.'

Although in placing the Daimler-Benz block of shares the bank was basically acting in its capacity as an issuing house and was concluding a transaction which also served overriding interests, the size of the deal alone attracted public attention. A transaction announced on 4 December 1985 gained similar public interest. This involved the bank's takeover of Friedrich Flick Industrieverwaltung KGaA, Düsseldorf. The Flick Group holdings in Dynamit Nobel, Feldmühle, Buderus, Daimler-Benz, W.R. Grace & Co., New York, and Gerling-Versicherungsgruppe were to be sold at the turn of the year 1985–86 for tax reasons on the part of the owner.

The holdings included in Friedrich Flick Industrieverwaltung KGaA were bought by the bank with the intention of broadly placing these companies' shares on the stock market or finding another solution in the interest of these companies. The transaction was carried out in several stages. The precondition for this was the conversion of Flick Industrieverwaltung in December 1985 into a joint stock corporation, Feldmühle Nobel AG. Through Alma Beteiligungsgesellschaft, a subsidiary, the bank bought Feldmühle Nobel at a fixed price of 5 billion DM in another 'midnight deal' on 31 December 1985/1 January 1986. These holdings were then sold: the stake in Grace was repurchased on 10 December 1985 because of the company's pre-emptive right; the Daimler-Benz block of 3.397 million shares was placed by a Euro-syndicate; the holding in Gerling was sold on the basis of a pre-emptive right to its senior partner Gerling, and the remaining shares in Feldmühle Nobel were widely placed in April 1986.

This deal was considered extremely sophisticated and attracted much publicity – firstly because of its amount of more than 5 billion DM, and secondly because of the tax credit of around 1 billion DM due to the bank as a result of the corporate and tax laws applying to this deal. This led to renewed, but unfounded, public criticism of Deutsche Bank's power. In both cases customers placed orders with the bank, which partly involved the bank adding certain holdings to its own portfolio for a limited period, but mainly entailed it acting as an issuing house.

A different situation again arose in October 1988 when the International Crude Oil and Related Product Trading Department at Klöckner & Co. KGaA, Duisburg, turned in a loss of between 600 and 700 million DM, more than the company's capital, due to signatory powers being exceeded and controlling procedures circumvented. Very quickly, in a decision-making process *par excellence*, the bank resolved to provide equity funds in the amount of 400 million DM to keep Klöckner alive. Here, with great public approval, the bank helped to avoid the company's bankruptcy by its financial involvement in the form of an equity holding, and it subsequently developed and realized a restructuring strategy. At the same time as announcing the injection of capital, the bank emphasized that a permanent equity holding was not intended, but that this was a short-term involvement.

After conversion of Klöckner into a joint stock corporation, the bank's stake was 100 per cent, held through a holding company and with no concrete prospects at the time of further placement. The bank's restructuring concept was implemented: the trading activities of the former Klöckner & Co. AG were hived off to a new company which was sold to VIAG-Bayernwerk-Beteiligungsgesellschaft mbH in 1989. The Klöckner stake in Klöckner-Humboldt-Deutz AG, Cologne, was not hived off; it was still in the bank's portfolio at the start of the 1990s.

Later the losses from oil futures, which were lower than expected owing to the market development, and the proceeds from the sale of Klöckner's trading activities helped to solve a problem of a special kind: to offset the loss incurred by holders of Klöckner participatory rights due to the capital write-down. The bank's position here was unusual in that it had lead-managed the issue of these participatory rights and placed a third of them with preferred customers in 1988. This provoked negative reactions from the public – particularly in view of the bank's conflict of interests. In July 1989 the bank offered participatory certificate-holders 112 DM cash per certificate of 100 DM nominal value. This 'voluntary' payment was equal to the market value of the certificates before the loss at Klöckner was announced.

Public scepticism concerning the bank's holdings also stemmed largely from its traditionally tight-lipped information policy on this subject. According to Abs' sibylline remark at the 1964 Balance Sheet Press Conference on the bank's tax-privileged minority holdings: 'That is what can be understood from the Annual Report. There is a third group which comes under the dividend-bearing securities, and we do not wish to say much about it. We are saying nothing misleading ... Of course equity holdings also include tax-privileged minority stakes.'

In the Annual Report for 1965, new regulations were complied with and a list of holdings where the bank's stake exceeded 25 per cent was published. More precise details on the size of each interest were not published. At the 1966 Balance Sheet Press Conference, Abs was again vague: 'If you now look at holdings of over 50 per cent ... HAPAG ... We have made repeated statements on this point, namely that we would not hesitate to sell HAPAG ... You are aware that, at the time, we made the acquisition at the request of the city state of Hamburg for specific political reasons relating to Hamburg ... Over the years, when it was not publicized, we have often held tax-privileged minority holdings and resold them – when certain dangers disappeared – by placing them widely.'

The decision to abandon such a restrictive information policy was not taken until the Annual Reports for 1986 and 1987, which gave specific details on the size of equity participations, albeit only those which exceeded the 25 per cent tax-privileged minority-holding limit. A further improvement of information on equity stakes in non-banks came when the Deutsche Bank share was listed on the Tokyo Stock Exchange in November 1989. Local listing regulations required the bank to disclose its shareholdings of over 10 per cent in listed companies.

In contrast to the bank's deliberate equity stakes, some holdings stemmed from capital increases or companies going public. Unfavourable market developments could cause an underwriting bank to take the underwritten shares into its portfolio for a definite or indefinite period. It was such a situation that led, for example, to the bank's roughly 2 per cent stake in Fiat S.p.A., Turin, when the placement of a share package at the end of the 1980s failed completely owing to the bank's misjudgement of the market (pp. 688–9).

These examples show that the reasons behind the bank's equity stakes in industrial companies were very diverse – in some cases at a company's or government agency's request, for overriding reasons or, in addition to pure investment, with the aim of rescuing companies, to support medium-sized companies with weak capital resources or to place shares with third parties. Further reasons were changes in law – for example, the tax privilege on minority holdings of at least 25 per cent. These could lead to an increase in existing holdings which, from the bank's point of view, were classified as medium- to long-term investments and were not intended to secure a majority or entrepreneurial influence.

Nevertheless, the substantial value of such holdings, which is controlled in line with the bank's above-mentioned participation policy, should not be underestimated and will probably continue to be the target of considerable public criticism – particularly when companies which have the bank as a shareholder are involved in the restructuring of individual industries. This problem became evident in 1989, when Daimler-Benz AG merged with Messerschmitt-Bölkow-Blohm. In a special report on this merger, the Monopolies Commission was very critical of the bank's holding in Daimler-Benz and hence its role in engineering the merger. This criticism led to the Monopolies Commission calling for banks' shareholdings in non-banks to be limited to 5 per cent of share capital.

In an interview with *Euromoney*[20] early in 1994, Kopper commented with regard to future policy on shareholdings that he would like them to be smaller, but that he would like to have more of them. Some of the present holdings were too big, he said, and he would like to see them split up and with a new geographical mix. But, he continued: 'I do not wish to reduce the overall size of our holdings, because this is an important part of what this bank does ... they are a very good and steady contributor to earnings. The influence and power they are said to give us I find totally uninteresting. They are supposed to give us power to influence and stay as the house bank. That may be a terrific disservice to the bank.'

This statement was of particular relevance, since it coincided with the Metall-gesellschaft disaster: this company completely unexpectedly reported losses of at least 3.8 billion DM. Deutsche Bank, alongside Dresdner Bank, with which it alternated tenure of the supervisory board chairmanship (most recently Röller and Schmitz), was a major shareholder and the largest lender, with at least 540 million DM invested.

While the problems at Metallgesellschaft led to extensive public discussion both about the German supervisory board system in general and, specifically, about the role of banks in this context and focused on possible defects, not always correctly, ignoring the bank's efforts to find a solution, the bank again became a target of public criticism in spring 1994 in connection with the bankruptcy of the Schneider property group. The collapse of the Schneider group, with Deutsche Bank as its biggest single lender (with outstanding loans of one billion DM) through its mortgage bank subsidiary Deutsche Central-bodenkredit AG – where two executive board members had to leave – led to the media being permeated, according to Kopper, by 'a kind of Schneider fever and a good helping of feverish hallucination'. Although as far as Deutsche Bank was concerned the claims affected accounted for only about 0.3 per cent of its total assets and were secured against property charges, discussions and speculation about a property and banking crisis began. Over and above that, the universal banking system was once again questioned, even though the system as such was not an explanation for the defaults – fraud and defaults occur in every banking system.

In the public eye, Deutsche Bank was forced into the role of guilty party, although it was actually the victim. The only criticism of the bank which is justified is that it allowed itself to be duped because the Schneider companies had submitted incorrect documentation for the loan examination, and the reports by external experts required under German mortgage bank law falsely reported excessive property values. Be that as it may, as Kopper told the press, the bank was the target of endless 'scorn and mockery' out of a sort of malicious pleasure that 'the top of the class has finally been caught out'. This widespread public criticism proved to Kopper 'what dimensions the negative attitude towards banks has reached in Germany'.

b) Relations with the (former) Soviet Union

The involvement of Deutsche Bank in trade with Eastern Europe, as a financial partner to German companies, has a long tradition. After 1957, the bank played a role in the beginnings of trade with the East, its structuring and realization, which did not stem merely from personal economic interests. Christians went to Moscow in December 1969 for the first time, as the member of the board of managing directors responsible for East European business, to negotiate a German–Soviet industrial project. Christians published the results of this and other events, including the facts surrounding them, in a highly acclaimed book.[21]

These talks resulted in the first German–Soviet trade agreement, signed on 1 February 1970 in Essen in the presence of the German economics minister and the Soviet foreign trade minister, which documented its great political importance. The German–Soviet contracts, known as the 'pipeline agreements', were conceived as a business triangle between German steel companies, German banks and, on the Soviet side, the respective government agencies. The German steel companies were to deliver pipes to the USSR for the construction of natural gas pipelines, and the Soviets were to deliver natural gas to German power utilities for up to 20 years and up to the value of the pipes.

A German syndicate led by the bank financed these transactions by providing loans to the Soviet Bank for Foreign Trade in Moscow. The loan linked to the first pipeline agreement, amounting to 2.5 billion DM, was for 1.5 billion DM and was followed by further similar loans – in 1972 for 1.2 billion DM, in 1974 for 1.5 billion DM and in 1975 for 1.2 billion DM – reflecting the greater intensity of German–Soviet trade relations in this period. Deutsche Bank's share of these loans, a total of 5.4 billion DM extended up to the mid-1970s in connection with the four pipeline agreements, was 900 million DM. The bank assumed a similar amount of exposure with the financial settlement of East European trade. In 1976 West Germany's total volume of trade with Eastern Europe was 11.6 billion DM, roughly 20 per cent of which was financed by the bank.

Another example of the intensification of German–Soviet trade in the early 1970s was a loan agreement for 790 million DM, signed in Moscow on 28 October 1974 between AKA Ausfuhrkredit-Gesellschaft (German Export Credit Guarantee Corporation) and a syndicate led by Deutsche Bank, on the one hand,

and the Soviet Bank for Foreign Trade, on the other. The loan was used to finance the supply of roughly 9,000 Magirus heavy trucks from Klöckner-Humboldt-Deutz AG to the Soviet Union.

It is no surprise that, with the intensification of relations between the Federal Republic and the Soviet Union, there were fears particularly on the part of the United States that Western European countries could become dependent on Soviet natural gas supplies, which might be used to apply pressure in political negotiations. Besides this, there was the criticism that western currency was providing the Soviet Union with war funds. In 1978 this situation led to an informal agreement between the German government, German power utilities, steel companies and Deutsche Bank, as head of the syndicate, to limit Soviet gas deliveries to 5 per cent of Germany's primary energy needs and 30 per cent of its total natural gas requirements up to the end of the 1980s.

At the end of the 1970s political relations between East and West cooled again following the debate on the deployment of new missiles, so that German industry representatives were exposed to considerable political criticism. However, the lack of East-West contact at the political level was partly offset by a less-publicized exchange of information between western business representatives and the Soviets. Christians acted here as a contact person, in particular for the Soviets, although it would appear that they misjudged the extent of his influence or even decision-making powers at the political level.

In 1977, at the Academy of Sciences in Moscow, Herrhausen highlighted the potential problems of East–West trade. One of the problems discussed was the creditworthiness of a country, at that time not (yet) seen as a serious matter for the Soviet Union owing to its raw materials reserves, as the Soviet Union did not publish any of the economic data which, in western countries, provide the basis for lending. It was realized that the danger of having to make estimates and assumptions about the Soviet economy could depress financial market sentiment. Such effects could be seen, for example, in German–Soviet credit relations in the late 1980s, by which time the creditworthiness of the USSR had deteriorated considerably as a result of accrued interest and redemption payments. In May 1988, on a state visit by Chancellor Kohl to the Soviet Union, a global loan facility for 3 billion DM was signed by representatives of German banks (including Herrhausen), German companies and a Soviet delegation; it was to be the last one for the time being.

The importance of the interrelationships between economic and political interests in trade with Eastern Europe became apparent once again in the late 1970s and early 1980s. Events such as the debate on the deployment of new arms in Western Europe, the Soviet invasion of Afghanistan in 1979, the boycott of the 1980 Olympic Games in Moscow and the exaggerated Cold War debate revived by the Reagan administration in the USA all had a profound impact on economic relations between East and West.

The bank's specific involvement was reflected in the fact that, in December

1979, Christians was asked by the Soviet Union to negotiate another pipeline agreement worth 20 billion DM. Negotiations on this 'Yamal project'[22] were impeded by political developments. Hence, in the months that followed, the Soviets tried to make up for the lack of political contact by forging links with representatives of Western industry and banks. In January 1980, at another round of negotiations on the Yamal project in Moscow, the bank's spokesman could not avoid this visit being used by the Soviets for publicity purposes in order to give the world a false picture of normality in East–West relations. Similarly, the Soviet Union tried, in spring 1980, to get Christians to intervene at the political level – again misjudging his influence in the Federal Republic's democratic system – to avert a boycott of the Olympic Games by West Germany. It was not until 1982 that the Yamal pipeline agreement was concluded after a renewed intensification of talks at the business level led by Christians. Left over from the original financing volume for the Yamal project was a global loan agreement for 3.3 billion DM, signed in Leningrad on 13 July 1982.

In the mid-1980s, the East–West political climate improved, especially due to the appointment of Gorbachev as General Secretary of the Communist Party of the Soviet Union, and his 'new ideology'. The importance attached by the Soviet Union to economic relations as a basis for political *détente* was apparent in the fact that Christians was one of the first Western business leaders to be invited to a meeting with Gorbachev, on 18 March 1985.[23] Christians explained the bank's motivation to sustain economic relations with the Soviet Union as follows: 'I consider economic integration as being a very important means of preventing war. This is one of the major reasons why the bank has specifically maintained talks with its Soviet partners even when the politicians of both countries were no longer speaking to each other because of the well-known events. Moreover, the Federal Republic is not only a reliable partner in political terms, but also economically, and is known world-wide for fulfilling the contracts it enters into.'[24]

Political *détente* led to a marked intensification of German–Soviet economic relations and also stimulated discussion on economic problems and possible solutions. Hence, for example, the German–Soviet Banks' Working Group, which had existed since 1982, met in September 1987 in Düsseldorf under Christians' chairmanship. In the same year, the bank established an internal working group called 'Project Development USSR' to revive German–Soviet business relations. The goal of this working group was to enhance the economic environment of German–Soviet relations over and above purely banking interests. One of the main foundations of this was the co-operation agreement signed in 1987 by Deutsche Bank, the Bank for Foreign Trade and the Soviet State Bank, providing for intensified bank supervision of German–Soviet economic projects, from exports to joint ventures.

The working group was especially to promote contacts between the bank's corporate customers and economic agencies in the Soviet Union. What was important here was the fact that the agreement created the first legal foundation for regular customer service at the bank's Moscow representative office. At the end of 1987, Kopper explained this commitment as follows: 'It has always been Deutsche Bank's policy to think long term and in large dimensions. This was the case even in the early years of economic relations with the Soviet Union. We believe that this more recent commitment will be welcomed by the Soviets and by German industry.'

A year later, at a German–Soviet meeting, one of Christians' initiatives was discussed: to establish 'special economic zones' in the Soviet Union where private foreign investors could operate under market conditions. In 1992 the Centre for German–Russian Economic Co-operation was set up in Düsseldorf and was expanded into a supra-regional advisory and information bureau for German–Russian economic relations. It was headed by a former staff member of the bank who had spent many years as its representative in Moscow.

When the Commonwealth of Independent States (CIS) was set up at the end of 1991, the assumption of the former Soviet Union's old debts by the new republics was an important issue. After the Bank for Foreign Trade had suspended its redemption payments on the former Soviet Union's foreign debts at the end of 1991, a steering committee was established, led by Deutsche Bank. It consisted of representatives of ten Western creditor banks and was to develop and implement strategies for solving the debt crisis in negotiations with CIS representatives. This committee co-ordinated the interests of around 400 Western creditor banks, among whom the estimated debt of $80 billion was divided. The German banks formed the largest creditor group, with roughly $22 billion, of which, however, all but $5 billion was covered by government guarantees. Deutsche Bank estimated its Soviet Union exposure at the end of 1991 to be less than 1.4 billion DM, for 70 per cent of which risk provisions had been formed. In mid-1992 it became increasingly obvious that the long-term deferral of interest and redemption payments until 1997 had to be the prime element in any solution to the Soviet Union's foreign debt problem.

Since the early 1980s, art has formed an important link within German–Soviet relations, promoted particularly by the bank's activities.[25] On the basis of a 1981 agreement between the Soviet Ministry of Education and the Arts and the bank, joint efforts have been made to further the exchange of art between the two countries.

c) Business relations with South Africa under public criticism

In the mid-1970s a resolution passed by the Ecumenical Council of Churches in Geneva precipitated a campaign which was to discredit banks and companies maintaining business ties with South Africa because of the apartheid policy there. In 1975 the Council's Executive Committee decided in Nairobi not to deposit any assets with certain international banks, including Deutsche Bank, and further recommendations were made to step up public pressure on banks which had business links with South Africa. In 1981 the Ecumenical Council closed its accounts with Dresdner Bank and two Swiss banks.

Although the Council of the Protestant Church in Germany merely acknowledged this decision, but did not follow it, the issue itself and the measures taken in the years following presented the basis for a series of demonstrations by diverse interest groups, particularly aimed at Deutsche Bank. Demonstrations were mounted outside the bank's branches and there were calls for customers to withdraw their deposits and close their accounts. It was suggested that, by providing loans and issuing bonds for South Africa, the bank was partly responsible for the effects of apartheid. In an open letter to the public service workers' union (ÖTV) in 1982 – in response to the union's public criticism of the bank's issuance of a DM-denominated bond for a South African company – Deutsche Bank clarified its position:

'The underwriting and placing of bonds is a service which forms part of our international business. It is not the job of an issuing house to attach political demands to the transaction of such a banking deal, or to make it conditional upon their fulfilment . . . The Republic of South Africa is an important economic partner for the Federal Republic. We are convinced that the development and continuation of good business relations is the most effective way to bring about an improvement in the living conditions of all groups in South Africa.'

In 1987 the controversial issue of South African relations received more publicity when the German Protestant Church Congress closed its accounts and withdrew its deposits with Deutsche Bank in protest at the bank's business relations with South Africa. International criticism of apartheid at the time led to many multinational companies selling or closing their production plants in South Africa. This caused the bank to reiterate its position on 14 May 1987:

'As an international bank, Deutsche Bank AG maintains business ties with almost all countries in the world, regardless of their political orientation. It is not compatible with the bank's approach to use its activities in either a positive or negative sense for political aims. Deutsche Bank regards its financing for South African borrowers . . . also from the viewpoint of South Africa's economic development, which has been proven to benefit all groups there. Deutsche Bank AG has always condemned apartheid and has emphasized this position publicly and also in many discussions with South African politicians. The abolition of racial discrimination and the granting of more rights for the black population in South Africa are urgently necessary. A permanent solution to the racial problem can only be found in the country itself, and through special co-operation between all sections of the population. It is doubtful whether trade embargoes can bring about a rapid solution.'

This stance revealed an attempt to distinguish as clearly as possible between the economic successes to be gained from business relations and the political strategies of governments. A difficult situation arose here for the bank in the sense that a specific problem was mixed with a general one. Critics, simply because of the general scepticism towards the big banks, received great publicity, whereas the bank's arguments were given less attention and less credence.

It was not until 1991 that South Africa regained its international credit-worthiness after having been unable to issue international bonds for six years, and floated a bond for 300 million DM under the bank's lead management. This especially underlined the fact that the gradual lifting of apartheid was reviving willingness for economic and financial involvement in South Africa. In recognition of the new political climate, the bank provided concrete financial support in 1990. A cash donation was given to the Johannesburg Urban Foundation, which had been founded as a private initiative in 1977 to speed up the social and economic integration of the black community and to improve their education. This money was used for ongoing educational and training schemes and to set up new businesses.

d) Position on the international debt crisis

Apart from its own specific business interests, Deutsche Bank's commitment to the economic development of Third World countries can, in retrospect, be interpreted as commitment in the sense of global responsibility. One example of such commitment over and above personal interests in the world economic environment was the regulation of Indonesia's debts in 1968/69.

Representatives of the seven governments in the Paris Club appointed Abs as an independent expert to draw up a report on how to solve the Indonesian debt problem. From the beginning, Abs envisaged the preservation of Indonesia's financial standing as a central point in the debt rescheduling. This meant in particular not reducing old debts, but rather suspending or waiving interest payments and stretching redemption payments over 30 years. Through the additional limitation of debt service payments after the debt rescheduling to between 15 and 25 per cent of export proceeds, the country's economic recovery was to be self-supporting. Even if the quantitative scope of this debt rescheduling was smaller than in subsequent Latin American cases, this approach showed parallels with later proposals for solving the international debt crisis.

It is significant that, in the late 1970s, Deutsche Bank was not alone in misjudging the economic prospects in Latin America. With hindsight this is probably the only explanation for the volume of loans extended by commercial banks to these countries. In January 1978, at a press conference marking the beginning of a tour of South America by bank representatives, among them Herrhausen and Thierbach, reference was made to the supposedly increasing economic importance of Latin America. The outlook for this economic region, with 330 million inhabitants and a national product of more than $350 billion, was assessed as extremely positive. These cheerful expectations were reflected in the extensive international capital flows into Latin America – a 'jumbo' loan for

Mexico of $1.2 billion in 1977 and a Brazilian loan of 200 million DM in 1978.

In spite of these countries' inflation rates, which by European standards were unimaginably high – Argentina 170 per cent, Brazil 40 per cent – there were no concrete scenarios whatsoever at the lending banks, which had to deal with the consequences of a development that ran counter to their positive expectations – and was soon to materialize – in these countries. The second international oil crisis completely belied the assumptions on which these positive expectations were based, and in the wake of the world economic recession the developing countries in particular could not complete the restructuring they had begun, which had been based on economic growth. This also had considerable repercussions for Deutsche Bank.

In the 1970s the external debt of developing and newly industrializing countries increased rapidly. With total debt of $91 billion, Mexico discontinued its payments on foreign debts in 1982, thereby triggering the debt crisis still in progress today. Deutsche Bank and many other domestic and foreign banks were hit by this development as lenders. As Mertin said in 1984, the banks had been caught off-guard by the debt crisis in the sense that the accumulation of individual risks relating to the total debt of a nation or a few nations had not been taken into consideration in the banks' risk management.

This led, at first, to the banks showing considerable solidarity and resolving unanimously on debt rescheduling agreements. At the same time, however, the banks in question became more sensitive to the situation and increasingly matched their sovereign risk to their individual business situation. Mertin, for example, mentioned that his first warnings came in 1978, but that the tax authorities could not at the time be convinced of the need to increase risk provisioning for country risk. He proposed as a guiding maxim of risk policy that no single credit risk should be larger than the cover that could be provided from earnings plus undisclosed reserves, should that risk materialize. In 1984 Werner Blessing also commented on the banks' position before the debt crisis broke out:

'If criticism is to be levelled at banks, then it should concern the fact that – naturally for competitive reasons – they have made it too easy for borrowers to obtain loans. It should also be remembered, though, that the German banks' growing exposure in other countries stems mainly from industry's need and urgent requests for additional export financing ... If one sees the increase in developing countries' debt ... in relation to their economic development, then this increase cannot be considered unusual. During this time, many Third World countries attained growth rates which substantially exceeded those in industrialized countries ... Since the second oil crisis in 1979/80, however, the environment has changed dramatically to the detriment of the developing countries, i.e. ... lower commodity prices, ... lower export revenues, ... high oil prices ... and ... a sharp rise in interest rates ... As a result of these factors the debt service ratio deteriorated rapidly.'

The *ad hoc* solutions typical of the early 1980s for avoiding a global escalation of the financial crisis were later replaced by initiatives – named after the initiators: Baker Initiative, Brady Initiative and Herrhausen Proposal – which sought a general solution to the debt crisis. As early as 1987, Herrhausen referred to the fact that reductions in debt and debt service were vital instruments in solving the debt crisis; but there was strong disagreement with this in the banking community.

In September 1988, at the International Monetary Fund meeting in Berlin, he pleaded for a more long-term debt strategy to replace increasingly frequent reschedulings and to come a step closer to solving the debt problem effectively by combining different instruments, including partial debt forgiveness. The prerequisite for this, he insisted, was co-operation between all parties involved – in particular, effective economic policies on the part of the indebted countries.

In 1989, at the Annual Meeting of the International Monetary Fund in Washington, Herrhausen outlined a new solution. His suggestion was mainly based on the realization that the debtor countries' debt volume, originally seen as a liquidity problem, had developed more and more into a solvency problem. According to Herrhausen, the countries could not be helped by fresh money and constant debt rescheduling; what was required was the gradual reduction of debt through the rescheduling of old bank debts into new loans – at an appropriate discount – the repurchasing of bank debts or the conversion of loans into equity (debt-to-equity swaps).

In addition, Herrhausen saw the need for a concerted effort by creditor banks, governments and bank supervisory authorities and, on the other side, by the debtor countries. The goal of his concrete proposal was to conceptualize a general offer on the part of the creditor banks which would be acceptable to their governments and supervisory authorities, and which would be available to all debtor countries which qualified for such a solution.

Herrhausen's proposal highlighted both the complexity of the situation and the difficulties of its successful implementation. In particular, the significantly divergent international requirements concerning the inclusion of sovereign risk in banks' balance sheets made a uniform approach by the banks involved seem less realistic in view of their differing vested interests. Moreover, the obligation on the part of the debtor countries to qualify for such support remained the decisive criterion of success, since sound economic policy could not be replaced by concessions on the part of banks. Neither this Herrhausen Plan – as it was soon called – nor other initiatives have been fully implemented to date. In practical terms they were hardly feasible either.

A concrete initiative for Poland was taken by Deutsche Bank at the International Monetary Fund Meeting in 1990. Poland's foreign debt of $45 billion was to be reduced, it suggested, by using various instruments such as the reduction of debt and debt service, extending loan periods and new loans. It had to be ensured that Poland could pay its foreign debts and, at the same time, that no damage was done to Poland's future international financial standing. Since around 80 per cent of Poland's foreign debt was accounted for by the public sector, besides which there was considerable divergence in risk provisioning by the commercial banks involved, the suggestion did not meet with unanimous agreement. In June 1991 the public-sector creditors agreed to halve Polish foreign debt, with the commercial banks agreeing to a debt remission of between 35 and 40 per cent.

The bank also showed flexibility in individual cases concerning debt rescheduling. It used a debt-to-nature swap to enable developing countries to reduce their debts: in 1989 it converted a partial loan claim on Sudan with a nominal value of 5 million Swiss francs into the country's currency and donated it to UNICEF. This money was used in co-operation with Sudan to develop health services and improve rural water supply, and for reafforestation projects.

A similar agreement was made in the same year with the World Wildlife Fund for Nature, to which the bank donated $1.6 million over eight years for environmental protection measures in Madagascar. This amount was equivalent to Madagascar's redemption payments up to 1996 on a loan from the bank. As a prerequisite for the remission of these payments, the bank expected Madagascar to comply with the rescheduling agreements in question. The money was used for environmental projects, which – though on a very limited scale – were to prevent further destruction of tropical rain forests and preserve the region's unique flora and fauna. Even if these measures, from a quantitative point of view, have not come any closer to solving the overall debt crisis, they are a clear indication of the bank's goodwill.

II. Deutsche Bank in the Market:
A Full-Service Bank for all Types of Customer

1. Developments in market positioning

The period since 1957 has been one in which Deutsche Bank's business expansion has been rapid and, at times, turbulent. This is in line with the bank's business policy, since growth has always been one of its objectives, even if its importance has varied over time. This is because the bank's public image and the security it offers its depositors are seen as being closely related to the bank's size. It is therefore considered to be too big to fail.

As an indication of this size, albeit an incomplete one, the total assets of Deutsche Bank AG grew from 8.4 billion DM in 1957 to 373 billion DM in 1992 (Figure 5.7). If we compare this with the growth of GNP at market prices, we can see that the bank was growing, even allowing for factors which artificially inflated the balance sheet. During the same period in which the bank's total assets increased by 44 times, GNP increased 'only' twelvefold.

Figure 5.7 Total assets of Deutsche Bank AG and Deutsche Bank Group

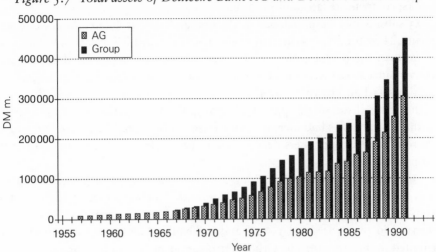

This growth, however, did not progress at an even pace: whereas total assets increased by two and a half times in the 1960s and threefold in the 1970s, they merely doubled in the 1980s. But this slowdown does not mean that business was lagging behind the development of the economy as a whole, since the German economy's production of goods and services also slowed. Compared to the other two big banks in Germany, Deutsche Bank's growth since the mid-1970s is particularly remarkable. In 1975 it had total assets of 57 billion DM, closely followed by Dresdner Bank, with total assets of 49 billion DM, and Commerzbank, with 39 billion DM. By the early 1990s, Deutsche Bank's total assets almost matched those of Dresdner and Commerzbank combined. The more pronounced growth in the bank's total assets in the early 1990s was largely attributable to German unification; Deutsche Bank-Kreditbank was merged with the parent company in 1990, and Deutsche Bank Berlin followed suit in 1991.

In 1967, ten years after the first annual financial statements were drawn up for Deutsche Bank AG, the bank's first consolidated financial statements were drawn up in accordance with the provisions contained in the amended Joint Stock Companies Act. These consolidated financial statements included 20 domestic subsidiaries. With Group assets totalling 22.1 billion DM, however, the Group was only 1.7 billion DM larger than the parent company (Figure 5.7).

In 1974 the bank's Luxemburg subsidiary became the first foreign subsidiary to be included in the consolidated financial statements. This move on the part of the bank, according to its 1974 Annual Report, was intended as a signal that it 'of course feels fully responsible for its subsidiary, which it virtually wholly owns'. After the remaining foreign subsidiaries and financing companies were included, the 1980 consolidated financial statements met the requirements of an international group's financial statements. This represented a first among the big banks; competitors later followed suit.

23 subsidiaries were included in the first global consolidated financial statements. Their total assets came to 174.6 billion DM, which was 70.4 billion DM more than the parent company. Ten years later, over 70 major domestic and foreign subsidiaries were included in the consolidated financial statements, whose total assets had grown to over 400 billion DM and were 144.8 billion DM higher than those of the parent company. Within a period of 23 years, the Group's total assets had increased by a factor of over 18. The parent company's share of total Group assets declined continuously from 92 per cent in 1967 to 67 per cent in 1993.

One reason for the Group's stronger growth than that of the parent company was the expansion in the number of consolidated companies. In addition, the consolidated specialized banks, whose financial services were increasingly in demand in the 1970s and 1980s, and the bank's Luxemburg subsidiary contributed to this growth. The Group's stronger growth than the parent company also shows that external growth via participating interests was more important than internal growth or the incorporation of participating interests in the form of mergers.

The significance of payment flows *within* the Group as an expression of the interdependence of Group companies is illustrated by the difference between the Group's combined and consolidated total assets. In 1967, the year in which the first consolidated financial statements were drawn up, this figure amounted to 748 million DM and combined total assets to 22.8 billion DM. This meant that 3.2 per cent of all payment flows took place within the Group. These intra-Group payment flows increased substantially during the 1980s and almost quadrupled from 5 per cent in 1980 to 20 per cent in 1991. Although the bank's business policy-makers increasingly tended to think in Group dimensions, the world-wide organization still had its central and stable base in the parent company.

The bank's objective of growth has always been seen in terms of expansion of its market share. The growth of the parent company and of the Group must therefore be put into the perspective of market growth as a whole. This induced Herrhausen to demand at the bank's 1989 General Meeting: 'We have to grow at least as much as our markets if we are not to fall behind, and we must invest and diversify, otherwise our customers around the world will turn to those banks who do – and rightly so.' Market share, often regarded as an indicator of power, is none the less difficult to define and quantify. Abs put this problem in a nutshell by trying to illustrate the relative size of Deutsche Bank and the other private banks in Germany: 'Take a look at the bill that the USA pays for imported oil. In 1971 it cost 4.5 billion dollars, and in 1980 it will be 20 billion dollars. If the USA did not have any exports to offset this, it would have to pay the Arab countries an amount equal to General Motors' total assets in order to pay this annual bill. This amount would be sufficient to buy up all the shares listed on the German stock exchange. Just look at these proportions. What poor, insignificant creatures we are, and that also goes for the so-called 'power' of Germany's private banks that is so often talked about.'

Deutsche Bank's market share – i.e. the ratio of its total assets to the total assets of all German banks – has been fluctuating between roughly 4 per cent and a good 5 per cent since 1957 (Figure 5.8), which seems a small percentage for what is by far the largest bank. However, it has always operated on various markets, some of which have differed substantially in nature, and in each case it has occupied a different and changing market position, which is not reflected by this figure.

Figure 5.8 The market share of Deutsche Bank AG (as a proportion of total assets of all German banks)

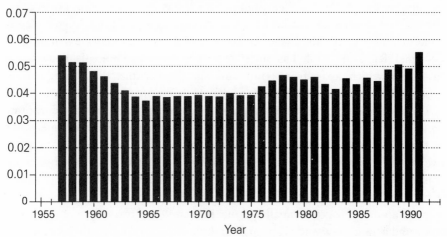

Moreover, because the Group has grown steadily compared to the parent company, it is more the Group's total assets – 578.6 billion DM in mid-1994 – which give an impression of the size of the bank, rather than the parent company's total assets alone. To enable these figures to be compared internationally, holdings in industrial and trading companies would also have to be included in the consolidated financial statements, as is the case in the USA. Owing to the strong growth in off-balance-sheet business, which since 1990 has exceeded business on the balance sheet, this should also be included in the calculation of market share. In mid-1994 the nominal value of this off-balance-sheet business was 1,651 billion DM for Deutsche Bank Group.

In 1991 Deutsche Bank was the largest listed bank and the twelfth-largest listed company in Europe. It was one of the 20 largest banks in the world. In that year, Krumnow outlined the relationship between expansion of business and capital requirements: 'In the early 1980s Deutsche Bank needed five years to acquire one billion deutschmarks of capital and reserves. Subsequently it only needed two years, later on only nine months, and by 1990 only six months.'

2. Trends in traditional domestic business with corporates and institutions

a) Target group expansion over time

Throughout most of its history, Deutsche Bank has been an institution that focused its activities on business with large corporate customers, and therefore developed its self-image accordingly. When the bank resumed business following the remerger of the three regional institutions in 1957, the bank's only customers, apart from large industrial companies, were private institutional investors such as insurance companies and banks engaged in foreign business.

Since the mid-1960s there has been increasingly strong competition with foreign banks for big-ticket customers, which has led to growing pressure on the interest margin earned from this customer group. By no longer merely concentrating on certain customer groups, and thus gradually expanding its customer base, the bank has since developed from a wholesale bank to an institution which, apart from retail banking, also occupies the leading market position with small and medium-sized corporate clients.

The main reason for the bank's decision to expand its target group in corporate banking is likely to have been the discovery of small and medium-sized enterprises in the mid-1970s. This process of diversification, which has been taking place over the last couple of decades as part of the bank's Group-oriented strategy, was largely a result of the realization that the bank could maintain the positions it had attained in wholesale and international business only if it successfully stepped up its exposure to small and medium-sized enterprises.

To understand how and why small and medium-sized enterprises became so important to the bank, we must first take a look at a measure which seemed primarily to be of an organizational nature, but was unique in terms of its significance for the bank's entire corporate business. In 1976 the bank set up an organizational unit geared to corporate customers at its central office, which it called the Central Corporate Customer Department. This had been preceded in 1974 by the establishment of a new organizational model for the regional head branches (pp. 526–9).

After decades of what had been an organizational system based on type of business, so-called corporate-customer relationship managers were introduced, an almost revolutionary organizational innovation in those days. These officers, whose remit has remained almost unchanged to the present day, were responsible for systematically managing customer relationships in all relevant areas. According-ing to the minutes of a meeting with the heads of the Corporate Customer Departments on 19 December 1976 in Frankfurt, their job was to 'apply their expert banking know-how, ideas and initiative to provide the customer with solutions to his problems'. By talking to their customers, ideally with their managements, the relationship managers had the task of finding out the company's needs in as much detail as possible and, in the overall interest of the bank, ensuring that the bank's various departments made use of these contacts in order to win new business. The definition of the job of corporate relationship manager was based on the realization that the wide variety of tasks involved in looking after a corporate customer took up so much of the relationship managers' time that they could not belong to any other specific department.

The department at the branches responsible for business with corporates, which included all services offered to corporate customers, was now called the Department for Corporate Customers. The decision on the allocation of customers to the various relationship managers was made by the management of the regional head branch according to local conditions. The Department for Corporate Customers was responsible for general business matters within the branch region, such as questions concerning loan conditions which exceeded the discretionary powers of the relationship manager or branch manager. According to the organization model, this department co-ordinated all activities directed at corporate customers.

To support the regional head branches in this task, a new organizational unit was set up at the central office in Frankfurt in 1976, and was joined to what was then called Central Credit Department; this was the above-mentioned Central Corporate Customer Department which, in addition to similar long-standing organizational arrangements for retail banking and portfolio investment, had the job of promoting the business potential of the branches, subsidiaries and affiliates, and of evaluating their experiences to help make business policy decisions at central office. To ensure a continuous close link between business in the branch regions and the Central Corporate Customer Department, regular contact was established after it was set up with the Departments for Corporate Customers at regional head branches.

Details of the organization and responsibilities of the Central Corporate Customer Department – mentioned for the first time in this form – were contained in a paper approved by the board of managing directors at its meeting on 9–10 October 1976 in Kronberg. Under the heading 'General matters' was an early assessment of the potential importance of business with small and medium-sized enterprises: 'Our competitors for small and medium-sized companies are primarily the savings banks, the people's banks (*Volksbanken*) and credit co-operatives. We still have substantial potential for acquiring new business here owing to our extensive range of services.'

Information on the bank's market position and ambitions as far as business with small and medium-sized corporates was concerned can be obtained from the minutes of the first meeting with the branch heads of Corporate Customer Departments in Frankfurt on 19 November 1976:

'Dr Kleffel opened his remarks by pointing out that the market survey "Our business with corporate customers" revealed that there was a large number of enterprises, particularly in the small and medium-sized sector, with which we do not have a relationship. We have observed that our competitors are going about this in a hurried fashion, particularly as far as small and medium-sized enterprises are concerned. Rather than simply following suit, Deutsche Bank intends to proceed systematically and with a firm strategy to stabilize and expand our market share. This will make it necessary to organize the Corporate Customer Departments, including those below regional head branch level, more efficiently, which will mean bringing the organizational model, which is geared to the regional head branches, into line with the requirements of the regional branches ... Past analysis has shown that the imbalanced customer structure of many branch regions, i.e. the predominance of big-ticket customers, means that Deutsche Bank's services are used relatively little in times of high macroeconomic liquidity and relatively frequently in times of a liquidity squeeze. If the customer structure were more balanced, the differences in behaviour between whole-sale and medium-sized customers could produce more consistent demand for Deutsche Bank's services. The less well-balanced branches in particular should attempt to acquire more medium-sized customers with their typical non-hectic behaviour.'

The activity reports produced by the Central Corporate Customer Department provide evidence of the bank's activities for small and medium-sized corporates. The activity report for 1977/78, for example, recommended that in 1978 the branches should 'place more emphasis on internal business acquisition – particularly with a view to small and medium-sized customers – without neglecting external acquisition. A survey of our customer structure revealed that the proportion of corporate customers with turnover of up to 25 million DM is considerably lower than the proportion of large enterprises. At around 27 per cent, however, it is better than we expected; none the less, these firms made relatively little use of our product range.' In 1978, the Central Corporate Customer Department provided the branches with the first ever marketing plan to support them in their corporate banking activities. This plan, which is still drawn up once a year, laid down a time-frame for the concrete policy measures to be introduced by the branches as well as the basic strategies and advertising methods to be used by central office. The 1981 marketing plan contained a list of objectives related directly to small and medium-sized customers:

'We are aiming to counter the loss of market share in high-yielding short- and medium-term lending business that has been observed to date in the cyclical downswing and, in doing so, at least maintain our market position. This will mean that the regional markets will have to be worked on individually, and that specific measures will have to be implemented to acquire new business from the target groups

– large enterprises
– small and medium-sized firms.

Above all, the income and volume reserves evident in the available customer potential must be mobilized through internal business acquisition.'

The marketing plan called for a 'systematic broadening of the bank's customer base in terms of deposits, especially those of small and medium-sized enterprises' and the 'greater involvement of the bank in the foreign commercial business of medium-sized customers and non-customers'. This also contained the first corporate customer marketing manual (*FM-Leitfaden*), which the Central Corporate Customer Department provided for the regional head branches to assist them in the planning and implementation of marketing in corporate banking.

The regional marketing measures also contained several activities aimed exclusively at small and medium-sized enterprises. If one assumes optimistically that the information contained in these marketing plans was regularly revised and not simply taken over wholesale with only marginal changes and extrapolated, a number of objectives that have remained virtually unchanged until very recently give the impression that – even more than the bank's measures aimed at small and medium-sized enterprises – the deficits that the bank perceived in its business with these clients reveal a high degree of stability over time.

As part of the restructuring of responsibilities in retail and corporate banking, in 1979 the Corporate Customer Departments were given responsibility for all companies – customers and non-customers alike – entered in the Commercial Register. In addition to retail banking in the narrow sense, the Private Customer Departments were also allocated responsibility for all other businesses and self-employed persons – for example, enterprises entered in the Register of Craftsmen – unless, on the basis of the allocation criteria applied to date, it appeared more sensible for the business concerned still to be serviced by the Corporate Customer Department. The result of this was that a number of smaller firms entered in the Commercial Register could not be catered for by the Corporate Customer Departments, either because these departments did not (yet) have sufficient advisory and servicing capability, because the nature and volume of the business in question did not, over the long term, require the sort of know-how, experience or financing offered by corporate banking, or because the potential of the customer relationship did not yet warrant having it transferred to the Corporate Customer Department.

The minutes of the board of managing directors' meeting on 2 June 1978 stated that the 'strategy devised by the Central Corporate Customer Department was discussed in detail. All agreed that the existing systematic servicing and acquisition of new small and medium-sized enterprises as customers should be supported by a training programme for our staff. The implementation of measures relating to corporate banking requires that targets are set and that feedback is provided in order to determine what sort of result, e.g. income, has been achieved. It is desirable for managers of branches and sub-branches to be better integrated into the social environment of their branches. Initiatives of this kind are to be promoted. The Central Corporate Customer Department is to provide our staff with a manual, devised together with the branches, in which questions of particular interest to small and medium-sized enterprises are summarized and explained. The Corporate Customer Department at each regional head branch is to have one staff member with regional responsibility for fundamental questions concerning medium-sized enterprises; the head of this department is responsible to central office for this business. The limit on the medium-sized commercial loan (*Gewerblicher Anschaffungskredit*) is to be increased with immediate effect from 250,000 DM to 750,000 DM. The normal conditions for this kind of loan as well as other rates for cash and bills of exchange can be reduced for small and medium-sized enterprises with the consent of the relevant regional head branch if the competitive situation in the area appears to justify it.'

Shortly after that, central office reiterated to regional head branch managers why and how they should intensify their service for small and medium-sized businesses: 'The greater scope you now have in lending business is intended to underpin your efforts to capture new customers among typically middle-sized manufacturing companies with annual turnover of up to roughly 20 million DM or trading companies with turnover of up to 40 million DM. Our job is to stress the importance that small and medium-sized enterprises have in our business policy and to outline the measures planned as far as management responsibility for your region is concerned.'

A milestone in the development of the bank's relationship with small and medium-sized enterprises was the so-called *Mittelstandsermächtigung* (authorization for small and medium-sized business) of 1980. With a view to consolidating and expanding the bank's position *vis-à-vis* middle-sized businesses, it allowed the branches to give certain customer groups preferential conditions – provided that certain specific limits were observed. This arrangement was limited, as two years previously, to manufacturing and service companies with annual sales of up to approximately 20 million DM and trading companies with up to 40 million DM; individual limits applied to certain types of business.

Corporate customers, which were becoming increasingly discerning, required special, tailor-made products over and above traditional standard services. While corporate customers preferred traditional short- and medium-term loans until the 1950s, the mid-1960s saw a tendency towards more long-term financing. In the 1990s, and particularly after about 1980, a number of new instruments were developed which extended the traditional range of banking services to cover bank-related and, in some cases, non-bank products.

Early steps in this direction were taken in the mid-1960s with the inclusion of services such as leasing, factoring and forfaiting, which were offered by subsidiaries without being actively promoted by the bank initially. The growing need for advisory services, particularly on the part of small and medium-sized corporate customers, in what were becoming increasingly complex financial questions, gradually went beyond these bank-related services. The bank was now no longer merely a financier, since the financial services it offered also comprised a complementary advisory capability for corporates and businesses (consulting banking).

A significant change in the bank's corporate customer business was brought about by internationalization. Only with the gradual removal of foreign exchange controls in the post-war period and the full convertibility of the deutschmark at the end of 1958 could foreign trade be resumed. In addition to the growing volume of foreign trade, the greater interdependence with overseas countries and the progress of European integration presented the bank with an increasingly diverse field of activity.

The emergence of the Euromarkets, the closer political and economic co-operation within the EEC and the growth in German companies' activities abroad from the early 1970s meant that the bank increasingly had to concentrate on the international dimension of its business to enable it to provide its customers with services at all major financial centres world-wide. Financing needed abroad, for example, could often be better arranged locally at the usual international conditions; credit exposures in the host country, which could not always be assessed from abroad according to German criteria owing to the great distances involved or differences in language and legislation, could be better judged in the locality of the borrower.

In addition to the provision of services for German customers abroad, particularly in connection with their growing direct capital investment, the cultivation and intensification of relations with major foreign enterprises world-wide were equally important for the bank. By operating globally under its own name, the bank was able to achieve a competitive edge over its German and European competitors, which initially concentrated more on forms of co-operation.

The bank's corporate banking continued to dominate its business until well into the 1960s, since its new business with the mass of retail customers only became more important after some time, and up to this point the bank's personnel and organizational structure were geared towards corporate banking. Thereafter, this naturally had to be seen, on the one hand, within the context of retail business, which was becoming increasingly important; and on the other, in terms of changes in the structure of the bank's business and macroeconomic influences, which often brought a shift of emphasis in the different areas of the bank's corporate activities.

The big banks' increasing trend away from corporate business towards more business with other customer groups was illustrated by the fact that the proportion of corporate loans on the average big bank's balance sheet declined from over 86 per cent in 1970 to 75 per cent in 1977. The main reason for this lay in companies' longer-term financing requirements, which savings banks and credit co-operatives could easily cover owing to their more appropriate funding structure, which contained high volumes of funds for lending over the long term.

None the less, in 1991 Deutsche Bank captured a 7 per cent market share in corporate lending; with 140,000 out of roughly 400,000 enterprises, its customer ratio was over 30 per cent.

It is interesting that in 1993 the bank enhanced its examination of customers' credit standing – which, although traditional in nature, had been developed and refined over the years – by setting up a Credit Control Division as a risk management unit within the Group. It was located at head office and mandated to examine how credit risks were managed at branches, mainly – but not only – for corporate loans. One of the main objectives here was to gather sufficient empirical information to allow the bank's risk management to be improved.

The universal banking system typical of Germany used to be one of the main reasons why corporates maintained particularly close relations with their bank throughout their history, thus forming an intimate relationship with their house bank. Deutsche Bank had to try to attain this house bank status in order to promote its relationship management. As far as the banks' relationships with their major corporate clients were concerned, however, the 1980s can be regarded as a deal-based phase. Deutsche Bank, for example, lost the lead management of a financing deal for Daimler-Benz to Dresdner Bank after the company had asked for a binding offer over the telephone from all the major banks at very short notice, and the offer made by Deutsche's competitor was slightly cheaper.

However, there was a marked turnaround in this trend towards transactional banking in Germany after the economy started to weaken. During the deal-based phase, the bank was always very reticent whenever customers demanded excessive price concessions, which also meant that it lost some of its former house-bank relationships. In certain cases, this was no doubt the result of the bank's internal workflows, which compared to its competitors were too expensive. But it was also because of the bank's fundamental attitude to risk, which always demanded margins commensurate with the risk involved. Owing to the superior quality of its advisory services, it sometimes managed to justify higher prices and therefore escape this trend; only seldom was it aggressive in its pricing for strategic reasons. After the turnaround in the trend, it managed again to become one of the core banks wherever it aimed to do so. In 1992 Deutsche Bank was named by 90 per cent of the 350 or so largest German companies as one of the core banks.

The large group of organizations described as *institutional investors* are characterized, by virtue of their business activity, by the fact that practically the only services they require from the bank are short-, medium- and long-term deposits and, on a large scale, payment facilities, but they do not have an impact on the bank's lending business. If, for example, government agencies borrow to cover their short-term liquidity requirements, these transactions – as normal money-market business – are not treated as belonging to any specific customer group, but are settled in the money-markets department; no all-round customer service is provided here. The bank's business with domestic institutional investors, on the other hand, mainly involves securities business and has been closely linked to the development of Deutsche Gesellschaft für Fondsverwaltung mbH.

The *social insurers* have always played a very small part in the bank's payments business. This is because these institutions have traditionally had links with the public sector banks, from which they have often been able to obtain special conditions that, for the bank, would have meant losses on such a scale that they could not have been offset by follow-up business. Only in individual cases was the bank able to acquire larger customer relationships as a result of payment facilities, particularly relating to electronic banking, which at local level were seen as innovative.

Since the beginning of the 1990s, however, growing cost awareness on the part of the public sector banks has increasingly caused savings banks in particular to start charging account-keeping fees to cover their costs. As a result of this, some institutions, particularly health insurance agencies, have closed their accounts. As a consequence of its aggressive pricing and occasionally subsidized prices for payments business, Deutsche Bank was able to win new customer relationships. In the same way, it was able, in a few cases, to establish account relationships with churches and church-related institutions, whose increasingly sophisticated payment requirements could only be covered insufficiently or not at all by the specialized institutions, mainly small credit co-operatives, with which they were traditionally linked.

Public authorities at national, state and local-authority level and related – mainly privately organized – commercial companies, particularly local-authority utilities, are one group which, until the early 1990s, was somewhat neglected by the bank. The main reason for this was, and still is, their personal relationship with the public-sector credit institutions, namely the regional banks and savings banks, which was often institutionalized and usually strengthened by political influence. Only in isolated cases were Deutsche Bank's local branches able to penetrate the local market owing to their new financing concepts or innovative payment facilities, or simply as a result of the limited financing capability of the often small savings banks. Although whenever there has been a strong rise in public sector budget deficits the bank certainly helped to reduce these shortfalls, its lending exposure here was always on a modest scale; its loans to public sector authorities never amounted to more than 10 per cent of its total lending volume.

Since 1988, however, the bank's business with local authorities and related enterprises has provided good potential for these institutions to be defined as a separate target group, and for tailor-made services to be developed for their requirements, mainly as a result of the increasing importance of environmental issues. On an organizational level, this was finally also reflected in the bank's new structure at the beginning of the 1990s, when the name of the responsible department at head office was changed from Corporate Customer Department to Corporate Banking.

Besides its traditional medium- and long-term book loans to public sector entities, which from 1988 were added to the earlier placements of bonds and Schuldschein loans, but which did not promise any new potential owing to their established customer relations with other institutions, the bank saw good potential in property finance, in innovative financing instruments for specific forms of financing, and in the trend towards the privatization of public sector enterprises, in addition to its usual large-scale financing relating to water supply and treatment, energy supply and hospitals.

The considerable investment volumes needed for environmental protection and clean-up by far exceeded the financial resources of the public authorities responsible. Ideas such as leasing financing of public sector projects, which had already been propagated in the late 1960s by the bank's real-estate leasing subsidiary, but which remained largely unsuccessful due to the lack of acceptance on the part of the target group concerned, were increasingly taken on board by those in charge. The local-authority credit institutions were often too small and too inflexible – owing to legal restrictions and the intentionally or unintentionally sluggish behaviour of their managements and ruling bodies – to be able to match the bank's ideas. In contrast to its usual policy, the bank even hired a specialist from outside to make up for its own in-house lack of expertise. In 1993 the bank set up an organizational unit at its Berlin regional head branch known as 'db-kommunal'. This was to act as a centre of competence to bundle the know-how dispersed throughout the Group. Although fairly late, the bank was the first of the big banks to make use of its available expertise to acquire local authorities as new customers and to steal market share from the public sector banks.

In 1991 the bank's business with local authorities received a further fillip from the necessity to build a new infrastructure in eastern Germany. The under-developed structure of the public banking sector and the substantial delay in the savings bank associations' business start-up in eastern Germany owing to polit-ical controversies enabled the bank to gain a strong foothold in local authority business and to prepare the ground for substantial business activity with newly developed forms of financing, for example to clean up the environment, before local institutions were anywhere near able to develop similar products.

b) Trends in the product range for corporates

In the period following the Second World War, during which Deutsche Bank was reconstituted, the bank initially only offered account-keeping and payment facilities and was involved in traditional lending and deposit-taking business. During the last four decades, however, the demands of the diverse range of corporates have grown both in terms of quantity and, particularly, in terms of quality. There has been an increasing demand for greater lending volumes with longer maturities and more flexible interest and redemption terms. Financing cost advantages, made possible for both the bank and its customers by the use of swaps, and the demand for interest-capping instruments have placed more sophisticated demands on the bank, which has been looking to maintain its substantial market position in corporate business.

From roughly the mid-1970s onwards, deposits business tended to become more important than lending as a result of companies' higher liquidity; innovatively structured services, such as liquidity management, became necessary. As early as the 1960s, beginning with the growing importance of the Euromarket, it became increasingly necessary to offer both traditional and new financing and investment facilities in conjunction with supranational financial markets. This all took place against the background of greater price awareness on the part of customers.

In contrast to very small, regional banks, the bank could not withdraw to a niche that was only partly exposed to the market. Although it initially took a critical attitude – sometimes explicitly so – to many innovations and was also largely able to resist the narrowing in margins, in the longer term it had no option but to follow market trends and find ways of offsetting the decline in income from traditional business by using new products.

Although later than others, the bank none the less managed to maintain its substantial – in many cases, leading – market position in corporate business mainly through its concerted efforts to market the new concepts. Here, it benefited from the fact that, in contrast to other banks, particularly big ones, it was already able to provide its customers with much more sophisticated products than its competitors owing to its experience with the newly emerging markets and its lower market and product development costs.

In hindsight it is often impossible to tell whether the bank's initial reticence was due to a deliberate business policy of averting risks – as the bank would have us believe – or whether the opportunities available were simply not recognized. Likewise, it is often impossible for the observer, and probably also for the bank itself, to tell whether the cost of entering the market at a later date and having to regain market share was in the end perhaps not greater than the product development and default costs of its more innovative competitors.

Throughout the history of the bank, there have only been a few genuine innovations in corporate business, by far the largest part of this market being governed by financing forms which have changed only marginally, or not at all, in their basic structure. The development of traditional lending business has been determined not so much by the bank's business strategies as by companies' financial behaviour, which complemented their business activities and was naturally to be seen within the context of fluctuations in the economic cycle.

If one looks at typical phases in corporate business, it becomes evident that the bank's activities in this market segment initially amounted to no more than orthodox lending business. This merely consisted of the customer applying for the loan, which was then granted by the bank; anything over and above this, particularly payments business, was merely an added extra or, at best, to be seen as intentional or unintentional sales promotion for the bank's lending. Business took place on a personal level, the local branch manager being the determining factor. The pricing of loans was not yet of any significance; as far as the average customer was concerned, the bank fixed the amount and price of its loans. Business itself consisted of the traditional textbook types of loan.

The advent of retail banking saw the bank's business develop two areas: private business and lending business. These areas underline the tremendous importance at the time of the traditional corporate loan within non-private-customer business. At the same time, loans involving smaller amounts were given special names, which had not been customary for the usual types of loan. Totally uninfluenced by the standardization of smaller loans, however, traditional lending business for larger amounts developed at the same time into various types of loan which could be tailored to the customer's individual requirements. It was only after around 1970 that there were signs of a dual trend: on the one hand making the Euroloan available for smaller amounts, while on the other attempting to standardize larger loans in traditional domestic business.

Until the late 1960s, the bank's (formally) short-term loan was the traditional form of credit line for financing corporates. Long-term loans were not yet of any great importance; this sector was left to the savings banks, mortgage banks and specialized institutions. In addition, insurance companies provided long-term *Schuldscheindarlehen* (loans against promissory notes). This composition of the bank's lending volume was very much in line with its refinancing structure, and until well into the 1960s long-term loans were primarily funds from Reconstruction Loan Corporation (Kreditanstalt für Wiederaufbau) passed on by Deutsche Bank. Including these, long-term loans made up less than 10 per cent of the bank's total lending volume until 1966. In line with industry's financing requirements, the substantial increase in savings deposits subsequently gave rise to double-digit growth rates in long-term lending and underscored the fact that many companies had a latent need to consolidate their short- and medium-term borrowing, which the bank only now started to cover.

While in the 1970s corporate banking was strongly influenced by foreign business and domestic influences, such as the decline in companies' equity ratios, were partly due to the greater investment demand from foreign business, the second half of the decade was marked by a greater market and marketing orientation, including corporate business. In addition to organizational changes, this was intended to shape the attitude of the bank's staff towards their customers. The division of lending business into business acquisition and business settlement according to the organization model (see pp. 526–9) and the advent of the Central Corporate Customer Department in 1976 were aimed at bringing the bank's business more into line with market demands. Loans – in official parlance, at least – were now no longer granted but 'sold'. By the 1990s, however, this mental adjustment process had still not been completed in those places where it needed to be implemented.

In 1974 a systematic survey by the new Planning Department on the bank's position in the corporate market, broken down by sector, region and company size, painted a clear picture. The bank's involvement in business with small and medium-sized enterprises was still too low, but its business with big-ticket customers had also been declining for many years. The bank was not involved at all – either as the house bank or as a secondary banking connection – in 64 of Germany's 350 largest companies. The relatively unfavourable sector profile of the bank's borrowers also revealed that they were well represented in low-potential markets and considerably underrepresented in more promising sectors. A survey of the bank's value added per staff member revealed the worst figure of all the big banks and pointed to alarming deficits in its new business acquisition.

As a result, the bank's marketing activities commenced by devising new lending programmes. Based on the older small personal loan – up to 2,000 DM for all customer groups, including commercial clients – the commercial medium-sized loan (*Gewerblicher Anschaffungskredit*), mainly aimed at small and medium-sized enterprises, was introduced in 1976. In addition to offering larger amounts, this was also more favourably priced than the small loan to maintain the bank's position in the face of the more favourable offerings of other banks. The bank quickly achieved substantial growth in its commercial medium-sized loans, which in 1977 amounted to an average of approximately 100,000 DM.

The product 'db-industriedarlehen' was born in 1977 as a collective name for the loans also offered by the bank's subsidiaries – for example, the mortgage banks – in their business with big-ticket customers. This did not, however, represent a fundamentally new type of product. The forerunner of the first marketing plan for corporate business in 1978 brought the bank's business policy objectives and activities, particularly with respect to small and medium-sized enterprises, closely into line with market realities in a way previously unknown in corporate banking.

In November 1977 an internal circular dealt for the first time with the need to introduce systematic group account management. Until then, the various subsidiaries of large groups had their accounts managed decentrally by the nearest branch, without there being any consultation on their business volumes or conditions, let alone their income. This group account management was finally introduced in 1984. The reasons for this change of attitude were the bank's jeopardized and, in some cases, declining customer relationships and its change of direction – necessitated by the limited growth potential in its lending portfolio and narrowing margins – away from the maximization of its lending volume, which had long been regarded as sufficient, and towards the optimization of existing customer relationships.

However, conflicts between the branches managing the accounts of individual group companies decentrally had to be resolved through the allocation of costs and income resulting from the overall customer relationship, which influence the success of a branch and for which there were no suitable instruments available up to that point. Moreover, it was not possible to make use of cross-selling potential without the bank having an effective form of internal communication regarding its customer relationships.

As a rule, the new system of group account management stipulated that overall responsibility for the entire relationship should be given to the branch already managing the account of the parent company or holding company. This task naturally entailed a high degree of communication both within the bank itself and also with the customer. It was initially largely carried out manually owing to the bank's inadequate customer information systems. The bank first started its group account management with only 40 customers whom it felt justified the costs involved, and increased this number to over 100 by 1992.

The bank saw its potential customers among the 500 to 600 multinationals world-wide with which it already had business relations with at least parts of the Group, and among which it viewed roughly 200 to 300 as potential candidates for its Group account management after the bank's internal communications had been partly automated in the form of an EDP-aided reporting system. The development towards one-stop account management found its logical continuation in early 1992, when the internationalized financial engineering services were bundled in account management teams of highly qualified staff in the newly created Corporate Finance Division, who were responsible for certain multinational customers or customer groups. These staff members were fully able to meet their customers' substantial global advisory needs in all areas.

Although the bank had been engaged since the late 1960s in chattel and real-estate leasing, forms of financing such as leasing and factoring, which supplement traditional lending business, were only offered half-heartedly. Consequently, misconceptions about competition within the bank and people's inability to think on a Group level meant that what were initially regarded as alternative products to the traditional corporate customer loan were offered only when informed customers approached the bank themselves – which in those days rarely happened.

Following the delayed implementation of the bank's market orientation, such forms of financing were offered on a substantial scale only after 1983; international leasing for big-ticket real estate (cross-border leasing) began only in 1985. The bank's reticence to introduce innovative services – which at least it did quickly once the decision was taken – was none the less often vindicated by market developments. Especially on the international money and capital markets many complex innovations were devised, the vast majority of which disappeared from the market after just a few years or even months. Some of them, however, attained lasting importance for national lending business.

Mention should be made at this juncture of a specific development of particular importance to Deutsche Bank which cannot easily be allocated to any of the above-mentioned periods, namely *Schuldscheine* (promissory notes) as a financing instrument. A central problem during the economic recovery of German industry after the Second World War was the mobilization of capital. The incomes and assets of West German citizens during the post-war period were still too low, and the unpleasant memory of their money's loss of value as a result of inflation and the currency reform was still too painful, for the government to allow securities to be sold directly to private individuals. Instead, there was a preference for indirect investments, particularly with life insurance companies.

The *Schuldscheindarlehen* (loan against a promissory note) – a form of credit invented as early as the mid-1930s – offered a favourable method of channelling funds held by institutional investors to companies requiring capital. Most banks initially regarded this as unwelcome competition for the industrial bond. Despite the dismissive attitude of its Frankfurt head office, however, Deutsche Bank right from the outset played an important mediating role between lenders and borrowers by virtue of the fact that its Mannheim branch, which had been traditionally strong in trading and sales and was keen to guard its independence, was quick to secure itself a substantial market position.

The first *Schuldschein* transaction at head office was a 60 million DM tranche borrowed by Gelsenkirchener Bergwerks-AG. Although this transaction, which the trader responsible carried out without consulting his superiors, provided the bank with a sound, risk-free margin of 4 per cent, the trader was admonished for his actions. After all, the bank's official attitude to such instruments was still strictly dismissive.

A significant milestone in the history of the *Schuldscheindarlehen* and for the bank, especially its Mannheim branch, was the first *Schuldscheindarlehen* to be taken up by the Federal Republic of Germany in 1968, with a total volume of 1 billion DM. The bank managed to persuade the mortgage banks to start buying *Schuldscheine* by assuring them that the bank, in turn, would place *Kommunalobligationen* (public mortgage bonds) issued by the mortgage banks. In the mid-1960s, increasing demand for *Schuldscheindarlehen*, particularly from foreign investors, induced the bank to buy up foreign *Schuldscheine* from domestic clients and sell them abroad.

After the bank's Cologne branch, in addition to Mannheim, had temporarily secured itself a substantial market position in *Schuldschein* trading, in 1970 *Schuldschein* business became fully accepted at the bank's head office in Frankfurt and was then systematically transacted. This change of attitude, however, was not for economic reasons, but was more the result of a change on the board of managing directors, when Robert Ehret replaced Hans Feith as the board member responsible for bond trading. Activities were concentrated on initial placements and subsequent repositionings when, once the oil crises had been overcome, there was a turnaround in the oil-exporting countries' financial situation, and it became necessary to sell *Schuldscheine* from OPEC portfolios.

Since the early 1970s there has been increasing competition in referral business;

the regional banks and mortgage banks in particular have been increasing their own placement capabilities. Although the greater competition led to a narrowing of margins and a decline in loan interest to just above capital market rates, the bank managed to continue the referral of *Schuldscheindarlehen* as a profitable business owing to its experience and sufficiently high turnover. This was the case even after life insurers increasingly began to issue *Schuldscheindarlehen* direct, without the mediation of banks.

The borrowing requirements of the new federal states were such that they, too, soon began to use *Schuldschein* loans. At the beginning of 1992, the first *Schuldschein* loans to be issued by the federal state of Brandenburg were placed through Deutsche Bank Mannheim and, as part of the efforts to rebuild the eastern German economy, were settled by the Land Central Bank of North Rhine-Westphalia.

The wide range of *securities business* so typical of universal banks has always been of central importance to Deutsche Bank's activities. Fluctuations in the income generated by this sector compared to other lines of business are the result of changes in interest rates. Compared to other institutions and specialized banks, however, these fluctuations are relatively small. The bank has been able to draw on its considerable underwriting know-how in such a way that even minor transactions can be settled at a profit, or at least show sufficient medium-term potential as a result of follow-up transactions for the bank to maintain its underwriting on a sound footing. When setting up national or international underwriting syndicates, it has always benefited from its considerable placement capability resulting from its extensive branch network and fine reputation, so that in the early 1980s it was still involved in roughly 90 per cent of primary-market placement volume in Germany.

Historically, the bank's Mannheim branch has always played an important part in bond trading and underwriting. Owing to its creativity, innovativeness and new business acquisition, the branch was quick to regain its major position after the war and, although not always the branch with the highest income, by 1991 it was one of the bank's most important bond trading units, with an annual volume of approximately 100 billion DM. Between 80 and 90 per cent of all placements abroad were routed through Mannheim.

It benefited in this respect from what was at least optically its distance from the banking centre of Frankfurt in the sense that decisions driven by business policy – for example, the bank's official cautious approach towards innovations – did not have the same impact in Mannheim as at head office. Other institutions' unplaceable underwriting shares from head office issues were sometimes inconspicuously brought back to the market via the Mannheim branch for reasons of standing. This branch's underwriting capability at the same time automatically gave it a significant market-maker position in secondary trading. In 1991, for example, the branch traded over 500 securities daily, many of them not listed, and practically the entire German market in Japanese convertible bonds and warrant issues was handled by Mannheim.

The bank's securities and underwriting business can be divided up into a few major phases. Following the re-emergence of what were at least the beginnings of an efficient capital market, the bank's forerunner institutions began at an early stage to co-operate with each other in their underwriting activities and visibly to work together in syndicates – if not as one bank, then at least as a banking group. In 1952 one of the predecessor banks underwrote the first bond for the Federal Republic of Germany for 500 million DM, which carried a 5 per cent coupon and ran for five years. From 1955 the expiration of the Capital Markets Acts allowed a genuine capital market to develop. One of the first issues on this market was the 1956 Bosch bond, which was well placed by another of the bank's predecessor institutions.

The buyers of paper issued by public authorities, industry and mortgage banks were almost exclusively institutional investors until well into the 1960s. The reconstituted bank was able to benefit from its excellent contacts with these institutions. There were only a few significant competitors on the market, since the regional banks did not yet have any major underwriting capability, and most private bankers had not yet recommenced their activities.

On the whole, the 1960s could be described as a decade of foreign business. During this period, the bank began to consolidate its pioneering role in internationalization. Its special position on the market for Japanese international DM bonds dates from 1962 when, as a result of the personal contacts between Abs and German Chancellor Adenauer, the first of two bonds issued by the City and Prefecture of Osaka for 100 million DM each and with a 6.5 per cent coupon was placed by the bank on the German market, at first somewhat sluggishly, but in the end very successfully after a good deal of public relations work. This was followed in 1964 by a 6 per cent bond issued by the Japanese government for 200 million DM.

One of the major developments of the 1960s was the emergence of the Euromarket. Abs had declared as late as November 1963 – when the Euromarket was already worth between $16 billion and $18 billion – that the bank had neither debts nor claims in Eurodollars, but that it would 'follow with interest the development of this market without participating in it'. By 1968 the Euro money and capital markets were in full swing – also as a result of speculations surrounding the revaluation of the deutschmark – and were outperforming the traditional market in international DM bonds.

The 1970s was a decade of crisis, and the capital markets were dominated by oil, the sheiks and their petrodollars. The Eurobond market received an extra fillip when the sale of domestic bonds to foreigners was made subject to authorization, introduced to prevent foreigners from getting around the so-called cash deposit requirement. High interest rates and low share prices practically brought the capital market to a standstill. During this period the bank was mainly engaged – also as a form of substitute business – in the sale of DM Eurobonds as well as warrant issues and convertible bonds of Japanese clients. Also worth mentioning is the bank's first issue of its own bonds since the late 1970s, which for a long time had been looked down upon. However, the decreasing attractiveness of traditional investment facilities for private customers meant that more and more funds were flowing into securities, and the bank thus felt it was forced to shore up this potential by issuing its own bonds.

The so-called remaining liberalization of the capital market in 1985 and the abolition of coupon tax in 1984 helped make it possible to issue internationally customary financing instruments on the German market. The bank was somewhat reticent here, since an issuing house is usually expected, after it has successfully placed an issue, to assist the security concerned, for example, by supporting the market. The incalculable risks of innovative instruments, particularly with regard to secondary-market liquidity, make prudence advisable here. Especially important for the bank was its issue of BMW abos (annuity bonds) – several tranches of zero bonds with staggered maturities. Despite the poor conditions on offer due to the interest rate situation and their lack of transparency, the bank was able – with some effort – to sell the issue. For the first time, however, this necessitated intensive marketing to win over potential private buyers.

The bank played a pioneering role with shorter-term forms of financing, which until then were not very widespread owing to statutory and minimum reserve requirements. After DM medium-term notes were admitted in July 1989, the bank arranged a programme for Volkswagen AG. In hindsight, the bank's reserved attitude towards many other innovations on the financial markets has in many respects proved to be farsighted.

After 1991, the market was characterized by substantial DM commercial paper programmes following the repeal of legislation preventing their issuance. Deutsche Bank was practically the first of the German banks to start launching DM commercial paper programmes for corporate customers with good credit standing. In 1991 alone, DM commercial paper programmes were arranged for such varied customers as Daimler-Benz, Südzucker, BMW, Herlitz, G. Haindl'sche Papierfabriken, Heraeus Holding and Korea's Samsung Group. In March 1992 the bank arranged a 2 billion DM programme for the German Post Office. By far the largest issuer in the early 1990s was the Treuhandanstalt, the government agency set up to privatize former East German enterprises. Its programme initially totalled 2 billion DM and subsequently, after several increases, 10 billion DM, and was co-arranged by Deutsche Bank and Dresdner Bank.

As far as developments in German companies' *equity financing* immediately after the currency reform are concerned, shares could only be issued, if at all, at par value owing to their low stock market valuation, and were therefore not very attractive for issuers. The recommencement of the issuance of equity was therefore marked by *convertible bonds*, starting in 1952 with a Deutsche Bank issue for Maschinenfabrik Augsburg-Nürnberg (MAN), with a right to convert the bonds into preference shares. The conditions governing these convertible bonds, however, was such that after a few years the entire debt issue had been converted into equity.

The bank's activities in what in those days was considered issuing business initially concentrated on the unbundling of existing groups and the merger of broken-up groups, and it arranged equity swaps aimed at simplifying participating interests. The late 1950s thus brought a sea change in the sense that the first bullish equity market, which peaked in 1958/59, signalled the start of equity issues.

The enactment of the Treaty of Rome on 1 January 1958 and the full convertibility of the deutschmark from December 1958 gave the equity markets a stronger international dimension. Deutsche Bank used this opportunity to float foreign companies on German stock exchanges, initially largely to establish contacts and improve its image. The first foreign share to be listed in Germany was that of Anglo American Corporation which, after its convertible bond was placed by Deutsche Bank in 1958, had both its bonds and equity listed.

The first pure equity listing was also in 1958, when Dresdner Bank handled the flotation of the Dutch group Philips on five German stock exchanges; the listing of Royal Dutch/Shell was the first to be managed by Deutsche Bank. This transaction was remarkable since any technical problems arising from the company's dual headquarters and the registered nature of the shares could be solved by tradable securities. This was followed by Deutsche Bank's listing of Banque Paribas, which in return managed the flotation of numerous German shares, such as BASF, Siemens, Mannesmann and Hoechst, in France. Further companies such as General Motors, Ford, Nestlé and Péchiney followed suit. However, not all of these listings involved new placements, since the shares in question were already in circulation and were obtained at stock exchanges world-wide.

A central problem was making the securities deliverable, especially in business with the USA. The listing of the Italian group Fiat in the early 1960s by Deutsche and Dresdner Bank together illustrated this, since the shares were actually certificates signed by the banks. It was only in the late 1970s that the global certificate came into use, and was later also utilized in domestic business as a replacement for the *Jungschein* (scrip). By the end of the 1970s, more than 50 per cent of all foreign stocks listed and placed in Germany had been managed by Deutsche Bank.

The late 1950s and early 1960s were marked by a wave of *Volksaktien* (shares for the small investor) from privatized or partly privatized federal government assets. The first *Volksaktie* in March 1959 resulted from a 30 million DM capital increase by Preussag AG, a subsidiary of Vereinigte Elektrizitäts- und Bergwerks-AG (VEBA), and thus indirectly a government holding, with VEBA renouncing its subscription right. A syndicate led by Deutsche Bank together with Commerzbank and Dresdner Bank underwrote the shares and sold them at 145 per cent of their nominal value at a par value of no more than 400 DM per subscriber. The placement was several times oversubscribed and terminated prematurely; none the less, the federal government had to instruct VEBA to bring far more shares than originally intended to market.

The bank managed a minor revolution on the market for regular equity issues with its first capital increase for BASF in 1961. In contrast to previous BASF capital increases in 1955, 1957 and 1959, this was not only carried out considerably above par value at a price of 300 per cent, but also gave the subscription right a substantial trading value.

In 1960 a law obliged the federal government, as the owner of Volkswagenwerk GmbH, to turn the firm into a joint stock company and place 60 per cent of its capital – 360 million DM – with the general public. A Deutsche Bank-led syndicate, based on the federal bond syndicate, sold the shares for 350 per cent at a social discount graded according to marital status and income. The issue was roughly 100 per cent oversubscribed; the first share prices were quoted at between 693 and 780 per cent on the unlisted securities market on 7 April 1961. This does not mean, however, that the bank priced the shares badly at the expense of the seller, since a low price had been deliberately stipulated for political reasons, as was the case with the Preussag placement.

The third issue of *Volksaktien* – this time without any social discount – when 64 per cent of VEBA was privatized in 1965, was carried out at an issue price of 210 per cent by a syndicate led by Dresdner Bank and co-managed by Deutsche Bank. The issue was preceded by months of advertising by the federal government and the banks involved in order to bring the largely unknown company into the public eye. The volume of approximately 1.2 billion DM did not allow it to be fully allocated. However, the share was first quoted at only 226 per cent, and at year-end the share was quoted below its issue price. Severe criticism was levelled at the two syndicate leaders in particular for their failure to support the share price sufficiently.

In 1966 a nominal 55 million DM capital increase by Lufthansa, as part of its partial privatization, was initially attempted without the involvement of banks. When this encountered difficulties, however, a syndicate led by Deutsche Bank was set up. A Vereinigte Elektrizitätswerke Westfalen (VEW) placement of 75 million DM under its lead management was also successful. The pricing debate inevitably following almost all issues presents the serious analyst with the problem of having to assess the reasons for the bank's decisions; a hindsight analysis of the share price's development, however, does not justify the accusation that the bank discriminated against either the issuers or investors, or even that its analysis was flawed.

Many convertible bond issues were only briefly popular before being overtaken by warrant issues in the early 1970s. The year 1964 saw the emergence of a new type of convertible bond which allowed additional, staggered payments to be made on top of the nominal amount upon conversion, so that there was only yield potential in future and not, as previously, immediately after their issue. The bank issued such bonds for BASF, DEMAG and Siemens, among others. The relatively low volume of capital increases was due to the fact that equity was regarded as too expensive as late as the mid-1960s, and the concept of leverage had become popular with many managers.

At the beginning of 1970 – the first quotation was on 6 January – the sale of Horten AG out of family ownership was the first flotation which did not also involve privatization. A syndicate led by Deutsche Bank and Commerzbank had no problems placing the shares in the market, although the share price subsequently fell owing to the company's credit standing. Foreign institutions were also in the syndicate for the first time. A major problem of the issue was the valuation of the company and the pricing, since the seller, Horten, was naturally interested in the share price being as high as possible, while the bank had to try to balance the interests of both issuer and investors.

In 1975 the bank's underwriting was dominated by the first sale of Daimler-Benz AG shares from the Flick Group's holdings. The 29 per cent block of share capital out of the total 39 per cent held by the Flick Group appeared to be in jeopardy after there was talk of Iran buying it. Probably primarily for political reasons and with the support of the federal government, the bank looked for a way of keeping this shareholding in German hands. After ten days of decision-making and negotiation, it bought the shares for an actual amount of almost exactly 2 billion DM, which amounted to a premium of roughly 10 per cent, under an agreement dated 13 January 1975, but effective from 1 January 1976 at 0:00 hours. The reasons for this forward purchase agreement were mainly of a tax nature, but also so that the bank had plenty of time to sell the shares again before it would be obliged to report them to the Federal Cartel Office (see pp. 592–4). The transaction was concluded in April 1976 by the issue of the bank's bonds with warrants attached, with a subscription right on Mercedes-Automobil-Holding's nominal 50 million DM worth of shares that were not placed in December 1975. Shares could be bought for 310 DM up to 1 April 1977 and then at gradually higher prices until 1 April 1979. The terms offered by the bond were clearly intended to ensure that the subscription right was exercised as soon as possible; the subscription right was not separately tradable either. Subsequent estimates put the bank's profit from this transaction at approximately 30 million DM, which seems small indeed compared to the estimated profit made by Dresdner Bank from its placement of the Quandt family's Daimler shareholding in Kuwait.

The 1980s will go down in capital market history as the going-public decade owing to low corporate equity ratios against the background of a very strong income situation and good stock market sentiment. An important stage here was an amendment to the Income Tax Act, which induced many proprietors of family-owned businesses to sell their companies, just as Flick disposed of his industrial shareholdings at the end of 1985. From these holdings, the bank placed the Daimler shares, worth approximately 3.8 billion DM, with the general public, as it did the Feldmühle shares following a reorganization of the family-owned group on 24 April 1986; this stock market listing was the largest to date, with proceeds of approximately 2 billion DM.

In 1984 the placement of 4.4 million VEBA shares marked the beginning of a new wave of privatizations – which was justified both on fiscal and general political grounds – in which the bank was always involved. In summer 1986, following a widespread information campaign, shares in the previously largely unknown VIAG Aktiengesellschaft, Bonn, with a market value of 1.5 billion DM were sold by the federal government and placed with the general public, and in March 1987 the remaining 10.1 million shares in VEBA were sold for 2.5 billion DM. A further 16 per cent block of Volkswagen shares worth 1.1 billion DM was sold in March 1988, and in May 1988 the last major partial privatization for the time being involved the federal government's remaining VIAG holding of almost 1.5 billion DM.

Following moves to reform the structure of the German Post Office into private companies, and after it had been decided to issue shares in the hived-off Telekom company in 1996, Deutsche Bank was chosen to lead-manage this most lucrative and prestigious project. The bank then did something which cast doubt on the venture: in 1993 it acquired a 25 per cent stake, together with RWE (25 per cent) and Mannesmann (50 per cent) in a new company set up to run corporate networks, primarily for corporates, on the German and European telecommunications markets. Post Minister Bötsch and the Telekom management were irritated and even angry at this, especially as they had only learned of it from the press. Telekom's management commented that the sale of its shares would now 'have to be reconsidered'.

As early as the late 1970s, Deutsche Bank started to promote an equity culture and equity financing in the form of share placements for private investors, and considered ways of using the capital markets more efficiently for both listed and unlisted companies. In the case of non-customers, the bank's initial 80–90 per cent market share of flotations offered good acquisition prospects. At this stage, 25–35 per cent of the flotation candidates looked after by the bank were not yet customers and, in addition to improving the bank's image, it offered the bank good income prospects over the medium term at least.

After the bearish stock market sentiment beginning in late 1987 had brought issuing activity to a standstill, it took some time for new stock-market candidates to appear. However, the bank's successful placements at this time were nowhere near as spectacular as in the mid-1980s, and the competition for mandates had become stronger. While until the mid-1980s the bank had been the undeniable market leader and in 1986 had arranged 15 out of 26 new issues, by 1988 it managed only 2 out of 14; in 1990, however, 9 out of 23; and in 1991, 9 out of

25. The rising issuing prices presented a much greater risk of incomplete placements or at least lower share price increases, if they rose at all.

Moreover, there were occasionally companies planning to go public whose financial situation – at least at the time in question – made this step inadvisable. In the case of Co op, the retail chain, the bank saw no other option after lengthy negotiation and detailed analyses but to refuse the company's underwriting mandate, which turned out to be the right decision. In autumn 1987, Co op's shares were placed by Swiss Bank Corporation, which had been seeking a sizeable mandate in Germany for some time. This bank – as an observer commented with a slight touch of malicious pleasure – 'fell flat on its face'. Less than a year later, Co op was insolvent and was forced to file for bankruptcy.

But Deutsche Bank also made errors. The shares of Volksfürsorge were placed by the bank and on 19 July 1991, despite massive purchasing to support their price, were quoted for the first time at practically their issue price of 800 DM. They then dropped so considerably shortly after they were issued that the bank had to ask itself if it might not have been better to reject this mandate.

The 1980s also saw a brief wave of participatory certificate issues: for example, for Klöckner & Co. AG, Duisburg. Although the bank repeatedly expressed its disapproval of hybrid instruments, which are partly a substitute for equity, it was accused of not having sufficiently pointed out their risks when the company collapsed a short time later in October 1988 (see p. 595). After these participatory certificates lost their value, however, one could not accuse the bank of failing to shoulder its responsibility for the company's considerable speculative blunders resulting from its oil transactions; on the contrary, it was more lenient with the ailing participatory certificate holders than was legally required.

A new trend was set in motion by the incorporation of the former East Germany into the Federal Republic. The first stock-market candidate from there, at the end of 1991, was Sachsenmilch AG, which used the bank's services to bring just under 50 per cent of its capital of 75 million DM to market. Although this first East German stock was intended as a long-term investment which would not pay a dividend until 1996 at the earliest and was generally regarded as very favourably priced, the placement failed to achieve the desired success, despite early termination of the subscription period. The first quotation of the share was only at its issue price of 80 DM, presumably supported by Deutsche Bank.

At the time of this placement, the bank was already talking to further potential flotation candidates in the new federal states. However, the bank was very cautious here – and rightly so, as events in 1993 proved. Sachsenmilch, whose equity had been so highly praised, became insolvent. Threatened with legal consequences, Deutsche Bank was finally forced to make those outside shareholders who had bought shares before their quotation was suspended on 15 July 1993 a repurchase offer at the original subscription price – a courageous step indeed.[26]

There are probably only few business lines that during the history of the bank have undergone so many fundamental structural changes as the *investment of corporate and institutional funds*. However, the possibility to outsource this business to specialized institutions within the Group was used to full advantage, and much earlier than in most other types of business. While in international investment the Euromarkets were closely looked after by subsidiaries, particularly in Luxemburg, Deutsche Gesellschaft für Fondsverwaltung mbH (DEGEF) started as early as 1967 to set up special-purpose funds for investment in securities. The activity of Deutsche Bank itself was largely restricted to acquiring new business and rounding off the forms of investment on offer, especially at the short end, although here, too, the trend towards investment funds reduced the volume of traditional time deposits through the arrival of money-market and money-market-related funds. Although this business was outsourced, primarily to DEGEF, the portfolio investment know-how was retained by the bank, since its fund management for DEGEF, for example, was carried out decentrally by the larger trading centres within the bank.

During the post-war period, the bank's principal investment customers were the institutional investors, particularly life insurers and social insurance agencies, as institutional investors for the increasing financial assets of private individuals. After the early to mid-1960s, households' wealth formation grew to such an extent that they started to deposit increasing amounts directly with banks as well. Since the customer structures meant that these funds were initially deposited with savings banks and commercial credit co-operatives, particularly in the form of savings deposits, and these banks had not yet developed their lending business sufficiently to be able to lend the funds to customers themselves, these institutions' search for alternative borrowers led them to Deutsche Bank, which in turn was not yet able to acquire its own deposits on the same scale and needed refinancing for its mainly short-term loans. In the 1970s, however, these funds from other banks declined substantially, instead of which the bank increasingly managed to obtain its own long-term deposits. After 1957, sight and time deposits, especially from interbank business, which at times accounted for up to 30 per cent of total assets, grew continually and rapidly. At the short end, repurchase agreements – which, although in use since the 1920s, were not very widespread – became increasingly popular after 1960 for optimizing returns on existing portfolios. Out of the approximately 330 institutions actively involved in repurchase agreements, the bank was one of the 15 most prolific borrowers and lenders, and one of the 25 institutions that accounted for three-quarters of the liabilities and two-thirds of the claims of all repurchase agreements.

In 1977 the first money-market transactions with large non-bank customers, particularly from the industrial sector, marked a milestone in investment business. Money-market dealing, primarily call money at interbank terms and conditions, had long been spurned by Deutsche Bank, since it regarded this as breaking into a traditional domain. Only after it was pressured by several customers, who were already doing such business with reputable competitors, did the bank enter this business, initially with only a few industrial customers.

The 1980s were then largely characterized by the unabated growth in deposits after 1983, particularly those of large industrial companies, which on balance switched from being borrowers to lenders thanks to the more favourable market conditions and their own high liquidity. American banks operating in Germany already had more experience in this sector, and Deutsche Bank was therefore faced by competition that was trading oriented by tradition as well. However, the bank was able to counter the more professional, sales-oriented behaviour of its competitors with its experience of special-purpose funds, so that in most cases it was able to maintain its customer relationships.

In recent years, the general financial market trends have contributed to greater volatility on the markets and a rise in innovations. This soon made it imperative for the bank to introduce instruments that could be used to plan and manage the volume of its deposits more precisely. Liquidity management and treasury were developed as international services for large corporates. After 1986, there was also an increasing tendency for corporates to buy securities which were frequently managed by DEGEF as special-purpose funds. After money-market and money-market-related funds were made legal in the 1990s, especially in other European countries, this trend away from sight and time deposits was intensified, and in 1994 money-market funds were also legalized in Germany.

The development of Deutsche Bank's *payment services* has been marked, on the one hand, by the emergence of new products and, on the other, by the rationalization and automation of existing payment services. Owing to its size and thus its considerable share of national payments business, however, the bank is naturally never the first to introduce innovations throughout its network; it prefers to wait for a while to see whether a development or trend is likely to last before fully implementing it in its own institution.

For a long time, the bank's payments business was handled manually, needed considerable labour and generated exceedingly high costs. The enormous rise in the number of items handled following the introduction of cashless payment for private customers led to ongoing rationalization within the departments handling payments, but not yet in business with customers. Long processing times for amounts handled within the bank allowed it to make substantial float profits, which partly covered the cost of its payments. The bank was therefore cautious towards innovations in business with customers. Only with big-ticket customers did the bank conclude initial agreements on a data carrier exchange for a number of small transfers; however, these could only be used for bulk payments owing to the data format's lack of standardization, incompatible computer systems, the inflexible burden of proof resting on customers and, not least, unattractive pricing.

A typical example of Deutsche Bank's attitude was the development of cash management systems. Since the 1970s, the Group's customers had been calling for their decentrally held accounts to be combined into one central account, mainly so that they would earn more interest. Only against its will and as a result of pressure from customers did the bank carry out such concentration processes manually, which reduced its float profits and entailed disproportionately high handling costs. The argument occasionally put forward by the bank nowadays that good liquidity management improves the customer's income and also the security of the loans extended has only been developed over the past few years to overcome internal resistance.

Although strategies for stepping up computerization within the bank were already being devised by middle management, in 1981 the board of managing directors – through its narrow interpretation of income – blocked attempts to develop such programmes since it feared that more customers might demand such a service in future. The bank changed its attitude in the early 1980s, when there was increasing demand from customers for comprehensive cash management systems, which had already been offered for some time by competitors, particularly American institutions. The board member responsible for corporate business had a sudden change of heart. In 1983 a working group was set up to look into the development of electronic banking services. A milestone generating substantial publicity came in 1986, when the bank became the first ever to attend the CeBiT computer trade fair in Hanover with a range of 15 electronic banking services.

As part of 'db-electronic banking', a service which had been offered under this collective heading since 1983, the existing magnetic tape clearing system, which at the time handled over 40 per cent of payments for corporate customers, was joined by other data carriers, especially diskettes, and offered to corporates as 'db-rationell'. In the mid-1980s, however, not all regional head branches were able to process all data carriers or even, in some cases, all customary diskette formats. The system was obviously still geared towards magnetic tapes, which only large corporates usually had.

Cash management, the only electronic banking product aimed solely at large corporates, was introduced at the end of 1984 in the form of 'db-direct', an international business information and transfer system which also included the branches abroad. The system's advantage over those of quicker competitors was its more sophisticated protection against unauthorized use. The manual account transfer system, a forerunner of the cash management system and solely geared to domestic business, was replaced by the 'db-transfer' national system, which enabled account balances at Deutsche Bank branches to be combined on the same value date.

The year 1991 saw the introduction of an electronic cash payment system (point of sale), initiated by the bank, which it called an online direct debit system. This procedure, which was first introduced by the retail chain Peek &

Cloppenburg and was therefore called the 'P & C system' in the industry, merely involved checking the customer's name against the German banking industry's central blocking list for eurocheque and, subsequently, suitable customer cards. A voucherless debit was generated for the respective amount on the basis of the card's data, and this amount was then credited to the retailer on the same day. In view of the bank's own actual costs, the fees charged to the retailer already more than covered the costs; moreover, crediting the turnover amount daily produced a larger volume of sight deposits than with other payment media. The bank's original intention was to introduce this system on its own, but since this would have created an unfair competitive advantage and the bank was intending to use the banking industry's blocking list, it was found advisable to include the other bank groups.

By the end of 1992, Deutsche Bank had the most comprehensive electronic data network in Germany, if not world-wide. This was then spun off into the new Deutsche Gesellschaft für Netzwerkdienste mbH. This was intended not to perform carrier functions for third parties, but to provide service functions for the bank's various products. The network was offered to customers to make the bank's electronic services more attractive. The new subsidiary did not necessarily have to make a profit, since competitors did not have anything similar. The most important thing was the efficiency of its service function and the prospect of follow-up business. To improve the efficiency of its cross-border payments in Europe, at the end of 1993 the bank introduced a standardized Euro form for transfers which could be read and processed electronically.

It is a fair assumption that Deutsche Bank, as a constant partner to its corporate customers, has throughout its history assisted in the *buying and selling of companies, parts of companies and participating interests* and, in particular, in the financing of such transactions. Probably Germany's first major takeover transaction involving the bank – although with a less than favourable outcome – was an attempt by Daimler-Benz AG in the early 1960s to take over BMW AG, which was in financial difficulty. Hans Feith pulled out all the stops to ensure that the takeover would go ahead, but in the end the Bavarian government managed to assert its own, very different interests. After what for the bank turned out to be an embarrassing BMW general meeting, the Quandt industrial dynasty acquired a stake in the car-maker in place of Daimler.

Only in about 1967 did the bank start attempting to make a direct profit from mergers and acquisitions by taking on a form of organized agency function. For this purpose, the so-called Industrial Agency Service was set up at central office in Frankfurt. Its task was to collect information on companies to be bought or sold, and regularly to send the branches an overview in the form of simple lists indicating supply and demand; it did not provide any advisory services. The list of companies was restricted to small and medium-sized enterprises.

The foundation of DB Consult GmbH in 1984 was born of the somewhat late realization that, without a more professional approach to the business opportunities offered by mergers and acquisitions, the bank would still fail to make a profit from this sector. After large industrial groups had begun as early as the 1970s to set up their own mergers and acquisitions departments, DB Consult's prime target group were the somewhat neglected small and medium-sized companies. In a few cases there were foreigners who were interested in buying into the German market. However, cross-border business was not actively carried out. Group responsibility for this lay with the working group within Deutsche Bank Capital Corporation, New York (DBCC), which was set up at about the same time.

After DB Consult was renamed DB Mergers & Acquisitions GmbH (DBM& A) at the beginning of 1989, the group in New York was spun off from DBCC as a subsidiary of DBM&A, and offered German customers systematic help in finding American companies to buy. Asian business was also settled in New York for a transition period. In line with the strategy of its forerunner, DBM&A concentrated mainly on small and medium-sized corporates, but also handled larger companies. Out of the roughly 70 mandates received by the company up to 1991, roughly 40 of which were actually concluded, the largest transaction came in 1988, when RWE took over Texaco for around 1 billion DM, a transaction in which the bank represented the interests of the seller; a further substantial transaction was the sale of Co op to Asko Deutsche Kaufhaus AG in 1989.

Although DBM&A had already begun to open representative offices abroad in 1989, the demands of German customers looking to enter markets abroad required a more substantial international presence. The opportunity at the end of 1989 for the bank to acquire the UK merchant bank Morgan Grenfell therefore seemed like a gift from heaven, since the British bank's traditionally weak German business could easily be integrated into DBM&A and, likewise, Morgan Grenfell's large international network and high reputation could make up for the bank's severe lack of experience on international markets. Consequently, Morgan Grenfell's Frankfurt activities were integrated into DBM&A, which in mid-1990 was renamed DB Morgan Grenfell GmbH.

A central question for both the bank and its corporate identity was its involvement in, and especially financing of, hostile takeovers. In 1988 Alfred Herrhausen described these as 'misguided American capitalism', and as early as 1983 the board of managing directors passed a resolution rejecting the bank's involvement in such takeovers. However, there was evidence of an increasing world-wide trend towards hostile rather than friendly takeovers, which was an almost inevitable result of the sharp rise in takeovers. The takeover of Morgan Grenfell Group was sufficient proof, if indeed any were needed, that the bank did not take part only in friendly takeovers.

Potential was seen on the German market following the country's unification. Initially, however, the bank was very cautious compared to its competitors, particularly non-banks, since the bank did not believe it was possible (at this stage) to carry out satisfactory company and market analyses. None the less, this argument by the bank was rejected by others, who pointed out that the Treuhand, which was engaged in the privatization of former East German enterprises, had been using the services of international investment banks on a substantial scale since mid-1991 in its search for potential investors around the world.

c) Trends in business with small and medium-sized corporates

Deutsche Bank's business with small and medium-sized corporates is not really a historical subject in the sense that this clientele did not become an integral part of the bank's business strategy until around the mid-1970s. There is no doubt that the bank was already doing business with medium-sized enterprises before this time, and that it also had a house-bank relationship with certain such enterprises that had evolved over time. However, its identification and treatment of this sector as a separate target group developed in the late 1970s and, especially, in the 1980s. With the benefit of hindsight, the bank's orientation towards small and medium-sized corporates could be favourably interpreted as the result of strategic market planning, which provided these companies, as a separate market component, with a product range conceived and continually developed in line with their typical requirements: 'db-Unternehmens-Service'.

Of the roughly 230,000 corporate customers in western Germany at the beginning of the 1990s, 95 per cent were small or medium-sized enterprises. Firms with annual turnover of up to 50 million DM accounted for over half of all deposits and loans in Deutsche Bank's corporate business, and including corporates with turnover of between 50 and 250 million DM, this figure was as high as 75 per cent. In addition, the bank also looked after over 400,000 self-employed people.

These figures alone underline the fact that the traditional popular image of the bank as 'a big bank for big customers' gives a one-sided and incomplete picture, and that it is certainly also a bank for small and medium-sized businesses. This is also the image the bank has of itself. Zapp commented in Magdeburg in 1991 that the bank saw itself 'as a bank that sees co-operation with small and medium-sized enterprises as a major part of its activity – both in western Germany and in the new federal states'.

The importance placed on small and medium-sized corporates is illustrated by the 1984 Annual Report. An article entitled 'On the Middle Classes' looked in detail at their significance – numerically, economically and politically. The bank has also been keen to draw a link between the financial importance of small and medium-sized enterprises and the bank's economic and social responsibility for this clientele. Zapp commented on this in 1985: 'This orientation towards small and medium-sized corporates is of great importance for the bank, since this customer group accounts for a substantial proportion of our business, and it is also commensurate with our concept of economic and social responsibility that we should strengthen the potential of this important industrial sector. It is for this reason that we have devoted the leader in our latest Annual Report to this group.'

As far as the bank's actual financing of small and medium-sized enterprises is concerned, the share revealed by market analyses in the mid-1970s was regarded as unsatisfactory by the bank, especially since the trend over the previous few years had been falling. For the first time, this was seen as evidence of the need for a market policy geared specifically to this segment. An internal circular put it as follows: 'In view of the growing importance of both lending and deposit business with small and medium-sized corporates, it is necessary for us to tap this market potential more successfully and systematically than in the past. To achieve this, we will have to recognize the particular requirements of these customers and take these into account in our assessment of the business prospects.'[27]

A special loan model for investment financing with fixed annuity was devised by central office to help the branches in their locality expand their business with small and medium-sized corporate customers and establish new business relationships with this target group. This was soon introduced throughout the bank as the medium-sized commercial loan (*Gewerblicher Anschaffungskredit*). The handling, technical and organizational settlement and monitoring of this loan were made as simple as possible to reduce the time and effort traditionally associated with smaller loans. A constantly updated break-even point was listed in margin tables.

Depending on the customer and the amount of the credit involved, applications for the commercial medium-sized loan were handled either by the Corporate or Retail Banking Department. At the smaller branches, these loans were processed by the department or group responsible for loans of the respective size. The branches were given detailed guidelines on how to apply this loan model. Central office left no doubt as to the intention behind this type of loan: 'We would ask you to fully utilize the business opportunities offered by the new model, so that we can achieve suitable market share in this sector as well.' In line with the trend to prefix the bank's services with 'db-', this loan was renamed 'db-Investitionsdarlehen' in 1988.

After 1957, the bank did not settle loans stemming from public support programmes that were to be passed on to customers on its own premises, but instead channelled them to Industriekreditbank AG. Since these mainly long-term loan programmes also required the necessary long-term collateral to be pledged to IKB, however, there was a danger that further business with these customers that did not stem from support programmes might also be acquired by IKB. The realization that public support programmes were still very important and were becoming even more so changed this situation fundamentally when the support programme database, 'db-select', was introduced around 1980. This enabled the bank to concoct a tailor-made financing package from its roughly 300 online programmes, and the complex knowledge of the various programmes previously reserved for specialists was now available at all branches via the bank's mainframe and its hooked-up terminals.

In addition to the 'db-select' database, which was installed on mainframes as a purely centralized database and at the end of 1991 contained almost 700 support programmes, 1987 saw the introduction of the advisory and settlement support system of the same name. This enabled every corporate relationship manager to put together financing packages on the basis of conventional programme techniques and, therefore, on personal computers. Whereas up to 1987 the referral of public support funds had been carried out more as a sideline, the bank was now able, within a short period, to expand its market share to 12 per cent, at times even 14 per cent. In the relatively new field of environmental loan programmes, aimed at cleaning up environmental waste and financing environmentally friendly technologies with new investments, the bank's market share even reached 40 per cent at one point, which was thanks to its know-how being better and more widely available than that of its competitors.

In contrast to 'db-select', the 'euro-select' database, which had been on offer since the spring of 1991 and contained information on support programmes offered around Europe, was only of interest to a smaller target group. 'db-select' and 'euro-select' were used almost exclusively by large corporates. This was in the bank's interests, since smaller customers were usually provided with information in a personal discussion, which increased the bank's chances of also being able to carry out the agreed financing solution itself.

A market research study conducted by the bank in 1980 helps to explain some of its later measures – some of them driven by business considerations and some by Group strategy.[28] First of all, the survey revealed that an unexpectedly high proportion of small and medium-sized enterprises were interested in receiving financial advice from banks. Deutsche Bank customers not only showed above-average interest in such advice, they were also more willing to pay for it. As far as the ability to provide such advice is concerned, Deutsche Bank achieved the best result of all its competitors on the basis of its customers' replies.

'db-Unternehmens-Service' was devised in response to this obvious need for counselling on the part of small and medium-sized corporate customers, and to enable companies to gain a competitive edge by using a range of products to enhance their core businesses. This service is divided into two components: while EDP-based services help entrepreneurs to analyse their company's performance and plan future business, databases provide them with quick and cheap access to the facts and figures they need to make their decisions.

Since the end of 1985, the bank has been offering a service named 'db-data', which it developed for the use of existing external databases. This was mainly intended for small and medium-sized enterprises for which it would cost too much time and money to obtain the information themselves. 'db-data' represented a new direction for the bank in the application of databases in the banking industry and contributed substantially to developing an electronic information market.

The most important criterion in the selection of databases offered by db-data was how economical, quick and up to date their information was. In 1983 the bank set up its Business database ('your international exchange for business relationships') in co-operation with a partner to provide a quick and cheap method of finding business partners in Germany and abroad. Other banks are now also involved in this system. In response to the growing number of enquiries as to the best location in the EC member states and the public support programmes they might offer, the bank decided in 1989 to set up a further database which, in addition to the EC programmes, was to contain all national support programmes in the EC. 'euro-select-Datenbank GmbH', Frankfurt, was therefore founded and included partners from other EC countries.

By the mid-1980s, the environmental aspect had become an increasingly important investment criterion, especially for small and medium-sized enterprises. In order to resolve the information deficit here, the bank devised an 'environmental database' as an information pool on producers of environmentally friendly technologies, products and processes. This information could be used, for example, to avoid environmental clean-up costs or to utilize market opportunities. The EDP-based service 'db-plan', introduced in 1985, was also part of the bank's philosophy to provide a corporate service to small and medium-sized customers without their own controlling and planning capability. The idea behind 'db-plan' was to help such companies implement a more practicable planning system.

A further service devised primarily for small and medium-sized corporates is 'db-report', which the bank developed together with its majority-owned management consultancy Roland Berger & Partner. 'db-report' provided its customers with a user-friendly instrument for analysing the company's development. As far as the bank is concerned, 'db-report' was a means of achieving several goals. It not only provided customers with advice and enhanced their image along the lines of db-Unternehmens-Service; the information it provided could also be used to spot additional business opportunities with a view to improving the profitability of the customer relationship through cross-selling.

'db-dialog' was a payments programme, developed between 1984 and 1986, for videotext-compatible PCs. 'db-dialog' was composed on a modular basis from a number of sub-services. 'db-rationell' was the collective term for all the electronic payments services offered by the bank which are tailored to each customer's existing payments system. 'db-expert: rationell' is a computer-based consultancy for optimizing a company's payments system.

A study carried out by the bank in 1988 revealed a substantial information deficit and need for counselling on the part of small and medium-sized enterprises against the background of the emerging single European market. The bank thus decided at an early stage to give the single European market a pivotal role in its business with small and medium-sized corporates. Of the existing products making up the bank's corporate service, the 'db-data', 'db-select' and Business databases were tailored to the European market. Information packages on relevant subjects devised by the bank were taken from the more comprehensive 'db-Auslands-Service'.

German unification added a new dimension to the bank's business with small and medium-sized corporates. After existing private enterprises in the former German Democratic Republic had been transferred to state ownership and many smaller companies had been merged into large industrial conglomerates, by the 1970s only about 1 per cent of industrial output was produced by enterprises with up to 100 employees, and small and medium-sized industrial companies were almost non-existent. Private craft trades, workshops, retailers, bars and restaurants, etc. were only tolerated under very restrictive conditions. Consequently, the number of self-employed people was also very low (in the late 1980s there were approximately 180,000 self-employed persons in the GDR compared to 2.5 million in the Federal Republic).

Unification triggered the rebirth of middle-sized enterprises. By early 1990, approximately 330,000 of these businesses had been newly registered. In lending to such enterprises in eastern Germany, the bank realized that the traditional methods it used in western Germany to assess counterparty risk and analyse the borrower's standing definitely had their limitations. Rolf-E. Breuer illustrated this point: 'If a company from east Germany approaches us and says that it wants to produce sausages for export, we as bankers will lend it money because we believe it has good prospects. Logically enough, this enterprise does not have a history of borrowing or of being an enterprise, for that matter. This means that the plain-vanilla personal loan will again become important. We will then again be bankers in the original sense. We will have to prove that we can still act as bankers in the original sense.'[29] The importance attached by the bank to small and medium-sized enterprises in eastern Germany was underlined by Zapp when he opened the bank's Magdeburg branch: 'I would go so far as to say that small and medium-sized businesses will not only be the driving force behind the recovery in the new federal states, by replacing "from below" those jobs at the *Kombinate* [industrial conglomerates] that are destroyed in the restructuring process; they will also be *the* social driving force.'

The bank was therefore quick to develop further activities aimed at small and medium-sized enterprises in the new federal states. In autumn 1990, Deutsche Bank-Kreditbank AG and relevant organizations staged information roadshows for the craft trades throughout the former GDR, thus continuing the commitment the bank had already shown towards small businesses at the Leipzig Trade Fair in spring of that year. In addition to demand for the traditional banking services, the bank found that these enterprises required information and advisory services that differed substantially in terms of intensity and range from those in western Germany, which was hardly surprising.

The bank reacted to this demand and, at the same time as a nationwide branch network was being established, it joined forces with some of its subsidiaries to set up special institutions to provide one-stop advisory services for the specific needs of potential small and medium-sized corporate customers. The first of these 'advisory centres for middle-sized corporates' was opened in Dresden in 1991. Its range of services included the planning of business start-ups and privatizations by Deutsche Gesellschaft für Mittelstandsberatung (DGM), investment financing and the leasing of vehicles and machinery by GEFA, and the purchase, rental or sale of factories. In autumn 1991 Deutsche Beteiligungsgesellschaft rounded off this range by introducing its special forms of equity financing.

Zapp put this market strategy in a nutshell when he said: 'You can see that our philosophy is the same in the new federal states as in the old federal states, namely to base our thinking and behaviour on our customers and their needs, and to analyse and solve problems with them in order to build a long-term relationship and help them generate their own success.'

'db-Unternehmens-Service: Neue Bundesländer' comprised a number of different services specially devised by the bank with a view to the situation in the new federal states, and these products could be combined with the existing elements of db-Unternehmens-Service and tailored to individual needs.

The importance generally attached by Deutsche Bank to small and medium-sized corporates was highlighted in recent years by its introduction of an outstanding measure which, as a programme of action aiming at corporate customers, was unprecedented. In spring 1991 the board of managing directors passed the so-called *Mittelstandskonzept* (business strategy for small and medium-sized enterprises). There were many reasons for this. For example, although there was believed to be considerable business potential in this sector, there were also signs of competitors stepping up their activities. A further reason for the need to tighten up the bank's market strategy for small and medium-sized corporates was the greater competitive pressure on traditional markets, particularly in wholesale and retail banking.

The starting point for this strategy was the bank's image as revealed by surveys; it was perceived by the general public very much as a 'bank for large corporates', and was not regarded as *the* partner for small and medium-sized enterprises, particularly by multipliers and the media. This may be somewhat surprising in view of the number of measures taken by the bank and the successes it at least claims to have achieved in this sector. The prime objective of this strategy was therefore to make the bank more attractive for small and medium-sized corporates, without the bank losing its clearly defined image.

Compared to previous, isolated measures, greater emphasis was placed on the positioning and support of corporate relationship managers in each locality. The intention was to strengthen the bank's position and image as a large, nationally and internationally successful bank, and thus to conserve and enhance the attractive features mentioned by small and medium-sized corporates, while at the same time the bank's staff were encouraged to be more pro-active and high-profile in their dealings with such companies than had previously been the case. A further intention was for the bank to win more trust and credibility in its relationship with the media and multipliers. The short-term objectives as far as communication was concerned were therefore to improve contact with the customer, transfer the competitive edge the bank was said to have in its business with large customers to its business with small and medium-sized corporates, use the market proximity and image advantages of other organizations dealing with small and medium-sized enterprises, and draw more heavily on Deutsche Bank Group companies related to this sector as communicators and multipliers.

These activities were centred on communicative (public relations) measures, which offered an opportunity for people to meet and talk to each other. This gave the head of Corporate Banking and his staff at each branch an important role in implementing these measures. There were plenty of opportunities for approaching this target group directly, ranging from roadshows and meetings, workshops, lectures and seminars held by individual branches and case studies with DGM, to lectures held by members of the board of managing directors on the subject of small and medium-sized corporates and weekend meetings held in a leisurely atmosphere.

The so-called *Kronberger Unternehmergespräche* (small and medium-sized business forums) were introduced as a special attraction for a select group of particularly interesting small and medium-sized entrepreneurs, and were to give them the opportunity to inform themselves and discuss a wide range of current topics. Only highly qualified speakers – the best in their field – were chosen to provide this information. The Public Relations Department at head office compiled a pool of suitably qualified speakers, who were given contracts. In order to be included in this pool, speakers had to fulfil five personal criteria: they had to be experts in their particular field, be excellent public speakers, have a certain charisma, have an uncomplicated personality and, last but not least, be affordable.

Members of the bank's board of managing directors held lectures at branches and outside the bank at high-profile events for small and medium-sized enterprises – including in other European countries, especially Italy, Spain and Portugal – and for associations, institutions and the press. Branch managers were also increasingly asked to hold lectures on a current topic. From 1990, the lecture documentation developed by head office was made available to the branches for a fee. Apart from the material provided by head office, the branches also started holding seminars on subjects of interest to small and medium-sized businesses. For certain topics – such as environmental protection, equity financing or communication – experts from head office or Group subsidiaries could be provided by the Public Relations Department at head office.

The establishment and intensification of co-operation with organizations relevant to small and medium-sized businesses took place in three stages. After the relevant organizations had been found, responsibility for their counselling had to be delegated (head office, branch, region, etc.), the individual corporate relationship manager had to be allocated and, finally, the appropriate measures had to be devised. The social commitment of senior staff at the branches has helped foster new contacts and strengthen existing relationships. Membership fees are borne by the branch. Once a month, a lunch is held where the Corporate Banking head of a particular branch invites 20 or 30 current or potentially lucrative small or medium-sized corporate customers either to the branch or to a suitable venue outside, and a lunch-time speaker gives a talk on a topic of particular interest.

In spring 1991, a series of advertisements was introduced as part of a new advertising campaign aimed primarily at the proprietors of small or medium-sized enterprises, leading figures in finance, industrial and trading companies and multipliers. The central message behind this was that Deutsche Bank was also a bank for small and medium-sized corporates, and that it offered a wide range of products to help solve the client's problems. These advertisements showed a photograph of one of the bank's genuine clients as a testimonial together with the bank products that he or she had successfully used.

d) Institutional developments in corporate banking

Over time there was a continual increase in the number of Deutsche Bank Group companies operating independently on the market and in business with small and medium-sized corporates. In some cases, legal restrictions forced the bank to set up independent subsidiaries, but the bank also preferred to offer certain products via subsidiaries in cases where non-banking services were concerned, where it seemed premature to add what were basically bank-compatible services to its range, or if the forecast market development involved such imponderables that the possibility of failure could not be excluded.

Most of these Group companies were *consultancies*. In a press interview in Frankfurt in 1987, Herrhausen announced the bank's participation in the Munich-based management consultancy Roland Berger & Partner Holding GmbH. The intention already at this stage was to raise the bank's initial stake of 24 per cent to a qualified majority. This was duly increased to 75.01 per cent at the end of 1987, and this holding was fixed by contract until 2001. After the takeover of Roland Berger, many observers expressed scepticism as to whether the consultancy would maintain its independence.

For the bank, this participation was anything but a chance purchase as part of an opportunistic acquisition strategy, as the bank's acquisitions in other parts of Europe were often called by official sources. It had always regarded management consultancy as an integral part of its corporate business, and this was commensurate with its traditionally relationship-driven client approach. Whereas the advice given to corporate customers by members of the board, relationship managers at the branches and specialists at head office had for a long time been largely restricted to banking matters, these customers were now increasingly articulating the need for competent advisory services for many areas of their business, over and above purely financial questions.

Especially from today's perspective, at a time when leading representatives of the bank like to play down its global ambitions and strategies, Herrhausen's comments on the bank's intention to integrate Roland Berger into an all-round, global strategy appear to be of particular historical interest: 'Our stake in Roland Berger & Partner provides us with the sort of advisory capability that in the not-too-distant future will be an integral part of the product range of any international bank. As part of our global strategy, this acquisition therefore represents a further decisive step towards making our bank a universal, multinational services group which, in addition to financing in its various forms, also offers management consultancy. This illustrates the shift of emphasis taking place in relationship banking.'

Not only the incorporation of this acquisition into a global strategy, but also the characterization of the management consultancy offered by the Group as consulting banking – in other words, a further arm of a multinational financial services group – in addition to the traditional business lines, appeared at the time to be an indication of an almost revolutionary change in the bank's self-image. This trend appears to have been abruptly reversed following Herrhausen's assassination. Nowadays not only does the bank's global strategy seem to have been put on the back burner, but consulting banking is no longer emphasized in this form as one of the bank's major fields of activity.

Just as important as the international dimension of the bank's stake in Roland Berger was its objective to meet the growing demand for advisory services from small and medium-sized enterprises. For this purpose, Deutsche Gesellschaft für Mittelstandsberatung mbH (DGM), Munich, was founded in 1988. The bank described DGM as being 'jointly founded by Roland Berger & Partner and Deutsche Bank', but in actual fact DGM had already been set up by Berger before the bank acquired its stake in the management consultancy. On acquiring its first holding in Berger, the bank automatically took over 100 per cent of DGM.

The reason behind DGM's formation was the bank's perception of a classical gap in the market: namely, a discrepancy between the management consultancy needed by small and medium-sized corporates, and what was available. The dividing line between banking and management consultancy was increasingly disappearing – first, because there was a tendency to tie financial questions into ever more complex entrepreneurial decisions; and second, because the selling of what used to be unproblematic banking services demanded a more pro-active advisory approach. At the same time, an ongoing transformation was taking place in the profile of the corporate relationship manager from an adviser on primarily banking issues to a consultant also covering general business management and entrepreneurial questions, a development that the bank had been tracking closely since the late 1970s through its db-Unternehmens-Service.

The idea behind DGM was to offer advisory services specially tailored to small and medium-sized enterprises, which in terms of price and quality met the requirements of this target group. In order to provide the desired high-quality and, therefore, inevitably cost-intensive and expensive advisory services at prices acceptable to smaller enterprises, a new kind of strategy was needed. This was to develop EDP-based advisory systems for selected problem areas which, although requiring substantial investment, generated only minor project costs for each advisory service, in relation to its quality, as a result of their widespread use. This idea was realized using what at the time was a new computer-aided advisory approach. On a public relations level, the bank's objective was to devise advisory services along the lines of a brand-name product that provide individual solutions.

In addition to its traditional management consultancy, mergers and acquisitions started to account for an increasing share of DGM's business. Here, it began to encounter more and more representatives of a new generation of entrepreneurs who were building up businesses within a few years and then selling them relatively quickly and profitably.

A further group of subsidiaries comprises the *specialized institutions offering venture capital*. In the mid-1960s, many small or medium-sized enterprises without direct access to the capital markets could only partly finance their rapid growth with their own capital. Against this background, capital-financing companies were established by banks to provide medium-sized businesses with equity. In the mid-1970s, these institutions were joined by venture capital companies, whose main task was to improve the unsatisfactory levels of equity at young and innovative enterprises. Since the mid-1980s, these two groups of institutions have been drawing closer together.

Deutsche Beteiligungsgesellschaft mbH (DBG) der Deutschen Bank started business in 1966. The main reason for the bank setting up DBG on its own was to ensure that the firm's name included the word 'Deutsche'. Immediately after its foundation, however, a number of other banks acquired stakes in it. During the first few years of its existence, until the early 1970s, DBG achieved no more than rudimentary success. The company found itself confronted by latent aversions of the typical small German enterprise, and was also seen as too expensive. Moreover, its interests inevitably conflicted with those of the bank's branches, which preferred to make loans.

During the first expansion phase in the early 1970s, DBG stepped up its market activities and adopted a pro-active approach towards companies. It was during this time that some of its most lucrative participations came about. In 1971/72, however, it also posted substantial losses for the first time, which caused considerable irritation on the part of its eight shareholders. Consequently, in 1972 the five private banks involved sold their shares to the bank at book value.

The venture capital market came to life when the capital requirements of small and medium-sized enterprises began to grow visibly following the start of the general economic upturn in 1982. The market became more attractive and competitive as a result of greater succession problems in small businesses. Today, one of DBG's explicit business policy objectives is to provide creative entrepreneurs looking to tap the potential of an expanding market with financial strategies for the various consecutive company stages from its formation until it is ready to go public.

DBG's offering covers the provision of capital and know-how. The company sees itself within Deutsche Bank Group as a specialist in providing equity. To build up this service, it was necessary to devise comprehensive strategies which took economic, tax and company-law aspects into account. This also involved advising and supporting clients in general questions of management. On a limited scale, DBG also provides subsidiaries of German companies with financial assistance and advice in tapping new markets abroad. In order to step up its activities in the new federal states, in 1991 DBG founded DBG Beteiligungsgesellschaft mbH in Frankfurt am Main. It is the market leader.

In the early 1970s, the federal ministries responsible for education, science, research and technology, together with German industry started discussing the need for a system of venture capital which should be financed privately. This was followed in 1973, after initial talks, by the formation of a working group comprising several banks under the chairmanship of Deutsche Bank 'in recognition of our obligation towards the national economy' (press release). After more than two years of negotiations, approximately 30 banks of various types put their signatures to shares in Deutsche Wagnisfinanzierungs-Gesellschaft mbH (WFG), which was founded in 1975 with share capital of 10 million DM. At the time of its formation there was little doubt that losses would have to be expected, at least in the initial phase. To partly offset these difficulties and to promote WFG's business development, the Federal Republic of Germany concluded a risk participation agreement with WFG and its shareholders.

WFG assisted mainly small and medium-sized enterprises with insufficient equity and management experience by providing them with venture or risk capital. This was primarily intended to promote technological innovations that were likely to raise the efficiency of German industry. Once they had been realized, these innovations were intended to be self-supporting. If potential buyers decide to exercise their pre-emption right, the participating interests are sold back to them and the funds resulting from this sale are used to acquire new interests.

At the end of its tenth financial year in 1984, WFG's shareholders and supervisory board decided to terminate its acquisition activity. Since then, WFG's portfolio has been continually reduced. Also in view of the fact that the necessary adjustment and expansion of WFG's business would have overstepped the limits of the risk participation agreement, the five bank shareholders, each holding at least 10 per cent of WFG's share capital, decided to set up WFG Deutsche Gesellschaft für Wagniskapital mbH, in which the existing organization was subsumed. It now looked after the former WFG, which continued unchanged, as a management company. Deutsche Bank held 30 per cent of the 'new' WFG's capital. It was agreed with the federal government to terminate the risk participation agreement, and since then WFG has been totally in private hands.

Resources for new business are provided in the form of an investment fund. In 1984 WFG therefore founded WFG Deutsche Gesellschaft für Wagniskapital mbH & Co. KG as a limited partnership with a fund volume of 100 million DM. After the fund capital raised by the co-operation partners had been fully invested, WFG's shareholders decided to wind up the joint venture from 1988. As the largest single shareholder, the bank took over the other shareholders' stakes. At the beginning of 1988, the staff and organization were taken over by Deutsche Beteiligungsgesellschaft mbH. Since then, it has also carried out WFG's business.

At the end of 1984 the bank founded Deutsche Beteiligungs AG Unternehmens-beteiligungsgesellschaft (DBAG) together with Schmidt-Bank (Hof). This company provided unlisted medium-sized enterprises unable to issue securities with indirect access to organized capital markets. The refinancing of its activities via the stock market at the same time offered a broad range of investors the opportunity to acquire an indirect holding in small or medium-sized corporates whose prospects met the stringent criteria of DBAG.

The idea of financing participations on the stock market was not repeated; although there are now 16 such companies in Germany, DBAG is the only listed one. Even at its inception it was structured in such a way that it conformed with the newly presented draft of a law on equity finance companies. DBAG was also listed before the new law had been passed. By taking over equity stakes or acting as a silent partner, the company was aiming to achieve longer-term participations, its partners being granted a repurchase right if so desired. Its investment principles stipulated that its acquisitions should be spread over as many sectors as possible and, in the case of new acquisitions, required that the companies concerned should be successfully managed with sound equity relationships and offer the prospect of an above-average, sustainable return on capital employed. DBAG's business was run by DBG on the basis of an agency agreement.

At the end of 1992 the bank reorganized its equity financing and bundled it in the newly founded DBG-Vermögensverwaltungsgesellschaft, Frankfurt. In the wake of this reorganization, the Gerling and Nürnberger insurance companies, part of the same group, each acquired 22.5 per cent of the share capital; Deutsche Bank held 45 per cent and Schmidt-Bank 10 per cent.

In autumn 1991 Deutsche Bank floated an initiative to speed up the privatization of former East German state-owned enterprises, which until then had been left to the Treuhand. To this end, it arranged with a partner the formation of DIH Deutsche Industrie-Holding Verwaltungs-GmbH & Co. KG which, concentrating on certain sectors, had the task of taking over complete enterprises and groups of companies from Treuhand ownership and then restructuring and developing them as private enterprises by providing special management support. The company worked closely with DBG. In addition to its exclusive concentration on eastern Germany, the major difference between it and DBG was the extent of their participating interests: while DBG, as an experienced partner to enterprises, and particularly managements, only entered into minority participations, DIH usually acquired 100 per cent stakes and even took over entire industrial conglomerates. Its main task, after all, was to devise and implement individual restructuring packages. None the less, DIH was sceptical about the chances of reselling the companies at a later date, possibly on the stock exchange.

As specialized institutions for *investment and instalment financing and factoring*, GEFA Gesellschaft für Absatzfinanzierung mbH, Wuppertal, a wholly owned subsidiary of the bank, and its subsidiaries GEFA-Leasing GmbH and EFGEE Gesellschaft für Einkaufs-Finanzierung mbH, Düsseldorf, enhance the bank's range of services. GEFA and GEFA-Leasing, which is only responsible for chattel leasing, are run by the same management. EFGEE specializes in lending to private individuals wanting to buy consumer goods. With a market share of approximately 8 per cent, its subsidiary ALD Autoleasing D GmbH is the largest non-captive German vehicle-leasing company. Together with Nürnberger Versicherung and two other partners, the bank in 1992 founded Garanta Fijynanzdienst GmbH to offer financial services such as car financing and leasing, insurance as well as purchase, warehouse and investment financing for German car dealers and their clients.

Deutsche Bank's *real-estate leasing* has a chequered history. In 1968 the board of managing directors ordered a survey on the potential offered by real-estate leasing. The market analysis came up with positive findings and, after initial activities as early as October 1968, Deutsche Gesellschaft für Immobilien-Leasing mbH (DIL) was founded in Cologne in 1969. Owing to the unpredictable development of this business, DIL was instructed not to publicize its business activities as those of the bank. In 1976, Deutsche Gesellschaft für Immobilien- und Anlagen-Leasing mbH, the 'second DIL', was founded as a subsidiary of Deutsche Bank and Commerzbank. Allianz, actually the bank's chosen partner, was forbidden from participating by the Insurance Supervisory Act. By 1985

DIL had become the market leader in real-estate leasing. After 1986 it operated under the originally intended name of Deutsche Immobilien Leasing GmbH.

When dealing with customers, DIL was flexible in its identity, acting as a subsidiary of either Deutsche Bank or Commerzbank, depending on which of the two banks was the house bank of the customer concerned. Surprisingly, this co-operation was terminated in 1991 and DIL split up. In order to prevent the joint venture agreement from having to be terminated, which might have attracted bad publicity, a mutual, extra-contractual solution was found. The official reason given for the demerger of DIL was 'changes in the strategic approach' of the two banks concerned. However, the decision to go separate ways, which was strongly encouraged by Deutsche Bank, is likely to have been for much more tangible reasons. Quite clearly there was a considerable discrepancy between the two banks' equity participations on the one hand, and their relative contribution to the company's business on the other. Commerzbank refused to accept any amendments to the agreement, particularly any profit sharing, to remedy this situation. In any case, the split from Commerzbank was also more in line with Deutsche Bank's declared strategy to go it alone as far as its other participations and takeovers were concerned, especially within the context of the single European market. DIL's third phase therefore began on 1 October 1992. Since then, the banks have gone their separate ways in this sector.

Another sizeable group of Deutsche Bank subsidiaries comprises the *mortgage banks*. One of these is Schiffshypothekenbank zu Lübeck AG (SHL). Since the former Deutsche Schiffspfandbriefbank, an institution owned by a number of banks with a dominant market position prior to the Second World War, failed to regain its importance, the substantial financing required to build a merchant fleet led to the formation of Schiffshypothekenbank zu Lübeck, formerly in Kiel, and Deutsche Schiffahrtsbank in Bremen. Their major competitors in ship financing were Deutsche Bank's Hamburg branch and the regional banks in Kiel, Bremen and Hamburg.

At first, the ship mortgage banks achieved constant growth. A boom was triggered by the 1973 oil crisis, which for cost and supply reasons produced substantial demand for large tankers and suitable financing. In the wake of the first shipping crisis ('tanker crisis') in the mid-1970s, however, the value of used ships fell to 10 per cent of their purchase price, the legal lending limit being 60 per cent, which is usually fully utilized. Since the ship mortgage banks had hardly formed any provisions against loan losses, owing to their tight margins as a result of the competitive situation and, probably, their lack of risk awareness, their reserves were eaten up by these defaults, which were not covered by collateral. This was not the case with their universal bank competitors. Eckart van Hooven, who was responsible for the Hamburg region, was therefore able to declare that, even in the worst-case scenario, the bank would 'not have to make any sacrifices'.

When in the late 1970s there were signs of problems arising in the ship mortgage industry, Deutsche Bank made efforts to reorganize it. These were thwarted, however, by the various political vested interests of the federal states, who were looking to use the ship banks to maintain their influence on the support given to the politically sensitive shipping industry, and who refused to relinquish their participating interests. The second crisis in liner shipping, which started at the beginning of the 1980s, again caught the cumbersome ship mortgage banks unprepared, although it had been foreseeable. Their financial situation cast doubt on their survival.

After 1985, all of these institutions were able to draw up their annual accounts only after having received financial assistance amounting to hundreds of millions of marks; for Schiffshypothekenbank zu Lübeck, there was talk of a figure of 30 million DM for 1986 alone. However, the banks involved restricted themselves to describing the amounts mentioned in the press as incorrect, without naming the actual sums involved. It was only in 1988 that there was finally agreement on the need to restructure them from top to bottom. At first, a merger of all three ship banks engineered by the three big banks plus Vereins- und Westbank seemed to be the most sensible solution, but this proved to be impracticable. The stumbling block here may well have been that Deutsche Bank believed that it should own the relative majority of the shares in the new institution, as befitted its status. This was unacceptable to the other institutions. The often-heard claim – which the bank did not contest – that it wanted to 'go its own way' right from the outset may seem to make sense with hindsight, but it is not really understandable in the context of the bank's acquisition policy at the time.

In 1989 the Kiel regional bank sold its SHL stake to Deutsche Bank which, after taking over the remaining minority shareholdings, then owned 100 per cent. Now that SHL's products complemented the ship financing offered by the bank's Hamburg branch, it was easily able to maintain its position on a market which was growing again. These two lines, which shared the same management, were thus able to offer financing solutions which a ship mortgage bank alone would not have been able to as a result of legal restrictions.

As far as the mortgage banks are concerned, after the reorganization of the stakes held in these banks at the end of 1970, Deutsche Bank had majority holdings in Deutsche Centralbodenkredit AG (93.28 per cent), Frankfurter Hypothekenbank AG (94.10 per cent, of which 0.01 per cent indirectly) and Lübecker Hypothekenbank AG (100 per cent, of which 75 per cent indirectly via Deutsche Bank Lübeck AG vormals Handelsbank). Smaller tax-privileged minority holdings in Deutsche Hypothekenbank in Bremen, Hypothekenbank in Hamburg and Pfälzische Hypothekenbank in Ludwigshafen were sold to other banks as part of a reorganization of these participating interests. Whereas Lübecker Hypothekenbank was traditionally more involved in residential construction, Frankfurter Hypothekenbank and Centralboden, merged in 1995 to form Frankfurter Hypothekenbank Centralboden AG, mainly financed commercial property.

The mortgage banks' business is characterized, on the whole, by a very steady development. The policy towards the services they offer is extremely consistent. Special lending programmes have usually involved co-operation with other institutions or pure marketing campaigns, rather than the addition of new items to the product range. Private customer programmes offering one-stop property finance in co-operation with banks or building societies find their equivalent in the commercial sector in the form of network financings, which were provided from the late 1960s along the lines of Deutsche Kreditbank für Baufinanzierung.

After 1978 this institution was wholly owned by Deutsche Bank and specialized in the financing of residential property, particularly in the form of developer models. Erroneous decisions on the part of its board of managing directors, which for a long time went undetected by the supervisory board provided by Deutsche Bank, the bankruptcy of big-ticket customers and the abolition of tax privileges were later to place the institution in such a desperate situation that the only way of avoiding an embarrassing bankruptcy was to merge it with Deutsche Bank and continue its business as one of the bank's branches.

In addition to property finance, a second arm of the mortgage banks' business is the financing of public entities in the form of local-authority loans and *Schuldscheindarlehen* (see pp. 622–4) and their own refinancing via *Öffentliche Pfandbriefe* (bonds secured by loans to the public sector). Public sector business is unproblematic compared to mortgages, although it offers relatively low margins.

A special role in the corporate business of Deutsche Bank's subsidiaries is performed by Deutsche Gesellschaft für Fondsverwaltung mbH (DEGEF). The idea to found this institution came about in 1967 as a result of discussions between the bank and the German subsidiary of IBM Corporation on how to invest funds from the IBM benevolent fund. It had long been the practice of big US corporations to take funds out of the companies' assets and invest them separately for the payment of old-age pensions and staff benefits. For this purpose, IBM Deutschland had participated in equity mutual funds. However, it was agreed that the volume of assets to be managed justified setting up a special fund. This was prohibited by law, which only allowed funds for a larger group of investors.

In talks with the Federal Insurance and Property Finance Supervisory Office, the bank devised a theory which stipulated that, as the fund was geared to its beneficiaries, this special-purpose fund was to be seen financially as a public fund. DEGEF was therefore set up in 1967 and commenced business in April of the following year with two special-purpose funds. The bank had obviously found a gap in the market, since this model became widespread without needing much marketing, so that by the end of 1969 21 funds with capital of approximately 200 million DM were under management. Despite DEGEF's success, initial scepticism on the part of competitors was such that they did not start to set up such companies of their own until 1969.

At the time that DEGEF commenced its business in special-purpose funds, the main market potential was believed to be in company pension schemes. In the early 1970s, however, life insurers were pinpointed as a new target group. But various events, especially the initial success of a fraudulent, exotic investment firm, gave rise to the idea of offering fund-linked life insurance as the bank's own product. In the end, however, this fund strategy was not pursued any further.

Following developments on the European insurance market – above all, the aggressive growth strategy of Equity & Law in the late 1980s – this idea regained popularity with German companies as well. The rump funds set up at DEGEF by insurance companies, in which ten companies had each invested 1 million DM as start-up capital, were initially not replenished from further investment funds. But DEGEF already had considerable experience of pension funds, and the insurance companies were interested in a reorganization of the investment funds for several reasons. Some insurers were already setting up their own fund management companies for this purpose, when in late 1971 DEGEF came up with the idea of offering insurance customers expiration funds for the investment of funds from matured insurance policies. Shortly after this, Allianz brought its own fund management company on to the market. The reason for this, according to market insiders, was not so much the prospect of good returns as the reluctance of Allianz to be seen in co-operation with a banking group. This was also underlined by the fact that, initially at least, all big banks were involved. None the less, smaller insurers chose to follow Allianz's example and founded their own fund management companies.

Deutsche Bank's decision to include life insurance in its product range also caused some of its customers to set up their own companies. For example, the bank's announcement of its new 'savings plan with insurance cover', first offered in 1983, brought a reduction in allocations to its investment funds. When it announced at the end of 1988 that it would set up Lebensversicherungs AG der Deutschen Bank, certain investment funds were wound up and billions of marks withdrawn, in contrast to the bank's other business lines, such as bond trading, which were only affected on a minor scale.

DEGEF's other traditional target groups are churches, associations and public-law foundations. For example, it looks after the Max Planck Foundation and the Volkswagen Foundation. However, one target group that was excluded right from the outset were so-called 'millionaire funds' for wealthy individuals, who used them to circumvent tax speculation periods. Owing to the initial uncertainty as to the legal status of special-purpose funds, the benevolence of legislators was so important to DEGEF that this group of investors was not targeted. The few investment funds for family foundations were soon wound up for similar reasons.

The growing income and substantial liquidity of large corporates from the early 1980s onwards has also increased their significance as investors, primarily over the short and medium term. Corporate funds held as financial investments rather than pension reserves accounted for 24 per cent of DEGEF's fund volume in 1991. As in the insurance industry, the most likely reasons for the rapid growth of these investments were window-dressing of balance sheets and tax breaks. Another significant factor was the trend towards allocating pension funds, i.e. deliberately removing funds of equal value to the pension reserves from the companies' assets and managing them separately. By 1991, pension and benevolent funds accounted for 18 per cent of the assets managed by DEGEF. However, this was much more the case among large corporates than among small and medium-sized enterprises. The late 1960s witnessed the introduction of staff funds to enable employees to acquire productive capital and to offer a voluntary method of circumventing legislation, for example the Wehner Plan. These investment funds were usually financed from part of the annual bonus received by all staff members. DEGEF saw new potential in these staff funds, which accounted for only about 1 per cent of its assets under management in 1991.

Last but not least, Deutsche Bank Group's *specialized institutions providing corporate customers with insurance products* are of growing importance. On 27 December 1990, Firmen-Lebensversicherungs-AG der Deutschen Bank was founded in Wiesbaden. The co-founder was Gerling Lloyd Allgemeine Betei-ligungs-GmbH. Deutsche Bank Group further expanded its range of financial consulting when DEUBA Verwaltungs-GmbH acquired a majority stake in the Wiesbaden-based PBG Pensions-Beratungs-Gesellschaft mbH on 21 August 1991. In 1992 the bank held 54 per cent of PBG's capital. PBG added to the range of services provided by Firmen-Lebensversicherungs-AG, which had recently commenced business. It advised mainly medium-sized and large cor-porates on all questions of company old-age pensions and related legal and business problems. Its core competences were actuarial reports and the develop-ment of pension schemes. The bank was both directly and indirectly involved in the insurance holding company Nürnberger-Beteiligungs-AG (23.15 per cent, of which approximately 7.5 per cent via Consortia Versicherungs-Beteiligungs-gesellschaft mbH), which held a diversified portfolio of insurance companies.

Damage insurance is not offered directly by Deutsche Bank Group. There are, however, co-operation agreements with insurers, and the bank will play a mediating role here if desired by the customer. Such activities are left to the discretion of the respective branch and are not subject to head office approval.

In summer 1992 Deutsche Bank acquired a majority holding in Deutscher Herold (see p. 730). With 60 branches throughout Germany, 12,000 staff and a life insurance portfolio amounting to approximately 45 billion DM, Deutscher Herold is one of Germany's medium-sized insurance companies. Deutscher

Herold Group also includes Bonnfinanz Aktiengesellschaft für Vermögens-beratung und Vermittlung, a well-established distribution company. (For further information, see the section on retail business, p. 730).

A substantial Deutsche Bank participation in the Cologne-based Gerling-Konzern Versicherungs-Beteiligungs-AG was announced to the public on 10 July 1992 in the form of a casual ten-line press release: 'Deutsche Bank and Dr Rolf Gerling hereby announce that they have agreed on the acquisition by Deutsche Bank of a 30 per cent stake in Gerling-Konzern Versicherungs-Beteiligungs-AG. The agreement is subject to the usual necessary approval by the respective domestic and foreign authorities, including the Federal Cartel Office. The bank's participation is intended to maintain the character of Gerling-Konzern as the only remaining family-owned, international large German insurance group and strengthen its role as an independent partner to German industry. The bank, which in 1993 also acquired 10 per cent of the Aachen-based insurance holding company AMB, was at pains to stress that the Gerling investment was to be seen as a financial participation. To what extent this was also intended to bring about greater co-operation with the subordinated companies within the Gerling Group was not evident to the outsider.

In setting up Lebensversicherungs-AG, however, the bank had entered the sacred terrain of life insurance on its own. Start-up help was given by the Gerling Group, which could not only provide db-Leben with reinsurance in the form of Gerling-Konzern Globale Rückversicherungs-AG and Frankona Rückver-sicherungs-AG, but also supplied the bank, at the time not very well versed in actuarial matters, with its know-how. However, the obvious next step of closer co-operation between db-Leben and Gerling Leben was denied by the bank as mere speculation – something which even at the time was hard to believe. There were finally tangible signs of co-operation at the end of 1990, when Gerling presented itself as a 30 per cent shareholder in the newly founded Firmen-Lebensversicherungs-AG der Deutschen Bank. These contacts in the late 1980s and early 1990s, however, were not the first between Deutsche Bank and Gerling; the foundations for the traditionally good relations had been laid as early as the 1930s, when Hermann Josef Abs helped Hans Gerling solve some inheritance problems.

In contrast to many other of the bank's strategic coups, the announcement of its stake in the Gerling Group did not exactly come as a surprise. It had been almost universally expected in financial and press circles for some time. As early as January 1992 there had been rumours that Gerling was forced to sell a substantial part of the group to be able to pay the death duties amounting to half a billion marks following the death of his father, the founder of the group. The traditionally publicity-shy company replied by stating that it was indeed negotiating with several reputable German banks on the possibility of co-operation, the aim being to devise a strategy which would give it access to new distribution channels: for example, the branch network of a major bank. The company expressly pointed out that it was prepared, in return, to grant the prospective partner a stake of up to 10 per cent of the Gerling Group's capital. These takeover rumours are also likely to have been fuelled by the fact that Gerling's subsidiaries would probably have needed more equity capital in the foreseeable future.

In view of the difficulties the company was having in procuring capital, the economic expediency of the bank's investment in Gerling could not exactly be described as obvious. A financial journal wished the bank 'plenty of patience until a profit is turned in'. The investment was also remarkable in another respect. The originality of attempting to preserve the character of the Gerling Group as a family-run business by seeking a major participation on the part of the bank was indeed considerable. 'We have entered into an arranged marriage with Deutsche Bank that has our blessing, but we could also be divorced one day',[30] commented the current Gerling boss, Kracht.

3. International business: cautious expansion and innovation

In 1870 Deutsche Bank had already stipulated in §2 of its Articles of Association that one of the main aims of its activities was to 'promote and facilitate trade relations between Germany, the other European countries and overseas markets'. As far as the period under discussion here is concerned, the beginnings of what from now on became an increasingly international range of banking services only emerged following the normalization of political and economic relations between the Federal Republic and other exporting and importing nations, and the gradual convertibility of the deutschmark in the 1950s. Historically speaking, the bank was only entering new business territory in the sense that the environmental conditions, such as the monetary system, banking supervision and competition, had changed considerably since the beginning of the century. The process of providing products and services, however, had largely remained the same.

In 1957, the year of its remerger, the bank had practically no assets abroad; it had also lost its foreign branch network, which it had built up since the late nineteenth century. Apart from the unfavourable external conditions prevailing, a further obstacle was that there were also psychological barriers to the sort of business strategy geared towards optimizing a company's success on the basis of business management principles. In particular, the experiences and consequences of the two world wars made the expansion of international business in the 1950s, and to some extent in the 1960s, an arduous process. This and other factors were the reasons for the bank's somewhat late entry to these markets.

The bank's product range gained both breadth and depth, especially after its international expansion as an independent institution. In addition to changing customer requirements, the main influences on this development were progress in the application of communications and information technologies, and more liberal financial market regulation in all major industrialized countries. After all, the bank's current products are a reflection of the financial markets, which have developed from international to global.

The following provides a summary of the bank's international business policy. Although internationally oriented banking services are also required to a certain extent by private customers, particularly high-net-worth individuals, international business is placed here in the context in which it has always really belonged: namely, in corporate banking and business with sovereign states, government agencies, supranational organizations and so on.

a) Partner to exporters and importers

The significance of the services provided by Deutsche Bank in connection with foreign trade is illustrated by two sets of figures. West Germany's export ratio for goods increased from 8.5 per cent in 1950 to 16.6 per cent in 1957, 18.5 per cent in 1970, and almost 30 per cent by 1990. Throughout the period under review, the bank was by far the most involved German foreign trade bank. In both payments and export and import finance, it handled far more business than any of its competitors. In 1957 it settled roughly 30 per cent, and over the course of time this share fell to between 20 and 25 per cent.

In the late 1950s the bank was most keen to re-establish as quickly as possible the correspondent banking relationships it had lost as a result of the war, and to expand its correspondent banking network over and above its pre-war level. Even before 1957, the three successor institutions had concentrated on certain economic areas and trade with their respective regions. This regional division was retained after the bank's remerger, so that the regional relationship manager at Hamburg branch mainly looked after South America and Asia, the officer in Düsseldorf took care of the Near and Middle East, and the one in Frankfurt handled the rest of the world.

Correspondent banking relationships met the full requirements of foreign-trade-oriented customers at that time. The satisfactory quality of these relationships induced the bank to pursue a defensive foreign policy, i.e. one which did without the bank's own institutional expansion. At the 10th German Banking Conference in 1963, Abs stated that an international expansion of the banks' branch networks did not make economic or business sense and was unattractive, since the tried-and-tested correspondent banking relations provided 'a sound basis on which to build greater co-operation in all business lines'. This view was soon to prove in need of revision.

For the time being, however, the bank pursued its correspondent banking strategy further and expanded its network. The zenith was reached in 1980, when the bank had connections with over 4,000 banks in 152 countries. Since then this figure has been stagnating. The reasons for this were the world-wide network it had built up and its own institutional expansion starting in the early

1970s. In this way, the bank was increasingly able to utilize the advantages of intra-bank clearing. However, progressive technologies allowed multinationals to implement their own efficient cash management systems, with the result that the bank lost some of its non-documentary payments business. When the SWIFT system (Society for Worldwide Interbank Financial Telecommunication) was introduced in 1977, the bank immediately benefited from its automation and standardization, since it was able to hook up 200 domestic branches with their own access to the network, and thus created considerable cost-cutting potential in international payments.

Owing to the ongoing improvement in communications and information technology and their application in the settlement of cross-border trade, documentary payments have lost much of their importance, although even in the 1990s they still play a certain role for the bank. In its 1965 Annual Report it discussed a trend that had been evident for some years to shift payments from the documentary credit to cash against documents, and then from cash against documents to clean payments.

There was a further increase in the use of documentary payments during the first oil crisis in 1973–4 and during the years when the debt crisis emerged between 1982 and 1984, when the bank registered a sharp rise in this business. In this respect it was complying with the wishes of German exporters, who wanted to have the greater risk of exporting to big debtor countries secured by guarantees. Following the rescheduling agreements and the onset of a consolidation period in the debtor countries, payments could also be settled unproblematically, which caused a decline in documentary credits.

Apart from the developing countries, the former Comecon countries were the only remaining group of trading partners for which the documentary credit still played a major role in such transactions. The bank carried out the follow-up financing of sight documentary credits by providing the East European foreign trade banks with unsecured cash advances with maturities of one to two years. With the collapse of the Soviet Union, there was also a change in the form of payment settlements with trading partners in the CIS from 1990 onwards. The bank registered an almost explosive increase in the number of documentary credits, since German exporters no longer trusted the credit standing of their customers and also wanted to include the Moscow Bank for Foreign Trade as guarantor. Deutsche Bank recommended to exporters that they insist on the opening of a documentary credit when doing business with the former Soviet Union.

The constantly increasing number of payments to be settled internationally induced the bank to look for ways of rationalizing the settlement of these payments as well. By using the rapidly progressing possibilities offered by electronic data processing, in the mid-1980s it came up with 'db-expert: rationell', which was geared to the settlement of international payments and integrated both documentary and non-documentary forms of payment. Following a recommendation by the EU Commission to the European banking industry to make European payments quicker, cheaper and more transparent, in 1993 the bank introduced forms for Euro transfers which could be electronically processed.

In *foreign trade financing* itself, the late 1950s saw the bank establishing the focal point of its business policy in its offering of trade-related international financing facilities at the *short* end, its loans seldom running for more than 12 months. The medium- and long-term financings for customers' foreign business were mainly in connection with capital investments by German companies and plant construction by German capital goods manufacturers on behalf of foreign investors. In isolated cases, foreign trade financings were also carried out to shore up German raw materials supplies. Other longer-term import financings, on the other hand, played a very minor role.

Covering the financing requirements of exporters was institutionalized at an early stage in the Federal Republic. In 1952, 28 strongly foreign-trade-oriented banks founded Ausfuhrkredit-Aktiengesellschaft, a consortium led by Deutsche Bank, to finance medium- and long-term export business (in 1966 the joint stock company was turned into a private limited company and operated as AKA Ausfuhrkredit-Gesellschaft mbH). Subsequent to this, Deutsche Bank, as consortium leader, held 26 per cent of the company's capital; this share rose slightly to 26.893 per cent after it took over Deutsche Kreditbank in the wake of German unification.

In 1958 the (state-owned) Reconstruction Loan Corporation extended the first tied financial loans, in line with what was to become international practice. Deutsche Bank was not without its reservations about the financing of foreign customers. In 1957 Abs justified the bank's cautious attitude towards investment financings by pointing out, among other things, the continually high domestic demand for capital and the banks' responsibility to cover this first. In addition, he believed that the risk inherent in such financings would cause German companies to provide funds from their own cash flow, or to borrow these funds on the capital markets. Finally, Abs saw potential dangers resulting from the long-term nature of the necessary refinancing and from the liquidity risk, which was to be borne initially by the bank, despite the Hermes cover.

The conviction that large companies could obtain risky financing better on the capital markets than in the form of bank loans consequently led to the bank concentrating the resources it had available for the financing of foreign trade on the provision of financing facilities for small and medium-sized plant exporters. The bank's entry to the consumer loan market in 1959 was thus in favour of Braunschweigische Maschinenbauanstalt, which was a medium-sized enterprise. This company had won an order to build a sugar factory in Greece, but owing to the large investment volume involved and the relatively long completion period, it did not want to bloat its balance sheet with a supplier loan. Consequently, it approached Deutsche Bank's Braunschweig branch and applied for export financing in the form of a consumer loan. The order value of 50 million DM, a substantial volume at that time, caused the bank, which shortly before had taken part for the first time in a consumer loan lead-managed by Reconstruction Loan Corporation, to seek Hermes cover. It thus lead-managed the first ever Hermes-backed, purely private financial or consumer loan.

A noteworthy project in the late 1960s was the financing of a steelworks complex in northern Spain on behalf of Unión de Siderugicas Asturianas SA (UNINSA). Mannesmann won the 300 million DM order to construct the complex, and approached AKA about the financing. The funds were provided through what at the time was an unusual financing mix of supplier and consumer loan. Internally, the funds were raised by Reconstruction Loan Corporation, AKA and a syndicate outside AKA led by Deutsche Bank. The internally raised funds were then bundled and disbursed externally via Reconstruction Loan Corporation as sole lender.

The 1970s were marked by the period of *détente* between East and West and the willingness on the part of the former Soviet Union – forced by its lack of hard currency – to develop its enormous natural gas reserves, not only for its own requirements and those of the other Comecon countries, but also to provide the west European countries with long-term supplies of natural gas. Of particular importance here was the first 'pipeline loan' (see p. 598), signed on 1 February 1970, which revived business relations from the 1920s between Russia, Mannesmann and the credit institutions Deutsche Bank, Disconto-Gesellschaft and Mendelssohn.

This tripartite transaction stipulated that the syndicate led by the bank was to grant a supply-related financial loan of 1.2 billion DM to the Foreign Trade Bank of the former Soviet Union, that Mannesmann and other pipe producers in the syndicate were to supply pipes to W/O Promsyrjoimport, and that Ruhrgas AG was to obtain natural gas for 20 years from the Soviet conglomerate Sojusnefteexport. At the time the agreement was signed, this was the largest earmarked financial loan granted by West German banks to date. It was to run for 12 years. The amount contributed by the bank was 18.4 per cent – approximately 220 million DM – and the interest on the loan was 6 per cent p.a. over its entire life. This presented the banks involved with certain interest rate risks, which actually became relevant later on.

Fifty per cent of the loan was backed by Hermes. At the beginning, this was a controversial point among the banks involved, since the Soviet Union presented itself as a creditworthy borrower, and the annual guarantee fee, which was to be borne by the German suppliers, had a substantial impact on the overall pricing of the loan owing to its size. The bank syndicate was provided with further collateral for this first pipeline loan in the form of an irrevocable instruction for Sojusnefteexport to transfer all proceeds from the sale of its natural gas to a special account at Deutsche Bank in favour of the Foreign Trade

Bank of the Soviet Union until the loan was fully serviced, as stipulated by the agreement. This arrangement was waived in the following pipeline loans.

In 1972 the second pipeline loan for a further 1.2 billion DM was arranged in two tranches under the lead management of the bank, also as an earmarked financial loan. Again, 50 per cent of the loan was guaranteed by Hermes. The third pipeline loan, arranged in 1974 for 1.5 billion DM, differed from the others in that the German firms were exempted from assuming liability for the part of the claims not covered by Hermes. In return, Hermes increased its cover to 85 per cent. For the fourth pipeline loan in 1975, the Hermes cover was raised to 95 per cent. Deutsche Bank, which lead-managed the loan, also succeeded in raising the interest rate to 7.35 per cent. The difference between the fourth pipeline loan and its predecessors was the inclusion of Iran as a gas supplier. In terms of settlement, this meant that only the transport proceeds were to be transferred to the Soviet Union, while the proceeds from the supply of gas were to be credited to Iran. The fact that the fourth loan was not utilized by the Soviet Union was due to the delay in laying the gas pipelines from the Iranian gas fields to the Soviet border, and because in future the Soviet Union did not want to link the supply of gas and pipes too closely, since the offers for pipelines from Italy and Japan were cheaper.

On the whole, these pipeline and gas transactions had a profound impact on the bank's considerable exposure to eastern Europe. Within the framework of this exposure, it was often the leader of bank syndicates. In 1974 it lead-managed an export transaction for Klöckner-Humboldt-Deutz for 9,000 trucks worth 1 billion DM. In 1977 it again led a syndicate that provided a tied financial loan of 86 million DM to the Soviet Foreign Trade Bank, the funds being used to build off-shore haulage equipment in Astrakhan supplied by the Hamburg company Blohm & Voss AG.

In the meantime, the technique of the parallel transaction was still being used: for example, in the 1976 loan agreement between Bank Indonesia and a syndicate led by Deutsche Bank. The total loan amounted to 1.175 billion DM, followed later by supplementary financings. The funds were used to convert an old scrap-processing plant in Indonesia into a state-of-the-art steelmaking complex. The plant was supplied and structural alterations carried out by reputable German companies. At the same time as the steelmaking complex was being constructed, the Saarberg plant of VEBA AG agreed to purchase Indonesian oil. The supplier loan to Bank Indonesia was extended in two tranches, Deutsche Bank's share being 20 per cent in both cases.

Pertamina, the Indonesian oil supplier, undertook to transfer all payments from the oil purchase agreements to a special account at the bank's Munich branch. The agreement also stipulated that Bank Indonesia had to maintain funds of at least the same amount as the next redemption instalment, plus the difference between the accumulated oil proceeds and accumulated redemption instalments on a deposit account at the bank's London branch. This meant that the debt service could be deducted from the deposit account and, if necessary, from the special account as well. Moreover, disbursement of the loan could be refused or repayment of disbursed amounts demanded if the cover funds were not maintained, or if they were seized by a third party.

The bank was involved not only in pure export financings, but also financed foreign investment projects aimed at shoring up West Germany's supplies of raw materials over the long term. One example of this was advance financing for copper in the form of loans provided by a Deutsche Bank-led syndicate to Poland, which were to be used to build up the copper-mining industry there, followed by a smelting plant in Upper Silesia. The German buyers, primarily the copper-processing industry, undertook to pay the copper proceeds into a special account at the bank, to which the latter, however, had no actual right of access (in the case of Poland this would have contravened international agreements).

In 1979 a second loan for the same purpose was again extended by a syndicate led by the bank. In contrast to the first 'copper loan', this one was not backed by the federal government, which in hindsight was a mistake, and the redemption instalments were not fixed beforehand, but depended on specific price/quantity ratios in copper mining and on the world market price. The syndicate did not insist that a transmission account be set up. Both loans remained outstanding, since Poland did not make any repayments as a result of the debt crisis, which had become increasingly acute since 1980.

None the less, the bank continued to provide more tied financing for the export of German capital goods. Its lead management functions for the construction of power stations and heavy industry in South Africa, power station financing in Turkey, energy projects in Brazil and the construction of a steelmaking plant in Nigeria represented highlights in the bank's export financing, which dominated its untied balance-of-payments financings in the wake of the debt crisis. At the height of the debt crisis in 1984, however, Herrhausen was forced to state before the bank's advisory board: 'At present, there is no financing of exports to problem countries.'

The situation was different with the export of plant to financially relatively healthy countries. One example of this was the Yamal/Urengoi project, which continued the tradition of the bank's business with the Soviet Union. Since 1978, the Soviet Union had been planning to build a pipeline from western Siberia through Czechoslovakia to West Germany, which would branch off through Hungary to Austria. Instead of the natural gas fields on the Yamal peninsula, however, the more conveniently situated Urengoi reserves were tapped first.

In 1982, after arduous negotiations, the Urengoi framework loan was signed by the Foreign Trade Bank of the USSR and the syndicate led by Deutsche Bank. Although the original fears about the 7.8 per cent fixed interest rate proved to be unfounded owing to a fall in interest rates and the improved refinancing model (the involvement of mortgage banks provided longer-term refinancing at fixed rates), problems were increasingly posed by the redemption process in

1992. Whereas the pipeline-loan tranche had been repaid by October 1991, as agreed, repayment of the last two instalments of the compressor tranche was suspended under the 'G7 deferral'.

In 1988 there was a substantial change in the technique of export financing. In recent years there had been a growing indication that the glamour transactions of the 1960s, 1970s and 1980s were a thing of the past. What was now in demand was not so much the export of complete industrial complexes as the supply of individual parts, which was a result of the greater division of labour worldwide. The bank broke new ground here as the leader of a German syndicate when it signed a framework loan agreement with the Foreign Trade Bank following Chancellor Kohl's trip to the Soviet Union in autumn 1988.

The loan amount, which was initially 3 billion DM and then 2.5 billion DM, and had been fully utilized by the beginning of 1992, was provided without Hermes cover. The aim of this agreement was to create a form of standardization that could quickly be filled out with individual loans as and when German exporters needed Russian consumer loans, without restricting it beforehand to specific investment projects. The largest individual loan was provided for the construction of a biscuit factory ('crackers for the Russians') and amounted to almost 300 million DM. Similar framework agreements were also concluded with, among others, the former GDR and Algeria.

As far as the use of more modern financing instruments is concerned, the bank included *forfaiting* in its product range in 1965 under pressure from its exporting customers and after much hesitation. None the less, the bank still had its reservations about the risks involved. This is illustrated by, among other things, the very low annual volume in the 1960s – roughly 50 million DM – and the fact that this service was only embedded in the bank's organization in the early 1970s, after it set up a separate department dealing primarily with forfaiting. In the 1980s, the annually forfaited volume stabilized at between 750 million DM and 1 billion DM. In terms of volume, Deutsche Bank was therefore the leader on the German primary market. Owing to a decline in the provision of bank guarantees, however, long-term forfaiting played only a minor role in the early 1990s.

Since the early 1980s, the bank's forfaiting portfolio has comprised claims on importers from between 40 and 60 states. Some time ago it also started to buy claims from foreign customers maintaining an account relationship with its foreign branches. The bank usually places 50 per cent of the forfaited claims directly in the secondary market and puts the other 50 per cent in its own portfolio. However, it makes active purchases on the secondary markets only if claims of its own customers are traded on the secondary market and they are to be taken out of the market in their interests.

Cross-border *sales or export leasing* became an integral part of the bank's product range in the mid-1970s. However, it entered the market not alone, but in close co-operation with its EBIC (European Banks' International Company) partners. This business was institutionalized by the foundation of EBICLEASE, a pool of interests comprising the leasing companies belonging to the EBIC banks. On the whole, EBIC's leasing strategy – as well as other EBIC co-operations and EBIC itself (see pp. 758–9) – has proved not to be a viable concept.

Deutsche Bank's export leasing business attained substantial proportions only after it had set up its own instalment financing and leasing companies abroad. Deutsche Credit Corporation in Deerfield, founded in 1982 as a wholly owned subsidiary, entered the American leasing market in the mid-1980s. However, the standard model of export leasing, whereby leasing business in the true sense is a purely domestic affair involving transaction partners based in the same country, was maintained.

Deutsche Credit Corporation, which by the early 1990s had a widespread branch network in the USA, purchased German exporters' products and leased them to American importers. Particularly important was the support given to the sales efforts of Deutsche Bank Group's customers. The same settlement procedure was also used for leasing transactions involving Leasing Bancotrans SA, BAI Factoring S.p.A., P.T. Euras Buana Leasing and the bank's branches abroad. None of these companies, however, was engaged in cross-border leasing.

This changed in 1985 with the foundation of DB Export-Leasing GmbH, Frankfurt. Although this company was primarily set up to deal with property finance, instalment financing was soon also included in its product range. In 1986 DB Export-Leasing signed a framework agreement with a Chinese state-run leasing company. Under this agreement, DB Export-Leasing leased German capital goods to the Chinese company, which in turn granted Chinese users right of disposal over these properties on the basis of sub-leases. A similar co-operation agreement was signed in 1987 with a Bulgarian state-owned leasing company. None the less, the clear focal point of DB Export-Leasing's business was on tax-oriented leasing transactions.

Since the mid-1980s, *countertrade* had been developing into an integral part of the bank's product range. In the broadest sense of the term, the pipeline loans arranged with the Soviet Union could also be regarded as countertrade. This development was reflected in the bank's organization in 1985, when the countertrade group was set up; this group was staffed by people with experience in pure commodity trade financings. It was soon discovered, however, that trading in commodities was alien to the bank's mentality and corporate culture. In contrast, countertrade was characterized not so much by its trading aspect as by its financing.

The Federal Republic's strong foreign trade and payments, which are characterized by a substantial current account surplus, mean that the efficiency of the foreign exchange markets is extremely important for both microeconomic and macroeconomic reasons. This is ensured especially by the constant market presence of trading partners. Deutsche Bank has traditionally been such a market maker in the major currencies. However, its remerger in 1957 did not have any initially visible impact on the 'new' big bank's business policy or its market position in *foreign exchange*. Owing to its low turnover in this business, it also regarded smaller banks as equal partners. There was therefore no immediate need to reorganize the bank's forex dealing departments. The forex trading offices at the branches in Düsseldorf, Hamburg and Frankfurt retained their independence and were at pains to ensure that none of them attained an unassailable lead over the others. In certain cases, this in-house competition went so far that other banks were given foreign exchange orders that could have been settled internally.

The first organizational changes did not come until 1967, when overall responsibility for foreign exchange was given to Frankfurt. The other offices contributed the know-how they had gained in specific areas to the joint profit centre. This reorganization was primarily driven by the market, since the growing volatility on the foreign exchange markets and rising transaction volumes meant that the risks inherent in trading were reaching new dimensions.

During the Bretton Woods system, the bank's business was for some time focused on spot exchange deals. Until the late 1960s, the turnover from its trading for customer account largely developed parallel to the Federal Republic's increasing foreign trade relations. Jumps in turnover were triggered only by purely financially induced foreign exchange transactions not connected with foreign trade. Various subsequent events raised the risk awareness of foreign-trade-oriented market players. Consequently, there was also a substantial rise in the bank's turnover from forward exchange trading. As a result, the demands placed on staff engaged in forex trading and their technical equipment grew sharply.

Against the background of an increasingly volatile environment and the more turbulent foreign exchange markets themselves, the bank had already started in the early 1970s gradually to expand its capability in forward exchange business. Subsequently, it largely managed to meet its customers' growing hedging requirements. During the early and mid-1970s, it slowly overcame its reticence, which mainly resulted from its consideration towards the EBIC banks and their jointly founded organizations (see pp. 752–9), to expand its institution into Europe and beyond. Subsidiaries or branches in Luxemburg, London, Tokyo and New York either had already been opened or were planned for the near future, which meant that the bank was departing from the centralization principle it had applied to forex trading since 1967: namely, that the central trading office was Frankfurt, even though trading was still carried out via its Düsseldorf and Hamburg branches. This increasingly enabled the Group's foreign branches to develop their own foreign exchange activities, initially on a modest scale, but later also in larger amounts.

The period under review also includes the implementation of the bank's foreign exchange business philosophy, which remains valid to the present day. This stresses, on the one hand, the importance of the service component and, on the other, the need to develop this business into an efficient profit centre. The bank claims that it does not generally transact purely speculative business. The objective of its forex trading has always been to avoid any conflict of interests between its proprietary trading and trading for customer account.

Despite the bank's supposedly reserved or cautiously speculative proprietary trading, it is none the less by far the biggest income earner in the bank's forex trading, outperforming its trading for customer account by a ratio of roughly 9:1. Despite the greater volume and income generated by own-account trading, the bank gives priority to trading for customer account, mainly as a result of its client orientation. This is illustrated by, among other things, the business principle which stipulates that call and put orders given by customers are also matched. The bank does not enter the market itself, and thus does not take advantage of the opportunity to make a profit through arbitrage.

In addition to the deutschmark/dollar swap book that had been run since 1983, the subsequent expansion of the bank's product range meant that it now also ran swap books in Swiss francs/deutschmarks, Swiss francs/dollars, yen/deutschmarks, yen/dollars, pounds sterling/deutschmarks, pounds sterling/dollars, etc. In particular, foreign exchange options also became an integral part of the bank's product range in 1983 because of their considerable popularity with customers, despite certain teething problems they had had.

Information systems provided an important service. A company that has decided to hedge its currency positions can call up the full range of relevant forex market data online by using the 'db-rates' database. All the latest quotations from the spot and forward markets can be obtained from the internal DDO system ('direct forex ordering'), which enables the bank's branches to contact the teams of traders by computer at the request of their customers, and from the forex and country information system 'db-forex'.

b) Trends in international lending

International lending played only a minor role in the first few years after the reamalgamation of Deutsche Bank. None the less, it was approached by international customers with requests for loans, and the gradual convertibility of the deutschmark from the late 1950s fulfilled the necessary monetary preconditions for international lending. There were several reasons why this international lending rarely came about. First, the loss of the bank's foreign assets made it sceptical towards new international exposure. In addition, foreign loans were subject to several imponderables, and the lack of staff and institutions made it difficult to check credit standings and monitor loans in the country concerned. At the same time, the bank's traditional domestic borrowers required only small-scale international financing for foreign direct investment. A further reason was probably the initial lack of long-term refinancing. The bank therefore encouraged companies investing abroad to tap the capital markets as a source of long-term funding.

These factors meant that international lending was restricted to a very narrow group of borrowers – usually sovereign states – and that they were generally *short term*. Typical examples of this were loans to Belgium and the Netherlands in 1957. The bank provided the loans by discounting Treasury notes, and in line with the maturities of this paper the loans were restricted to one or two years. Further lending followed, but instead of entering the full amounts in its own books, the bank sometimes syndicated them to other domestic banks. A loan was given directly to a foreign borrower which was neither a sovereign state nor a bank for the first time in 1968.

Even at the end of the 1960s, the bank was only sporadically engaged in international lending. The participating interests it acquired within the context of EBIC had only a minor impact here. The bank's commencement of Euroloan business, if only indirectly through the EBIC banks and the finance companies they founded, was probably much more significant. Over the following decades, Euroloans were to have a lasting impact on international lending.

Moreover, when lending to sovereign states, the bank no longer assumed that sovereign risk did not involve default risk costs, since it realized that this was a fiction. Over time, sovereign risks confronted the bank with a risk dimension that was new in terms of type and amount. In 1978 the bank was also the first in Germany to form provisions and value adjustments for sovereign risk. Owing to the considerable scope offered in the assessment and structuring of risk provisioning, which as a result of generous regulations was also largely tax deductible, the bank seems to have always been more cautious than was really necessary. In 1989, for example, 78 per cent of its foreign claims involving sovereign risk were covered by value adjustments. This valuation procedure not only illustrated its cautious policy towards risk, but was also evidence of the bank's considerable earning power.

After Dresdner Bank, in 1967, and Commerzbank, in 1968, had founded subsidiaries in Luxemburg and were able to exert pressure on margins by extending Euroloans to domestic borrowers, Deutsche Bank also saw the need to enter the Euromarket under its own name. This resulted in the foundation of Compagnie Financière de la Deutsche Bank AG (CFDB). At the time, Luxemburg was not the bank's first choice as the location for its first wholly owned foreign subsidiary; it would have preferred London. Out of consideration for its EBIC partner Midland Bank, however, the bank decided not to set up a subsidiary there at first. Having obtained a Luxemburg licence for 'toutes opérations bancaires', on 12 August 1970 it became the thirty-sixth foreign and third German bank to commence business there. Its first premises were in an apartment next to the railway station, and it had 11 members of staff.

In the early 1970s, CFDB managed to achieve a remarkable expansion on the Euroloan market. Its total assets rose from the equivalent of 2 billion DM in 1971 to 4.1 billion DM in 1973 and 5.8 billion DM in 1974. It focused on wholesale banking with, for example, 1 million DM being the minimum loan amount before any business relationship could be established. CFDB's objective was to provide mainly German industrial clients with financial loans. Their loan requests were routed to CFDB through the bank's domestic branches. Loans were provided primarily at medium term and on a roll-over basis. Further borrowers during CFDB's first few years of activity were the Eastern bloc countries, South Africa and Iran, but loans were also extended as financing facilities to assist exports.

However, pure balance-of-payments loans were rarely extended. The reason for this was that the bank believed that its main priority, in view of the increasing exports in industry, was to provide its export clients with customer loans funded in Germany. As a result, Group-wide country guarantee limits are often likely to have prevented large-scale balance-of-payments financing through the Euro-market. In addition, the severe mismatch between the maturities of funds offered and loans demanded implied substantial currency procurement risks in the case of dollars, to which the bank did not wish to be fully exposed. Instead, CFDB was pursuing a consistent strategy to make Luxemburg – in contrast to London, which was a dollar-dominated location – the centre of the Euro deutschmark market.

After about 1973, CFDB modified the traditional method of extending individual loans such that, although loans were still negotiated bilaterally between itself and the borrower, other banks were granted undisclosed sub-participations on conclusion of the agreement or during the course of the relationship. For CFDB, the advantage of such arrangements was that the claim disappeared from its books and therefore did not affect internal country guarantee or maturity transformation limits. After 1981 – following the International Harvester case, in which the sub-participating company of the same name defaulted on such a transaction on a guarantee basis – the Deutsche Bank subsidiary concentrated on undisclosed sub-participation on a trust basis only.

Despite the substantial growth in its total assets, at the end of this first phase the bank still demonstrated what was, in relation to its position on the domestic lending market, a cautious attitude on the Euroloan market. In 1974, Ulrich gave the following reasons for this:

- incalculable procurement risks for creditors upon roll-over;
- low margins compared to the risks assumed;
- the often insufficient internal guarantee limits of individual banks which had lent several times their own capital;
- the lack of opportunity for the banks, in contrast to supranational organizations, to place effective conditions on loans, and thus the danger of financing economic laxity;

– the inherent lack of control over the market and the lack of a general information centre.

Especially in response to the last point, the bank was in favour of self-discipline. With CFDB's own capital and reserves reported at 1.1 billion LF, the bank set the internal limit for Euroloans at 3 billion DM, a figure which was substantially higher than its lendings to customers of 2.2 billion DM, of which 1.8 billion DM was in the form of roll-over loans. Despite CFDB's aversion to risk, its Euroloan business subsequently experienced a considerable upturn.

Whereas individual loans and undisclosed sub-participations were the major products of the first phase of the bank's Euroloan business, after 1975 syndicated loans and loans used not only for direct investments or trade financing, but also to finance temporary and, later on, structural balance-of-payments deficits, took on an important role. The shift in the borrower structure, evident since about 1976, from western industrialized countries to developing countries, and the continually growing volumes of individual loans, increased the qualitative and quantitative risk potential for banks involved in Euroloans, especially since, on the one hand, their deposits were growing substantially but, on the other, there was a lack of first-class borrowers.

At the same time, however, CFDB was obliged to meet the demands placed on it by the market, including the need to recycle the oil billions. The bank thus decided to widen its lending, which meant a deterioration in the quality of its portfolio. Consequently, the Luxemburg subsidiary's total assets had jumped to 9 billion DM by the end of 1975 and had risen further to 15.5 billion DM by 1979. This was mainly attributable to large loans to Mexico, the UK, Spain, Argentina and Sweden, and to state-run enterprises such as Société Nationale Elf Aquitaine, Abu Dhabi Corporation, Montreal Urban Community, Ente Nazionale Idrocarburi and others.

The extent to which the bank's policy varied according to the borrowers' estimated credit standing was clearly illustrated by the loans to the UK ($600 million) and Mexico ($1.2 billion). The UK loan in February 1977 for the first time involved the four German banks heavily engaged in Luxemburg Euroloans (Deutsche Bank, Dresdner Bank, Commerzbank and Westdeutsche Landesbank) in the form of a club deal. There was no intention of making the syndicate bigger. In contrast, the 'jumbo' loan to Mexico involved 33 managers, 12 co-managers and 68 participants. As co-ordinating manager, Deutsche Bank played a very important part. At the signing of the agreement, Herrhausen commented: 'We shall be putting our signatures to a loan agreement which ought to be seen as proof of the international banking community's confidence in Mexico and its promising future development ... The efficiency of the Euromarket as an instrument of financing high-priority investments in a flexible manner and, at the same time, on a very large scale has been proved again.'

In addition to the increasing syndication of Euroloans and the trend towards longer maturities while margins narrowed, this period is also notable for the risks taken by foreign subsidiaries of German banks. These risks were also discussed publicly. In 1977 Deutsche Bank commented as follows in its Interim Report: 'Although industrial and commercial lending has recovered, it is increasingly being financed through the Euromarket. The growth in this area is therefore primarily reflected in our subsidiary's balance sheet.' The subsidiary's equity capital was to be steadily increased as a precaution against default and interest rate and exchange rate risks. The Luxemburg subsidiary's formation of reserves was accelerated by the bank's agreement to waive dividend payments until 1987. It also raised its subsidiary's capital in 1973, 1975, 1977 and 1979.

The following years until the outbreak of the international debt crisis were marked by a bountiful supply of liquidity on the Euromarket and a tighter competitive situation on the Euroloan markets, caused mainly by a number of newcomers and by sluggish domestic demand for Euroloans. While in the 1977/78 financial year the bank, which had recently been renamed Deutsche Bank Compagnie Financière Luxembourg (DBCF), had lead-managed 47 syndicated loans for a total equivalent of 23 billion DM, the figures for 1978/79 had fallen to 31 loans with a volume of 11 billion DM. This development also illustrates that the scale of the loans was again declining. This trend continued in 1979/80, when DBCF lead-managed 38 Euroloans with a countervalue of 12 billion DM. Notable highlights during this period – owing to their size but also, in some cases, due to special features in their syndication – were loans to Istituto Mobiliare Italiano, Mexico, Ente Nazionale per l'Energia Elettrica and Venezuela.

At the 1980 International Monetary Conference in New Orleans, Guth highlighted four particularly noteworthy changes in the market conditions for Euro-loans:

1. The world monetary system was subject to new tensions and disturbances, which were reflected in high interest rate and exchange rate volatilities.
2. The regional distribution of borrowers had changed; newly developing countries accounted for a growing proportion of lending volume.
3. Balance-of-payments financing was not carried out in the form of bonds; roll-over loans provided by multinational syndicates represented the main source of financing for deficit countries.
4. The banks had made a 'dialectic leap', which was illustrated by the fact that they had become an integral part of the world financial and monetary system, side by side with the official monetary and development institutions. They would have to shoulder their responsibility to meet these tasks.

Logically enough, the bank – interested in offsetting the higher risks involved by seeking higher margins – therefore imposed spreads of at least 75 basis points above LIBOR as part of its minimum spread policy. Euro roll-over loans became less important for the bank as a result of the flood of liquidity after the second oil price shock and the continuing erosion of margins.

In the early 1980s, the bank only allowed margins below the agreed minimum in the case of export financings, where in some cases it accepted margins of 50 basis points. In addition to its export financing, it also stepped up its participation in club deals. In 1982 it led nine of these and, as the leading German bank, was twenty-second world-wide. On the whole, its Luxemburg subsidiary entered the new era following the debt crisis, which had left behind many bad experiences, with a reduced product range as far as some borrowers were concerned. During the following years, however, the bank consolidated its position in Luxemburg and became the leading player in international lending.

The year 1983 saw a further increase in the world economy's current-account imbalances. Growing budget and current-account deficits in the USA, recessions in almost all industrialized countries, high interest rates, substantial interest rate volatility and the Mexican debt moratorium gave a clear indication of the increasingly difficult climate in international lending. There was also the threat of the bank losing a major business field in which considerable resources had been invested through the expansion of its international branch network: in addition to Luxemburg and London, it had also been represented in New York since 1981 with international banking facilities for the Euromarket. This situation made it necessary for the bank to expand its product range – up to that point consisting of fixed-interest and roll-over loans – and to gear its business to private companies as a borrower target group.

After 1982, DBCF added a new feature to the granting of export loans as supplier or customer loans. Through its Luxemburg subsidiary, the bank offered financing facilities which, in terms of their financing, collateralization, conditions or sovereign risk structure, did not fit into the AKA models. In addition, DBCF also had to assume the risk of loans accompanying Hermes-backed customer loans – for example, in the financing of down-payments and interim payments and, occasionally, local costs – since passing the liability on to the exporter would have contravened Hermes regulations. The bank provided accompanying financing, especially for exports and for direct investments in Turkey, South Africa and other African countries.

In addition to export loans, loans to the Eastern bloc became significant from the mid-1980s. Particularly important here were the loans extended to the German Foreign Trade Bank of the GDR (DABA) in November 1984. These loans must be seen in connection with the so-called 'Strauss billions'. The first tranche of this loan package, which was guaranteed by the Bavarian government, was lead-managed by Bayerische Landesbank. Notwithstanding the loans initiated by Bavarian prime minister Strauss, DABA did not achieve market maturity until the end of 1994 as far as Euromarket players were concerned. The initial problem was not so much the economic aspect of these loans, since the federal government was willing to guarantee them, as the political and legal factors.

Euroloans lead-managed by German Euro banks had hitherto been granted on the basis of federal German law, which went against DABA's ideologically determined business principles. For this reason, the syndicate leaders Bayerische Landesbank and DBCF chose Luxemburg law which meant, however, that the economic aspect of the transaction, namely the federal government's guarantee, would have to be renegotiated. The federal government was only allowed to back financial claims based on federal German law. A trick was finally used to enable the agreement to be signed: it was based on the law valid at the place of execution, although this place was not specifically named. None the less, it was agreed with DABA that only Frankfurt am Main or Munich could be considered as places of execution. An additional problem was that the federal government was only allowed to back transactions with domestic clients, but neither the GDR nor the banks acting through their foreign subsidiaries were domestic clients in the true sense. A solution was presented in the form of the Jenninger model, which categorized the GDR as domestic on the basis of prevailing German law, so that the federal government was able to guarantee the debt service to foreign banks.

In 1984 a further Eastern bloc loan was extended to the National Bank of Hungary. The Jenninger model could not be applied here. Consequently, since Hungary was not a first-class borrower, a guarantee had to be obtained in some other way, since Deutsche Bank wanted to obtain cheaper refinancing through the Euromarket or its Luxemburg subsidiary, and therefore did not qualify as a domestic lender. The problem was solved by the bank functioning as lender, and since it was bearing the loan risk, it was also able to act as guarantee. The more favourable financing through the Euromarkets was arranged bilaterally via DBCF. Subsequently, such bilateral refinancing structures were always used whenever federal government guarantees were deemed necessary for loans. In 1986 the National Bank of Hungary became a regular borrower on the Euromarket. Under the lead management of Deutsche Bank, syndicated loans were provided in 1986 for $300 million, in 1987 for $400 million, in 1988 for $200 million and in 1989 for $240 million. This lending was politically sensitive and produced different reactions from the economics and finance ministries. The latter only approved cover of 90 per cent of the loan amount instead of the usual 95 per cent cover.

The bank had established close relations with Ceskoslovenská Obchodní Banka similar to those with the National Bank of Hungary. Deutsche Bank, which also had personal contacts with this bank and was impressed with its disciplined performance on the capital market, played a leading part in the formation of international lending syndicates, which in 1987 provided $220 million, in 1988 $150 million and in 1989 $240 million. Substantial publicity was also generated by the signing of a framework loan for 3 billion DM between the lead manager, Deutsche Bank, and, for the Soviet Union, the Foreign Trade Bank, following Chancellor Kohl's trip to the USSR in mid-1988. This loan, which was not backed by the federal government, was settled along the lines of the Hungarian model. Deutsche Bank Luxembourg S.A. acted as lead manager and agent.

The provision of loans to eastern European countries, which had gained a certain momentum of its own, slowed down when it became clear that the funds granted in the mid- and late 1980s were not being used efficiently enough. Moreover, the implementation of planned reforms was often being delayed or even suspended, while old planning structures remained, and, consequently, new mechanisms could not take effect.

Following the unilateral moratorium announced by Bulgaria in March 1990 – in 1989 the bank had lead-managed a $250 million loan to the Bulgarian Bank for Foreign Trade – Deutsche Bank decided not to take on any further exposure to eastern Europe, which became evident when it did not participate in a 2 billion DM Euro facility for the Soviet Union in September 1990. Thereafter, loans were extended only if they were almost 100 per cent guaranteed by the federal government, as in mid-1990 with the 5 billion DM granted to the Soviet Foreign Trade Bank, and in 1991 for the 500 million DM lent to the National Bank of Hungary, or if they were guaranteed by the European Community, as in December 1991 for a 500 million ECU framework loan to the Soviet Union. The bank continued to be involved in medium- and long-term trade financing, but only in cases where 95 per cent of the loan amount was backed by Hermes. The bank was prepared to accept the remaining risk, since it was able to obtain risk compensation in the form of higher risk premiums on the uninsured parts of the loan, and these would not produce any fresh-money demands in rescheduling agreements.

Since the mid-1980s, however, the international banks had been assuming quite different risks in the financing of their big-ticket customers. Owing to the experience gained during the debt crisis that pure book claims were difficult to trade and the gearing of this business line towards privately organized enterprises, which wanted to utilize the benefits of all Euromarket segments in one package, newer forms of financing were devised to remove the dividing line between commercial and investment banking, namely Euronote facilities and the related back-up facilities.

In 1986 Deutsche Bank acted for the first time as lead manager and agent on the strongly growing market for these new instruments, primarily through London and in full awareness of the risks involved. In view of this strong demand from German companies, the bank's reputation would have suffered and the continuation of long-standing customer relationships could have been jeopardized had the bank still refused to trade Euronotes. None the less, it restricted its revolving underwriting and note issuance facilities to the absolute minimum.

It was, however, heavily involved in the *Baukasten-Finanzierungen* (modular financings) offered from 1986 in the form of multi-option financing facilities and multi-instrument financing programmes. Owing to the complex structure of such financing and their relatively high up-front premiums for the arranger, the bank decided to offer this product, especially to improve its income. In mid-1986 it lead-managed its first multi-instrument financing programme for the German company Metallgesellschaft. Further mandates followed. The year 1990 saw another boom in these complex financings when the bank arranged several facilities: 1.5 billion DM for Volkswagen, 1.6 billion DM for Solvay Deutschland GmbH, $1.2 billion for Thyssen, 750 million DM for Hoesch and a 600 million DM dual-option revolving credit facility for PWA Papierwerke Waldhof Aschaffenburg.

c) Trends in international issuing

The deutschmark's full convertibility at the end of 1958 provided a new basis for the issuance and placement of foreign bonds in West Germany. Germany regained the acceptance as a creditor that it had lost over previous decades.

Recognizing the trends of the time and the needs of investors looking for attractive forms of investment, at the beginning of October 1958 Deutsche Bank floated a convertible bond for the Anglo American Corporation of South Africa Ltd without forming a syndicate. This meant that after almost four decades of inactivity, the bank on its own placed this first issue of a foreign bond denominated in German currency. In view of the small issue amount of 50 million DM and the shortage of material, however, the risks did not seem to be particularly great. The 5.5 per cent coupon was above that of purely domestic issues and facilitated the bond's complete and immediate placement. After five redemption-free years, repayment was to be made by 1973. Its official listing on the Frankfurt Stock Exchange was admitted at the same time as the company's ordinary shares were listed on 18 March 1959. With hindsight, one can see that the flotation of the Anglo American Corporation's foreign DM bond triggered a process that culminated in 1969, only 11 years later, with foreign DM bond net sales of 6.4 billion DM and a total outstanding volume of just under 16 billion DM.

In April 1959 the bond market interest rate reached a post-war low owing to the continuing rise in West Germany's current account surpluses and, with exchange rates still fixed, the liquidity inflow this produced. This market situation persuaded the World Bank, which up to then had mainly refinanced itself by issuing dollar bonds and borrowing directly from selected central banks, to test the resilience of the German capital market by issuing debt for 200 million DM.

Owing to the risks involved with such placement volumes and the World Bank's desire to place its bonds as widely as possible, the option of Deutsche Bank being sole issuer was excluded. The syndicate formed was similar in composition to the federal bond syndicate and was led by Deutsche Bank. The bond's 5 per cent interest rate was just above the effective rate paid by the World Bank in the USA and just under that applied to first-class German borrowers of 5.2 per cent.

Nevertheless there were no substantial difficulties with the placement, since investors found the risk/return ratio acceptable owing to the borrower's credit standing. However, on the secondary market the bond revealed its weaknesses. Continuing inflation caused the Bundesbank to introduce a restrictive monetary policy. This quickly raised interest rates on the bond market. By the end of 1959, domestic borrowers were already issuing at 6 per cent. The price of the World Bank bond began to fall ominously.

An unsuccessful issue on the secondary market would have damaged the reputation not only of the World Bank, but also of Deutsche Bank as a lead manager. Owing to the vested interests of the other underwriters and the lack of customary practices that would have committed all underwriters to purchase in support of the price, Deutsche Bank felt obliged to support the price itself. Finally, almost two-thirds of the bond amount was incorporated into its port-folio. Although critical voices within the bank saw this as confirmation of their misgivings, it cannot be denied that the support action taken by the bank on its own had revealed it, as far as the World Bank was concerned, to be a particularly competent and reliable partner on the capital market. This is one reason why since then Deutsche Bank and World Bank have had a lasting relationship in deutschmark issues.

A bond for the city of Oslo at the end of 1959 was the first foreign local-authority bond to be placed by the bank on the German capital market since 1914. However, the low issue amount revealed the uncertainty surrounding the further development of interest and exchange rates. This uncertainty and the underwriting banks' fears that, if capital market interest rates were to rise further, they would have to maintain the paper placed by them at an acceptable price level, were the main reasons why issuing activity in foreign DM bonds was at a virtual standstill until February 1962.

It was therefore not until February 1962 that the bank lead-managed a bond for the prefecture and city of Osaka, whose issue amount of 100 million DM was substantial compared to the Oslo bond. This was Japan's first ever bond issue in Germany and its first bond in Europe since the war. Right from the outset, the Japanese planned to tap the resilient German capital market in future years as well, provided the placement of the first tranche went successfully. Owing to the slight possibility of a renewed rise in interest rates in the spring of 1962, the bank recommended that the interest rate be fixed at 6.5 per cent, just above the rate for first-class domestic borrowers. The recommendation of the Central Capital Market Committee on 13 June 1963 to return to the 6 per cent bond finally guaranteed the success of this issue. Osaka again tapped the German market in 1963, 1964 and 1965 with further bonds lead-managed by the bank for 100 million DM each. This was to set a precedent. In the following years, the Japanese city of Kobe tapped the German capital market annually, with Deutsche Bank as the lead manager of its issues.

In 1963, after the 1959 World Bank issue, the European Investment Bank became the second supranational borrower to tap the German capital market, once again under the lead management of Deutsche Bank which, owing to its handling of the 1959 World Bank issue, had earned the reputation of a competent and reliable issuer. In 1965 the bank further diversified its product range for international underwriting by lead-managing its first bond issues for foreign private companies. Transocean Gulf Oil, DuPont and British Petroleum each tapped the market for 100 million DM, and IBM World Trade for 120 million DM.

All the issues mentioned so far were brought to the German market by purely domestic syndicates. For various reasons, foreign banks, which in 1963 had given Deutsche Bank access to the dollar bond sector, wanted to be involved in syndicates issuing foreign DM bonds. Bond syndicates and placements were becoming internationalized, and the Euro DM bond was born. None the less, the traditional foreign DM bond also remained an integral part of the bank's product range. The European Investment Bank (EIB) and the World Bank in particular remained regular issuers of foreign DM bonds.

In 1965 the World Bank continued its policy of resorting to the German market with an external bond for 250 million DM, and in 1968 with a further one for 120 million DM, both of them lead-managed by Deutsche Bank. In the mid-1970s, individual World Bank bond issues reached volumes of 650 million DM. In 1985 the World Bank raised 1 billion DM by issuing a zero bond, interestingly enough still underwritten by a purely German syndicate led by Deutsche Bank. This 30-year zero bond was very popular with German investors. By the early 1990s it was the only interest-rate benchmark for such long maturities owing to its trading volume on the secondary market.

The World Bank's purely German syndicate for foreign DM bonds continued until 1987. In that year, three big Swiss and US banks were invited to join the syndicate for a 600 million DM issue. Although changes to the usual syndicate structure had been expected for some time, it was ultimately the practices of smaller German banks – some of the paper was placed not with private investors on a permanent basis but with financial intermediaries, whose investment decisions are more short termist, and with speculative institutional investors – that persuaded the World Bank to reorganize the traditional structure of the syndicate; however, the issue was still lead-managed by Deutsche Bank.

By the mid-1960s it had become clear that national capital markets could no longer handle the volume of bond issues. However, the bank had misgivings about internationalizing syndicates, partly because institutional investors would then occasionally be forced to purchase foreign-currency paper and would thus be contravening statutory investment regulations. To prevent this, Abs was in favour of a new type of bond, the 'European parallel loan'.[31]

Under this concept, an issue would be divided into various tranches and floated on the European capital markets in the respective local currency. The tranches would be largely uniform in terms of nominal interest rate, so that only their volumes would differ according to the capacity of the national markets.

Abs believed that this type of bond, which would be issued by national syndicates, would help gradually to integrate national capital markets to form a uniform European capital market.

The suggestion was implemented in 1965 for an issue by Ente Nazionale per l'Energia Elettrica (ENEL), an Italian state-owned electricity company with traditionally close ties to Deutsche Bank. This was to be the first and last issue of its kind, especially owing to the lack of success of ENEL's issue. Its pricing, which was intended to offset the differences in interest rates, proved somewhat laborious; the uniform interest rate on the bond made it look as though it had been forced into a corset. Moreover, the number of potential issuers was very limited from the outset, since only few companies have need of liabilities in so many different currencies. The fact that the 'European parallel loan' was introduced (albeit unwillingly) against the advice of the experts can probably be attributed to Abs' dominant position at the time on the bank's board of managing directors.

The 200 million DM bond issued by the Japanese government in 1964 can be described as the first Euro DM bond. This had two special features. First, it was the first time that Deutsche Bank, the lead manager of the issue, invited foreign banks to join the syndicate. This ensured that the loan would also be placed outside the German currency area. Second, it was also the first time in Germany that a bond had been issued and listed at the same time. This procedure was largely continued in future.

Since the 1960s, big German companies had been stepping up their direct investments abroad. Since German banks did not have sufficient presence there, these companies improved their contacts with foreign banks in the relevant country. Consequently, the foreign banks started to urge their new customers to allow them to participate in their issues. This development was irreversible, especially since Deutsche Bank itself was increasingly being invited to participate in dollar issues, an invitation which was expected to be reciprocated. This cleared the way for international syndicates.

At the same time, more and more big German corporations were starting to float bond issues through financing companies which they had specially set up at off-shore centres for capital procurement purposes. The process was started in 1965 by BASF, whose subsidiary BASF Holding Luxembourg issued a loan for 80 million DM, which was lead-managed by the bank. This avoided having to pay withholding tax in Germany. This example was followed in 1966 by financing companies of AEG, Thyssen and Siemens. After having to fight for these mandates, Deutsche Bank was once again lead manager of these issues.

In 1966 the bank diversified its product range further. For the first time in several decades it helped finance the formation of a foreign company, Highveld Steel and Vanadium Corporation in South Africa. The company floated a warrant issue for 100 million DM, with Deutsche Bank as lead manager. The warrants became a hit, but the performance of the ordinary share price was somewhat disappointing.

Over the next few years, the internationalization of underwriting syndicates continued. Although foreign banks had been syndicate members before 1967, they had not been co-managers of Euro DM bonds. This changed with a bond issued by Argentina, which because of its considerable capital requirement wanted to float separate dollar, Swiss franc and deutschmark tranches. Argentina, with which Deutsche Bank had long had close links, favoured international syndicates, partly for prestige reasons and partly to limit the number of banks involved in the negotiations. Recognizing the risk inherent in this 100 million DM issue, the bank deliberately started looking for strong underwriting houses as co-managers. The deutschmark tranche of the Argentina loan became the first Euro DM issue, with an international management group consisting of seven co-managers. The bank used the same procedure when issuing a 100 million DM bond for Mexico in December 1968. That year also saw the bank's second lead management of a Japanese issue (100 million DM) in the deutschmark sector.

Between 1969 and 1972 the bank was the most active underwriter on the international capital markets. The main reason for this was its strong position in the deutschmark sector. In 1976 the bank again demonstrated its strength in lead-managing bonds of public sector issuers by structuring and issuing loans for the European Communities (EC) in favour of Italy and Ireland. The EC had originally intended to raise the funds in the form of floating rate notes. The regulated German capital market and its lack of experience with floating rate notes did not give the bank much hope of becoming lead manager. However, the EBIC organization had good prospects of obtaining a management mandate in the deal.

In the course of negotiations between EC representatives and banks interested in winning a mandate, it emerged that the volume of over $1 billion was too big for one currency and for the placement of floating rate notes. The division of the total amount into individual tranches also brought Deutsche Bank into play; the bank lead-managed the seven-year, 500 million DM tranche in what for the Euromarket at the time was an unusual combined underwriting and issuing syndicate. The placement, which came a relatively short time after the oil crisis, did not prove easy, and so the bank initially retained parts of the issue.

Up to 1985, deutschmark issues led by the bank, including the traditional external bonds for the World Bank, reached annual volumes of between 1.3 billion and 4.5 billion DM. With a market share of between 30 and 60 per cent between 1976 and 1985, Deutsche Bank maintained its leading position in the issuance of DM-denominated bonds. In DM bonds, whose issuance since 1976 had largely done without the three-tier syndicate structure, the bank lead-managed issues for countries such as Sweden, Argentina, Australia, Mexico and Norway, and for supranational organizations such as the World Bank, the EIB and the Asian Development Bank – the latter still preferring three-tier syndicate structures – as well as for private issuers.

On 12 April 1985, the Bundesbank announced deregulations in the market for foreign DM bonds – the so-called liberalization of the rest of the German capital market. The new conditions had a marked impact on Deutsche Bank's position. On the one hand, this enabled it to introduce bond types to the DM sector which it had already used as the lead manager of deutschmark-denominated bonds – more so than other German banks – and of which it therefore already had experience. On the other hand, there was a danger of lower fee income because from now on more banks would be competing for attractive underwriting mandates. Finally, the new principle of reciprocity gave the bank the opportunity to expand its product range abroad.

In addition to the above-mentioned lead management of the World Bank's zero bond, in 1985 Deutsche Bank introduced two further DM bond innovations to the Euromarket: Sweden's 1.5 billion DM floating rate note and the first German dual-currency loan for the Canadian Export Development Corporation. The latter proved to be a mistake, since it was not accepted by investors and therefore remained a one-off experiment. Despite its efforts in connection with the floating rate note for Sweden, which generated a good deal of publicity owing to its volume, the bank did not lead-manage any substantial floating rate note programmes for a while, primarily because borrowers were increasingly attempting to obtain rates below LIBOR or FIBOR, and the problems resulting from this would be too great for the underwriting banks to bear. Moreover, stock transfer tax was substantially hindering the market success of deutschmark floating rate notes. When the abolition of this tax was announced in 1990, however, the bank successfully placed a 1.2 billion DM floating rate note for Lufthansa International Finance (Nederlands) N.V.

By the early 1990s, therefore, the bank's DM bond business still focused on *fixed-income* bonds. The bank claims that it does not place junk bonds. However, some of the bonds brought to market by the bank – some of them in lead manager capacity – in effect became junk bonds soon after they were issued. Thus there was never any question of the bank lead-managing the underwriting of two loans for the Australian Bond Finance Corporation in 1988 which turned out to be a super-flop; on 20 May 1988 and 6 September 1988 Bond Finance (DM) Ltd issued two deutschmark-denominated bonds for 150 million and 175 million DM at 6.25 and 6.5 per cent respectively.

In 1983 Alan Bond became a sort of national hero in Australia after he and his yacht (*Australia II*) won back the world's most prestigious yachting trophy, the 'America's Cup', from the Americans after 132 years. At the time of the first issue in May 1988, Australian Ratings had classified Bond Corporation's credit standing as 'BB-'. In contrast to almost all other foreign banks in Australia, Deutsche Bank Australia did not make any loans to Bond. Shortly after the issue of the second bond, for which, as for the first one, BHF-Bank (which lost some of its standing on the Euromarket as a result of the Bond catastrophe) acted as lead manager – without having had close relations with the Bond group either as lender or shareholder – there were initial rumours about difficulties in Bond's business empire and about dishonest behaviour. As a result, his rating was further downgraded.

Nine months after the issue of the first bond, Bond Finance Ltd and Bond Corporation Holdings Ltd, which guaranteed the loan, signed the issuing prospectus. This prospectus, which the underwriting banks – including Deutsche Bank – all signed, did not reveal the desperate financial situation of the issuer. In March 1989 the company was officially listed on the Frankfurt Stock Exchange. A little later there was a drastic deterioration in the company's situation, which was also evident to the general public. At the end of 1989, the company's bonds, which were not collateralized by real property but merely carried a guarantee from the parent company, which in such cases is worthless, were trading at 20 per cent of nominal value.

In 1990 there was growing unrest among bondholders, who accused the underwriting banks of having given false information in their investment counselling and of having neglectfully signed the issuing prospectus – and rightly so, as the underwriting banks were informed in a court ruling following a 1992 prospectus liability lawsuit on behalf of the German Association for Protection of Securities Holdings. Gradually, the banks involved – including Deutsche Bank – compensated bondholders who had acquired the bonds before the prospectus was published. The bank either repurchased the bonds at their issue price or exchanged them for Deutsche Bank bonds. Although the bank had not occupied a leading position as underwriter, it was still represented in the managing group. It should also be mentioned, as the bank likes to point out, that it only gives investment recommendations for AAA issues. The reality looks different: for all issues in which the bank acts as an underwriter, Frankfurt head office sends the branches a list of these securities, which are then recommended to the client in the course of investment counselling.

The bank was also involved in other problematic issues. In 1988, for example, the UK financial group National Home Loans Corporation plc issued two bonds directly and through its financing company NHL Finance (Nederland) B.V., both with Deutsche Bank as lead manager. The two issues became non-performing, and at their lowest point in 1992 were trading at between 40 and 30 DM. The buyers of the bonds were not informed of the substantial risk involved. Moreover, the interest rate chosen at the time, which was close to the interest rate on government bonds, suggested that they were a safe investment. These bonds were not collateralized by real property either, and only carried a guarantee from the parent company.

When bondholders demanded that their securities be exchanged, the lead manager replied that it would be uncustomary to swap these broadly placed bonds since they were still being serviced, and at the time the bonds were issued

NHL's commercial paper programmes had been given the top P1 rating by Moody's and the good A-2 rating by Standard & Poor's. After that, the NHL investors were unable to get any more information out of the bank, which was also involved as a direct lender, but had already written off its exposure at an early stage. However, they were fortunate: the first bond was repaid on schedule, and in 1993 the price of the second one recovered to a normal level as a result of restructuring measures at NHL.

The foreign DM bond issued by Heron International Finance B.V., The Hague – a dubious financing company owned by the UK Heron Corporation, which was engaged in real estate – also turned out to be a flop. The lead manager, Deutsche Bank, floated the 100 million DM loan – which carried a 7.25 per cent coupon and was issued at 99.5 per cent – in 1988 on the international DM bond market. At the end of March 1992, Heron applied for a payment extension and rescheduling of its long-term liabilities. In 1992 after Credit Suisse, the lead manager of four Heron bonds for 600 million Swiss francs, had called in the loans, the trading and listing of the DM bond in Frankfurt were also suspended at Deutsche Bank's request on 8 April 1992, and have not been resumed since. On 7 April the bond was quoted at 57.50 DM after trading had been suspended from 27 March to 6 April.

In the market for Eurodollar straight bonds, Deutsche Bank participated in 1957 in an issue for Petrofina S.A., Brussels, for $25 million. Despite its dollar denomination and the attempt to involve several European banks, the issue was not a genuine Eurodollar issue. Petrofina needed several currencies and so the banks involved paid the countervalue of those parts of the bond underwritten by them in their respective local currencies. The issue was settled in the form of a club deal. Deutsche Bank was invited to participate as a result of its close relationship with Société Générale de Belgique, Petrofina's house bank.

The Eurodollar bond market only really emerged in 1963, when President Kennedy, who was very much a layman in economic matters, introduced an interest equalization tax. For Deutsche Bank, this development meant that an issuing market that was difficult to locate had, as it were, appeared right in front of its nose. When in 1963 the London merchant bank S.G. Warburg & Co. agreed to lead-manage an issue for AUTOSTRADE Concessioni e Costruzioni Autostrade, Italy, for $15 million, Deutsche Bank and three other banks agreed to be managers. The risk seemed to be acceptable since the issue was guaranteed by Istituto per la Ricostruzione Industriale, a holding company wholly owned by the Italian government. Owing to the international composition of its syndicate, this issue was the first genuine Eurodollar bond issue. The bank is therefore one of the founders of the Eurodollar bond market.

Over the following years, the bank continued to participate in Eurodollar issues. The relatively insignificant issue volumes could, in hindsight, substantiate the assumption that in carrying out these issues the bank was still not trying to achieve a lasting presence on the Euromarket. Its participation looked more like a testing of the market, as did its subsequent infrequent participation in the flotation of dollar bonds. In addition to its uncertainty about the development of the Eurodollar market, the main reason was the uncertainty on the part of the bank and the general public about the future development of the dollar.

In 1975 the dollar consolidated, and in 1976 a new record for Eurodollar bond issues was set with a volume of approximately $10 billion. The bank now also considered that the time had come for it to become more active in Eurodollar bonds. Although in 1975 it had already lead-managed the issue of two dollar loans for $150 million each for Ontario Hydro, the high-profile entry to the Eurodollar market it had always sought did not actually come until 1976, when it lead-managed an issue by the EC. The bank's lead management of the deutschmark tranche came as no surprise to market observers. However, leading international investment banks from the USA and the UK had applied for the mandate for the dollar tranches. Despite their market know-how and placement strength in dollar issues, Deutsche Bank – which, though already known as a founding member of Eurodollar bond business (see Petrofina, p. 681), was merely considered an outsider – was preferred to the other banks by the EC bodies.

The bank's management style in this prestigious, six-year Eurodollar bond issue for $300 million attracted particular attention. Traditional, professional issuing banks know how to fine-tune the bond's conditions to the market situation and, after careful selection of the banks participating as underwriters and sellers, to place it world-wide. On the one hand, this fine-tuning prevents the banks from pricing too aggressively, but on the other the premiums paid to the underwriters increase the EC's financing costs. The bank got rid of such restrictions by simply eliminating the underwriting group. The EC, as issuer, therefore saved itself an underwriting fee, which was probably the decisive factor in Deutsche Bank's receiving the mandate.

The bank's decision to exclude the underwriting group, however, was not only to cut down on the issuer's costs. The bank tried to impose a certain discipline on individual underwriters. These had earned fairly substantial fees from previous issues. For this reason, the managing group expected them to take parts of the issue into their own portfolio in the event that the issue could not be fully placed. In practice, however, some underwriters get rid of parts of the bond they have underwritten at dumping prices on the secondary market, so that the lead manager – because of its duty to support the price of the security – is forced to take up these securities, which usually trade at a discount. By transferring national underwriting techniques to the Euromarket, Deutsche Bank was aiming to teach the underwriters first that their involvement in Euromarket transactions was not absolutely essential to the issue and second, and more indirectly, that underwriting involved fairly substantial risks and that the not ungenerous 0.5 per cent up-front premium was paid as compensation for assuming these.

A further highlight of 1976 was the Australian 'jumbo' issue. With a volume of $300 million, the issue could claim to be the largest to date in terms of volume of any one country on the Euromarket. Morgan Stanley made great efforts to win the leading mandate for this issue and, after having lead-managed other Australian bonds previously, was the favourite to win the position. In order to ensure that the US institution was not overlooked – so rumour has it – even US Secretary of State Henry Kissinger declared his support for Morgan Stanley to the Australian government. None the less, Deutsche Bank won the mandate, again mainly owing to its pricing. Although insiders claimed that the bank had to support the price substantially, even Morgan Stanley had to admit that 'given the size of the financing and aggressive offering terms, the opening quotes were respectable'.[32]

At the beginning of 1977 the bank diversified its international issuing programme by introducing *Schuldscheine* (promissory notes) to the Euromarket. The Australian Shipping Commission had announced that it needed $50 million. A loan of that amount was to be guaranteed by the Australian government. However, these funds would have been subject to tax. The bank therefore received the mandate to handle this financing transaction, and it was suggested that the *Schuldschein* used on the German market could be applied to the Euromarket dollar sector – a successful undertaking despite the lack of a listing.

In mid-1977 the EC announced it was to issue another jumbo bond. At first, the bank kept out of the competition for mandates, since the EBIC subsidiary EBC (European Banking Company) for a long time looked certain to win the mandate. Only after the issue structuring suggested by EBC had been rejected by the EC Council of Ministers did the bank get involved, acting as lead manager of the five-year tranche for $200 million and the seven-year tranche for $300 million. This was conclusive proof that the bank was now fully established on the Eurodollar bond market. Although it had already topped several league tables in the early 1970s, this was mainly due to the larger volume of its Euro deutschmark issues. The bank was aware of the need to enter the market aggressively – especially as its domestic customers were showing increasing demand for dollar-denominated securities – and at the end of 1978, at the first time of asking, it won a market share of almost 26 per cent. Subsequently, however, it lost market share, which remained at around 10 per cent in the following years.

The bank remained top lender for supranational issuers and no. 2 for issues whose funds were used for public investment projects. However, its product range was limited almost exclusively to the management of straight bonds with volumes of more than $100 million per issue. One example was the bank's lead management of a $750 million bond for Canada in April 1982. Within half an hour, bank representatives reached agreement with the government on this issue, the largest single transaction to date, without even consulting the board of managing directors. Canada, which was interested in a functioning, liquid secondary market, chose the bank as lead manager, first, because its retail placing system allowed it to give the bond a broad placement and second, because the flat hierarchy in the department dealing with international bond issues ensured quick decision-making.

In mid-1989 there was growing unrest again among major players on the Eurobond market about the underwriting practices used. A solution was to be found by transferring the underwriting and placement methods used on the US domestic bond market to the Euro primary market. Deutsche Bank did all it could to support the introduction of this new regime. On 30 August 1989, Deutsche Bank Capital Markets (DBCM), London, brought to the market a five-year, $300 million bond for the Reconstruction Loan Corporation according to US practices. Just under three weeks later, the bank again used this pricing procedure. Together with Salomon Brothers, it acted as lead manager for the World Bank's $1.5 billion global bond. The idea behind this was to link domestic and off-shore dollar markets, i.e. to ensure that the bond could be traded world-wide in such a way that market participants could trade on their original markets. Euroclear and Cedel, the international clearing centres, were intregrated into the transaction at the European end. The global bond was the first registered bond to be issued on the Euromarkets since the 'Carter bonds' of the late 1970s.

The bank was also quick to enter the market for Eurodollar bonds with warrants. In 1967 it acted as lead manager for De Beers, Highveld Steel and Renault. More surprising was the awarding of mandates for dollar warrant issues by big German corporations; for tax reasons, these companies transferred their capital-raising measures to their off-shore financing companies. In 1969, Siemens, Bayer and BASF came to the market with a total issue volume of $190 million. The motives behind this step were, first, to find the most cost-effective way of procuring capital for direct investment abroad and, second, to put an end to the traditional under-representation of large German corporations on the international capital market. While Deutsche Bank was certainly credited with the capability to meet the first requirement, American investment banks in particular saw the second as their domain and so did all they could to win the mandate. The bank won it nevertheless, but included a few foreign banks as co-managers.

There was further diversification in dollar bond issues in the form of floating rate notes and bonds linked to interest rate swaps. Because of the legal situation and a gentlemen's agreement between the German banks and the Bundesbank, the use of both of these forms of bond was initially restricted to foreign currencies or, to be more precise, to dollars, owing to their longer market tradition. At first the bank did not have sufficient experience of swaps, and so for its first trans-action in 1982 it drew on the services of its partner Morgan Guaranty. For tax reasons, the funds were raised through its subsidiary DB Finance N.V., Curaçao, which passed the funds on to the Luxemburg subsidiary. In August, DB Finance N.V. issued 14.5 per cent, seven-year dollar *Schuldscheine* as part of an overall issue of swap-related bonds amounting to $710 million. The issuing volume was $300 million. The bank had therefore carried out what until then was the largest swap-related issue on the capital market in terms of volume.

Initially, the bank was somewhat sceptical about floating rate note issues. In view of rising dollar interest rates, however, which made long-term fixed-interest periods unattractive for issuers, it was forced to follow market trends. After having gained experience as a co-manager in a few floating rate note issues in the early 1980s, in September 1983 it won the mandate for a floating rate note of Crédit Foncier de France for $500 million. Two further mandates for floating rate note issues followed in the same year. However, the bank had not changed its fundamentally sceptical attitude, so that it substantially reined in its floating rate note activities following a renewed fall in interest rates. An exception to this was the above-mentioned jumbo issue for Sweden and, in 1986, the $200 million for China. In 1992 the bank launched its first floating rate note for 1 billion DM, the interest rate based on one-month FIBOR.

Many innovative forms of debt instrument introduced in the interests of issuers and, in some cases, investors have proved unviable as long-term prospects. Kopper summarized such developments in the 1980s as follows: 'From euphoria to new realism, to a new sobriety, or: from illusion to disillusion – that is how I would describe the general line pursued by Eurobond investment banking in the 1980s. In terms of quantity, the 1980s were certainly impressive; with the Euro-issue volumes, turnover on the secondary markets exploded out of all proportion owing to the performance- and trading-oriented institutional investors. Since about 1985, however, we have increasingly seen an alarming erosion of quality in terms of yield, ethos and style – the conduct of business – in Euro securities business.' His recommendation was: 'Reconsideration, repositioning and, in some cases, painful redimensioning after the hypertrophy are needed if we are to get back to realistic, sensible and manageable levels. During the 1980s, the word "innovation" acquired a clearly negative connotation and undertone; there are three main reasons for this. First, many innovations lacked a sense of balance with respect to the interests of borrowers, investors and banks; they are too debt oriented. Second, many innovations reveal too large a discrepancy between practicability on the primary market and containability on the secondary market. And third, many banks go overboard on innovation simply to attract non-customers and, sometimes, do business with them.' Finally he gave a view of the bank's product range in bond issuing of the 1990s: 'We are definitely reverting to products which are simple, comprehensible, fair to all and controllable. This does not exactly mean only plain vanilla – but innovation as an end in itself is over.'[33]

Customer demand in the 1980s, and probably in the 1990s too, was broadly developing towards investment in high-interest-rate currencies. The bank was at first slow to follow this trend, since exchange rate weaknesses in the bond currency can easily give rise to hopes of better returns. However, after other domestic banks had successfully placed bonds denominated in Australian dollars, Canadian dollars and pesetas, Deutsche Bank had no option but to follow suit. It was supported in this by its world-wide branch network. Diversification into the ECU and Swiss franc markets was also significant here.

The ECU bond market was neglected for some time. The Euromarkets have always been sceptical about bonds denominated in artificial currencies, since more than almost any other instrument they are influenced more by political factors than by economic ones. However, driven by a number of ECU-denominated government bond issues and the conviction of many institutional investors that the ECU would become Europe's common currency after economic unification, the ECU established itself on the Eurobond market in the early 1990s.

Although initially various difficulties – such as the Bundesbank's refusal to recognize the ECU as a currency until 1990 – prevented Deutsche Bank from issuing ECU-denominated paper, it was able to enter the market with greater resources following the Bundesbank's announcement on 13 June, which allowed ECU-denominated liabilities to be assumed. In 1990 it lead-managed a Reconstruction Loan Corporation bond for 200 million ECU and in 1991 a 200 million ECU issue for Daimler-Benz of North America through its subsidiary Deutsche Bank Capital Markets. This was the first time that a German industrial borrower had raised funds on the ECU market. In January 1992 the bank also established itself as a market-maker in ECU bond futures on the Marché à Terme International de France in Paris. Since June 1991 it has been acting as a broker for ECU bond futures on the London International Financial Futures Exchange. In subsequent years, however, the private ECU market became less interesting for market participants.

Since the beginning of the 1990s, the bank has been aiming to become a market-maker in government securities at the major financial centres. This process was begun in 1989, when the bank acquired its primary dealership in the USA. London and Paris followed. The main aim of its market-maker function, which initially entailed substantial costs, was to underline its trading competence. It also provided certain institutionalized benefits; in the case of government securities auctions in France, for example, it enabled the bank to order securities later in the event of brief, usually marginal changes in the interest rate. One result of its market-maker activity in the UK is an online link with the Bank of England which speeds up and facilitates the procurement of information on latest events on the London financial market. The bank's market-maker function also improved its block trading of financial securities with institutional investors.

The bank set up a European trading network based on its activity as a government bond-dealer or market-maker on all major European bond markets. In 1993 the bank transferred its business with supranational organizations and the syndication of all capital market products to its new Capital Markets Division, for which Rolf-E. Breuer is responsible. This division also has direct responsibility for the financing of government agencies world-wide and for the issuance of innovative financial instruments.

d) Trends in Euro equities business

Euro equities business did not really start until the mid-1980s. Although Deutsche Bank had floated a number of shares for foreign issuers on the German stock markets, there were no placements by international syndicates. The first step in this direction resulted from its acquisition of shares in the Flick Group. In December 1985, the industrialist Friedrich Flick offered the bank the opportunity to purchase Friedrich Flick Industrieverwaltung KGaA after its conversion into a joint stock company. The bank took up the offer with the intention of placing the shares widely, thereby giving as many people as possible the chance to acquire them. The subject of the transaction was the industrial core of Flick's business empire, which comprised Buderus, Dynamit Nobel and Feldmühle, and its participating interests in Daimler-Benz and W.R. Grace & Co., New York.

The central features of the entire transaction were, first, the takeover of Friedrich Flick Industrieverwaltung at a fixed price of 5 billion DM, which was then to be converted into a joint stock company and, second, the subsequent broad placement of the shares, which covered three separate transactions. On 2 January 1986, the 26 per cent holding in the US conglomerate W.R. Grace & Co., which was valued at 1.5 billion DM, was taken over by Grace itself. Although this part of the deal could be described as international, there was no broad placement of the shares. The second part, the third chronologically, consisted of merging the three companies Feldmühle, Dynamit Nobel and Buderus to form Feldmühle-Nobel AG. Finally, in January 1986, 3.397 million Daimler-Benz shares – 10 per cent of the company's share capital, with a market value of 3.8 billion DM – were widely placed by an international syndicate.

The placement went so successfully that Deutsche Bank, the lead manager, was later accused of having underpriced the shares. Indeed, on 14 January 1986, the Daimler-Benz share price reached 1,440 DM, which was well above the subscription price of 1,120 DM. In addition to the scale of this deal, its technical settlement was probably its most significant feature. Flicksche Industrieverwaltung KGaA, having been converted into a joint stock company, was transferred to the bank's ownership at a fictitious time, namely after 24:00 hours on 31 December 1985 and before 0:00 hours on 1 January 1986. This meant that no wealth or trade capital tax was payable, as was intended by the so-called 'midnight directive', invented for such cases.

Moreover, the bank was not subject to any restrictions imposed by the Federal Banking Supervisory Office, since the Flick holdings had disappeared again from its books by the end of 1986. The German Banking Act stipulates that this institution had to examine whether the bank's stake in its long-standing borrower Flick should not have been treated as a large loan. Strictly speaking, the bank should not have been allowed to take over the Flick package, but the Federal Banking Supervisory Office supported the overall transaction right from the beginning. Finally, the Office did not have any objections either to the subsequent trustee construction, on the basis of which the fiduciary – not defined as a bank by the Banking Act – acquires the shares for the bank's account and then resells them.

The most remarkable international equities transaction took place in the summer of 1986 and brought the bank much criticism. Almost ten years previously, Colonel Gaddafi's Libyan government had acquired 10 per cent of the car-making group Fiat (purchase price: $415 million) through the state-owned Libyan Arab Foreign Investment Corporation, and had therefore become the second-largest shareholder after the Agnelli family. In 1986 Fiat was competing for orders from the US Department of Defense, among other things in connection with the development of the Strategic Defense Initiative. The Pentagon was not willing to give Fiat production orders as long as the Libyans held their Fiat stake.

After tough negotiations, the Libyans were finally prepared to sell their holding. The selling price was to be 16,000 lire per ordinary share, 10,000 lire per preference share and 9,550 lire per non-voting share – the equivalent of $3.1 billion, payable in dollars. This was almost seven times the amount Libya had originally paid. $1.1 billion was raised through transactions involving the state-owned Italian Mediobanca, and the other $2 billion was to be obtained through the public placement of part of Libya's shareholding.

After Mediobanca and Lazard Frères, which had a sort of house-bank relationship with the Fiat Group, declared that they were unable to handle a placement of this magnitude, Deutsche Bank took the initiative. Deutsche Bank Capital Markets, London, was appointed co-ordinator of the entire transaction. On 23 September 1986, the day it was announced that Libya was to sell its stake, Fiat's ordinary share price shot up to 16,600 lire, primarily owing to positive earnings expectations announced shortly beforehand, possibly contrary to better knowledge. The price had therefore risen eightfold from its pre-year low of 2,000 lire. Together, Deutsche Bank and Mediobanca, which had agreed to purchase the package, paid $2 billion to Fiat. Of this, Mediobanca underwrote $500 million worth of shares, so that it could then place them in the Italian market. Deutsche Bank underwrote the lion's share of the package – worth $1.5 billion – with a view to placing it internationally. The equity to be placed amounted to 8.5 per cent of Fiat's entire share capital, 13 per cent of the preference shares issued and 13 per cent of its non-voting shares. The latter had warrants attached which later entitled the holder to subscribe to the shares of a Fiat subsidiary.

On the afternoon of 23 September, investment bankers at DBCM began to look for potential co-lead managers for the deal to underwrite a portion of Deutsche Bank's package. By midnight, ten underwriters had agreed to take $100 million worth of equity each. The deadline for the members of the sub-underwriting group to agree to underwrite part of the package was 10 a.m. on 25 September 1986. The bank itself agreed to place equity worth $600 million. It priced the ordinary shares at $11.28, the preference shares at $7.08 and the non-voting preference shares at $6.75, thus granting discounts of only 4–5 per cent on the Fiat share's top price.

After being too conservative in the Daimler deal, the bank appears in hindsight to have been too relaxed with Fiat. In the case of Daimler, the discount was too high as a result of fears that such a large number of shares might be impossible to place, and because of the bank's failure to recognize the stability of the bullish market at the time. With Fiat, on the other hand, the discount was not big enough considering the substantial volume and Fiat's low standing.

On the evening of 23 September, the first problems with the settlement began to arise. When putting together the underwriting group, the bank had stipulated 7 October as the date for payment and delivery of the shares. Settlement of the transaction was to be handled by the clearing systems Centrale de livraison de valeurs mobilières (Cedel) or Euroclear. Further details were not stipulated. On 24 September, 14 days prior to payment and delivery of the shares, the Fiat share opened lower. Because of this, the underwriters, who were tied to the fixed price negotiated with the bank, saw their fees disintegrate and were unable to dispose of any securities – which would not have been the purpose of their inclusion anyway – because they were still not available to them. The Fiat share price fell to 15,000 lire, while the offering price fixed by the bank had been 15,939 lire.

The banks were forced to hold on to huge amounts of Fiat shares. Deutsche Bank, in some cases criticized by its own underwriters, did its utmost to avert a disaster. It reduced the amount that the underwriters had agreed to take on, and attempted to support the share price and set up a secondary market for Fiat shares outside Italy. This was necessary because it had omitted to publicize the fact that the shares, which had originally been purchased at a 4 per cent discount on the top price, could not be sold in Italy.

This deal once again reveals that the bank was not very sophisticated when it came to pricing, complicated as it was. This is why the bank is still one of the main Fiat shareholders. By contrast, placements geared to the German market over the next few years were largely successful, despite their occasionally substantial volumes. This gave the bank the opportunity to display the expertise it had acquired in issues involving international placements. The privatization of the British Gas Corporation in 1986 was successful. The bank led the German sub-syndicate. Shares of Volkswagen AG and Feldmühle-Nobel – stemming from the Flick transaction – were largely placed without any problems. In the privatization of the French Banque Paribas, the bank was involved as the regional underwriter of the German tranche.

It was less successful, however, with the privatization of British Petroleum. The events of 19 October 1987 ('Black Monday') came between the bank's agreement to underwrite the issue and the beginning of the placement. It became obvious that it was going to be very difficult to achieve the minimum price from the placement. Since the bank did not know the allocation price, which was only revealed at the auction, it was impossible for it to get out of the transaction by selling the equity immediately on the grey market. On the other hand, the UK government was unable to withdraw the privatization deal since such action would have implied an obvious bias in favour of the bank and, at the same time, would have disadvantaged all other investors. In the end, Kuwait benefited from the BP shares' weak opening prices by buying up substantial holdings.

In mid-1991, the bank received the mandate to place just under one million shares of the trade-union-owned insurance company Volksfürsorge throughout Europe, a transaction which had a total volume of almost 800 million DM. For the first time in a German equity issue, the bank used the so-called 'New York syndication procedure' instead of the usual quota procedure. It intended to place 50 per cent of the new issue in other European countries. However, the actual placement abroad could hardly be carried out, since, according to the New York procedure, it was not intended to publish the book. The disappointing performance of the Volksfürsorge share price (subscription price 800 DM, first quotation 802 DM, after the first week 780 DM, by July 1992 only 545 DM) does, however, suggest that there had possibly been substantial selling pressure from abroad, particularly from institutional investors.

A particularly noteworthy event of 1993 is that Deutsche Bank was the only German institution in the global syndicate that privatized the UK government's remaining stake in British Telecom. This was the first time that a global issue had been launched by only *one* syndicate, which placed the shares with institutional investors world-wide.

e) Trends in international asset management

The foundation of Capital Management International GmbH of Deutsche Bank (CMI), Frankfurt, in 1983 can be regarded as one of the first signs of the bank's commitment to international asset management for institutional investors. Its task was to manage institutional funds of non-German customers on all the world's major markets. This formation was prompted by a change in the legal provisions governing the investment policy of US pension funds (Employee Retirement Income Security Act, or ERISA).

CMI registered itself as a money manager with the US Securities and Exchange Commission (SEC). However, CMI was forced to transact its business as an independent asset manager of Deutsche Bank Group, since the SEC did not allow the bank to be used as a broker or custodian for ERISA funds. Although in 1983 it was not long before the bank won its first customer, which brought in $20 million and six months later added to its managed funds as a result of the positive performance of its assets, the fact that there were only two further mandates up to 1985 demonstrated that it would be very difficult to enter the

US market from Germany. For this reason, the company opened a representative office in New York in 1985.

On the whole, it was faced by a number of problems during the first few years. First of all, it did not have any track record. Second, the American methods of measuring performance were very different to those in Germany, and it was not possible to devise a suitable mathematical model from one day to the next. Third, CMI did not have an investment committee of bank staff, which was again due to the regulations of the SEC. Until 1989, the company's successes remained modest.

The bank's takeover of Morgan Grenfell Group at the end of 1989 changed the competitive situation within asset management. Morgan Grenfell had already begun with portfolio management for UK pension funds in the 1950s, and since then had constantly expanded its customer base. As far as institutional portfolio management was concerned, Morgan Grenfell Asset Management Ltd. had acquired substantial, global expertise with respect to the special demands of institutional customers.

Meanwhile, the bank had renamed CMI as Deutsche Asset Management GmbH. The management of institutional customers still took place on an individual basis and according to certain guidelines. The main target group here was institutional investors who had decided not to set up their own research and portfolio management capabilities, but who did not want to forgo individual, tailor-made securities investment.

Since the beginning of 1992, Deutsche Bank has been increasing its efforts to attract private clients' assets by setting up a number of units within the Group. In addition to the traditional German location, asset management services are provided, also for private investors, from Paris, Hong Kong, Milan (Banca d'America e d'Italia), Luxemburg (Deutsche Bank Luxembourg, DB Investment Management), Amsterdam (de Bary), Vienna, Lisbon, Geneva, Zurich, Lugano, Singapore and New York. Since the early 1970s, other international activities – with the exception of Luxemburg – have largely been managed centrally from Germany.

By the mid-1980s, the Euro euphoria of the 1970s at what used to be Deutsche Bank Compagnie Financière had disappeared as a result of occasional sharp drops in margins, sluggish growth and the international debt crisis. The continuing need for risk provisioning forced the bank to think more in terms of yield. The bank believed that one way to do this was to increase its retail banking activities, which was to put an end to the bias in its business towards Euroloans and the Euro money market. The bank's diversification into retail business was also supported by the farsighted Luxemburg government, which did much to market its location. The necessary technology, premises and staff were initially provided by Banque de Luxembourg, in which DBCF held a 25 per cent stake. By 1987, the bank had set up sufficient capacity to enable it to work independently. Deutsche Bank Luxembourg offered portfolio management for amounts of

500,000 DM and above. The bank was given its new name after its product range had been expanded accordingly.

f) Corporate finance: a new international business line

The integration of corporate finance into Deutsche Bank's international product range took place gradually, at times hardly noticeably, primarily in the second half of the 1980s. Ultimately, this also necessitated organizational changes, which were reflected in the bank's 1990 structural reform in the shape of a separate business division. One thing common to all corporate finance services is that they could be described as sophisticated. Because of this greater sophistication and, as far as the bank is concerned, their better return on investment, they stand out from the standard services on offer.

As early as the turn of the century, Deutsche Bank had been involved in the financing of big-ticket projects, especially the construction of railways. The world wars and, in particular, the restrictions on capital movements put an end to their activities in this area. Even until well into the 1960s and 1970s, the bank was hardly involved at all in the financing of major projects not related to foreign trade. The reasons for this inactivity were the bank's insufficient presence abroad, which lasted until the mid-1970s and made it difficult to carry out controls and risk analyses on the projects being financed, and the lack of technical capabilities and know-how for discovering and managing the sort of risk inherent in such big projects. This meant that, by the early 1980s, the bank was a considerable way behind Anglo-Saxon banks in *project finance*. Against this background, Christians pointed out at the 1981 General Meeting that 'we are being confronted by a largely new and fascinating task that will place considerable demands, especially on our powers of imagination and creativity. By this I mean the financing of large-scale energy projects, such as those emerging in those continents with plentiful supplies of raw materials. What is new about these project financings is, first, their dimension and, second, the need to take account of more than just the traditional credit risks. We are aware that the international competitiveness of our economy depends largely on our ability to develop the necessary forms of financing. As is our custom, we will therefore play a constructive role in meeting this major challenge in future.'

In 1987 the conclusion of the £5 billion loan agreement to finance the Channel Tunnel represented a major milestone in project finance. In contrast to the recently completed Seikan Tunnel in Japan, which had been financed under government guarantee, the French and UK governments stipulated at the time the concession to build the tunnel was granted that it should be purely privately financed, without any state guarantee. The loans taken up were to be repaid from the cash flow resulting from the tolls paid for use of the tunnel. Owing to the long duration of the project, American institutions were hardly represented in this financing, so that the group of underwriters was composed primarily of

European and Japanese banks. One of these was Deutsche Bank, which in turn passed on certain amounts of its underwriting share to other banks. The unusually wide spread of underwriters proved in hindsight to be necessary, and the financing was guaranteed despite the enormous additional costs during the construction phase. By 1992 the bank had provided £109 million for the project.

The bank's commitment to this project – at times half the staff working in the bank's Project Finance Department were involved in the risk analysis and subsequent structuring of the financing – achieved two things from its own point of view. On the one hand, it became evident that it was also possible to devise privately based financings for other types of investment project; in the following years, the bank did indeed diversify in terms of the kinds of investment project it financed (raw materials, co-generation and infrastructure). On the other, it could use the know-how gained from this project diversification to win more mandates as lead manager or co-lead manager.

At the beginning of the 1990s, the bank's Project Finance Department was largely run as a decentrally organized unit operating in Frankfurt, London, New York and, on a more limited scale, in Los Angeles, Melbourne and Singapore. The major projects managed from Frankfurt were the financing of the cellular phone network, Berlin's Schönefeld Airport, a power station and a gas pipeline in Portugal, and a plant for smelting aluminium in Iceland. Further projects financed were the Brenner Railway Tunnel and the Fehmarn Belt Crossing. In spring 1991 the bank also became involved in the financing of Euro Disneyland near Paris.

Compared, for example, with merchant banks in the UK and the USA, Deutsche Bank's *mergers and acquisitions* (M&A) activities only developed considerably later. Owing to the mainly small and medium-sized nature of German enterprises, which required less reorganization than their counterparts in the UK and the USA as a result of the energy demonstrated by the pioneering generation that emerged after the Second World War, there was not sufficient demand to justify the bank stepping up its mergers and acquisitions activities. It therefore had little opportunity to gain the sort of experience and technical know-how relevant to such transactions.

The bank's cautious attempts to enter the market through the Industrial Agency Service, which was founded in 1967 and was primarily nationally oriented, and its participation in European Financial Associates N.V., Amsterdam, in 1970 as one of seven founder banks, were largely unsuccessful. The bank attempted to provide those of its customers seeking participating interests abroad with the sort of know-how it did not possess itself by finding them competent contact persons. Looking back, it must be said that the low level of business in this area was primarily attributable to the continued lack of interest in international participations and, even where there was a certain amount of interest, to the policy of big German companies, which usually used the services of British and American M&A specialists for cross-border acquisitions.

The first substantial, high-profile transactions involving the bank did not therefore materialize until it had formulated its own international expansion strategy. Starting with the UBS–DB Corporation joint venture in New York, which in 1978 was renamed Atlantic Capital Corporation and in 1985 became Deutsche Bank Capital Corporation, the bank managed to build up its own capacities on the US market. This also made the bank more interesting for large German corporations, which had often used Goldman Sachs, Morgan Stanley and others as advisers and financiers for acquisitions in North America. However, the bank's lack of M&A staff in the USA initially allowed it to do no more than gain experience and score minor successes; it would be an exaggeration to talk of market share.

Instead, the bank aimed to import into Germany the experience gained in the USA and the mentality and organizational patterns needed for successful M&A consulting. This was reflected at an institutional level by the foundation of the Industrial Agency Service in 1984 and in the same year the formation of DB Consult GmbH, Frankfurt, which in 1989 was renamed DB Mergers & Acquisitions GmbH. Despite the fact that its business was conducted in English, its outlook was still national, again a result of its lack of market acceptance. The aim of setting up an international network of mergers and acquisitions specialists was only slowly put into practice. Small representative offices in Paris, London and Tokyo – often with only one or two staff – were intended to start the international expansion of DB Mergers & Acquisitions. Quicker progress was prevented by the shortage of qualified M&A staff. The only remaining option to achieve strategic market access was to buy an internationally renowned M&A house. In this connection, the bank's participation in and subsequent complete takeover of Morgan Grenfell appears to have been a stroke of luck. As a leading international merchant bank, Morgan Grenfell also possessed a network of mergers and acquisitions specialists both in the UK and beyond. This immediately removed the bottleneck in this business line and became a great strategic success. Morgan Grenfell was made into a centre of competence and given overall responsibility for Deutsche Bank Group's M&A business. The M&A activities of Mergers & Acquisitions GmbH and Morgan Grenfell Deutschland were merged under the name DB Morgan Grenfell GmbH (DBMG) in Frankfurt. Morgan Grenfell's John Craven became the first member of the bank's board of managing directors with English as his mother tongue.

The cornerstone of the bank's international strategy was its presence in the major triad markets. From these bases, M&A transactions could be tailored to the local market. Responsibility for business within the M&A organization was governed by the regional principle. German Desks were set up in London and New York to underline the importance of the Germany-related business and to raise its transparency. In addition, all M&A units are in contact with the German parent company, which helps ensure easier referral of potential M&A candidates to the specialized units. The units in Frankfurt and London acquire new business unusually quickly, contrary to the customary long incubation period in such transactions.

A joint venture with Gleacher & Co. Inc. in mid-1990 substantially increased the bank's American capability, since even Morgan Grenfell had previously had considerable problems to contend with on the US market. It was not long before market successes materialized. While Knorr-Bremse's acquisition of the New York Air Brake Corporation in 1991 was more of a début, the successful advice given by the bank to RWE-DEA in its acquisition of Vista Chemical Company, Texas, in June 1991 won it a permanent place on the American market. With an acquisition volume of $1.1 billion, this transaction was one of the largest German–American corporate takeovers.

Meanwhile, Deutsche Bank Group's mergers and acquisitions activities were not merely restricted to advising buyers. In 1991 DBMG played an important part in defending Continental AG against a takeover bid from Pirelli. DBMG's mandate was to ensure that a possible merger between Pirelli and Continental was in the interests of all Continental shareholders – among them Deutsche Bank, which was represented on the company's supervisory board – in other words, not only those shareholders who also owned Pirelli shares (especially the industrialist Pirelli and dummies financed by him). Moreover, the interests of customers, sub-contractors and employees were also to be safeguarded. In the end, the merger did not come about owing to Pirelli's conditions, which were unacceptable to Continental's other major shareholders.

A further aspect of corporate finance is *derivatives*. Since the early 1970s, there had been increasing volatility in interest rates and exchange rates. Deutsche Bank and its customers maintained a largely defensive attitude towards this scenario during the 1970s. At the beginning of the 1980s, however, various developments caused the bank to change its attitude towards the new risk structures. First, the strong fluctuation of the dollar against the deutschmark jeopardized its domestic placement power in Eurodollar loans and its frequent role as lead manager of Eurobond issues. Second, the bank's domestic big-ticket customers were afraid of losing some of their international competitiveness. US firms in particular reined in their financing costs considerably by using swaps. Third, the bank was forced to restructure its Luxemburg subsidiary's liabilities-side business to maintain its own competitiveness on the Euroloan market. Short-term money market paper was to be replaced by longer-term refinancing securities, which did, however, have variable rates. At first, though, the bank's lack of expertise induced it to carry out swaps as a customer. The first of a total of four dollar fixed-rate loans issued by its Luxemburg subsidiary in 1982 was swapped into floating rate, sub-LIBOR positions with the help of the investment bank Morgan Guaranty.

At the time, the bank regarded open interest rate positions as a risk factor and therefore tried to avoid them. For this reason, its swap activity was initially restricted to the *referral* of interest rate swaps. Its lack of expertise and experience compared to other international institutions was to be rectified by the involvement of American and UK experts. After a transitional phase, which was mainly intended to give the bank time to learn about swap book management – although the first interest rate swap was transacted as early as 1982 with great publicity by DB Luxembourg – the bank started to run a book for dollar interest rate swaps at the beginning of 1986. As a result of its strong position in international bond business, these interest rate swaps were often accompanied by currency swaps. The expertise it had gained with dollars was put to good use in the following years. At the beginning of 1987, the bank diversified its swaps into deutschmarks and ran an interest rate swap book in this currency as well. Further interest rate swap books followed: in 1987 for yen, in 1989 for ECU and Swiss francs, in 1990 for Australian dollars, pound sterling and guilders, and in 1991 for French francs.

Starting in 1989, activities related to currency swaps were centralized in London. While at the end of 1987, roughly the time at which the bank's learning phase had ended, the bank had about 400 contracts with a swap volume of the equivalent of 7 billion DM in its books (US dollars, deutschmarks and yen), this business line always attained growth rates of more than 50 per cent p.a. during the following years, and with 11,000 contracts and a volume of 250 billion DM by the end of 1991 it had become an important part of the bank's international business. According to *Euromoney*, the bank was one of the world's five leading swap banks in 1990. Pure referrals accounted for less than 1 per cent of its swaps, which meant that over 99 per cent went into its own swap books.

Diversification in the form of new swap books in additional currencies was always carried out decentrally. In contrast to other swap-trading banks, Deutsche Bank applied the regional principle of 'exclusive product responsibility' and thus followed a different procedure from that in forex trading. It was of the opinion that operating locally would create greater market awareness of interest rate developments and allow more qualified consulting for its customers in their respective locality. The chosen form of swap trading required a complete infrastructure to be built up at major financial centres, and increased the danger of selfish behaviour in the various swaps departments as a result of the profit-centre mentality. The bank therefore sought to offset these negative trends by making a compromise: the settlement of swap transactions – the back-office activity – was carried out centrally from Frankfurt, so that only front-office tasks, such as market observation, new customer acquisition and trading, were decentralized.

As far as derivatives were concerned, at the end of 1992 Deutsche Bank London and Morgan Grenfell merged their futures and options activities to form DBMG Futures & Options Ltd. This company was primarily to handle business related to interest rates, share indices, currencies, energy, raw materials and precious metals. DB Capital Markets (Deutschland) GmbH had already been issuing warrants for bonds, the Deutscher Aktienindex (DAX), interest rates, currencies and precious metals for some time.

As part of the safety standards applied throughout Deutsche Bank Group nowadays, new products are introduced only after careful examination by the bank's Risk Management and Controlling groups (according to its 1993 Annual Report). This applies particularly to its growing business in derivatives, for which it has also had to modify its accounting.

By the end of the 1980s, the integration of Europe and the ever closer inter-relationships between European currencies and interest markets no longer allowed banks to take an isolated national approach towards interest rate developments. Against this background, at the end of 1988 Deutsche Bank set up a Liquidity Management Group whose main task was to manage the interest rate affairs of its 100 largest customers in Germany. The major reason for setting up this group, which was founded as a sort of joint venture between Corporate Finance and the bank's Trading and Sales Division, was the realization that, although big corporations had substantial amounts of liquidity, they had insufficient knowledge of new products on the international markets. At the same time, the bank did not have a department that was able to provide customers with information and meet their requirements for yield-enhancing and, if possible, low-risk forms of investment.

Over time, the Liquidity Management Group developed into a combination of management consulting, trading and, especially, an extended arm of the Swap Group, and it took over the latter's sales assignment *vis-à-vis* large customers. By the beginning of 1992 it was based in Frankfurt and several European centres. The Liquidity Management Group also aimed to gear its activities to local markets. In addition to being present on the European swap markets, it also intended to establish a permanent presence on the money markets – in 1993, for example, the bank became the first institution to offer interest rate swaps for a call money index – as well as on bond and futures markets. In addition, it pursued the development of tax-oriented investments and, eventually, borrowing instruments aimed at optimizing tax payments. At the beginning of the 1990s, the complete management of big-ticket customers' interest rate activities was also extended to their liabilities-side business.

4. Revolutionary at first: retail banking in Germany

a) Roots and changing importance of retail banking

After reamalgamation of the three successor institutions in 1957, retail business at Deutsche Bank gradually took on unexpected importance. The bank's venture into broad retail banking dates from 2 May 1959, when the 'small personal loan' (PKK) was introduced at the initiative of the bank's 'Hamburg board', Ulrich, Klasen and Manfred O. von Hauenschild. Involved from the start was van Hooven, later a member of the board of managing directors and responsible for developing this business line into a comprehensive standardized banking service programme to meet the typical requirements of wage-earning households. Until then, the bank had been perceived as the bank for firms, big corporates and institutions. But even as far back as 1870, the year of its foundation, it had supplied banking services to company representatives, wealthy private individuals and high income earners – including freelancers and independent businesspeople.

The product range offered to a small set of private individuals was substantial, but not standardized. Before 1957 savings deposit boxes had been donated to clubs and savings certificates had been given to private clients to celebrate births, confirmations, school-leaving, weddings, etc. The aim was to stimulate the inflow of private deposits. In 1957/58, the bank launched pioneer standardized services to a broader banking public, albeit hesitantly and in just a few regions. But the 'man in the street' was nervous about entering the bank's sumptuous, sacred halls. Its imposing counters were insurmountable barriers between customer and clerk. Initially, the bank seemed to have little interest in supplying banking services to wage-earners and low-income individuals. Abs was openly dismissive in his stated attitude towards broad retail business. Fears that the bank's image with traditional corporate clients might suffer and the relatively low profit potential per small customer made management reluctant at first to enter this sector.

Today, retail banking is one of the bank's core business divisions. It generates about 60 per cent of total non-bank business and contributed 5.3 billion DM to 1993 income with attributable costs of 4 billion DM; the division's operating profit was about DM 750 million. The bank has 7 million retail customers in united Germany. They are served by roughly 1,500 branches with 20,500 staff. Roughly 10,000 service division employees are also allocated to retail banking. A field service is under formation and numerous self-service facilities are available 24 hours a day. The bank's national shares of the retail banking market are 7 per cent of customers, 5 per cent of savings deposits and 4 per cent of consumer loans. This puts Deutsche Bank among Germany's biggest retail bankers.

The bank's decision to enter what, at the time, was still known as mass business led to a far-reaching change in the bank's client structure. Management must have had good reasons to offer simple standardized banking products to a general retail population alongside the traditionally successful corporate business. It was basically the changes in Germany's post-war economic and social environment that induced Deutsche Bank to enter retail banking. As van Hooven said: 'Viewed with hindsight, the decision to enter mass business was totally logical. It was rooted in and explained by major changes in the "market", though this term sounded most unusual at the time.'[34]

The German economic miracle, which began in the early 1950s and provided one and a half decades of steady economic growth of roughly 10 per cent p.a., turned the Federal Republic from a war-ravaged, economically idle country into the world's third-largest industrial nation. Strong economic expansion – GNP trebled between 1950 and 1960 – caused massive upheavals in income and social structures. Households' disposable income rose nearly threefold from 1950 to 1960.

There were also structural changes: the share of wages and salaries (wage ratio) rose substantially at the expense of incomes from entrepreneurial activity and assets. In the same period, households sharply increased their proportion of gross annual saving in the economy. The emphasis in the capital formation process shifted to these savers, who had not originally been big-bank customers. At the same time, corporate clients adjusted their liquidity management by reducing deposits repayable on demand, which meant that banks could no longer tap this segment for their funding. On the other hand, corporate demand for medium- to long-term capital investment loans increased. So an important motive for the bank's entering broad retail banking – as surprising as this may seem at first glance – was to protect the long-term refinancing of its traditional corporate lending.

A further motive was the rising demand for finance in many households. At that time, after years of want and deprivation, people wished to see something for their efforts. This was reflected in waves of consumption spending centred on key needs. But many wage and salary earners only had limited funds available. Household propensity to borrow became greater, and the bank rightly sensed that there was great potential here for instalment loans. As the profit margin per loan was relatively low owing to the high administrative workload, it was clear right from the start that retail lending could be viable only with a large number of customers. The bank therefore concentrated its marketing activities on capturing and keeping such clients, while constantly improving its technical processing standards in this area.

The bank's activities from 1957 in broad retail banking were also an important step towards a conscious orientation to markets and marketing and to target or customer groups. The bank evolved separate strategies for retail customers, i.e. the general population with no commercial register entry, for wealthy private clients and traditional corporate customers. Manfred O. von Hauenschild listed nine principles – still valid today – for retail lending and deposits business:

1. The business has its own rules and its own language.
2. The same basic rules apply to retail lending and retail deposits business.
3. The bank's services form a bouquet. Both loan and deposits products must be diversely structured and offered in package form.
4. The basic internal settlement principle is standardization of workflows. Retail business does not tolerate exceptions. Every deviation from this harbours dangers for organization and quality.

5. This business requires control and support from a central point.
6. Retail business advertising is subject to different laws from those in traditional business. Uniform appearance and mass appeal are required, with marketing research to establish measures needed and possibilities.
7. Technical implementation must be handled by high-quality staff dedicated to retail business.
8. Branches must attract retail lending and deposits business.
9. The large number of transactions can only be handled sensibly using electronic data processing.

Up to 1959, however, broad retail banking had next to no importance for the bank. A circular distributed by Rheinisch-Westfälische Bank in 1953 explicitly stated that small and very small transactions were not to be accepted. In the next six years, in which the bank achieved extremely strong growth, it revised this policy position, but saw no need for further segmentation of the retail banking market into specific customer groups, i.e. for separate strategies aimed at retail market segments. The range of products for these customers comprised an almost identical universal programme marketed through an increasingly dense network of outlets. The number of domestic branches, for example, rose from 364 in 1959 to 1,132 in 1976. At the same time, many new employees had to be recruited, with the bank even having to hire staff from other industries.

At the beginning of the 1970s, a new philosophy began to pervade the bank. It became increasingly clear that there were limits to growth in the economy and also in banking. The bank noted that the strong volume expansion of previous years did not automatically mean rising earnings. The reasons were rising costs in retail banking, high market penetration and, as a result of that, ever keener competition. This led, among other things, to more intensive market research, a reduction in the number of new products, new procedures for analysing branches from market and yield standpoints, and EDP-based cross-selling programmes to make greater use of customer relationships.

The stronger customer orientation was also reflected in a more client-friendly branch design. From 1974 onwards, the big regional head branches were gradually converted in line with the Mannheim model (p. 528). In particular, the savings, private and corporate account and personal loan sections, which had formerly been organizationally and spatially segregated, were combined into service groups. Each one served a certain group of customers – mostly split up by letters of the alphabet – and had a separate area with a generally more relaxed atmosphere, thanks to carefully positioned seating groups and advisory desks. More specialized departments such as property finance, asset management, securities, corporate banking and international were not incorporated into the service groups; at the same time, walls and other elements separating these departments from the others were removed, since they were often seen not only as physical barriers, but also as psychological ones.

An important step towards a differentiated approach to the retail banking market was the OM model dating from 1975 (pp. 526–7). The bank's objective with this reorganization of regional head branches was to be able to adjust more closely to changing market conditions at short notice, and to keep expected cost increases within bounds. The instruments offered by EDP were used for this purpose in retail business. Important corporate and private customers were henceforth served from one point.

Customer services were differentiated by market criteria. The Portfolio Management Department, set up at the beginning of the 1970s, was responsible for providing a full service to private customers who had a mainly individual investment advisory relationship with the bank. On the other hand, Retail Banking handled business with general retail banking clients besides retail securities business and property finance. It was also responsible for serving firms in the consumer retail sector, trade and craftspeople, other small businesspeople and professionals, where an individual Corporate Banking service seemed inappropriate. Overall, the OM model already reflected the bank's growing market orientation.

In the 1980s, keener competition forced the bank to concentrate even more strongly on target groups. Non-banking companies (near-banks and non-banks) began to offer financial services on a growing scale. While financial services had previously been provided by banks, insurance companies and building and loan associations on a largely segregated basis, there was now a tendency to offer as much as possible from one source. A more sophisticated target-group orientation emerged; tailored financial service packages were offered to customers with almost identical financial service requirements.

As competition toughened in the 1980s for the individual customer, the upper-segment private client and the high-net-worth individual as target groups – they were extremely attractive to all financial service suppliers – the bank had to defend its strong market position (about 30 per cent market share) with a greater resource input. One response was to enhance its securities service, which was especially attractive to well-to-do clients. It also developed a tailored service package for the self-employed, a group with specific financial problems which the bank tried to solve by supplying the desired advisory services in conjunction with information and financial packages. In the 1980s, besides introducing new communication forms, the bank adjusted its overall service more closely to self-employed persons' needs with respect to financing, payments, risk protection, electronic banking and general help, suggestions and ideas.

Another target group gained importance over time: young people and young adults. Their special significance for business policy stemmed from the realization that new potentially attractive customers were becoming harder to find. Most people already had a bank account and few were ready to change their bank. To counteract the ageing tendency in its customer structure, the bank differentiated and extended its product offering for adolescents and young adults, and aimed at a more individual and life-cycle-based service for this customer group. Besides special communication vehicles (Youth Forum, etc.), it developed, for example, the 'Young Account' – a set of free banking services for young people including the under-14s. This was a response to young people's changed demands and their new penchant for individuality, acceptance and independence.

This retail customer-group approach peaked in the early 1990s. In 1991 there was an almost total reorganization of the bank. The private banking group was split into two divisions: 'Private Customers I' (today: 'Retail Banking') and 'Private Customers II' (today: 'Private Banking'), each with a clear target group mission. 'Retail Banking' was responsible for wage and salary earners and the self-employed, unless they were served by other business divisions; small undertakings and small institutions differing from corporate customers in terms of requirements and size were also included here. To guarantee a better service to the highly heterogeneous retail customer group through more efficient marketing management, the division was further subdivided by customer and service categories into the Retail Customers A (PKa) and Retail Customers B (PKb) sub-sectors. PKa customers – wage and salary earners with low to medium-sized incomes, comparable self-employed persons and small traders – were offered a broad, basic product range comprising largely standardized services (savings agreements, life insurance, building and loan agreements, property finance, personal loans, mutual funds, etc.). PKb customers, i.e. self-employed persons and small traders with higher incomes – in 1993, one million customers supplying 15 per cent of the division's profits – received an individual service from specially trained account officers. The bank also installed specialized advisers for self-employed persons and small traders to answer questions on going into business, financing, leasing, etc. The products for well-to-do clients were mainly qualified portfolio investment advisory and management; the Retail Banking Division product range was also available for this segment.

The extensive reorganization also triggered a restructuring in the branch network. Overall responsibility for the branch network lay with the Retail Banking Division. To give due consideration to different customer structures at city branches and branches in separate communities ('market branches') while at the same time ensuring clear cost responsibility, the bank applied three branch management models. Branches with predominantly retail business and little corporate banking (in 1991, 713 branches) had the 'P model'. Branches and small market branches with largely retail and substantial corporate business used the 'P/F model'. Medium to large market branches and branches with significant corporate and private banking business applied the 'market branch model'. These models differed mainly in terms of the areas of responsibility of the branch/market branch manager. For the well-to-do client and high-net-worth customer target groups (clients with safe custody accounts from 100,000 DM to 5 million DM), for whom the Private Banking Division was responsible, the bank set up 350 'investment centres' in 1991 with about 430 'investment units'. The more than 2,000 employees working here were responsible for delivering an all-round service to the more than 200,000 private clients in this category. In this way, the bank tried to adjust efficiently, using new data-processing technology, to the growing demands of these clients. The private banking service was meant to ensure that wealthy private clients were served from one source. The board member initially responsible for this business line was Carl L. von Boehm-Bezing and since 1994 Tessen von Heydebreck. The bank described its 'demand-oriented private banking', emphasized from 1992 onwards, as a new philosophy. This strategy was known as 'ADAM' (*Anleger-Diagnose im Anlage-Management*, or investor diagnosis in private banking) and comprised co-ordinated elements intended to guarantee a full-spread, demand-oriented service to portfolio investment customers in the long term. For a separate highly sophisticated target group with assets exceeding 5 million DM (high-net-worth individuals), there was Grunelius, a private banking house experienced in managing large asset portfolios. The bank had acquired Grunelius in 1989 with this customer group specifically in mind (p. 723).

b) Trends in the financial services programme

Deutsche Bank's entry into broad retail banking came with the introduction of the 'small personal loan' (PKK) as the first form of 'personal loan' (P loan),[35] subsequently developed in a step-by-step process. The launching of this product coincided – probably by chance – with a programmatic statement by Ludwig Erhard, Federal Economics Minister, who wrote in a letter to Robert Pferdmenges (read out at the 9th German Banking Conference in Cologne in 1958): 'In my view, it is one of the banker's tasks that a private person should be able to borrow a few hundred marks from him without having to pledge his entire worldly possessions.' Anyone could obtain a small personal loan up to 2,000 DM against presentation of a wage or salary slip. The standard conditions (0.4 per cent interest per month, 2 per cent front-end fee) were fixed for the customer when the contract was signed; repayment was in regular monthly instalments, and the maturity was limited to 24 months. Collateral was not required as it would have caused excessive costs; the borrower had to pledge his or her assignable wage and salary claims. Disbursement was in cash and how the funds were used was at the borrower's discretion, by contrast with traditional instalment loans.

The terms and conditions were identical with those of competitor banks owing to the debit and credit interest rate regulation still in force at that time. This convenient situation, which impeded competition, was defended vehemently by the bank: in a letter to the Federal Association of Private Banks in 1962, it argued with great conviction in favour of retaining the controls on interest rates. Be that as it may, despite the efforts of other banks with arguments which subsequently proved incorrect, the state interest rate regulation was abolished in 1967 under pressure from liberal market quarters.

When the small personal loan was launched, it was accompanied by a much-criticized publicity campaign, described as untypical of banks, involving widely spread newspaper advertisements. The criticism that this product would simply encourage households to overborrow still gets media and parliamentary attention today. In actual fact, the consumer loan volume per member of the population rose from 100 to 3,341 DM between 1959 and 1988, while the per capita savings balance increased from 800 to 11,579 DM over the same period. In the 1980s, however, the number of indebted and overindebted households rose strongly: in 1989 in the old federal states 9.7 million households (37 per cent) were debtors; 1.2 million households, mainly young low-income families and single mothers, were no longer able to meet their payment commitments. To protect borrowers, the German Parliament passed the Consumer Credit Act in 1990.

The small personal loan was marketed largely via Deutsche Bank's stationary branch network which, with 364 offices, did not yet offer full geographical coverage, but also through mobile outlets (*Depositenkassen*). Within the first five years, the bank extended well over one million loans totalling 1.3 billion DM, giving it a market share of 22 per cent; over 700,000 new customers were acquired through small personal loans.

The savings banks recognized the challenge and took the market by surprise with a more attractive 'personal loan'. The big banks reacted promptly: on 1 June 1962 Deutsche Bank introduced the 'personal loan for specified purposes' (PAD) as a new form of instalment loan. It offered repayment in instalments, higher amounts than the small personal loan, longer maturities, lower interest rates and specific purpose – the loan amount was remitted directly to the seller – and it also provided for different forms of security (ownership of the financed asset was transferred for collateralization purposes). The rapid and simple PAD drawdown procedure was made possible by extensive standardization and uniform terms and conditions; but the loan amount, maturity and repayment instalments were variable and could be adjusted to borrowers' needs and income. In the first two years, personal loans for specified purposes were granted for 178 million DM and attracted 20,000 new customers, most of whom also opened a current account. It was not until the 1970s that PKK and PAD were combined to form the 'personal loan'.

In 1968 (which marked the end of a recession), the bank broadened its programme for private customers to include further loan variants: beginning in September it offered a larger circle of customers more flexible short-term over-draft facilities on current account. Customers with regular income and whose creditworthiness was visible from the development of their accounts were informed that without prior arrangement or other formalities they could get a short-term loan ('Dispo-Kredit') and could overdraw their wage or salary account. The credit line, introduced as the 'personal disposition loan' (PDK), was limited initially to 1,000 DM. It could be increased at the customer's request – taking into account his or her net income. Today the PDK forms an integral part of the bank's product range for private customers.

Surprisingly at first sight, the bank introduced another 'P' loan in September 1968, the 'personal mortgage loan' (PHD) – surprising because in doing so it was competing with mortgage banks in which it held an interest, and whose building finance facilities were referred through its branch network. In fact, the PHD closed the gap *vis-à-vis* the 'traditional' long-term property loans given by the mortgage banks. It could be geared individually to the customer's financial strength and ability to repay the loan. With this innovative product, the bank entered a market niche. It was only when it realigned its entire property finance product range in 1992 that the PHD was replaced by the Deutsche Bank mortgage.

For members of the liberal professions, with their high capital requirements above all when setting up practices and extending their businesses, the bank introduced in 1968 the 'doctor's and chemist's loan', later known as the 'personal practice loan' (PPD). It was structured like the PAD. In 1986 it was modified and renamed the 'small-business loan'.

In reaction to other market developments, the bank supplemented its range of loan products for private customers in 1984 with the 'personal loan with variable utilization'. As customers had generally become more critical and were looking more and more closely at the price, quality and real benefit of the financial services on offer, the bank adopted this new type of loan which, in its view, was particularly suited to customer needs and therefore customer-friendly. For example, a loan facility of up to 50,000 DM had to be agreed only once, and could then be drawn on at any time at the customer's discretion; individual repayment instalments and variable interest rates were further features.

This variant was intended to give more financial convenience and independence to customers who, in the light of their income and wealth, were used to a more generous credit line. Since, however, after the introduction of the 'anniversary loan' it turned out that private customers with higher income and assets – such as managers and civil servants – had no or very little demand for credit, the bank successfully offered this new loan product to its normal instalment loan clients. To reduce the loan-processing workload, the bank developed an EDP-based credit-scoring system in 1988. Competence and independent discretionary power on the part of the account officer remained unaffected. The bank expected this additional instrument to reduce the workload on its staff, lower the loan default risk and improve the quality of its instalment loan portfolio. The system was introduced together with terminal-based loan processing in February 1991 (Figure 5.9).

In the 1980s, a stronger target-group orientation also began in retail banking business. The bank no longer concentrated merely on broad retail banking as such, but displayed a more pro-active approach towards lucrative retail banking market segments. It was the financial service requirements of self-employed

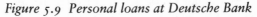

Figure 5.9 Personal loans at Deutsche Bank

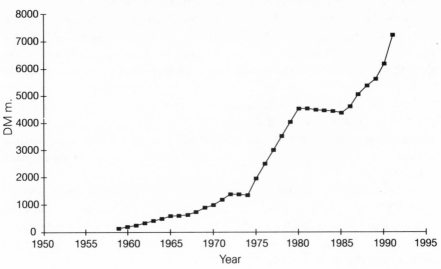

persons, but also of small to medium-sized corporates which induced it to introduce new products aimed specifically at target groups. A product package was offered in 1988 as 'our banking service for the self-employed – practice and firm' which, alongside the small-business loan, comprised credit line, practice and firm account, appropriate insurance and electronic banking services, such as 'db-rationell' for the electronic settlement of payments, 'db-Bildschirmtext' for the retrieval of account and safe custody account data, and 'db-dialog' for multibank access to videotext accounts. Taken in total, standardized loan business with smaller companies and the self-employed developed very well; within only 11 years the bank more then tripled its lending business with this group of customers (Figure 5.10).

The bank has also shown particular interest in the financing of private residential property in the last 25 years. It had intensive competition right from the beginning, often on terms and conditions. Despite the strong market position of savings banks and credit co-operatives, it captured important market share in a short time and defended – even expanded – it over the years by steadily developing its range of products (Figure 5.11).

Its own property finance business really began in the early 1970s. An important factor behind the favourable economic climate until then was the flourishing building industry: besides the construction of commercial properties, private home building in particular gained in importance. This created good business prospects for the banks, and the income and growth opportunities were used by Deutsche Bank to develop its property finance activities. It had numerous holdings in domestic banks already transacting retail banking or with market-

Figure 5.10 Deutsche Bank loans to self-employed persons

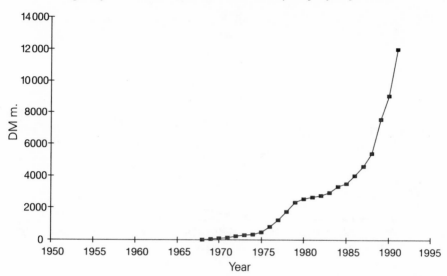

policy relevance for this sector. Its subsidiaries Berliner Disconto Bank (restyled Deutsche Bank Berlin in 1978 and merged with the bank in 1991), Saarländische Kreditbank (Deutsche Bank Saar since 1978; the bank's share in 1991, 69.24 per cent), and Deutsche Bank Lübeck vormals Handelsbank, in which the bank had a stake of more than 50 per cent from 1979 (in 1991, 92.47 per cent), offered private customers services largely identical with Deutsche Bank's. Deutsche Kreditbank für Baufinanzierung (DKB) in Cologne, a member of the Group since 1967, operated as a specialized bank in the field of property and home-building finance. Subsequently, though, this almost bankrupt institution was practically wound up: DKB, to whose management serious errors were attributed, was merged with the bank in 1988 and continued as a (relatively insignificant) branch.

At the end of the 1960s, Deutsche Bank also had stakes of 25 per cent or less in numerous mortgage banks. Due to their shareholder structures – other banks besides Deutsche Bank, above all Dresdner and Commerzbank, were also shareholders – the mortgage banks were able to determine their business policy more or less independently. Property-finance business came chiefly from their own acquisition efforts and only occasionally through referral by shareholder banks.

With good growth prospects in the early 1970s, the bank sought a reorganization in the mortgage bank sector. It came in 1970/71 following difficult negotiations on equity holding swaps. First of all, at the turn of 1970–71 it received Commerzbank's 10 per cent stake in Frankfurter Hypothekenbank in a (tax-driven) 'midnight deal'; in return, Commerzbank got Deutsche Bank's stakes in Rheinische Hypothekenbank (at 25.1 per cent) and Westdeutsche

Figure 5.11 Deutsche Bank property loans

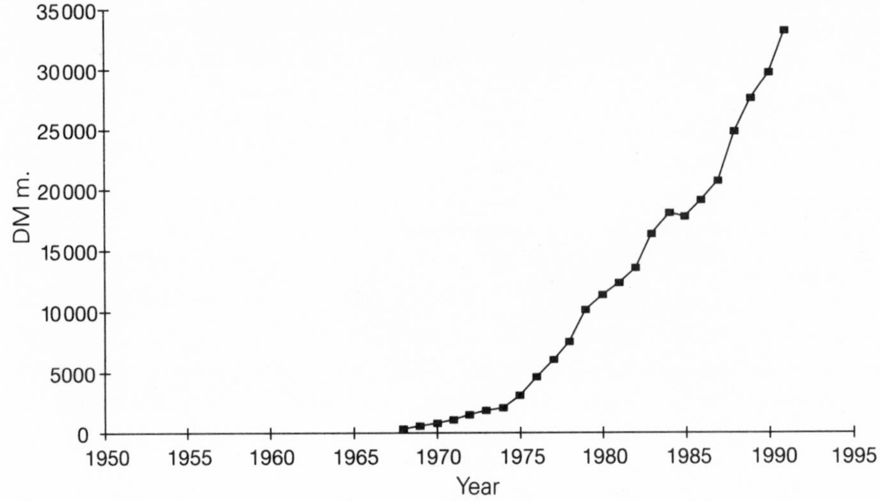

Bodenkreditanstalt (25.1 per cent). In 1971 Dresdner Bank, in return for its holdings in Frankfurter Hypothekenbank (33.4 per cent) and Centralboden, got Deutsche Bank's tax-privileged shares in Deutsche Hypothekenbank, Hypothekenbank in Hamburg and Pfälzische Hypothekenbank. The bank thus raised its holdings in Centralboden and Frankfurter Hypothekenbank from 25.1 per cent to 63.7 per cent and 75.7 per cent respectively. In 1995, after serious mistakes connected with a property firm's billion-mark bankruptcy (the 'Schneider case'), Centralboden was merged with the apparently uninvolved Frankfurter Hypothekenbank, after two members of the Centralboden board, who took responsibility, had to resign from their positions. Since the changing market situation had for some time persuaded the Group of the need to reorganize its real-estate activities, the merger of the two mortgage banks into Frankfurter Hypothekenbank Centralboden AG (FHC) was now speeded up, and Lübecker Hypothekenbank was included in the form of an association agreement.

The rising aspirations of growing segments of the population with increasing income and prosperity, and their greater interest in buying property and home building, induced Deutsche Bank to use the special abilities and knowledge of its subsidiaries to adjust its product range; it also developed models, in co-operation with its mortgage bank subsidiaries, to solve the practical property finance problems of private customers. While this created more intensive co-operation with the mortgage bank subsidiaries, care was taken to ensure that their traditional business links were not disturbed, and that they could access new customer circles through the bank's branch network. In the following years, this closer co-operation was reflected in a strong expansion of property finance business.

The product range for prospective home-building clients was extended by the bank in 1968/69 with the 'personal mortgage loan' and the 'bank preliminary loan', available for bridging finance. In 1972, supplementing the product range of the acquired mortgage banks, Deutsche Bank introduced the 'personal building loan'. This was a standardized, simplified loan for 50,000 to 300,000 DM with a maturity of close on 30 years; it could be used to finance up to 80 per cent of building costs or purchase price. This new product enabled the bank for the first time to offer its customers one-stop property finance.

This was improved again in 1975: under the trademark 'BauKreditSystem der Deutschen Bank', the various forms of property finance were combined. This was based on co-operation with the bank's mortgage bank subsidiaries and the savings and loan institutions (Beamtenheimstättenwerk, Wüstenrot, Leonberger). In line with customers' wishes, the individual financial building blocks were combined to form tailored property finance with which low-priced funds from other sources, such as savings and loan agreements, employer loans and public funds could be linked.

In the following years, the BauKreditSystem was adjusted repeatedly to changing customer demand. Furthermore, the bank introduced life insurance products for property finance in 1987. Deutsche Bank Bauspar-AG was set up in the same year. This rounded off the bank's one-stop property finance product range with attractive savings and loan schedule systems and innovative products, and meant that it was no longer dependent on co-operation with other savings and loan institutions.

In 1992 the bank totally reorganized its property finance product range. Instead of the BauKreditSystem, since then it has offered only a comprehensive personal mortgage loan under the title 'db-Baufinanzierung'. This loan can be adjusted to customers' wishes with regard to maturity, fixed interest period and redemption. Over and above that, the bank introduced alternative terms and conditions incorporating an interest rate ceiling (cap). Taken in total, this gave the bank an efficient and competitive property finance product range. In 1991 property finance accounted for roughly 50 per cent of total loans to private individuals. Estate agency activities were concentrated in 'db-Immobilien' in 1993.

A further important development in Deutsche Bank's retail banking business concerned its *payment facilities*. In 1960, against the background of the economic and sociodemographic structural changes taking place with increasing clarity in the Federal Republic at the end of the 1950s, which were reflected, among other things, in strong income growth among workers and employed persons, the bank introduced wage and salary accounts for employees and pensioners. The bank's corporate customers provided the impulse here, too. In 1959/60, companies approached the bank and asked it to open salary accounts for their employees for rationalization reasons. The idea was that the account holder's remuneration should be remitted monthly by the employer to these accounts, and that the account holder should be able to draw on this money according to his or her current needs.

Deutsche Bank was relatively late in complying with this request. While the savings banks already had 1.5 million salary accounts at the end of 1956 and 3 million in 1960, the bank did not introduce wage and salary accounts until 1960. Before that, it had to solve substantial technical and organizational problems. There were also particular questions to be answered, not least with regard to account charges, the subject of recurring controversy ever since. At that time, private banks, savings banks and credit co-operatives – within the framework of a quasi-trust agreement – set an account charge of 1 per cent of credit turnover on the account. This was to be paid by employers, since cashless wage and salary payments would give them substantial rationalization benefits. However, competition for new customers caused the bank initially to maintain the accounts free of charge.

It was not until 1972 that almost the entire banking industry decided to ask account holders to pay account charges; the Federal Association of German Banks had to justify their introduction ideologically. Owing to the much more frequent utilization of wage and salary accounts than had been expected at the time, the costs incurred were rising faster than anticipated. Deutsche Bank was thus subsequently compelled, despite rationalization efforts such as the development of large EDP capacities for electronic processing of payments, the introduction of automated cash dispensers, account statement printers and self-service terminals in the 1980s, to increase its account charges repeatedly, often as part of a restructuring (Figure 5.12).

The frequent price increases for account-keeping and payments at practically

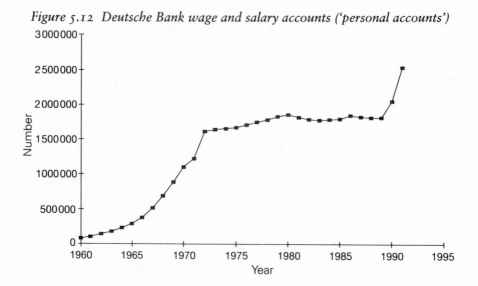

Figure 5.12 Deutsche Bank wage and salary accounts ('personal accounts')

all banks met with massive public criticism; banking prices became a kind of political matter. Deutsche Bank's conduct was often criticized directly – not surprisingly for a market leader. Under the heading: 'The trap closes', *Der Spiegel* reported in 1977 that from 1 July Deutsche Bank 'intends to increase its charges again – although the industry had seldom reported better earnings'; the report mentioned 'a total of seven partly well-disguised price increases'. Representatives of all political parties spoke out against further increases, and the German Trades Union Congress warned urgently in 1977 against further increases. The Consumer Working Group appealed in 1977: 'Don't just accept account charge increases ... – compare prices', and wrote: 'Deutsche Bank says nothing about its profits ... With this announcement, Deutsche Bank is not only demonstrating a lack of instinct for stable policy, but ... an attitude ... which can only be described as impudent.'

On 1 June 1977, even Bundesbank President Klasen, member of Deutsche Bank's board of managing directors from 1957 to 1969 and supervisory board member from 1978 to 1984, criticized the banks' price increases. This criticism culminated in the action taken by the Consumer Protection Association in Hesse, which organized a demonstration on 23 July 1977 outside Deutsche Bank's Wiesbaden branch and distributed pamphlets with the heading 'Consumers feel cheated', and in the press conference held by the Baden-Württemberg Consumer Association on 28 July 1977, in which an appeal was made to boycott the big banks. Such strong reactions caused the bank to undertake more intensive public relations work, the efficiency of which, however, remained very limited.

The banks' pricing policy even occupied the courts in the 1980s. After the Federal Supreme Court in 1988 severely criticized the banks' value-dating practices, and in 1987 the Federal Association of German Industry, in a letter to the Central Credit Committee, also criticized the differences in the value dating of credits and debits, the Baden-Württemberg Consumer Association called up the Federal Supreme Court in 1989 and instituted proceedings against the method of value dating used for cash payments to private current accounts. The Federal Supreme Court granted the petition in its ruling of 17 January 1989, and the banking industry changed its value-dating practice – in some cases fairly hesitantly. To improve – in its own words – transparency for customers, Deutsche Bank introduced a new price model in 1990 with so-called cost-covering prices.[36]

Despite the manifold price increases, the bank still described its payment business – as usual in the industry – as loss-making. Here, the cross-selling opportunities resulting from the leader merchandise function of wage and salary accounts were, misleadingly, not taken into account. In November 1993 Deutsche Bank – after winning in two lower instances – lost a case before the Federal Supreme Court filed by the Berlin Consumer Association: it was instructed not to charge its private current-account customers fees for deposits or withdrawals over the counter.

In 1972 the bank combined its wage and salary accounts with the other current accounts of private customers under the heading 'personal accounts'. The main reasons for this were firstly the scope for rationalization inside the bank itself, and secondly the interest of customers who use the various types of account largely in the same way in a simple and transparent banking service. Until today, the bank has offered an increasingly diverse service to increase the attraction of personal accounts, which in the meantime are used by customers from all sections of the population.

With regard to payment instruments, Deutsche Bank has improved its services since entering broad retail banking. It was particularly closely involved in the development of the eurocheque. Van Hooven in particular, sometimes called the 'payments pope' and 'father of the eurocheque' – titles he was not averse to hearing – initiated the development of the European eurocheque system in the mid-1960s. It took off on 10 May 1968 at the bank's premises in Frankfurt. Representatives of the banking industry from 15 European countries attended a conference to negotiate European co-operation between the various countries' isolated payment systems. After a further two conferences, agreement was reached on a standardized redemption system for cheques guaranteed by special cards. The final realization and internationalization of the eurocheque system, in which 150,000 banks from 18 European countries now participate, began in 1969. By 1993 more than 1.5 million of the bank's customers had a eurocheque card, which now had several different uses.

Although the main reason for the introduction of the eurocheque system was that in Germany the development of a confusing diversity of credit card systems – as had happened in the USA – was to be prevented, the banking industry veered away from this philosophy after 1977. Jointly with other German banks, Deutsche Bank bought the right to issue a travel and entertainment card, Euro-card, from the Swedish Wallenberg Group. However, the decision to introduce Eurocard in Germany did not meet with universal approval. Be that as it may, the bank substantially increased its supposed 'own competition' in 1989: mainly due to the costs of eurocheque – primarily voucher-based processing – two new credit cards were introduced bearing the name 'Deutsche Bank'. The bank not only put its name on the cards, but was also responsible for fixing their prices and linked the card with individual products. Owing to the attractive price/benefit ratio, the bank saw demand leap by 60 per cent in 1989. In 1991, 280,000 of the bank's customers had a Eurocard. At the beginning of 1992 the bank held talks with Citibank Group, evidently concerning the purchase of the 'smallest' credit card company, Diners Club Deutschland GmbH; these discussions did not bear fruit, however, and were sold to the general public as merely being 'card-marketing talks'.

The rapid development of tourism in Europe and, as prosperity increased, the Germans' growing taste for travel caused Deutsche Bank, in unison with the rest of the banking industry, to intensify its efforts in the late 1970s to introduce a further cashless payment medium in foreign travel: a Euro traveller's cheque modelled on the eurocheque. Until then, the German banks had only had the deutschmark-denominated German traveller's cheque, which lacked global acceptance and was therefore not competitive. The Euro traveller's cheque was to be a way for the German banks to participate in the growing traveller's cheque market, which was largely in American hands. As van Hooven said at the time: 'If nothing happens, it is only a question of time before the European banks' traveller's cheque business is forced into insignificance by the increasingly powerful competition.'[37]

To avoid this, a European bank syndicate in which Deutsche Bank, Dresdner Bank, Commerzbank, savings banks and credit co-operatives participated bought most of the traveller's cheque business of the Thomas Cook travel group on 31 March 1980. To begin with, though, differences of opinion impeded the creation of a Euro traveller's cheque system. In June 1981 the banks from 12 European countries that were combined in Euro Travellers Cheque International (ETCI), Brussels, made a renewed attempt to issue a joint Euro traveller's cheque. Again, the project failed, it was reported, for profitability reasons. The German savings banks and credit co-operatives left the group and reached agreement with the American Express Corporation (Amexco) to market the latter's traveller's cheques. Deutsche Bank thereupon left the group as well, to the irritation primarily of the British ETCI members. The rest of the German banking industry decided to sell Amexco traveller's cheques. But this project failed in 1982 owing to the objection of the Federal Cartel Office. The other ETCI banks agreed, in February 1982, to issue an 'ETC traveller's cheque'. Arrangements were made with Deutsche Bank to market this instrument in Germany. However, the German banks, including Deutsche Bank, did not join the ETCI system at first and it took years for the new ETC traveller's cheque to become established in Germany. The bank today offers ETC traveller's cheques in many currencies, including ECU.

In the past four decades, technological progress and technical developments have had a strong influence on Deutsche Bank's retail banking business. With the introduction of automation in the early 1960s, it was already clear to the bank that electronic data processing would have a considerable impact on future retail banking. It told its employees in 1963: 'Only with the help of automation will it be possible to tackle certain new tasks ahead of us. In the last few years, our bank's circle of customers has steadily expanded ... And the tendency for growing segments of the population to take an interest in banking services should become even stronger in the coming decade, as shown by the development in the United States. Automation will allow us to handle the bulk turnover we shall be facing ... Electronic data processing will give us all kinds of valuable information which we do not have at the moment to help us market our services. It can tell us immediately how many workers or employed persons have a wage or salary account at our bank. It will show us how many of our safe custody account holders belong to the liberal professions. With such information at our fingertips, we shall make even more selective and effective use of our personal and institutional advertising in future.'

Moreover, it was EDP which made it possible in the first place for the bank to handle the flood of data and transactions which expanded dramatically in the years that followed. Its consistent use brought the bank substantial rationalization gains. In the early 1980s – roughly 20 years after the introduction of punch-card machines – new and improved communication and information technology found its way into the customer processing sectors. The bank began to introduce electronic services for private customers. While some competitors – the savings banks, above all – had installed ATMs and account statement printers earlier on, Deutsche Bank's ATM service did not take off until 1982. The bank's caution was due to the high capital investment costs entailed by a comprehensive ATM network. Furthermore, the investment risk was high, since at the beginning of the 1980s little was yet known about the acceptance of technology among customers and employees, and cash dispensers were profitable only if they were sufficiently utilized.

The bank saw substantial cost economies due to the customer's involvement in producing the machine-based services. At the same time, employees were relieved of laborious routine jobs. The time now available was used for more intensive customer service and advisory work. Private customers profited from shorter queuing times and longer business hours, as self-service machines were frequently installed outdoors and hence were available around the clock. Furthermore, the bank made it cheaper to use ATMs, account statement printers and customer terminals to induce customers to use them. The bank has meanwhile issued 3.5 million customer cards, of which 1.9 million are eurocheque cards giving access to electronic banking services at all European branches. In 1993 it recorded a total of roughly 6.2 million withdrawals per month at more than 1,500 ATMs for a total amount of roughly 1.9 billion DM. It also had 2,400 account statement printers in operation in 1991. Over and above that, the bank signed a co-operation agreement with the American Express credit card organization giving AMEX customers access to the bank's cash dispensers; AMEX has over one million cards in issue in Germany and 36 million internationally.

The bank's range of electronic banking services for private customers has been extended in various ways. In 1984, to improve the self-service programme for private customers, it supplemented its range of products with a videotext account service, the precursor of home banking, enhanced in 1993 by telephone banking. The steady growth of payment transactions caused the bank to seek further rationalization potential in the 1980s. This explains why it participated in building up a multibank point-of-sale (POS) system allowing cashless payment by eurocheque at electronic counters. During the pilot phase, the project almost failed on a number of occasions owing to the high costs. It was not until the summer of 1990 that the banking industry reached agreement with well-known trading and services companies to launch a cashless payment system called 'electronic cash', technically comparable with the enhanced POS system, initially in department stores and at petrol stations. It provided the bank with considerable cost savings, as cash withdrawals and voucher-based cheque payments were no longer needed. Be that as it may, continuing high costs and the technical structure of electronic cash caused some companies to develop their own cashless and chequeless payment systems. For example, Peek & Cloppenburg – in cooperation with Deutsche Bank – developed its own payment system in 1990 involving a eurocheque card, but no cheque: the electronic direct debit.

Since the mid-1980s, the bank has offered self-employed customers its own innovative electronic banking services, chiefly to handle their payments business. It developed numerous programmes specifically for personal computers, which have become increasingly popular. This service, offering *inter alia* a more efficient structuring of routine payments ('db-rationell', 'db-dialog', 'db-gateway'), balance enquiries also for accounts in Germany and abroad not kept by the bank ('db-direct', 'db-dialog'), world-wide access to databases ('db-data') and an EDP-based advisory service on public subsidy programmes for the commercial sector and liberal professions ('db-select'), was aimed not only at the self-employed, but primarily at corporate customers. This is why responsibility for these electronic banking services lies not with Private Banking Division, but with Corporate Banking.

Deposits and capital investment facilities for private customers have developed into a very important field of business. Even before it entered retail banking, Deutsche Bank managed a high volume of savings deposits. At the end of 1957, for example, it already had roughly 1.1 billion DM in savings deposits on 550,000 accounts (Figure 5.13).

In the 1950s, households' share in overall monetary wealth formation rose from 20 per cent in 1950 to 30 per cent in 1959; total financial asset formation expanded from 3.15 billion DM in 1950 to 16.32 billion DM in 1960. The bank first offered private customers only simple *savings accounts* for the investment of their savings.[38] When state savings promotion started in 1959, it gradually expanded its range of products to include appropriate variants of account saving. In 1959, for example, premium-bearing savings agreements were introduced following the Savings Premium Act, and in 1961 capital formation savings accounts were introduced after the Wealth Formation Act ('DM 312 Act'). While the state promoted wealth formation by households for reasons of *social policy*, the bank had a vested *business policy* interest in increasing savings deposits: the monies deposited for wealth formation purposes were an important and above all – because interest was not paid at market rates – very cheap funding base for its lending business. The bank therefore added new forms and techniques to its savings products, also in response to numerous subsequent

Figure 5.13 Development of deposits at Deutsche Bank

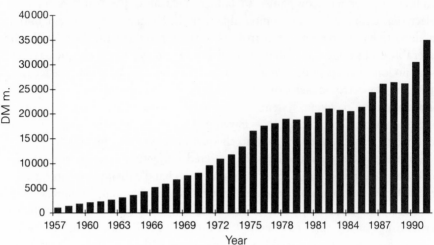

changes in state savings promotion. It also reacted to the changed behaviour of savers due, among other things, to the inflation rate, which leaped from 1.9 per cent (1969) to 6.9 per cent (1973).

Retail customers' *propensity* to save did not let up; although inflation influenced saving *motives*, households' savings *ratio* remained high. However, the choice of saving *forms* changed: savers proved increasingly interest sensitive. Consequently, annual growth in the volume of savings deposits halved in 1973 after reaching 12 to 14 per cent 'with the regularity of a natural law' in the years before.[39] On the other hand, the share of higher interest-bearing savings certificates and fixed-term deposits rose markedly; hence the launch in 1973 of the first 'Deutsche Bank savings certificate'.

In order to counteract the growing withdrawals of savings deposits in favour of securities purchases and investments in fixed-term accounts, the bank simplified its savings-book saving in 1974 by introducing 'end-of-month saving' as a form of automated saving. In 1977 it supplemented its range of products in this field with the discounted 'Deutsche Bank Savings Certificate A'. It was similar to the type of savings certificate issued in the late 1920s by Deutsche Bank und Disconto-Gesellschaft. Today the bank has a complete savings certificate range with various maturities and interest payment schemes.

A new savings plan era began in 1983: together with the associated insurance company Berlinische Leben, the bank developed what today is the almost legendary 'Deutsche Bank savings plan with insurance cover', where the savings target could be covered by an inexpensive risk life insurance policy. The product was an attempt to regain lost shares of wealth formation by households using a traditional banking service, for in the years before, the insurance industry above

From the imperial eagle to the current logo;
Deutsche Bank's various symbols through the ages

König der Sparer *)
ist der
steuerbegünstigte Sparer!

Wir beraten Sie DEUTSCHE BANK

WERTPAPIERE AUCH FÜR SIE

DEUTSCHE BANK

Bank advertising in the 1960s

Genießen Sie
Ihren Traumurlaub
unbeschwert

Fragen Sie
die DEUTSCHE BANK

INVESTA illustriert 1-1966

The Spokesmen of the Board of Managing Directors
from 1957 to 1988 (*from left to right*):
Hermann J. Abs (1957–1967)
Karl Klasen (1967–1969)
F. Wilhelm Christians (1976–1988)
Franz Heinrich Ulrich (1967–1976)
Wilfried Guth (1976–1985)

Alfred Herrhausen, Spokesman of the Board of Managing Directors
from 1985 to 1989

Hilmar Kopper, Spokesman of the Board of Managing Directors
since December 1989

Deutsche Bank S.p.A. in Milan
(until 1994 Banca d'America e d'Italia S.p.A.)

The headquarters of Morgan Grenfell Group in London

The headquarters of Deutsche Bank Sociedad Anónima Española
(until 1993 Banco Comercial Transatlántico S.A.)
in Sant Cugat del Vallés (Barcelona)

Deutsche Bank in Boulevard Konrad Adenauer, Luxemburg

In 1989 the bank resumed operations in east Germany;
here is the head branch in Leipzig

Der richtige Partner für Ihre Geldanlage kann nur eine Bank mit Erfahrung sein.

Ihr Einsatz im Beruf ist hoch - entsprechend ist Ihr Lebensstandard. Auch bei der Wahl Ihrer Bank stellen Sie hohe Ansprüche. Bei der Geldanlage ebenso wie bei der Beratung und beim Service.

Die richtige Adresse für Sie kann deshalb nur eine Bank sein, die in allen Fragen der Vermögensanlage kompetent ist - wie die Deutsche Bank.

Wir beraten Sie nach wirtschaftlichen und steuerlichen Gesichtspunkten. Bei in- und ausländischen Aktien, bei Rentenpapieren und anderen Anlageformen. Wir gehören zu den führenden Emissionshäusern der Welt und haben auf diesem Gebiet ein umfassendes Know-how.

Sprechen Sie mit uns. Denn unser Service ist es wert.

Wenn Sie Hausbank mal wörtlich nehmen,

könnten Sie zum Beispiel mit unseren elektronischen Dienstleistungen in Ihrem Betrieb eine eigene Bank-filiale eröffnen.

Doch das ist nur eine Möglichkeit, unseren Bank-Service für Selbständige geschäftlich und privat zu nutzen. Wir beraten Sie ganz individuell bei Ihren Finanzierungen, Ihrem Ver-mögensaufbau, Ihrer Altersvorsorge oder dem richtigen Versicherungsschutz. Darüber hinaus haben wir für Sie ein umfangreiches Informationsangebot. Denn wir sind an Ihrem langfristigen Erfolg genauso interessiert wie Sie. Nehmen Sie uns als Ihre Hausbank beim Wort.

■ Reden wir darüber.

Deutsche Bank

Bank advertising in the 1980s and 1990s

Vertrauen ist die Basis jeder guten Partnerschaft.

Mit Freude erleben Sie, wie Ihre Kinder groß werden. Sich selbstbewußt und phantasievoll bewegen. Das verlangt Vertrauen – auf beiden Seiten. Kinder erkennen schon früh, daß Eltern auch die besten Freunde sind. Und damit Ihre Kinder später einmal gute Voraussetzungen für die eigene Zukunft haben, planen Sie voraus. Dabei helfen wir Ihnen. Wir nennen das: Deutsche Bank-Service für Privatkunden. Mit dem finanziellen Vorsorgeprogramm, das Ihren Kindern einen guten Berufseinstieg möglich macht.

Fragen Sie die Deutsche Bank.

Deutsche Bank

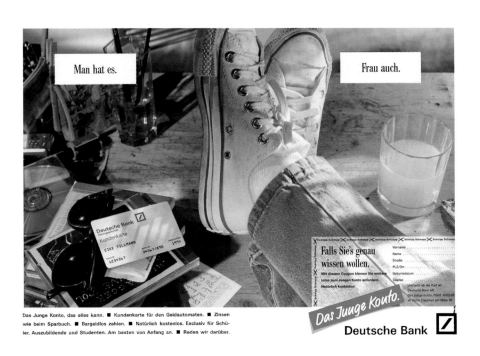

Man hat es.

Frau auch.

Das Junge Konto, das alles kann. ■ Kundenkarte für den Geldautomaten. ■ Zinsen wie beim Sparbuch. ■ Bargeldlos zahlen. ■ Natürlich kostenlos. Exclusiv für Schüler, Auszubildende und Studenten. Am besten von Anfang an. ■ Reden wir darüber.

Das Junge Konto.

Deutsche Bank

Since 1984 the bank's head office in Frankfurt am Main;
the twin towers and the *Trianon* building (*left*),
completed in 1993

all had profited from greater changes in wealth formation habits at the expense of savings deposits. This trend, which has lasted until today, though weakening slightly, was rooted in the growing importance of *private* provision for retirement and other typical existential risks. Confidence in *state* retirement pension schemes was disappearing, and broad sections of the population were thinking more intensively about how to ensure financial security for the latter part of their lives. With the savings plan with insurance cover, the bank tried to offer such customers an alternative to traditional capital-sum life insurance policies which was superior to them in terms of transparency and flexibility. However, this caused substantial problems: although the bank did not use comparative or aggressive advertising compared with traditional capital-sum life insurance products, it experienced a lot of trouble.[40]

The life insurance companies in particular, for which competition, and especially non-sector competition, was something unknown, saw their dominant position in the market for capital-forming life insurance policies under threat. The previously rather co-operative relations between Deutsche Bank and insurance companies deteriorated, with many 'battle cries' from the latter. Furthermore, members of the boards of managing directors of insurance companies resigned from the bank's regional advisory councils. The situation escalated when life insurance companies began to withdraw deposits from the bank. Moreover, its bond and *Schuldschein* (promissory note) trading suffered substantial setbacks, as many large insurers shifted the buying and selling and administration of fixed-income securities and *Schuldscheine* to other banks: while up to 1982 the bank's bond-trading turnover had increased markedly, this business declined in 1983 by 8.45 billion DM (–16.37 per cent) on the previous year. But turnover in this sector rose again sharply in the following years (in 1990, 88 billion DM). *Schuldschein* turnover also fell between 1983 and 1985 from 22.8 billion to 15.7 billion DM; after that, it increased continuously and came to roughly 24 billion DM in 1990.

The strong reactions of some insurance companies came as a surprise to the bank: for one thing, the savings plan with insurance protection was not totally new to the market; savings targets had long been securable by means of risk life insurance policies. For another, it was not the bank or one of its subsidiaries that provided the insurance cover, but Berlinische Lebensversicherungsgesellschaft, in which the Allianz and Munich Re insurance groups had stakes. Over and above that, the savings plan with insurance cover suffered a tax disadvantage.

In the 'battle for the piggy-bank',[41] the bank brought several new products to the market in the following years. In line with its retail customers' greater awareness of yield, it introduced the 'Deutsche Bank fixed-rate saving' product in 1985, today one of the most important investment forms in its savings business. This reflected its particularly strong efforts in these years to bring its funding into line with the development of long-term lending and to stabilize it. Here, it accepted higher funding costs and at the same time accommodated the interest of savers, articulated with increasing vocality, in higher-yielding forms of investment.

In 1986 and 1987 a kind of savings plan inflation set in, including those with which its private customers could include the mutual funds of its subsidiary Deutsche Gesellschaft für Wertpapiersparen. The deposit and withdrawal programmes provided investment alternatives for funds disbursed under life insurance policies maturing on a growing scale since the 1980s; it is estimated that by the year 2000 the funds available from this source will total roughly 360 billion DM. And of that, as the bank stated programmatically in 1989, 'we want to have a reasonable share'.[42]

In 1989, in view of the great diversity which had meanwhile arisen, the bank streamlined its range of savings-plan products and repositioned them: 'savings plan with bonus', 'savings plan with insurance cover' and 'savings plan for young adults' were combined in the 'Deutsche Bank savings plan'. This new product was intended to serve private customers' more medium-term wealth formation, especially that under 12 years, which was tax privileged. The retirement-provision motive was no longer covered by the savings plan, but primarily by a capital-sum life insurance policy from the bank's own life insurance company, formed in 1989 (pp. 729–30). With savings deposits amounting to 35.25 billion DM, the bank called itself the 'biggest German savings bank' in 1991. However, this was not correct: in fact, the German Post Office's 'Postbank' (much unloved by the banks) had more.

The bank's interest policy in savings business – like that of other banks as well – was often criticized in public. Christians, for example, speaking at the bank's press conference in April 1984, admitted that savers had 'not exactly come off too well', above all during the period of high interest rates in 1980–82. Nothing has changed since.

Within the scope of Deutsche Bank's investment facilities, *securities business* has had a long tradition. Today, securities commission business and, in the same context, custody account business are among the very profitable business divisions. This is shown indirectly by the following figures: from 1957 to 1991, the number of custody accounts held for private customers increased from 259,407 to 1.49 million; the market value of securities under management increased from less than 7 billion DM at the end of 1957 to 93 billion DM at the end of 1991. Securities turnover amounted to 4.1 billion DM in 1957 compared with more than 138.5 billion DM in 1990. Commissions (and allowances) rose from 16.62 million to 662.5 million DM.

Securities commission and custody account business at the bank, including with *broad* retail customers, began in the late 1950s, though it was only of minor importance. At that time, both sectors were included internally under 'C business', which was segregated in organizational terms from retail deposits and lending business. Owing to the substitutional relationship between securities and deposits business, there were pronounced rivalries between these departments – a conflict of interests typical of universal banks. It was not until 1991 that the distinction between interest-related retail banking and fee-based securities business was abandoned within the bank as a result of the new organizational structure.

Important stimuli for the securities sector emanated from the privatizations of Preussag AG (1959), Volkswagenwerk (1961) and VEBA (1965). Many people with low incomes were ready to buy these *Volksaktien* (people's shares) owing to the incentives provided, but were not intellectually ready for it.[43] The number of custody accounts maintained by the bank rose between 1959 and 1961 from 284,934 to 405,328 (+42 per cent). With hindsight, however, this programme did not produce the desired success – promotion of productive asset formation for broad sections of the population. At the end of the 1960s, the bank noted that 90 per cent of customers' custody accounts had a value of less than 50,000 DM, and that the *sum total* of the securities held in these accounts amounted to only 10 per cent of the value of all customers' securities accounts. Cost calculations revealed that 90 per cent of custody account customers could not be served profitably in a traditional manner – at least according to the bank's costing.

Furthermore, very little was done to trigger growth in saving through equities. The custody accounts of small shareholders were in many cases characterized by a lack of movement and low account values. Hence, the bank continued to feel called upon to increase the attraction of the equity to the general population. At the same time, it had to defend itself against the criticism often voiced in public that, as a typical universal bank, it had no interest in promoting the equity as a financing instrument on the one hand, or as an investment alternative on the other, since this would be possible only at the expense of its lending or deposits.

Ulrich, Christians and Ehret in particular repeatedly supported the promotion of the equity and the conditions governing it; Christians' personal efforts brought him the name 'Mr Equity'. In 1973 he replaced Ulrich on the board of directors of the Working Group for the Promotion of the Equity (today, the German Equity Institute e.V.) and retained this position until 1991. He was succeeded by Breuer, who in 1991 came out in support of state promotion of household saving through equities. However, Breuer described as appropriate a substantial increase in minimum commissions in securities business for small investors, followed by an increase in custody account charges, because he regarded these investors as speculators.[44]

In the field of investment advisory, closely linked with securities business, Deutsche Bank turned in a relatively mediocre performance, despite certain successes: in a 1991 survey carried out by the magazine *Das Wertpapier* of the advisory services provided by 17 banks, it came only fifteenth. It was also occasionally said to have conflicts of a typical universal banking nature. Not least to counteract this tendency, in 1968 the bank formed, at the laudable initiative of Christians, the (legally independent) Deutsche Gesellschaft für Anlageberatung mbH, Frankfurt (degab), which was largely shaped by Christians in the following 25 years. One year after the formation of degab, Deutsche Bank transferred to it the bank's entire financial analysis.

Degab was conceived above all as a service company for the bank: the results of its research served branches as a basis and advisory aid for investment in securities. In addition, it provided services for the bank's issuing and under-writing. Its analytical work was performed with the tools of modern securities analysis. The advisory services given at branches and based on the findings of the analysis team were incomparably more credible than before. It also appeared easier than before to avoid conflict situations.

The bank underlined the desired independence of degab by appointing inde-pendent experts to its supervisory board. Breuer, degab's last supervisory board chairman, had the honour of putting an end to Christians' favourite 'child': in 1991, as part of the overall reorganization of the bank, degab, together with the Economics Department, including 'Information and Documentation' and 'Fixed Income Research/Investment Research' from the 'Trading and Sales' Division, were merged with the newly founded DB Research GmbH. The reason given by the bank for combining its entire investment research activities in a legally and economically independent company was the need to be quicker in reacting to market changes and informing customers. Furthermore, it considered the approach in its research activities and in the sale of research to be no longer up to date. Its objective was to offer customers better, quicker and cheaper advisory services.

In terminating the independence of degab, the bank also had to manage without independent experts on the supervisory board of DB Research. Whether the quality and objectivity of its research were improved substantially is, however, not clear. DB Research was criticized in 1992 in connection with the valuation of the Allianz and Commerzbank equities for 'shooting first and asking questions later'.[45] Today, DB Research's main customers are the bank itself and its sub-sidiaries, which (have to) buy the company's research at market prices. In addition, the company offers its services to third parties, taking account of client wishes regarding service and price. It was believed that conflicts of interest could be avoided by installing a compliance officer (p. 724). In 1994 the Securities Trading Act created the formal legal basis for these requirements.

Despite certain efforts by the banking industry to promote an equity culture, equities investment as a proportion of total monetary wealth formation remained small. It was not until the 1980s that a more positive attitude towards the equity emerged: the almost uninterrupted rise in share prices from 1982 to 1987 induced investors to buy more equities. The stock market crash of October 1987 and the mini crashes in October 1989, August 1990 and August 1991 and the resulting loss of confidence caused many investors to withdraw again from equities. The bank noted a temporary decline in its securities commissions and custody accounts. Employees' lack of experience with the phenomenon of a crash also made it more difficult to carry out customer advisory work.

Taken in total, however, the bank was able to expand its securities commissions and custody account business considerably. They were among the most profitable business divisions: from 1957 to 1993, the number of private customers' securities accounts rose from 259,407 to 1.47 million; the market capitalization of securities under management increased from less than 7 billion DM at the end of 1957 to 111 billion DM at the end of 1993. Securities turnover came to 4.1 billion DM in 1957 and 98 billion DM in 1993. Commissions (and allowances) rose from 16.6 million DM to 1.02 billion DM. However, only a fraction of this was attributable to equities business among the bank's retail clientele, which showed little change in its negative attitude towards equities and continued to invest only a very small part of its assets in shares.

In the Federal Republic, households' monetary wealth formation in equities has actually turned negative in the last few years, and its share in German equities has fallen in recent decades. By contrast, there has been growing interest in fixed-income securities: their share in households' financial asset creation has shown steady growth for a long time and now stands at almost 40 per cent. This is why the lion's share of the bank's securities turnover is accounted for by such paper. In 1990 the bank's bond turnover stood at 87.973 billion DM (its share in total securities turnover was more than 50 per cent).

New securities business potential with (wealthy) private customers arose for the bank with the opening of Deutsche Terminbörse (DTB), computerized the German Futures and Options Exchange, in 1990. The bank had strongly supported the establishment of a futures and options exchange to raise the competitiveness of Germany as a financial centre and had played an important role in the development of the DTB. Over and above that, it assumed significant market-maker functions. So far, however, the bank's private customers have made little use of the possibilities offered by the DTB. Risk, a lack of understanding and not inconsiderable security requirements have apparently frightened off many prospective clients. High minimum charges have prevented small investors from participating in the DTB.

The bank's restructuring in 1991 (pp. 530–3) also set new accents in its securities commission and custody account business. The Retail Banking Division, for example, was responsible for customers with securities accounts below 100,000 DM. The Private Banking Division was responsible for the 200,000 wealthy private customers with custody accounts above this figure, with whom the bank transacted securities business of more than 50 billion DM in the 1990 financial year alone. For this purpose, it set up the investment centres mentioned earlier, which were equipped with the necessary technology. They provided a clear distinction between the Private Banking Division and Retail Banking.

Asset management is transacted by the bank only above substantial minimum investment amounts owing to the high administrative expenses entailed by this business. It is only since 1968 – later than some of its competitors – that the bank has consistently developed asset management with private customers, which today includes estate management, the setting up of foundations, and the administration of foundation and pension fund assets.

The introduction of asset management was preceded by controversial debate. The Legal Department above all pointed out potential liability risks which the bank could face as a result of this business. But to avoid the danger of wealthy private customers drifting off to competitors, the bank set up asset management departments at various regional head branches. The minimum sum for this business was initially 500,000 DM; this could be reduced in exceptional cases, though not below 100,000 DM.

The 1980s saw the beginning of keener competition for wealthy private customers. At that time, the bank already had an impressive share in this lucrative market segment, and in the years that followed it had to tackle the problem of defending its market position. Competitors proved to be not only other big banks, but also non-bank asset management companies. The latter were increasingly successful at capturing the owners of large private fortunes, high income earners, companies and institutional investors as customers. However, their deliberate confrontation with the (big) universal banks proved to be the downfall of many: in some cases they had to wind up their business or were taken over by banks.

One reason for rising competition in the field of asset management was the continued strong increase in households' monetary assets, which amounted to 20 billion DM after the currency adjustment in 1948. From 1967 to 1992 they rose from 314 billion to 3,500 billion DM. Most of this was held by older people and was transferred to generations of heirs because, since the currency reform of 1948 – and for the first time this century over so long a period – there has been no state-imposed open destruction of wealth. This has allowed the transfer of assets from generation to generation without any disturbance by exogenous influences. By the 1980s, the total volume of annual inheritances was 80 billion DM, and in the 1990s it has risen to roughly 200 billion DM per year. At the same time, the number of asset portfolios of more than 1 million DM has risen continuously.

The need for professional asset management, linked with executor services and estate management, will thus – in the bank's assessment – continue to rise strongly in the 1990s. The bank has therefore set itself the goal of offering its wealthy private clients modern asset management which is more than just traditional custodial services. High-net-worth individuals with assets of up to 5 million DM are handled by the Asset Management Department of the Private Banking Division. For the restructuring of existing or the development of new custody accounts, the bank devised its new services 'db-privat' and 'db-profil', which have also been used to handle smaller securities accounts of 100,000 DM or more.

The growing desire in the past of owners of particularly large asset portfolios for individually tailored services induced the bank to acquire the majority in the Frankfurt private banking house Grunelius in 1989. While conventional asset management is restricted to a certain set of services, Grunelius is not limited in this sense and has operated – since 1990 as Grunelius KG Privatbankiers – individually and on a problem-oriented basis (to quote the bank itself) for a fairly small group of customers with disposable assets of 5 million DM and more. Grunelius offers these top customers an all-round service.

Incorporated in the investment strategy, apart from securities, were high-potential real-estate holdings in unlisted undertakings, precious metals, works of art and antiques. Over and above that, in 1992 the bank introduced the 'Grunelius DVG' mutual fund, thus expanding its range of products for high-net-worth individuals to include a standardized form of asset management. This step was surprising inasmuch as Grunelius could also offer customers the mutual funds launched by the fund management companies. Taken in total, Deutsche Bank's private-banker strategy seems to have been unsuccessful initially: in the first few years, Grunelius had to report substantial losses.

At the end of 1990, Deutsche Bank Group managed assets of 124.7 billion DM world-wide. Of this sum, 43.3 billion DM was attributable to retail funds, 3.2 billion DM to property, 62.6 billion DM to institutional asset management and 15.5 billion DM to individual asset management. By 1995 the bank was seeking to double its assets under management. For this purpose, it reorganized the divisions operating in asset management and integrated them into the Bank Trust Group.

After the merger with Morgan Grenfell Asset Management, it was one of the world's 15 biggest asset managers in 1991. At the time, it was one of the top five among the universal banks, and at the same time was the largest asset manager in the European Community; the foreign share of the assets under its management was 48 per cent. By the end of 1993 the volume of private assets managed by Deutsche Bank institutions stood at 230 billion DM. What from the bank's perspective is seen as the positive development of its asset management has been overshadowed in the past by various – occasionally criminal – activities on the part of bank employees. In most cases, the bank dismissed the employees concerned; court proceedings were the exception. *Der Spiegel* reported on this subject in 1992: 'The boards of managing directors of German banks refused to speak of a "scandal" when dubious securities trades by employees were revealed last year. The so-called insider affair ended with "first-class not-guilty verdicts", as Kopper, spokesman of Deutsche Bank's board of managing directors, noted. No customer had suffered as a result. But now that the internal auditors have looked more closely, Kopper probably sees the case differently, too. He had two members of staff at the Frankfurt branch sacked on the spot. They are suspected of having profited from securities deals to the detriment of several big customers. The bank also instituted court proceedings against them.' By installing a compliance officer in 1992 (pp. 540, 720) – hailed by *Der Spiegel* as the bank's 'watchdog' – the bank hoped to prevent abuse of the system by its employees. In 1994 further precautions were institutionalized by the new Securities Trading Act.

Finally, Deutsche Bank transacts *mutual fund business* with private customers, which can be termed 'standardized asset management', primarily via its subsidiaries Deutsche Gesellschaft für Wertpapiersparen mbH (DWS), DB Investment Management SA (DBIM), Deutsche Grundbesitz-Investmentgesellschaft mbH (DGI) and Deutsche Gesellschaft für Fondsverwaltung mbH. It acts as custodian bank for its mutual fund subsidiaries and sells their shares through its branch network. While DEGEF launches specialized funds for institutional investors in accordance with the provisions of the Fund Management Company Act, the funds launched by DWS, DBIM and DGI are retail funds for private customers.

The bank's investment fund business had its origins in December 1956 when, in co-operation with 12 other banks, the predecessor institutions – after controversial internal discussions – founded Deutsche Gesellschaft für Wertpapiersparen. For business policy reasons the pre-merger bank did not wish to set up its own fund management company. It therefore took a stake of only 30 per cent in DWS. In the course of time it noted that over 90 per cent of the fund units were being sold through its branch network, but that its share of DWS earnings only corresponded to its small participating interest in the company's capital; starting in the late 1960s, therefore, it made efforts to take it over. The other shareholders were initially unwilling to sell their shares in the profitable company. It was not until 1986 that the bank was able to increase its stake to 51.5 per cent; since 1988 it has held 93 per cent.

Ulrich – the founding father and for many years supervisory board chairman of DWS – stressed at the press conference to mark the launching of the first fund, 'Investa', that the investment fund unit was 'not only an instrument to mobilize idle savings capital', but also had 'eminent importance as a sociopolitical equalizer'. The promotion of private individuals' participation in productive capital was then, as now, one of the major social policy objectives. In accordance with this, laws were enacted at the time which created the legal basis for investment funds.

'Investa', the first DWS fund, was launched on 17 December 1956, before the first Fund Management Company Act was passed, at a first-issue price of 100 DM per unit. The fund assets were invested primarily in the equities of sound German companies. In 1959 DWS launched 'Intervest' as the first fund for international equities. In 1961 it rounded off its range of funds with the reinvesting equity fund 'Akkumula', which made no cash distributions and was geared exclusively to the realization of capital gains.

In the mid-1960s, funds concentrating on fixed-income securities became popular with investors: the reasons were a sharp fall in the prices of German equities in the early 1960s, the alleged poor performance of fund managers – in many cases they were even 'beaten' by representative share indices – and attractive capital market interest rates. So DWS launched its first bond fund, 'Inrenta', on 25 January 1966 at 80 DM per unit. At the end of the 1960s, the higher international level of interest rates made foreign bonds an attractive investment. DWS reacted in July 1969 with 'Inter-renta', an international bond fund. In 1992, with fund assets totalling 22.8 billion DM and 671.2 million units in issue, this was the world's biggest fund.

To let customers participate in the burgeoning construction boom and the rise in property values the bank, in co-operation with the parent company of the building and loan association GdF Wüstenrot, formed Deutsche Grundbesitz-Investmentgesellschaft mbH in 1970. It floated an open-ended property fund called 'Grundbesitz-Invest' in 1970 with an issue price per unit of 50 DM. The fund invested chiefly in commercial properties such as office blocks and shopping centres in attractive central locations. The investor profited both from the fund's regular rental income and from what in some cases were strong capital gains from the fund assets. 'Grundbesitz-Invest' developed successfully: in 1991 its assets were valued at 4 billion DM. The bank raised its stake to 60 per cent in 1990.

Clients' interest in mutual funds waned across the board in the 1970s due, among other things, to the negative experience of many mutual fund investors in the years between 1970 and 1980. This was caused by the weak state of national and international capital markets and the poor performance of fund managers. But the 1980s saw a renaissance. DWS gave support in the form of innovative fund constructions, and developed expiry funds specifically for private customers' matured life insurance policies.

The 1980s provided a good environment for such funds: after more than a generation following the end of the Second World War, a growing number of life insurance policies were coming up for disbursement; the number and amounts paid out were becoming bigger and bigger. Of 12.4 billion DM paid by life insurance companies in 1981, 8.4 billion DM were payments due to expiry. In 1990 a substantial share of the 35 billion DM disbursed related to expiry payments. Owing to their age structure, the beneficiaries were looking for a portfolio investment that was safe and profitable, would remain fungible and would incur little administrative expense. The expiry funds tried to meet this demand profile. In the 1980s, private customers became more sophisticated, partly because of the bank's own advisory activities, and increasingly turned into shrewd investors. DWS reacted to this by deepening its product range – though relatively unsuccessfully – to include speciality funds.

The more favourable legal framework in Luxemburg caused DWS and Deutsche Bank to form a subsidiary called IIM Internationale Investment Management Gesellschaft in the Grand Duchy, where the bank had been represented since 1970. The company – styled DB Investment Management S.A. (DBIM) from 1 September 1991 – launches investment funds under Luxemburg law whose units are marketed largely through the bank's branch network, the first one being 'Eurorenta' in November 1987. It was a hit: in just under 14 months, its fund assets leaped to 8 billion DM (90 million units in issue).

In the following years the attraction of Luxemburg funds was that Luxemburg allowed great flexibility in investment policy, but above all offered German tax exiles a supposedly safe haven. It is typical that quasi money market funds could appear early on in Luxemburg as competition for pure money market funds. The performance guarantee, also developed in Luxemburg in the form of a minimum repurchase price, made it possible to offer a product comparable with the money market fund. In Luxemburg investment funds could also be offered in foreign currency, including ECU. DBIM has made full use of the scope offered by Luxemburg to extend its range of funds; it is seen partly as innovative but also, due to the confusing diversity of customers and investment advisors, as no longer manageable.

In 1991 DWS group and DGI, taken in total, managed assets of more than 52 billion DM in more than 65 funds. It is interesting that, in almost all funds launched by DWS and DBIM in the last few years, their volume has grown only in the first year and in many cases has fallen considerably in the following years: the bank's customer advisers are mostly only prepared to offer their clients units of *one* new fund. The confusing diversity of various investment funds undoubtedly overtaxes the individual adviser, and units of existing funds are hardly included in the advisory service or sold. Moreover, the second year after a fund is launched often sees a large volume of units returned. But since the assets under management expand continually, it can be assumed that the steady expansion of the fund range not only covers but more than makes up for the outflows in older funds. The bank can be satisfied with this trend owing to the very lucrative front-end load of 3–5 per cent on the issue of new units.

c) Development into a national financial conglomerate

In 1986 the board of managing directors of Deutsche Bank resolved to reposition its retail banking strategically and to develop it in the direction of *Allfinanz*, a one-stop financial service. The fashionable word *Allfinanz* did not, however, find much sympathy in the bank. As Kopper said clearly in an interview: 'Everyone is talking about Allfinanz, and I say loud and clear: I hate the word, because I don't know what it means … It reminds me of Baufinanz, building finance. Maybe it means insurance plus finance. But that would be confusing money with finance. Risk insurance has absolutely nothing to do with finance. I don't know who invented the term. And I shall never say that the bank is occupied with Allfinanz.'[46] This is surprising, since Hans Janberg had already given a clear definition of the word in a lecture in 1969: 'So, as I would like to show you today, a variety of parts are emerging which will lead in future to a one-stop financial offering. Wealth formation, provision for old age and family, home building or buying will in future be offered in the most diverse forms and combinations by banks and insurance companies together – from one source, as it were.'

In the early 1980s new competitors from the non-bank and near-bank sectors pursued aggressive growth strategies: large building and loan associations founded banks and life insurance companies, insurance groups acquired banks or signed co-operation agreements with them, and vice versa; credit card companies and department store groups followed similar courses. Car manufacturers no longer restricted their financial service products to the referral of financings for their own products, but gradually expanded them. Even Daimler-Benz, where the bank held a stake of 28.19 per cent and supplied the chairman of the supervisory board, decided to enter banking business. The bank had to react to such challenges.

When in the 1980s households showed an increasing desire for time-saving and comprehensive advice as well as the provision of financial services from one source, and the bank noted that 80 per cent of its retail clients expected an all-round advisory product, the board of managing directors resolved, in December 1986, to expand the bank's product range and to set up a building and loan association – Deutsche Bank Bauspar-AG. In line with its philosophy, shaped largely by Herrhausen, the bank deliberately refrained from intensifying its co-operation with building and loan associations, which had existed since the early 1970s, as there was a lack of reciprocity: while the bank had referred substantial new business to them, the building and loan associations were unable to refer new customers to the bank on the same scale.

The acquisition of a building and loan association was out of the question for the bank, because there was nothing available on the market. The decision to set up its own institution was at the time a surprise to many observers. Just a few years before, the sector had been confronted with a more difficult market and operating environment, which resulted in a deterioration in building and loan business. Several building and loan associations were actually pleased that the bank had given building and loan business its stamp of approval, and thus new stimulus.

The strong demand for residential property at the end of the 1980s, high interest rates and above all German unification in 1990 led to a rapid increase in the building and loan subsidiaries' contract portfolio, which stood at 381,375 agreements in 1991 with a property finance total of 11.123 billion DM. This put it among the big private building and loan associations within just three years of its foundation. The development in earnings was also positive just two years after the company was founded. Property finance agreements were marketed in the initial phase exclusively through the bank's branch network. In accordance with supervisory stipulations it built up a field service to visit customers at home as well as advising them in the branches.

In 1991, to co-ordinate its services in the property sector, Deutsche Bank founded Deutsche Immobilien Anlagegesellschaft mbH (DIA) in Frankfurt. The task of DIA is to strengthen property investment business by developing new types of product in order to offer present and potential customers of the bank new options for portfolio investment. In view of the complexity of property investment decisions, the rapid change in the relevant legal, especially tax-law, conditions surrounding an investment in property, and not least the desire of many investors to have global investment alternatives, DIA intended to contribute to the utilization of new market opportunities through its all-round professionalism in the property field and by management flexibility.

Within the Group, DIA was given the task of steering the bank's entire domestic and foreign property business, including open-ended and closed-end property funds and property equity funds. It took responsibility for all project development and property fund companies within the Group; the basis for this was the strong domestic presence, market know-how and market experience of its various allocated subsidiaries. Furthermore, the bank combined its property-broking activities in 1993 in its wholly-owned subsidiary Deutsche Immobilienvermittlungs-Holding GmbH, the successor to hitherto independently operating companies.

In the last few days of December 1988, the important decision was taken at the bank's central office to set up a *life insurance company*. This anything but simple decision was apparently preceded by a tough decision-making process. In 1987 the bank knew in principle that it would have to extend its product range for retail customers to include attractive services to help provide for the future: their desire for one-stop financial services, rising demand for comprehensive provision for old age and ways to protect their standard of living, the resulting good growth prospects in life insurance and increasing competition underlined this fact.

Despite the introduction of Deutsche Bank's savings plan with insurance cover (pp. 716–17), it was not able to participate on the desired scale in households' monetary asset formation. To be able to offer the right product combination for each specific demand profile, it decided not only to refer life insurance as a product providing for the future, but also to develop it itself. The only problem was how to do it: the bank had to decide between an integration (group) strategy and a co-operation strategy. In earlier years it had chosen the second route: standardized residual debt and risk life insurance policies of independent insurers, which could be handled without any specific advisory work, with the use of EDP and hence inexpensively, were sold over the bank counter. But the problems of a co-operation strategy (frictional and time losses in structuring products, advertising, pricing, etc.) induced the bank, as in the case of property finance, not to transact insurance business in this way, particularly as 'experience shows that the acceptance of our own products among our own employees is far greater than that of external products',[47] as Krupp stressed.

While the majority of its competitors were following co-operation strategies, the bank's objective was to develop its own new marketing channels and to offer its customers new, inexpensive and transparent insurance premiums. To begin with, the option of buying an existing life insurance company was considered; it was mainly the absence of suitable candidates that led to the decision to take the more time-consuming route of setting up an independent company. The advantages of this going-it-alone policy were considered to be the uniformity and speed of business policy formulation, freedom of action, the opportunity to recognize and fully exploit synergies, and above all the chance to increase the gross profit contribution from the client relationship by keeping the entire profit generated by the insurance services.

However, the bank's decision, as previously upon introduction of the savings plan with insurance cover in 1983, precipitated strong reactions from the insurance industry, which has meanwhile been finally calmed. The bank's board of managing directors received warnings from some companies with which it had business relations to the effect that it should not set up its own insurance company. The then chairman of the board of managing directors of Allianz-Holding, Wolfgang Schieren – already known in public for being excessively 'standing-conscious' – terminated his membership of the bank's Advisory Council.

Ultimately, despite all the threats, the bank did not experience a substantial withdrawal of deposits by insurance companies or a decline in its bond and *Schuldschein* business: although bond turnover fell to 72.7 billion DM in 1989 from 78.8 billion DM in 1988, the decline was more than recouped in the following year (turnover: 88 billion DM). This minor quantitative effect was also due to the fact that the bank's angry insurance company clients had already scaled back their business relations after the introduction of the savings plan with insurance cover.

The actual establishment of Lebensversicherungs-AG der Deutschen Bank took place within a short time: only about nine months passed between the formal decision to set the company up and the introduction of new life insurance products. In this time, experts and know-how had to be hired quickly, supervisory requirements had to be met, new insurance products and appropriate premium systems had to be worked out and, last but not least, more than 10,000 employees at branches had to be trained. On 1 September 1989 the company – abbreviated to 'Deutsche Bank-Leben' or 'db-Leben' – began to sell life insurance through the bank's branch network.

The product range first comprised endowment, risk life, supplementary risk and supplementary incapacitation insurance policies. In terms of the products it offered, the 'db-Leben' range was in line with what was available in the rest of the German insurance industry. On some points – above all where life insurance as a sector, which until then had operated without any serious competition, had often been criticized – its endowment life insurance policy differed clearly from that of competitors in its value added for customers. It fulfilled long-standing demands for more transparency from the consumer protection associations, who believed that the usual types of insurance policy failed to take sufficient account of consumer interests. The new life insurance was awarded the 'Silver DM' by the *DM* magazine. It was successful in both the old and new federal states: at the end of 1991 it had 158,278 insurance policies amounting to almost 12.2 billion DM in its portfolio; there were also supplementary incapacitation insurances with capitalized pension payments in the amount of 4.1 billion DM.

The bank took a major step forward in this field in September 1992 when it acquired a 56 per cent stake in Deutscher Herold AG, which brought in 2 million insured persons in the life and non-life insurance sectors of retail banking, and had been seeking a financially strong partner for some time. The bank intends to increase its holding, if possible, to 100 per cent, having raised it to 65.3 per cent at the beginning of 1993. Experts estimated that the holding was a bargain for the bank at 200 million DM, as Herold had annual premium revenues of 1.9 billion DM;[48] this was explained by tax reasons relating to the 20 people from 6 families who last owned the shares (besides 8.9 per cent held by Swiss Re, which passed to the bank in 1992).

Special insurance counters – at first 110, later 200 – were opened at the bank's branches for the sale of Herold insurance products; 'db-Leben' retained its counter marketing strategy, and its products were supplemented by fund-based life insurance, private pension insurance and the insurance mortgage offered by Herold. The Herold sales organization markets all types of financial services for Deutsche Bank Group. A decisive point is that the former, besides its own field service of more than 10,000 people, gained about 3,000 from Bonnfinanz. Bonnfinanz AG für Vermögensberatung und Vermittlung was practically part of the package bought by the bank, so that through the deal as a whole it also obtained a strong distribution network for its one-stop financial product range.

In mid-1993 the bank reorganized its insurance activities to give them a management structure in line with its normal principle, which put similar functions under uniform management: 'db-Leben' was transferred in full to the Deutscher Herold holding company, and the bank's insurance activities were combined under one roof. They were joined by health and litigation insurance products: the Globale Krankenversicherung, founded with Gerling, was then held by Gerling and Herold with 45 per cent each, and by Deutsche Bank directly with 10 per cent; the also new Deutscher Herold Rechtsschutz-Versicherungs-AG was held by the Herold Group with 70 per cent, and Gerling with 30 per cent. Krupp, the member of the bank's board of managing directors responsible for this sector, was reserved in his assessment of their insurance power: 'All these diverse activities are steps towards realizing a uniform concept for serving our retail customers. The aim here is to bind these customers to the bank in what is a changing market with a marked decline in customer loyalty by enhancing our own products and marketing channels. This means that the "traditional" banking products will be joined by bank-related financial services covering the retail customer's entire personal requirements ... Customers expect these products to be part of our range of services and consider the banks to be highly competent to supply them.'[49]

d) The new challenge: retail banking in the former GDR

German unification provided Deutsche Bank with a virtually untapped financial services market practically on its own doorstep. In the GDR there were only about 550 bank branches for 16 million people. These could not be compared with those in the West and, as a result of the system, only offered their private customers a very narrow range of services. Moreover, banks in the GDR had neither well-trained staff nor an efficient organization.

Right from the outset, Deutsche Bank's aim was to establish a nationwide network as quickly as possible in East Germany. It started to think along these lines immediately after the fall of the Berlin Wall. Only a few days before he was assassinated, Alfred Herrhausen set up a GDR Working Group to look into the business potential offered by the still existing GDR. However, the almost daily changing situation prevented any kind of strategic planning. Owing to legal restrictions, the bank was not allowed to build up its own branch network.

At the beginning of 1990, the bank started to send teams of staff to East Germany to examine the local market and get an impression of the situation in the various cities and locations. At the same time, it developed initial contacts with the State Bank of the GDR. Edgar Most, at the time vice president of the East German State Bank and since 1991 a member of the management of Deutsche Bank's Berlin branch, met secretly with representatives of Deutsche Bank to discuss how the East German banking system could be restructured and what part Deutsche Bank could play in this process.

On 1 April 1990, a two-tier banking system was introduced, and Deutsche Kreditbank AG was founded. The latter took over almost the entire branch network from the State Bank and all the loans the State Bank had extended to the state-owned enterprises and industrial conglomerates. However, Deutsche Bank wanted to avoid taking on such a debt portfolio, since the East German companies could not be expected to repay these loans in their desperate situation. The bank's acquisition of a direct holding in Deutsche Kreditbank was therefore out of the question.

The idea was then floated in March 1990 to set up a joint venture with what was to become Deutsche Kreditbank. A framework agreement to this effect was concluded on 18–21 March 1990, and on 17 April a declaration of intent was signed. The bank promised to provide the necessary capital, the technical, organizational and staff capabilities, and its know-how. Deutsche Kreditbank was to contribute its branches in the former GDR as well as their staff. In March, the first 100 staff from East Germany were sent to the bank's western branches for training on the job.

The necessary legal framework for the joint venture was not created by the GDR government until spring 1990. The majority of Deutsche Kreditbank's branches were in very poor condition, with bars in front of the windows and lacking the necessary technical infrastructure. The staff had not been adequately trained, so that they needed to undergo rigorous training after they were taken on. At the same time, the bank worked out several scenarios, including the establishment of its own branch network without a joint venture, but the growing time pressure forced it to continue the policy it had already started and to stick to the joint venture with Kreditbank.

When in spring 1990 the West German government indicated that it wanted to set up an economic, monetary and social union with the GDR as soon as possible, it became clear that the bank did not have much time to seek alternatives. The state treaty between the Federal Republic and the GDR of May 1990 stipulated that this union would come into force on 1 July, when the deutschmark would also be introduced in the GDR. The conversion from East German marks to deutschmarks was to be carried out via credit balances held in accounts at East German banks. This provided the West German banks with excellent access to GDR households. The precondition for this, however, was for the bank to expand its network as much as possible.

Had the bank taken over the entire branch network of Deutsche Kreditbank as planned, it could have commenced business in the GDR with 184 outlets on 1 July 1990. However, the Federal Cartel Office raised objections. Most, by this time a member of Deutsche Kreditbank's management board, thus entered into negotiations with other banks. After initial hesitation, agreement was reached with Dresdner Bank. In the joint venture with Dresdner Bank (Dresdner Bank-Kreditbank AG), Deutsche Kreditbank contributed 72 branches, and in the joint venture with Deutsche Bank (Deutsche Bank-Kreditbank AG), it provided 112 branches. Deutsche Bank had the benefit of having first choice of the outlets. However, it allowed Dresdner Bank to acquire its former headquarters in Dresden as a gesture of goodwill.

On the day the economic, monetary and social union came into effect, Deutsche Bank was represented in the GDR with a total of 140 more or less functioning outlets – including 12 provisional ones in buses and 6 belonging to Deutsche Bank Berlin in East Berlin. The bank managed to link up all these branches via an online data network. Prior to this, hundreds of lorry-loads of furniture, second-hand telephones, building materials, terminals, wallpaper and payment forms had to be transferred to the GDR. The staff was made up of approximately 8,500 employees of the former State Bank and 500 West German staff from Deutsche Bank. Deutsche Bank-Kreditbank's Berlin-Alexanderplatz branch was the only bank to open on Sunday, 1 July at 0:00 hours to pay out the new deutschmarks to GDR citizens. Huge crowds of people thronged into the branch to collect their money. During the course of this day, the bank paid out 120 million DM. Hundreds of journalists, photographers and television reporters came to the 'Alex' to cover this historic event, and their reports were beamed around the world.

On 1 July 1990 Deutsche Bank virtually had to start from scratch in the GDR. It had not taken over any customers, i.e accounts, or any deposits or loans from Deutsche Kreditbank, so that it was solely dependent on new business. Right from the beginning, the product range it offered was virtually the same as the one offered in the West. The various advantages and disadvantages of the bank's different services had to be explained to the customers in some detail. Since customers were not familiar with many of these services, the staff had to demonstrate a high degree of tact and understanding. At first, the new customers were understandably rather suspicious of the new products on offer, but these fears were soon allayed.

The bank had always been aware that the joint venture with Deutsche Kreditbank could only be of a temporary nature. In the months preceding German unification, the bank operated as Deutsche Bank Berlin, Deutsche Bank-Kreditbank and Deutsche Bank. It was therefore keen to standardize its image as soon as possible. Thus, on 17 July 1990, the bank raised its stake in Deutsche Bank-Kreditbank to 85 per cent in the form of a capital increase. In August 1990 it started to devise a strategy for the restructuring of its East German branches. After the formal unification of Germany on 3 October 1990, the bank had already decided that it was imperative to reorganize the branch regions in the new federal states as quickly as possible.

On 27 November 1990, the bank's board of managing directors decided to introduce the new branch structure with two new regional head branches in Berlin and Leipzig. Deutsche Bank-Kreditbank and Deutsche Bank Berlin were therefore merged with Deutsche Bank AG. At the end of 1990 the bank acquired the remaining 15 per cent of Deutsche Bank-Kreditbank from the Treuhandanstalt in Berlin, and for tax reasons carried out the merger during the last few days of December. Deutsche Bank Berlin was merged with the bank on 18 June 1991.

Retail business in the eastern federal states developed well after 1 July 1990. Some 11,500 staff were employed at the bank's 280 or so outlets in 1991. By 31 December 1991, the bank had almost 1.2 million private customers in the new federal states (including Berlin) with 955,000 savings accounts and 600,000 current accounts. At the end of 1991, the bank's loan portfolio for retail customers totalled 5.7 billion DM. Since many east Germans saw the privatization of their economy as a challenge and wanted to become self-employed, the bank supported many such projects by providing ERP funds and loans for setting up new businesses. Another substantial part of the bank's retail business was accounted for by personal loans for the financing of cars, furniture, etc. Property finance, on the other hand, was much slower to develop in the new federal states. This was largely due to the unclear property ownership situation in the former GDR and the overworked land registry offices and other authorities, which at first made it virtually impossible to register mortgages or land charges. By the end of 1991, however, the volume of property finance loans to private customers had risen to 1.9 billion DM.

Right from the outset the bank's deposit business developed gratifyingly in the new federal states and Berlin; by the end of 1991, retail customer deposits had reached 11.6 billion DM, of which 6.0 billion DM were savings deposits and 2.8 billion DM time deposits, including savings certificates. These savers soon proved to be aware of the uses of interest rates and increasingly started investing their money in higher-yielding instruments. The bank was surprised by the substantial growth in securities commissions, custody accounts and investment funds. By December 1991 it had opened 184,000 securities accounts with a market value at the end of 1991 of 6.7 billion DM. At approximately 65 million DM, the monthly securities turnover of private customers was amazingly high.

During the first few months there were considerable difficulties with payments in the new federal states. The duration of transfers was in some cases more than four weeks. Although the bank was able to effect entries within its own branch network without great delay, since the outlets were all hooked up to each other, the settlement of cashless payments with other banks in some cases had to be carried out manually. Only after the Bundesbank had established its giro system did the speed of cashless payments reach western German levels. New features such as cash-dispensing machines and account statement printers were surprisingly quickly accepted by the bank's eastern German private customers. By the end of 1991 the bank had issued 25,000 Eurocards and over 184,000 eurocheque cards.

The products offered by Deutsche Bank's building and loan and life insurance companies were also successful; by 31 December 1991 the former had achieved an amount of 1.6 billion DM (53,000 policies) and the latter 1.1 billion DM (17,000 policies).

Such positive figures conceal the problems with which the bank was confronted initially in the new federal states. First of all, the bank was forced to admit that it had set its market share targets too high. On entering the retail market in the ex-GDR, the bank had assumed that it would be able to obtain a substantially greater market share than in western Germany. In particular, the bank had anticipated that the former East German savings banks would lose a lot of their customers. These banks were in a bad situation, since they had formerly been part of the state authorities – an extended arm of the GDR State Bank, so to speak – and therefore had a negative image. As it was, however, the ex-GDR savings banks managed to maintain their market share at a high level. The eastern German retail customers proved to be surprisingly loyal; many people believed that the 1989 revolution had placed them in an uncertain situation as far as living and work were concerned, and were therefore reticent and cautious in financial matters. Many people were more worried about losing their job than about changing their bank.

The bank's lack of profile in the new federal states also turned out to be a disadvantage. While Dresdner Bank was familiar to many eastern Germans as a result of its advertising on television and also benefited from its name and the generally positive image enjoyed by the western German banks, Deutsche Bank was less well known at the time of the East German revolution and did not have an immediately identifiable name. Moreover, criticism was levelled at its image by many eastern Germans. When the bank moved into the former State Bank buildings without immediately renovating and redecorating them, many customers were reminded of the old GDR days. The bank was even said to have a certain 'Stasi ambience' about it. There was also initial criticism of the bank's personal advisory services.

As a result of this, the bank was forced to review the market share targets it had set itself. In 1991 it was content with a slightly higher market share in the new federal states than in western Germany. Nonetheless, the criticisms levelled at it by its eastern German private customers induced Deutsche Bank to iron out some of its weaknesses, raise its market profile and clean up its image. The first step in this direction was the new branch structure introduced in 1991. More than 70 buildings housing branches of the bank were purchased and renovated from top to bottom. In addition, the bank improved the quality of its customer advisory services by organizing comprehensive training aimed especially at those staff members taken over from Deutsche Kreditbank, who were described by Krupp, the member of the board of managing directors responsible for the former GDR, as the bank's 'most valuable dowry'. The aim here was to raise standards to western levels. In certain areas the bank managed to achieve this target fairly quickly. In 1992 Deutsche Bank Chemnitz became the bank's first branch to be awarded the distinction of 'Friendliest Bank of the Year' by a business magazine.

III. Becoming a Global Financial Conglomerate

1. Trends in globalization as a strategic concept at Deutsche Bank

On the threshold of the third millennium, the globalization of mankind is one of the principal megatrends. In the financial world[50] globalization denotes a process of far-reaching change which began in the early 1980s and is still in progress today: the development of the international financial market – or at least some of its sub-markets – into a single global market. The globalization of financial markets has led to the settlement of banking business at the world's financial centres 'around the clock' and 'around the world'.

As for most banks operating in such assimilated markets, globalization has also impacted on the corporate objectives of Deutsche Bank, with its traditional international character. A bank working in globalized markets faces special demands on its organization and, logically enough, on its ability to think strategically.[51] As Mertin already said in 1987:

'What is decisive for the long-term business success of banks operating on the global financial stage is, ultimately, a coherent strategy which does not neglect their strengths and foundations in domestic business, but rather consciously cultivates them. Apart from that, an international strategy must be based on as realistic a view as possible of prospects in specific business fields and diverse financial markets – which is not always easy in this transitional phase and might require adjustment over the years. Moreover – and this should be less difficult – one's own bank's potential must be objectively assessed. For this, besides personnel capacities, a bank's financial strength and placement power have, in my view, key importance – a fact which may easily go under in today's trading climate with its short-term profit opportunities.'[52]

This already addressed the key questions which have until today dominated debate on the bank's positioning. These questions started with the vision[53] of the bank as a global financial services supplier, as articulated by Herrhausen soon afterwards, which soon caused a furore under the catchword 'global player'. They concern the need for a consistent and cohesive strategy – to be formulated not only for the bank, but also for the entire Deutsche Bank Group – the problem of determining the attraction of banking business areas, and the necessity of continued reflection on personnel and capital, resources which are fundamentally scarce and thus critical to the bank's business success.

For Deutsche Bank, which includes globalization in its entrepreneurial philosophy, the main question must be whether bank services or bank service packages can be created whose relevant market is 'the world'. In its global strategy and international self-perception, Deutsche Bank tries intensively to identify which traditional and promising business sectors have global potential, which customer groups can be regarded as global demanders, and which financial services can be offered world-wide.[54] For example, the bank considers a certain segment of investment banking to be already globalized. In the words of Krumnow: 'We are convinced that investment banking with institutional investors can only be conducted on a global basis. Institutional investors buy and sell around the clock. At every moment, be it night or day in Germany, one of the world's principal financial centres is in operation; prices and values are changing somewhere at all times and as an investment bank we must be part of this process'.[55]

Indeed, the bank came to the conclusion at the beginning of the 1990s, on the basis of surveys of corporate customers' demand and willingness to pay for tailored problem solutions, that a global offering in the form of service packages aimed at specific customer groups would be economically viable.[56] Meanwhile, however, the existing range of basically globalizable bank products is viewed not just as a latent need, but rather as the direct starting point for strategic concepts. Notable in this context is the bank's step-by-step approach to the globalization – used here to mean global marketing – of complex product configurations: 'Although such a product combines the entire know-how of a universal group, we only proceed gradually when marketing it internationally. The first condition is widespread acceptance of the product package in a regional market, let's say the home market. Once we have it, we introduce the service package selectively in foreign markets, i.e. gradually "internationalize" it. We don't think about globalization until we have found acceptance in a number of markets.'[57]

This led – as part of a market strategy that could be called target group banking – to concentration on certain customer groups classified by specific demand profiles. 'With our limited equity capital resources, especially "human capital", we shall concentrate globally on customer groups for whom we can reconcile the advantages of a global business system with a certain homogeneity in our clients' demand to produce benefits for both sides'.[58]

The many statements on the bank's attitude towards the theoretical glo-balizability and/or practical globalization of services reflect how far theoretical considerations formed the basis of its corporate policy, be it in the formulation of an overriding Group corporate strategy or in comparatively elementary categories such as internal profit and loss calculation. In a global context, therefore, the bank emphasizes the benefits deriving from the links between its own added value creation process and that of corporate customers, for example, when Schmitz says: 'Benefits . . . that a global financial services supplier can offer clients if top ratings give it access to money and capital markets at special terms and conditions.'[59]

The 'effects, only partially visible to the customer, of technology and know-how transfer inside a global financial group' are similarly emphasized.[60] On the other hand, a more concrete formulation was chosen by Schmitz for the question – and its answer in the form of a heuristic suggestion – of the economic utility of the types of bank service to be globalized: 'The deciding factor when choosing products to be globalized is whether or not money can be made from them. The answer is not given solely by a calculation of product profitability. In the end, how far we, as a universal bank, push ahead with globalization depends on our relationship with clients.'[61]

As the main prospective clients for financial services world-wide, the bank has specifically identified multinational companies seeking greater flexibility and improved efficiency for their liquid assets to minimize short-term borrowing and reduce the cost of foreign exchange and other transactions. It has also identified large insurance companies wishing to diversify their investments by country, currency and issuer. Internationalization and globalization are ways in which the bank has been able to vary its offering; in Kopper's words: 'Please do not regard the internationalization of the bank as an end in itself. It serves to make us more attractive to German corporate customers wanting to work with us abroad, but they will turn to competitors if we cannot help them outside Germany. Our internationalization,[62] which has taken only 12 years to engineer, has given us a popularity lead over German and European competitors. This also applies to foreign corporate clients who are happy to work with the bank in Italy, Spain, the UK and other countries, and whose subsidiaries in Germany we can also serve.'[63]

For the bank, therefore, every customer segment, including private customers and small and medium-sized companies, is a potential target group for global financial services, provided the bank succeeds in providing a long-term competitive advantage. In Schmitz' words: 'Important for global products, therefore, besides homogenous demand, is at least one other criterion, namely, the special benefit to the customer. So those products can, in theory, be globalized which offer the customer unparalleled terms and conditions, or such special advantages that, in the end, price only plays a minor role.'[64] In practice, however, this hypothesis has had to be qualified: 'The particularly inexpensive offer will come solely from the financial services supplier that can establish price leadership among its competitors. Such price leadership inevitably has a negative effect on the individuality of the offer.'[65]

Despite the publicity that the vision of the bank as a global player owes chiefly to Herrhausen's many formulations, it would seem wrong to identify the bank's fundamentally global perspective solely with him. Statements and implications can be found in the bank's Annual Reports since the 1960s, especially in the 1980s, which indicate that a global strategy was being pursued, at least implicitly. The 1963 Annual Report addressed in parts the question of institutional internationalization:

'The intensification of international economic relations ... also confronts credit institutions with new responsibilities. The Bank which has watched this development with great attention for years, felt itself called upon, especially in the interest of its customers, to examine how the challenges could best be met. Having been placed before the alternative whether allowance for existing requirements should be made by establishing branch offices or acquiring part interests in neighbouring countries or whether preference should be given to an appropriate form of co-operation extending to special fields of activity with correspondent banks in the respective countries, we have chosen the latter. We feel, the industrial countries in Europe already maintain a highly developed banking system and a sufficiently dense network of credit institutions so that an extension of the national branch networks beyond the borders does not seem to be a goal worth striving for. At the same time, however, our attitude was also determined by the endeavour not only to maintain the existing close relationships with all our banking friends but to develop them further. The long-standing close connections of the Bank with its correspondents in Europe and throughout the world will remain unchanged.'

Two years later, however, another course was already being pursued in view of the growing economic relations with developing countries, as can be gathered from the Annual Report for 1965: 'In view of the growing interest which our customers have shown in trade relations with, and investments in, developing countries, we have acquired participations in commercial and investment banks in these territories. Such holdings also facilitate an insight into the life and conditions in the countries concerned so that we may give our customers pertinent advice. The acquisition of minority interests proved to be particularly suitable. The institutions in which we hold participations always employ predominantly native personnel and capital.'

In 1970 the bank's need to adjust its organization to the increasing globalization of corporate clients was noted:

'The growing importance of multinational companies is causing increasingly marked structural changes in the world economy. These companies have a worldwide business policy and are tending more and more to shift their production to those countries where they sell most, or to their most important sources of raw materials, with the result that the financing of investment projects is gaining in importance over export financing, which was dominant up to now. The multinational companies expect their banks to provide them with as comprehensive a service as possible in all important countries ... We are meeting the challenge of these structural changes in the world economy and of the steadily growing requirements in the foreign business in general through increased contacts with multinational companies, regular visits to all important industrial and financial centres and especially through continued expansion of our foreign network. This is taking place mainly on two levels: through the setting up of new representative offices of the Deutsche Bank or branches of our subsidiary, the Deutsche Ueberseeische Bank, which is predominantly active in Latin America, and through greater co-operation with our partner banks in Europe and the establishment of joint new bases outside Europe. As a result of this policy, we are already in a position to be directly active for our customers in most international business centres.'

This aspect received greater emphasis in 1971: 'This expansion of the Deutsche Bank Group, which has been proceeding for years, must be seen as a parallel development to important changes in our economic and social structure and the growing integration in the world economy ... Institutionally and in our organisation we have met this continual challenge in four ways: by a continuous expansion and improvement of our own services ... By founding subsidiaries to which special functions are transferred ... By acquiring majority participations or joining in the establishment of specialised institutions, where the bank may work in fruitful combination with the particular knowledge and ability of qualified partners ... By working with other European banks in founding joint subsidiaries in Europe and overseas. This shows the main principles according to which the Deutsche Bank Group has been built up and which will also determine future decisions: quick reaction to indications of new needs on the part of our customers, the choice of the most appropriate organizational form in each case, and work in partnership wherever this promises the best performance. It is obvious that in the course of this development of the Group the central management problems also become greater and more difficult, but that at the same time growing demands are made on those in responsible positions in all parts of the Group to be ready to take responsibility and to make independent decisions.'

In the following years these aspects were discussed in greater depth. The 1985 Annual Report emphasized the need to exploit synergy potential in the considerably bigger group: 'Our aim is for all Group units to complement and support each other in their activity, thereby optimizing the use of our entire resources. From the point of view of efficiency and result. For this purpose, we further improved the instruments in our management information system.' The greater importance of investment banking, which dominated international financial markets in the 1980s, is also included in the strategic statement: 'We made good progress with the implementation of our international investment banking strategy. Our aim is to be represented by our own securities houses at all centres where international business is concentrated. These are London as the centre of the euromarket, New York for the US market, Tokyo for the Pacific region as well as Frankfurt am Main, Geneva and Zurich for the Continental European market.'

In the Annual Report for 1986, the bank contrasted the global perspective with a reiteration of the significance of domestic business: 'The globalization and internationalization of the bank do not, however, mean an abatement in our concern for our domestic customers. Our domestic business is still *the* backbone of our earning power. Without our domestic business we could not sustain our international activities on their present scale. On the other hand, our foreign branches and subsidiaries support the results of our domestic organization through their services to German customers ... In the year under review, we supplemented and expanded our international network of bases in those regions world-wide which we consider to be particularly growth oriented. Our strategic thinking was concentrated on three large regions: the Pacific Basin, Europe and North America.' In 1989, finally, consolidation and the identification of new challenges re-appeared in equal measure: 'We have accepted the challenges emerging for the nineties. The main focus is on securing our competitiveness and market position in the future single European market and positioning ourselves on the ever more closely interlinked financial markets. In addition, there are the preparations for our future business presence in the GDR and the countries of Eastern Europe after they have turned to systems based on market economics.'

The global vision itself was based ultimately on such ideas as the following: 'Deutsche Bank, as its name suggests, was originally a bank in and for German national and international business. Then it became a Deutsche Bank, operating not only from within the borders of the Federal Republic, but also in foreign positions. What is the next step? Well, it will have to change from being a German bank with international business into a multinational institution with its home base in Germany.'[66]

Long before Deutsche Bank began to discuss its own globalization, it recognized the significance of developments affecting the global economy in particular and their implications for the formulation of corporate strategies which were, however, primarily intended for international corporate customers. In 1977 Abs already pointed out, in a speech on 'Global economic trends as the overall framework of corporate strategies', that the state and prospects of the world economy were among the most important parameters for successful corporate strategies: 'The important aspect for corporate management and economic policy makers is to recognize global economic tendencies and trends as swiftly and accurately as possible, and to incorporate them as exogenous data in their own strategies.'

With historical hindsight, the institutional internationalization of Deutsche Bank AG, later on in a Group context, was a continuous process, which makes it difficult to pinpoint its origin in a comprehensive, consistently formulated strategy. 1957 can be seen as the year in which internationalization began, when Abs assumed management responsibility for the reamalgamated bank. The process was continued by Ulrich, under whose aegis the number of subsidiaries in central European markets rose continually from the late 1950s onwards. At the end of the 1970s the bank, under Christians and Guth, ventured cautiously into international markets. This came about primarily within the framework of the EBIC bank club through the formation of consortium banks. In the course of the rapid expansion of international financial markets, which began in the 1970s, interest in joint ventures waned again for various reasons. More and more partners began to open their own branches outside their national borders; consortium banks lost significance.

More than ten years were to pass after Abs' forecast before Herrhausen in 1988 broached the subject of 'The strategic implications of globalization for German banks' and outlined its definition for the bank: 'On the basis of the broadly positive macroeconomic and political parameters, German banks, while objectively assessing their resources and market opportunities, have broadened their range of products and become more international without letting themselves be seduced into overinflating their ambitions by the many temptations in the historical and unique "securitization boom". We kept our feet on the ground while others got carried away.'

While this first stage of globalization was primarily concerned with investment banking, the creation of a single European financial market in conjunction with the impending realization of the single European market also had repercussions for traditional commercial banking. In Herrhausen's words: 'This second phase flies the "Europe 1992" banner and concerns the other big field of activity of German-style universal banks which temporarily surrendered the limelight to investment banking: traditional commercial banking.'

At the same time, the spokesman of the board of managing directors warned against the possible dangers of one-sided concentration on the European financial services market: 'The predominance of "Europe", which was addressed with 1992, could lead to the conclusion that European banks are restricting themselves largely to our continent and, in a certain sense, narrowing their global perspective – if only temporarily – while the Americans and the Japanese are maintaining theirs.' The global perspective was referred to in the following passage: 'None the less, exclusive concentration of power in Europe would not be without risk in the medium and long term because it would mean that in global terms we would remain a "demi-monde". Although we must work hard to keep the European end as our home-turf in the field of global development, we still have to try hard not to lose sight of the global objective. Otherwise, in the end, we will not be globalized but just re-provincialized, be it at a higher or European level ... In correctly understanding the phenomenon of globalization, our strategic and structural considerations must extend beyond the Europe which was the focus of attention in 1992. The Americans and Japanese are showing us how to do it.'

As justified as the emphasis on American and Japanese banks' exemplary function may seem to be as things stood then, their global ambitions have been scaled down considerably for specific national reasons, in favour of greater concentration on and business policy re-orientation to domestic markets. The consequence for the bank – both ambitious and pragmatic (Herrhausen 1988): 'We have to position ourselves globally ... We are not bent on global conquest. We are simply considering, in rational and businesslike manner, the global financial networks which, visible to all, will develop towards the end of this century, and are trying to adjust our own strategies accordingly.'

The global perspective, the global objective, the idea of a globalized bank or global player, remained imprecise in such formulations. It became clear, however, that the European dimension, the bank's European strategy as a European bank, would play a major role in any global strategy. Even at this European level, management had to change its thinking. In Herrhausen's words: 'But I am convinced that even this Europe cannot be developed using traditional means. We need ... a new corporate policy approach, new strategies. These new strategies require new structures which, in turn, require new management mechanisms; all three require a new culture – corporate culture – and this ultimately calls for a new kind of communication, i.e. new PR internally and externally.' It was obvious that the development of the European financial services market was identified and internalized as a challenge to the bank's strategic management going beyond the pure formulation of strategy. In the light of Herrhausen's diagnosis of the global trend towards the universal banking system, the bank's global range of services should not be in any way restricted: 'Investment banking, commercial banking and more recently consulting banking are the universal bank's typical menu approach to serving international customers. They are bundled in the person of the only sovereign known to the market economy: the customer. Whenever we view the bank from his angle, supposed opposites start to complement each other. Of course, we cannot be everywhere in the world with all products at the same time, but must be selective. We must try, however, to continually enlarge the product range offered. To do this will require systems allowing us to steer global activities and universal products and services.'

An analysis of the bank's own self-perception as a European bank, reflected principally in statements by members of the board of managing directors, should differentiate between the bank's quasi-natural quality of being a European bank by virtue of its domicile, and an assessment of its overall European significance. Here, in the light of the single European market, it may be said that the bank's domestic market, since implementation of the single market programme, has no longer been the nation-state within whose geographical borders one is domiciled, and which can serve in comparisons as the benchmark for such indicators as market share. The domestic market is rather the complete single market as an 'area without internal borders, in which the free movement of goods, people, services and capital ... is guaranteed'.[67] Within this structure there is a regional presence – at least the geographical position of the branches or distribution systems – which, even for the largest banks, can at best be compared to those of traditional regional banks.

In planning its European, international or global strategy, Deutsche Bank works from the strategic premise that it should maintain its traditionally strong position in the domestic market – which in itself is not a sufficient, but a necessary condition for any international expansion – and, if possible in the face of growing competition, strengthen it. As a basis for its European and global strategy, the bank aims, at the national level, to protect its market position and profitability – especially in the new federal states – by expanding its range of services. In institutional terms this concerns – as in European strategy – Group strategy, and from a marketing perspective diversification strategy – known generally as the *Allfinanz* or all-round financial service strategy.

With the acquisition of an initial 24 per cent stake, raised to a qualified majority of 75.1 per cent, in Roland Berger Verwaltungsgesellschaft mbH, Deutsche Bank entered consulting banking in 1987, later described as the third future element of national, European and global banking business alongside commercial and investment banking. The bank's Annual Report for 1987 under-lined the greater corporate importance attributed to consulting banking: 'We shall make every effort to expand our consultancy business and to establish it as a standard part of our Group's range of services.'

For the bank, extending the Group service programme was not an end in itself, but the result of objective entrepreneurial thinking; it was 'not a vision, but a very pragmatic step in the expansion of our product range. We saw that it made sense – for example, in the services area – to offer our more demanding customers, using the same marketing strategy, life insurance, property finance and portfolio investment products. Capacities can thus be fully utilized and additional profits generated, which we also need to cover the high cost of our branch network. This is why we entered the property finance business and life insurance. It could be termed the *Allfinanz* or all-round financial service strategy. I would call it diversifying our product range.'[68]

It is clear that the bank has a problem with the definition of the popular term *Allfinanz*: 'Is Allfinanz a must, an opportunity or simply a passing fashion? Although the term crops up everywhere these days and has been adopted into the English language, I don't particularly like this word, because it has so many possible interpretations and conveys a misleading picture of banking. We at Deutsche Bank prefer the expression "Everything from one source".'[69]

It may be left open – because it is irrelevant – whether the preferred circumlocution of the strategy of product range expansion or diversification is actually superior to the *Allfinanz* concept; but it is surprising that one word can cause such excitement.

The measures taken with a view to the single European market have affected many legally independent companies operating within Deutsche Bank Group as independent suppliers in their respective markets. In line with the structural features of banking business, the European strategy is primarily a strategy of institutional growth taking into account special features – regional in a European context, but initially more national.

The bank's European strategy is based on thoughts which, in the context of strategic development, can be described as strategic premisses. The bank assumes, when planning the adjustment of its objectives and the regulations considered sufficient to achieve these targets in a single European market, that the potential danger to national business should be seen as greatest during, and most definitely after, realization of the single market; in Kopper's words: 'Our initial thought is: the more strongly a business is conducted at national level, the greater the risk. The most secure sectors are those which are strongly internationalized and can adapt flexibly to customer demands. Anyone wishing to sustain his position in the domestic market in the long term must expand his activities in the single European market.'[70] This formulation, which appears contradictory only at first glance – 'the realization that a business cannot maintain its strong position on the domestic market in the long term without holding an equally strong position in foreign markets'[71] – may at the same time be accepted as the essence of the bank's European strategy, and as the grounds for the acquisitions made in the second half of the 1980s. The explanation is plausible, 'because the customers themselves often work globally or in global regions. Furthermore, we wish to be present where the highest growth rates are expected, where we can find a stable currency and political situation, and also where our industrial partners will settle in the future – a triad consisting of Asia-Pacific, Europe and North America.'[72]

According to an analysis of its position in a still fictitious single European market, the bank had to accept that, given the enormous enlargement of the potential domestic market, a new assessment of its own position was inevitable: 'We are still the leading universal bank in Germany with more than 1,300 branches and a market share of around 5 per cent.'[73] 'At home we are a universal bank with a comprehensive wholesale and retail product range. De facto we are a regional bank with a mere 5 per cent market share in loans and deposits in our German home market.'[74]

Even though the bank, with this market share, is market leader in Germany, its market share in the European Union is only slightly over 2 per cent. Nevertheless it is one of Europe's largest banks.[75] However, an assessment of its own importance, based solely on on-balance-sheet business, does not match the bank's self-perception as a traditional universal bank. Despite the problem of the quantitative comparability of various activities in commercial and investment banking, the bank, in both respects, has a very high estimate of its own importance, as Krumnow said: 'Taking our investment banking activities into account, Deutsche Bank is probably number one among all European banks.'[76]

Assuming a potential threat to its competitive position in a European context,[77] ideas are put forward on strategic business planning: 'We know, of course, that we must not lose our way. For all our diversification, concentration on our strengths and a careful analysis of available profit potential in Germany and abroad are important prerequisites in the development of business strategy in the 1990s. We must keep asking ourselves critically what customers in individual markets expect from us, and whether and how we can best meet our customers' needs. It makes no sense, for example, to create a branch network from scratch in another country and to offer our retail customers products already being sold by other local banks. Why would a French retail customer suddenly decide to go to a more distant branch of a German bank? It does, however, make sense to handle corporate business and provide advisory services through just a few branches in a country with which we do a large proportion of our foreign trade.'[78]

From an organizational point of view, the bank's European strategy has followed the old saying 'structure follows strategy'. The primacy of the following strategic concept derived from entrepreneurial vision has been recognized and accepted: 'The strategic implication which has emerged here is clear: structures follow strategy. A group of subsidiaries and participating interests has a different structure than one consisting of legally dependent branches. Mutual relationships based on co-operation and integration lead to constructions – or, I fear, to dependence – different from autonomous solutions.'[79] A more concrete formulation of the relationship between strategy and structure in the bank came from Herrhausen's successor as spokesman of the board of managing directors: 'First of all you have to know where you want to go. You need an idea of your objective. The next question is how to get there. Only then can you consider what kind of ship and crew are needed.'[80]

In expanding into the EU member states, the bank differentiates in institutional terms between three strategic possibilities or alternative institutional strategies as basic options to be considered for the bank as well as for its national and European competitors:

'1. Expansion of our own network beyond German borders by setting up subsidiaries and affiliated companies.

2. Acquisition of banks in other countries and expansion of existing branches.

3. Co-operation and possible integration with neighbour banks in the European environment.'[81]

According to Herrhausen, there are three factors of special importance for the choice of strategy: 'The path taken depends, of course, on the resources available or which could become available – capital and personnel – but also on one's vision of the bank in future. All strategies start with visions: that is, with a target which can be projected into an assumed pattern of development as an objective.'[82]

Since it is the bank's acknowledged intention to take up an independent European position, the co-operation approach, which has also led to frictional losses and time wasting in decision-making processes, as well as dependence, has ceased to be an option. The reason for not extending its own branch network has been the need for prompt use of human and capital resources. The immediate availability of a well-adjusted organization and the limited resources needed in capital and management capacity are factors in favour of acquiring existing banks, an option which has been given basic preference and put into practice: 'The cost of an acquisition, and that means full capital backing in accordance with the Banking Act, can be considerable. The suitable alternative from case to case always depends on the specific circumstances. Whenever suitable takeover candidates have appeared, we have so far chosen the quicker path of acquisition because our capital resources have allowed us to do so.'[83]

It is unclear whether and on what scale the bank intended to transfer the *Allfinanz* concept, already implemented in Germany, to Europe. Statements by board members in 1989 did not convey a clear concept. In the areas of insurance and property, Krupp had 'no concrete thoughts in this direction. I think it is improbable that we will act along these lines. More probable, however, is that we will, at a given time, provide our foreign sales networks with policies "produced" in Germany or choose the road of co-operation with German or foreign companies abroad. In any case we will have to observe cultural and legal factors carefully in any given country. Certainly that could mean that German standards and especially German products might not be easily transferred to other European markets.'[84] According to Krumnow, however: 'In retail banking we aim to use our strength as domestic Allfinanz suppliers abroad. On the road to Europe, more and more customers will not just confine themselves to their respective domestic markets, but will make more intensive use than ever of opportunities in European capital markets. We want to take advantage of these changes, on the one hand, as a starting point for intensifying existing business relations, on the other for stimulating new customer contacts, above all in the other EC countries.'[85]

More recent statements suggest a selective procedure: 'The single European market will open up a new dimension in the evolution of Allfinanz strategies. Can a national Allfinanz strategy also be applied to the total European market? An Allfinanz strategy which aims to offer the entire range of products and services in every market is doomed to failure from the start. For example, Deutsche Bank's domestic product range is already a quantitative challenge. Cross-border activities, in particular, demand selectivity not only in products, but also in geographical areas and markets.'[86]

Finally, mention should be made of the most recent explicit programmatic statement. Kopper's answer to a question on strategy in an interview with *Euromoney* in 1994: 'To be the market leader at home ... The second is to become a European bank ... It means we want to be a retail bank in Italy and Spain, and to be a corporate bank across Europe, where we want to be strong in corporate finance, and in trading money, currencies, fixed-income, equities and derivatives ... We are a European corporate bank, or a European trading bank, in the best traditions of a universal bank.'[87]

While it appears that the single European market has occupied a large part of the bank's business policy and strategic attention since it was first recognized as having secular opportunity and risk potential, it has never been forgotten – judging by many statements by members of the board of managing directors – that even the extended single European market cannot be a closed self-sufficient system, and that the bank's horizons can never be limited to Europe's borders. All measures serving the implementation of the European strategy and of, in Kopper's words, 'the strategy of opportunistic, selective acquisition'[88] are to be seen as embedded in a (still) more extensive strategic framework. A long-term European strategy has to be integrated into the bank's overall strategy; apart from the question of how far concrete ideas regarding the bank's role as global player can be developed, its perspective is a global one. Together with its European strategy, the bank's path towards its present global positioning can be understood by tracing the principal institutional steps in its development.

2. The international institutional development of Deutsche Bank

All in all, Deutsche Bank's policy of going international or institutional internationalization has been both long and successful to date. This process must be seen in conjunction with the ongoing development of its services programme

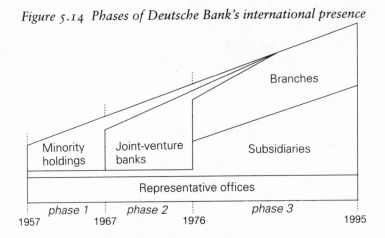

Figure 5.14 *Phases of Deutsche Bank's international presence*

(see pp. 726–31). Apart from this, two further elements are of interest: location policy and the structural organization of its international presence.

Three partially overlapping phases can be seen in its international institutional development (Figure 5.14). The first one, from 1957 to 1967, is characterized by a rather sparse international presence with a few representative offices and minority holdings (low profile). The second one, from 1967 to 1976, featured the intensification of the bank's presence abroad through many (minority) holdings (still low profile due to indirect representation) in banks, founded within EBIC. In the third phase, since 1976, the bank has adopted the policy of "going it alone"; in this phase it has used every form of foreign representation in order to achieve a global presence, and has dispensed where possible with minority holdings if they were only able to offer little scope for influence (high profile).

At the beginning of the first phase in 1957, the bank reported some early international holdings in its Annual Report. It had held a 15 per cent stake in Banco Español en Alemania S.A., Madrid, (up to 1983) since the bank's foundation initiated by Deutsche Bank and Banco Exterior de España in 1953. It also had a 16.6 per cent shareholding in Consafrique – Consortium Européen pour le Développement des Ressources Naturelles de l'Afrique S.A., Luxemburg. The bank had a 3.7 per cent stake in Deltec Panamericana S.A., founded in 1947, with its legal domicile in Panama and business headquarters in Nassau/Bahamas. Its articles of association allowed Deltec to own a very extensive body of corporations complete with numerous subsidiaries in almost every country in South America, Mexico, the USA, Canada and throughout Europe. At that time, the areas of trade finance and consulting were of particular interest to Deutsche Bank. In addition, the bank had acquired another shareholding in 1957 – for historical reasons – of 19.6 per cent in Handel-Maatschappij H. Albert de Bary & Co. N.V., Amsterdam, a 49.4 per cent shareholding in Société

Européenne de Développement Industriel S.A., Paris, and in Transoceanic Development Corporation Ltd, Toronto. It also had a 52.5 per cent shareholding in Deutsche Ueberseeische Bank AG, Berlin-Hamburg (DUB), originally founded as a subsidiary in 1886 to handle only foreign business, especially in Latin America.

By taking over the offices of its three predecessors in 1957, the bank was present in only a few centres in the form of representative offices. One representative office was set up in Turkey (Istanbul) in 1954. Others were in Argentina (Buenos Aires) from 1954, Mexico (Mexico City) from 1955, Venezuela (Caracas) from 1955, Brazil (São Paulo from 1955, Rio de Janeiro from 1956) and Chile (Santiago) from 1956. The offices in Latin America were representative offices both for the bank itself and for its subsidiary DUB. The latter tried in this way to link up with its network of subsidiaries which had existed before the Second World War.

Branches and subsidiaries had not yet been set up abroad; with the exception of DUB, domiciled in Germany, the bank had to date only taken up minority holdings. However, it may be noted that in 1957 there was regional concentration in South and Central America in the form of holdings in banks and via representative offices. The network of representative offices and minority holdings – and later of branches and subsidiaries – was extended through the already expanded system of correspondent banks.

Deutsche Bank's philosophy and strategy in international business and international representation in the 1950s were reflected clearly in the regional presence and business emphasis of minority-held banks and representative offices. It saw itself as a German bank with international activities geared to financing foreign trade in goods and services and settlement of the documentary and clean payment transactions associated with it. In this context its foreign representation was adequate for advising customers on questions of foreign trade, and the extensive network of correspondent banks could handle payments business.

During the 1950s and 1960s, the network of foreign representative offices abroad was extended in accordance with the expected development of German foreign trade. In 1958 a representative office was set up for the Middle East in Egypt (Cairo); in 1961 a joint office of DUB and Deutsche Bank was founded in Colombia (Bogotá); a joint representative office in Japan (Tokyo) followed a year later. The representative office in the Lebanon (Beirut), opened in 1966 and closed in 1981 due to the civil war, supplemented the activities of the bank's offices in Cairo, and served the Lebanon, Jordan, Iran, Iraq, Syria, Kuwait, Afghanistan and Cyprus.

At the end of the 1950s, increasingly important challenges arose in the expectation of ongoing European integration and growing economic links between the German economy and overseas. The main activities were advising customers on foreign business and helping them establish new business contacts. Here, the bank's foreign holdings which were intensifed, proved helpful. Several more interests were acquired: in 1959, Euroalliance Luxembourg (32.7 per cent); in 1960, Foreign Trade Bank of Iran (14.5 per cent); in 1964, Banque Commerciale du Maroc (10 per cent, up to 1989).

Later on, Banco Comercial Transatlántico ('Bancotrans'), Barcelona, was to play a special role for the bank. It goes back to the branches of DUB (Banco Alemán Transatlántico) founded in 1904 (Barcelona) and 1907 (Madrid). After the Second World War, German assets in Spain were frozen by the Allies, and were confiscated without compensation in 1949. The Spanish state, as the new owner, sold the remaining assets to the shareholder group Banco Comercial Transatlántico. Deutsche Bank's stake of 22 per cent was created in 1968 from the takeover of the DUB interest which first became possible, after lengthy negotiations, with 10 per cent.

In the late 1950s and 1960s, capital investment by German companies in the developing countries gained new significance. In order to guarantee them the best possible service, the bank acquired minority holdings in developing banks in these states (e.g. in Tehran, Bombay, Karachi, Rabat, Bogota, Kuala Lumpur and Seoul). They were to enable the bank – according to Abs in 1964 – 'to hop slowly from country to country, without actually entering a foreign country, from a country in which we have a stake in a development bank'. In addition, since 1962 the bank had taken over minority holdings in the French-speaking countries of Black Africa (in Abidjan, Yaoundé, Coutonou, Dakar, Lomé, Brazzaville and Fort Lamy). These had been chiefly brought about by Crédit Lyonnais, which during the process of decolonization had withdrawn from the former French territories, inviting Italian, American and German banks to acquire stakes in their companies in the emerging states.

Deutsche Bank assumed that the former French – and then EC-associated – areas would become increasingly interesting for German exporters; initially, they were not taken on for reasons of profitability, but rather as contact points for the bank's customers and the development of the local economy. Before they were acquired, it was agreed that no long-term credit requests within these companies should be submitted to the bank; Abs, at a press conference in 1963, said: 'We did not acquire these holdings without first making sure that we don't become the father of children.'

Minority holdings were a preferred form of foreign presence because they made it possible to gain an insight into regional conditions so that customers could be advised appropriately. In addition, the bank could, through individual minority-held banks, fulfil loan requests of German companies with subsidiaries in these countries. At the minority-held institutions, local personnel and capital always played a significant role, which made co-operation with that country's business community easier. In addition, the bank aimed to grant the banks, especially those in developing countries, support and encouragement; for this reason, the number of such holdings was restricted.

The main problem, however, was the scarcity of capital, which did not allow a more closely woven network of minority or even majority holdings. They were also rejected because they were seen as a burden on relations with local correspondent banks. A major problem with this kind of holding is that it is very difficult systematically to build up such a presence abroad. The same applies to correspondent banks. Attracting customers to a bank with a foreign name, the relatively high expenditure in return for limited influence, and the fact that the share in the affiliate's profit did not correspond to the share of business obtained were the major obstacles to such a strategy.

For the same reasons that did not favour minority holdings, the loose network of representative offices, established chiefly in co-operation with DUB anyway, was not expanded or supplemented with branches. Moreover, the bank regarded branches as largely obsolete in view of technological developments: 'Nowadays, telephones and planes have replaced the formerly difficult personal contact,' said Abs in London in 1963.

In this first phase, the transfer of information between the bank and its few foreign bases was guaranteed by a system in which employees were recalled to Germany to report at three-year intervals; these employees were available to the bank's customers. With regard to internal organization, it proved expedient to combine the managements of the foreign departments of the three central offices in Frankfurt, and to create a 'Central Foreign Department'. This went into operation in 1969.

The multinationalization of large companies took on clearer contours in the 1960s, and involved a corresponding structural change in the world economy. International *investment* finance gained further importance compared with the hitherto dominant *export* finance. These companies expected their banks to offer them a comprehensive on-the-spot service in the major countries. In the second phase of internationalization, this required Deutsche Bank's presence at the investment locations of its customers, and the bank also had to be represented at important financial centres in order to strengthen the acquisition of new customers abroad. In addition, important changes took place in its international business sector: the advancement of American banks all over the world, especially in Europe, and the development of the Euromarket as an exterritorial financial and capital market; account was also taken of the expected rapid assimilation of European economies.

The bank allowed for structural change by constantly expanding its foreign network. Starting in the late 1960s, the bank stepped up its foreign presence simultaneously at three different levels: by setting up new representative offices and branches of its subsidiary DUB, which had the bulk of its activity in Latin America; through the establishment of a Luxemburg subsidiary for the Euromarket; and especially through considerably intensified co-operation with partner banks in Europe and the formation of joint bases outside of Europe.

Faced with the question of whether to adjust to the changed overall conditions in international business by setting up its own branches and/or acquiring holdings of shares, or to give preference to certain areas of extensive co-operation with other banks, Deutsche Bank chose the latter alternative. The explanation given, which was to change considerably later on, was that a highly developed banking apparatus and a sufficiently dense branch network already existed in the industrial countries of Europe, and thus reciprocal expansion of national branch networks beyond national borders did not appear desirable. In addition, an essential consideration was that in this way one could strengthen the expected rapidly progressing political and economic development in the EC, as well as co-operation between the leading European banks, while at the same time operating together in important regions of the world.

The bank's decision was guided by its traditional intention not only to maintain relations with other banks, but to deepen them, and not to endanger traditional contacts with correspondent banks all over the world. An aspect not to be underestimated was the experience of twice losing many foreign branches after the world wars. Abs summarized this at the 10th German Banking Conference in 1963, while not mentioning the scarcity of capital, which was the main factor behind the decision in favour of co-operation: 'Reliable partnerships are a stable foundation for growing co-operation in all areas of the bank. One cannot identify national economic reasons for a supranational expansion of the bank's branch network, nor do they appear sensible and attractive from a private economic perspective.'

The first discussions on the possibility of co-operation took place in 1958 between Amsterdamsche Bank, Banque de la Société Générale de Belgique and Deutsche Bank. The co-operation which followed at first remained behind the scenes: the 'club des célibataires' reached an agreement to work partly together, but did not want it made public, so as not to endanger correspondent bank connections and business relations. The final result was an agreement with the aforementioned institutions plus Midland Bank, and was announced by Deutsche Bank in 1963. Disclosure of the co-operation followed because the impending European integration was seen as a fact, because co-operation between banks was accepted, and because competitors had announced similar agreements.

A European Advisory Council was founded, in which two members of the bank and the other banks were represented. In 1971 two more partners from France and Austria joined, and in 1973 an Italian partner. The aim of the agreement was to establish mutual consultation, exchange experiences, hold regular discussions on matters of common interest, and create a joint starting point for specific types of business, especially large-scale international financing. In addition, they wanted to co-operate on economic studies and to exchange their findings in order to improve customer services. As they believed in rapid European integration, a future merger into a 'European Bank' was seen as an objective. There are few examples of such misjudgement.

Up to 1970 co-operation led to the formation of joint subsidiary banks, and representative offices were opened in Indonesia and South Africa. This induced the partners to form a more solid institutional framework for their co-operation: in October 1970 they founded the European Banks' International Company S.A. (EBIC) with capital of $2 million and its headquarters in Brussels. EBIC's terms of reference, in addition to functioning as a management company for the group, were to co-ordinate co-operation within the scope of the targets pursued by the European Advisory Council, and to prepare new activities, including the establishment of joint representative offices and further subsidiaries abroad. Creditanstalt-Bankverein in Vienna and Société Générale, Paris, which joined the European Advisory Council in 1971, also became EBIC members. Banca Commerciale Italiana joined in 1973.

While the capital of the four founding members was privately owned, the banks that joined in 1971 and 1973 were mostly state owned. Since, on the one hand, the co-operation was to be extended to include the latter but, on the other hand, the long-term objective of 'European Bank', including state or state-controlled institutions, appeared neither viable nor desirable, the expansion of EBIC was preceded by many discussions. In the end, the state partner banks also agreed in principle with the target of merger, with the reservation that they could decide to participate either not at all or only partly in its realization. The decisive point, however, was that, in view of the very slow pace of European integration, the original partners, too, meanwhile saw the merger as a very distant prospect, as more of a theoretical option.

The management of EBIC rested with the board of directors, which was chaired in rotation by each institution; this board was made up of members of the European Advisory Council, to which two members from each partner bank belonged. In 1977 the European Advisory Council was renamed the 'Board of EBIC', and was responsible for fundamental questions. The 'Management Committee' took care of routine affairs. In addition, there were also committees and working groups.

Co-operation in EBIC was influenced greatly by its international institutional development. This was based on product-related co-operation, which extended from a joint offering in international finance and mutual funds to co-operation in the services sector, organizational and security questions, and macroeconomic analyses. Various 'programmes' were developed as joint products of the group: EBICREDIT, for example, was to accelerate and simplify customers' borrowing in partner countries; every branch of the bank was to be in a position to have loans granted by the appropriate EBIC bank to German customers' branches and subsidiaries domiciled in other EBIC countries; EBICLEASE was to offer exporters additional financing options; and EBICEM was to help train internationally orientated employees, who could then work in partner banks or joint ventures.

In 1967, three years before the formation of EBIC in Brussels, Banque Européenne de Crédit à Moyen Terme (BEC) was founded by Amsterdam-

Rotterdam Bank, Midland Bank, Société Générale de Banque, Samuel Montagu & Co. and Deutsche Bank. That same year Banca Commerciale Italiana, Crédit Lyonnais and Société Générale joined as well. In 1970 Creditanstalt-Bankverein acquired a stake in BEC; at the end of 1971 Crédit Lyonnais withdrew, owing to its membership of another European group.

BEC was to function as a specialized bank dealing in longer-term loan business with companies operating in Europe and requiring borrowed funds for international investment; public institutions were, however, also financed. Subsequently BEC became more and more involved in long-term international syndicated lending business. It established a leading position as a consortium bank, especially for medium and long-term Euro-credit. In 1968 BEC Finance N.V., Amsterdam, was founded as a subsidiary for Euromarket finance. From 1970 on, BEC began more and more to compete with Deutsche Bank's Luxemburg subsidiary, which had been formed in the meantime.

In 1973 it was renamed Banque Européenne de Crédit (BEC). Deutsche Bank held its stake in BEC until 1986, from 1982 to 1985 indirectly through the European Banking Group Ltd., London. In 1986 the EBIC partners liquidated BEC: firstly, the international debt crisis had caused such a high adjustment requirement at BEC that only a new capital injection could secure its existence; and secondly, BEC's services for the EBIC partners were now handled by their own Euromarket subsidiaries, so that BEC was no longer important enough to justify such capital contributions.

European Banking Company Ltd., as a further EBIC joint venture, came into being in London in 1973. It operated in international finance and issuing business, particularly in Eurodollar lending. As a merchant bank it also set up financial consulting services. In the late 1970s it became involved in project finance, leasing and asset management, and also in foreign exchange.

In 1982 EBC and BEC were combined to form European Banking Group Ltd., London. As far as business policy was concerned, this did not mean a significant change. Hence, Deutsche Bank, in conjunction with the establishment of its own subsidiary in London, was able to sell its 14.1 per cent stake in EBC in 1985 to Amsterdam-Rotterdam Bank, which took over the whole of the former EBC from the EBIC partners and, in doing so, ended the union of the two banks after just three years.

On 1 May 1968, the member banks of the European Advisory Council decided in New York to establish the first consortium bank in the form of European American Banking Corporation and European American Bank & Trust Company (EAB banks). The foundation consisted of Deutsche Bank, Amro-Bank and Midland Bank entering partnerships with Belgian American Banking Corporation and Belgian American Bank & Trust Company, which originated in 1927 and had hitherto belonged to Société Générale de Banque. Deutsche Bank had a $20 million holding. The circle of shareholders expanded subsequently with the admission of new partners to the European Advisory Council and EBIC. These two institutions had been Deutsche Bank's most significant foreign holdings until then, and EBIC's most important joint ventures.

To be at customers' disposal with its own financial commitment and to give them local banking support, the bank set up a German department staffed largely with Deutsche Bank people. Much of EAB Group's business was handled by this 'German desk'. The partners offered Euro-currency loans via EAB's off-shore branch – European American Banking Corporation in Nassau (Bahamas) – set up in 1969. Special attention was devoted here to financing the subsidiaries of European companies in the USA. Also in 1969, EAB set up European American Finance (Bermuda) Ltd. The reasons behind the branches opened in Los Angeles and San Francisco in 1972 were to make better use of business opportunities in the Californian market and give better access to the Pacific region.

The total assets of EBIC's two New York entities exceeded $4 billion in 1974. The growth was due mainly to the takeover of large parts of Franklin National Bank, New York. This bank was insolvent due to big losses, especially in foreign exchange trading, and was publicly auctioned in October 1974; EAB Group won the bidding. It thereby entered retail banking and substantially widened its business base. The European American Banks together were now among the 25 biggest US banks.

But the takeover was a substantial burden on EAB. It was only when the decrease in customers was turned around and the number of employees strongly cut that EAB's profits improved again from 1978. Also a thing of the past was the pressure on profits resulting from the default on a large loan to the Colocotronis oil tanker shipping group. In 1976, EAB and Deutsche Bank were sued for having obtained the plaintiff syndicate members' participation in the loan on the basis of false information. The dispute was resolved out of court in 1978, but write-downs and payments to the plaintiffs substantially reduced EAB profits up to 1978.

In 1977 European American Banking Corporation and European American Bank & Trust Company were combined in a holding company, European American Bancorp. All the EBIC partners, apart from the Italian member, had stakes in the company. Deutsche Bank continued to hold 20.1 per cent, and from 1985, in connection with the reorganization of EBIC holdings, 23.2 per cent, through German American Capital Corporation, Baltimore, set up in 1971. To obtain the permit for a joint holding company, EAB had to close its offices in San Francisco and Los Angeles within two years. European American Bank & Trust Company was admitted to the New York Clearing House Association in 1978, the first foreign-owned bank to receive this privilege.

The further institutional development at EAB Group was as follows: in 1977 a subsidiary was formed in Chicago, in 1979 a branch in Luxemburg for foreign exchange trading and Euromarket business; in 1980 the subsidiary EAB Venture Corporation in New York, the purpose of which was to promote smaller growth-oriented enterprises by providing high-quality technological systems and equipment; 1981 saw the opening of a subsidiary in Miami for the intensification of international business; in 1981 the acquisition of Dorman & Wilson Inc., White Plains, which was engaged in mortgage intermediation and administration, and offered a full-range property consulting service; in 1982 a 20 per cent holding in Banque Européenne pour L'Amerique Latine S.A., Brussels, was acquired, along with branches and representative offices in Latin America. By 1980, thanks to these acquisitions and new companies, EAB was also operating in the intermediation of long-term financings, corporate intermediation and property consulting.

In February 1978 Deutsche Bank announced what had been the subject of speculation since 1975: that it was planning its own network of representative offices in the USA for American big-loan business. The first presence came in New York in 1978, in branch form right from the start. This was followed in 1982 by representative offices in Los Angeles and Chicago; at the same time, Deutsche Bank intensified its presence through subsidiaries. There were frequent rumours from 1978 onwards that the bank planned to divest its EAB shares; but this was denied with equal regularity, although it can be noted that EAB was seen increasingly from a yield aspect and less from the perspective of business representation. In 1988 agreement was reached with Amro Bank that the latter would receive the 23.15 per cent share in the European American Bancorp holding company in return for Amro Bank's remaining 50 per cent in H. Albert de Bary & Co. Midland Bank also sold its share in EAB to Creditanstalt-Bankverein.

The reason for Deutsche Bank holding on to EAB for so long was its business structure at the time: its portfolio contained a large number of problem loans, especially to South American borrowers. Though these were transferred to the holding company, reducing the adjustment requirement to be reported in the bank's balance sheet, the result on the one hand was that for a long time no EBIC partner or external party was ready to increase its stakes or buy shares. On the other hand, the US bank regulator was not prepared to release a solvent EBIC partner from its responsibility. The concentration of the circle of shareholders in 1988 made it easier for the bank to focus on its future tasks. At the same time, this step meant the end of EAB as the strongest and last symbol of club banking within the framework of EBIC co-operation.

Euro-Pacific Finance Corporation Ltd., Melbourne, set up in 1970, was founded by the four EBIC banks in co-operation with other institutions (Fuji Bank, Commercial Bank of Australia, United California Bank) for the medium- and long-term financing and advising of Australian subsidiaries of companies from EBIC countries and Australia, as well as domestic and foreign deposits business and underwriting, including the Eurodollar market. The institution could also operate outside Australia through the branch in Port Vila/New Hebrides. This off-shore company was used above all for international loan syndication. In 1978 a branch was set up in Hong Kong for off-shore business.

In 1985 the bank sold its holding as part of the run-up to formation of its own Australian subsidiary.

Deutsche Bank brought Deutsch-Asiatische Bank AG (DAB), Hamburg, into the European Asian Bank AG joint venture, set up in 1972 by what at the time had still been six EBIC banks. DAB had been formed in 1889 with its domicile in Shanghai by leading German banks. In the wake of the two world wars, it had lost its foreign branch network; in 1945 its Berlin office was closed and in 1953 its domicile changed to Hamburg. From 1958, DAB had rebuilt its foreign branch network: branches were opened in Hong Kong (1958), Karachi (1962), Kuala Lumpur (1968) and Jakarta (1969).

In 1972 – after the withdrawal of other shareholders – Deutsche Bank remained with 36 per cent, Dresdner Bank 22 per cent, Bleichröder 10 per cent and Commerzbank 10 per cent as large shareholders. In the reorganization of the big banks' holdings, Deutsche Bank took over most of DAB. While the other shareholders sold their shares to Deutsche Bank, Dresdner Bank received DAB's recently opened Singapore branch. But by the end of 1972, a new branch of European Asian Bank was already doing business there.

When Euras Bank was founded by EBIC, the initial intention was only close co-operation with DAB. The merger in December 1972 by transfer of the branches and business of DAB, in which the other EBIC partners had meanwhile taken stakes, to Euras Bank became possible because agreement was reached with the countries in which DAB had branches that the latter could be maintained by Euras. Subsequently Euras opened further branches (Manila, Seoul, Bangkok, Bombay, Colombo, Taipei and Macao) and representative offices (Sydney, Tokyo and Lahore) in the Far East. Through its branch network, therefore, Euras Bank was thus represented in all states of the expanding ASEAN (Association of South-East Asian Nations) community, a total of 11 countries, and thus had one of the most comprehensive presences in the region among all the European banks. In 1977 it was restyled European Asian Bank AG.

The objective of Euras Bank was to promote trade and financial relations between Europe and Asia, and within Asian countries, and the participation of EBIC in these relations. It proved to be an increasingly efficient international commercial bank and at the same time a qualified business intermediary for customers of EBIC banks in the East Asian economic area. It was particularly active in the syndication of international loans for South-East Asia, and was considered to be a specialist in the financing of trade between Asia and Europe.

In the middle of 1983 there was a reorganization of holdings because the activities of the EBIC partners in the region were developing differently, and some of them wanted to establish a presence there under their own names. Deutsche Bank's holding after reorganization was 60 per cent. In 1984, in view of the negative development at Euras Bank, Deutsche Bank issued a guarantee on its behalf for 300 million DM. Nevertheless, there was a high adjustment requirement until 1986. The reasons given by the bank for this negative development were economic problems in individual countries in the region and – put most diplomatically despite the massive losses involved – management errors, over-hasty expansion and lack of risk awareness.

On 1 January 1986, the holding structure was again reorganized: Amro Bank and Société Générale sold their stakes to Creditanstalt-Bankverein and Deutsche Bank, which thereby held 25 per cent and 75 per cent respectively. The latter took most of the bad loans into its portfolio in order to square the balance sheet at Euras Bank. It was agreed that it would shortly take over Euras Bank entirely (see p. 764).

European Arab Holding S.A. and its subsidiaries – Eurab group – were founded in 1972 by EBIC and 14 leading Arab banks under Luxemburg law. In 1975 the number of shareholders was raised to include two further Arab banks and Swiss Bank Corporation, Fuji Bank and Industrial Bank of Japan. Deutsche Bank had a stake of 5.7 per cent to begin with, from 1983 12.8 per cent. All partners transferred parts of their business to the Eurab subsidiaries. These – as working units of the holding company – were European Arab Bank S.A., Brussels (1972), Europäisch-Arabische Bank GmbH, Frankfurt (1972), European Arab Bank Ltd., London (1976) and European Arab Bank (Middle East) E.C., Manama (1978/79).

After the international debt crisis had become apparent in 1982, there was a high adjustment requirement for the Eurab banks resulting from South American problem loans. In 1985 the group discontinued its new business; business still to be wound up was transferred to the London company; the other companies were liquidated between 1989 and 1991, and so too subsequently was the Luxemburg holding company. In 1987 the London company was restyled European Arab Finance Ltd. after surrendering its banking licence, and after that administered its residual portfolio.

There was also institutional expansion in EBIC through joint representative offices. It opened one in Jakarta in 1969, European Banks International, which was merged in 1972 with the Jakarta branch of European Asian Bank. A joint office of the EBIC partners was also set up in 1969 in Johannesburg as European Banks International with the additional task of representing the interests of EAB. In 1980 Deutsche Bank took over the representative office. As the final joint representative office, EBIC partners set up an office in Canada in 1971 under the name European Banks International Representative Office Toronto. In 1975 the office was taken over by Deutsche Bank as its own representative office.

At the beginning of the 1980s, EBIC was represented by subsidiaries, minority holdings, offices and representative offices at all important international financial centres. Accordingly, the bank could serve its customers directly or indirectly in the major segments of international business. But the banking landscape had changed substantially, and the partners agreed that it would benefit the group if, besides their active participation in the joint ventures, they were also to build up their own presence at important international financial centres so as to keep pace with the growing competition. This retreat – which basically heralded the approaching demise of co-operation – was given makeshift legitimacy by formulation of a two-tier strategy: what is good for one bank is good for EBIC too.

The (changed) policy of pushing ahead with the expansion of the partners under their own names was indicated in 1980 by Christians, spokesman of the board of managing directors: the joint institutions supplemented geographically and functionally the international business of the individual EBIC banks; the danger that the two-tier strategy could lead to tension in the co-operation was openly admitted. But reference was made to regulative arrangements, e.g. by Christians on 3 December 1980 in the *Financial Times*, to the effect that it was not intended to expand the bank's own activities in retail banking to the countries of the EBIC partners. And so the reasons quoted by the bank for the decline of EBIC – and generally for European banks' 'club banking' in general – were:

– The strongest partners were willing and able from the end of the 1970s to assume themselves the risks and the costs, the distribution of which among several partners when starting operations in overseas regions had formerly been quoted as the main reason for club banking.
– The strong partners wanted to fly their own flags.
– The stakes in joint ventures, and thus the profit shares, were becoming increasingly disproportionate to the business referrred to the joint ventures (Kopper in 1988).

Looking back, the decline of EBIC was also due to the fact that it was not possible to control the consortium banks' own momentum through standardization of the tasks assigned to EBIC. The scope that arose made it possible for EBIC joint ventures to operate largely autonomously.

A major reason frequently cited today for the formation of EBIC was its character as a counter-offensive to the advance of American banks into Europe. This seems to contain an opportunistic element inasmuch as the decline of EBIC – and of club banking in general – in the 1980s came about because it had fulfilled its original task. But if one assumes a further motive in addition to co-operation, namely to merge into a Europe bank, then EBIC failed completely to achieve its target. In Deutsche Bank's present, more pragmatic view, however, the EBIC co-operation was not a mistake, but a sensible interim step in its institutional development. In the case of Euras Bank, which was taken over in full along with its subsidiaries by Deutsche Bank, the co-operation was actually an essential driving force behind the development of its own presence, as Kopper stressed in 1988.

After 1975 it proved to be increasingly necessary for the bank, as a now truly international bank – i.e. as a bank not only with German customers in Germany and abroad – to operate under its own name at international financial centres. Institutionally, this meant – as a third phase in the process of internationalization – setting up branches and/or subsidiaries and acquiring majority holdings. The objective was to gain strong access to international financial centres and to open up markets with growth potential in lending and securities business.

Here, strategic thinking focused on three main areas, namely the so-called Triad: the Pacific Basin, Europe and North America. Great importance was assumed here – after the establishment of branches world-wide for investment banking and corporate finance as part of the globalization of financial markets – by the European region with the implementation, starting in 1986, of the single EC-wide market. As Krumnow clearly stated: 'One day, Europe is to become for us what the Federal Republic already is today: our home market.'

But Europe-wide retail banking was not the target here. Investment banking bases were set up at the financial centres, and additionally a broader retail banking clientele was generated in some countries selected for their market and income opportunities through the acquisition of subsidiaries: the bank became a 'European player'.

A main reason for the strategic change was the ongoing integration of the world economy, which made it essential to adjust in good time to new horizons and challenges in international business – in terms of know-how as well as magnitudes and tougher competition. Speed and flexibility in the response to customer wishes, careful cultivation of foreign contacts and steady development of the services offering in this area were necessary but not sufficient preconditions for the sustainment of the bank's high share of international business. Also essential to maintaining the efficiency of a universal bank in the world economic environment are a strong financial capacity, broad placement potential in issuing business, highly efficient systems for the settlement of all foreign exchange and payments transactions, comprehensive advice and service, and thus a comprehensive institutional presence in international business and financial activities. As Kopper stated in 1990 in a lecture at the Institut für Bankwirtschaft at the University of Cologne: 'Banks are therefore compelled, in the interest of their customers, to maintain an efficient infrastructure which allows them – directly or indirectly – to be present at all important financial centres and in all important currencies. In future, every bank will have to be an international bank if it is to survive.'

In accordance with this target, the bank has achieved unparalleled systematic expansion of its foreign organization to date. In the third phase, therefore, the focus was no longer exclusively on accompanying and supporting German companies in 'going abroad'; the bank was now increasingly interested in intensifying its links with local customers and with non-German international corporations. The question of funding also made it necessary to use the opportunities available on international and local financial markets. Furthermore, the search for a foreign presence in the bank's own name was stimulated in the 1980s by the approaching single European market. The starting point for the bank's

European strategy was that the more nationally a business activity is conducted, the greater the danger to it. With regard to its positioning in the (future) single market, therefore, it was guided by the objective of a network of locations characterized by regional equilibrium and – as mentioned above – encompassing retail business. The European strategy was to be implemented chiefly by capturing market share, so as to implement the concept of Europe-wide distribution with supranational market penetration in selected customer and product groups.

The strategic shift towards 'going it alone', which was preceded by a period of intensive research, was reflected first in two measures taken in 1976. First, there was the conversion of the London representative office, founded in 1973, into a branch. The bank was thus represented again in the City, as it had been from 1873 to 1914, with its first foreign branch since 1914. It was intended to serve international customers rather than do purely British business, and was not to compete directly with EBIC partner Midland Bank. Second, the integration of Deutsche Ueberseeische Bank (DUB) into the group also had the target of letting the bank conduct international business more strongly in its own name.

The foundation of DUB as a subsidiary for foreign business dates back to 1886. It built up a foreign branch network which it lost in the aftermath of the world wars. In 1957 Deutsche Bank had 52.5 per cent of DUB. In 1967 the bank made a takeover bid to shareholders to give them a chance to sell their shares, as they could not be satisfied with the dividends paid by DUB in view of the rebuilding of its foreign branch network and the currency risks. By 1975, the bank's stake had risen to 97.4 per cent.

In 1976 DUB's foreign bases comprised a branch in Buenos Aires with ten city branches, since the restitution in 1960 of the branch confiscated in 1945 – subject to the condition that a true bank was to be set up and not simply a representative office – and further branches in São Paulo from 1969, Asunción from 1971 and in Tokyo from 1971. Over and above that, DUB had representative offices in Bogotá, Caracas, Mexico, Rio de Janeiro, La Paz and Santiago de Chile, and an office in Luxemburg from 1974. With the integration of DUB into Deutsche Bank Group in 1976, its business activity was restricted to South America. The reason given by Ulrich for this in 1976 at the General Meeting of DUB was the new strategy of Deutsche Bank, namely to be present abroad in its own name and under its own management, but also the wish to achieve synergy effects in terms of know-how, administration and managing borrowers' total exposures and country risks.

DUB's successful Tokyo branch became Deutsche Bank's second foreign branch after the integration. On the other hand, the South American branches continued to operate for the time being under the traditional names Banco Alemán Transatlántico in Argentina (Buenos Aires and Rosario) and Banco Alemão Transatlântico in São Paulo, as did the subsidiaries in Luxemburg (Succursale de Luxembourg) and Paraguay (Banco Alemán Transatlántico). It was not until 1978 that the DUB subsidiaries in Argentina, Brazil and Paraguay became

Deutsche Bank branches. The Rosario branch was sold to Bank of America in 1978, as its business development did not meet expectations. The Asunción branch was spun off in 1989 as Banco Alemán Paraguayo, converted into a joint stock corporation under Paraguayan law, and sold. The integration of DUB into Deutsche Bank also increased the latter's holding in Adela Investment Company S.A., Luxemburg, and led to the takeover of several South American stakes, some of them becoming subsidiaries.

If one looked back over important stages in the corporate activity of majority holdings and subsidiaries in the third phase of Deutsche Bank's expansion, one would have to begin with Compagnie Financière de la Deutsche Bank AG in the commercial bank subsidiary sector. Founded in Luxemburg in 1970, it had a full bank licence and membership of the Luxemburg Bank Association, and existed purely as a Eurobank without local or counter transactions. Again, Deutsche Bank was not a pioneer: in institutional terms, it was the last of the German big banks to take account of the development of the Euromoney market in the late 1960s, with Luxemburg at the centre.

Placing the Luxemburg subsidiary in the third phase is factually, but not temporally accurate, because it was set up in 1970 before some EBIC banks. It must therefore be viewed in the light of the developments in the late 1950s: the European corporate market was already significant which, under the aspect of competition, required its own presence in Luxemburg and therefore excluded other solutions – for example, a further EBIC venture. Even in 1973/74 the Luxemburg subsidiary reported higher total assets than the EBIC bank Banque Européenne de Crédit à Moyen Terme, and this clearly indicated Deutsche Bank's changing interest.

The Luxemburg subsidiary was primarily formed to handle the bank's Euro-financing business; other activities were added in the course of time. The emphasis was still on the syndication of international loans. Amounts repayable to other banks were the funding basis for its lending business. Long-term funds were raised in the form of loans from Deutsche Bank Finance N.V., Curaçao, under guarantee from the parent company. With the securitization fashion starting roughly in 1986, traditional medium-term lending business slackened but remained an important component. Innovative instruments had always been issued chiefly by the bank's London branch and, to a lesser extent, by Luxemburg.

Developments at the Luxemburg subsidiary were reflected in changes in its style: in the late 1970s it was renamed Deutsche Bank Compagnie Financière de Luxembourg, and in 1987 Deutsche Bank Luxembourg S.A. In view of the increasing significance of private banking in Luxemburg, it incorporated this business and also asset management and portfolio management for institutional customers into its product range, and thus developed significantly beyond its original character as a Eurofinancing bank. Through its Luxemburg subsidiary, Deutsche Bank took a 5 per cent stake in Banque de Luxembourg S.A., raising it to 25 per cent in 1981 in view of the increasing significance of private banking, and 7.4 per cent of Société Européenne des Satellites S.A., Luxemburg, set up in 1985. In 1991 DB Lux entered spacious new premises designed by Gottfried Böhm, the Cologne architect, thereby documenting its view that Luxemburg would remain a financial centre over the longer term.

DB U.K. Finance Ltd., London, founded in 1976, operated as a commercial bank; however, it was a bank only under German law, while under the British legal system it was a financing company and therefore not subject to bank legislation. This provided tax and supervisory law advantages. Although it was affiliated with the London branch and shared the same management, it used only the abbreviated style 'DB' to document its non-bank character. Accordingly, DB U.K. Finance remained unaffected by the restructuring of the bank's activities in London in 1991/92.

Singapore was the centre of the Asian dollar market and was a very important financial centre; therefore, great significance was attached to Deutsche Bank (Asia Credit) Ltd., founded in 1978. It operated mainly in the syndicated loan division in the East Asian region in their short-, medium- and long-term financing business, as well as in foreign exchange and money dealing. Hence the ASEAN countries were to be accessible for the bank, because otherwise it could only operate indirectly through Euras Bank. During the reorganization of company activities in Asia in 1988, the so-called merchant banking division was transferred to the Singapore branch of the bank; it did not actively participate in business after that.

Deutsche Bank (Canada), Toronto, was founded in 1981 following the spin-off from the representative office. The establishment of the subsidiary was possible after permission was granted to foreign banks, under banking legislation, to conduct business fully in Canada. Branches, which the bank actually preferred, were not permitted, and so a subsidiary had to be chosen. As a subsidiary of Deutsche Bank (Canada), the securities house McLean McCarthy Ltd., Toronto, was wholly acquired in 1988. The operational sector of Deutsche Bank (Canada) included commercial banking with corporate and retail customers, with special emphasis on foreign trade as well as money and foreign exchange trading, and in addition it dealt with project financing specifically in the energy and extractive industry and in international payment transactions.

Deutsche Bank Australia Ltd. (DBAL), Melbourne, originated in 1986 when Deutsche Bank, as the only Continental European bank to do so, received permission to set up a trading bank which corresponds to a universal bank. In 1985 the holding in Euro-Pacific Finance Corporation Ltd., held through EBIC, was sold. The new institution took over the representative office in Sydney and had subsidiaries in the form of Deutsche Capital Management Australia Ltd., Melbourne – active since 1987 in mutual fund and portfolio management business for Australian institutions – and European Asian of Australia Ltd., Sydney, set up in 1982 as a merchant bank by European Asian Bank and State

Bank of New South Wales. Other subsidiaries were Deutsche Capital Markets Australia Ltd., Sydney, supplementing the parent's functions in investment banking from 1988, and Bain & Company Ltd., from 1988 with a holding of initially 50 per cent, acquired to be able to fulfil the merchant and investment banking requirements for Australian customers in the Anglo-Saxon style. Client relationships with leading Australian, German and multinational groups were continuously expanded, with domestic Australian business being the pre-dominant sector, interestingly enough, until today. A positive impulse came from the cautious business policy on participation in speculative acquisition financings. As part of the liberalization of the Australian financial system, Deutsche Bank received permission to open a branch in Sydney in 1994.

Deutsche Bank (Asia) AG, Hamburg, was the former European Asian Bank AG, founded in 1972 by EBIC. In 1987 Deutsche Bank acquired the remaining 25 per cent from Creditanstalt-Bankverein, the last EBIC partner in Euras Bank. While the latter wanted to obtain at least the book value of its holding, this appeared too high to Deutsche Bank, given the special risk structure of Euras Bank and the help it had already received. But it did not exploit its strong negotiating position. The bank's tradition of solving conflicts of interest as far as possible on a partner-like basis was greater than its desire to avoid a perhaps slightly excessive purchase price. Bankverein was able to end its participation, according to Androsch, chairman of the board of managing directors, 'after years of fluctuation, with neither a profit nor a loss'.

Deutsche Bank (Asia) was represented in Asia by 20 branches and subsidiaries. An interesting detail here is that the bank considerably simplified the transfer of business in Hong Kong from Deutsche Bank (Asia) to Deutsche Bank AG. For this purpose, a special act was passed in Hong Kong at its instigation – with a Chinese banker representing the bank as lobbyist. In the course of the restruc-turing of the group in South-East Asia, much of the business of Deutsche Bank (Asia) AG, Hamburg, and Deutsche Bank (Asia Credit) Ltd., Singapore, was transferred to the branch of the bank operating at the respective centre. The two institutions' former branches were maintained as branches of Deutsche Bank after the integration, and the activities of the former Euras head office in Hamburg were transferred to Singapore. The 'Regional Head Office' set up there in 1988 steers and co-ordinates the operating business of the acquired branches and subsidiaries in 13 Asian countries. The bank has thus been able to reorganize its presence in this area so as to increase the efficiency of the branches and achieve better penetration of markets with high growth potential. Thanks to its central position, political stability and excellent infrastructure, Singapore was preferred to Hong Kong and Bangkok. As in the USA, the management of the Asian and Australian activities was concentrated further in 1992. Management is deployed at the Singapore, Tokyo and Sydney centres.

Rumours that the bank intended to enter Italy by taking over a commercial bank came up repeatedly from 1984. Within the framework of its European strategy, it did indeed plan to create a stronger presence in that country. Deutsche Bank's management recognized that opening branches at several preferred centres was not sufficient for truly entrepreneurial activity, especially in other European countries. In this environment, it was considered time and again, sporadically rather than systematically, that the acquisition of intact units was a possible course of action if the bank wanted to take a real step into international business. Furthermore, the history of the bank showed that it had achieved its position – if one looks at the big steps – by acquisition rather than by organic growth.

In September 1986 the opportunity arose to acquire Banca d'America e d'Italia S.p.A. (BAI), Milan, from Bank of America (BoA) with its substantial problems. At first there was much scepticism, and it was only with great caution and hesitation that the bank took up the idea of operating in the south of Europe. So the first step was not enthusiastic at all. Kopper, responsible for Europe at that time, submitted the concept at the end of September 1986. Negotiations began under great time pressure, as the deal was to be concluded by the end of 1986. Deutsche Bank and Bank of America reached agreement – first by telephone under great time pressure due to the problems at BoA – on $603 million. On 1 December 1986 the supervisory board of Deutsche Bank and the board of BoA approved the deal, and on 18 December there was a final resolution by the board of managing directors of Deutsche Bank. The latter examined various models for integrating BAI institutionally into Deutsche Bank Group; the main aspect was taxation: the closing day was 23 December 1986, when the contract was signed in Frankfurt. The optimum venue for the signing was also vetted carefully. The staff of the two banks were informed about the acquisition shortly before the general public.

Before the end of the year, the shares of BAI previously owned by BoA – 98.3 per cent of voting capital – were brought to Frankfurt in physical certificates. Italian law requires investments by non-residents to be registered; the acquisition of BAI was such an investment. The purchase price therefore had to be converted into lire in Frankfurt, transferred to Milan for registration and from there to New York, where it was converted into dollars and credited to BoA in good time.

BAI had existed since 1917; it conducted mainly lending business with small and medium-sized companies and had a considerable market position in retail banking. The acquisition – according to Kopper in 1990 – laid 'the foundations for a comprehensive service to local, German and other foreign private and corporate customers in Italy'. BAI retained adequate independence and an Italian top management; however, in October 1994 – following Deutsche Bank's general line – its name was changed to Deutsche Bank S.p.A.; the traditional corporate style disappeared. Subsidiaries of BAI are BAI Leasing S.A. (1987), especially for commercial customers, BAI Factoring S.p.A. (1988), BAI Luxembourg S.p.A. and DB Finanziaria S.p.A. (1989), formed after the acquisition by Deutsche Bank. In September 1989 the bank bought from Barclays Group the latter's

Italian financial brokerage subsidiary Barclays Commissionaria S.p.A. (Barcom) – later Bank Commissionaria S.p.A., and from 1991 Deutsche Bank Commissionaria S.p.A. (DB Com). Barcom, with eight offices at Italian financial centres, was to support BAI in securities business. In 1991 DB Com became the first securities trading house in Italy to have a foreign capital stake. Through Bank Finanziaria S.p.A., Deutsche Bank held more than 50 per cent. The securities trading house was to conduct securities and bond business in the Italian market in close co-operation with BAI. Apparently it did not succeed: at the end of 1991 it was resold. In 1993 Deutsche Bank strengthened its position as the biggest foreign bank in Italy by acquiring – through BAI – 58.1 per cent of the capital of the Lombardian Banca Popolare di Lecco. The purchase price was 20 per cent above market price.

DB (Belgium) Finance S.A./N.V., which started operations in 1986, rounded off the product range of the bank's branches in Brussels and Antwerp. Its activities specifically comprise international lending business and the extension of longer-term loans to companies domiciled in Belgium, as well as securities trading.

H. Albert de Bary & Co. N.V., Amsterdam, had traditional links with the bank dating back to Disconto-Gesellschaft's holding in 1919. In 1945 Deutsche Bank held more than 95 per cent, which was confiscated by the Dutch state. In 1954 it repurchased 19.6 per cent and increased its holding to 20 per cent in 1960. The same interest was held by Amro Bank, Société Générale, Paris, Société Générale de Banque, Brussels, and Crédit Suisse. In 1977 the holdings were reorganized, and since the end of 1988 Deutsche Bank has had 100 per cent, with 50 per cent taken over in return for simultaneous transfer of the stake in European American Bancorp, New York, in favour of Amro Bank. The full acquisition rounded off Deutsche Bank's position in the Benelux states. De Bary specializes in financing and serving European and overseas foreign trade business. In 1992 Deutsche Bank became the third-largest market party on the Amsterdam Stock Exchange through de Bary.

In Spain, Deutsche Bank already took a 22.9 per cent stake in Banco Comercial Transatlántico S.A. (BCT) in 1968. This was increased to 25.2 per cent, then 28.8 per cent (1978), 29.5 per cent (1979) and on to 39 per cent (1988). Irrespective of the size of the holding, BCT remained, in its own perception and that of the Catalan public in the tradition of the pre-war period, Banco Alemán, subsidiary of Deutsche Ueberseeische Bank and Deutsche Bank. The holding in BCT was not undertaken right from the start, with a view to acquiring a majority; on the contrary, sale of the shares was considered on several occasions. In the middle of the 1980s, however, the bank wanted to safeguard its influence and from 1988, under the leadership of Kopper, the member of the board of managing directors with regional responsibility, acquire the majority. However, Banco de España refused to allow foreign banks to do so with regard to Spanish institutions before 1992.

Probably, in view of this situation, to secure influence for Deutsche Bank, Baden-Württembergische Bank – in which the former has a stake – bought 10 per cent of BCT. That the acquisition had been agreed with the bank was disputed by both sides; be that as it may, the Spanish central bank would not accept it. After clarifying discussions, *inter alia* between Herrhausen and Kopper and Central Bank President Rubio, and the depositing of its own shares in BCT, Deutsche Bank first obtained approval to acquire the majority in BCT in 1992/93. But in March 1989 it was already able to make a public takeover offer – the first one for a bank in Spanish financial history. Deutsche Bank succeeded in increasing its stake to more than 97 per cent up to 1992. The Madrid branch of Deutsche Bank remained in place for participation in underwriting syndicates and large loans, while the Barcelona branch was closed or rather transferred to BCT in May 1989.

After taking over BCT, Deutsche Bank began to restructure it. In particular there was a substantial cut in personnel to secure the company's competitiveness. Besides developing new business areas – e.g. business with large customers and corporate finance – and the renewal of the technical and organization areas, an element of Deutsche Bank's strategy was to supplement BCT's product range institutionally by means of specialized suppliers. In this vein, Leasing Bancotrans S.A. was founded as a subsidiary in 1989. The second stage was the establishment of Deutsche Bank Crédit S.A. in 1991. This company, domiciled in La Florida, is a kind of consumer loan bank. 1992 saw the emergence of DB Carplan, the objective of which is to finance and administer entire car fleets.

A further step in Deutsche Bank's positioning in Spain came in 1991 with the foundation of DB Morgan Grenfell S.A., Madrid, as a joint venture within the group covering a broad segment of investment banking; the company's business focused on mergers and acquisitions and securities trading, for which DB Securities, set up in 1992, also acquired a seat on the Madrid stock exchange. At the same time BCT extended its range of products organically in the direction of 'all-round financial service' *(Allfinanz)*, in particular as a supplier of insurance products. Under the trade name DB Seguros, the company markets both its own life insurances produced by its subsidiary DB Vida S.A., and offers intermediation and consulting services for other insurance fields. DB Gestión was also set up as an investment company. In 1993 Deutsche Bank became the biggest foreign bank in Spain when, after long and tough price negotiations, it acquired 98 per cent of Banco de Madrid from Banco Español de Crédito via BCT. BCT and Banco de Madrid merged in 1994 to form Deutsche Bank Sociedad Anónima Española.

Deutsche Bank (Austria) AG came into being in 1989 through the acquisition of Antoni, Hacker & Co., Vienna, a private banking house founded in 1896, with which Deutsche Bank had had business relations for many years. The restyling of the company reflected its integration into the Group, but was not linked with a move away from its typical private bank character. The new subsidiary is a merchant bank operating in portfolio management, securities and foreign exchange trading, issuing business and corporate finance, and selectively approaches the 500 biggest Austrian subsidiaries of German companies. It is to become – according to Endres in 1991 – an 'important node in Deutsche Bank's European network'.

In the field of *capital market institutions* in the broadest sense of the term, Deutsche Bank Capital Corporation, New York, was set up originally in 1970 by Union Bank of Switzerland as American UBS Corporation. Deutsche Bank joined at the end of 1971 as an equal partner with a capital contribution of $4 million (henceforth UBS-DB Corporation). The co-operation with Union Bank of Switzerland was arranged in such a way that it had no influence on competition between the two institutions in Europe. At first the company was an important addition to the service already offered to Deutsche Bank customers since 1968 by European American Banking Corporation and European American Bank & Trust Company. UBS-DB Corporation was designated as the bank's securities and issuing house in America. Later on, the product range was extended to include leasing and the intermediation of equity participations. In 1978 Union Bank of Switzerland and Deutsche Bank ended the partnership – amicably, as they said – with the latter taking over the other partner's 50 per cent. In 1978 the company was restyled Atlantic Capital Corporation, with the name beginning with the letter 'A', giving it a high-profile position in tombstones. In 1985 the name was changed to Deutsche Bank Capital Corporation (DBCC), as the bank expected more from emphasizing the parenthood than from just coming first in the alphabet.

As an issuing house, DBCC participated in inner-American and international capital market financings. In this context it had a leading position among non-American investment firms in initial public offerings (IPOs). As a broker, it transacted securities business in American stocks. From 1986 it became more involved in the Group's swap operations, and from 1988 its asset management and property investment business was intensified, as was business in mergers and acquisitions, despite tough competition. Close co-operation was developed with the Canadian broker company McLean McCarthy, also a member of the Group, especially in trading in Canadian and US securities.

Subsidiaries of DBCC were Deutsche Portfolio Corporation and Deutsche Bank Government Securities Inc., founded in 1988; in 1991 DBCC set up DBCC Asset Management Ltd., another 100 per cent subsidiary. The latter, domiciled in the international financial services centre in Dublin, initially had the job of mediating investment business for DBCC. It was, however, planned right from the start to expand its range of business activities. In 1989 DBCC, some of its subsidiaries and DB Capital Management (USA) Corporation – which emerged from the New York branch of the Deutsche Bank subsidiary Capital Management International GmbH, Frankfurt – as well as Deutsche Credit Corporation's international leasing department and Deutsche Bank's New York branch moved together into high-quality premises in the centre of Manhattan in an office building which – typical of this financial centre – was renamed 'Deutsche Bank Building'.

Deutsche Bank Government Securities operates in the US Treasury bond market and has the function of a primary dealer, with securities lending and repo business as other core activities. Business in Treasuries has been developed systematically, giving Deutsche Bank Group a highly efficient unit in the world's biggest bond market. The bank is the only German institution in the USA to have the status of primary dealer in this, the biggest market for Treasury bonds.

The beginning of the 1980s saw the end of a gentlemen's agreement between the Swiss and German big banks that they would not compete directly on each other's respective home markets. At the end of 1980 Deutsche Bank set up Deutsche Bank (Suisse) S.A., Geneva, a subsidiary. At the time of this foundation, the bank stressed that its Swiss subsidiary should comply with local conditions. At the same time it was pointed out when business started that 'much patience would be needed' for this undertaking, and it was emphasized that there was no prime intention of acquiring local business – according to Christians at the opening ceremony. A branch was opened in Zurich in 1981, Deutsche Bank (Schweiz) AG, and in mid-1988 in Lugano, Deutsche Bank (Svizzera) S.A.

The Swiss subsidiary was conceived as a specialized unit for portfolio management, especially for international private customers seeking a service under Swiss law and in accordance with Swiss practice going beyond the normal German service. The bank's activities in Switzerland supplement those of its Luxemburg subsidiary in private banking. The presence in Geneva is dedicated more to international investment business – it also fills a gap in Near and Middle East business, since Deutsche Bank (Suisse) actively seeks new business in that area – while the Zurich branch focuses on commercial business.

Since it was founded, Deutsche Bank's Swiss unit has participated in Swiss bond syndicates. In 1988 Deutsche Bank (Suisse) joined the Swiss big bank syndicate for Swiss franc bonds of foreign issuers; for certain Swiss-franc-denominated paper, it acts as market-maker. With Deutsche Bank's acquisition of Morgan Grenfell in 1989, Deutsche Bank (Suisse) took all the shares of Banque Morgan Grenfell en Suisse. After the merger that followed, the bank licence for the English bank's Swiss subsidiary was returned and its staff were taken over.

DB Capital Markets (Asia) Ltd. (DBCMA) was set up in Hong Kong in 1985 as a subsidiary for investment banking in Asia. It concentrated on wholesale banking, but also supplemented the range of products for private customers offered by the branches and subsidiaries in the region. DBCMA opened a branch in Tokyo in 1985 which shifted its business emphasis to Japan. But it was not possible to become active on the Tokyo Stock Exchange owing to the conditions of the Japanese authorities relating to issuance of a licence until Deutsche Bank had sold half of the shares of this subsidiary to Bayer and Siemens; it retained a 54.5 per cent stake in DBCMA, but only 50 per cent of voting capital. Deutsche Bank was thus the first foreign bank to cover all areas of banking business. Initially, the bank intended to refrain from taking a seat on the Tokyo Stock Exchange so as to maintain good relations with local securities dealers. But in 1988, DBCMA actually bought for about 16 million DM direct access to the stock exchange and thus responded to the growing importance of the centre for the bank. In view of the liberalization of the Japanese financial markets, DBCMA was restyled Deutsche Bank Capital Markets Asia in 1991; it was the first foreign securities house to include the word 'bank' in its name. Its business activity was extended by representative offices to Singapore, South Korea and Taiwan.

DB Asia Finance (HK) Ltd., Hong Kong, operates in investment banking and was originally founded in 1975 as European Asian Finance (HK) Ltd. by the Euras Group. In 1985 Deutsche Bank acquired all shares from the EBIC partners. The relocation of its domicile to Singapore was completed by mid-1990, and from there its objective was to supplement, as a merchant bank, the business activities of the branches in the Far East. In this relocation, a role was played first and foremost by the presence of the regional head office in Singapore, but also by the uncertain future of Hong Kong. The company is now styled Deutsche Bank (Asia Pacific) Ltd.

Deutsche Bank Capital Markets Ltd. (DBCM) commenced its business in London in 1985 as a 100 per cent Deutsche Bank subsidiary. It was to supplement the bank's investment banking and issuing business conducted in Germany and that of the other Group companies. London had developed into the most important investment banking centre in Europe, which meant that its own presence for this type of business in the City – besides the branch, which was responsible for commercial banking – was indispensable for the bank. The previous indirect presence through the holding in the EBIC consortium bank European Banking Company was given up by the bank in 1985.

The business activity of DBCM mainly comprised the syndication of Euro issues not denominated in deutschmarks as well as trading and placing Euro securities. In the middle of 1992 there was an institutional restructuring. The basic idea, as Krumnow stated, was to strengthen the bank there systematically from inside and to give it the possibility of income-oriented growth using its own strength through the combination of joint operating functions, particularly as the earning power of the London units left a lot to be desired. On the other hand, Deutsche Bank wanted to have a visible presence as a universal bank wherever it was legally possible. This latter point in particular induced it to merge its London units operating under the bank's own name. Investment banking and commercial banking were united in Deutsche Bank AG London. Morgan Grenfell Group was unaffected.

In 1984 Deutsche Bank acquired 4.99 per cent of Morgan Grenfell Holdings, the parent of the London merchant bank Morgan Grenfell & Co. Ltd. This stake, which was just below the mandatory approval limit, was intended to provide the basis for co-operation between the two companies, from which the bank hoped to gain access to London investment banking know-how. The bank subsequently examined the possibility of taking the majority. The process had to be speeded up suddenly in November 1989 under Kopper's leadership, being the responsible member of the board of managing directors, when the French Indosuez financial group took 14.9 per cent of the shares of Morgan Grenfell Group plc from the British insurance company Willis Faber, with an option for a further 10 per cent. Morgan Grenfell feared a full takeover by Indosuez and saw a threat to its character and independence. Deutsche Bank offered to play the role of 'white knight', making substantial promises to Morgan Grenfell in this connection. It could thus count on management's approval in the event of a takeover bid. The preparation of an offer to shareholders – preceded by discreet and detailed examination and valuation of the investment bank's largely intangible and human assets – took place under great time pressure, as the offer had to be made before the Willis Faber General Meeting. On 26 November 1989 – a Sunday – the supervisory board, following the board of managing directors of Deutsche Bank, approved the project codenamed 'Magic'. Great discretion was needed, as most of the Morgan Grenfell shares were traded on the stock exchange and rumours would have triggered off strong price fluctuations. Trading was therefore suspended on Friday.

On 27 November, the day the deal was officially announced, press conferences were held simultaneously in London and Frankfurt before the start of trading. Here, an offer was made to shareholders to buy their shares at £5.50 per share. Previously, mergers and acquisitions specialists commissioned by Deutsche Bank had received promises from larger-scale shareholders over the weekend, so that they could buy a further 10 per cent on Monday. The bank thus caught up with Indosuez. On Thursday, 30 November, the day Herrhausen was murdered by Red Army Faction terrorists, the French group sold its 15 per cent to the bank at the takeover price and netted a substantial profit. The bank subsequently bought more shares via the stock exchange before, on 7 December 1989 (document day), the official written offer went out to shareholders. Shortly before year's end, the Willis Faber General Meeting, meanwhile postponed, resolved to sell the remaining 10 per cent to the bank. This gave Deutsche Bank the majority with 59.5 per cent. In January 1990 there was a takeover bid for option rights of the directors and employees of Morgan Grenfell, and on 29 June 1990 the takeover was formally completed by acquisition of the final shares.

The transaction had a volume of roughly 2.7 billion DM and was the bank's biggest post-war investment. Most of the holding was held through DB Investments (GB) Ltd., London. The takeover was effected in the expectation of a further intensification of the already good co-operation between the two companies. The objective of the transaction was to reinforce the bank's position in the U.K. corporate banking market, and specifically its position in mergers and acquisitions, as well as in asset management for institutional investors. The takeover gave the bank not only Morgan Grenfell & Co. itself, a merchant bank operating for more than 150 years, but also its subsidiaries in the USA, Japan, Australia, Hong Kong, Singapore, as well as in Switzerland and on the Channel Islands, a total of 30 foreign presences.

Kopper justified the takeover at the 1990 General Meeting on four levels: Morgan Grenfell significantly strengthened the bank's position in London, undisputably the leading financial centre in Europe, and thus in Anglo-Saxon investment banking. The takeover fitted perfectly into the bank's European strategy by allowing it to cover the interesting business in the United Kingdom with companies and institutions. The takeover was also an optimum supplement to the group's range of products, as there was hardly any overlapping. There were also cultural reasons for the takeover: international investment banking thought, spoke and acted in Anglo-Saxon fashion. During the takeover, Herrhausen had already stressed: 'What we admire and don't have is an Anglo-Saxon culture in the money business.' Morgan Grenfell itself gained stability as a result of the takeover after apparently serious problems following a period of rapid expansion between 1984 and 1987 – e.g. the entry into securities business and the so-called 'Guinness affair' – had been overcome.

The takeover of Morgan Grenfell made it advisable to concentrate international investment banking in Deutsche Bank Group. Hence there were smaller restructurings in 1990/91, where Morgan Grenfell, partly for organizational reasons, partly due to market developments, gave up certain business fields or transferred them to other subsidiaries of the bank. Neutral analysts, too, confirmed that the takeover was a success for the bank: Morgan Grenfell in particular profited from fast expansion, while the bank's return from the new subsidiary tended to be on the low side given the decline in profits in 1990; but the long-term prospects are assessed positively. The integration of the company into the Group represented a tightrope walk inasmuch as, on the one hand, the independence and traditional character of the London bank were to be maintained but, on the other, synergy and complementary effects could only be gained from intensive co-operation.

In July 1990, Morgan Grenfell and Gleacher & Co., New York, a company specializing in mergers and acquisitions, signed a co-operation agreement. Since then, Gleacher has carried out all mergers and acquisitions deals of Deutsche Bank in the USA and between the USA and other countries. In April 1992 the bank formed a subsidiary, Deutsche Bank Gilts Ltd., London, as market-maker for business in U.K. government bonds. This function – comparable in the USA to that of Deutsche Bank Government Securities – became attractive for the bank after a period of inactivity when the market, following a period of institutional oversupply, had again become profitable as a whole. The bank thus returned to a business field given up four years previously by Morgan Grenfell.

At the end of 1992, Deutsche Bank and Morgan Grenfell & Co. combined their futures and options business in the new DBMG Futures and Options Ltd. At the end of 1993, Deutsche Bank also bought the London precious metal trading company Sharps Pixley from Kleinwort Benson Group.

MDM Sociedade de Investimento, S.A., Lisbon, was set up in 1978 in equal parts by Deutsche Bank, Morgan Guaranty International Finance Corporation and the industrialist José de Mello at the latter's instigation as a consulting company, initially under the style M.D.M. - Estudos Técnicos e Financeiros Lda. In the course of liberalization in Portugal, its conversion into an investment bank became possible in 1984. Deutsche Bank was thus one of the first foreign banks to be present in the Portuguese market. The increase of its stake to 100 per cent came in 1988. In 1989 Deutsche Bank de Investimento, S.A. (DBI), Lisbon, took over MDM's business. It now became possible to take in customers' deposits, obtain funding on the money market, transact short-term lending business, portfolio management and custody account business. Up to 1990, only one other institution obtained permission for such a conversion into a bank. In the course of the residual liberalization of the Portuguese financial services market, in anticipation of the single European market, Deutsche Bank took the opportunity to review the positioning of DBI, as its unique position would be lost: all banks, including all other foreign institutions, would be able to conduct all business. The beginning of 1992, therefore, saw the beginning of the universalization of the Portuguese subsidiary.

IIM Internationale Investment Management Gesellschaft S.A. was set up in Luxemburg in 1987. The shares were distributed equally between DWS Deutsche Gesellschaft für Wertpapiersparen and Deutsche Bank Luxembourg. As an investment company, IIM engages in the administration and distribution of shares of the mutual funds which it floats in Luxemburg. Since 1991 it has borne the style DB Investment Management S.A.

McLean McCarthy Ltd., Toronto, formed in 1972, operates in institutional securities business, but also transacts corporate finance business, and through its subsidiary McLeanco Realty Services is engaged in real estate agency business. Deutsche Bank (Canada) acquired all shares in 1988; they are held by subholding companies – DB Holdings Canada Inc. and McLeanco Holdings Ltd. The securities broker was fully integrated into Deutsche Bank Group in 1988.

In 1988 the bank acquired 50 per cent of the capital of Bain & Company Ltd., Sydney, through its subsidiary Deutsche Bank Australia. Bain & Co. is one of the oldest and most important investment banking groups in Australia, with branches there and bases abroad. In 1991 the bank increased its stake by an all-important percentage point to 51 per cent and made the institution a subsidiary in formal terms, too. Bain & Co. was fully integrated into the Group in the middle of 1992, when the residual shares were acquired. This participation confirmed – according to the managing director of Deutsche Bank Australia, Beck – that 'the highly developed and innovative capital and investment banking markets in Australia are an important part of the growing presence of Deutsche Bank in the Asia-Pacific region'.

In the field of *sales financing and leasing companies*, Deutsche Credit Corporation (DCC), Deerfield, was created in 1982 as a 100 per cent subsidiary of Deutsche Bank. The shares were originally held via the holding company Deutsche Credit Services Inc., the former Fiat Credit Services Inc., a joint venture between the bank and Fiat, which was intended to serve the sales financing activities of the Italian company; the bank's 50 per cent holding in this company was held via DB Luxembourg. Owing to changed organizational conditions, Credit Corporation and Credit Services were merged at the end of 1988. DCC specialized in sales financing, primarily in the form of asset-based dealer and final consumer loans, especially tailored to small and medium-sized German exporters. From 1986 the company was also active in leasing, subsequently in the financing of data-processing equipment and office machinery, passenger aircraft and helicopters. As the unit responsible for international leasing, a department was located in New York at the end of 1989.

Some sales financing and leasing companies have already been mentioned as subsidiaries of other subsidiaries of the bank – e.g. Leasing Bancotrans S.A. and BAI Factoring S.p.A. Over and above that, the leasing company P.T. Euras Buana Leasing Indonesia (subsequently: P.T. DB Leasing), Jakarta, should also be mentioned: in 1985 the bank first acquired 60 per cent of the shares of the company, which previously – from its foundation in 1983 – had been a minority holding of European Asian Bank, which was subsequently also taken over by the bank. Apart from that, some of the international subsidiaries in the group of commercial banks – such as Deutsche Bank Australia – also conduct leasing and sales financing business.

In the field of *mortgage banks*, Europäische Hypothekenbank der Deutschen Bank – subsequently Europäische Hypothekenbank S.A. (EHB) – was formed in 1989 in Luxemburg by Deutsche Bank (33.3 per cent), its three mortgage bank subsidiaries – Frankfurter Hypothekenbank (33.3 per cent), Deutsche Centralbodenkredit (20.0 per cent), Lübecker Hypothekenbank (10.0 per cent) – and Deutsche Bank Luxembourg (3.3 per cent). The intention was to create a basis from which to enter the European property loan market. In the first two years, communal loan business, and later also property loan business as such, was expanded and funded by appropriate issues. The idea behind the foundation was, on the one hand, to retain the high credit rating of German mortgage banks, the structure of which is largely unknown abroad, by making high demands on borrowers and, on the other, both to internationalize this business and also to circumvent certain restrictions in German law. EHB complies voluntarily with many provisions of German mortgage bank law and can thus obtain favourable international funding as a first-class borrower. This is particularly important against the background that in the common European banking market there is no special protection for the traditional German mortgage bank. In 1991 the ownership structure was marginally altered.

With regard to *international financing companies*, probably the most important purely off-shore funding institution of the bank is Deutsche Bank Finance N.V., Curaçao, established in 1981 and profiting from 'exotic' tax advantages. It acts as a Group funding vehicle by issuing bonds in deutschmarks and in foreign currencies. Here, numerous issues have been floated with interest rate swap agreements in order to hedge the interest risk of Deutsche Bank Luxembourg in roll-over loans extended by the latter bank. The funds taken up are placed at its disposal, and it guarantees the bond issues.

Deutsche Finance (Netherlands) B.V., Amsterdam, is also used for the tax-privileged raising of long-term financing funds. Short-term funding, on the other hand, is generated by Deutsche Bank Financial Inc., Dover/USA, set up in 1985, mainly on the commercial paper market in the USA. These funds are placed for the most part at the disposal of Deutsche Bank Group companies in the USA.

Typical of its third expansion phase is that since 1976 Deutsche Bank has also systematically broadened its *branch network* world-wide. Although it was repeatedly emphasized, especially at the beginning of the 1980s, that this development was largely over, further branches are still being opened, or old or more recent representative offices converted into branches. This shows how flexibly the bank responds with this form of presence to changing economic and political conditions in individual countries and regions. The bank's lack of representation in Scandinavia may be explained by the fact that business there can be settled without problems from Germany and especially from London. For this reason, and owing to the difficult situation for banks in the region, it also decided not to acquire any one of the banks which could easily have been taken over in the Scandinavian banking crisis at the beginning of the 1990s. The situation is similar in large parts of Africa, where the bank has hardly any presence except for a few representative offices. The presence there of some European competitors must be seen more as a colonial heritage and can hardly be regarded as a competitive advantage in international business.

In the Far East, a branch was opened in Tokyo in 1971 as an office of Deutsche Ueberseeische Bank (DUB); it replaced the joint representative office of Deutsche Bank and DUB, which had been there since 1962. In opening the branch, Deutsche Bank resumed an old tradition: once before – roughly 100 years earlier – it had had a branch in Japan. Following the integration of DUB into Deutsche Bank in 1976, the branch was again operated under the name of 'Deutsche Bank'. Customers – above all German companies and their subsidiaries as well as German-Japanese joint ventures – are given access to loans and Japanese facilities in foreign trade financing. The branch also offers support with the business projects of German enterprises in Japan. In this way, the bank participated in the construction of two industrial centres for German enterprises in Yokohama (1987, 1989). By opening a branch of DB Capital Markets (Asia) in 1985 in Tokyo, to transact securities business separately, the branch was the first foreign bank in Japan to cover both business sectors.

A branch was opened in Osaka in 1982 as this city, besides Kobe, was regarded as one of the Japanese windows to China and South-East Asia. The conversion of the representative office, in place since 1978, into a branch was intended as a response to the growing number of corporate customers in south-western Japan. The Nagoya representative office was also converted into a branch in 1989 to ensure a balanced presence in all Japanese business centres.

In India, alongside the branch in Bombay taken over with Euras Bank, a second one was opened in 1989 in New Delhi. The motive here was the expected intensification of German-Indian economic relations and the development of this region into one of the growth centres in India. The branch was not only to promote German-Indian joint ventures, but also to give Indian companies access to the European market. A company founded in 1991 as DB Finance India Ltd. and soon restyled DB Financial Services (India) Ltd. in Bangalore – one of the biggest centres for the services sector in India and suppliers of modern technology – was constituted as a joint venture with Unilever. The company was to offer the products which the bank's branches in New Delhi and Bombay could not supply owing to legal restrictions. Their business activity extended correspondingly to leasing and bill business as well as to money market business and consulting. The bank had a share of 30 per cent.

The Surabaya branch, founded in 1989, was intended to pave the way for German and European investors into the interesting growth region of East Java, which is characterized by above-average growth, good infrastructure, diversified industry and a high level of education among the labour force, and thus to supplement the activities of the Jakarta branch, which was founded by Deutsch-Asiatische Bank in 1969 and, with the integration of Euras Bank into Deutsche Bank, became the latter's first office in Indonesia.

The Hong Kong branch emerged in 1979 by conversion of the representative office existing there since 1976. In 1984 all commercial and other bank services aimed at private customers were withdrawn from its programme and transferred to the Euras Bank branch located there since 1958. The branch was left with the existing business with large institutional clients. It remained the bank's main base for this investment banking activity in the South-East Asian region until 1987. In that year it was closed and replaced by a new branch of the bank in Hong Kong – from the takeover of Euras Bank. Working in co-ordination with DB Capital Markets (Asia), the new branch devoted its efforts to commercial business.

Besides the bank's own branches set up since 1976 in South-East Asia, it took over through the acquisition of the majority in Euras Bank in 1986 – and as a result of the latter's integration as Deutsche Bank (Asia) AG into Deutsche Bank in 1988 – the branches of the former EBIC in Hong Kong, Jakarta, Karachi, Kuala Lumpur, Singapore, Manila, Seoul, Bangkok, Bombay, Colombo, Taipei, Pusan and Macao. The business activity of these branches in South-East Asia is very heterogeneous.

As far as Europe is concerned, the opening of Deutsche Bank's first foreign branch in its own name after the First World War came in 1976 in London through conversion of the representative office open there since 1973. Its activities subsequently served to develop business with international companies and U.K. firms, also export and import financings, especially for commodity transactions, and business with foreign banks and foreign exchange trading. Through its branch in the City, the bank played a growing role as lead manager and agent in the strongly expanding market for new financing instruments. Over and above that, it participated in the syndication of long-term loan facilities.

In 1987, as a supplement to its London branch, the bank opened a representative office in Manchester, which had gained importance as the centre of the north-west of England, which was important for future industry and trade, and was also a financial centre of supraregional significance. Later though, a change in the business activities of the London branch became apparent: it made more and more efforts to obtain British customers, and its original restraint in deference to its British EBIC partner became less pronounced. This business accounts for 80 per cent of the London branch's business. On 1 July 1992 the 'old' branch and Deutsche Bank Capital Markets (London) were combined to form Deutsche Bank AG (London).

The foundation of the branch in Paris came in 1977 by conversion of the representative office open there since 1970. In the foreground of its business activity were loans to French companies and subsidiaries of German companies in France as well as the financing of German-French trade. The opening of the branch at the traditional Place Vendôme was effected in agreement with the (then) French EBIC partner Société Générale, which in turn opened a branch in Frankfurt. Since 1987 the bank has had a second branch in Strasburg to round off its presence in France, but subordinated in organizational and business terms to the Paris branch. Be that as it may, France continued to be a problem in the implementation of the bank's European strategy, which was reflected also in assessments published by the bank – by Kopper, for example, in 1989 at the General Meeting. While the extension of EBIC to include a French partner had been difficult owing to the state control of banks in France, an acquisition in France continued to depend at this point on progress with privatization. Over and above that, however, the bank was not prepared to pay an excessive price or to acquire a bank which did not fit into its overall business strategy. Nevertheless, there has been repeated speculation in the past about an immediately impending acquisition – e.g. in 1989 when the bank (for no reason) was mentioned in connection with Banque Indosuez.

Parallel to the opening of the Brussels and Antwerp branches in autumn 1978, the bank's shares were listed on the stock exchanges in these cities. This double opening, which resumed the bank's presence in Brussels and the presence of Disconto-Gesellschaft in Antwerp[89] before the First World War, matches the economic ties between the Federal Republic and its neighbouring country. The new branches, managed jointly from Brussels, concentrated on corporate banking business; in Antwerp, a special role was played in this connection by port business. Points of emphasis were, among other things, local short- and medium-term lending business, Eurocredit business, foreign exchange and money market business. DB (Belgium) Finance S.A./N.V. was added to them. In 1992 the Belgian Ministry of Finance granted the bank's Brussels branch the status of primary dealer for the sale of government debt instruments; it was the only German bank outlet to be awarded this honour.

The bank has no further Benelux branches in Luxemburg or the Netherlands owing to its subsidiaries there. The Brussels branch does, however, operate a liaison office with the European Union.

The Madrid branch, which in 1979 – along the lines of many other branches – stemmed from the representative office founded in 1973, operates in particular in corporate banking and foreign business. Its customers are chiefly the subsidiaries of German and international companies in Spain as well as Spanish undertakings. The branch is responsible for both Spain and Portugal; it became particularly important in the run-up to and after completion of the admission of Spain and Portugal to the European Union. From 1981 it was supplemented by an office in Barcelona, which was responsible initially for corporate banking only and served as a contact office with BCT. With the takeover of Bancotrans by the bank in 1989, the hierarchy between the branches in Madrid and Barcelona was reversed. Since then BCT in Barcelona has been the head office for Spain. It took over the business of the branch there which was closed in May 1989. The Madrid branch, on the other hand, was maintained until 1990 – when its business was taken over by the BCT head branch there, as it had loans in its portfolio which BCT could not handle in terms of magnitude. For this reason, and as an institutional bracket for the Marbella branch allocated to it, the branch has continued to exist as a legal shell after discontinuation of its business activities. This branch – Deutsche Bank AG Sucursal en España; for private asset management on the Costa del Sol – is a unique element in the bank's European network: for one thing, it operates in a region where BCT is also present; its *raison d'être* results from the lack of expertise at BCT in the sophisticated business with high-net-worth private customers. For another, it is controlled by the bank's head branch in Mannheim, at the initiative of which it was founded in the first place; all other foreign offices report to head office in Frankfurt.

In Italy, the emphasis in the business activity of the Milan branch, which emerged in 1979 from the representative office established in 1977, alongside money market business and foreign exchange trading, was on foreign and lending business, above all with large and medium-sized companies in Lombardy. The bank's acquisition of Banca d'America e d'Italia in 1988 resulted in the branch's business being sold to an Italian regional savings bank. Initially it remained in existence in formal terms so that, until implementation of the single European market, corporation tax credits paid on dividends to Deutsche Bank – mainly from the latter's packet of Fiat shares – could be imputed (pp. 688–9).

On the American continent, the opening of a branch in the USA did not take place until 1979 in New York. This year is therefore an important one for the bank's American activities owing to the complete takeover of UBS-DB Corporation (p. 768). It was thus the last of the German big banks to come to New York with a branch of its own. The reasons for this long hesitation, the subject of critical comment, were the existence of a presence in the form of the European American Banks, which 'owed their existence from the very start to a perhaps excessive caution and restraint on the part of the bank and then to consideration for this successful joint venture'.[90] This consideration is striking inasmuch as the bank itself established a presence in regions where EBIC was also active. In the middle of 1977 Christians said at the General Meeting, talking about the 'two-tier strategy EBIC/own branches': 'We do not, however, want to open our own branches in the USA. Here, we feel we have optimum representation by the successful EABs.' But in 1986 even the business of the German desk at the European American Banks was transferred to the branch; in 1989 the bank ended its participation completely.

The New York branch and the representative offices – subsequently converted into representative offices – in Los Angeles (founded 1982, branch from 1990) and Chicago (1982/1988) were intended to stimulate the development of the big American market. A more closely knit network of representative offices and branches in the USA, however, was dispensed with for cost reasons. From 1978 the branch had a subsidiary as a branch of the bank in Georgetown, Grand Caymans. From 1981 the New York branch had an international banking facility for certain international off-shore ('out-out') business.

1992 saw the completion of a restructuring of the bank's activities in North America. A new Deutsche Bank North America Holding Corporation comprised Deutsche Bank Capital Corporation with its subsidiaries, Deutsche Credit Corporation, Deutsche Bank (Canada), McLean McCarthy Ltd., DB Capital Management (USA) Corp. and brokers C.J. Lawrence Inc., New York, which was acquired as a subsidiary of Morgan Grenfell and transferred to the bank. The intention behind this measure was to create a more streamlined hierarchy corresponding to American custom and practice with only one decision-maker. The holding company, however, functioned exclusively as an organizational unit; it did not constitute a bank holding under American law. It was the head office for a total of 1,200 employees and responsible for Deutsche Bank companies with total assets of $14 billion (1992). The bank expected it to bring advantages in the management of its North American presence as a 'distant time zone'. Furthermore, it underlined its character as a universal bank and, through the new organizational structure, laid the foundations for the planned strong expansion especially in corporate banking business, but also in the hitherto neglected business with high-net-worth private customers in the USA.

In South America, the branches and merged subsidiaries in Argentina (Buenos Aires), Brazil (São Paulo) and Paraguay (Asunción) of Deutsche Ueberseeische Bank, fully integrated in 1978, were maintained as branches of the bank. Hitherto joint representative offices in Chile, Mexico and Venezuela were also continued. Over and above that, Brazilian branches were opened in 1988 in Porto Alegre and Campina, regions in which German industrial corporations were strongly represented. A further point with regard to Porto Alegre is the high proportion of people of German origin, the basis of the traditional commercial links with Germany. Both branches rounded off the bank's presence in São Paulo, to which they are subordinated. The main emphasis in the bank's Brazilian business was on local corporate finance, as a rule in the form of short-term working capital loans, deposits and foreign trade business, as well as retail banking business.

In Argentina, the bank saw massive expansion of its presence in greater Buenos Aires in 1989 through the acquisition of 29 city branches from Bank of America. This gave it 43 branches in and around Buenos Aires. By strengthening its presence in this way, it assumed that the enormous economic problems of the country could be solved and that South America as a whole would again become a growth region. Herrhausen said as much in 1988: 'You can't write off Latin America either. The obstinate debt crisis will one day be overcome there or diffused, I'm sure of that. That's why this part of the world must be incorporated into globalization strategies in good time – and for me that means now – and the potential there must be used. Banking around the globe, around the clock certainly doesn't exclude the South American continent.' For the bank's business activity in Argentina, the branch network gave it access to deposits outside the interbank market as well and to lending business with smaller and medium-sized companies, which offered better spreads than lending business with large corporations, but could not be provided by the previous branch due to information problems. In Argentina the bank was thus able to solve the usual Latin American problem of not being able to achieve adequate volumes through branches. It is against this background that the closure of branches and representative offices in Rosario (sold in 1978), Asunción (sold in 1989), Rio de Janeiro (transferred in 1988 to São Paulo) and Bogotá (closed in 1989[91]) should be seen.

Despite the world-wide expansion of Deutsche Bank's own network of foreign branches and subsidiaries, the co-operation in EBIC remained for the time being – at least officially – an important part of its foreign strategy. In particular it was repeatedly emphasized that the expansion of the bank's own foreign organization did not represent a move away from the 'proven' EBIC co-operation, but ultimately benefited the partners within the framework of the 'two-tier strategy'. In fact, the co-operation became increasingly weak: rather than expanding the institutional network, it was now more geared to providing a forum for exchanging views and experiences and for training each other's staff.

Although it was still emphasized optimistically in the bank's Annual Reports at the beginning of the 1980s that the EBIC co-operation contributed to improving its product range for the benefit of customers, this contrasted with the fact that at that time the bank had hardly any more co-operative arrangements. Either EBIC holdings were sold or shares were taken over from partner banks. In 1984, for the first time, there was no separate section on 'EBIC holdings' or the 'EBIC Group' in the Annual Report for the Group. In 1985 the restructuring of the holdings was then discussed again. The end had come for EBIC.

Parallel to the development of its own network of branches and subsidiaries and to the co-operation in EBIC, the bank also acquired further minority holdings and opened representative offices. The assumption of minority holdings came to an end, by and large, in the middle of 1975, i.e. with the beginning of the third phase. A regional concentration of the relatively unimportant holdings was not apparent; in most cases they were holdings in development banks. In the foreground, therefore, was the transfer of know-how for the development of foreign economies, coupled with the target of obtaining insight into the economies concerned and initiating business relationships.

From the end of the 1970s, the bank continually streamlined its minority holdings in banks and quasi-bank institutions; from today's – not only external – view, it seems as if they were not the result of a clear strategy anyway. The reasons for this streamlining lay in the reformulation of strategy and in business considerations. On the one hand, some companies did not develop in line with the bank's expectations when acquiring the holdings; on the other, some companies were able to report a good local performance which the bank was unable to realize, however, owing to exchange rate changes and capital controls.

In such situations it proved difficult to sell a holding, first because few foreign investors had any interest and, second, because domestic buyers were rare. A further point is that for banks themselves in developing countries, as well as for the local administration, a bank participation counted as a symbol of solvency and confidence not willingly given up. In such cases, Deutsche Bank's delegates in Asia could point to the closely knit branch network, which made minority holdings appear obsolete even to external parties, while in Africa an appeal was made to the growing independence of states and their emancipation from Europe.

Thus, the reason for the bank's move away from minority holdings is that, on the one hand, they were out of date as a form of foreign presence, as the bank now had access to all relevant markets in its own name and comprehensive know-how in international business, which explains why minority holdings, especially when no further-reaching co-operation agreement was reached in the sense of co-ordinated business policy, could only be an investment undertaken for reasons of return. On the other hand, the yield opportunities decreased owing to the rising prices of shares in banks, the administrative costs and the possible necessity of divestment. For the bank, therefore, according to Kopper in February 1990, minority holdings only made strategic sense in the international sector if they were acquired as a necessary preliminary step to a planned majority holding or merger – a clearly defined policy, consistently pursued since then.

Throughout all phases of its international expansion, however, the bank consistently developed its network of representative offices world-wide, for example in former Eastern bloc and present-day reforming countries. The opening of the office in Moscow in 1973 opposite the Bolshoi Theatre was in the tradition of the bank's business relations with the Soviet Union. They were considered capable of development, but the specific problems connected with them made a local presence absolutely essential. The task of the representative office, therefore, was to intensify contacts with Soviet authorities and to create new links with German business. From 1986 the bank's representative office was the only representation of a Western bank to be housed in its own building. With the demise of the Soviet Union, the office remained the representation for Russia. 1993 saw the opening of a further representative office for Russia in St. Petersburg[92], for Kazakhstan in Almaty, for Ukraine in Kiev, for Uzbekistan in Tashkent, and for Georgia in Tbilisi (1993), in each case as the first German bank.

The representative office in Beijing, the first of a German bank in the People's Republic of China, was opened in 1981 at the invitation of the Chinese authorities. Its main task was to intermediate, within the framework of the traditional relations between China and the bank, contacts between German companies and Chinese organizations, and to help with business initiation and – as far as possible – to transact its own business. During the suppression of the student protest against the Chinese régime in 1989, the representative office was closed as a sign of protest or, to be more precise, the two representatives were recalled to Hong Kong, although a setback had to be expected for the development of business.

The decision to go to Hungary was taken soon after the political upheaval: a representative office was opened in Budapest in 1990. Owing to the more liberal economic stance towards the West, which had begun during the Communist era, the bank saw a lead here compared with the neighbouring countries on the road to a market economy. To support this process, and to let the bank participate in it, was to be the task of the office. For the representative office in Prague (1990) the bank expected growth in bilateral trade in the wake of the economic and political upheaval in the Czechoslovakia of that time, a process which made a local presence seem sensible. In February 1994, the Prague representative office was converted into a branch, thus becoming the first branch in the former Eastern bloc. The representative office in Warsaw (1990) was intended to play a role in the privatization process in the Polish economy and to provide an advisory service to the authorities.

The two representative offices in Ho Chi Minh City and Hanoi (1992/93) were intended to round off the bank's presence in Asia. In the project stage for these two offices, it was already planned to convert them soon into branches.

It is clear that representative offices have played a role in all phases of the bank's international presence; but the reasons for opening them have changed: the frequent conversion of representative offices into branches has shown that the former no longer had the same function as in the first phase, namely as the only and relatively seldom used way of being represented in the bank's own name, but operated in a market-monitoring capacity only as a preliminary step towards a more efficient and committed positioning.

If one examines the opening of representative offices by country of domicile, there is no sign of regional concentration. Looking at the present list of representative offices, it can only be said that they exist primarily in developing and newly industrializing countries as well as in the former state trading nations currently in a process of change, i.e. in states where a more committed presence could also be necessary soon. In this sense, it is difficult to allocate the new representative offices in the 1970s and 1980s in material terms to the first phase. On the contrary, they appear to a large extent to be a necessary step in the conception of the third phase, and may thus reflect the future international positioning of the bank in the form of new branches.

3. On the evaluation of the institutional lines of development

Taken in total, it may be noted that, compared with the other big banks, Deutsche Bank's internationalization in the various sectors and phases under its own name has begun in most cases relatively late and that the bank has often been the last one to move in the early phase – although less so today. This cannot be generally explained by the existence of EBIC, because other German banks also belonged to similar groupings; on the contrary, the bank seems to have had more faith in the sustainability of consortium banking. With regard to its international presence, above all compared with the other big banks, the bank 'held back at first, but then entered the market on a massive scale with all its strength'.[93] This is why the bank today has the most closely knit world-wide branch network of all the German banks. It is not only represented at all important financial centres in the world, but over and above that at locations which are still in the process of economic development. There, in many cases it (still) operates in isolation – as the only local German bank.

Even if the three phases of the bank's international institutional development since 1957 cannot be pinpointed without some overlapping, it is possible, as Figure 5.14 shows, to give a systematic presentation of the development. If one looks at the institutional *options* for presence abroad, it may be said that minority holdings played an important role until the middle of the 1970s in the bank's strategic concept, quickly losing their relative importance with the beginning of the co-operation in EBIC. But since, strictly speaking, holdings in consortium banks are also (modified) minority stakes, the breach between the second and the third phase from 1976 appears more striking than that between the first and the second. The third phase – presence through the bank's own branches and subsidiaries – represents a complete turnaround of the previous concept of extensive risk-averse presence abroad.

Regarding representative offices as a further institutional option, opened by the bank throughout the entire period, it is important to note the low intensity of this form of presence, which makes it compatible with all strategic phases: where representative offices in the first and second phase serve as the only – and thus in relative terms perhaps the most intensive – form of foreign presence in the bank's own name, they serve today in most cases as preliminary stages to a more committed positioning. If one describes the first phase as 'low profile', Deutsche Ueberseeische Bank can be seen as a subsidiary with much importance for the bank's early international business; the Hamburg domicile, however, gave DUB an ambivalent position. A clear pioneer role for subsidiaries abroad was played, on the other hand, by Compagnie Financière de la Deutsche Bank in Luxemburg from 1970.

An evaluation of the three phases indicates, both in a separate consideration of the individual developments and in a more general analysis of the entire period, that the early phases – even for the simple reason that the institutional strategy was turned around from 1976 – must be seen as less successful or the decisions they were based on as wrong. Such an evaluation may seem clear from today's point of view; but it presupposes knowledge at that time that there were other correct alternative courses of action. But if one measures the early concepts for the bank's international presence against the situation in which the decisions were taken, it is soon clear that not all options were available to the bank at that time.

Especially at the beginning, it did not have the resources to set up subsidiaries and branches abroad, apart from political animosity which it met with in the early post-war years. On the other hand, though, despite reconstruction and the economic miracle, international business in the first phase was still a long way from the dimensions and importance it gained later on. Consideration must also be given to experiences which the bank's decision-makers gathered during two world wars and the National Socialist régime, developments which isolated Germany, excluded it from world trade, and in the wake of which the banks lost their foreign networks. That the bank began cautiously, in spite of all that, to establish a footing abroad through Deutsche Ueberseeische Bank, representative offices and minority holdings – especially in development banks – points to a far-sighted anticipation of the growing importance of international banking business.

The subsequent phase of club banking in EBIC, from today's point of view, does not present a convincing picture, even in conceptual terms, as on the one hand problems had to arise in connection with the development of a joint policy, and on the other such a co-operative arrangement completely ignored the competitive relations between the partner banks and also between the banks themselves and their joint ventures. Seen from the 1960s standpoint, they appeared to offer a possibility of, on the one hand, excluding by means of higher profile and more efficient presence, the disadvantages of more or less unsystematic minority holdings, and on the other of using the latter's advantages – spreading the risk and resource input over several partners. The fact that consortium banks were just a passing phase for the bank, primarily because of the steering and distribution problems, but also on account of general developments – e.g. the debt crisis – and thus remained an episodic phenomenon, should not hide the fact that in this phase positive and negative experience was gathered, organizations were created and business generated, which helped to make it possible for the bank to go abroad under its own name from 1976 onwards. It would be mere speculation to consider how the bank would have developed without its participation in EBIC. Perhaps it would have built up its own presence abroad at an earlier stage, but it might have been dragged more deeply into the international debt problem.

At the present time, the third phase is still in progress. The previous phases were dominated by the criteria of flexibility and manageability at institutional level in the international sector. Neither is possible in minority holdings and consortium banks; in this sense, the strategy of building up a global network under the bank's own name, despite the high resource input, seems logical. Although the bank's success especially in international business indicates that the strategy is correct, the present-day concept must stand the test of time and be open to assessment against future criteria possibly reflecting quite different questions which are not foreseeable today.

4. 'Global playing' under discussion

Despite the positive connotation of the concept of 'global player', its material content remains strangely unclear; it is difficult, on the basis of the sophisticated formulations, to form a picture of what it means for the future structure of Deutsche Bank Group. Even the attempt at linguistic clarification embedded in an obituary for the murdered spokesman of the board of managing directors, Herrhausen, is far from giving an answer. 'Thought through to its logical conclusion, this may have been Herrhausen's concept: Deutsche Bank Group as a global economic all-round potential of unique structure and volume with a corporate culture that does not constantly have to seek justification.'[94] Notwithstanding this, the development of the bank into a global or globalized financial services supplier is almost necessarily linked with continuous growth in its corporate size and thus in the complexity of Deutsche Bank as a system. Given the problem of co-ordination resulting from this steadily rising systemic complexity, there is a clear need to draft concepts and measures for *managing* it: 'Even the best of strategies and the most efficient of structures will not help us if we don't develop management instruments which allow us to stabilize our course and, if necessary, change it, and quickly. The most important implications of globalization therefore include an appropriate accounting, information and management system.'[95]

Independent of the concrete definition of the object to be managed, the demands on the bank's internal information system have grown as well as the relevance of this information system for the controllability of the whole. For the ever more complex task of information management, the availability of quantitatively adequate and qualitatively sophisticated information technology has become a decisive factor behind success: 'The complexity of our banks is increasing steadily. To control it, we must be able to express it in information terms. That means getting a grip on an incredible volume of data which is also changing quickly. Obviously that would be impossible without the latest electronic equipment.'[96]

In the nature of the characterization of German and international banks, as related to their prospective international role, and the classification of Deutsche Bank by the members of its board of managing directors that regularly follows, one can see on the one hand entrepreneurial vision and self-perception, but on the other – especially in view of the consistent implementation of strategic projects – the probably unique potential available on the German banking market and particularly at the big banks in the critical resources personnel and capital. At Deutsche Bank too, though, resources are not unlimited. The visionary ambition formulated mainly by Herrhausen to push ahead with the development of the bank into a member of the very exclusive group of 'global players'[97] is critically questioned, modified, relativized – if not revised – under the aegis of spokesman Kopper, his successor, in many partly direct, partly indirect comments on the role of 'global player', restricted in terms of content to selected fields of investment banking: 'Yes, we are a global player. But only in certain areas and certainly not in retailing. In that quarter, we don't even want to be a European player. It is not our intention to enter other European industrial nations in this field. Global are all trading activities involving money, foreign exchange and securities. What we call "corporate finance" must also be global today. We are making very great efforts there, but are not where we would like to be everywhere in the world.'[98] It may be supposed that after Herrhausen it may possibly have become unmodern in the bank to use the term 'global player', that a different – standard – 'post-Herrhausen formulation' may have been introduced. Another statement by Kopper – in response to the question as to whether 'global player' had been abandoned – even reflects aversion: 'No, not at all. Only we first have to define what a global player is. It's a buzzword which doesn't mean much to me. But irrespective of that, we have always been international and will continue to be so in future.'⁹⁹ The question of whether the bank finds it desirable to be among the five to twenty institutions – depending on the definition – which in future will be in a position to play a global role, however you define it, is negated by Kopper: 'I have read too many such studies in my life. I don't believe in it any more. On the contrary, I believe that the idea of the global mega-bank is relatively dead. Just look at the ten biggest banks in the world, almost all of them Japanese institutions. They are stagnating, and for domestic reasons.'¹⁰⁰

More objective, but at the same time all the more clear, is the formulation of the bank's position targets in a national, European and global context: 'What do we want to achieve? In Germany we want to remain a fully integrated supplier of all financial services and develop our market share. In Europe we are operating in the wholesale sector with the emphasis on investment banking/corporate finance in countries with high potential, but also as a branching bank with a broad retail offering. Otherwise we use our regional opportunities wherever possible through subsidiaries operating throughout Europe. Overseas we wish to supply a wholesale product range in selected countries and regions with the emphasis on investment banking and corporate finance.'¹⁰¹

Acquisitions on a global scale, in particular a stronger universal bank positioning in the USA and Japan as the other parts of the Triad, are viewed sceptically: 'In Japan, I don't see that you could buy a bank, especially a small one. Because they don't exist. It's different in America. There, one could certainly buy a whole series of institutions at the moment. Only we don't believe that these banks, even if they are cheap, are at present desirable acquisitions for us. Moreover, as a bank you have to know what you can and can't do on the world market.'¹⁰²

The bank's international strategy – not called global – is summarized by Kopper as follows: 'Our international strategy includes, on the one side, providing services to international corporate customers, trading in securities and foreign exchange and money market business, and, on the other, going beyond that, corporate finance including mergers and acquisitions, project finance and international leasing. For this we need world-wide connections and bases and – where necessary – an international crew. We have that already, and we shall continue to invest and expand in these areas, but not necessarily through acquisitions. It is completely unrealistic that Deutsche Bank should become a world-wide universal bank with the full span of its domestic product range.'¹⁰³ This means a clear rejection by the bank – or rather by its present spokesman – at least of the vision of 'global player' as global and universal bank. Possible advantages of insiders on national markets and the present structure of customers' needs may be accepted as an explanation:

'The pursuit of a world-wide and, at the same time, universal strategy ultimately brings nothing but losses, for

- many of our customers want an individual and local full-range offering rather than world-wide specialities,
- to want to be better than competition everywhere would mean losing sight of the realities of one's own resources.'[104]

Over and above this, the bank sees a fundamental dilemma owing to different competitive advantages specific to individual business fields: 'The world-wide development of a local presence for all customer groups with simultaneous cost and quality leadership is a Gordian knot which no bank has yet been able to cut.'[105]

This seems to mean, surprisingly, that the need, emphasized frequently by Herrhausen, to embed the bank's European strategy in an overriding strategic framework is not upheld by Kopper. This would suggest that a global strategy as a consistent blueprint compatible with the European strategy is in fact no longer being formulated, let alone pursued, reflecting a reduction of the strategic perspective to the *European* level, that – in other words – the results of strategic analysis seem to allow global interdependences to be excluded from consideration or a purely defensive attitude to be taken *vis-à-vis* global developments.

Since the fundamental elements of the European strategy have been established and major acquisitions carried out, one could talk of the bank's abandonment of a global strategy in so far as the latter includes regional expansion or concentration. On the other hand, it is surprising that, especially in the recent past[106], an apparently intensive process of examining global product configurations has been initiated, the provisional results of which – the status of discussion mentioned at the beginning – shed a different light on the statements by the spokesman of the board of managing directors. Furthermore, Kopper writes elsewhere: 'We have no doubt that our strategy in and for Europe must be integrated into our global strategy. A European strategy can only be part of an overall strategy.'[107]

Kopper also emphasizes the intention, in connection with the takeover of Morgan Grenfell (pp. 770–3), to abandon the image of the bank as a purely German institution and underlines the need, especially in investment banking, to resort to human resources that are only available abroad: 'Success in investment banking has always been determined not only by capital, but primarily by people. The German reservoir is not big enough. In order to grow successfully and internationally, we shall have to go abroad to a far greater extent for human resources. This will increase our acceptance, effectiveness and credibility in the market. International merchant banking thinks, talks and acts in English. We must accept this culture as ours, integrate it as a multinational element, allow it to develop and use it. Only in this way will we be truly able to call ourselves Deutsche Bank Group and not be seen as a purely German institution.'

On the other hand, the assessment of the importance of international investment banking by today's spokesman reveals ambivalences: 'I have never been one of those who believe that so-called investment banking is the big business of the future. We as a universal bank cannot believe that, because for 120 years we have been transacting both sides of the business and know precisely how important classical lending business is.'[108]

In fact, the bank – for example in 1990 – expanded its business in Japan and the USA well beyond classical lending business – a sign that much of the growth in lending has to do with foreign corporate customers. And hence Kopper's clear statement in a *Euromoney* interview at the beginning of 1994 about the result of the bank's international expansion: on a net basis, Deutsche Bank's 1993 profits from outside Germany were probably greater than domestic profits. Alongside Europe, South-East Asia was a terrific success. Proprietary trading plus straightforward banking grew, with an ever increasing value added in lending. Structured finance was the future.

Only the future will show to what extent Herrhausen's visions have been abandoned, whether this has meant at least the temporary end of a period of acquisitional growth, and whether its financial and, above all, organizational integration will continue to allow even the retention of the 'strategy of opportunistic, selective acquisition'.[109] In an obituary on Herrhausen, it is stated that: 'Deutsche Bank may have to be measured against the visions and certainly the investments of the Herrhausen period. That will be a continuous link with the coming years without Herrhausen. All eyes are trained on Hilmar Kopper, the new spokesman of the board of managing directors. The transition is a return from charisma and toil to normality.'[110]

It is certainly convenient to interpret successful acquisitions in hindsight as the active implementation of previously explicitly formulated strategies. It could well be more difficult, however, to fulfil the expectation induced by permanent public articulation of strategic policy by means of measures which are recognizably connected in terms of time and materially compatible. Even if adequate resources are available, the absence, due to various factors, of adequate acquisition targets may often be observed. This raises the question of whether the announcement of a 'strategy of opportunistic, selective acquisition'[111] – irrespective, for example, of the material consistency of such a strategic formulation – serves to sustain the positive connotation of the term 'strategy' and its use, at the same time keeping open the option of exploiting *ad hoc* opportunities arising in the short term.

More convincing, on the other hand, is the assessment of the chances of seeking market leadership in segments of foreign – national – financial markets in specific fields of business: 'Our bank has deliberately refrained from catching up everywhere with market leaders on important foreign markets and competing, say, with Nomura or with Morgan Stanley or Goldman Sachs in the USA in securities issuing. These competitors develop their strengths from their position of "niche supplier", while our bank tries to achieve comparative competitive advantages by doing a balancing act between traditional universal bank and focused specialist at selected financial centres and in core markets.'¹¹²

It may be that a stock-taking and critical prognosis of the resources available to the bank could be followed by the insight – and then possibly conflict with the bank's entrepreneurial self-perception and the never considered target of sustaining independence – that a policy of going it alone, analogous to that in Europe, on a global scale and especially in other sub-markets of the triad – in the USA and the South-East Asian area dominated by Japan – is burdened with a large number of imponderables and risks, and may eventually prove to be illusory. The principle of independence in particular, in conjunction with the resulting flexibility, is in the bank's self-perception a *conditio sine qua non* for its entrepreneurial existence: 'Our strategy is to maintain the strength and thus the independence which allows us to respond flexibly to different developments. We shall never start something which takes up so much of our strength that we lose this flexibility.'¹¹³

For Deutsche Bank, then, strategic alliances of any kind with banks it sees as being comparable or its peers are presumably out of the question. As Kopper says quite clearly: 'If a co-operation is to be successful, it must ultimately end up in a merger.'¹¹⁴ The volume of investment which the bank considers necessary to be able to accompany its customers into all areas of the world in which they do business and make investments, and at the same time to give them a universal service in 'core markets', is gigantic: 'In the development of our presence at world financial centres, the adaptation of regional expertise and links through majority holdings in interesting European and overseas markets and the acquisition of global know-how in M&A and asset management (Morgan Grenfell), we have invested roughly 6.5 billion DM in the last few years alone.'¹¹⁵ Seen in this light, only a very small number of banks world-wide do indeed have the resources – and the capabilities to use them – to be able to operate globally at the leading financial centres by building up relations with customers in individual countries and by setting up a world-wide network. Furthermore, it is clear at many international competitors that the income situation is not positive in all global fields of business.

The bank strongly disputes the existence of an – at least theoretically conceivable – connection between the recognizable (temporary) end of the series of acquisitions abroad and the building up of a branch network in the new federal states: 'This new development has in no way impeded our international and especially our European business. For this is an effort which for once, if I may say so, we have not made with our international team. Their work was done in the past few years. This time the pressure is on the traditional domestic bank; and even today it has done the job to an extent that none of us could have ever imagined.'¹¹⁶

Recently, however, it can be observed that there is less and less diffidence about using concepts involving the stem 'global'. Various fields of business are being examined with regard to their level of globalization, and the plausibility of global strategies is investigated:

'Unlike the situation with corporate finance, global strategies in private banking are still in their infancy. Naturally the traditional private banking centres such as Switzerland, Liechtenstein and more recently Luxemburg serve a chiefly international clientele. A main reason for making deposits in these banking centres is the desire to reduce tax payments. This traditional investor motive has been joined by new forms of behaviour. More and more frequently we can see the internationally oriented investor who would like to use the know-how at international financial centres. But it is probably too early to talk about a "global trend". I believe, though, that we shall have to accept at least a certain degree of internationalization in certain segments of private banking business, or rather be able to generate it. The aim of the bank is to extend private banking in the 1990s to Europe and to certain selected non-European financial centres.'[117]

As far as Deutsche Bank Group's position target at the end of the millennium is concerned, the sustainment and – where possible – the expansion of its traditionally undoubtedly very strong market and income position in its home market, now extended to include the new federal states, as a precondition for European and, especially, for any kind of global ambition seems to be of essential importance as the basis of the bank's earning power – not only with retention of its universal-bank character, but within the framework of the Group as a 'fully integrated supplier of all financial services'.[118] In the perhaps somewhat drastic words of a British financial journalist, 'the enlarged home market ... is the cash machine that pays the bills for the bank's foreign push. More than four out of every five deutschmarks that Deutsche takes in as profit come from domestic operations.'[119]

Certainly in the competitively organized economic order of the Federal Republic, the bank cannot assume that it can retain this position, as it were, automatically. Thus, the insight that the implemented European financial services market has facilitated not only the possibility of banking activity in other European countries, but has made it correspondingly easier to enter the German market, and that over and above that a large number of developments tending to increase competition on the German core market have been observed, could result in a shift in the emphasis of strategic conceptions and business policy measures towards the home market. It remains to be seen how far the bank succeeds in getting a grip on the new and still developing competitive dynamism in the banking market.

The paradigm valid today differs from the European position target originally formulated by Herrhausen in the face of the single European market and the vision of 'global player' in the abandonment of the target of being present in all member countries of the European Union with a comprehensive branch network, linked with the fundamental strategic concentration on wholesale banking, with the focus on investment banking and corporate finance.[120] The bank intends to concentrate on retail banking as mass business in selected countries only, for example, in Italy and Spain. Not clear so far is the formulation regarding further typical universal-bank activities – in other words corresponding acquisitions in European countries where this is (not) yet the case. Schmitz, for example, using a term that Herrhausen liked, talks about a 'vision' of proceeding 'universally in our (future) home market Europe, wherever possible.'[121]

At the balance sheet press conference at the end of 1992, Kopper stressed that the bank did not think either nationally or internationally in market shares; the bank had no additional retail ambitions in Europe; on the contrary, its target was to be represented everywhere and appropriately in three segments: in trading, asset management and corporate finance. And at the beginning of 1994 he stated in detail in an interview that Deutsche Bank should develop into a European bank. It wanted to be market leader in Germany, in Italy and Spain an institution for individual customers, and throughout Europe a corporate and trading bank with the focus on corporate finance, money market business, foreign exchange, fixed income, equities and derivatives. This included asset management and the sale of mutual funds. On the other hand, the bank did not want to become a bank with customer business throughout Europe. For this reason, the bank had never participated in takeover plans concerning Lloyds Bank, Midland Bank or Credito Italiano. The bank did not want to be the tenth-biggest bank in a European country where they made no money. Italy and Spain had been different at the time the bank entered these countries, which the bank believed were behind in professionalism when it came to retailing. He could see no other countries.

The new European strategy for the bank can be described as having three characteristics:[122]

1. Individual country strategies of the bank aim at regional coverage of attractive core markets by the acquisition of market shares.

2. Within the framework of a strategy of pan-European distribution, the largest possible supranational development of selected customer groups through the conception of European products – European marques – with centralized production is sought.

3. In the development of competitive advantages specific to business fields, the bank is guided by its view of Europe as a whole.

In the European core countries, the United Kingdom and France in particular, the lack of a branch network implies the question as to how the bank assesses the appropriateness of its strategic positioning. The bank has no further discernible ambitions in the United Kingdom where, after the acquisition of Morgan Grenfell, it considers itself to be very well represented. It probably does not intend to engage in mass retail business alongside the four big English banks. The bank makes no secret of the absence of an appropriate market position in France. It would like to strengthen its position here in securities business and corporate banking; hence, it appears to be permanently interested in an acquisition in

France. 'Part of our strategy is that we should have an appropriate position in the country of our largest foreign trade partner in the EC. Ideal would be the acquisition of an investment bank ... If we found a suitable object where the cost/benefit ratio was right and which suited our business philosophy, we would snap it up immediately, especially in France.'[123] Kopper, however, talks in different terms: 'In France we want to buy neither a bank nor an insurance company. We are building up our business in France organically. That may take longer, but it's much cheaper.'[124]

If one asks which institution would be among the preferred partners, the bank has so far said absolutely nothing. The co-operation strategy pursued by some German and French banks in various forms – with and without capital backing – is not a strategic option for the bank in France, either. As Kopper again says critically in the *Euromoney* interview on co-operation between banks such as that between Dresdner Bank and Banque Nationale de Paris: he had seen consortium banks breaking apart because at some time it was a question of who would bear which risk and the responsibility. Difficulties in the acquisition of a French bank also arise through the self-formulated desire to have an appropriate positioning in every case: the bank did not wish to be no. 30 or 50 in the French national ranking after an acquisition. With regard to its French ambitions, it certainly does not seem to be in a hurry. In view of the largely distributed market, it probably no longer intends to conduct mass business with private customers. One can only speculate about the motives behind this decision. As a large number of disadvantages linked with the building up of its own branch network – capital and personnel requirements, time intensity – would not play a role here, it may be asked whether the explanation of such a refusal may be related in some way to the recognition of historical animosity on the part of the French: 'For us, France is not a retail market in which we wish to operate, no more than in the United Kingdom. In Europe we can really only see two retail markets which we consider to be interesting. We are in both of them, that is Italy and Spain.'[125] In Portugal, too, the bank's medium-term planning does not foresee the commencement of retail business: 'Retail banking in Portugal is something for the Portuguese, who know the market, rather than for foreigners.'[126]

In the recent past, the business field defined with an eye to the European private customer has been given the name 'private banking', which is somewhat irritating when translated directly into German. That this cannot refer to retail banking business in the sense of mass business is made quite clear in view of the market segmentation applied by the bank. As Kopper says: 'For our private banking products Europe-wide, we have defined roughly 2.5 million high-income individuals as a target group, all of them earning more than 200,000 DM p.a.'[127] A future focal point for the bank's activities within the framework of European private banking is to be asset management in selected individual countries; here, on the one hand, it will offer individual portfolio management to appropriately big customers – 'discretionary accounts' – and otherwise international mutual funds of its subsidiaries active in mutual fund business. The need to develop and trademark bank services for European private customers is regarded as increasingly urgent: 'In Europe, the name Deutsche Bank has a high quality: it stands for solidity, quality, internationality and professionalism. Parallel to Frankfurt's campaign as the "natural location for the European central bank", we want to reach a situation where Deutsche Bank products – and presumably that will often mean DM products – have a European positioning as the natural choice in private banking.'[128]

Besides Switzerland and Luxemburg, the traditional centres for international high-net-worth private customers, the Netherlands, Italy and Spain are the major target markets for the bank in private banking; it has developed tailored concepts for these markets: 'It will hardly be possible to offer bank services in all European markets on an identical basis. Different cultures and consumer expectations force us to proceed individually.'[129]

In particular, the fundamental concentration on Italy and Spain remains unaffected by the conception of the private banking business field. On the contrary: the assessment so far of individual national markets appears to have been confirmed by observations of the development of demand structures: 'We are pinning great hopes on the Italian and Spanish markets, as the need there for internationally oriented financial services is relatively high. In these countries we expect a gradual move towards the demand structure of the German market and see a genuine opportunity of getting an appropriate slice of the cake through our already well-established subsidiaries BAI and BCT. We are well represented in the attractive U.K. market with Morgan Grenfell. The bank has a prominent position in asset management for private customers. We have no definitive concept for France. A concentration of private banking on one or two locations (Paris and Strasburg) makes little sense in our experience. It would seem more desirable to develop private banking in France through an acquisition or some other form of co-operation. Should this not be possible in the foreseeable future, we shall – if necessary – set up our own offices in various centres.' The intention to extend the regional boundaries of private banking beyond the borders of Europe is probably especially interesting: 'These thoughts about private banking apply similarly, by the way, to selected financial centres in Asia. Here, our branch network in South-East Asia is a good starting point for our international private banking aspirations.'[130]

Every claim not to want to be a 'global player' must be understood, in the face of such new formulations, as referring to the past or as an understatement. In 1991 the bank describes the typical qualities of a 'global player' in what may be regarded as the latest and most concrete definition of this concept:

'Important elements of a globally oriented bank in the 1990s are ...
– centres of competence for customers
– development of global core products
– creation of inexpensive structures and

– use of information technology for customer products and our own management.'¹³¹

For complex service configurations such as corporate finance or mergers and acquisitions – 'product-oriented functions'¹³² – where the decisive competitive factor is probably human resources in view of the need for creative, but also scarce and expensive specialists, the bank is seeking a concentration in centres of competence and their installation at local offices. The concept of centres of competence – for example, Morgan Grenfell – can be described as the organizational reflection of globalization, on the basis of which the bank is planning to develop a global product range and offer it in selected core markets: 'Such core products make it possible not only to achieve competence advantages and scope for differentiation through the specialization of products in the form of our own marque profiles, but at the same time offer approaches to the exploitation of rationalization potential. At the present time we are working more intensively on so-called Euro-products, e.g. European payments business or European M&A services. In risk and portfolio management, too, core products can be built up by supra-disciplinary analysis competence, but also in consulting or in specialized financings.'¹³³

The formulation of and response to distribution policy questions, especially the probable reorientation of the distribution network, characterized by the end of the monopoly of stationary distribution through branches and the growing popularity of alternative distribution forms, such as home banking, and new distribution media, such as cards or telephone, will probably have outstanding market-political importance in the national, European and, only in third place, in the global context. A more differentiated market segmentation and more strongly cost-oriented pricing within the framework of market policy, as well as lean management and cost management in the field of internal operations have been identified by the bank as challenges in its preparation for competition in the 1990s. Tackling them across the increasingly blurred boundaries of the German market is to allow the creation and sustainment of competitive advantages:

'1. As in any mature market, a stronger segmentation of products – by customer – is necessary. How did Ludwig Erhard put it: "Market economics is something for consumers." And the banks should take note.

2. The subsidizing of one product by another cannot be maintained. The saver will not accept that he has to receive a lower interest rate so that property finance can be carried out at less than capital market costs. The big portfolio investor will not be prepared to subsidize the loss-making business with small investors.

3. The standardization of bank services will carry the banks into new cost dimensions. Here, they must learn to think in industrial categories.'¹³⁴

The preconditions for this may – all in all – be regarded as fulfilled, as external observers also believe: 'Poised at the gates of Eastern Europe, Deutsche Bank holds a regional edge that its larger European, Japanese and American rivals do not possess. Add to that its well-deployed assets, its drive and sense of purpose, and there is no reason to doubt that the aggressive bank is ready to grow, grow, grow.'

That this might not happen at the pace expected in many quarters is viewed calmly by the bank. As Kopper says: 'It may well be that our strategy for international banking appears too cautious to some. There are presumably other banks pursuing a more aggressive policy. Nevertheless, I prefer a more evolutionary approach. It's part of my understanding of prudent banking to give priority, even in competition for future markets, to the interests of depositors and shareholders.'[135]

Notes

The Deutsche Bank
from its Founding to the Great War
1870–1914

[1] See *Deutsche Bankengeschichte*. Edited by the Wissenschaftliche Beirat des Instituts für bankhistorische Forschung, vol. 2, (Frankfurt a.M. 1982), pp. 171–94, 223–70. Karl Erich Born, *International Banking in the 19th and 20th Centuries* (Leamington Spa 1983), pp. 82–92.

[2] Obituary in Deutsche Bank Business Report 1890, p. 4.

[3] On what follows, see *Neue Deutsche Biographie*. Edited by the Historische Kommission der Bayerischen Akademie der Wissenschaften, vol. 3 (Berlin 1957), pp. 574ff.; Historisches Archiv Deutsche Bank (HADB), file: Supervisory Board, Delbrück.

[4] Adelbert Delbrück, *Aufzeichnungen unseres Vaters Adelbert Delbrück. Für die Enkel und Urenkel gedruckt* (Leipzig 1922), p. 175.

[5] Ludwig Bamberger, *Erinnerungen*. Edited by Paul Nathan (Berlin 1989), p. 385.

[6] See Marie-Lise Weber, *Ludwig Bamberger* (Stuttgart 1987); Stanley Zucker, *Ludwig Bamberger. German Politician and Social Critic 1823–1899* (Pittsburgh 1975); Erich Achterberg and Maximilian Müller-Jabusch, *Lebensbilder deutscher Bankiers aus fünf Jahrzehnten* (Frankfurt a.M. 1963), pp. 193–216; HADB, file: Supervisory Board, Bamberger.

[7] Achterberg and Müller-Jabusch, *Lebensbilder*, p. 205.

[8] Quoted in Achterberg and Müller-Jabusch, *Lebensbilder*, p. 211.

[9] See Manfred Pohl, 'Selected Documents on the History of the Deutsche Bank', *Studies on Economic and Monetary Problems and on Banking History*, 22 (1988), pp. 35ff.; Fritz Seidenzahl, *100 Jahre Deutsche Bank 1870–1970* (Frankfurt a.M. 1970), pp. 8f.

[10] Born, *International Banking*, pp. 171ff.

[11] HADB, J 20; the memorandum is reprinted in Manfred Pohl, 'Documents on the History of the Deutsche Bank', *Studies on Economic and Monetary Problems and on Banking History*, 21 (1986), pp. 75ff.

[12] Articles of Association of the Deutsche Bank Aktien-Gesellschaft, 10 March 1870, pp. 3f., HADB.

[13] Delbrück, *Aufzeichnungen*, p. 178; Deutsche Bank Business Report 1871, p. 4.

[14] Delbrück, *Aufzeichnungen*, p. 175.

[15] The memorandum is reprinted in Karl Helfferich, *Georg von Siemens*, vol. 1 (Berlin 1921), pp. 215f.

[16] Geheimes Staatsarchiv Preussischer Kulturbesitz (GStA Merseburg), Rep. 120, Ministry for Trade and Industry, dept XI.2, no. 24, vol. 1, fol. 21.

[17] Ibid.

[18] Ibid., fol. 24.

[19] Ibid., fol. 27.

[20] Letter from founding committee, 24 February 1870, HADB, file: 1870.

[21] Letter from provisional administrative board, 24 February 1870, in which the members of the founding committee inform potential subscribers about the further development of the project, HADB, file: 1870; the provisional administrative board to Trade Minister von Itzenplitz, 25 February 1870, GStA Merseburg, Rep. 120, Ministry for Trade and Industry, dept. XI.2, no. 24, vol. 1, fol. 41ff.

[22] See esp. Friedrich List, *Der internationale Handel, die Handelspolitik und der deutsche Zollverein*, 2nd edn (Stuttgart 1842), Introduction.

[23] See Richard Tilly, 'Los von England: Probleme des Nationalismus in der deutschen Wirtschaftsgeschichte', *Zeitschrift für die gesamte Staatswissenschaft*, 124 (1968), pp. 179–196.

[24] The patriotic argument comes out particularly clearly in Wallich's case: 'The Deutsche Bank was founded with the object of conducting overseas banking in Germany and releasing Germany's overseas trade from British mediation. Up until 1870, not a single bale of cotton could be imported into Germany without being financed by a British agency ... These unnecessary agency fees cost Germany many millions annually, and it was a happy notion to free the fatherland from this tribute and make our commerce independent.' Hermann Wallich, 'Aus meinem Leben', in Hermann Wallich and Paul Wallich, *Zwei Generationen im deutschen Bankwesen 1833–1914* (Frankfurt a.M. 1978), p. 116.

[25] *Hermes, Informationsblatt für Volkswirtschaft und Finanzwesen*, 7 April 1910, HADB, press cuttings.

[26] Michalowsky to Centralverband des Deutschen Bank- und Bankiergewerbes, 5 November 1913, HADB, file: 1913.

[27] HADB, file: Erste Zeichner; the list of subscribers is reprinted in Pohl, *Studies*, 22, pp. 42ff.

[28] HADB, press cuttings; the first financial advertisement of the Deutsche Bank in the *Frankfurter Zeitung*, 24 and 25 March 1870, is also reprinted in Pohl, *Studies*, 22, p. 46.

[29] Seidenzahl, *100 Jahre*, p. 25.

[30] *Der Aktionär*, 30 January 1870.

[31] *Der Aktionär*, 27 March 1870.

[32] *Frankfurter Zeitung*, 25 March 1870.

[33] *Der Aktionär*, 17 December 1871.

[34] HADB, file: 1870.

[35] Articles of association of the Deutsche Bank Aktien-Gesellschaft, 10 March 1870, section 22, p. 13, HADB.

[36] Ibid., section 17, p. 11.

37 Helfferich, *Siemens*, vol. 1, p. 217f.

38 Wallich, 'Aus meinem Leben', p. 116.

39 Ibid., p. 123.

40 See Manfred Pohl, 'Vom Bankier zum Manager', in Hanns Hubert Hofmann (ed.), *Bankherren und Bankiers* (Limburg 1978), pp. 149ff.

41 See Karl Helfferich, *Georg von Siemens. Ein Lebensbild aus Deutschlands grosser Zeit*, 3 vols. (Berlin 1921–23); see also Achterberg and Müller-Jabusch, *Lebensbilder*, pp. 227–40; HADB, file: Siemens.

42 Siemens to Elise Görz, 9 March 1872, quoted in Helfferich, *Siemens*, vol. 3, p. 269.

43 Helfferich, *Siemens*, vol. 1, p. 226.

44 Quoted in Helfferich, *Siemens*, vol. 3, p. 243.

45 Erich Achterberg, 'Hermann Wallich', *Zeitschrift für das gesamte Kreditwesen*, 16 (1963), p. 228.

46 See Wallich, 'Aus meinem Leben'; Erich Achterberg, *Berliner Hochfinanz. Kaiser, Fürsten, Millionäre um 1900* (Frankfurt a.M. 1965), pp. 115–26; HADB, file: Wallich.

47 Bamberger, *Erinnerungen*, p. 386.

48 Wallich, 'Aus meinem Leben', p. 124.

49 Ibid., pp. 135f.

50 *Berliner Börsen-Zeitung*, 2 May 1928.

51 Helfferich, *Siemens*, vol. 1, p. 228.

52 Bamberger, *Erinnerungen*, p. 386.

53 On what follows, see below, pp. 49ff, for greater detail.

54 Wallich's memorandum for the administrative board, probably written shortly after he joined the Deutsche Bank in the autumn of 1870, p. 1, HADB, file: 1870.

55 Ibid., p. 4; see also Helfferich, *Siemens*, vol. 1, pp. 232f., 241ff.

56 Manfred Pohl, 'Deutsche Bank London Agency founded 100 years ago', *Studies on Economic and Monetary Problems and on Banking History*, 10 (1973), pp. 17–35.

57 On what follows, see below, pp. 51ff, for greater detail.

58 See Deutsche Bank Business Report 1872, p. 4.

59 See Helfferich, *Siemens*, vol. 1, pp. 248f.; the share capital was in the amount of 3 million talers, with the Deutsche Bank holding 1 million (see Deutsche Bank Business Report 1874, p. 4).

60 Deutsche Bank Business Report 1888, p. 4.

61 'Setting up a general overseas bank seems to us, according to our experience, impossible for a wide variety of technical reasons (different currencies in individual countries and so on). What would, however, be useful is to establish such banks for the purpose of supporting overseas trade in particular areas' (Deutsche Bank Business Report 1886, p. 4).

62 In 1889, for example, it founded (in conjunction with a consortium of thirteen well-known joint stock and private banks) the Deutsch-Asiatische Bank with branches in China, Japan and India. The same year saw the founding of the Madrid-based Banco Hispano Alemán, which in 1894 was converted into the limited partnership Guillermo

Vogel & Co. and eventually, in 1906, into a branch of the Deutsche Ueberseeische Bank. Its participation in the Banco Central Mexicano, entered into in 1899, was sold off again by the Deutsche Bank in 1908. In 1905 it participated in the founding of the Zentralamerika-Bank in Guatemala, although in the very next year this was turned into the Aktiengesellschaft für ueberseeische Bauunternehmungen. In Africa it was involved in setting up the Deutsch-Ostafrikanische Bank in 1905, and finally in 1911 there was the participation in the Handelsbank für Ostafrika. In this connection, see Karl Strasser, *Die deutschen Banken im Ausland* (Munich 1924).

[63] See Deutsche Bank Business Report 1890, p. 5.

[64] Memorandum from Wallich, p. 1, HADB, file: 1870.

[65] Ibid., p. 2.

[66] See Walter Hook, *Die wirtschaftliche Entwicklung der ehemaligen Deutschen Bank im Spiegel ihrer Bilanzen* (Heidelberg 1954), pp. 112f.

[67] See Jacob Riesser, *Die deutschen Grossbanken und ihre Konzentration mit der Entwicklung der Gesamtwirtschaft in Deutschland*, 4th edn (Jena 1912), pp. 64, 166ff.

[68] Helfferich, *Siemens*, vol. 1, p. 303.

[69] Deutsche Bank Business Report 1870, p. 5.

[70] In 1899 company capital stood at 150 million marks while deposits totalled 155.5 million marks; in 1901 total equity amounted to 199.3 million marks and deposits had risen to 214.5 million marks (see balance sheets in Deutsche Bank Business Reports 1899 and 1901).

[71] Riesser, *Konzentration*, pp. 177ff.

[72] The first deposit office outside Berlin was set up on the premises of a private banker in Dresden in 1889; see Hook, *Die wirtschaftliche Entwicklung*, p. 113. In 1900 the Deutsche Bank had six deposit offices outside Berlin; see Adolf Weber, *Depositenbanken und Spekulationsbanken. Ein Vergleich deutschen und englischen Bankwesens*, 4th edn (Munich 1938), p. 120.

[73] Weber, *Depositenbanken und Spekulationsbanken*, p. 120.

[74] See Riesser, *Konzentration*, p. 178.

[75] For a general view of this subject, see Hans Rosenberg, *Grosse Depression und Bismarckzeit. Wirtschaftsablauf, Gesellschaft und Politik in Mitteleuropa* (Berlin 1967).

[76] Helfferich, *Siemens*, vol. 1, pp. 212f.; Born, *International Banking*, p. 86.

[77] Friedrich Gneist, *Die nationale Rechtsidee von den Ständen und das preussische Dreiklassenwahlsystem* (Darmstadt 1962), p. 254.

[78] Wallich, 'Aus meinem Leben', p. 127.

[79] See Pohl, *Konzentration im deutschen Bankwesen 1848–1980* (Frankfurt a.M. 1982), pp. 130ff.; Manfred Pohl, 'Deutsche Bank during the "Company Promotion" Crisis (1873–1876)', *Studies on Economic and Monetary Problems and on Banking History*, 11 (1973), pp. 19–33.

[80] Wallich, 'Aus meinem Leben', p. 128.

[81] See balance sheets in Deutsche Bank Business Reports 1875 and 1880.

[82] Carl Fürstenberg, *Die Lebensgeschichte eines deutschen Bankiers*. Edited by Hans Fürstenberg (Berlin 1931), p. 212.

[83] Seidenzahl, *100 Jahre*, pp. 51ff.

[84] Paul Model, *Die grossen Berliner Effektenbanken* (Jena 1896), p. 106.

[85] *Die Bank*, 1914, pp. 415ff.

[86] Ibid., p. 424.

[87] Pohl, *Konzentration*, pp. 202ff., esp. pp. 210f.

[88] Ibid., pp. 231ff.

[89] Therese Krupp née Wilhelmi to her father, 12 May 1819, quoted in Wilhelm Bredow, *Friedrich Krupp der Erfinder und Gründer. Leben und Briefe* (Berlin 1923), p. 187; on this subject in general, see Jürgen Lindenlaub and Renate Köhne-Lindenlaub, 'Unternehmensfinanzierung bei Krupp 1811–1848. Ein Beitrag zur Kapital- und Vermögensentwicklung', *Beiträge zur Geschichte von Stadt und Stift Essen*, 102 (1988), pp. 83ff.

[90] See Knut Borchardt, 'Zur Frage des Kapitalmangels in der ersten Hälfte des 19. Jahrhunderts in Deutschland', in Rudolf Braun *et al.* (eds), *Industrielle Revolution. Wirtschaftliche Aspekte* (Cologne/Berlin 1972), p. 221.

[91] See Toni Pierenkemper, 'Zur Finanzierung von industriellen Unternehmensgründungen im 19. Jahrhundert – mit einigen Bemerkungen über die Bedeutung der Familie', in Dietmar Petzina (ed.), *Zur Geschichte der Unternehmensfinanzierung* (Berlin 1990), p. 77.

[92] See Otto Hübner, *Die Banken* (Leipzig 1854), pp. 170 ff.

[93] Quoted from Bertrand Gille, 'Banking and Industrialisation in Europe 1730–1914', in Carlo M. Cipolla (ed.), *The Fontana Economic History of Europe, vol. 3. The Industrial Revolution* (Glasgow 1973), p. 272.

[94] In this connection, see Pohl, *Konzentration*, pp. 44ff.

[95] Karl Erich Born, 'Die Hauptentwicklungslinien des mitteleuropäischen Universalbankensystems', in *Universalbankensystem als historisches und politisches Problem* (= *Bankhistorisches Archiv*, Beiheft 2), (Frankfurt a.M. 1977), p. 14.

[96] See Pohl, *Konzentration*.

[97] See Weber, *Depositenbanken und Spekulationsbanken*.

[98] See Riesser, *Konzentration*, p. 388.

[99] Pohl, *Konzentration*, p. 153; see also Deutsche Bank Business Report 1873, p. 5.

[100] See Pohl, *Studies*, 11, pp. 26ff.

[101] The management vehemently opposed this plan, and it was eventually thrown out at an extraordinary shareholders' meeting on 31 January 1876 by 6,169 votes to 1,902 (Wilckens' motion at the extraordinary shareholders' meeting of 31 January 1876, HADB, file: 1873–75); see also Helfferich, *Siemens*, vol. 1, p. 297.

[102] HADB, file: 1873–75, pp. 11ff.

[103] Deutsche Bank Business Report 1876, p. 5.

[104] On the significance of the current account loan, see Otto Jeidels, *Das Verhältnis der deutschen Grossbanken zur Industrie mit besonderer Berücksichtigung der Eisenindustrie*, 2nd edn (Munich/Leipzig 1913), pp. 121ff.

[105] Riesser, *Konzentration*, p. 302.

[106] See Wilfried Feldenkirchen, 'Banken und Stahlindustrie im Ruhrgebiet. Zur Entwicklung ihrer Beziehungen 1873–1914', *Bankhistorisches Archiv*, 5 (1979), p. 30; see also Riesser, *Konzentration*, p. 292f.

[107] The first Krupp loan is generally regarded in the literature as an expression of the strong position occupied by the banks *vis-à-vis* industry (see, for example, Feldenkirchen, 'Banken und Stahlindustrie', p. 30). On the other hand, Wellhöner rates the redemption of the loan in 1879 as a sign of how Krupp was able to turn competition between the banks to his own advantage. See Volker Wellhöner, *Grossbanken und Grossindustrie im Kaiserreich* (Göttingen 1989), pp. 155ff.

[108] Copies of consortium agreements for Krupp bonds from 1874, HADB, S633.

[109] See Helfferich, *Siemens*, vol. 2, pp. 29f.

[110] It was from this sector that Siemens & Halske (founded in 1847) began its dramatic expansion.

[111] On what follows, see Hubert Kiesewetter, *Industrielle Revolution in Deutschland 1815–1914* (Frankfurt a.M. 1989), pp. 219ff.

[112] See Helfferich, *Siemens*, vol. 2, pp. 52f., 62ff.

[113] See Manfred Pohl, *Emil Rathenau und die AEG*, (Berlin/Frankfurt a.M. 1988) pp. 56ff.; Helfferich, *Siemens*, vol. 2, pp. 70ff.; Felix Pinner, *Emil Rathenau und das elektrische Zeitalter* (Leipzig 1918), pp. 146ff.

[114] HADB, S76. Key sources are reprinted in Pohl, *AEG*, pp. 65ff., 235–40; see also Helfferich, *Siemens*, vol. 2, p. 80. The reorganization of the Edison-Gesellschaft as AEG was entered in the Berlin Commercial Register on 12 July 1887, HADB, S76.

[115] Stock exchange prospectus of October 1887, reprinted in Pohl, *AEG*, pp. 241f.; the subscription took place on 25 October 1887. See *Berliner Börsen-Courier*, 22 October 1887.

[116] See Hugh Neuburger and Houston H. Stokes, 'German Banks and German Growth 1883–1913. An Empirical View', *Journal of Economic History*, 34 (1974), p. 713.

[117] Jeidels, *Grossbanken*, p. 49.

[118] See Manfred Pohl, 'Überlebenschancen von Unternehmensgründungen in der Zeit von 1870–1918', in Hans Pohl (ed.), *Überlebenschancen von Unternehmensgründungen* (= *Zeitschrift für Unternehmensgeschichte*, Beiheft 63), (Stuttgart 1991), p. 42.

[119] Rathenau and Deutsch to the Deutsche Bank, 8 May 1887, HADB, S76; reprinted in Pohl, *AEG*, p. 67.

[120] Landau to Deutsche Edison-Gesellschaft, 9 May 1887, HADB, S76; reprinted in Pohl, *AEG*, p. 67.

[121] Friedmann to the Deutsche Bank, 12 May 1887, Deutsche Bank to Friedmann, 14 May 1887, HADB, S76; reprinted in Pohl, *AEG*, p. 68.

[122] See Sontag, 'Die Geschäfts-Bedingungen im Verkehr der Banken und Bankiers mit ihrer Kundschaft', *Bank-Archiv*, 3 (1903/04), p. 187; Walter Hartmann, 'Das Stimmrecht der Depotaktie', *Bank-Archiv*, 24 (1924/25), p. 486–91.

[123] General Terms of Business of the Deutsche Bank, 2 February 1900, p. 3, HADB, file: Allgemeine Geschäftsbedingungen – Giroverkehr und diverse Geschäfte.

[124] See HADB, S77. The causes and unfolding of the conflict are described in Pohl, *AEG*, pp. 117ff. For the following years, too, there are copies of some of the correspondence between Siemens & Halske and AEG in the files of the Deutsche Bank. In other words, AEG kept the bank fully informed about such events.

[125] See Pohl, *AEG*, pp. 117ff.; Allgemeine Elektricitäts-Gesellschaft (ed.), *50 Jahre AEG*, Berlin 1956, pp. 79ff.; HADB, S77–8.

[126] Pohl, *AEG*, pp. 141f.

[127] Carbon copy of founders' report, undated, HADB, S1346; see also Georg Siemens, *Geschichte des Hauses Siemens*, vol. 1, (Munich 1947) pp. 192, 236ff.

[128] Helfferich, *Siemens*, vol. 2, p. 128.

[129] List of capital increases and subscribers 1897–99, HADB, S1346.

[130] Minutes of board meeting of 26 and 27 April 1898, HADB, S1346; see also Hugh Neuburger, 'The Industrial Politics of the Kreditbanken 1880–1914', *Business History Review*, 51 (1977), p. 195.

[131] On the development of trams, see Siemens, *Geschichte*, vol. 1, pp. 223ff.; HADB, S304–5.

[132] For a description of the post-1901 crisis in the electrical industry, see Siemens, *Geschichte*, vol. 1, pp. 278–82; see also HADB, S1320.

[133] In this connection, see Wilfried Feldenkirchen, 'Die Rolle der Banken bei der Sanierung von Industrieunternehmen (1850–1914)', *Die Rolle der Banken bei der Unternehmenssanierung* (= *Bankhistorisches Archiv*, Beiheft 22), (Frankfurt a.M. 1993), pp. 34f.; see also Pohl, *Konzentration*, pp. 268ff.

[134] See Yorck Dietrich, *Die Mannesmannröhren-Werke 1888 bis 1920* (= *Zeitschrift für Unternehmensgeschichte*, Beiheft 66), Stuttgart 1991, p. 30.

[135] HADB, S879.

[136] See Heinrich Koch, *75 Jahre Mannesmann. Geschichte einer Erfindung und eines Unternehmens* (Düsseldorf 1965), pp. 45f.

[137] Quoted in Koch, *75 Jahre Mannesmann*, p. 47.

[138] HADB, S876 Actien-Vertheilung; see also Horst A. Wessel, 'Finanzierungsprobleme in der Gründungs- und Ausbauphase der Deutsch-Österreichischen Mannesmannröhren-Werke AG. 1890–1907', in Dietmar Petzina (ed.), *Zur Geschichte der Unternehmensfinanzierung* (Berlin 1990), p. 127. Dietrich sees the reason for this distribution of shares not primarily in the assessment of the profits resulting from the patents but in a condition of the Mannesmann family to have a 50 per cent holding in all companies based on their invention. See Dietrich, *Mannesmannröhren-Werke*, p. 25.

[139] See HADB, S877; there is a distribution list of Mannesmann shares dated 11 September 1896 in HADB, S876.

[140] Julius Franken joined the Deutsch-Österreichische Mannesmannröhren-Werke on 1 July 1892, initially at the Komotau factory. He had previously headed an agency in Milan that represented the interests of a number of steel companies (Mannesmann included) in Italy. On the retirement of the inventors in the following year he became sole managing director.

[141] HADB, S953.

[142] For more detail see the Deutsch-Österreichische Mannesmannröhren-Werke Business Report for 1897/98, p. 7, HADB, S888. Copy of a statement by the Mannesmann brothers to the syndicate of the Deutsch-Österreichische Mannesmannröhren-Werke, HADB, S879 – Prozess Material Diverses. Max and Reinhard Mannesmann to Deutsche Bank, 27 December 1892, ibid. See also Wessel, 'Finanzierungsprobleme', p. 129.

[143] Horst A. Wessel, *Kontinuität im Wandel. 100 Jahre Mannesmann 1890–1990* (Düsseldorf 1990), p. 74.

[144] Deutsch-Österreichische Mannesmannröhren-Werke Business Report, 1895/96, p. 5, HADB, S888.

[145] This arrangement forms the basis of a share purchase agreement of 5 June 1897. See HADB, S879.

[146] Dietrich sees 1896/97 as the point where the fortunes of the Deutsch-Österreichische Mannesmannröhren-Werke began to improve. The loss that continued to be shown on the balance sheet was intended primarily to force the Mannesmann family out of the company. See Dietrich, *Mannesmannröhren-Werke*, p. 44.

[147] The Mannesmanns returned shares with a face value of 9 million marks and were paid 2 million in cash for them. They received a further 800,000 marks in 4.5 per cent bonds of Deutsch-Österreichische Mannesmannröhren-Werke AG; see Deutsch-Österreichische Mannesmannröhren-Werke Business Report, 1899/1900, p. 7, HADB, S888.

[148] Ibid., p. 27.

[149] See Deutsche Bank Business Reports 1889 and 1890.

[150] Pohl, *Konzentration*, pp. 261f.

[151] Seidenzahl, *100 Jahre*, p. 180.

[152] See Achterberg and Müller-Jabusch, *Lebensbilder*, pp. 241–52.

[153] See Walther Däbritz, *Denkschrift zum fünfzigjährigen Bestehen der Essener Credit-Anstalt in Essen* (Essen 1922), p. 172.

[154] Unfortunately, the correspondence has survived only for the period 1900 to 1905, HADB, file: Klönne.

[155] Thyssen to Klönne, 18 December 1902, ibid.

[156] Klönne to Thyssen, 19 December 1902, ibid.

[157] Thyssen to Klönne, 10 December 1903, ibid.

[158] Klönne to Thyssen, 6 July 1900, ibid.; Thyssen to Klönne, 9 July 1900, ibid.

[159] Klönne to Thyssen, 4 August 1902, ibid.

[160] Thyssen to Klönne, 7 August 1902, ibid.

[161] Klönne to Thyssen, 19 February 1903, ibid.

[162] Thyssen to Klönne, 20 February 1903, ibid.

[163] Thyssen to Klönne, 12 January 1902, ibid.

[164] Thyssen to Klönne, 16 July 1902, ibid.

[165] Thyssen to Klönne, 23 June 1902, HADB, S3610.

[166] Ibid.

[167] See Ulrich Wengenroth, 'Iron and Steel', in Rondo Cameron and V.I. Bovykin (eds), *International Banking 1870–1914* (New York/Oxford 1991), p. 488.

[168] Jeidels, *Grossbanken*.

[169] Rudolf Hilferding, *Das Finanzkapital. Eine Studie über die jüngste Entwicklung des Kapitalismus*. Reprint of the 1st edn of 1910 (Berlin 1947), p. 144.

[170] See Riesser, *Konzentration*.

[171] Jeidels, *Grossbanken*, p. 2.

[172] Alexander Gerschenkron, 'Wirtschaftliche Rückständigkeit in historischer Perspektive', in Rudolf Braun *et al.* (eds), *Industrielle Revolution. Wirtschaftliche Aspekte* (Cologne/Berlin 1972), p. 71.

[173] See, for example, Wellhöner, *Grossbanken und Grossindustrie*, pp. 66ff.; see also Jürgen Kocka, *Unternehmensverwaltung und Angestelltenschaft am Beispiel Siemens 1847–1914, Zum Verhältnis zwischen Kapitalismus und Bürokratie in der deutschen Industrialisierung* (Stuttgart 1969), p. 287.

[174] Neuburger, 'Kreditbanken', p. 198.

[175] Kocka, *Unternehmensverwaltung*, pp. 432ff.

[176] See also OMGUS, *Ermittlungen gegen die Deutsche Bank 1946/47* (Nördlingen 1985), p. 103; Dietrich, *Mannesmannröhren-Werke*, pp. 28f. Jeidels, *Grossbanken*, pp. 204f. For a critical account, see Volker Wellhöner and Harald Wixforth, 'Unternehmensfinanzierung durch Banken – ein Hebel zur Etablierung der Bankenherrschaft? Ein Beitrag zum Verhältnis von Banken und Schwerindustrie während des Kaiserreiches und der Weimarer Republik', in Dietmar Petzina (ed.), *Zur Geschichte der Unternehmensfinanzierung* (Berlin 1990), p. 22.

[177] In this connection, see also Dietrich, *Mannesmannröhren-Werke*, pp. 31ff.

[178] Ibid., pp. 26ff.

[179] Ibid., pp. 57f.

[180] Forgoing interest payments on share capital for years on end represents a measure of financial backing for the company that would hardly seem to justify Dietrich's view (*Mannesmannröhren-Werke*, p. 50) that provision by the banks of financial support for Deutsch-Österreichische Mannesmannröhren-Werke began only in 1897.

[181] This is the view put forward at least by Dietrich, *Mannesmannröhren-Werke*, p. 44.

[182] Klönne to Thyssen, 3 November 1903, HADB, file: Klönne.

[183] Thyssen to Klönne, 12 November 1903, ibid.

[184] Gille, 'Banking and Industrialisation in Europe 1730–1914', pp. 287ff., 294ff. Another reason was French company law, the restrictive provisions of which inhibited the formation of joint stock companies; in this connection, see Claude Fohlen, 'France 1700–1914', in Carlo M. Cipolla (ed.), *The Fontana Economic History of Europe, vol. 4. The Emergence of Industrial Societies, part 1* (Glasgow 1973), pp. 32–7.

[185] This process is described in great detail so far as Germany is concerned in Knut Borchardt, 'Germany 1700–1914', in Carlo M. Cipolla (ed.), *The Fontana Economic History of Europe, vol. 4. The Emergence of Industrial Societies, part 1* (Glasgow 1973), pp. 124f., 142–5.

[186] Wallich, 'Aus meinem Leben', p. 135.

[187] Jeidels, *Grossbanken*, p. 197.

[188] Ibid., p. 186.

[189] See also Helfferich, *Siemens*, vol. 3, p. 273.

[190] Wolfgang Zorn, 'Wirtschaft und Politik im deutschen Imperialismus', in Wilhelm Abel et al. (eds), *Wirtschaft, Geschichte und Wirtschaftsgeschichte. Festschrift zum 65. Geburtstag von Friedrich Lütge* (Stuttgart 1966), p. 342.

[191] HADB, J 20; see also Pohl, *Studies*, 21, pp. 75ff.

[192] On what follows, see also Pohl, *Studies*, 10, pp. 17ff.

[193] Deutsche Bank Business Report 1873, p. 3.

[194] HADB, J 20; see also Pohl, *Studies*, 21, p. 81.

[195] J.A. Hobson, *Imperialism. A Study*, 3rd edn (London/Boston/Sydney 1988), pp. 240f.

[196] Mammelsdorf report, HADB, file: Shanghai/Yokohama, p. 5.

[197] Ibid., p. 6.

[198] Quoted in Helfferich, *Siemens*, vol. 1, p. 242.

[199] Ibid., pp. 266f.

[200] Deutsche Bank Business Report 1875, p. 4.

[201] See Ernst Klein, 'The Deutsche Bank's South American Business before the First World War', *Studies on Economic and Monetary Problems and on Banking History*, 16 (1978), p. 12.

[202] Quoted in Model, *Berliner Effektenbank*, p. 117.

[203] Deutsche Bank Business Report 1879, p. 4.

[204] Georg Bessell, *Norddeutscher Lloyd 1857–1957. Geschichte einer bremischen Reederei* (Bremen 1957), pp. 49ff.

[205] See Hans-Ulrich Wehler, *Bismarck und der Imperialismus* (Cologne/Berlin 1969), pp. 235ff.; specifically on steamship subsidies, ibid., pp. 239ff.; Bessell, *Norddeutscher Lloyd*, pp. 49ff.

[206] The subsidizing of the steamship line was by no means viewed in an unreservedly positive light by Norddeutscher Lloyd. On conclusion of the negotiations with Postmaster General Heinrich von Stephan and Home Secretary Karl Heinrich von Boetticher, on 4 July 1885, the man who headed the company for many years, Lohmann, is said to have described the agreement to his daughter in the following terms: 'Today, the anniversary of the United States' Declaration of Independence, I am signing the agreement of our [the company's] enslavement.' See Bessell, *Norddeutscher Lloyd*, p. 53.

[207] Ludwig Raschdau, *Unter Bismarck und Caprivi. Erinnerungen eines deutschen Diplomaten 1885–1894*, 3rd edn (Berlin 1939), p. 18.

[208] Manfred Pohl, *Deutsche Bank Buenos Aires 1887–1987* (Mainz 1987), p. 24 suggests this; Wehler, *Bismarck und der Imperialismus*, p. 237 disagrees.

[209] Waldemar Hummer, 'Wirtschaft', in *Argentinien. 100 Jahre Deutsche Bank am Rio de la Plata. Katalog zur Ausstellung der Deutschen Bank AG* (Mainz 1987), p. 52.

[210] See Pohl, *Deutsche Bank Buenos Aires*, p. 20.

[211] Articles of association of the Deutsche Ueberseeische Bank, Berlin, 1897, section 2, HADB, file: Deutsche Ueberseeische Bank.

[212] See Pohl, *Deutsche Bank Buenos Aires*, pp. 26ff.; see also Klein, 'South American Business', pp. 19f.

[213] Pohl, *Deutsche Bank Buenos Aires*, p. 46.

[214] Klein, 'South American Business', pp. 21f.

[215] Pohl, *Deutsche Bank Buenos Aires*, p. 48.

[216] Klein, 'South American Business', p. 17.

[217] Quoted in Pohl, *Deutsche Bank Buenos Aires*, p. 52.

[218] See Fritz Seidenzahl, 'The Beginnings of the Deutsch-Ueberseeische Electricitäts-Gesellschaft', *Studies on Economic and Monetary Problems and on Banking History*, 7 (1968), pp. 15–21.

[219] See Maximilian Müller-Jabusch, *Fünfzig Jahre Deutsch-Asiatische Bank 1890–1939* (Berlin 1940), p. 31.

[220] See Peter Hertner, 'German banks abroad before 1914', in Geoffrey Jones (ed.), *Banks as Multinationals* (London/New York 1990), p. 110.

[221] Ibid.; Wilfried Feldenkirchen, 'Deutsches Kapital in China vor dem Ersten Weltkrieg', *Bankhistorisches Archiv*, 9 (1983), 2, p. 75.

[222] In a letter to Villard, Siemens noted on 29 July 1887 'that a major party that has the ear of the government is hostile, from what it calls the national viewpoint, to any overseas business (except it be a colonial swindle)'. Quoted in Helfferich, *Siemens*, vol. 2, p. 238.

[223] See Mira Wilkins, *The History of Foreign Investment in the United States to 1914* (Cambridge, Mass./London 1989), pp. 190ff.

[224] Siemens to Steiner, 28 June 1883, quoted in Helfferich, *Siemens*, vol. 2, p. 232.

[225] See Vincent P. Carosso, *The Morgans. Private International Bankers 1854–1913* (= *Harvard Studies in Business History*, 38), (Cambridge, Mass./London 1987), p. 383.

[226] Helfferich, *Siemens*, vol. 2, p. 247.

[227] Ibid., p. 255.

[228] His letter of resignation is reprinted in Arthur von Gwinner, *Lebenserinnerungen*. Edited by Manfred Pohl on behalf of the Historische Gesellschaft der Deutschen Bank, 2nd edn (Frankfurt a.M. 1992), pp. 127ff.

[229] Ibid., pp. 62, 121ff.

[230] This judgement was confirmed shortly afterwards by the United States Supreme Court. See Carosso, *The Morgans*, p. 384.

[231] Deutsche Bank Business Report 1897, p. 4.

[232] Moritz Bauer, Wiener Bankverein, to Steinthal, 10 February 1901, HADB, S1676.

[233] Gwinner to Stillman, 25 November 1902, Gwinner to Wiener Bankverein, 12 November 1902, Stillman to Gwinner, 28 April 1903, Gwinner to Stillman, 29 June 1903, HADB, S1676.

[234] Agreement of 27 June 1903, HADB, S1676.

[235] Gwinner to James Stillman, 29 June 1903, HADB, S1676.

[236] According to Hans Pohl, 'The Steaua Romana and the Deutsche Bank (1903–1920)', *Studies on Economic and Monetary Problems and on Banking History*, 24 (1989), pp. 86f.

[237] See HADB, S1676.

[238] Pohl, 'Steaua Romana', pp. 86f.

[239] The sole exception being the oil interests in Mesopotamia, where through its subsidiary, the Anatolian Railway Company, the Deutsche Bank had a preliminary concession to exploit the Mossul oil field.

[240] Pohl, 'Steaua Romana', pp. 86f.

[241] *Handels-Signale*, No. 289, 11 August 1903.

[242] Gwinner, *Lebenserinnerungen*, p. 99.

[243] Confidential message from Gwinner to Georg Spiess, Chairman of Steaua Romana, 3 July 1907, HADB, S1677.

[244] Gwinner, *Lebenserinnerungen*, p. 99.

[245] Wilhelm Pressel, 'Das Anatolische Eisenbahnnetz', offprint from *Zeitschrift für Eisenbahnen und Dampfschiffahrt der österreichisch-ungarischen Monarchie*, HADB, OR5. That the hopes associated with the building of the railways were subsequently only in part fulfilled has been shown by Donald Quataert, 'Limited Revolution. The Impact of the Anatolian Railway on Turkish Transportation and the Provisioning of Istanbul 1890–1908', *Business History Review*, 51 (1977), pp. 139–60.

[246] For a general view of this subject, see S. Pamuk, The *Ottoman Empire and European Capitalism 1820–1913. Trade, Investment and Production* (Cambridge 1987); H. Islamoglou-Inan (ed.), *The Ottoman Empire and the World Economy* (Cambridge 1987).

[247] For a general view of German foreign policy under Wilhelm II, see Gregor Schöllgen, *Flucht in den Krieg? Die Aussenpolitik des kaiserlichen Deutschland* (Darmstadt 1991).

[248] Foreign Office to Deutsche Bank, 2 September 1888, copy in HADB, OR5.

[249] In this connection, see Gregor Schöllgen, *Imperialismus und Gleichgewicht. Deutschland, England und die orientalische Frage 1871–1914* (Munich 1984), pp. 43f.

[250] In this connection, see Bernd Schmiale's (albeit ideologically slanted) dissertation, *Zur Tätigkeit der Philipp Holzmann AG im Rahmen der Nahostexpansion der Deutschen Bank AG. Eine wirtschaftshistorische Betrachtung unter besonderer Berücksichtigung des Zeitraumes zwischen 1888 und 1918*, unpublished thesis (East Berlin 1987).

[251] Stenographische Berichte über die Verhandlungen des Deutschen Reichstages, VIII. Legislaturperiode, I. Session 1890–91, 2 vols., fortieth sitting on 12 December 1890, p. 887.

[252] See Schmiale, *Philipp Holzmann*, p. 65.

[253] See Manfred Pohl and Jürgen Lodemann, *Die Bagdadbahn. Geschichte und Gegenwart einer berühmten Eisenbahnlinie* (Mainz 1989), p. 28.

[254] See Helmut Mejcher, 'Die Bagdadbahn als Instrument deutschen wirtschaftlichen Einflusses im osmanischen Reich', *Geschichte und Gesellschaft*, 1 (1975), p. 454.

[255] See Born, *International Banking*, pp. 140f.

[256] Ibid., p. 142.

[257] Telegram of 24 December 1899, HADB, OR17 (where there is also a contemporary copy of the agreement).

[258] Quoted in Helfferich, *Siemens*, vol. 3, pp. 104f.

[259] Quoted in ibid., p. 90.

[260] Klaus Hildebrand, *Deutsche Aussenpolitik 1871–1918* (= *Enzyklopädie Deutscher Geschichte* 2), (Munich 1989) p. 36.

[261] Schöllgen, *Imperialismus und Gleichgewicht*, p. 114.

[262] Notes by Bülow, 26 April and 5 May 1899, quoted in Schöllgen, *Imperialismus und Gleichgewicht*, p. 115.

[263] The bank went back to Junius Spencer Morgan, father of John Pierpont Morgan, with whom the Deutsche Bank collaborated in the USA and who founded the J.P. Morgan bank that still exists today.

[264] See Schöllgen, *Imperialismus und Gleichgewicht*, p. 239ff.

[265] Gwinner, *Lebenserinnerungen*, p. 81.

[266] See Fritz Seidenzahl, 'The Agreement concerning the Turkish Petroleum Company. The Deutsche Bank and the Anglo-German Understanding of the 19th March 1914', *Studies on Economic and Monetary Problems and on Banking History*, 5 (1967), pp. 14–36.

[267] *Frankfurter Zeitung*, 16 July 1940.

[268] Schöllgen, *Imperialismus und Gleichgewicht*, p. 177.

[269] Report by Siemens to the management of Deutsche Bank, 28 April 1900, HADB, OR293.

[270] Siemens to Foreign Minister Prince von Bülow, 11 September 1900, copy, HADB, OR295.

[271] Gerhard Wiegand (ed.), *Halbmond im letzten Viertel. Briefe und Reiseberichte aus der alten Türkei von Theodor und Marie Wiegand 1895 bis 1918* (Munich 1970), p. 29.

[272] Mejcher, 'Bagdadbahn', pp. 455f.

[273] See John G. Williamson, *Karl Helfferich 1872–1924. Economist, Financier, Politician* (Princeton, New Jersey 1971), pp. 78f.

[274] *Frankfurter Zeitung*, 5 March 1914.

[275] Quoted in Hartmut Berghoff and Roland Müller, 'Unternehmer in Deutschland und England', *Historische Zeitschrift*, 256 (1993), p. 381; for a general view of this subject, see esp. Hans Jaeger, *Unternehmer in der deutschen Politik 1890–1918* (Bonn 1967).

[276] Berghoff and Müller, 'Unternehmer', pp. 382f.

[277] Servaes to Heinrich Hermann Rentzsch, General Secretary of the Union of German Iron and Steel Manufacturers, 6 November 1875, quoted in Helmut Böhme, *Deutschlands Weg zur Grossmacht. Studien zum Verhältnis von Wirtschaft und Staat während der Reichsgründungszeit 1848–1881*, 2nd edn (Cologne 1972), p. 388.

[278] See Fritz Seidenzahl, 'Das Spannungsfeld zwischen Staat und Bankier im wilhelminischen Zeitalter', *Tradition*, 13 (1968), pp. 142ff.

[279] Bamberger, *Erinnerungen*, pp. 386f.

[280] Helfferich, *Siemens*, vol. 3, pp. 160f.

[281] Ibid., p. 163.

[282] Jacob Riesser, 'Dr Georg von Siemens', *Bank-Archiv*, 1 (1901–02), p. 21.

[283] Published by Julius Springer, Berlin, 1874; in this connection, see also Fritz Seidenzahl,

'A Forgotten Pamphlet by Georg Siemens', *Studies on Economic and Monetary Problems and on Banking History*, 8 (1969), pp. 17–21.

[284] Stenographische Berichte über die Verhandlungen des Deutschen Reichstages, II. Legislaturperiode, II. Session 1874–75, vol. 1, pp. 216ff., vol. 2, pp. 1371ff.

[285] Ibid., vol. 1, p. 220.

[286] Ibid., vol. 1, p. 217; see also Helfferich, *Siemens*, vol. 3, p. 165.

[287] Quoted in Helfferich, *Siemens*, vol. 3, p. 166.

[288] Ibid., p. 167.

[289] Stenographische Berichte über die Verhandlungen des Deutschen Reichstages, VI. Legislaturperiode, I. Session 1884–85, vol. 2, p. 767; see also Helfferich, *Siemens*, vol. 3, pp. 170ff.

[290] In this connection, see Johann Christian Meier, *Die Entstehung des Börsengesetzes vom 22. Juni 1896* (St Katharinen 1992), pp. 32ff.

[291] Stenographische Berichte über die Verhandlungen des Deutschen Reichstages, VI. Legislaturperiode, I. Session 1884–85, vol. 2, p. 769.

[292] Quoted in Helfferich, *Siemens*, vol. 3, pp. 174f.

[293] Ibid., p. 179.

[294] Stenographische Berichte über die Verhandlungen des Deutschen Reichstages, VIII. Legislaturperiode, II. Session 1892–93, vol. 1, p. 583.

[295] Ibid., p. 584.

[296] Quoted in Helfferich, *Siemens*, vol. 3, p. 191.

[297] Thomas Nipperdey, *Deutsche Geschichte 1866–1918, vol. 2. Machtstaat vor der Demokratie* (Munich 1992), p. 706.

[298] Stenographische Berichte über die Verhandlungen des Deutschen Reichstages, X. Legislaturperiode, II. Session 1900–02, vol. 2, pp. 2355f.

[299] Helfferich, *Siemens*, vol. 2, p. 157.

[300] For comparison, see also Hans-Ulrich Wehler, *Bismarck und der Imperialismus*, pp. 158ff.

[301] HADB, S193, Deutscher Kolonialverein.

[302] Helfferich, *Siemens*, vol. 2, p. 219.

[303] Mommsen to Friedrich Imhoof-Blumer, 24 October 1901; by kind information of Mr von Kaenel, Frankfurt a.M., who is preparing an edition of this very interesting correspondence.

[304] Jaeger, *Unternehmer*, p. 167.

[305] Ibid., pp. 35, 44, 65.

[306] On Gwinner in general, see HADB, files: Gwinner 1–4; Achterberg, *Berliner Hochfinanz*, pp. 33ff.; Gwinner, *Lebenserinnerungen*.

[307] Gwinner, *Lebenserinnerungen*, p. 106.

[308] The letter of appointment is in HADB, file: Gwinner 2.

[309] Schöllgen, *Imperialismus und Gleichgewicht*, pp. 253ff.

[310] Gwinner, *Lebenserinnerungen*, pp. 104ff.

[311] Bundesarchiv, Abteilung Potsdam (BAP), Reichskanzlei, No. 1065, fol. 164–7.

[312] Ibid., fol. 168ff.

[313] Bülow to Gwinner, 31 January 1910, HADB, file: Gwinner 3.

[314] See *Die Bank*, 1 (1908), I, pp. 194f.

[315] *Plutus*, 5 February 1910, p. 104.

[316] Gwinner, *Lebenserinnerungen*, p. 107.

[317] Gwinner to Kautz, Chairman of the Anatolian Railway Company, 24 January 1910, HADB, file: Gwinner 2.

[318] Stenographische Berichte über die Verhandlungen des Herrenhauses, 12. Sitzung, 30 May 1910, pp. 239, 241.

[319] Ibid., 10. Sitzung, 27 May 1910, p. 173.

[320] Ibid., p. 239.

[321] A.L. [Alfred Lansburgh], 'Bankdirektor und Regierung', *Die Bank*, 3 (1910), I, p. 534.

[322] Stenographische Berichte über die Verhandlungen des Herrenhauses, 9. Sitzung, 7 April 1911, p. 179.

[323] Ibid., 10. Sitzung, 8 April 1911, p. 199.

[324] Ibid., 30. Sitzung, 26 April 1913, p. 1312.

[325] HADB, file: Gwinner 2.

[326] HADB, file: Gwinner 4.

[327] HADB, file: Gwinner 1.

[328] On Helfferich in general, see HADB, files: Helfferich 1 and 2; *Neue Deutsche Biographie*, vol. 8 (Berlin 1969), pp. 470ff; Achterberg, *Berliner Hochfinanz*, pp. 197ff; Williamson, *Karl Helfferich*.

[329] Gwinner to Bülow, 9 June 1905, HADB, file: Helfferich 1.

[330] Helfferich to Deutsche Bank head office, 9 October 1908, in HADB, file: Helfferich 2.

[331] Gwinner, *Lebenserinnerungen*, p. 86.

[332] According to Riesser on Helfferich's death, in *Bank-Archiv*, 23 (1923/24), p. 188.

[333] *Verhandlungen des IV. Allgemeinen Deutschen Bankiertages zu München am 17. und 18. September 1912* (Berlin 1912), p. 74.

[334] See Fritz Blaich, *Staat und Verbände in Deutschland zwischen 1871 und 1945* (Wiesbaden 1979), pp. 49ff.; Jaeger, *Unternehmer*, pp. 153ff.

[335] Felix Pinner, *Deutsche Wirtschaftsführer* (Berlin 1925), pp. 170ff.

[336] HADB, file: Siemens.

[337] Helfferich, *Siemens*, vol. 3, pp. 87f.

[338] Ibid., p. 359.

[339] Ibid., pp. 89, 359.

[340] Helfferich, *Siemens*, vol. 3, pp. 229f.

[341] Diary entry, 6 March 1899, quoted in Helfferich, *Siemens*, vol. 3, p. 106.

[342] Marie Siemens to Josef Görz, her grandfather, quoted in ibid., pp. 367f.

[343] Wilhelm II to Gwinner, 25 October 1904, HADB, file: Gwinner 1.

[344] Wilhelm von Gwinner to Arthur von Gwinner, 20 December 1909, HADB, file: Gwinner 3.

[345] According to Jaeger, *Unternehmer*, p. 178.

[346] In this connection, see the collection of newspaper cuttings about his death, in HADB; offers of a ministry are mentioned frequently.

[347] *Berliner Volks-Zeitung*, 24 October 1901.

[348] *Vorwärts*, 2 December 1900; the article is in the files of the Deutsche Bank, GStA Merseburg, Rep. 120, Ministry for Trade and Industry, dept XI.2, no. 24, vol. 1, fol. 108.

[349] Siemens to his wife, 28 October 1900, quoted in Helfferich, *Siemens*, vol. 3, p. 376; his wife to their daughter, 29 January 1900, ibid., p. 371.

[350] Theodor Barth, 'Nachruf auf Siemens', *Die Nation*, 26 October 1901.

[351] Jaeger, *Unternehmer*, p. 168.

[352] Helfferich, *Siemens*, vol. 3, pp. 178f.

[353] Ibid., p. 286.

[354] Ibid., p. 351.

[355] In this connection, see letters and cards from Bülow to Gwinner from the period 1902 to 1915, HADB, file: Gwinner 3.

[356] Gwinner to Bülow, 9 June 1905, HADB, file: Helfferich 1.

[357] Bülow to Gwinner, 21 July 1907 and 4 December 1908, HADB, file: Gwinner 3.

[358] Bernhard Fürst von Bülow, *Denkwürdigkeiten*, vol. 3 (Berlin 1930), p. 352.

[359] Fritz Fischer, *Griff nach der Weltmacht. Die Kriegszielpolitik des kaiserlichen Deutschland 1914–18* (Düsseldorf 1961), pp. 107f.

[360] Ibid., p. 109.

[361] Gerhard Besier, *Die Mittwochs-Gesellschaft im Kaiserreich* (Berlin 1990), pp. 354, 309.

[362] In this connection, see Egmont Zechlin, 'Deutschland zwischen Kabinettskrieg und Wirtschaftskrieg. Politik und Kriegsführung in den ersten Monaten des Weltkrieges 1914', *Historische Zeitschrift*, 199 (1964), p. 394.

[363] Letter from Gwinner to *Vossische Zeitung*, 21 October 1926, in which he commented on the value of the 'Tirpitz documents' and corrected a number of statements that Tirpitz had made about him in his collection of documents *Deutsche Ohnmachtspolitik im Weltkrieg* (Berlin 1926).

[364] *Bank-Archiv*, 1 (1901/02), p. 1.

[365] Riesser at the first conference; see *Verhandlungen des I. Allgemeinen Deutschen Bankiertages zu Frankfurt am Main am 19. und 20. September 1902* (Frankfurt 1902), p. 2.

[366] *Bank-Archiv*, 1 (1901/02), p. 191.

[367] This law, prohibiting forward operations and preferring cash operations, which called for substantially larger amounts of capital, was one by which all banks felt threatened. It also contained a provision whereby banks had to hold the shares of new companies for at least a year in their own portfolios and were only then allowed to list them on the stock exchange – a rule that again only banks with a great deal of capital were able to comply with. Private bankers and the smaller local joint stock banks were particularly affected by the new law, while the beneficiaries (not that this was the intention of the legislator at the time) were to be the big banks. In this connection, see Meier, *Entstehung des Börsengesetzes*, pp. 316ff.

[368] See Kurt Wagner, *Stationen deutscher Bankengeschichte. 75 Jahre Bankenverband* (Cologne 1976), pp. 11ff.

[369] George Hallgarten, *Imperialismus vor 1914*, vol. 1, 2nd edn (Munich 1963), pp. 195ff.

[370] Helfferich, *Siemens*, vol. 3, p. 6.

[371] *Hermes*, 7 April 1910.

[372] *Der Aktionär*, 1 April 1906.

[373] *Berliner Börsen-Courier*, 27 February 1898 (third supplement).

[374] *Effekten-Kursblatt*, 30 April 1906.

[375] *Berliner Börsen-Zeitung*, 5 March 1911.

[376] *Frankfurter Zeitung*, 9 March 1907.

[377] *Frankfurter Zeitung*, 7 March 1912.

[378] Theodor Barth, 'Nachruf auf Siemens', *Die Nation*, 26 October 1901.

[379] *Vorwärts*, 25 October 1901.

[380] *Fremdenblatt*, Berlin 1911.

[381] *Die Bank*, 5 (1912), II, pp. 1211f.

[382] Siemens on 15 February 1900 in the debate in the Reichstag about the East African railway; quoted in Helfferich, *Siemens*, vol. 2, p. 281.

[383] Helfferich, *Siemens*, vol. 1, p. 227.

[384] Ibid.

[385] Quoted in Helfferich, *Siemens*, vol. 2, p. 194.

[386] Hallgarten, *Imperialismus*, vol. 1, p. 483.

[387] Deutsche Bank Business Report 1914, p. 7.

[388] Quoted in Helfferich, *Siemens*, vol. 2, p. 158.

[389] 'The Deutsche Bank after proposed absorption will not only remain largest bank in Germany, but become world's biggest bank'. Gwinner to Adams, 6 March 1914, HADB, file: 1914.

[390] *Frankfurter Zeitung*, 5 March 1914.

[391] Maximilian Müller-Jabusch, *Franz Urbig*, 2nd edn (1954), pp. 65f.

[392] There is a collection of early photographs in Manfred Pohl, 'Die Gebäude der Deutschen Bank. Ein Rückblick', in Bernhard Leitner, Manfred Pohl and Gilbert Becker, *Taunusanlage 12* (Frankfurt a.M. 1985).

[393] Helfferich, *Siemens*, vol. 1, p. 225.

[394] Karl Wichmann, 'Unser älteste Lehrling erzählt. Eine Lehrzeit in der Deutschen Bank, 1872–1875', *Monatshefte für die Beamten der Deutschen Bank*, March 1928, pp. 37–9.

[395] Ibid., p. 38.

[396] Ibid.; Max Fuchs, the first archivist of the Deutsche Bank, says on the other hand that the bank already employed a staff of 50 in 1871. See Fuchs, 'Die Deutsche Bank in Berlin', *Jahrbuch der Schiffbautechnischen Gesellschaft* (1910), p. 849, HADB, picture archive.

[397] 'Deutsche Bank', in *Unser Kaiserpaar. Gedenkblätter zum 27. Februar 1906* (Berlin 1906), p. 284, HADB, press cuttings.

[398] See Deutsche Bank Business Reports 1896, 1898, 1900 and 1914.

[399] See Pierenkemper, *Arbeitsmarkt und Angestellte im deutschen Kaiserreich 1880–1913. Interessen und Strategien als Elemente der Integration eines segmentierten Arbeitsmarktes* (= Vierteljahrschrift für Sozial- und Wirtschaftsgeschichte, Beiheft 82), (Stuttgart 1987), p. 221.

[400] See Hans Janberg, *Die Bankangestellten. Eine soziologische Studie* (Wiebaden 1958), p. 23.

[401] See Jürgen Kocka, 'Angestellter', in Otto Brunner, Werne Conze and Reinhart Koselleck (eds), *Geschichtliche Grundbegriffe. Historisches Lexikon zur politisch-sozialen Sprache in Deutschland*, vol. 1 (Stuttgart 1972), p. 112.

[402] See Jürgen Kocka, *Die Angestellten in der deutschen Geschichte 1850–1980* (Göttingen 1981), p. 70.

[403] Kocka, *Unternehmensverwaltung*, p. 155.

[404] See Kocka, 'Angestellter', p. 121f.

[405] See Günther Schulz, *Die Arbeiter und Angestellten bei Felten & Guilleaume* (Zeitschrift für Unternehmensgeschichte, Beiheft 13), (Wiesbaden 1979), p. 117.

[406] Oskar Stillich, 'Die Schulbildung der Bankbeamten', *Zeitschrift für die gesamte Staatswissenschaft*, 72 (1916) p. 103. The study is based on data collected during a survey carried out in 1914.

[407] Oskar Stillich, *Soziale Strukturveränderungen im Bankwesen* (Berlin 1916), p. 10.

[408] Ibid., p. 12.

[409] Ibid.

[410] See Pierenkemper, *Arbeitsmarkt und Angestellte*, p. 222.

[411] Verband Deutscher Handlungsgehilfen, founded in Leipzig in 1881, Deutsche Privat-Beamten-Verein, founded in Magdeburg in 1881, Verein der deutschen Kaufleute, founded in Berlin in 1884, and Deutscher Gruben- und Hüttenbeamten Verein, founded in Bochum in 1890. See Pierenkemper, *Arbeitsmarkt und Angestellte*, p. 224.

[412] Emil Lederer, *Die Privatangestellten in der modernen Wirtschaftsentwicklung* (Tübingen 1912), p. 166.

[413] Ibid., pp. 158f.

[414] In this connection, see Deutsche Bank (ed.), *Unsere Wohlfahrtseinrichtungen* (Berlin 1927), p. 50.

[415] See Lederer, *Die Privatangestellten*, pp. 176f. It is no longer possible to ascertain how these questions were settled at the Deutsche Bank, since neither the statutes nor the terms of insurance of this pension and welfare fund have survived.

[416] Deutsche Bank (ed.), *Unsere Wohlfahrtseinrichtungen*, p. 50.

[417] Max Fuchs, 'Die Deutsche Bank in Berlin', *Jahrbuch der Schiffbautechnischen Gesellschaft* (1910), p. 849, HADB, picture archive.

[418] Ibid., p. 862.

[419] Ibid., p. 864.

[420] See Deutsche Bank (ed.), *Unsere Wohlfahrtseinrichtungen*.

[421] HADB, press-cuttings collection, October 1913–April 1914.

[422] *Frankfurter Zeitung*, 2 April 1914.

[423] See Karl Erich Born, 'Vom Beginn des Ersten Weltkrieges bis zum Ende der Weimarer

Republik (1918–1933)', in *Deutsche Bankengeschichte*. Edited by the Wissenschaftliche Beirat des Instituts für bankhistorische Forschung, vol. 3 (Frankfurt a.M. 1983), p. 54; 'Der Berliner Bankenstreik', *Die Bank*, 12 (1919), I, pp. 269–71; 'Der Beamtencharakter des Bankangestellten', *Die Bank*, 12 (1919), II, pp. 478–80.

[424] Even the Deutscher Bankbeamten-Verein was still, in 1916, awarding apprenticeships only to those who had completed secondary schooling (*Realschule* or *Gymnasium*). See Stillich, 'Schulbildung', p. 104.

[425] Michalowsky to court chaplain D. Rogge, 17 December 1906, HADB, file: 1906.

[426] Georg Obst, *Der Bankberuf. Stellungen im Bankwesen, Ausssichten im Bankberuf, Fortbildung der Bankbeamten* (Stuttgart 1921), p. 4.

[427] Karl Wichmann, 'Unser älteste Lehrling erzählt. Eine Lehrzeit in der Deutschen Bank, 1872–1875', *Monatshefte für die Beamten der Deutschen Bank*, March 1928, p. 37.

[428] Ibid., p. 39.

[429] Michalowsky to court chaplain D. Rogge, 17 December 1906, HADB, file: 1906.

[430] See Pierenkemper, *Arbeitsmarkt und Angestellte*, p. 150.

[431] The consumer price index rose (with slight fluctuations) from 76 in 1876 to 77 in 1900. The price rise that then set in pushed the index up to 100 in 1913 and 1914. See Deutsche Bundesbank (ed.), *Deutsches Geld- und Bankwesen in Zahlen 1876–1975* (Frankfurt a.M.), p. 6.

[432] Janberg, *Bankangestellte*, p. 55.

[433] Obst, *Bankberuf*, p. 7.

[434] Stillich, *Schulbildung*, pp. 104ff.

[435] See Martin Peteranderl, *Die Welt der Deutschen Bank 1870–1914. Ein Beitrag zur Betriebs-Organisation im deutschen Kaiserreich*. Unveröffentlichte Magisterarbeit im Fach Neuere und Neueste Geschichte an der Ludwig-Maximilians-Universität (Munich 1993), pp. 12f.

[436] See Stillich, *Strukturveränderungen*, p. 44.

[437] Deutsche Bank Business Report 1914, p. 10.

[438] See Käthe Lövinson, *Frauenarbeit in Bankbetrieben. Ein Beitrag zur Wirtschaftsgeschichte unserer Zeit* (Berlin 1926); Günther Schulz, 'Die weiblichen Angestellten vom 19. Jahrhundert bis 1945', in Hans Pohl (ed.), *Die Frau in der deutschen Wirtschaft. Referate und Diskussionsbeträge des 8. Wissenschaftlichen Symposiums der Gesellschaft für Unternehmensgeschichte am 8. und 9. Dezember 1983 in Essen* (= *Zeitschrift für Unternehmensgeschichte*, Beiheft 35), (Stuttgart 1985).

[439] Lövinson states that the percentage of women among those employed in banking rose from 0.76 in 1875 to 4.66 in 1907. See Lövinson, *Frauenarbeit*, p. 9. Schulz puts the percentages of woman employed in all sectors of the economy at 5.5 in 1882 and 12.4 in 1907. See Schulz, 'Die weiblichen Angestellten', p. 185.

[440] Letter from Michalowsky to Weber, 6 October 1910, HADB, file: 1910.

[441] See Stillich, *Strukturveränderungen*, pp. 44f.

[442] See Obst, *Bankberuf*, p. 7.

[443] Articles of association of the Deutsche Bank Aktien-Gesellschaft, 10 March 1870, pp. 10, 16, HADB.

[444] Quoted in Helfferich, *Siemens*, vol. 1, p. 321.

[445] Wallich, 'Aus meinem Leben', p. 123.

[446] Ibid.

[447] Richard H. Tilly, *Vom Zollverein zum Industriestaat. Die wirtschaftlich-soziale Entwicklung Deutschlands 1834–1914* (Munich 1990), p. 85.

[448] See the address list of the adjacent streets also, in Achterberg, *Berliner Hochfinanz*, p. 44f.

[449] Articles of association of the Deutsche Bank Aktien-Gesellschaft, 10 March 1870, section 21, HADB. Members of the administrative board had to deposit twice as many shares (i.e. 50) with the bank. See ibid., section 24.

[450] Wallich, 'Aus meinem Leben', p. 124.

[451] See Ernst Wilhelm Schmidt, *Männer der Deutschen Bank und der Disconto-Gesellschaft* (Düsseldorf 1957); Manfred Pohl and Wilhelm Treue, 'Deutsche Bank. Ein Teil deutscher Wirtschaftsgeschichte. Berichte und Biographien', unpublished manuscript, part II, HADB.

[452] Helfferich, *Siemens*, vol. 3, p. 153.

[453] Gwinner to the editor of *Berliner Tageblatt*, 13 May 1912, HADB, file: Gwinner 2.

[454] Note by Gwinner, 1 November 1922, HADB, file: Gwinner 2.

[455] Max Fuchs, 'Max Steinthal zu seinem achtzigsten Geburtstage', *Monatshefte für die Beamten der Deutschen Bank und Disconto-Gesellschaft*, December 1930, p. 186.

[456] See Rudolf Martin, *Handbuch des Vermögens und Einkommens der Millionäre in Preussen* (Berlin 1912), pp. 317ff.; in addition to his salary and bonus from the Deutsche Bank, his income included the sums he received as chairman of the advisory boards of five companies and as a member of the advisory boards of six other companies.

[457] Ibid.

[458] Fuchs, 'Max Steinthal', p. 185.

[459] Ibid.

[460] Bamberger, *Erinnerungen*, p. 386.

[461] Wallich, 'Aus meinem Leben', p. 124.

[462] *Der Aktionär*, 1 April 1906.

[463] On the significance of Jews in the context of Germany's economic development, see Werner E. Mosse, *Jews in the German Economy. The German–Jewish Economic Elite 1820–1935* (Oxford 1987).

[464] Gerd Hohorst, Jürgen Kocka and Gerhard A. Ritter, *Sozialgeschichtliches Arbeitsbuch, vol. 2. Materialen zur Statistik des Kaiserreichs 1870–1914*, 2nd edn (Munich 1978), pp. 54–5.

[465] Arthur Prinz, *Juden im Deutschen Wirtschaftsleben 1850–1914* (= *Schriftenreihe wissenschaftlicher Abhandlungen des Leo Baeck Instituts*, 43), (Tübingen 1984), p. 133.

[466] There were 2,733 directors or proprietors of banks in Prussia in 1882, 1,182 of whom (43.25 per cent) were Jews; in 1895 there were 2,982, including 1,122 Jews (37.63 per cent). See Prinz, *Juden im Deutschen Wirtschaftsleben*, p. 134.

[467] Rolf Walter, 'Jüdische Bankiers in Deutschland bis 1932', in Werner E. Mosse and Hans Pohl (eds), *Jüdische Unternehmer in Deutschland im 19. und 20. Jahrhundert* (= *Zeitschrift für Unternehmensgeschichte*, Beiheft 64), (Stuttgart 1992), pp. 78–99.

[468] Wallich, 'Aus meinem Leben', p. 132.

[469] Ibid., p. 133.

[470] See Paul Wallich, 'Lehr- und Wanderjahre eines Bankiers', in Hermann Wallich and Paul Wallich, *Zwei Generationen im deutschen Bankwesen 1833–1914* (Frankfurt a.M. 1978); Werner E. Mosse, 'Problems and Limits of Assimilation. Hermann and Paul Wallich 1833–1938', *Leo Baeck Institute Year Book*, 33 (1988), pp. 43–65.

[471] Quoted in Helfferich, *Siemens*, vol. 3, p. 246.

[472] Ibid.

[473] Emil Georg von Stauss, *Georg von Siemens. Ein Gedenkblatt zu seinem 100. Geburtstag*, BAP, R 8119 F, 24455.

[474] Letter to Gwinner, 9 October 1910, HADB, file: Gwinner 3.

[475] On the foundation and collection of donations, see Lothar Burchardt, *Wissenschaftspolitik im Wilhelminischen Deutschland. Vorgeschichte, Gründung und Aufbau der Kaiser-Wilhelm-Gesellschaft zur Förderung der Wissenschaften* (Göttingen 1975).

[476] Max Fuchs, 'Die Deutsche Bank in Berlin', *Jahrbuch der Schiffbautechnischen Gesellschaft* (1910), p. 849, HADB, picture archive.

[477] See John Booker, *Temples of Mammon. The Architecture of Banking* (Edinburgh 1990).

[478] See Bernhard Leitner, 'Geld und Raum', in Bernhard Leitner, Manfred Pohl and Gilbert Becker, *Taunusanlage 12* (Frankfurt a.M. 1985), p. 19.

[479] Werner Sombart, *Die deutsche Volkswirtschaft im Neunzehnten Jahrhundert* (Berlin 1903), p. 195.

[480] In connection with this and what follows, see Pohl, 'Die Gebäude der Deutschen Bank', pp. 99ff.

[481] Deutsche Bank legal department to the Berlin municipal authorities (*Magistrat*), 3 May 1907, HADB, file: 1907.

The Deutsche Bank
from World War to World Economic Crisis
1914–1933

[1] *Frankfurter Zeitung*, 3 March 1914, and Deutsche Bank Prospectus, May 1914, HADB, file: Deutsche Bank 1914.

[2] Deutsche Bank Business Report 1918, p. 12.

[3] P. Barrett Whale, *Joint Stock Banking in Germany. A Study of the German Creditbanks Before and After the War* (London 1930), p. 196.

[4] Theodore Balderston, 'War Finance and Inflation in Germany 1914–1918', *Economic History Review*, 42 (1989), pp. 222–44, and Theodore Balderston, *The Origins and Course of the German Economic Crisis 1921–1932* (Schriften der Historischen Kommission zu Berlin, vol. 2. Beiträge zu Inflation und Wiederaufbau in Deutschland und Europa 1914–1924) (Berlin 1993), pp. 277–8.

[5] This discussion is based on Gerald D. Feldman, *The Great Disorder. Politics, Economics, and Society in the German Inflation, 1914–1924* (Oxford 1993), pp. 29–32.

[6] The discussion which follows is taken from the protocol in BAP, RB, No. 6474, fol. 399ff. It is reprinted in Reinhold Zilch, 'Zum Plan einer Zwangsregulierung im deutschen Bankwesen vor dem ersten Weltkrieg und zu seinen Ursachen. Dokumentation', in B.A. Aisin and W. Gutsche (eds), *Forschungsergebnisse zur Geschichte des deutschen Imperialismus vor 1917* (Berlin 1980), pp. 229–56.

[7] Gwinner to Walter Bürhaus, 22 July 1914, HADB, S83.

[8] Deutsche Bank to the General Direction of the Anatolian Railway Corporation, 12 Aug. 1914, HADB, file: Deutsche Bank 1914.

[9] Michalowsky to Director Jötten of the Essener Credit-Anstalt, 6 Aug. 1914, and circular of the Deutsche Bank to its branches, 8 Aug. 1914, HADB, S630.

[10] See the correspondence with Wallenberg in HADB, file: Krieg 1914–1918I.

[11] Gwinner to Edward D. Adams, 7 Nov. 1914, HADB, file: Arthur v. Gwinner, 2.

[12] Gwinner to the editors of the *Norddeutschen Allgemeinen Zeitung*, 18 Dec. 1917, HADB, S83.

[13] Deutsche Bank to Reichshauptbank für Wertpapiere, 1 July 1919, HADB, S2682, and Whale, *Joint Stock Banking*, p. 199.

[14] See Michalowsky's report of 19 Sept. 1916, HADB, S130.

[15] BAP, Reichslandbund, Pressearchiv, No. 5935, fol. 20.

[16] Michalowsky report of 8 Dec. 1916, HADB, file: Deutsche Bank 1917.

[17] Minute by Michalowsky, 7 Feb. 1917, ibid.

[18] *Berliner Börsen Courier*, 7 Feb. 1917, HADB, Presseauschnitte 1917.

[19] Directors' meeting, 2 May 1917, HADB, file: Deutsche Bank 1917.

[20] Ballin to Gwinner, 21 July 1917, HADB, S435.

[21] On Salomonsohn and Gwinner, see Peter Krüger, *Deutschland und die Reparationen 1918/19. Die Genesis der Reparationsproblems in Deutschland zwischen Waffenstillstand und Versailler Friedensschluss* (Stuttgart 1973), p. 75. See also Georges-Henri Soutou, *L'or et le sang. Les buts de guerre économiques de la Premiére Guerre mondiale* (Paris 1989), pp. 25–6. On Weigelt and Millington-Herrmann, see Dieter Fricke (ed.), *Die bürgerlichen Parteien in Deutschland*, 2 vols (Berlin 1970), I, pp. 390, 399. See also the interesting comments on the correspondence between Max Steinthal and General Director Eich of Mannesmann in Hartmut Pogge von Strandmann, *Unternehmenspolitik und Unternehmensführung. Der Dialog zwischen Aufsichtsrat und Vorstand bei Mannesmann 1900 bis 1919* (Düsseldorf/Vienna 1978), pp. 122–3. On the warnings to the Reichsbank, see Mankiewitz to Bergmann, 26 Nov. 1921, HADB, file: Carl Bergmann.

22 Alfred Lansburgh, 'Zur Kapitalsherhöhung der Deutschen Bank', *Die Bank*, 10 (1917), pp. 185–96, quote on pp. 194–5.

23 As Volker Wellhöner shows in his *Grossbanken und Grossindustrie im Kaiserreich* (Kritische Studien zur Geschichtswissenschaft, vol. 85) (Göttingen 1989), the Hilferding thesis on the role of finance capital was highly exaggerated even for the prewar period.

24 Arthur von Gwinner, *Lebenserinnerungen*. Edited by Manfred Pohl on behalf of the Historische Gesellschaft der Deutschen Bank, 2nd edn (Frankfurt a.M. 1992), p. 84.

25 Günther to Direktor von Stauss, 24 July 1924, HADB, file: Karl Helfferich, 2.

26 Helfferich to Muehlon, 2 July 1914, HADB, OR1090.

27 Telegram to the General Direction, Anatolian Railway Corporation, 29 July 1914, ibid.

28 This argument is convincingly made by Ulrich Trumpener, *Germany and the Ottoman Empire 1914–1918* (Princeton 1968), which is the best single study of the subject.

29 Ibid., pp. 271–84. A record of the Deutsche Bank's early role in the transmission of wartime subsidies to the Turks is to be found in BAP, R 8119 F, P7743.

30 Günther to Gwinner, 15 Sept. 1915, HADB, OR1083.

31 The details are discussed in Trumpener, *Ottoman Empire*, pp. 285–316, which is a good source on these wartime negotiations.

32 Günther to Gwinner, 17 Aug. 1915, HADB, OR1704.

33 Günther to Gwinner, 30 Oct. 1915, ibid.

34 Report by Günther, 5 Nov. 1918, ibid.

35 See Trumpener, *Ottoman Empire*, pp. 200–70.

36 Unpublished memoirs of Director Peter Brunswig, HADB, file: Peter Brunswig, pp. 27–8.

37 Günther to Gwinner, 9 May 1917, HADB, OR303.

38 Ibid.

39 A copy, which is dated June 1917, is in HADB, OR303.

40 Gwinner to Günther, 25 May 1917, HADB, OR303.

41 Trumpener, *Ottoman Empire*, pp. 305–16.

42 Michalowsky to Norddeutsche Creditanstalt, 31 Jan. 1916, and minute of Michalowsky, 8 Sept. 1916, HADB, file: Deutsche Bank 1916.

43 See his letters to Müller of 24 Dec. 1914 and 20 Jan. 1915, HADB, S567.

44 Gwinner to Wassermann, 29 March 1917, HADB, file: Reichsbank MA282.

45 Warburg to Gwinner, 21 Nov. 1915, HADB, file: Verhältnis zwischen Deutscher Bank und Disconto-Gesellschaft, for this and other documents discussed here.

46 Gwinner to Stinnes, 13 July 1917, ACDP, I-220, No. 118/1.

47 See the newspaper reports on his appointment in BAP, Reichslandbund, Pressearchiv, No. 5934, fol.85–6 and Ernst Wilhelm Schmidt, *Männer der Deutschen Bank und der Disconto-Gesellschaft* (Düsseldorf 1957), p. 120. Stauss was apparently 'discovered' by Siemens, who employed him as his personal secretary and contact with the board of directors between his retirement in January 1901 and death ten months later. See the letter of Alfred Schulze, 27 Feb. 1951 in HADB, file: Arthur von Gwinner, 2. See

also Friedrich Glum, *Zwischen Wissenschaft und Politik. Erlebtes und Erdachtes in vier Reichen* (Bonn 1964), p. 165.

[48] See Gwinner to Ministeraldirektor Fl. Lusensky, 28 May 1915, and the DPAG supervisory board meetings of 1915–18 in HADB, S1597 and S1602. See also Stauss's secret report of 23 May 1921 on 'Die Bedeutung der deutschen Beteiligung an der Steaua Romana während des Krieges', BAP, R 8119 F, P8364, fol. 146–7. More generally, see Hans Pohl, 'The Steaua Romana and the Deutsche Bank (1903–1920)', *Studies on Economic and Monetary Problems and on Banking History*, 24 (1989), pp. 77–94.

[49] Felix Pinner, 'Wenn Banken sich streiten...', BAP, Reichslandbund, Pressearchiv, No. 5935, fol. 21–2.

[50] Ballin to Stinnes, 14 Jan. 1918, ACDP, I-220, 272/6. This volume contains the detailed correspondence on which this discussion is based.

[51] Stinnes to Cuno, 31 March 1918, ibid.

[52] Fritz Fischer, *Griff nach der Weltmacht. Die Kriegszielpolitik des kaiserlichen Deutschland 1914/18* (Düsseldorf 1961), pp. 689–90.

[53] See his lengthy report on the negotiations for a consortium of 22 March 1918, ACDP, I-220, 272/6.

[54] Nöllenburg memorandum of 5 March 1918, ibid.

[55] Georg Münch, 'Krieg und Banken', *Westfälische Zeitung*, 10 Dec. 1916, BAP, Reichslandbund, Pressearchiv, No. 5934, fol. 95. See also HADB, S693 and S699.

[56] Gwinner to Ballin, 18 July 1917, HADB, S435.

[57] Undated Haeften memorandum of 1918, HADB, S3614. See also the account in Klaus Kreimeier, *Die Ufa Story. Geschichte eines Filmkonzerns* (Munich and Vienna 1992), pp. 28ff.

[58] Grau to Stauss, 19 March 1921, HADB, S3614.

[59] Grau to Stauss, 19 March 1921, and Ludendorff to the War Ministry, 15 Dec. 1917, HADB, S3614, and Stauss's Aktennotiz of 19 Dec. 1917, HADB, S3637.

[60] Arbeitsausschuss Sitzung, 15 Jan. 1918, HADB, S3632.

[61] Arbeitsausschuss, 29 Jan. 1918, ibid.

[62] Stauss *Notiz* for Kiehl, 3 Oct. 1918, HADB, S3621. On the agreement with Deulig, see the report of 24 April 1918, HADB, S3615, and the Arbeitsausschuss report of 29 Jan. 1918 as well as the report on the expansion in the Balkans of May 1918, HADB, S3632.

[63] The relevant materials are in HADB, S501.

[64] Meeting in the RWA of 22 Feb. 1918, HADB, file: Deutsche Bank 1918.

[65] Letter to Gwinner, 29 Dec. 1916, HADB, file: Deutsche Bank 1916; see also Gwinner to Adams, 7 Nov. 1914 and 26 Feb. 1915, HADB, file: Deutsche Bank 1915–1916.

[66] On the Lehigh transaction, see HADB, A465, A563, A565, and Gwinner to Schmidt, 17 Jan. 1916, file: Deutsche Bank Krieg 1914–1918, II.

[67] Meeting of 7 Nov. 1917, HADB, file: Deutsche Bank Krieg 1914–1918, II.

[68] Heinemann to the Deutsche Wirtschaftsverband für Süd- und Mittelamerika, e.V., 24 March 1917, HADB, S196.

[69] Peltzer to Stapelfeldt, 20 Dec. 1917, HADB, file: Deutsche Bank 1917. Obviously

Peltzer did not intend this letter to fall into the hands of the Deutsche Bank.

[70] Heinemann to Director Eich of Mannesmann, 22 Nov. 1917, HADB, file: Deutsche Bank 1917.

[71] Deutsche Bank, Berlin, to Deutsche Bank, Hamburg, 7 Nov. 1917, ibid.

[72] Heinemann to the Deutsche Bank directors, 24 Nov. 1917, ibid.

[73] Minute by Mankiewitz, 27 Nov. 1917, ibid.

[74] Warburg to Mankiewitz, 29 Nov. 1917, ibid.

[75] Heinemann to Eich, 29 Nov. 1917, ibid.

[76] Deutsche Bank, Sofia, to Deutsche Bank, Berlin, 8 June 1918, HADB, S2473.

[77] Mankiewitz to Gwinner, 24 July 1918, HADB, Georgische Staatsanleihe 1918, S629. On the Deutsche Bank's financial position with respect to Russia, see also Soutou, *L'or et le sang*, pp. 644–5, 696.

[78] Steinthal to Eich, 28 Sept. 1918, quoted in Pogge von Strandmann, *Unternehmenspolitik*, p. 122.

[79] Report of 14 Oct. 1918, HADB, S3633.

[80] Kreimeier, *Ufa*, p. 58.

[81] Wassermann to Warburg, 11 Jan. 1919, Warburg Papers, M.M. Warburg & Co., Hamburg.

[82] Report on a reception held by Arndt von Holtzendorff, 5 Jan. 1919, Hapag Archiv, StA Hamburg.

[83] Kurt Sorge to Alfred Hugenberg, 6 Dec. 1918, BAK, NL Hugenberg, No. 27, fol. 172–6.

[84] Wassermann to Warburg, 11 Jan. 1919, Warburg Papers, M.M. Warburg & Co., Hamburg.

[85] Mankiewitz to Klaproth, 30 Jan. 1920, HADB, file: Hannoversche Bank. See also the Deutsche Bank Business Reports 1918, p. 13, and 1919, pp. 15f.

[86] 'Die Deutsche Bank und ihre Bedientesten', Sept. 1918, BAP, Reichslandbund, Pressearchiv, No. 5935, fol.23. For an excellent general discussion, see Emil Lederer, 'Kritische Uebersichten der Sozialen Bewegung. Die Bewegung der Privatangestellten seit dem Herbst 1918, die Entwicklung der Organisationen, die Gestaltung der Lebenshaltung und der Besoldung; die Umformung des sozialen Habitus und der Ideologien', *Archiv für Sozialwissenschaft*, 47 (1920–21), pp. 585–619.

[87] Declaration of 27 Nov. 1918, BAP, R 8119 F, P8891.

[88] See the tendentious but sociologically revealing statement, 'Der drohende Bankbeamtenstreik', in BAP, R 8119 F, P8890.

[89] See the informative newspaper reports in BAP, Reichslandbund Pressearchiv, No. 5935, fol. 26–7.

[90] *Vorwärts*, 3 July 1919.

[91] *Neue Zürcher Zeitung*, 1 July 1919. HADB, Zeitungsberichte Sammlung. See also the other reports in this collection and in BAP, Reichslandbund, Pressearchiv, No. 5935, fol. 41–2.

[92] Confidential memorandum of the Deutsche Bank, 15 Nov. 1919, BAP, R 8119 F, P8887, fol. 86–9.

[93] Deutsche Bank to Reichsregierung, 26 Jan. 1920, ibid., fol. 97–100.

[94] See the Cabinet meetings of 16 June and 2 Nov. 1922, *Akten der Reichskanzlei. Die Kabinette Wirth I und II* (Boppard am Rhein 1973), II, pp. 882–3, 1147.

[95] See the Deutsche Bank to Generaldirektor Brennecke of the Oberschlesische Eisenbahn-Bedarfs-Aktien-Gesellschaft, 18 Nov. 1921, HADB, file: Deutsche Bank 1921. More generally, see Knut Wolfgang Nörr, *Zwischen den Mühlsteinen. Eine Privatrechtsgeschichte der Weimarer Republik* (Tübingen 1988), p. 114.

[96] See Feldman, *Great Disorder* and Carl-Ludwig Holtfrerich, *The German Inflation 1914–1923. Causes and Effects in International Perspective* (Berlin/New York 1986) for general discussions of the inflation here.

[97] Deutsche Bank Business Report 1919, p. 13.

[98] Circular to the branches signed by Mankiewitz and Millington-Herrmann, 30 Sept. 1919, BAP, R 8119 F, P8871.

[99] Materials for the conference of the banking associations adhering to the 'general conditions', 12 and 13 Dec. 1919, BAP, R 8119 F, P8870, fol. 85–105, quote on fol. 106.

[100] Circular of 22 Jan. 1919, BAP, R 8119 F, P8871.

[101] Circular of 29 March 1920 and Carl Wuppermann, 'Vorsicht im Kreditgeschäft', ibid.

[102] Meeting of 1 Oct. 1920 in the Reich Economics Ministry, Archiv preussischer Kulturbesitz Merseburg, Rep. 120, AX No. 43.

[103] For a detailed discussion of these plans, see Feldman, *Great Disorder*, pp. 255–72.

[104] Circular of 10 Nov. 1920, BAP, R 8119 F, P8871.

[105] Mankiewitz to Klaproth, 10 May 1920, HADB, Hannoversche Bank, K4/13.

[106] Michalowsky to Jahr, 6 Nov. 1920, HADB, file: Rheinische Creditbank, Schriftwechsel 1911–1920.

[107] Millington-Herrmann to Director Kluge, 15 March 1921, HADB, Hannoversche Bank, K4/13.

[108] Minute by Bonn on his discussions with Nöllenburg in Interlaken, 3 and 5 Sept. 1920, HADB, S1620.

[109] Minute by Mankiewitz, 4 Nov. 1920, ibid.

[110] Willi Strauss, *Die Konzentrationsbewegung im deutsche Bankgewerbe. Ein Beitrag zur Organisationsentwicklung der Wirtschaft unter dem Einfluss der Konzentration des Kapitals. Mit besonderer Berücksichtigung der Nachkriegszeit* (Berlin/Leipzig 1928), pp. 31–2, 65–7, 85–6.

[111] Deutsche Bank Business Reports, 1919–23. There are useful discussions of the Deutsche Bank in the inflation by Karl Erich Born, 'Deutsche Bank during Germany's Great Inflation after the First World War', *Studies on Economic and Monetary Problems and on Banking History*, 17 (1979), pp. 11–27, and in Manfred Pohl, 'Die Situation der Banken in die Inflationszeit', in Otto Büsch and Gerald D. Feldman, *Historische Prozesse der Deutschen Inflation 1914–1924* (Berlin/New York 1978), pp. 83–95, 115–26. On concentration in Banking, see Manfred Pohl, *Konzentration im Deutschen Bankwesen (1848–1980)* (Frankfurt a.M. 1982).

[112] Deutsche Bank to the Bergisch Märkische Bank branch of the Deutsche Bank, 14 April

1920; petition to the Deutsche Bank, 22 April 1920; and Bergisch Märkische Bank to the Ministry of Commerce, 17 May 1920, HADB, file: Elberfelder Bankverein.

[113] Schlitter to Schleifenbaum, 30 April 1921, HADB, file: Siegener Bank.

[114] Wassermann to Klaproth, 15 May 1920, HADB, Hannoversche Bank, K4/13.

[115] Klaproth to Mankiewitz, 2 Oct. 1920, ibid.

[116] Klaproth to Mankiewitz, 3 Nov. 1920, ibid.

[117] Meeting of 31 May 1920, HADB, file: Württembergische Vereinsbank.

[118] Meeting of 20 Oct. 1920, ibid.

[119] Circular of 17 Sept. 1921, BAP, R 8119 F, P8871.

[120] Manfred Pohl, *Baden-Württembergische Bankgeschichte* (Stuttgart/Berlin/Cologne 1992), p. 195.

[121] Meeting of the shareholders of the Pfälzische Bank, 9 Jan. 1922, p. 48, HADB, file: Pfälzische Bank, Zusammenbruch II.

[122] Michalowsky memorandum of 6 Dec. 1921, HADB, file: Pfälzische Bank, Zusammenbruch I.

[123] Deutsche Bank to its Frankfurt branch, 8 Dec. 1921, ibid.

[124] See the interesting letter from Heinrich Emden to Mankiewitz, 13 Jan. 1922, and Mankiewitz's careful and thoughtful reply of 17 Jan. 1922, HADB, file: Pfälzische Bank, Zusammenbruch II.

[125] *Die Bank*, 15 (1922), pp. 469–70.

[126] See the DPAG supervisory board meetings, especially those of 1919–20, HADB, S1602, and the report of an interview with Dr Weigelt of 3 June 1965 in HADB, file: Deutsche Bank 1922. This parallels the discussion of Born, *Beiträge* (1979), pp. 15–16.

[127] Günther to Deutsche Bank, 22 Oct. 1922, HADB, file: Deutsche Bank 1922; also discussed and partially quoted in Born, *Beiträge* (1979), p. 18.

[128] Marginal notation on a minute of 7 Nov. 1922, HADB, file: Deutsche Bank 1922.

[129] There is an excellent record of the negotiations in HADB, S99. See especially Gwinner to the directors of the Compania Alemana Transatlatica de Electricidad, Buenos Aires, 22 March 1920, ibid.

[130] Gwinner to F. Kautz, 13 Aug. 1921, ibid.

[131] Gwinner to Frey, 31 March 1920, ibid.

[132] Frey to Gwinner, 5 Jan. 1921, HADB, file: Arthur v. Gwinner, 2.

[133] Gwinner to Frey, 27 Jan. 1921, ibid.

[134] Cambó to Gwinner, 21 June 1922 and Gwinner to Cambó, 6 July 1922, HADB, S100.

[135] James Speyer to Gwinner, 16 Feb. 1920, HADB, file: Arthur v. Gwinner, 1.

[136] Blinzig to the board of managing directors, 23 April 1927, HADB, file: Alfred Blinzig.

[137] Mankiewitz to Klaproth, 30 Jan. 1920, HADB, Hannoversche Bank, K4/13.

[138] Krüger, *Deutschland und die Reparationen*, pp. 170, 207.

[139] Peter Wulf, *Hugo Stinnes. Wirtschaft und Politik 1918–1924* (Stuttgart 1979), p. 150.

[140] Ibid., p. 249.

[141] Statement at a Reich Economic Council Finance Committee meeting of 3 June 1921, cited in Feldman, *Great Disorder*, p. 349.

[142] Wassermann to Klaproth, 18 May 1920, HADB, Hannoversche Bank, K4/13.

[143] Schmidt, *Männer*, p. 102.

[144] Bergmann to the managing directors of the Deutsche Bank, 20 Oct. 1921, HADB, file: Carl Bergmann.

[145] Bergmann report of 10 Nov. 1921, ibid.

[146] Bergmann to the Deutsche Bank, 19 Oct. 1921, ibid.

[147] Bergmann to Deutsche Bank, 12 Nov. 1921, ibid. On the so-called credit action, see Feldman, *Great Disorder*, pp. 358–76.

[148] Marginal comment on Bergmann to Deutsche Bank, 12 Nov. 1921, HADB, file: Carl Bergmann.

[149] Mankiewitz to Bergmann, 26 Nov. 1921, ibid.

[150] Minute by Mankiewitz, Dec. 1921, ibid.

[151] While there were a number of occasions on which hope was placed in Morgan in 1922, this is the most likely instance. For Bergmann's reports of this period, see ibid. For the meeting, see Brunswig memoirs in HADB, file: Peter Brunswig, p. 21.

[152] Minute by Osius, 27 Nov. 1922, ACDP, I–220, No. 046/3.

[153] The quotations and discussion are from Wassermann to Cuno, 30 Nov. 1922, BAK, R 43I/33, fol. 3–10. Various drafts are also to be found in HADB, file: Oscar Wassermann.

[154] Bergmann to Deutsche Bank, 12 Nov. 1921, HADB, file: Carl Bergmann.

[155] Holtfrerich, *Inflation*, p. 68; Deutsche Bank Business Report 1922, p. 1.

[156] Ibid., and see the documents in HADB, S86.

[157] Deutsche Bank Business Report 1922, p. 21; Deutsche Bank to Jakob Wassermann, 7 Oct. 1924, HADB, file: Deutsche Bank 1923.

[158] Deutsche Bank Business Report 1922, p. 18.

[159] Ibid., p. 19.

[160] Schlitter to Silverberg, 2 Aug. 1922, BAP, R 8119 F, 24371, fol. 4–6.

[161] See the circulars of 27 March, 10 April, 13 July 1922, in BAP, R 8119 F, P8872.

[162] Meeting at Reichsbank of 22 June 1922, BAP, RB, No. 6460, fol. 81–96.

[163] Circular of 23 Aug. 1922, BAP, R 8119 F, P8872.

[164] Ibid.

[165] Ibid., and circular of 26 Oct. 1922, ibid.

[166] See the discussion at the Reich Economic Council (Reichswirtschaftsrat) meeting of 21 Feb. 1923, BAP, RWR, No. 396, vol. 12, fol. 132–204.

[167] Circular of 5 March 1923, BAP, R 8119 F, P8873. On the Reichsbank concern over the quality of the commercial bills it was getting in late 1922 and in 1923, see Feldman, *Great Disorder*, pp. 591–2.

[168] Circular of 29 Aug. 1923, BAP, R 8119 F, P8873.

[169] Deutsche Bank Business Report 1923, p. 17. On the banks and the currency reform, see Feldman, *Great Disorder*, pp. 752–3, 794, 804. It is worth noting that at least one high official of the Deutsche Bank did play a significant role in the currency reform, namely the head of the Berlin head office, Peter Brunswig, who had experienced inflation in Chile while serving for the bank before the war and was asked by Helfferich to draw up the Statute for the Rentenbank. He was invited to serve on the Rentenbank Directory but declined because his ambition was to become a Deutsche Bank managing

director, which he was in 1933–34. See his unpublished memoirs, HADB, file: Peter
Brunswig, pp. 23–5.

[170] Bergmann to Blinzig, 27 March 1924, HADB, file: Carl Bergmann.

[171] Expert Report by Leitner, 27 April 1925, BAP, R 8119 F, P6178 and Deutsche Bank
Business Report 1924, p. 22.

[172] There is an important collection of reports on profiteering prosecution efforts and
legal briefs in defence of the bank in BAP, R 8119 F, P8819–P8820. On the cartel
question, BAP, R 8119 F, P9269. See *Untersuchung des Bankwesens 1933*. Part I,
vol. 2. (Berlin 1933), pp. 203–4.

[173] See the materials collected for the *Bank-Enquête* in BAP, R 8119 F, P418, fol. 42–6,
60–77.

[174] See the materials in BAP, R 8119 F, P8824.

[175] For an illustration of this formulaic approach, see Deutsche Bank, Berlin, to Deutsche
Bank, Saarbrücken, 21 Jan. 1924, BAP, R 8119 F, P7495, and the other materials in
this file.

[176] Minute of 3 Jan. 1924, BAP, R 8119 F, P10330.

[177] Whale, *Joint Stock Banking*, chs. 7–8 and the interesting report by the Deutsche Bank's
Economic Section of 1934, BAP, R 8119 F, P8903. Deutsche Bank Business Report
1924, p. 22. More generally, see Carl-Ludwig Holtfrerich, 'Auswirkungen der Inflation
auf die Struktur des deutschen Kreditgewerbes', in Gerald D. Feldman and Elisabeth
Müller-Luckner, *Die Nachwirkungen der Inflation auf die Deutsche Geschichte*
(Munich 1985), pp. 187–209; see also the comments of Manfred Pohl and Karl Erich
Born in Büsch/Feldman, *Historische Prozesse*, pp. 83–95, 122f. On the sale of the
shares, see the correspondence in HADB, file: Deutsche Bank 1925. On its position
among corporations, see Born, *Beiträge* (1979), p. 29.

[178] *Verhandlungen des VI. Allgemeinen Deutschen Bankiertages zu Berlin in der 'Oper
am Königsplatz' (Kroll), am 14., 15. und 16. September 1925* (Berlin/Leipzig 1925),
p. 12.

[179] See the revealing letter by Ernst Hoppe to Carl Wuppermann, 29 Oct. 1968, HADB,
file: Deutsche Bank 1929.

[180] *Bankiertag 1925*, p. 44. This discussion is based on the materials in HADB, file: Oscar
Wassermann.

[181] *Bankiertag 1925*, p. 25.

[182] Ibid., pp. 29–30.

[183] The consequences of the inflation for the Essener Credit-Anstalt are well demonstrated
by Manfred Pohl, 'The Deutsche Bank's Entry into the Industrial Area in the Rhineland
and Westphalia. The Merger with the Bergisch Märkische Bank and the Essener
Credit-Anstalt in 1914 and 1925', *Studies on Economic and Monetary Problems and
on Banking History*, 20 (1983), pp. 13–24.

[184] Deutsche Bank to Dr Felix Hirsch of the 8-Uhr Abendblatt, 22 Nov. 1927, HADB,
file: Personalbestand, 1927–29.

[185] Newspaper reports of late April 1927, HADB, Presseausschnitte 1927.

[186] See the internal memorandum for 1929 in HADB, file: Personalbestand, 1927–29.

[187] Meeting of the branch directors, 11 March 1926, file: Deutsche Bank 1926.

[188] Leaflet of the Reich Association of Bank Managers (Reichsverband der Bankleitungen) on the 'contract dispute in the banking sector' ('Zum Tarifstreit im Bankgewerbe'), 26 Jan. 1925, BAP, R 8119 F, P8758, fol. 228.

[189] Newspaper reports on general shareholders' meeting of 4 April 1928, HADB, Zeitungsausschnitte 1928.

[190] Schlitter to August Thyssen, 11 Feb. 1925, BAP, R 8119 F, 24368.

[191] Fritz Thyssen to Schlitter, 18 July 1926, ibid., fol. 94.

[192] Wuppermann to Kehl, 17 Feb. 1925, ibid., fol. 75.

[193] Minute of 2 Feb. 1933, BAP, R 8119 F, 24342, fol. 177. See also 'Die Stinnes'sche Befreiungsanleihe', in *Magazin der Wirtschaft* (14 Oct. 1926), pp. 1314–26. On the Deutsche Bank participation, see HADB, S1839–S1841.

[194] Meeting of 17 April 1926, HADB, S1897.

[195] Meeting of the branch directors, 11 March 1926, HADB, file: Deutsche Bank 1926.

[196] Stauss to Arndt von Holtzendorff, 10 Feb. 1921, HADB, S3624.

[197] See the report by the Amerika-Institut in New York, 23 Feb. 1922, and the report on a trip to America by Dr Fellner, 28 Dec. 1922, HADB, S3626; the reports by the Foreign Division (Auslands-Abteilung) of 3 March 1925, and from Paris of 9 Feb. 1925, and the analysis of the American public by Fritz Lang of 27 Feb. 1925, HADB, S3628.

[198] Kiehl to Stauss, 21 July 1925, HADB, S3628.

[199] Stauss to Lang, 17 Dec. 1925, HADB, S3629; Stauss to Lang, 26 Sept. 1925, HADB, S3636; and Lang to Stauss, 14 Sept. 1926, ibid.

[200] See the AR meeting of 29 March 1927 and the memorandum by Stauss of the same date, in HADB, S3673.

[201] Felix Pinner, 'Autorität und Prestige', *Berliner Tageblatt*, 31 March 1927, in HADB, S1847. Wassermann may not have been as 'collegial' as he sounded. As the publicist Ernst Feder noted in his diary on 29 March 1927, 'Wassermann (who gets on so badly with Stauss that he only deals with him through intermediaries) still claimed at the press conference yesterday that one cannot make a single person responsible for the Ufa bankruptcy …'. Ernst Feder, *Heute sprach ich mit … Tagebücher eines Berliner Publizisten 1926–1932* (Stuttgart 1971), p. 116.

[202] *Berliner Börsen-Courier*, 16 April 1927.

[203] The correspondence of 1919–24 and the Jahr memorandum of 30 Jan. 1924 are to be found in HADB, S179 and S181.

[204] Pohl, *Baden-Württembergische Bankgeschichte*, pp. 206–8.

[205] Jahr to Abshagen, 22 Aug. 1928, BAP, R 8119 F, P3197, fol. 121.

[206] Stauss to Kissel, 30 Sept. 1928, BAP, R 8119 F, P3197, fol. 216–19.

[207] Stauss to Kopp, 26 March 1929, BAP, R 8119 F, P3198, fol. 185–6.

[208] On 24 September 1930, Stauss reported to Schlitter that the Daimler debts had dropped from 8 to 4.5 million marks, during the previous few months, ibid., BAP, R 8119 F, P14, fol. 41.

[209] Enquête Auschuss, 20 March 1929, BAP, R 8119 F, P3198, fol. 276, pp. 28–29.

[210] Wassermann to Stauss, 11 July 1928, BAP, R 8119 F, P3197, fol. 71/1–5. The sarcastic remark about alphabetical order probably refers to an incident where the Reichsbank had summoned a consortium to assist the agricultural banks (*Landschaften*), in the course of which Wassermann exploded when Goldschmidt claimed the traditional right to be listed first since the DANAT-Bank came ahead in the alphabet. Schacht became so furious at the unseemly behaviour of the D-Banks that he sent them packing and announced, to the horror of his subordinates, that the Reichsbank and Seehandlung would do the business themselves. See HADB, file: Peter Brunswig, memoirs, pp. 36–8.

[211] Report by the Frankfurt branch of the Disconto-Gesellschaft to the Chef-Cabinet, 16 April 1928, HADB, S582.

[212] Hergt of the Disconto-Gesellschaft, Munich branch, to Theodor Frank, 17 April 1928, ibid.

[213] Hergt to Frank, 20 July 1928, ibid.

[214] For an illustration of the patriotic airs, see Wilhelm Opel to Schlieper, 16 July 1927, and for the identification with General Motors, see the minute of 30 June 1928, ibid.

[215] Popp to Stauss, 26 March 1929, BAP, R 8119 F, P3198, fol. 194–8.

[216] See the reports of Dr Pinner of 14 Dec. 1929 and of Otto Max Müller of 30 Dec. 1929, BAP, R 8119 F, P3080, fol. 396–401, 419/1–6.

[217] Minute of 17 Nov. 1928, BAP, R 8119 F, P3197, fol. 362; for the negotiations with van Roggen, ibid., fol. 331/1–6, 389; on the military, ibid., fol. 360–3. See also Otto Wolff to Director Serruys, 13 April 1929, BAP, R 8119 F, P3198, fol. 245.

[218] Reich Transportation Minister Koch to Stauss, 17 March 1928, BAP, R 8119 F, P3130, fol. 42–3.

[219] Ministerial Director Brandenburg to Stauss, 18 Nov. 1929, BAP, R 8119 F, P3080, fol. 328–9.

[220] Stauss to Brandenburg, 7 Dec. 1929, ibid., fol. 385–6.

[221] A good collection of documents on the founding is in HADB, S104. There is a good account by Martin Wronsky, 'Deutscher Luftverkehr', in BAP, R 8119 F, P5004, fol. 309–14.

[222] Supervisory board meeting of 6 Aug. 1927, BAP, R 8119 F, P5049, fol. 45. This discussion is based on the protocols of 1926–29 in this volume.

[223] Meeting of 9 April 1929, ibid., fol. 79/1–12.

[224] Meeting of 6 May 1929, ibid., fol. 86/1–11.

[225] Stauss to Mamroth, 13 April 1929, BAP, R 8119 F, P5038, fol. 147.

[226] Weigelt to Stauss, 13 July 1929, ibid., fol. 175.

[227] Stauss to Weigelt, 16 July 1929, ibid., fol. 177–8.

[228] For the basic details, see Manfred Pohl, *Geschäft und Politik. Deutsch-russisch/sowjetische Wirtschaftsbeziehungen 1850–1988* (Mainz 1988), pp. 76–100.

[229] Minute by Schlieper, 13 Oct. 1925, HADB, S3140.

[230] Minute by Boner, 1 Oct. 1925, ibid.

[231] Minute by Schacht, Feb. 1926, ibid.

[232] Disconto-Gesellschaft to Norddeutsche Bank, 31 Oct. 1925, ibid.

[233] Minute by Niedermeyer, 19 Nov. 1925 (italics omitted), ibid.

[234] Bonn to Wassermann, 9 April 1926, BAP, R 8119 F, P7142, fol. 25–35.

[235] Notation by Urbig, 13 July 1927, HADB, S3840.

[236] See the circular to the bank branches of 24 June 1927 in HADB, file: Deutsche Bank 1927.

[237] See the memo by Blinzig of 21 Feb. 1928 in HADB, file: Deutsche Bank 1927, Blinzig Reise. On the Chandler Plan, see HADB, file: Deutsche Bank 1921.

[238] 'Was wir meiner Ansicht nach ohne Danger sagen können natürlich ohne irgendwelche Folgerungen daran zu knüpfen ist dass einem people auf lange decades wohl eine leichte burden nicht aber eine Abgabe aufgeladen werden kann die einen sehr grossen wenn nicht den grössten Teil der National Jahres Savings absorb das erträgt das einzelne individual das ja letzten Endes zahlen muss auf keinen Fall stop Soweit es älteren Generationen angehört fühlt es sich not guilty soweit es jüngeren oder zukünftigen Generationen angehört ist es ja unter allen Umständen auch im Urteil der Americans sicher not guilty.' Wassermann to Blinzig, 18 June 1927. For this and the correspondence on Alfred Blinzig's trip to the United States in 1927, see HADB, file: Deutsche Bank 1927. Blinzig Reise nach USA.

[239] Blinzig to the managing board, 23 April 1927, ibid.

[240] Ibid.

[241] See William C. McNeil, *American Money and the Weimar Republic. Economics and Politics on the Eve of the Great Depression* (New York 1986), pp. 149–52; Balderston, *Origins*, pp. 208–9; Rolf E. Lüke, *Von der Stabilisierung zur Krise* (Zurich 1958), pp. 232–40. See also the Deutsche Bank circular of 2 June 1927 trying to allay currency anxieties, HADB, file: Deutsche Bank 1927.

[242] Lüke, *Stabilisierung*, p. 235.

[243] Branch Conference of the Disconto-Gesellschaft, 24th meeting, 8 Sept. 1927, BAP, R 8119 F, P10579, fol. 210–11.

[244] See the thoughtful and revealing letter by Oswald Rösler to Müller-Jabusch, 10 June 1959, HADB, file: Bankenkrise 1931.

[245] Wassermann to Speyer & Co., 13 Sept. 1927, HADB, file: Deutsche Bank 1927, Anleihe über $25.000.000. The discussion which follows is based on the material in this volume.

[246] Blinzig to Leffingwell, 7 Jan. 1928, HADB, file: Deutsche Bank 1928. Of the 172 loans, 138 were below $150,000. Deutsche Bank Business Report 1927, p. 19.

[247] Leffingwell to Blinzig, 26 Jan. 1928, HADB, file: Deutsche Bank 1928.

[248] Ibid.

[249] A basic account and some of the important documents are provided by Manfred Pohl, 'The Amalgamation of the Deutsche Bank and the Disconto-Gesellschaft in October 1929', *Studies on Economic and Monetary Problems and on Banking History*, 18 (1980), pp. 27–52.

[250] Wassermann to Salomonsohn, 29 April 1926, and the other relevant correspondence, in HADB, file: Disconto-Gesellschaft.

[251] Minute, probably by Salomonsohn, of 26 April 1926, HADB, A. Schaaffhausen'scher Bankverein, K2/15.

[252] Minutes by Michalowsky, 11 Oct. 1926 and 21 Jan. 1927, HADB, file: Deutsche Bank 1929, Verschmelzung.

[253] There is an analysis of Goldschmidt in HADB, file: Georg Solmssen.

[254] Felix Pinner, 'Der Banken-Koloss', *Berliner Tageblatt*, 27 Sept. 1929. The role played by generational difference and snobbism in the treatment of Goldschmidt is evident from a report by Theodor Wolff of an evening at Goldschmidt's home in January 1927: 'At Jakob Goldschmidt's all the, so to speak, old established Jewish financiers like Schwabach, Fürstenberg, then also Wassermann, were presented like chained beasts, flattering on the outside, seething over the upstart on the inside ...'. Feder, *Heute sprach ich mit*, p. 101.

[255] 'Der Kampf zwischen der Deutschen Bank und der Danatbank. Hie Werner Kehl – hie Jakob Goldschmidt', *Der Metallmarkt*, 2 July 1929, BAP, R 8119 F, P8757, fol. 110–11. See Rösler to Müller-Jabusch, 10 June 1959, HADB, file: Bankenkrise.

[256] The memorandum was handwritten, and there are a number of transcriptions in the HADB. The one used here is from the file: Georg Solmssen, and is misdated 16 Sept. 1926. From internal evidence, it was obviously written in 1929 and, in this writer's judgement, is more reliable than some of the later ruminations by others found in the bank's file on the fusion. The quotes and discussion which follow are from this document.

[257] This is reported in Lüke, *Stabilisierung*, p. 243 (note 36), but no source is provided.

[258] See also the letters of Herbert C. Dicke of 19 Oct. 1968, Ernst Hoppe of 29 Oct. 1968, and the other relevant documents in HADB, file: Verschmelzung. On Mosler, see Schmidt, *Männer*, p. 64. See also Rösler to Müller-Jabusch, 10 June 1959, HADB, file: Bankenkrise.

[259] See the protocol of the meeting of 13 Sept. 1929 in HADB, file: Hans Rummel. On Rummel, see also Schmidt, *Männer*, pp. 135–8. For Rummel's critique of the accounting methods employed in banking after the war, and his reform proposals, many of which he carried out between 1929 and 1933, see Hans Rummel, 'Die Rentabilitätsfrage der Banken, ihre Unkosten und die Kalkulation', in *Untersuchung des Bankwesens 1933*. Part 1, vol. 1, pp. 421–75.

[260] *Berliner Boursen-Courier*, 26 Sept. 1929.

[261] 'Deutsche Bank-Disconto-Gesellschaft' trade supplement of the *Berliner Börsen-Zeitung*, 27 Sept. 1929.

[262] For a general account, see Pohl, *Studies*, 18 (1980), pp. 27–52.

[263] Remarks by Katzenstein, 'Stenographic Protocol of the Extraordinary General Assembly of the Deutsche Bank on 29 October 1929', ('Stenographische Niederschrift über die ausserordentliche Generalversammlung der Deutschen Bank am 29. Oktober 1929'), HADB, file: Verschmelzung.

[264] Fehr to Carl Boschwitz, 25 Oct. 1929, HADB, file: Deutsche Bank 1929.

[265] For the propaganda campaign, see the circulars of 13 Nov. 1929 and the brochures in BAP, R 8119 F, P8876. See also the material and newspaper articles in HADB, file:

Deutsche Bank 1929, and the newspaper file: for November 1929.

[266] 'Die neue Auslandsgründung der Deutschen Bank', *Magazin der Wirtschaft*, 19 Sept. 1929. For the correspondence on the United States and Overseas Corporation, see HADB, S1822.

[267] Granbery to Kehl, 27 Dec. 1929, ibid.

[268] Kehl to Granbery, 16 Jan. 1930, ibid.

[269] Solmssen to Schlitter, 20 Jan. 1930, BAP, R 8119 F, 24362. For Goldschmidt's speech of 1928, see *Verhandlungen des VII. Allgemeinen Deutschen Bankiertages zu Köln am Rhein am 9., 10. und 11. September 1928* (Berlin/Leipzig 1928), pp. 129–68. For Goldschmidt's report to the Macmillan Committee and testimony, see *Minutes of Evidence taken before the Committee on Finance and Industry*, 2 vols (London 1931), II, pp. 147–62. It is interesting to note that Greenwood accompanied Goldschmidt when he gave testimony on 25 July 1930. A useful if obviously tendentious appraisal of Goldschmidt was written by Maximilian Müller-Jabusch under the pseudonym Andreas Weitenweber, 'Das System Goldschmidt', *Die Bank*, 34 (1941), pp. 549–66, 576–82.

[270] Georg Solmssen, 'Entwicklungstendenzen und weltwirtschaftliche Aufgaben der deutschen Grossbanken', *Monatshefte für die Beamten der Deutschen Bank und Disconto-Gesellschaft* (February 1930), pp. 17–26, quote on p. 24.

[271] See Deutsche Bank und Disconto-Gesellschaft Berlin to Director Kraemer, 2 Dec. 1930, BAP, R 8119 F, 24048. On the banker teas, see the note to Abshagen, 11 Nov. 1930, BAP, R 8119 F, 23990, fol. 177. Wassermann, Nathan, Gutmann, Goldschmidt and Bodenheimer are specifically mentioned as attending the first of these.

[272] Meeting of the Club von Berlin, 2 April 1932, BAK, NL Luther, No. 340, fol. 266. On Palyi's appointment, see *Magazin der Wirtschaft*, 39 (September 1928), p. 1508. For Goldschmidt's views on economists and economics, see *Bankiertag 1928*, pp. 131ff. See also Melchior Palyi, *The Twilight of Gold 1914–1936. Myths and Realities* (Chicago 1972), which contains some interesting comments reflecting his work at the bank.

[273] Most of these were printed in expanded form by Deutsche Bank und Deutsche Bank and Disconto-Gesellschaft employees by the *Monatshefte*.

[274] Bonn to Rothschild, 11 Dec. 1928, HADB, S233.

[275] Minute by Bonn, 20 Aug. 1929, HADB, S236.

[276] Minute by Mosler, 1 Nov. 1929, ibid.

[277] Minute, 30 Jan. 1930, HADB, S241.

[278] Minute of 15 March 1930 and press conference of 12 March 1930, HADB, S242.

[279] For materials on the Aktiengesellschaft für Osthandel, see HADB, S689–90. See also BAP, R 8119 F, 24048 for the discussion in the press and the correspondence of the bank.

[280] See the materials in ibid. There is a good explanation of the bank's policy in an unsigned letter of 22 Nov. 1930.

[281] Georg Bernhard, 'Anklagen in der Generalversammlung', *Magazin der Wirtschaft*, 23 May 1930, pp. 970–1.

[282] Balderston, *Origins*, p. 312. See also Harold James, 'Did the Reichsbank draw the Right Conclusions from the Great Inflation?', in Feldman and Müller-Luckner, *Nachwirkungen*, pp. 211–31.

[283] Materials prepared in response to the Bank-Enquête, 1933, in BAP, R 8119 F, P418, fol. 140–1.

[284] Kehl to Schlitter, 21 Aug. 1930, BAP, R 8119 F, P11, fol. 8–11.

[285] Frederic M. Sackett to the US Secretary of State, 20 Jan. 1931, US National Archives, Record Group 39, Box 64.

[286] Schäffer diary, 14 Oct. 1930, kindly supplied to me by Prof. Harold James.

[287] See the note from Wassermann's office of 29 Oct. 1930, and Gottfried Feder, 'Das Programm der NSDAP', BAP, R 8119 F, 24046, fol. 8–36. Like Wassermann, Solmssen seems to have toyed with taming the Nazis through collaboration. At the end of 1930, Theodor Wolff had to calm Max Warburg down about 'Solmssen, who is flirting with National Socialism'. See Feder, *Heute sprach ich mit ...*, p. 280.

[288] See the newspaper reports and letters in BAP, R 8119 F, 24048, especially the letter of the bank to Frau Justizrat Helene Meyer of 21 Oct. 1930. On Stauss's lifestyle, see Glum, *Zwischen Wissenschaft und Politik*, pp. 260–1. For the contacts with Göring, see Müller-Jabusch to Waldemar Besson, 25 Oct. 1960, HADB, NL Müller-Jabusch.

[289] See the excellent discussion in W.E. Mosse, *Jews in the German Economy. The German-Jewish Economic Elite 1820–1935* (Oxford 1987), ch. 8, esp. pp. 329–39. Schlitter's attitude may be gathered from his letter to the banker Anton Brüning of 27 Feb. 1931: 'Frederick II was not called the Great because of his victorious wars but because he rebuilt a totally wasted Prussia in a short time. He attracted foreign capital along with – horrible dictu even at that time – Jews, treated them very well, and granted them tax exemption for many years to the great good of his country.' BAP, R 8119 F, 24342, fol. 31–2.

[290] Urbig to Pfeiffer, 22 Feb. 1930, BAP, R 8119 F, 24474, and the correspondence between Duisberg and Schlitter, 8 March–31 March 1932, BAP, R 8119 F, 24357. More generally, see the interesting analysis by Erich W. Abraham, 'Grossbanken und Politik', *Die Welt am Montag* (18 Nov. 1929), BAP, RB, No. 1130, fol. 64. On the DNVP committee, see Henry A. Turner, Jr, *German Business and the Rise of Hitler* (New York/Oxford 1985), p. 297.

[291] Schlitter to Niehues, 9 Feb. 1931, BAP, R 8119 F, 24341, fol. 309–11.

[292] Wassermann's speech of 17 April 1931, HADB, file: Oscar Wassermann. It is noteworthy that the speech was translated into English and appeared in brochure form in both languages.

[293] On the negotiations with the French, see Director Brüning to Schlitter, 25 Feb. BAP, R 8119 F, 24342, fol. 29–30. On Kehl's trip, see Edward W. Bennett, *Germany and the Diplomacy of the Financial Crisis 1931* (Cambridge, Mass. 1962), pp. 37–8.

[294] Solmssen's Zurich speech of 5 Feb. 1930 in *Monatshefte*, Feb. 1930, p. 23.

[295] On the cuts in Rhineland-Westphalia, see the Revisions-Kommission meeting of 10 Sept. 1930, BAP, R 8119 F, P42, fol. 28; on the cuts of the branch directors, see the

detailed lists in ibid., P10942, fol. 22–102. On Solmssen's pay cut, see HADB, personnel file: Dr Solmssen.

[296] Discussion between Brüning and Wassermann, 14 Nov. 1930, *Akten der Reichskanzlei. Kabinette Brüning*, 3 vols (Boppard am Rhein 1990) I, p. 621, n.12.

[297] Aurel Schubert, *The Credit-Anstalt Crisis of 1931* (Cambridge 1991), pp. 85–6. Wassermann evidently did a splendid job of answering critics of this move at the supervisory board, see Abshagen to Michalowsky, 24 March 1931, BAP, R 8119 F, 23991, fol. 12–13.

[298] Minute of 18 March 1930, BAP, R 8119 F, P146, fol. 1–5.

[299] Ibid., fol. 25.

[300] Circulars of 5 July and 6 Aug. 1930, BAP, R 8119 F, P10603.

[301] Auditing Commission of the Rhenish-Westphalian Committee, 10 Sept. 1930, BAP, R 8119 F, P42, fol. 29.

[302] Meeting of 10 Oct. 1930, ibid., fol. 44.

[303] See, for example, his 16-page letter to Karl Stollwerck of 24 Feb. 1931 and the other relevant documents in BAP, R 8119 F, P4784, fol. 270/1–16.

[304] Report of the Board of Directors (1930), undated, BAP, R 8119 F, P3217, fol. 269, and the correspondence in BAP, R 8119 F, P3248 and P3199.

[305] Abshagen to Frahne, 27 Sept. 1930, BAP, R 8119 F, P3978, fol. 15–16.

[306] Abshagen to Frahne, 15 Oct. 1930, ibid., fol. 42/1–4.

[307] Deutsche Bank und Disconto-Gesellschaft to Methner & Frahne, 31 Oct. 1930, ibid., fol. 81–4.

[308] The process can be followed in BAP, R 8119 F, P3979.

[309] Director Maser of the Deutsche Bank und Disconto-Gesellschaft, Augsburg, to von Stauss, 1 Dec. 1930, BAP, R 8119 F, 24449, fol. 159.

[310] For the breakdown of the engagements, see ibid., fol. 192; for the quotes, see Stauss to Lindenmeyer, 19 Jan. 1931, ibid., fol. 193–4 and Stauss to Kehl, 19 Feb. 1931, ibid., fol. 207.

[311] See the correspondence of May–June 1930, in BAP, R 8119 F, P413, fol. 333–49.

[312] See the minute by Urbig, 2 Feb. 1930, BAP, R 8119 F, 24472, and the adjacent correspondence in this volume for this discussion.

[313] *Kabinette Brüning*, I, p. 175f.

[314] Schlitter to Anton Brüning, 27 Feb. 1931, BAP, R 8119 F, 24342, fol. 30–2.

[315] Documented remarks by Solmssen, 26 Feb. 1930, BAP, R 8119 F, 24046, fol. 49–51. Schacht had made the commitment in question in a letter to the Committee of Experts on 6 June 1929. He there promised to place in force paragraph 31, asserting the obligation to redeem Reichsmark in gold or foreign exchange, of the Banking Law of 1924 no later than when the new reparations plan came into force. Minute of 28 April 1930, BAP, RB, No. 6742, fol. 477–83.

[316] The fullest scholarly study, now out of date, is Karl Erich Born, *Die deutsche Bankenkrise 1931. Finanzen und Politik* (Munich 1967). For newer analyses, see Harold James, 'The Causes of the German Banking Crisis of 1931', *Economic History Review*, 45 (1984), pp. 68–87; Theo Balderston, 'German Banking Between the Wars: The

Crisis of the Credit Banks', *Business History Review*, 65 (1991), pp. 554–605, and Theo Balderston, 'The Banks and the Gold Standard in the German Financial Crisis of 1931', *University of Manchester Working Papers in Economic and Social History*, 24 (1993). Two partisan blow-by-blow accounts are H.E. Priester, *Das Geheimnis des 13. Juli. Ein Tatsachenbericht von der Bankenkrise* (Berlin 1932) and Rolf E. Lüke, *13. Juli 1931. Das Geheimnis der deutschen Bankenkrise* (Frankfurt a.M. 1981). On the Deutsche Bank's efforts to wrestle with Brüning's memoirs and the history of the banking crisis, see Gerald D. Feldman, 'Jakob Goldschmidt, The History of the Banking Crisis of 1931, and, the Problem of Freedom of Manoeuvre in the Weimar Economy', in Christoph Buchheim, Michael Hutter and Harold James (eds), *Zerissene Zwischenkriegszeit: Wirtschaftshistorische Beiträge. Knut Borchardt zum 65. Geburtstag* (Baden-Baden 1994).

[317] This discussion is based on the lengthy description provided in a letter from Doerner to Solmssen, 6 Nov. 1956, HADB, file: Georg Solmssen, and file: Bankenkrise 1931.

[318] Silverberg to Stolper, 19 July 1931, BAK, NL Silverberg, No. 707. On the crisis, see Peter Krüger, *Die Aussenpolitik der Republik von Weimar* (Darmstadt 1985), pp. 531ff.

[319] For the international and domestic context of the banking crisis, see Gerhard Schulz, *Von Brüning zu Hitler. Zwischen Demokratie und Diktatur*, Vol. 3 (Berlin/New York 1992), ch. 8.

[320] Balderston, *Origins*, pp. 311–12. See also the report of the Reichsbank Statistical Department, 'Zur Deutschen Kreditkrise', 31 July 1931, BAK, NL Luther, No. 359.

[321] Lüke, *Von der Stabilisierung*, p. 274 in which he follows H. Priester, *Das Geheimnis des 13. Juli*, p. 25.

[322] Erich Freudenberg to the *Frankfurter Allgemeine Zeitung*, 14 Dec. 1970, and Hermann J. Abs to Volkmar Muthesius, 29 Dec. 1970, HADB, Abs, Bankenkrise 1931. Abs had unsuccessfully tried to block a Delbrück, Schickler credit to the Lahusens at the turn of 1930–31 after Lahusen refused information on his financial status on the grounds that it was insulting to request it from so established a businessman!

[323] Luther diary, 13 June 1931, BAK, NL Luther, No. 365, fol. 32.

[324] Reichsbank Statistical Department, 'Zur deutschen Kreditkrise', 31 July 1931, BAK, NL Luther, No. 359.

[325] Brüning Cabinet meeting of 1 July 1931, *Kabinette Brüning*, II, pp. 1264–8. The discussion which follows is based on the documents for July 1931 published in this volume as well as the discussion in Schulz, *Von Brüning zu Hitler*, ch. 8, and Gerhard Schulz, *et al.*, *Politik und Wirtschaft in der Krise. Quellen zur Ära Brüning*, 2 vols (Düsseldorf 1980), I, pp. 727ff.

[326] The phrase is that of Director Vocke, see Schäffer notations, ibid., p. 825.

[327] Meeting of 6 July 1931, *Kabinette Brüning*, II, p. 1294.

[328] Schäffer notations, *Politik und Wirtschaft*, II, pp. 825–6 and the severe but just criticism of Silverberg in his letter to Stolper of 19 July 1931, BAK, NL Silverberg, No. 707. In this account, I follow the day-by-day compilation of Müller-Jabusch, developed in the late 1950s from the extant sources and his investigations, without,

however, accepting all his judgements and conclusions. See HADB, NL Müller-Jabusch.

329 Schäffer notations, *Politik und Wirtschaft*, II, p. 827.

330 On this important distinction, which is based on the Deutsche Bank und Disconto-Gesellschaft memorandum to the Chancellor of 1 Oct. 1931 in the HADB, see Müller-Jabusch to Schäffer, 1 Aug. 1960, HADB, NL Müller-Jabusch. For a rundown of Wassermann's treatment of the DANAT-Bank in July, see Schäffer to Müller-Jabusch, 30 June 1960, ibid.

331 Heinrich Brüning, *Memoiren 1918–1934* (Stuttgart 1970), pp. 312ff. See Brüning to Goldschmidt's brother, 31 Oct. 1955, where he asks for copies of the accounts, especially those relating to the shipping companies, which Wassermann was allegedly 'greedy' to have: Brüning Papers, Harvard University. The accounts are actually in the HADB, file: Deutsche Bank 1931.

332 Schäffer to Müller-Jabusch, 22 July 1960, HADB, NL Müller-Jabusch.

333 Minute by Solmssen, sent to Oswald Rösler, 7 Jan. 1954, HADB, file: Bankenkrise 1931.

334 The most reliable account of this change of Reichsbank attitude is provided by State Secretary Pünder's 'Gestaltung der aussen-, innen und wirtschaftlichen Lage seit Sonntag, den 5. Juli 1931,' BAK, NL Pünder, No. 139, fol. 166–70. The Reichsbank decision to sharpen its credit restrictions on 10 July is given a rather tendentious interpretation by Heinz Habedank, *Die Reichsbank in der Weimarer Republik. Zur Rolle der Zentralbank in der Politik des deutschen Imperialismus* (East Berlin 1981), p. 212.

335 Minute by Solmssen, sent to Oswald Rösler, 7 Jan. 1954, HADB, file: Bankenkrise 1931, and meeting of 11 July 1930 in *Kabinette Brüning*, II, pp. 1324–37.

336 Schäffer to Müller-Jabusch, 30 June 1960, HADB, NL Müller-Jabusch.

337 Frisch to Müller-Jabusch, 27 May 1959, HADB, NL Müller-Jabusch.

338 Meeting of 12 July 1931 in *Kabinette Brüning*, II, pp. 1338–43.

339 Born, *Bankenkrise*, p. 110ff.

340 On the aftermath of the crisis, see ibid, p. 110ff.

341 See its circular of 21 July 1931, BAP, R 8119 F, P42, fol. 78–82.

342 'Denkschrift über die Juli-Ereignisse im Bankgewerbe', 1 Oct. 1931, HADB, file: Deutsche Bank 1931. An abbreviated version is printed in *Politik und Wirtschaft*, I, pp. 843–54.

343 Ministerial discussion, 20 June 1931, *Kabinette Brüning*, II, p. 1229.

344 Head of Department discussion, 14 July 1931, ibid, p. 1357.

345 See his remarks at the meeting of 3 Aug. 1931, ibid., II, p. 1508. For the Reichsbank reform proposals, see 'Zur deutschen Kreditkrise', 31 July 1931, BAK, NL Luther, No. 359.

346 Meeting of 18 Sept. 1931, *Kabinette Brüning*, II, p. 1704, and meeting of 28 July 1931, p. 1442.

347 Meeting at the Club von Berlin, 1 Feb. 1932, BAK, NL Luther, No. 340, fol. 264.

348 Notations, *Politik und Wirtschaft*, I, p. 817.

[349] Report of Reichsbank Statistical Section, 7 Oct. 1931, BAP, RB, No. 6493, fol. 285–6.

[350] BAP, R 8119 F, P415, fol. 101.

[351] Minute by Redelmeier, 21 Aug. 1931, BAP, R 8119 F, 24343, fol. 35.

[352] See the Deutsche Bank Business Reports for 1931 and 1932 and HADB, personnel file: Solmssen. On the contractual employee cuts, see the circular of 29 Dec. 1931 in BAP, R 8119 F, P11, fol. 97–8. See the branch directors' meeting of 2 Sept. 1931, HADB, file: Direktorensitzungen.

[353] Report on the status of the Deutsche Bank und Disconto-Gesellschaft, Feb. 1932, BAK, NL Luther, No. 340, fol. 1–23. For a valuable discussion of the role of the Deutsche Bank und Disconto-Gesellschaft and its leaders in dealing with the aftermath of the crisis, see Karin Lehmann, 'The Reaction of the Deutsche Bank and Disconto-Gesellschaft to the banking crisis of 1931', unpublished mauscript. For the record of the profits and losses of the bank, Figure 3.3 on p. 288 of this book.

[354] Silverberg to Schlitter, 5 March 1932, BAK, NL Silverberg, No. 81, fol. 58–63.

[355] On the Schultheiss case, see the reports in BAP, R 8119 F, P4649.

[356] See Silverberg to Urbig, BAK, NL Silverberg, No. 81, fol. 78–80, and Steinthal to Silverberg, 8 Dec. 1932, ibid., fol. 124–5, and newspaper articles on Schäfer and Kehl in HADB, file: Werner Kehl.

[357] Kimmich to Hager, 2 Oct. 1931, BAP, R 8119 F, P2468, fol. 357–8.

[358] Protocol of the meeting of the Economic and Administrative Committee of the Rhein-Main-Donau AG, 21 Jan. 1932, BAP, R 8119 F, P4989, fol. 203.

[359] Johannes Jeserich AG to Deutsche Bank Director Ottmar Benz, chairman of the supervisory board, 26 Jan. 1932, BAP, R 8119 F, P2373, fol. 347–59. Unemployment in the construction industry in May 1932, the height of the construction season, was to be 82 per cent, BAP, R 8119 F, P2363, fol. 198.

[360] Solmssen speech of 12 March 1932, HADB, file: Georg Solmssen.

[361] Solmssen to Springorum, 17 Jan. 1933, BAP, R 8119 F, P1220, fol. 251–6.

[362] See the excellent discussion in Karin Lehmann, 'Reaction of the Deutsche Bank und Disconto-Gesellschaft'.

[363] Kiehl to Reemtsma, 6 Jan. 1932, BAP, R 8119 F, P2876, fol. 228–9.

The Deutsche Bank and the Dictatorship
1933–1945

[1] Thomas Balogh, *Studies in Financial Organization* (Cambridge 1947), p. 78: 'a secular tendency for the demand for bank loans to decline'. See also *Frankfurter Zeitung*, 3 June 1934: the state had financed new credit through work creation programmes, but 'The credit created in this way did not stay in the economy, because important sectors still preferred to liquidate inventories in order to repay credit'.

[2] From October 1929 to October 1937 the official name of the corporation was 'Deutsche Bank und Disconto-Gesellschaft'. It will be referred to below simply as 'Deutsche Bank'.

[3] To branch managers, 22 Aug. 1933, Bundesarchiv Potsdam (BAP), R 8119 F, 24000.

[4] Directors' meetings of 6 Oct. 1936 and 30 Aug. 1938, HADB, file: Directors' Meetings.

[5] Deutsche Bank special circulars, S62/33, 16 August 1933, HADB.

[6] Cited in Rainer Zitelmann, *Hitler. Selbstverständnis eines Revolutionärs*, 2nd edn (Stuttgart 1991), pp. 260–1. In general, on Hitler's economic views, see Henry A. Turner, 'Hitlers Einstellung zu Wirtschaft und Gesellschaft vor 1933', *Geschichte und Gesellschaft*, 2 (1976), pp. 89–117; and Avraham Barkai, 'Sozialdarwinismus und Antiliberalismus in Hitlers Wirtschaftskonzept. Zu Henry A. Turner Jr "Hitlers Einstellung zu Wirtschaft und Gesellschaft vor 1933"', *Geschichte und Gesellschaft*, 3 (1977), pp. 406–17. More extensively, Avraham Barkai, *Das Wirtschaftssystem des Nationalsozialismus* (Stuttgart 1988), pp. 27ff.

[7] Cited in Klaus Kreimeier, *Die Ufa-Story. Geschichte eines Filmkonzerns* (Munich 1992), p. 306.

[8] Eduard Rosenbaum/A.J. Sherman, *M.M. Warburg & Co. 1798–1938. Merchant Bankers of Hamburg* (London 1979), p. xi.

[9] Wilhelm Keppler in Bank Inquiry Meeting, 6 September 1933, Bundesarchiv Koblenz (BAK), R2/13682, fol. 15–21.

[10] Gottfried Feder in Bank Inquiry Meeting, 6 Sept. 1933, BAK, R2/13682, fol. 23; Feder in Bank Inquiry on 23 November 1933, R2/13683, fol. 69–70.

[11] 23 and 24 Nov. 1933, BAK, R2/13683, fol. 65f., 76.

[12] G.H. Pinsent's notes on interview with Schacht, 6 Oct. 1933, Bank of England Archive, OV34/5.

[13] Reich Deputy in Braunschweig and Anhalt Leeper to Deputy of Führer Rudolf Hess, 13 March 1934, BAK, R43II/243, fol. 74–5.

[14] Mosler's note for board of managing directors, 5 Dec. 1934, BAP, R 8119 F, 24004.

[15] Reich Finance Ministry, note of 25 May 1939, BAK, R2/13685, fol. 64.

[16] Mosler and Kimmich note (only for the board of managing directors), 21 Feb. 1934, HADB, Crisis of the Bank 1931–34.

[17] 'The Development of Banking Since the Seizure of Power', May 1938, Bundesbank Archive, Reichsbank file 6520.

[18] 'Prospectus: Conversion of Daimler-Benz Bonds', BAP, R 8119 F, P3191, fol. 260 ff.

[19] See Manfred Pohl, *Die Finanzierung der Russengeschäfte zwischen den beiden Weltkriegen* (Frankfurt a.M. 1975), pp. 44–8.

[20] Note of 10 Feb. 1938, BAK, R2/3847. In general, see Rudolf Stucken, *Deutsche Geld und Kreditpolitik 1914–1953* (Tübingen 1953), p. 143.

[21] Figures from BAP, R 8119 F, P294.

[22] Reichsbank to Reich Finance Minister, 29 Dec. 1938, BAK, R2/3847. See Heinz Pentzlin, *Hjalmar Schacht. Leben und Wirken einer umstrittenen Persönlichkeit* (Berlin 1980), p. 250. Wilhelm Vocke, *Memoiren* (Stuttgart 1973), p. 110.

[23] Meeting of Reich Loan Consortium, 10 Jan. 1939, BAP, R 8119 F, P296, fol. 68 ff.

[24] Reichsbank to Reich Finance Minister, 29 Dec. 1938, BAK, R2/3847.

[25] Kimmich's note of 19 July 1939, BAP, R 8119 F, P3359, fol. 198.

[26] Peter Hayes, *Industry and Ideology. IG Farben in the Nazi Era* (New York 1987), pp. 176, 184.

[27] Mosler's memorandum of 27 Jan. 1938, BAP, R 8119 F, P1775, fol. 423 ff.

[28] Mosler's memorandum of 25 May 1939, BAP, R 8119 F, P1767 fol. 106 ff.

[29] Deutsche Bank to Deutsche Bank supervisory board, 24 Nov. 1933, BAK, NL Silverberg 83, fol. 169–70. See Manfred Pohl, *Konzentration im deutschen Bankwesen 1848–1980* (Frankfurt a.M. 1980), p. 353.

[30] Rhineland-Westphalian Advisory Council, 27 Nov. 1935, BAP, R 8119 F, P41, fol. 31; Advisory Council, 5 May 1936, fol. 43f.

[31] Rhineland-Westphalian Advisory Council, 11. Nov. 1936, BAP, R 8119 F, P41, fol. 62; Advisory Council, 28 Oct. 1937, fol. 98.

[32] Rhineland-Westphalian Advisory Council, 30 April 1940, BAP, R 8119 F, P41, fol. 137.

[33] Eckard Wandel, *Hans Schäffer. Steuermann in wirtschaftliche und politischen Krisen* (Stuttgart 1974), pp. 160–1. 4 December 1931 diary entry, Institut für Zeitgeschichte, Munich, Schäffer diary, ED93/16.

[34] *Frankfurter Zeitung*, 9 Dec. 1932.

[35] Deutsche Bank (signed Solmssen and Schlitter) to Silverberg, 19 March 1932, BAK, NL Silverberg 83, fol. 72–3.

[36] Silverberg to Urbig, 22 March 1932, BAK, NL Silverberg 83, fol. 78–80.

[37] Urbig cable to Silverberg, 28 May 1933, BAK, NL Silverberg 83, fol. 151.

[38] Report of Urbig, July 1933, BAP, R 8119 F, P55, fol. 18–19.

[39] Report of Urbig, July 1933, BAP, R 8119 F, P55. See also Christopher Kopper, 'Zwischen Marktwirtschaft und Dirigismus. Staat, Banken und Bankenpolitik im "Dritten Reich" von 1933 bis 1939', Ruhr-University Bochum Ph.D. thesis 1992, pp. 138–40.

[40] *Frankfurter Zeitung*, No. 398–400, 31 May 1933.

[41] Urbig to Russell, 18 Jan 1934, HADB, personnel file: Solmssen.

[42] Solmssen to Urbig, 9 April 1933, HADB, personnel file: Solmssen.

[43] Martin H. Sommerfeldt, *Ich war dabei. Die Verschwörung der Dämonen 1933–1939* (Darmstadt (n.d.)), p. 41. I owe this reference to Professor Gerhard Schulz.

[44] Kiehl to Philipp Reemtsma, 19 April 1934, BAP, R 8119 F, P4746.

[45] Notice on meeting with Schlieper, 3 May 1935, HADB, RWB, 54.

[46] Kimmich to Schlegelberger, 4 Jan 1939, BAP, R 8119 F, 24008, fol. 13.

[47] *Monatshefte für die Beamten der Deutschen Bank und Disconto-Gesellschaft*, November–December 1933, p. 88, speech of Pg. Hertel.

[48] ibid., pp. 84–5.

[49] Kranefuss (office of Wilhelm Keppler) to Sippell, 7 July 1934, HADB, RWB, 57; note of Sippell, 19 Dec. 1933, HADB, RWB, 57.

[50] Reichsbank Directorate to Reich Economics Minstry, 23 March 1933, BAK, R43II/244, fol. 7–8.

[51] Kaiser's notice, 14 March 1933, BAP, R 8119 F, 24001; Berndts (Hirschberg) to May, 28 June 1935, BAP, R 8119 F, 24001.

[52] Letter to Chief of Special Service, SS Gruppenführer Heydrich (with membership list), 22 Aug. 1934, Berlin Document Center (BDC), Society of Friends special file; 2 October 1934 Reichsführer SS, Head of Chief Reich Security Office to Supreme Party Court of NSDAP, 2 Oct. 1934, BDC, Society of Friends special file.

[53] Sippell's note for Kimmich, 29 Sept. 1934, HADB, RWB, 54.

[54] See in general Robert Gellately, *The Gestapo and German Society. Enforcing Racial Policy 1933–1945* (Oxford 1990), especially pp. 130–58.

[55] Winkelmann to managing board, 3 Sept 1934, HADB, RWB, 54; Winkelmann to Sippell, 9 Sept. 1934, HADB, RWB, 54.

[56] Memorandum by Sippell, 6 Dec. 1935, HADB, RWB, 54; also letter from Rösler to Maximilian Müller-Jabusch, 1 March 1951, HADB, RWB, 54.

[57] Von Halt had joined the NSDAP in May 1933: party membership number 3204950 (BDC).

[58] Hermann Hess, *Ritter von Halt. Der Sportler und Soldat* (Berlin 1936), pp. 126–9. I owe this reference to Carl-Ludwig Holtfrerich.

[59] BDC, file: Von Halt.

[60] Dohmen interview with Frau von Halt (25 August 1982, HADB, interviews) gives an extreme version: 'The board of managing directors asked my husband, who was after all quite fit and slim, to give them classes in gymnastics. My husband said yes.'

[61] *Schwibbogen*, 7/2, February 1937, p. 22, HADB.

[62] Rösler's declaration under oath, 20 March 1950, HADB, RWB, 31.

[63] *Schwibbogen*, 7/11, November 1937, pp. 250–1, HADB.

[64] *Mitteilungen für die NSBO Deutsche Bank und Disconto-Gesellschaft*, 1934, 12, p. 12, HADB.

[65] *Deutsche Juristenzeitung*, 1929, 23, Column 1597.

[66] Rhineland-Westphalian Advisory Council, BAP, R 8119 F, P41, fol. 93.

[67] Pfeiffer (Kassel) to Head Office, 13 July 1933, BAP, R 8119 F, 24001.

[68] Hutschenreuther AG to Urbig, 1 Dec. 1933, BAP, R 8119 F, P4295, fol. 106.

[69] Eugen Schweisheimer to Urbig, 15 Nov. 1933, BAP, R 8119 F, P4295, fol. 96.

[70] Rudolf Sies memorandum on negotiations in Braunes Haus, Selb, 5 Nov. 1934, BAP 80, Ba 2, P4295, fol. 223.

[71] Joh. Jeserich AG to Benz (Deutsche Bank), 3 April 1933, BAP 80, Ba 2, P2372, fol. 2–4.

[72] Benz note of 20 April 1933, BAP, R 8119 F, P2372, fol. 94.

[73] Memorandum from Benz, 29 May 1933, fol. 139; Feuchtmann to Benz, 10 July 1933, BAP, R 8119 F, P2372, fol. 177–8; Feuchtmann to Benz, 24 July 1933, BAP, R 8119 F, P2372, fol. 187–8.

[74] Hertie-Kaufhaus-Beteiligungs-G.m.b.H. to Advisory Council, 30 Aug. 1933, BAP, R 8119 F, P5218, fol. 9–10.

[75] Avraham Barkai, *From Boycott to Elimination*, pp. 69–72.

[76] Avraham Barkai, 'Die deutschen Unternehmer und die Judenpolitik im Dritten Reich', *Geschichte und Gesellschaft*, 15 (1989), p. 232.

[77] Rhineland–Westphalian Advisory Council meeting, 11 Nov. 1936, BAP, R 8119 F, P41, fol. 63.

[78] See Peter Hayes, 'Big Business and "Aryanization" in Germany 1933–1939', *Jahrbuch für Antisemitismusforschung*, 3 (1994), pp. 254–81.

[79] Reich Economic Chamber to Reich Economic Groups, 7 Jan 1938, BAP, R 8119 F, P2947, fol. 114–15.

[80] Memorandum on visit of Dr Schacht, 25 Sept. 1935, BAP, R 8119 F, 24002.

[81] See Hayes, 'Big Business', p. 264.

[82] Mannheim branch to Head Office, Branch Department, BAP, R 8119 F, 24003.

[83] Deutsche Bank to branch managers, 14 Jan. 1938, BAP, R 8119 F, P2947, fol. 112–13.

[84] Memorandum on meeting of branch managers in Nuremberg, 21 June 1938, BAP, R 8119 F, 24330.

[85] Letter to Berlin head office, branch department, 29 Dec. 1938, Saxon State Archive, Deutsche Bank files 623 (I owe this reference to Peter Hayes).

[86] Rhineland–Westphalian Advisory Council meeting, 2 Nov. 1938, BAP, R 8119 F, P41, fol. 126.

[87] Memorandum of Rodolfo Löb (previously a partner of Mendelssohn & Co.), 20 Dec. 1947, HADB, RWB, 31.

[88] See Kopper, 'Zwischen Marktwirtschaft und Dirigismus', pp. 290–3.

[89] Reich Security Chief Office report, BAK, R58/717, fol. 165.

[90] BAK, R7/1010 and 1011 for negotiations. The critical meeting was on 28 June 1939 in the Reich Economics Ministry: R7/1011, fol. 323–8.

[91] Note of 18 Oct. 1948, Rheinbraun Archive, 210/328. 'Supreme Finance President Hanover: Security Decree under Paragraph 37a of Law on Foreign Exchange', 19 Oct. 1938, Rheinbraun Archive, 374/328.

[92] Hubertus Braunkohlen AG to Reich Economics Ministry, 11 March 1939, BAP, R 8119 F, P964, fol. 101–4. The valuation is set out in Dr Josef Abs to H.J. Abs, 30 March 1939, BAP, R 8119 F, P964, fol. 108–17.

[93] Verdict 2077, Bad Godesberg, 30 December 1950, Rheinbraun Archive, 378/328.

[94] Deutsche Bank special circulars, S25/38, 'Strictly Confidential: To Branch Managers', 19 May 1938, HADB.

[95] Deutsche Bank, Bamberg branch to head office, legal department, 24 Jan. 1938, BAP, R 8119 F, P7403, fol. 385; Deutsche Bank, Frankfurt a.M. branch, to legal department, BAP, R 8119 F, P2947, fol. 408–9.

[96] Deutsche Bank Frankfurt a.M., to head office, personnel department, 10 Dec. 1938, BAP, R 8119 F, 24151.

[97] Dingeldey to Dieckmann, 27 April 1933, BAK, NL Dingeldey. Larry E. Jones, *German Liberalism and the Dissolution of the Weimar Party System* (Chapel Hill 1988), p. 474. (I owe this reference to Professor Henry Turner.)

[98] Telegram from Deputy of Führer to NSDAP Reich Treasurer, Munich, 19 May 1938,

BDC, file: Papen. Tiessler (Propaganda Ministry) to Schmidt-Römer, Party Chancellery Munich, 2 Oct. 1942, BAK, NS 18/579. The OMGUS report is clearly mistaken in claiming that von Stauss had joined the party before the National Socialist seizure of power (Report on the Investigation of the Deutsche Bank, November 1946, p. 35, National Archives, Washington, DC, RG 360, OMGUS, BICO, Box 71).

[99] Stauss's note of 11 March 1933, BAP, R 8119 F, 24404.

[100] Securities Office: Universum-Film Aktiengesellschaft, 24 Nov. 1933, BAP, R 8119 F, P6014, fol. 378.

[101] Kreimeier, *Ufa-Story*, pp. 244, 248.

[102] Ibid, p. 265.

[103] Attachment to 6 April 1934 letter from Klitzsch to Stauss, BAP, R 8119 F, P6015, fol. 82.

[104] UfA AG to Stauss, 14 May 1934, BAP, R 8119 F, P6015, fol. 138/2.

[105] Development of Star Remuneration, 16 Nov. 1936, BAP, R 8119 F, P6016, fol. 236ff. Contract with Hans Albers of 8 April 1933, BAP, R 8119 F, P6014, fol. 332; contract with Zarah Leander of 5 Nov. 1936, BAP, R 8119 F, P6016, fol. 227.

[106] Meeting of supervisory board of Filmkredit-Bank GmbH, 16 July 1936, BAP, R 8119 F, P5360, fol. 159.

[107] Memorandum from Kiehl, 'Filmkredit-Bank GmbH', 14 Aug. 1936, BAP, R 8119 F, P5359, fol. 93. David Welch, *Propaganda and the German Cinema 1933–1945* (Oxford 1983), p. 32.

[108] Kiehl's note: Ufa, 28 July 1938, BAP, R 8119 F, P6017, fol. 308–10; decision of 14 May 1942, BAP, R 8119 F, P6020, fol. 32ff.

[109] Stauss to Klitzsch (Ufa), 1936, BAP, R 8119 F, P6016, fol. 165.

[110] Riedel to Stauss, 9 May 1939, BAP, R 8119 F, P6018, fol. 194; Ernst H. Correll to Stauss, 5 Aug. 1938, BAP, R 8119 F, P6017, fol. 316.

[111] Siebert to Stauss, 25 Aug. 1940, BAP, R 8119 F, P5953, fol. 142.

[112] Siebert to Stauss, 13 Aug. 1940, BAP, R 8119 F, P5953, fol. 135; Siebert to Lammers, 22 July 1941, BAP, R 8119 F, P5953, fol. 522–6.

[113] Siebert to Stauss, 25 Aug. 1940, BAP, R 8119 F, P5953, fol. 142.

[114] Meeting of Small Council, 22 Feb. 1939, BAP, R 8119 F, P5956, fol. 70.

[115] Siebert to Stauss, 6 July 1939, BAP, R 8119 F, P2952, fol. 251; memorandum from Siebert, 7 May 1940, BAP, R 8119 F, P5953, fol. 53–4.

[116] Memorandum from Siebert, 4 Nov. 1940, BAP, R 8119 F, P5953, fol. 208.

[117] Supervisory board meeting, 9 June 1933, BAP, R 8119 F, P5052, fol. 95.

[118] Hans Pohl, Stephanie Habeth and Beate Brüninghaus, *Die DaimlerBenz AG in den Jahren 1933 bis 1944* (Wiesbaden 1986), p. 44.

[119] Werlin, 'Confidental Information', 29 Nov. 1933, BAP, R 8119 F, P3297, fol. 151.

[120] Werlin to Kissel, 5 March 1935, BAP, R 8119 F, P3297, fol. 173.

[121] Lewinski (Secretariate of Stauss) to Werlin, 12 May 1934, BAP, R 8119 F, P3297, fol. 165.

[122] BMW to Stauss, 15 Feb. 1938, BAP, R 8119 F, P3075, fol. 321–3.

[123] Statement of Hermann Kaiser, 19 March 1946, NA, OMGUS, Exhibit 12: 'The other

members of the Kreditausschuss were not in favor of these credits but could not intervene as von Stauss was obviously collaborating with the Reich government in these matters' (interrogation by Charles E. Bancroft).

[124] Stauss to Daimler–Benz managing board, 23 Nov. 1934, BAP, R 8119 F, P3228, fol. 434.

[125] Benrath to Stauss, 12 Jan. 1934, BAP, R 8119 F, P7276, fol. 134.

[126] Decision of Wuppertal Court, 14 Sept. 1933, BAP, R 8119 F, P7276, fol. 123–4.

[127] AKU supervisory board, 17 May 1933, BAP, R 8119 F, P7284, fol. 73ff.

[128] *Berliner Börsen Zeitung*, 13 Dec. 1934. AKU to L.J.A. Trip (President of Nederlandsche Bank), 6 Feb. 1935, BAP, R 8119 F, P7277.

[129] Oberst Löb to Stauss, 11 March 1937, BAP, R 8119 F, P7278, fol. 106; Stauss to Löb, 19 March 1937, BAP, R 8119 F, P7278, fol. 107–8.

[130] Delegates' Committee, where these arguments were repeated again, 17 March 1939, BAP, R 8119 F, P7278, fol. 374.

[131] Meeting with State Secretary Körner, 5 May 1939, BAP, R 8119 F, P7329, fol. 57ff.

[132] Kiehl to Philipp Reemtsma, 1939, BAP, R 8119 F, P7329, fol. 102–3.

[133] Halt to Himmler, 20 Jan. 1941, BAK, NS19/1043.

[134] Fritz Kranefuss to Himmler, 21 April 1943, BAK, NS19/2219, fol. 36–8.

[135] NSDAP membership number 4245867 (BDC).

[136] Speech to Reich Chamber of Labour, 24 Nov. 1936, BAP, R 8119 F, 24534, fol. 190 ff.

[137] Klaus Hildebrand, *Vom Reich zum Weltreich. Hitler, NSDAP und koloniale Frage 1919–1945* (Munich 1969), pp. 189–200.

[138] Weigelt note for Schlieper, 16 Jan. 1936, BAP, R 8119 F, 24526, fol. 277.

[139] Hans–Erich Volkmann, 'Die NS–Wirtschaft in Vorbereitung des Krieges', *Das Deutsche Reich und der Zweite Weltkrieg*, vol. I (Stuttgart 1979), p. 329.

[140] Federal Reserve System, Board of Governors, Preliminary Draft (September 1944), 'German Banking Penetration of Continental Europe', p. iv.

[141] Abs's note of 8 Oct. 1938, NA, OMGUS, FINAD 2/47/2; also Abs's statement of 10 Oct. 1945, NA, OMGUS, Exhibit 195. See also Kopper, 'Zwischen Marktwirtschaft und Dirigismus', pp. 345–8.

[142] Stauss to Fritz Krebs, 7 March 1939, BAP, R 8119 F, 24419.

[143] Volkmann, 'Die NS-Wirtschaft', p. 331.

[144] Pohle to Deutsche Bank, 22 May 1939, HADB, file: Böhmische Union-Bank.

[145] The Deutsche Bank to Reich Economics Ministry, 14 Nov. 1939, BAK, R2/13533, fol. 136.

[146] Statement of Hermann J. Abs, 10 Oct. 1945, NA, OMGUS, Exhibit 195.

[147] Memorandum of 30 March 1939, BAK, R2/13532, fol. 20.

[148] Deutsche Bank to Reich Finance Ministry, 13 Nov. 1939, BAK, R2/13533, fol. 119f.

[149] Memorandum from Kimmich, 28 June 1939, BAP, R 8119 F, P5351, fol. 147–8.

[150] Reich Finance Ministry note, BAK, R2/14087, fol. 342; Deutsche Bank to Reich

Economics Ministry, 14 Nov. 1939, R2/13533, fol. 141; Reich Finance Ministry memorandum of Jan. 1942, R2/13535, fol. 300–3; Deutsche Bank to Reich Finance Ministry, 3 May 1940, R2/13536, fol. 124–5.

[151] Reich Economics Ministry (Kehrl) to Reich Finance Ministry, 15 May 1940, BAK, R2/13536, fol. 136–7. Reich Finance Ministry memorandum, 28 April 1939, R2/13532, fol. 43–4.

[152] Reich Economics Ministry to Berlin Currency Office, 18 April 1940, BAK, R2/13536, fol. 96–7; Pohle to Benz, 25 Aug. 1939, R2/14894, fol. 6; memorandum from Benz, 31 Aug. 1939, R2/14894, fol. 8–9.

[153] Kiehl's note on conversation with Rasche and Rinn (Dresdner Bank), 18 Oct. 1937, BAP, R 8119 F, P1418, fol. 36–7.

[154] Kimmich's note of 28 July 1937, BAP, R 8119 F, P1416, fol. 11–13.

[155] Kimmich's note of 28 June 1939, BAP, R 8119 F, P1416, fol. 91–2; Reich Economics Ministry (Kehrl), BAK, R7/2268, fol. 7–9.

[156] Memorandum from Dr Müller, 12 June 1943, BAK, R2/17830.

[157] Jonathan Steinberg, *All or Nothing. The Axis and the Holocaust* (London 1990), p. 171.

[158] Kimmich to Pohle, 26 June 1940, BAP, R 8119 F, P1416, fol. 116.

[159] Deutsche Bank (Kiehl) to Böhmische Union-Bank, 23 June 1939, BAP, R 8119 F, P1417, fol. 84.

[160] Willi A. Boelcke, *Die deutsche Wirtschaft 1930–1945* (Düsseldorf 1983), p. 265. Hans Umbreit, 'Auf dem Weg zur Kontinentalherrschaft', *Das Deutsche Reich und der Zweite Weltkrieg*, vol. V/1 (Stuttgart 1988), pp. 213–15.

[161] Veltjens (Luftwaffe colonel), 'Report on Capital Penetration in Holland and Belgium Since the Occupation', 1941, BAK, R7/3158, fol. 4–5. Also NA, OMGUS, p. 169.

[162] Note of 1 April 1941, HADB, file: Holland.

[163] In general, BAP, R 8119 F, P6875; see also Böhmische Union-Bank to Rösler, 5 March 1942, BAP, R 8119 F, P6854, fol. 349.

[164] Pohle to Rösler, 16 Oct. 1940, BAP, R 8119 F, P6853.

[165] Lippmann, Rosenthal & Co. to Deutsche Bank, 20 April 1944, BAP, R 8119 F, P6876, fol. 321; Deutsche Bank to Böhmische Union-Bank, 9 Aug. 1944, BAP, R 8119 F, P6876, fol. 528.

[166] Pohle to Bechtolf, 11 June 1942, BAP, R 8119 F, P6931, fol. 28–30.

[167] Pohle to Rösler, 9 June 1942, BAP, R 8119 F, P6876, fol. 571–2.

[168] Note of 6 June 1942, BAP, R 8119 F, P6931, fol. 1–5.

[169] Beate Ruhm von Oppen (ed.), *Helmuth James von Moltke. Briefe an Freya 1939–1945* (Munich 1988), p. 369.

[170] Letter from Bechtolf to Berghütte supervisory board, 28 June 1943, BAP, R 8119 F, P6932, fol. 60–1. Rolf-Dieter Müller, 'Von der Wirtschaftsallianz zum kolonialen Ausbeutungskrieg', *Das Deutsche Reich und der Zweite Weltkrieg*, vol. IV (Stuttgart 1983), p. 140.

[171] Pott to Kiehl, 30 Oct. 1940, BAP, R 8119 F, P7236, fol. 33; Kiehl's note of 29 Jan. 1941, BAP, R 8119 F, P7236, fol. 43–8.

[172] Bechtolf to Pohle, 5 May 1943, BAP, R 8119 F, P6932; Rohde and Pohle to Bechtolf, 3 March 1943, BAP, R 8119 F, P6931, fol. 315–16.

[173] Deutsche Bank board of managing directors to Dresdner Bank, 19 Oct. 1944, BAP, R 8119 F, P1416, fol. 141.

[174] Rösler to Böhmische Union-Bank, 18 Aug. 1941, BAP, R 8119 F, P6854, fol. 204; Böhmische Union-Bank to Rösler, 30 Aug. 1943, BAP, R 8119 F, P6855, fol. 188–93.

[175] Memorandum, 14 March 1941, BAP, R 8119 F, P6854, fol. 35; Böhmische Union-Bank to Mannesmann Pipes Works, 13 June 1941, BAP, R 8119 F, P 6894, fol. 131.

[176] Rösler's note of 20 July 1943, BAP, R 8119 F, P6855, fol. 179.

[177] Accounts, 20 Nov. 1942, BAP, R 8119 F, P11013, fol. 4.

[178] Accounts, 28 Feb. 1945, BAP, R 8119 F, P11013, fol. 136.

[179] Memorandum from E.W. Schmidt, 5 Oct. 1940, BAP, R 8119 F, P10913, fol. 345.

[180] Reichsbank Bourse Committee, 25 Sept. 1941, BAP, R 8119 F, P5182.

[181] Kimmich's note of 24 July 1940, HADB, file: Holland.

[182] Kimmich's note of 29 Aug. 1940, HADB, file: Holland.

[183] Mojert 'Links of Dutch and German Economy', 15. Oct. 1941, HADB, file: Holland.

[184] Memorandum from Ulrich, 'On Foreign Business', 14 Aug. 1941, BAP, R 8119 F, 24151.

[185] Memorandum from Kimmich, 13 Aug. 1940, HADB, file: Belgium.

[186] See Etienne Verhoeyen, 'Les grands industriels belges entre collaboration et résistance. Le moindre mal', *Centre de Recherches et d'études historiques de la seconde guerre mondiale*, 10 (1986), pp. 57–114.

[187] Ibid, p. 67.

[188] Kurzmeyer, 'Notice on Events in Brussels 26–29 August 1940', 29 Aug. 1940, HADB, file: Belgium.

[189] Kimmich's notice of 17 Oct. 1940, HADB, file: Belgium; Schacht to Reich Economics Minister, 17 Oct. 1940, HADB, file: Belgium.

[190] Verhoeyen, 'Les grands industriels', p. 69; John Gillingham, 'The Baron de Launoit. A Case Study in the "Politics of Production" of Belgian Industry during Nazi Occupation', *Revue belge d'histoire contemporaine*, V (1974), pp. 1–59.

[191] Verhoeyen, 'Les grands industriels', p. 71.

[192] Pollems' note of 3 March 1941, HADB, file: Belgium.

[193] VIAG supervisory board meeting, 20 May 1942, BAP, R 8119 F, P5620, fol. 115–18. OMGUS, p. 189.

[194] Abs to Joham, 24 May 1939, BAP, R 8119 F, P6503, fol. 39.

[195] Hasslacher to Abs, 7 July 1939, BAP, R 8119 F, P6503, fol. 77–8; Abs to Hasslacher, 11 July 1939, BAP, R 8119 F, P6503, fol. 80–2.

[196] Abs's note, 10 June 1941, BAP, R 8119 F, 24158.

[197] Creditanstalt Working Committee, 3 Sept. 1940, BAP, R 8119 F, P6504, fol. 20–5; Joham to Abs, 27 Oct. 1941, BAP, R 8119 F, P6504, fol. 311; Creditanstalt to Reich Economics Ministry, 26 Sept. 1940, BAP, R 8119 F, P6504, fol. 59–60.

[198] Abs's note of 14 Nov. 1940, BAP, R 8119 F, P6504, fol. 110–11; Joham, 'Memorandum on Meeting with Abs and Rummel', 4 Dec. 1941, BAP R 8119 F, P6504, fol. 359.

[199] Memorandum from Ulrich to Abs, citing Abs's notice of 23 January 1942, 27 Aug. 1943, BAP, R 8119 F, P67, fol. 54–5.

[200] Memorandum from Joham, 29 Oct. 1940, BAP, R 8119 F, 24158.

[201] Memorandum, 'Meeting in Badgastein', 10 Aug. 1940, BAP, R 8119 F, 24158.

[202] Pilder to Abs, 5 June 1941, BAP, R 8119 F, 24158; Pilder to Abs, 22 July 1941, BAP, R 8119 F, 24158.

[203] 'Meeting in Badgastein', 10 Aug. 1940, BAP, R 8119 F, 24158.

[204] Memorandum from Weigelt, 3 May 1935, BAP, R 8119 F, P6968, fol. 268–9.

[205] Memorandum from Weigelt, 7 May 1935, BAP, R 8119 F, P6968, fol. 270–1; Supervisory Office for Petroleum to Deutsche Bank, 24 April 1936, BAP, R 8119 F, P6968, fol. 290.

[206] David E. Kaiser, *Economic Diplomacy and the Origins of the Second World War. Germany, Britain, France and Eastern Europe 1930–39* (Princeton 1980), p. 144; Andreas Hillgruber, *Hitler, König Carol und Marschal Antonescu. Die deutsch-rumänischen Beziehungen 1938–44* (Wiesbaden 1954), pp. 28–34.

[207] German–Romanian Society, 11 May 1939, BAP, R 8119 F, 24527, fol. 44.

[208] Memorandum from Schmidt: 'Banks in German–Romanian Economic Relations', 26 Jan. 1943, BAP, R 8119 F, P10880, fol. 419.

[209] Ilgner to Abs, 'Draft: Recommendations on an Intensification of German–Romanian Economic Relations', 17 Feb. 1942, BAP, R 8119 F, P6974, fol. 25ff.

[210] Memorandum from Ulrich, 'On Foreign Business', 14 Aug. 1941, BAP, R 8119 F, 24151. In general, P. Marguerat, *Le IIIe Reich et le pétrole roumaine. 1938–1940. Contribution à l'étude de la penetration économique allemande dans les Balkans à la veille et au début de la seconde Guerre Mondiale* (Geneva 1977).

[211] Minute by Sippell, 'Meeting with Director Schroeder', 11 Nov. 1941, BAP, R 8119 F, P8586, fol. 263–6; note of 22 Nov. 1942, BAP, R 8119 F, P8586, fol. 338–9; Sippell to Schroeder, 23 Nov. 1942, BAP, R 8119 F, P8586, fol. 340.

[212] 11 December 1942, BAP, R 8119 F, P8586, fol. 342.

[213] Walter Funk, 'Die Länder des Südostens und die Europäische Wirtschaftsgemeinschaft. Rede, gehalten vor der Südosteuropa–Gesellschaft in Wien am 10. März 1944', p. 15, BAK, R63/281.

[214] BAK, R11/271, fol. 84ff. For examples of how widely differing interpretations can be made of the same speech, see Dietrich Eichholtz, *Geschichte der deutschen Kriegswirtschaft 1939–1945*, vol. I (East Berlin 1971), pp. 176–8; and Ludolf Herbst, *Der Totale Krieg und die Ordnung der Wirtschaft* (Stuttgart 1982), pp. 142–4. East Germany printed this speech selectively in a collection: D. Eichholtz and W. Schumann (eds), *Neue Dokumente zur Rolle des deutschen Monopolkapitals bei der Vorbereitung und Durchführung des zweiten Weltkrieges* (East Berlin 1969), Document No. 173.

[215] Reichsbank Advisory Council Foreign Trade Sub-Committee, 19 Dec. 1939, BAP, R 8119 F, P349, fol. 126ff.

[216] Diary of Per Jacobsson, 45, entries of 14–15 May and 2 June 1943, University of Basle. The Dresdner Bank representative is called Görg in the diary: it is almost certain that this man was Carl Goetz, and that Jacobsson misheard or misremembered the

name. See also: Erin J. Jacobsson, *A Life for Sound Money. Per Jacobsson, His Biography* (Oxford 1979), pp. 178–9.

[217] Reichsbank Advisory Council, 24 June 1943, BAP, R 8119 F, P349, fol. 27.

[218] List of debtors, HADB, Filialbüro, file: Günkel.

[219] Memorandum from Bechtolf, 11 Feb 1942, BAP, R 8119 F, P4969, fol. 2–3; Bechtolf's note: 'Strictly Confidential', 20 Oct. 1941, BAP, R 8119 F, P4968. The acrimonious correspondence between Philip Reemtsma and Emil Helfferich, the chairman of the Hapag supervisory board, is reproduced in: Emil Helfferich, *Tatsachen 1932–1946. Ein Beitrag zur Wahrheitsfindung* (Oldenburg 1968), pp. 245–55.

[220] Memorandum from Kimmich, 1 Sept. 1941, BAP, R 8119 F, P1563.

[221] See Alan S. Milward, *The German Economy at War* (London 1965), pp. 59–85, and Herbst, *Der Totale Krieg*, pp. 171–241.

[222] To the dismay of BMW's management, which complained about 'conditions which … always give the Reich the occasion to intervene in the affairs of BMW': Hille to Rummel, 27 Feb. 1940, BAP, R 8119 F, P3076, fol. 430.

[223] 'BMW: Development of Credits' (n.d.), BAP, R 8119 F, P3167; Financial Report, 18 Nov. 1941, BAP, R 8119 F, P3078.

[224] Rummel's note of 12 Aug. 1942, BAP, R 8119 F, P3078, fol. 336.

[225] Junkers Flugzeug– und Motorenwerke AG Dessau, Credit Report, 7 Jan. 1941, BAP, R 8119 F, P3336.

[226] See the discussion of the Reichsbank Advisory Council Credit Sub-Committee, 28 Nov. 1939, BAP, R 8119 F, P350, in which the commercial banks complained about their disadvantaged position.

[227] Reich Supervisory Office for Credit, 3 June 1941, BAK, R2/13551, fol. 16. *Frankfurter Zeitung*, No. 463/4, 12 September 1941.

[228] *Deutsche Allgemeine Zeitung*, No. 384, 12 August 1942, Wirtschaftsblatt.

[229] 'Gehören die Banken in die Aufsichtsräte', *Völkischer Beobachter*, No. 9, 9 January 1943.

[230] Security Service Reports, 5 Aug. 1943, BAK, R58/187, fol. 106.

[231] Memorandum from E.W. Schmidt, 'News Reports for the Works Leader', 12 Jan. 1944, BAP, R 8119 F, P10882, fol. 630–1.

[232] Memorandum from Schmidt, 26 Oct. 1944, BAP, R 8119 F, P10883, fol. 121–2. The Supervisory Office had tried to argue for simplification, but ineffectively. In 1941 it had stated: 'Since the state reorganization of the credit apparatus, in other words since 1935, credit has been extended more widely, and in part the administrative machinery has also been simplified; but fundamentally the organization of credit still depends on the economic ideas of a past age' (memorandum of 3 June 1941, BAK, R2/13551).

[233] Jens van Scherpenberg, *Öffentliche Finanzwirtschaft in Westdeutschland 1944–1948* (Munich 1984), pp. 51ff.

[234] Meeting of 19 Feb. 1942, BAK, R2/13686, fol. 241–2.

[235] Reich Finance Ministry note of Dec. 1942, BAK, R2/13530, fol. 269–70.

[236] Note (meeting in Reich Supervisory Office for Credit), 12 June 1942, BAK, R2/13551, fol. 62; 'Meeting with Press', 15 Oct. 1942, BAP, R 8119 F, P10879, fol. 280–2.

[237] Circular of Reich Economics Ministry for Reich Defence Commissars, 16 Feb. 1943, BAK, R2/13551, fol. 210–11.

[238] Deutsche Bank special circulars, S31/43, 17 Nov. 1943, HADB.

[239] Wilhelm Zangen, 'Industry and Banks', Dec. 1942, BAP, R 8119 F, P10879, fol. 67–77.

[240] Memorandum from Schmidt, 10 Jan. 1944, BAP, R 8119 F, P10882, fol. 640.

[241] Working Committee minutes, 11 March 1943, BAP, R 8119 F, P31, fol. 8.

[242] Rösler's declaration under oath, 20 March 1950, HADB, RWB, 31.

[243] NSDAP membership number 6927011 (BDC).

[244] Deutsche Bank to Gau Economic Chamber, Berlin, 15 Feb. 1945, HADB, personnel file: Frowein.

[245] 'Berlin: Meeting with Reich Minister Walter Funk', 18 Feb. 1943, BAK, R43II/245 b, fol. 1.

[246] NSDAP membership number 91273 (BDC).

[247] Heinrich Hunke, 'Verstaatlichung der Grossbanken', *Die Deutsche Volkswirtschaft*, 3 (1934), 1, pp. 3–6.

[248] NA, OMGUS, Deutsche Bank, p. 61; and information collected by Carl-Ludwig Holtfrerich.

[249] Working Committee, 16 Sept. 1943, BAP, R 8119 F, P31, fol. 27–32.

[250] Memorandum from Dr Hanel, 6 Oct. 1943, BAK, R63/198, fol. 12.

[251] This list is contained in the HADB, Filialbüro, file: Günkel: it is undated, but must be from 1944 or later. It may even have been prepared as part of a deNazification exercise, although I have not seen a copy of this document in the extensive material collected by OMGUS.

[252] Rösler to Frowein, 14 Feb. 1944, HADB, personnel file: Frowein.

[253] Hunke, 'Zehn Thesen zur Wirtschaftspolitik', published in *Der neue Tag*, No. 257, 17 September 1943.

[254] In general BAP, R 8119 F, P4653; P4654, memorandum, 27 March 1941, fol. 28–30.

[255] Rath (Deutsche Bank, Cologne) to Kurt von Schroeder, 19 Sept. 1942, BAP, R 8119 F, 24133; Abs's note of 24 Sept. 1942, BAP, R 8119 F, 24133.

[256] Supervisory board meeting, 21 Dec. 1933, BAP, R 8119 F, P3073, fol. 304–7.

[257] Note of 5 Feb. 1934, BAP, R 8119 F, P3073, fol. 343.

[258] Stauss to Rummel, 11 June 1936, BAP, R 8119 F, P3075, fol. 25.

[259] 'Secret: Bayerische Motoren Werke', 7 May 1942, BAP, R 8119 F, P3146, fol. 462.

[260] Popp to Stauss, 11 Nov. 1936, BAP, R 8119 F, P3075, fol. 90–1.

[261] Siemens & Halske to Reich Air Ministry, 31 March 1936, BAP, R 8119 F, P3167, fol. 10.

[262] 'The BMW Concern: Organizational Questions', 12 April 1940, BAP, R 8119 F, P3076, fol. 465.

[263] Popp to Lucht (Reich Air Ministry), 8 Feb. 1941, BAP, R 8119 F, P3146, fol. 252.

[264] Memorandum for Stauss and Rummel, 17 May 1939, BAP, R 8119 F, P3167, fol. 107–8.

[265] Meeting of managing board, 11 Nov. 1941, BAP, R 8119 F, P3078, fol. 96ff.

[266] Popp to Admiral Lahs, 19 April 1940, BAP, R 8119 F, P3136, fol. 302: 'In the end, in the case of a long war the new production capacity will determine the size of the air fleet.'

[267] Göring to Popp, 25 Nov. 1940, BAP, R 8119 F, P3077, fol. 199.

[268] Popp to Lucht, 6 Feb. 1941, BAP, R 8119 F, P3146, fol. 235.

[269] Popp to Stauss, 22 March 1941, BAP, R 8119 F, P3146, fol. 349.

[270] Reich Air Ministry (LC3), 14 Feb. 1941, BAP, R 8119 F, P3146, fol. 285.

[271] For example, Stauss to Frau Eva von Schröder, National Socialist Welfare Office (NSV) Berlin, 11 Oct. 1938, BAP, R 8119 F, P6132, fol. 128: 'In particular, I was very pleased that the automobile and parts industry in the end exceeded 2.5 million marks, after I convinced BMW to go up by 50,000 marks, even though Opel had failed to pay.'

[272] Rummel's note of 12 August 1942, BAP, R 8119 F, P3078, fol. 336.

[273] Hille to Rummel, 20 Sept. 1944, BAP, R 8119 F, P3114, fol. 191.

[274] Rummel's note (Hille's letter of 9 December is appended), 12 Dec. 1944, BAP, R 8119 F, P3114, fol. 248–51.

[275] Memorandum from Rummel, 15 Dec. 1944, BAP, R 8119 F, P3114, fol. 254–5.

[276] Deutsche Bank to Rummel, 20 Dec. 1944, BAP, R 8119 F, P3114, fol. 266–7.

[277] BMW AG to BMW Flugmotorenwerke Brandenburg, 2 Feb. 1945, BAP, R 8119 F, P3114, fol. 319.

[278] Working Committee meeting, 4 Nov. 1943, BAP, R 8119 F, P31, fol. 38.

[279] People's Court judgment, 8 Oct. 1943, BAK, R60I/548; People's Court judgment, 14 Sept. 1943, R60I/369.

[280] Finance Group, Misc. Reports and Publications: 'Preliminary Study of the Deutsche Bank, prepared by Program Planning Section, Treasury Department, Foreign Funds Control', NA, RG260, Box 71, Folder 3.

[281] Note of 27 June 1940, BAP, R 8119 F, 24130.

[282] Giles MacDonogh, *A Good German. Adam von Trott zu Solz* (London 1989), p. 164.

[283] Ruhm von Oppen (ed.), *Helmuth James von Moltke*, pp. 261, 265, 481.

[284] Note of 15 Oct. 1943, BAP, R 8119 F, P68, fol. 7–8.

[285] Hans-Adolf Jacobsen, '*Spiegelbild einer Verschwörung*'. *Die Opposition gegen Hitler und der Staatsstreich vom 20. Juli 1944 in der SD–Berichterstattung*, vol. I (Stuttgart 1984), p. 60.

[286] Telegram from Dr Lorenzen to Bormann, 14 Nov. 1944, BAK, NS6/19, fol. 68–70.

[287] Personnel records, HADB; Working Committee meeting, 15 April 1942, BAP, R 8119 F, P41, fol. 161.

[288] Fritz Scholtz (Deutsche Bank, Cottbus) to Karl Günkel, Berlin, 9 Feb. 1944, BAP, R 8119 F, P10972.

[289] Working Committee, 8 July 1943, BAP, R 8119 F, P31, fol. 22–3.

[290] Meeting of directors, 5 Nov. 1942, HADB, Deutsche Bank 1941–44.

[291] Working Committee, 16 Sept. 1943, BAP, R 8119 F, P31, fol. 29.

[292] Schmidt to Rosentreter, 26 Feb. 1944, BAP, R 8119 F, P10882, fol. 459; BAP, R 8119 F, P10883; circular of Deutsche Bank (to branch managers), 29 Nov. 1943, P11127, fol. 1–2.

²⁹³ Rummel 'The German Banking Business in 1943', 20 Jan. 1944, BAP, R 8119 F, P10882, fol. 602.

²⁹⁴ Discussion of Reich Group Banking, 31 July 1944, BAP, R 8119 F, P10952.

²⁹⁵ To branch managers, 27 March 1945, BAP, P10914, fol. 53.

²⁹⁶ Minutes of great bank meetings, 22 Sept. 1944, HADB, RWB, 441.

²⁹⁷ Rösler to Wuppermann, 27 March 1945, HADB, RWB, 50.

²⁹⁸ Board of managing directors to Gau Economic Chamber, Hamburg, 28 March 1945, HADB, RWB, 50.

²⁹⁹ Deutsche Bank to branch managers, 25 March 1945, BAP, R 8119 F, P10914, fol. 43–4; Deutsche Bank to branch managers, 27 March 1945, fol. 52.

³⁰⁰ This paragraph is based primarily on the contemporary diary notes of Rosenbrock, April/September 1945, HADB.

³⁰¹ Statement of Hermann J. Abs, 22 April 1950, NA, RG 319–X8001750.

The Deutsche Bank 1945–1957:
War, Military Rule and Reconstruction

¹ Interrogation protocol of Heinrich Hunke, IfZ, OMGUS FINAD 2/234/7.

² Report Liermann dated 10 October 1945 and addressed to Abs, HADB, personnel file: Sippell.

³ Hermann Hess, *Ritter von Halt. Der Sportler und Soldat* (Berlin 1936), pp. 129, 183.

⁴ Ibid., p. 126.

⁵ NA, RG 260 (OMGUS), Finance Group, BICO. Miscellaneous Reports and Publications, Box 72, Folder No. 1: Exhibit 27 to Report on the Deutsche Bank.

⁶ 'Beschluss des Präsidiums des Aufsichtsrates der Deutschen Bank in seiner Eigenschaft als Personalausschuss', 5 September 1938, HADB, RWB, 432. Oswald Rösler also describes von Halt's role in the bank in a positive light in his affidavit of 20 March 1950, for the denazification trial of von Halt, located in HADB, RWB, 31.

⁷ On 12 April 1945, he attended a board meeting, but a day later he was excused from the same such meeting due to the *Volkssturm*, as it was noted. HADB, RWB, 434.

⁸ Letter from von Halt to Oesterlink, 23 August 1950, HADB, Aufsichtsrat der Deutschen Bank, vol. III.

⁹ As to Hunke's education as a primary school teacher, his doctoral studies, and his occupation before 1933, see Chapter 3 in this volume. See also: Willi A. Boelcke (ed.), *Kriegspropaganda 1939–1941* (Stuttgart 1966), p. 74. Personal data on H. Hunke, IfZ, OMGUS FINAD 2/232/1.

¹⁰ Ludolf Herbst, *Der totale Krieg und die Ordnung der Wirtschaft. Die Kriegswirtschaft im Spannungsfeld von Politik, Ideologie und Propaganda 1939–1945* (Stuttgart 1982), p. 248, note 331.

[11] Herbst, *Der totale Krieg*, pp. 248–51. The German version of the Monroe Doctrine had originally been presented by the constitutional law professor Carl Schmitt, *Völkerrechtliche Grossraumordnung mit Interventionsverbot für raumfremde Mächte. Ein Beitrag zum Reichsbegriff im Völkerrecht* (Berlin/Vienna 1939).

[12] OMGUS, *Ermittlungen gegen die Deutsche Bank 1946/47* (Nördlingen 1985), p. 61.

[13] See his NSDAP file at the Berlin Document Center.

[14] OMGUS, *Ermittlungen gegen die Deutsche Bank*, p. 60. OMGUS, *Ermittlungen gegen die Dresdner Bank, 1946* (Nördlingen 1986), p. LXI–LXIII. Christopher Kopper, 'Zwischen Marktwirtschaft und Dirigismus: Staat, Banken und Bankenpolitik im "Dritten Reich" vom 1933 bis 1939', Ph.D. thesis (Bochum 1992), pp. 381–5.

[15] Aufstellung Kaiser, 1 February 1946, HADB, Abgegebene Aufstellungen an die amerikanische Militärregierung (Tätigkeit der Deutsche Bank im 'Dritten Reich'). The list shows that party membership was nearly twice as great among employees at the bank's branches as among those at the Berlin head office; among the top managers of the branches the rate was 60 per cent, the highest rating for any group of employees.

[16] Memo by von Halt on the 'Unterredung im Fürstenhof am 17. November 1942, 1 bis 3 Uhr' as well as more precise information on the individuals attending: 'Eidesstattliche Erklärung' of Oswald Rösler, 20 March 1950, for the denazification trial of Ritter von Halt, HADB, RWB, 31.

[17] 'Eidesstattliche Erklärung' of Oswald Rösler, 20 March 1950, HADB, RWB, 31. For information on Bormann's own opposition to this plan, see Chapter 3 and OMGUS, *Ermittlungen gegen die Dresdner Bank*, p. LXII.

[18] For more on these events, see: IfZ, OMGUS FINAD 2/234/11 and 2/234/7. The meeting of Abs, Rösler and Hunke in the sleeping car on the way to Vienna is also found in HADB, RWB, 31, letter from Hunke during his imprisonment in Nuremberg to Wintermantel, 2 February 1947. On Hunke's moderate economic *Weltanschauung* during the final years of the war, see also: Herbst, *Der totale Krieg*, pp. 249–50.

[19] OMGUS, *Ermittlungen gegen die Deutsche Bank*, pp. 60–1, and HADB, personnel file: Frowein.

[20] For more on the entire issue of Hunke's appointment, see: IfZ, OMGUS FINAD 2/234/1.

[21] Letter from Deputy Minister Gutterer at the Reich Propaganda Ministry to Hunke, 16 November 1943, HADB, personnel file: Hunke.

[22] HADB, personnel file: Hunke.

[23] OMGUS, *Ermittlungen gegen die Dresdner Bank*, pp. LIX–LX, LXIII–LXV.

[24] NA, RG 260 (OMGUS), Finance Group, BICO. Miscellaneous Reports and Publications, Box 72, Folder No. 1: Exhibit 28 to Report on Deutsche Bank.

[25] OMGUS, *Ermittlungen gegen die Deutsche Bank*, p. 61.

[26] Document no. 2, 20 June 1945, p. 1, HADB, Filiale Litzmannstadt/Lodz, Führungsstab/Vorstand Hamburg.

[27] Investigation report dated 20 August 1945, IfZ, OMGUS FINAD 2/232/1.

[28] More on this and the blocking of assets that automatically followed such a dismissal (Law No. 52) in section I.3.

[29] Report by Dr Günter Keiser on 'Die Lage der Banken im anglo-amerikanischem Raum nach dem Stande von Mitte Juli 1945', p. 11, HADB, RWB, 51.

[30] IfZ, OMGUS FINAD 2/234/1.

[31] 'Aufsichtsratsmandate des Vorstandes der Deutschen Bank', HADB, RWB, 31.

[32] HADB, personnel file: Hunke.

[33] HADB, RWB, 31.

[34] HADB, Aufsichtsrat der Deutschen Bank, vol. III.

[35] HADB, personnel file: Hunke. His former colleagues on the board decided, on 14 October 1951, on the compensation payment that Hunke was to receive. See protocol for the respective bank board meeting, HADB, RWB, 434.

[36] Herbst, *Der totale Krieg*, p. 248. Boelcke, *Kriegspropaganda*, p. 75.

[37] HADB, personnel file: Wintermantel.

[38] 'Aufenthaltsgenehmigung Polizeipräsidium Leipzig' and file: Führungsstab Vorstand Hamburg, with a list of 34 auxiliary offices, HADB, Filiale Litzmannstadt/Lodz.

[39] Letter from directing office, Hamburg, to the Creditanstalt-Bankverein in Vienna, dated 15 October 1947, HADB, RWB, 7.

[40] HADB, RWB, 441. This file also contains the circular from the head office with instructions for the branches, should they have to be evacuated.

[41] Deutsche Bank special circular 25/1943, 16 September 1943, HADB, Sonderrundschreiben 1940–1945.

[42] Notarial act bestowing general power of attorney to J.B. Rath, 26 October 1943, HADB, file: Direktoren bis 1945.

[43] Deutsche Bank press release, 18 September 1943, over an article in the *Deutsche Allgemeine Zeitung*, HADB, Presse 1940–1945.

[44] NA, RG 260 (OMGUS), Finance Group, BICO. Miscellaneous Reports and Publications, Box 72, Folder No. 1: Exhibit 28 to Report on Deutsche Bank. See also Exhibit 37 and Kopper, 'Bankenpolitik im Dritten Reich', p. 382. For more on the Nazi Party's efforts to regionalize the banking system, see Chapter 3.

[45] Ibid., Exhibit 28.

[46] 'Bericht über Erläuterungen zum Jahresabschluss 31.12.1944 und über die Lage der Deutschen Bank bei Kriegsende', BAP, R 8119 F, 24555, f. 696. That 12 top managers were charged with the responsibility for the future of the Deutsche Bank just prior to the end of the war was also mentioned by Abs to the author Andrew Shonfield, *Modern Capitalism. The Changing Balance of Public and Private Power* (London 1967), p. 242. Wuppermann retired at the age of 65 just as the war ended. Apparently Simon had already died because his wife in Munich was the one who suffered from the consequences of confusion in pension regulations in the spring of 1946; see letter from Else Liermann in Garmisch-Partenkirchen to Wintermantel in Hamburg, dated 5 April 1946, file 1946 A–L, Papers of F. Wintermantel, private property of the Gröning family, Essen. The case of Kurt Weigelt (b. 4 June 1884) is also noteworthy. He co-managed Abs's foreign business department. Under the guise of a business trip to Hungary and without Abs's knowledge and consent, he fled Berlin on 11 March 1945, allegedly after a friend in a ministry had warned him of the Gestapo. He

returned from Hungary in early April to his private estate Huberhof in Hochberg bei Traunstein (Bavaria). From there he telephoned Abs, who insisted that he return to Berlin. According to Weigelt's account, there was no longer a way to reach Berlin. Consequently, Abs convinced the board of managing directors on 12 April 1945 to impose forced retirement on Weigelt. In the chaos of the end of the war, the letter informing Weigelt of this decision was never delivered to him. In July 1946 he was arrested and spent a full year in American custody. Once his denazification process had been successfully completed, he succeeded in having the directing office in Hamburg repeal the board's decision on his forced retirement. Starting on 1 July 1948, he received temporary financial support, later a regular pension. On 6 January 1953, he became chairman of the supervisory board of the AG für Luftverkehrsbedarf, Cologne. He died in 1968. HADB, personnel file: Weigelt.

[47] Memo by Hermann Kaiser, 4 May 1946, HADB, Abgegebene Aufstellungen an die amerikanische Militärregierung (Tätigkeit der Deutsche Bank im 'Dritten Reich'); also quoted in Theo Horstmann, *Die Alliierten und die deutschen Grossbanken. Bankenpolitik nach dem Zweiten Weltkrieg in Westdeutschland* (Bonn 1991), p. 43.

[48] As decided by the European Advisory Commission of the three major Allied powers with regard to the Soviet zone on 12 September 1944, and with regard to the English and American zones in a supplementary protocol on 14 November 1944. Not until the Yalta Conference in the first half of February 1945 were these plans for the partition of Germany definitely accepted by all three Allied governments.

[49] NA, RG 260 (OMGUS), Finance Group, BICO. Miscellaneous Reports and Publications, Box 73, Folder No. 1: Exhibit Nos. 183–295 to Report on Deutsche Bank. Exhibit 285: memo from Schmidt, Frankfurt a.M. branch, 12 April 1946. Also in the HADB, RWB, 4. For more on the early evacuation to Wiesbaden, see: speech manuscript by Wintermantel for a meeting of the Deutsche Bank supervisory board on 14 October 1948, in Wuppertal, HADB, RWB, 409.

[50] Circular no. 1 from Erfurt, HADB, Filiale Litzmannstadt/Lodz, Verbindungsstelle Vorstand Erfurt.

[51] Letter from the Wiesbaden branch to the management of the Saarbrücken branch, 27 May 1945, HADB, Deutsche Bank 1945.

[52] Tom Bower, *The Pledge Betrayed. America and Britain and the Denazification of Postwar Germany* (Garden City, NY 1982), p. 104.

[53] Memo from Ermisch to Director Ulbricht, 26 August 1950, HADB, Fortführung der alten Bank.

[54] Letter to Reichsbankdirektorium, 10 February 1945, BAP, R 8119 F, 23989. Industrial firms which also had their home offices in Berlin and plants throughout Germany, such as Siemens, decided in late January and early February 1945 'to establish independent management groups in southern and western Germany'. Klaus-Dietmar Henke, *Die amerikanische Besetzung Deutschlands* (Munich 1995) p. 455.

[55] Statement by Abs to British officiers in May 1945, as quoted in Horstmann, *Die Alliierten*, p. 45.

[56] Memo by Deutsche Bank Director Erhard Ulbricht, 31 October 1947, p. 6, HADB, RWB, 7.

[57] Memo from Ermisch to 'Herrn Direktor Ulbricht zur Verwertung', 26 August 1950, HADB, Fortführung der alten Bank.

[58] Memo by Rösler, 2 March 1945, HADB, RWB, 50.

[59] Letter from Frowein to Rösler, 3 March 1945, HADB, RWB, 50.

[60] HADB, RWB, 50.

[61] Pocket calendar of Plassmann 1945, HADB, Fortführung der alten Bank; see also Horstmann, *Die Alliierten*, p. 46.

[62] Letter from Plassmann in Erfurt to Rösler in Berlin, 29 March 1945, HADB, RWB, 50.

[63] Letter from Plassmann in Erfurt to the Deutsche Bank board in Berlin, 9 April 1945, HADB, Fortführung der alten Bank; also in HADB, Deutsche Bank 1945.

[64] All letters located in HADB, RWB, 50.

[65] Circular no. 1 from Erfurt, 22 May 1945, HADB, Filiale Litzmannstadt/Lodz, Verbindungsstelle Vorstand Erfurt.

[66] Minutes of meeting with Reichsbank President and Reich Minister Funk on 16 March 1945, HADB, RWB, 50.

[67] Meeting with Ministerialdirektor Riehle on 20 March 1945, in the Reich Economics Ministry, HADB, RWB, 50.

[68] HADB, RWB, 50.

[69] Ibid.

[70] Letter from Bechtolf in Hamburg to Rösler in Berlin, 5 April 1945, HADB, RWB, 50.

[71] Manfred Pohl (ed.), *Hermann J. Abs. A Biography in Text and Pictures* (Mainz 1983), p. 51.

[72] HADB, transcript of an interview of Abs with Manfred Pohl in December 1992.

[73] Namely the Wirtschaftsgruppe Privates Bankgewerbe. See HADB, report by Rosenbrock, p. 25. This was the successor organization to the traditional Centralverband des Deutschen Bank- und Bankiergewerbes.

[74] Circular letter from the directing office in Hamburg to the branches, 25 May 1945, and a letter from Dr Günter Keiser to Dr Erich Trost, managing director of the Wirtschaftsgruppe Privates Bankgewerbe, Berlin, 19 July 1945, HADB, RWB, 51. Although this correspondence ended with the notation 'sgd: Dr Günther Kaiser', it has to be concluded from the circumstances that the man in question was actually Dr Günter Keiser. During the war, Keiser was head of the Statistical Department of the *Wirtschaftsgruppe* of Private Banking Business. After the war, he reappeared as a member of the Special Committee on Money and Credit, as head of the Department for Economic Planning in the Bizonal Economic Administration and as head of the department handling principle policy issues in the Federal Ministry of Economics.

[75] Statement of Hermann J. Abs, 22 April 1950, NA, RG 319, X800 1750. I owe the use of this file to Harold James.

[76] Pocket calendar of Plassmann 1945, HADB, Fortführung der alten Bank. On 4 June 1945, the Soviets put an end to the rumours and speculations concerning the final

borders of the occupation zones by making the formerly secret Allied agreement over Germany's partition public.

77 Document no. 2, 20 June 1945, p. 1, HADB, Filiale Litzmannnstadt/Lodz, Führungsstab/Vorstand Hamburg; pocket calendar of Plassmann 1945, HADB, Fortführung der alten Bank.

78 Circular no. 7, 9 June 1945, HADB, Filiale Litzmannstadt/Lodz, Verbindungsstelle Vorstand Erfurt. For more on the ordinances of the British and American military governments, including the blocking of personal assets which automatically followed suspension (Law. No. 52), see section I.3.

79 Pohl, *Abs*, p. 52.

80 Document no. 2, 20 June 1945, pp. 1–2, HADB, Filiale Litzmannstadt/Lodz, Führungsstab/Vorstand Hamburg; also in Führungsstab Hamburg 1945–1948, Rundschreiben.

81 HADB, Filiale Litzmannstadt/Lodz, Führungsstab/Vorstand Hamburg.

82 Letter from Dr Günter Keiser to Dr Erich Trost, 19 July 1945, HADB, RWB, 51. As to the misspelling of Keiser's name see note 74.

83 Protocol of the Hamburg meetings from 10/11 December 1946, HADB, RWB, 440.

84 Correspondence between Wintermantel and von Schenk in August and September 1948, in the papers of F. Wintermantel, private property of the Gröning family, Essen.

85 For more on the changes after April 1946, see the papers of F. Wintermantel.

86 For the make-up of the directing office in April 1946, see NA, RG 260 (OMGUS), Finance Group, BICO. Miscellaneous Reports and Publications, Box 73, Folder No. 1: Exhibit Nos. 183–295 to Report on Deutsche Bank. Exhibit No. 285: memo by Schmidt, Filiale Frankfurt a.M., 12 April 1946.

87 Speech manuscript by Wintermantel for a meeting of the supervisory board on 14 October 1948, HADB, RWB, 409.

88 HADB, Führungsstab Hamburg 1945–1948, Rundschreiben.

89 The banks were informed in early March 1946 through either the *Land* finance ministries or the Reichsbank head offices that the military governments in the three Western zones prohibited sending directions concerning bank policy to branches outside of each respective zone. This and the many consequences it had on the organization are examined in greater detail in section II.2.

90 Horstmann, *Die Alliierten*, p. 71, note 88.

91 Both quotations from: Bower, *Pledge Betrayed*, pp. 8, 12.

92 Horstmann, *Die Alliierten*, p.72. The British authorities thereafter imposed a travel ban on the three interrogated bankers as well as on Bechtolf and Plassmann, which meant they were not allowed to leave Hamburg. See letter from Walter Schmidt, Wiesbaden, to Rummel, 22 October 1945, and letter from Abs, Bechtolf and Plassmann in Hamburg to Wintermantel in Berlin, 5 October 1945, HADB, RWB, 442.

93 Memorandum, 5 October 1945, 'Vetting of German Bankers', BEA, OV 34/11.

94 Statement of Hermann J. Abs, 22 April 1950, NA, RG 319, X800 1750.

95 Horstmann, *Die Alliierten*, pp. 72, 74.

96 Department of State, Division of Biographic Information. Report on Hermann J. Abs,

February 1950, NA, RG 319, X800 1750. The accusations levelled against Abs were based on the events connected with 'Aryanization', especially in occupied Czechoslovakia. Abs was later exonerated from these charges due to testimony on his behalf by involved Jewish citizens. See Chapter 3.

[97] The complete text of the law is printed in *Die Berliner Konferenz der Drei Mächte/Der Alliierte Kontrollrat für Deutschland/Die Alliierte Kommandantur der Stadt Berlin*, Sammelheft 1, 1945 (Berlin 1946), pp. 71–6.

[98] The supervisory board positions held by Abs and other members of the board of the Deutsche Bank are listed in HADB, RWB, 31.

[99] Bower, *Pledge Betrayed*, p. 13. Also for the previous quotation.

[100] For more on this complicated topic, see HADB, Urteile und Anlagen im Czichon-Prozess.

[101] Henke, *Besetzung Deutschlands*, pp. 531, 565.

[102] Statement of Hermann J. Abs, 22 April 1950, NA, RG 319, X800 1750.

[103] Pohl, *Abs*, p. 52.

[104] HADB, RWB, 432. Also: pocket calendar of Plassmann 1946, HADB, Fortführung der alten Bank.

[105] Letter from Plassmann to Oesterlink, 28 January 1948, HADB, Aufsichtsrat der Deutschen Bank, vol. III.

[106] Manuscript of Wintermantel's speech at the supervisory board meeting on 14 October 1948, in Wuppertal, HADB, RWB, 409.

[107] Report by Günkel, p. 14, HADB, Fortführung der alten Bank. See also Papers of F. Wintermantel, private property of the Gröning family, Essen.

[108] Letter from Wintermantel in Hamburg to Amanda Boehnert, Berlin, his former housekeeper, 8 June 1946, in the papers of F. Wintermantel.

[109] Pocket calendar of Plassmann 1946, HADB, Fortführung der alten Bank.

[110] Ernst Wilhelm Schmidt, *Männer der Deutschen Bank und der Disconto-Gesellschaft* (Düsseldorf 1957), p. 10.

[111] Horstmann, *Die Alliierten*, p. 76.

[112] Papers of F. Wintermantel.

[113] Ibid.

[114] Letter from Wintermantel, Hamburg, to Alfred Kurzmeyer, Zurich, 29 March 1947, in the papers of F. Wintermantel, 1947, K–Z.

[115] Statement of Hermann J. Abs, 22 April 1950, NA, RG 319, X800 1750.

[116] Letter from the Zentralstelle für Berufungsausschüsse, Hamburg, to Plassmann, 8 December 1947, HADB, Aufsichtsrat der Deutschen Bank, vol. III; also in HADB, file: Plassmann.

[117] HADB, file: Führungsstab Hamburg 1945–1948 Rundschreiben. Also in Anlage zum Protokoll der Vorstandssitzung, 19 January 1948, HADB, RWB, 434.

[118] Department of State. Division of Biographic Information. Report on the investigation of Abs, February 1950, NA, RG 319, X800 1750.

[119] Minutes of a secret meeting in Hamburg on 11–12 March 1948, HADB, RWB, 434. The same stipulation was applied to Rummel.

120 What was at issue was the value of stock of the Rheinische AG für Braunkohlenbergbau und Brikettfabrikation, a lignite mining and briquette manufacturer on whose supervisory board Abs had sat as a representative of the Deutsche Bank, and claims against the Vereinigte Glanzstoff-Fabriken AG (VGF) with regard to Algemeene Kunstzijde Unie (AKU), Arnhem, on whose supervisory board Abs had served as vice-chairman and chairman. References to this are in the papers of F. Wintermantel, correspondence between Wintermantel and Dr Ernst Helmut Vits, chairman of the board of VGF, 3 August and 3 September 1949. Minutes of the meeting of branch managers on 29 August 1946, p. 4, HADB, RWB, 440. Konrad Adenauer, *Briefe 1945–1947* (Berlin 1983), pp. 121, 390. On the AKU issue in general, see IfZ, OMGUS FINAD, 2/188/2, Final Report [of the Decartellization Branch] on the Investigation of the Allgemeene Kunstzijde Unie N.V., Arnhem, Holland, and Vereinigte Glanzstoff-Fabriken AG, Wuppertal-Elberfeld, Germany, 1 August 1946. These reports confirm that Abs conducted the takeover of AKU stock for the Deutsche Bank in an orderly business-like fashion following the occupation of Holland in 1940.

121 Hans-Peter Schwarz, *Adenauer. Der Aufstieg: 1876–1952* (Stuttgart 1986), pp. 652, 666, 702–3, 724, 909. For the role that Abs played in the London negotiations on Germany's foreign debt, see: Hans-Peter Schwarz, *Die Wiederherstellung des deutschen Kredits. Das Londoner Schuldenabkommen* (Stuttgart/Zurich 1982), and Hermann J. Abs, *Entscheidungen 1949–1953. Die Entstehung des Londoner Schuldenabkommens* (Mainz/Munich 1991).

122 HADB, personnel file: Rummel.

123 'Betriebswirt der Banken. Hans Rummel 70 Jahre alt', *Der Tagesspiegel*, 8 March 1952; two essays by Rummel were included in the published papers of the 1933 official bank inquiry.

124 HADB, personnel file: Rummel.

125 On the day of Rummel's arrest, Col. H.G. Sheen, SHAEF Headquarters, G–2, sent a notice, dated 20 June 1945, to all army units stating that an arrest list of leading individuals from German industry and banking would soon be issued. Although the men whose names were on the list had not been active 'Nazis', they were dangerous and, he claimed, had to be arrested because they had held positions of responsibility and thus stabilized the system. The list was distributed exactly one week later. The names of 24 men from the Deutsche Bank were on it, including eight members of the board of managing directors (only the names of Rösler and Hunke(!) were missing), 9 of the original 14 executive vice-presidents, and from the supervisory board, Karl Kimmich as well as Ernst Enno Russell. NA, RG 260 (OMGUS), FINAD. Records Relating to Financial Institution Policy 1945–1949, Box 132, Folder: Arrests.

126 OMGUS, *Ermittlungen gegen die Deutsche Bank*, pp. 334–5.

127 Bank-Untersuchungen in Frankfurt a.M., 31 January 1946, HADB, RWB, 4.

128 HADB, personnel file: Rummel; HADB, RWB, 442.

129 Letter from Wintermantel, Hamburg, to G. Tinnemann, Bremerhaven, 3 May 1947, with an order of herring for Rummel, in the papers of F. Wintermantel.

130 Letter from Heinrich Klöckers, Südwestbank, to Dr Joachim Kessler, directing office,

Hamburg, 14 October 1947, HADB, RWB, 7. With this law for 'the liberation from National Socialism and militarism', 5 March 1946, the US military government had transferred the responsibility for the denazification trials to special German courts (*Spruchkammern*).

[131] HADB, personnel file: Rummel.

[132] Manuscript of speech given by Wintermantel at the meeting of the Deutsche Bank supervisory board on 14 October 1948, in Wuppertal, HADB, RWB, 409.

[133] Report probably by Dr Günter Keiser in an English translation, 17 July 1945, 'The Fate of the Berlin Banks up to 22 June 1945', in BEA, OV 34/10.

[134] HADB, Rosenbrock report, p. 50.

[135] 'Eidesstattliche Erklärung' of Oswald Rösler on 20 March 1950; for the denazification trial of Ritter von Halt, p. 1, HADB, RWB, 31.

[136] HADB, personnel file: Rösler.

[137] Ibid.

[138] Manuscript of speech given by Wintermantel at the supervisory board meeting on 14 October 1948, HADB, RWB, 409.

[139] See the job reference written for his chauffeur in Hamburg, F. Ratzko, 17 September 1948, in the papers of F. Wintermantel, file: house personnel.

[140] HADB, personnel file: Wintermantel. For more on the role of the custodians, see section III.2.

[141] Letter from Frowein to Wintermantel, 28 December 1948, HADB, RWB, 442; HADB, Rosenbrock report, pp. 11, 53.

[142] Unpublished manuscript of Wilhelm Treue and Manfred Pohl, 'Biographien der Vorstandsmitglieder und Aufsichtsratsvorsitzenden der Deutschen Bank von 1870–1945', part 2, HADB; for the date on which he assumed his position as a managing director of the Hessische Bank, see the letter from Plassmann to Oesterlink, 25 October 1949, HADB, Aufsichtsrat der Deutschen Bank, vol. III.

[143] Comments of Oesterlink at the supervisory board meeting on 14 October 1948, in Wuppertal, HADB, RWB, 409.

[144] Deutsche Bank Business Report for 1944, BAP, R 8119 F, 24555, f. 677. Also in file: Deutsche Bank (Altbank) Hauptversammlung, 12 December 1974.

[145] OMGUS, *Ermittlungen gegen die Deutsche Bank*, pp. 36, 56–7, 359.

[146] Lutz Niethammer, *Entnazifizierung in Bayern. Säuberung und Rehabilitierung unter amerikanischer Besatzung* (Frankfurt a.M. 1972). Clemens Vollnhals (ed.), *Entnazifizierung. Politische Säuberung und Rehabilitierung in den vier Besatzungszonen 1945–1949* (Munich 1991).

[147] Circular from the directing office in Hamburg to the Deutsche Bank's supervisory board members, 5 January 1948, HADB, Aufsichtsrat der deutschen Bank, vol. III.

[148] For this and other information concerning the supervisory board members, see OMGUS, *Ermittlungen gegen die Deutsche Bank*, pp. 49–57, 301–52, 474. In 1945, the following names were listed in the commercial register of the central city of Berlin as deputy supervisory board members 'for the duration of incapacitation': Walther

Graemer for Zangen, Dr Fritz Jessen for von Siemens, and Clemens Lammers for Russell. See HADB, Aufsichtsrat der Deutschen Bank, vol. II.

[149] Comments by Osterlink at the supervisory board meeting on 14 October 1948, in Wuppertal, HADB, RWB, 409. As to the fate of Otto Fitzner, an active Nazi and as such economic consultant for the *Gau* of Lower Silesia and head of the Wirtschaftsgruppe Metallindustrie, see Walter Laqueur and Richard Breitman, *Breaking the Silence* (New York 1986).

[150] Documents for Oesterlink for the supervisory board meeting on 7 April 1952, in Düsseldorf, HADB, RWB, 409.

[151] See documents for the supervisory board meeting on 7 April 1952, HADB, Aufsichtsrat der Deutschen Bank, vol. III.

[152] Ibid., and Plassmann report to the supervisory board, 19 December 1949, HADB, Aufsichtsrat der Deutschen Bank, vol. III.

[153] Letter from E.W. Schmidt to Oesterlink, 19 February 1948, HADB, Aufsichtsrat der Deutschen Bank, vol. III.

[154] HADB, Günkel report, p. 7. See also memorandum dated 17 July 1945, probably by Dr Günter Keiser from the Wirtschaftsgruppe Privates Bankgewerbe in Berlin, translated into English, 'The Fate of the Berlin Banks up to 22 June 1945', BEA, OV 34/10. According to this, Keiser left Berlin on 22 June 1945.

[155] *Verordnungsblatt der Stadt Berlin*, vol. 1, no. 1 (1945).

[156] The names of these people, the addresses of the relatives who were to be notified in the case of emergency, and the guard duty schedule are found in BAP, R 8119 F, 24555, ff. 664–73.

[157] HADB, Rosenbrock report, pp. 12–13.

[158] BAP, R 8119 F, 24555, f. 663.

[159] HADB, Günkel report, p. 11.

[160] Memomorandum from Deutsche Bank Senior Vice-President Richard Ahlborn and Assistant Vice-President Martin Rosenbrock for Wintermantel, 24 July 1945, BAP, R 8119 F, 24555, ff. 247–9.

[161] HADB, Rosenbrock report, p. 25.

[162] HADB, Günkel report, p. 4.

[163] HADB, Rosenbrock report, p. 19.

[164] Ibid., p. 18.

[165] Ibid., p. 23.

[166] HADB, Günkel report, p. 4. See also Bericht zur Altbankenrechnung, 1 February 1960, file B, Banken, inländisch, Deutsche Bank Berlin, until Dec. 1961. Included in this file are many details on the activities of the old bank until 1960.

[167] HADB, Rosenbrock report, p. 29.

[168] Ibid., p. 31.

[169] HADB, Günkel report, p. 8; see also the report of the manager of the Deutsche Bank's deposit-taking branch V, Schönhauser Allee 8, to the executive management of the Berlin branch head office, 16 May 1945, on a discussion about this between rep-

resentatives of the various banks and Dr Siebert that day, BAP, R 8119 F, 24555, f. 630.

[170] HADB, Rosenbrock report, pp. 34–5.

[171] Ibid., pp. 38–9.

[172] *Verordnungsblatt der Stadt Berlin*, vol. 1, no. 1 (1945).

[173] However, it was not dependent on the Collection Commission, founded in 1947. For more on this in general, see Hans Weber, *Der Bankplatz Berlin* (Cologne/Opladen 1957), pp. 114, 171–3, 190.

[174] HADB, Rosenbrock report, p. 46; for the content of the letter, see Weber, *Bankplatz*, p. 172.

[175] HADB, Rosenbrock report, pp. 47–8.

[176] Ibid., p. 49.

[177] Ibid., p. 14.

[178] Ibid., p. 29.

[179] Letter from Wintermantel to directing office, Hamburg, 18 July 1945, HADB, RWB, 51. For the following, see numerous letters in HADB, RWB, 442.

[180] HADB, Rosenbrock report, p. 54.

[181] Ibid., p. 58.

[182] HADB, Günkel report, p. 10.

[183] HADB, RWB, 51. HADB, Günkel report, p. 12. Gesetz Nr. 52 usw., HADB file: Meldungen an die Alliierte Kommandantur.

[184] Oliver J. Frederiksen, *The American Military Occupation of Germany 1945–1953*. Historical Division, Headquarters, United States Army, Europe (1953), p. 23.

[185] HADB, Rosenbrock report, p. 63.

[186] *Verordnungsblatt der Stadt Berlin*, vol. 1, no. 4 (1945).

[187] HADB, Rosenbrock report, p. 71.

[188] Josef Deckers, *Die Transformation des Bankensystems in der sowjetischen Besatzungszone/DDR* (Berlin 1974), p. 29.

[189] Ibid., pp. 130–1.

[190] Ibid., pp. 28, 130.

[191] Ibid., pp. 26–7. The Americans estimated the monthly issue of military notes by the Soviets in 1945 to be 1 billion RM. See Manuel Gottlieb, 'Failure of Quadripartite Monetary Reform 1945–1947', *Finanzarchiv*, 17 (1956/57), pp. 398–417.

[192] Earl F. Ziemke, *The US Army in the Occupation of Germany, 1944–1946* (Washington, DC 1975), p. 60.

[193] Deckers, *Transformation*, pp. 25–7.

[194] NA, RG 260 (OMGUS), Finance Group, BICO, Miscellaneous Reports and Publications, Box 73, Folder No.1: Exhibit Nos. 183–295 to Report on Deutsche Bank, Exhibit 293.

[195] Remarks by Wintermantel on occasion of the supervisory board meeting on 14 October 1948, in Wuppertal, HADB, RWB, 409.

[196] Deckers, *Transformation*, pp. 31, 160.

[197] Bericht der Treuverkehr Wirtschaftsprüfung-AG, 28 August 1952, on the ten regional

banks, p. 2, HADB, file B, Banken, inländisch, Deutsche Bank Berlin, until Dec. 1961.

[198] There are several memoranda on this in HADB, RWB, 4. See also pp. 411–12.

[199] HADB, Günkel report, pp. 11, 12, 14 and appendix 2.

[200] Deckers, *Transformation*, pp. 31–2.

[201] Weber, *Bankplatz*, p. 173.

[202] HADB, Günkel report, p. 13 and appendix 1.

[203] See the ordinance of the Allied Military Government – Berlin, 14 June 1949, BK/L(49)4, 'Betrifft: Ausschuss für die ruhenden Berliner Kreditinstitute', *Verordnungsblatt für Gross-Berlin*, vol. 5, part I, no. 48/1949.

[204] HADB, Günkel report, pp. 13–15 and appendix 2.

[205] *Verordnungsblatt für Gross-Berlin*, vol. 3, no. 28/1947. Weber, *Bankplatz*, p. 174.

[206] Weber, *Bankplatz*, p. 175.

[207] NA, RG 260 (OMGUS), FINAD. Records Relating to Financial Institution Policy 1945–1949, Box 155, Folder: Removal of Papers Out of Berlin Banks. An official protest by the French against the Soviet removal of bank records in late 1946–early 1947 is located in DFIN/P(47)59, 1 April 1947, in RG 260 (OMGUS), Allied Control Authority, Finance Directorate (DFIN), Box 344, Folder: DFIN/P(47)41–89.

[208] Pertaining to these events, see: NA, RG 260 (OMGUS), FINAD. Records Relating to Financial Institution Policy 1945–1949, Box 131, Folder: Activity of Closed Banks in Berlin; as well as NA, RG 260 (OMGUS), Allied Control Authority. Finance Directorate (DFIN), Box 346, Folder: DFIN/MISC(47)1–103; (48)1–13.

[209] HADB, Günkel report, p. 16.

[210] Weber, *Bankplatz*, p. 175.

[211] Allied Military Government – Berlin BK/L (49) 4, 14 June 1949, 'Betrifft: Ausschuss für die ruhenden Berliner Kreditinstitute', *Verordnungsblatt für Gross-Berlin*, vol. 5, part 1, no. 48 (1949).

[212] Weber, *Bankplatz*, p. 176.

[213] In October 1965, for example, there were only 26 employees there. See HADB, Günkel report, pp. 20, 33.

[214] HADB, Günkel report, pp. 15–16. The securities settlement issue is summarized in Bernd Rudolph, 'Effekten- und Wertpapierbörsen, Finanztermin- und Devisenbörsen seit 1945', in Hans Pohl (ed.), *Deutsche Börsengeschichte* (Frankfurt a.M. 1992), pp. 293–375, here pp. 296–7.

[215] Weber, *Bankplatz*, p. 202.

[216] Ordinance of the Allied Military Government – Berlin BK/o (50) 63, 16 June 1950, 'Betrifft: Zulassung von Privatbanken', *Verordnungsblatt für Gross-Berlin*, vol. 6, part 1, no. 40 (1950).

[217] For more on its organization, tasks and status with respect to Allied agencies, on the one hand, and the Bank deutscher Länder, on the other, see: Rodney C. Loehr, *The West German Banking System*. Edited by the Office of the US High Commissioner for Germany, Office of the Executive Secretary, Historical Division (1952), pp. 104–9. On the topic of the 'Currency Commission', headed by Friedrich Ernst, see Michael W. Wolff, *Die Währungsreform in Berlin 1948/49* (Berlin/New York 1991), p. 75.

[218] Weber, *Bankplatz*, pp. 191–4. On the rather heated debate with the British representative in the Allied Bank Commission about whether the public sector alone should supply the needed capital or whether the majority of it should come from the private sector, see Loehr, *West German Banking System*, pp. 113–17.

[219] Weber, *Bankplatz*, p. 180.

[220] On the numerous drafts of the Handbook until it was published and the points of contention, see Ziemke, *US Army*, pp. 83–90. For regulations governing the financial sector in particular, see BEA, OV 34/22 B.

[221] Allied Forces, Supreme Headquarters, G–5 Division, *Handbook for Military Government in Germany prior to Defeat or Surrender*, December 1944.

[222] Allied Forces, Supreme Headquarters, G–5 Division, *Financial and Property Control Technical Manual*, October 1944.

[223] Allied Forces, Technical Manual, p. 16.

[224] Ibid., p. 17. See also Allied Forces, Handbook, item 339 (b).

[225] Allied Forces, Technical Manual, p. 144, contains not only the English original, but also the German translation. The English text was included word-for-word in the classified 'secret' document of the US Group Control Council, Finance Division 'Basic Preliminary Plan. Tripartite Control Council and Occupation of Germany', Annex XIV: Finance, 15 February 1945. NA, RG 260 (OMGUS), Finance Group, BICO, Miscellaneous Reports and Publications, Box 76, Folder: Basic Preliminary Plan. Also in FINAD. Records Relating to Financial Institution Policy 1945–1949, Box 137, Folder: Basic Plan.

[226] Allied Forces, Technical Manual, p. 144.

[227] The text of such a questionnaire is reprinted in Frank S.V. Donnison, *Civil Affairs and Military Government in North-West Europe, 1944–1946* (London 1961), pp. 492–7.

[228] Allied Forces, Technical Manual, pp. 149–50.

[229] The list, accompanied by a letter dated 27 June 1945, by Colonel H.G. Sheen, SHAEF Headquarters, G–2, was sent to the various army headquarters. NA, RG 260 (OMGUS), FINAD. Records Relating to Financial Institution Policy 1945–1949, Box 132, Folder: Arrests.

[230] Allied Forces, Technical Manual, p. 152.

[231] Ibid., p. 65.

[232] Ibid., p. 101.

[233] *Notenknappheit*, or a shortage of bills, was a problem at several branches of the Deutsche Bank, e.g. in late May 1945 in Halle. Verbindungsstelle Vorstand in Erfurt, circular no. 5, 1 June 1945, HADB, RWB, 51. See also HADB, file: Deutsche Bank 1945, with several reports from various branches to the directing office, Hamburg, especially from the summer of 1945.

[234] This is the profit earned from issuing money that has a lesser intrinsic value than its nominal value.

[235] I am not aware of any quantification of the seigniorage profit earned by the Allies by issuing military marks. In order to evaluate fully the German reparation payments after the Second World War, these sums could be of great significance due to the

uncontrolled printing and circulation of such notes by the Soviets, estimated at about 1 billion RM per month in 1945. See Gottlieb, *Failure*, p. 400.

[236] See note 154.

[237] Enclosure with letter from Dr Günter Keiser to Dr Erich Trost, managing director of the Association of Private Banking Business, 19 July 1945, HADB, RWB, 51. In the document, which is not signed by Keiser personally, his name is misspelled as Dr Günther Kaiser. After having participated in the work of the Bizonal Economics Administration under Ludwig Erhard and in the planning of West Germany's currency reform, Keiser held a leading position in the Economics Ministry of the Federal Republic.

[238] Horstmann, *Die Alliierten*, pp. 52–3. For the number of Deutsche Bank branch operations in each of the Western zones in May 1946 compared with the end of 1944, see NA, RG 260 (OMGUS), Finance Group, BICO. Miscellaneous Reports and Publications, Box 73, Folder No. 1: Exhibit Nos. 183–285 to Report on Deutsche Bank. Exhibit No. 294. The Günkel report, p. 1, HADB, states that the number of Deutsche Bank branches outside of the Western zones lost due to the war was 73, which closely correlates with the figures cited above.

[239] Paul Y. Hammond, 'Directives for the Occupation of Germany. The Washington Controversy', in Harold Stein (ed.), *American Civil-Military Decisions. A Book of Case Studies* (Birmingham, Alabama 1963), pp. 311–364, here p. 328.

[240] Ziemke, *US Army*, pp. 59–60.

[241] Hammond, *Directives*, p. 389.

[242] Summaries of this debate are included in John Lewis Gaddis, *The United States and the Origins of the Cold War 1941–47* (New York/London 1972), pp. 117–32; Wolfgang Krieger, *General Lucius D. Clay und die amerikanische Deutschlandpolitik 1945–1949* (Stuttgart 1987), pp. 28–53.

[243] Matthias Peter, 'John Maynard Keynes und die deutsche Frage', Ph.D thesis (Giessen 1992) p. 201.

[244] See Hammond, *Directives*, pp. 421–3; Günther Moltmann, 'Zur Formulierung der amerikanischen Besatzungspolitik in Deutschland am Ende des Zweiten Weltkrieges', *Vierteljahrshefte für Zeitgeschichte* 15 (1967), pp. 299–322. Churchill had agreed to the plans proposed by Morgenthau and Roosevelt to turn Germany into an agrarian country perhaps only in an effort to create a more benevolent mood with the Americans for his financial demands. On this see Harry G. Gelber, 'Der Morgenthau-Plan', *Vierteljahrshefte für Zeitgeschichte* 13 (1965), pp. 372–402, specifically pp. 389–92.

[245] Jean Edward Smith, *Lucius D. Clay. An American Life* (New York 1990), p. 98. One publication among others in which the JCS 1067 is printed is Carl J. Friedrich, *American Experiences in Military Government in World War II* (New York 1948), appendix A, pp. 381–402.

[246] Ibid., pp. 398–9.

[247] Hammond, *Directives*, p. 396.

[248] Ibid., pp. 437–8.

[249] Ibid., p. 429. For a comprehensive depiction of the events leading up to the Potsdam Agreements and the outcome, see Hermann Graml, *Die Alliierten und die Teilung*

Deutschlands. Konflikte und Entscheidungen 1941–1948 (Frankfurt a.M. 1985), pp. 61–104.

[250] Hajo Holborn, *American Military Government. Its Organization and Policies* (Washington, DC 1947), p. 200. The text of the document can be found in Beate Ruhm von Oppen (ed.), *Documents on Germany under Occupation 1945–1954* (London 1955), pp. 40–50, at 46; and also in Henry Morgenthau Jr, *Germany Is Our Problem* (New York/London 1945), appendix C, pp. 213–29.

[251] All quotes have been taken from Ruhm von Oppen, *Documents*, pp. 44–5.

[252] The overwhelming French concern for military security was the reason why one of the central goals of French occupation policy was to prevent centralized political and economic structures and institutions. See F. Roy Willis, *France, Germany and the New Europe 1945–1967* (Stanford 1968), p. 15; Krieger, *Clay*, pp. 104–9.

[253] Gaddis, *Cold War*, pp. 316–52.

[254] Hammond, *Directives*, pp. 438–43. The wording of the directive can be found in US Department of State, *Documents on Germany 1944–1985* (Washington, DC 1985), pp. 124–35.

[255] Lucius D. Clay, *Decisions in Germany* (London 1950), p. 19.

[256] Hans-Peter Schwarz, *Vom Reich zur Bundesrepublik. Deutschland im Widerstreit der außenpolitischen Konzeptionen in den Jahren der Besatzungsherrschaft 1945–1949*, 2nd ed. (Stuttgart 1980), p. 99.

[257] Gaddis, *Cold War*, p. 96.

[258] Clay, *Decisions*, p. 18.

[259] Horstmann, *Die Alliierten*, p. 54.

[260] Robert Murphy, *Diplomat Among Warriors* (London 1964), p. 308.

[261] Horstmann, *Die Alliierten*, pp. 58–9.

[262] NA, RG 260 (OMGUS), FINAD. Records Relating to Financial Institution Policy 1945–49, Box 153, Folder: Potsdam Agreement. Memorandum dated 5 September 1945, 'Implementation of the Potsdam Agreement' by Major E.C. Ophuls, Financial Institution Section of the Financial Branch, G–5 Division, USFET. The three concepts for restructuring the German banking system mentioned here were also noted in a historical report on 'Financial Institutions – SHAEF Period' from 29 August 1945. NA, RG 260 (OMGUS), FINAD. Records Relating to Financial Institution Policy 1945–1949, Box 131, Folder: Administration of Military Government in the US Zone in Germany, July 1945.

[263] Horstmann, *Die Alliierten*, pp. 61–2.

[264] For more on the impact of the 'home model' on American banking policy in Germany, see Loehr, *West German Banking System*, pp. 124–6.

[265] See Chapter 3, as well as Kopper, *Bankenpolitik im Dritten Reich*.

[266] Horstmann, *Die Alliierten*, pp. 65, 79.

[267] NA, RG 260 (OMGUS), FINAD. Correspondence and Other Records Maintained by Joseph M. Dodge 1945–6, Box 10, Folder: Financial Institutions. With arguments similar to those supporting his banking reform plans of autumn 1945, Dodge presented his modified proposals for decentralizing the banks on the four-power basis to the

Finance Directorate of the Allied Control Council on 5 April 1946. His one concession to the British was the proposal to create a Länder Union Bank. NA, RG 260 (OMGUS), Allied Control Authority. Finance Directorate (DFIN), Box 340, Folder: DFIN/M (46) 1–15: 'Statement to the Finance Directorate by Joseph M. Dodge', Appendix 'A' to DFIN/M (46) 11. The Dodge proposal can also be found in ibid., FINAD. Records Relating to Financial Institution Policy 1945–1949, Box 135, Folder: Banking Committee – Elimination of Excessive Concentration of Economic Power in Banking; and in BEA, OV 34/11. And in IfZ, US Military Government in Germany, Historical Division, Manuscript 'Financial Policies and Operations' by Robert P. March, Karlsruhe, 1950, appendix B. This roughly 300-page manuscript offers a good summary of the planning and actual development of US occupation policy in the area of banks and finance.

[268] Letter by Rosewick and Bacher from the Deutsche Bank branch in Stuttgart to the directing office, Hamburg, 19 December 1945, including a copy of the newspaper article from *Die Neue Zeitung*, in HADB, RWB, 4.

[269] Ibid.

[270] NA, RG 260 (OMGUS), FINAD. Records Concerning Proposals for Control Council Regulations 1946–1948, Box 79, Folder: Elimination of Excessive Concentration of Economic Power in Banking. The German translation of the Dodge Plan can be found in Büro der Militär Regierung für Deutschland (US), Finanz Abteilung, 1 November 1945 (Dodge-Plan in Übersetzung), HADB, RWB, 4.

[271] In 1946, exports from the British zone earned a total of $145 million, as opposed to $350 million spent on imported goods, of which $291 million went for the importation of food alone. HADBB, Monatsberichte der Reichsbankleitstelle Hamburg, Nr 11 (for April 1947).

[272] Horstmann, *Die Alliierten*, p. 69.

[273] Ibid., pp. 78–9. For more details on the criteria for arrest and the arrest waves, as well as on the denazification trials and their frequency in the US zone, see Rolf Steiniger, *Deutsche Geschichte 1945–1961. Darstellung und Dokumente*, 2 vols (Frankfurt a.M. 1983), pp. 128–31.

[274] See BEA, OV 34/87, for details on the organization of the chief office of the Reichsbank during its initial phase.

[275] Willi A. Boelcke, *Die deutsche Wirtschaft 1930–1945. Interna des Reichswirtschaftsministeriums* (Düsseldorf 1983), p. 217.

[276] There were meetings held regularly in the Reichsbank chief office with bank representatives. For a description of the topics addressed at these meetings from 1946 to 1948, see HADB, RWB, 441. The Reichsbank chief office interjected its disapproval twice (on 16 August and 6 September 1946) during the Allied discussion on decentralization of the Reichsbank and the big banks. The English wording of these can be found in BEA, OV 34/12.

[277] Reichsbankhauptstelle Hamburg, circular no. 93, 1 March 1946, 'An alle finanziellen Unternehmen', HADB, RWB, 4.

[278] Cited in Horstmann, *Die Alliierten*, p. 105. The orders of the American military

government were dated 6 March 1946; NA (OMGUS), FINAD. Records Relating to Financial Institution Policy 1945–1949, Box 151, folder: Military Government Law No. 57, the memorandum from OMGUS, Finance Division, 'Decentralization of Banking in the American Zone of Occupation', 14 March 1947, in which Jack Bennett presents the events leading up to the opposition of the Germans with regard to bank decentralization. See also the memorandum by Suchsland 'Betr.: Dezentralisierung der Grossbanken', 11 March 1946, HADB, RWB, 4. There are also other documents here on the reorganization of the head offices under zonal partitioning.

[279] See memorandum from 15 March 1946, HADB, RWB, 4. Klöckers organized meetings regularly for the managers of the Deutsche Bank branches in the French zone at which primarily business policies were discussed. The minutes of meetings held in 1946 and 1947 are located in HADB, Fortführung der alten Bank.

[280] See the reports of the censorship office of the American military government on letters and telephone calls between branches of the Deutsche Bank and the directing office in Hamburg in 1947: NA, RG 260 (OMGUS), FINAD. Records Relating to Financial Institution Policy 1945–1949, Box 143, Folder: Decentralization of Banking – US Zone (Except Land Central Bank).

[281] NA, RG 260 (OMGUS), Allied Control Authority. Finance Directorate (DFIN), Box 342, Folder: DFIN/P(45)1–62. The two Dodge proposals are numbered DFIN/P(45)29 and DFIN/P(45)33.

[282] See the minutes for the tenth meeting of the Finance Directorate, NA, RG 260 (OMGUS) Allied Control Council. Finance Directorate (DFIN), Box 340, Folder: DFIN/M(45)1–15. For the following: NA, RG 260 (OMGUS), FINAD. Records Concerning Proposals for Control Council Regulations 1946–1948, Box 79, Folder: Elimination of Excessive Concentration of Economic Power in Banking. This folder includes a three-page summary of the discussion as it developed until the proposals were finally rejected by the Allied Control Council on 18 October 1946. This summary clearly shows how greatly the British concepts differed from those of the other three powers. See also Theo Horstmann, 'Um "das schlechteste Bankensystem der Welt". Die interalliierten Auseinandersetzungen über amerikanische Pläne zur Reform des deutschen Bankwesens 1945/46', *Bankhistorisches Archiv* 11 (1985), pp. 3–27. Horstmann, *Die Alliierten*, pp. 84–94.

[283] NA, RG 260 (OMGUS), FINAD. Records Relating to Financial Institution Policy 1945–1949, Box 135, Folder: Banking Committee – Elimination of Excessive Concentration of Economic Power in Banking. UK memorandum, 31 January 1946, 'Elimination of Excessive Concentration of Economic Power in Banking' (= Appendix 'B' to DFIN/BC/MEMO(46)4 (2nd Revise)).

[284] NA, RG 260 (OMGUS), FINAD. Records Relating to Financial Institution Policy 1945–1949, Box 151, Folder: Military Government Law No. 57. Secret memorandum, 14 June 1947, 'Financial Trends in the British Zone'.

[285] NA, RG 260 (OMGUS), FINAD. Records Relating to Financial Institution Policy 1945–1949, Box 135, Folder: Banking Committee – Elimination of Excessive Concentration of Economic Power in Banking. DFIN/P(46)39, 5 April 1946, Paper Sub-

mitted by US Member: 'Proposal for a New Länder Union Bank'. Also located in BEA, OV 34/11.

[286] The paper that the representatives of the four powers agreed upon is filed under the reference number DFIN/BC/MEMO(46)15. It is located in NA, RG 260 (OMGUS), FINAD. Records Relating to Financial Institution Policy 1945–1949, Box 135, Folder: Banking Committee – Elimination of Excessive Concentration of Economic Power in Banking. See also the minutes of the meeting of the Finance Directorate on 24 July 1946, ibid., Box 144, Folder: Elimination of Power of Banks, etc. A reconstruction of the events and all of the important documents can also be found in BEA, OV 34/11 and 34/12.

[287] Werner Weber and Werner Jahn, *Synopse zur Deutschlandpolitik 1941 bis 1973* (Göttingen 1973), pp. 15–18.

[288] Conrad F. Latour and Thilo Vogelsang, *Okkupation und Wiederaufbau. Die Tätigkeit der Militärregierung in der amerikanischen Besatzungszone Deutschlands 1944–1947* (Stuttgart 1973), pp. 158–60; Krieger, *Clay*, pp. 139–43.

[289] The papers presented to this committee contained the proposals unanimously passed by the Banking Committee and a notation of the differences that arose in the Finance Directorate. See NA, RG 260 (OMGUS), Allied Control Authority, Finance Directorate (DFIN), Box 342, specifically DFIN/Memo(46)161, 30 September 1946, with DFIN/Memo(46)130 (2nd Revise) as supplement [identical with DFIN/BC/MEMO(46)15].

[290] These failed attempts at reaching a common banking policy are described in detail in Appendix B of DFIN/BC/MEMO(47)1 'Subject: Banking', in BEA, OV 34/13.

[291] For example, see DFIN/Memo(47)113, 27 August 1947: 'Elimination of power to engage in stock exchange transactions and to invest in certain securities', in NA, RG 260 (OMGUS). Allied Control Authority. Finance Directorate (DFIN), Box 346, Folder: DFIN/Memo(47)85–130. For the description of the discussion on this in 1946, see DFIN/P(46)23, 35, 95 and 179 in Boxes 341 to 343.

[292] NA, RG 260 (OMGUS), FINAD. Records Relating to Financial Institution Policy 1945–1949, Box 133, Folder: Bank Decentralization. Page 1 of the memorandum on 'Decentralization of the German Banks', 28 March 1949. See also the letters from the Kommission der Deutschen Zentral-Finanzverwaltung zur Sicherstellung der Geschäftsunterlagen und Wertpapiere der Hauptsitze geschlossener deutscher Banken,7 and 20 November 1947, to the lower district court of central Berlin, Dept Commercial Register (Amtsgericht Berlin-Mitte, Abt. Handelsregister bzw. Geschäftsstelle), in Berlin-Charlottenburg, HADB, Fortführung der alten Bank. The issue revolved around registering the commission as the administrator of the Deutsche Bank's assets in the Soviet sector of Berlin and in the Soviet occupation zone.

[293] NA, RG 122 (Federal Trade Commission), Box 29, Folder: Germany – General – 1945–1949. See also Graham D. Taylor, 'The Rise and Fall of Antitrust in Occupied Germany 1945–48', *Prologue. The Journal of the National Archives* 11 (1979), pp. 23–39, and HICOG, Historical Division, manuscript 'Deconcentration and

Decartellization in West Germany 1945–1953' by J.F.J. Gillen (1953), Library of Congress, Washington, DC.

[294] NA, RG 260 (OMGUS) FINAD, Records Concerning Proposals for Control Council Regulations 1946–1948, Box 79, Folder: Elimination of Excessive Concentration of Economic Power in Banking. Memorandum from J.M. Dodge, 1 November 1945, 'Subject: Central Banking and Bank Supervision'. Despite the title, this paper included his concepts for decentralization of the entire banking system. On the corresponding instructions from the American military government to the Minister-Presidents of Bavaria, Greater Hesse and Württemberg-Baden, see the article from *Die Neue Zeit*, 17 December 1945, HADB, RWB, 4.

[295] Memorandum by Luttitz, Wiesbaden branch, on this meeting, HADB, RWB, 4.

[296] By the end of June 1944, the three big banks held only about 10 per cent of the 150 billion RM in Reich bonds in circulation. See the letter from the Freiburg branches of the Deutsche Bank and the Dresdner Bank to the French military government, 18 January 1947, HADB, RWB, 5. See also memorandum of the Reichsbank chief office in Hamburg, 22 September 1947, 'The Development of the German Banking System', p. 8, BEA, OV 34/17.

[297] Quoted in Horstmann, *Die Alliierten*, p. 100.

[298] See letter from Dr Walter Schmidt, Wiesbaden, to Plassmann, Hamburg, 11 January 1946, HADB, RWB, 4.

[299] Horstmann, *Die Alliierten*, pp. 100–2. The legislative proposal with the letter from the ministry and documentation of the Deutsche Bank's strong opposition to the proposal – including a letter written in conjunction with the other two banks on 28 January 1946 to the finance minister of Hesse, expressing opposition to the Hessian solo venture in decentralization – are located in HADB, RWB, 4. Abs also wrote a personal letter on 12 January 1946 to Hesse Minister-President Dr Geiler, concerning his reservations about American decentralization policy, HADB, Dezentralisierung, Korrespondenz, 024/1.

[300] NA, RG 260 (OMGUS), Finance Group, BICO. Miscellaneous Reports and Publications, Box 73, Folder No. 1: Exhibit Nos. 183–295 to Report on Deutsche Bank. Exhibit 284: Letter from directing office, Hamburg, to the executive management of the Filiale Frankfurt, 11 January 1946. This letter was sent to 17 Deutsche Bank head offices in the British zone at once and to the Kassel office, which was also 'put in stocks', as it were. See HADB, RWB, 4.

[301] NA, RG 260 (OMGUS), FINAD. Records Concerning Proposals for Control Council Regulations 1946–1948, Box 79, Folder: Elimination of Excessive Concentration of Economic Power in Banking. Minutes from the meeting on 24 July 1946, DFIN/M(46)21, p. 5.

[302] See an article by Cahn-Garnier in the *Stuttgarter Wirtschaftszeitung*, 15 November 1946, quoted in minutes of the Hamburg meeting on 10–11 December 1946, HADB, RWB, 440. See also Fritz Cahn-Garnier, 'Dekartellierung der Banken', *Deutsche Finanzwirtschaft* 1 (1947), 6, pp. 9–14.

[303] For more on this specific issue, see the Deutsche Bank memorandum 'Depotstimmrecht

der Banken', 21 January 1946, supplement 26 January 1946, HADB, RWB, 4 and 8. Here it was argued that even the National Socialists had not touched the proxy voting power, although they had included in their party programmes the call for 'fighting against the banks' and 'weakening the influence of the banks'. But it is improbable that they would have let this stand untouched after a victorious war.

[304] This 13-page memorandum was signed by Arnold Maser for the Deutsche Bank. It is located in the HADB, RWB, 5. See also the minutes of the meeting on 11 July 1946, with representatives of the big banks and the finance ministers of the three *Länder* involved, at which this memo was prepared, HADB, RWB, 4.

[305] Memorandum by Gunston, 17 January 1947, 'Reichsbank chief office in Hamburg', BEA, OV 34/13.

[306] This was published in *Journal Officiel*, 23 February 1947. A copy is located in HADB, RWB, 5.

[307] Horstmann, *Die Alliierten*, p. 115.

[308] Letter from General Lucius D. Clay to Abs, 19 April 1971, HADB, verdicts and additional documents from the Czichon trial.

[309] Note of Freiburg branch on this meeting, 28 December 1946, HADB, RWB, 5.

[310] HADB, RWB, 5.

[311] Minutes of the Hamburg meeting, 10/11 December 1946, HADB, RWB, 440.

[312] HADB, RWB, 5. See also the detailed memorandum by Deutsche Bank Executive Vice-President Arnold Maser on 5 February 1947, on a meeting between the vice-president of the Munich Land Central Bank Hartlieb, the bank commissioner from the Bavarian finance ministry Dr Kreuser, and representatives of the three big banks in Munich the previous day. It is evident here that the US military government was placing the *Land* governments under considerable political pressure on this issue. The decentralization model favoured by both of the Bavarian officials called for the creation of legally independent shareholding banks on the *Land* basis, the shares of which were to be taken over by the big banks on the condition that they forfeit their voting rights for a certain period; these would be safeguarded temporarily by the Bavarian Land Central Bank or the finance ministry as a proxy. Maser did not consider this plan realistic due to the enormous capital transaction requirements between the zones and because the chances were good that the Allies would reject such a solution. However, the Bavarian officials were still advocating this plan in the second half of March. See the report on the meeting in the Bavarian finance ministry with Dr Kessler from the Deutsche Bank directing office and Maser, 20 March 1947, HADB, RWB, 6. The unrelenting refusal of the Deutsche Bank to submit its own decentralization proposal can be discerned in a series of other documents in HADB, RWB, 5. A ten-page translation of the complete statement submitted by the three big banks on 14 March 1947 was telegraphed to London by the British military government and is located also in BEA, OV 34/14.

[313] All three events mentioned in this and the next paragraph are documented in HADB, RWB, 5.

[314] Appendix 'A' to BIFIN/P(47)36, 26 February 1947: Statement of the British Position, BEA, OV 34/90.

[315] NA, RG 260 (OGMUS), FINAD. Records Relating to Financial Institution Policy 1945–1949, Box 151, Folder: Military Government Law No. 57. Memorandum by Jack Bennett, 14 March 1947, 'Decentralization of Banking in the American Zone of Occupation'.

[316] HADB, RWB, 6.

[317] Ibid.

[318] Memorandum by Sir O.E. Niemeyer, 13 August 1947, BEA, OV 34/90.

[319] See the speech written by E.W. Schmidt for Bechtolf for the Deutsche Bank supervisory board meeting on 14 October 1948, 'Zu der durch die Dezentralisation geschaffenen Rechtslage', HADB, RWB, 409.

[320] There was controversy over terminology between General Clay and the War Department, on one hand, and the State Department, on the other, in connection with the 1948 Bi-Zone legislation to decartellize the iron and steel industry. Clay wanted to label the appointed German general managers 'trustees', in German *Treuhänder*, meaning someone to guarantee the rights of the property owners, as opposed to 'custodian', meaning someone entrusted with the rights divested from the owner. See Dörte Winkler, 'Die amerikanische Sozialisierungspolitik in Deutschland 1945–1948', in Heinrich A. Winkler (ed.), *Politische Weichenstellungen im Nachkriegsdeutschland 1945–1953* (Göttingen 1979), p. 105. Contrary to the case of the iron and steel industry, the decision was made to use the word 'custodian' for banking in order to clarify that the former owners had been deprived of their rights. It was also a conscious decision officially to translate 'custodian' into German as *Verwalter* instead of *Treuhänder*. The latter would have been an equally correct translation of 'trustee'. On this, see the letter from the Deutsche Bank branch in Frankfurt a.M. to Kessler in the directing office in Hamburg, 10 May 1947, in HADB, RWB, 6.

[321] Letter E.J.W. Hellmuth, Banking Branch, Berlin, to Montford, Foreign Office, London, 16 August 1947, BEA, OV 34/16.

[322] BEA, OV 34/15. Concrete examples of the shortcomings of the foreign trade bureaucracy are included in the memorandum, 'Germany. Shortcomings of the Joint Export–Import Agency', 11 December 1947, BEA, OV 34/18.

[323] The exact German translation of Ordinance No. 25 can be found in HADB, RWB, 6 and in HADB, file: Neuordnung der Grossbanken nach dem Kriege.

[324] See HADB, RWB, 7. Not until autumn did the court battles end in the US zone, finally settling the differences between the stipulated tasks of a 'board of management/board of directors' in American English and of a *Vorstand/Aufsichtsrat* in German stock company law. The issue was whether the custodian was to assume only the role of the *Vorstand*, or also that of the supervisory board, the *Aufsichtsrat*. This was not settled until General Order No. 3 of Law No. 57 was issued on 19 September 1947, in Württemberg-Baden (as in Bavaria and Hesse), in which a council was created to exercise supervisory board rights; the custodian was also a member of the council. NA, RG 260 (OMGUS), FINAD, Records Relating to Financial Institution Policy 1945–1949, Box 151, Folder: Military Government Law No. 57, and Box 143, Folder: Decentralization of Banking – US Zone (Except Land Central Bank).

[325] Memorandum by Bechtolf, 'Geheim, Betr.: Künftige Struktur der Grossbanken', 9 January 1948, HADB, RWB, 7.

[326] BEA, OV 34/19. For a description of the events leading to this treaty, beginning with the request from London for financial aid from Washington on 23 August 1947, see the telegram from Washington to the Foreign Office, 11 September 1947, and a memorandum from 26 August 1947, in BEA, OV 34/17, as well as another telegram on this matter from 2 August 1947, in BEA, OV 34/16.

[327] This proposed partition was presented to the Deutsche Bank as a type of map exercise in a memorandum with the notation St/Mg 'Betr.: Dezentralisierung der drei Grossbanken', 12 December 1947. Once again, Wintermantel and Bechtolf rejected Hülse's plan in an extensive letter addressed to him. Both events are documented in HADB, RWB, 7.

[328] Memorandum by Bechtolf, 9 January 1948, HADB, RWB, 7.

[329] Enclosure to letter from the three big banks to Hülse, 15 January 1948, HADB, RWB, 7.

[330] Abs to Mayor R. Petersen, Hamburg, 17 February 1948, HADB, RWB, 7.

[331] Memorandum, p. 2, HADB, RWB, 7.

[332] Ibid., p. 4.

[333] Abs to Mayor R. Petersen, Hamburg, 17 February 1948, HADB, RWB, 7.

[334] 'Secret' minutes of this meeting, HADB, RWB, 434.

[335] See the complete collection of the minutes of these board meetings, the last being on 31 October 1953, HADB, RWB, 434.

[336] Herbert Wolf, 'Die Dreier-Lösung. Marginalien zum Niederlassungsgesetz von 1952', *Bankhistorisches Archiv* 19 (1993) pp. 1, 30.

[337] See letter from the Hanover branch to Finance Minister Dr Strickrodt, Hanover, 27 February 1948, suggesting the name 'Nordwestbank' and his later custodian Dr Hans Fiehn, HADB, RWB, 49. In the French zone, the proposals for bank names and custodians put forth by the banks were also accepted. See the letter of Deutsche Bank Executive Vice-President Heinrich Klöckers, whom the Deutsche Bank had put in charge of this zone, from Mannheim, to Kessler at the directing office, Hamburg, 20 September 1947, HADB, RWB, 6. For the more serious conflicts between the Germans and the American military government in selecting custodians for the US zone, see NA, RG 260 (OMGUS), FINAD. Records Relating to Financial Institution Policy 1945–1949, Box 143, Folder: Decentralization of Banks. Memorandum Richard P. Aikin, 3 July 1947, 'Appointment of custodians for Deutsche, Dresdner and Commerzbank under Law No. 57'.

[338] Memorandum, 'Aufgaben der Verwalter', 18 January 1949, HADB, RWB, 8.

[339] Wintermantel to Oesterlink, 12 April 1948, HADB, RWB, 7.

[340] Ibid.

[341] Neuburger to Deutsche Bank directing office, Hamburg, 13 April 1948, HADB, RWB, 7.

[342] Memorandum, 'Fragen für die nächste Vorstandssitzung', 11 August 1948, HADB, Deutsche Bank-Führungsstab Hamburg 1945–1948 Rundschreiben. Information on

how work was delegated and districts and departments set up in the RWB is also documented in HADB, Aufsichtsrat der Deutschen Bank, vol. III.

[343] 76-page manuscript from July 1951, 'Die Rheinisch-Westfälische Bank', p. 4, HADB, file: Deutsche Bank Nachfolgebanken 1947–1952 (I).

[344] Deutsche Bank directing office, Hamburg, special circular 10/48 to the branches in North Rhine-Westphalia, HADB, Aufsichtsrat der Deutschen Bank, vol. III.

[345] 'Die Rheinisch-Westfälische Bank', p. 4, HADB, file: Deutsche Bank Nachfolgebanken 1947–1952 (I).

[346] HADB, Aufsichtsrat der Deutschen Bank, vol. III.

[347] Diagram of the structural organization of the bank in HADB, Aufsichtsrat der Deutschen Bank, vol. III.

[348] 'Die Rheinisch-Westfälische Bank', p. 3, HADB, file: Deutsche Bank Nachfolgebanken 1947–1952 (I).

[349] Horstmann, *Die Alliierten*, p. 147.

[350] E.W. Schmidt, 'Die Kreditbanken nach der Währungsreform', *Industriekurier*, 30 August 1949, p. 5.

[351] Enclosure with letter from Plassmann to Oesterlink, 20 December 1949, HADB, Aufsichtsrat der Deutschen Bank, vol. III.

[352] Hermann Herold, 'Die Neuordnung der Großbanken im Bundesgebiet', *Neue Juristische Wochenschrift* 5 (1952), pp. 481–4, 566–8.

[353] The papers of Fritz Wintermantel, file 1947 A–Z, private property of the Gröning family, Essen.

[354] This and the following are from Horstmann, *Die Alliierten*, pp. 123–34.

[355] Ibid., p. 134. For more on the British arguments in the controversy with the US military government during the establishment of the Bank deutscher Länder, see BEA, OV 34/90.

[356] Telegram quoted in Jean Edward Smith (ed.), *The Papers of General Lucius D. Clay* (Bloomington, Indiana 1974), pp. 429–31.

[357] Law No. 60 of the American military government and Ordinance No. 129 of the British. For the history leading up to its founding, see Theo Horstmann, 'Die Entstehung der Bank deutscher Länder als geldpolitische Lenkungsinstanz in der Bundesrepublik Deutschland', in Hajo Riese/Heinz-Peter Spahn (eds.), *Geldpolitik und ökonomische Entwicklung. Ein Symposion* (Regensburg 1990), pp. 202–18. Theo Horstmann, 'Kontinuität und Wandel im deutschen Notenbanksystem. Die Bank deutscher Länder als Ergebnis alliierter Besatzungspolitik nach dem Zweiten Weltkrieg', in Theo Pirker (ed.), *Autonomie und Kontrolle. Beiträge zur Soziologie des Finanz- und Steuerstaates* (Berlin 1989), pp. 135–54.

[358] Eckhard Wandel, *Die Entstehung der Bank deutscher Länder und die deutsche Währungsreform 1948* (Frankfurt a.M. 1980), p. 81. A more detailed account of the policies of the Allied Bank Commission can be found in Loehr, *West German Banking System*, pp. 21–40.

[359] Memorandum, 'Germany: Proposed Banking Reorganisation in Anglo-US Joint Zones', C.A. Gunston for Siepmann and Sir O.E. Niemeyer, BEA, OV 34/90.

[360] Resolution proposal of 19 February 1948, Neuordnung des Bankwesens, rapporteur: Schmidt, HADB, RWB, 7.

[361] With the exact wording of the letter of rejection, 4 May 1948, BEA, OV 34/228.

[362] Wandel, *Entstehung*, pp. 74–6; Pohl, *Abs*, pp. 57–8.

[363] Report of the Department of State, Division of Biographic Information, February 1950, NA, RG 319, X800 1750.

[364] Ibid., memo from Carver to Harris, 16 March 1950. Wandel may also have implied a political reason for the failure of the election in *Entstehung*, p. 75. For more detail on the controversy among the Allies over the appointment of Abs (and Schniewind), see also IfZ, OMGUS POLAD 808/10 with numerous documents, and OMGUS FINAD 2/188/2, memorandum W.E. McCurdy, Legal Div., to Clay, 17 April 1948.

[365] Horstmann, *Die Alliierten*, p. 136. The ideas did not originate from Abs, as is argued by Manfred Pohl, *Wiederaufbau. Kunst und Technik der Finanzierung. Die ersten Jahre der Kreditanstalt für Wiederaufbau* (Frankfurt a.M. 1973), p. 21, and Pohl, *Abs*, p. 61.

[366] For more detail, see Pohl, *Wiederaufbau*; see also Pohl, *Abs*, pp. 61–74.

[367] The reasons for this are presented in Graml, *Die Alliierten*, pp. 203–7. Michael Brackmann, *Vom totalen Krieg zum Wirtschaftswunder. Die Vorgeschichte der westdeutschen Währungsreform 1948* (Essen 1993), pp. 239–43.

[368] Memorandum from Gunston 'Germany: Financial Reform', 15 January 1948, to Sir O.E. Niemeyer and Mr Siepmann, BEA, OV 34/19. This file contains other interesting details on the preparation phase of currency reform. See also Hans Möller (ed.), *Zur Vorgeschichte der Deutschen Mark. Die Währungsreformpläne 1945–1948* (Tübingen 1961), and Hans Möller, 'Die westdeutsche Währungsreform von 1948', in Deutsche Bundesbank (ed.), *Währung und Wirtschaft in Deutschland 1876–1975* (Frankfurt a.M. 1976), pp. 433–83. For the more recent discussion on the political impact of currency reform on stability and growth and on the significant German contribution to shaping this reform, see numerous articles by C. Buchheim and R. Klump, including those in Wolfram Fischer (ed.), *Währungsreform und Soziale Marktwirtschaft. Erfahrungen und Perspektiven nach 40 Jahren* (Berlin 1989), pp. 391–422. Rainer Klump (ed.), *40 Jahre Deutsche Mark. Die politische und ökonomische Bedeutung der westdeutschen Währungsreform von 1948* (Wiesbaden 1989). Brackmann, *Vom totalen Krieg*. Several documents showing the influence of German experts on shaping currency reform, e.g. the final report of the 'Konklave im Rothwesten' and two memoranda of Central Bank Council President Bernard about meetings with the military governors, are located in HADB, file: Währungsreform 1948. More on currency reform in HADB, RWB, 7.

[369] See Wolff, *Währungsreform*.

[370] Eugen Langen, *Die neuen Währungsgesetze* (Essen 1948), p. 5. The technical details of currency reform are to be found here and also in Rudolf Stucken, *Deutsche Geld- und Kreditpolitik 1914 bis 1963*, 3rd edn (Tübingen 1964), pp. 201–8.

[371] On the discussion within the Allied Bank Commission about these quotas, see Loehr, *West German Banking System*, pp. 24–6.

[372] A detailed conversion table, i.e. a comparison of the RM closing balance sheet and the DM opening balance sheet of the RWB is located in the manuscript by Erhard Ulbricht, 'Die Rheinisch-Westfälische Bank', July 1951, HADB, file: Nachfolgebanken 1947–1952 (I).

[373] Stucken, *Geld- und Kreditpolitik*, p. 209.

[374] E.W. Schmidt, 'Kreditbanken nach der Währungsreform', p. 5.

[375] Christoph Buchheim, 'Marshall Plan and Currency Reform', in Jeffrey Diefendorf *et al.* (eds.), *American Policy and the Reconstruction of West Germany, 1945–1955* (Cambridge 1993), pp. 69–83.

[376] Letter from the Allied Bank Commission ABC/DIR(48)12, June 1948, BEA, OV 34/228, with which this authority was transferred to the Bank deutscher Länder. See also Christoph Buchheim, *Die Wiedereingliederung Westdeutschlands in die Weltwirtschaft 1945–1958* (Munich 1990), pp. 62–3.

[377] The currency reform and its consequences, as well as the reasons for the continuing dollar gap, were described with impressive clarity by Hermann J. Abs, 'The Structure of the Western German Monetary System', *Economic Journal*, 80 (1950), pp. 481–8.

[378] Langen, *Währungsgesetze*, p. 37.

[379] Horstmann, *Die Alliierten*, pp. 223–5; Abs/Goetz/Marx memorandum, 'Vorschlag betreffend die zukünftige Struktur der deutschen Aktienbanken', pp. 23–6, HADB.

[380] Memorandum by Vallenthin, 'Wiedervereinigung der Grossbanken', 8 March 1956, HADB, RWB, 89; memorandum by Vallenthin, 'Aufhebung des Grossbankengesetzes', 23 May 1956, HADB, RWB, 90.

[381] Memorandum by E.W. Schmidt, 'Die Währungsreform und ihre Auswirkungen', 30 August 1948, HADB, RWB, 8. A recent depiction of production development following currency reform is offered by Albrecht Ritschl, 'Die Währungsreform von 1948 und der Wiederaufstieg der westdeutschen Industrie: Zu den Thesen von Mathias Manz und Werner Abelshauser über die Produktionswirkungen der Währungsreform', *Vierteljahrshefte für Zeitgeschichte*, 33 (1985), pp. 136–63.

[382] For a more detailed presentation, see John Gimbel, *The Origins of the Marshall Plan* (Stanford 1976), pp. 220–33.

[383] On the controversy over reparations, the amount taken out of current production and by demontage, as well as other reparation payments, see Jörg Fisch, *Reparationen nach dem Zweiten Weltkrieg* (Munich 1992). Rainer Karlsch, *Allein bezahlt? Die Reparationsleistungen der SBZ/DDR 1945–53* (Berlin 1993).

[384] Letter from Schmidt to Abs, 18 March 1949, with enclosure, and Abs's response to Schmidt, 22 March 1949, in HADB, RWB, 8. The articles from the British economic press are also located here.

[385] Abs to E.W. Schmidt, 16 August 1949, HADB, RWB, 8. For the following, see HADB, Dezentralisierung, Korrespondenz, 024/1. The committee statement is also located here.

[386] Several of the proposals discussed by the Allies at the time are located in NA, RG 260 (OMGUS), FINAD. Records Relating to Financial Institution Policy 1945–1949, Box

134, Folder: Banking (Decentralization); folder: Banking and Decentralization. See also Loehr, *West German Banking System*, p. 55.

[387] Horstmann, *Die Alliierten*, pp. 192–3.

[388] Loehr, *West German Banking System*, p. 58.

[389] Horstmann, *Die Alliierten*, p. 196.

[390] Quoted in ibid., p. 199.

[391] Ibid., p. 204.

[392] Loehr, *West German Banking System*, p. 55.

[393] HADB, file: Neuordnung der Grossbanken nach dem Kriege; and HADB, RWB, 8.

[394] Memorandum by E.W. Schmidt, 7 November 1949, 'Betr. Denkschrift: Dezentralization der Grossbanken', 7 November 1949, HADB, RWB, 8; also in HADB, RWB, 64.

[395] Horstmann, *Die Alliierten*, p. 205 (note 63), pp. 206–7.

[396] Ibid., p. 202.

[397] For a detailed account of these events including the statements of a series of witnesses exonorating Abs, see: NA, RG 319, X800 1750. The answers submitted by Abs to the questions concerning his past are also located here.

[398] Horstmann, *Die Alliierten*, p. 208 (note 67); on the press campaign in general, ibid., pp. 208–10.

[399] HADB, RWB, 64.

[400] Horstmann, *Die Alliierten*, p. 209.

[401] HADB, RWB, 64. Both versions of the memorandum are found in the file: HADB, Dezentralisierung, Korrespondenz, Protokolle, Presse 1947–1950, 024/2.

[402] NA, RG 260 (OMGUS), FINAD. Records Relating to Financial Institution Policy 1945–1949, Box 134, Folder: Banking. Memorandum, 'Recentralization of German Banking', by Fred H. Klopstock, 2 February 1950, p. 7. The minority British vote and numerous memoranda from 1950 on the big banks issue (including some of their drafts) are located in HADB, Dezentralisierung, Korrespondenz, Protokolle, Presse 1947–1950, 024/2. The minutes of relevant meetings are also here, including those of the Federal Finance Ministry on the important meeting in Unkel on 28 July 1950, with a list of those who were present.

[403] NA, RG 260 (OMGUS), FINAD. Records Relating to Financial Institution Policy 1945–1949, Box 134, Folder: Banking, p. 7 of the memorandum.

[404] Ibid., p. 4 of the memorandum.

[405] Horstmann, *Die Alliierten*, pp. 214–15.

[406] Ibid., pp. 212–13.

[407] Ibid., p. 219. Hans Booms (ed.), *Die Kabinettsprotokolle der Bundesregierung, vol. 1, 1949* (Boppard am Rhein 1982), pp. 189–90.

[408] Memorandum by E.W. Schmidt, 'Betr. Dezentralisation', 16 January 1950, HADB, RWB, 64.

[409] Horstmann, *Die Alliierten*, p. 220–1.

[410] I thank Knut Borchardt, Munich, for this information.

[411] Letter from Boston, 22 February 1950, HADB, RWB, 43.

[412] NA, RG 319, X800 1750. Department of State, Division of Biographic Information, Progress Report No. 2 on Case of Hermann J. Abs, 28.3.1950. The chairman of the Council on Foreign Relations decided to organize the dinner to honour Abs after Kempner had recommended Abs to him.

[413] This is evident from a list Abs submitted to the Allies during their investigation of him. This list included the names of contacts he made during visits abroad. Located in NA, RG 319, X800 1750.

[414] Letter from Dr F. Kempner to Bechtolf, 4 April 1950, HADB, RWB, 64. See also IfZ, OMGUS POLAD 808/10, ten-page assessment of Otto Schniewind by F.C. Kempner in connection with the election of Schniewind as president of the Central Bank Council of the Bank deutscher Länder, 2 April 1948. Kempner was then Special Assistant to the Economic Adviser of OMGUS.

[415] Horstmann, *Die Alliierten.*, p. 236.

[416] Letter from Cahill, Gordon, Zachry and Reindel to Abs, 25 October 1951, with the final bill, HADB, RWB, 392, No. 31.

[417] HADB, RWB, 64. The terms 'successor banks' and 'regional banks' were often mixed up. For the sake of clarity, the institutions decoupled in 1952 should be labelled 'successor banks', while those at the *Länder* level which were still not legally independent are to be called 'regional banks'.

[418] See HADB, RWB, 64.

[419] Horstmann, *Die Alliierten*, pp. 220, 222.

[420] Ibid., p. 216.

[421] Ibid., pp. 225–6.

[422] Wolf, 'Dreier-Lösung', p. 31.

[423] Letter from Vocke to the presidents of the Central Bank Council, 2 March 1950, HADB, RWB, 64.

[424] 'Vorschläge zur Neuordnung der Grossbanken', 27 February 1950, HADB, RWB, 64.

[425] From the minutes of the meeting, quoted in Horstmann, *Die Alliierten*, p. 232.

[426] Quoted in Wolf, 'Dreier-Lösung', p. 32.

[427] Ibid., p. 33.

[428] HADB, RWB, 64.

[429] Minutes in HADB, RWB, 64.

[430] Minutes by Dr Herold, in HADB, RWB, 64.

[431] Abs to State Secretary Alfred Hartmann, Federal Finance Ministry, 7 June 1950, HADB, RWB, 64. The lists of the Allied and German bank experts and politicians who received a copy of either the English or German version of the memorandum are located in HADB, Dezentralisierung, Korrespondenz, 024/1 and 024/3–I,II.

[432] On the position of the Land Central Banks and the HICOG, see Horstmann, *Die Alliierten*, pp. 238–45.

[433] Ibid., p. 248.

[434] See Loehr, *West German Banking System*, p. 62.

[435] Wolf, 'Dreier-Lösung', p. 35.

[436] Quoted in Horstmann, *Die Alliierten*, p. 251.

[437] Loehr, *West German Banking System*, p. 58.

[438] Memorandum by E.W. Schmidt on the meeting in Unkel and letter Abs to Rösler, 2 September 1950, HADB, RWB, 65. The meeting in Unkel was preceded by a discussion between Schäffer and the finance ministers of the *Länder* and members of the Central Bank Council in the 'Haus der Länder' in Königstein on 15 June 1950. For more on this and on the meeting in Unkel, see Wolf, 'Dreier-Lösung', pp. 34–6.

[439] Horstmann, *Die Alliierten*, p. 243. For more on the thoroughly constructive rounds of negotiation between the Germany government and Allied financial experts at the administrative headquarters of the Allied High Commission at Petersberg from June until September 1950, see the notes of the Deutsche Bank delegate Dr Hermann Herold and those of the head of the bank division of the Bank deutscher Länder Dr Rudolf Eicke, in HADB, Dezentralisierung, Korrespondenz, 024/3-I.

[440] Loehr, *West German Banking System*, p. 59.

[441] Quoted in Horstmann, *Die Alliierten*, p. 253.

[442] Ibid., p. 255. For the response of the Allies to the various German draft laws during this period, see Loehr, *West German Banking System*, pp. 59–65.

[443] See Horstmann, *Die Alliierten*, pp. 255–6, and especially HADB, RWB, 65.

[444] The entire course of events is documented in HADB, RWB, 65.

[445] In a letter dated 6 September 1950, HADB, RWB, 65. For the following, see also RWB, 65, and HADB, Dezentralisierung, Korrespondenz, 024/3-I.

[446] HADB, RWB, 65.

[447] Memorandum by Herold, 11 September 1950, HADB, RWB, 65.

[448] Horstmann, *Die Alliierten*, p. 257.

[449] Memorandum by E.W. Schmidt, 'Betr. Rezentralisierung der Grossbanken', 3 October 1950, HADB, RWB, 65. Following this meeting, the Deutsche Bank Group discontinued its press campaign in order to avoid angering the 'Bavarian lion'. See letter E.W. Schmidt to Hunscha, 2 October 1950, ibid.

[450] Memorandum by Frowein, 'Betr.: Neuordnung der Grossbanken', 16 October 1950, HADB, RWB, 65.

[451] Ibid.

[452] On this and the following, see Horstmann, *Die Alliierten*, pp. 261–4.

[453] Loehr, *West German Banking System*., pp. 60–1.

[454] Horstmann, *Die Alliierten*, pp. 265–6; Loehr, *West German Banking System*, pp. 61–2.

[455] For a list of the participants at this meeting, see Pohl, *Abs*, p. 120.

[456] Minutes of the meeting of the Allied Bank Commission in Frankfurt on 19 January 1951, with the plan proposed by Beerensson and his proposals for limiting the investment of successor banks in each other and their proxy voting rights; all dated 20 January 1951, HADB, file: Neuordnung der Grossbanken nach dem Kriege.

[457] Loehr, *West German Banking System*, p. 63.

[458] On this and the following, see Horstmann, *Die Alliierten*, pp. 275–8.

[459] Memoranda dated 29 February 1952, Dr Herold, 'Neuordung der Grossbanken' and

Dr E.W. Schmidt, 'Verabschiedung des Bankengesetzes durch den Bundestag am 28.2.1952', HADB, RWB, 67.

460 Memorandum of 1 November 1947, 'Betr.: Ausstattung der aus den Grossbank-niederlassungen neu entstandenen Regionalinstitute mit Kapital', pp. 3, 5, HADB, RWB, 7.

461 Horstmann, *Die Alliierten*, p. 281. Memorandum by Dr Herold, 29 February 1952, HADB, RWB, 67.

462 A statement on capital resources in Manfred Pohl, *Konzentration im deutschen Bankwesen 1848–1980* (Frankfurt a.M. 1982), p. 450.

463 Memorandum by Schäffer, 25 January 1952, quoted in Horstmann, *Die Alliierten.*, p. 281.

464 According to the FDP member of the Bundestag Dr Preusker in the parliamentary debate on 28 February 1952. See memorandum by Dr Herold, 29 February 1952, HADB, RWB, 67.

465 Manuscript of an article by E.W. Schmidt, 'Bankengesetz verabschiedet', 3 March 1952, HADB, RWB, 67.

466 Newspaper reports on this are located in HADB, RWB, 67.

467 *Bundesgesetzblatt* (1952), part I, pp. 217–20.

468 See the enclosure accompanying the letter from Bechtolf to Abs and Rösler, 3 August 1954, HADB, RWB, 88.

469 This and other legal details are summarized well in Hermann Herold, 'Die Neuordnung der Grossbanken im Bundesgebiet', *Neue Juristische Wochenschrift* 5 (1952), pp. 481–4, 566–8.

470 The entire old bank balance sheet for the Deutsche Bank is located in HADB, file: Deutsche Bank (Altbank) Hauptversammlung, 12 December 1974.

471 Ibid.

472 So the title of a memorandum quoted in Horstmann, *Die Alliierten*, p. 282.

473 This assurance was included in Art. 3 'Big Banks', part two of the Bonn Conventions of 27 May 1952; Pohl, *Abs*, p. 122. Not only were the responsible ministries informed of the Allied demand for a three-year moratorium, but also the Bundestag Committee for Money and Credit, which had debated the bill in a closed-door session on 14 February 1952. Wolf, 'Dreier-Lösung', p. 40.

474 Memoranda by Dr Herold, 26 March 1952, 'Zeitpunkt der Verkündung des Grossbankengesetzes im Bundesgesetzblatt' and Dr E.W. Schmidt, 31 March 1952, 'Bankengesetz', as well as a letter from Ministeraldirigent Dr Gessler, Federal Ministry of Justice, to Senior Vice-President Snowadzki, Rheinisch-Westfälische Bank, in Düsseldorf, HADB, RWB, 67. On 6 September 1954, Abs sent a copy of Adenauer's letter to Rösler in Düsseldorf. The cover letter and Adenauer's letter are located in HADB, RWB, 88, the latter also in HADB, file: Deutsche Bank (Altbank) Hauptversammlung, 12 December 1974, and in HADB, Rezentralisierung, Pool Vertrag, 024. The letter from the Auswärtiges Amt is also located here.

475 See Hermann-Josef Rupieper, *Die Wurzeln der westdeutschen Nachkriegsdemokratie. Der amerikanische Beitrag 1945–1952* (Opladen 1993).

[476] Notes by Manfred Pohl, 'Allgemeine Entwicklung der Deutschen Bank', HADB, file: Deutsche Bank (Altbank) Hauptversammlung, 12 December 1974. The letter itself is located in the HADB, Dezentralisierung, Korrespondenz, 024/3–I.

[477] See the respective meeting minutes, memoranda and letters in HADB, RWB, 67, and HADB, file: Deutsche Bank Neuordnung der Grossbanken nach dem Kriege.

[478] Pohl, *Abs*, p. 122.

[479] Memorandum by Dr Barkhausen, 29 November 1956, HADB, file: Deutsche Bank (Altbank) Hauptversammlung, 12 December 1974. The extensive analysis of the balance sheet items, on which the calculation of the capital resources of the decoupled banks was based, are located in HADB, Dezentralisierung, Korrespondenz, 024/3–II.

[480] Franz Seidel, *Die Nachfolgebanken in Westdeutschland. Ihre Entstehung und Entwicklung auf Grund ihrer Bilanzen* (Vienna 1955), p. 19. For the accounting side of the decoupling process, see also Walter Bauer, 'Die westdeutsche Bankreform. Eine Studie zur Entwicklung des Grossbank- und Zentralbankwesens seit dem Jahre 1945 bis zur Gegenwart', Ph.D. thesis (Tübingen 1954), pp. 189–208.

[481] Seidel, *Nachfolgebanken*, p. 24.

[482] HADB, Frowein, 21.

[483] Supervisory board minutes for the Süddeutsche Bank, in HADB, Frowein, 21, and HADB, files: R. Merton.

[484] Minutes of the joint sessions from 1 October 1952 to 30 April 1957, HADB, Frowein, 23.

[485] 'Probleme zum Zusammenschlusse der Nachfolgeinstitute der Deutschen Bank', in HADB, RWB, 87, and HADB, file: Neuordnung der Grossbanken nach dem Kriege.

[486] Memorandum by Rösler, 2 July 1954, HADB, RWB, 87.

[487] Memorandum by Wienands and Vallenthin, 'Wiedervereinigung der Nachfolgeinstitute der Deutschen Bank', 26 July 1954, HADB, RWB, 87. The other alternatives are also debated here; in the end it was concluded that an amalgamation of the three successor institutions would be the best solution.

[488] Abs to Rösler, 16 September 1954, with memorandum from Winden to Abs, 6 September 1954, HADB, RWB, 87.

[489] Memorandum by Vallenthin, 5 December 1955, HADB, file: Neuordnung der Grossbanken nach dem Kriege.

[490] This treaty was practically a revised version of the Bonn Conventions of 26 May 1952: Steiniger, *Deutsche Geschichte 1945–1961*, pp. 403–4.

[491] Memorandum by Vallenthin, 27 October 1954, HADB, RWB, 87.

[492] Memorandum by Winden, 3 November 1954, HADB, file: Deutsche Bank (Altbank), Hauptversammlung, 12 December 1974.

[493] Rösler to Plassmann, 12 July 1955, HADB, RWB, 87.

[494] HADB, RWB, 87.

[495] Minutes of the *Gemeinschaftssitzungen* from 1 October 1952 until 4 April 1957, HADB, Frowein, 1. The minutes of all nine syndicate meetings are located there, each with an outline of the credit transactions that were discussed.

[496] Memorandum by Vallenthin, 4 August 1955, HADB, RWB, 87.

[497] Memorandum by Vallenthin, 22 September 1955, HADB, RWB, 88.

[498] Ibid.

[499] Ibid.

[500] HADB, RWB, 88.

[501] Memorandum by Siara, 22 October 1955, HADB, RWB, 88.

[502] Ibid.

[503] Vallenthin to Janberg, 11 November 1955, HADB, RWB, 88. This file contains the first drafts of the banks for the long-sought law. See also HADB, file: Rezentralisierung, Pool Vertrag, 024.

[504] Memorandum by Vallenthin, 23 November 1955, HADB, RWB, 88.

[505] Ibid. The draft sent to Dr Schäfer and Prof. Möhring on 23 November 1955 for their evaluation, and other revised drafts, are located in HADB, RWB, 88.

[506] Vallenthin to Dr Schäfer and Prof. Möhring, 5 January 1956, HADB, RWB, 88.

[507] Invitation Dr vom Hofe, 21 January 1956, HADB, RWB, 88.

[508] Memorandum by Vallenthin, 2 February 1956, with legislative draft of the Economics Ministry as enclosure, HADB, RWB, 89.

[509] Memorandum by Vallenthin, 17 February 1956, HADB, RWB, 89.

[510] Memorandum by Vallenthin, 24 February 1956, HADB, RWB, 89.

[511] Letter from Plassmann/Vallenthin to Süddeutsche and Norddeutsche Bank, 21 February 1956, HADB, RWB, 89.

[512] HADB, RWB, 89.

[513] Letter from Plassmann/Vallenthin to the boards of managing directors of the Süddeutsche Bank and Norddeutsche Bank, 29 February 1956, HADB, RWB, 89.

[514] Letter from the Rheinische-Westfälische Bank to the board of managing directors of the Berliner Disconto Bank, 12 March 1956, HADB, RWB, 89.

[515] Letter from the Rheinische-Westfälische Bank to the Norddeutsche Bank and the Süddeutsche Bank, 27 March 1956, HADB, RWB, 89.

[516] HADB, RWB, 89.

[517] Memorandum by Vallenthin on a visit by the Berlin Senator for Federal Affairs, Dr Klein, to RWB Managing Director Janberg, 21 April 1956, HADB, RWB, 89.

[518] Letter from the Deutsche Bank AG West to the board of managing directors of the Norddeutsche Bank, 23 May 1956, HADB, RWB, 90.

[519] Memorandum by Vallenthin, 17 May 1956, letter from Vallenthin to Prof. Möhring, 16 May 1956, and letter from Vallenthin to Frowein, 11 May 1956, HADB, RWB, 89.

[520] Vallenthin to Prof. Möhring, 18 May 1956, HADB, RWB, 90.

[521] Memorandum by Vallenthin, 23 May 1956, and letter from Vallenthin to Abs, 23 May 1956, HADB, RWB, 90.

[522] Letter from Deutsche Bank West to the boards of managing directors of the Norddeutsche Bank and the Süddeutsche Bank, 25 May 1956, HADB, RWB, 90.

[523] Letter from Vallenthin to Abs, 25 May 1956, HADB, RWB, 90.

[524] Ibid. The minutes are located in HADB, file: Wiedervereinigung, Grossbankengesetz, 7 June 1955. Many of the cited documents are also here, specifically from the files RWB, 87–91.

525 The letter is located in HADB, RWB, 90.

526 Now all three successor institutions carried the same name, except for the differing suffixes indicating geographic directions. The Nord- and Süddeutsche Banks had already fought this battle against the opposition of the Allied financial advisers when the original firm names were chosen. See memorandum by Dr Barkhausen, 'Betr.: Firma DEUTSCHE BANK', 10 December 1956, HADB, file: Neuordnung der Grossbanken nach dem Kriege.

527 Vallenthin to Abs, 12 June 1956, and 13 June 1956, HADB, RWB, 90.

528 Memorandum by Vallenthin, 14 June 1956, HADB, RWB, 90.

529 Letter from Deutsche Bank West to the boards of managing directors of the Norddeutsche Bank and Süddeutsche Bank, 20 June 1956, HADB, RWB, 90.

530 Memoranda by Vallenthin, 26 June 1956 and 30 June 1956, on his telephone conversations with Senator Klein, HADB, RWB, 90.

531 Letter from the Deutsche Bank West to the boards of managing directors of the Norddeutsche Bank and the Süddeutsche Bank, 9 July 1956, HADB, RWB, 90.

532 Janberg/Vallenthin to Abs, 10 September 1956, with a memorandum on the discussion enclosed, HADB, RWB, 90.

533 Abs to Janberg, 17 September 1956, HADB, RWB, 90.

534 Memorandum by Dr Schäfer, 'Betr.: Grossbankengesetz', 5 July 1956, HADB, RWB, 90.

535 Various memoranda and letters on this in HADB, RWB, 90.

536 *Bundesgesetzblatt* (1956), part I, p. 1073.

537 Memorandum by Vallenthin, 28 May 1956, HADB, RWB, 90.

538 Memorandum by Vallenthin, 30 June 1956, HADB, RWB, 90.

539 HADB, RWB, 90.

540 Ibid.

541 Janberg to Tron, 19 November 1956, HADB, RWB, 90.

542 Memorandum by Vallenthin, 30 November 1956, HADB, RWB, 90.

543 Memorandum by Siara, 9 January 1957, on this meeting, HADB, RWB, 91.

544 Vallenthin to Siara, 6 November 1956, HADB, RWB, 90.

545 HADB, RWB, 90.

546 Memorandum by Vallenthin, 30 November 1956, HADB, RWB, 90. The draft assessment of the banks for tax exemption is located in HADB, RWB, 91.

547 HADB, RWB, 91.

548 Memorandum by Siara, 1 March 1957, HADB, RWB, 91.

549 Several memoranda on this in HADB, RWB, 91.

550 Letter from the Norddeutsche Bank to the board of managing directors of the Deutsche Bank West, 12 February 1957, with the tax law expert opinion from 11 February 1957 as enclosure, HADB, RWB, 91.

551 A copy of the contract is included in HADB, RWB, 93. It is also printed in the Deutsche Bank business report for 1956.

552 HADB, Frowein, 2, and HADB, RWB, 91.

553 See the amalgamation agreement in HADB, RWB, 93 and the memoranda in HADB,

file: Deutsche Bank (Altbank), Hauptversammlung, 12 December 1974.

554 For the reasons why this happened, see Manfred Pohl, *Baden-Württembergische Bankgeschichte* (Stuttgart 1992), p. 260.

555 HADB, file: Deutsche Bank Regionalbanken 1952–1957.

556 Calculated from statistics cited in Pohl, *Konzentration*, p. 413, and Deutsche Bundesbank (ed.), *Deutsches Geld- und Bankwesen in Zahlen 1876–1975* (Frankfurt a.M. 1976), p. 74.

557 Ibid., p. 127.

558 Ibid., pp. 136, 166.

559 NA, RG 260 (OMGUS), FINAD, Records Relating to Financial Institutions Policy 1945–1949, Box 134, Folder: Banking, memorandum from A.J. Warner to L.M. Pumphrey, 'Decentralization of Banking', 9 February 1950.

560 'All of the sister banks exchange their most important business figures with each other every month', stated Plassmann in his talk to supervisory board members of the old Deutsche Bank on 19 December 1949. HADB, Aufsichtsrat der Deutschen Bank, vol. III. The special committee for bank supervision at the bizonal Länderrat had passed a resolution explicitly to permit this; it stated that 'mutual instructions' would not be tolerated, but 'a certain exchange of experience is considered safe'. Quoted in Wolf, 'Dreier-Lösung', p. 30.

561 HADB, RWB, 440, with minutes.

562 Minutes of the meetings of the board of managing directors from 19 January 1948 to 31 October 1953, HADB, RWB, 434.

563 Wolfgang Stützel, 'Banken, Kapital und Kredit in der zweiten Hälfte des 20. Jahrhunderts', in Fritz Neumark (ed.), *Strukturwandlungen einer wachsenden Wirtschaft*, vol. 2 (Berlin 1964), pp. 527–75, at 527.

564 Carl-Ludwig Holtfrerich, 'Zur Entwicklung der deutschen Bankenstruktur', in Deutscher Sparkassen- und Giroverband (ed.), *Standortbestimmung. Entwicklungslinien der deutschen Kreditwirtschaft* (Stuttgart 1984), pp. 13–42.

565 Calculated from statistics cited in Pohl, *Konzentration*, pp. 413, 437, 455–9.

566 Wolf, 'Dreier-Lösung', p. 29.

567 Speech by Plassmann at the extraordinary general meeting of the Deutsche Bank in Berlin, 25 September 1952, HADB, file: Clemens Plassmann.

568 Pohl, *Konzentration*, p. 413. Due to the war, the business report for 1944 is a short, typewritten report located in HADB, file: Deutsche Bank (Altbank), Hauptversammlung, 12 December 1974.

569 See section I.3.

570 Memorandum by Suchsland, 15 November 1946, HADB, RWB, 5.

571 Monthly report of the Reichsbank chief office in Hamburg for August 1946 with monthly statistics on the development of deposits at the big banks and savings banks in the British zone, HADBB. See also the corresponding reports for the following months. Since nearly a third of all deposits were blocked as part of the denazification measures (at the Deutsche Bank only a quarter, see Report No. 5) the relative decrease camouflages the actual degree to which deposits shrank. Monthly data on the entire

deposits of all credit institutions in the British zone from July 1946 (93.3 billion RM) until May 1947 (87.3 billion RM) show that deposits dropped especially rapidly by 2 billion RM both in September 1946 and April 1947. Memorandum by the Reichsbank chief office in Hamburg, 'The Development of the German Banking System', p. 13, 22 September 1947, BEA, OV 34/17. Knut Borchardt has explained the withdrawal of deposits in that period before the currency reform as follows: 'To a large degree taxes were paid not only out of current income, which was hardly sufficient for that purpose, but by depleting financial wealth.' See his 'Realkredit- und Pfandbriefmarkt im Wandel von 100 Jahren', *100 Jahre Rheinische Hypothekenbank* (Frankfurt a.M. 1971), p. 145.

[572] Minutes of the Hamburg meeting from 10–11 December 1946, HADB, RWB, 440.

[573] Copy of the *Zeit* article and other information on it, in HADB, RWB, 5.

[574] Available in HADBB.

[575] Ibid., Economic Report No. 2.

[576] Ibid., Economic Report No. 1.

[577] Ibid., Economic Report No. 2.

[578] Monthly report of the Reichsbank chief office in Hamburg, Nos. 1 and 8, HADBB. Rudolph, 'Effekten- und Wertpapierbörsen', pp. 294–6.

[579] Monthly report of the Reichsbank chief office in Hamburg, Nos. 17, 19, 20, HADBB.

[580] Rheinisch-Westfälische Bank (ed.), *Die deutschen Börsen im Jahre 1948, HADB.*

[581] As Table 7 illustrates, by the end of the second quarter in 1955, the market price of the Deutsche Bank successor bank shares had risen to 226 per cent, to which 60 percentage points must be added again for the subscription ex rights. This 286 per cent of the nominal value for a 1,000 RM share of the Deutsche Bank Group, converted originally into 625 DM, equals 1,787.50 DM.

[582] Speech by Plassmann on 25 September 1952, HADB, file: Clemens Plassmann.

[583] See the progress report by A. Neuburger, custodian of the Südwestbank, to the finance ministry of Württemberg-Baden, 12 January 1949, in NA, RG 260 (OMGUS), FINAD, Records Relating to Financial Institution Policy 1945–1949, Box 133, Folder: Bank Decentralization.

[584] Ibid.

[585] Harald Winkel, *Die Wirtschaft im geteilten Deutschland 1945–1970* (Wiesbaden 1974), p. 59. Gerold Ambrosius, *Die Durchsetzung der Sozialen Marktwirtschaft in Westdeutschland 1945–1949* (Stuttgart 1977), p. 183.

[586] Schmidt, 'Kreditbanken nach der Währungsreform', p. 5.

[587] Despite this it still continued to rise rapidly. See Schmidt, 'Kreditbanken nach der Währungsreform', p. 5.

[588] Enclosure for letter from Plassmann to Oesterlink, 20 December 1949, HADB, Aufsichtsrat der Deutschen Bank, vol. III.

[589] Siegfried C. Cassier, *Biographie einer Unternehmerbank* (Frankfurt a.M. 1977), pp. 157–80, and Herbert Wolf, 'Geld und Banken nach dem Zweiten Weltkrieg', in Hans Pohl (ed.) *Europäische Bankengeschichte* (Frankfurt a.M. 1993), pp. 517–50, at 518–9.

[590] Schmidt, 'Kreditbanken nach der Währungsreform', had already presented a similarly positive evaluation of the banks' foreign business on 30 August 1949.

[591] Manuscript of Plassmann's speech at the meeting of the supervisory board of the Deutsche Bank, 7 April 1952, HADB, RWB, 409.

[592] Ibid.

[593] On this see Heiner R. Adamsen, *Investionshilfe für die Ruhr. Wiederaufbau, Verbände und soziale Markwirtschaft 1948–1952* (Wuppertal 1981), pp. 199–235.

[594] A complete, but indicatively short list of issued securities, in which the Rheinisch-Westfälische Bank was involved after the currency reform, with the corresponding nominal volume, the underwriting share and the percentage placed is located in the HADB, RWB, 409. A thorough study of the Federal Republic's capital market, including its regulation by the government, especially in the period from the currency reform to the mid-1950s, has been presented by Borchardt, 'Realkredit', pp. 157–84.

[595] Joachim Christopeit, *Hermes-Deckungen* (Munich 1968), p. 12.

[596] HADB, personnel file: Rösler.

[597] HADB, RWB, 390.

[598] 76-page manuscript by Erhard Ulbricht, 'Die Rheinisch-Westfälische Bank' from July 1951, HADB, file: Nachfolgebanken 1947–1952 (I).

[599] Ibid.

[600] Werner Abelshauser, *Wirtschaftsgeschichte der Bundesrepublik Deutschland 1945–1980* (Frankfurt a.M. 1983), p. 74.

[601] Annual figures for all ten regional banks are located in the report of the Treuverkehr Wirtschaftsprüfung-AG, 28 August 1952, pp. 15–20, HADB, file B, Banken, inländisch, Deutsche Bank Berlin, until December 1961.

[602] Detailed information on this can be found in Kurt Pritzkoleit, *Bosse, Banken, Börsen. Herren über Geld und Wirtschaft* (Vienna 1954), pp. 114–46.

[603] Statistics on tax benefits for savings deposits, 7 February 1955, HADB, Frowein, 27. For all savings deposits: SDB Business Report for 1954.

[604] Deutsche Gesellschaft für Wertpapiersparen m.b.H., Hamburg, minutes of the meeting of the consortium on 27 July 1956, HADB, Frowein, 3. In the summer of 1953, there was only one such capital investment company in the Federal Republic, namely the Allgemeine Deutsche Investment G.m.b.H. in Munich, with two funds: FONDRA (stocks and bonds) and FONDAK (just stocks); see enclosure to confidential memorandum, 20 August 1953, HADB, Frowein, 1. The Deutsche Bank group was not involved in this.

[605] Comprehensive data on the personnel structure and the percentage of women in the workforce in the ten regional banks, including the occupational status, are located in the report of the Treuverkehr Wirtschaftsprüfung-AG, 28 August 1952, 25–7, HADB, file B, Banken, inländisch, Deutsche Bank Berlin, until December 1961.

[606] Evaluation of the balance sheet and the profit and loss account of the Deutsche Bank for the business year 1957, p. 45, HADB, Frowein, 18.

[607] A summary of the most important balance sheet items and profit and loss accounts of the successor institutions for 1952–56 is located in HADB, RWB, 47.

608 Compilation of results from the profit and loss accounts of the Deutsche Bank Group for the period between 1 January 1952 and 31 December 1956, HADB, Frowein, 16.

609 Memorandum by Frowein on the meeting of the board of managing directors in Düsseldorf on 11 June 1952, HADB, RWB, 434.

610 Memorandum, 'Betr.: Zinsmarge/Pressemitteilung', 12 May 1953, HADB, Frowein, 27. Minutes on the fifth meeting of the supervisory board of the Süddeutsche Bank in Munich on 5 November 1953, HADB, Frowein, 21.

611 Evaluation of the balance sheet and the profit and loss account of the Deutsche Bank for the business year 1957, p. 40, HADB, Frowein, 18.

612 Gerald Epstein/Thomas Ferguson, 'Monetary Policy, Loan Liquidation, and Industrial Conflict. The Federal Reserve and the Open Market Operations of 1932', *Journal of Economic History* 44 (1984), pp. 957–83.

613 Memorandum by R. Merton, 4 May 1953, HADB, Frowein, 21.

614 The currency reserves of the Bundesbank rose from 0.7 billion DM in 1950 to 5.6 billion DM in 1953. Deutsche Bundesbank (ed.), *40 Jahre Deutsche Mark. Monetäre Statistiken 1948–1987* (Frankfurt a.M. 1988), p. 26.

615 Business Report of the Süddeutsche Bank for 1953.

616 The profit shares from non-profit housing firms were also exempted from taxation, as was, retroactively, the interest from fixed-interest securities that had been officially recognized as financing for promotable projects. See *Bundesgesetzblatt* (1952), part I, pp. 793–6, and (1953), part I, p. 190. The effects of the Federal Government's measures to promote the development of the capital market have been studied in detail by Borchardt, 'Realkredit', pp. 165–84. See also Rudolph, 'Effekten- und Wertpapierbörsen', pp. 297–9.

617 A table listing the various individual loans of this sort issued by the Rheinisch-Westfälische Bank (total value 29.3 million DM) and the Norddeutsche Bank (total value 14.5 million DM) between the end of 1952 and the end of 1954 is located in HADB, 'Unterlagen zur Gemeinschaftssitzung', 1 October 1956, Frowein, 3. See also memorandum by Walther, 4 December 1952, 'Betr.: Buchmässige Behandlung der 7c Darlehn', HADB, Frowein, 27.

618 See the identically worded section I in each of the 1953 Business Reports of the Rheinisch-Westfälische Bank, the Süddeutsche Bank and the Norddeutsche Bank.

619 Ibid. Exact figures starting in July 1948 on a monthly basis are available in *Statistisches Handbuch der Bank deutscher Länder 1948–1954* (Frankfurt a.M. 1955), pp. 232–41. According to this source, the turnover of tax-free, fixed-interest securities in 1953 amounted to a total value of 2,435 million DM, compared with a total value of only 467 million DM in taxable bonds and 269 million DM in stock.

620 Minutes on the sixth supervisory board meeting of the Süddeutsche Bank, HADB, Frowein, 21. Abs used similar arguments in his address at the fifth supervisory board meeting, ibid.

621 See the identically worded section I of the 1954 Business Reports of the Rheinisch-Westfälische Bank, the Süddeutsche Bank and the Norddeutsche Bank.

622 It is indicative of this new situation that the 1955 Business Reports include for the

first time long lists of shares taken, issued or introduced by the bank group.

[623] Minutes of the eighth meeting of the supervisory board of the Süddeutsche Bank, 1 October 1954, HADB, file: Dr Richard Merton, Aufsichtsrat-Süddeutsche Bank, 1 September 1952–31 March 1955.

[624] See the summarized statements of principal securities taken, issued and introduced by the banks in the Business Reports of 1954 for the Rheinisch-Westfälische Bank, the Süddeutsche Bank and the Norddeutsche Bank.

[625] 1956 Business Report for the Deutsche Bank Group.

[626] 'Statistische Erfassung des Rentengeschäfts im Jahre 1957', HADB, Frowein, 27.

[627] The most comprehensive summary of the participations of the Deutsche Bank Group, including data on the capital of each of the firms and usually the participation percentages, is found in Commerzbank (ed.), *Wer gehört zu Wem? Mutter- und Tochtergesellschaften von A–Z*, 1954–57.

[628] Paper by Erhard Ulbricht, 'Betr.: Auswirkungen der Fusion', p. 11, 22 November 1956, HADB, RWB, 90. See also ibid., 'Wertpapiere der Trinitas Vermögensverwaltung GmbH', as of 23 November 1956. There are 45 types of company share with a pro memoria value of 1 DM. The largest among the seven other values totalling 12.2 million DM in the balance sheet was the value of Deutsche Bank salvage shares, which equalled 8.6 million DM.

[629] Minutes of this meeting of the board of managing directors for the entire bank group are located in HADB, RWB, 434.

[630] See the comments by Abs at the eighth meeting of the supervisory board of the Süddeutsche Bank on 1 October 1954, and the ninth meeting of the same board on 24 March 1955, in HADB, file: Dr Richard Merton, Aufsichtsrat-Süddeutsche Bank, 1 September 1952–31 March 1955. During the German occupation of the Netherlands, the Deutsche Bank had had control of over 96 per cent of the share capital of de Bary. See Deutsches Wirtschaftsinstitut (ed.), *Konzentration*, p. 17. At a meeting of the board of managing directors of the Deutsche Bank on 10 August 1951, the topic of the de Bary shares, which had been confiscated by the Dutch government, was addressed. It was also decided to pay out pensions in needy cases to former employees of de Bary, for whom de Bary itself refused to make any payments, evidently because these people had collaborated with the Germans. Minutes of the above-mentioned meeting, HADB, RWB, 434.

[631] Papers pertaining to item 4 of the joint board meeting of the Deutsche Bank Group on 7 February 1953, HADB, Frowein, 1.

[632] Comments by Abs at the eighth meeting of the supervisory board of the Süddeutsche Bank on 1 October 1954, HADB, file: Dr Richard Merton, Aufsichtsrat-Süddeutsche Bank, 1 September 1952–31 March 1955. For more on the recall, see minutes of the meeting of the board of managing directors for the entire Deutsche Bank, 29 January 1951, HADB, RWB, 434.

[633] A summary of these numerous holdings in mortgage banks and shipping banks is included in papers pertaining to item 3 of the joint board meeting of the Deutsche Bank Group on 3 May 1955, HADB, Frowein, 1.

[634] An overview of the most important holdings is available in the stock exchange pamphlets on the various capital increases, in HADB, file: Regionalbanken 1952–1957.

[635] Plassmann's speech, 'Unsere Bank', given at the 'community hour' of the Rheinisch-Westfälische Bank on 4 November 1950, pp. 29–30, HADB, file: Clemens Plassmann.

[636] A copy of the charter is located in HADB, Aufsichtsrat der Deutschen Bank, vol. III.

[637] Plassmann, 'Unsere Bank', p. 22, HADB, file: Clemens Plassmann.

[638] For more on the demands from Berlin and the legal status, see HADB, RWB, 10; and HADB, Aufsichtsrat der Deutschen Bank, vol. III.

[639] Speech manuscript of 3 April 1954, for the supervisory board meeting in Düsseldorf on 7 April 1952, HADB, RWB, 409; manuscript of Erhard Ulbricht, 'Die Rheinisch-Westfälische Bank', pp. 35–6, HADB, file: Nachfolgebanken 1947–1952 (I).

[640] Compilation by Erhard Ulbricht, 25 January 1956, HADB, RWB, 88.

[641] Compilation of the contributions over 1,000 DM made by the head office of the Süddeutsche Bank in 1956, HADB, Frowein, 27.

Deutsche Bank from 1957 to the Present: The Emergence of an International Financial Conglomerate

[1] A responsibility for international sectors was established solely at central office in Düsseldorf within the scope of the Foreign Department, but only at deputy level. There was no differentiation between international competences.

[2] In a paper at the Bank and Stock Exchange Department of the University of Cologne in 1993.

[3] Ulrich Weiss, 'Aufbauorganisation einer Europabank', *Mitteilungen und Berichte des Instituts für Bankwirtschaft und Bankrecht der Universität zu Köln*, Abt. Bankwirtschaft 21 (1990), no. 63, pp. 1ff.

[4] Meeting on 13 September 1929, minutes of the discussion, HADB, file: Rummel.

[5] Klaus Mertin, 'Das Rechnungswesen einer Großbank im Spannungsbereich veränderter Umfeldbedingungen', *Wirtschaft und Wissenschaft im Wandel*, anniversary publication for Dr Carl Zimmerer on his 60th birthday (Frankfurt a.M. 1986), pp. 233–45.

[6] Jürgen Krumnow, 'Das Betriebsergebnis der Banken – ein aussagefähiger Erfolgsindikator?', *Zeitschrift für das gesamte Kreditwesen* 46 (1993), part 2, pp. 64–8.

[7] See Jürgen Krumnow, 'Operatives Controlling im Bankkonzern', in Jürgen Krumnow, *Rechnungswesen im Dienste der Bankpolitik* (Stuttgart 1987), p. 129.

[8] See Jürgen Krumnow, 'Strategisches Bankencontrolling – organisatorische und instrumentelle Führungsunterstützung in einem Bankkonzern', in Peter Horvarth (ed.),

Strategieunterstützung durch das Controlling. Revolution im Rechnungswesen? (Stuttgart 1990).

[9] Jürgen Krumnow, 'Controlling im Konzern Deutsche Bank', paper given at the agplan Arbeitsgemeinschaft für Planung e.V. on 19 September 1990 in Frankfurt.

[10] Alfred Herrhausen, 'Zielvorstellungen und Gestaltungsmöglichkeiten einer Langfristplanung in Kreditinstituten', *Bank-Betrieb* 11 (1971), no. 10, p. 354.

[11] Hilmar Kopper, 'Die Zeit ist reif. Neue Leitlinien und Ziele für die Deutsche Bank', *Forum* (1993), no. 1, p. 3.

[12] Ulrich Weiss, 'Warum brauchen wir die Leitlinien?', *Forum* (1993), no. 1, p. 5.

[13] Ulrich Weiss, 'Menschen in der Bank', *Zeitschrift für das gesamte Kreditwesen* 43 (1990), part 17, pp. 872–6.

[14] Padraic Fallon, 'The battle plans of Hilmar Kopper' (Interview), *Euromoney* (January 1994), pp. 34ff.

[15] As at 31 December.

[16] The analysis as at the end of 1991 was carried out by the 'Investor Relations' department for the first time. The department could give no reasons for the rather strong decline in numbers of institutional investors in 1991 – as compared to the figures for the two previous years; a possible reason may lie in the shortcomings of earlier surveys.

[17] Quoted according to *Wirtschaftswoche*, no. 48, 26 November 1993.

[18] Wilfried Guth, 'Verantwortung der Banken – heute', Wilfried Guth, *Weltwirtschaft und Währung, Aufsätze und Vorträge 1967–1989*, (Mainz 1989), pp. 389ff.

[19] In connection with the unbelievable mistakes by the Chairman of Metallgesellschaft, Supervisory Board Chairman Ronaldo Schmitz, a member of Deutsche Bank's board of management, is heavily criticized by the public for having 'strongly neglected his supervisory duty' and having learned 'about the group's impending insolvency much earlier than hitherto known'.

[20] Fallon, 'The battle plans of Hilmar Kopper', pp. 29ff.

[21] See Friedrich Wilhelm Christians, *Wege nach Russland. Bankier im Spannungsfeld zwischen Ost und West*, 2nd edition (Hamburg 1990), for what follows.

[22] On the Yamal project see ibid, pp. 81 ff.

[23] Ibid., pp. 142 ff.

[24] Ibid., p. 146.

[25] Ibid., pp. 99 ff.

[26] According to 'Geste an den Kapitalmarkt', *Börsen-Zeitung*, 11 November 1993.

[27] Circular no. 11/76, 20 October 1976.

[28] This refers, on the one hand, to product policy measures – expansion of db-Unternehmens-Service – and, on the other hand, to classical strategic 'coups' such as the takeover of Roland Berger & Partner and the related foundation of Deutsche Gesellschaft für Mittelstandsberatung.

[29] Rolf-E. Breuer, 'Europa ist total overbanked' (Interview), *Finanz und Wirtschaft*, (1990), pp. 33f.

[30] Quoted according to *Capital* (1993), no. 12, p. 167.

[31] See Hermann J. Abs, 'Parallel loans to mobilize continental funds', *The Times*, 11 March 1964.

[32] An unnamed member of the Morgan Stanley executive board in *Institutional Investor*, December 1976.

[33] Hilmar Kopper, *Entwicklungen und Perspektiven des Investment Banking*, paper given to the Working Group of European Students in St Gallen on 17 January 1989.

[34] See Eckart van Hooven, 'Wandlungen im Bankgeschäft mit der privaten Kundschaft', *Beiträge zu Wirtschafts- und Währungsfragen und zur Bankgeschichte* 12 (1974), p. 3 (reprinted Mainz 1988).

[35] Although it appears – at first glance – that the term 'P' was chosen to designate a group of the bank's services, it must be noted that the choice of the term 'P' was rather a random one.

[36] Krupp chose as the heading for an article relevant to the subject in *Die Bank* (1993), no. 2, 'Bankpreise zwischen wirtschaftlichen und "politischen" Notwendigkeiten' and lamented a 'communication deficit'.

[37] Eckart van Hooven, quoted according to W. Kohler, 'Dem Reisescheckmarkt steht ein heisser Kampf bevor', in *FAZ*, 4 October 1979, p. 10.

[38] Today, owing to a sharp decline in significance, often belittled as 'grandfather's savings account'.

[39] Ulrich Weiss, 'Sparmarketing in der Inflation', part 1, *Bank-Betrieb* 14 (1974), no. 12, p. 495.

[40] Eckart van Hooven, in a discussion on 'Wachstumschancen der Banken im Privatkundengeschäft' in the Bank and Stock Exchange Department of the University of Cologne on 11 January 1989.

[41] Headline in *Wirtschaftswoche*, 20 March 1987.

[42] Deutsche Bank, *30 Years of Private Banking*, special issue, p. 15.

[43] See Robert Ehret, 'Strukturwandel der Effektenkundschaft', paper given at the 17th Kreditpolitische Tagung in Frankfurt in 1971.

[44] Even the *Handelsblatt*, known for its friendly attitude towards the (big) banks, is critical of such a measure because it does not fit a time of high inflation rates, in particular on account of increasingly expensive services and the good economic situation of the banks.

[45] Breuer, as the responsible member of the board of managing directors, disputed this (see *FAZ*, 1 September 1992) and also described Deutsche Bank's 100 per cent subsidiary located at head office as independent. The latter point is at least not undisputed. *Der Spiegel* (1994), no. 8, p. 90, for example, noted in connection with the Metallgesellschaft affair: 'It is, after all, strange that a study done by DB Research at the end of 1992 and critical of the company's situation and capital consumption was never published.' After complaints by MG's management board chairman to Schmitz of Deutsche Bank's board of managing directors, 'a discussion took place between MG top management and DB's – actually independent – analysts. Official result: the study was not published as some questions were still open.' In 1993 MG was on the verge of bankruptcy.

[46] Hilmar Kopper, 'Wir verkaufen, was dem Kunden Freude macht', *Cash* (1991), no. 6, p. 19.

[47] Georg Krupp, 'Bankstrategien im Versicherungsgeschäft', *Die Bank* (1993), no. 6, p. 334.

[48] It is usual for this business to pay 1 DM for every premium mark.

[49] Krupp, 'Bankstrategien im Versicherungsgeschäft', p. 334.

[50] See Ronaldo H. Schmitz, 'Global Financial Services', paper given at the spring conference of the ICC on 13 May 1991 in Berlin.

[51] Alfred Herrhausen, 'Strategische Führung – Mehr als nur Strategie', in Herbert A. Henzler (ed.), *Handbuch Strategische Führung* (Wiesbaden 1988), p. 62; Alfred Herrhausen, 'Die Zukunft des Universalbankensystems', paper given in Stuttgart-Hohenheim on 25 May 1988.

[52] Klaus Mertin, 'Globalisierung der Finanzmärkte – Chancen und Risiken der Banken', *Börsenzeitung* (13 June 1987).

[53] This term, too, is no longer in favour today; when asked 'Do you have a vision for this bank?' Kopper replied 'No. A vision often turns into an illusion.' Fallon, 'The battle plans of Hilmar Kopper', p. 29.

[54] See Hilmar Kopper, 'Neue Aufgaben und Ziele im Marketing einer internationalen Bank', in Rosemarie Kolbeck (ed.), *Bankmarketing vor neuen Aufgaben* (Frankfurt a.M. 1992), pp. 107–17.

[55] Jürgen Krumnow, 'Die Deutsche Bank auf dem Weg in die 90er Jahre', paper given to the Europe India Foundation e.V. on 28 July 1989 in Oberursel.

[56] See Schmitz, 'Global Financial Services'.

[57] Ibid.

[58] Ibid.

[59] Ibid.

[60] Ibid.

[61] Ibid.

[62] Since this statement was made on 23 October 1989 in Cologne, it suggests that Kopper puts the beginning of internationalization roughly in 1977. He seems to refer here to the third phase of the bank's internationalization, during which – from around 1976 onwards – it is increasingly represented by branches and subsidiaries on the international bank and financial markets.

[63] Hilmar Kopper, 'Die Deutsche Bank auf dem Weg in die Zukunft', remarks during the 'db intern' meeting on 23 October 1989 in Cologne.

[64] Schmitz, 'Global Financial Services'.

[65] Ibid.

[66] Alfred Herrhausen, 'Die strategischen Implikationen der Globalisierung für die deutschen Banken', paper given at the Institut für Kapitalmarktforschung at the Johann Wolfgang Goethe-Universität Frankfurt on 18 February 1988, pp. 177–92.

[67] Legal definition of the single European market in article 8a included in the EEC Treaty by the Single European Act.

[68] Jürgen Krumnow, 'Ideal wäre eine französische Investmentbank' (Interview), in *Börse Online* (1990), no. 40, pp. 25–6.

[69] Burkhardt Pauluhn, 'Everything from one source – a strategy for the future', in *Bank und Markt und Technik* 20 (1991), no. 6, pp. 21–3.

[70] Hilmar Kopper, 'Strategische Ausrichtung einer Universalbank auf einen gemeinsamen EG-Finanzmarkt', in Österreichisches Bank-Archiv 38 (1990), no. 2, pp. 67–72.

[71] Krumnow, 'Die Deutsche Bank auf dem Weg in die 90er Jahre', p. 9.

[72] Ibid., p. 10.

[73] Ibid.

[74] Kopper, 'Strategische Ausrichtung einer Universalbank', p. 68.

[75] See Jürgen Krumnow, 'Strategische Herausforderungen an einen Finanzkonzern mit Blick auf Europa 1992', paper given on 13 June 1989 in Gracht castle, Erftstadt.

[76] Jürgen Krumnow, 'Ideal wäre eine französische Investmentbank', p. 25.

[77] See Jürgen Krumnow, 'Finanzdienstleistungen und EG-Binnenmarkt', paper given at the Research Institute for Leasing at the University of Cologne on 2 November 1989.

[78] Krumnow, 'Die Deutsche Bank auf dem Weg in die 90er Jahre', p. 14.

[79] Herrhausen, 'Die strategischen Implikationen'.

[80] Hilmar Kopper in Sybille Zehle, 'Der Erbe', *Manager Magazin* 20 (1990), no. 9, p. 77.

[81] Herrhausen, 'Die strategischen Implikationen', pp. 177–92.

[82] Ibid.

[83] Krumnow, 'Finanzdienstleistungen und EG-Binnenmarkt'.

[84] Georg Krupp, 'Strategien der Deutschen Bank im Markt für Finanzdienstleistungen', paper given during the seminar 'Globalization of Markets and Individualization of Customer Demands' on 9 September 1989 in Lisbon.

[85] Krumnow, 'Finanzdienstleistungen und EG-Binnenmarkt'.

[86] Pauluhn, 'Everything from one source', p. 23.

[87] Fallon, 'The battle plans of Hilmar Kopper', p. 29f.

[88] Kopper, 'Strategische Ausrichtung einer Universalbank'.

[89] This presence of Disconto-Gesellschaft consisted in a participation in the Belgian predecessor of the later Dutch bank Albert de Bary.

[90] According to *Börsen-Zeitung* in February 1978.

[91] The closure was a formal one; a small representative office was maintained and was served from Caracas.

[92] In 1993, with the help of Deutsche Bank, one of the most important new Russian private banks, Pomstrojbank in St Petersburg, opened a representative office in Berlin.

[93] According to *Die Bank* in February 1988.

[94] Bernd Baehring, 'Der Meister und sein Instrument? Die Deutsche Bank vor, mit und nach Alfred Herrhausen', in *Börsen-Zeitung*, no. 30, 13 February 1990.

[95] Herrhausen, 'Die strategischen Implikationen', pp. 177–92.

[96] Ibid.

[97] 'Relatively few banks will have EC-European horizons. And only a small minority will

aim at global dimensions', Alfred Herrhausen, 'Die strategischen Implikationen', pp. 179f.

[98] Bolke Behrens/Mario Müller, 'Insel der Seligen. Interview: Kopper über Konjunktur und Banken', *Wirtschaftswoche* 44 (1990), no. 39, p. 230.

[99] Anton Hunge/Reinhold Müller, 'Die Funkstille war nicht gewollt' (Interview with Hilmar Kopper), *Industriemagazin* (1991), no. 2, pp. 25–8.

[100] Ibid.

[101] Kopper, 'Strategische Ausrichtung einer Universalbank', p. 68.

[102] Hunge/Müller, 'Die Funkstille war nicht gewollt', pp. 25–8.

[103] Ibid.

[104] Schmitz, 'Global Financial Services', p. 12.

[105] Ibid., p. 10.

[106] See ibid., pp. 7ff.

[107] Kopper, 'Strategische Ausrichtung einer Universalbank', p. 72.

[108] Hunge/Müller, 'Die Funkstille war nicht gewollt', pp. 25–8.

[109] Kopper, 'Strategische Ausrichtung einer Universalbank', p. 70.

[110] Baehring, 'Der Meister und sein Instrument?'.

[111] Kopper, 'Strategische Ausrichtung einer Universalbank', p. 70.

[112] Schmitz, 'Global Financial Services', p. 12.

[113] Behrens/Müller, 'Insel der Seligen', p. 230.

[114] Kopper, 'Strategische Ausrichtung einer Universalbank', p. 70.

[115] Schmitz, 'Global Financial Services', p. 12.

[116] Hunge/Müller, 'Die Funkstille war nicht gewollt', pp. 25–8.

[117] Kopper, 'Neue Aufgaben und Ziele', p. 111.

[118] Kopper, 'Strategische Ausrichtung einer Universalbank', p. 68.

[119] Kevin Muehring, 'The Kopper era at Deutsche Bank', *Institutional Investor* (December 1990), p. 43.

[120] Kopper, 'Strategische Ausrichtung einer Universalbank', p. 68.

[121] Schmitz, 'Global Financial Services', p. 13.

[122] Kopper, 'Strategische Ausrichtung einer Universalbank', p. 68.

[123] Krumnow, 'Ideal wäre eine französische Investmentbank', p. 25.

[124] Kopper in Paris to the Association for Supranational Co-operation, quoted according to *FAZ*, 13 December 1992.

[125] Hilmar Kopper, 'Zu warten, daß ein Kunde kommt – das hat sich längst geändert' (Interview), *Cash* (1992), no. 1, pp. 21–5.

[126] Ulrich Weiss, 'Banca de retalhlo deve ser para os portugueses', *Expresso* (Lisbon), 16 November 1991.

[127] Kopper, 'Neue Aufgaben und Ziele', p. 113.

[128] Ibid., p. 10.

[129] Ibid., pp. 11ff.

[130] Ibid., p. 12.

[131] Schmitz, 'Global Financial Services', p. 17.

[132] Ibid.

[133] Ibid., p. 18.

[134] Michael Endres, 'Die europäische Bankenwelt – Entwicklungslinien und Zukunfts-trends', Österreichisches Bank-Archiv 38 (1990), no. 9, p. 660.

[135] Kopper, 'Neue Aufgaben und Ziele', p. 115.

Abbreviations

ACDP	Archiv für Christlich-Demokratische Politik
ADAM	Anleger-Diagnose im Anlagenmanagement [Investor Diagnosis in Private Banking]
AEG	Allgemeine Elektrizitäts-Gesellschaft
AKA	Ausfuhrkredit-Gesellschaft mbH
AKU	Algemeene Kunstzijde Unie
ALD	Autoleasing D GmbH
AMB	Aachener und Münchener Beteiligungs-Aktiengesellschaft
Amexco	American Express Corporation
Arbed	Aciéries Réunies de Burbach-Eich-Dudelange
ASEAN	Association of South-East Asian Nations
ATM	automated teller machine
BAI	Banca d'America e d'Italia
BAK	Bundesarchiv Koblenz
BAP	Bundesarchiv Potsdam
Barcom	Barclays Commissionaria
BASF	Badische Anilin- & Soda-Fabrik AG
BAT	Banco Alemán Transatlántico
BCT	Banco Comercial Transatlántico
BDC	Berlin Document Center
BDI	Bundesverband der deutschen Industrie [Federation of German Industries]
BEA	Bank of England Archive
BEC	Banque Européenne de Crédit à Moyen Terme
BHF-Bank	Berliner Handels- und Frankfurter Bank
BICO	Bipartite Control Office
BMW	Bayerische Motoren Werke AG
BoA	Bank of America
Btx	Bildschirmtext
Bufa	Bild- und Filmamt
BVV	Beamtenversicherungsverein
CCS	Combined Chiefs of Staff
CDU	Christlich-Demokratische Union
Cedel	Centrale de livraison de valeurs mobilières
CFDB	Compagnie Financière de la Deutsche Bank

CHADE	Compañía Hispano Americana de Electricidad
CIA	Central Intelligence Agency
CIS	Confederation of Independent States
CMI	Capital Management International GmbH of Deutsche Bank
CMS	cash management system
Comecon	Council for Mutual Economic Assistance
CROWCASS	Central Registry of War Criminals and Security Suspects
CSU	Christlich-Soziale Union
DAB	Deutsch-Asiatische Bank
DABA	Deutsche Außenhandelsbank
DAF	Deutsche Arbeitsfront [German Labour Front]
DANAT-Bank	Darmstädter und Nationalbank
DAX	Deutscher Aktienindex
DB	Deutsche Bank
DBAG	Deutsche Beteiligungs AG Unternehmensbeteiligungsgesellschaft
DBAL	Deutsche Bank Australia Ltd
DBCC	Deutsche Bank Capital Corporation
DBCF	Deutsche Bank Compagnie Financière Luxembourg
DBCM	Deutsche Bank Capital Markets
DBCMA	DB Capital Markets (Asia)
DB Com	Deutsche Bank Commissionaria
DBG	Deutsche Beteiligungsgesellschaft mbH
DBI	Deutsche Bank de Investimento
DBIM	DB Investment Management
DB Lux	Deutsche Bank Luxembourg
DBM&A	DB Mergers & Acquisitions
DBMG	DB Morgan Grenfell
DCC	Deutsche Credit Corporation
DD Bank	Deutsche Bank und Disconto-Gesellschaft [official name of Deutsche Bank from 1929 to 1937]
DDO	Devisen-Direktes-Ordern
DEAG	Deutsche-Erdöl-Aktiengesellschaft
DeDi Bank	Deutsche Bank und Disconto-Gesellschaft [official name of Deutsche Bank from 1929 to 1937]
DEG	Deutsche Edison-Gesellschaft für angewandte Electrizität
degab	Deutsche Gesellschaft für Anlageberatung mbH
DEGEF	Deutsche Gesellschaft für Fondsverwaltung mbH
DEMAG	Deutsche Maschinenbau Aktien-Gesellschaft
Deulig	Deutsche Lichtbild-Gesellschaft
DFIN	Directorate of Finance
DGB	Deutscher Gewerkschaftsbund [German Trades Union Congress]
DGI	Deutsche Grundbesitz-Investmentgesellschaft mbH
DGM	Deutsche Gesellschaft für Mittelstandsberatung mbH
DHV	Deutschnationaler Handlungsgehilfenverband [German National Commercial Assistants' Association]
DIA	Deutsche Immobilienanlagegesellschaft mbH
DIH	Deutsche Industrie-Holding Verwaltungs-GmbH
DIHT	Deutscher Industrie- und Handelstag [Association of German Chambers of Industry and Commerce]
DIL	Deutsche Gesellschaft für Immobilien-Leasing mbH

DKB	Deutsche Kreditbank für Baufinanzierung
DLG	Deutsche Lichtbild-Gesellschaft
DM	Deutsche Mark
DNVP	Deutschnationale Volkspartei
DPAG	Deutsche Petroleum-Aktiengesellschaft
DTB	Deutsche Terminbörse
DUB	Deutsche Ueberseeische Bank
DUEG	Deutsch-Ueberseeische Elektricitäts-Gesellschaft
DVP	Deutsche Volkspartei
DWS	Deutsche Gesellschaft für Wertpapiersparen mbH
DZFV	Deutsche Zentralfinanzverwaltung [Division of German Central Finance]
EAB	European American Banks
EBC	European Banking Company
EBIC	European Banks' International Company
EC	European Community
ECU	European Currency Unit
EDP	electronic data processing
EEC	European Economic Community
EFGEE	Gesellschaft für Einkaufs-Finanzierung mbH
EHB	Europäische Hypothekenbank
EIB	European Investment Bank
ENEL	Ente Nazionale per l'Energia Elettrica
Eos	Erdöl-Syndikat
ERISA	Employee Retirement Income Security Act
ERP	European Recovery Programme
ETCI	Euro Traveller's Cheque International
EU	European Union
EWG	Europäische Wirtschaftsgemeinschaft
EZU	Europäische Zahlungsunion
FAVAG	Frankfurter Versicherungsgesellschaft
FAZ	Frankfurter Allgemeine Zeitung
FDP	Freie Demokratische Partei
FHC	Frankfurter Hypothekenbank Centralboden
FIBOR	Frankfurt Interbank Offered Rate
FINAD	Office of the Finance Adviser & Finance Division
FRUS	Foreign Relations of the United States
GAK	Gewerblicher Anschaffungskredit [commercial medium-sized loan]
GDR	German Democratic Republic
GEFA	Gesellschaft für Absatzfinanzierung mbH
Gestapo	Geheime Staatspolizei [Secret State Security Police]
GM	General Motors
GStA	Geheimes Staatsarchiv
HADB	Historisches Archiv der Deutschen Bank
HADBB	Historisches Archiv der Deutschen Bundesbank
HICOG	US High Commissioner for Germany
ICC	International Chamber of Commerce
IFAGO	Industriefinanzierungs-AG Ost [Industry Finance Corporation East]
IfZ	Institut für Zeitgeschichte
IKB	Industriekreditbank

IMF	International Monetary Fund
IOC	International Olympic Committee
JCS	Joint Chiefs of Staff
JEIA	Joint Export–Import Agency
JFEA	Joint Foreign Exchange Agency
KfW	Kreditanstalt für Wiederaufbau [Reconstruction Loan Corporation]
LIBOR	London Interbank Offered Rate
MAN	Maschinenfabrik Augsburg-Nürnberg
MG	Metallgesellschaft
Misc.	Miscellaneous
Mitropa	Mitteleuropäische Schlaf- und Speisewagen-AG [Central European Sleeping and Dining Car Corporation]
NA	National Archives, Washington DC
NDB	Norddeutsche Bank
NL	Nachlaß [Bequest]
NSBO	Nationalsozialistische Betriebszellenorganisation [National Socialist Factory Cell Organization]
NSDAP	Nationalsozialistische Deutsche Arbeiterpartei [National Socialist German Workers' Party]
NS-HAGO	Nationalsozialistische Handwerks-, Handels- und Gewerbe-Organisation [National Socialist Artisan and Commercial Organization]
OECD	Organization for Economic Co-operation and Development
OEEC	Organization for European Economic Co-operation
OM	Organisation und Management
OMGUS	Office of Military Government for Germany, United States
OPEC	Organization of Petroleum Exporting Countries
ÖTV	Gewerkschaft Öffentliche Dienste, Transport und Verkehr
PAD	Persönliches Anschaffungs-Darlehen [personal loan for specified purposes]
PBG	Pensions-Beratungs-Gesellschaft mbH
PDK	Persönlicher Dispositions-Kredit [personal disposition loan]
Pg.	Parteigenosse [Member of the National Socialist German Workers' Party]
PHD	Persönliches Hypotheken-Darlehen [personal mortgage loan]
PKK	Persönlicher Klein-Kredit [small personal loan]
POLAD	Office of the Political Adviser
POS	point of sale
PPD	Persönliches Praxis-Darlehen [personal practice loan]
PWA	Papierwerke Waldhof-Aschaffenburg
RKG	Reichs-Kredit-Gesellschaft
RM	Reichsmark
RWA	Reichswirtschaftsamt
RWB	Rheinisch-Westfälische Bank
RWE	Rheinisch-Westfälisches Elektrizitätswerk
RWR	Reichswirtschaftsrat
SA	Sturmabteilung [Storm Troopers]
SDB	Süddeutsche Bank
SEC	Securities and Exchange Commission
SED	Sozialistische Einheitspartei Deutschlands

SHAEF	Supreme Headquarters Allied Expeditionary Force
SHL	Schiffshypothekenbank zu Lübeck
SMAD	Soviet Military Administration
SPD	Sozialdemokratische Partei Deutschlands
SS	Schutzstaffel [Guard Echelon]
StA	Staatsarchiv
SWIFT	Society for Worldwide Interbank Financial Telecommunication
Tobis	Tonbild-Syndikat
UBS	Union Bank of Switzerland
UEG	Ungarische Erdgas-Gesellschaft
UfA	Universum-Film Aktiengesellschaft
UNICEF	United Nations International Children's Emergency Fund
UNINSA	Unión de Siderugicas Asturianas
USA	United States of America
USFET	United States Forces, European Theater
USSR	Union of Soviet Socialist Republics
VEBA	Vereinigte Elektrizitäts- und Bergwerks-AG
VEW	Vereinigte Elektrizitätswerke Westfalen
VfZ	Vierteljahrshefte für Zeitgeschichte
VGF	Vereinigte Glanzstoff-Fabriken
VIAG	Vereinigte Industrie-Unternehmungen Aktiengesellschaft
WFG	Deutsche Wagnisfinanzierungs-Gesellschaft mbH

List of Visited Archives

Archiv für Christlich-Demokratische Politik (ACDP), St. Augustin
Bank of England Archive (BEA), London
Berlin Document Center (BDC), Berlin (now Bundesarchiv, Aussenstelle Berlin-Zehlendorf)
Bundesarchiv Koblenz (BAK)
Bundesarchiv Potsdam (BAP)
Geheimes Staatsarchiv Preussischer Kulturbesitz (GStA), Merseburg (files are now in Geheimes Staatsarchiv Preussischer Kulturbesitz, Berlin)
Historisches Archiv der Deutschen Bank (HADB), Frankfurt am Main
Historisches Archiv der Deutschen Bundesbank (HADBB), Frankfurt am Main
Houghton Library, Harvard University, Cambridge, Massachusetts
Institut für Zeitgeschichte (IfZ), Munich
National Archives (NA), Washington DC
Personal Papers Fritz Wintermantel, private property of the family of Dr Dietrich Gröning, Essen
Sächsisches Staatsarchiv, Leipzig
Staatsarchiv (StA), Hamburg
University of Basel
M.M. Warburg & Co., Hamburg
Zentralarchiv der Rheinischen Braunkohlenwerke AG (Rheinbraun-Archiv), Bergheim-Pfaffendorf

Bibliography

Abelshauser, Werner: *Wirtschaftsgeschichte der Bundesrepublik Deutschland 1945–1980.* Frankfurt a.M. 1983

Abelshauser, Werner: *Die langen fünfziger Jahre. Wirtschaft und Gesellschaft der Bundesrepublik Deutschland 1945–1966.* Düsseldorf 1987

Abs, Hermann J.: 'The Structure of the Western German Monetary System'. In: *Economic Journal,* 80 (1950), pp. 481–8

Abs, Hermann J.: *Zeitfragen der Geld- und Wirtschaftspolitik. Aus Vorträgen und Aufsätzen.* Frankfurt a.M. 1959

Abs, Hermann J.: 'Deutschlands wirtschaftlicher und finanzieller Aufbau'. In: Carstens, Karl *et al.* (eds): *Franz Josef Strauss. Erkenntnisse, Standpunkte, Ausblicke.* Munich 1985, pp. 351–70

Abs, Hermann J.: 'Der Weg zum Londoner Schuldenabkommen'. In: Mückl, Wolfgang J. (ed.): *Föderalismus und Finanzpolitik. Gedenkschrift für Fritz Schäffer.* Paderborn 1990, pp. 81–93

Abs, Hermann J.: *Entscheidungen 1949–1953. Die Entstehung des Londoner Schuldenabkommens.* Mainz/Munich 1991

Achterberg, Erich: 'Hermann Wallich'. In: *Zeitschrift für das gesamte Kreditwesen,* 16 (1963), pp. 228–31

Achterberg, Erich: *Berliner Hochfinanz. Kaiser, Fürsten, Millionäre um 1900.* Frankfurt a.M. 1965

Achterberg, Erich/Müller-Jabusch, Maximilian: *Lebensbilder deutscher Bankiers aus fünf Jahrhunderten.* Frankfurt a.M. 1963

Adamsen, Heiner R.: *Investitionshilfe für die Ruhr. Wiederaufbau, Verbände und soziale Marktwirtschaft 1948–1952.* Wuppertal 1981

Adenauer, Konrad: *Briefe 1945–1947.* Berlin 1983

Adler, Hans A.: 'The Post-War Reorganization of the German Banking System'. In: *Quarterly Journal of Economics,* 63 (1949), pp. 322–41

Akten der Reichskanzlei. Die Kabinette Brüning. 3 vols. Boppard am Rhein 1990

Akten der Reichskanzlei. Die Kabinette Wirth I und II. 2 vols. Boppard am Rhein 1973

Allgemeine Elektricitäts-Gesellschaft (ed.): *50 Jahre AEG.* Berlin 1956

Ambrosius, Gerold: *Die Durchsetzung der Sozialen Marktwirtschaft in Westdeutschland 1945–1949.* Stuttgart 1977

Aubin, Hermann/Zorn, Wolfgang (eds): *Handbuch der Deutschen Wirtschafts- und Sozialgeschichte.* Vol. 2. Stuttgart 1976

Backer, John H.: *Priming the German Economy. American Occupational Policies 1945–1948.* Durham, NC 1971

Balderston, Theodore: 'War Finance and Inflation in Germany 1914–1918'. In: *Economic History Review*, 42 (1989), pp. 222–44

Balderston, Theodore: 'German Banking Between the Wars. The Crisis of the Credit Banks'. In: *Business History Review*, 65 (1991), pp. 554–605

Balderston, Theodore: *The Origins and Course of the German Economic Crisis 1923– 1932* (= Schriften der Historischen Kommission zu Berlin 2). Berlin 1993

Balogh, Thomas: *Studies in Financial Organization*. Cambridge 1947

Bamberger, Ludwig: *Erinnerungen*. Edited by Paul Nathan. Berlin 1899

Bank deutscher Länder (ed.): *Statistisches Handbuch der Bank deutscher Länder 1948– 1954*. Frankfurt a.M. 1955

Barkai, Avraham: 'Sozialdarwinismus und Antiliberalismus in Hitlers Wirtschaftskonzept. Zu Henry A. Turner Jr. "Hitlers Einstellung zu Wirtschaft und Gesellschaft vor 1933"'. In: *Geschichte und Gesellschaft*, 3 (1977), pp. 406–17

Barkai, Avraham: *Das Wirtschaftssystem des Nationalsozialismus*. Frankfurt a.M. 1988

Barkai, Avraham: *From Boycott to Elimination. The economic struggle of German Jews, 1933–1943*. Hanover/London 1989

Barkai, Avraham: 'Die deutschen Unternehmer und die Judenpolitik im Dritten Reich'. In: *Geschichte und Gesellschaft*, 15 (1989), pp. 227–47

Bauer, Walter: 'Die westdeutsche Bankreform. Eine Studie zur Entwicklung des Grossbank- und Zentralbankwesens seit dem Jahre 1945 bis zur Gegenwart'. Ph.D. thesis, Tübingen 1954

Behrens, Bolke/Müller, Mario: 'Insel der Seligen. Interview: Kopper über Konjunktur und Banken'. In: *Wirtschaftswoche*, 44 (1990), No. 39, pp. 226–30

Bennett, Edward W.: *Germany and the Diplomacy of the Financial Crisis 1931*. Cambridge, Mass. 1962

Benz, Wolfgang: *Von der Besatzungsherrschaft zur Bundesrepublik. Stationen einer Staatsgründung 1946–1949*. Frankfurt a.M. 1984

Berghahn, Volker: *Unternehmer und Politik in der Bundesrepublik*. Frankfurt a.M. 1985

Berghahn, Volker: *The Americanisation of West German Industry 1945–1973*. Leamington Spa 1986

Berghoff, Hartmut/Müller, Roland: 'Unternehmer in Deutschland und England'. In: *Historische Zeitschrift*, 256 (1993), pp. 353–86

Bernhard, Georg: 'Anklagen in der Generalversammlung': In: *Magazin der Wirtschaft* (Mai 1930), pp. 970–1

Besier, Gerhard: *Die Mittwochs-Gesellschaft im Kaiserreich*. Berlin 1990

Bessell, Georg: *Norddeutscher Lloyd 1857–1957. Geschichte einer bremischen Reederei*. Bremen 1957

Blaich, Fritz: *Staat und Verbände in Deutschland zwischen 1871 und 1945*. Wiesbaden 1979

Blume, Herbert: *Gründungszeit und Gründungskrach mit Beziehung auf das deutsche Bankwesen*. Danzig 1914

Boelcke, Willi A. (ed.): *Kriegspropaganda 1939–1941*. Stuttgart 1966

Boelcke, Willi A.: *Die deutsche Wirtschaft 1930–1945. Interna des Reichswirtschaftsministeriums*. Düsseldorf 1983

Böhme, Helmut: *Deutschlands Weg zur Grossmacht. Studien zum Verhältnis von Wirtschaft und Staat während der Reichsgründungszeit 1848–1881*. 2nd edn. Cologne 1972

Booker, John: *Temples of Mammon. The Architecture of Banking*. Edinburgh 1990

Booms, Hans (ed.): *Die Kabinettsprotokolle der Bundesregierung*. Vol. 1. 1949. Boppard am Rhein 1982

Borchardt, Knut: 'Realkredit- und Pfandbriefmarkt im Wandel von 100 Jahren'. In: *100*

Jahre Rheinische Hypothekenbank. Frankfurt a.M. 1971, pp. 105–96

Borchardt, Knut: 'Zur Frage des Kapitalmangels in der ersten Hälfte des 19. Jahrhunderts in Deutschland'. In: Braun, Rudolf *et al*. (eds): *Industrielle Revolution. Wirtschaftliche Aspekte*. Cologne/Berlin 1972, pp. 216–36

Borchardt, Knut: 'Germany 1700–1914'. In: Cipolla, Carlo M. (ed.): *The Fontana Economic History of Europe*. Vol. 4. *The Emergence of Industrial Societies*, part 1. Glasgow 1973, pp. 76–160

Borchardt, Knut: *Perspectives on Modern German Economic History and Policy*. Cambridge 1991

Born, Karl Erich: *Die deutsche Bankenkrise 1931. Finanzen und Politik*. Munich 1967

Born, Karl Erich: 'Die Hauptentwicklungslinien des mitteleuropäischen Universalbankensystems'. In: *Universalbankensystem als historisches und politisches Problem*. (= Bankhistorisches Archiv Beiheft 2). Frankfurt a.M. 1977, pp. 13–18

Born, Karl Erich: 'Deutsche Bank during Germany's Great Inflation after the First World War'. In: *Studies on Economic and Monetary Problems and on Banking History*, 17 (1979), pp. 11–27. Reprinted Mainz 1988, pp. 495–514

Born, Karl Erich: *International Banking in the 19th and 20th Centuries*. Leamington Spa 1983

Born, Karl Erich: 'Vom Beginn des Ersten Weltkrieges bis zum Ende der Weimarer Republik (1918–1933)'. In: *Deutsche Bankengeschichte*. Edited by the Wissenschaftliche Beirat des Instituts für bankhistorische Forschung. Vol. 3. Frankfurt a.M. 1983, pp. 11–146

Bower, Tom: *The Pledge Betrayed. America and Britain and the Denazification of Postwar Germany*. Garden City, NY 1982

Brackmann, Michael: *Vom totalen Krieg zum Wirtschaftswunder. Die Vorgeschichte der westdeutschen Währungsreform 1948*. Essen 1993

Bredrow, Wilhelm: *Friedrich Krupp der Erfinder und Gründer. Leben und Briefe*. Berlin 1923

Breuer, Rolf-E.: 'Europa ist total overbanked' (interview). In: *Finanz und Wirtschaft* (1990), no. 41, pp. 33–9

Brüning, Heinrich: *Memoiren 1918–1934*. Stuttgart 1970

Buchheim, Christoph: 'Der Ausgangspunkt des westdeutschen Wirtschaftswunders. Zur neueren Diskussion über die Wirkungen von Währungs- und Bewirtschaftungsreform 1948'. In: *IFO- Studien*, 34 (1988), pp. 69–77

Buchheim, Christoph: 'Die Währungsreform 1948 in Westdeutschland'. In: *Vierteljahrshefte für Zeitgeschichte*, 36 (1988), pp. 189–231

Buchheim, Christoph: 'Die Währungsreform in Westdeutschland im Jahre 1948. Einige ökonomische Aspekte'. In: Fischer, Wolfram (ed.): *Währungsreform und Soziale Marktwirtschaft. Erfahrungen und Perspektiven nach 40 Jahren*. Berlin 1989, pp. 391–402

Buchheim, Christoph: *Die Wiedereingliederung Westdeutschlands in die Weltwirtschaft 1945–1958*. Munich 1990

Buchheim, Christoph: 'Marshall Plan and Currency Reform'. In: Diefendorf, Jeffry *et al*. (eds): *American Policy and the Reconstruction of West Germany 1945–1955*. Cambridge 1993, pp. 69–83

Bührer, Werner: *Ruhrstahl und Europa. Die Wirtschaftsvereinigung Eisen- und Stahlindustrie und die Anfänge der europäischen Integration 1945–1952*. Munich 1986

Bülow, Bernhard Fürst von: *Denkwürdigkeiten*. Vol.3. Berlin 1930

Bungeroth, Rudolf: *50 Jahre Mannesmannröhren 1884–1934*. Berlin 1934

Burchardt, Lothar: *Wissenschaftspolitik im Wilhelminischen Deutschland. Vorgeschichte, Gründung und Aufbau der Kaiser-Wilhelm-Gesellschaft zur Förderung der Wis-

senschaften (= Studien zu Naturwissenschaft, Technik und Wirtschaft im Neunzehnten Jahrhundert 1). Göttingen 1975

Büschgen, Hans E.: *Universalbanken oder spezialisierte Banken als Ordnungsalternativen für das Bankgewerbe der Bundesrepublik Deutschland unter besonderer Berücksichtigung der Sammlung und Verwertung von Kapital.* 2 parts. Cologne 1970

Büschgen, Hans E.: *Die Grossbanken.* Frankfurt a.M. 1983

Büschgen, Hans E.: 'Zeitgeschichtliche Problemfelder des Bankwesens der Bundesrepublik Deutschland'. In: *Deutsche Bankengeschichte.* Edited by the Wissenschaftliche Beirat des Instituts für bankhistorische Forschung. Vol. 3. Frankfurt a.M. 1983, pp. 351–405

Büschgen, Hans E.: 'Entwicklungsphasen des internationalen Bankgeschäftes'. In: Büschgen, Hans E./Richolt, Kurt (eds): *Handbuch des internationalen Bankgeschäfts.* Wiesbaden 1989, pp. 1–23

Büschgen, Hans E.: *Bankbetriebslehre. Bankmanagement.* 4th edn. Wiesbaden 1993

Büschgen, Hans E.: 'Geld und Banken nach dem Zweiten Weltkrieg. Internationale Kapitalbewegungen, Bankensysteme, grenzüberschreitende Kooperation'. In: Pohl, Hans (ed.): *Europäische Bankengeschichte.* Frankfurt a.M. 1993, pp. 455–85

Büschgen, Hans E.: *Internationales Finanzmanagement.* 2nd edn. Frankfurt a.M. 1993

Cahn-Garnier, Fritz: 'Dekartellierung der Banken'. In: *Deutsche Finanzwirtschaft,* 1 (1947), no. 6, pp. 9–14

Carosso, Vincent P.: *The Morgans. Private International Bankers 1854–1913* (= Harvard Studies in Business History 38). Cambridge, Mass./London 1987

Cassier, Siegfried C.: *Biographie einer Unternehmerbank.* Frankfurt a.M. 1977

Christopeit, Joachim: *Hermes-Deckungen.* Munich 1968

Clay, Lucius D.: *Decision in Germany.* London 1950

Commerzbank (ed.): *Wer gehört zu Wem? Mutter- und Tochtergesellschaften von A–Z.* Jge. 1954–57

Däbritz, Walther: *Denkschrift zum fünfzigjährigen Bestehen der Essener Credit-Anstalt in Essen.* Essen 1922

Deckers, Josef: *Die Transformation des Bankensystems in der sowjetischen Besatzungszone/DDR.* Berlin 1974

Delbrück, Adelbert: *Aufzeichnungen unseres Vaters Adelbert Delbrück. Für die Enkel und Urenkel gedruckt.* Leipzig 1922

Deutsche Bank (ed.): *Sonderausgabe '30 Jahre Privatkundengeschäft'.* Frankfurt a.M. 1989

Deutsche Bankengeschichte. Edited by the Wissenschaftliche Beirat des Instituts für bankhistorische Forschung. 3 vols. Frankfurt a.M. 1982–83

Deutsche Bundesbank (ed.): *Deutsches Geld- und Bankwesen in Zahlen 1876–1975.* Frankfurt a.M. 1976

Deutsche Bundesbank (ed.): *Währung und Wirtschaft in Deutschland 1876–1975.* 2nd edn. Frankfurt a.M. 1976

Deutsche Bundesbank (ed.): *40 Jahre Deutsche Mark. Monetäre Statistiken 1948–1987.* Frankfurt a.M. 1988

Diefendorf, Jeffry M./Frohn, Axel/Pupieper, Hermann-J. (eds): *American Policy and the Reconstruction of West Germany 1945–1955.* Cambridge 1993

Dietrich, Yorck: *Die Mannesmannröhren Werke 1888 bis 1920* (= Zeitschrift für Unternehmensgeschichte, Beiheft 66). Stuttgart 1991

Donnison, Frank S.V.: *Civil Affairs and Military Government North-West Europe 1944–1946.* London 1961

Dorendorf, Annelies: *Der Zonenbeirat der britisch besetzten Zone. Ein Rückblick auf seine Tätigkeit.* Göttingen 1953

Dormanns, Albert: 'Die amerikanischen Banken – das System und die derzeitigen Reform-bestrebungen'. In: *Bank-Betrieb*, 6 (1976), pp. 191–6, 241–5

Eichengreen, Barry: *Golden Fetters. The Gold Standard and the Great Depression 1919–1939*. Oxford 1991

Eichholtz, Dietrich: *Geschichte der deutschen Kriegswirtschaft 1939–1945*. Vol. 1. East Berlin 1971

Eichholtz, D./Schumann, W.: *Neue Dokumente zur Rolle des deutschen Monopolkapitals bei der Vorbereitung und Durchführung des Zweiten Weltkrieges*. East Berlin 1969

Emminger, Otmar: *D-Mark, Dollar, Währungskrisen. Erinnerungen eines ehemaligen Bundesbankpräsidenten*. Stuttgart 1986

Endres, Michael: 'Die europäische Bankenwelt – Entwicklungslinien und Zukunftstrends'. In: *Bank-Archiv*, 38 (1990), no. 9, pp. 658–64

Epstein, Gerald/Ferguson, Thomas: 'Monetary Policy, Loan Liquidation, and Industrial Conflict. The Federal Reserve and the Open Market Operations of 1932'. In: *Journal of Economic History*, 44 (1984), pp. 957–83

Erhard, Ludwig: *Deutschlands Rückkehr zum Weltmarkt*. Düsseldorf 1953

Erhard, Ludwig: 'Die deutsche Wirtschaftspolitik im Blickfeld europäischer Politik'. In: Hunold, Albert (ed.): *Wirtschaft ohne Wunder*. Erlenbach-Zurich 1953, pp. 128–57

Erhard, Ludwig: *Deutsche Wirtschaftspolitik. Der Weg der Sozialen Marktwirtschaft*. Düsseldorf/Vienna 1962

Eschenburg, Theodor: 'Deutschland in der Politik der Alliierten'. In: Foschepoth, Josef (ed.): *Kalter Krieg und Deutsche Frage. Deutschland im Widerstreit der Mächte 1945–1952*. Göttingen/Zurich 1985, pp. 35–197

Eschenburg, Theodor/Bracher, Karl Dietrich et al. (eds): *Geschichte der Bundesrepublik Deutschland*. 5 vols. Stuttgart/Wiesbaden 1981–87

Fallon, Padraic, 'The battle plans of Hilmar Kopper' (interview). In: *Euromoney* (January 1994), pp. 28–44

Feder, Ernst: *Heute sprach ich mit ... Tagebücher eines Berliner Publizisten 1926–1932*. Stuttgart 1971

Feldenkirchen, Wilfried: 'Deutsches Kapital in China vor dem Ersten Weltkrieg'. In: *Bankhistorisches Archiv*, 9 (1983), no. 2, pp. 64–80

Feldenkirchen, Wilfried: 'Banken und Stahlindustrie im Ruhrgebiet. Zur Entwicklung ihrer Beziehungen 1873–1914'. In: *Bankhistorisches Archiv*, 5 (1979), no. 2, pp. 26–52

Feldenkirchen, Wilfried: 'Die Rolle der Banken bei der Sanierung von Industrie-unternehmen (1850–1914)'. In: *Die Rolle der Banken bei der Unternehmens-sanierung* (= Bankhistorisches Archiv Beiheft 22). Frankfurt a.M. 1993, pp. 14–39

Feldman, Gerald D.: *The Great Disorder: Politics, Economics, and Society in the German Inflation 1914–1924*. Oxford 1993

Feldman, Gerald D.: 'Jakob Goldschmidt, the History of the Banking Crisis of 1931, and the Problem of Freedom of Manoeuvre in the Weimar Economy'. In: Buchheim, Christoph/Hutter, Michael/James, Harold (eds): *Zerrissene Zwischenkriegszeit. Wirt-schaftshistorische Beiträge. Knut Borchardt zum 65. Geburtstag*. Baden-Baden 1994, pp. 307–27

Fisch, Jörg: *Reparationen nach dem Zweiten Weltkrieg*. Munich 1992

Fischer, Fritz: *Griff nach der Weltmacht. Die Kriegszielpolitik des kaiserlichen Deutsch-land 1914/18*. Düsseldorf 1961

Fohlen, Claude: 'France 1700–1914'. In: Cipolla, Carlo M. (ed.): *The Fontana Economic History of Europe*. Vol. 4. *The Emergence of Industrial Societies*, part 1. Glasgow 1973, pp. 7–75

Frederiksen, Oliver J.: *The American Military Occupation of Germany 1945–1953.* Edited by the Historical Division, Headquarters, United States Army, Europe. 1953

Fricke, Dieter (ed.): *Die bürgerlichen Parteien in Deutschland.* 2 vols. Berlin 1970

Friedjung, Heinrich: *Das Zeitalter des Imperialismus 1884–1914.* 3 vols. Berlin 1919–22

Friedrich, Carl J.: *American Experiences in Military Government in World War II.* New York 1948

Fürstenberg, Carl: *Die Lebensgeschichte eines deutschen Bankiers.* Edited by Hans Fürstenberg. Berlin 1931

Gaddis, John Lewis: *The United States and the Origins of the Cold War 1941–1947.* New York/London 1972

Gall, Lothar: *Bismarck. The white revolutionary.* London 1986

Gall, Lothar: *Europa auf dem Weg in die Moderne 1850–1890* (= Oldenbourg-Grundriss der Geschichte 14). 2nd edn. Munich/Vienna 1989

Gelber, Harry G.: 'Der Morgenthau-Plan'. In: *Vierteljahrshefte für Zeitgeschichte,* 13 (1965), pp. 372–402

Gellately, Robert: *The Gestapo and German Society. Enforcing Racial Policy 1933–1945.* Oxford 1990

Gerhards, Michael: 'Die westdeutschen Banken'. In: *WSI Mitteilungen,* 28 (1975), pp. 391–8

Gerschenkron, Alexander: 'Wirtschaftliche Rückständigkeit in historischer Perspektive'. In: Braun, Rudolf *et al.* (eds): *Industrielle Revolution. Wirtschaftliche Aspekte.* Cologne/Berlin 1972, pp. 59–78

Giersch, Herbert/Paqué, Karl-Heinz/Schmieding, Holger: *The Fading Miracle. Four Decades of Market Economy in Germany.* New York 1992

Gille, Bertrand: 'Banking and Industrialisation in Europe 1730–1914'. In: Cipolla, Carlo M. (ed.): *The Fontana Economic History of Europe.* Vol.3. *The Industrial Revolution.* Glasgow 1973, pp. 255–300

Gillingham, John: 'The Baron de Launoit. A Case Study in the "Politics of Production" of Belgian Industry during Nazi Occupation'. In: *Revue belge d'histoire contemporaine,* 5 (1974), pp. 1–59

Gimbel, John: *Amerikanische Besatzungspolitik in Deutschland 1945–1949.* Frankfurt a.M. 1971

Gimbel, John: *The Origins of the Marshall Plan.* Stanford 1976

Glum, Friedrich: *Zwischen Wissenschaft und Politik. Erlebtes und Erdachtes in vier Reichen.* Bonn 1964

Gneist, Rudolf: *Die nationale Rechtsidee von den Ständen und das preussische Drei-klassenwahlsystem.* Darmstadt 1962

Gottlieb, Manuel: 'Failure of Quadripartite Monetary Reform 1945–1947'. In: *Finanzarchiv,* 17 (1956–57), pp. 398–417

Graml, Hermann: 'Zwischen Jalta und Potsdam. Zur amerikanischen Deutsch-landplanung im Frühjahr 1945'. In: *Viertelsjahrshefte für Zeitgeschichte,* 24 (1976), pp. 308–23

Graml, Hermann: *Die Alliierten und die Teilung Deutschlands. Konflikte und Ent-scheidungen 1941–1948.* Frankfurt a.M. 1985

Grotkopp, Wilhelm *et al.* (eds): *Germany 1945–1954.* Cologne 1955

Guth, Wilfried: 'Verantwortung der Banken – heute'. In: Guth, Wilfried: *Weltwirtschaft und Währung. Aufsätze und Vorträge 1967–1989.* Mainz 1989, pp. 373–98

Gwinner, Arthur von: *Lebenserinnerungen.* Edited by Manfred Pohl on behalf of the Historische Gesellschaft der Deutschen Bank. 2nd edn. Frankfurt a.M. 1992

Habedank, Heinz: *Die Reichsbank in der Weimarer Republik. Zur Rolle der Zentralbank in der Politik des deutschen Imperialismus*. East Berlin 1981

Hallgarten, George: *Imperialismus vor 1914*. Vol. 1. 2nd edn. Munich 1963

Hammond, Paul Y.: 'Directives for the Occupation of Germany: The Washington Controversy'. In: Stein, Harold (ed.): *American Civil–Military Decisions. A Book of Case Studies*. Birmingham, Alabama 1963, pp. 311–64

Härtel, Lia: *Der Länderrat des amerikanischen Besatzungsgebietes*. Stuttgart/Cologne 1951

Hayes, Peter: *Industry and Ideology. IG Farben in the Nazi Era*. New York 1987

Hayes, Peter: 'Big Business and "Aryanization" in Germany 1933–1939'. In.: *Jahrbuch für Antisemitismusforschung, 3 (1994), pp. 254–81*

Helfferich, Emil: *Tatsachen 1932–1946. Ein Beitrag zur Wahrheitsfindung*. Oldenburg 1968

Helfferich, Karl: *Georg von Siemens. Ein Lebensbild aus Deutschlands grosser Zeit. 3* vols. Berlin 1921–23

Henke, Klaus-Dietmar: *Die amerikanische Besetzung Deutschlands*. Munich 1994

Henning, Friedrich-Wilhelm: *Die Industrialisierung in Deutschland 1800 bis 1914*. Paderborn *et al*. 1989

Herbst, Ludolf: *Der totale Krieg und die Ordnung der Wirtschaft. Die Kriegswirtschaft im Spannungsfeld von Politik, Ideologie und Propaganda 1939–1945*. Stuttgart 1982

Herbst, Ludolf (ed.): *Westdeutschland 1945–1955. Unterwerfung, Kontrolle, Integration*. Munich 1986

Herbst, Ludolf/Bührer, Werner/Sowade, Hanno (eds): *Vom Marshallplan zur EWG. Die Eingliederung der Bundesrepublik Deutschland in die westliche Welt*. Munich 1990

Herold, Hermann: 'Die Neuordnung der Grossbanken im Bundesgebiet'. In: *Neue Juristische Wochenschrift*, 5 (1952), pp. 481–4, 566–8

Herrhausen, Alfred: 'Zielvorstellungen und Gestaltungsmöglichkeiten einer Langfristplanung in Kreditinstituten'. In: *Bank-Betrieb*, 11 (1971), no. 10, pp. 354–9.

Herrhausen, Alfred: 'Strategische Führung – Mehr als nur Strategie'. In: Henzler, Herbert A. (ed.): *Handbuch Strategische Führung*. Wiesbaden 1988, pp. 59–68

Hertner, Peter: 'German Banks abroad before 1914'. In: Jones, Geoffrey (ed.): *Banks as Multinationals*. London/New York 1990, pp. 99–119

Hess, Hermann: *Ritter von Halt. Der Sportler und Soldat*. Berlin 1936

Hildebrand, Klaus: *Vom Reich zum Weltreich. Hitler, NSDAP und koloniale Frage 1919–1945*. Munich 1969

Hildebrand, Klaus: *Deutsche Aussenpolitik 1871–1918*. (= Enzyklopädie Deutscher Geschichte 2). Munich 1989

Hilferding, Rudolf: *Das Finanzkapital. Eine Studie über die jüngste Entwicklung des Kapitalismus*. Reprint of the 1st edition of 1910. Berlin 1947

Hillgruber, Andreas: *Hitler, König Carol und Marschal Antonescu. Die deutsch-rumänischen Beziehungen 1938–44*. Wiesbaden 1954

Hilpert, Werner/Stahlberg, Max: 'Wirtschaftsfreiheit und Bankpolitik'. In: *Frankfurter Hefte*, 4 (1951), pp. 101–12

Hintner, Otto: 'Der amerikanische Einfluss auf die Organisation des deutschen Bankwesens'. In: *Österreichisches Bankarchiv*, 1 (1953), pp. 332–9

Hobson, J. A.: *Imperialism. A Study*. 3rd edn. London/Boston/Sydney 1988

Hohorst, Gerd/Kocka, Jürgen/Ritter, Gerhard A.: *Sozialgeschichtliches Arbeitsbuch*. Vol.2. *Materialien zur Statistik des Kaiserreichs 1870–1914*. 2nd edn. Munich 1978

Holborn, Hajo: *American Military Government. Its Organization and Policies.* Washington, DC 1947

Holtfrerich, Carl-Ludwig: *Die deutsche Inflation 1914–1923. Ursachen und Folgen in internationaler Perspektive.* Berlin/New York 1980

Holtfrerich, Carl-Ludwig: 'Zur Entwicklung der deutschen Bankenstruktur'. In: Deutscher Sparkassen- und Giroverband (ed.): *Standortbestimmung. Entwicklungslinien der deutschen Kreditwirtschaft.* Stuttgart 1984, pp. 13–42

Holtfrerich, Carl-Ludwig: 'Auswirkungen der Inflation auf die Struktur des deutschen Kreditgewerbes'. In: Feldman, Gerald D./Müller-Luckner, Elisabeth: *Die Nachwirkungen der Inflation auf die Deutsche Geschichte.* Munich 1985, pp. 187–209

Hook, Walter: *Die wirtschaftliche Entwicklung der ehemaligen Deutschen Bank im Spiegel ihrer Bilanzen.* Heidelberg 1954

Hooven, Eckart van: 'Changes in Banking Business with Personal Customers'. In: *Studies on Economic and Monetary Problems and on Banking History,* 12 (1974), pp. 3–13. Reprinted Mainz 1988, pp. 297–309

Horstmann, Theo: 'Die Angst vor dem finanziellen Kollaps. Banken- und Kreditpolitik in der britischen Zone 1945–1948'. In: Petzina, Dietmar/Euchner, Walter (eds): *Wirtschaftspolitik im britischen Besatzungsgebiet.* Düsseldorf 1984, pp. 215–33

Horstmann, Theo: 'Um "das schlechteste Bankensystem der Welt". Die interalliierten Auseinandersetzungen über amerikanische Pläne zur Reform des deutschen Bankwesens 1945/46'. In: *Bankhistorisches Archiv,* 11 (1985), pp. 3–27

Horstmann, Theo: 'Kontinuität und Wandel im deutschen Notenbanksystem. Die Bank deutscher Länder als Ergebnis alliierter Besatzungspolitik nach dem Zweiten Weltkrieg'. In: Pirker, Theo (ed.): *Autonomie und Kontrolle. Beiträge zur Soziologie des Finanz- und Steuerstaates.* Berlin 1989, pp. 135–54

Horstmann, Theo: 'Die Entstehung der Bank deutscher Länder als geldpolitische Lenkungsinstanz in der Bundesrepublik Deutschland'. In: Riese, Hajo/Spahn, Heinz-Peter (eds): *Geldpolitik und ökonomische Entwicklung. Ein Symposion.* Regensburg 1990, pp. 202–18

Horstmann, Theo: *Die Alliierten und die deutschen Grossbanken. Bankenpolitik nach dem Zweiten Weltkrieg in Westdeutschland.* Bonn 1991

Hübner, Otto: *Die Banken.* Leipzig 1854

Hummer, Waldemar: 'Wirtschaft'. In: *Argentinien. 100 Jahre Deutsche Bank am Rio de la Plata. Katalog zur Ausstellung der Deutschen Bank AG.* Mainz 1987

Hunger, Anton/Müller, Reinhold: 'Die Funkstille war nicht gewollt' (interview with Hilmar Kopper). In: *Industriemagazin* (1991), no. 2, pp. 25–8

Hunke, Heinrich: 'Verstaatlichung der Grossbanken'. In: *Die Deutsche Volkswirtschaft,* 3 (1934), no. 1, pp. 3–6

Islamoglu-Inan, H. (ed.): *The Ottoman Empire and the World Economy.* Cambridge 1987

Jacobsen, Hans-Adolf: *'Spiegelbild einer Verschwörung'. Die Opposition gegen Hitler und der Staatsstreich vom 20. Juli 1944 in der SD-Berichterstattung.* Vol. 1. Stuttgart 1984

Jacobsson, Erin J.: *A Life for Sound Money. Per Jacobsson. His Biography.* Oxford 1979

Jaeger, Hans: *Unternehmer in der deutschen Politik 1890–1918.* Bonn 1967

James, Harold: 'The Causes of the German Banking Crisis of 1931'. In: *Economic History Review,* 45 (1984), pp. 68–87

James, Harold: *The Reichsbank and Public Finance in Germany 1924–1933. A Study of the Politics of Economics during the Great Depression* (= Schriftenreihe des Instituts für bankhistorische Forschung 5). Frankfurt a.M. 1985

James, Harold: 'Did the Reichsbank draw the Right Conclusions from the Great Inflation?' In: Feldman, Gerald D./Müller- Luckner, Elisabeth: *Die Nachwirkungen der Inflation auf die Deutsche Geschichte.* Munich 1985, pp. 211–31

James, Harold: *The German Slump. Politics and Economics, 1924–1936.* Oxford 1986

Janberg, Hans: *Die Bankangestellten. Eine soziologische Studie.* Wiesbaden 1958

Jeidels, Otto: *Das Verhältnis der deutschen Grossbanken zur Industrie mit besonderer Berücksichtigung der Eisenindustrie.* 2nd edn. Munich/Leipzig 1913

Jelinek, Yeshayahu A.: 'Die Krise der Shilumim/Wiedergutmachungs-Verhandlungen im Sommer 1952'. In: *Vierteljahrshefte für Zeitgeschichte,* 38 (1990), pp. 113–39

Jerchow, Friedrich: *Deutschland in der Weltwirtschaft 1944–1947. Alliierte Deutschland- und Reparationspolitik und die Anfänge der westdeutschen Aussenwirtschaft.* Düsseldorf 1978

Jones, Larry E.: *German Liberalism and the Dissolution of the Weimar Party System.* Chapel Hill 1988

Kaiser, David E.: *Economic Diplomacy and the Origins of the Second World War. Germany, Britain, France and Eastern Europe 1930–39.* Princeton 1980

Kampen, Wilhelm von: 'Studien zur deutschen Türkeipolitik in der Zeit Wilhelms II'. Ph.D. thesis, Kiel 1968

Karlsch, Rainer: 'Die Garantie- und Kreditbank AG – Hausbank der Besatzungsmacht in der SBZ/DDR von 1946 bis 1956'. In: *Bankhistorisches Archiv,* 18 (1992), pp. 69–84

Karlsch, Rainer: 'Allein bezahlt? Die Reparationsleistungen der SBZ/DDR 1945–53'. Berlin 1993

Kent, Bruce: *The Spoils of War. The Politics, Economics, and Diplomacy of Reparations 1918–1932.* Oxford 1989

Kern, Werner: 'Zentralismus und Föderalismus im Bankwesen'. Thesis, Darmstadt 1957

Kiesewetter, Hubert: *Industrielle Revolution in Deutschland 1815–1914.* Frankfurt a.M. 1989

Klein, Ernst: 'The Deutsche Bank's South American Business before the First World War'. In: *Studies on Economic and Monetary Problems and on Banking History,* 16 (1978), pp. 11–22. Reprinted Mainz 1988, pp. 471–83

Klopstock, Fred H.: 'Monetary Reform in Western Germany'. In: *Journal of Political Economy,* 57 (1949), pp. 277–92

Klump, Rainer: 'Die Währungsreform von 1948. Ihre Bedeutung aus wachstumstheoretischer und ordnungspolitischer Sicht'. In: Fischer, Wolfram (ed.): *Währungsreform und Soziale Marktwirtschaft. Erfahrungen und Perspektiven nach 40 Jahren.* Berlin 1989, pp. 403–22

Klump, Rainer (ed.): *40 Jahre Deutsche Mark. Die politische und ökonomische Bedeutung der westdeutschen Währungsreform von 1948.* Wiesbaden 1989

Koch, Heinrich: *75 Jahre Mannesmann. Geschichte einer Erfindung und eines Unternehmens.* Düsseldorf 1965

Kocka, Jürgen: *Unternehmensverwaltung und Angestelltenschaft am Beispiel Siemens 1847–1914. Zum Verhältnis zwischen Kapitalismus und Bürokratie in der deutschen Industrialisierung.* Stuttgart 1969

Kocka, Jürgen: 'Angestellter'. In: Brunner, Otto/Conze, Werner/Koselleck, Reinhart (eds): *Geschichtliche Grundbegriffe. Historisches Lexikon zur politisch-sozialen Sprache in Deutschland.* Vol. 1. Stuttgart 1972, pp. 110–28

Kocka, Jürgen: *Die Angestellten in der deutschen Geschichte 1850–1980.* Göttingen 1981

Kopper, Christopher: 'Zwischen Marktwirtschaft und Dirigismus. Staat, Banken und Bankenpolitik im "Dritten Reich" von 1933 bis 1939'. Unpublished Ph.D. thesis, Bochum 1992. Published Bonn 1995

Kopper, Hilmar: 'Strategische Ausrichtung einer Universalbank auf einen gemeinsamen EG-Finanzmarkt'. In: *Bank-Archiv*, 38 (1990), no. 2, pp. 67–72

Kopper, Hilmar: 'Wir verkaufen, was dem Kunden Freude macht'. In: *Cash* (1991), no. 6, pp. 19–25

Kopper, Hilmar: 'Zu warten, dass ein Kunde kommt – das hat sich längst geändert' (interview). In: *Cash* (1992), no. 1, pp. 21–5

Kopper, Hilmar: 'Neue Aufgaben und Ziele im Marketing einer internationalen Bank'. In: Kolbeck, Rosemarie (ed.): *Bankmarketing vor neuen Aufgaben*. Frankfurt a.M. 1992, pp. 107–17

Kopper, Hilmar: 'Die Zeit ist reif. Neue Leitlinien und Ziele für die Deutsche Bank'. In: *Forum* (1993), no. 1, pp. 2–3

Krebs, Paul: 'Schuldenabkommen'. In: Seischab, Hans/Schwantag, Karl (eds): *Handwörterbuch der Betriebswirtschaft*. Vol. 3. Stuttgart 1960, cols. 4816–29

Kreimeier, Klaus: *Die Ufa-Story. Geschichte eines Filmkonzerns*. Munich/Vienna 1992

Krieger, Leonard: 'The Inter-Regnum in Germany: March–August 1945'. In: *Political Science Quarterly*, 64 (1949), pp. 507–32

Krieger, Wolfgang: *General Lucius D. Clay und die amerikanische Deutschlandpolitik 1945–1949*. Stuttgart 1987

Krüger, Peter: *Deutschland und die Reparationen 1918/19. Die Genesis des Reparationsproblems in Deutschland zwischen Waffenstillstand und Versailler Friedensschluss*. Stuttgart 1973

Krüger, Peter: *Die Aussenpolitik der Republik von Weimar*. Darmstadt 1985

Krumnow, Jürgen: 'Operatives Controlling im Bankkonzern'. In: Krumnow, Jürgen/Metz, Matthias (eds): *Rechnungswesen im Dienste der Bankpolitik*. Stuttgart 1987, pp. 127–43

Krumnow, Jürgen: 'Finanzdienstleistungen und EG-Binnenmarkt'. In: Büschgen, Hans E. (ed.): *Der Finanzdienstleistungsmarkt in der Europäischen Gemeinschaft*. Frankfurt a.M. 1990, pp. 67–79

Krumnow, Jürgen: 'Strategisches Bankencontrolling. Organisatorische und instrumentelle Führungsunterstützung in einem Bankkonzern'. In: Horvarth, Peter (ed.): *Strategieunterstützung durch das Controlling. Revolution im Rechnungswesen?* Stuttgart 1990, pp. 333–51

Krumnow, Jürgen: 'Ideal wäre eine französische Investmentbank' (interview). In: *Börse Online* (1990), no. 40, pp. 25–6

Krumnow, Jürgen: 'Das Betriebsergebnis der Banken – ein aussagefähiger Erfolgsindikator?' In: *Zeitschrift für das gesamte Kreditwesen*, 46 (1993), no. 2, pp. 64–8

Krupp, Georg: 'Bankpreise zwischen wirtschaftlichen und "politischen" Notwendigkeiten'. In: *Die Bank* (1993), no. 2, pp. 78–81

Krupp, Georg: 'Bankstrategien im Versicherungsgeschäft'. In: *Die Bank* (1993), no. 6, pp. 332–7

Langen, Eugen: *Die neuen Währungsgesetze*. Essen 1948

Lanner, J.: 'Changes in the Structure of the German Banking System'. In: *Economica*, 18 (1951), pp. 169–83

Lansburgh, Alfred: 'Zur Kapitalserhöhung der Deutschen Bank'. In: *Die Bank*, 10 (1917), pp. 185–96

Laqueur, Walter/Breitman, Richard: *Breaking the Silence*. New York 1986

Latour, Conrad F./Vogelsang, Thilo: *Okkupation und Wiederaufbau. Die Tätigkeit der Militärregierung in der amerikanischen Besatzungszone Deutschlands 1944–1947*. Stuttgart 1973

Lederer, Emil: *Die Privatangestellten in der modernen Wirtschaftsentwicklung*. Tübingen 1912

Lederer, Emil: 'Kritische Übersichten der Sozialen Bewegung. Die Bewegung der Privat-angestellten seit dem Herbst 1918, die Entwicklung der Organisationen, die Ge-staltung der Lebenshaltung und der Besoldung; die Umformung des sozialen Habitus und der Ideologien'. In: *Archiv für Sozialwissenschaft*, 47 (1920–21), pp. 585–619

Leitner, Bernhard: 'Geld und Raum'. In: Leitner, Bernhard/Pohl, Manfred/Becker, Gilbert: *Taunusanlage 12*. Frankfurt a.M. 1985, pp. 11–95

Lindenlaub, Jürgen/Köhne-Lindenlaub, Renate: Unternehmensfinanzierung bei Krupp 1811–1848. Ein Beitrag zur Kapital- und Vermögensentwicklung. In: *Beiträge zur Geschichte von Stadt und Stift Essen*, 102 (1988), pp. 83–164

List, Friedrich: *Der internationale Handel, die Handelspolitik und der deutsche Zollver-ein*. 2nd edn. Stuttgart 1842

Loehr, Rodney C.: *The West German Banking System*. Edited by the Office of the US High Commissioner for Germany, Office of the Executive Secretary, Historical Division. 1952

Lövinson, Käthe: *Frauenarbeit in Bankbetrieben. Ein Beitrag zur Wirtschaftsgeschichte unserer Zeit*. Berlin 1926

Lüke, Rolf E.: *Von der Stabilisierung zur Krise*. Zurich 1958

Lüke, Rolf E.: *13. Juli 1931. Das Geheimnis der deutschen Bankenkrise*. Frankfurt a.M. 1981

MacDonogh, Giles: *A Good German. Adam von Trott zu Solz*. London 1989

Maier, Charles/Bischof, Günter (eds): *The Marshall Plan and Germany. West German Development within the Framework of the European Recovery Program*. New York/Oxford 1991

Marguerat, Philippe: *Le IIIe Reich et le pétrole roumaine 1938–1940. Contribution à l'étude de la pénétration économique allemande dans les Balkans à la veille et au début de la Seconde Guerre Mondiale*. Geneva 1977

Martin, Rudolf: *Handbuch des Vermögens und Einkommens der Millionäre in Preussen*. Berlin 1912

McNeil, William C.: *American Money and the Weimar Republic. Economics and Politics on the Eve of the Great Depression*. New York 1986

Meier, Johann Christian: *Die Entstehung des Börsengesetzes vom 22. Juni 1896*. St Katharinen 1992

Mejcher, Helmut: 'Die Bagdadbahn als Instrument deutschen wirtschaftlichen Einflusses im Osmanischen Reich'. In: *Geschichte und Gesellschaft*, 1 (1975), pp. 447–81

Merkl, Peter-Hans: *Die Entstehung der Bundesrepublik Deutschland*. Stuttgart 1965

Mertin, Klaus: 'Das Rechnungswesen einer Grossbank im Spannungsbereich veränderter Umfeldbedingungen'. In: *Wirtschaft und Wissenschaft im Wandel. Festschrift für Dr. Carl Zimmerer zum 60. Geburtstag*. Frankfurt a.M. 1986, pp. 233–45

Meyer, F.W.: 'Der Aussenhandel der westlichen Besatzungszonen Deutschlands und der Bundesrepublik 1945–1952'. In: Hunold, Albert (ed.): *Wirtschaft ohne Wunder*. Erlen-bach-Zurich 1953, pp. 258–85

Meyer, Ulrich: 'Die Verwalter der Grossbanken'. In: *Deutsche Rechts-Zeitschrift*, 4 (1949), no. 2, pp. 25–9

Milward, Alan S.: *The German Economy at War*. London 1965

Minutes of Evidence taken before the Committee on Finance and Industry (Macmillan Committee). 2 vols. London 1931

Model, Paul: *Die grossen Berliner Effektenbanken*. Jena 1896

Möhring, Philipp: 'Rechtsprobleme der Grossbanken-Dezentralisation'. In: *Zeitschrift für das gesamte Kreditwesen*, 5 (1949), pp. 14–16

Möller, Hans (ed.): *Zur Vorgeschichte der Deutschen Mark. Die Währungsreformpläne 1945–1948*. Tübingen 1961

Möller, Hans: 'Die westdeutsche Währungsreform von 1948'. In: Deutsche Bundesbank (ed.): *Währung und Wirtschaft in Deutschland 1876–1975.* 2nd edn. Frankfurt a.M. 1976, pp. 433–83

Moltmann, Günther: 'Zur Formulierung der amerikanischen Besatzungspolitik in Deutschland am Ende des Zweiten Weltkrieges'. In: *Vierteljahrshefte für Zeitgeschichte*, 15 (1967), pp. 299–322

Mommsen, Hans: *Die verspielte Freiheit. Der Weg der Republik von Weimar in den Untergang 1918–1932.* Frankfurt a.M./Berlin 1989

Mommsen, Hans *et al.* (eds): *Industrielles System und Politische Entwicklung in der Weimarer Republik.* Düsseldorf 1974

Morgenthau, Henry, Jr: *Germany Is Our Problem.* New York/London 1945

Morsey, Rudolf: *Die Bundesrepublik Deutschland. Entstehung und Entwicklung bis 1969.* Munich 1987

Moser, Hubertus: 'Von der Sparkasse der Stadt Berlin zur Landesbank Berlin. Geschichte der Sparkasse in Berlin seit dem Ende des Zweiten Weltkriegs'. In: Fischer, Wolfram/Bähr, Johannes (eds): *Wirtschaft im geteilten Berlin 1945–1990. Forschungsansätze und Zeitzeugen.* Munich 1994, pp. 289–99

Mosse, Werner E.: *Jews in the German Economy. The German-Jewish Economic Elite 1820–1935.* Oxford 1987

Mosse, Werner E.: 'Problems and limits of assimilation. Hermann and Paul Wallich 1833–1938'. In: *Leo Baeck Institute Year Book*, 33 (1988), pp. 43–65

Muehring, Kevin: 'The Kopper era at Deutsche Bank'. In: *Institutional Investor* (December 1990), pp. 43–51

Müller, Rolf-Dieter: 'Von der Wirtschaftsallianz zum kolonialen Ausbeutungskrieg'. In: *Das Deutsche Reich und der Zweite Weltkrieg*, vol. IV. Edited by the Militärgeschichtliche Forschungsamt Freiburg. Stuttgart 1983

Müller-Jabusch, Maximilian: *Fünfzig Jahre Deutsch-Asiatische Bank 1890–1939.* Berlin 1940

Müller-Jabusch, Maximilian: *Franz Urbig.* 1954.

Murphy, Robert: *Diplomat Among Warriors.* London 1964

Neebe, Reinhard: 'Technologietransfer und Aussenhandel in den Anfangsjahren der Bundesrepublik Deutschland'. In: *Vierteljahrschrift für Sozial- und Wirtschaftsgeschichte*, 76 (1989), pp. 49–75

Neuburger, Hugh: 'The Industrial Politics of the Kreditbanken 1880–1914'. In: *Business History Review*, 51 (1977), pp. 190–207

Neuburger, Hugh/Stokes, Houston H.: 'German Banks and German Growth, 1883–1913. An Empirical View'. In: *Journal of Economic History*, 34 (1974), pp. 710–31

Neue Deutsche Biographie. Edited by the Historische Kommission der Bayerischen Akademie der Wissenschaften. Vols. 1–17. Berlin 1953–94

Niethammer, Lutz: *Entnazifizierung in Bayern. Säuberung und Rehabilitierung unter amerikanischer Besatzung.* Frankfurt a.M. 1972

Nipperdey, Thomas: *Deutsche Geschichte 1866–1918. Vol. 1. Arbeitswelt und Bürgergeist.* Munich 1990

Nipperdey, Thomas: *Deutsche Geschichte 1866–1918. Vol. 2. Machtstaat vor der Demokratie.* Munich 1992

Nörr, Knut Wolfgang: *Zwischen den Mühlsteinen. Eine Privatrechtsgeschichte der Weimarer Republik.* Tübingen 1988

Obst, Georg: *Der Bankberuf. Stellungen im Bankwesen, Aussichten im Bankberuf, Fortbildung der Bankbeamten.* Stuttgart 1921

OMGUS: *Ermittlungen gegen die Deutsche Bank 1946/47.* Nördlingen 1985

OMGUS: *Ermittlungen gegen die Dresdner Bank 1946*. Nördlingen 1986

Osthoff, Michael: 'Das Bankwesen in den USA'. In: *Die Bank*, 8 (1980), pp. 371–5

Ott, Hugo/Schäfer, Hermann (eds): *Wirtschafts-Ploetz. Die Wirtschaftsgeschichte zum Nachschlagen*. 2nd edn. Freiburg/Würzburg 1984

Palyi, Melchior: *The Twilight of Gold 1914–1936. Myths and Realities*. Chicago 1972

Pamuk, S.: *The Ottoman Empire and European Capitalism 1820–1913. Trade, Investment and Production*. Cambridge 1987

Panten, Hans-Joachim: 'The Growth and Activity of the West German Successor Banks'. In: *The Bankers' Magazine*, 177 (1954), pp. 113–22

Panten, Hans-Joachim: 'The Come-back of the German Big Three Banks'. In: *The Bankers' Magazine*, 184 (1957), pp. 280–3

Pauluhn, Burkhardt: 'Everything from one Source – a Strategy for the Future'. In: *Bank und Markt und Technik*, 20 (1991), no. 6, pp. 21–3

Pentzlin, Heinz: *Hjalmar Schacht. Leben und Wirken einer umstrittenen Persönlichkeit*. Berlin 1980

Peter, Matthias: 'John Maynard Keynes und die deutsche Frage. Strukturprobleme der britischen Deutschlandpolitik zwischen politischem Machtanspruch und ökonomischer Realität in der ersten Hälfte des 20. Jahrhunderts'. Ph.D. thesis, Giessen 1992.

Peteranderl, Martin: 'Die Welt der Deutschen Bank 1870–1914. Ein Beitrag zur "Betriebs-Organisation" im deutschen Kaiserreich'. Unveröffentlichte Magisterarbeit im Fach Neuere und Neueste Geschichte an der Ludwig-Maximilians-Universität, Munich 1993

Pierenkemper, Toni: *Arbeitsmarkt und Angestellte im Deutschen Kaiserreich 1880–1913. Interessen und Strategien als Elemente der Integration eines segmentierten Arbeitsmarktes* (= Vierteljahrschrift für Sozial- und Wirtschaftsgeschichte Beiheft 82). Stuttgart 1987

Pierenkemper, Toni: 'Zur Finanzierung von industriellen Unternehmensgründungen im 19. Jahrhundert – mit einigen Bemerkungen über die Bedeutung der Familie'. In: Petzina, Dietmar (ed.): *Zur Geschichte der Unternehmensfinanzierung*. Berlin 1990, pp. 69–97

Pingel, Falk: 'Politik deutscher Institutionen in den westlichen Besatzungszonen 1945–1948'. In: *Neue politische Literatur*, 25 (1980), pp. 341–59

Pingel, Falk: '"Die Russen am Rhein?" Zur Wende der britischen Besatzungspolitik im Frühjahr 1946'. In: *Vierteljahrshefte für Zeitgeschichte*, 30 (1982), pp. 98–116

Pinner, Felix: *Emil Rathenau und das elektrische Zeitalter*. Leipzig 1918

Pinner, Felix: *Deutsche Wirtschaftsführer*. Berlin 1925

Plischke, Elmer: *The Allied High Commission for Germany*. Edited by the Office of the US High Commissioner for Germany, Office of the Executive Secretary, Historical Division. 1953

Pogge von Strandmann, Hartmut: *Unternehmenspolitik und Unternehmensführung. Der Dialog zwischen Vorstand und Aufsichtsrat bei Mannesmann 1900 bis 1919*. Düsseldorf/Vienna 1978

Pohl, Hans: 'The Steaua Romana and the Deutsche Bank (1903–1920)'. In: *Studies on Economic and Monetary Problems and on Banking History*, 24 (1989), pp. 77–94

Pohl, Hans/Habeth, Stephanie/Brüninghaus, Beate: *Die Daimler-Benz AG in den Jahren 1933 bis 1944*. Wiesbaden 1986

Pohl, Manfred: *Wiederaufbau. Kunst und Technik der Finanzierung 1947–1953. Die ersten Jahre der Kreditanstalt für Wiederaufbau*. Frankfurt a.M. 1973

Pohl, Manfred: 'Deutsche Bank London Agency founded 100 years ago'. In: *Studies on Economic and Monetary Problems and on Banking History*, 10 (1973), pp. 17–35. Reprinted Mainz 1988, pp. 233–53

Pohl, Manfred: 'Deutsche Bank during the "Company Promotion" Crisis (1873–1876)'. In: *Studies on Economic and Monetary Problems and on Banking History*, 11 (1973), pp. 19–33. Reprinted Mainz 1988, pp. 277–93

Pohl, Manfred: 'Dismemberment and Reconstruction of Germany's Big Banks, 1945–1957'. In: *Studies on Economic and Monetary Problems and on Banking History*, 13 (1974), pp. 18–27. Reprinted Mainz 1988, pp. 343–53

Pohl, Manfred: *Die Finanzierung der Russengeschäfte zwischen den beiden Weltkriegen. Die Entwicklung der 12 grossen Russlandkonsortien* (= Tradition Beiheft 9). Frankfurt a.M. 1975

Pohl, Manfred: *Einführung in die Deutsche Bankengeschichte*. Frankfurt a.M. 1976

Pohl, Manfred: 'Deutsche Bank's East Asia Business (1870–1875). A Contribution to the Economic History of China and Japan'. In: *Studies on Economic and Monetary Problems and on Banking History*, 15 (1977), pp. 25–57. Reprinted Mainz 1988, pp. 423–59

Pohl, Manfred: 'Die Situation der Banken in der Inflationszeit'. In: Büsch, Otto/Feldman, Gerald D. (eds): *Historische Prozesse der Deutschen Inflation 1914–1924. Ein Tagungsbericht* (= Einzelveröffentlichungen der Historischen Kommission zu Berlin 21). Berlin 1978, pp. 83–95, 115–26

Pohl, Manfred: 'Vom Bankier zum Manager'. In: Hofmann, Hans Hubert (ed.): *Bankherren und Bankiers* (= Büdinger Vorträge 10). Limburg 1978, pp. 145–59

Pohl, Manfred: 'The Amalgamation of Deutsche Bank and Disconto-Gesellschaft in October 1929'. In: *Studies on Economic and Monetary Problems and on Banking History*, 18 (1980), pp. 27–52. Reprinted Mainz 1988, pp. 543–70

Pohl, Manfred: *Konzentration im deutschen Bankwesen 1848–1980* (= Schriftenreihe des Instituts für bankhistorische Forschung 4). Frankfurt a.M. 1982

Pohl, Manfred: 'The Deutsche Bank's Entry into the Industrial Area in the Rhineland and Westphalia. The Merger with the Bergisch Märkische Bank and the Essener Credit-Anstalt in 1914 and 1925'. In: *Studies on Economic and Monetary Problems and on Banking History*, 20 (1983), pp. 13–24. Reprinted Mainz 1988, pp. 637–54

Pohl, Manfred: 'Die Entwicklung des privaten Bankwesens nach 1945. Die Kreditgenossenschaften nach 1945'. In: *Deutsche Bankengeschichte*. Edited by the Wissenschaftliche Beirat des Instituts für bankhistorische Forschung. Vol. 3. Frankfurt a.M. 1983, pp. 207–76

Pohl, Manfred (ed.): *Hermann J. Abs. A Biography in Text and Pictures*. Mainz 1983

Pohl, Manfred: 'Die Gebäude der Deutschen Bank. Ein Rückblick'. In: Leitner, Bernhard/Pohl, Manfred/Becker, Gilbert: *Taunusanlage 12*. Frankfurt a.M. 1985, pp. 97–131

Pohl, Manfred: 'Documents on the History of the Deutsche Bank'. In: *Studies on Economic and Monetary Problems and on Banking History*, 21 (1986), pp. 73–84. Reprinted Mainz 1988, pp. 727–39

Pohl, Manfred: *Entstehung und Entwicklung des Universalbankensystems. Konzentration und Krise als wichtige Faktoren* (= Schriftenreihe des Instituts für bankhistorische Forschung 7). Frankfurt a.M. 1986

Pohl, Manfred: *Deutsche Bank Buenos Aires 1887–1987*. Mainz 1987

Pohl, Manfred: *Emil Rathenau und die AEG*. Berlin/Frankfurt a.M. 1988

Pohl, Manfred: 'Selected Documents on the History of the Deutsche Bank'. In: *Studies on Economic and Monetary Problems and on Banking History*, 22 (1988), pp. 35–55. Reprinted Mainz 1988, pp. 769–91

Pohl, Manfred: *Geschäft und Politik. Deutsch-russisch/sowjetische Wirtschaftsbeziehungen 1850–1988*. Mainz 1988

Pohl, Manfred: 'Die Überlebenschancen von Unternehmensgründungen in der Zeit von 1870 bis 1918'. In: Pohl, Hans (ed.): *Überlebenschancen von Unternehmensgründungen* (= Zeitschrift für Unternehmensgeschichte Beiheft 63). Stuttgart 1991, pp. 29–47

Pohl, Manfred: *Baden-Württembergische Bankgeschichte.* Stuttgart/Berlin/Cologne 1992

Pohl, Manfred/Lodemann, Jürgen: *Die Bagdadbahn. Geschichte und Gegenwart einer berühmten Eisenbahnlinie.* Mainz 1989

Pollock, James K.: *Besatzung und Staatsaufbau nach 1945. Occupation Diary and Private Correspondence 1945–1948.* Edited by Ingrid Krüger-Bulcke. Munich 1994

Pollock, James K./Meisel, James H.: *Germany under Occupation. Illustrative Materials and Documents.* Ann Arbor, Michigan 1947

Priester, H.E.: *Das Geheimnis des 13. Juli. Ein Tatsachenbericht von der Bankenkrise.* Berlin 1932

Prinz, Arthur: *Juden im Deutschen Wirtschaftsleben 1850–1914* (= Schriftenreihe wissenschaftlicher Abhandlungen des Leo Baeck Instituts 43). Tübingen 1984

Pritzkoleit, Kurt: *Bosse, Banken, Börsen. Herren über Geld und Wirtschaft.* Vienna 1954

Pritzkoleit, Kurt: *Männer, Mächte, Monopole. Hinter den Türen der westdeutschen Wirtschaft.* 2nd edn. Düsseldorf 1960

Quataert, Donald: 'Limited Revolution. The Impact of the Anatolian Railway on Turkish Transportation and the Provisioning of Istanbul 1890–1908'. In: *Business History Review,* 51 (1977), pp. 139–60

Raschdau, Ludwig: *Unter Bismarck und Caprivi. Erinnerungen eines deutschen Diplomaten 1885–1894.* 3rd edn. Berlin 1939

Riesser, Jacob: *Die deutschen Grossbanken und ihre Konzentration im Zusammenhang mit der Entwicklung der Gesamtwirtschaft in Deutschland.* 4th edn. Jena 1912

Ritschl, Albrecht: 'Die Währungsreform von 1948 und der Wiederaufstieg der westdeutschen Industrie. Zu den Thesen von Mathias Manz und Werner Abelshauser über die Produktionswirkungen der Währungsreform'. In: *Vierteljahrshefte für Zeitgeschichte,* 33 (1985), pp. 136–63

Rosenbaum, Eduard/Sherman, A.J.: *M.M. Warburg & Co. 1798–1938. Merchant Bankers of Hamburg.* London 1979

Rosenberg, Hans: *Grosse Depression und Bismarckzeit. Wirtschaftsablauf, Gesellschaft und Politik in Mitteleuropa.* Berlin 1967

Rostow, Walt Whitman: *Stadien wirtschaftlichen Wachstums. Eine Alternative zur marxistischen Entwicklungstheorie.* Göttingen 1960

Ruhl, Hans-Jörg (ed.): *Neubeginn und Restauration. Dokumente zur Vorgeschichte der Bundesrepublik Deutschland 1945–1949.* Munich 1982

Ruhm, von Oppen, Beate (ed.): *Documents on Germany under Occupation 1945–1954.* London 1955

Ruhm von Oppen, Beate (ed.): *Helmuth James von Moltke. Briefe an Freya 1939–1945.* Munich 1988

Rummel, Hans: 'Die Rentabilitätsfrage der Banken, ihre Unkosten und die Kalkulation'. In: *Untersuchung des Bankwesens 1933.* Part I. Vol. 1. Berlin 1933, pp. 421–75

Rupieper, Hermann-Josef: *Der besetzte Verbündete. Die amerikanische Deutschland-Politik 1949–1955.* Opladen 1991

Rupieper, Hermann-Josef: *Die Wurzeln der westdeutschen Nachkriegsdemokratie. Der amerikanische Beitrag 1945–1952.* Opladen 1993

Schaffner, Peter F.: 'Die Regelung der verbrieften Auslandsschulden des Deutschen Reichs innerhalb des Londoner Schuldenabkommens – ein taugliches Modell zur Bereinigung gouvernementaler Auslandsschulden?' Thesis, Würzburg 1987

Scharf, Claus/Schröder, Hans-Jürgen (eds): *Die Deutschlandpolitik Grossbritanniens und die Britische Zone 1945–1949.* Wiesbaden 1979

Scherpenberg, Jens van: *Öffentliche Finanzwirtschaft in Westdeutschland 1944–1948.* Munich 1984

Schieder, Theodor (ed.): *Handbuch der Europäischen Geschichte. Vol. 6. Europa im Zeitalter der Nationalstaaten und Europäische Weltpolitik bis zum Weltkrieg.* Stuttgart 1968. Reprinted 1973

Schlarp, Karl-Heinz/Windelen, Markus: 'Das Dilemma des westdeutschen Osthandels und die Entstehung des Ost-Ausschusses der Deutschen Wirtschaft 1950–1952'. In: *Vierteljahrshefte für Zeitgeschichte,* 41 (1993), pp. 223–76

Schmiale, Bernd: 'Zur Tätigkeit der Philipp Holzmann AG im Rahmen der Nahostexpansion der Deutschen Bank AG. Eine wirtschaftshistorische Betrachtung unter besonderer Berücksichtigung des Zeitraumes zwischen 1888 und 1918'. Unpublished thesis, East Berlin 1987

Schmidt, Ernst Wilhelm: *Männer der Deutschen Bank und der Disconto-Gesellschaft.* Düsseldorf 1957

Schmitt, Carl: *Völkerrechtliche Grossraumordnung mit Interventionsverbot für raumfremde Mächte. Ein Beitrag zum Reichsbegriff im Völkerrecht.* Berlin/Vienna 1939

Schöllgen, Gregor: *Imperialismus und Gleichgewicht. Deutschland, England und die orientalische Frage 1871–1914.* Munich 1984

Schöllgen, Gregor (ed.): *Flucht in den Krieg? Die Aussenpolitik des kaiserlichen Deutschland.* Darmstadt 1991

Schöllgen, Gregor: *Das Zeitalter des Imperialismus* (= Oldenbourg Grundriss der Geschichte 15). 3rd edn. Munich 1994

Schröder, Hans-Jürgen (ed.): *Marshallplan und westdeutscher Wiederaufstieg.* Stuttgart 1990

Schubert, Aurel: *The Credit-Anstalt Crisis of 1931.* Cambridge 1991

Schulz, Gerhard: *Von Brüning zu Hitler. Zwischen Demokratie und Diktatur.* 3 vols. Berlin/New York 1992.

Schulz, Gerhard et al: *Politik und Wirtschaft in der Krise. Quellen zur Ära Brüning.* 2 vols. Düsseldorf 1980

Schulz, Günther: *Die Arbeiter und Angestellten bei Felten & Guilleaume* (= Zeitschrift für Unternehmensgeschichte Beiheft 13). Wiesbaden 1979

Schulz, Günther: 'Die weiblichen Angestellten vom 19. Jahrhundert bis 1945'. In: Pohl, Hans (ed.): *Die Frau in der deutschen Wirtschaft. Referate und Diskussionsbeiträge des 8. Wissenschaftlichen Symposiums der Gesellschaft für Unternehmensgeschichte am 8. und 9. Dezember 1983 in Essen* (= Zeitschrift für Unternehmensgeschichte Beiheft 35). Stuttgart 1985, pp. 179–215

Schwartz, Thomas Alan: *America's Germany. John J. McCloy and the Federal Republic of Germany.* Cambridge/London 1991

Schwarz, Hans-Peter: *Vom Reich zur Bundesrepublik. Deutschland im Widerstreit der aussenpolitischen Konzeptionen in den Jahren der Besatzungsherrschaft 1945–1949.* 2nd edn. Stuttgart 1980

Schwarz, Hans-Peter (ed.): *Die Wiederherstellung des deutschen Kredits. Das Londoner Schuldenabkommen.* Stuttgart/Zurich 1982

Schwarz, Hans-Peter: *Adenauer. Der Aufstieg: 1876–1952.* Stuttgart 1986

Seidel, Franz: *Die Nachfolgebanken in Westdeutschland. Ihre Entstehung und Entwicklung auf Grund ihrer Bilanzen.* Vienna 1955

Seidel, Franz: 'Die Nachfolgebanken in Westdeutschland'. In: *Österreichisches Bankarchiv,* 3 (1955), pp. 398–409

Seidenzahl, Fritz: 'The Agreement concerning the Turkish Petroleum Company. The Deutsche Bank and the Anglo-German Understanding of the 19th March 1914'. In: *Studies on Economic and Monetary Problems and on Banking History*, 5 (1967), pp. 14–36. Reprinted Mainz 1988, pp. 95–120

Seidenzahl, Fritz: 'The Beginnings of the Deutsch-Überseeische Elektricitäts-Gesellschaft'. In: *Studies on Economic and Monetary Problems and on Banking History*, 7 (1968), pp. 15–21. Reprinted Mainz 1988, pp. 163–9

Seidenzahl, Fritz: 'Das Spannungsfeld zwischen Staat und Bankier im wilhelminischen Zeitalter'. In: *Tradition*, 13 (1968), pp. 142–50

Seidenzahl, Fritz: 'A Forgotten Pamphlet by Georg Siemens'. In: *Studies on Economic and Monetary Problems and on Banking History*, 8 (1969), pp. 17–21. Reprinted Mainz 1988, pp. 187–92

Seidenzahl, Fritz: *100 Jahre Deutsche Bank 1870–1970*. Frankfurt a.M. 1970

Sewering, Karl: 'Zum Neubau der Banken'. In: *Betriebswirtschaftliche Forschung und Praxis*, 1 (1949), pp. 449–60, 708–11

Shonfield, Andrew: *Modern Capitalism. The Changing Balance of Public and Private Power*. London 1967

Siemens, Georg: *Geschichte des Hauses Siemens*. 3 vols. Freiburg/Munich 1947–51

Smith, Jean Edward (ed.): *The Papers of General Lucius D. Clay. Germany 1945–1949*. 2 vols. Bloomington, Indiana 1974

Smith, Jean Edward: *Lucius D. Clay. An American Life*. New York 1990

Sombart, Werner: *Die deutsche Volkswirtschaft im Neunzehnten Jahrhundert*. Berlin 1903

Sommerfeldt, Martin H.: *Ich war dabei. Die Verschwörung der Dämonen 1933–1939*. Darmstadt n.d.

Soutou, Georges-Henri: *L'or et le sang. Les buts de guerre économiques de la Première Guerre Mondiale*. Paris 1989

Steinberg, Jonathan: *All or Nothing. The Axis and the Holocaust*. London 1990

Steininger, Rolf: *Deutsche Geschichte 1945–1961. Darstellung und Dokumente*. 2 vols. Frankfurt a.M. 1983

Stern, Fritz: *Gold and Iron. Bismarck, Bleichröder and the Building of the German Empire*. New York 1977

Stillich, Oskar: *Soziale Strukturveränderungen im Bankwesen*. Berlin 1916

Stillich, Oskar: 'Die Schulbildung der Bankbeamten'. In: *Zeitschrift für die gesamte Staatswissenschaft*, 72 (1916), pp. 103–13

Stolper, Gustav/Häuser, Karl/Borchardt, Knut: *Deutsche Wirtschaft seit 1870*. Tübingen 1966

Strasser, Karl: *Die deutschen Banken im Ausland*. Munich 1924

Strauss, Willi: *Die Konzentrationsbewegung im deutschen Bankgewerbe. Ein Beitrag zur Organisationsentwicklung der Wirtschaft unter dem Einfluss der Konzentration des Kapitals. Mit besonderer Berücksichtigung der Nachkriegszeit*. Berlin/Leipzig 1928

Stucken, Rudolf: *Deutsche Geld- und Kreditpolitik 1914 bis 1963*. 3rd edn. Tübingen 1964

Stützel, Wolfgang: 'Banken, Kapital und Kredit in der zweiten Hälfte des 20. Jahrhunderts'. In: Neumark, Fritz (ed.): *Strukturwandlungen einer wachsenden Wirtschaft*. Vol. 2. Berlin 1964, pp. 527–75

Taylor, Graham D.: 'The Rise and Fall of Antitrust in Occupied Germany 1945–48'. In: *Prologue. The Journal of the National Archives*, 11 (1979), pp. 23–39

Tilly, Richard H.: 'Geschäftsbanken und Wirtschaft in Westdeutschland seit dem Zweiten

Weltkrieg'. In: Schremmer, Eckart (ed.): *Geld und Währung vom 16. Jahrhundert bis zur Gegenwart.* Stuttgart 1993, pp. 315–43

Tilly, Richard H.: 'Los von England. Probleme des Nationalismus in der deutschen Wirtschaftsgeschichte'. In: *Zeitschrift für die gesamte Staatswissenschaft*, 124 (1968), pp. 179–96

Tilly, Richard H.: *Vom Zollverein zum Industriestaat. Die wirtschaftlich-soziale Entwicklung Deutschlands 1834 bis 1914.* Munich 1990

Treue, Wilhelm: 'Die Juden in der Wirtschaftsgeschichte des rheinischen Raumes 1648–1945'. In: Treue, Wilhelm: *Unternehmens- und Unternehmergeschichte aus fünf Jahrzehnten* (= Zeitschrift für Unternehmensgeschichte Beiheft 50). Stuttgart 1989, pp. 113–60

Trumpener, Ulrich: *Germany and the Ottoman Empire 1914–1918.* Princeton 1968

Turner, Henry A., Jr: 'Hitlers Einstellung zu Wirtschaft und Gesellschaft vor 1933'. In: *Geschichte und Gesellschaft*, 2 (1976), pp. 89–117

Turner, Henry A., Jr: *German Business and the Rise of Hitler.* New York/Oxford 1985

Turner, Jan D. (ed.): *Reconstruction in Post-War Germany. British Occupation Policy and the Western Zones 1945–55.* Oxford 1989

US Department of State: *Foreign Relations of the United States. Diplomatic Papers. The Conferences of Malta and Yalta 1945.* Washington, DC 1955

US Department of State: *Documents on Germany 1944–1985.* Washington, DC 1985

Umbreit, Hans: 'Auf dem Weg zur Kontinentalherrschaft'. In: *Das Deutsche Reich und der Zweite Weltkrieg.* Vol. V/1. Edited by the Militärgeschichtliche Forschungsamt Freiburg. Stuttgart 1988

Untersuchung des Bankwesens 1933. Part I. Vol. 2. Berlin 1933

Varain, Heinz Josef: 'Verbändeeinfluss auf Gesetzgebung und Parlament'. In: Varain, Heinz Josef (ed.): *Interessenverbände in Deutschland.* Cologne 1973, pp. 305–19

Verhandlungen des I. Allgemeinen Deutschen Bankiertages zu Frankfurt am Main am 19. und 20. September 1902. Frankfurt a.M. 1902

Verhandlungen des IV. Allgemeinen Deutschen Bankiertages zu München am 17. und 18. September 1912. Berlin 1912

Verhandlungen des VI. Allgemeinen Deutschen Bankiertages zu Berlin in der 'Oper am Königsplatz' (Kroll), am 14., 15. und 16. September 1925. Berlin/Leipzig 1925

Verhandlungen des VII. Allgemeinen Deutschen Bankiertages zu Köln am Rhein am 9., 10. und 11. September 1928. Berlin/Leipzig 1928

Verhoeyen, Etienne: 'Les grands industriels belges entre collaboration et résistance. Le moindre mal'. In: *Centre de Recherches et d'études historiques de la seconde guerre mondiale*, 10 (1986), pp. 57–114

Vocke, Wilhelm: *Memoiren.* Stuttgart 1973

Volkmann, Hans-Erich: 'Die NS-Wirtschaft in Vorbereitung des Krieges'. In: *Das Deutsche Reich und der Zweite Weltkrieg.* Vol. I. Edited by the Militärgeschichtliche Forschungsamt Freiburg. Stuttgart 1979

Vollnhals, Clemens (ed.): *Entnazifizierung. Politische Säuberung und Rehabilitierung in den vier Besatzungszonen 1945–1949.* Munich 1991

Wagner, Kurt: *Stationen deutscher Bankengeschichte. 75 Jahre Bankenverband.* Cologne 1976.

Wallich, Henry C.: *Triebkräfte des deutschen Wiederaufstiegs.* Frankfurt a.M. 1955

Wallich, Hermann: 'Aus meinem Leben'. In: Wallich, Hermann/Wallich, Paul: *Zwei Generationen im deutschen Bankwesen 1833–1914* (= Schriftenreihe des Instituts für bankhistorische Forschung 2). Frankfurt a.M. 1978, pp. 29–158

Wallich, Paul: 'Lehr- und Wanderjahre eines Bankiers'. In: Wallich, Hermann/Wallich, Paul: *Zwei Generationen im deutschen Bankwesen 1833–1914* (= Schriftenreihe des Instituts für bankhistorische Forschung 2). Frankfurt a.M. 1978, pp. 159–426

Walter, Rolf: 'Jüdische Bankiers in Deutschland bis 1932'. In: Mosse, Werner E./Pohl, Hans (eds.): *Jüdische Unternehmer in Deutschland im 19. und 20. Jahrhundert* (= Zeitschrift für Unternehmensgeschichte Beiheft 64). Stuttgart 1992, pp. 78–99

Wandel, Eckhard: *Hans Schäffer. Steuermann in wirtschaftlichen und politischen Krisen.* Stuttgart 1974

Wandel, Eckhard: *Die Entstehung der Bank deutscher Länder und die deutsche Währungsreform 1948.* Frankfurt a.M. 1980

Weber, Adolf: *Depositenbanken und Spekulationsbanken. Ein Vergleich deutschen und englischen Bankwesens.* 4th edn. Munich 1938

Weber, Hans: *Der Bankplatz Berlin.* Cologne/Opladen 1957

Weber, Marie-Lise: *Ludwig Bamberger. Ideologie statt Realpolitik.* Stuttgart 1987

Weber, Werner/Jahn, Werner: *Synopse zur Deutschlandpolitik 1941 bis 1973.* Göttingen 1973

Wehler, Hans-Ulrich: *Bismarck und der Imperialismus.* Cologne/Berlin 1969

Wehler, Hans-Ulrich: *Das Deutsche Kaiserreich 1871–1918.* 5th edn. Göttingen 1983

Weiss, Ulrich: 'Sparmarketing in der Inflation'. Part 1. In: *Bank-Betrieb*, 14 (1974), no. 12, pp. 490–5

Weiss, Ulrich: 'Aufbauorganisation einer Europabank'. In: *Mitteilungen und Berichte des Instituts für Bankwirtschaft und Bankrecht der Universität zu Köln. Abt. Bankwirtschaft*, 21 (1990), no. 63

Weiss, Ulrich: 'Menschen in der Bank'. In: *Zeitschrift für das gesamte Kreditwesen*, 43 (1990), no. 17, pp. 872–6

Weiss, Ulrich: 'Warum brauchen wir die Leitlinien?' In: *Forum* (1993), no. 1, pp. 4–5

Weitenweber, Andreas (= Müller-Jabusch, Maximilian): 'Das System Goldschmidt'. In: *Die Bank*, 34 (1941), pp. 549–66, 576–82

Welch, David: *Propaganda and the German Cinema 1933–1945.* Oxford 1983

Wellhöner, Volker: *Grossbanken und Grossindustrie im Kaiserreich* (= Kritische Studien zur Geschichtswissenschaft 85). Göttingen 1989

Wellhöner, Volker/Wixforth, Harald: 'Unternehmensfinanzierung durch Banken – ein Hebel zur Etablierung der Bankenherrschaft? Ein Beitrag zum Verhältnis von Banken und Schwerindustrie während des Kaiserreiches und der Weimarer Republik'. In: Petzina, Dietmar (ed.): *Zur Geschichte der Unternehmensfinanzierung.* Berlin 1990, pp. 11–33

Wengenroth, Ulrich: 'Iron and Steel'. In: Cameron, Rondo/Bovykin, V.I. (eds): *International Banking 1870–1914.* New York/Oxford 1991, pp. 485–98

Wessel, Horst A.: *Kontinuität im Wandel. 100 Jahre Mannesmann 1890–1990.* Düsseldorf 1990

Wessel, Horst A.: 'Finanzierungsprobleme in der Gründungs- und Ausbauphase der Deutsch-Österreichischen Mannesmannröhren-Werke AG. 1890–1907'. In: Petzina, Dietmar (ed.): *Zur Geschichte der Unternehmensfinanzierung.* Berlin 1990, pp. 119–71

Whale, P. Barrett: *Joint Stock Banking in Germany. A Study of the German Creditbanks Before and After the War.* London 1930

Wiegand, Gerhard (ed.): *Halbmond im letzten Viertel. Briefe und Reiseberichte aus der alten Türkei von Theodor und Marie Wiegand 1895 bis 1918.* Munich 1970

Wilkins, Mira: *The History of Foreign Investment in the United States to 1914.* Cambridge, Mass./London 1989

Williamson, John G.: *Karl Helfferich 1872–1924. Economist, Financier, Politician.* Princeton 1971

Willis, F. Roy: *France, Germany, and the New Europe 1945–1967.* Stanford 1968

Winkel, Harald: *Die Wirtschaft im geteilten Deutschland 1945–1970.* Wiesbaden 1974

Winkler, Dörte: 'Die amerikanische Sozialisierungspolitik in Deutschland 1945–1948'. In: Winkler, Heinrich A. (ed.): *Politische Weichenstellungen im Nachkriegsdeutschland 1945–1953.* Göttingen 1979, pp. 88–110

Winkler, Heinrich August: *Weimar 1918–1933. Die Geschichte der ersten deutschen Demokratie.* Munich 1993

Wolf, Herbert: *30 Jahre Nachkriegsentwicklung im deutschen Bankwesen.* Mainz 1980

Wolf, Herbert: 'Die Dreier-Lösung. Marginalien zum Niederlassungsgesetz von 1952'. In: *Bankhistorisches Archiv,* 19 (1993), pp. 26–42

Wolf, Herbert: 'Geld und Banken nach dem Zweiten Weltkrieg. Internationale Kapitalbewegungen, Bankensysteme, grenzüberschreitende Kooperation. Länderkapitel Deutschland'. In: Pohl, Hans (ed.): *Europäische Bankengeschichte.* Frankfurt a.M. 1993, pp. 517–50

Wolff, Michael W.: *Die Währungsreform in Berlin 1948/49.* Berlin/New York 1991

Wulf, Peter: *Hugo Stinnes. Wirtschaft und Politik 1918–1924.* Stuttgart 1979

Zechlin, Egmont: 'Deutschland zwischen Kabinettskrieg und Wirtschaftskrieg. Politik und Kriegführung in den ersten Monaten des Weltkrieges 1914'. In: *Historische Zeitschrift,* 199 (1964), pp. 347–458

Zehle, Sybille: 'Der Erbe'. In: *Manager Magazin,* 20 (1990), no. 9, p. 77

Ziemke, Earl F.: *The US Army in the Occupation of Germany 1944–1946.* Washington, DC 1975

Zilch, Reinhold: 'Zum Plan einer Zwangsregulierung im deutschen Bankwesen vor dem ersten Weltkrieg und zu seinen Ursachen. Dokumentation'. In: Aisin, B.A./Gutsche, W. (eds): *Forschungsergebnisse zur Geschichte des deutschen Imperialismus vor 1917.* East Berlin 1980, pp. 229–56

Zink, Harold: *The United States in Germany 1944–1955.* Princeton 1957

Zitelmann, Rainer: *Hitler. Selbstverständnis eines Revolutionärs.* Stuttgart 1991

Zorn, Wolfgang: 'Wirtschaft und Politik im deutschen Imperialismus'. In: Abel, Wilhelm et al. (eds): *Wirtschaft, Geschichte und Wirtschaftsgeschichte. Festschrift zum 65. Geburtstag von Friedrich Lütge.* Stuttgart 1966, pp. 340–54

Zschaler, Frank: 'Von der Emissions- und Girobank zur Deutschen Notenbank. Zu den Umständen der Gründung einer Staatsbank für Ostdeutschland'. In: *Bankhistorisches Archiv,* 18 (1992), pp. 59–68

Zucker, Stanley: *Ludwig Bamberger. German Politician and Social Critic 1823–1899.* Pittsburgh 1975

Index of Persons

Index of Companies and Institutions

Although Deutsche Bank AG and Deutsche Bank Group are not mentioned here, the index lists the bank's subsidiaries and affiliates, as well as the successor institutions which operated from 1948 to 1957. Superscript figures refer to the Notes.

Members of the Board of Managing Directors

The following lists the members of the board of managing directors of:

the Deutsche Bank, Berlin (1870–1945)
the regional banks:
Süddeutsche Bank AG, Frankfurt am Main/Munich (1952–57)
Norddeutsche Bank AG, Hamburg (1952–57)
Rheinisch-Westfälische Bank AG/Deutsche Bank AG West, Düsseldorf
(1952–57)
Deutsche Bank AG, Frankfurt am Main, from 1957

Abs, Hermann J.: 1938–45; 1952–57;
1957–67; spokesman 1957–67
Bechtolf, Erich: 1942–45; 1952–57;
1957–59
Blessing, Werner: 1981–87
Blinzig, Alfred: 1920–34
Boehm-Bezing, Carl L. von:
since 1990
Boner, Franz: 1929–32
Bonn, Paul: 1928–30
Breuer, Rolf-E.: since 1985
Brunswig, Peter: 1933–34
Burgard, Horst: 1971–93
Cartellieri, Ulrich: since 1981
Christians, F. Wilhelm: 1965–88;
spokesman 1976–88
Craven, John A.: since 1990
Ehret, Robert: 1970–85
Endres, Michael: since 1988
Fehr, Selmar: 1923–30
Feith, Hans: 1959–76
Frank, Theodor: 1929–33
Frowein, Robert: 1943–45; 1952–57;
1957–58
Gröning, Fritz: 1953–57; 1957–68
Guth, Wilfried: 1968–85;
spokesman 1976–85

Gwinner, Arthur von: 1894–1919;
spokesman 1910–19
Halt, Karl Ritter von: 1938–45
Hauenschild, Manfred O. von: 1959–72
Heinemann, Elkan: 1906–23
Helfferich, Karl: 1908–15
Herrhausen, Alfred: 1970–89;
spokesman 1985–89
Heydebreck, Tessen von: since 1994
Hooven, Eckart van: 1972–91
Hunke, Heinrich: 1943–45
Janberg, Hans: 1953–57; 1957–70
Jonas, Paul: 1881–87
Kaiser, Hermann: 1872–75
Kehl, Werner: 1928–32
Kiehl, Johannes: 1938–44
Kimmich, Karl: 1933–42;
spokesman 1940–42
Klasen, Karl: 1952–57; 1957–69;
spokesman 1967–69
Kleffel, Andreas: 1963–82
Klönne, Carl: 1900–14
Koch, Rudolph von: 1878–1909,
spokesman 1901–09
Kopper, Hilmar: since 1977;
spokesman since 1989
Krumnow, Jürgen: since 1988

Krupp, Georg: since 1985
Leibkutsch, Hans: 1968–79
Mankiewitz, Paul: 1898–1923;
    spokesman 1919–22
Mertin, Klaus: 1971–88
Michalowsky, Carl: 1908–27
Millington-Herrmann, Paul: 1911–28
Mölle, Andreas Friedrich: 1871–72
Mosler, Eduard: 1929–39;
    spokesman 1934–39
Naphtali, Berthold: 1911
Osterwind, Heinz: 1953–57; 1957–71
Plassmann, Clemens: 1940–1945;
    1952–57; 1957–60
Platenius, Wilhelm A.: 1870
Rath, Jean Baptist: 1952–57; 1957–58
Rösler, Oswald: 1933–45; 1952–57;
    spokesman 1943–45
Roland-Lücke, Ludwig: 1894–1900;
    1901–03; 1905–07
Rummel, Hans: 1933–45
Schlieper, Gustaf: 1929–37

Schlitter, Oscar: 1912–32
Schmitz, Ronaldo H.: since 1991
Schneider-Lenné, Ellen R.: since 1988
Schröter, Gustav: 1906–25
Siemens, Georg von: 1870–1900;
    spokesman 1870–1900
Sippell, Karl: 1933–45
Solmssen, Georg: 1929–34;
    spokesman 1933
Stauss, Emil Georg von: 1915–32
Steinthal, Max: 1873–1905
Thierbach, Hans-Otto: 1971–80
Tron, Walter: 1952–57; 1957–62
Ulrich, Franz Heinrich: 1952–57;
    1957–76; spokesman 1967–76
Vallenthin, Wilhelm: 1959–75
Wallich, Hermann: 1870–94
Wassermann, Oscar: 1912–33;
    spokesman 1923–33
Weiss, Ulrich: since 1979
Wintermantel, Fritz: 1933–45
Zapp, Herbert: 1977–94

The Authors

Lothar Gall, born 1936, is professor of modern history at the University of Frankfurt am Main. He is chairman of the Association of Historians in Germany, vice-president of the Deutsche Forschungsgemeinschaft, member of the Bayerische Akademie der Wissenschaften and numerous academic societies as well as editor of *Historische Zeitschrift*.

Publications: *Benjamin Constant. Seine politische Ideenwelt und der deutsche Vormärz*. Wiesbaden 1963; *Der Liberalismus als regierende Partei*. Wiesbaden 1968; *Bismarck. The White Revolutionary*. London 1986 (first German edition 1980); *Europa auf dem Weg in die Moderne 1850–1890*. Second edition, Munich 1989 (first edition Munich 1984); *Bürgertum in Deutschland*. Berlin 1989; *Von der ständischen zur bürgerlichen Gesellschaft*. Munich 1993; *Fragen an die deutsche Geschichte*. 18th edition, Berlin 1994 (first edition Berlin 1971).

Gerald D. Feldman, born 1937, is professor of history and director of the Center for German and European Studies at the University of California at Berkeley. He has held scholarships from the Historisches Kolleg in Munich, the Wissenschaftskolleg in Berlin and the Woodrow Wilson Center in Washington, DC.

Publications: *Army, Industry and Labor in Germany, 1914–1918*. Princeton 1966 (reprint 1992, German edition 1985); *Iron and Steel in the German Inflation, 1916–1923*. Princeton 1977 (with Heidrun Homburg); *Industrie und Inflation*. Hamburg 1977; *Vom Weltkrieg zur Weltwirtschaftskrise*. Göttingen 1984; *Industrie und Gewerkschaften 1918–1924* (with Irmgard Steinisch). Stuttgart 1985; *The Great Disorder. Politics, Economics, and Society in the German Inflation, 1914–1924*. New York/Oxford 1993.

Harold James, born 1956, was a fellow of Peterhouse College, Cambridge, UK, from 1978 to 1986 and since 1986 has been professor of history at Princeton University, USA.

Publications: *The Reichsbank and Public Finance in Germany 1924–1933*. Frankfurt am Main 1985; *The German Slump*. Oxford 1986 (German edition 1988); *A German Identity 1770–1989*. London 1989 (German edition 1989);

Vom Historikerstreit zum Historikerschweigen. Berlin 1993; also numerous essays on international economic history between the world wars. He is currently working on a history of the world monetary order since 1945, which is due to appear in autumn 1995.

Carl-Ludwig Holtfrerich, born 1942, is professor of economics and economic history at the Free University of Berlin.

Publications: *Quantitative Wirtschaftsgeschichte des Ruhrkohlenbergbaus im 19. Jahrhundert.* Dortmund 1973; *Die deutsche Inflation 1914–1923.* Berlin 1980; *Alternativen zu Brünings Wirtschaftspolitik in der Weltwirtschaftskrise.* Wiesbaden 1982; *Vom Weltgläubiger zum Weltschuldner: USA.* Frankfurt am Main 1988; as editor: *Interactions in the World Economy: Perspectives from International Economic History.* New York 1989; *Economic and Strategic Issues in U.S. Foreign Policy.* Berlin 1989; *Wirtschaft USA: Strukturen, Institutionen und Prozesse.* Munich 1991.

Hans E. Büschgen, born 1932, is professor of business administration at the University of Cologne. He heads the department of general business economics and banking, the banking department at the Institute of Banking and Bank Law and the Leasing Research Institute at the University of Cologne, and sits on the management board of Düsseldorf Stock Exchange.

Publications: *Die Großbanken.* Frankfurt am Main 1983; *Zinstermingeschäfte.* Frankfurt am Main 1988; *Grundlagen betrieblicher Finanzwirtschaft – Unternehmensfinanzierung.* Third edition, Frankfurt am Main 1991; *Das kleine Bank-Lexikon.* Düsseldorf 1992; *Internationales Finanzmanagement.* Second edition, Frankfurt am Main 1993; *Bankbetriebslehre: Bankgeschäfte und Bankmanagement.* Fourth edition, Wiesbaden 1993.

Photo Sources

AEG catalogue, 1892: AEG company archives, Frankfurt am Main
John McCloy: Ullstein Bilderdienst, Berlin
The Spokesmen of the Board of Managing Directors, 1957–1988:
    Lutz Kleinhans, Frankfurt am Main
Alfred Herrhausen: Wolf P. Prange, Berlin
Hilmar Kopper: Martin Joppen, Frankfurt am Main
Morgan Grenfell's headquarters: Morgan Grenfell, London
Deutsche Bank's headquarters in Spain: Deutsche Bank Sociedad Anónima
    Española, Barcelona
Deutsche Bank's premises in Luxemburg: Dieter Leistner, Mainz
Trianon and the twin towers of Head Office: Jutta Hofmann, Frankfurt am
    Main

All other photographs: Deutsche Bank, Frankfurt am Main